SCOTT FORESMAN

READING STREET

COMMON CORE 

Program Authors

Peter Afflerbach
Camille Blachowicz
Candy Dawson Boyd
Elena Izquierdo
Connie Juel
Edward Kame'enui
Donald Leu
Jeanne R. Paratore
P. David Pearson
Sam Sebesta
Deborah Simmons
Susan Watts Taffe
Alfred Tatum
Sharon Vaughn
Karen Kring Wixson

SAVVAS
LEARNING COMPANY

We dedicate Reading Street to
Peter Jovanovich.

His wisdom, courage,
and passion for education
are an inspiration to us all.

RENAISSANCE
Accelerated Reader

Copyright © 2013 by Savvas Learning Company LLC. All Rights Reserved. Printed in the United States of America.

This publication is protected by copyright, and permission should be obtained from the publisher prior to any prohibited reproduction, storage in a retrieval system, or transmission in any form or by any means, electronic, mechanical, photocopying, recording, or otherwise. The publisher hereby grants permission to reproduce the Day 5 Monitor Progress pages, the Day 1 Small Group Advanced Selections, and the Day 5 Small Group Read Alouds, in part or in whole, for classroom use only, the number not to exceed the number of students in each class. Notice of copyright must appear on all copies. For information regarding permissions, request forms, and the appropriate contacts within the Savvas Learning Company Rights Management group, please send your query to the address below.

Savvas Learning Company LLC, 15 East Midland Avenue, Paramus, NJ 07652

The Acknowledgments page appears in the back of the book immediately following the Small Group section and constitutes an extension of this copyright page.

Common Core State Standards: © Copyright 2010. National Governors Association Center for Best Practices and Council of Chief State School Officers. All rights reserved.

Savvas™ and **Savvas Learning Company**™ are the exclusive trademarks of Savvas Learning Company LLC in the U.S. and other countries.

Savvas Learning Company publishes through its famous imprints **Prentice Hall**® and **Scott Foresman**® which are exclusive registered trademarks owned by Savvas Learning Company LLC in the U.S. and/or other countries.

Reading Street® and **Savvas Realize**™ are exclusive trademarks of Savvas Learning Company LLC in the U.S. and/or other countries.

Unless otherwise indicated herein, any third party trademarks that may appear in this work are the property of their respective owners, and any references to third party trademarks, logos, or other trade dress are for demonstrative or descriptive purposes only. Such references are not intended to imply any sponsorship, endorsement, authorization, or promotion of Savvas Learning Company products by the owners of such marks, or any relationship between the owner and Savvas Learning Company LLC or its authors, licensees, or distributors.

ISBN-13: 978-0-328-72509-0
ISBN-10: 0-328-72509-9
14 21

Program Authors

Peter Afflerbach, Ph.D.
Professor; Department of Curriculum and Instruction, University of Maryland; College Park, Maryland
Areas of Expertise: Common Core State Standards English Language Arts Work Team, Assessment, and Comprehension

Camille L. Z. Blachowicz, Ph.D.
Professor; National College of Education, National-Louis University; Skokie, Illinois
Areas of Expertise: Vocabulary and Comprehension

Candy Dawson Boyd, Ph.D.
Professor, School of Education; Saint Mary's College; Moraga, California
Areas of Expertise: Children's Literature and Professional Development

Elena Izquierdo, Ph.D.
Associate Professor, University of Texas at El Paso
Area of Expertise: English Language Learners

Connie Juel, Ph.D.
Professor of Education; Stanford University; Stanford, California
Areas of Expertise: Phonics, Oral Vocabulary, and Intervention

Edward J. Kame'enui, Ph.D.
Dean-Knight Professor of Education and Director, Institute for the Development of Educational Achievement, and the Center on Teaching and Learning; College of Education; University of Oregon
Areas of Expertise: Assessment, Intervention, and Progress Monitoring

Donald J. Leu, Ph.D.
John and Maria Neag Endowed Chair in Literacy and Technology Board of Directors, International Reading Association; University of Connecticut; Storrs, Connecticut
Areas of Expertise: Comprehension, Technology, and New Literacies

Jeanne R. Paratore, Ed.D.
Professor of Literacy, Language, and Cultural Studies; Boston University School of Education; Boston, Massachusetts
Areas of Expertise: Intervention and Small Group Instruction

P. David Pearson, Ph.D.
Professor of Language, Literacy and Culture, and Human Development; Graduate School of Education; University of California; Berkeley, California
Areas of Expertise: Common Core State Standards English Language Arts Work Team, Comprehension

Sam L. Sebesta, Ph.D.
Professor Emeritus; Curriculum and Instruction College of Education, University of Washington; Seattle, Washington
Areas of Expertise: Children's Literature, Reader Response, and Motivation

Deborah Simmons, Ph.D.
Professor in the Department of Educational Psychology, College of Education and Human Development, Texas A&M University
Areas of Expertise: Literacy Development, Phonics, and Intervention

Susan Watts Taffe, Ph.D.
Associate Professor and Program Coordinator, Literacy and Second Language Studies, School of Education; University of Cincinnati; Cincinnati, Ohio
Areas of Expertise: Vocabulary, Comprehension, and New Literacies

Alfred Tatum, Ph.D.
Associate Professor and Director, UIC Reading Clinic, University of Illinois at Chicago
Areas of Expertise: Adolescent Literacy, Reader Response, and Motivation

Sharon Vaughn, Ph.D.
H. E. Hartfelder/The Southland Corporation Regents Professor; University of Texas; Austin, Texas
Areas of Expertise: Literacy Development, Intervention, Professional Development, English Language Learners, Vocabulary, and Small Group Instruction

Karen Kring Wixson, Ph.D.
Dean of Education, University of North Carolina, Greensboro
Areas of Expertise: Common Core State Standards English Language Arts Work Team, Assessment, Small Group Instruction

Consulting Authors

Jeff Anderson, M.Ed.
Author and National Literacy Staff Developer

Jim Cummins, Ph.D.
Professor; Department of Curriculum, Teaching and Learning; University of Toronto

Tahira A. DuPree Chase, Ed.D.
Director of Curriculum and Instruction, Mt. Vernon City School District, New York

Lily Wong Fillmore, Ph.D.
Professor Emerita; Graduate School of Education, University of California, Berkeley

Georgia Earnest Garcia, Ph.D.
Professor; Language and Literacy Division, Department of Curriculum and Instruction, University of Illinois at Urbana-Champaign

George A. Gonzalez, Ph.D.
Professor (Retired); School of Education, University of Texas-Pan American, Edinburg

Adria Klein, Ph.D.
Professor Emeritus; School of Education, California State University, San Bernadino

Lesley Maxwell, M.S., CCC-SLP
Director of Clinical Education, Clinical Associate Professor; Department of Communication Sciences and Disorders, MGH Institute of Health Professions

Valerie Ooka Pang, Ph.D.
Professor; School of Teacher Education, San Diego State University

Sally M. Reis, Ph.D.
Board of Trustees Distinguished Professor; Department of Educational Psychology, University of Connecticut

Jon Scieszka, M.F.A.
Children's Book Author and Founder of GUYS READ, First National Ambassador for Young People's Literature 2008

Grant Wiggins, Ed.D.
President of Authentic Education, coauthor of *Understanding by Design*

Nurture the love of reading.

Help students learn to read *and* love to read. *Reading Street Common Core* supports reading, writing, and language development. Amazing literature on amazing devices inspires students in a whole new way.

Literature students love

The best literary and informational text

On devices they crave!

Whiteboards, tablets, computers, mobile devices

Build a foundation for reading.

Reading Street Common Core helps students develop foundational skills for reading more complex text. Common Core experts helped design the plan. Classroom results prove it works.

Early Reading Success

Reading Street students outperformed their peers by 15 percentile points, even though they started below the comparison students.

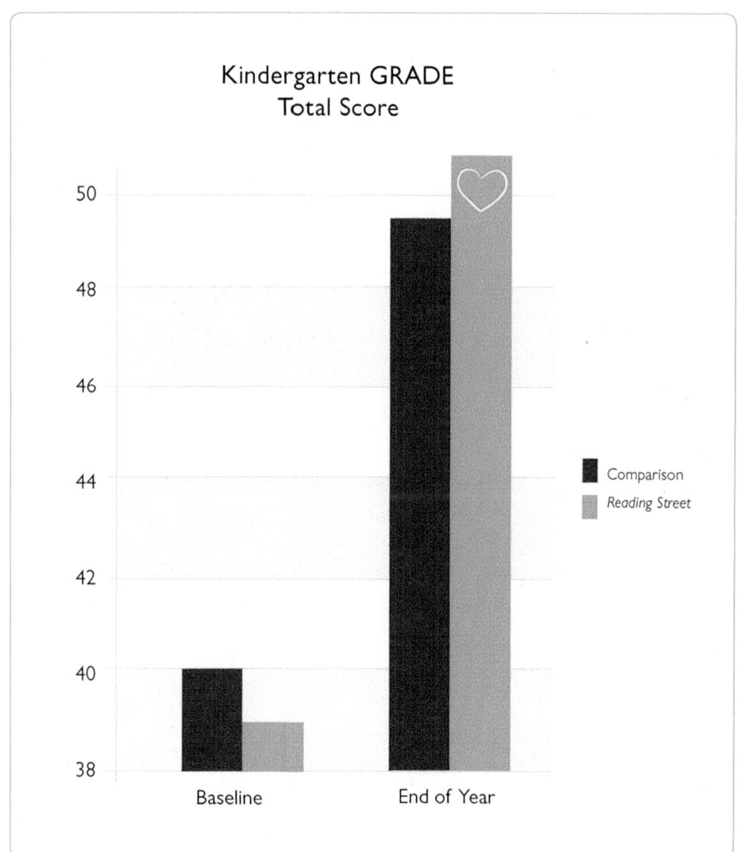

Greater Reading Enjoyment Later

Fourth-grade *Reading Street* students had more positive attitudes toward reading.

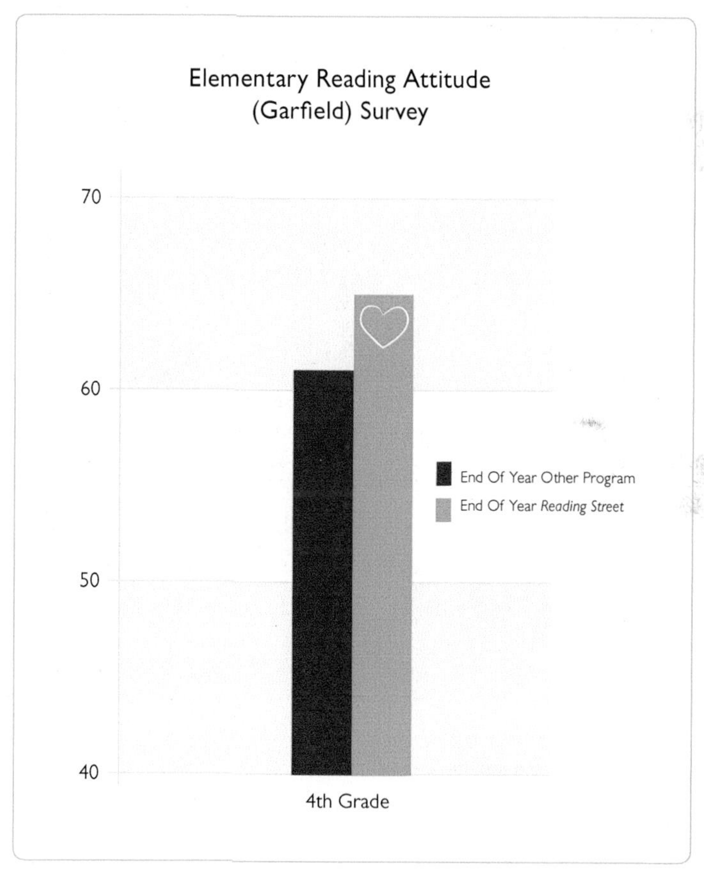

"The texts children read provide them with a foundation not just for what they're going to read, but also for what they're going to write and talk about."

Jeanne R. Paratore, Ed.D.
Program Author

Grow student capacity.

Reading Street Common Core builds students' capacity to read complex texts. Zoom in on elements critical to the Common Core State Standards.

Text-Based Comprehension

Modeling, analysis, and guided practice prepare students for more demanding text.

DAYS 2 & 3

1ST READ

Access Text If children need help, then...

CONNECT TO CONCEPT Look at the pictures on page 147. Look at the chipmunk. Describe what it looks like. Encourage children to answer the question in complete sentences. Yes, the chipmunk is light brown with dark brown stripes. I think it is eating something. Ask children to describe the ant, raccoon, and bird.

AUTHOR'S PURPOSE What is the author's purpose for writing this selection? How do you know? (The author's purpose is to give information about animals and plants in a forest. These pages tell facts about bugs and leaves.)

Life in the Forest

by Claire Daniel

Genre **Expository text** tells facts about real places. Next you will read about the plants and animals in a forest.

Question of the Week

How are plant and animal communities important to each other?

146 147

Student Edition, pp. 146–147

We can find life in the forest. It is a busy place!

Sun shines on the leaves and helps them grow. Bugs like munching on them. Yum, yum! Bugs can eat lots and lots.

Sun helped these leaves get wide and flat.

148 149

Student Edition, pp. 148–149

DAYS 2 & 3

Common Core State Standards

Informational Text 1. Ask and answer questions about key details in a text. **Informational Text 3.** Describe the connection between two individuals, events, ideas, or pieces of information in a text. **Informational Text 8.** Identify the reasons an author gives to support points in a text. **Also Informational Text 7.**

2ND READ

Close Reading

INFERENCE • TEXT EVIDENCE Look at the pictures on page 147. How can you tell what kinds of animals and plants you are going to read about? Point to the pictures where you found this information.

SYNTHESIS What if the sun never shined on leaves? How would this change the community? (If the sun never shined, the leaves would never grow. There would be no leaves for the bugs to munch on.)

CONNECT TO SCIENCE Different parts of a plant help it get what it needs to live. Roots take in water from the soil. Leaves use sunlight and a green pigment called chlorophyll to make food.

ELL

Academic Language Have pairs find other things in their environment that are *wide* and *flat*, like the leaf on page 148.

146–147 Communities • Unit 2 • Week 5

Life in the Forest **148–149**

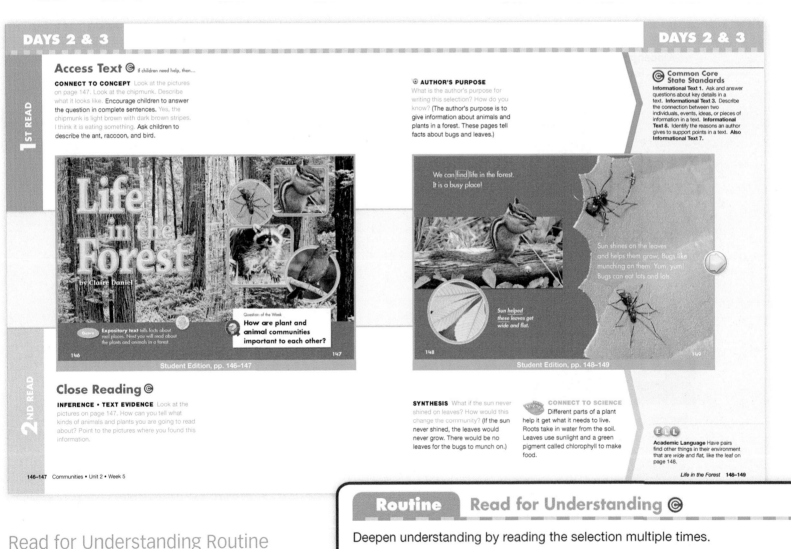

Read for Understanding Routine

Routines provide weekly opportunities to develop deep understanding and build higher-order thinking skills through Close Reading.

Routine **Read for Understanding**

Deepen understanding by reading the selection multiple times.

1. **First Read**—use the **Access Text** notes to help children clarify understanding.
2. **Second Read**—use the **Close Reading** notes to help children draw knowledge from the text.

Content Knowledge

Weekly and unit instruction is built around science and social studies concepts. These concepts connect every piece of literature, vocabulary, and writing, allowing students to develop deep knowledge.

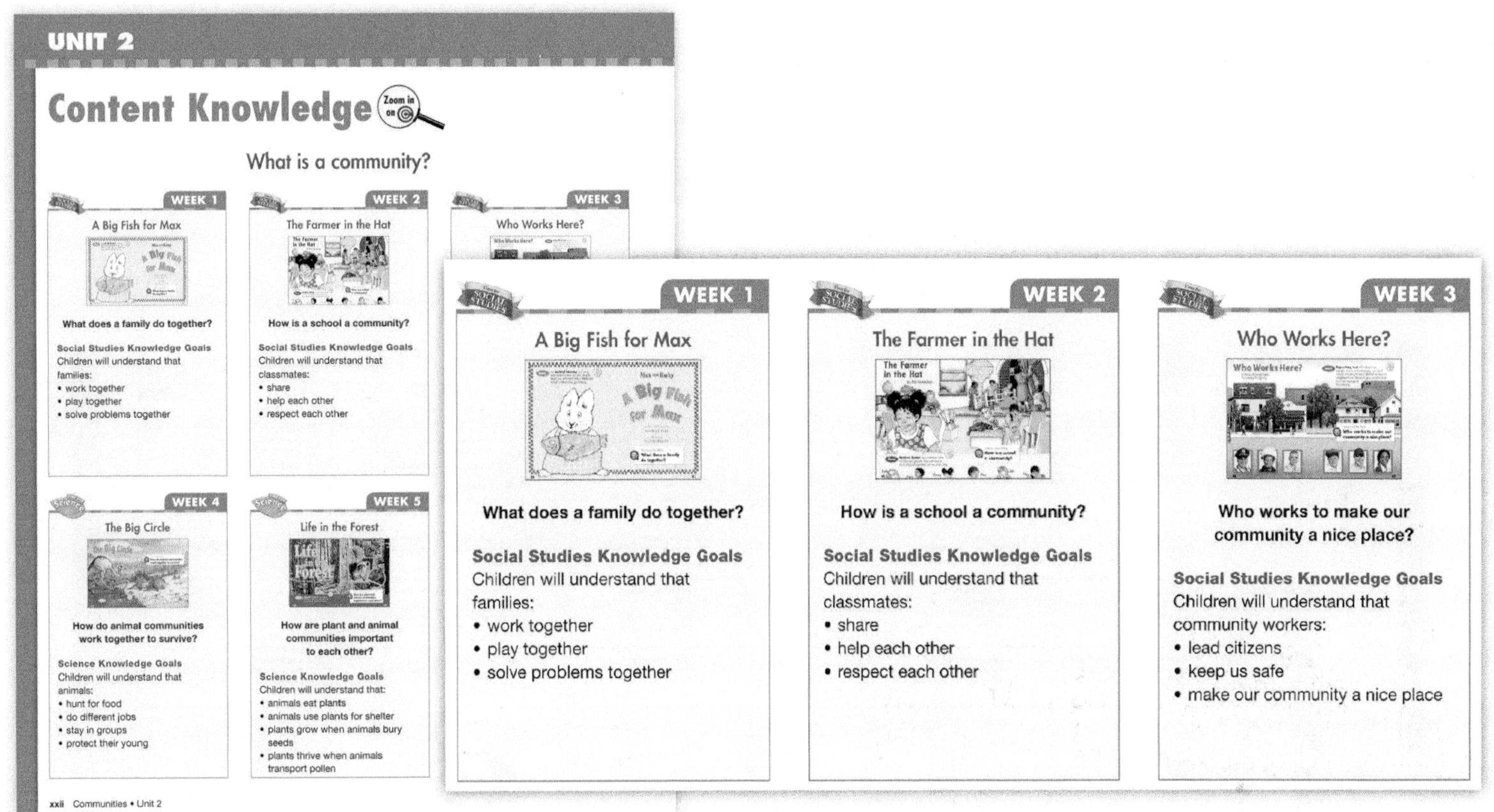
UNIT 2

Content Knowledge

What is a community?

WEEK 1

A Big Fish for Max

What does a family do together?

Social Studies Knowledge Goals

Children will understand that families:
- work together
- play together
- solve problems together

WEEK 2

The Farmer in the Hat

How is a school a community?

Social Studies Knowledge Goals

Children will understand that classmates:
- share
- help each other
- respect each other

WEEK 3

Who Works Here?

Who works to make our community a nice place?

Social Studies Knowledge Goals

Children will understand that community workers:
- lead citizens
- keep us safe
- make our community a nice place

WEEK 4

The Big Circle

How do animal communities work together to survive?

Science Knowledge Goals

Children will understand that animals:
- hunt for food
- do different jobs
- stay in groups
- protect their young

WEEK 5

Life in the Forest

How are plant and animal communities important to each other?

Science Knowledge Goals

Children will understand that:
- animals eat plants
- animals use plants for shelter
- plants grow when animals bury seeds
- plants thrive when animals transport pollen

xxii Communities • Unit 2

Writing

Varied writing tasks help students write to inform or explain.

DAILY
- 10-minute mini-lessons on writing traits and craft allow students to write in response to their reading
- Quick Write routine for writing on demand

WEEKLY
- Different writing product each week
- Writing mini-lessons and organizational models
- Mentor text to exemplify good traits

UNIT
- One- or two-week Writing Workshops
- Writing process lessons

Inspire confidence.

"What do I do in group time?" Follow the simple 3-step plan. *Reading Street Common Core* provides a road map to help you teach with confidence. You'll know exactly where to go and what to do next.

1 Teacher-Led Small Groups

See how to differentiate instruction day by day.

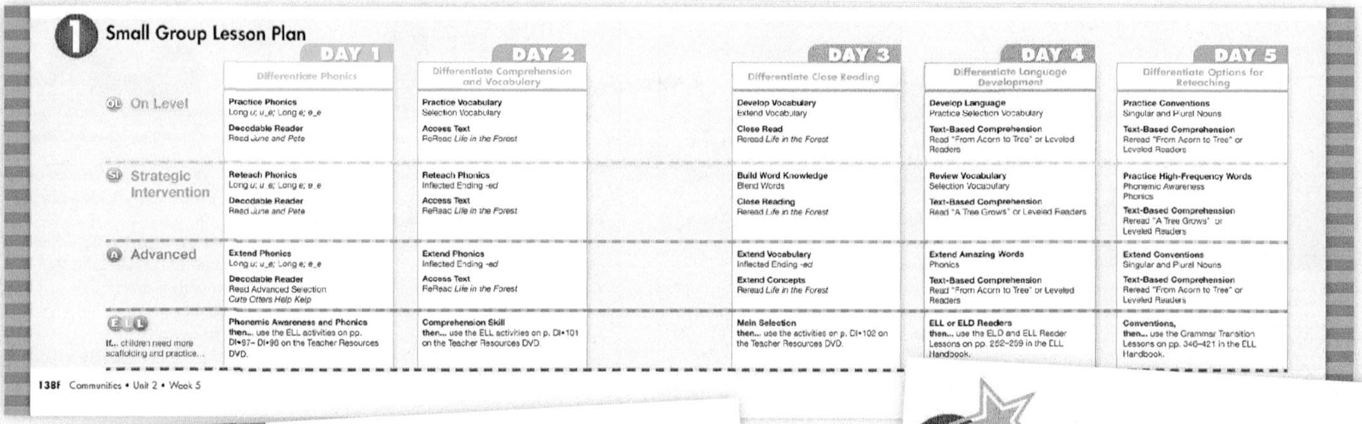

1 Small Group Lesson Plan

	DAY 1 Differentiate Phonics	DAY 2 Differentiate Comprehension and Vocabulary	DAY 3 Differentiate Close Reading	DAY 4 Differentiate Language Development	DAY 5 Differentiate Options for Reteaching
OL On Level	**Practice Phonics** Long *u*; *u_e*; Long *e*; *e_e* **Decodable Reader** Read *June and Pete*	**Practice Vocabulary** Selection Vocabulary **Access Text** ReRead *Life in the Forest*	**Develop Vocabulary** Extend Vocabulary **Close Read** Reread *Life in the Forest*	**Develop Language** Practice Selection Vocabulary **Text-Based Comprehension** Read "From Acorn to Tree" or Leveled Readers	**Practice Conventions** Singular and Plural Nouns **Text-Based Comprehension** Reread "From Acorn to Tree" or Leveled Readers
SI Strategic Intervention	**Reteach Phonics** Long *u*; *u_e*; Long *e*; *e_e* **Decodable Reader** Read *June and Pete*	**Reteach Phonics** Inflected Ending *-ed* **Access Text** ReRead *Life in the Forest*	**Build Word Knowledge** Blend Words **Close Reading** Reread *Life in the Forest*	**Review Vocabulary** Selection Vocabulary **Text-Based Comprehension** Read "A Tree Grows" or Leveled Readers	**Practice High-Frequency Words** Phonemic Awareness Phonics **Text-Based Comprehension** Reread "A Tree Grows" or Leveled Readers
A Advanced	**Extend Phonics** Long *u*; *u_e*; Long *e*; *e_e* **Decodable Reader** Read Advanced Selection *Cute Otters Help Kelp*	**Extend Phonics** Inflected Ending *-ed* **Access Text** ReRead *Life in the Forest*	**Extend Vocabulary** Inflected Ending *-ed* **Extend Concepts** Reread *Life in the Forest*	**Extend Amazing Words** Phonics **Text-Based Comprehension** Read "From Acorn to Tree" or Leveled Readers	**Extend Conventions** Singular and Plural Nouns **Text-Based Comprehension** Reread "From Acorn to Tree" or Leveled Readers
ELL **If...** children need more scaffolding and practice...	**Phonemic Awareness and Phonics** **then...** use the ELL activities on pp. DI•97– DI•98 on the Teacher Resources DVD.	**Comprehension Skill** **then...** use the ELL activities on p. DI•101 on the Teacher Resources DVD.	**Main Selection** **then...** use the activities on p. DI•102 on the Teacher Resources DVD.	**ELL or ELD Readers** **then...** use the ELD and ELL Reader Lessons on pp. 252–259 in the ELL Handbook.	**Conventions,** **then...** use the Grammar Transition Lessons on pp. 340–421 in the ELL Handbook.

13BF Communities • Unit 2 • Week 5

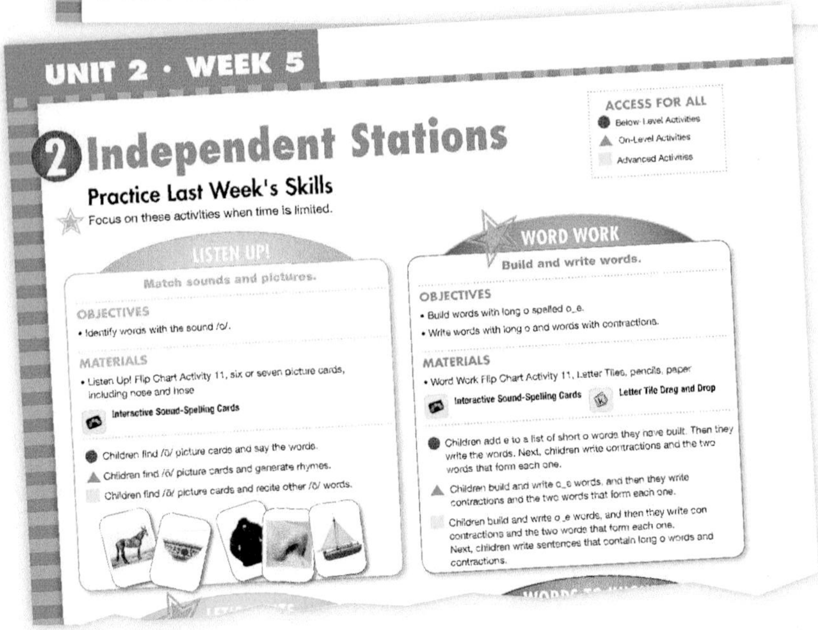

UNIT 2 • WEEK 5

2 Independent Stations

Practice Last Week's Skills

Focus on these activities when time is limited.

ACCESS FOR ALL
- Below-Level Activities
- On-Level Activities
- Advanced Activities

LISTEN UP!

Match sounds and pictures.

OBJECTIVES
- Identify words with the sound /ō/.

MATERIALS
- Listen Up! Flip Chart Activity 11, six or seven picture cards, including nose and hose

Interactive Sound-Spelling Cards

- Children find /ō/ picture cards and say the words.
- Children find /ō/ picture cards and generate rhymes.
- Children find /ō/ picture cards and recite other /ō/ words.

WORD WORK

Build and write words.

OBJECTIVES
- Build words with long o spelled o_e.
- Write words with long o and words with contractions.

MATERIALS
- Word Work Flip Chart Activity 11, Letter Tiles, pencils, paper

Interactive Sound-Spelling Cards | Letter Tile Drag and Drop

- Children add e to a list of short o words they have built. Then they write the words. Next, children write contractions and the two words that form each one.
- Children build and write o_e words, and then they write contractions and the two words that form each one.
- Children build and write o_e words, and then they write con contractions and the two words that form each one. Next, children write sentences that contain long o words and contractions.

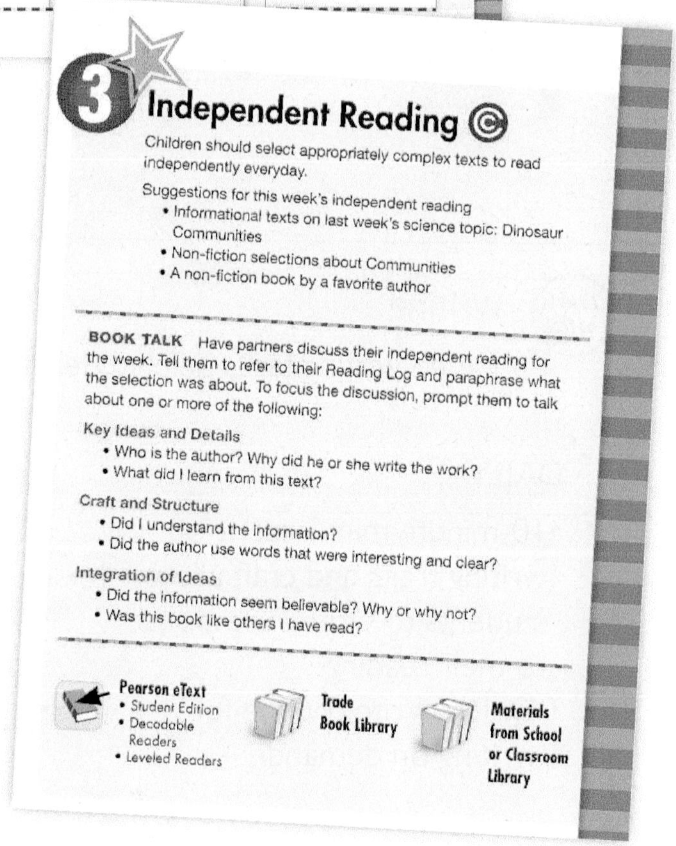

3 Independent Reading

Children should select appropriately complex texts to read independently everyday.

Suggestions for this week's independent reading
- Informational texts on last week's science topic: Dinosaur Communities
- Non-fiction selections about Communities
- A non-fiction book by a favorite author

BOOK TALK Have partners discuss their independent reading for the week. Tell them to refer to their Reading Log and paraphrase what the selection was about. To focus the discussion, prompt them to talk about one or more of the following:

Key Ideas and Details
- Who is the author? Why did he or she write the work?
- What did I learn from this text?

Craft and Structure
- Did I understand the information?
- Did the author use words that were interesting and clear?

Integration of Ideas
- Did the information seem believable? Why or why not?
- Was this book like others I have read?

Pearson eText
- Student Edition
- Decodable Readers
- Leveled Readers

Trade Book Library

Materials from School or Classroom Library

2 Independent Practice Stations

Level activities and provide focus when time is limited.

3 Independent Reading

Suggest concept-related reading and partner activities.

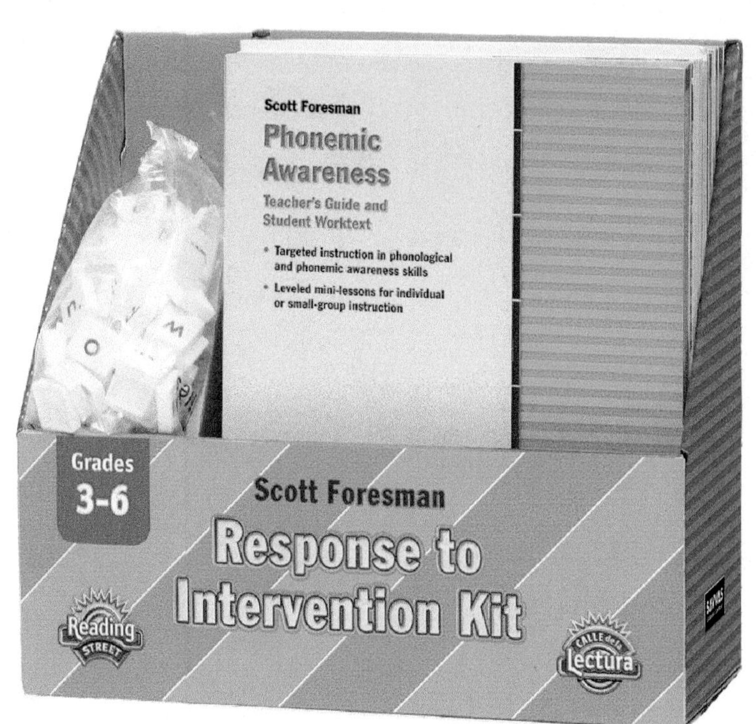

Response to Intervention Kit

Tier 2 RTI Kit provides a targeted focus and leveled mini-lessons for individuals and small groups.

Intensive Intervention

My Sidewalks Intensive Intervention

Conceptually related to *Reading Street, My Sidewalks* provides 30 weeks of instruction for struggling readers.

"What we need to do is to increase the support strategies to help students cope with complex text."

P. David Pearson
Program Author

TABLE OF CONTENTS

YOU ARE HERE

UNIT 1 All Together Now

UNIT 2 Look at Us!

TABLE OF CONTENTS

UNIT 3 Changes All Around Us

UNIT 4 Let's Go Exploring

UNIT 5 Going Places

UNIT 6 Putting It Together

eSTREET INTERACTIVE
www.ReadingStreet.com

All Together Now

How do we live, work, and play together?

The Little School Bus

ANIMAL FANTASY

How do children get to school?

We Are So Proud!

REALISTIC FICTION

How do school children work and play together?

Plaidypus Lost

REALISTIC FICTION

How do families cooperate?

Miss Bindergarten Takes a Field Trip

ANIMAL FANTASY

How do people in a community cooperate?

Smash! Crash!

FANTASY

What do you like to do with your friends?

Dig Dig Digging

NONFICTION

How do machines help people work?

Skills Overview

Key
T Tested Skill
◎ Target Skill

		WEEK 1	WEEK 2	WEEK 3
		The Little School Bus Animal Fantasy, pp. 60–75	**We Are So Proud!** Realistic Fiction, pp. 161–171	**Plaidypus Lost** Realistic Fiction, pp. 258–277
Build Content Knowledge	Integrate Science and Social Studies	Time for Social Studies: Economics; History; Government	Time for Social Studies: Working Together; Belonging to a Group; Rules at School	Time for Social Studies: Culture
	Weekly Question	*How do children get to school?*	*How do school children work and play together?*	*How do families cooperate?*
	Knowledge Goals	Children understand that riding the bus together: • helps them get to school • helps them arrive safely	Children understand that working together with classmates: • helps them share tools and supplies • helps them solve problems	Children understand that support from their families: • helps them take care of themselves • helps them take care of their friends
Get Ready to Read	Phonological/ Phonemic Awareness	**T** Rhyming Words	**T** Syllables **T** Sound Discrimination	**T** Initial Sounds **T** Initial Sound Discrimination
	Letter Recognition/ Phonics	**T** ◎ Letters *Aa, Bb, Cc, Dd, Ee*	**T** ◎ Letters *Ff, Gg, Hh, Ii, Jj, Kk, Ll, Mm, Nn*	**T** ◎ Letters *Oo, Pp, Qq, Rr, Ss,*
	High-Frequency Words	**T** *I, am*	**T** *I, am*	**T** *the, little*
Read and Comprehend	Comprehension	**T** ◎ **Skill** Character	**T** ◎ **Skill** Setting **Review Skill** Character	**T** ◎ **Skill** Sequence **Review Skill** Setting
Language Arts	Writing	Song	Invitation	Poem
	Conventions	Say Our Names	Write Our Names	What We Look Like
	Listening and Speaking	Follow Directions	Respond to Literature: Drama	Listen for Rhyme and Rhythm
	Vocabulary	Words for Transportation	Color Words	Words for Shapes

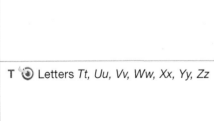

 WEEK 4	 WEEK 5	 WEEK 6
Miss Bindergarten Takes a Field Trip Animal Fantasy, pp. 364–383	**Smash! Crash!** Fantasy, pp. 469–485	**Dig Dig Digging** Nonfiction, pp. 572–583
Social Studies: Economics; Government; Culture; Citizenship	Social Studies: Culture; Responsibility	Science: Physical Science; Earth Science
How do people in a community cooperate?	*What do you like to do with your friends?*	*How do machines help people work?*
Children understand that cooperating with others: • helps them have a fun time • helps them learn new things	Children understand that playing with others: • helps them share fun experiences • helps them share a common goal	Children understand that working with machines: • helps get a lot of work done • helps with many different jobs
T Initial Sounds	**T** Initial and Final /m/	**T** Initial and Final /t/
T Letters *Tt, Uu, Vv, Ww, Xx, Yy, Zz*	**T** /m/ Spelled *Mm* **Review** Letter Recognition	**T** /t/ Spelled *Tt* **Review** /m/ Spelled *Mm*
T *the, little*	**T** *a, to*	**T** *a, to*
T **Skill** Classify and Categorize **Review Skill** Setting	**T** **Skill** Character **Review Skill** Sequence	**T** **Skill** Classify and Categorize **Review Skill** Setting
Instructions	Caption	Story
What We Can Do	Nouns for People and Animals	Nouns for Places and Things
Talk About Me	Announcements/Messages	Respond to Literature: Drama
Location Words	Position Words	Words for Sizes

Assessment

5 Steps to Success on Reading Street

RIGHT IN YOUR TEACHER'S EDITION

Step 1

Begin the Year

The Assessment Handbook provides ideas and support to begin the school year and beyond.

The Baseline Group Test helps identify where children are. Use the Baseline Test results to make initial grouping decisions and to differentiate instruction based on ability levels.

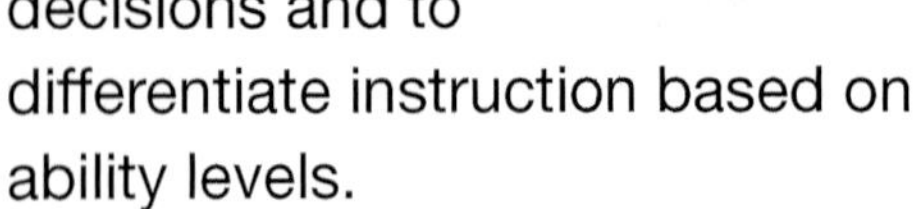

Step 2

Every Day

During the day, use these tools to monitor student progress.

- **Corrective Feedback** provides point of use support.

Corrective feedback	If... students are unable to answer the comprehension questions, then... use the Reteach lesson in *First Stop*.

- **Monitor Progress** boxes each day check phonemic awareness, phonics, retelling, and oral vocabulary.

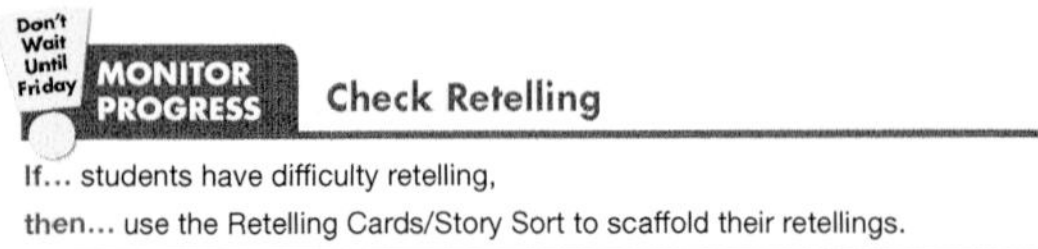
Don't Wait Until Friday MONITOR PROGRESS Check Retelling

If... students have difficulty retelling,
then... use the Retelling Cards/Story Sort to scaffold their retellings.

Step 3

Every Week

- **Weekly Assessments** on Day 5 check phonics, high-frequency words, and comprehension.

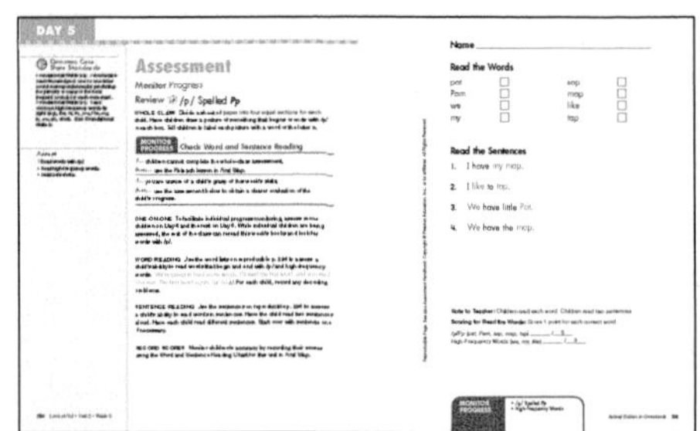

- **Reading Street Sleuth** assesses children's ability to find clues in text through close reading.

- **Writing to Sources** assesses children's ability to write an argumentative, narrative, or explanatory paragraph in response to one source and then across two sources.

Step 4

Every Unit

- **Unit Benchmark Assessments** assess mastery of unit skills: phonemic awareness, phonics, comprehension, high-frequency words, and writing.

- **Unit Benchmark Assessments** provide professional development and support with performance-based assessment.

- **Performance-Based Assessments** assess children's ability to demonstrate text-based comprehension and application of higher-order thinking skills.

Step 5

End the Year

- **End-of-Year Benchmark Assessments** measures student mastery of skills covered in all six units with options for performance-based assessment.

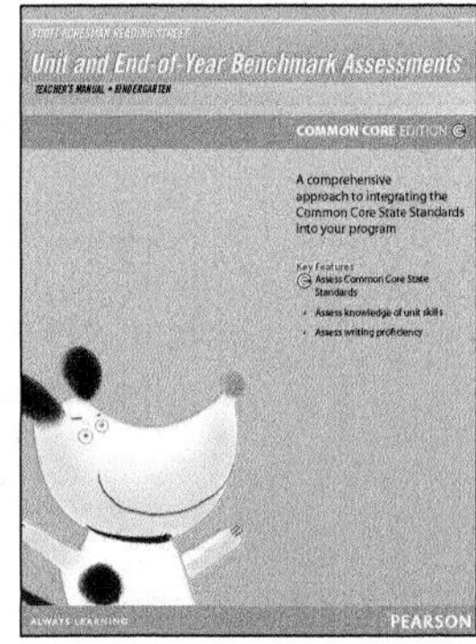

5 Steps to Success on Reading Street

1. Begin the Year
2. Every Day
3. Every Week
4. Every Unit
5. End the Year

Implementing eStreet Interactive

Power up your classroom and put time back on your side!

eStreet Interactive
www.ReadingStreet.com

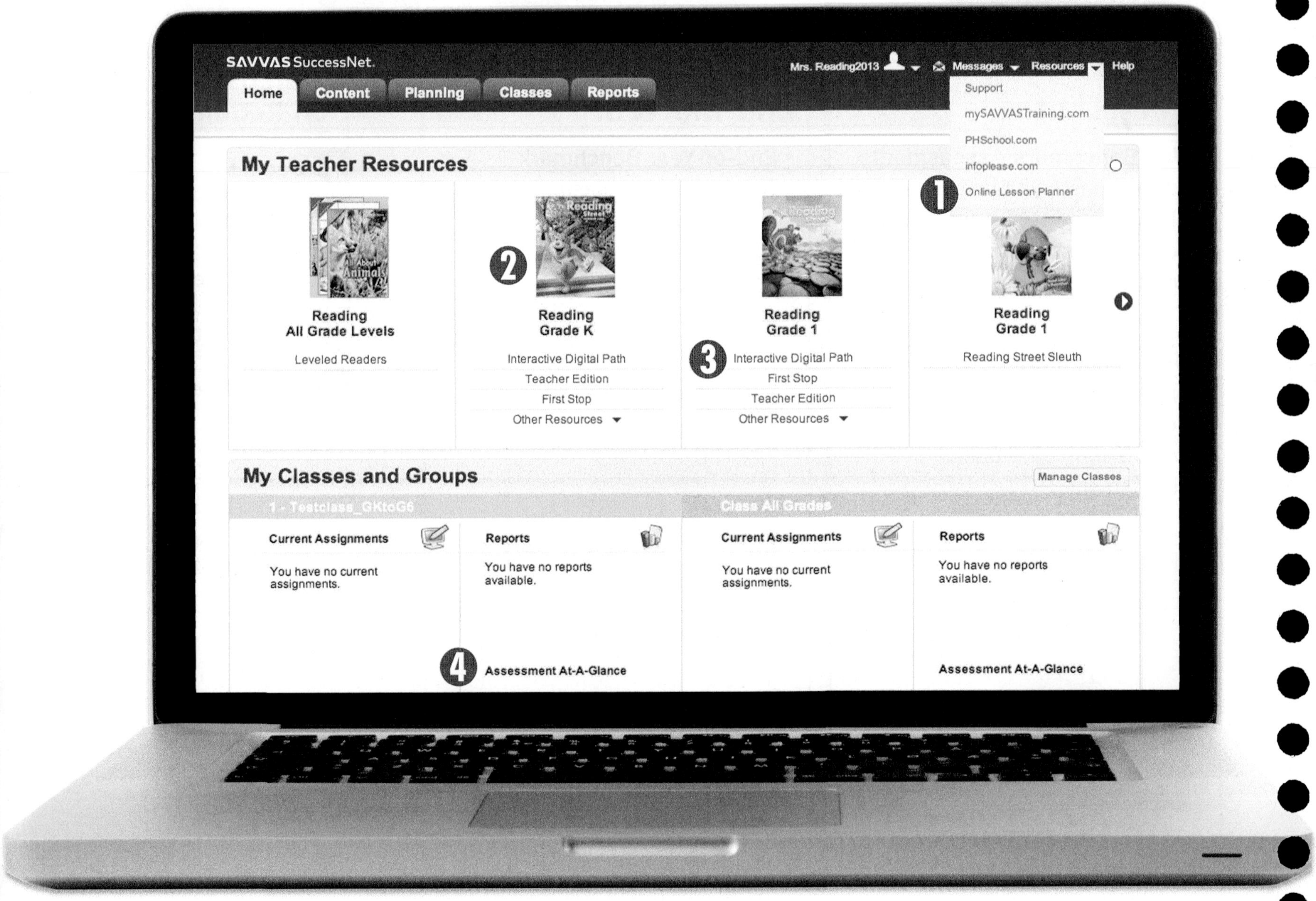

Additional Digital Support

AudioText CD
Sing with Me CD
Background Building CD
Teacher Resources DVD

Plan

Customize your daily plan by clicking, dragging, and posting!

- Online Lesson Planner
- Online Teacher's Edition

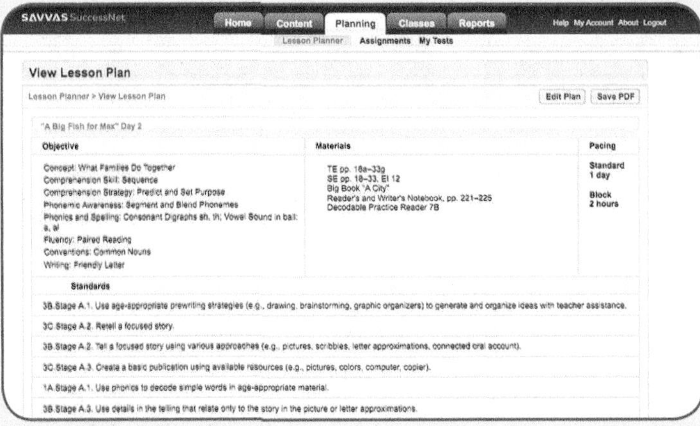

Online Lesson Planner

Teach

Engage through interactive media!

- Concept Talk Videos
- Interactive Sing with Me Chart
- Letter Tile Drag and Drop
- Envision It! Animations
- Grammar Jammer

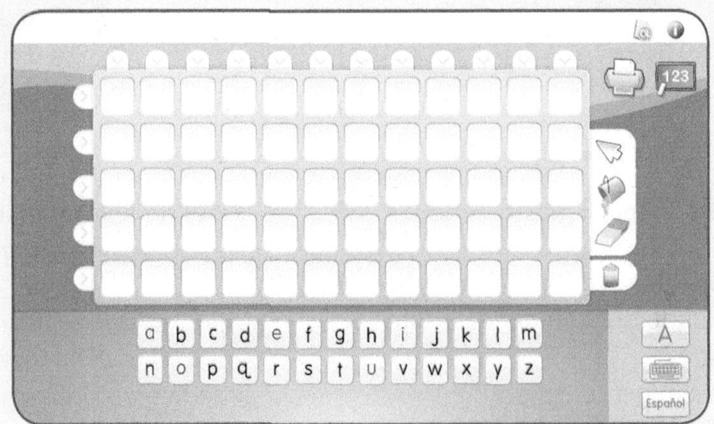

Letter Tile Drag and Drop

Practice

Motivate through personalized practice activities!

- Story Sort
- Savvas eText
- Vocabulary Activities
- Leveled Reader Database

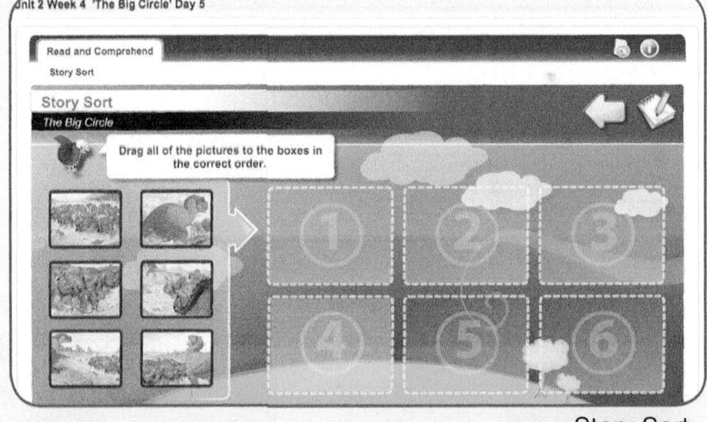

Story Sort

Manage

Respond to individual needs!

- Monitor Student Progress
- Assign

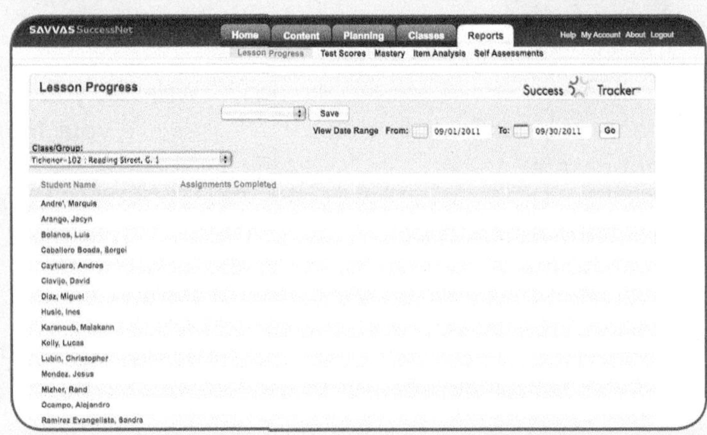

Class Management

Content Knowledge

How do we live, work, and play together?

WEEK 1

The Little School Bus

How do children get to school?

Social Studies Knowledge Goals

Children understand that riding the bus together

- helps them get to school
- helps them arrive safely

WEEK 2

We Are So Proud!

How do school children work and play together?

Social Studies Knowledge Goals

Children understand that working together with classmates

- helps them share tools and supplies
- helps them solve problems

WEEK 3

Plaidypus Lost

How do families cooperate?

Social Studies Knowledge Goals

Children understand that support from their families

- helps them take care of themselves
- helps them take care of their friends

WEEK 4

Miss Bindergarten Takes a Field Trip

How do people in a community cooperate?

Social Studies Knowledge Goals

Children understand that cooperating with others

- helps them have a fun time
- helps them learn new things

WEEK 5

Smash! Crash!

What do you like to do with your friends?

Social Studies Knowledge Goals

Children understand that playing with others

- helps them share fun experiences
- helps them share a common goal

WEEK 6

Dig Dig Digging

How do machines help people work?

Science Knowledge Goals

Children understand that working with machines

- helps get a lot of work done
- helps with many different jobs

Teaching the Common Core State Standards This Week

The Common Core State Standards for English Language Arts are divided into strands for **Reading** (including **Foundational Skills**), **Writing**, **Speaking and Listening**, and **Language**. The chart below shows some of the content you will teach this week, strand by strand. Turn to this week's 5-Day Planner on pages 10–11 to see how this content is taught each day.

Reading Strand

- **Phonological Awareness:** Rhyming Words
- **Letter Recognition:** *Aa, Bb, Cc, Dd, Ee*
- **Text-Based Comprehension:** Character
- **High-Frequency Words:** *am, I*
- **Genre:** Animal Fantasy

Common Core State Standards for English Language Arts

Writing Strand

- **Wonderful, Marvelous Me**
- **Respond to Literature**
- **Genre:** Song
- **Extend the Concept**
- **This Week We...**

Speaking and Listening Strand

- **Content Knowledge:** Build Oral Language
- **Listening and Speaking:** Follow Directions

Language Strand

- **Oral Vocabulary: Amazing Words** *first, second, third, fourth, fifth, sixth*
- **Vocabulary:** Words for Transportation
- **Academic Vocabulary:** *character, name, rhyme, song, directions, myth, alphabet, beginning, ending, drawing, letter sound relationship, picture book, story, print, title, word, read*
- **Conventions:** Say Our Names

Text-Based Comprehension

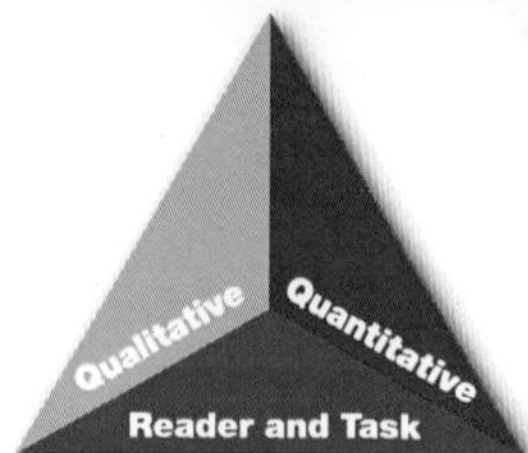

Text Complexity Measures

Use the rubric to familiarize yourself with the text complexity of ***The Little School Bus.***

Bridge to Complex Knowledge

Qualitative Measures		
	Levels of Meaning	understand what makes each animal in the story unique; personification
	Structure	simple rhyme; predictable structure
	Language Conventionality and Clarity	humor; close alignment between images and text; sentences that include lists
	Theme and Knowledge Demands	a basic understanding of why some students ride a school bus; common experiences

Reader and Task Suggestions

FORMATIVE ASSESSMENT Based on assessment results, use the **Reader and Task Suggestions** in Access Main Selection to scaffold the selection or support independence for children as they read ***The Little School Bus.***

READER AND TASK SUGGESTIONS	
Preparing to Read the Text	**Leveled Tasks**
• Review the Amazing Words and have children use them to talk about the selection. • Discuss the use of rhyming words and repetition in this predictable story.	• **Structure** If children have difficulty remembering the order in which the animal characters boarded the bus, they can reread pages 22–23, emphasizing the rhyming descriptions. • **Language Conventionality and Clarity** If children need reinforcement of the connection between the illustrations and the text, have them look at the illustration on pages 14–15 and name and describe each character.

Recommended Placement This text is appropriate for placement as a read aloud at this level due to the qualitative elements of the selection.

Focus on Common Core State Standards

Text-Based Comprehension

 **Character**
CCSS Literature 1., CCSS Literature 2., CCSS Literature 3.

Letter Recognition

 ***Aa, Bb, Cc, Dd, Ee***
CCSS Foundational Skills 1., CCSS Foundational Skills 1.d.

Writing and Conventions

Genre: Song
CCSS Writing 2.

Conventions: Say Our Names
CCSS Speaking/Listening 1.a.

Oral Vocabulary

Amazing Words

first	second
third	fourth
fifth	sixth

CCSS Language 6.

Phonological Awareness

Rhyming Words
CCSS Foundational Skills 2.a.

High-Frequency Words

I am

CCSS Foundational Skills 3.c.

Listening and Speaking

Follow Directions
CCSS Speaking/Listening 1.a., CCSS Speaking/Listening 3.

Preview Your Week

How do children get to school?

Genre: Animal Fantasy

Letter Recognition: *Aa, Bb, Cc, Dd, Ee*

Text-Based Comprehension: Character

Build Content Knowledge

KNOWLEDGE GOALS
Children will learn that riding the bus together

- helps them get to school
- helps them arrive safely

BUILD ORAL VOCABULARY
This week, children will acquire the following academic vocabulary/ domain-specific words.

Amazing Words

first	second
third	fourth
fifth	sixth

BUILD INDEPENDENT READERS
Children will enjoy becoming independent readers as they build decoding skills.

Get Set, Roll! Reader

Decodable Reader

OPTIONAL CONCEPT-BASED READING Use the Digital Path to access readers offering different levels of text complexity.

Concept Literacy

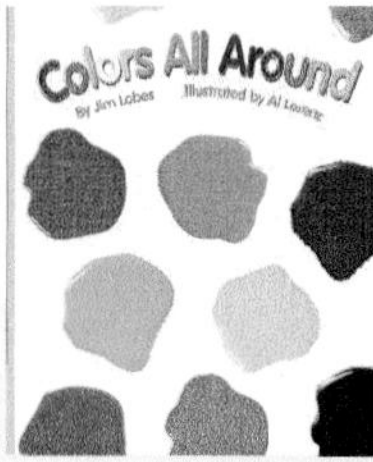

Listen to Me Reader

Student Reader

Independent Reader

This Week's Digital Resources

eStreet Interactive
www.ReadingStreet.com

Get Ready to Read

Big Question Video This video on the Digital Path introduces children to the unit question, *How do we live, work, and play together?*, and provides background for the reading children will do throughout the unit.

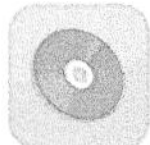
Background Building Audio CD This audio CD provides valuable background information about the ways that people cooperate to help children read and comprehend the weekly texts.

Concept Talk Video Use this video on the Digital Path to build momentum and introduce the weekly concept of how children get to school.

Interactive Sing with Me Chart and Audio "How We Get to School," sung to the tune of "Mary Had a Little Lamb," introduces the Amazing Words with a catchy, concept-related song.

Phonics Songs and Rhymes Audio "A Bus Comes Along Every Day," sung to the tune of "If You're Happy and You Know It," helps children recognize *Aa, Bb, Cc, Dd,* and *Ee*.

Letter Tile Drag and Drop Using this interactive tool, children click and spell words to enhance their newly learned phonics skills.

Savvas eText For phonics and fluency support, use the eText of the Decodable Reader; the Student Reader; and the Get Set, Roll! Reader on the Leveled Reader Database.

Read and Comprehend

Envision It! Animations Use this colorful animation on the Digital Path to explain the target comprehension skill, Character.

Savvas eText Go to Savvas SuccessNet and use the eText of the many student edition pages in *My Skills Buddy* with audio support.

Story Sort Use the Story Sort Activity on the Digital Path after reading *The Little School Bus* to involve children in retelling.

Language Arts

Grammar Jammer Choose a whimsical animation on the Digital Path to provide an engaging lesson on Say Our Names that will capture children's attention.

Additional Resources

Teacher Resources DVD-ROM Use the following resources on the TR DVD or on Savvas SuccessNet throughout the week:

- Amazing Word Cards
- High-Frequency Word Cards
- Daily Fix-It Transparencies
- Reader's and Writer's Notebook
- Scoring Rubrics

This Week's Skills

Letter Recognition
Aa, Bb, Cc, Dd, Ee

Comprehension
Skill: Character

Language
Vocabulary: Words for Transportation
Conventions: Say Our Names

Writing
Wonderful, Marvelous Me!
Respond to Literature
Genre Writing
Extend the Concept
This Week We …

5-Day Planner

DAY 1

Get Ready to Read

Content Knowledge 16
Oral Vocabulary: *first, second, third, fourth, fifth, sixth*

Phonological Awareness 18
Rhyming Words
Monitor Progress
Check Phonological Awareness

Letter Recognition 20
Aa

Handwriting 22
A and *a*

High-Frequency Words 23
I, am

READ Decodable Story 1 24
I Am!

Read and Comprehend

Text-Based Comprehension 26
Character

Language Arts

Conventions 28
Say Our Names

Writing 29
Wonderful, Marvelous Me!
Daily Handwriting

Listening and Speaking 30
Follow Directions

Extend Your Day! 31

DAY 2

Get Ready to Read

Content Knowledge 32
Oral Vocabulary: *first, second*

Phonological Awareness 34
Rhyming Words

Letter Recognition 36
Bb
Monitor Progress
Check Letter Recognition

Handwriting 38
B and *b*

High-Frequency Words 39
I, am

READ Decodable Reader 1 40
Who Am I?

Read and Comprehend

Text-Based Comprehension 42
READ *The Little School Bus*—1st Read
Think, Talk, and Write
Monitor Progress Check Retelling

Language Arts

Conventions 45
Say Our Names

Writing 46
Respond to Literature
Daily Handwriting

Vocabulary 47
Words for Transportation

Extend Your Day! 49

DAY 3

Get Ready to Read

Content Knowledge 50
Oral Vocabulary: *third, fourth*

Phonological Awareness 52
Rhyming Words

Letter Recognition 54
Cc

Monitor Progress
Check Word Reading
High-Frequency Words

READ Kindergarten Student Reader 56
Cat and Dog at School

Read and Comprehend

Text-Based Comprehension 58
READ *The Little School Bus*—
2nd Read

Language Arts

Conventions 76
Say Our Names

Writing 77
Song
Daily Handwriting

Listening and Speaking 78
Follow Directions

Extend Your Day! 81

DAY 4

Get Ready to Read

Content Knowledge 82
Oral Vocabulary: *fifth, sixth*

Phonological Awareness 84
Rhyming Words

Monitor Progress
Check Phonological Awareness

Letter Recognition 86
Dd

Get Set, Roll! Reader 1 87
READ *Jack and Max*

Read and Comprehend

Text-Based Comprehension 88
Character
READ *The Little School Bus*—
3rd Read

Language Arts

Conventions 90
Say Our Names

Writing 91
Extend the Concept
Daily Handwriting

Vocabulary 92
Words for Transportation

Extend Your Day! 93

DAY 5

Get Ready to Read

Content Knowledge 94
Review Oral Vocabulary

Monitor Progress
Check Oral Vocabulary

Phonological Awareness 96
Review Rhyming Words

Letter Recognition 96
Ee

Assessment 98

Monitor Progress
Letter Recognition and Word Reading

Read and Comprehend

Let's Practice It! 100
Myth

Assessment 102
Review Character

Language Arts

Conventions 104
Review Say Our Names

Writing 105
This Week We ...
Daily Handwriting

Wrap Up Your Week! 106

Extend Your Day! 107

Access for All

What do I do in group time?
It's as easy as 1-2-3!

1 TEACHER-LED SMALL GROUPS → 2 INDEPENDENT PRACTICE STATIONS → 3 INDEPENDENT READING

Small Group Time

SKILL DEVELOPMENT

Rhyming Words
Aa, Bb, Cc, Dd, Ee
Character

DEEP UNDERSTANDING

This Week's Knowledge Goals
Children will learn that riding the bus together
- helps them get to school
- helps them arrive safely

1 Small Group Lesson Plan

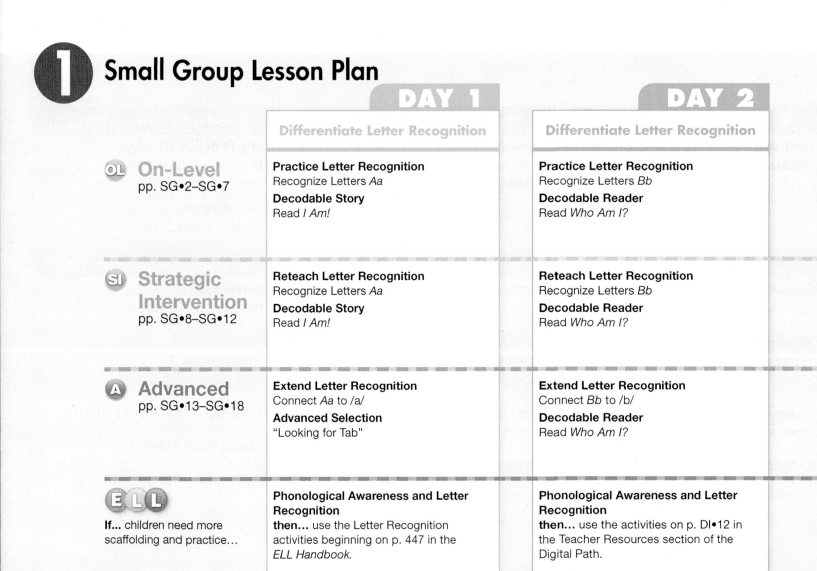

	DAY 1: Differentiate Letter Recognition	DAY 2: Differentiate Letter Recognition
On-Level pp. SG•2–SG•7	**Practice Letter Recognition** Recognize Letters *Aa* **Decodable Story** Read *I Am!*	**Practice Letter Recognition** Recognize Letters *Bb* **Decodable Reader** Read *Who Am I?*
Strategic Intervention pp. SG•8–SG•12	**Reteach Letter Recognition** Recognize Letters *Aa* **Decodable Story** Read *I Am!*	**Reteach Letter Recognition** Recognize Letters *Bb* **Decodable Reader** Read *Who Am I?*
Advanced pp. SG•13–SG•18	**Extend Letter Recognition** Connect *Aa* to /a/ **Advanced Selection** "Looking for Tab"	**Extend Letter Recognition** Connect *Bb* to /b/ **Decodable Reader** Read *Who Am I?*
ELL If... children need more scaffolding and practice...	**Phonological Awareness and Letter Recognition** then... use the Letter Recognition activities beginning on p. 447 in the *ELL Handbook.*	**Phonological Awareness and Letter Recognition** then... use the activities on p. DI•12 in the Teacher Resources section of the Digital Path.

Reading Street Sleuth Read Aloud

- Provides access to grade-level text for all students
- Focuses on finding clues in text through close reading
- Builds capacity for complex text

Build Text-Based Comprehension

The Little School Bus

Optional Leveled Readers

Concept Literacy

Below Level

On Level

Advanced

Get Set, Roll! Reader

Decodable Reader

DAY 3	DAY 4	DAY 5
Differentiate Vocabulary	**Differentiate Language**	**Differentiate Close Reading**
Develop Vocabulary Practice Words for Transportation **Student Reader** Read *Cat and Dog At School*	**Build** Sentences and Words **Get Set, Roll! Reader** Read *Jack and Max*	**Practice Letter Recognition** Recognize Letters *Cc, Dd, Ee* **Text-Based Comprehension** Read "Riding Mr. Frank's Bus"
Develop Vocabulary Reteach Words for Transportation **Student Reader** Read *Cat and Dog At School*	**Talk About** Sentences and Words **Get Set, Roll! Reader** Read *Jack and Max*	**Reteach Letter Recognition** Recognize Letters *Cc, Dd, Ee* **Text-Based Comprehension** Read "Riding Mr. Frank's Bus"
Develop Vocabulary More Words for Transportation **Student Reader** Read *Cat and Dog At School*	**Extend** Sentences and Words **Get Set, Roll! Reader** Read *Jack and Max*	**Extend Letter Recognition** Connect Letters to Sounds **Text-Based Comprehension** Read "Riding Mr. Frank's Bus"
Vocabulary **then...** use the ELL activities on p. DI•14 in the Teacher Resources section of the Digital Path.	**Developing Language** **then...** use the Language Workshops beginning on p. 306 in the *ELL Handbook.*	**Comprehension** **then...** use the ELL activities on pp. DI•13–DI•14 in the Teacher Resources section of the Digital Path.

Independent Stations

Practice This Week's Skills

Focus on these activities when time is limited.

ACCESS FOR ALL

- Below-Level Activities
- On-Level Activities
- Advanced Activities

LISTEN UP!

Identify words that rhyme.

OBJECTIVES

- Listen to and identify words that rhyme.

MATERIALS

- *Listen Up!* Flip Chart Activity 1
- Picture Cards: *man, fan, cat, hat, jet, net*
- paper, pencils, crayons

 **Modeled Pronunciation Audio CD**

- ● Children name each Picture Card.
- ▲ Children name each Picture Card and find two Picture Cards that rhyme.
- ■ Children name each Picture Card and match all the Picture Cards that rhyme.

WORD WORK

Identify letters *Aa, Bb, Cc, Dd, Ee.*

OBJECTIVES

- Identify letters *Aa, Bb, Cc, Dd, Ee.*

MATERIALS

- *Word Work* Flip Chart Activity 1
- Alphabet Cards: *Aa, Bb, Cc, Dd, Ee*
- Letter Tiles
- paper, pencils

 **Interactive Sound-Spelling Cards** 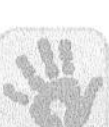 **Letter Tile Drag and Drop**

- ● Children find Alphabet Cards for letters *Aa, Bb, Cc, Dd,* and *Ee.*
- ▲ Children match Alphabet Cards *Aa, Bb, Cc, Dd,* and *Ee* with Letter Tiles.
- ■ Children match Alphabet Cards *Aa, Bb, Cc, Dd,* and *Ee* with Letter Tiles and write each letter.

LET'S WRITE!

Write our names.

OBJECTIVES

- Write our names.

MATERIALS

- *Let's Write!* Flip Chart Activity 1
- paper, pencils, crayons

 **Grammar Jammer**

- ● Children draw a picture of themselves and write their names.
- ▲ Children draw a picture of themselves going to school and write their names.
- ■ Children draw a picture of themselves going to school and write their first and last names.

WORDS TO KNOW

Practice vocabulary.

OBJECTIVES

- Identify words for transportation.

MATERIALS

- *Words to Know* Flip Chart Activity 1
- Picture Cards: *bus, boat, box, taxi, tiger, tub, train, van*
- Teacher-made word cards: *bus, boat, box, taxi, tiger, tub, train, van*
- paper, crayons

 **Vocabulary Activities**  **Teacher Resources**
- High-Frequency Word Cards for Unit 1, Week 1

- ● Children choose Picture Cards for ways people go places.
- ▲ Children choose Picture Cards for ways people go places. Then they draw a picture that shows how they go somewhere.
- ■ Children match the Picture Cards and word cards that show how people go places.

READ FOR MEANING

Use text-based comprehension tools.

OBJECTIVES

- Identify and describe a story character.

MATERIALS

- *Read for Meaning* Flip Chart Activity 1
- Little Book *The Little School Bus*
- paper, pencils, crayons

Envision It! Animations
- Leveled eReaders

● Children look at the book and draw a picture of a character in the story.

▲ Children look at the book and draw a picture of a character in the story. Then they write the name of that character.

■ Children look at the book and draw a picture of a character in the story. Then they write something about the character.

LET'S MAKE ART!

Use art to demonstrate understanding.

OBJECTIVES

- Decorate a school bus.

MATERIALS

- *Let's Make Art!* Flip Chart Activity 1
- Teacher-made outline of a school bus
- crayons, construction paper scraps, safety scissors, glue

● Children decorate the school bus and draw themselves on the bus.

▲ Children decorate the school bus and draw themselves on the bus. Then they write their names.

■ Children decorate the school bus and draw themselves and someone else on the bus. Then they write their names.

Manage the Stations

Use these management tools to set up and organize your Practice Stations:

Practice Station Flip Charts

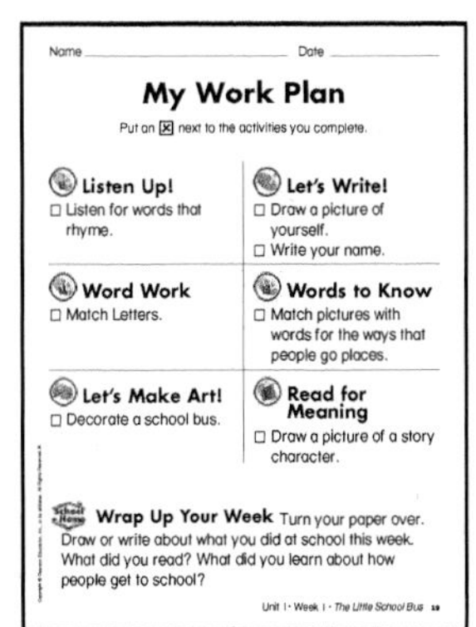
Name Date

My Work Plan

Put an ☒ next to the activities you complete.

Listen Up! ☐ Listen for words that rhyme.	**Let's Write!** ☐ Draw a picture of yourself. ☐ Write your name.
Word Work ☐ Match Letters.	**Words to Know** ☐ Match pictures with words for the ways that people go places.
Let's Make Art! ☐ Decorate a school bus.	**Read for Meaning** ☐ Draw a picture of a story character.

Wrap Up Your Week Turn your paper over. Draw or write about what you did at school this week. What did you read? What did you learn about how people get to school?

Unit 1 • Week 1 • The Little School Bus

Classroom Management Handbook for Differentiated Instruction Practice Stations, p. 19

3 Independent Reading

Help children choose complex texts so that they can engage in paired and group reading and writing activities every day before, during, and after school.

Suggestions for this week's independent reading:

- *Fluffy's School Bus Adventure* by Kate McMullan
- *The Boy on the Bus* by Penny Dale

BOOK TALK Have pairs or groups of children actively engage in reading activities through a discussion of their independent reading for the week. Focus their discussions with the following ideas:

Key Ideas and Details
- Retell the text to your partner or group.
- Identify the main idea and one detail of the text.

Craft and Structure
- Name the title and author of the text.
- Talk about illustrations in the text.

Integration of Ideas
- With support, describe text/illustration relationships.
- Was this book like others I have read?

Savvas eText
- Student Edition
- Decodable Readers
- Get Set, Roll! Readers
- Leveled Readers

Materials from School or Classroom Library

DAY 1 at a Glance

Content Knowledge
Oral Vocabulary

Phonological Awareness
Rhyming Words

Letter Recognition
Letters *Aa*

Handwriting
A and *a*

High-Frequency Words
I, am

Text-Based Comprehension
Character

Conventions
Say Our Names

Writing
Wonderful, Marvelous Me!

Listening and Speaking
Follow Directions

Materials

- Student Edition
- Truckery Rhymes
- Talk with Me/Sing with Me Chart
- Reader's and Writer's Notebook
- Alphabet Cards
- Picture Cards
- Phonics Songs and Rhymes Chart

Bridge to Common Core

INTEGRATION OF KNOWLEDGE/IDEAS
This week children read, write, and talk about how children get to school together.

Texts This Week

- "How We Get to School"
- "At the Bus Stop"
- *The Little School Bus*
- *Cat and Dog at School*
- "Mary Had a Little Lamb"

Social Studies Knowledge Goals
Children will understand that riding the bus together

- helps them get to school
- helps them arrive safely

Start your engines!
Display p. 5 of *Truckery Rhymes.*

- Read aloud "Jack Be Nimble" and track the print.
  - Reread the rhyme and have children chime in as they wish.
    - Ask children to identify rhyming words. (*quick, brick*)

Truckery Rhymes

Content Knowledge

Getting to School Together

CONCEPT TALK To explore the unit concept of All Together Now, tell children that this week they will listen, talk, sing, read, and write about how children cooperate. Write the Question of the Week on the board, *How do children get to school?* Track each word as you read.

Build Oral Language

TALK ABOUT GOING TO SCHOOL TOGETHER Display Talk with Me Chart 1A. This week we will learn about how people cooperate while living, working, and playing together. One way we cooperate is by taking turns. The chart shows the six children standing in order. The numbers tell the order of the children. Let's point to the child with the number 1.

We are going to learn six Amazing Words that will help us talk about taking turns. Listen as I say each word: *first, second, third, fourth, fifth, sixth.* Point to the child who is first. Continue with the other Amazing Words. Have children say each Amazing Word as you point to the picture.

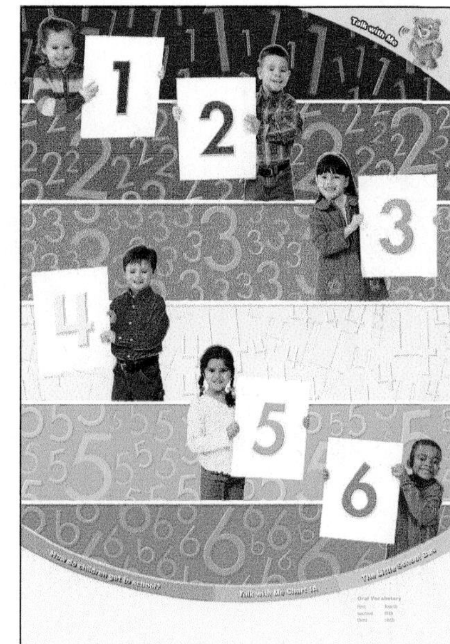

Talk with Me/Sing with Me Chart 1A

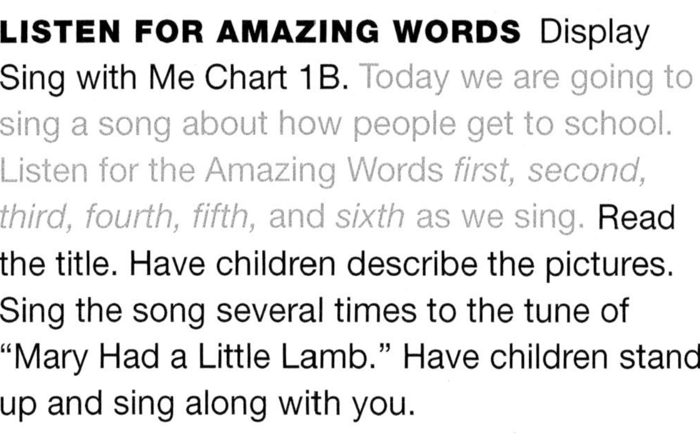

LISTEN FOR AMAZING WORDS Display Sing with Me Chart 1B. Today we are going to sing a song about how people get to school. Listen for the Amazing Words *first, second, third, fourth, fifth,* and *sixth* as we sing. Read the title. Have children describe the pictures. Sing the song several times to the tune of "Mary Had a Little Lamb." Have children stand up and sing along with you.

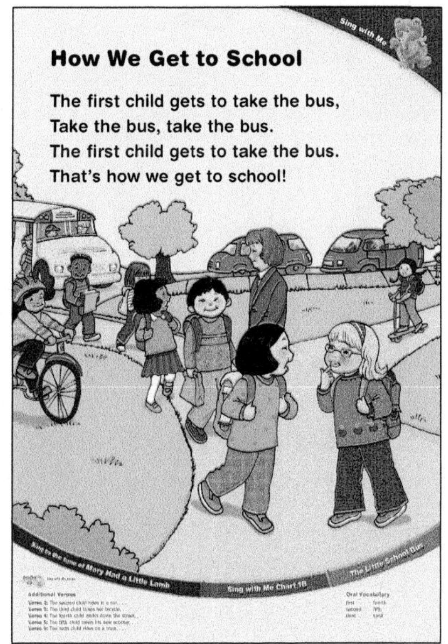

The first child gets to take the bus,
Take the bus, take the bus.
The first child gets to take the bus.

Talk with Me/Sing with Me Chart 1B

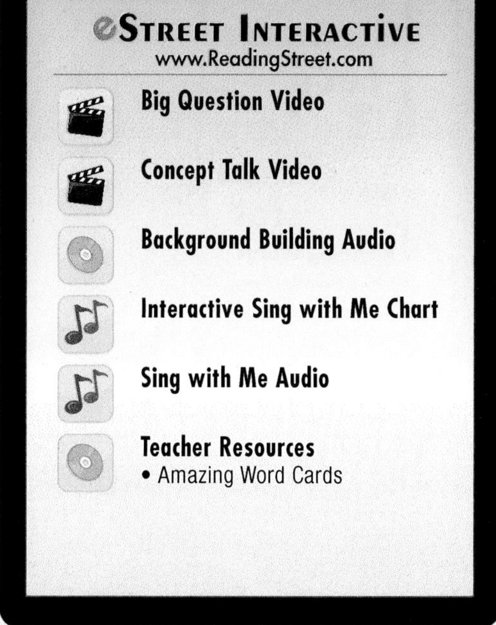

eStreet Interactive
www.ReadingStreet.com
Big Question Video
Concept Talk Video
Background Building Audio
Interactive Sing with Me Chart
Sing with Me Audio
Teacher Resources
• Amazing Word Cards

Amazing Words

You'll learn 216 words this year.

You'll learn 006 words this week!

first	second
third	fourth
fifth	sixth

Access for All

SI Strategic Intervention

Review Concept Review numbers 1–6 with children. Write the numbers on the board and have children copy them on their Write-On Boards.

ELL

Access Content Have English learners say the name of each ordinal number in their home languages as they show the appropriate number of fingers.

ELL Support Additional ELL support and modified instruction is provided in the *ELL Handbook* and in the ELL Support lessons on the *Teacher Resources DVD-ROM.*

Preteach Concepts Use the Day 1 instruction on ELL Poster 1 to assess and build background knowledge, develop concepts, and build oral vocabulary.

Common Core State Standards
Foundational Skills 2.a. Recognize and produce rhyming words.

Phonological Awareness

Let's Listen for Rhyming Words

- Find things that rhyme.
- What rhymes with *man?* with *mop?* with *coat?* with *book?*
- Which word pairs rhyme: *nap/lap, cook/coat, boat/goat?*

READING STREET ONLINE
BIG QUESTION VIDEO
www.ReadingStreet.com

12 13

My Skills Buddy, pp. 12–13

Foundational Skills 2.a. Recognize and produce rhyming words.

Access for All

Advanced

Extend Language Help children make a rhyming picture book. Have them draw a picture that shows rhyming words, such as a *cat* wearing a *hat.* Write the rhyming words on children's pictures. Assemble and display the group book.

Phonological Awareness

Rhyming Words

TEACH Today we will learn about rhyming words. Listen as I say some rhyming words: *pig, dig, wig, big.* Say the words with me: *pig, dig, wig, big.* These are rhyming words because the middle and ending parts of the words sound the same.

MODEL Have children look at the picture on pp. 12–13 of *My Skills Buddy.* Tell them that they will be looking for pictures of rhyming words. I see a paint can in this picture. What do you see that rhymes with *can?* I see a pan. *Pan* has the same middle and ending parts as *can.*

GUIDE PRACTICE As children name example words from the picture, guide them in stating that the words have the same middle and ending parts. Discuss with children the first bulleted item on p. 12 of *My Skills Buddy.* Save the other bulleted items for discussion on Day 2.

Corrective feedback	**If...** children cannot hear the rhyming words, **then...** say each word and stretch the ending part: /k/ /a/ /a/ /a/ /n/ /n/ /n/ and /p/ /a/ /a/ /a/ /n/ /n/ /n/.

DISCRIMINATE RHYMING WORDS To identify rhyming words, I say the words and listen to their middle and ending parts. My words are *big, cat,* and *pig.* I say the words *big, cat, pig.* I listen to the middle and ending parts. The words *big* and *pig* have the same middle and ending parts, so *big* and *pig* are rhyming words.

Display Picture Cards *cat, dog,* and *bat.* Let's say the words together as we listen to the middle and ending parts of the words. Say the words several times together as children listen for the rhyming words. Have children identify the rhyming words *cat* and *bat.* Continue with the following sets of Picture Cards: *cap, map, boat; can, mask, man; fox, top, mop.*

Picture Card

Picture Card

REVIEW Say three words and have children identify the words that rhyme. Listen: *cab, jam, tab; vet, cap, nap; bed, hop, mop; mouse, house, mom.*

Picture Card

Teacher Tip

Help children separate the initial consonant in each word so that they identify the ending part of the word as the part that rhymes.

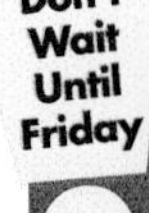

MONITOR PROGRESS Check Phonological Awareness Rhyming Words

FORMATIVE ASSESSMENT Say the words *hop, cat,* and *top.* Ask children to identify the two words that rhyme. Continue with these word groups: *hay, day, see; cat, men, bat; cap, red, bed.*

If... children cannot identify rhyming words,

then... use the small-group Strategic Intervention lesson, p. SG•8, to reteach rhyming words.

Support Phonological Awareness
Some children may have difficulty identifying and pronouncing some English sounds. Isolate the sounds in the rhyming word parts and help children listen to and say the sounds.

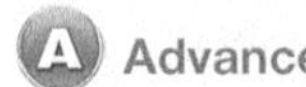

Common Core State Standards

Foundational Skills 1.d. Recognize and name all upper- and lowercase letters of the alphabet. **Foundational Skills 2.c.** Blend and segment onsets and rimes of single-syllable spoken words. **Foundational Skills 2.e.** Add or substitute individual sounds (phonemes) in simple, one-syllable words to make new words. **Also Foundational Skills 1.**

Access for All

Advanced

Letter Recognition Have children use clay to form the letters and then trace the letters to remember the uppercase *A* and lowercase *a* letter forms. Have children say the letter names as they trace the clay letters.

Academic Vocabulary

alphabet all the letters of a language; in English, the alphabet is *a, b, c, d, e, f, g, h, i, j, k, l, m, n, o, p, q, r, s, t, u, v, w, x, y,* and *z.*

Letter Recognition

Teach/Model

Letters *Aa*

INTRODUCE Display the *Aa* Alphabet Card. Point to uppercase *A*. This is uppercase letter *A*. What is this letter? Point to lowercase *a*. This is lowercase letter *a*. What is this letter? Explain that the letter *a* is the first letter of the alphabet.

Aa
astronaut
Alphabet Card

MODEL Write "A Bus Comes Along Every Day" on the board. Point to the first *A*. This is uppercase *A*. Point to *Along*. This word begins with uppercase letter *A* too. Point to the *a* in *Day*. This word has a lowercase letter *a* in it. These words tell the song we are going to sing: "A Bus Comes Along Every Day."

Guide Practice

GROUP PRACTICE Display Phonics Songs and Rhymes Chart 1. Teach children the song "A Bus Comes Along Every Day" sung to the tune of "If You're Happy and You Know It." Play the CD and sing the song several times. When children are familiar with the song, have them sing it with you. Then have them come up and point to each uppercase *A* and lowercase *a* on the chart.

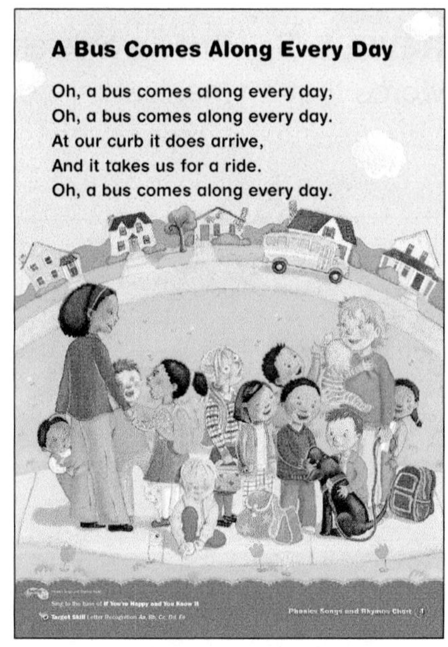
A Bus Comes Along Every Day
Oh, a bus comes along every day,
Oh, a bus comes along every day.
At our curb it does arrive,
And it takes us for a ride.
Oh, a bus comes along every day.
Phonics Songs and Rhymes Chart 1

ON THEIR OWN Have children look around the room and find examples of uppercase *A* and lowercase *a*. As each letter is found, have the group say the name of the letter.

Blend Words

REVIEW Write the following letters in a row on the board: *A, C, D, A, A, V, A, A.* Have children point to and circle each uppercase *A.* Repeat the process with these letters for lowercase *a: c, a, d, a, a, g, a, o.*

CONNECT Say the word *at.* Have children say the word with you. Now say /b/ and ask children what the word would be if you add /b/ and /at/ together. Blend the sounds with children to make the word *bat.* Repeat the blending several times so that children understand how to blend the sounds together.

MODEL When I say the word *bat,* it begins with /b/. If I want to make a new word that begins with /h/, I say /h/ and /at/ to make the word *hat.* Have children blend the sounds with you and repeat the blending several times.

GUIDE PRACTICE Let's make some more words. When I say a new sound, add the sound to /at/ to make a word. Use the following sounds: /m/, /k/, /p/, /r/, /s/. Have children blend the sounds and say the new words.

Corrective feedback	**If...** children have trouble blending sounds, **then...** model blending any of the sounds from words used in the lesson. Have children blend the sounds with you and say the new word.

Teacher Tip

Have children repeat the sounds several times as they do the blending routine: /b/ /b/ /b/ /at/ /at/ /at/. Continue with /h/ /h/ /h/ /at/ /at/ /at/.

Letter Names Children whose home languages share the characters *Aa* may know the letters by different names or pronunciations. Emphasize that this letter name is pronounced /ā/ in English, and have children say the letter name with you several times.

Common Core State Standards

Foundational Skills 3.c. Read common high-frequency words by sight (e.g., *the, of, to, you, she, my, is, are, do, does*). **Language 1.a.** Print many upper- and lowercase letters. **Also Foundational Skills 1.b.**

Handwriting

INTRODUCE Write *Aa* on the board and point to *A.* This is uppercase *A.* We use uppercase letters at the beginning of sentences and for the first letter in a person's name.

MODEL UPPERCASE *A* Write *Ann* on the board. This is the name *Ann.* I use an uppercase letter for the first letter in a name. *Ann* begins with uppercase *A.* Watch as I trace the uppercase *A* with my finger. Follow the stroke instructions given below.

GUIDE PRACTICE Have children practice tracing the uppercase *A* in the air. Use your finger to make an uppercase *A* in the air. Now write it on your hand.

MODEL LOWERCASE *a* Write *ant* on the board. This is the word *ant.* I use a lowercase letter at the beginning of *ant.* See how I make the lowercase *a.* Write another *a* on the board, following the stroke instructions below. Again, have children write lowercase *a* in the air and on their hands.

GUIDE PRACTICE Have children use their Write-On Boards to write a row of uppercase *A* and a row of lowercase *a.*

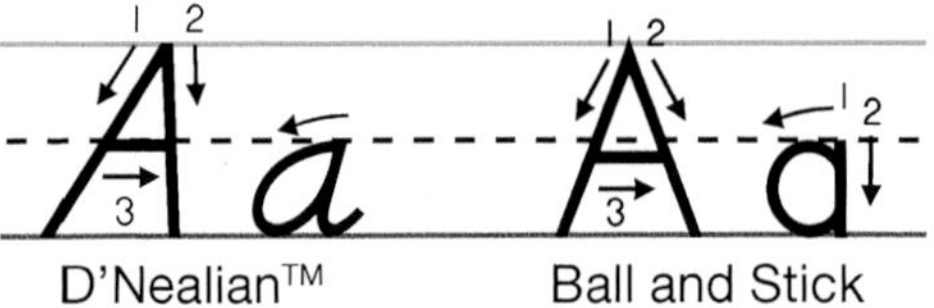

ON THEIR OWN Use *Reader's and Writer's Notebook,* pp. 3 and 4, for additional practice with initial *a.* Return to these pages on Day 2 to practice *Bb.*

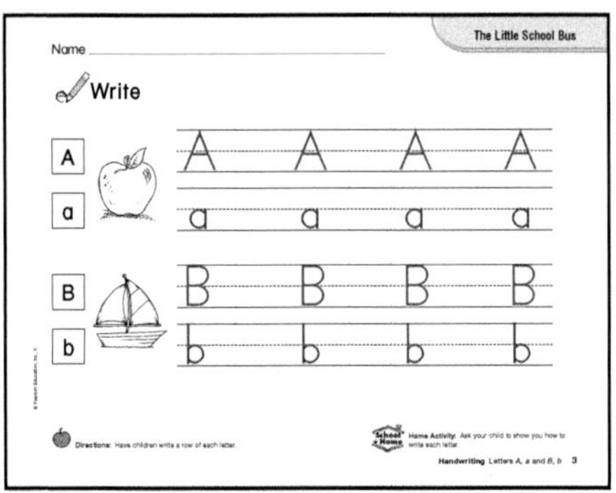

Reader's and Writer's Notebook, p. 3

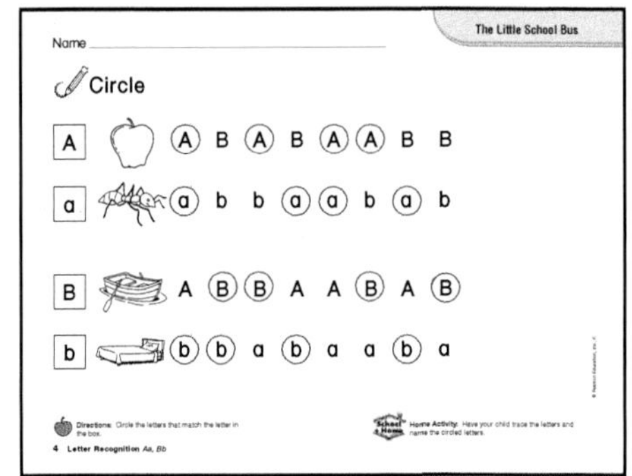

Reader's and Writer's Notebook, p. 4

High-Frequency Words

INTRODUCE Use the routine below to teach high-frequency words *I* and *am.*

Routine Nondecodable Words

1. **Say and Spell** Some words we have to learn by remembering the letters rather than saying the sounds. We will say and spell the words to help learn them. Write *I* on the board. This is the word *I*. It has one letter. The letter in the word is uppercase *I*. Have children say and spell the word with you.
2. **Demonstrate Meaning** I can use the word *I* in lots of sentences. Here is one sentence: *I like the color red.* Now you use the word in a sentence.

Repeat the routine with the word *am.*

Add *I* and *am* to the Word Wall.

Routines Flip Chart

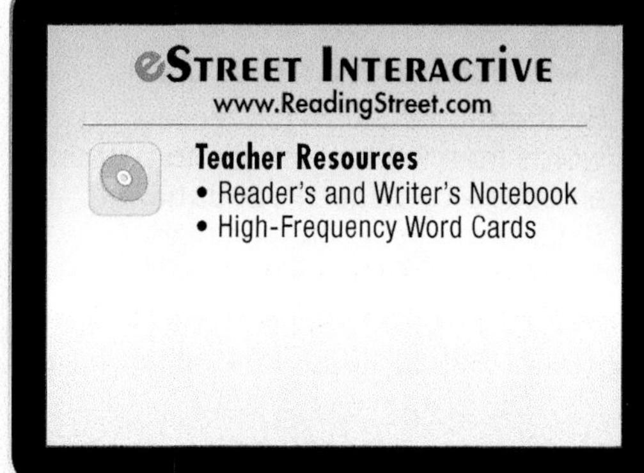

Teacher Resources

- Reader's and Writer's Notebook
- High-Frequency Word Cards

Access for All

A Advanced

High-Frequency Words Write the words *I* and *am* on the board. Ask children to point to the word you say while several children write the word on the board.

High-Frequency Words In some languages, forms of *be,* including *am,* are omitted. Speakers of Arabic, Chinese, Khmer, Russian, and Vietnamese may need extra support to understand the use of *am.* Help children by saying sentences that contrast the subjects *I* and *you,* such as *I* ***am*** *a teacher. You* ***are*** *a student.*

Common Core State Standards

Foundational Skills 1.a. Follow words from left to right, top to bottom, and page-by-page. **Foundational Skills 3.c.** Read common high-frequency words by sight (e.g., *the, of, to, you, she, my, is, are, do, does*). **Also Foundational Skills 1.**

Access for All

Strategic Intervention

Decodable Story Before children read *I Am!,* review the high-frequency words on the Word Wall with them. Have children point to the word you say.

Decodable Story 1

Read *I Am!*

REVIEW Review the following high-frequency words by having children read each word as you point to it on the Word Wall: *I, am.*

TEACH REBUS WORDS Show the *ant* Picture Card. Write the word *ant* on the board. Tell children to look at the picture and say the word with you. Look for the word *ant* in our story today. You will see the word with a picture above it to help you read the word. Continue the routine with Picture Cards for *dog* and *cat.* Use a similar routine for *bear.*

READ Tear out Decodable Story *I Am!* on pp. 5–6 of *Reader's and Writer's Notebook.* Then fold the pages to form a book. Repeat this process with each child's *Reader's and Writer's Notebook.* Distribute the self-cover books to each child.

Reader's and Writer's Notebook, pp. 5–6

Today we will read a story about some animals. First let's look at our story. This is the right way to hold the book. Model how to hold the book. Point to the letter *A* in *Am.* We know it is right side up because the letter *A* looks right. Turn the book upside down. This is the wrong way to hold a book; the letter *A* looks funny. We cannot read letters and words if they are upside down! Turn the book right side up. Pick up your copy of the book and hold it right side up. Check to see that you are holding it correctly by making sure the letter *A* is right side up. Check to see that all children are holding their books correctly.

Point to the front cover. This is the front cover of our book. *Front* means the side that faces us. Open the book. These are the pages in our story. We turn the pages from right to left. Demonstrate how to turn the pages. Now you turn the pages from right to left. Observe and make sure all children are turning the pages correctly. This is the back cover. It is the part of the book we look at last. Point to the title of the story. What is the title of our book? The title of the story is *I Am!* These are our high-frequency words! Have children read the story, holding the book right side up and turning the pages correctly.

Use the routine for reading decodable books to read Decodable Story 1.

eStreet Interactive
www.ReadingStreet.com

Teacher Resources
- Reader's and Writer's Notebook

Routine Reading Decodable Books

1. **Read Silently** Have children whisper read the story page by page as you listen in.
2. **Model Fluent Reading** Have children finger point as you read a page. Then have children reread the page without you.
3. **Read Chorally** Have children finger point as they chorally read the page. Continue reading page by page, repeating steps 1 and 2.
4. **Read Individually** Have children take turns reading aloud a page.
5. **Reread and Monitor Progress** As you listen to individual children reread, monitor progress and provide support.
6. **Reread with a Partner** Have children reread the story page by page with a partner.

Routines Flip Chart

Visual Support Books in some children's home languages may be read from right to left and back to front. Reiterate the locations of front and back covers by showing children other English-language books. Turn the pages and track the print as you read sentences from left to right.

Day 1 SMALL GROUP TIME • Differentiate Letter Recognition, p. SG•1

OL On-Level	SI Strategic Intervention	A Advanced
• **Practice Letter Recognition** Recognize Letters *Aa*	• **Reteach Letter Recognition** Recognize Letters *Aa*	• **Extend Letter Recognition** Connect *Aa* to /a/
• **Read** Decodable Story *I Am!*	• **Read** Decodable Story *I Am!*	• **Read** Advanced Selection "Looking for Tab"

Place English Language Learners in the groups that correspond to their reading abilities in English.

If... children need more support with **Letter Recognition,**
then... use the Letter Recognition activities beginning on p. 447 in the *ELL Handbook.*

Comprehension

Envision It! Literary Elements

READING STREET ONLINE
ENVISION IT! ANIMATIONS
www.ReadingStreet.com

Characters

Setting

Plot

START

FINISH

My Skills Buddy, pp. 14–15

Zoom in on

Common Core State Standards

Literature 1. With prompting and support, ask and answer questions about key details in a text.
Literature 3. With prompting and support, identify characters, settings, and major events in a story.

Skills Trace

Character

Introduce U1W1D1; U1W5D1; U4W4D1; U6W2D1

Practice U1W1D2; U1W1D3; U1W1D4; U1W5D2; U1W5D3; U1W5D4; U4W4D2; U4W4D3; U4W4D4; U6W2D2; U6W2D3; U6W2D4

Reteach/Review U1W1D5; U1W2D4; U1W5D5; U3W4D4; U4W4D5; U5W4D4; U6W2D5

Assess/Test Benchmark Assessment U1; U6

KEY: U=Unit W=Week D=Day

Text-Based Comprehension

Character

READ Remind children of the weekly concept—Getting to School Together. Have children listen as you read aloud "At the Bus Stop" on p. 27.

MODEL A CLOSE READ Model how to identify the characters in a story as a tool to build comprehension.

When I read a story, I ask myself: *Who is this story about?* At the start of this story, I learn that there are two children named Jay and Ana. I learn that Ana usually holds Jay's hand while they wait for the bus. What else will I learn about Jay and Ana?

TEACH CHARACTER A story is usually about someone or something. It can be a person or an animal. The people or animals in a story are called **characters.** Good readers pay attention to whom or what the story is about to help them better understand the story and what happens in the story.

Have children turn to pp. 14–15 in *My Skills Buddy* and tell them the story "The Tortoise and the Hare." Direct them to the Characters box. Guide children as they tell about the picture.

- Who are the characters in this story? (the tortoise and the hare)
- What are the characters doing? (The tortoise and the hare are in a race.)

GUIDE PRACTICE Now I will reread the story about two children. Ask children to name the characters in "At the Bus Stop" and to tell about each one.

- Which character seems to forget things? (Jay)
- Which character seems to have good ideas? (Ana)
- How do the characters help each other? (Jay helps Ana carry things. Ana helps Jay remember what he needs.)

Teacher Read Aloud

At the Bus Stop

Jay and his sister Ana are waiting for the school bus. Usually Ana holds Jay's hand, but today her hands are full.

"I forgot my backpack!" said Jay. He ran home to get his backpack.

The next day Jay and Ana are waiting for the bus again.

"I forgot my lunch!" said Jay. He ran home to get his lunch.

When Jay got back, Ana said, "Here's an idea. Each morning I'll help you remember what you need. You can help me too. When my hands are full, you can carry my lunch."

"Okay," Jay said.

After that, Jay never forgot anything, and Ana always had a free hand for Jay to hold.

Access for All

 Advanced

Character Have children describe a familiar fairy tale. Have them identify the characters in the story. Ask children to describe the characters and tell what they do.

Academic Vocabulary 

character a person or an animal in a story

Bridge to Common Core

KEY IDEAS AND DETAILS

As children identify and describe the characters in a story, they are determining key details in the story. Answering questions about characters helps children use evidence from the text and illustrations to support the conclusions they draw about the story.

Support Listening Comprehension Use the modified Read Aloud from the ELL Support lessons (p. DI•13) on *Teacher Resources DVD-ROM* to build background knowledge. Preview new vocabulary and support understanding of complex text with visuals from *My Skills Buddy* and online sources.

Common Core State Standards

Speaking/Listening 1. Participate in collaborative conversations with diverse partners about *kindergarten topics and texts* with peers and adults in small and larger groups. **Speaking/ Listening 1.a.** Follow agreed-upon rules for discussions (e.g., listening to others and taking turns speaking about the topics and texts under discussion). **Language 1.a.** Print many upper- and lowercase letters. **Also Writing 1., Speaking/ Listening 3.**

Academic Vocabulary 

name a word or group of words by which a person or animal is known

Daily Fix-It

I am rafael
I am Rafael.

This week's practice sentences appear on *Teacher Resources DVD-ROM.*

Conventions

Say Our Names

MAKE CONNECTIONS Today we listened to a story about two children named Jay and Ana. Who can tell me his or her name? Who can tell me the name of a friend?

TEACH We all have names. A **name** is a word or group of words that stands for a person or an animal. A person or an animal is called by his or her name.

MODEL I am (your name). (Your name) is my name. Point to someone in the class. What is your name? Continue going around the class, calling on other children to tell their names.

Write your name on the board. Point to the words. This is my name. I am (your name). Say my name with me. Continue by writing a child's name on the board and having the class read the name with you as they point to the child with that name.

GUIDE PRACTICE Tell children to listen to clues you give and ask them to name the person: This person is wearing a blue shirt. Who is it? Have children with blue shirts stand to confirm correct answers. Continue to give clues and have children identify classmates by name.

Write the following sentences on the board: *What is your name? My name is* ______. Help children practice asking and answering questions using these sentences. Read the question and the sentence frame with children. Choose one child to ask the question and another child to answer it using the sentence frame. The child who answers then asks another classmate the question. Continue until everyone has had a turn to ask and answer a question.

Team Talk **APPLY** Pair children and have them introduce themselves using complete sentences. Have them follow this sentence frame: *Hello! My name is* ______. Have partners shake hands after stating their names.

Wonderful, Marvelous Me! I Am Special...

INTRODUCE Talk with children about how everyone is special. Everyone in this room is special. What makes us special? Lots of wonderful, marvelous things make each of us special. We are special because of who we are on the inside, what we can do, or even how we look. Someone may be special because she can run very fast. Someone else may be special because he has a great smile. Encourage children to share their thoughts and ideas about things that make each of us special.

MODEL Today we're going to write about something we do that makes us special. I'm going to close my eyes and think about things I can do. One special thing I can do is I can whistle all kinds of songs. Whistle a short tune. Another special thing about me is I have freckles on my nose. Draw a picture of yourself with freckles on your nose and write *freckles* below. I am also special because I am a good listener.

GUIDE PRACTICE Encourage children to help you name other things that make you special. Write their ideas and draw pictures.

INDEPENDENT WRITING Now you're going to share something special about you. Close your eyes and think about wonderful, marvelous you. What is something that makes you special? Remember, there are many things about you that are special, but today pick just one. Have children dictate their ideas and then illustrate them.

Daily Handwriting

Write uppercase *A* and lowercase *a* on the board. Review correct letter formation of uppercase *A* and lowercase *a.*

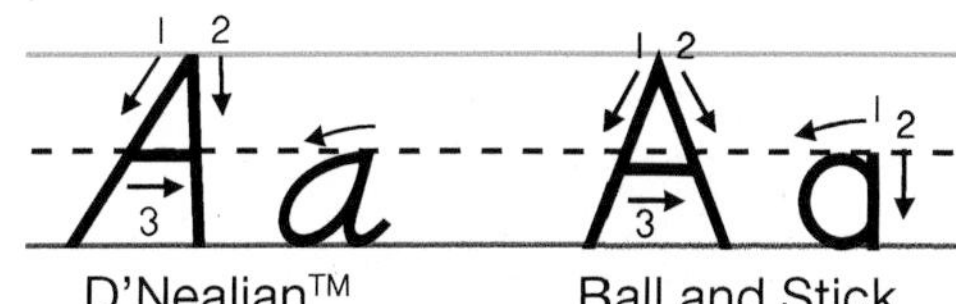

Have children write uppercase *A* and lowercase *a* on their Write-On Boards. Remind them to use proper left-to-right and top-to-bottom progression and proper spacing between letters when writing *A* and *a.*

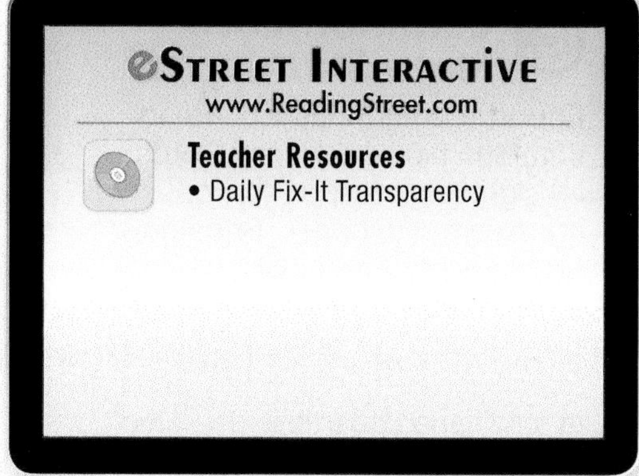

Write Guy *by Jeff Anderson*

What Do You Notice?

When children are examining the model text, ask, "What do you notice?" By giving children the responsibility of commenting on what they find effective in the text, they build self-confidence and often begin to notice features of the writing they might not have otherwise.

Bridge to Common Core

TEXT TYPES AND PURPOSES

Today children draw and write about things that make them special.

Opinion Writing

Children are learning to write for a particular purpose: to offer an opinion and support it with valid reasons.

Throughout the week, children will have opportunities to write varied text types for different purposes.

5-Day Plan

DAY 1	Wonderful, Marvelous Me!
DAY 2	Respond to Literature
DAY 3	Genre Writing
DAY 4	Extend the Concept
DAY 5	This Week We...

Support Writing Encourage children to discuss their ideas for writing with you. Supply any English words with which they may be unfamiliar.

Common Core State Standards

Foundational Skills 3.c. Read common high-frequency words by sight (e.g., *the, of, to, you, she, my, is, are, do, does*). **Speaking/Listening 1.** Participate in collaborative conversations with diverse partners about *kindergarten topics and texts* with peers and adults in small and larger groups. **Also Speaking/Listening 1.a., 3., 5.**

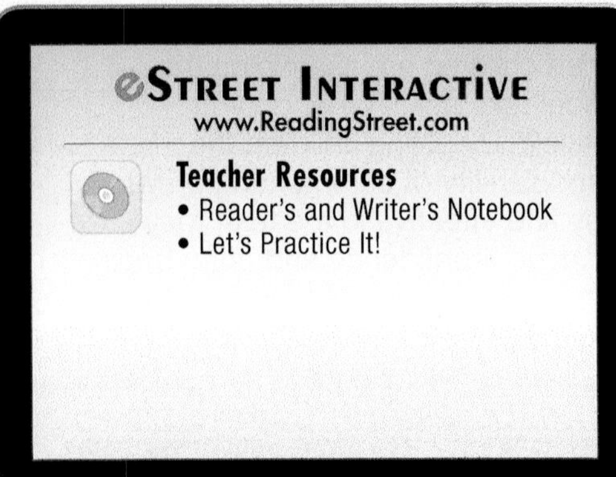

Listening and Speaking

Follow Directions

TEACH Directions are instructions or steps that tell us how or what to do. We must listen carefully to understand and follow directions. Good listeners face the person who is speaking and ask questions if they do not understand something.

MODEL I will read directions for a stretching exercise. Listen carefully: *Stand up. Raise your arms over your head. Bend down to touch your toes. Stand up straight.* What do these directions tell me? They tell me how to stretch. How can I follow these directions? Perform the actions as you say: I need to stand up. I need to raise my arms. I need to touch my toes. I need to stand up straight.

GUIDE PRACTICE Have children follow sets of simple directions, such as how to line up properly. Guide children by acting out the directions with them. Refer children to the Rules for Listening and Speaking on pp. 1–2 of the *Reader's and Writer's Notebook.* Remind them to face the speaker when they are listening and to ask any questions after the speaker has stopped speaking.

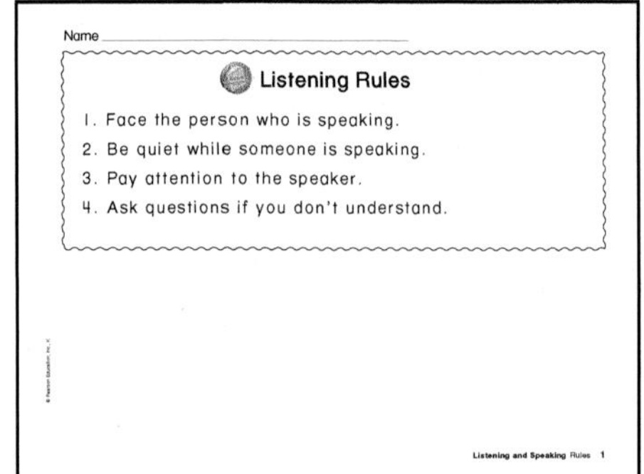
Name

Listening Rules

1. Face the person who is speaking.
2. Be quiet while someone is speaking.
3. Pay attention to the speaker.
4. Ask questions if you don't understand.

Reader's and Writer's Notebook, pp. 1–2

Wrap Up Your Day!

- **Content Knowledge** This week we are going to talk about cooperation—living, working, and playing together. What did we learn about cooperation today?
- **Phonological Awareness** Today we learned about rhyming words. Which word rhymes with *cat: cup* or *bat?*
- **Homework Idea** Send home the Family Times Newsletter from Let's Practice It! pp. 1–2 on the *Teacher Resources DVD-ROM.*

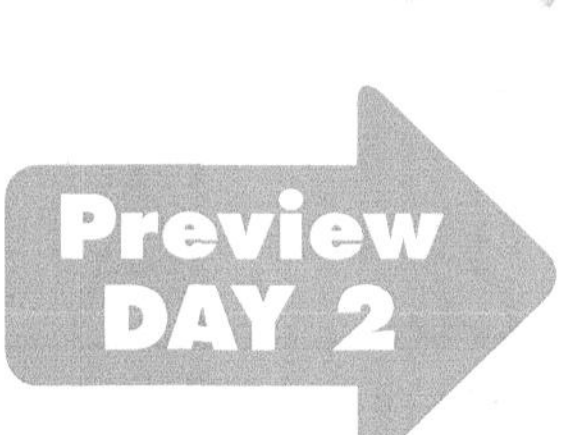

Tomorrow we will read about animals that ride a bus to school together.

Extend Your Day!

Social Studies

Cooperating

MATERIALS: paper, glue, chart or mural paper

LET'S COOPERATE Remind children that there are many things they do each day that involve other people and that they have to work together to get the job done. Tell them that when they work together, they are cooperating. Ask children to think of times when they cooperate with others to solve a problem, find something, or do something.

CREATE A COOPERATION POSTER Have children draw pictures that show how people cooperate. Write the word *Cooperating* at the top of the chart paper. Have children glue their pictures to the page and write or dictate their names by their pictures. Have children take turns telling about their picture and how it shows people cooperating.

High-Frequency Words

I Am...

MATERIALS: paper, crayons or markers

MAKE A BOOK Have children fold a sheet of paper in half to make a book. Write the following sentence frames on the board and read them aloud.

Cover: I Am ______! **Page 2: I eat ______.**

Page 1: I like ______. **Page 3: I play ______.**

Have children copy the first sentence frame and complete it by writing their name. Tell them to copy the other sentence frames and complete them with pictures. Then have children illustrate their books. Ask children to read their books to the class.

Conventions

Names

MATERIALS: shallow pan, paint, paper, crayon

ILLUSTRATE NAMES Have children dip one hand in a flat pan of paint and make a handprint on a sheet of paper. Ask them to write or dictate their names next to the handprints. Arrange the handprints in a bulletin board display.

DAY 2 at a Glance

Content Knowledge
Oral Vocabulary

Phonological Awareness
Rhyming Words

Letter Recognition
Letters *Bb*

Handwriting
B and *b*

Text-Based Comprehension
Character

Conventions
Say Our Names

Writing
Respond to Literature

Vocabulary
Words for Transportation

Materials

- Student Edition
- Truckery Rhymes
- Talk with Me/Sing with Me Chart
- Picture Cards
- Alphabet Cards
- Reader's and Writer's Notebook
- Big Book

Common Core State Standards

Speaking/Listening 1. Participate in collaborative conversations with diverse partners about *kindergarten topics and texts* with peers and adults in small and larger groups. **Language 6.** Use words and phrases acquired through conversations, reading and being read to, and responding to texts.

TRUCKTOWN on Reading Street

Start your engines!
Display p. 5 of *Truckery Rhymes.* Point to "Jack Be Nimble." Who remembers which truck this rhyme is about? Yes, it's about Jack. Let's read the rhyme together. Have a child point to the rhyming words as the class reads the rhyme again. Give additional children the opportunity to point to the rhyming words as you repeat the rhyme.

Truckery Rhymes
Truckery Rhymes

Content Knowledge

Zoom in on

Getting to School Together

TALK ABOUT GOING TO SCHOOL TOGETHER Write the Question of the Week on the board, *How do children get to school?,* and track the print as you read it aloud. Ask children to answer the question in complete sentences. To reinforce the concept and focus children's attention, display Sing with Me Chart 1B. Tell children that they are going to sing a song about children getting on a bus.

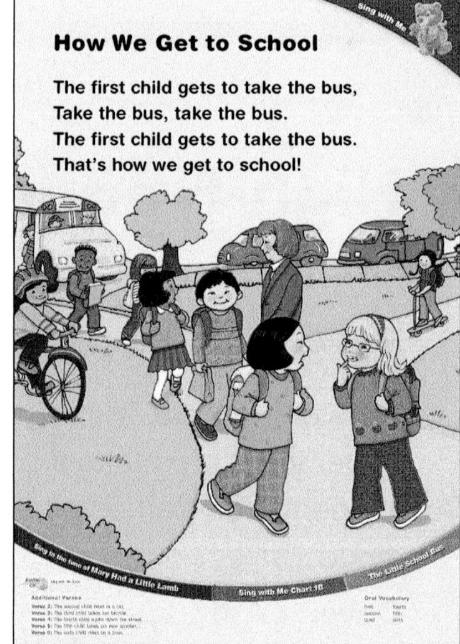
How We Get to School
The first child gets to take the bus,
Take the bus, take the bus.
The first child gets to take the bus.
That's how we get to school!
Talk with Me/Sing with Me Chart 1B

Build Oral Language

LISTEN FOR AMAZING WORDS The Amazing Words *first* and *second* are in the song "How We Get to School." Read the title and have children describe the children in the picture. Sing the song several times to the tune of "Mary Had a Little Lamb" until children become familiar with the words and can sing along. Have children clap when they hear the Amazing Words *first* and *second.*

Build Oral Vocabulary

Amazing Words — Robust Vocabulary Routine

1. **Introduce the Word** The child who gets on the bus before all other children is the *first* child. The word *first* tells that something happens or someone does something before all others. What is our new Amazing Word that tells about the child who gets on the bus before all others? Say it with me: *first.*

2. **Demonstrate** Provide examples to show meaning. *When several children are standing in line, the child at the beginning of the line is the first child.*

   Repeat steps 1 and 2.

   Introduce the Word The child who gets on the bus after the first child is the *second* child. The word *second* tells that something happens or someone does something right after the first. What is our new Amazing Word that tells about the child who gets on the bus after the first child? Say it with me: *second.*

   Demonstrate *If Ella stands behind the first person in line, she is second in line.*

3. **Apply** Have children line up in groups facing the front of the classroom. Have the first and second children in line state their position (*first, second*) and then move to the back of the line. Continue until every child has had a chance to be first or second in line.

4. **Display the Words** Point to and name the beginning letters in *first* and *second.* Have children repeat the letter names. Then ask them if they see the letter *s* in *first.*

Routines Flip Chart

USE AMAZING WORDS To reinforce the concept and the Amazing Words, have children supply the appropriate Amazing Word for each sentence.

I am at the beginning of the line. I am _______. (first)
I am behind the first person in line. I am _______. (second)

Amazing Words

first	second
third	fourth
fifth	sixth

Access for All

Strategic Intervention

Sentence Production If children have difficulty completing the sentences, give examples with various choices and let children select the correct words.

Access Content Ask children to say the words *first* and *second* in their home languages.

Reinforce Vocabulary Use the Day 2 instruction on ELL Poster 1 to reinforce the meanings of high-frequency words.

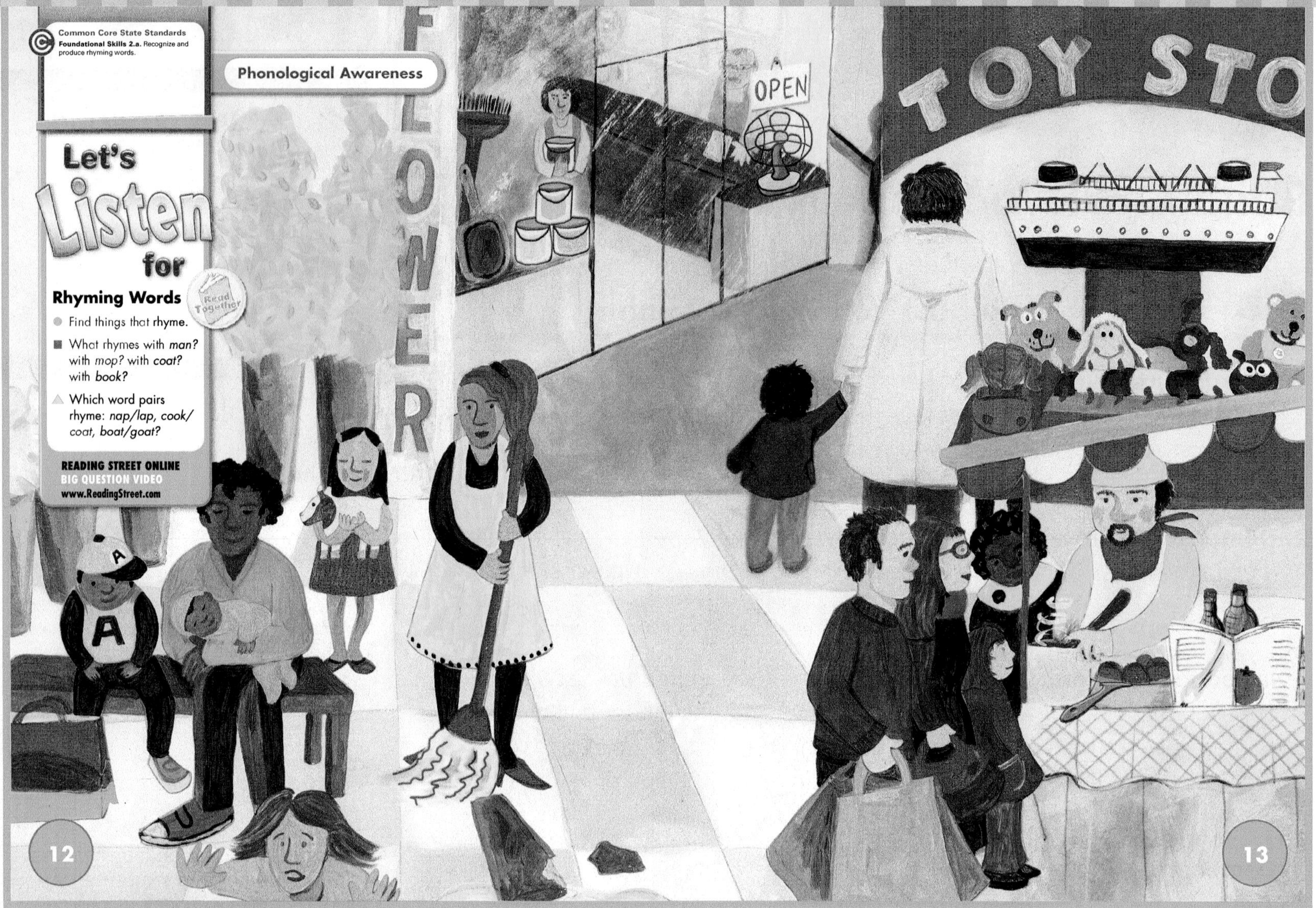

Common Core State Standards
Foundational Skills 2.a. Recognize and produce rhyming words.
Phonological Awareness
Let's Listen for
Rhyming Words
Read Together
Find things that rhyme.
What rhymes with man? with mop? with coat? with book?
Which word pairs rhyme: nap/lap, cook/coat, boat/goat?
READING STREET ONLINE
BIG QUESTION VIDEO
www.ReadingStreet.com
FLOWER
OPEN
TOY STO
A
A
U
12
13
My Skills Buddy, pp. 12–13

Common Core State Standards

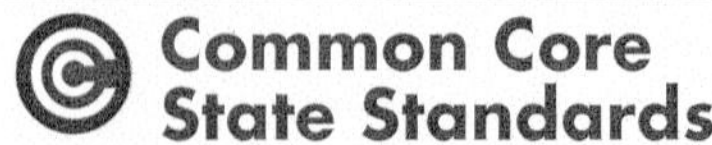

Foundational Skills 2.a. Recognize and produce rhyming words.

Academic Vocabulary

rhyme to have the same middle and ending sounds

Phonological Awareness

Rhyming Words

TEACH Display the *cap, dog,* and *map* Picture Cards. Have children say the picture names together. Say the words again, emphasizing the middle and ending parts. Ask children to tell which words rhyme. Let's say the rhyming words: *cap, map.* Continue with the following sets of Picture Cards: *bed, cat, bat; pen, jet, hen; box, web, fox.*

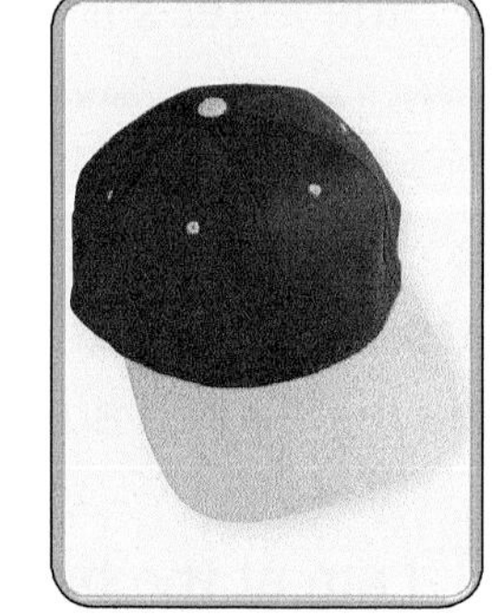

Picture Card

MODEL Display Big Book *The Little School Bus.* Remember, rhyming words are words that have the same middle and ending sounds. Open to p. 4 and read the page. Do you hear words that rhyme? *Goat* and *coat* have the same middle and ending parts. *Goat* and *coat* rhyme. Continue the routine with *pig* and *wig* on p. 7.

GUIDE PRACTICE Have children look at the picture on *My Skills Buddy,* pp. 12–13. Remember that we saw a can in this picture. *Can* rhymes with *pan.* What other things did we find that rhyme with *can* and *pan?* Can we find other things that have the same middle and ending sounds? Discuss with children those bulleted items on p. 12 not discussed on Day 1.

Corrective feedback	**If...** children cannot identify rhyming words, **then...** say the words, isolating the middle and ending parts of each word. Listen as I say the words *boat* and *coat.* Say the words with me: /b/-*oat,* /k/-*oat.* The words have the same middle and ending sounds. Continue with the following words: /n/-*ap,* /k/-*ap;* /m/-*all,* /f/-*all;* /m/-*op,* /t/-*op.*

ON THEIR OWN Draw and label a picture of a cat on the board. Read the label aloud to children and have them repeat it. Then ask them to draw a picture of something that rhymes with *cat.* Have them share their drawings with the class. Continue the routine with *bug, pen,* and *log.*

SOUND SUBSTITUTION Say the word *an.* Ask children to make a new, rhyming word by adding /p/ to *-an.* Say the words with me: *an, pan.* Let's make a new word with /t/ and *-an.* Say /t/ /an/. What is the word? (*tan*) Continue with *can, fan, man, ran,* and *van.*

Access for All

Support Phonological Awareness
Say a word followed by a beginning sound, such as *wig,* /f/. Have children practice forming rhyming words by replacing the beginning sound of each word with the given new sound.

Support Phonological Awareness
English learners may need extra practice with rhyming word pairs such as *pig/wig* and *fall/mall* that may contain vowel and final consonant sounds unfamiliar to them.

Common Core State Standards

Foundational Skills 1.d. Recognize and name all upper- and lowercase letters of the alphabet. **Also Foundational Skills 1.**

Alphabet Card

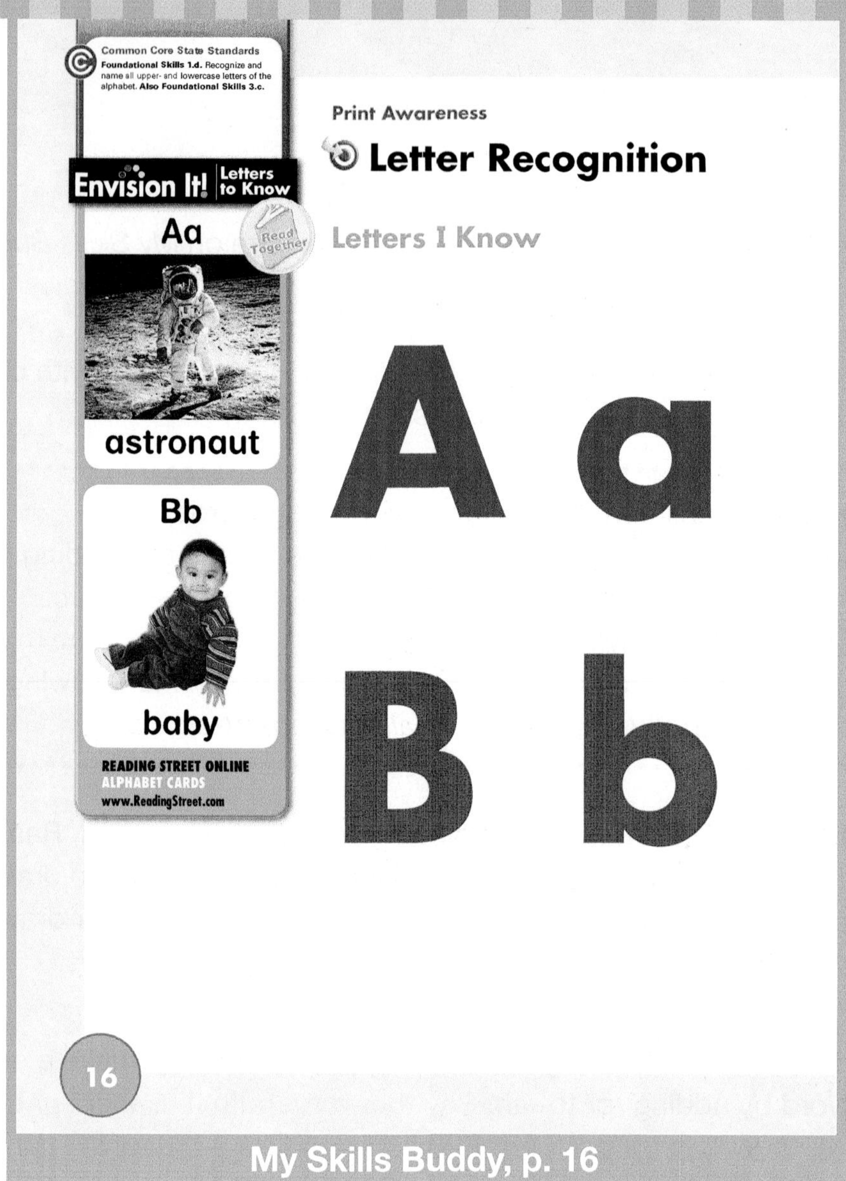

My Skills Buddy, p. 16

Letter Recognition

Teach/Model

Letters *Bb*

INTRODUCE Display the *Bb* Alphabet Card. Point to the picture of the baby. This is a baby. The word *baby* begins with the letter *b*. Point to the letters on the card. This is uppercase *B*, and this is lowercase *b*.

MODEL Write several uppercase and lowercase *Aa* and *Bb* on the board. Randomly call on children to come to the board and cross out a specific letter. Put an *X* on an uppercase *A*. Continue until all letters have been crossed out.

Guide Practice

GROUP PRACTICE Have children turn to p. 16. Point to the top row. These purple letters are uppercase *A* and lowercase *a.* Repeat the routine with the red letters *Bb.* Point to the lowercase *a.* Is this uppercase *A* or lowercase *a?* Point to the uppercase *A.* What is this letter? (uppercase *A*) Repeat the routine with *Bb.* Have children say the letters as you point to them.

Apply

CONNECT Say the name *Barbara.* Have children say the name with you. Listen as I say the name: *Bar-ba-ra.* Now say the parts of the name with me: *Bar-ba-ra.* Blend the sounds with children to make the name *Barbara.* Repeat the blending several times so that children understand how to blend the sounds together.

MODEL When I say *Bet-ty,* I say the sounds in a name. Then I blend the sounds together to make the name *Betty.* Have children blend the sounds with you and repeat the blending several times.

GUIDE PRACTICE Let's make some more names. When I say the sounds in the name, repeat the sounds with me. Then we can blend the sounds to make a name. Use the following names: *Bil-ly, Bob-by, Bud.*

Access for All

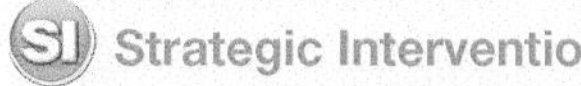

Letter Recognition Write children's names that start with *B* on the board. Have children take turns circling *B* in the names on the board. Remind children to look for lowercase *b* in the middle of some names, such as *Bobby.*

Check Letter Recognition Letter Names

FORMATIVE ASSESSMENT Write a row of uppercase *B* and lowercase *b* on the board. Have children point to each letter and name it.

If... children cannot recognize *B* or *b,*

then... use the small-group Strategic Intervention lesson, p. SG•9, to reteach *Bb.*

Continue to monitor children's progress during the week so that children can be successful with the Day 5 Assessment.

Common Core State Standards

Foundational Skills 3.c. Read common high-frequency words by sight (e.g., *the, of, to, you, she, my, is, are, do, does*). **Language 1.a.** Print many upper- and lowercase letters.

Access for All

A Advanced

Handwriting Display Phonics Songs and Rhymes Chart 1. Point out that the picture contains words that start with *b*, such as *baby, blue,* and *bus*. Write these words on the board. Read the words and have children copy one onto their Write-On Boards.

Handwriting

INTRODUCE Write *Bb* on the board and point to *B*. This is uppercase *B*. We use uppercase letters at the beginning of sentences and for the first letter in a person's name.

MODEL UPPERCASE *B* Write *Ben* on the board. This is the name *Ben*. I use an uppercase letter for the first letter in a name. *Ben* begins with uppercase *B*. Watch as I trace the uppercase *B* with my finger. Follow the stroke instructions given below.

GUIDE PRACTICE Have children write the uppercase *B* in the air. Use your finger to make an uppercase *B* in the air. Now write it on your hand.

MODEL LOWERCASE *b* Write *bug* on the board. This is the word *bug*. I use a lowercase letter at the beginning of *bug*. See how I make the lowercase *b*. Write another *b* on the board, following the stroke instructions below. Again, have children write *b* in the air and on their hands.

GUIDE PRACTICE Have children use their Write-On Boards to write a row of uppercase *B* and a row of lowercase *b*.

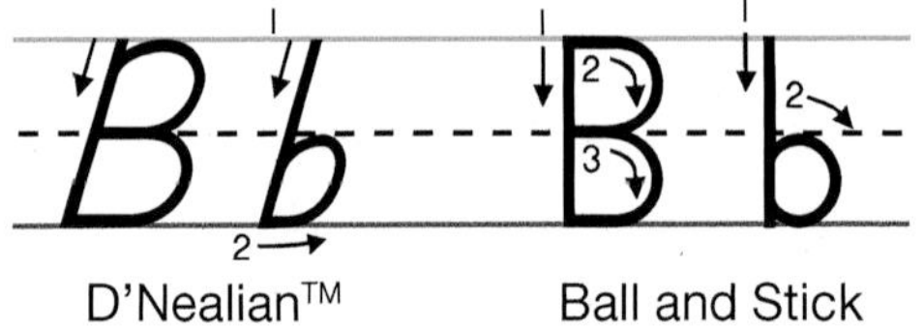

D'Nealian™ Ball and Stick

ON THEIR OWN Use *Reader's and Writer's Notebook,* pp. 3 and 4, for more practice with *Bb*.

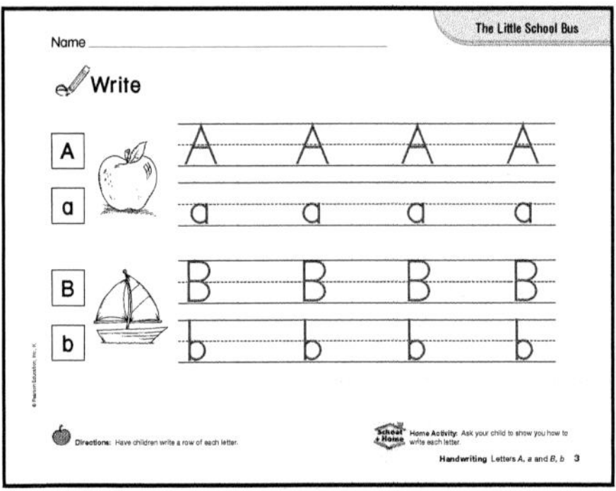

Reader's and Writer's Notebook, p. 3

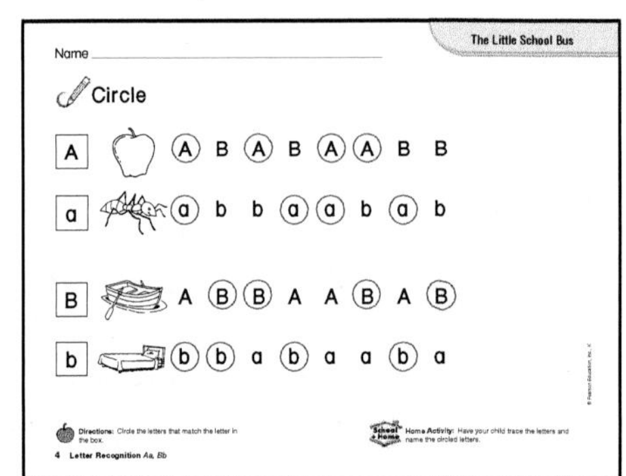

Reader's and Writer's Notebook, p. 4

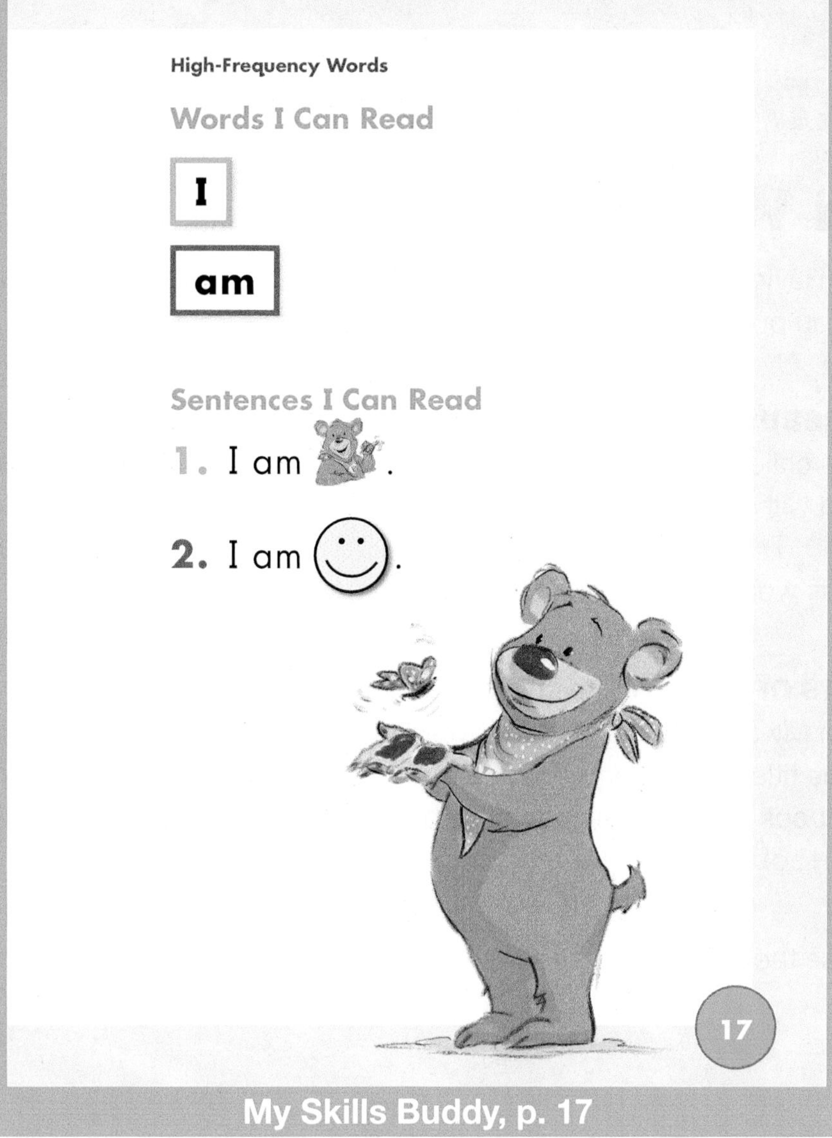

My Skills Buddy, p. 17

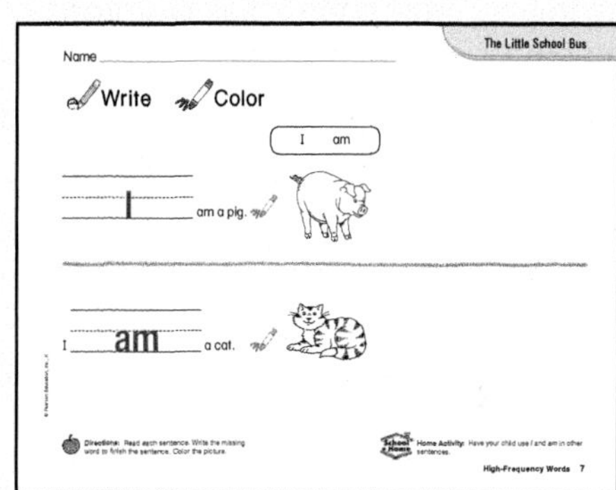

Reader's and Writer's Notebook, p. 7

High-Frequency Words

READ WORDS Have children turn to p. 17 of *My Skills Buddy.* Read the high-frequency words *I* and *am* together. Then have children point to each word and read it themselves.

READ SENTENCES Read the sentences on the *My Skills Buddy* page together to read the high-frequency words in context.

Team Talk Pair children and have them take turns reading each of the sentences aloud.

ON THEIR OWN Use *Reader's and Writer's Notebook,* p. 7, for additional practice with this week's high-frequency words.

Find and Trace Letters Ask children to find examples of *Aa* and *Bb* in printed classroom materials. Have children trace the letters using stroke instructions. Read aloud the words they find, providing definitions when necessary.

 Common Core State Standards

Foundational Skills 4. Read emergent-reader texts with purpose and understanding. **Also Foundational Skills 1.a., 1.d., 3.c.**

Access for All

SI Strategic Intervention

Decodable Reader Before reading the story, page through it and have children tell about the small pictures and how they are related to the big pictures.

Decodable Reader 1

Read *Who Am I?*

REVIEW Review this week's high-frequency words. Have children read each word as you point to it on the Word Wall: *I, am.*

TEACH REBUS WORDS Write the name *Ann* on the board. This is the name *Ann.* Have children say the name with you. Look for this word in our story today. You will see the word with a small picture of a girl above it. The girl is named Ann. The small picture helps you read the word *Ann.* Continue with the other rebus words: *Ben, Cam, Dot, Ed, Emma, Dad.*

CONCEPTS OF PRINT Have children turn to Decodable Reader 1, *Who Am I?,* on p. 18 of *My Skills Buddy.* Today we will read a story about some children. Point to the title of the story. The title of this story is *Who Am I?* Review the parts of a book with children, identifying the front cover, pages, and back cover. Now let's read!

READ Use the routine for reading decodable books to read Decodable Reader 1.

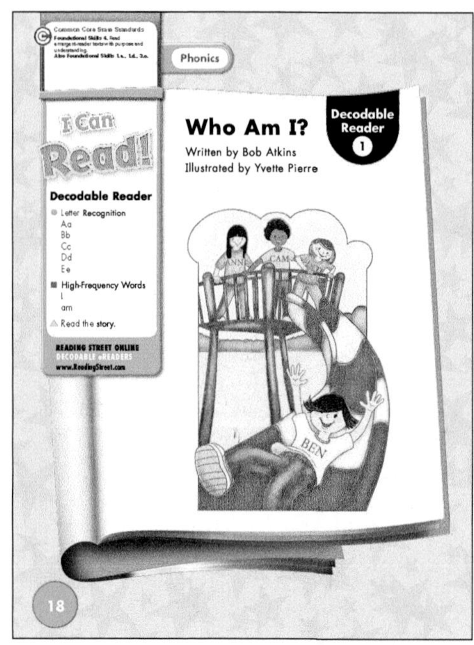

My Skills Buddy, pp. 18–25

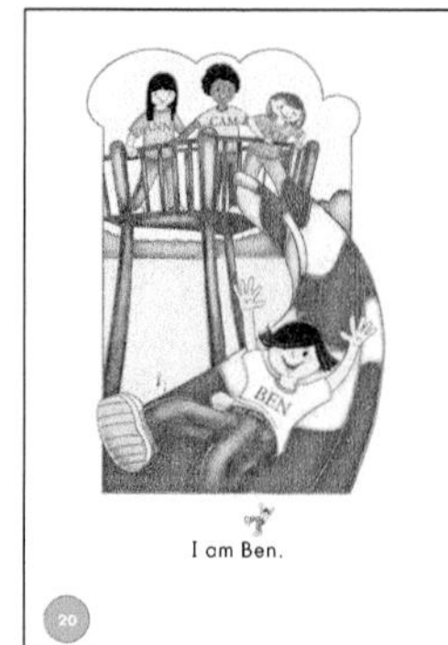

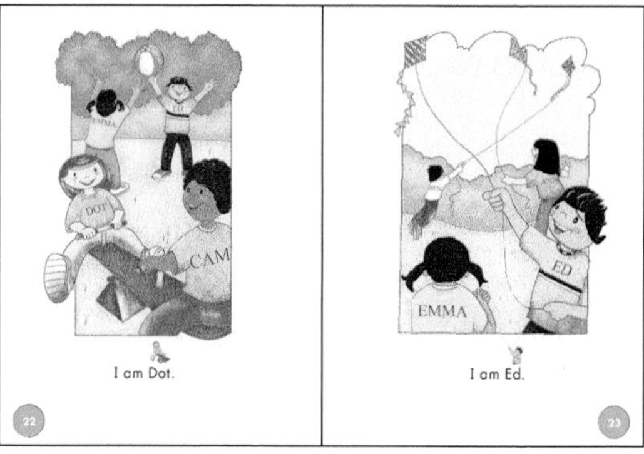

eStreet Interactive
www.ReadingStreet.com

Savvas eText
- Student Edition

Routine Reading Decodable Books

1. **Read Silently** Have children whisper read the book page by page as you listen in.
2. **Model Fluent Reading** Have children finger point as you read a page. Then have children reread the book without you.
3. **Read Chorally** Have children finger point as they chorally read the page. Continue reading page by page, repeating steps 1 and 2.
4. **Read Individually** Have children take turns reading aloud a page.
5. **Reread and Monitor Progress** As you listen to individual children reread, monitor progress and provide support.
6. **Reread with a Partner** Have children reread the book page by page with a partner.

Routines Flip Chart

Find and Name Letters Page through the Decodable Reader with children. Have them point to examples of *Aa* and *Bb* in the story. Encourage children to say the letter names with proper pronunciation as they point.

Day 2 SMALL GROUP TIME • Differentiate Letter Recognition, p. SG•1

OL On-Level
- **Practice Letter Recognition** Recognize Letters *Bb*
- **Read** Decodable Reader *Who Am I?*

SI Strategic Intervention
- **Reteach Letter Recognition** Recognize Letters *Bb*
- **Read** Decodable Reader *Who Am I?*

A Advanced
- **Extend Letter Recognition** Connect *Bb* to /b/
- **Read** Decodable Reader *Who Am I?*

Place English Language Learners in the groups that correspond to their reading abilities in English.

If... children need more support with **Letter Recognition,** **then...** use the activities on p. DI•12 in the Teacher Resources section of the Digital Path.

Common Core State Standards

Literature 2. With prompting and support, retell familiar stories, including key details. **Literature 3.** With prompting and support, identify characters, settings, and major events in a story. **Also Literature 5., 7., 10., Foundational Skills 1.a., Speaking/ Listening 5.**

Text-Based Comprehension

Introduce Main Selection

CONCEPTS OF PRINT Display p. 3 of *The Little School Bus.* Remind children to begin at the top of the page and to move from left to right to the bottom.

GENRE An animal fantasy is a story about animal characters that talk and act like people. We will read about these young animals and their school bus.

PREVIEW AND PREDICT Display *The Little School Bus.* What do you see on the cover? I see young animals and a school bus. The title is *The Little School Bus.* What do you think the book will be about? Take children on a walk through the book. Have them tell about what they see in each picture.

SET PURPOSE Remind children of the Question of the Week: *How do children get to school?* Have children listen as you read.

MODEL Read *The Little School Bus* with expression to build interest in the text.

Routine Read for Understanding 

Deepen understanding by reading the selection multiple times.

1. **First Read**—Read the entire selection aloud to build interest in the text.
2. **Second Read**—Use the **Develop Vocabulary** notes on pages 60–75.
3. **Third Read**—Use the **Develop Comprehension** notes on pages 60–75.

Retell

CHECK RETELLING Have children turn to p. 26 of *My Skills Buddy.* Walk through the retelling boxes as children retell *The Little School Bus.* After they retell the story as a group, have children draw a picture to retell a favorite part. Have them dictate a word or sentence to go with their picture.

Check Retelling

If... children have difficulty retelling the story,

then... go through the story one page at a time, and ask children to tell what happens in their own words.

My Skills Buddy, p. 26

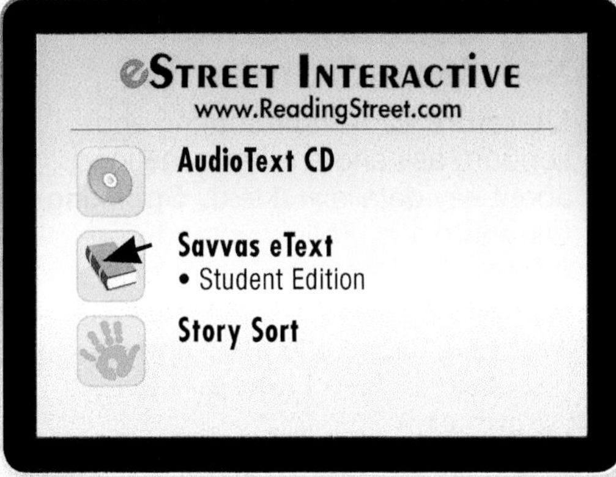

Retelling Plan

- [x] **This week assess Advanced students.**
- [ ] **Week 2** Assess On-Level students.
- [ ] **Week 3** Assess Strategic Intervention students.
- [ ] **Week 4** Assess Advanced students.
- [ ] **Week 5** Assess On-Level students.
- [ ] **Week 6** Assess Strategic Intervention students.

Scoring Rubric Narrative Retelling

	4	3	2	1
Connections	Makes connections and generalizes beyond the text	Makes connections to other events, stories, or experiences	Makes a limited connection to another event, story, or experience	Makes no connection to another event, story, or experience
Author's Purpose	Elaborates on author's purpose	Tells author's purpose with some clarity	Makes some connection to author's purpose	Makes no connection to author's purpose
Characters	Describes the main character(s) and any character development	Identifies the main character(s) and gives some information about them	Inaccurately identifies some characters or gives little information about them	Inaccurately identifies the characters or gives no information about them
Setting	Describes the time and location	Identifies the time and location	Omits details of time or location	Is unable to identify time or location
Plot	Describes the events in sequence using rich detail	Tells the plot with some errors in sequence that do not affect meaning	Tells parts of plot with gaps that affect meaning	Retelling has no sense of story

Access Content Take children on a picture walk through *The Little School Bus,* pointing out characters. Have children name each character in their home languages.

Common Core State Standards

Literature 1. With prompting and support, ask and answer questions about key details in a text. **Speaking/ Listening 1.a.** Follow agreed-upon rules for discussions (e.g., listening to others and taking turns speaking about the topics and texts under discussion). **Also Literature 3.**

Access for All

 Strategic Intervention

Support Discussion Display pp. 24–25 of *The Little School Bus.* Have children point to the way they get to school.

Think, Talk, and Write
Read Together
1. How do you get to school? Text to Self
2. Which is a character from The Little School Bus? Character
3. Look back and write.
27

My Skills Buddy, p. 27

Think, Talk, and Write

DISCUSS CONCEPT We're learning about how children get to school. Think about the animals in our story and how they get to school.

- Which animals are going to school?
- In what order do the animals get on the bus?
- How are these animals like us?

CONFIRM PREDICTIONS Ask children to recall their predictions before you read *The Little School Bus.*

- What did you think the story would be about?
- Was your prediction correct?

Have children turn to p. 27 of *My Skills Buddy.* Read the questions and directives and have children respond.

1. **TEXT TO SELF** How do you get to school? Do you ride a school bus like these animals do? Which animal are you most like?

2. **CHARACTER** Which is a character from *The Little School Bus?* (the pig) What does the pig look like? (She is pink and wears a wig.) How does the pig act? (She is proud of her wig.) Whose hair does the pig brush at the end? (the bear's)

3. **LOOK BACK AND WRITE • TEXT EVIDENCE** Let's look back at our story and write about it. The characters in our story ride a bus to school. Let's look at pictures to learn some more ways to get around. Turn to pp. 24–25. Now let's write our ideas. Discuss with children other ways the animals are getting to school and record children's responses on chart paper. (A duck walks. Some rabbits bike. Some birds drive.)

Conventions

Say Our Names

TEACH Remind children that a name is the word or words that stand for a person or an animal. We call a person or an animal by his or her name.

GUIDE PRACTICE Display p. 4 of *The Little School Bus.* Look at the picture. The goat is getting on the bus. Let's give the goat a name.

I will choose a name for the goat. I will call the goat *Gary Goat.* What name would you choose for the goat?

Write children's suggestions on the board and help the group decide on one name for the goat. Continue choosing names for the animals that get on the bus. After giving each animal a name, have children take turns saying their own names.

ON THEIR OWN Use *Reader's and Writer's Notebook,* p. 8, for more practice with names.

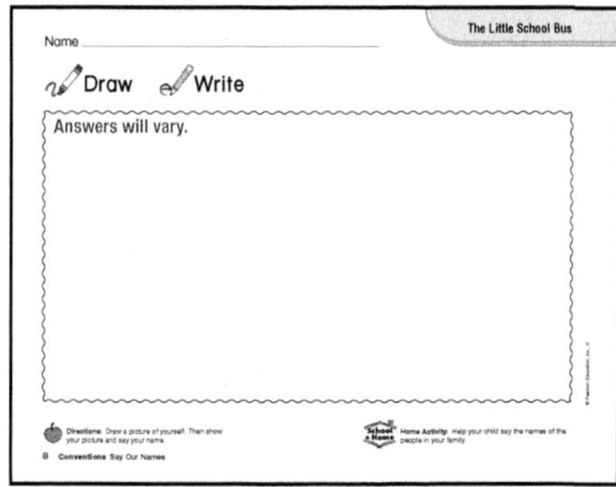

Reader's and Writer's Notebook, p. 8

Writing to Sources

Use Write Like a Reporter on pp. 6–7 to guide children in writing text-based responses using one source.

Daily Fix-It

My name is bob

My name is Bob.

This week's practice sentences appear on *Teacher Resources DVD-ROM.*

Bridge to Common Core

CONVENTIONS OF STANDARD ENGLISH

Children demonstrate their command of the conventions of standard English grammar and usage when they recognize and use frequently occurring nouns such as people's and animals' names.

Extend Vocabulary As children discuss methods of transportation shown on pp. 24–25 of *The Little School Bus,* monitor English learners. Identify and define words such as *school, bus, car, bike, walk,* and *skateboard.*

Common Core State Standards

Writing 2. Use a combination of drawing, dictating, and writing to compose informative/explanatory texts in which they name what they are writing about and supply some information about the topic. **Language 1.a.** Print many upper- and lowercase letters. **Language 5.c.** Identify real-life connections between words and their use (e.g., note places at school that are *colorful*). **Also Language 5.a., 6.**

Respond to Literature

DISCUSS Display *The Little School Bus.* In the story, the animals get on the bus in a special order. Write the Amazing Words *first, second, third, fourth, fifth,* and *sixth* on chart paper. Ask children to name the animals that get on the bus. List their responses next to the ordinal number words.

first	goat
second	pig
third	fox...

MODEL The goat is the first animal to get on the bus. I want to write a sentence that tells that the goat is first. Here is what I write:

The goat gets on first.

GUIDE PRACTICE Have children choose one of the other animals and dictate a complete sentence telling when that animal gets on the bus.

The pig gets on second.

INDEPENDENT WRITING Have children dictate their own complete sentences about the animals in *The Little School Bus.* Then have children illustrate their sentences.

Daily Handwriting

Write uppercase *B* and lowercase *b* on the board and review correct letter formation.

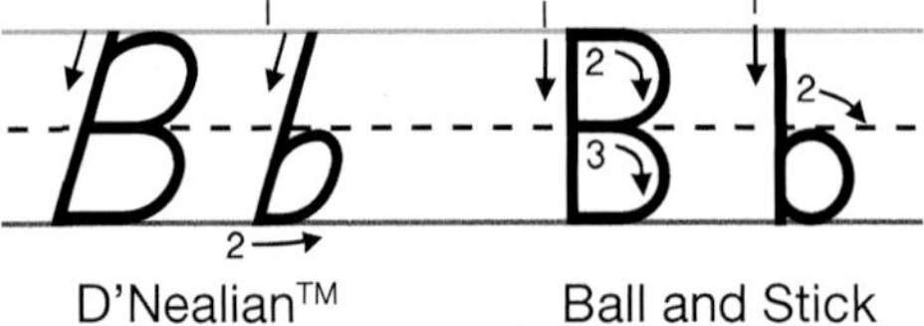

D'Nealian™ Ball and Stick

Have children write a row of uppercase *B* and a row of lowercase *b* on their Write-On Boards. Remind children to use proper left-to-right and top-to-bottom progression when writing *B* and *b.*

Writing to Sources Use More Connect the Texts on pp. 222–293 to guide children in writing text-based responses within various forms and modes.

Common Core State Standards
Speaking/Listening 1.a. Follow agreed-upon rules for discussions (e.g., listening to others and taking turns speaking about the topics and texts under discussion).
Also Language 6.
Let's Learn It!
Vocabulary
Talk about the pictures.
Which do you use?
Listening and Speaking
Point to the picture of the bus.
Cover the picture of the bus with your hand.
Pretend to drive a bus.
Vocabulary
Words for Transportation
bus
car
van
bike
28

My Skills Buddy, p. 28

Vocabulary

Words for Transportation

TEACH Have children turn to p. 28 of *My Skills Buddy.* Use the first Vocabulary bullet to guide the discussion of the transportation words *bus, car, van,* and *bike.* Have children point to the pictures, identify them, and tell how they are alike and different.

GUIDE PRACTICE Write the words *bus, car, van,* and *bike* on the board. Point to each word as you read it.

Give children clues, such as "Only one person can fit on this," and have them name the transportation word (*bike*) and point to the appropriate picture.

ON THEIR OWN Have children draw pictures of the transportation words *bus, car, van,* and *bike.* Tape their illustrations to the board under the proper headings: *bus, car, van, bike.*

Access for All

A Advanced

Extend Vocabulary After discussing the vocabulary words, ask children to suggest other vehicles used for transportation with which they are familiar, such as airplanes, trains, boats, or motorcycles.

Bridge to Common Core

VOCABULARY ACQUISITION AND USE
Learning about transportation words helps children understand the relationships among words in a specific category as well as expand their vocabulary by using frequently occurring nouns.

ELL

Support Vocabulary Review the words for transportation with children. Display toy vehicles so that children can identify the vehicles in their home languages.

Common Core State Standards

Foundational Skills 1.d. Recognize and name all upper- and lowercase letters of the alphabet. **Speaking/ Listening 2.** Confirm understanding of a text read aloud or information presented orally or through other media by asking and answering questions about key details and requesting clarification if something is not understood.

Wrap Up Your Day!

- ✔ **Content Knowledge** Today we read about the animals getting on the bus. How do the animals cooperate as they get on the bus?
- ✔ **Phonological Awareness** I am going to say three words. Tell me which two words rhyme: *bus, Gus, bat.* Why do *bus* and *Gus* rhyme?
- ✔ **Vocabulary Skill** Today we talked about the words *bus, car, van,* and *bike.* How are these words alike?
- ✔ **Homework Idea** Have children draw a picture of one of the words for transportation.

Preview DAY 3

Tomorrow we will read more about animals on a school bus.

Extend Your Day!

Science
Animals We Know

MATERIALS: Big Book *The Little School Bus,* paper, crayons, chart paper

ALL ABOUT ANIMALS Show the first animal in the book. The first animal is a goat. Look at the goat. What do you know about a goat? Write the animal name in a chart. Fill in the chart with information about the animal. Continue with the other animals. Ask children to tell what they know about the animals. Give clues that identify characteristics to compare the animals.

WRITE ABOUT AN ANIMAL Ask children to choose an animal and draw its picture. Have them dictate a sentence that tells about their picture.

Animal	Characteristics
goat	two horns, four legs, hooves
pig	curly tail, eats a lot, short nose or snout, says "oink, oink"
bear	
hen	
dog	
cat	
sheep	

Comprehension
Character

MATERIALS: Picture Cards: *bat, cat, crab, dog, elephant, fox, frog, goat, pig, koala*

IDENTIFY CHARACTERS Display the *fox* and *koala* Picture Cards. This is a fox. This is a koala. One of these two animals was a character in *The Little School Bus.* Which animal was a character in the story? The fox was a character. Tell me about the fox. Continue with the following pairs of Picture Cards: *cat, crab; dog, goat; elephant, frog; pig, bat.*

Letter Recognition
Find the Letters

MATERIALS: index cards with the letter *A, a, B,* or *b* on each

LETTER MATCH First, provide each child with a letter card. Have children find a partner who has the other form of their letter. Then when all the uppercase and lowercase letters are matched, have partners look for words in the classroom that have the letter on their cards. They can also look for words in books.

Each time children find a word, have them copy it on a sheet of paper. Allow time for children to share the *Aa* or *Bb* words they found.

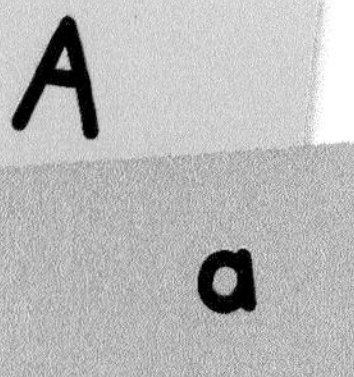

DAY 3 at a Glance

Content Knowledge
Oral Vocabulary

Phonological Awareness
Rhyming Words

Letter Recognition
Letters *Cc*

Text-Based Comprehension
Character

Conventions
Say Our Names

Writing
Song

Listening and Speaking
Follow Directions

Materials

- Student Edition
- Truckery Rhymes
- Talk with Me/Sing with Me Chart
- Picture Cards
- Alphabet Cards
- Reader's and Writer's Notebook
- Student Reader K.1.1
- Big Book

Common Core State Standards

Speaking/Listening 1. Participate in collaborative conversations with diverse partners about *kindergarten topics and texts* with peers and adults in small and larger groups.
Language 6. Use words and phrases acquired through conversations, reading and being read to, and responding to texts.

TRUCKTOWN
on Reading Street

Start your engines!
Display p. 5 of *Truckery Rhymes.* Do you know the original "Jack Be Nimble"? Recite the rhyme together:

Jack be nimble, Jack be quick.
Jack jump over a candlestick.

Truckery Rhymes
Truckery Rhymes

Content Knowledge

Zoom in on

Getting to School Together

Write the Question of the Week on the board, *How do children get to school?* Read the question as you track the print. Talk with children about how to get to school. Remind them to respond in complete sentences.

Build Oral Language

LISTEN FOR AMAZING WORDS Display Sing with Me Chart 1B. Remind children that yesterday they sang "How We Get to School" and listened for the words *first* and *second.* Today we are going to listen for the words *third* and *fourth.* Sing the song several times to the tune of "Mary Had a Little Lamb." Have groups of six children make lines to act out the song.

How We Get to School
The first child gets to take the bus,
Take the bus, take the bus.
The first child gets to take the bus.
That's how we get to school!
Talk with Me/Sing with Me Chart 1B

Build Oral Vocabulary

Amazing Words Robust Vocabulary Routine

1. **Introduce the Word** The child that gets on the bus after the second child is the *third* child. What is our new Amazing Word for the child that gets on the bus after the second child? Say it with me: *third.*

2. **Demonstrate** Provide examples to show meaning. Imagine you are in line for lunch. *If Kim is standing right behind the second person, she is third in line.*

   Repeat steps 1 and 2.

   Introduce the Word The next child that gets on the bus after the third child is the *fourth* child. What is our new Amazing Word for the child that gets on the bus after the third child? Say it with me: *fourth.*

   Demonstrate Ann is third in line to play kickball. Jim is right behind Ann. *Jim is fourth.*

3. **Apply** Tell children to use *third* and *fourth* in complete sentences. Have them arrange books, pencils, or crayons in a line and identify the objects that are *third* and *fourth.*

4. **Display the Words** Point to and name the beginning letters in *third* and *fourth.* Have children repeat the letter names. Then ask them if they see the letter *t* in *fourth.*

Routines Flip Chart

USE AMAZING WORDS To reinforce the concept and the Amazing Words, have children supply the appropriate Amazing Word for each sentence.

The person after the second person is ______. (third)
The person after the third person is ______. (fourth)

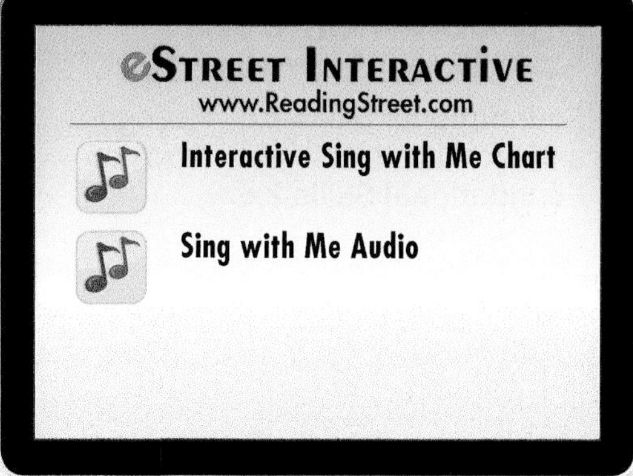

Amazing Words

first	second
third	fourth
fifth	sixth

Visual Support Provide opportunities for children to place sets of objects in an order and to count them using the ordinal numbers *first, second, third,* and *fourth* in English and in their home languages.

Expand Vocabulary Use the Day 3 instruction on ELL Poster 1 to help children expand their use of the lesson vocabulary.

Common Core State Standards

Foundational Skills 2.a. Recognize and produce rhyming words. **Also Foundational Skills 2.e.**

Phonological Awareness

Rhyming Words

REVIEW Remember, rhyming words are words that have the same middle and ending sounds. Say three words and have children identify the two words that rhyme. Use the following sets of words: *dog, hog, hat; goat, boat, mouse; hen, pig, ten; train, truck, rain; cake, vase, bake; cat, dog, rat.*

Picture Card

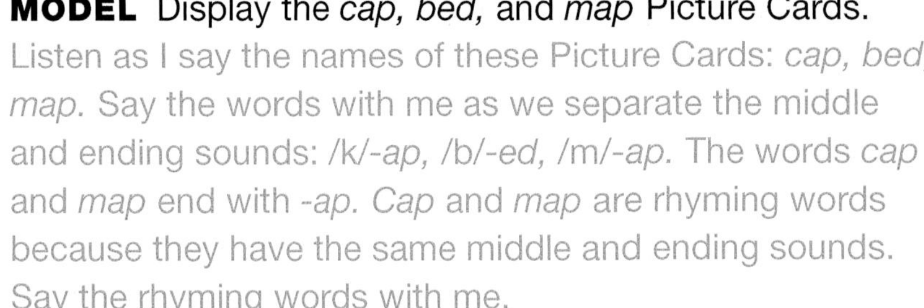

MODEL Display the *cap, bed,* and *map* Picture Cards. Listen as I say the names of these Picture Cards: *cap, bed, map.* Say the words with me as we separate the middle and ending sounds: /k/-*ap*, /b/-*ed*, /m/-*ap*. The words *cap* and *map* end with *-ap. Cap* and *map* are rhyming words because they have the same middle and ending sounds. Say the rhyming words with me.

Picture Card

ON THEIR OWN Place the following Picture Cards in a row: *box, hen, cat, pen, bat, fox.* Look for two picture names that rhyme. Draw the two rhyming picture names on your paper. Allow time for children to work. Then have them show their pictures.

Picture Card

Picture Card

IDENTIFY NUMBER OF WORDS Listen to this sentence: *The cat with the hat had a bat.* Have children repeat the sentence with you and clap as they say each word. Repeat the sentence again and have children count the words. How many words are in the sentence? Continue with these sentences: *The pig in the wig likes to dig. The dog by the log saw a hog.*

Corrective feedback	**If...** children cannot identify the number of words in a sentence, **then...** write a short sentence on the board. Read the sentence with children. Point to each word as children count the words.

SUBSTITUTE INITIAL SOUNDS Remind children that rhyming words have the same middle and ending parts. If we change the beginning sound, we make a new word. Our new word will rhyme with the old word because they will have the same middle and ending parts. I am going to say a word. Listen carefully for the middle and ending part: *top.* What are the middle and ending parts of *top?* (*-op*) Now change the beginning sound in *top* to /m/. What is our new word? (*mop*) Does *mop* rhyme with *top?* Why? Have children supply their own beginning sounds to make new words from *tap, bun, ten,* and *sit.*

Access for All

 Advanced

Extend Phonological Awareness
Display the *hen* Picture Card. Have children take turns generating words that rhyme with *hen.* List their words on the board.

Teacher Tip

Ask children to name rhyming words for a quick transition activity.

Support Phonological Awareness
Distinguishing the /ō/ sound in the rhyming words *goat, coat,* and *boat* may be difficult for speakers of Arabic and Korean, as these languages do not have /ō/. Help children by drawing out the /ō/ sound when pronouncing the words *goat, coat,* and *boat.*

Common Core State Standards

Foundational Skills 1.d. Recognize and name all upper- and lowercase letters of the alphabet.

Letter Recognition

Teach/Model

Letters *Cc*

INTRODUCE/MODEL Display the *Cc* Alphabet Card. Point to the uppercase *C.* The name of this letter is uppercase *C.* What is the name of this letter? (uppercase *C*) Point to the lowercase *c.* The name of this letter is lowercase *c.* What is the name of this letter? (lowercase *c*) Point out to children that uppercase *C* and lowercase *c* look alike except for their sizes.

Alphabet Card

Guide Practice

GROUP PRACTICE Write *b* on the board. Have a child trace the letter and say its name. Continue with several uppercase *B* and lowercase *b.* Continue the routine with *Aa.* Display the *Bb* Alphabet Card. Point to the uppercase letter. What is the name of this letter? (uppercase *B*) Point to the lowercase letter. What is the name of this letter? (lowercase *b*) Continue the routine with *Aa* and *Cc.*

ON THEIR OWN Use *Reader's and Writer's Notebook,* p. 9, for additional practice with *Cc.* Return to this page on Days 4 and 5 for practice with *Dd* and *Ee.*

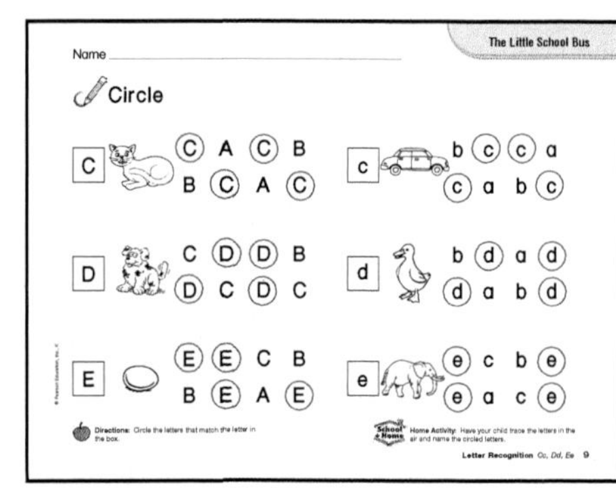

Name

The Little School Bus

Circle

C — C A C B / B C A C
c — b c c a / c a b c
D — C D D B / D C D C
d — b d a d / d a b d
E — E E C B / B E A E
e — e c b e / e a c e

Letter Recognition *Cc, Dd, Ee* 9

Reader's and Writer's Notebook, p. 9

REVIEW LETTER RECOGNITION Write the following row of letters on the board: *C, b, A, a, c, B, B, c, a, C, A, b.* Name a letter and have a child circle an example of that letter from the row on the board. Continue until all the letters have been circled. Repeat the activity until every child has had a turn to identify a letter on the board.

REVIEW HIGH-FREQUENCY WORDS Write the word *I* on the board. Then write this sentence: *I go to school.* Read the sentence and have children repeat it. Have a child circle the word *I.* Continue with the word *am* and the following sentence: *I am a fox.*

Access for All

Strategic Intervention

Letter Recognition Have children find one example of uppercase *C* or lowercase *c* in the classroom.

MONITOR PROGRESS Check Word Reading High-Frequency Words

FORMATIVE ASSESSMENT Write *I* and *am* on the board. Have children take turns reading the words. These words are used in Kindergarten Student Reader K.1.1, *Cat and Dog At School.*

If... children cannot read the high-frequency words,

then... write the words on cards for them to practice at home.

If... children can successfully read the high-frequency words,

then... have them read Kindergarten Student Reader K.1.1, *Cat and Dog At School.*

Letter Recognition Write and read this sentence: *Cam and Carl can find the cat.* Ask children to point to each uppercase *C* and lowercase *c* in the sentence. Explain that *Cam* and *Carl* begin with uppercase *C* because they are people's names.

Common Core State Standards

Literature 7. With prompting and support, describe the relationship between illustrations and the story in which they appear (e.g., what moment in a story an illustration depicts). **Foundational Skills 4.** Read emergent-reader texts with purpose and understanding. **Also Literature 10., Foundational Skills 3.c.**

Access for All

Advanced

High-Frequency Words Write this sentence frame on the board: *I am* ________. Have children copy the sentence frame and draw a picture of themselves to complete the sentence.

Student Reader

Read *Cat and Dog At School*

REVIEW Review the high-frequency words children learned this week. Have children read each word as you point to it on the Word Wall: *I, am.*

TEACH REBUS WORDS Children may be unfamiliar with rebus words. Show p. 2 of Kindergarten Student Reader K.1.1, *Cat and Dog At School.* Point to the word *Cat.* This is the word *Cat.* This picture of a cat will help you read the word. Say the letters with me: *c, a, t, cat.* Repeat the routine with *Dog* on p. 3.

READ Display Kindergarten Student Reader K.1.1. Today we are going to read a new book. Point to the title. *Cat and Dog At School* is the title. It was written by Nikki Chase. It was illustrated by Mike Dammer.

Use the reading decodable books routine to read the Kindergarten Student Reader.

Routine Reading Decodable Books

1. **Read Silently** Have children whisper read the book page by page as you listen in.
2. **Model Fluent Reading** Have children finger point as you read a page. Then have children reread the page without you.
3. **Read Chorally** Have children finger point as they chorally read the page. Continue reading page by page, repeating steps 1 and 2.
4. **Read Individually** Have children take turns reading aloud a page.
5. **Reread and Monitor Progress** As you listen to individual children reread, monitor progress and provide support.
6. **Reread with a Partner** Have children reread the book page by page with a partner.

Routines Flip Chart

Kindergarten Student Reader K.1.1

eSTREET INTERACTIVE
www.ReadingStreet.com

Savvas eText
- Kindergarten Student Reader

Day 3 SMALL GROUP TIME • Differentiate Vocabulary, p. SG•1

OL On-Level

- **Develop Vocabulary** Practice Words for Transportation
- **Read** Student Reader *Cat and Dog At School*

SI Strategic Intervention

- **Develop Vocabulary** Reteach Words for Transportation
- **Read** Student Reader *Cat and Dog At School*

A Advanced

- **Develop Vocabulary** More Words for Transportation
- **Read** Student Reader *Cat and Dog At School*

ELL

Place English Language Learners in the groups that correspond to their reading abilities in English.

If... children need more scaffolding and practice with **Vocabulary,** **then...** use the ELL activities on p. DI•14 in the Teacher Resources section of the Digital Path.

Common Core State Standards

Literature 2. With prompting and support, retell familiar stories, including key details. **Literature 3.** With prompting and support, identify characters, settings, and major events in a story. **Literature 10.** Actively engage in group reading activities with purpose and understanding.

Access for All

Ⓐ Advanced

Character Make a graphic organizer for the characters and have children add what they know about each character.

Bridge to Common Core

CRAFT AND STRUCTURE

As children retell the story, they are analyzing how the parts of the story relate to each other and to the whole. Reading the story to children a second time and using the Develop Vocabulary notes will help children learn how to interpret words and phrases as they are used in the text.

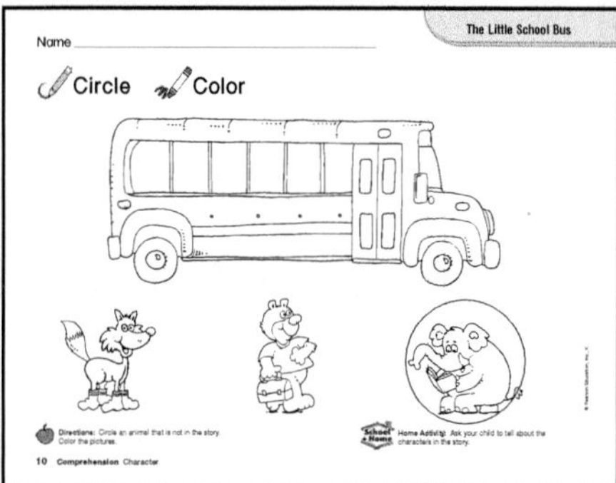

Reader's and Writer's Notebook, p. 10

Text-Based Comprehension

Read Main Selection

RETELL THE SELECTION Have children turn to p. 26 of *My Skills Buddy* and use the retelling boxes to retell the story *The Little School Bus.*

Direct children to the first retelling box. This is when the first animal gets on the bus. Where is the bus going? Tell me about the bus.

Continue reviewing the retelling boxes and having children retell the story.

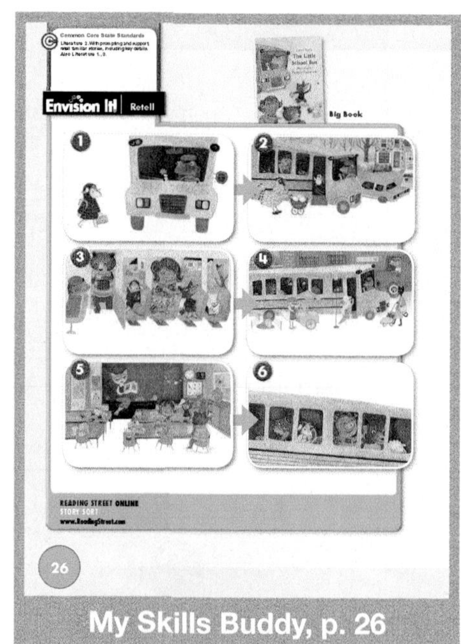

My Skills Buddy, p. 26

REVIEW CHARACTER Display *The Little School Bus.* The characters are the people or animals that the story is about. Let's review the characters of this story.

- Who is the first to get on the bus? (the goat in the coat)
- What can you tell about the goat? (The goat is carrying his lunchbox and is ready to get on the bus.)
- Who is the second character to get on the bus? (the pig in a wig)
- What can you tell about the pig? (The pig is brushing her hair and spraying hairspray. She is wearing a very fancy dress. She is very busy.)

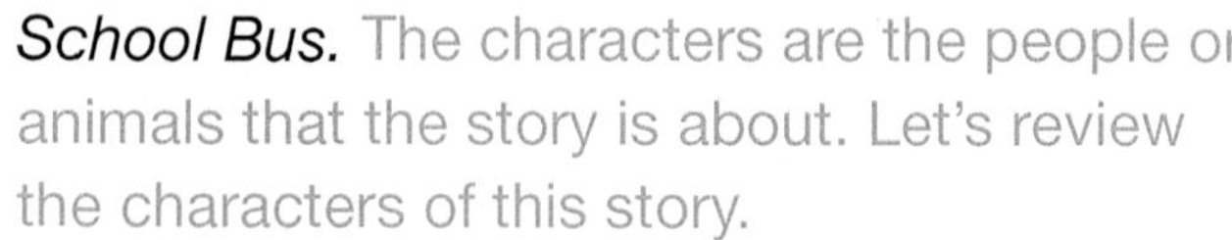

MORE PRACTICE Use *Reader's and Writer's Notebook,* p. 10, for additional practice with character.

Access Main Selection

READER AND TASK SUGGESTIONS	
Preparing to Read the Text	**Leveled Tasks**
• Review the Amazing Words and have children use them to talk about the selection. • Discuss the use of rhyming words and repetition in this predictable story.	• **Structure** If children have difficulty remembering the order in which the animal characters boarded the bus, they can reread pages 22–23, emphasizing the rhyming descriptions. • **Language Conventionality and Clarity** If children need reinforcement of the connection between the illustrations and the text, have them look at the illustration on pages 14–15 and name and describe each character.

See Text Complexity Measures for *The Little School Bus* on the tab at the beginning of this week.

READ Reread *The Little School Bus.* Follow the **2nd Read** beginning on p. 60, and use the **Develop Vocabulary** Notes to prompt conversations about the story.

Routine Read for Understanding

Deepen understanding by reading the selection multiple times.

1. **First Read**—Read the entire selection aloud to build interest in the text.
2. **Second Read**—Use the **Develop Vocabulary** notes on pages 60–75.
3. **Third Read**—Use the **Develop Comprehension** notes on pages 60–75.

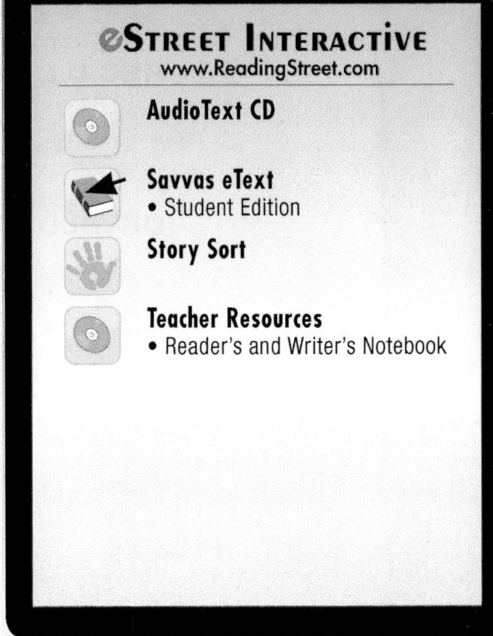

Character Go on a picture walk through the story to review characters with children. Point to each character as he or she is introduced. Say the animal name for the character and have children repeat after you.

2ND READ

Develop Vocabulary

RECALL Point to the bus on p. 3. What is this? (a school bus)

- This is a school bus. Who sits on this bus?

DEVELOP VOCABULARY bus, school

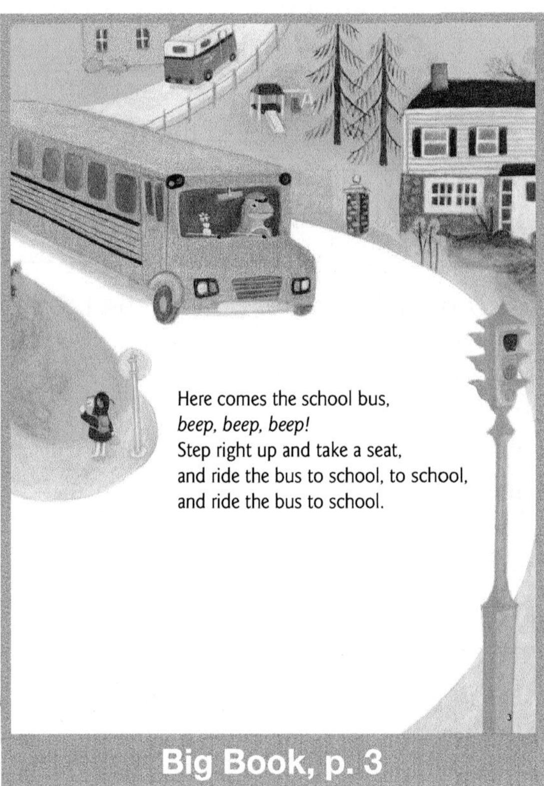

Here comes the school bus,
beep, beep, beep!
Step right up and take a seat,
and ride the bus to school, to school,
and ride the bus to school.

Big Book, p. 3

3RD READ

Develop Comprehension ©

OPEN-ENDED What is this bus used for? (This bus takes children to school.)

RECALL What is the first animal to get on the bus? (a goat)

- The goat is the first animal on the bus. What is the goat wearing?

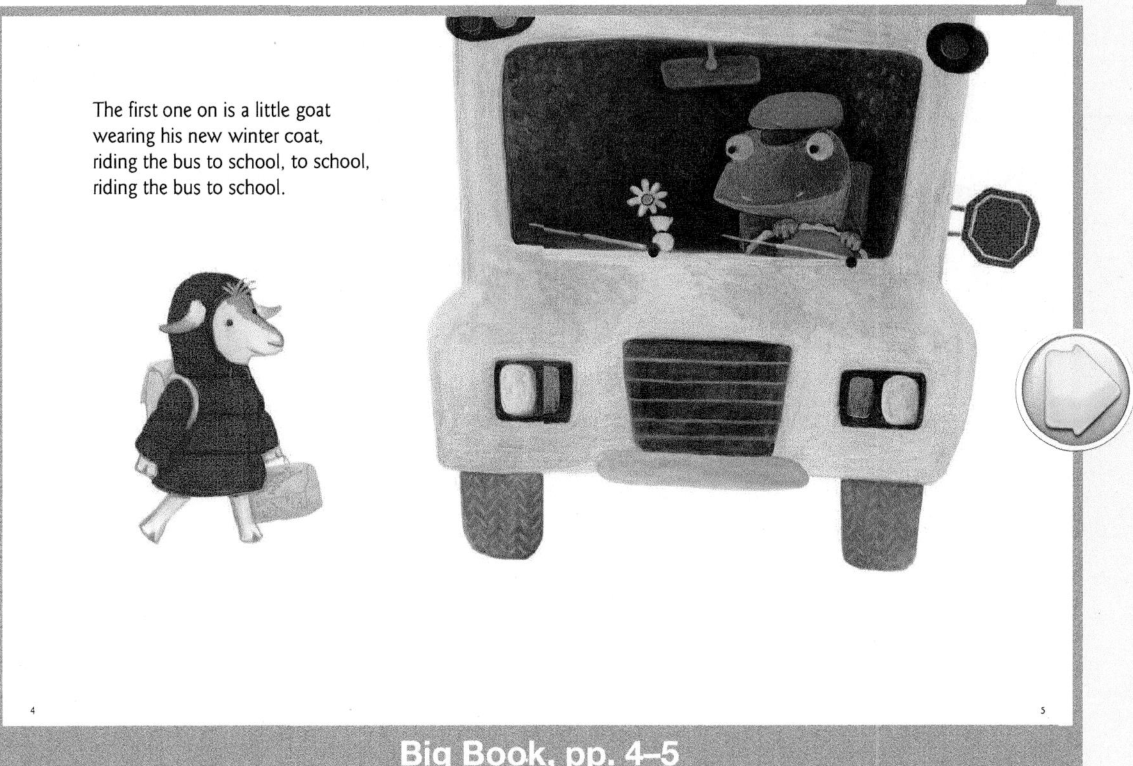

The first one on is a little goat
wearing his new winter coat,
riding the bus to school, to school,
riding the bus to school.

Big Book, pp. 4–5

***WH-* QUESTION** What is the goat waiting for? (The goat is waiting for the bus.)

Why does the goat want to get on the bus? (The goat wants to get on the bus to go to school.)

Common Core State Standards

Literature 1. With prompting and support, ask and answer questions about key details in a text. **Literature 2.** With prompting and support, retell familiar stories, including key details. **Literature 3.** With prompting and support, identify characters, settings, and major events in a story.

2ND READ

Develop Vocabulary

RECALL What is the second animal to get on the bus? (a pig)

- The pig is the second animal to get on the bus. What is the pig wearing on her head?

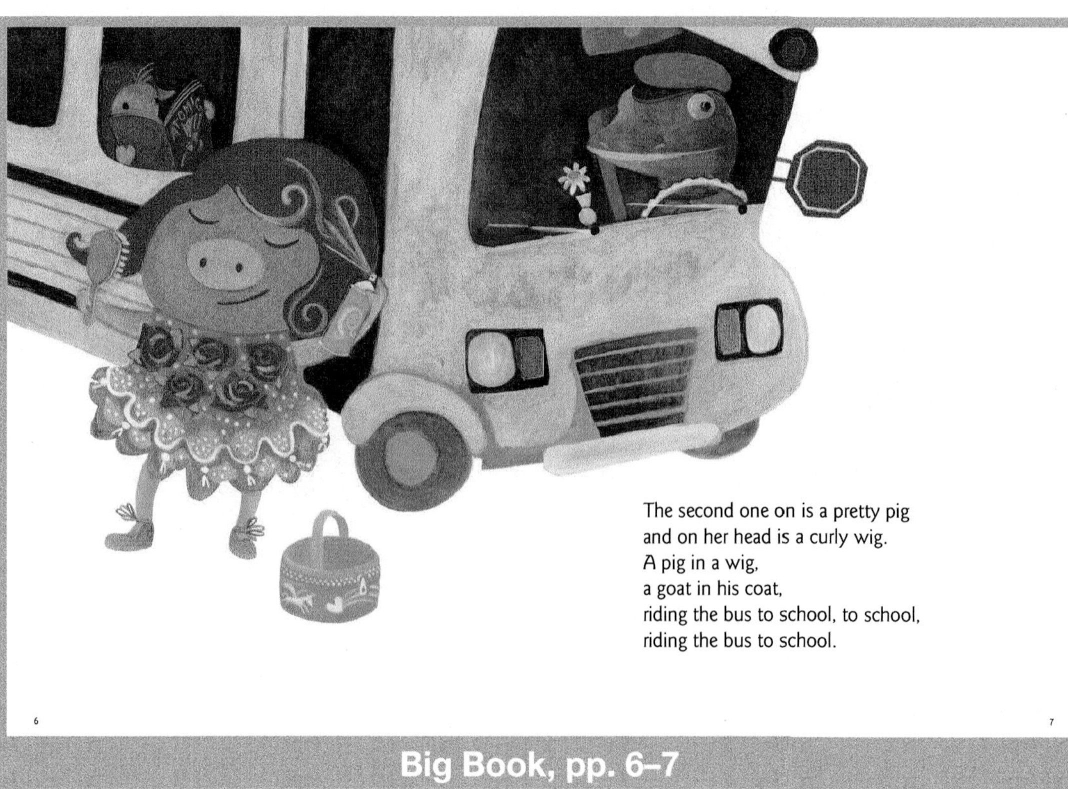

The second one on is a pretty pig
and on her head is a curly wig.
A pig in a wig,
a goat in his coat,
riding the bus to school, to school,
riding the bus to school.
6
7

Big Book, pp. 6–7

3RD READ

Develop Comprehension ©

OPEN-ENDED Why does the pig look so different? (The pig is wearing a wig.) Tell me what you think a wig might be.

RECALL What is the third animal to get on the bus? (a fox)

- The fox is the third animal to get on the bus. What is he wearing on his feet? What is he missing?

EXPAND VOCABULARY sly

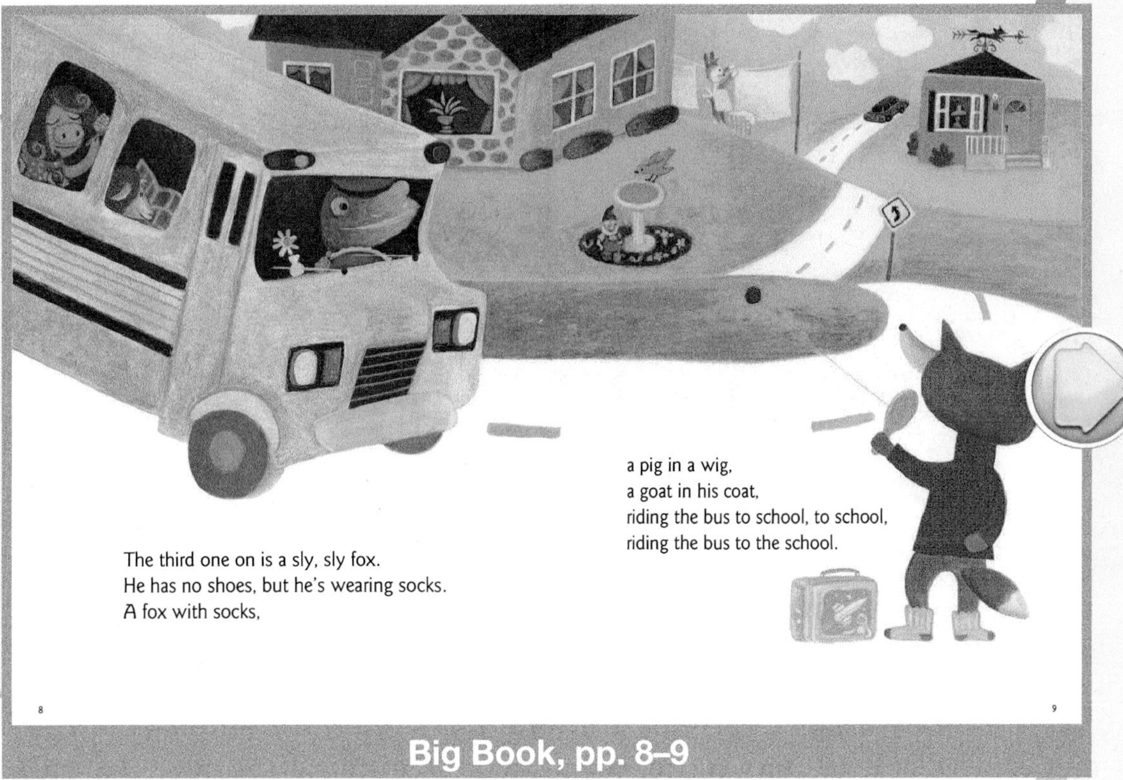

The third one on is a sly, sly fox.
He has no shoes, but he's wearing socks.
A fox with socks,
a pig in a wig,
a goat in his coat,
riding the bus to school, to school,
riding the bus to the school.
8
9

Big Book, pp. 8–9

INFERENCE What does the fox have on his feet? (The fox is wearing socks.) Why do you think the fox is wearing socks? (I think his feet might be cold.)

Common Core State Standards

Literature 1. With prompting and support, ask and answer questions about key details in a text. **Literature 2.** With prompting and support, retell familiar stories, including key details. **Literature 3.** With prompting and support, identify characters, settings, and major events in a story. **Literature 7.** With prompting and support, describe the relationship between illustrations and the story in which they appear (e.g., what moment in a story an illustration depicts). **Also Literature 4., Language 4.**

2ND READ

Develop Vocabulary

***WH-* QUESTION** What is the fourth animal to get on the bus? (a chick)

- The chick is the fourth animal to get on the bus. Who takes the fuzzy chick to the bus stop?

DEVELOP VOCABULARY bus stop

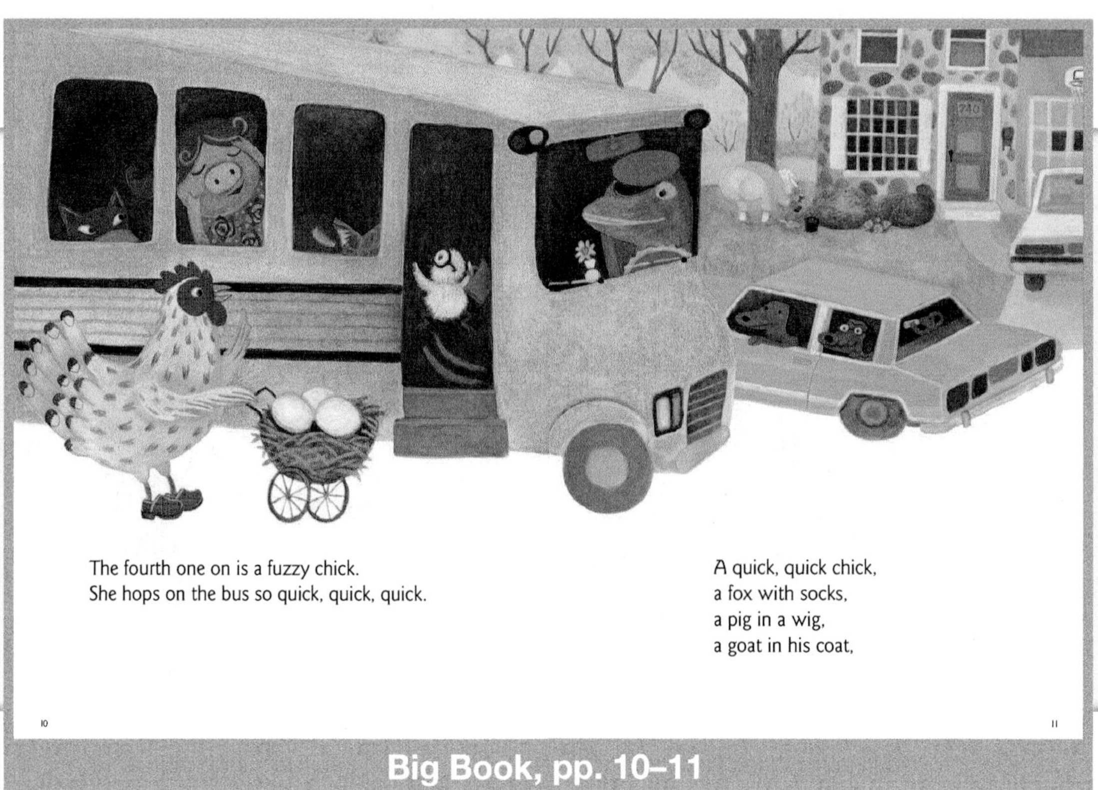

The fourth one on is a fuzzy chick.
She hops on the bus so quick, quick, quick.
A quick, quick chick,
a fox with socks,
a pig in a wig,
a goat in his coat,

Big Book, pp. 10–11

3RD READ

Develop Comprehension ©

MONITOR AND FIX UP Who walks with the chick to the bus stop? (a hen) If you can't answer the question, look at the picture to see what it shows. It will help you figure out who walks with the chick.

WH- QUESTION Where is the bus driver taking the animals? (to school)

- The bus driver is taking the animals to school. What is each animal doing while riding on the bus?

DEVELOP VOCABULARY driver

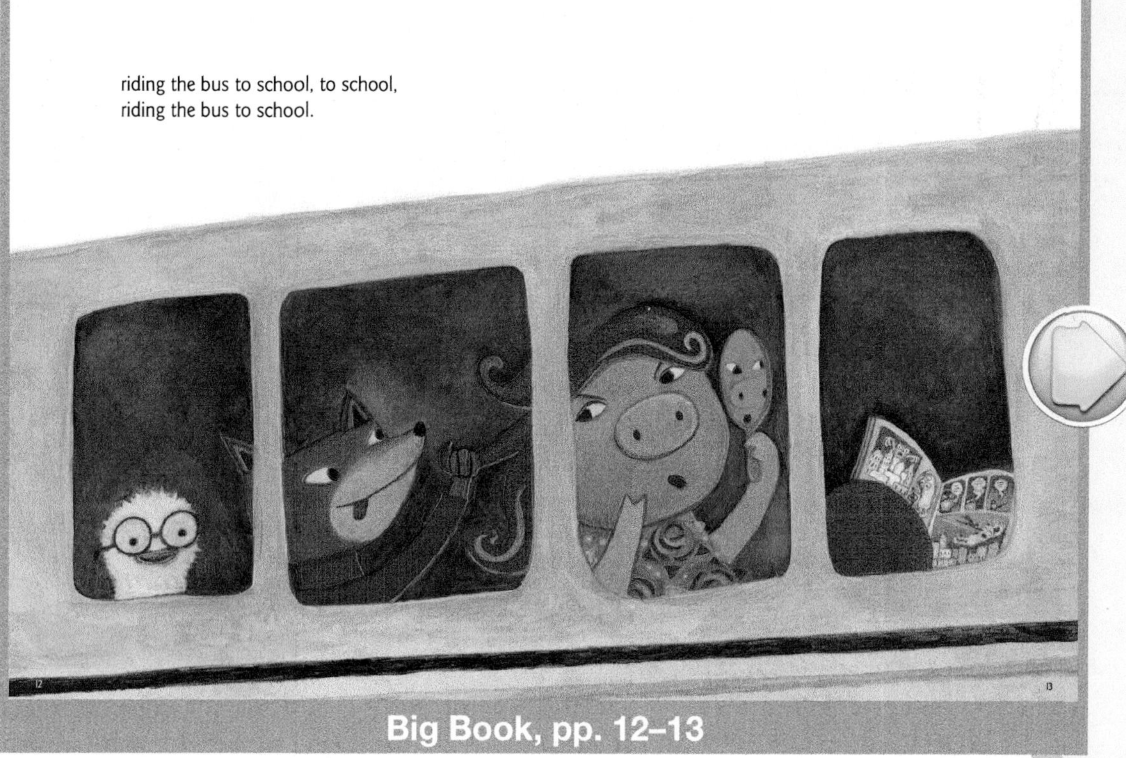

riding the bus to school, to school,
riding the bus to school.

Big Book, pp. 12–13

SEQUENCE Look at the animals in the windows on the bus. Who gets on the bus first? second? third? fourth? (Children should recognize that the animals are sitting on the bus in the order they got on the bus.)

Common Core State Standards

Literature 1. With prompting and support, ask and answer questions about key details in a text. **Literature 2.** With prompting and support, retell familiar stories, including key details. **Literature 3.** With prompting and support, identify characters, settings, and major events in a story. **Literature 7.** With prompting and support, describe the relationship between illustrations and the story in which they appear (e.g., what moment in a story an illustration depicts).

2ND READ

Develop Vocabulary

OPEN-ENDED Which animal gets on at the fifth bus stop? (a bear)

- The bear is the fifth animal on the bus. The bear is called a hairy bear. Why would that be a good name for the bear?

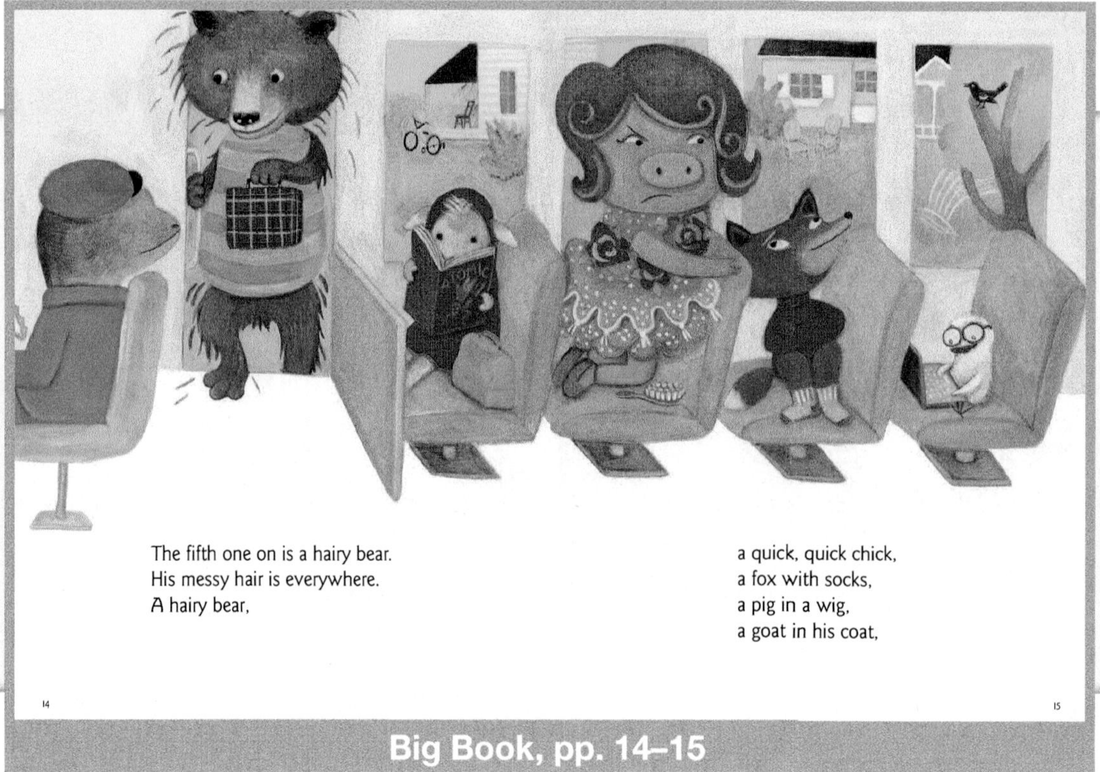
The fifth one on is a hairy bear.
His messy hair is everywhere.
A hairy bear,
a quick, quick chick,
a fox with socks,
a pig in a wig,
a goat in his coat,
14
15

Big Book, pp. 14–15

3RD READ

Develop Comprehension ©

***WH-* QUESTION** Which animals on the bus are reading? (The goat and the chick are reading.)

COMPLETION After the bus picks up the bear, what do the animals do? (ride the bus to school)

- The animals ride the bus to school. Read the words with me.

Common Core State Standards

Literature 1. With prompting and support, ask and answer questions about key details in a text. **Literature 2.** With prompting and support, retell familiar stories, including key details. **Literature 3.** With prompting and support, identify characters, settings, and major events in a story. **Literature 7.** With prompting and support, describe the relationship between illustrations and the story in which they appear (e.g., what moment in a story an illustration depicts). **Also Literature 4., Language 4.**

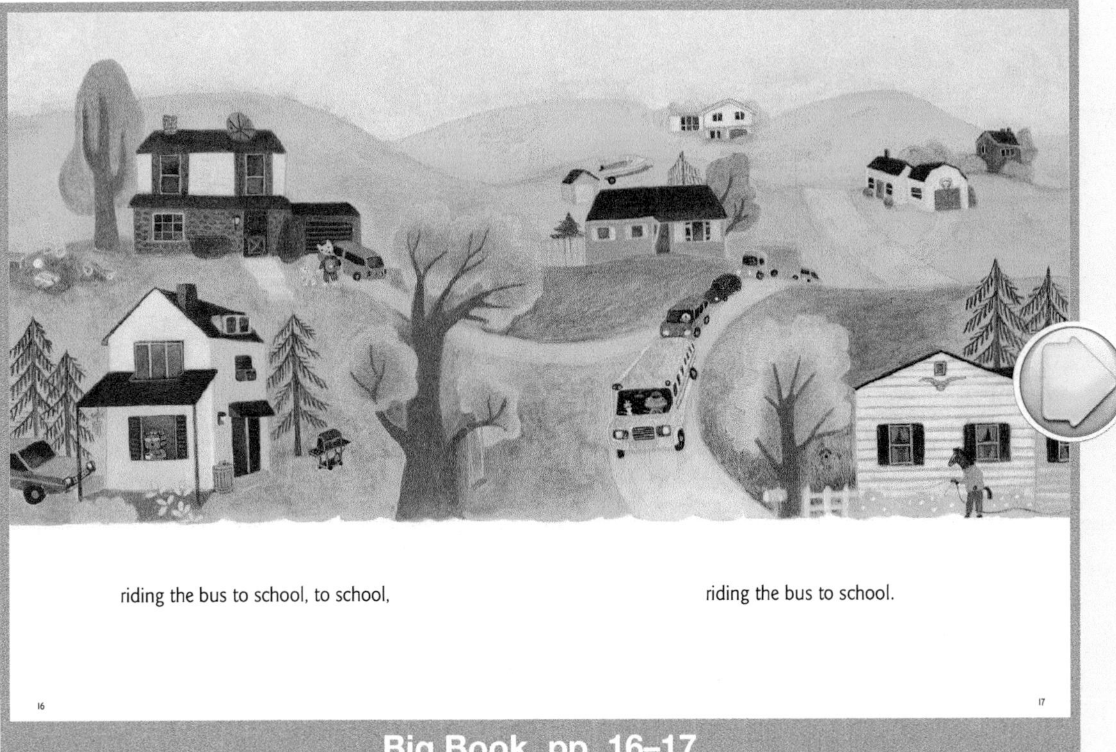

riding the bus to school, to school,
riding the bus to school.
16
17

Big Book, pp. 16–17

OPEN-ENDED Is the bus on a city road or a country road? How do you know? (The bus is on a country road. The houses are far apart, and there are lots of trees and grass.)

2ND READ

Develop Vocabulary

RECALL What is the sixth animal to get on the bus? (a worm)

- The worm is the sixth animal to get on the bus. What does the worm look like?

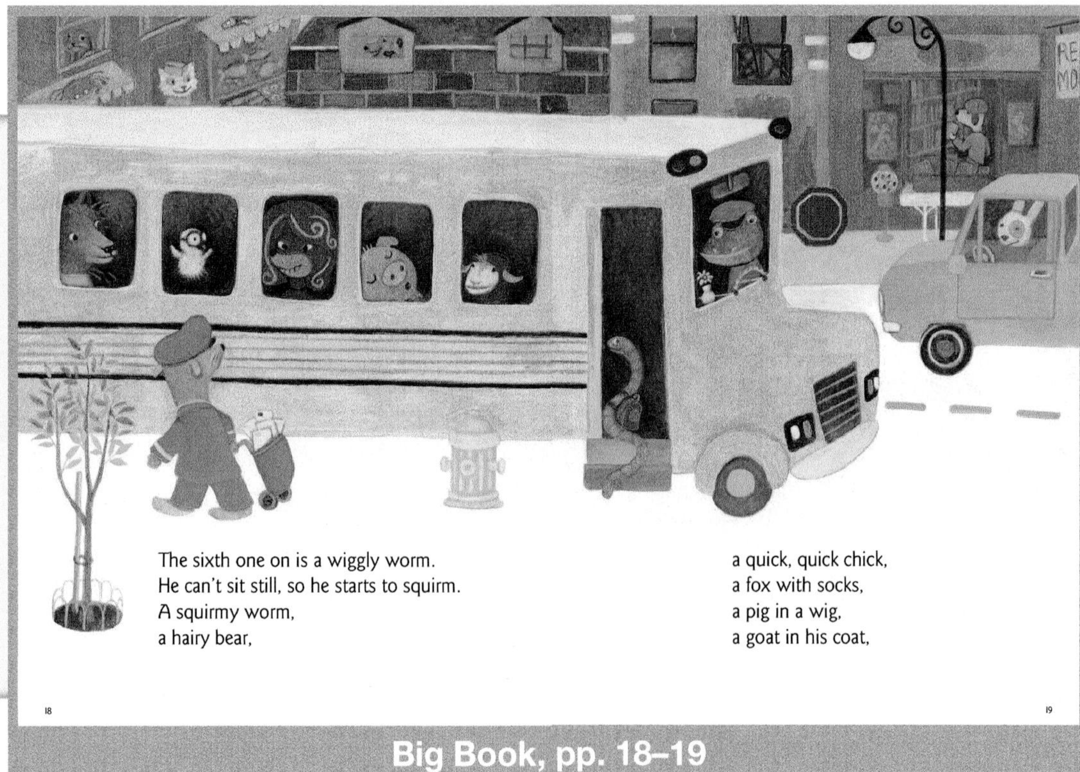

The sixth one on is a wiggly worm.
He can't sit still, so he starts to squirm.
A squirmy worm,
a hairy bear,
a quick, quick chick,
a fox with socks,
a pig in a wig,
a goat in his coat,
18
19

Big Book, pp. 18–19

3RD READ

Develop Comprehension ©

***WH-* QUESTION** Where is the bus now? How can you tell? (The bus is in a town. It is on a street, and the street is lined with buildings.)

WH- QUESTION After the bus picks up the worm, where does it go? (to school)

- The school bus is taking the animals to school. What animals and places do you see in the town?

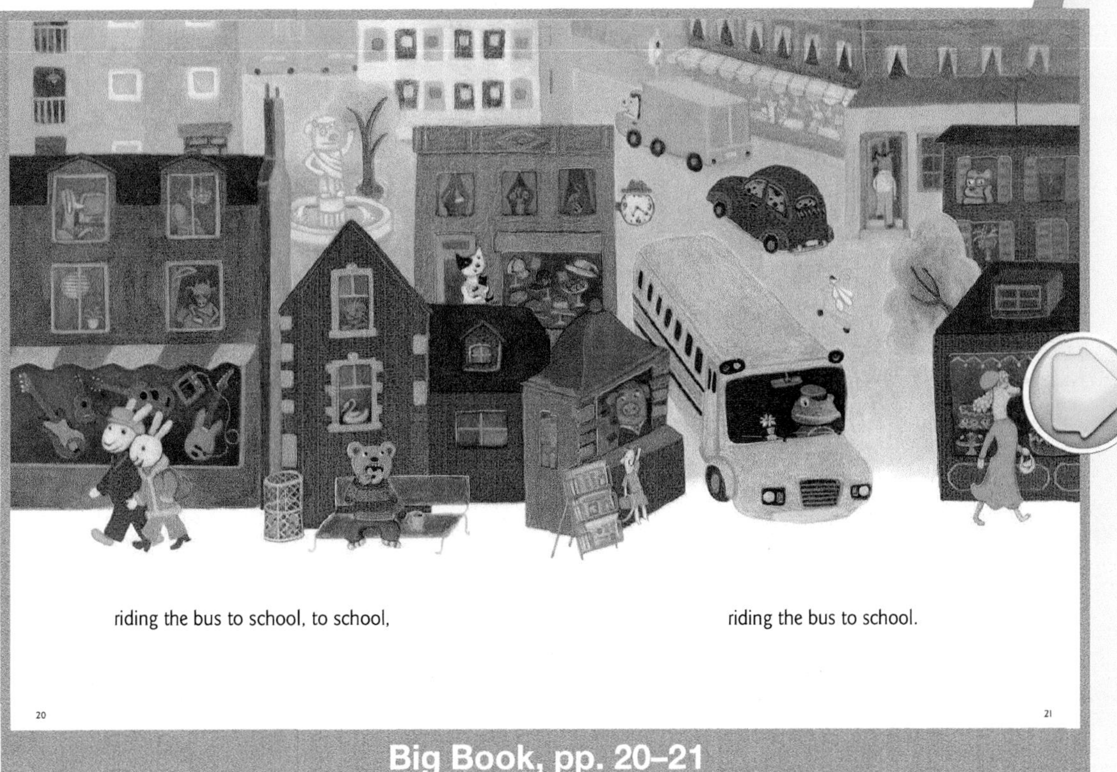

riding the bus to school, to school,
riding the bus to school.
20
21

Big Book, pp. 20–21

OPEN-ENDED What kinds of places are on this street? (Help children identify and describe several places, such as the guitar store, the restaurant, or the newsstand.)

Common Core State Standards

Literature 1. With prompting and support, ask and answer questions about key details in a text. **Literature 2.** With prompting and support, retell familiar stories, including key details. **Literature 3.** With prompting and support, identify characters, settings, and major events in a story. **Literature 7.** With prompting and support, describe the relationship between illustrations and the story in which they appear (e.g., what moment in a story an illustration depicts).

2ND READ

Develop Vocabulary

RECALL What is the last animal to get on the bus? (a sheep)

- The sheep is the last animal to get on the bus. What does the sheep do that is very different from the other animals?

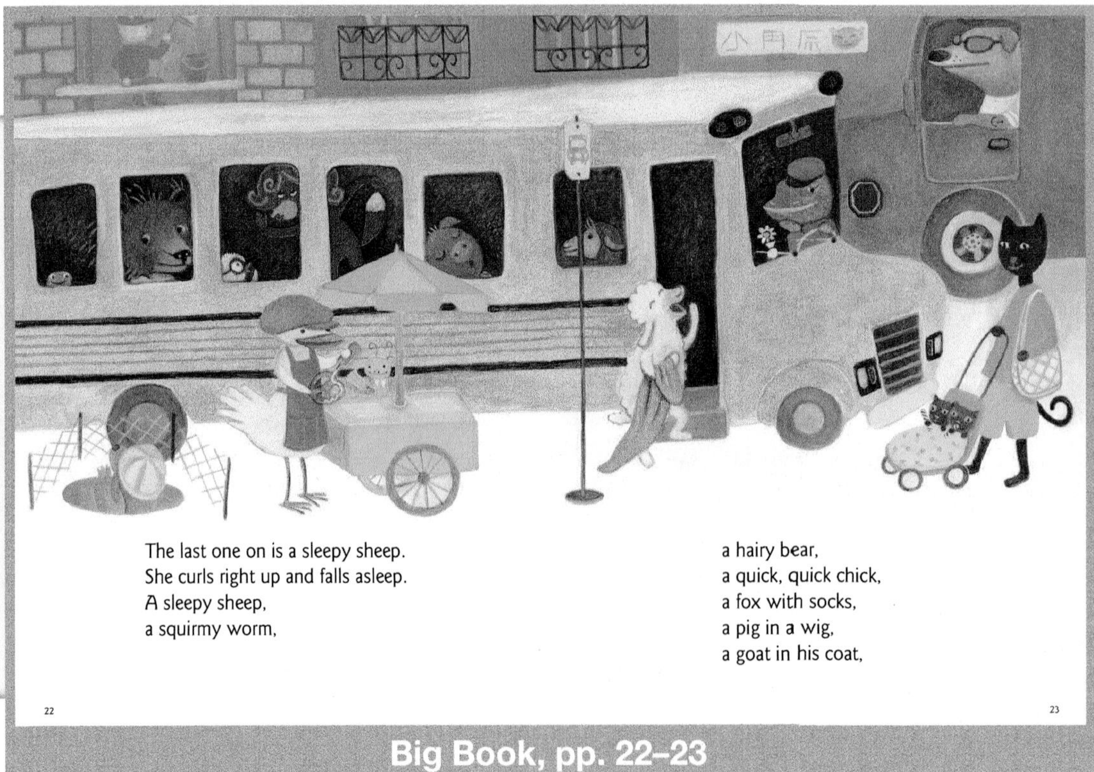
The last one on is a sleepy sheep.
She curls right up and falls asleep.
A sleepy sheep,
a squirmy worm,

a hairy bear,
a quick, quick chick,
a fox with socks,
a pig in a wig,
a goat in his coat,

22

23

Big Book, pp. 22–23

3RD READ

Develop Comprehension ©

***WH-* QUESTION** What is at the bus stop where the sheep gets on? (Children should describe the food stand, the lady with the baby carriage, and the man working underground.)

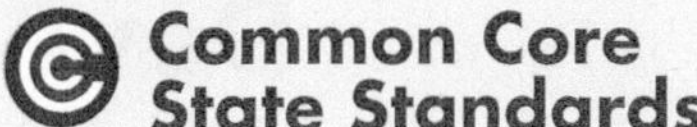

***WH-* QUESTION** Where is the next stop the bus makes? (at school)

- The bus stops at school. What do the animals do when the bus gets to school?

riding the bus to school, to school,
riding the bus to school.
24
25

Big Book, pp. 24–25

COMPLETION How do the animals get to school? (Some animals come by car, some come by bus, and some walk to school.)

How did you get to school today? Point to the picture that shows how. (Children should indicate what method of transportation they used to get to school today.)

Common Core State Standards

Literature 1. With prompting and support, ask and answer questions about key details in a text. **Literature 2.** With prompting and support, retell familiar stories, including key details. **Literature 3.** With prompting and support, identify characters, settings, and major events in a story. **Literature 7.** With prompting and support, describe the relationship between illustrations and the story in which they appear (e.g., what moment in a story an illustration depicts).

2ND READ

Develop Vocabulary

COMPLETION What do the animals do during the school day? (learn and play)

- The animals do several things, and the bus does something. Let's read these pages together to find out what the animals do and what the bus does.

During school they learn and play,
while the little bus sits and waits all day.
26
27

Big Book, pp. 26–27

3RD READ

Develop Comprehension ©

***WH-* QUESTION** What are the animals doing at school? (The teacher is reading a story, and the animals are listening to the story.)

What other things are in this classroom? (Have children name objects they see in the illustration.)

OPEN-ENDED What does the bus driver do when the school day ends? (starts up the bus)

- The bus driver starts the bus at the end of the day. Why do the animals need to ride the bus again?

And when the school day finally ends,
the little bus starts right up again.
28
29

Big Book, pp. 28–29

OPEN-ENDED What do the animals do at the end of the school day? What do you do after school is out? (The animals rush to the school bus. Children's responses to the second question will vary.)

Common Core State Standards

Literature 1. With prompting and support, ask and answer questions about key details in a text. **Literature 2.** With prompting and support, retell familiar stories, including key details. **Literature 3.** With prompting and support, identify characters, settings, and major events in a story. **Literature 7.** With prompting and support, describe the relationship between illustrations and the story in which they appear (e.g., what moment in a story an illustration depicts).

2ND READ

Develop Vocabulary

RECALL What do the animals do when they get on the bus? (sit down)

- The animals sit down in their seats. Which animals are riding the bus home?

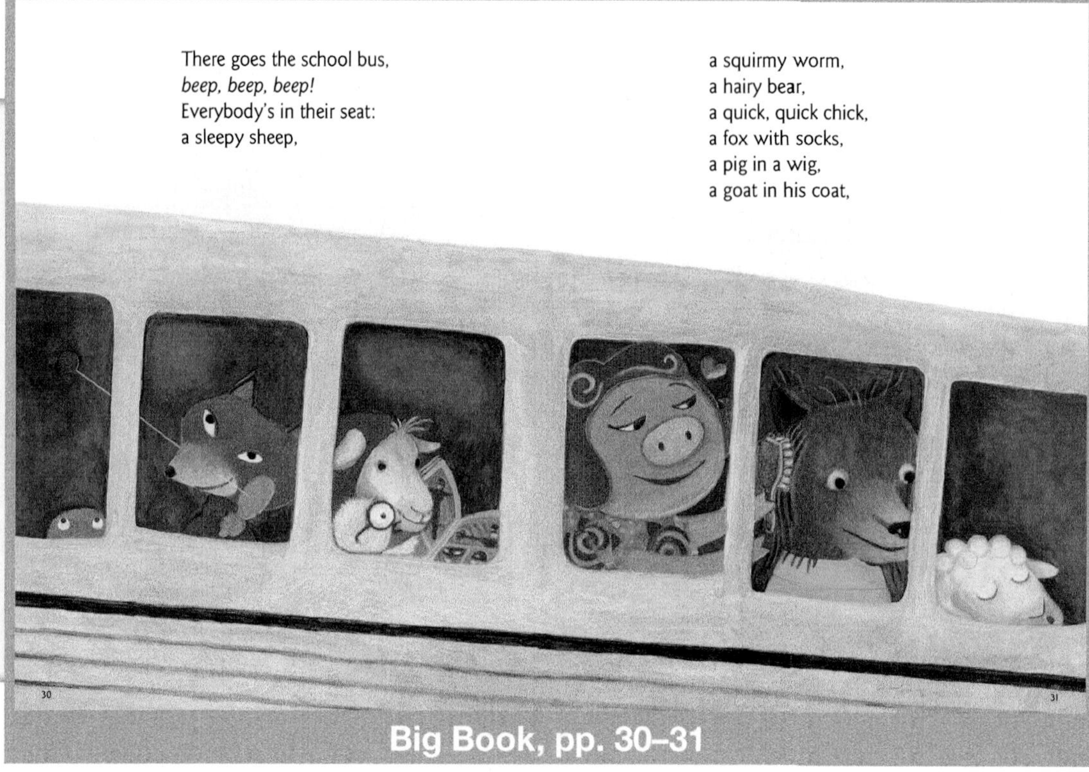

There goes the school bus,
beep, beep, beep!
Everybody's in their seat:
a sleepy sheep,
a squirmy worm,
a hairy bear,
a quick, quick chick,
a fox with socks,
a pig in a wig,
a goat in his coat,
30
31

Big Book, pp. 30–31

3RD READ

Develop Comprehension ©

COMPLETION Look at the pictures. What animals are first, second, third, fourth, fifth, sixth, and last, moving from right to left? (The sheep is first, the bear is second, the pig is third, the chick is fourth, the goat is fifth, the fox is sixth, and the worm is last.)

RECALL Where are all the animals going now? (home)

- All the animals on the bus are going home from school. Which animals are waving to us?

Continue with DAY 3
Conventions
p. 76

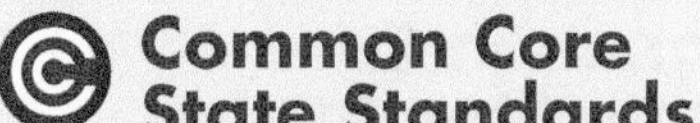

Common Core State Standards

Literature 1. With prompting and support, ask and answer questions about key details in a text. **Literature 2.** With prompting and support, retell familiar stories, including key details. **Literature 3.** With prompting and support, identify characters, settings, and major events in a story. **Literature 7.** With prompting and support, describe the relationship between illustrations and the story in which they appear (e.g., what moment in a story an illustration depicts).

riding home from school, from school,
riding home from school.

32

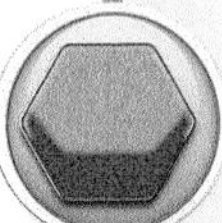

Big Book, p. 32

OPEN-ENDED What are the animals at the back of the bus doing? Why do you think the animals wave? (The animals at the back are waving. I think the animals are waving goodbye to the reader.)

Skip to DAY 4
Conventions
p. 90

Common Core State Standards

Writing 2. Use a combination of drawing, dictating, and writing to compose informative/explanatory texts in which they name what they are writing about and supply some information about the topic. **Speaking/Listening 1.a.** Follow agreed-upon rules for discussions (e.g., listening to others and taking turns speaking about the topics and texts under discussion). **Language 1.a.** Print many upper- and lowercase letters.

Daily Fix-It

I am pam
I am Pam.

This week's practice sentences appear on *Teacher Resources DVD-ROM.*

Conventions

Say Our Names

TEACH Point to one of the children and say the child's name. A name is the word that tells who this is. What is the word that tells who this is? Point to other children in the class and have the group say the child's name.

Picture Card

GUIDE PRACTICE Show the *cat* Picture Card. Look at the cat. What do you think would be a good name for this cat? List children's answers on the board, calling attention to the uppercase and lowercase letters. Continue with these Picture Cards: *dog, fox, elephant, frog.*

ON THEIR OWN Use *Reader's and Writer's Notebook,* p. 8, to continue practice with names.

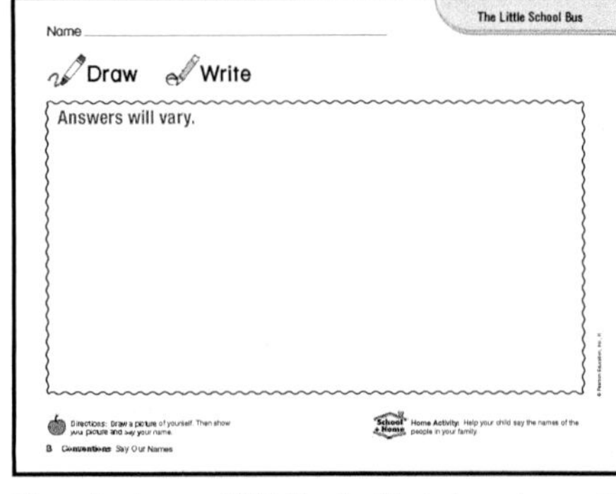
The Little School Bus

Name

Draw Write

Answers will vary.

Reader's and Writer's Notebook, p. 8

Song

TEACH A **song** is a short piece of music, or a tune, with words for singing. People sometimes sing songs to show they are happy. Do you know any songs about being happy? I know one. Hum the tune of "If You're Happy and You Know It." Do not sing the words. What part are we missing? That's right, we are missing the words to the song! We need to have words to sing a song.

MODEL I remember the first words to this song because they are the same as the title of the song. Listen carefully: *If you're happy and you know it...* That is the first part of our song. We can use our imaginations to write the rest. This song is about telling how we show that we are happy. When I am happy, I clap my hands. I am going to draw a picture of clapping to remember what to sing. Draw a picture of yourself clapping on the board. Now I can sing more words to the song. Sing the new verse to the song.

GUIDE PRACTICE Have children suggest things they do when they are happy. List the activities on the board and practice singing about these activities.

INDEPENDENT WRITING Have children turn to p. 11 of *Reader's and Writer's Notebook.* Have them draw a picture of something they do when they are happy. Then sing the song using the children's activities.

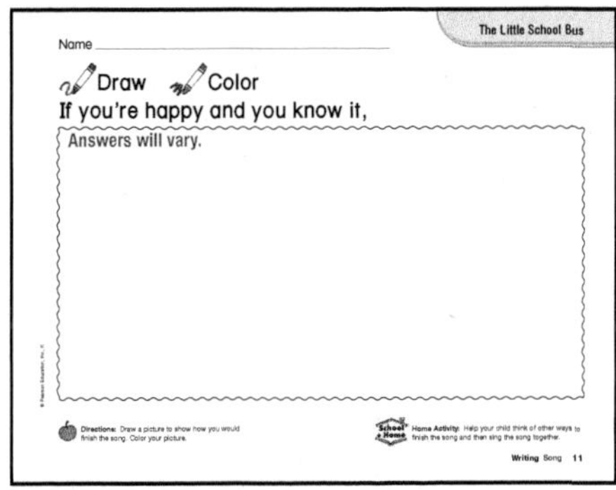
The Little School Bus

Name

Draw Color

If you're happy and you know it,

Answers will vary.

Reader's and Writer's Notebook, p. 11

Daily Handwriting

Write letters *Aa* and *Bb* on the board. Review correct letter formation.

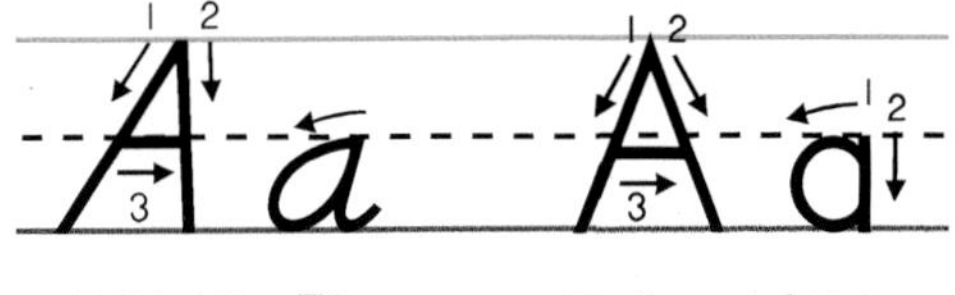
D'Nealian™ Ball and Stick

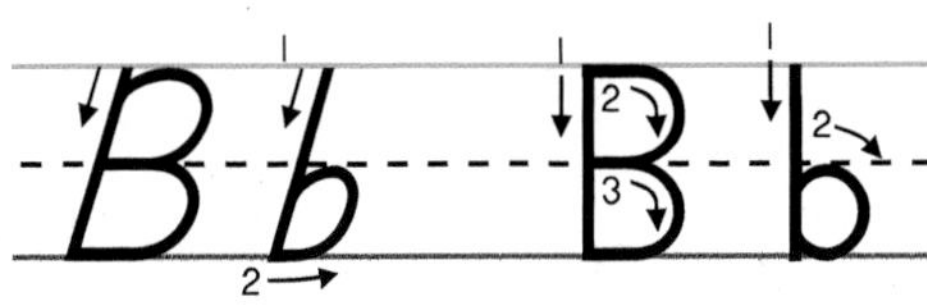
D'Nealian™ Ball and Stick

Have children write *Aa* and *Bb* on their Write-On Boards. Remind them to use proper left-to-right and top-to-bottom progression and proper spacing between the letters.

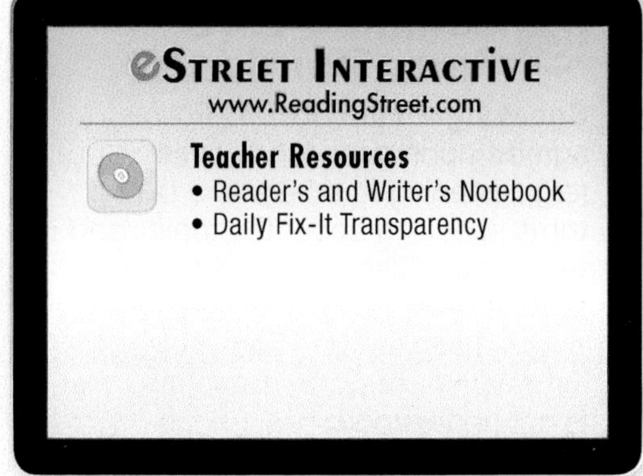

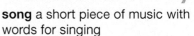

Academic Vocabulary 

song a short piece of music with words for singing

Access Content If children are unfamiliar with the song "If You're Happy and You Know It," sing the song for them. Encourage them to sing along after they have listened to the song several times.

Common Core State Standards

Speaking/Listening 1.a. Follow agreed-upon rules for discussions (e.g., listening to others and taking turns speaking about the topics and texts under discussion). **Speaking/Listening 3.** Ask and answer questions in order to seek help, get information, or clarify something that is not understood.

Academic Vocabulary

directions sentences that tell what to do or how to do something

Bridge to Common Core

COMPREHENSION AND COLLABORATION

As children follow and give directions, they are learning to participate in a structured collaboration, to follow agreed-upon rules, and to request clarification if they don't understand something.

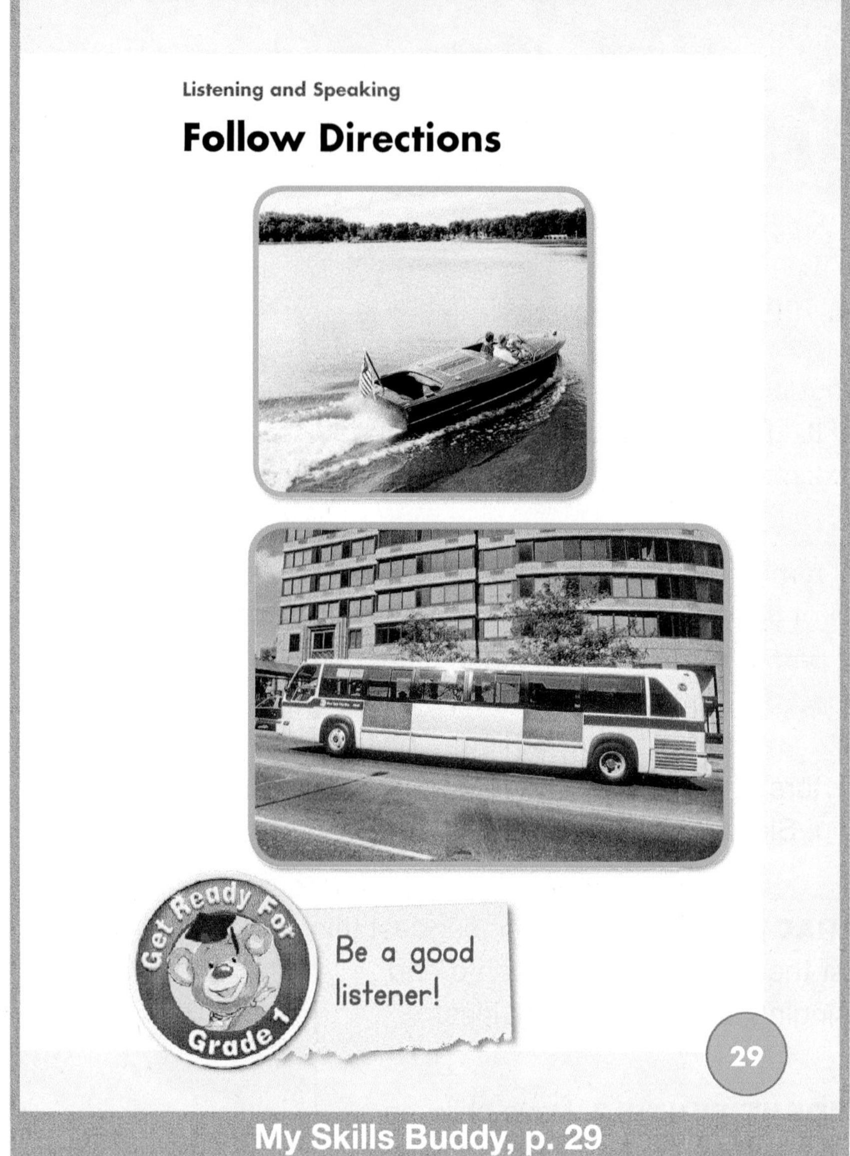

My Skills Buddy, p. 29

Listening and Speaking

Follow Directions

TEACH When we do things at school, we often have to follow directions. **Directions** tell us what to do or how to do something. We need to listen carefully to directions so we can follow them and do them correctly. Discuss the Listening and Speaking bullets on p. 28 of *My Skills Buddy.*

MODEL If I am told to turn around, this is what I do. Show children how you turn around. The direction told me to turn around, so that's what I did. Turn around again. Did I follow the direction? Now you do it with me. Remind children that good listeners face the speaker and ask questions if they need help understanding something.

GUIDE PRACTICE AlphaBuddy is going to tell you some things to do. Listen carefully to what AlphaBuddy says. AlphaBuddy will give each direction once.

- Raise your hand.
- Touch your head with your hand.
- Touch your desk with your elbow.

Continue with other directions until children are able to follow more complicated sentences.

INDEPENDENT PRACTICE Have one child give a simple direction to the class, such as *Touch your toes.* Have the class practice listening to and following one direction from each child. Remind children that good listeners face the speaker. Refer children to their Rules for Listening and Speaking from pp. 1–2 of the *Reader's and Writer's Notebook.* Remind children that it is very important to ask questions if they do not understand a direction. Tell them to raise their hands if they have questions or need help.

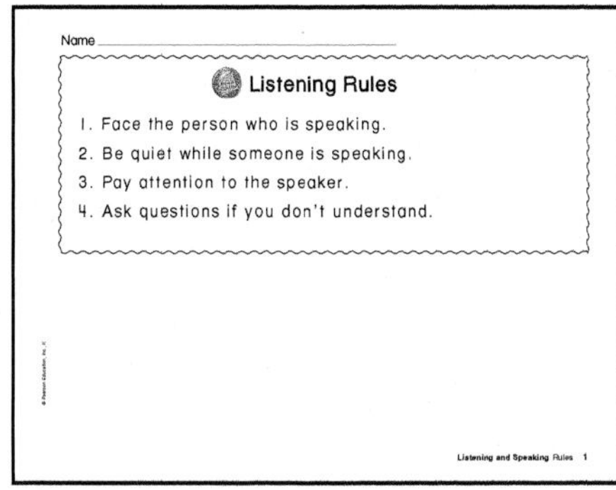
Name

Listening Rules

1. Face the person who is speaking.
2. Be quiet while someone is speaking.
3. Pay attention to the speaker.
4. Ask questions if you don't understand.

Listening and Speaking Rules 1

Reader's and Writer's Notebook, pp. 1–2

Be a Good Listener!

1. Face the person who is speaking.
2. Be quiet while someone is speaking.
3. Pay attention to the speaker.
4. Ask questions if you don't understand.

Follow Directions Point out and name body parts in English to help children understand activity directions.

Common Core State Standards

Foundational Skills 1.d. Recognize and name all upper- and lowercase letters of the alphabet. **Speaking/ Listening 1.** Participate in collaborative conversations with diverse partners about *kindergarten topics and texts* with peers and adults in small and larger groups. **Also Language 5., 5.a.**

Wrap Up Your Day!

- ✔ **Content Knowledge** Today we learned how people get to school. Did everyone come to school by bus? How else do people get to school?
- ✔ **Comprehension** Today we read about Cat and Dog. Who are they? What did they do?
- ✔ **Listening and Speaking** Listen carefully to my directions and try to do what I say. Tell children a simple set of directions quietly so they have to listen carefully.
- ✔ **Homework Idea** Have children write the letters *Aa, Bb,* and *Cc.* Have them find and circle examples of these letters in text at home (for example, from magazines, ads, newspapers).

Preview DAY 4

Tomorrow we will read about one of our Trucktown friends.

Extend Your Day!

Science
Fast, Faster, Fastest

MATERIALS: paper; crayons; glue; photographs of buses, cars, and walkers

BUS, CAR, OR WALKING We get to school in different ways. Some walk, some ride in a car, and some ride a bus. Which is the fastest way?

Divide the class into three groups: Walkers, Bus Riders, and Car Riders. Choose a familiar landmark in your community. Have each group decide which group of children will get from that landmark to school fast, faster, and fastest.

RECORD YOUR RESULTS Have each child complete a *Fast, Faster, Fastest* log. Children can either draw or glue pictures to show which modes of transportation belong with each label. Gather children's logs to create a bulletin board.

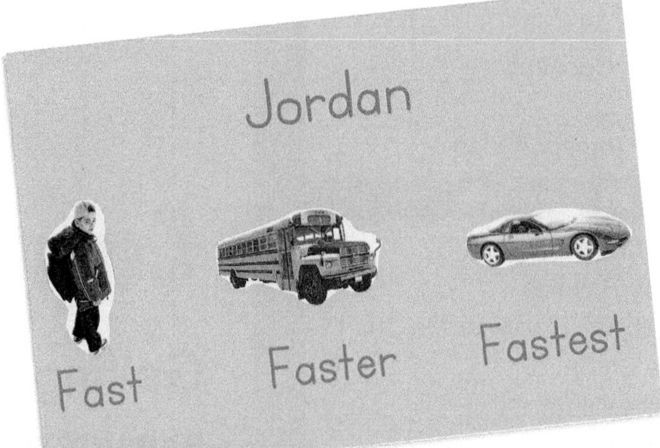

Letter Recognition
Match Letters

MATERIALS: Alphabet Cards—*Aa, Bb, Cc;* index cards with words such as *Ann, Abby, am, ant, Bob, Ben, bat, bus, Cam, Cal, cat, car*

LETTER SEARCH When children are not in the room, hide the word cards in easily reachable places. Tape the Alphabet Cards *Aa, Bb,* and *Cc* on the board. Ask children to search the room and each find one card. After the search is complete, have children show the cards they found and tape them on the board under the matching letter. Review letters and pictures together.

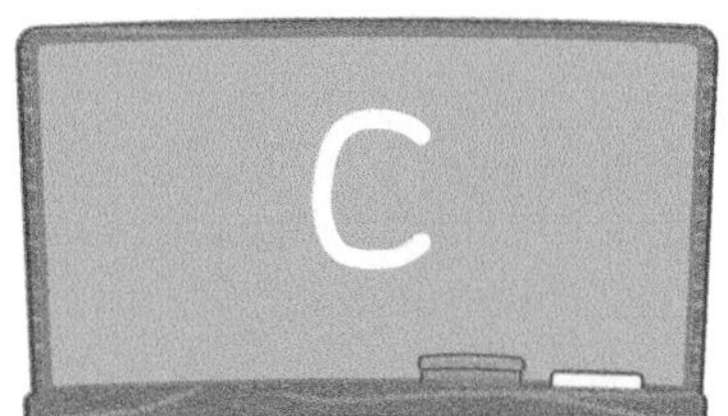

Conventions
Names

MATERIALS: index cards

INTRODUCE ME Have each child write his or her name on an index card. Collect the cards and place them in a stack at the front of the room. Begin the game by taking a card and giving the following clue about the child so the others can guess the name: *It is a boy's name. He is wearing a green shirt.* The child whose name was on the card gets the next turn to take a card. Assist children in reading the names and giving hints as necessary.

Clint Tyrone Lynne Marie Sonja

DAY 4
at a Glance

Content Knowledge
Oral Vocabulary

Phonological Awareness
Rhyming Words

Letter Recognition
Letters *Dd*

Text-Based Comprehension
Character

Conventions
Say Our Names

Writing
Extend the Concept

Vocabulary
Words for Transportation

Materials

- Student Edition
- Truckery Rhymes
- Talk with Me/Sing with Me Chart
- Picture Cards
- Alphabet Cards
- Phonics Songs and Rhymes Chart
- Get Set, Roll! Reader 1
- Reader's and Writer's Notebook
- Big Book

Common Core State Standards

Speaking/Listening 2. Confirm understanding of a text read aloud or information presented orally or through other media by asking and answering questions about key details and requesting clarification if something is not understood. **Language 6.** Use words and phrases acquired through conversations, reading and being read to, and responding to texts.

TRUCKTOWN on Reading Street

Start your engines!

- Display "Jack Be Nimble" and lead the group in saying the rhyme a few times.
- Have the group clap the rhythm as they recite the rhyme.
  - When children have mastered the rhythm, have them march around the room as they say the rhyme.

Truckery Rhymes
Truckery Rhymes

Content Knowledge

Zoom in on

Getting to School Together

EXPAND THE CONCEPT Write the Question of the Week on the board, *How do children get to school?* Read the question as you track the print. Tell children to respond in complete sentences. Display Sing with Me Chart 1B.

How We Get to School
The first child gets to take the bus,
Take the bus, take the bus.
The first child gets to take the bus.
That's how we get to school!
Talk with Me/Sing with Me Chart 1B

Build Oral Language

LISTEN FOR AMAZING WORDS We are going to sing this song again. Listen for the Amazing Words *fifth* and *sixth.* Sing the song several times with children to the tune of "Mary Had a Little Lamb." Have them hop when they hear *fifth* and *sixth.*

Build Oral Vocabulary

Amazing Words Robust Vocabulary Routine

1. **Introduce the Word** The child that gets on the bus after the fourth child is the *fifth* child. What is our new Amazing Word to tell about a child that gets on the bus after the fourth child? Say it with me: *fifth.*

2. **Demonstrate** *If there is a group of people waiting to buy lunch and you are right behind the fourth person, you are fifth in line.*

   Repeat steps 1 and 2.

   Introduce the Word The child that gets on the bus after the fifth child is the *sixth* child. What is our new Amazing Word to tell about a child that gets on the bus after the fifth child? Say it with me: *sixth.*

   Demonstrate Pretend you are in a line of people waiting to see a movie. *If you are right behind the fifth person, you are sixth in line.*

3. **Apply** Have children use *fifth* and *sixth* in complete sentences. Have them arrange books, pencils, or crayons in a line and identify the objects that are *fifth* and *sixth.*

4. **Display the Words** Point to and name the beginning letters in *fifth* and *sixth.* Have children repeat the letter names. Then ask them what they notice about the last two letters in both words.

Routines Flip Chart

USE AMAZING WORDS To reinforce the concept and the Amazing Words, have children supply the appropriate Amazing Word for each sentence.

The _______ person comes after the fourth person. (fifth)
The _______ person comes after the fifth person. (sixth)

Amazing Words

first	second
third	fourth
fifth	sixth

Access for All

SI Strategic Intervention

Amazing Words Display a line of six objects. Label the objects with index cards numbered from 1 to 6. Point to each object and say its ordinal number. Have children supply the ordinal numbers for the *fifth* and *sixth* objects.

Access Content Ask children to share the words in their home languages for the ordinal number words *first, second, third, fourth, fifth,* and *sixth.*

Produce Oral Language Use the Day 4 instruction on ELL Poster 1 to extend and enrich language.

Common Core State Standards

Foundational Skills 2.a. Recognize and produce rhyming words.

Phonological Awareness

Rhyming Words

PRACTICE Read p. 4 from *The Little School Bus.* Remind children that rhyming words are words with middle and ending parts that sound the same. Ask children to identify the rhyming words in the sentence (*goat, coat*). Continue the activity with p. 6 for *pig* and *wig.*

Say the words *pig* and *wig* with children. Remember, rhyming words have the same middle and ending parts. Let's make a new rhyming word. I can change /p/ in *pig* to /d/: /d/ *-ig, dig. Dig* rhymes with *pig.* They both have the same middle and ending sounds. Continue with *big* and *jig.*

REVIEW COUNTING WORDS Reread the page from *The Little School Bus* about the goat getting on the bus. Repeat the sentence and have children clap and count as you say each word. Continue with several other sentences from the book.

Corrective feedback	**If...** children cannot count words, **then...** say the sentence slowly, clapping once for each word. Have children imitate your actions. Repeat several times.

GUIDE PRACTICE Display the *dog* Picture Card. This is a dog. What are the middle and ending parts in the word *dog?* The middle and ending parts in *dog* are *-og.* Can you think of other words that have the same middle and ending parts as *dog?* List children's suggestions on the board.

Picture Card

ON THEIR OWN Read each word on the list with the following sentence frame: _______ *rhymes with dog.* Have children choose a rhyming word from the list and illustrate it.

Don't Wait Until Friday **MONITOR PROGRESS**

Check Phonological Awareness

FORMATIVE ASSESSMENT Say the following sentences two times each: *The goat wears a coat. The pig has a pretty wig.* Ask children to clap when they hear rhyming words the second time you read the sentences.

If... children cannot distinguish rhyming words,

then... say the sentences slowly, drawing out the words that rhyme: *goat, coat; pig, wig.*

Continue to monitor children's progress during the week so that they can be successful with the Day 5 Assessment.

Access for All

 Advanced

Phonological Awareness Display the following Picture Cards: *can, fan, man, pan, van.* Have children identify the middle and ending parts of these words. Then have them generate their own rhyming words.

Common Core State Standards

Foundational Skills 1.d. Recognize and name all upper- and lowercase letters of the alphabet. **Also Foundational Skills 1.a., 3.c.**

Letter Recognition

Teach/Model

Letters *Dd*

INTRODUCE/MODEL Display the *Dd* Alphabet Card. Point to the uppercase letter. The name of this letter is uppercase *D.* What is the name of this letter? Continue the routine with lowercase *d.*

Dd
dolphin
Alphabet Card

Guide Practice

GROUP PRACTICE Display Phonics Songs and Rhymes Chart 1. Do you remember the song we learned about a bus? Let's look at the chart and find words that have a *d* in them. Have children point to words that have uppercase *D* and lowercase *d.* Have children say the word with you for each letter they find. List the words with *d* on the board and have children take turns circling the letter.

A Bus Comes Along Every Day
Oh, a bus comes along every day,
Oh, a bus comes along every day.
At our curb it does arrive,
And it takes us for a ride.
Oh, a bus comes along every day.
Phonics Songs and Rhymes Chart 1

ON THEIR OWN Have children use *Reader's and Writer's Notebook,* p. 9, for more practice with letters *Dd.* Save the *Ee* section of the page for Day 5.

REVIEW LETTER RECOGNITION Write *a* on the board. Have children write the letter with their fingers on their hands and say its name. Continue with uppercase *A.* Continue the review routine with *Bb* and *Cc.*

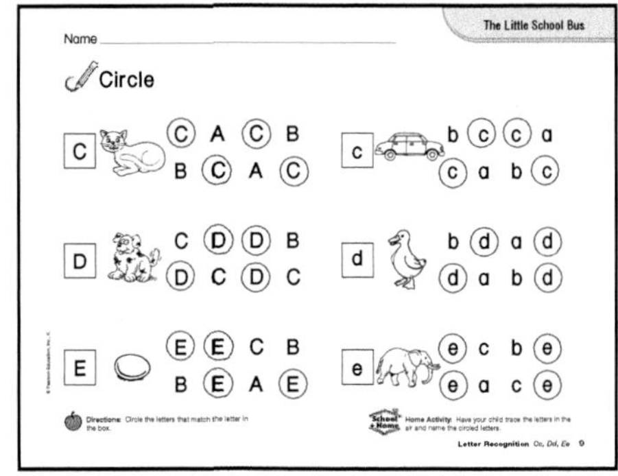
The Little School Bus
Name
Circle
C C A C B B C A C
c b c c a c a b c
D C D D B D C D C
d b d a d d a b d
E E E C B B E A E
e e c b e e a c e
Reader's and Writer's Notebook, p. 9

Get Set, Roll! Reader 1

Read *Jack and Max*

REVIEW Review the high-frequency words *I* and *am.* Have children read each word as you point to it on the Word Wall.

TEACH REBUS WORDS Write the word *Jack* on the board. This is the name *Jack.* Have children say the name with you. Look for this word in our story today. You will see the word with a small picture of a truck above it. This is the truck that is called Jack. The small picture will help you read the word *Jack.* Continue with the other rebus words: *Max, wet, up, down.*

Get Set, Roll! Reader 1

READ Today we will read a book about two of our Trucktown friends. Point to the title of the story. The title of this story is *Jack and Max.* Look at how I am holding the book. The *a* in *Jack* is right-side up. This is the right way to hold a book. Remind children how to correctly turn pages.

Use the routine for reading decodable books in the Routines Flip Chart to read Get Set, Roll! Reader 1.

Day 4 SMALL GROUP TIME • Differentiate Language, p. SG•1

OL On-Level	SI Strategic Intervention	A Advanced
• **Build** Sentences and Words • **Read** Get Set, Roll! Reader *Jack and Max*	• **Talk About** Sentences and Words • **Read** Get Set, Roll! Reader *Jack and Max*	• **Extend** Sentences and Words • **Read** Get Set, Roll! Reader *Jack and Max*

eSTREET INTERACTIVE
www.ReadingStreet.com

Savvas eText
• Get Set, Roll! Reader

Phonics Songs and Rhymes Audio

Teacher Resources
• Reader's and Writer's Notebook

Access for All

A Advanced

Rebus Words Have children discuss the character Jack. Prompt discussion by asking them what Jack is and what he is like. Have children write about Jack using rebus words and the following sentence frame: *Jack is* ________. Have them draw pictures to complete the sentence.

Access Content Define the word *truck* for English learners and point out examples of specialized trucks in Get Set, Roll! Reader 1.

Place English Language Learners in the groups that correspond to their reading abilities in English.

If... children need more practice **Developing Language,**
then... use the Language Workshops in the *ELL Handbook* beginning on p. 306.

Text-Based Comprehension

Character

PRACTICE Have children turn to the Literary Elements pictures on pp. 14–15 of *My Skills Buddy.* As you look at the Characters picture, remind children that all stories have characters.

My Skills Buddy, pp. 14–15

Team Talk Pair children and have them take turns describing the characters in "The Tortoise and the Hare," as featured on pp. 14–15 of *My Skills Buddy.* Characters are the animals or people in a story. Good readers pay attention to the characters so they know who the story is about. We can understand the characters better when we tell what they are like and when we pay attention to what they are doing. Review the story of "The Tortoise and the Hare."

- Who are the characters in the picture? (the tortoise and the hare)
- What does the hare do? (He takes a nap and loses the race.)
- What does the tortoise do? (He works hard and wins the race.)

MORE PRACTICE For more practice with character, have children discuss their favorite characters in *The Little School Bus.*

Common Core State Standards

Literature 1. With prompting and support, ask and answer questions about key details in a text. **Literature 3.** With prompting and support, identify characters, settings, and major events in a story. **Literature 10.** Actively engage in group reading activities with purpose and understanding.

Read Main Selection

GUIDE COMPREHENSION Display *The Little School Bus.* Show the cover of the book. Have children identify the characters on the cover.

- What can you tell about the fox? (He has on socks.)
- What can you tell about the pig? (She is wearing a wig.)
- What can you tell about the bear? (He is hairy.)

READ Reread *The Little School Bus.* Return to p. 60. Follow the **3rd Read** and use the **Develop Comprehension** notes to give children the opportunity to gain a more complete understanding of the story.

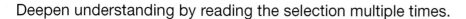

Routine Read for Understanding

Deepen understanding by reading the selection multiple times.

1. **First Read**—Read the entire selection aloud to build interest in the text.
2. **Second Read**—Use the **Develop Vocabulary** notes on pages 60–75.
3. **Third Read**—Use the **Develop Comprehension** notes on pages 60–75.

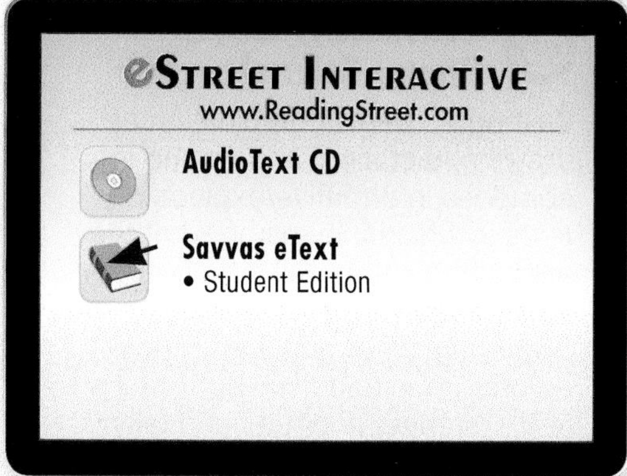

eStreet Interactive
www.ReadingStreet.com
AudioText CD
Savvas eText
• Student Edition

Access for All

Strategic Intervention

Support Discussion Have children draw pictures of the characters and use the pictures to guide their answers to the Develop Comprehension questions.

RANGE OF READING AND LEVEL OF TEXT COMPLEXITY

Using the Develop Comprehension notes as you read the text a third time will help you assess how well children are comprehending the authentic literary text in *Reading Street.* As the year progresses, children will improve as independent, proficient readers of complex text.

Extend Vocabulary When discussing the chick character in the story, explain to children that *chick* is the word for a baby bird. Point out that a chick can be any baby bird but often is a baby chicken, as in this story.

Common Core State Standards

Writing 2. Use a combination of drawing, dictating, and writing to compose informative/explanatory texts in which they name what they are writing about and supply some information about the topic. **Speaking/Listening 1.a.** Follow agreed-upon rules for discussions (e.g., listening to others and taking turns speaking about the topics and texts under discussion). **Language 1.a.** Print many upper- and lowercase letters. **Also Writing 5.**

Access for All

Strategic Intervention

Support Conventions Remind children that names begin with uppercase letters.

Advanced

Amazing Words After children have lined up under their names, have others use the Amazing Words *first, second, third, fourth, fifth,* and *sixth* to describe children's positions.

Daily Fix-It

My name is dan

My name is Dan.

This week's practice sentences appear on *Teacher Resources DVD-ROM.*

Conventions

Say Our Names

TEACH Remind children of what they learned about names. Say several names. Listen as I say the names again. Let's point to the people whose names I say. Repeat with several other names.

GUIDE PRACTICE Write six names across the board. Point to and read the first name and have a volunteer find the child with that name. Have the child stand under his or her name. Continue until the six children are standing in a row. Repeat with other names, letting children find the child for each name.

ON THEIR OWN Use *Reader's and Writer's Notebook,* p. 12, for more practice with names.

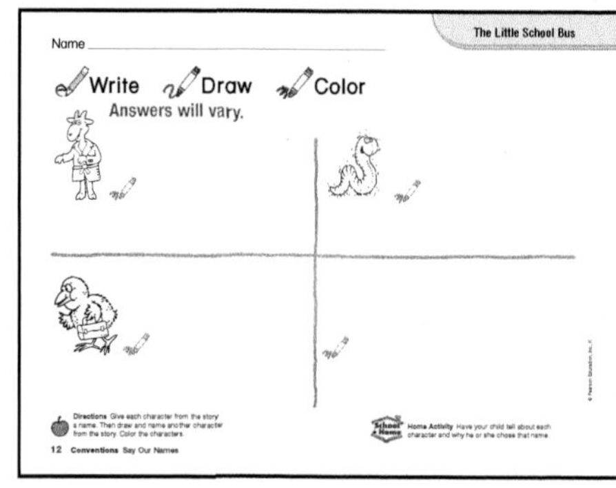

Reader's and Writer's Notebook, p. 12

Extend the Concept

DISCUSS We just read a story about how some animals get to school. Most of the animals we read about ride a school bus. Some people have different ways of getting to school. I drive my car to school each morning. How do you get to school?

Have children discuss ways to get to school. Expand the discussion by describing other ways children get to school in different parts of the country, such as taking a train, a city bus, or skateboarding.

GUIDE PRACTICE Use children's contributions to the discussion to write sentences using the following sentence frame: *We can* _______ *to school.*

We can bike to school.
We can walk to school.

INDEPENDENT WRITING Copy the following sentence frame on a sheet of paper for each child: *I can* _______ *to (rebus: schoolhouse).* Explain that the drawing of a schoolhouse is a rebus word: *school.* Pictures can help us understand writing. Have children complete the sentence frame by drawing their own rebus word for how they get to school. Then have children share their sentences with the class.

Daily Handwriting

Write uppercase *A,* lowercase *a,* uppercase *B,* and lowercase *b* on the board. Review correct letter formation with children.

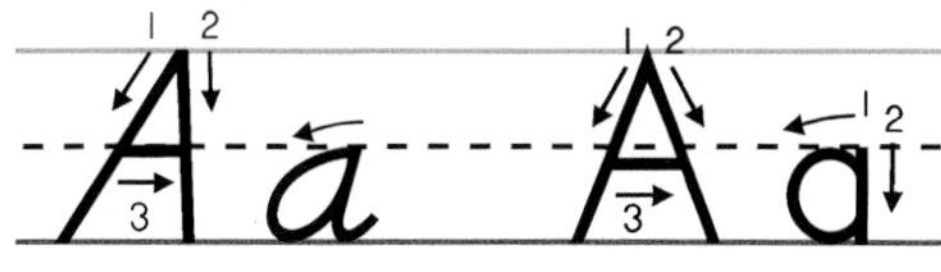
D'Nealian™

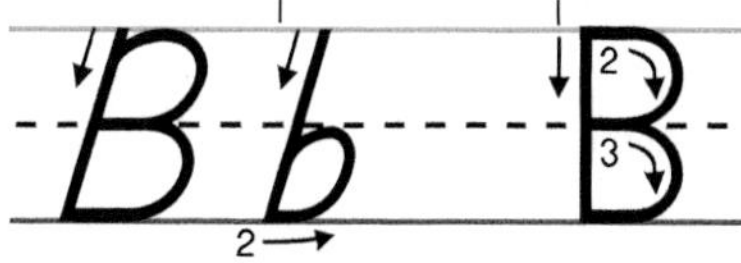
Ball and Stick

D'Nealian™

Ball and Stick

Have children write a row of uppercase *A,* lowercase *a,* uppercase *B,* and lowercase *b* on their Write-On Boards. Remind them to use proper left-to-right and top-to-bottom progression when writing letters.

Bridge to Common Core

PRODUCTION AND DISTRIBUTION OF WRITING
With your guidance and support, children add details to complete sentences, demonstrating their understanding of the subject and task.

Common Core State Standards

Foundational Skills 1.d. Recognize and name all upper- and lowercase letters of the alphabet. **Foundational Skills 2.a.** Recognize and produce rhyming words. **Language 5.c.** Identify real-life connections between words and their use (e.g., note places at school that are *colorful*).

Vocabulary

Words for Transportation

bus car van bike

TEACH Write the words *bus, car, van,* and *bike* on the board. Point to each word as you read it. These words show ways we can go places. Have children turn to p. 28 of *My Skills Buddy.* Use the second Vocabulary bullet in the discussion. Direct children to the picture of a school bus. Is this a bus or a car? (*bus*) Continue with the pictures of the bike, van, and car.

Team Talk Pair children and have them take turns describing the bus, car, van, and bike on p. 28.

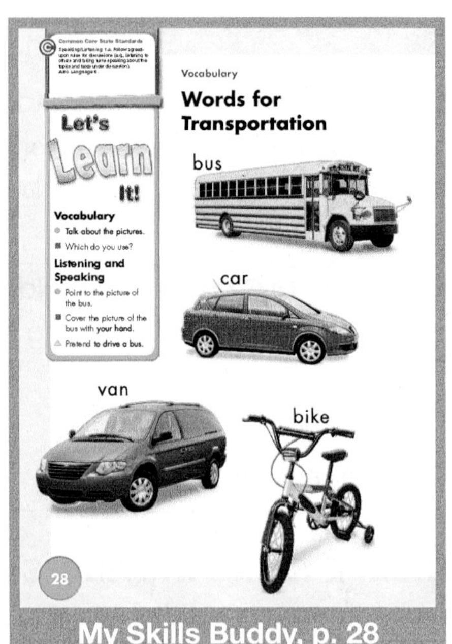

My Skills Buddy, p. 28

Wrap Up Your Day!

✔ **Oral Language** Today we read about the animals in *The Little School Bus.* What do the animals do when they get on the bus?

✔ **Phonological Awareness** Today we worked with rhyming words. What rhyming words can we make for *goat* and *pig?*

✔ **Conventions** Point to a child and ask the child to give his or her name. Have that child point to someone else for the next turn.

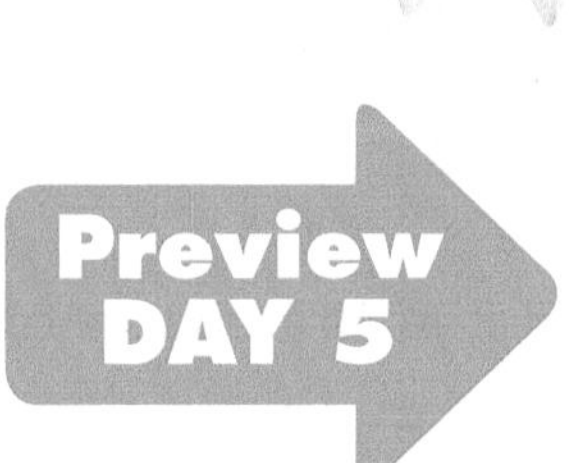

Tell children that tomorrow they will review some of the books and stories they have read this week.

Extend Your Day!

Social Studies
Finding the Way

MATERIALS: *The Little School Bus,* chart paper, markers, paper, crayons

PUT PLACES ON A MAP Show children the pictures in *The Little School Bus.* Have them discuss and identify places that the bus passes as it picks up the animals on its way to school. The bus travels around the neighborhood. A neighborhood is made up of the streets, buildings, and places around your home or school. On chart paper, draw the streets around the school. Ask children to help you draw the school and other buildings and landmarks near the school in the correct positions on the map.

DRAW AND LABEL A MAP Help children draw a map of the neighborhood around their home. First, draw a picture of your home in the middle of your paper. Now think about things that are around your home. What streets, buildings, and other places do you know? Where will you draw them on your map? Once children have drawn as many details as they can on their maps, help them dictate labels such as *My Home, My School,* and *The Park.*

Comprehension
Character

DRAMATIZE *THE LITTLE SCHOOL BUS*
Designate an area as the bus using several rows of chairs. Choose children to be the six characters who get on the bus in the story. Have them stand in a line. Show the second page of the story and have the child who is the goat walk on the bus. Have the rest of the class say: *Riding the bus to school, to school, riding the bus to school.* Continue until all the animals have boarded the bus.

Letter Recognition
Letter Tic-Tac-Toe

MATERIALS: Tic-Toe-Toe pattern (3 x 3 grid), one for each child

WRITE LETTERS Give each child a Tic-Tac-Toe pattern. Then name a letter, selecting it from *Aa* through *Dd.* Tell children to write the letter in any box they choose. Continue until nine spaces are filled. Have children look at their cards to see if they have a vertical, horizontal, or diagonal row with the uppercase and lowercase forms of the same letter.

a	B	c
D	A	b
d	C	A

DAY 5 at a Glance

Content Knowledge
Oral Vocabulary

Phonological Awareness
Review Rhyming Words

Letter Recognition
Letters *Ee*

Assessment
Letter Recognition
High-Frequency Words
Comprehension

Text-Based Comprehension
Review Character

Conventions
Review Say Our Names

Writing
This Week We…

Materials

- Student Edition
- Truckery Rhymes
- Talk with Me/Sing with Me Chart
- Alphabet Cards
- Phonics Songs and Rhymes Chart
- Reader's and Writer's Notebook
- Read Aloud Anthology
- Student Reader K.1.1
- Get Set, Roll! Reader 1

Bridge to Common Core

INTEGRATION OF KNOWLEDGE/IDEAS
This week children have integrated content presented in diverse formats and analyzed how different texts address similar topics. They have developed knowledge about how children get to school together to expand the unit topic of Cooperation.

Social Studies Knowledge Goals
Children have learned that riding the bus together
- helps them get to school
- helps them arrive safely

TRUCKTOWN
on Reading Street

Start your engines!

- Display "Jack Be Nimble" and lead the group in saying the rhyme a few times.
- Have half the group recite the rhyme while the other half acts it out.
- Ask the halves to change roles.

Truckery Rhymes
Truckery Rhymes

Content Knowledge

Zoom in on ©

Getting to School Together

REVIEW THE CONCEPT Discuss with children what they have added to their knowledge about this unit of study, All Together Now. Encourage them to use the Amazing Words.

Build Oral Language

LISTEN FOR AMAZING WORDS Display Sing with Me Chart 1B. Let's sing "How We Get to School." I want you to listen for the Amazing Words we learned this week. Say them with me: *first, second, third, fourth, fifth, sixth.* Sing the song several times to the tune of "Mary Had a Little Lamb." Have children sing with you.

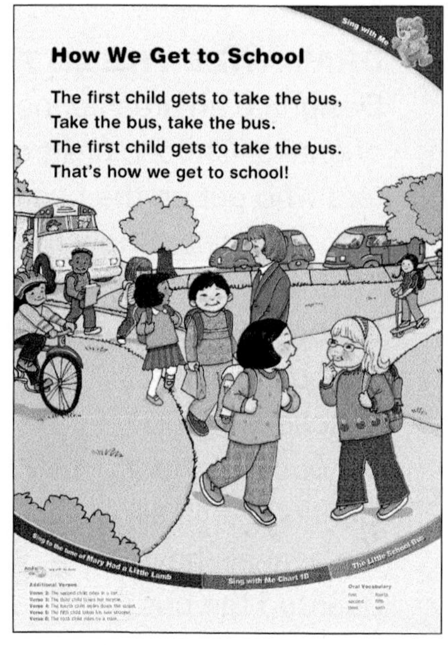
How We Get to School
The first child gets to take the bus,
Take the bus, take the bus.
The first child gets to take the bus.
That's how we get to school!
Talk with Me/Sing with Me Chart 1B

Build Oral Vocabulary

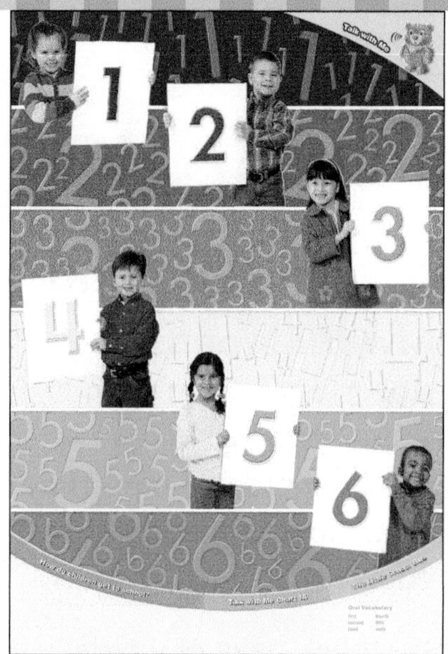

Talk with Me/Sing with Me Chart 1A

REVIEW AMAZING WORDS Display Talk with Me Chart 1A. Point to each child on the chart and say his or her position. Then have six children form a line. Have children use an Amazing Word to answer these questions in complete sentences:

Who is the first child in line?

Who is the third child in line?

What Amazing Word tells about the child before the third child?

Who is the fourth child in line?

What Amazing Word can be used to identify the last child in line?

What Amazing Word tells about the child in front of the last child?

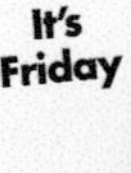

MONITOR PROGRESS Check Oral Vocabulary

FORMATIVE ASSESSMENT Demonstrate Word Knowledge Monitor the Amazing Words by asking the following questions. Encourage children to use the Amazing Words in their answers. Put six different objects in a line on a desk or table.

- **What is sixth in line?**
- **What is second in line?**
- **What is third in line?**
- **What is fifth in line?**
- **What is first in line?**
- **What is fourth in line?**

If... children have difficulty using the Amazing Words,

then... reteach the words using the Robust Vocabulary Routine on the Routines Flip Chart.

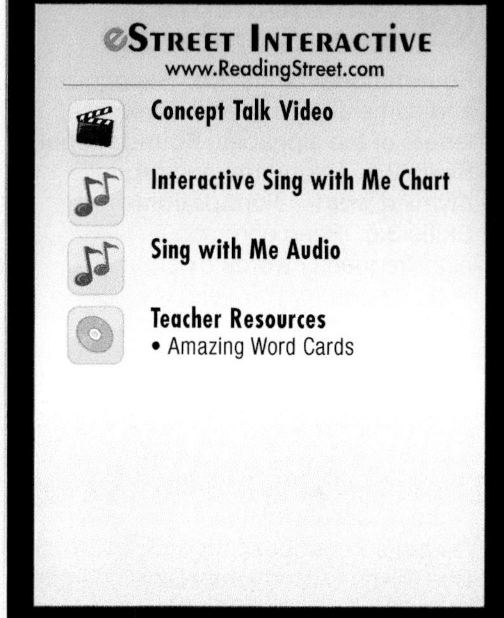

Amazing Words

first	second
third	fourth
fifth	sixth

ELL

Professional Development: Sheltering Instruction "[English learners] benefit when teachers shelter, or make comprehensible, their literacy instruction. Sheltered techniques include using consistent, simplified, clearly enunciated, and slower-paced oral language to explain literacy concepts or activities."
—Dr. Georgia Earnest García

Check Concepts and Language Use the Day 5 instruction on ELL Poster 1 to monitor children's understanding of the lesson concept.

Phonological Awareness

Review Rhyming Words

RHYMING WORDS Remember, rhyming words are words with the same middle and ending sounds. Listen: *The man with a fan ran to the van.* What are the rhyming words? After children name *man, fan, ran,* and *van,* ask them why the words rhyme. (They have the same middle and ending sounds.) Continue with these sentences: *Bill and Jill will go up the hill. Ned sat on the red sled with Ted.*

Say these pairs of words: *hat/cat, bad/tip.* Have children distinguish the rhyming pair from the nonrhyming pair. Continue with these word pairs: *bell/cab, back/tack; pass/grass, sad/top.*

What rhymes with *map?* Have children think of words that rhyme with *map,* such as *tap, cap, clap,* and *rap.*

Letter Recognition

Teach/Model

Letters *Ee*

INTRODUCE/MODEL Point to the escalator on the *Ee* Alphabet Card. This is an escalator. The word *escalator* begins with the letter *e.* Point to and name the letters on the card.

Alphabet Card

Guide Practice

GROUP PRACTICE Write "A Bus Comes Along Every Day" on the board. Point to *Every.* This word begins with uppercase letter *E.* Point to the lowercase *e* in *Every.* This word has a lowercase letter *e* in it. Display Phonics Songs and Rhymes Chart 1. Have children identify lowercase *e* on the chart. Then sing the song to the tune of "If You're Happy and You Know It."

ON THEIR OWN Have children find examples of uppercase *E* and lowercase *e* in the classroom. As each letter is found, have the group say the letter name. Then have children use *Reader's and Writer's Notebook,* p. 9, for more practice with *Ee.*

Common Core State Standards

Foundational Skills 1.d. Recognize and name all upper- and lowercase letters of the alphabet. **Foundational Skills 2.a.** Recognize and produce rhyming words. **Foundational Skills 3.c.** Read common high-frequency words by sight (e.g., *the, of, to, you, she, my, is, are, do, does*).

Access for All

SI Strategic Intervention

Access Content Explain the lyrics "at the curb it does arrive" from "A Bus Comes Along Every Day." Identify the curb in the picture and provide a simple definition of the word *arrive.*

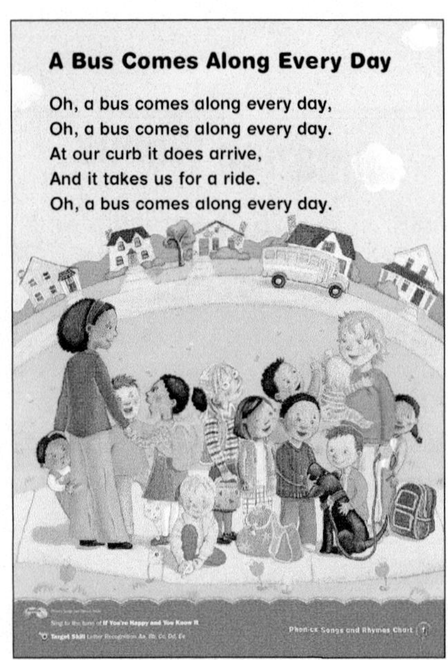

Phonics Songs and Rhymes Chart 1

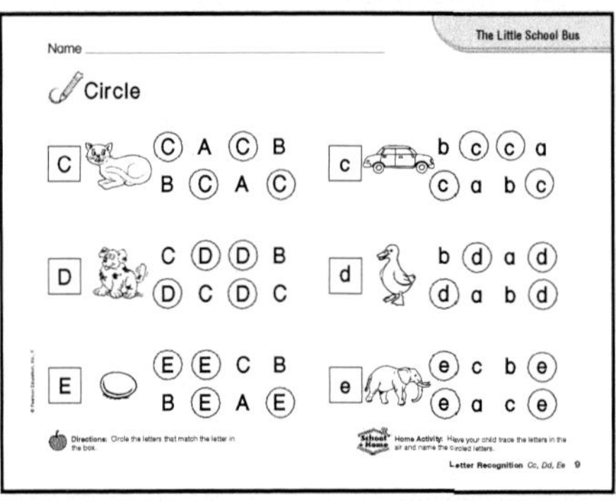

Reader's and Writer's Notebook, p. 9

REVIEW HIGH-FREQUENCY WORDS Write the word *am* on the board. This is the word *am.* Let's say it together. What is this word? Repeat with *I.*

REREAD Have children reread one of these books. You may wish to review the rebus words that appear in each book prior to rereading.

Decodable Reader 1
My Skills Buddy, p. 18

Kindergarten Student Reader K.1.1

Get Set, Roll! Reader 1

ELL

Pronunciation When saying the names of the letters *Ee,* be aware that speakers of Russian and Cantonese may not be familiar with the /ē/ sound. Repeat the letter names with children to practice this sound.

Day 5 SMALL GROUP TIME • Differentiate Close Reading, p. SG•1

OL On-Level	SI Strategic Intervention	A Advanced
• **Practice Letter Recognition** Recognize Letters *Cc, Dd, Ee*	• **Reteach Letter Recognition** Recognize Letters *Cc, Dd, Ee*	• **Extend Letter Recognition** Connect Letters to Sounds
• **Read** "Riding Mr. Frank's Bus"	• **Read** "Riding Mr. Frank's Bus"	• **Read** "Riding Mr. Frank's Bus"

ELL

Place English Language Learners in the groups that correspond to their reading abilities in English.

If... children need more support with **Comprehension,**
then... use the ELL activities on pp. DI•13–DI•14 in the Teacher Resources section of the Digital Path.

Common Core State Standards

Foundational Skills 1.d. Recognize and name all upper- and lowercase letters of the alphabet. **Foundational Skills 3.c.** Read common high-frequency words by sight (e.g., *the, of, to, you, she, my, is, are, do, does*).

Assess

- Identify letters *Aa, Bb, Cc, Dd,* and *Ee.*
- Read high-frequency words.

Assessment

Monitor Progress

Review Letter Recognition

WHOLE CLASS Display the following Alphabet Cards: *Aa, Ee, Cc, Bb, Dd.* Hold up the *Bb* card. What are the names of these letters? (*Bb*) Hold up the *Ee* card. What are the names of these letters? (*Ee*) Have children point to the *Aa* Alphabet Card. Continue the routine with the remaining letters.

MONITOR PROGRESS Check Letter Recognition and Word Reading

If... children cannot complete the whole-class assessment,
then... use the Reteach lesson in *First Stop.*

If... you are unsure of a child's grasp of this week's skills,
then... use the assessment below to obtain a clearer evaluation of the child's progress.

ONE-ON-ONE To facilitate individual progress monitoring, assess some children on Day 4 and the rest on Day 5. While individual children are being assessed, the rest of the class can practice finding the letters *Aa, Bb, Cc, Dd,* and *Ee* in the readers.

LETTER READING Use the letter list on reproducible p. 99 to assess a child's ability to name the letters *Aa, Bb, Cc, Dd,* and *Ee.* Have children name the letters in each row. For each child, record any problems with letter identification.

WORD READING Use the word list on reproducible p. 99 to assess a child's ability to read high-frequency words. Have each child read the words aloud.

RECORD SCORES Monitor children's accuracy by recording their scores using the Letter Recognition Chart for this unit in *First Stop.*

Name ______________________________

Name the Letters

A	b	C	d	B
e	D	a	E	c

Read the Words

I ☐

am ☐

Copyright © Savvas Learning Company LLC. All Rights Reserved.

Note to Teacher: Children name each letter. Children read words.

Scoring for Name the Letters/Read the Words: Score 1 point for each correct letter/word.

Letter Recognition (*Aa, Bb, Cc, Dd, Ee*) _______ /__10__

High-Frequency Words (*I, am*) _______ /__2__

MONITOR PROGRESS

- Letters *Aa, Bb, Cc, Dd, Ee*
- High-Frequency Words

Common Core State Standards
Speaking/Listening 2. Confirm understanding of a text read aloud or information presented orally or through other media by asking and answering questions about key details and requesting clarification if something is not understood. **Also Literature 3.**

King Midas and the Golden Touch

Let's Practice It!

Myth

- Listen to the myth.
- How does it begin?
- Who is King Midas?
- How does King Midas get the "golden touch"?
- What lesson does King Midas learn?

1 2 3 4 5

30 31

My Skills Buddy, pp. 30–31

Common Core State Standards

Literature 3. With prompting and support, identify characters, settings, and major events in a story. **Literature 5.** Recognize common types of texts (e.g., storybooks, poems). **Speaking/Listening 2.** Confirm understanding of a text read aloud or information presented orally or through other media by asking and answering questions about key details and requesting clarification if something is not understood.

Academic Vocabulary

myth a very old story about people or animals with special powers

Let's Practice It!

Myth

TEACH Tell children that today they will listen to a well-known myth. A **myth** is a very old story about people or animals with special powers. Discuss the features of a myth with children.

- A myth tells a story.
- A myth has people or animals with special powers.
- A myth can teach a lesson or explain something.

Have children turn to pp. 30–31 of *My Skills Buddy.* I am going to read a myth called "King Midas and the Golden Touch." Look at the pictures as I read. Read the text of "King Midas and the Golden Touch." As you read, direct children to look at the appropriate picture.

GUIDE PRACTICE Discuss the features of a myth and the bulleted text on *My Skills Buddy,* p. 30, with children.

- A myth tells a story. What happens in the story of King Midas? (King Midas can turn things to gold. He gives up the power when he turns his daughter into gold.)
- A myth has people or animals with special powers. Who has a special power in our story? (King Midas) What is his power? (He can turn things to gold.)
- A myth can teach a lesson or explain something. What lesson does this story teach? (Gold is not the most important thing.)

Writing to Sources

Use Connect the Texts on pp. 8–9 to guide children in writing text-based responses using two sources.

Teacher Read Aloud

King Midas and the Golden Touch

Once upon a time, there was a king named Midas. He loved his wife, and he loved his little daughter. But what he loved most of all was gold.

One day, while counting his gold, King Midas heard a voice say, "I will grant you whatever you most wish for." King Midas did not need to think long.

"I wish that everything I touch would turn to gold," he said.

The voice said, "You have your wish."

King Midas picked up a stone. It turned to solid gold. He touched the flowers in the garden. They turned to solid gold.

"How wonderful!" he cried.

King Midas sat down to eat his dinner, but when he touched the bread, the meat, the fruit, and the water, they all turned to gold. King Midas was hungry. Suddenly, the golden touch did not seem quite so wonderful.

Just then, Midas's little daughter ran to him. He bent to kiss her on the head, and she turned into a solid gold statue. The king cried bitterly.

continued on p. 108a

Access Content Encourage children to share myths or folk stories from their home languages. After they have summarized the stories, ask children questions that guide them to see how these stories are similar to and different from "King Midas and the Golden Touch."

Common Core State Standards

Literature 10. Actively engage in group reading activities with purpose and understanding.

Assess

Identify character.

Assessment

Monitor Progress

REVIEW CHARACTER Remind children that a story is usually about someone or something. It can be a person or an animal. The people or animals in a story are called characters. Good readers pay attention to the characters to help them understand the story.

READ "MARY HAD A LITTLE LAMB" Tell children you are going to read them a poem about Mary and her little lamb. As they listen, ask them to identify the characters in the poem. After I read the poem, I am going to ask you to identify and describe the characters. Read "Mary Had a Little Lamb" on p. 1 of *Read Aloud Anthology.*

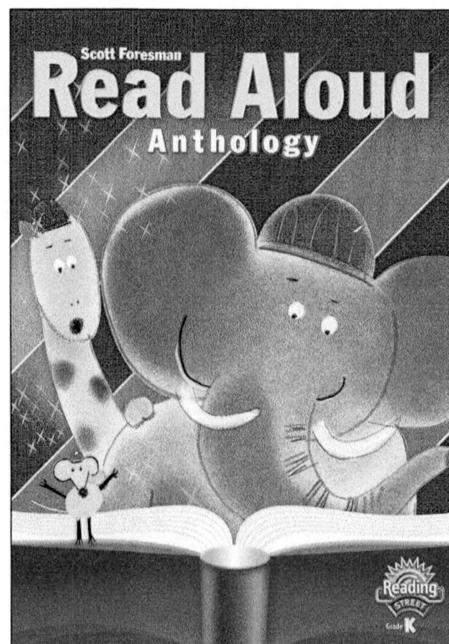

Read Aloud Anthology

CHECK CHARACTER After you read the poem, ask children to identify and describe the characters.

- Who are the characters in the poem? (Mary, her pet lamb, the teacher, the other children at school)
- What does it mean when the poem says the lamb is patient? (The lamb will wait for Mary as long as necessary.)
- Why does the teacher "turn out" the lamb? (The teacher knows that a lamb does not belong at school.)

Corrective feedback	**If...** children cannot identify and describe characters, **then...** reteach character using the Reteach lesson in *First Stop.*

ASSESS CHARACTER Use the blackline master on p. 103. Have children color the pictures that show the characters from "Mary Had a Little Lamb."

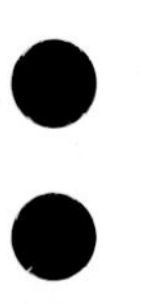
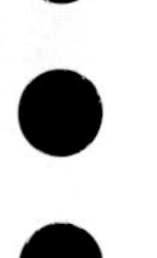

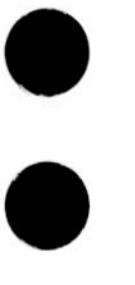

Name ______________________________

Character

Note to Teacher: Have children color the pictures that show characters from "Mary Had a Little Lamb."

Copyright © Savvas Learning Company LLC. All Rights Reserved.

MONITOR PROGRESS

- Character

Common Core State Standards

Writing 2. Use a combination of drawing, dictating, and writing to compose informative/explanatory texts in which they name what they are writing about and supply some information about the topic. **Speaking/Listening 1.a.** Follow agreed-upon rules for discussions (e.g., listening to others and taking turns speaking about the topics and texts under discussion). **Language 1.a.** Print many upper- and lowercase letters.

Daily Fix-It

Dan and nan ran fast
Dan and Nan ran fast.

This week's practice sentences appear on *Teacher Resources DVD-ROM.*

Conventions

Review Say Our Names

REVIEW Remind children of what they learned about names. Names are words we use to stand for people or animals. We all have names. We have names so others know what to call us.

MODEL Write the title "Mary Had a Little Lamb" on the board. Read the title with children. Choose a child to say his or her name to replace *Mary.* Write the new title on the board and read it aloud with children. Continue with other children saying their names.

GUIDE PRACTICE Make a two-column chart or use Graphic Organizer 4. Label the first column *Girls* and the second column *Boys.* Have children take turns saying their names and pointing to the appropriate column for their name. Write their name in the *Boys* or *Girls* column. When the chart is completed, read aloud the names in each column together.

ON THEIR OWN Distribute paper to children and write the following sentence frame on the board: *I am* _______. Have them draw a rebus self-portrait to stand for their own names. Then have each child present his or her drawing to the class, saying: *I am (child's name).*

This Week We...

REVIEW This week we read two stories about animals. We read about the animals getting on a bus in *The Little School Bus* and the lamb in "Mary Had a Little Lamb." Which of the animal characters was your favorite? What did you like about this character?

Team Talk Pair children and have them take turns telling which character was their favorite and why.

MODEL Think of an animal friend you would like to have. What would you write? Have children name their animal friend and dictate a sentence about it.

John has a gerbil named Squeaky.
Sonja has a tiger named Happy.
Robin has a snake named Slinky.

GUIDE PRACTICE Encourage all children to dictate a sentence about a pet they would want and the name they would give it.

ON THEIR OWN Have children dictate or copy the name of their pets from the board and draw pictures to illustrate their new animal friends.

Daily Handwriting

Write uppercase *A,* lowercase *a,* uppercase *B,* and lowercase *b* on the board. Review correct letter formation with children.

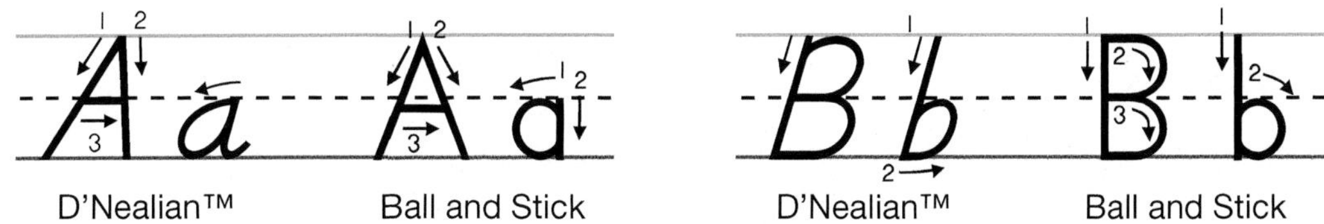

D'Nealian™ Ball and Stick D'Nealian™ Ball and Stick

Have children write a row of uppercase *A* and *B* and a row of lowercase *a* and *b* on their Write-On Boards. Remind them to use proper left-to-right and top-to-bottom progression.

Bridge to Common Core

PRODUCTION AND DISTRIBUTION OF WRITING
When children produce sentences about an animal they would like to have, they are learning to use writing to convey imagined experiences. They are also demonstrating their understanding of how to accomplish a particular task and purpose.

Support Writing Before they begin writing, encourage children who share the same home language to share their ideas for writing in that language and to talk about how they can express their ideas in English.

Common Core State Standards

Foundational Skills 1.d. Recognize and name all upper- and lowercase letters of the alphabet. **Speaking/ Listening 5.** Add drawings or other visual displays to descriptions as desired to provide additional detail.

Wrap Up Your Week!

Getting to School Together

How do children get to school?

MAKE A WORD WEB This week we talked about how children get to school.

- Make a word web like the one shown.
- Write *School* in the center oval. What are ways children get to school? Write children's ideas in the other ovals.
- Give each child art paper to draw a picture showing how one character gets to school.
- Attach the pictures to a bulletin board. Have children arrange the pictures based on how the characters get to school.

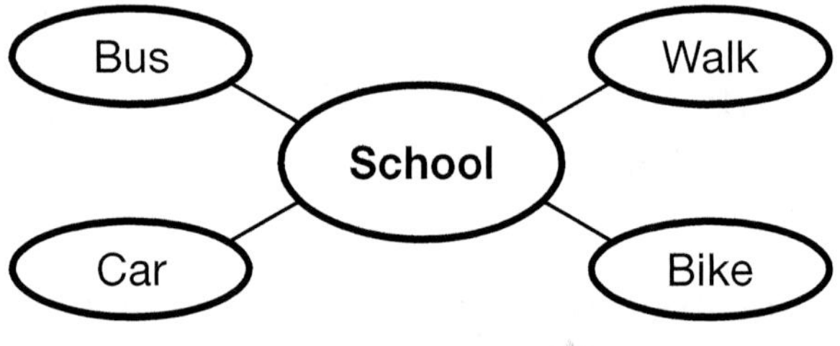

Amazing Words

You've learned 006 words this week!

You've learned 006 words this year!

Next Week's Concept

Working and Playing Together at School

How do school children work and play together?

Discuss next week's question. Guide children in making connections between how children get to school and how they work and play together.

Tell children that next week they will read about children working together.

Preview Next Week

Extend Your Day!

Conventions
Animal Names

MATERIALS: 4 sheets of paper stapled together for story booklets, one per child; crayons

ANIMAL STORYBOOK Help children make a list of animals on the board. Tell them to pick an animal they like and give the animal a name. Ask them to create a story about their animal by drawing pictures for each page of their story. Have them make a cover with a title and their name as the author. Allow time for children to "read" their stories to the group.

cat
dog
bear
kangaroo
gorilla
tiger
lion
giraffe

Math
Ordinal Number Lineup

MATERIALS: 6 index cards marked with numerals 1–6

GET IN ORDER Distribute cards to six children in the class. Tell them that when you say "Number Lineup!" the children with cards should walk up to form a line across the front of the room. Correct their order as needed. Have children name their places in line by ordinal number words *first, second, third, fourth, fifth,* and *sixth.* Repeat until all children stand in line.

Letter Recognition
ABC Hopscotch

MATERIALS: 2 large letter cards for each of the letters *A, B, C, D, E*

LETTER NAME GAME Arrange the set of letters in a hopscotch form on the floor as shown here. Have children take turns hopping through the form and naming each letter.

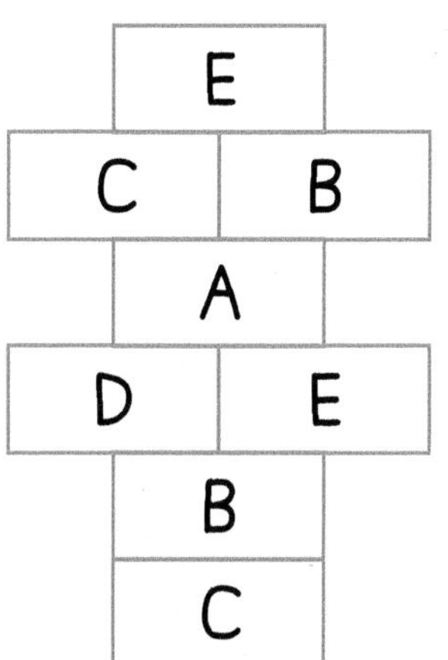

Assessment Checkpoints for the Week

Weekly Assessment

Use the whole-class assessment on pages 98–99 and 102–103 in this Teacher's Edition to check:

- **Letters *Aa, Bb, Ce, Dd, Ee***
- **Comprehension** *Character*
- **High-Frequency Words** *I* *am*

You will find the Weekly Assessments on Day 5 of this week's lesson.

Managing Assessment

Use the Assessment Handbook for:

- **Observation Checklists**
- **Record-Keeping Forms**
- **Portfolio Assessment**

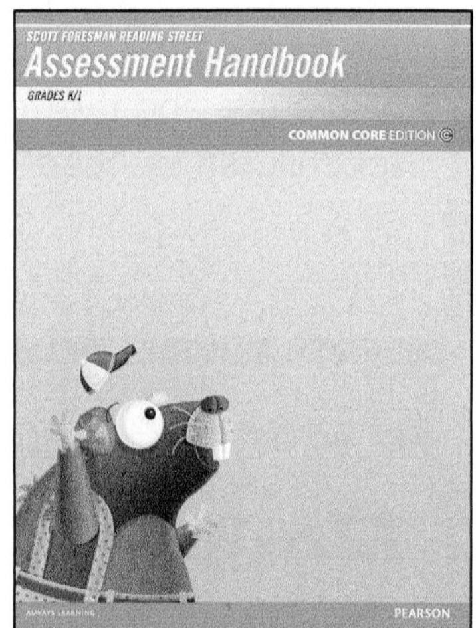
Assessment Handbook
COMMON CORE EDITION
PEARSON
Assessment Handbook

Let's Practice It!

Teacher Read Aloud continued from p. 101

King Midas and the Golden Touch

"Why did I make such a foolish wish?"

Now the voice said, "Go to the river and wash your hands. Then bring back water and sprinkle it over everything you have turned to gold."

King Midas hurried to do as he was told. He washed his hands in the river. Then he brought a pitcher of water and sprinkled it over his little daughter, who instantly came back to life.

King Midas had learned his lesson. He no longer valued gold above everything else.

TEACHER NOTES

DAY 1 Differentiate Letter Recognition

- Letters *Aa*
- Decodable Story
- Advanced Selection “Looking for Tab”

DAY 2 Differentiate Letter Recognition

- Letters *Bb*
- Decodable Reader

DAY 3 Differentiate Vocabulary

- Develop Vocabulary: Words for Transportation
- Kindergarten Student Reader

DAY 4 Differentiate Language

- Develop Language
- Get Set, Roll! Reader

DAY 5 Differentiate Letter Recognition/ Close Reading

- Letters *Cd, Dd, Ee*
- “Riding Mr. Frank’s Bus”

Place English Language Learners in the groups that correspond to their reading abilities.
If... children need scaffolding and practice,
then... use the ELL notes on the page.

Independent Practice

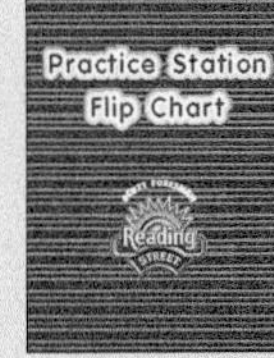

Independent Practice Stations

See pp. 14 and 15 for Independent Stations.

Reading Street Digital Path

Independent Practice Activities available in the Digital Path.

Independent Reading

See p. 15 for independent reading suggestions.

On-Level

Common Core State Standards

Literature 1. With prompting and support, ask and answer questions about key details in a text. **Literature 10.** Actively engage in group reading activities with purpose and understanding. **Foundational Skills 1.d.** Recognize and name all upper- and lowercase letters of the alphabet. **Foundational Skills 2.a.** Recognize and produce rhyming words. **Foundational Skills 3.c.** Read common high-frequency words by sight (e.g., *the, of, to, you, she, my, is, are, do, does*).

1 Build Word Knowledge

Practice Phonological Awareness

RHYMING WORDS Listen to these words: *cat, hat.* Do *cat* and *hat* rhyme? Help children conclude that because *cat* and *hat* have the same middle and ending sounds, they are rhyming words. Ask children to name other words that rhyme with *cat* and *hat.* Continue with the rhyming words *can* and *man.*

Practice Letter Recognition

RECOGNIZE LETTERS *Aa* Write an uppercase *A* on chart paper. Show children how to make the letter. Have several volunteers write the letter *A* on the chart paper. Repeat the routine with lowercase *a.*

2 Read

Decodable Story 1 *I Am!*

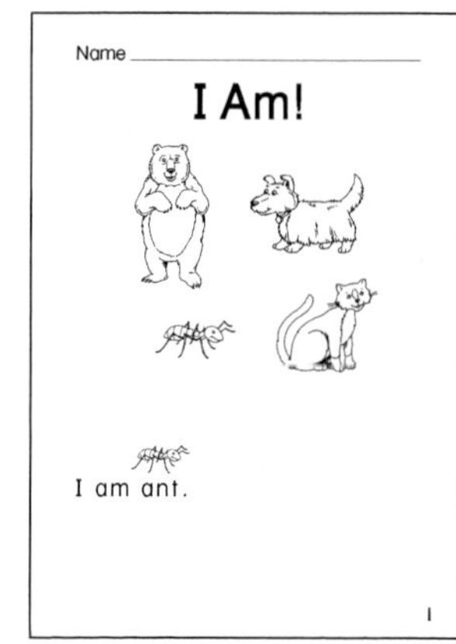

READ Have children read the story. Then have them reread the text to develop automaticity.

HIGH-FREQUENCY WORDS Have children return to the text and identify the high-frequency words *I* and *am.* Help children demonstrate their understanding of these words by completing sentence frames such as these: *You sit there, and _______ sit here.* (I) *You are my students, and I _______ your teacher.* (am)

3 Reread for Fluency

Have children reread the Decodable Story *I Am!* individually to develop fluency.

Independent Reading Options

Trade Book Library

eSTREET INTERACTIVE
www.ReadingStreet.com

Teacher's Guides available on the Leveled Reader Database.

On-Level

1 Build Word Knowledge

Practice Letter Recognition

RECOGNIZE LETTERS *Bb* Show the *Bb* Alphabet Card. Point to each letter. This is uppercase *B*. This is lowercase *b*. Write the letters on chart paper. Call on volunteers to write the letters. Continue until many children have had turns.

Practice High-Frequency Words

COMPLETE A SENTENCE Display the high-frequency word cards for *I* and *am.* Have children read each word as you hold up the card. Then write the following on chart paper: *I am* _______. Read the sentence adding your name. Have children take turns reading the sentence and adding their names. Have them point to the words as they read their sentences.

2 Read

Decodable Reader 1 *Who Am I?*

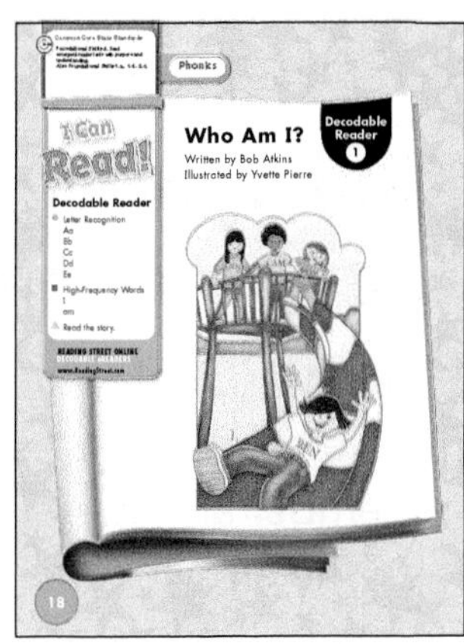

CONCEPTS OF PRINT Display Decodable Reader 1 in *My Skills Buddy.* Show children the illustrations and read aloud the title. What do you think the story is about?

READ Have children take turns reading the Decodable Reader. Pause at the end of each page to ask questions. What is this child's name? What is [child's name] doing?

3 Reread for Fluency

Have children reread the Decodable Reader *Who Am I?* individually to develop fluency.

SMALL GROUP TIME

More Reading for Group Time

CONCEPT LITERACY

- Concept Words
- High-Frequency Words

Use these suggested readers or other text at children's instructional level.

Street Interactive
www.ReadingStreet.com

Use the Leveled Reader Database for lesson plans and student pages for *Off to School*.

If... children need more scaffolding and practice with phonological awareness and letter recognition,
then... use the activities on p. DI•12 in the Teacher Resources section of the Digital Path.

On-Level

Common Core State Standards

Literature 1. With prompting and support, ask and answer questions about key details in a text. **Literature 10.** Actively engage in group reading activities with purpose and understanding. **Foundational Skills 3.c.** Read common high-frequency words by sight (e.g., *the, of, to, you, she, my, is, are, do, does*). **Language 5.a.** Sort common objects into categories (e.g., shapes, foods) to gain a sense of the concepts the categories represent. **Language 5.c.** Identify real-life connections between words and their use (e.g., note places at school that are *colorful*). **Language 6.** Use words and phrases acquired through conversations, reading and being read to, and responding to texts.

1 Build Word Knowledge

Develop Vocabulary

WORDS FOR TRANSPORTATION Have children return to p. 28 in *My Skills Buddy.* Review the transportation words *bus, car, van,* and *bike.* Remind children that *transportation* means ways to go somewhere. Point to each picture and ask questions. What is this? Is this a car or a bus? Is this a van or a bike? Give the following clues to children and have them say the appropriate transportation word.

- Many children can ride on this. It takes them to school. (bus)
- This is bigger than a car but smaller than a bus. (van)
- This is smaller than a van. (car)
- Only one person can ride on this. (bike)

Team Talk Have children work with a partner to use the words for transportation in sentences.

2 Read

Kindergarten Student Reader *Cat and Dog at School*

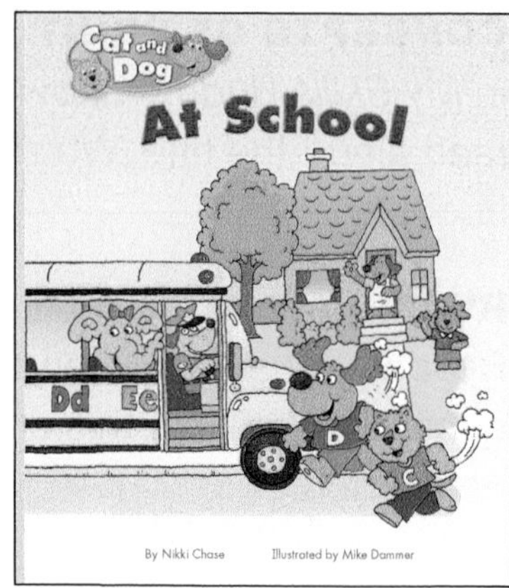

REREAD Display the reader and have children tell the title of the story. Have them tell what they remember about the story. Then have children read the story chorally. After reading each page, ask children to tell what they see. Who is this? What letter is this? To check children's understanding, have them take turns reading the story to a partner and then retelling the story to the partner.

On-Level

1 Build Word Knowledge

Develop Language

Display the Big Book *The Little School Bus* and read the text on pp. 26–27.

During school they learn and play,
while the little bus sits and waits all day.

- Ask children to read the text with you as you track the print.
- Point to the line, *while the little bus sits and waits all day.*
- What does the word *little* mean? What is another word for *little?* Why do you think the author chose the word *little?*
- Let's try some other words in place of *little.*
- Continue with the words *learn* and *play.* What else could the children do during the school day? What words could we use in place of *learn* and *play?*

2 Read

Get Set, Roll! Reader 1 *Jack and Max*

REVIEW HIGH-FREQUENCY WORDS Review the following high-frequency words with children: *I, am.* Ask children to use each word in a sentence.

REVIEW REBUS WORDS Distribute Letter Tiles to each child or use Letter Tile Drag and Drop in the Digital Path. Write the name *Max* on a card. This is the name *Max.* The letters in *Max* are *M, a, x.* Use your letters to build this word. What does this spell? Which character is Max? Continue the routine with the following words: *Jack, up, down, wet.*

REREAD Have children whisper read *Jack and Max* as you listen to each child. Then have children take turns reading the story aloud.

SMALL GROUP TIME

If... children need more scaffolding and practice with vocabulary, **then...** use the ELL activities on p. DI•14 in the Teacher Resources section of the Digital Path.

On-Level

Common Core State Standards

Literature 1. With prompting and support, ask and answer questions about key details in a text. **Literature 10.** Actively engage in group reading activities with purpose and understanding. **Foundational Skills 1.d.** Recognize and name all upper- and lowercase letters of the alphabet.

1 Build Word Knowledge

Practice Letter Recognition

RECOGNIZE LETTERS *Cc, Dd, Ee* Display the *Cc, Dd,* and *Ee* Alphabet Cards. Have children identify the letters as you say the letter names. Write a mixture of uppercase *C, D,* and *E* and lowercase *c, d,* and *e* on chart paper. Ask children to find the letter you name and circle it. Continue until all the letters have been circled.

REVIEW LETTERS *Aa–Ee* Display the *Aa, Bb, Cc, Dd,* and *Ee* Alphabet Cards in a row on the chalk ledge. Have children point to and name each letter. Mix the cards and place them in a different order. Have children find the letters you name.

Corrective feedback	**If...** children have difficulty naming letters, **then...** review the letter names using the Alphabet Cards.

2 Text-Based Comprehension

Read

READ ALOUD Read the Reading Street Sleuth Read Aloud, "Riding Mr. Frank's Bus," on p. SG•7 to children.

READ LIKE A SLEUTH! Encourage children to cite evidence from the text to support their answers. You may wish to reread sections of the text to verify children's answers.

Look for Evidence Why does the narrator like riding Mr. Frank's bus?

Ask Questions If you could meet Mr. Frank, what questions would you ask him?

Prove It! Performance Task Have children draw a picture of Mr. Frank's bus and its riders, focusing on how the riders feel about riding the bus. Ask children to label the picture with one or two key details they used from the text. Children may write or dictate a short phrase or sentence.

Reading Street Sleuth Teacher Read Aloud

Riding Mr. Frank's Bus

I was waiting for the school bus. It was my first day at another new school. I had butterflies in my stomach. I'm sure I had a terrible scowl on my face.

Rumble, rumble, rumble came the school bus. Well, it was yellow like a school bus. It was so clean and shiny that it made me squint when I looked at it. The front was flat with big windows.

The bus stopped, the door opened with a swoosh, and I was looking up at the driver. Suddenly, he bounded down the steps.

"Hello!" he boomed. "I'm Mr. Frank. Welcome to Bus 306."

Mr. Frank asked me my name and then shepherded me up the steps and into an empty seat. He hurried back to his seat, announced my name, checked the riders in his rearview mirror, and off we went. This was not like any school bus I'd ever ridden. He was not like any bus driver I'd ever known.

Mr. Frank was a stocky man with dark eyes and a voice that could be heard a block away. If you rode his bus, you followed his rules. And it really was *his* bus. He owned it. He kept it sparkling clean, and he expected his riders to do the same. Mr. Frank also kept his riders safe. There was no standing in the aisle, kneeling on the seats, or sitting backwards. There was no pushing, yelling, fighting, or bullying.

Mr. Frank was also a kind, friendly man, and his riders loved him. He led sing-alongs, told jokes, and shared stories. He celebrated all the holidays and all his riders' birthdays. He made riding the bus fun.

Two years later, my family moved again, and I went off to other new schools. But I never met another bus driver like Mr. Frank. That's why I've always remembered him.

Reproducible Page. Copyright © Pearson Education, Inc., or its affiliates. All Rights Reserved.

Literature 1. With prompting and support, ask and answer questions about key details in a text. **Literature 10.** Actively engage in group reading activities with purpose and understanding. **Foundational Skills 1.d.** Recognize and name all upper- and lowercase letters of the alphabet. **Foundational Skills 2.a.** Recognize and produce rhyming words. **Foundational Skills 3.c.** Read common high-frequency words by sight (e.g., *the, of, to, you, she, my, is, are, do, does*).

More Reading for Group Time

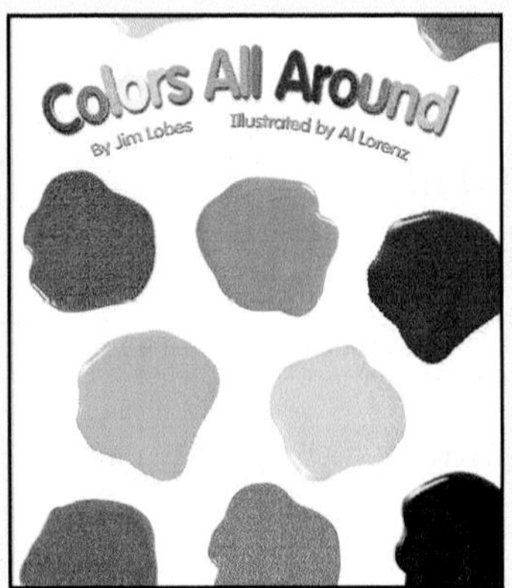

LISTEN TO ME READER

- Concepts of Print

Use these suggested readers or other text at children's instructional level.

eSTREET INTERACTIVE
www.ReadingStreet.com

Use the Leveled Reader Database to access an online version of *Colors All Around.*

If... children need more scaffolding and practice with phonological awareness and letter recognition, **then...** use the Phonics Transition lessons beginning on p. 447 in the *ELL Handbook.*

1 Build Word Knowledge

Reteach Phonological Awareness

RECOGNIZE RHYMING WORDS Tell children that rhyming words are words that have the same middle and ending sounds. *Cat* and *bat* both end with *-at.* They have the same middle and ending sounds, so they rhyme. Let's listen for more rhyming words. I will say two words, and I want you to tell me whether they rhyme. Use these word pairs: *wet, pet; tan, cup; can, man; hen, pen; hat, bed.*

Reteach Letter Recognition

RECOGNIZE LETTERS *Aa* Write *A* and *a* on chart paper. This is uppercase *A.* This is lowercase *a.* Ask several children to write the letters on the chart paper as you explain the steps. Have the other children write the letters in the air with their fingers. Continue until everyone has had a turn to write the letters on the chart paper.

2 Read

Decodable Story 1 *I Am!*

REVIEW HIGH-FREQUENCY WORDS Display the high-frequency word card for *I.* This is the word *I.* What word is this? Say the word with me. Listen for the word in the sentence I say. Clap when you hear the word. *I went to school.* Continue with the high-frequency word *am.*

Corrective feedback	**If...** children have difficulty reading the high-frequency words, **then...** say a word and have children point to the word. Repeat several times, giving assistance as needed.

READ Have children read the story.

3 Reread for Fluency

Have children reread the story *I Am!* chorally. Then have them reread the story several times individually to develop fluency.

1 Build Word Knowledge

Reteach Phonological Awareness

PRACTICE RHYMING WORDS Remind children that rhyming words are words that have the same middle and ending sounds. *Wet* and *let* are rhyming words. Both end with *-et.* They have the same middle and ending sounds. Let's listen for more rhyming words. I will say two words, and I want you to tell me whether they rhyme. Use these word pairs: *cat, bat; bear, hare; moon, cot; top, mop; big, pig.*

Reteach Letter Recognition

RECOGNIZE LETTERS *Bb* Cut the letters *B* and *b* out of felt or another material with texture. Glue the letters to poster board. Have children take turns running their fingers over the letters as they name them. This is uppercase *B.* This is lowercase *b.* Then have children write the letters on paper.

Reteach High-Frequency Words

REVIEW Have children read each previously taught high-frequency word as you point to it on the Word Wall.

I am

Corrective feedback **If...** children have difficulty reading the words, **then...** say a word and have children point to the word. Repeat several times, giving assistance as needed.

2 Read

Decodable Reader 1 *Who Am I?*

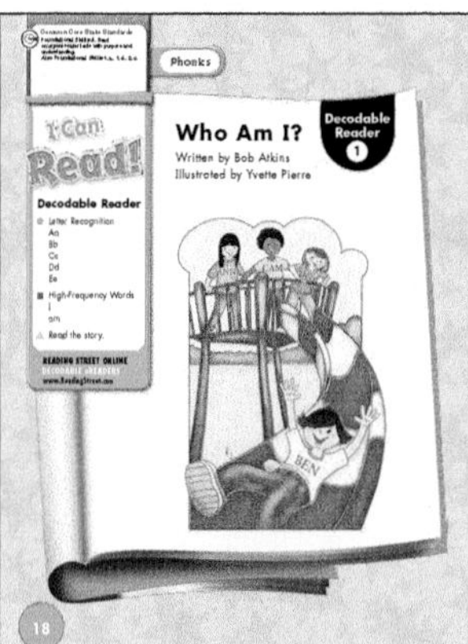

CONCEPTS OF PRINT Display Decodable Reader 1 in *My Skills Buddy.* The title of this story is *Who Am I?* The author is Bob Atkins. The illustrator is Yvette Pierre. Look at the picture on the cover. Look at the pictures inside. What do you think the story is about?

READ Let's read the story together. After reading chorally with children, have them reread the story several times with a partner and then independently.

SMALL GROUP TIME

Independent Reading Options

Trade Book Library

eStreet Interactive
www.ReadingStreet.com
Teacher's Guides available on the Leveled Reader Database.

If... children need more support with letter recognition,
then... use the ELL activities on p. DI•12 in the Teacher Resources section of the Digital Path.

Common Core State Standards

Literature 1. With prompting and support, ask and answer questions about key details in a text. **Literature 10.** Actively engage in group reading activities with purpose and understanding. **Foundational Skills 3.c.** Read common high-frequency words by sight (e.g., *the, of, to, you, she, my, is, are, do, does*). **Language 5.a.** Sort common objects into categories (e.g., shapes, foods) to gain a sense of the concepts the categories represent. **Language 5.c.** Identify real-life connections between words and their use (e.g., note places at school that are *colorful*). **Language 6.** Use words and phrases acquired through conversations, reading and being read to, and responding to texts.

1 Build Word Knowledge

Develop Vocabulary

RETEACH WORDS FOR TRANSPORTATION Have children return to p. 28 of *My Skills Buddy* to review the transportation words *bus, car, van,* and *bike.*

- Which picture shows a car? Where can a car go?
- Which picture shows a bus? Who rides on this kind of bus?
- Which picture shows a bike? Have you ridden on a bike?
- Which picture shows a van? Does a van hold more than a person?

Display other pictures of a bus, car, van, and bike. Write the words on index cards. Ask children to label the pictures with the cards.

2 Read

Kindergarten Student Reader *Cat and Dog at School*

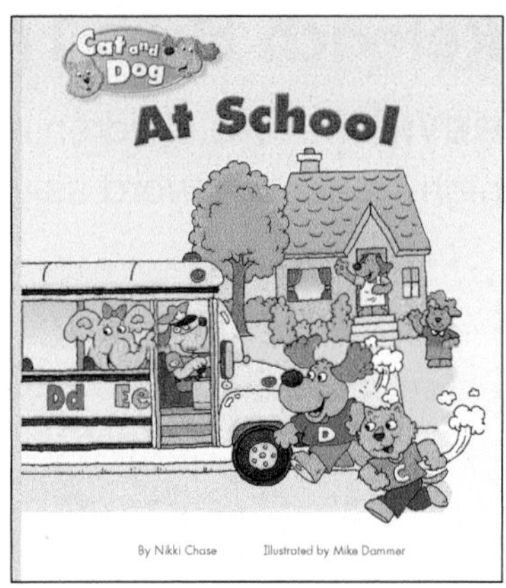

REVIEW REBUS WORDS Write *Cat* on chart paper. This is the word *Cat.* Name the letters with me: *C, a, t.* Repeat with the other rebus word *Dog.*

REVIEW HIGH-FREQUENCY WORDS Write *I* on chart paper. Ask children to read the word with you. Have a volunteer read the word. Continue with the other high-frequency word *am.*

REREAD STORY Display the reader. The title of this book is *Cat and Dog at School.* What do you think the story is about? Read the story chorally with children. Pause at the end of each page to ask: What animal do you see? What is the animal doing? Starting with p. 4, also ask: What letter do you see on the [animal's name]? What things do you see in the picture that begin like [animal's name]? Have children reread the story several times to build fluency.

If... children need more scaffolding and practice with vocabulary, **then...** use the ELL activities on p. DI•14 in the Teacher Resources section of the Digital Path.

Strategic Intervention

1 Build Word Knowledge

Develop Language

Display the Big Book *The Little School Bus* and read the text on pp. 26–27.

During school they learn and play,
while the little bus sits and waits all day.

- Ask children to read the text with you as you track the print.
- Point to the line, *while the little bus sits and waits all day.*
- What does the word *little* mean? What is another word that means the same as *little?*
- I am going to say three words. I want you to tell me which word means the same as *little: big, enormous, small; tiny, large, huge.*
- Continue with the words *learn* and *play.* What else could the children do during the school day? What words could we use in place of *learn* and *play?*

2 Read

Get Set, Roll! Reader 1 *Jack and Max*

REVIEW HIGH-FREQUENCY AND REBUS WORDS Review the high-frequency and rebus words (*I, am, down, Jack, Max, up, wet*) using the following routine.

1. Display and read the word.
2. Name the letters in the word.
3. Read the word. Use it in a sentence.

REREAD Have children chorally read aloud *Jack and Max* several times. Then ask them to take turns reading a page aloud.

SMALL GROUP TIME

Independent Reading Options

Trade Book Library

eStreet Interactive
www.ReadingStreet.com

Teacher's Guides available on the Leveled Reader Database.

Common Core State Standards

Literature 1. With prompting and support, ask and answer questions about key details in a text. **Literature 10.** Actively engage in group reading activities with purpose and understanding. **Foundational Skills 1.d.** Recognize and name all upper- and lowercase letters of the alphabet.

1 Build Word Knowledge

Reteach Letter Recognition

RECOGNIZE LETTERS *Cc, Dd, Ee* Write the letters *C, c, D, d, E,* and *e* on index cards. Place the cards in a box. Have a child take a card, name the letter, and write the letter on chart paper. The other children can write the letter in the air with their fingers. Continue until all cards have been used. Repeat until everyone gets a chance to write a letter on the chart paper.

REVIEW LETTERS *Aa–Ee* Write the letters *A, a, B,* and *b* on index cards. Add these cards to the cards from the activity above. Mix the cards and place them face up on a tabletop. First have children match the uppercase and lowercase forms of the letters. Then have children put the pairs of letters in alphabetical order.

Corrective feedback **If...** children have difficulty with matching or alphabetical order, **then...** place the *Aa–Ee* Alphabet Cards in order on the chalk ledge for children to refer to.

2 Text-Based Comprehension

Read

READ ALOUD Read the Reading Street Sleuth Read Aloud, "Riding Mr. Frank's Bus," on p. SG•7 to children.

READ LIKE A SLEUTH! Encourage children to cite evidence from the text to support their answers. You may wish to reread sections of the text to verify children's answers.

Look for Evidence How does the narrator feel about Mr. Frank?

Ask Questions If you could meet Mr. Frank, what questions would you ask him?

Prove It! Performance Task Have children draw a picture of Mr. Frank and his bus. Ask them to dictate a phrase or short sentence for the picture using one or two key details from the text. Read children's phrases or sentences to them as you track the print.

Advanced

1 Build Word Knowledge

Extend Letter Recognition

CONNECT *Aa* TO /a/ Display the *Aa* Alphabet Card. Ask children to name the letters and identify the picture. Point to the letters *Aa* and say the picture name *astronaut.* I am going to say a word. The word is *apple.* Do the words *astronaut* and *apple* begin with the same sound? Say the words with me: *astronaut, apple.* Because *astronaut* and *apple* both begin with /a/, let's write the letter *a* in the air with our fingers. Continue with these words: *ask, egg, ant, alligator, baby, cabin, answer, dirty.*

2 Read

"Looking for Tab"

Looking for Tab
I am sad.
My cat Tab ran.
Is Tab on the mat?
I look at the mat.
No Tab.
Is Tab in the cot?
I look at the cot.
No Tab.
Is Tab in the bin?
I look at the bin.
I see Tab!
She naps in the bin.

CONCEPTS OF PRINT Read aloud the title of the story, "Looking for Tab." Remember, the title of a story gives us clues to what the story is about. Ask children what the title tells them about the story. (The story has a character named Tab. Someone is looking for that character.)

TEACH STORY WORDS Present any story words that children may need help with, such as *my, is, the, mat, cot, bin,* and *naps.* Use the words in sentences that give clues to their meanings. For example, This is *my* book. This book belongs to me. She sleeps on the rug. She *naps* on the rug.

READ Distribute copies of "Looking for Tab" from p. SG•14, and have children read it on their own. Then have them take turns reading the story aloud. After reading, have children tell whom the story is about and what happens.

More Reading for Group Time

INDEPENDENT READER

- More Challenging Text

Use the suggested Leveled Reader or other text at children's instructional level.

eStreet Interactive
www.ReadingStreet.com

Use the Leveled Reader Database for lesson plans and student pages for *Max the Duck.*

If... children need more practice with letter recognition,
then... use the Phonics Transition lessons beginning on p. 447 in the *ELL Handbook.*

Looking for Tab

I am sad.
My cat Tab ran.
Is Tab on the mat?
I look at the mat.
No Tab.
Is Tab in the cot?
I look at the cot.
No Tab.
Is Tab in the bin?
I look at the bin.
I see Tab!
She naps in the bin.

Reproducible Page. Copyright © Pearson Education, Inc., or its affiliates. All Rights Reserved.

Advanced Phonics Selection 1

Advanced

1 Build Word Knowledge

Extend Letter Recognition

CONNECT *Bb* TO /b/ Display the *Bb* Alphabet Card. Ask children to name the letters and identify the picture. Point to the letters *Bb* and say the picture name *baby.* I am going to say a word. The word is *book.* Do the words *baby* and *book* begin with the same sound? Say the words with me: *baby, book.* Because *baby* and *book* both begin with /b/, let's write the letter *b* in the air with our fingers. Continue with these words: *bed, ask, box, boat, cape, desk, bag, elf.*

2 Read

Decodable Reader 1 *Who Am I?*

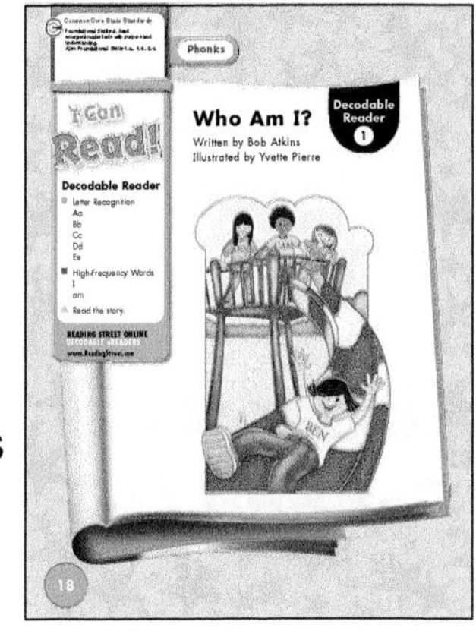

CONCEPTS OF PRINT Display Decodable Reader 1 in *My Skills Buddy.* Ask children to identify the author and illustrator.

READ Have children read the Decodable Reader quietly as you listen to them. Then have them take turns reading aloud one page at a time.

3 Reread for Fluency

Have children reread Decodable Reader 1 *Who Am I?* to develop fluency.

SMALL GROUP TIME

Independent Reading Options

Trade Book Library

eStreet Interactive
www.ReadingStreet.com
Teacher's Guides available on the Leveled Reader Database.

If... children need more support with letter recognition,
then... use the ELL activities on pp. DI•12, DI•15–DI•16 in the Teacher Resources section of the Digital Path.

Advanced

1 Build Word Knowledge

Develop Vocabulary

WORDS FOR TRANSPORTATION Review the transportation words *bus, car, van,* and *bike* with children. Have them use the words in sentences.

Let's learn more transportation words. Remember, these transportation words name things that can go somewhere. Have children identify the transportation words in these sentences.

- The *train* left the station at exactly three o'clock.
- People waved good-bye from the deck of the *ship.*
- The fastest way to get to Australia is by *plane.*

Team Talk Have children work in pairs to use *train, ship,* and *plane* in their own sentences. Ask them to illustrate one of the new transportation words and write a phrase or sentence to describe their picture.

2 Read

Kindergarten Student Reader *Cat and Dog at School*

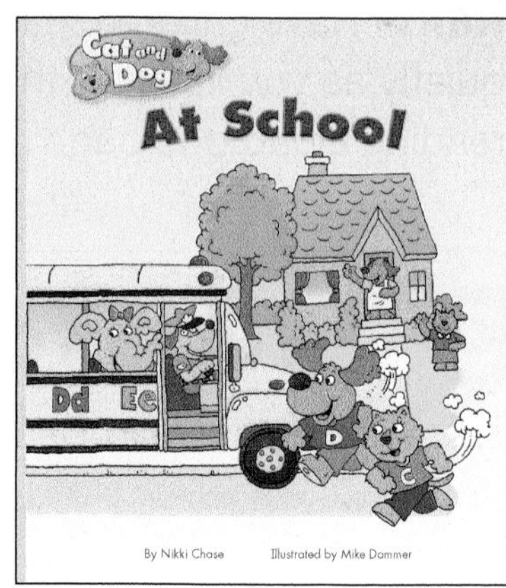

REREAD STORY Display the reader and have children read the title with you. Then have them read the story. Finally, have them reread the story aloud several times to build fluency.

EXTEND STORY Ask children to recall what the animals in the story do. What could happen next in the story? Encourage children to think of other animals and letters. Have them draw a picture and write the sentence to go with the picture. Put children's pages in alphabetical order, add them to the story, and then read the whole story together.

Common Core State Standards

Literature 1. With prompting and support, ask and answer questions about key details in a text. **Literature 10.** Actively engage in group reading activities with purpose and understanding. **Foundational Skills 3.c.** Read common high-frequency words by sight (e.g., *the, of, to, you, she, my, is, are, do, does*). **Language 5.a.** Sort common objects into categories (e.g., shapes, foods) to gain a sense of the concepts the categories represent. **Language 5.c.** Identify real-life connections between words and their use (e.g., note places at school that are *colorful*). **Language 6.** Use words and phrases acquired through conversations, reading and being read to, and responding to texts.

ELL

If... children need more scaffolding and practice with vocabulary, **then...** use the ELL activities on p. DI•14 in the Teacher Resources section of the Digital Path.

Advanced

1 Build Word Knowledge

Develop Language

Display the Big Book *The Little School Bus* and read the text on pp. 26–27.

During school they learn and play,
while the little bus sits and waits all day.

- Ask children to read the text with you as you track the print.
- Point to the line, *During school they learn and play.* Read this with me.
- What do the children do during school? Why did the author choose the words *learn* and *play?* (They tell things children do in school. *Play* rhymes with *day.*) What words could we use instead of *learn* and *play?*
- Continue the routine with the words *sits* and *waits.*
- Team Talk Have children work with a partner to replace key words in a sentence with simpler words or synonyms without changing the meaning of the sentence. Use sentence frames, such as the following.

During school they _______ and _______.
The little bus _______ and _______ all day.

2 Read

Get Set, Roll! Reader 1 *Jack and Max*

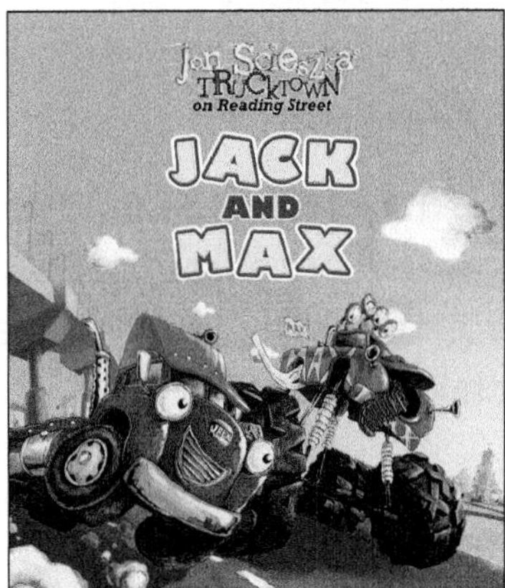

REVIEW HIGH-FREQUENCY AND REBUS WORDS Review the high-frequency and rebus words by asking children to spell the words with Letter Tiles. (*I, am, down, Jack, Max, up, wet*)

REREAD Have children whisper read *Jack and Max* as you listen to each child. Then have children take turns reading the story aloud.

3 Reread for Fluency

BUILD FLUENCY Have children read again with expression and accuracy. Encourage them to use self-correction techniques for any mistakes.

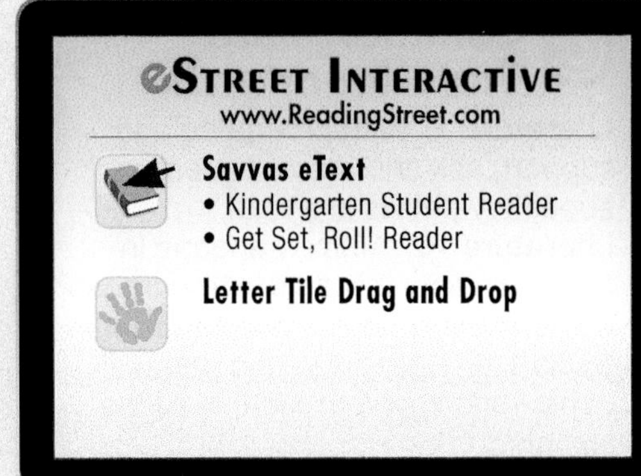

eStreet Interactive
www.ReadingStreet.com

Savvas eText
- Kindergarten Student Reader
- Get Set, Roll! Reader

Letter Tile Drag and Drop

SMALL GROUP TIME

Independent Reading Options

Trade Book Library

eStreet Interactive
www.ReadingStreet.com

Teacher's Guides available on the Leveled Reader Database.

Common Core State Standards

Literature 1. With prompting and support, ask and answer questions about key details in a text. **Literature 10.** Actively engage in group reading activities with purpose and understanding. **Foundational Skills 1.d.** Recognize and name all upper- and lowercase letters of the alphabet.

1 Build Word Knowledge

Extend Letter Recognition

CONNECT LETTERS TO SOUNDS Display the *Cc, Dd,* and *Ee* Alphabet Cards. Ask children to name the letters and identify the pictures. Point to each pair of letters in turn and say the picture names emphasizing each beginning sound. Now I am going to say two words. Tell me the sound at the beginning of both words and the letter that stands for that sound. Hold up the appropriate Alphabet Card and repeat the words together. Use these pairs of words: *donate, dinner; canyon, comet; educate, elevator.*

WRITE WORDS Distribute paper and pencils to children. Today we are going to use what we know about letters and the sounds they stand for to write words. I am going to say some words, and I want you to write them. Listen carefully.

1. bed **2.** cab **3.** dad

2 Text-Based Comprehension

Read

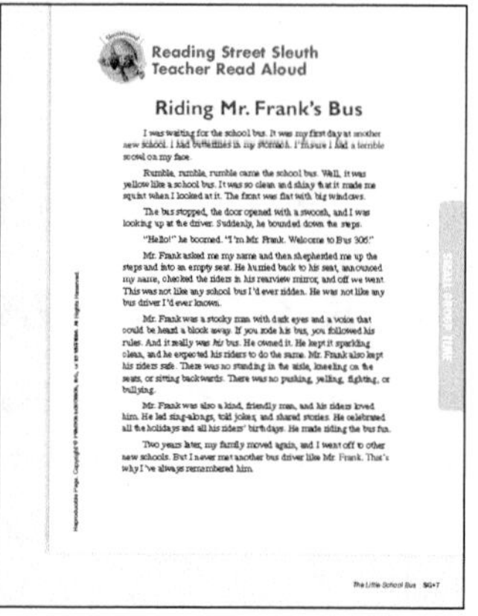
Reading Street Sleuth Teacher Read Aloud

Riding Mr. Frank's Bus

READ ALOUD Read the Reading Street Sleuth Read Aloud, "Riding Mr. Frank's Bus," on p. SG•7 to children.

READ LIKE A SLEUTH! Encourage children to cite evidence from the text to support their answers. You may wish to reread sections of the text to verify children's answers.

Look for Evidence Why does the narrator like riding Mr. Frank's bus?

Ask Questions If you could meet the narrator, what would you ask him or her? What do you still wonder about the narrator, Mr. Frank, or his bus?

Prove It! Performance Task Have children draw a picture of Mr. Frank's bus and its riders, focusing on how the riders feel about riding the bus. Ask children to write a sentence or two using key details from the text. Have them read their sentences to you.

Teaching the Common Core State Standards This Week

The Common Core State Standards for English Language Arts are divided into strands for **Reading** (including **Foundational Skills**), **Writing**, **Speaking and Listening**, and **Language**. The chart below shows some of the content you will teach this week, strand by strand. Turn to this week's 5-Day Planner on pages 112–113 to see how this content is taught each day.

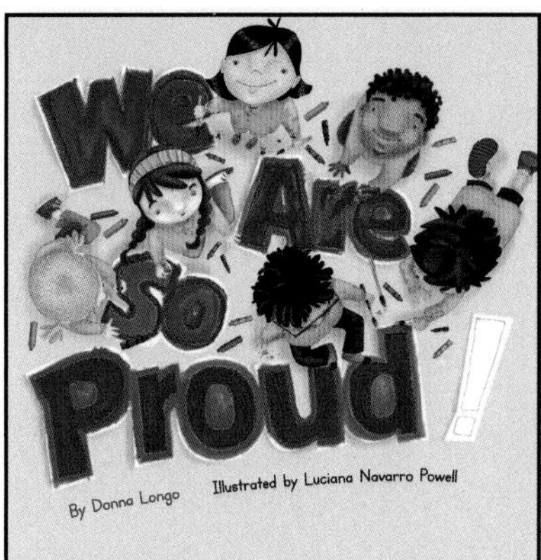

Reading Strand

- **Phonological Awareness:** Syllables
- **Letter Recognition:** *Ff, Gg, Hh, Ii, Jj, Kk, Ll, Mm, Nn*
- **Text-Based Comprehension:** Setting
- **High-Frequency Words:** *am, I*
- **Genre:** Realistic Fiction

Common Core State Standards for English Language Arts

Writing Strand

- **Wonderful, Marvelous Me**
- **Respond to Literature**
- **Genre:** Invitation
- **Extend the Concept**
- **This Week We…**

Speaking and Listening Strand

- **Content Knowledge:** Build Oral Language
- **Listening and Speaking:** Drama–Respond to Literature

Language Strand

- **Oral Vocabulary: Amazing Words** *proud, preparation, cooperation, creation, float, guide*
- **Vocabulary:** Color Words
- **Academic Vocabulary:** *uppercase, lowercase, setting, illustration, predict, invitation, retell, characters, expository text*
- **Conventions:** Write Our Names

Text-Based Comprehension 

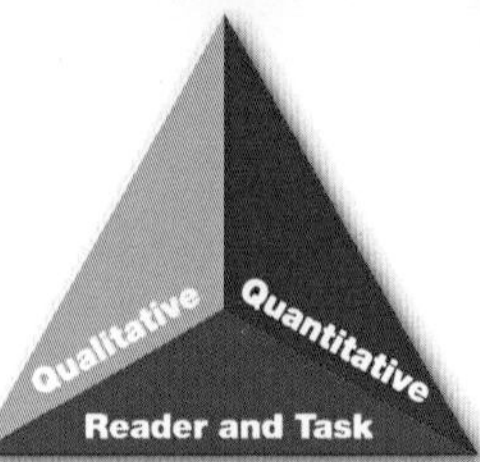

Text Complexity Measures

Use the rubric to familiarize yourself with the text complexity of ***We Are So Proud!***

Bridge to Complex Knowledge

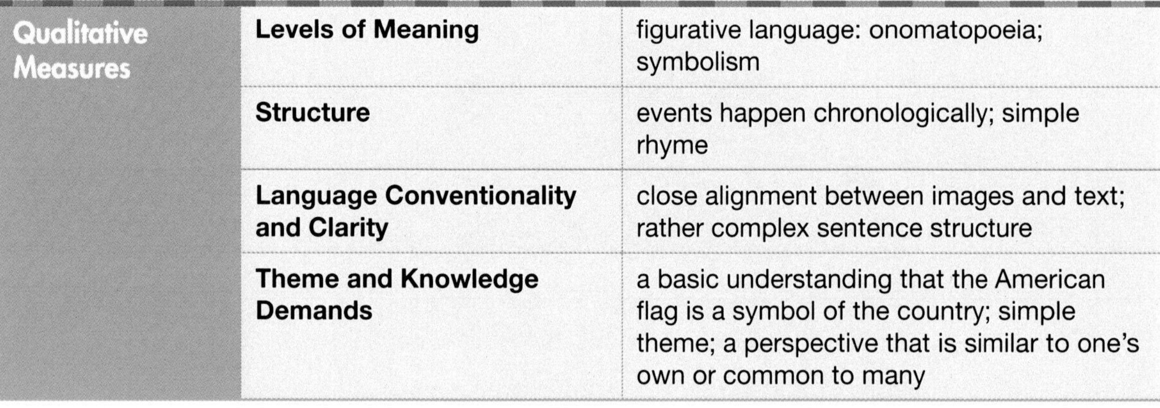

Qualitative Measures		
	Levels of Meaning	figurative language: onomatopoeia; symbolism
	Structure	events happen chronologically; simple rhyme
	Language Conventionality and Clarity	close alignment between images and text; rather complex sentence structure
	Theme and Knowledge Demands	a basic understanding that the American flag is a symbol of the country; simple theme; a perspective that is similar to one's own or common to many

Reader and Task Suggestions

FORMATIVE ASSESSMENT Based on assessment results, use the **Reader and Task Suggestions** in Access Main Selection to scaffold the selection or support independence for children as they read ***We Are So Proud!***

READER AND TASK SUGGESTIONS	
Preparing to Read the Text	**Leveled Tasks**
• Review the Amazing Words and have children use them to talk about the selection. • Discuss the author's use of setting in this story.	• **Levels of Meaning • Analysis** If children don't understand how words can stand for sounds, have them name the words for the sounds of the instruments in the story and talk about each.

Recommended Placement This text is appropriate for placement as a read aloud at this level due to the qualitative elements of the selection.

Focus on Common Core State Standards

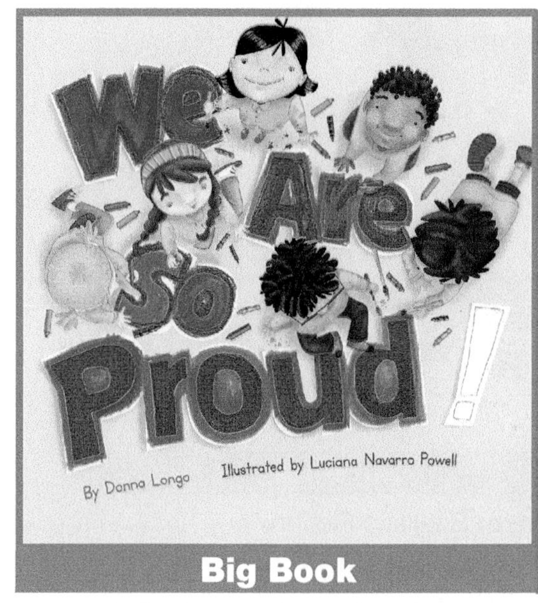

Big Book

Text-Based Comprehension

 **Setting**
CCSS Literature 3.

Letter Recognition

 ***Ff, Gg, Hh, Ii, Jj, Kk, Ll, Mm, Nn***
CCSS Foundational Skills 1.a., CCSS Foundational Skills 1.d.

Writing and Conventions

Genre: Invitation
CCSS Writing 2.

Conventions: Write Our Names
CCSS Language 1.a.

Oral Vocabulary

Amazing Words

proud	preparation
cooperation	creation
float	guide

CCSS Language 6.

Phonological Awareness

Syllables
CCSS Foundational Skills 2., CCSS Foundational Skills 2.b., CCSS Foundational Skills 2.d.

High-Frequency Words

I am

CCSS Foundational Skills 3.c.

Listening and Speaking

Drama—Respond to Literature
CCSS Speaking/Listening 1.a.

Preview Your Week

How do school children work and play together?

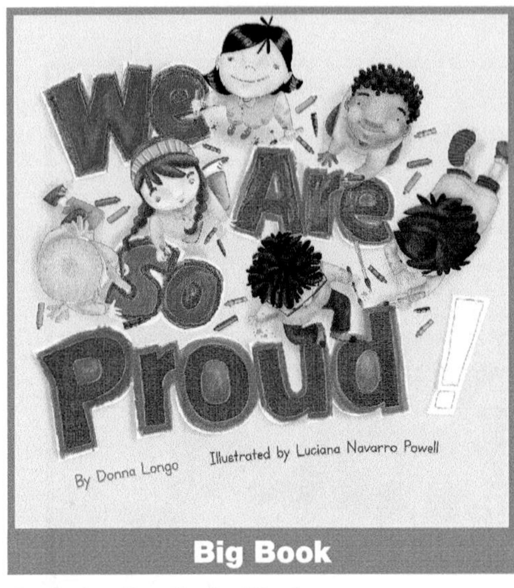

Big Book

Genre: Realistic Fiction

Letter Recognition: *Ff, Gg, Hh, Ii, Jj, Kk, Ll, Mm, Nn*

Text-Based Comprehension: Setting

Build Content Knowledge

KNOWLEDGE GOALS

Children understand that working together with classmates

- helps them share tools and supplies
- helps them solve problems

BUILD ORAL VOCABULARY

This week, children will acquire the following academic vocabulary/ domain-specific words.

Amazing Words

proud	preparation
cooperation	creation
float	guide

BUILD INDEPENDENT READERS

Children will enjoy becoming independent readers as they build decoding skills.

Get Set, Roll! Reader

Decodable Reader

OPTIONAL CONCEPT-BASED READING Use the Digital Path to access readers offering different levels of text complexity.

Concept Literacy

Listen to Me Reader

Student Reader

Independent Reader

This Week's Digital Resources

eSTREET INTERACTIVE
www.ReadingStreet.com

Get Ready to Read

Big Question Video This video on the Digital Path introduces children to the unit question, *How do we live, work, and play together?*, and provides background for the reading children will do throughout the unit.

Background Building Audio CD This audio CD provides valuable background information about the ways that children cooperate to complete a project to help children read and comprehend the weekly texts.

Concept Talk Video Use this video on the Digital Path to build momentum and introduce the weekly concept of working and playing together.

Interactive Sing with Me Chart and Audio "We're Proud of Our Nation," sung to the tune of "B-I-N-G-O," introduces the Amazing Words with a catchy, concept-related song.

Phonics Songs and Rhymes Audio "Jimmy Found a Leaky Faucet," sung to the tune of "Jack and Jill Went Up the Hill," helps children recognize *Ff, Gg, Hh, Ii, Jj, Kk, Ll, Mm,* and *Nn.*

Letter Tile Drag and Drop Using this interactive tool, children click and spell words to enhance their newly learned phonics skills.

Savvas eText For phonics and fluency support, use the eText of the Decodable Reader; the Student Reader; and the Get Set, Roll! Reader on the Leveled Reader Database.

Read and Comprehend

Envision It! Animations Use this colorful animation on the Digital Path to explain the target comprehension skill, Setting.

Savvas eText Go to Savvas SuccessNet and use the eText of the many student edition pages in *My Skills Buddy* with audio support.

Story Sort Use the Story Sort Activity on the Digital Path after reading *We Are So Proud!* to involve children in retelling.

Language Arts

Grammar Jammer Choose a whimsical animation on the Digital Path to provide an engaging lesson on Write Our Names that will capture children's attention.

Additional Resources

Teacher Resources DVD-ROM Use the following resources on the TR DVD or on Savvas SuccessNet throughout the week:

- Amazing Word Cards
- High-Frequency Word Cards
- Daily Fix-It Transparencies
- Reader's and Writer's Notebook
- Scoring Rubrics

This Week's Skills

Letter Recognition
Ff, Gg, Hh, Ii, Jj, Kk, Ll, Mm, Nn

Comprehension
Skill: Setting

Language
Vocabulary: Color Words
Conventions: Write Our Names

Writing
Wonderful, Marvelous Me!
Respond to Literature
Genre Writing
Extend the Concept
This Week We …

5-Day Planner

DAY 1

Get Ready to Read

Content Knowledge 118
Oral Vocabulary: *proud, preparation, cooperation, creation, float, guide*

Phonological Awareness 120
Introduce Syllables
Monitor Progress
Check Phonological Awareness

Letter Recognition 122
Ff and *Gg*

Handwriting 124
F, f, G, and *g*

High-Frequency Words 125
I, am

READ Decodable Story 2 126
Am I?

Read and Comprehend

Text-Based Comprehension 128
Setting

Language Arts

Conventions 130
Write Our Names

Writing 131
Wonderful, Marvelous Me!
Daily Handwriting

Listening and Speaking 132
Respond to Literature: Drama

Extend Your Day! 133

DAY 2

Get Ready to Read

Content Knowledge 134
Oral Vocabulary: *proud, preparation*

Phonological Awareness 136
Syllables

Letter Recognition 138
Hh and *Ii*
Monitor Progress
Check Letter Recognition

Handwriting 140
Write Words with *Hh* and *Ii*

High-Frequency Words 141
I, am

READ Decodable Reader 2 142
Am I?

Read and Comprehend

Text-Based Comprehension 144
READ *We Are So Proud*—1st Read
Think, Talk, and Write
Monitor Progress Check Retelling

Language Arts

Conventions 147
Write Our Names

Writing 148
Respond to Literature
Daily Handwriting

Vocabulary 149
Color Words

Extend Your Day! 151

DAY 3

Get Ready to Read

Content Knowledge 152
Oral Vocabulary: *cooperation, creation*

Phonological Awareness 154
Sound Discrimination

Letter Recognition 156
Jj and *Kk*

Monitor Progress
Check Word Reading
High-Frequency Words

READ Kindergarten Student Reader 158
Cat and Dog Work

Read and Comprehend

Text-Based Comprehension 160
READ *We Are So Proud!*—2nd Read

Language Arts

Conventions 172
Review Say Our Names

Writing 173
Invitation
Daily Handwriting

Listening and Speaking 174
Respond to Literature: Drama

Extend Your Day! 177

DAY 4

Get Ready to Read

Content Knowledge 178
Oral Vocabulary: *float, guide*

Phonological Awareness 180
Review Syllables, Words, and Rhymes

Monitor Progress
Check Phonological Awareness

Letter Recognition 182
Ll and *Mm*

Get Set, Roll! Reader 2 183
READ *Melvin*

Read and Comprehend

Text-Based Comprehension 184
Setting
Review Character
READ *We Are So Proud!*—3rd Read

Language Arts

Conventions 186
Write Our Names

Writing 187
Extend the Concept
Daily Handwriting

Vocabulary 188
Color Words

Extend Your Day! 189

DAY 5

Get Ready to Read

Content Knowledge 190
Review Oral Vocabulary

Monitor Progress
Check Oral Vocabulary

Phonological Awareness 192
Review Syllables

Letter Recognition 192
Nn

Assessment 194

Monitor Progress
Check Letter and Word Reading

Read and Comprehend

Let's Practice It! 196
Expository Text

Assessment 198
Review Setting

Language Arts

Conventions 200
Review Write Our Names

Writing 201
This Week We ...
Daily Handwriting

Wrap Up Your Week! 202

Extend Your Day! 203

Access for All

What do I do in group time?

It's as easy as 1-2-3!

1. TEACHER-LED SMALL GROUPS
2. INDEPENDENT PRACTICE STATIONS
3. INDEPENDENT READING

Small Group Time

Bridge to Common Core

SKILL DEVELOPMENT

- *Ff, Gg, Hh, Ii, Jj, Kk, Ll, Mm, Nn*
- Syllables
- Setting

DEEP UNDERSTANDING

This Week's Knowledge Goals

Children will understand that working together with classmates

- helps them share tools and supplies
- helps them solve problems

1 Small Group Lesson Plan

	DAY 1	DAY 2
	Differentiate Letter Recognition	Differentiate Letter Recognition
OL On-Level pp. SG•20–SG•25	**Practice Letter Recognition** Recognize Letters *Ff, Gg* **Decodable Story** Read *Am I?*	**Practice Letter Recognition** Recognize Letters *Hh, Ii* **Decodable Reader** Read *Am I?*
SI Strategic Intervention pp. SG•26–SG•30	**Reteach Letter Recognition** Recognize Letters *Ff, Gg* **Decodable Story** Read *Am I?*	**Reteach Letter Recognition** Recognize Letters *Hh, Ii* **Decodable Reader** Read *Am I?*
A Advanced pp. SG•31–SG•36	**Extend Letter Recognition** Connect *Ff* to /f/, *Gg* to /g/ **Advanced Selection** Read "Let's Get a Pet"	**Extend Letter Recognition** Connect *Hh* to /h/, *Ii* to /i/ **Decodable Reader** Read *Am I?*
ELL **If...** children need more scaffolding and practice...	**Phonological Awareness and Letter Recognition** **then...** use the Letter Recognition activities beginning on p. 447 in the *ELL Handbook.*	**Phonological Awareness and Letter Recognition** **then...** use the activities on p. DI•29 in the Teacher Resources section of the Digital Path.

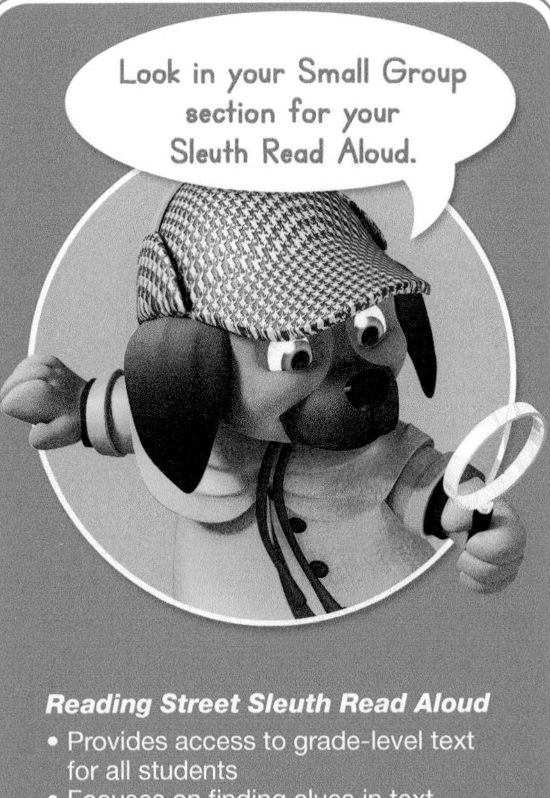

Reading Street Sleuth Read Aloud

- Provides access to grade-level text for all students
- Focuses on finding clues in text through close reading
- Builds capacity for complex text

Build Text-Based Comprehension

We Are So Proud!

Optional Leveled Readers

Concept Literacy

Below Level

On Level

Advanced

Get Set, Roll! Reader

Decodable Reader

DAY 3 Differentiate Vocabulary	DAY 4 Differentiate Language	DAY 5 Differentiate Close Reading
Develop Vocabulary Practice Color Words **Student Reader** Read *Cat and Dog Work*	**Build** Sentences and Words **Get Set, Roll! Reader** Read *Melvin*	**Practice Letter Recognition** Recognize Letters *Jj, Kk, Ll, Mm, Nn* **Text-Based Comprehension** Read "Gadget Is Gone!"
Develop Vocabulary Reteach Color Words **Student Reader** Read *Cat and Dog Work*	**Talk About** Sentences and Words **Get Set, Roll! Reader** Read *Melvin*	**Reteach Letter Recognition** Recognize Letters *Jj, Kk, Ll, Mm, Nn* **Text-Based Comprehension** Read "Gadget Is Gone!"
Develop Vocabulary More Color Words **Student Reader** Read *Cat and Dog Work*	**Extend** Sentences and Words **Get Set, Roll! Reader** Read *Melvin*	**Extend Letter Recognition** Connect Letters to Sounds **Text-Based Comprehension** Read "Gadget Is Gone!"
Vocabulary **then...** use the ELL activities on p. DI•31 in the Teacher Resources section of the Digital Path.	**Developing Language** **then...** use the Language Workshops beginning on p. 306 in the *ELL Handbook.*	**Comprehension** **then...** use the ELL activities on pp. DI•30–DI•31 in the Teacher Resources section of the Digital Path.

 Independent Stations

Practice Last Week's Skills

★ Focus on these activities when time is limited.

ACCESS FOR ALL
- ● Below-Level Activities
- ▲ On-Level Activities
- ■ Advanced Activities

LISTEN UP!

Identify words that rhyme.

OBJECTIVES
- Listen and identify words that rhyme.

MATERIALS
- *Listen Up!* Flip Chart Activity 2
- Picture Cards: *man, fan, cat, hat, jet, net*
- paper, pencils, crayons

 **Modeled Pronunciation Audio CD**

● Children name each Picture Card.

▲ Children name each Picture Card and find two Picture Cards that rhyme.

■ Children name each Picture Card and match all the Picture Cards that rhyme.

★ WORD WORK

Identify letters *Aa, Bb, Cc, Dd, Ee.*

OBJECTIVES
- Identify letters *Aa, Bb, Cc, Dd, Ee.*

MATERIALS
- *Word Work* Flip Chart Activity 2
- Alphabet Cards: *Aa, Bb, Cc, Dd, Ee*
- Letter Tiles
- paper, pencils

 **Interactive Sound-Spelling Cards** 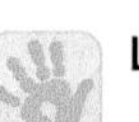 **Letter Tile Drag and Drop**

● Children find Alphabet Cards for letters *Aa, Bb, Cc, Dd,* and *Ee.*

▲ Children match Alphabet Cards *Aa, Bb, Cc, Dd,* and *Ee* with Letter Tiles.

■ Children match Alphabet Cards *Aa, Bb, Cc, Dd,* and *Ee* with Letter Tiles and write each letter.

★ LET'S WRITE!

Write our names.

OBJECTIVES
- Write our names.

MATERIALS
- *Let's Write!* Flip Chart Activity 2
- paper, pencils, crayons

 **Grammar Jammer**

● Children draw a picture of themselves and write their names.

▲ Children draw a picture of themselves going to school and write their names.

■ Children draw a picture of themselves going to school and write their first and last names.

WORDS TO KNOW

Practice vocabulary.

OBJECTIVES
- Identify words for transportation.

MATERIALS
- *Words to Know* Flip Chart Activity 2
- Picture Cards: *bus, boat, box, taxi, tiger, tub, train, van*
- Teacher-made word cards: *bus, boat, box, taxi, tiger, tub, train, van*
- paper, crayons

 **Vocabulary Activities**  **Teacher Resources**
- High-Frequency Word Cards for Unit 1, Week 1

● Children choose Picture Cards for ways people go places.

▲ Children choose Picture Cards for ways people go places. Then they draw a picture that shows how they go somewhere.

■ Children match the Picture Cards and word cards that show how people go places.

READ FOR MEANING

Use text-based comprehension tools.

OBJECTIVES

- Identify and describe a story character.

MATERIALS

- *Read for Meaning* Flip Chart Activity 2
- Little Book *The Little School Bus*
- paper, pencils, crayons

Envision It! Animations
- Leveled eReaders

● Children look at the book and draw a picture of a character in the story.

▲ Children look at the book and draw a picture of a character in the story. Then they write the name of that character.

■ Children look at the book and draw a picture of a character in the story. Then they write something about the character.

LET'S MAKE ART!

Use art to demonstrate understanding.

OBJECTIVES

- Decorate a school bus.

MATERIALS

- *Let's Make Art!* Flip Chart Activity 2
- Teacher-made outline of a school bus
- crayons, construction paper scraps, safety scissors, glue

● Children decorate the school bus and draw themselves on the bus.

▲ Children decorate the school bus and draw themselves on the bus. Then they write their names.

■ Children decorate the school bus and draw themselves and someone else on the bus. Then they write their names.

Manage the Stations

Use these management tools to set up and organize your Practice Stations:

Practice Station Flip Charts

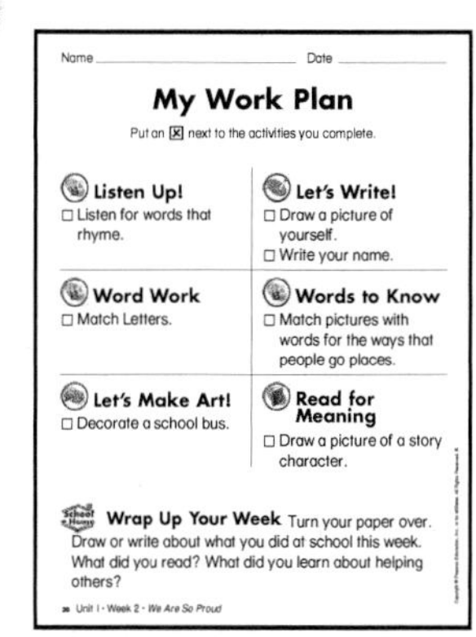
Name / Date

My Work Plan

Put an ☒ next to the activities you complete.

Listen Up! ☐ Listen for words that rhyme.	Let's Write! ☐ Draw a picture of yourself. ☐ Write your name.
Word Work ☐ Match Letters.	Words to Know ☐ Match pictures with words for the ways that people go places.
Let's Make Art! ☐ Decorate a school bus.	Read for Meaning ☐ Draw a picture of a story character.

Wrap Up Your Week Turn your paper over. Draw or write about what you did at school this week. What did you read? What did you learn about helping others?

Unit 1 • Week 2 • We Are So Proud

Classroom Management Handbook for Differentiated Instruction Practice Stations, p. 20

3 Independent Reading

Help children choose complex texts so that they can engage in paired and group reading and writing activities every day before, during, and after school.

Suggestions for this week's independent reading:
- *The House That Jill Built* by Phyllis Root
- *Count Down to Clean Up!* by Nancy Elizabeth Wallace

BOOK TALK Have pairs or groups of children actively engage in reading activities through a discussion of their independent reading for the week. Focus their discussions with the following ideas:

Key Ideas and Details
- Retell the text to your partner or group.
- Identify the main idea and one detail of the text.

Craft and Structure
- Name the title and author of the text.
- Talk about illustrations in the text.

Integration of Ideas
- With support, describe text/illustration relationships.
- Was this book like others I have read?

Savvas eText
- Student Edition
- Decodable Readers
- Get Set, Roll! Readers
- Leveled Readers

Materials from School or Classroom Library

DAY 1 at a Glance

Content Knowledge
Oral Vocabulary

Phonological Awareness
Introduce Syllables

Letter Recognition
Letters *Ff* and *Gg*

Handwriting
F, f, G, and *g*

High-Frequency Words
I, am

Text-Based Comprehension
Setting

Conventions
Write Our Names

Writing
Wonderful, Marvelous Me!

Listening and Speaking
Respond to Literature: Drama

Materials

- Student Edition
- Truckery Rhymes
- Talk with Me/Sing with Me Chart
- Reader's and Writer's Notebook
- Alphabet Cards
- Phonics Songs and Rhymes Chart

Bridge to Common Core

INTEGRATION OF KNOWLEDGE/IDEAS

This week children read, write, and talk about how children work and play together at school.

Texts This Week

- "We're Proud of Our Nation"
- "The Camping Trip"
- *We Are So Proud!*
- *Cat and Dog Work*
- "Mr. Spuffington Fixes It Himself"

Social Studies Knowledge Goals

Children will understand that working together with classmates

- helps them share tools and supplies
- helps them solve problems

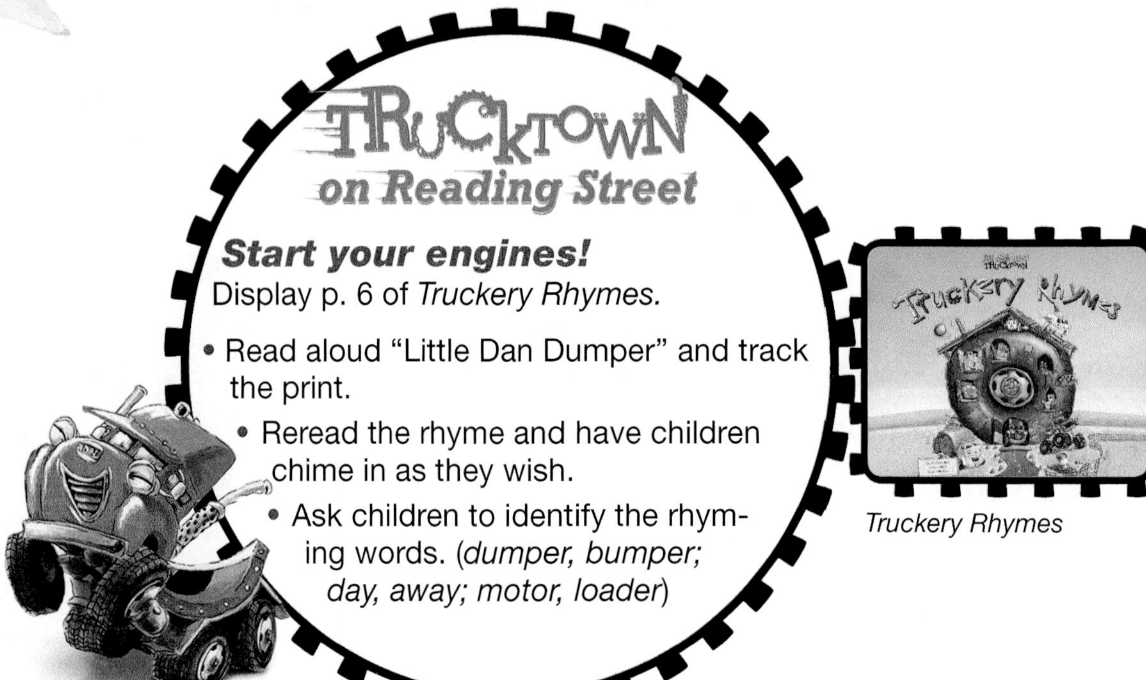

Start your engines!
Display p. 6 of *Truckery Rhymes.*

- Read aloud "Little Dan Dumper" and track the print.
    - Reread the rhyme and have children chime in as they wish.
        - Ask children to identify the rhyming words. (*dumper, bumper; day, away; motor, loader*)

Truckery Rhymes

Content Knowledge

Zoom in on ©

Working and Playing Together at School

CONCEPT TALK To explore the unit concept of All Together Now, tell children that this week they will listen, talk, sing, read, and write about how children work and play together. Write the Question of the Week on the board, *How do school children work and play together?* Track each word as you read.

Build Oral Language

TALK ABOUT COOPERATION Display Talk with Me Chart 2A. What do you see in the pictures? Point to the girl waving a flag. This girl is proud of her country. She is waving the flag. Look at the two pictures that show people working together. They are cooperating. How can we cooperate? We can take turns.

We are going to learn six new Amazing Words this week. Listen as I say each word: *proud, preparation, cooperation, creation, float, guide.* Have children say each word as you point to the picture.

LISTEN FOR AMAZING WORDS Display Sing with Me Chart 2B. Tell children that they are going to sing a song about being proud of our country. Read the title. *Nation* is another word for a country. Have children describe the picture. Sing the song several times to the tune of "B-I-N-G-O." Listen for the Amazing Words: *proud, preparation, cooperation, creation, float, guide.* Have children stand up and sing with you.

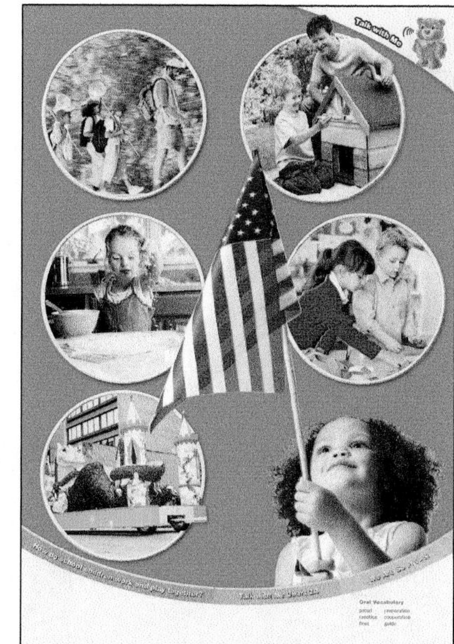

Talk with Me/Sing with Me Chart 2A

We're Proud of Our Nation
Here's our teacher as our guide
With plans and preparation,
P-R-O-U-D,
P-R-O-U-D,
P-R-O-U-D,
We've built a new creation.

Talk with Me/Sing with Me Chart 2B

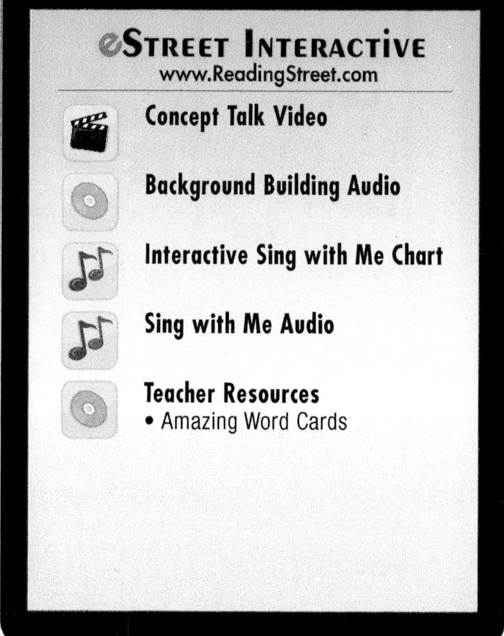
eStreet Interactive
www.ReadingStreet.com
Concept Talk Video
Background Building Audio
Interactive Sing with Me Chart
Sing with Me Audio
Teacher Resources
• Amazing Word Cards

Amazing Words

You've learned 006 words so far.

You'll learn 006 words this week!

proud	preparation
cooperation	creation
float	guide

Visual Support English learners will benefit from additional visual support to understand words in the song. For example, point to the float in the art to scaffold meaning.

ELL Support Additional ELL support and modified instruction is provided in the *ELL Handbook* and in the ELL Support lessons on the *Teacher Resources DVD-ROM.*

Preteach Concepts Use the Day 1 instruction on ELL Poster 2 to assess and build background knowledge, develop concepts, and build oral vocabulary.

Common Core State Standards Foundational Skills 2.b. Count, pronounce, blend, and segment syllables in spoken words. Also Foundational Skills 2.
Phonological Awareness
Let's Listen for
Syllables
Read Together
Point to a picture, say the word, and clap for each part, or syllable, you hear.
Which words have one part, or syllable?
Which words have more than one part, or syllable?
READING STREET ONLINE
BIG QUESTION VIDEO
www.ReadingStreet.com
32
33

My Skills Buddy, pp. 32–33

Common Core State Standards

Foundational Skills 2. Demonstrate understanding of spoken words, syllables, and sounds (phonemes). **Foundational Skills 2.b.** Count, pronounce, blend, and segment syllables in spoken words.

Phonological Awareness

Introduce Syllables

INTRODUCE Words have parts called syllables. Say *proud* and clap once. *Proud* has one syllable. Say *pa-rade,* clapping once for each syllable. *Parade* has two syllables. Listen again. Say *pa-rade* again and clap for each syllable. How many syllables are in *parade?* Clap with me. Repeat *pa-rade* several times. Have children clap syllables with you. Repeat for *honor, classes, plan,* and *nation.*

MODEL Have children look at the picture on pp. 32–33 of *My Skills Buddy.* Tell children they will point to a picture, say the word for the picture, and clap the number of syllables, or word parts, in the word. I see a flower. Say *flow-er* and clap twice. *Flower* has two syllables. Clap with me.

GUIDE PRACTICE As children name pictures, guide them in saying the word and clapping for each syllable. Discuss some of the bulleted items on p. 32 of *My Skills Buddy.* Save the other bulleted items for discussion on Day 2.

Corrective feedback	**If...** children cannot identify the syllables in a word, **then...** say *flower* again, pausing after each syllable.

BLEND SYLLABLES Say the word *super.* *Super* has two syllables: *su-per.* I am going to blend the syllables to make the word *super*: *su-per, super.* Repeat with *puddle.*

This time I will say the word parts, or syllables, first. I want you to help me blend the syllables to say the word: *lit-tle.* Now blend the syllables with me to say the word: *little.* Repeat with *repair, borrow,* and *rattle.*

Corrective feedback	**If...** children cannot blend syllables to say words, **then...** say the word *rabbit,* dividing the word into syllables: *rab-bit.* Have children say each syllable with you slowly and then say the syllables together quickly. Repeat with the words *monkey, duckling,* and *tiger.*

REVIEW Read a sentence from a book. Have children say the sentence with you as they clap once after saying each word. Count the number of words in the sentence. Repeat the sentence to check the number of words counted. Continue with other sentences from the book.

Check Phonological Awareness Syllables

FORMATIVE ASSESSMENT Say the word *forest.* Ask children to say the word with you and to count the number of syllables, or parts, the word has. Continue with these words: *trail, campsite, mountains, hike, dinner.*

If... children cannot identify the number of syllables,
then... use the small-group Strategic Intervention lesson, p. SG•26, to reteach syllables.

Access for All

 Advanced

Phonological Awareness Have children hold up a finger for each syllable in the word they find in the picture.

Teacher Tip

Throughout the day, stop and have children count the number of syllables in words being used in other content areas or activities.

Clapping Syllables Speakers of monosyllabic languages such as Cantonese, Hmong, Khmer, Korean, and Vietnamese may have difficulty understanding that multisyllabic words are single words. Reinforce children's understanding of the meanings of multisyllabic words before clapping syllables.

Common Core State Standards

Foundational Skills 1.d. Recognize and name all upper- and lowercase letters of the alphabet. **Foundational Skills 2.b.** Count, pronounce, blend, and segment syllables in spoken words.

Letter Recognition

Teach/Model

Letters *Ff* and *Gg*

INTRODUCE Display the *Ff* Alphabet Card. The name of this letter is uppercase *F.* What is the name of this letter? Continue with lowercase *f.* Repeat with the *Gg* Alphabet Card. Who can find the letters *Ff* in the classroom? Who can find the letters *Gg?*

Alphabet Card

MODEL Write "Jimmy Found a Leaky Faucet" on the board. Who can find an uppercase *F?* Yes, uppercase *F* is in the second word. Where is another uppercase *F?* The last word has an uppercase *F.* Write "Good Golly Miss Molly" on the board. Who can find uppercase *G?*

Alphabet Card

Guide Practice

GROUP PRACTICE Display Phonics Songs and Rhymes Chart 2. Teach children the song "Jimmy Found a Leaky Faucet" sung to the tune of "Jack and Jill Went Up the Hill." Play the CD and sing the song several times. When children are familiar with the song, have them sing along with you, clapping in time to the music. Then have children come up and point to uppercase *F* and lowercase *f* and *g* in the song lyrics. Encourage them to say the letter they identify.

Jimmy Found a Leaky Faucet
Jimmy found a leaky faucet,
And kindly tried to fix it.
He got a good look,
He jiggled the hook,
And lickety-split, he did it!

Phonics Songs and Rhymes Chart 2

ON THEIR OWN Display a page of a book and have children look for words with uppercase and lowercase *Ff* and *Gg.* Write the words on the board. Have children say each word with you.

Blend Words

REVIEW To review letter names, use the *Aa, Bb, Cc, Dd,* and *Ee* Alphabet Cards. Have children use their finger to write each letter on their hand as they say the name. Then use this process for blending syllables to have children blend new words.

CONNECT Say the word *remember.* Have children say the word with you. Now listen as I say the word: *re-mem-ber.* Say the parts of the word, or syllables, with me: *re-mem-ber.* Blend the syllables with children to make the word *remember.* Repeat the blending several times so that children understand how to blend the syllables together.

MODEL When I say *col-or,* I say the syllables in the word. Then I blend the syllables together to make the word *color.* Have children blend the syllables with you and repeat the blending several times.

GUIDE PRACTICE Let's make some more words. When I say the syllables in the word, repeat them with me. Then we can blend the syllables to make a word. Say *for-est, hi-ker, el-e-phant, ti-ger, bea-ver.* Have children blend the syllables and say the new words.

Corrective feedback	**If...** children have trouble blending the syllables to say a word, **then...** model blending the syllables for any word in the lesson and have children blend the syllables with you and say the word.

Access for All

SI Strategic Intervention

Support Letter Recognition Have children place letter cards on their desks that they can use to trace and name letters between lesson activities.

Teacher Tip

Begin the practice with easy words, such as *teacher* and *children.* Have children repeat each syllable with you and then blend the syllables to make the words.

Support Letter Recognition Have children use the Alphabet Cards to review the names of the new letters *Ff* and *Gg.*

Foundational Skills 3.c. Read common high-frequency words by sight (e.g., *the, of, to, you, she, my, is, are, do, does*). **Language 1.a.** Print many upper- and lowercase letters. **Also Foundational Skills 1.b.**

Access for All

Strategic Intervention

Handwriting Say uppercase *F.* Have children write the letter on their Write-On Boards. When they finish writing the letter, have them hold up their Write-On Boards. Repeat with uppercase *G* and lowercase *f* and *g.*

Academic Vocabulary 

uppercase in capital letters

lowercase in small letters, not capital

Handwriting

INTRODUCE Write *Ff* on the board and point to *F.* This is uppercase *F.* We use uppercase letters at the beginning of sentences and names. Write *Gg* on the board and repeat the routine.

MODEL UPPERCASE *F* AND *G* Write *Fay* on the board. Point to the uppercase *F.* This is uppercase *F.* Watch as I trace the uppercase *F* with my finger. Follow the stroke instructions pictured below. Repeat the routine for *G* with *Gil.*

GUIDE PRACTICE Have children write uppercase *F* in the air. Use your finger to make an uppercase *F* in the air. Now write it on your hand. Repeat the routine with uppercase *G.*

MODEL LOWERCASE *f* AND *g* Write *fan* on the board. Point to *f.* This is lowercase *f.* Watch as I trace the lowercase *f* with my finger. Write another lowercase *f* on the board, following the stroke instructions. Again, have children write *f* in the air and on their hands. Repeat the routine for *g* with *girl.*

GUIDE PRACTICE Have children use their Write-On Boards to write a row of uppercase *F* and *G* and a row of lowercase *f* and *g.*

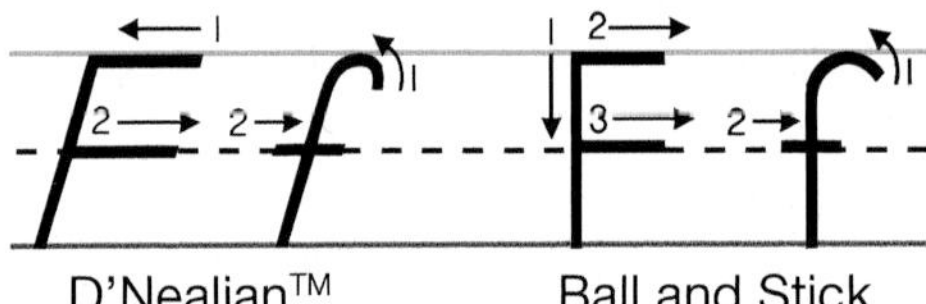

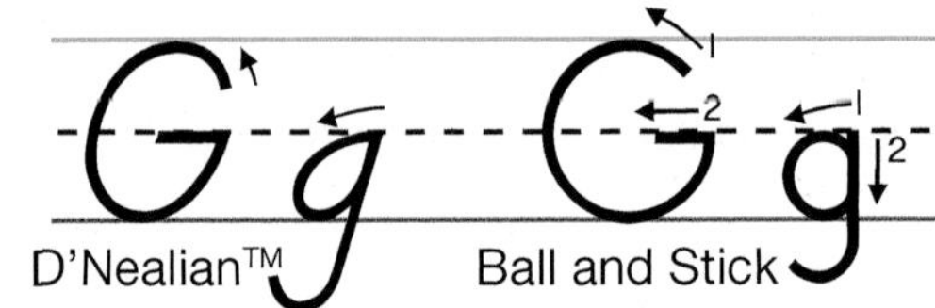

ON THEIR OWN Use *Reader's and Writer's Notebook,* pp. 13 and 14, for additional practice with *Ff* and *Gg.* Return to these pages on Day 2 to practice *Hh* and *Ii.*

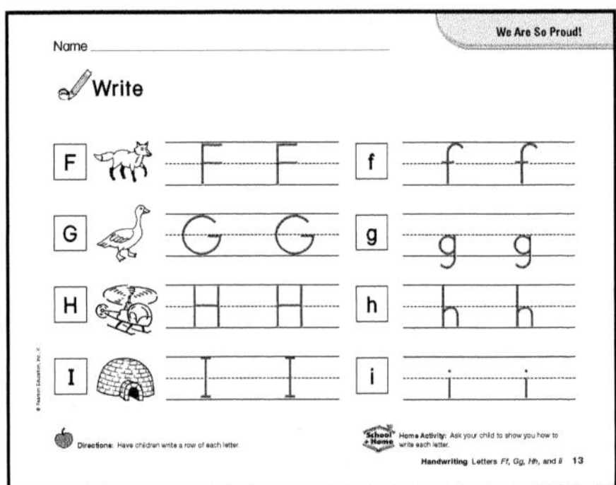

Reader's and Writer's Notebook, p. 13

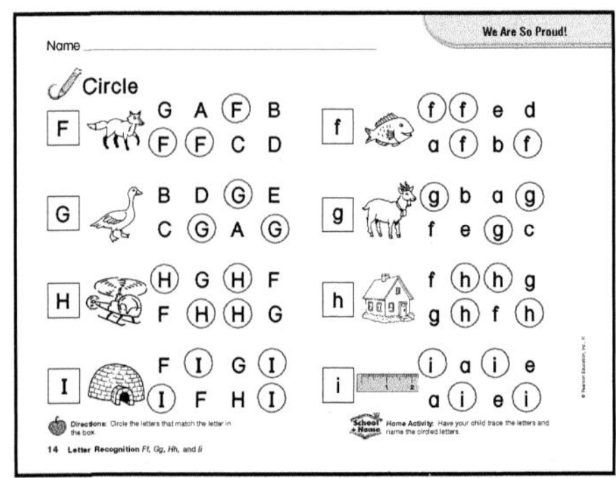

Reader's and Writer's Notebook, p. 14

High-Frequency Words

INTRODUCE Use the routine below to review high-frequency words *I* and *am.*

Routine Nondecodable Words

1. **Say and Spell** Some words we must learn by remembering the letters rather than saying the sounds. We will say and spell the words to help learn them. Write *am* on the board. This is the word *am.* It has two letters. The letters in *am* are *a* and *m.* Have children say and spell the word, first with you and then without you.
2. **Demonstrate Meaning** I can use the word *am* in lots of sentences. Here is one sentence: *I am at school.* Now you use the word in a sentence.

Repeat the routine with the word *I.*

Routines Flip Chart

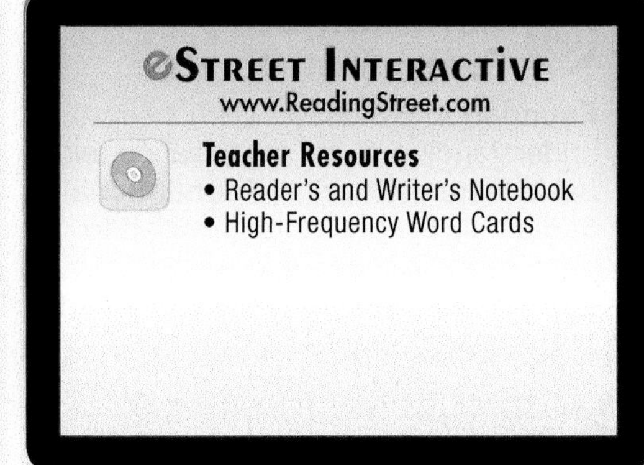

eStreet Interactive
www.ReadingStreet.com

Teacher Resources
- Reader's and Writer's Notebook
- High-Frequency Word Cards

Professional Development: Introduce Classroom Vocabulary Throughout the year, have children help you label the parts of the classroom and the objects in the classroom. Say the name of each item as you label it, and use the word in a sentence that explains the item. This can help children become more familiar with everyday English used in an academic setting.

Common Core State Standards

Foundational Skills 1. Demonstrate understanding of the organization and basic features of print. **Foundational Skills 1.a.** Follow words from left to right, top to bottom, and page-by-page. **Foundational Skills 3.c.** Read common high-frequency words by sight (e.g., *the, of, to, you, she, my, is, are, do, does*).

Access for All

Advanced

Use High-Frequency Words Write the words *I* and *am* on the board. Say the words. Ask several children to write the words on the board and use them in a sentence.

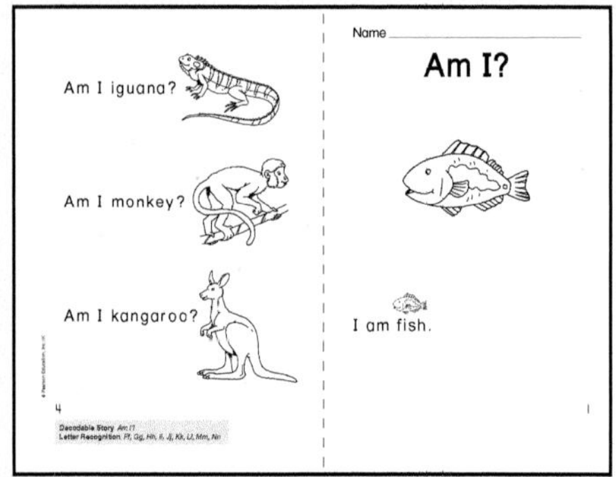

Reader's and Writer's Notebook, pp. 15–16

Decodable Story 2

Read *Am I?*

REVIEW Review the previously taught high-frequency words by having children read each word as you point to it on the Word Wall: *I, am.*

TEACH REBUS WORDS Draw a fish on the board and write the word *fish.* This is the word *fish.* Say the letters with me: *f, i, s, h, fish.* Continue with *horse, goose, iguana, monkey,* and *kangaroo.* We will see these words in our book today. There will be a picture above the word to help you read it.

READ Tear out Decodable Story *Am I?* on pp. 15–16 of each child's *Reader's and Writer's Notebook.* Fold the pages to form a book. Distribute the self-cover books.

Today we will read a story about some animals. First let's look at our book. This is the right way to hold the book. Model how to hold the book. Point to the fish on the cover. We know the book is right side up because the fish is right side up. Turn the book upside down. This is the wrong way to hold a book. The fish and the words are upside down. We cannot read upside-down words. Turn the book right side up. Now hold your book right side up. Make sure the letter *A* is right side up. Check to see that all children are holding their books correctly.

Point to the front cover. This is the front cover of our book. *Front* means the side that faces us. Open the book. These are the pages in our story. We turn the pages from right to left. Demonstrate how to turn the pages. Now you turn the pages from right to left. Observe and make sure all children are turning the pages correctly. This is the back cover. It is the part of the book we look at last. Point to the title of the story. What is the title of our book? The title of the story is *Am I?* Finally, draw children's attention to the final page of the story. Explain that reading moves from top to bottom. They should read the first question at the top of the page, then the question below it, and the one below that.

Have children read the story, holding the book right side up and turning the pages correctly. When they get to the final page, observe to ensure that children are reading from top to bottom.

Use the routine for reading decodable books to read Decodable Story 2.

Routine Reading Decodable Books

1. **Read Silently** Have children whisper read the story page by page as you listen in.
2. **Model Fluent Reading** Have children finger point as you read a page. Then have them reread the page without you.
3. **Read Chorally** Have children finger point as they chorally read the page. Continue reading page by page, repeating steps 1 and 2.
4. **Read Individually** Have children take turns reading aloud a page.
5. **Reread and Monitor Progress** As you listen to individual children reread, monitor progress and provide support.
6. **Reread with a Partner** Have children reread the story page by page with a partner.

Routines Flip Chart

eStreet Interactive
www.ReadingStreet.com

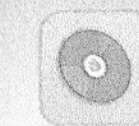

Teacher Resources
- Reader's and Writer's Notebook

Access Decodable Story Before children read *Am I?*, review the high-frequency words on the Word Wall. Have children point to the word you say.

Day 1 SMALL GROUP TIME • Differentiate Letter Recognition, p. SG•19

OL On-Level	SI Strategic Intervention	A Advanced
• **Practice Letter Recognition** Recognize Letters *Ff, Gg* • **Read** Decodable Story *Am I?*	• **Reteach Letter Recognition** Recognize Letters *Ff, Gg* • **Read** Decodable Story *Am I?*	• **Extend Letter Recognition** Connect *Ff* to /f/, *Gg* to /g/ • **Read** Advanced Selection "Let's Get a Pet"

Place English Language Learners in the groups that correspond to their reading abilities in English.

If... children need more support with **Letter Recognition,**
then... use the Phonics Transition lessons beginning on p. 447 in the *ELL Handbook.*

Common Core State Standards
Literature 3. With prompting and support, identify characters, settings, and major events in a story.

Comprehension

Envision It!
Literary Elements

READING STREET ONLINE
ENVISION IT! ANIMATIONS
www.ReadingStreet.com

Characters

Setting

Plot

START

FINISH

34

35

My Skills Buddy, pp. 34–35

Zoom in on

Common Core State Standards

Literature 3. With prompting and support, identify characters, settings, and major events in a story.

Skills Trace

Setting

Introduce U1W2D1; U2W2D1; U4W6D1; U6W5D1

Practice U1W2D2; U1W2D3; U1W2D4; U2W2D2; U2W2D3; U2W2D4; U4W6D2; U4W6D3; U4W6D4; U6W5D2; U6W5D3; U6W5D4

Reteach/Review U1W2D5; U1W3D4; U1W4D4; U1W6D4; U2W2D5; U2W4D4; U4W4D4; U4W6D5; U6W5D5

Assess/Test Benchmark Assessment U2; U6

KEY: U=Unit W=Week D=Day

Text-Based Comprehension

Setting

READ Remind children of the weekly concept—Working and Playing Together at School. Have children listen as you read aloud "The Camping Trip" on p. 129.

MODEL A CLOSE READ Model how to identify and describe the setting as a tool to build comprehension.

Where and when does this story take place? The story tells about a campsite in the mountains. The Garcias are getting ready to make dinner, so it must be late afternoon. The story takes place in the mountains in the late afternoon.

TEACH SETTING When we read a story, we pay attention to where the story happens and when it happens. When and where the story takes place is called the **setting.** Good readers identify when and where a story takes place because it helps them understand the story.

Have children turn to pp. 34–35 in *My Skills Buddy* and look at the pictures. Tell children the story of "The Tortoise and the Hare."

- Where does the story take place? (The animals are outside.)
- When does the story take place? (The story takes place during the daytime.) How do you know it is the daytime? (The sun is shining.)

GUIDE PRACTICE Reread "The Camping Trip" as children identify the clues that help them figure out the story's setting. Have children draw the setting on a sheet of paper as the mountains, trees, and lake are identified as parts of the setting of the story.

MORE PRACTICE Display the Big Book *The Little School Bus.* Help children recall and describe the setting of the story.

Teacher Read Aloud

The Camping Trip

The Garcias are camping. They pick a campsite in the mountains. They can hike on trails through the cool, green forests. They can fish and swim in the clear, blue lake. First, they have to set up their camp.

Carla is trying to put up the tent, but it keeps falling down. Juan helps her. He fixes the tent poles.

Mr. Garcia is trying to start a fire. Olivia helps him. She gets more wood.

Mrs. Garcia is trying to fix dinner, but she needs water. Tomas helps her. He goes to get the water.

Soon the tent is up, the fire is blazing, and dinner is cooking. This camping trip will be great!

Access for All

Support Setting Remind children that any place they go can be a setting. This classroom is a setting. How would you describe this setting?

Academic Vocabulary

setting the time (when) and place (where) of a story or play

Bridge to Common Core

KEY IDEAS AND DETAILS
When children identify and describe the setting of a story, they are determining key details in the story. Answering questions about setting helps children comprehend and make logical inferences about the text.

Check Understanding Stop after each paragraph and discuss it with children. Clarify their understanding by asking questions such as these: *Why did the Garcias choose this campsite? What is Carla doing? Who helps her?*

Common Core State Standards

Writing 3. Use a combination of drawing, dictating, and writing to narrate a single event or several loosely linked events, tell about the events in the order in which they occurred, and provide a reaction to what happened. **Language 1.a.** Print many upper- and lowercase letters. **Also Writing 8., Language 2.**

Daily Fix-It

my name is greg.
My name is Greg.

This week's practice sentences appear on *Teacher Resources DVD-ROM.*

Conventions

Write Our Names

MAKE CONNECTIONS Today we listened to a story about the Garcia family. The names of the Garcia children are Carla, Juan, Olivia, and Tomas. What is the name of someone in your family? Remind children that a name is a word or words that stand for a person or an animal.

TEACH My name is [say your first name]. Point to a child. What is your name? Have the child answer by saying "My name is _______." Then have children take turns telling another child their name using the sentence frame.

MODEL You know my name is [say your first name]. This is how I write my name. Write your name on the board. Point to the uppercase letter. I use an uppercase letter to begin my name. Then write one of the children's names. Whose name is this? How did I write the first letter in the name? Continue with other names.

GUIDE PRACTICE Have children come to the board to write or dictate their names. Help them identify and write each letter in their name. Remind them to begin their name with an uppercase letter.

Team Talk **APPLY** Pair children and have them write their own name on their Write-On Boards and show it to their partner. Then have them tell the letters in their name.

Wonderful, Marvelous Me! Today I Feel...

INTRODUCE Talk with children about feelings. We can have so many different feelings. We may feel happy when we sing our favorite song. We may feel sad when our dog runs away. We may feel shy when we meet someone new. Display the following list of emotion words and review it with children.

silly	excited	afraid	lonely	sad
proud	curious	happy	surprised	angry
scared	shy	nervous	confident	tired

All of our feelings are important. Why is it important to share our feelings with others? Encourage children to share their thoughts and ideas.

MODEL We're going to share how we feel today. I'm going to close my eyes and look inside at my feelings. I woke up this morning and thought about all of the things you and I will do today. I thought about all of the fun we have learning new things, and I couldn't wait to get to school this morning so we could start our day together. Today I am excited because we will spend the day learning new things.

INDEPENDENT WRITING Now you're going to share how you feel today. Close your eyes and look inside at your wonderful, marvelous feelings. What do you see? How do you feel? Why do you feel that way? Have children write or dictate their ideas and then illustrate them.

Daily Handwriting

Write uppercase *F* and *G* and lowercase *f* and *g* on the board. Review correct letter formation with children.

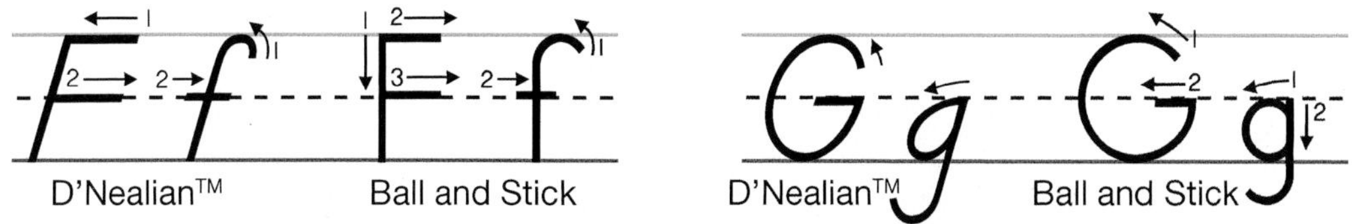

Have children write a row of uppercase *F* and *G* and a row of lowercase *f* and *g* on their Write-On Boards. Remind them to use proper left-to-right and top-to-bottom progression when writing *F, f, G,* and *g*.

Write Guy *by Jeff Anderson*

Conferencing Is Listening

Conferring about children's writing is more about teachers listening than teachers speaking. What is the child trying to say? What help does he or she need? We can ask questions to keep children speaking. "What do you want your reader to know?"

Bridge to Common Core

TEXT TYPES AND PURPOSES

Today children draw and write about their feelings.

Narrative Writing

Children are learning to use writing to convey personal experiences and events through well-chosen words and details.

Throughout the week, children will have opportunities to write varied text types for different purposes.

5-Day Plan

DAY 1	Wonderful, Marvelous Me!
DAY 2	Respond to Literature
DAY 3	Genre Writing
DAY 4	Extend the Concept
DAY 5	This Week We...

Common Core State Standards

Foundational Skills 1.d. Recognize and name all upper- and lowercase letters of the alphabet. **Speaking/ Listening 1.** Participate in collaborative conversations with diverse partners about *kindergarten topics and texts* with peers and adults in small and larger groups. **Speaking/ Listening 1.a.** Follow agreed-upon rules for discussions (e.g., listening to others and taking turns speaking about the topics and texts under discussion). **Also Speaking/ Listening 4., 5.**

Listening and Speaking

Respond to Literature: Drama

TEACH After we read a story, it's fun to think about the parts of the story we enjoyed. We can act out things that happen in the story that we think are funny or exciting.

MODEL In *The Little School Bus,* the animals get on the bus to go to school. Let's pretend we are the animals getting on a bus to go to school. Place six chairs in three rows for bus seats. Have six children pretend to be the animals boarding and sitting on the bus.

GUIDE PRACTICE Have children pretend to be the animals getting out of school. Have them tell what the animals do. Tell children to speak one at a time. Then choose a group of children to board the bus to ride home from school. Refer children to the Rules for Listening and Speaking on pp. 1–2 of *Reader's and Writer's Notebook.* Remind children to speak one at a time.

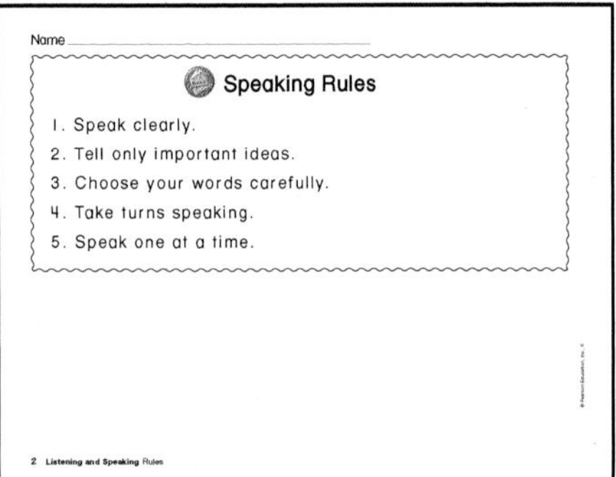
Name

Speaking Rules

1. Speak clearly.
2. Tell only important ideas.
3. Choose your words carefully.
4. Take turns speaking.
5. Speak one at a time.

Reader's and Writer's Notebook, pp. 1–2

Wrap Up Your Day!

✓ **Oral Language** Today we sang about a parade to show we are proud of our nation. Say the Amazing Words with me: *proud, preparation, cooperation, creation, float, guide.*

✓ **Conventions** Write the first letter of a child's name on the board. Whose name begins with this letter? Invite these children to write their names on the board. Repeat with other letters.

✓ **Homework Idea** Send home the Family Times Newsletter from Let's Practice It! pp. 3–4 on *Teacher Resources DVD-ROM.*

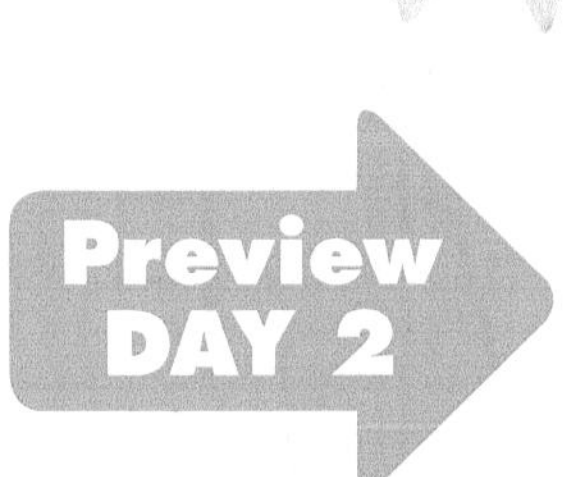

Tomorrow we will read about a class preparing for a celebration.

Extend Your Day!

Social Studies
Cooperation Station

MATERIALS: Sing with Me Chart 2B, chart paper, drawing paper, crayons

HOW DO WE COOPERATE? Discuss cooperation with children. Explain that cooperation is the way we work together. When we cooperate, we help one another. Show the pictures on Sing with Me Chart 2B. How do these pictures show people cooperating? We can have so much fun when we cooperate. We can cooperate at home and at school. How do you cooperate at home? How do you cooperate at school?

Make a two-column chart labeled *Cooperation at Home* and *Cooperation at School.* Write children's responses in the appropriate columns.

Cooperation at Home	Cooperation at School
clean my room help my mom and dad	share toys help friends read clean up my desk

DRAW PICTURES Give each child a sheet of paper divided in half. On one half, have children draw a picture of one way they cooperate at home. On the other half, have children draw a picture of one way they cooperate at school.

Letter Recognition
Letter Search

MATERIALS: paper, writing utensils

RECOGNIZE LETTERS Make a letter search page by writing uppercase and lowercase forms of the letters *Aa* through *Gg* in a list on a sheet of paper. Have children search around the room for the letters. When they find one of the letters, have them write it on their paper.

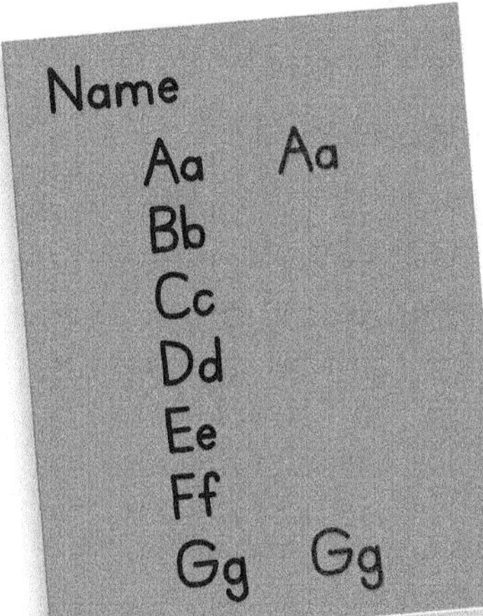

Conventions
Our Dazzling Names

MATERIALS: construction paper, glue, glitter

WRITE OUR NAMES Have children write their names in large letters on construction paper using glue or a glue stick. Then have them sprinkle glitter in different colors over their names. Carefully shake the excess glitter off the paper to reveal their names in dazzling colors.

DAY 2 at a Glance

Content Knowledge
Oral Vocabulary

Phonological Awareness
Syllables

Letter Recognition
Letters *Hh* and *Ii*

Handwriting
H, h, I, and *i*

Text-Based Comprehension
Setting

Conventions
Write Our Names

Writing
Respond to Literature

Vocabulary
Color Words

Materials

- Student Edition
- Truckery Rhymes
- Talk with Me/Sing with Me Chart
- Picture Cards
- Phonics Songs and Rhymes Chart
- Alphabet Cards
- Reader's and Writer's Notebook
- Big Book

Common Core State Standards

Speaking/Listening 2. Confirm understanding of a text read aloud or information presented orally or through other media by asking and answering questions about key details and requesting clarification if something is not understood. **Language 6.** Use words and phrases acquired through conversations, reading and being read to, and responding to texts. **Also Language 5.c.**

TRUCKTOWN
on Reading Street

Start your engines!

Display p. 6 of *Truckery Rhymes.* Point to "Little Dan Dumper." Who remembers the truck in this rhyme? Yes, it's Dump Truck Dan. Let's read the rhyme together. Have a child point to the rhyming words as the class reads the rhyme again. Give additional children the opportunity to say the rhyme aloud and track the print.

Truckery Rhymes

Truckery Rhymes

Content Knowledge

Zoom in on

Working and Playing Together at School

TALK ABOUT COOPERATION AT SCHOOL On the board, write the Question of the Week, *How do school children work and play together?,* and track the print as you read it aloud. Have children answer the question in complete sentences. To reinforce the concept and focus children's attention, display Sing with Me Chart 2B. Tell children that they are going to sing about a celebration for our nation.

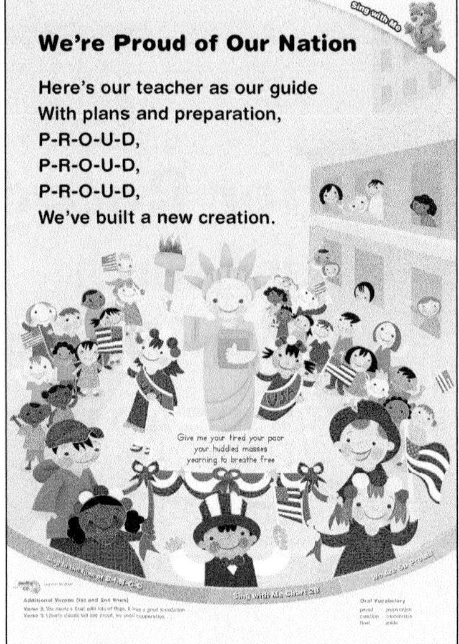
We're Proud of Our Nation
Here's our teacher as our guide
With plans and preparation,
P-R-O-U-D,
P-R-O-U-D,
P-R-O-U-D,
We've built a new creation.

Talk with Me/Sing with Me Chart 2B

Build Oral Language

LISTEN FOR AMAZING WORDS The Amazing Words *proud* and *preparation* are in the song "We're Proud of Our Nation." Have children describe the picture. Sing the song several times to the tune of "B-I-N-G-O." Ask children to sing along with you. Have them clap when they hear *proud* and *preparation.*

Build Oral Vocabulary

Amazing Words Robust Vocabulary Routine

1. **Introduce the Word** The title of the story we will read today is *We Are So Proud! Proud* means to think well of people and things. What's our new Amazing Word for thinking well of people and things? Say it with me: *proud.*

2. **Demonstrate** Provide examples to show meaning. *Jack is proud of his family.* What are things or people you are *proud* of?

   Repeat steps 1 and 2.

   Introduce the Word Some big projects take a lot of *preparation. Preparation* is the act of getting something ready. What's our new Amazing Word for the act of getting something ready? Say it with me: *preparation.*

   Demonstrate *It takes a lot of preparation to get the classroom ready for special visitors.*

3. **Apply** Tell children to use *proud* and *preparation* in complete sentences. Have them draw a picture of something they are *proud* of.

4. **Display the Words** Ask children where they see the letter *d* in *proud.* Have them point to the letter and say its name. Continue with the letters *a* and *e* in *preparation.*

Routines Flip Chart

USE AMAZING WORDS To reinforce the concept and the Amazing Words, have children supply the appropriate Amazing Word for each sentence.

He is _______ of the pictures he draws. (proud)
The play takes a lot of _______. (preparation)

Amazing Words

proud	preparation
cooperation	creation
float	guide

Access for All

 Strategic Intervention

Sentence Production If children have difficulty completing the sentences, say a sentence using both Amazing Words and ask children to choose the one that makes sense. Say the sentence together.

Reinforce Vocabulary Use the Day 2 instruction on ELL Poster 2 to reinforce the meanings of high-frequency words.

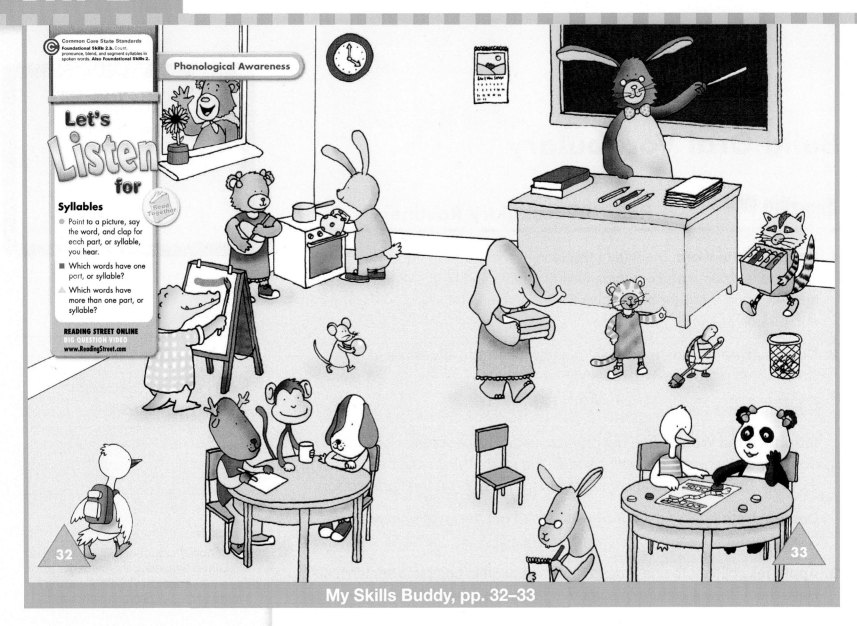

Common Core State Standards
Foundational Skills 2.b. Count, pronounce, blend, and segment syllables in spoken words. **Also Foundational Skills 2.**

Phonological Awareness

Let's Listen for

Syllables

Read Together

- Point to a picture, say the word, and clap for each part, or syllable, you hear.
- Which words have one part, or syllable?
- Which words have more than one part, or syllable?

READING STREET ONLINE
BIG QUESTION VIDEO
www.ReadingStreet.com

32

33

My Skills Buddy, pp. 32–33

Common Core State Standards

Foundational Skills 2. Demonstrate understanding of spoken words, syllables, and sounds (phonemes). **Foundational Skills 2.b.** Count, pronounce, blend, and segment syllables in spoken words. **Also Foundational Skills 2.a.**

Phonological Awareness

Syllables

IDENTIFY SYLLABLES Display the *kitten* Picture Card. This is a kitten. Have children clap the number of syllables as they say the word: *kit-ten.* How many syllables are in the word *kitten?* Repeat for the words *city, building,* and *corner.*

Picture Card

MODEL When I want to count the syllables in a word, I hold up a finger for each syllable I say: *rab* (show one finger) *bit* (show a second finger). I held up two fingers, so I know the word has two syllables. Say the word with me and hold up your fingers: *rab-bit, rabbit.*

Let's say a word and use our fingers to count the parts. The word is *crocodile.* Say it with me: *croc-o-dile.* Continue with these words: *alligator, tiger, hippopotamus, lion, elephant.*

GUIDE PRACTICE Have children look at the picture on *My Skills Buddy,* pp. 32–33. Remember we said *flower* and clapped for each syllable. Say *flow-er* with me and clap for each syllable. Name other things in the picture and clap for each syllable in the word. Discuss with children those bulleted items on p. 32 not discussed on Day 1.

Corrective feedback	**If...** children cannot identify the number of syllables, **then...** have them repeat the word as you say the parts. Then have them clap the syllables. Listen as I say *pencil: pen-cil.* Say the syllables with me. How many times should I clap? *Pencil* has two syllables, so I should clap two times. Continue to identify syllables in other words children say for the picture on pp. 32–33 of *My Skills Buddy.*

ON THEIR OWN Display Phonics Songs and Rhymes Chart 2. Remind children of the song "Jimmy Found a Leaky Faucet" sung to the tune of "Jack and Jill Went Up the Hill." Have them sing the song with you several times. This time I want you to tell me how many syllables are in some of the words in the song. The name *Jimmy* is in the title. How many syllables are in *Jimmy?* Clap the syllables with me. Continue clapping syllables with these words: *leaky, faucet, kindly, tried, good, jiggled, lickety-split.*

Jimmy Found a Leaky Faucet

Jimmy found a leaky faucet,
And kindly tried to fix it.
He got a good look,
He jiggled the hook,
And lickety-split, he did it!

Phonics Songs and Rhymes Chart 2

REVIEW RHYMING WORDS Say *steep* and *cheap.* Do *steep* and *cheap* rhyme? Yes, *steep* and *cheap* have the same middle and ending sounds. Listen to the words I say. If the words rhyme, clap your hands. Say the following pairs of words: *frog, pool; ladder, tune; rain, train; creation, nation; leak, peak; goat, boat; pride, hide.*

Access for All

 Advanced

Count Syllables Have children choose a word with several syllables and draw a picture of the word. Then have them show their picture as they say the word. Have children tell how many syllables their word has.

Support Syllables in Words Verify that children know what an alligator, tiger, hippopotamus, lion, and elephant are before saying the words in syllables. Provide visual support by showing pictures of the animals.

Common Core State Standards

Foundational Skills 1.b. Recognize that spoken words are represented in written language by specific sequences of letters. **Foundational Skills 1.d.** Recognize and name all upper- and lowercase letters of the alphabet. **Foundational Skills 2.b.** Count, pronounce, blend, and segment syllables in spoken words. **Also Foundational Skills 1., 1.a.**

Alphabet Card

Alphabet Card

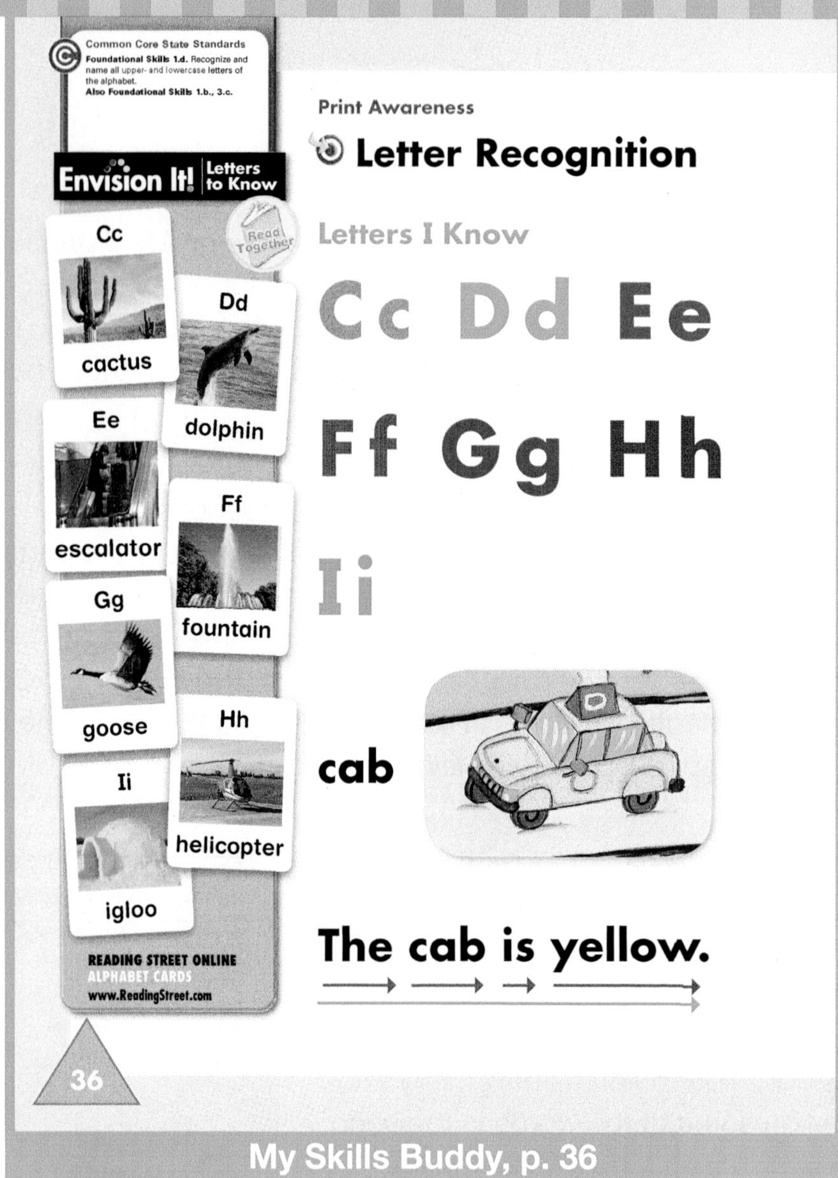

My Skills Buddy, p. 36

Letter Recognition

Teach/Model

Letters *Hh* and *Ii*

INTRODUCE Display the *Hh* Alphabet Card. Point to uppercase *H.* This is uppercase *H.* What is the name of this letter? Repeat for *h, I,* and *i.*

MODEL Display Phonics Songs and Rhymes Chart 2. Sing the song with children. Let's circle all the *Hh*'s in the song. Repeat with the letters *Ii.*

Guide Practice

GROUP PRACTICE Have children identify the letters at the top of p. 36. Look at the cab. The letters *c, a, b* spell the word *cab.* When we put letters together, we can spell words. Read the sentence as children point to the red arrow under each word. Each word I say matches a word in this sentence. Run your finger along the blue arrow from left to right. Reading always moves in this direction.

Apply

CONNECT Say the word *monkey.* Have children say the word with you. Listen as I say the word: *mon-key.* Say the syllables, or parts of the word, with me: *mon-key.* Blend the syllables with children to make the word *monkey.* Repeat the blending several times so that children understand how to blend the syllables together.

MODEL When I say *kan-ga-roo,* I say the syllables in the word. Then I blend the syllables together to make the word *kangaroo.* Have children blend the syllables with you and repeat the blending several times.

GUIDE PRACTICE Let's make some more words. When I say the syllables in the word, repeat them with me. Then we can blend the syllables to make a word. Say *ti-ger, li-on, el-e-phant,* and *hip-po-pot-a-mus.*

Don't Wait Until Friday

MONITOR PROGRESS — Check Letter Recognition Letters *Hh* and *Ii*

FORMATIVE ASSESSMENT Write *H, h, I,* and *i* on separate cards. Mix up the cards. As you display each card, have children name the letter. Show each letter several times.

If… children cannot name the letters,

then… use the small-group Strategic Intervention lesson, p. SG•27, to reteach *Hh* and *Ii.*

Continue to monitor children's progress during the week so that children can be successful with the Day 5 Assessment.

Access for All

Advanced

Blending Have children explain in their own words how to blend the syllables of a word together to make a word.

Common Core State Standards

Foundational Skills 3.c. Read common high-frequency words by sight. (e.g., *the, of, to, you, she, my, is, are, do, does*). **Language 1.a.** Print many upper- and lowercase letters.

Handwriting

Write Words with *Hh* and *Ii*

MODEL UPPERCASE *H* AND *I* Write *Hank* on the board. Point to the uppercase *H.* This is uppercase *H.* Watch as I trace this uppercase *H* with my finger. Follow the stroke instructions pictured below. Repeat the routine for *I* with *Ike.*

MODEL LOWERCASE *h* AND *i* Write *hat* on the board. Point to *h.* This is lowercase *h.* Watch as I trace this lowercase *h* with my finger. Write another lowercase *h* on the board, following the stroke instructions. Have children write *h* in the air and on their hands. Repeat the routine for *i* with *ink.*

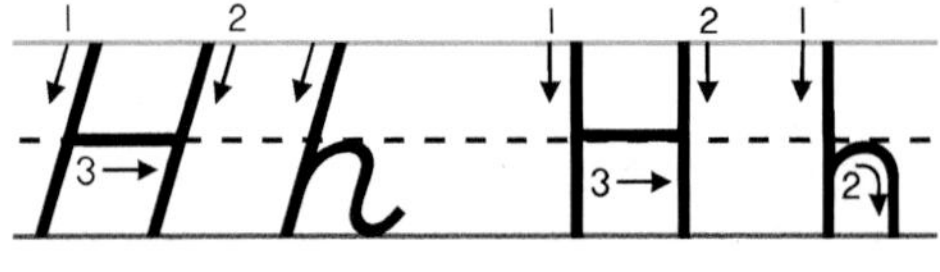

D'Nealian™ Ball and Stick

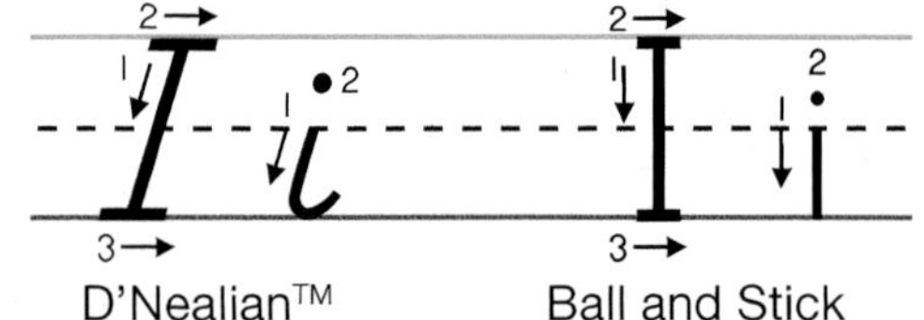

D'Nealian™ Ball and Stick

GUIDE PRACTICE Have children use their Write-On Boards to write a row of uppercase *H* and *I* and a row of lowercase *h* and *i.* Return to *Reader's and Writer's Notebook,* pp. 13 and 14, for more practice with letters *Hh* and *Ii.*

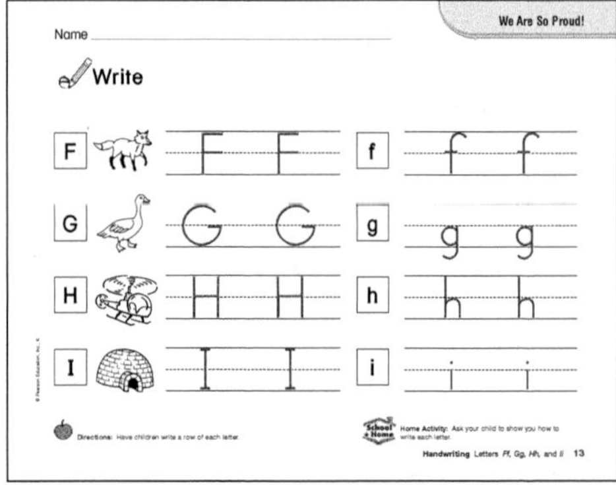

Reader's and Writer's Notebook, p. 13

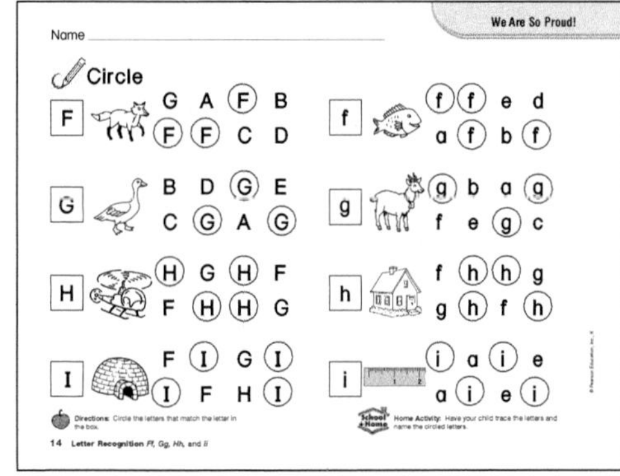

Reader's and Writer's Notebook, p. 14

My Skills Buddy, p. 37

High-Frequency Words

READ WORDS Have children turn to p. 37 of *My Skills Buddy.* Read the high-frequency words *I* and *am* together. Then have children point to each word and read it themselves.

READ SENTENCES Read the sentences on the *My Skills Buddy* page together to read the new high-frequency words in context.

Team Talk Pair children and have them take turns reading each of the sentences aloud.

ON THEIR OWN Use *Reader's and Writer's Notebook,* p. 17, for additional practice with this week's high-frequency words.

Access for All

A Advanced

High-Frequency Words After children read the sentences on p. 37 of *My Skills Buddy,* have them replace the feeling word and say new sentences, such as *I am happy. Am I happy?*

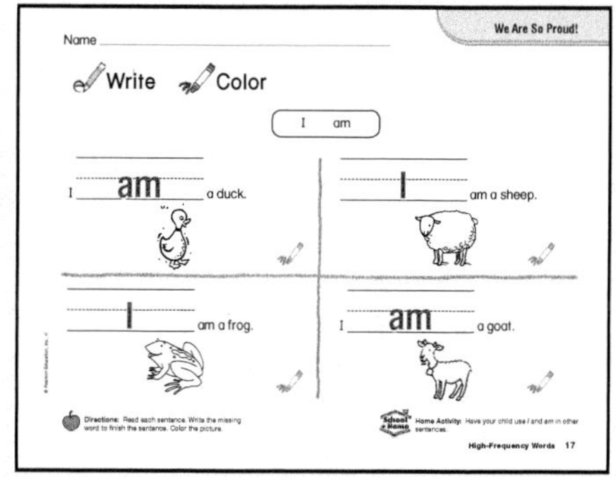

Reader's and Writer's Notebook, p. 17

ELL

High-Frequency Words After the Team Talk activity, have children continue to work in pairs to check understanding. Have one child read one of the sentences aloud while the other child makes a simple drawing to illustrate the sentence.

Common Core State Standards

Foundational Skills 1.a. Follow words from left to right, top to bottom, and page-by-page. **Foundational Skills 1.d.** Recognize and name all upper- and lowercase letters of the alphabet. **Foundational Skills 3.c.** Read common high-frequency words by sight. (e.g., *the, of, to, you, she, my, is, are, do, does*). **Foundational Skills 4.** Read emergent-reader texts with purpose and understanding. **Also Literature 6.**

Decodable Reader 2

Read *Am I?*

REVIEW Review the previously taught high-frequency words. Have children read each word as you point to it on the Word Wall: *I, am.*

TEACH REBUS WORDS Write *Jan* on the board. This is the name *Jan.* Say the letters with me: *J, a, n, Jan.* Continue with *Fran, Len, Ken, Kim, Hanna,* and *Gus.* These are names in the story we will read today. Each name has a small picture above it. The picture will help you read the name.

CONCEPTS OF PRINT Have children turn to Decodable Reader 2, *Am I?,* on p. 38 of *My Skills Buddy.* Today we will read a story about some children. Point to the title. The title of this story is *Am I?* The author's name is George Helm. What does the author do? The author writes the words in the story. What letter do you see at the beginning of the author's last name?

READ Use the routine for reading decodable books to read Decodable Reader 2.

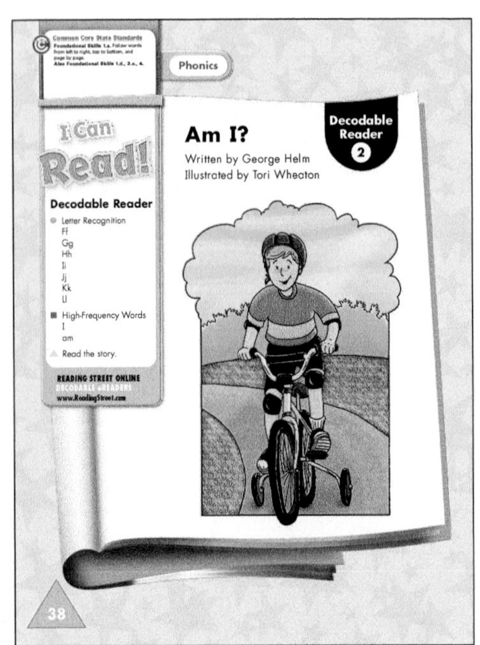

My Skills Buddy, pp. 38–45

Am I Fran?

Am I Ken?
I am Kim.

Am I Hanna?

Routine Reading Decodable Books

1. **Read Silently** Have children whisper read the book page by page as you listen in.
2. **Model Fluent Reading** Have children finger point as you read a page. Then have them reread the book without you.
3. **Read Chorally** Have children finger point as they chorally read the page. Continue reading page by page, repeating steps 1 and 2.
4. **Read Individually** Have children take turns reading aloud a page.
5. **Reread and Monitor Progress** As you listen to individual children reread, monitor progress and provide support.
6. **Reread with a Partner** Have children reread the book page by page with a partner.

Routines Flip Chart

Day 2 SMALL GROUP TIME • Differentiate Letter Recognition, p. SG • 19

OL On-Level	SI Strategic Intervention	A Advanced
• **Practice Letter Recognition** Recognize Letters *Hh, Ii*	• **Reteach Letter Recognition** Recognize Letters *Hh, Ii*	• **Extend Letter Recognition** Connect *Hh* to /h/, *Ii* to /i/
• **Read** Decodable Reader *Am I?*	• **Read** Decodable Reader *Am I?*	• **Read** Decodable Reader *Am I?*

eStreet Interactive
www.ReadingStreet.com

Savvas eText
• Student Edition

Access for All

SI Strategic Intervention

Support Letter Recognition Ask children to identify any uppercase and lowercase letters they know as they read *Am I?*

Access Decodable Reader Before children read *Am I?,* page through the book and have them match the rebus pictures to the parts of the big pictures.

Place English Language Learners in the groups that correspond to their reading abilities in English.

If... children need more support with **Letter Recognition,**
then... use the activities on p. DI•29 in the Teacher Resources section of the Digital Path.

Common Core State Standards

Literature 2. With prompting and support, retell familiar stories, including key details. **Literature 3.** With prompting and support, identify characters, settings, and major events in a story. **Literature 7.** With prompting and support, describe the relationship between illustrations and the story in which they appear (e.g., what moment in a story an illustration depicts). **Also Literature 5., Foundational Skills 1., 1.a.**

Access for All

 Strategic Intervention

Support Concepts of Print After you read one line of text, have children tell you where to continue reading. They should tell you to continue on the line below with the word on the left.

Academic Vocabulary 

illustration a picture in a book that helps tell the story

predict tell what might happen next

Zoom in on

Text-Based Comprehension

Introduce Main Selection

CONCEPTS OF PRINT Display p. 3 of *We Are So Proud!* As you read, run your finger under the first text line and then sweep back to the left and down to the next line. When we read, we move left to right and from top to bottom.

GENRE Realistic fiction is a made-up story that could happen in real life. Let's read about a class preparing for a celebration.

PREVIEW AND PREDICT Display *We Are So Proud!* The title of this book is *We Are So Proud!* Tell me what you see on the cover. What do you think this book will be about? Take children on a walk through the book. Have them tell about what they see in each picture.

SET PURPOSE Remind children of the Question of the Week: *How do school children work and play together?* Have children listen as you read.

MODEL Read *We Are So Proud!* with expression to build interest in the text.

Routine: Read for Understanding 

Deepen understanding by reading the selection multiple times.

1. **First Read**—Read the entire selection aloud to build interest in the text.
2. **Second Read**—Use the **Develop Vocabulary** notes on pages 161–171.
3. **Third Read**—Use the **Develop Comprehension** notes on pages 161–171.

Retell

CHECK RETELLING Have children turn to p. 46 of *My Skills Buddy.* Walk through the retelling boxes as children retell *We Are So Proud!* After they retell the story as a group, have them draw a picture to retell a favorite part. Have children write or dictate a word or sentence to go with their picture.

Check Retelling

If... children have difficulty retelling the story,

then... go through the story one page at a time, and ask children to tell what happens in their own words.

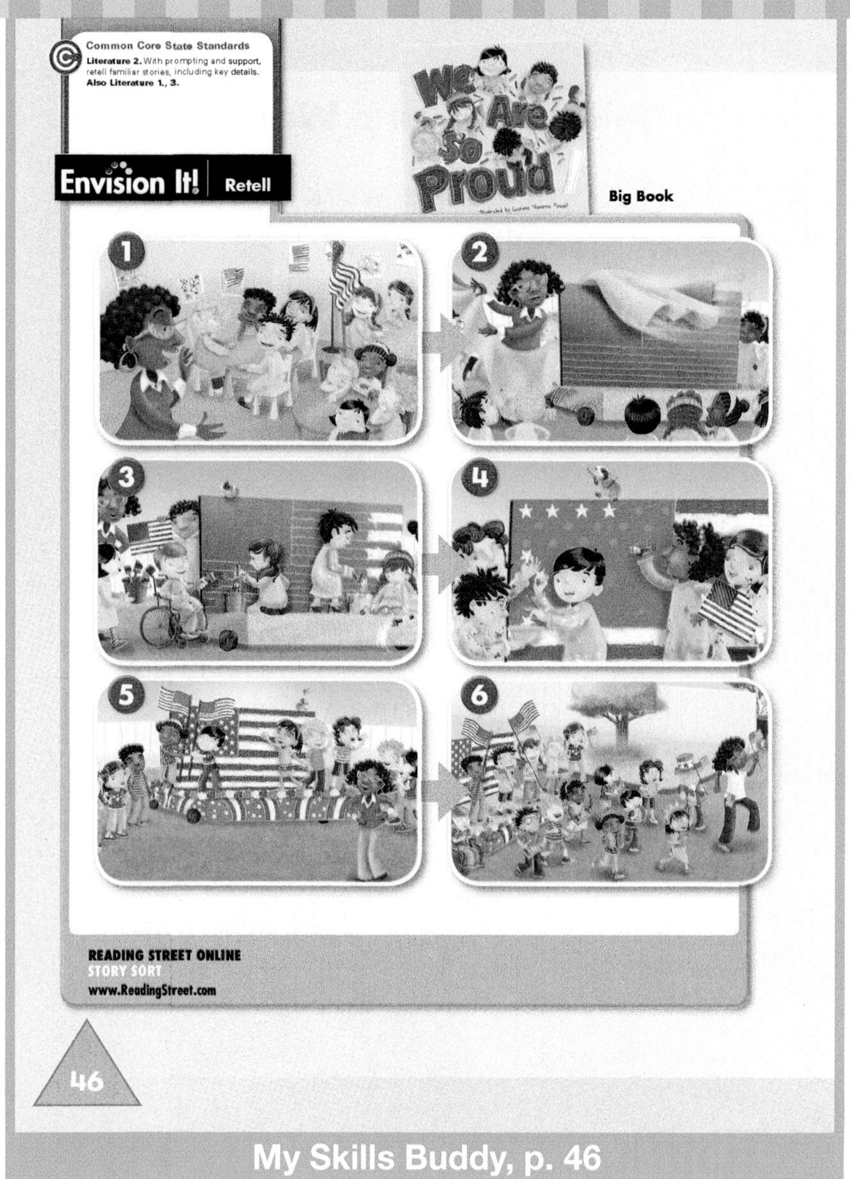

My Skills Buddy, p. 46

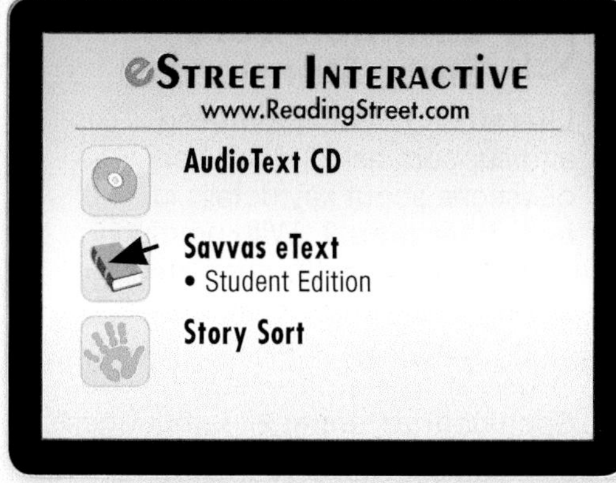

Retelling Plan

- ☑ **Week 1** Assess Advanced students.
- ☑ **This week assess On-Level students.**
- ☐ **Week 3** Assess Strategic Intervention students.
- ☐ **Week 4** Assess Advanced students.
- ☐ **Week 5** Assess On-Level students.
- ☐ **Week 6** Assess Strategic Intervention students.

Scoring Rubric Narrative Retelling

	4	3	2	1
Connections	Makes connections and generalizes beyond the text	Makes connections to other events, stories, or experiences	Makes a limited connection to another event, story, or experience	Makes no connection to another event, story, or experience
Author's Purpose	Elaborates on author's purpose	Tells author's purpose with some clarity	Makes some connection to author's purpose	Makes no connection to author's purpose
Characters	Describes the main character(s) and any character development	Identifies the main character(s) and gives some information about them	Inaccurately identifies some characters or gives little information about them	Inaccurately identifies the characters or gives no information about them
Setting	Describes the time and location	Identifies the time and location	Omits details of time or location	Is unable to identify time or location
Plot	Describes the events in sequence using rich detail	Tells the plot with some errors in sequence that do not affect meaning	Tells parts of plot with gaps that affect meaning	Retelling has no sense of story

Support Retelling Have children act out the events from *We Are So Proud!* and tell what they are doing.

 Common Core State Standards

Literature 1. With prompting and support, ask and answer questions about key details in a text. **Literature 3.** With prompting and support, identify characters, settings, and major events in a story. **Language 1.a.** Print many upper- and lowercase letters. **Also Speaking/Listening 2., Language 2.**

Access for All

 Strategic Intervention

Discuss Concept Remind children about activities they have done in groups or pairs. Tell them to think about how they worked with other children as they answer the questions.

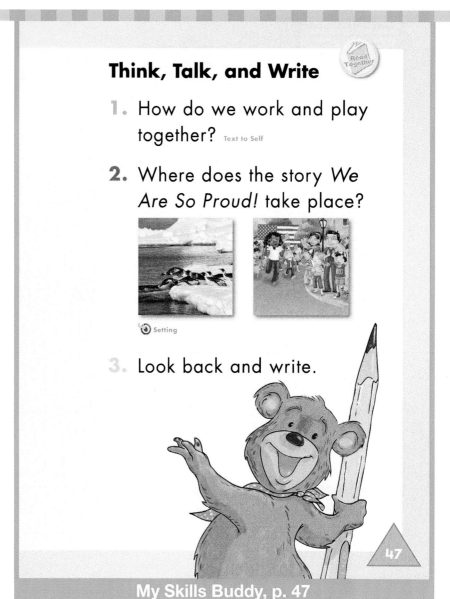

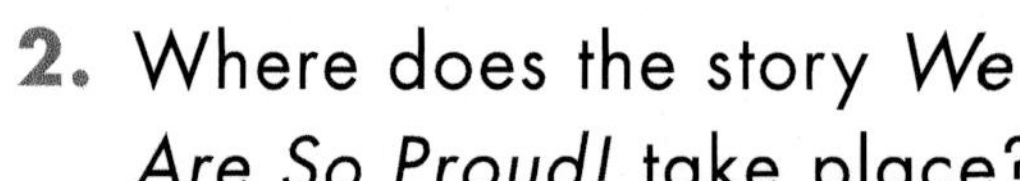

Think, Talk, and Write

1. How do we work and play together? Text to Self
2. Where does the story *We Are So Proud!* take place?

Setting

3. Look back and write.

47

My Skills Buddy, p. 47

Think, Talk, and Write

DISCUSS CONCEPT We're learning about how children cooperate. Think about how you work and play with other children.

- What kinds of things do you work on with other children?
- What do you like about working together?

CONFIRM PREDICTIONS Have children recall their predictions before you read *We Are So Proud!*

- What did you think the story would be about?
- Was your prediction correct?

Have children turn to p. 47 of *My Skills Buddy.* Read the questions and directives and have children respond.

1. **TEXT TO SELF** How do we work and play together? Do we follow rules? Can you have fun when you work with others?

2. **SETTING** Where does the story *We Are So Proud!* take place? What can you tell about the setting? What is the time of day?

3. **LOOK BACK AND WRITE • TEXT EVIDENCE** Let's look back at our story and write about it. We remember that the children in Ms. Vogel's class work together on a special project. Listen for ways they work on the float. Read pp. 8–12 of *We Are So Proud!* Now let's write our ideas. Discuss with children how Ms. Vogel's class decorates the float. Record their responses on chart paper. (The children paint with brushes. They use red, white, and blue paint. They paint stripes. They make roses.)

Conventions

Write Our Names

TEACH Remind children that each of them has a name. My name is [say your name]. Write your name on the board. Let's read my name together. What letter does my name begin with? Is it an uppercase or lowercase letter?

GUIDE PRACTICE Display Decodable Reader 2, *Am I?* The characters in this book have names. Point to Jan. Jan is one of the characters. Let's write Jan's name. Write *Jan* on the board. Point out that a name always begins with an uppercase letter.

We all have names. Point to a child. What is your name? Invite the child to come to the board and write his or her name. Repeat the routine with several other children. Remind children to begin their name with an uppercase letter.

ON THEIR OWN Use *Reader's and Writer's Notebook,* p. 18, for more practice writing our names.

Name

We Are So Proud!

Draw Write

Answers will vary.

10 Conventions Write Our Names

Reader's and Writer's Notebook, p. 18

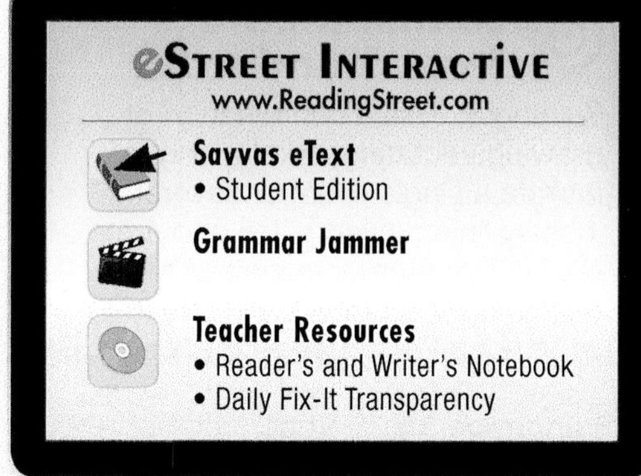

Writing to Sources

Use Write Like a Reporter on pp. 10–11 to guide children in writing text-based responses using one source.

Daily Fix-It

duck is a good Friend.
Duck is a good friend.

This week's practice sentences appear on *Teacher Resources DVD-ROM.*

CONVENTIONS OF STANDARD ENGLISH

When children write their own and other people's names with initial uppercase letters, they are demonstrating their command of one of the conventions of standard English capitalization.

Support Conventions If children have difficulty writing their names, encourage them to practice writing one letter at a time on their Write-On Boards. After they have mastered each letter, have children practice writing their entire name.

Common Core State Standards

Writing 3. Use a combination of drawing, dictating, and writing to narrate a single event or several loosely linked events, tell about the events in the order in which they occurred, and provide a reaction to what happened. **Language 1.a.** Print many upper- and lowercase letters. **Language 5.a.** Sort common objects into categories (e.g., shapes, foods) to gain a sense of the concepts the categories represent. **Also Literature 4., Writing 8., Language 5., 6.**

Respond to Literature

DISCUSS Display *We Are So Proud!* Discuss with children how the children in the story work together to plan and create a float for a parade.

MODEL In the story, the class plans a float as part of a celebration for our nation. They work and play together to make the float. I am going to write:

The children have fun painting stripes.

GUIDE PRACTICE Invite children to help you write more sentences about how the children in the story work and play together to celebrate our nation.

They make flowers.
They play music.

INDEPENDENT WRITING Have children write or dictate about other things the children in the story do together as they make the float. Some children may wish to use this sentence frame:

The children ______.

Daily Handwriting

Write uppercase *H* and *I* and lowercase *h* and *i* on the board. Review correct letter formation with children.

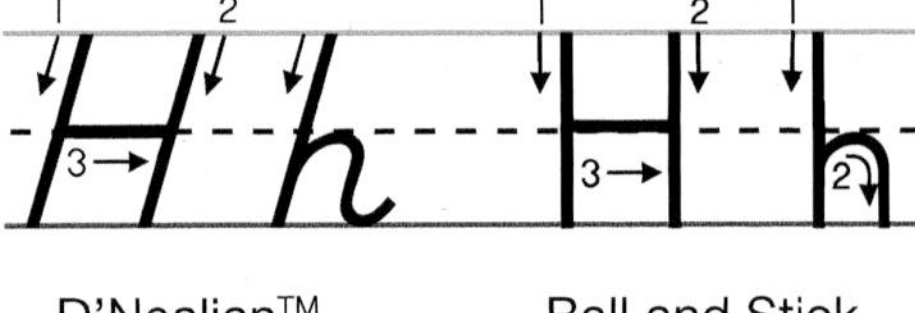

D'Nealian™ Ball and Stick

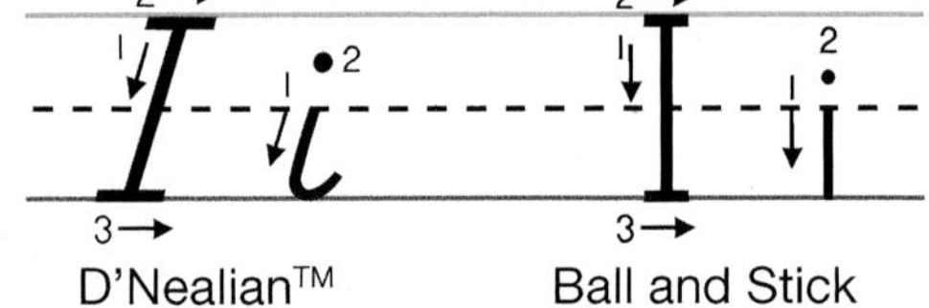

D'Nealian™ Ball and Stick

Have children write a row of uppercase *H* and *I* and a row of lowercase *h* and *i* on their Write-On Boards. Remind them to use proper left-to-right and top-to-bottom progression when writing *H, h, I,* and *i.*

Writing to Sources Use More Connect the Texts on pp. 222–293 to guide children in writing text-based responses within various forms and modes.

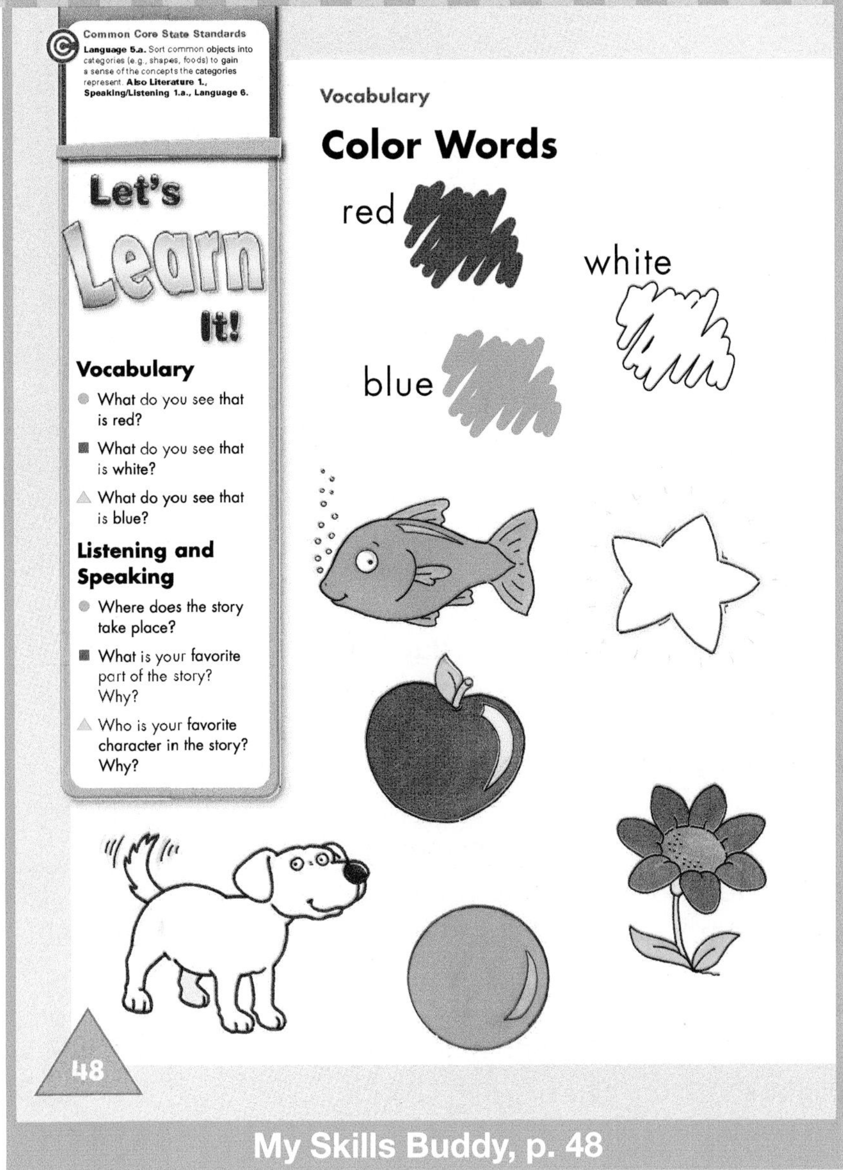

Common Core State Standards
Language 5.a. Sort common objects into categories (e.g., shapes, foods) to gain a sense of the concepts the categories represent. Also Literature 1., Speaking/Listening 1.a., Language 6.
Let's Learn It!
Vocabulary
What do you see that is red?
What do you see that is white?
What do you see that is blue?
Listening and Speaking
Where does the story take place?
What is your favorite part of the story? Why?
Who is your favorite character in the story? Why?
Vocabulary
Color Words
red
white
blue
48

My Skills Buddy, p. 48

Vocabulary

Color Words

TEACH Have children turn to p. 48 of *My Skills Buddy.* Use the first Vocabulary bullet to guide discussion about the colors red, white, and blue. Have children point to each color and tell where they see it on the page.

GUIDE PRACTICE Write the words *red, white,* and *blue* on the board. Point to each word as you read it.

Display p. 18 of *We Are So Proud!* Have children point to things in the picture that are red, white, or blue and say the appropriate color word.

ON THEIR OWN Have children find something in the classroom that is red, white, or blue. After they show and describe the object using the color word, collect all the objects and have children sort them into the three color groups.

Access for All

Advanced

Build Vocabulary Have children use a corresponding color crayon to copy the color words *red, white,* and *blue* onto cards. Have children use the cards to review the color words throughout the week.

Bridge to Common Core

VOCABULARY ACQUISITION AND USE
When children use color words correctly, they are demonstrating their comprehension of the words' meanings, of the relationships among words in a category, and of the connections between words and their use in describing.

Access Vocabulary Have children say the color words in their home languages as you point to each color word on the board.

Common Core State Standards

Foundational Skills 2. Demonstrate understanding of spoken words, syllables, and sounds (phonemes). **Foundational Skills 2.b.** Count, pronounce, blend, and segment syllables in spoken words.

Wrap Up Your Day!

- ✓ **Content Knowledge** Today we read a story about a class that works together to create something. What do they make for the parade?
- ✓ **Phonological Awareness** Today we talked about syllables. How many syllables are in the word *color?*
- ✓ **Vocabulary Skill** Today we talked about the color words *red, white,* and *blue.* Have children name the colors of red, white, and blue things you point to in the room.
- ✓ **Homework Idea** Ask children to find pictures of red, white, and blue things to share with the class.

Preview DAY 3

Tomorrow we will reread the story *We Are So Proud!*

Social Studies
Celebration Traditions

MATERIALS: chart paper, markers

DISCUSS CUSTOMS AND TRADITIONS Give a brief description of what we mean when we talk about traditions. A tradition is something people have been doing for a long time. One tradition people do to celebrate their nation is wave their country's flag.

Invite children to share traditions they do when they celebrate. Write their responses on chart paper. Review the list and discuss how these celebration traditions are alike and different. Why is it important to know about other people's traditions?

PERFORM A SKIT ABOUT TRADITIONS Arrange children in small groups. Ask each group to choose one tradition on the chart and create a skit about it. They should create dialogue that describes and explains the tradition.

Traditions
eat special food
light candles
sing songs
give gifts
dress up

Letter Recognition
Letter Forms

MATERIALS: geoboards, rubber bands

MAKE UPPERCASE LETTERS Have children use rubber bands and a geoboard to make uppercase letters *A, E, F, H,* and *I.* Encourage children to make each letter several times in different sizes.

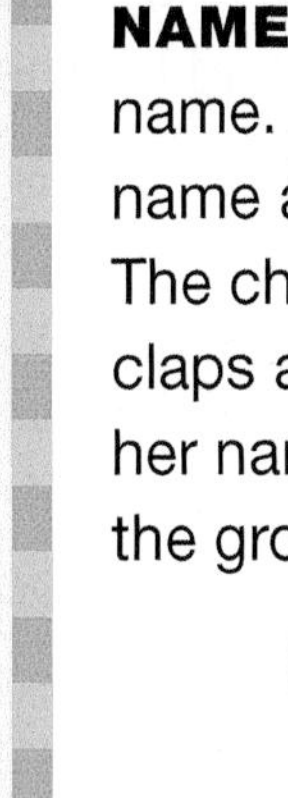

Phonological Awareness
Count Syllables

CLAP SYLLABLES IN CHILDREN'S NAMES Have a child stand up and say his or her name. Ask the other children to repeat the child's name and clap once for each syllable in the name. The child who is standing counts the number of claps and tells how many syllables are in his or her name. Repeat with the names of all children in the group if time allows.

Kim-ber-ly Ro-ber-to
Sam Ju-lie
E-liz-a-beth An-tho-ny

DAY 3 at a Glance

Content Knowledge
Oral Vocabulary

Phonological Awareness
Sound Discrimination

Letter Recognition
Letters *Jj* and *Kk*

Text-Based Comprehension
Setting

Conventions
Review Say Our Names

Writing
Invitation

Listening and Speaking
Respond to Literature: Drama

Materials

- Student Edition
- Truckery Rhymes
- Talk with Me/Sing with Me Chart
- Picture Cards
- Phonics Songs and Rhymes Chart
- Alphabet Cards
- Reader's and Writer's Notebook
- Student Reader K.1.2
- Big Book

Common Core State Standards

Speaking/Listening 1.a. Follow agreed-upon rules for discussions (e.g., listening to others and taking turns speaking about the topics and texts under discussion). **Language 6.** Use words and phrases acquired through conversations, reading and being read to, and responding to texts. **Also Speaking/Listening 6.**

TRUCKTOWN
on Reading Street

Start your engines!
Display p. 6 of *Truckery Rhymes.* Do you know the original "Little Miss Muffet"? Recite it first, and then have children repeat it with you:

Little Miss Muffet sat on a tuffet,
Eating her curds and whey.
Along came a spider who
sat down beside her,
And frightened Miss Muffet
away.

Truckery Rhymes

Content Knowledge

Zoom in on

Working and Playing Together at School

On the board, write the Question of the Week, *How do school children work and play together?* Read the question as you track the print. Talk with children about how children work and play together. Remind them to speak clearly and to take turns.

Build Oral Language

LISTEN FOR AMAZING WORDS Display Sing with Me Chart 2B. Remind children that yesterday they sang "We're Proud of Our Nation" and listened for the words *proud* and *preparation.* Today we are going to listen for the Amazing Words *cooperation* and *creation.* Sing the song several times to the tune of "B-I-N-G-O." Have children sing along with you, clapping their hands when they say the Amazing Word *cooperation* or *creation.*

We're Proud of Our Nation
Here's our teacher as our guide
With plans and preparation,
P-R-O-U-D,
P-R-O-U-D,
P-R-O-U-D,
We've built a new creation.

Talk with Me/Sing with Me Chart 2B

Build Oral Vocabulary

Amazing Words Robust Vocabulary Routine

1. **Introduce the Word** It takes a lot of *cooperation* to finish a big project. *Cooperation* is the way we work together. What's our new Amazing Word for working together? Say it with me: *cooperation.*
2. **Demonstrate** Provide examples to show meaning. *The class needs everyone's cooperation to finish the float.*

   Repeat steps 1 and 2.

   Introduce the Word A *creation* is something we make that is important and original. What's our new Amazing Word for something we make that has never been made before? Say it with me: *creation.*

   Demonstrate *Our creation takes hours to make.*
3. **Apply** Have children use *cooperation* and *creation* in complete sentences.
4. **Display the Words** Ask children where they see the letter *c* in *cooperation* and *creation.* Then ask them to point to the letters *e* and *a* in both words.

Routines Flip Chart

USE AMAZING WORDS To reinforce the concept and the Amazing Words, have children supply the appropriate Amazing Word for each sentence.

We all helped to make our ______. (creation)
We need your ______ to finish the float. (cooperation)

Amazing Words

proud	preparation
cooperation	creation
float	guide

Access for All

 Advanced

Build Vocabulary Have children discuss ways they cooperate with friends and family.

ELL

Visual Support Use the pictures on Talk with Me Chart 2A to help children complete the Amazing Word sentences.

Expand Vocabulary Use the Day 3 instruction on ELL Poster 2 to expand children's use of vocabulary about lesson concepts.

Common Core State Standards

Foundational Skills 2.d. Isolate and pronounce the initial, medial vowel, and final sounds (phonemes) in three-phoneme (consonant-vowel-consonant, or CVC) words.* (This does not include CVCs ending with /l/, /r/, or /x/.) **Also Foundational Skills 2.**

Phonological Awareness

Sound Discrimination

TEACH Today we are going to learn that some words start with the same sound and some words start with different sounds.

Display the *bag* and *bat* Picture Cards. This is a bag. This is a bat. Do these words begin with the same sound? Listen as I say the words: *bag, bat.* Yes, these words begin with the same sound.

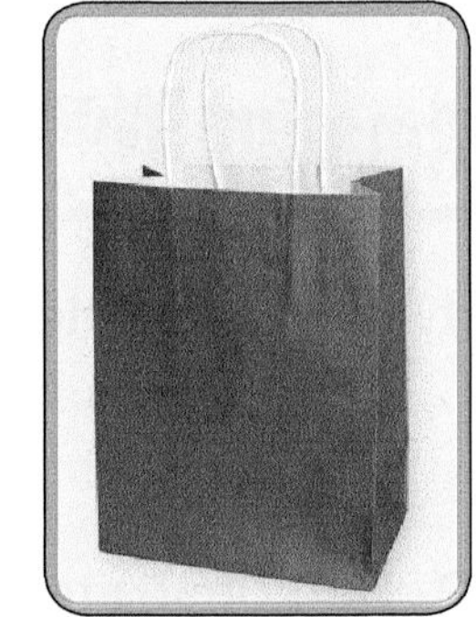

Picture Card

GUIDE PRACTICE Say the word *hen* with me. Now say the words *hen* and *hop: hen, hop.* Do the words begin with the same sound? Listen as I say the words: *hen, hop.* Say the words with me: /h/ /h/ /h/ *hen,* /h/ /h/ /h/ *hop.* Do the words begin with the same sound? (yes) Continue with the following pairs of words: *hat, bed; hand, head; house, ten; hose, hammer.*

Picture Card

ON THEIR OWN Display the following set of Picture Cards in random order: *fox, fan, cap, cat, hen, hat, man, mop.* Have children name each picture and repeat the picture name several times. Then ask them to find two pictures whose names begin with the same sound. Have children say the picture names to decide whether they begin with the same sound.

DISCRIMINATE INITIAL SOUNDS Display Phonics Songs and Rhymes Chart 2. Remind children of the song "Jimmy Found a Leaky Faucet." Sing the song with them several times. Then read the title of the song. What two words in the title begin with the same sound? (*Found, Faucet*) Read the next two lines of the song. What word begins with the same sound as *Found* and *Faucet?* (*fix*) Continue asking questions that guide children to find other words that have the same beginning sounds, such as *he/hook, got/good, Jimmy/jiggled,* and *leaky/look/lickety.*

Jimmy Found a Leaky Faucet
Jimmy found a leaky faucet,
And kindly tried to fix it.
He got a good look,
He jiggled the hook,
And lickety-split, he did it!

Phonics Songs and Rhymes Chart 2

Corrective feedback	**If...** children cannot identify the words that begin with the same sound, **then...** say the words again, isolating the initial sound in each word: /h/ *-op,* /b/ *-ed.* Have children echo you. Then have them tell whether the words begin with the same sound.

Access for All

 Advanced

Practice Sound Discrimination
Say a word and have children think of another word that begins with the same sound.

Common Core State Standards

Foundational Skills 1.d. Recognize and name all upper- and lowercase letters of the alphabet.

Letter Recognition

Teach/Model

Letters *Jj* and *Kk*

INTRODUCE/MODEL Display the *Jj* Alphabet Card. Point to the uppercase letter. The name of this letter is uppercase *J.* What is the name of this letter? Continue with lowercase *j.* Repeat for *Kk.*

Alphabet Card

Guide Practice

GROUP PRACTICE Display the *brick* Picture Card. Have children name the picture. Write the picture name on the board. Who can show me the letter *k* in the word *brick?* Continue having children find the letter *j* or *k* using the following Picture Cards: *jet, jug, juice, kangaroo, truck.* Write the word *jig* on the board. Have children identify the letters in *jig.* The letters *j, i, g* spell the word *jig.* When we put letters together, we can spell words. Repeat the activity with the word *Jack.*

Alphabet Card

ON THEIR OWN Use *Reader's and Writer's Notebook,* p. 19, for additional practice with letters *Jj* and *Kk.* Return to this page on Days 4 and 5 to practice *Ll, Mm,* and *Nn.*

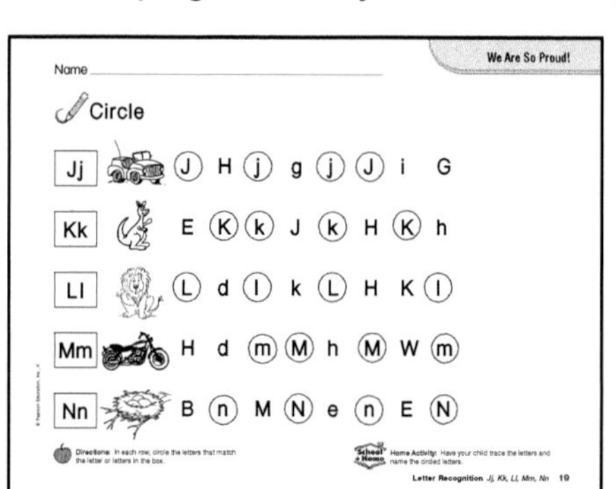
Name

We Are So Proud!

Circle

Jj J H j g j J i G

Kk E K k J k H K h

Ll L d l k L H K l

Mm H d m M h M W m

Nn B n M N e n E N

Letter Recognition *Jj, Kk, Ll, Mm, Nn* 19

Reader's and Writer's Notebook, p. 19

REVIEW LETTER NAMES Display the *Ff, Gg, Hh,* and *Ii* Alphabet Cards. Point to the uppercase and lowercase letters on the cards in random order. Ask children to identify each letter as you point to it. When children have identified all eight letters, display four different Alphabet Cards and continue in the same way.

REVIEW HIGH-FREQUENCY WORDS Write *I* on the board. This is the word *I*. What is this word? Continue the routine with *am.*

Access for All

Strategic Intervention

Access Content Have children look through books or magazines to find letters *Jj* and *Kk.* Have them cut out the letters and glue them to a sheet of paper.

MONITOR PROGRESS Check Word Reading High-Frequency Words

FORMATIVE ASSESSMENT Write the word *am* on the board. Have children say the word with you and find the word in a sentence you write. Continue with the word *I.* Then let children create sentences using the words *I* and *am.*

If... children cannot read the high-frequency words,
then... write the words on cards so they can practice at home.

If... children can successfully read the high-frequency words,
then... have them read Kindergarten Student Reader K.1.2, *Cat and Dog Work.*

Common Core State Standards

Literature 7. With prompting and support, describe the relationship between illustrations and the story in which they appear (e.g., what moment in a story an illustration depicts). **Literature 10.** Actively engage in group reading activities with purpose and understanding. **Also Foundational Skills 1., 1.a.**

Access for All

 Strategic Intervention

Access Content Have children point out the person who is called *I* in each picture.

Student Reader

Read *Cat and Dog Work*

REVIEW Review the previously taught high-frequency words. Have children read each word as you point to it on the Word Wall: *I, am.*

TEACH REBUS WORDS Write *cat* on the board. This is the word *cat*. Name the letters with me: *c, a, t, cat.* Repeat the routine with *dog, mom, hammering, painting,* and *happy.* Look for these words in the book we read today. There will be a picture above the word to help you read it.

READ Display Kindergarten Student Reader K.1.2. Today we are going to read a new book. Point to the title. The title of this book is *Cat and Dog Work.* The author's name is Lisa Walston. Take children on a picture walk. Look at the pictures. What do you think will happen in this book? Remind children to hold their book right side up and to turn the pages one at a time. When we finish reading the words on the page, we turn the page right to left.

Use the reading decodable books routine to read the Kindergarten Student Reader.

Routine Reading Decodable Books

1. **Read Silently** Have children whisper read the book page by page as you listen in.
2. **Model Fluent Reading** Have children finger point as you read a page. Then have them reread the page without you.
3. **Read Chorally** Have children finger point as they chorally read the page. Continue reading page by page, repeating steps 1 and 2.
4. **Read Individually** Have children take turns reading aloud a page.
5. **Reread and Monitor Progress** As you listen to individual children reread, monitor progress and provide support.
6. **Reread with a Partner** Have children reread the book page by page with a partner.

Routines Flip Chart

Kindergarten Student Reader K.1.2

eStreet Interactive
www.ReadingStreet.com

Savvas eText
- Kindergarten Student Reader

Day 3 SMALL GROUP TIME • Differentiate Vocabulary, p. SG•19

OL On-Level
- **Develop Vocabulary** Practice Color Words
- **Read** Student Reader *Cat and Dog Work*

SI Strategic Intervention
- **Develop Vocabulary** Reteach Color Words
- **Read** Student Reader *Cat and Dog Work*

A Advanced
- **Develop Vocabulary** More Color Words
- **Read** Student Reader *Cat and Dog Work*

ELL

Place English Language Learners in the groups that correspond to their reading abilities in English.

If... children need more scaffolding and practice with **Vocabulary,** **then...** use the ELL activities on p. DI•31 in the Teacher Resources section of the Digital Path.

Text-Based Comprehension

Common Core State Standards

Literature 1. With prompting and support, ask and answer questions about key details in a text. **Literature 2.** With prompting and support, retell familiar stories, including key details. **Literature 3.** With prompting and support, identify characters, settings, and major events in a story.

Bridge to Common Core

CRAFT AND STRUCTURE

When children retell the story, they are analyzing how story elements, such as setting, relate to the whole story structure. Using the Develop Vocabulary notes as you read the text a second time focuses children's attention on comprehending unknown words and word choices.

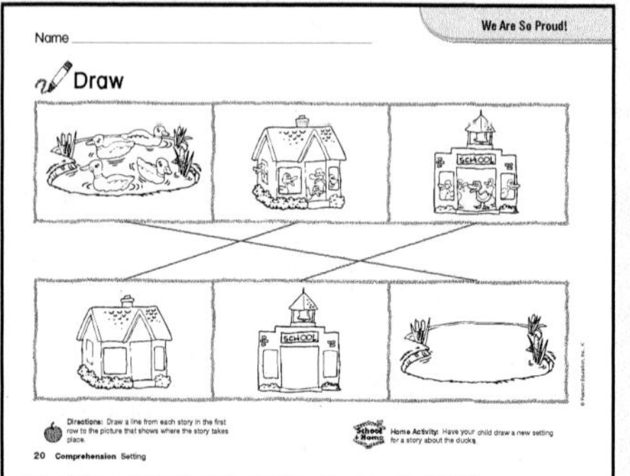

Reader's and Writer's Notebook, p. 20

Read Main Selection

RETELL THE SELECTION Have children turn to p. 46 of *My Skills Buddy* and use the retelling boxes to retell the story. Direct children to the first retelling box. Continue reviewing the retelling boxes and having children retell the story.

REVIEW SETTING Display illustrations in *We Are So Proud!* Let's review the setting of the story.

MORE PRACTICE Use *Reader's and Writer's Notebook,* p. 20, for more practice with setting.

My Skills Buddy, p. 46

Access Main Selection

READER AND TASK SUGGESTIONS	
Preparing to Read the Text	**Leveled Tasks**
• Review the Amazing Words and have children use them to talk about the selection. • Discuss the author's use of setting in this story.	• **Levels of Meaning • Analysis** If children don't understand how words can stand for sounds, have them name the words for the sounds of the instruments in the story and talk about each.

See Text Complexity Measures for *We Are So Proud!* on the weekly tab.

READ Reread *We Are So Proud!* Follow the **2nd Read** beginning on p. 161, and use the **Develop Vocabulary** notes to prompt conversations about the story.

Routine Read for Understanding

Deepen understanding by reading the selection multiple times.

1. **First Read**—Read the entire selection aloud to build interest in the text.
2. **Second Read**—Use the **Develop Vocabulary** notes on pages 161–171.
3. **Third Read**—Use the **Develop Comprehension** notes on pages 161–171.

2ND READ

Develop Vocabulary

DISTANCING What has the school planned for a celebration? (a parade)

- The school and all the classes will have a parade. Have you ever been to a parade? What was the parade like?

DEVELOP VOCABULARY parade

EXPAND VOCABULARY nation

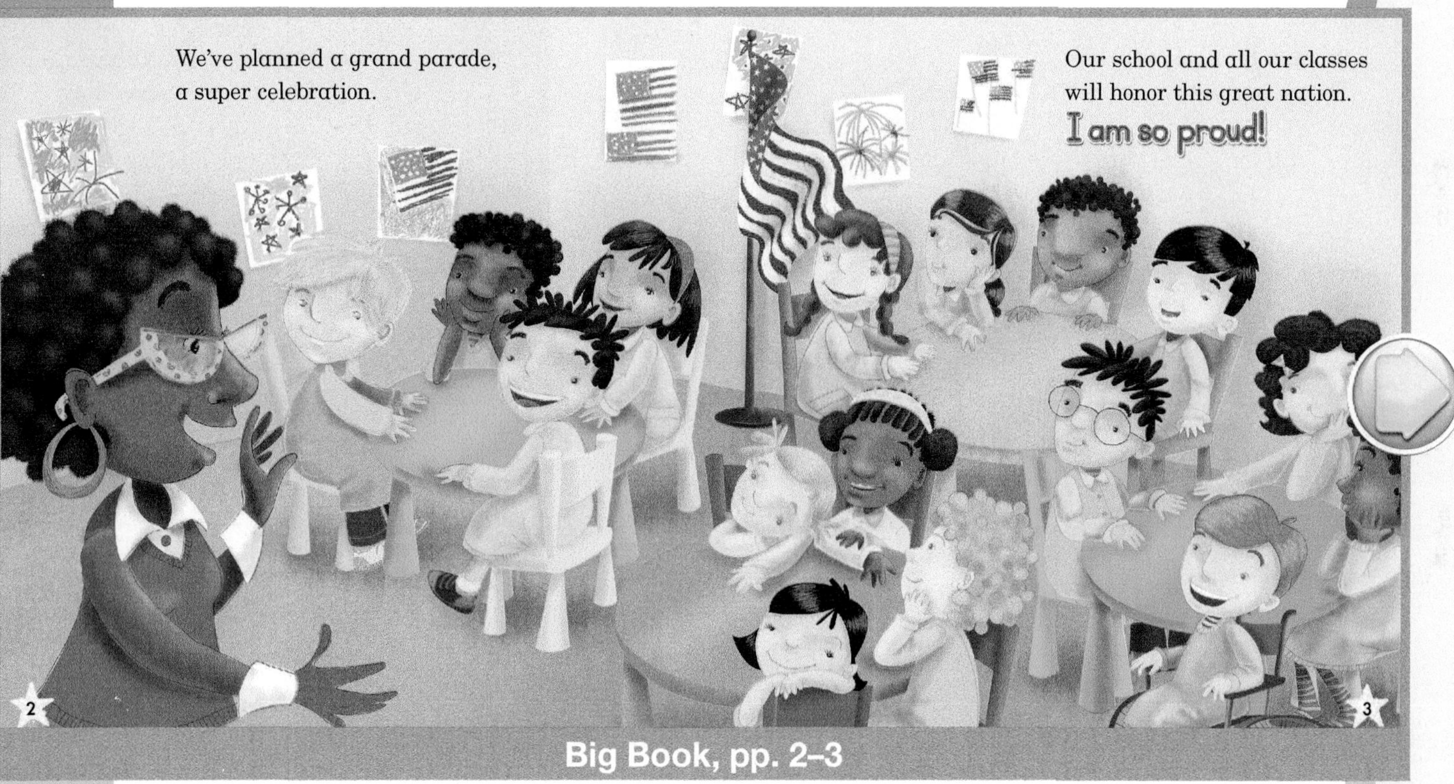

We've planned a grand parade,
a super celebration.
Our school and all our classes
will honor this great nation.
I am so proud!
2
3

Big Book, pp. 2–3

3RD READ

Develop Comprehension ©

OPEN-ENDED Point to Ms. Vogel. The teacher looks happy. Look at the children. How do you think the children feel about the parade? (They look excited.)

2ND READ

Develop Vocabulary

WH- QUESTION What are the children wearing? (They are wearing smocks.)

- The children are wearing gray shirts, or smocks, over their clothes. Why do you think they are wearing these smocks?

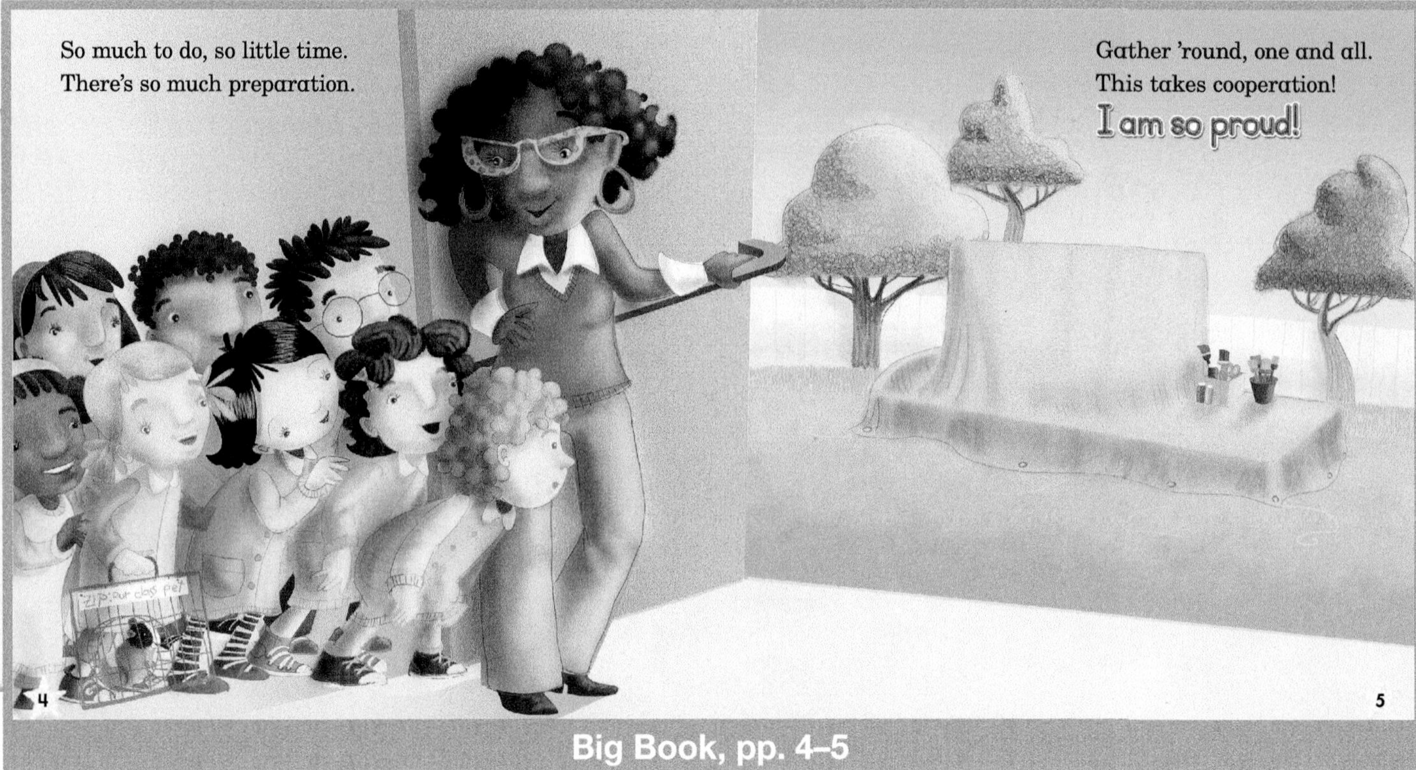

So much to do, so little time.
There's so much preparation.
Gather 'round, one and all.
This takes cooperation!
I am so proud!
4
5

Big Book, pp. 4–5

3RD READ

Develop Comprehension ©

OPEN-ENDED What do you think is under the sheet? (I think it is a big sign.) Why do you think so? How do you think children will work together to make something so big? (They will have to take turns and share supplies.)

Common Core State Standards

Literature 1. With prompting and support, ask and answer questions about key details in a text.
Literature 3. With prompting and support, identify characters, settings, and major events in a story.
Literature 7. With prompting and support, describe the relationship between illustrations and the story in which they appear (e.g., what moment in a story an illustration depicts).

INFERENCE How much time does the class have to make their creation? (three hours)

- The class has three hours to make their project for the parade. What do you think they have to do?

EXPAND VOCABULARY precious, whip up

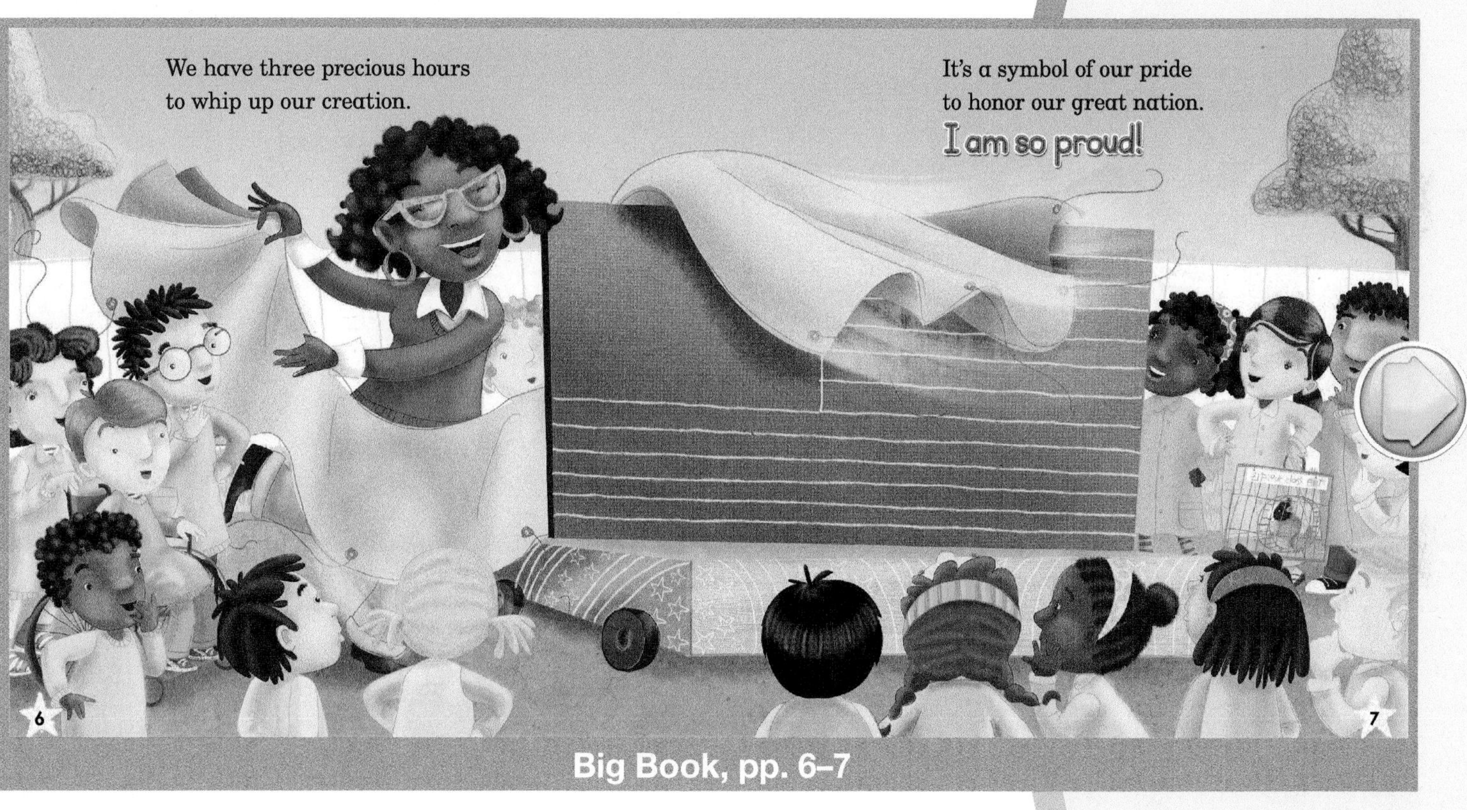

Big Book, pp. 6–7

***WH-* QUESTION** This story has rhyming words. Which words rhyme on these pages? (*creation* and *nation*)

2ND READ

Develop Vocabulary

OPEN-ENDED What colors of paint is the class using? (red and white)

- The children are painting with brushes along the border. Is it important to paint inside the lines?

DEVELOP VOCABULARY border

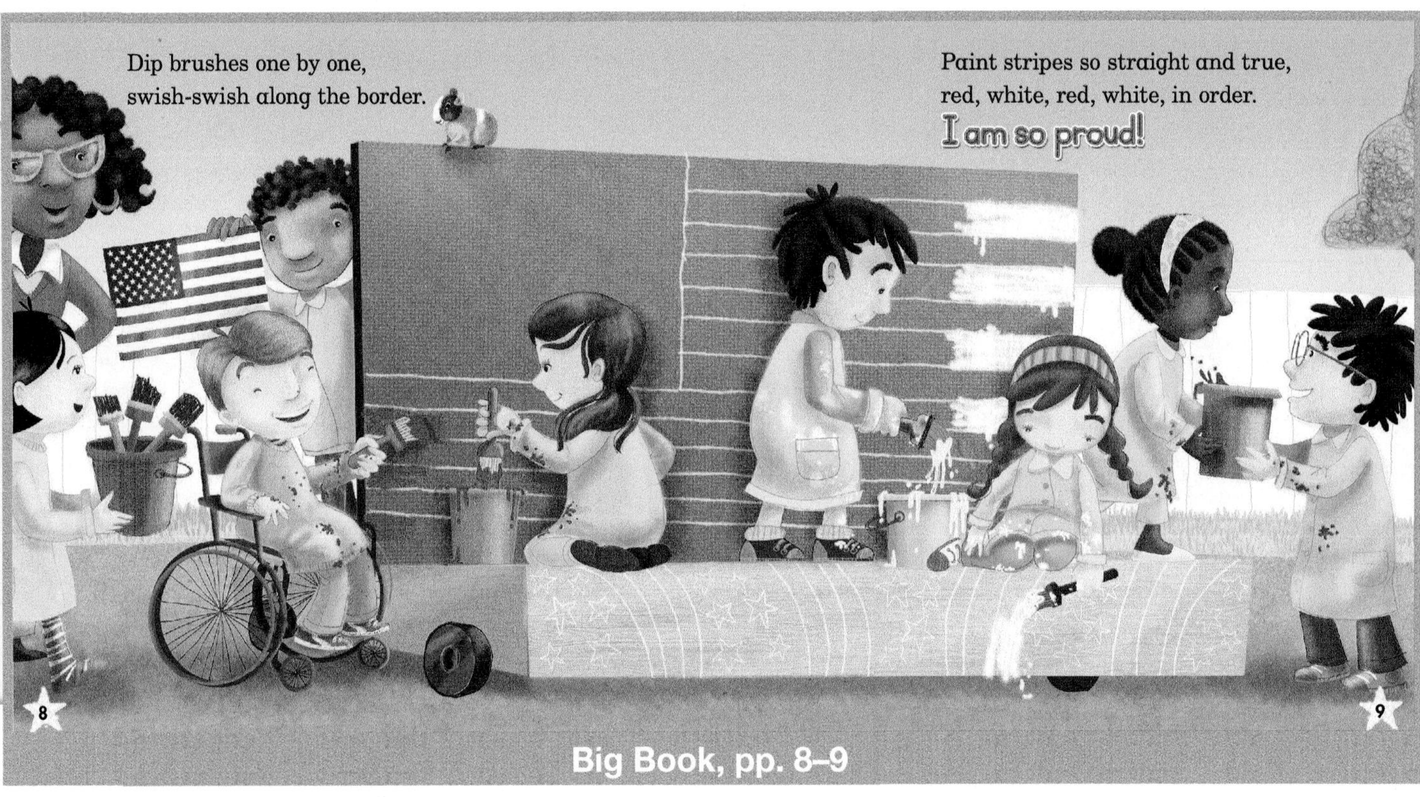

Dip brushes one by one,
swish-swish along the border.
Paint stripes so straight and true,
red, white, red, white, in order.
I am so proud!
8
9

Big Book, pp. 8–9

3RD READ

Develop Comprehension ©

INFERENCE How do you see the children cooperating in this picture? (Some children are carrying buckets and paintbrushes. Some children are taking turns. Another child is holding up a flag so the other children know what colors to paint.)

RECALL What do the children do here? (They mix buckets of blue paint.)

- The children mix blue paint in the buckets. What sound does the paint make?

DEVELOP VOCABULARY buckets

Common Core State Standards

Literature 1. With prompting and support, ask and answer questions about key details in a text.
Literature 3. With prompting and support, identify characters, settings, and major events in a story.
Literature 7. With prompting and support, describe the relationship between illustrations and the story in which they appear (e.g., what moment in a story an illustration depicts).

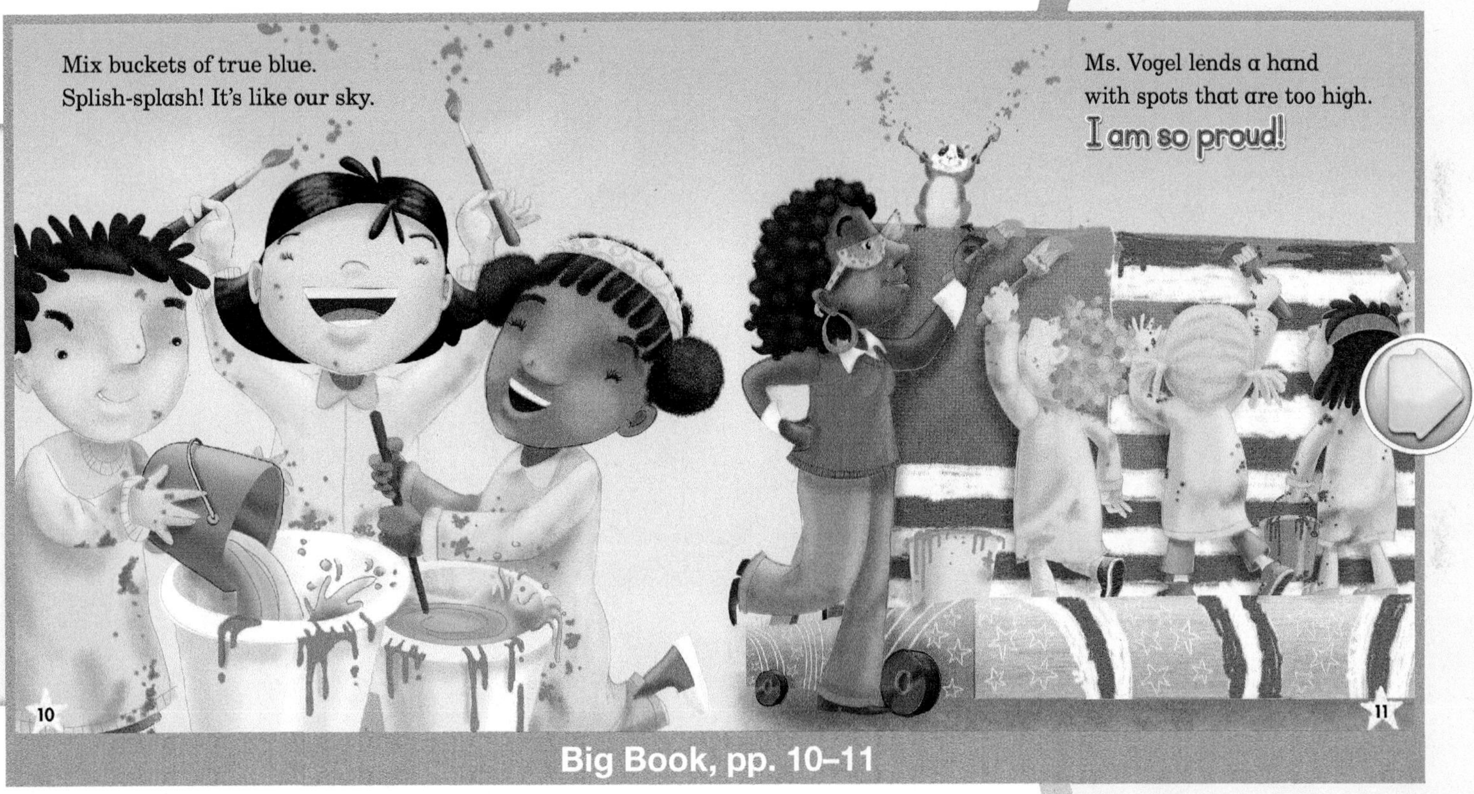

Mix buckets of true blue.
Splish-splash! It's like our sky.
Ms. Vogel lends a hand
with spots that are too high.
I am so proud!
10
11

Big Book, pp. 10–11

RECALL How does Ms. Vogel help the children paint? (She paints the parts up high that the children can't reach.)

2ND READ

Develop Vocabulary

RECALL How many stars do the children put on the flag? (fifty)

- The class puts fifty stars on the blue part. What color are the stars?

EXPAND VOCABULARY twinkle

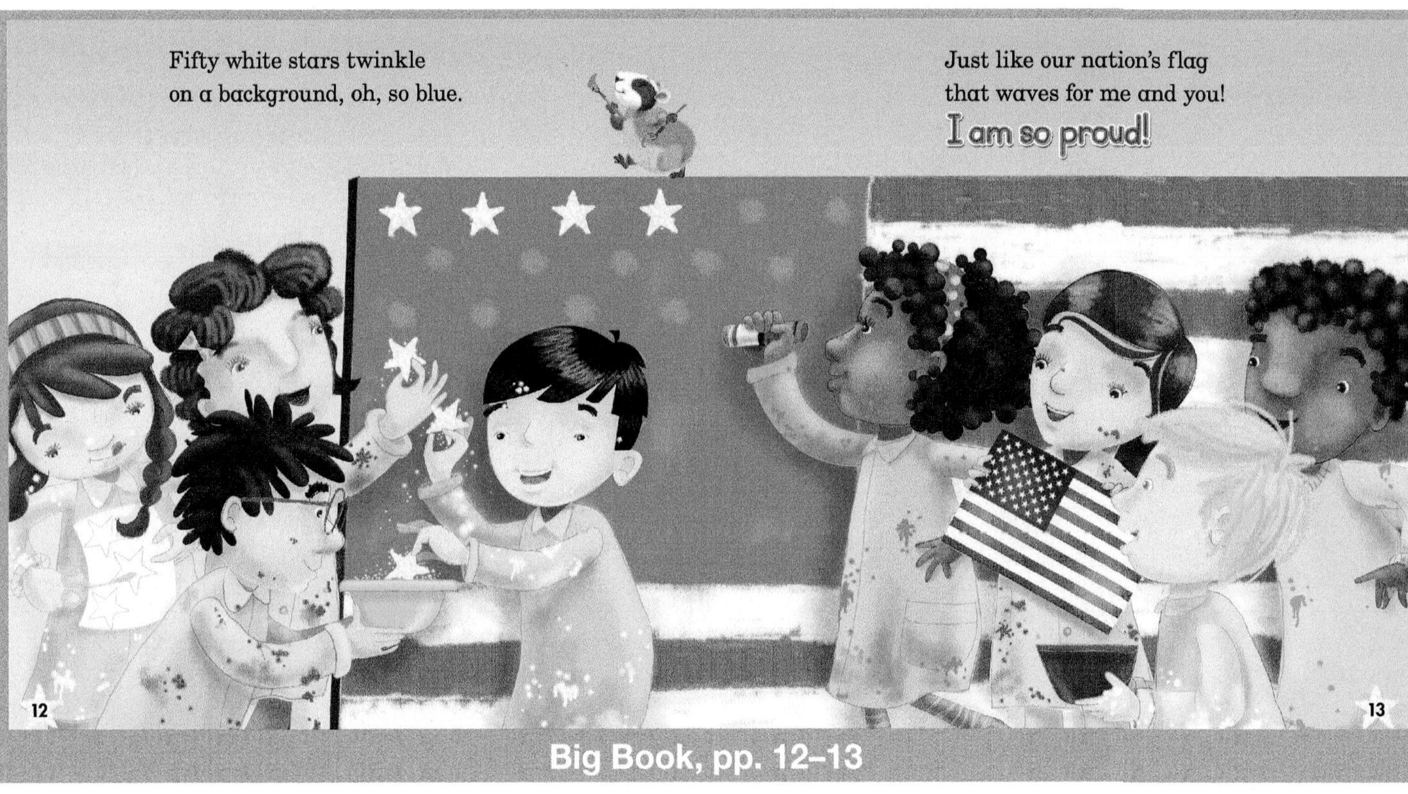

Fifty white stars twinkle
on a background, oh, so blue.
Just like our nation's flag
that waves for me and you!
I am so proud!
12
13

Big Book, pp. 12–13

3RD READ

Develop Comprehension ©

***WH-* QUESTION** What does the United States flag look like? (It has white stars on a blue background. It has red and white stripes.)

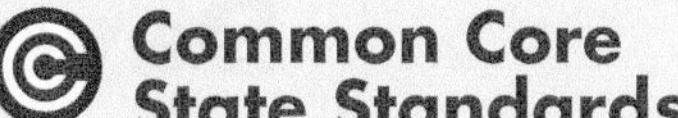

DISTANCING What do the children do with the paper roses? (They sniff them with their noses.)

- The children sniff the paper roses. Do paper flowers smell? What do real flowers smell like?

DEVELOP VOCABULARY sniff

Common Core State Standards

Literature 1. With prompting and support, ask and answer questions about key details in a text.
Literature 3. With prompting and support, identify characters, settings, and major events in a story.
Literature 7. With prompting and support, describe the relationship between illustrations and the story in which they appear (e.g., what moment in a story an illustration depicts).

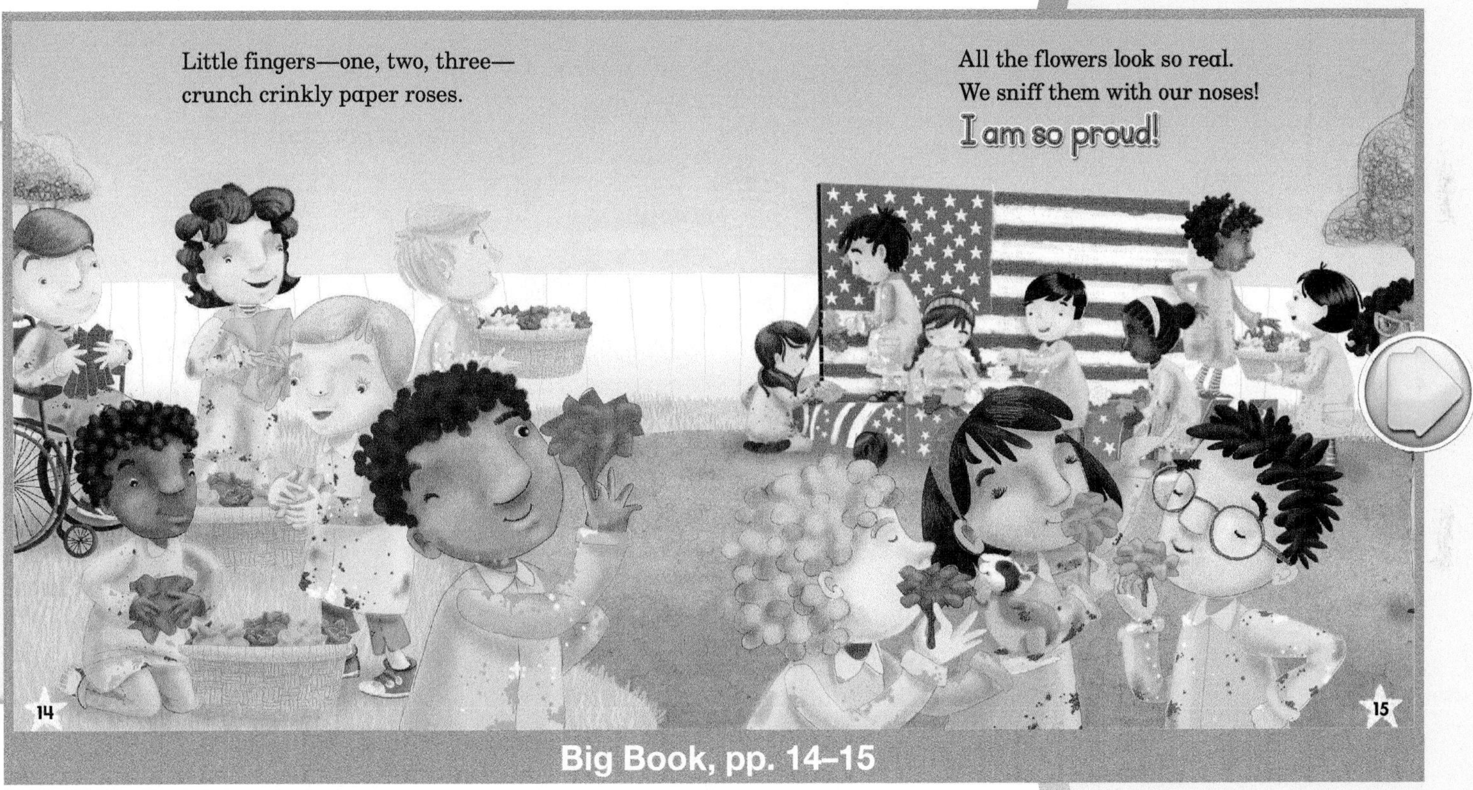

Little fingers—one, two, three—
crunch crinkly paper roses.
All the flowers look so real.
We sniff them with our noses!
I am so proud!
14
15

Big Book, pp. 14–15

INFERENCE Look at the gray smocks the class is wearing. Was it a good idea for them to cover their clothes while they painted? Why? (Yes, because they got the gray smocks dirty, not their clothes.)

2ND READ

Develop Vocabulary

WH- QUESTION What does the class do when the float is finished? (They stand at attention.)

- The class lines up. What do you think they will do next?

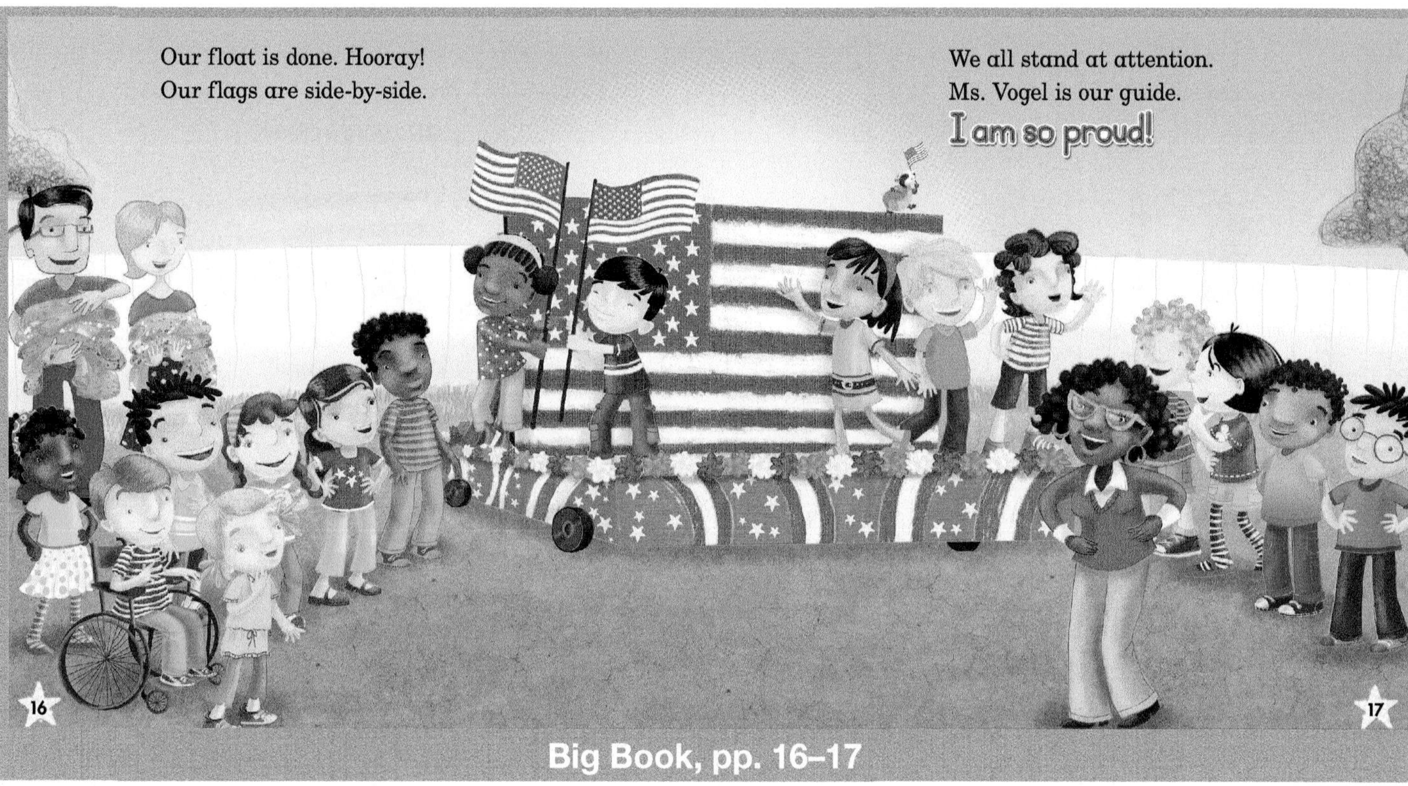

Our float is done. Hooray!
Our flags are side-by-side.
We all stand at attention.
Ms. Vogel is our guide.
I am so proud!
16
17

Big Book, pp. 16–17

3RD READ

Develop Comprehension ©

WH- QUESTION What are the children wearing now? (They are wearing red, white, and blue clothes.) What happened to the gray smocks they were wearing? (They don't need to wear them anymore because the float is done.)

Common Core State Standards

Literature 1. With prompting and support, ask and answer questions about key details in a text.
Literature 3. With prompting and support, identify characters, settings, and major events in a story.
Literature 7. With prompting and support, describe the relationship between illustrations and the story in which they appear (e.g., what moment in a story an illustration depicts).

***WH-* QUESTION** What are the children doing? (They are marching in the parade with the float. They are playing instruments.)

- The children are playing instruments. What sounds do the instruments make?

Tap-tap the rhythm sticks!
Crash the cymbals loudly!
Plink-plink the xylophone!
March with us, oh, so proudly!
18
19

Big Book, pp. 18–19

DISTANCING Tell me about the instruments the children are playing. (They are playing rhythm sticks, xylophones, and cymbals.) Have you ever played an instrument? What did it sound like?

2ND READ

Develop Vocabulary

OPEN-ENDED Who comes to watch the parade? (people in the community)

- The people in the community come out to watch the parade. Tell me about the people in the crowd.

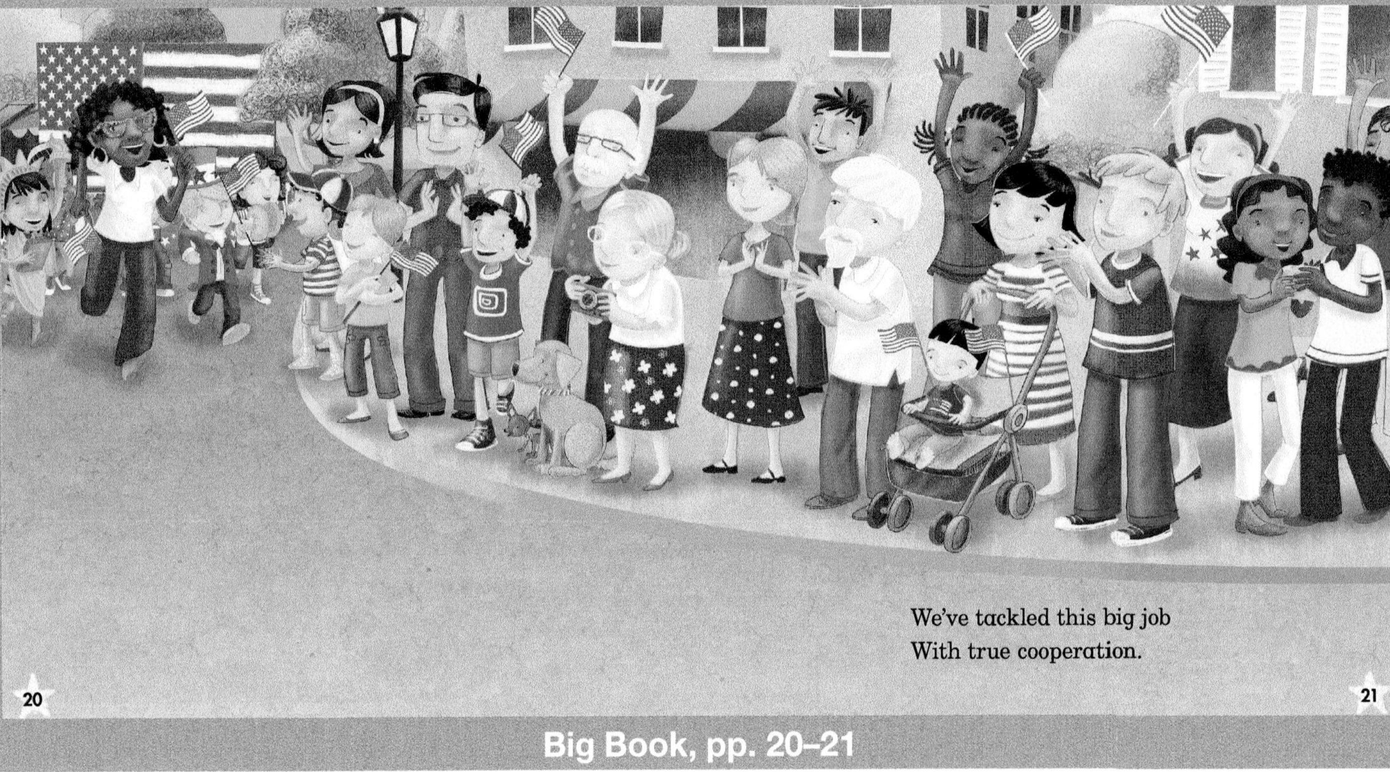

We've tackled this big job
With true cooperation.
20
21

Big Book, pp. 20–21

3RD READ

Develop Comprehension ©

SETTING The class is marching in a parade. When and where does a parade take place? (A parade happens during the day when the weather is nice. The floats and people in a parade move along the streets.)

***WH-* QUESTION** What does Ms. Vogel's class put on the back of the float? (their handprints)

- The class puts their handprints on the back of the float. What color of paint do they use?

Conventions
p. 172

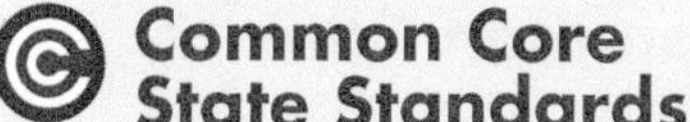

Common Core State Standards

Literature 1. With prompting and support, ask and answer questions about key details in a text.
Literature 3. With prompting and support, identify characters, settings, and major events in a story.
Literature 7. With prompting and support, describe the relationship between illustrations and the story in which they appear (e.g., what moment in a story an illustration depicts).

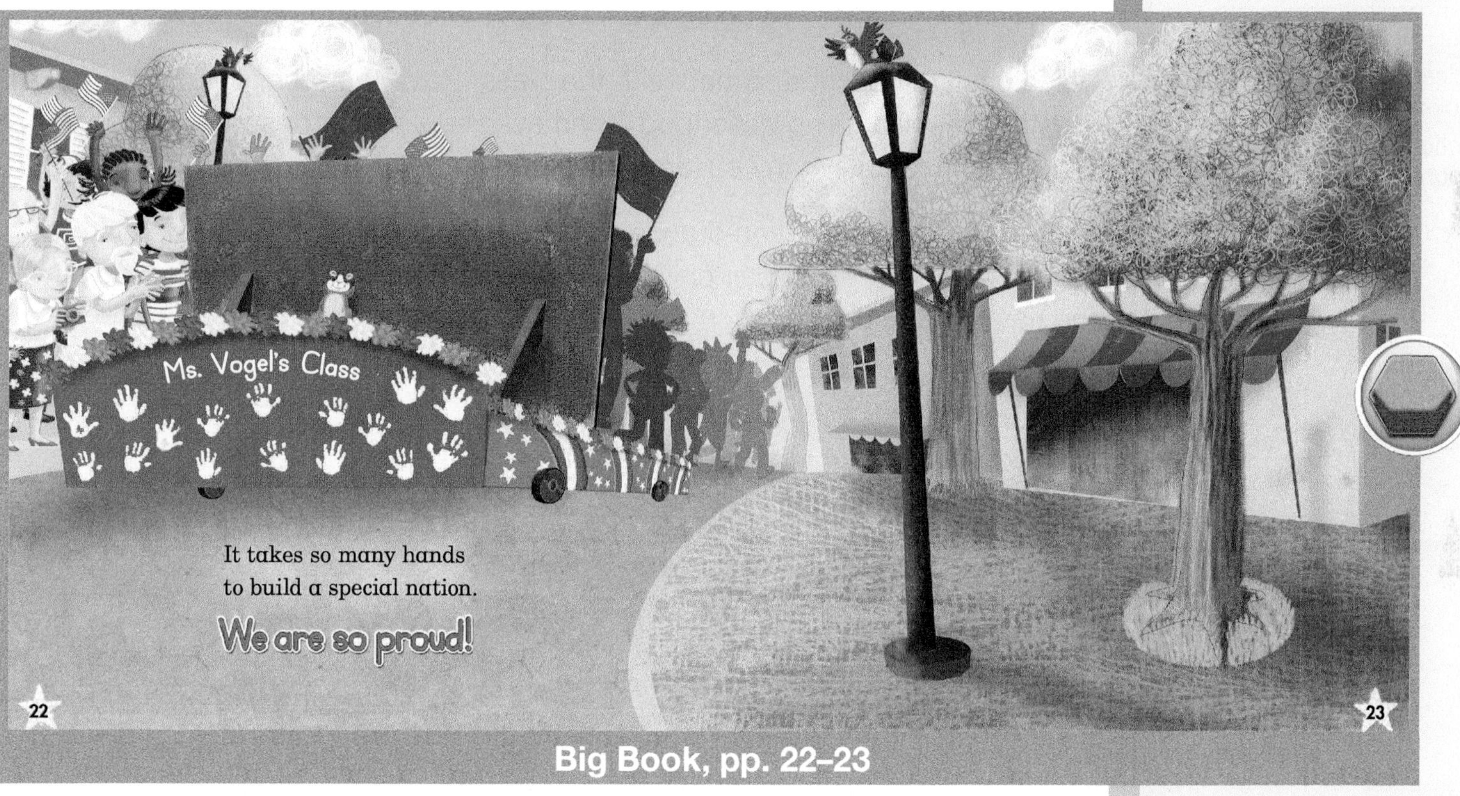

Ms. Vogel's Class
It takes so many hands
to build a special nation.
We are so proud!
22
23

Big Book, pp. 22–23

INFERENCE Where do you think the parade will end? (I think the parade will end back at the school where the class made the float.)

Conventions
p. 186

Common Core State Standards

Writing 2. Use a combination of drawing, dictating, and writing to compose informative/explanatory texts in which they name what they are writing about and supply some information about the topic. **Speaking/ Listening 1.a.** Follow agreed-upon rules for discussions (e.g., listening to others and taking turns speaking about the topics and texts under discussion). **Language 1.a.** Print many upper- and lowercase letters.

Daily Fix-It

i can help jack clean his room.
I can help Jack clean his room.

This week's practice sentences appear on *Teacher Resources DVD-ROM.*

Conventions

Review Say Our Names

TEACH Remind children that everyone has a name. My name is [say your name]. Point to a child in the class. What is your name? Encourage children to say their name in a complete sentence, using this sentence frame: *My name is* _______. After a child says his or her name, have the rest of the class repeat the name.

GUIDE PRACTICE I am going to describe a child in our room. When you know who I am describing, say that person's name. Describe a child by identifying his or her eye color and hair color or describing his or her clothing.

Ask a child to describe someone in the class. Have the other children identify the child being described. Then ask that child to describe someone else. Continue until many children have had a turn.

Team Talk Have children draw a picture of themselves. Display the pictures around the room. Then pair children and have them work together to identify the name of the child in each drawing.

ON THEIR OWN Use *Reader's and Writer's Notebook,* p. 21, for more practice with saying our names.

Reader's and Writer's Notebook, p. 21

Invitation

TEACH Write this invitation on the board:

> **Come to the school for a parade.**
> **It is on Saturday.**
> **It is at 1 o'clock.**

Read aloud the invitation. This is an invitation. An **invitation** is a polite request that asks someone to go somewhere or to do something. An invitation tells what will happen and when and where it will happen. Reread the invitation. What is this invitation for? When and where is the parade?

MODEL Write the invitation on the board with blanks for the underlined parts. Let's write an invitation to a celebration. The celebration will be in this room, so we will put our room number on the first line. Write *Room* and the room number. It is a celebration, so we will write *a celebration* on the next line.

GUIDE PRACTICE Have children provide information to fill in the rest of the invitation. Read aloud the finished invitation. Have children discuss to whom they could send the invitation.

INDEPENDENT WRITING Have children turn to p. 22 of *Reader's and Writer's Notebook.* Have children draw a picture for their invitation to a school activity. Then have them write or dictate the missing information.

Name ______ We Are So Proud!

Draw Write

Answers will vary.

Come to school for ______

It is on ______

It is at ______ o'clock.

Reader's and Writer's Notebook, p. 22

Daily Handwriting

Write uppercase *F* and *G* and lowercase *f* and *g* on the board. Review correct letter formation of uppercase *F* and *G* and lowercase *f* and *g.*

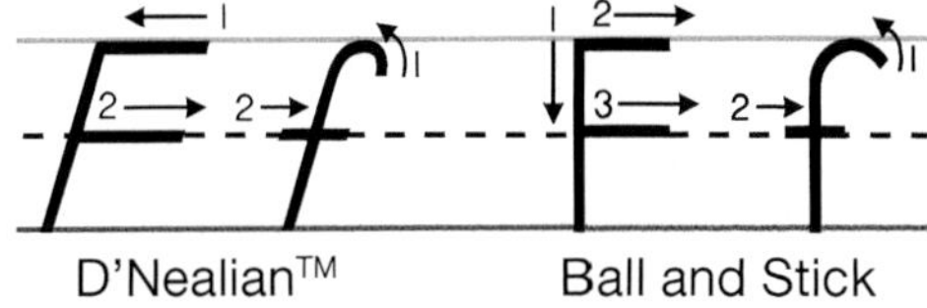

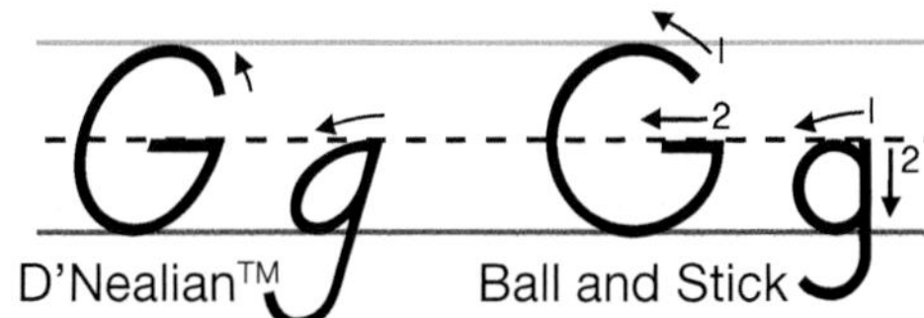

Have children write uppercase *F* and *G* and lowercase *f* and *g* on their Write-On Boards. Remind children to use proper left-to-right and top-to-bottom progression and proper spacing between letters when writing *F, f, G,* and *g.*

Access for All

Advanced

Extend Content Display a calendar. Tell children they can write a day of the week or a date on their invitation. Have children use the calendar to find a day or date to write.

Academic Vocabulary

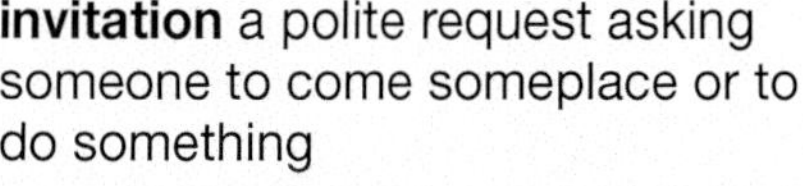

invitation a polite request asking someone to come someplace or to do something

Support Writing Explain to children that *where* in an invitation refers to a place and that *when* in an invitation refers to a time. The *when* and *where* in an invitation is like the setting of the activity.

Common Core State Standards

Literature 1. With prompting and support, ask and answer questions about key details in a text. **Speaking/Listening 1.a.** Follow agreed-upon rules for discussions (e.g., listening to others and taking turns speaking about the topics and texts under discussion). **Also Speaking/Listening 4., 6.**

Access for All

 Strategic Intervention

Respond to Literature Before children respond to *The Little School Bus,* display the pictures and allow children to retell what happens in the story based on the illustrations.

Academic Vocabulary

retell to state briefly the events in a story

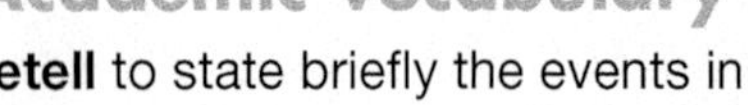

Bridge to Common Core

PRESENTATION OF KNOWLEDGE/IDEAS

When children summarize familiar stories and discuss their favorite parts and characters, they are learning to describe familiar people, places, things, and events; to speak audibly; and to express their thoughts, feelings, and ideas clearly.

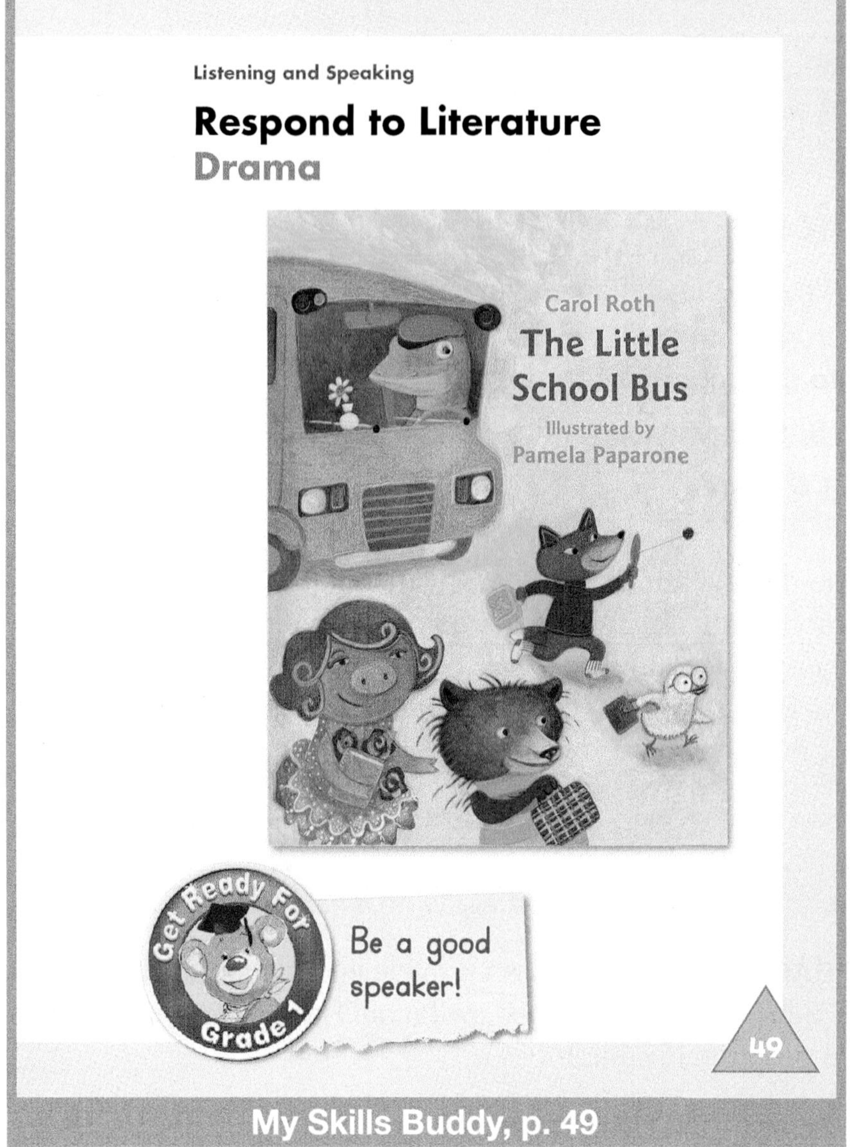

Listening and Speaking
Respond to Literature
Drama
Carol Roth
The Little School Bus
Illustrated by
Pamela Paparone
Get Ready For Grade 1
Be a good speaker!
49

My Skills Buddy, p. 49

Listening and Speaking

Respond to Literature: Drama

TEACH Remind children that when they respond to stories, they discuss what happens in a story and where and when it happens. They can also talk about their favorite parts and characters.

MODEL Have children turn to p. 49 of *My Skills Buddy.* Direct them to the picture of the cover of *The Little School Bus*. We read *The Little School Bus* last week. What happens in this story? Have children briefly retell the story. Remind them that good speakers speak one at a time and speak loudly and clearly. Who are the characters in the story? Use the picture on the cover to help you remember.

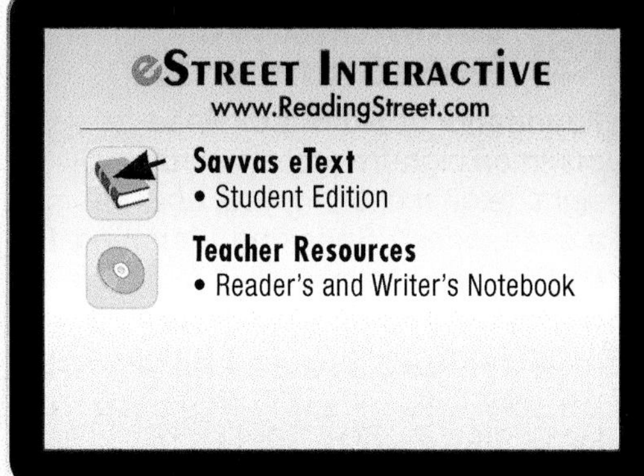

After children retell the story and identify the characters, use the Listening and Speaking bullets on p. 48 of *My Skills Buddy* to guide the discussion. Then ask children the following questions:

- Did you like the story? Why or why not?
- What word can you use to describe the story?

INDEPENDENT PRACTICE Write the names of familiar stories on the board, such as "Cinderella" and "Jack and the Beanstalk." For each story, have children briefly retell the story. Ask children to identify the setting of the story and to tell about their favorite part and favorite character. Refer children to their Rules for Listening and Speaking from pp. 1–2 of the *Reader's and Writer's Notebook.* Tell children to speak loudly and clearly and to listen politely when others are speaking. Remind children to take turns speaking.

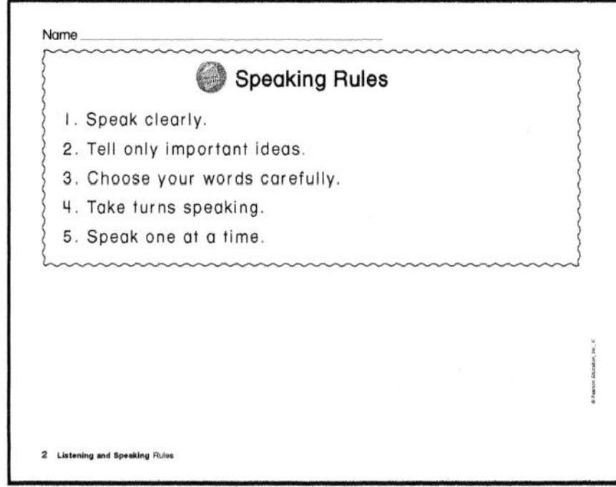
Name

Speaking Rules

1. Speak clearly.
2. Tell only important ideas.
3. Choose your words carefully.
4. Take turns speaking.
5. Speak one at a time.

2 Listening and Speaking Rules

Reader's and Writer's Notebook, pp. 1–2

Be a Good Speaker!

1. Speak loudly and clearly.
2. Tell only important ideas.
3. Choose your words carefully.
4. Take turns speaking.
5. Speak one at a time.

Scaffold Instruction Ask questions about *The Little School Bus* to guide children's thinking about characters and events. Show illustrations in the book to help children remember the events and to remind them of their favorite parts.

Foundational Skills 3.c. Read common high-frequency words by sight. (e.g., *the, of, to, you, she, my, is, are, do, does*). **Speaking/Listening 1.** Participate in collaborative conversations with diverse partners about *kindergarten topics and texts* with peers and adults in small and larger groups. **Also Speaking/ Listening 5.**

Wrap Up Your Day!

- ✔ **Content Knowledge** Today we talked about how we can work together. Tell about how you work with other children.
- ✔ **Phonological Awareness** Today we talked about words that begin with the same sound. Can you name two words that begin with the same sound?
- ✔ **Respond to Literature** Have children draw a picture of their favorite part of *We Are So Proud!*
- ✔ **Conventions** Point to children and ask them to say their name.
- ✔ **Homework Idea** Have children find pictures of things whose names begin with the same sound to share with the class.

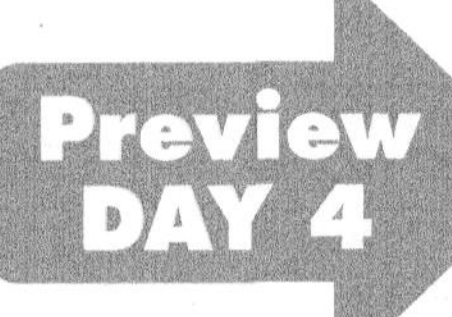

Tomorrow we will read a story about our Trucktown friend, Melvin.

Extend Your Day!

Social Studies
Class Parade

MATERIALS: Big Book *We Are So Proud!,* paper, crayons or markers

DISCUSS PARADES Have children think about a parade they have seen or been in, or have them think about the parade in *We Are So Proud!* People have parades to celebrate something. What are they celebrating in *We Are So Proud!?* What else can people celebrate by having a parade?

The class in *We Are So Proud!* makes a special float. What is on their float? They paint a United States flag. They also stand on their float. What else can be on a float? Write children's suggestions on the board.

DRAW PICTURES Have children choose something they want to show off on a float. Have them draw a picture of it on a sheet of paper. Remember, a float is on wheels. When people come to watch a parade, they want to see exciting floats, so add lots of detail and color to your pictures.

After children finish their drawings, have them hold their drawings and march around the classroom in a "parade." Tell them that parades move slowly so everyone gets a chance to look at the floats.

Vocabulary
High-Frequency Words

MATERIALS: paper, crayons

DESCRIBE YOURSELF Have children fold a sheet of paper in half and then in half again and then open up the paper. In each of the four sections, children are to describe themselves by completing this sentence frame:

I am ______.

Ask children to draw a self-portrait to illustrate each of their four sentences.

Letter Recognition
Letters *h, i, j,* and *k*

MATERIALS: set of Picture Cards, index cards

FIND LETTERS IN WORDS Write each of the letters *h, i, j,* or *k* on separate index cards. Distribute one card to each child. Then choose twenty Picture Cards, all of which contain one or more of the letters *h, i, j,* or *k* in them. Hold up the Picture Cards one by one and ask the following questions: What letter does this word begin with? What letter does this word end with? Is the letter *h* in this word? *i? j? k?* Ask children to hold up their card if they have a letter that answers the question.

DAY 4 at a Glance

Content Knowledge
Oral Vocabulary

Phonological Awareness
Review Syllables, Words, and Rhymes

Letter Recognition
Letters *Ll* and *Mm*

Text-Based Comprehension
Setting
Review Character

Conventions
Write Our Names

Writing
Extend the Concept

Vocabulary
Color Words

Materials

- Student Edition
- Truckery Rhymes
- Talk with Me/Sing with Me Chart
- Picture Cards
- Alphabet Cards
- Get Set, Roll! Reader 2
- Reader's and Writer's Notebook
- Big Book

Common Core State Standards

Speaking/Listening 1. Participate in collaborative conversations with diverse partners about *kindergarten topics and texts* with peers and adults in small and larger groups. **Language 4.a.** Identify new meanings for familiar words and apply them accurately (e.g., knowing *duck* is a bird and learning the verb *to duck*). **Also Language 4., 5.c., 6.**

Start your engines!

- Display "Little Dan Dumper" and lead the group in saying the rhyme a few times.
- Have the group clap the rhythm as they recite the rhyme.
- When children have mastered the rhythm, have them march around the room as they say the rhyme.

Truckery Rhymes
Truckery Rhymes

Content Knowledge

Zoom in on

Working and Playing Together at School

EXPAND THE CONCEPT On the board, write the Question of the Week, *How do school children work and play together?* Read the question as you track the print. Tell children to respond in complete sentences. Display Sing with Me Chart 2B.

We're Proud of Our Nation
Here's our teacher as our guide
With plans and preparation,
P-R-O-U-D,
P-R-O-U-D,
P-R-O-U-D,
We've built a new creation.
Talk with Me/Sing with Me Chart 2B

Build Oral Language

LISTEN FOR AMAZING WORDS We are going to sing this song again. Listen for the Amazing Words *float* and *guide.* Sing the song several times with children to the tune of "B-I-N-G-O." Have them stand up when they hear the Amazing Word *float* or *guide.*

Build Oral Vocabulary

Amazing Words Robust Vocabulary Routine

1. **Introduce the Word** When we watch a parade, we watch *floats* travel down the street. A *float* is a low, flat car that carries something to show in a parade. What's our new Amazing Word for a low, flat car in a parade? Say it with me: *float.*
2. **Demonstrate** Provide examples to show meaning. *The class works hard to decorate the float.* What kinds of *floats* have you seen in a parade?

   Repeat steps 1 and 2.

   Introduce the Word A person is a *guide* when he or she shows the way. A thing, such as a map, can also be a *guide.* What's our new Amazing Word for someone or something that shows the way? Say it with me: *guide.*

   Demonstrate *She asks the guide to tell her the way to go.*
3. **Apply** Have children use *float* and *guide* in complete sentences.
4. **Display the Words** Have children point to and name letters in *float* and *guide* that they recognize.

Routines Flip Chart

USE AMAZING WORDS To reinforce the concept and the Amazing Words, have children supply the appropriate Amazing Word for each sentence.

I can't wait to ride on the _______ in the parade. (float)

The _______ shows the group how to follow the trail. (guide)

MULTIPLE-MEANING WORDS Explain to children that some words can mean more than one thing. You know that the word *float* means "a low, flat car in a parade." *Float* can also mean "to stay on the surface of water." You know that the word *guide* means "someone or something that shows the way." *Guide* can also mean "to show the way." Use both meanings of each word in sentences and help children decide which meaning is being used.

Amazing Words

proud	preparation
cooperation	creation
float	guide

Access for All

 Advanced

Expand Vocabulary Remind children that the words *float* and *guide* mean more than one thing. The meanings of these words depend on how they are used in a sentence. Encourage children to use *float* and *guide* as both nouns and verbs in sentences.

Access Content Have children say the words *float* and *guide,* as defined in the Oral Vocabulary Routine, in their home languages.

Produce Oral Language Use the Day 4 instruction on ELL Poster 2 to extend and enrich language.

Common Core State Standards

Foundational Skills 2. Demonstrate understanding of spoken words, syllables, and sounds (phonemes). **Foundational Skills 2.a.** Recognize and produce rhyming words. **Foundational Skills 2.b.** Count, pronounce, blend, and segment syllables in spoken words.

Phonological Awareness

Review Syllables, Words, and Rhymes

PRACTICE Display the *kangaroo* Picture Card. Say *kan-ga-roo* and clap as you say each syllable. Have children echo you. How many times did we clap? How many word parts, or syllables, are in *kangaroo?* Repeat the activity with these Picture Cards: *apple, doll, feather, alligator, crayon, sandcastle, zipper, hippopotamus.*

Picture Card

Corrective feedback	**If...** children have difficulty counting syllables in words, **then...** say the syllables in a word slowly, showing one finger for each syllable, and have children count the number of fingers you are showing.

PRACTICE Reread a page from *We Are So Proud!* Have children read the sentence with you. Repeat the sentence and have them clap and count as you say each word. Continue with several other sentences from the book.

Corrective feedback	**If...** children have difficulty counting words, **then...** after reading the sentence, point to each word and count the words together.

PRACTICE Tell children you are going to say a word and then ask AlphaBuddy to say a word that rhymes with your word. If AlphaBuddy says a word that rhymes with my word, give him a round of applause. If his word does not rhyme with my word, say "Boo!" Use these pairs of words: *frog, dog; bus, truck; school, pool; goose, loose; tree, train; lamp, limp; goat, boat; rake, take; seal, meal; house, home.*

Check Phonological Awareness

FORMATIVE ASSESSMENT Say the following sets of words and have children identify the two words that rhyme: *cap, map, ten; bed, hop, mop; pin, pot, win.*

If... children cannot identify rhyming words,

then... say the words slowly, drawing out the words that rhyme.

Continue to monitor children's progress during the week so that children can be successful with the Day 5 Assessment.

Access for All

Strategic Intervention

Rhyming Words Remind children that rhyming words have the same middle and ending sounds. What words can you think of that rhyme with *cat?* What are the middle and ending sounds that make those words rhyme?

Common Core State Standards

Literature 10. Actively engage in group reading activities with purpose and understanding. **Foundational Skills 1.a.** Follow words from left to right, top to bottom, and page-by-page. **Foundational Skills 1.d.** Recognize and name all upper- and lowercase letters of the alphabet.

Letter Recognition

Teach/Model

Letters *Ll* and *Mm*

INTRODUCE/MODEL Display the *Ll* Alphabet Card. Point to the uppercase letter. The name of this letter is uppercase *L*. What is the name of this letter? Repeat for lowercase *l*. Does anyone have uppercase *L* in his or her name? Write names that contain the letter *L* on the board. Display the *Mm* Alphabet Card and repeat the activity.

Alphabet Card

Guide Practice

GROUP PRACTICE Display the *leaf* Picture Card. Have children name the picture. Write the picture name on the board. Who can show me the letter *l* in the word *leaf?* Continue having children find the letter *l* or *m* using the following Picture Cards: *doll, man, drum, mop.*

Alphabet Card

Display a page of a book and have children look for words with uppercase *L* or *M* and lowercase *l* or *m.* Write the words on the board. Have children say each word with you.

ON THEIR OWN Have children use *Reader's and Writer's Notebook,* p. 19, for more practice with letters *Ll* and *Mm.* Return to this page on Day 5 to practice *Nn.*

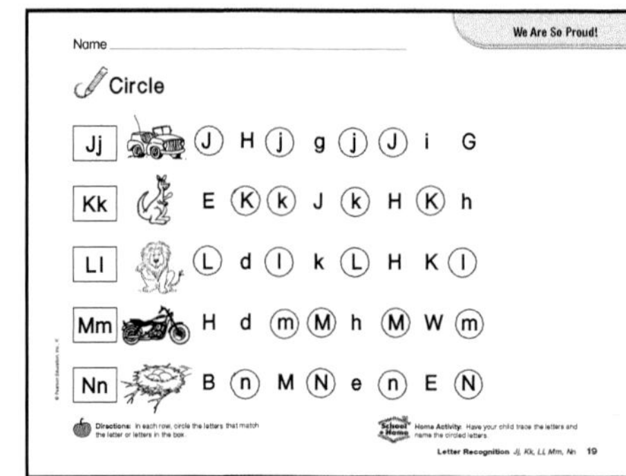

We Are So Proud!

Name

Circle

Jj J H j g j J i G

Kk E K k J k H K h

Ll L d l k L H K l

Mm H d m M h M W m

Nn B n M N e n E N

Directions: In each row, circle the letters that match the letter or letters in the box.

Home Activity: Have your child trace the letters and name the circled letters.

Letter Recognition *Jj, Kk, Ll, Mm, Nn* 19

Reader's and Writer's Notebook, p. 19

Get Set, Roll! Reader 2

Read *Melvin*

REVIEW Review the high-frequency words *I* and *am.* Have children find each word on the Word Wall.

Get Set, Roll! Reader 2

TEACH REBUS WORDS Write the word *Melvin* on the board. This is the name *Melvin.* Name the letters with me: *M, e, l, v, i, n, Melvin.* Repeat the procedure with *worried* and *glad.* Look for these words in the story today. A picture above the word will help you read it.

READ Today we will read a story about Melvin. Point to the title of the book. What is the title of the book? (*Melvin*) Where is the title of the book? Point to the front cover. This is the front cover of the book. Where is the back cover?

Use the routine for reading decodable books in the Routines Flip Chart to read Get Set, Roll! Reader 2.

eSTREET INTERACTIVE
www.ReadingStreet.com
Savvas eText
• Get Set, Roll! Reader
Teacher Resources
• Reader's and Writer's Notebook

Access for All

SI Strategic Intervention

Practice Retelling Have children draw pictures that retell Get Set, Roll! Reader 2, *Melvin.*

Access Reader Do a picture walk with children to preview the reader before starting the routine.

Day 4 SMALL GROUP TIME • Differentiate Language, p. SG•19

OL On-Level	SI Strategic Intervention	A Advanced
• **Build** Sentences and Words • **Read** Get Set, Roll! Reader *Melvin*	• **Talk About** Sentences and Words • **Read** Get Set, Roll! Reader *Melvin*	• **Extend** Sentences and Words • **Read** Get Set, Roll! Reader *Melvin*

Place English Language Learners in the groups that correspond to their reading abilities in English.

If... children need more practice **Developing Language,**
then... use the Language Workshops in the *ELL Handbook* beginning on p. 306.

Text-Based Comprehension

Setting

PRACTICE Have children turn to the Literary Elements pictures on pp. 34–35 of *My Skills Buddy.* As you look at the pictures, remind children that when and where a story takes place is called the setting.

My Skills Buddy, pp. 34–35

Team Talk Pair children and have them think of questions they have about the setting of *We Are So Proud!*

Review Character

PRACTICE Direct children to the Literary Elements pictures on pp. 34–35 of *My Skills Buddy.*

Characters are the animals or people in a story. Good readers pay attention to the characters so they know whom the story is about. Review the story "The Tortoise and the Hare."

- Who are the characters in the pictures? (the tortoise and the hare)

MORE PRACTICE For more practice with character, use *Reader's and Writer's Notebook,* p. 23.

Reader's and Writer's Notebook, p. 23

Common Core State Standards

Literature 1. With prompting and support, ask and answer questions about key details in a text.
Literature 3. With prompting and support, identify characters, settings, and major events in a story.

Access for All

Strategic Intervention

Practice Character Have children pretend that their classmates are in a story. Have them name the "characters."

Academic Vocabulary

characters the people or animals in a story

Read Main Selection

GUIDE COMPREHENSION Display *We Are So Proud!* There are many people in this story.

Display pp. 2–3. Point to Ms. Vogel.

- Who is this character? (This is the teacher, Ms. Vogel.)
- What does Ms. Vogel do in the story? (She helps the class make a float for a parade.)

Point to all the children in the class.

- Who are these characters? (They are the children in Ms. Vogel's class.)
- What does the class do in this story? (They make a float and march in a parade.)

READ Reread *We Are So Proud!* Return to p. 161. Follow the **3rd Read** and use the **Develop Comprehension** notes to give children the opportunity to gain a more complete understanding of the story.

Routine Read for Understanding

Deepen understanding by reading the selection multiple times.

1. **First Read**—Read the entire selection aloud to build interest in the text.
2. **Second Read**—Use the **Develop Vocabulary** notes on pages 161–171.
3. **Third Read**—Use the **Develop Comprehension** notes on pages 161–171.

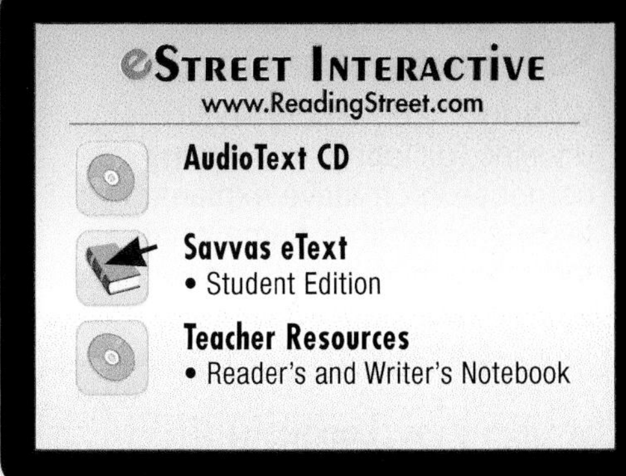

Bridge to Common Core

RANGE OF READING AND LEVEL OF TEXT COMPLEXITY
Using the Develop Comprehension notes as you read the text a third time will help you assess how well children are comprehending the authentic literary text in *Reading Street.* As the year progresses, children will improve as independent, proficient readers of complex text.

 Common Core State Standards

Writing 2. Use a combination of drawing, dictating, and writing to compose informative/explanatory texts in which they name what they are writing about and supply some information about the topic. **Language 1.a.** Print many upper- and lowercase letters. **Also Writing 5., 8., Language 2.**

Access for All

 Strategic Intervention

Support Conventions Have children practice writing the name of a family member, friend, or pet.

Daily Fix-It

my friend gabe is nice.

My friend Gabe is nice.

This week's practice sentences appear on *Teacher Resources DVD-ROM.*

Conventions

Write Our Names

TEACH Remind children that people have names and that a name always begins with an uppercase letter.

Write your name on the board. My name is [write your name]. When I write my name, I use an uppercase letter for the first letter. Point to the uppercase letter in your name.

GUIDE PRACTICE Have children draw a self-portrait and label their picture with their first and last names. Help children name and write each letter in their last name. Remind them to begin their first and last names with uppercase letters.

ON THEIR OWN Use *Reader's and Writer's Notebook,* p. 24, for more practice writing names.

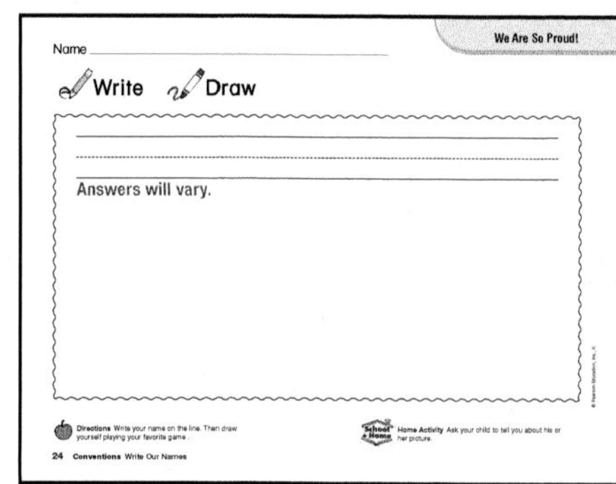
Name

We Are So Proud!

Write Draw

Answers will vary.

24 Conventions Write Our Names

Reader's and Writer's Notebook, p. 24

Writing

Extend the Concept

DISCUSS We just read a story about a class that works together to make a float for a parade. They look like they have fun working together. Like Ms. Vogel's class in the book, we work together every day.

Ask children to think about what kinds of things they work on with other children. Talk with children about why working together can be fun.

GUIDE PRACTICE Use children's contributions to the discussion to write sentences.

We work together when...	**we clean up.**
	we read new words.
Working together is fun because...	**we make new things.**
	we learn new things.

INDEPENDENT WRITING Have children write or dictate their own sentence about working together, or they may copy a sentence from the board. Invite children to read their sentences to the class.

Daily Handwriting

Write uppercase *H* and *I* and lowercase *h* and *i* on the board. Review correct letter formation with children.

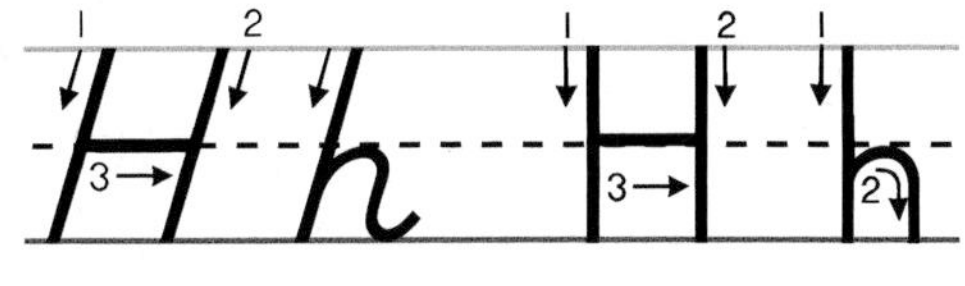

D'Nealian™ Ball and Stick

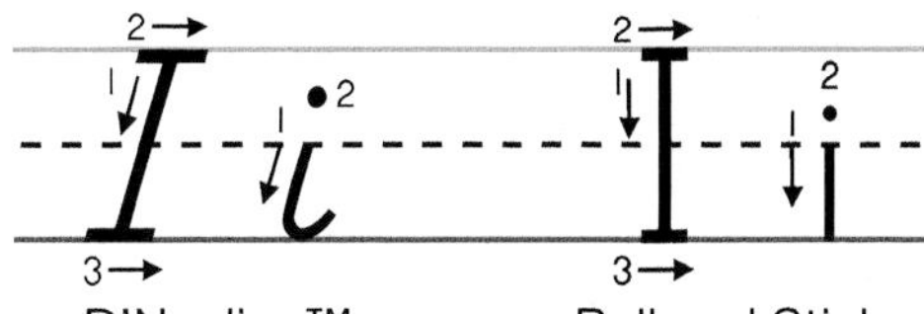

D'Nealian™ Ball and Stick

Have children write a row of uppercase *H* and *I* and a row of lowercase *h* and *i* on their Write-On Boards. Remind them to use proper left-to-right and top-to-bottom progression when writing *H, h, I,* and *i.*

eSTREET INTERACTIVE
www.ReadingStreet.com

Teacher Resources
- Reader's and Writer's Notebook
- Daily Fix-It Transparency

Bridge to Common Core

PRODUCTION AND DISTRIBUTION OF WRITING
With your guidance and support, children interact and collaborate with others to write sentences about working together.

Support Writing Before writing, children can state their ideas and you can restate them to model correct word usage.

Common Core State Standards

Foundational Skills 2.a. Recognize and produce rhyming words. **Language 5.a.** Sort common objects into categories (e.g., shapes, foods) to gain a sense of the concepts the categories represent. **Also Literature 4., Language 5.**

Vocabulary

Color Words

TEACH Write the words *red, white,* and *blue* on the board. Point to each word as you read it. These words name three colors. Have children turn to p. 48 of *My Skills Buddy.* Use the last two Vocabulary bullets to guide the discussion. Direct children to the colors at the top of the page. Which color is red? Direct them to the pictures below the colors. Which pictures are red? Repeat with white and blue.

Team Talk Pair children and have them take turns using the color words *red, white,* and *blue* in complete sentences.

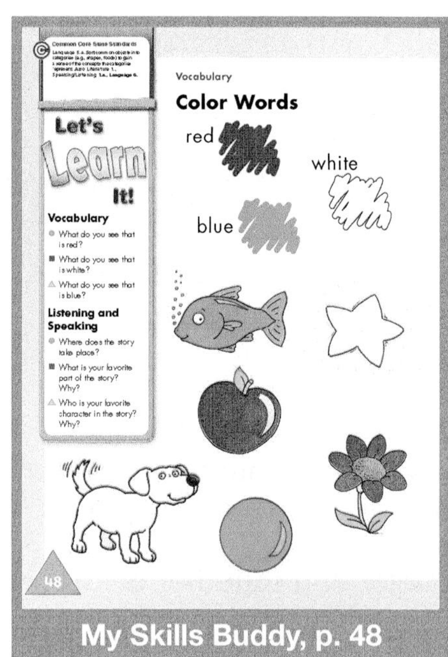

My Skills Buddy, p. 48

Wrap Up Your Day!

- ✔ **Oral Language** Sing "We're Proud of Our Nation" with me. Clap your hands when you hear an Amazing Word—*proud, preparation, cooperation, creation, float, guide.*
- ✔ **Phonological Awareness** Today we worked with rhyming words. What rhyming words can we think of for *goat* and *pig?*
- ✔ **Homework Idea** Ask children to tell a family member which of the two stories they like better and why.

Tell children that tomorrow they will review some of the books and stories they have read this week.

Extend Your Day!

Science
What Do I Look Like?

MATERIALS: large sheet of chart paper, objects to compare, index cards

DISCUSS PROPERTIES Display two balls: a baseball and a foam ball. Talk about the words you can use to describe the balls. Words that you can use to describe are also called *properties.* For example, point out that the baseball is hard, heavy, rough, solid, dry, and so on. Help children identify properties of each ball.

USING A VENN DIAGRAM Make a Venn diagram on chart paper and lay it flat. Place either a picture of a baseball or write *Baseball* above one circle and do the same for the foam ball and the other circle. Have children describe the properties of the balls. Write the properties named on index cards.

Place the cards in the appropriate circle in the Venn diagram. If the property applies to both balls, place the card in the section where the circles overlap.

Have children use the diagram to compare and contrast the two balls.

Ask them questions such as these:

- Are both balls rough?
- Which ball is round?

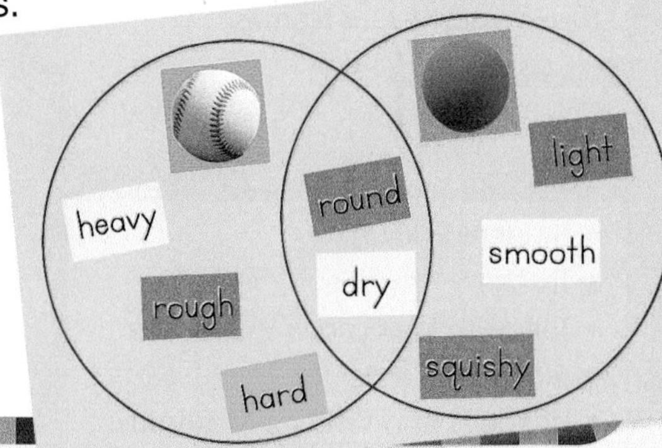

Phonological Awareness
Rhyming Words

MATERIALS: chart paper or Graphic Organizer 5, pencils

SORT WORDS INTO FAMILIES Write these word endings as separate headings at the top of a three-column chart: *-ap, -op, -an.* Distribute copies of the chart to children and together find rhyming words that belong in each column, such as *cap, tap; mop, hop;* and *man, ran.* Help children write the rhyming words in the correct column on the chart.

-ap	-op	-an
cap	mop	man
tap	hop	ran
gap	pop	can
lap	top	fan
map		pan
nap		tan
rap		van

Letter Recognition
Letters *A, B, M, L*

MATERIALS: construction paper with *LAMB* written in large letters, glue, cotton balls, crayons

MAKE WORD ART Give each child a sheet of paper with the word *LAMB* written on it in large letters. Have children name each of the letters. Then read the word for them. Have them glue cotton balls onto the letters and then glue bunches of cotton balls together to make a lamb. They can add legs, a tail, and ears using crayons.

DAY 5 at a Glance

Content Knowledge
Oral Vocabulary

Phonological Awareness
Review Syllables

Letter Recognition
Letters *Nn*

Assessment
Letter Recognition
High-Frequency Words
Comprehension

Text-Based Comprehension
Review Setting

Conventions
Review Write Our Names

Writing
This Week We…

Materials

- Student Edition
- Truckery Rhymes
- Talk with Me/Sing with Me Chart
- Alphabet Cards
- Reader's and Writer's Notebook
- Read Aloud Anthology
- Student Reader K.1.2
- Get Set, Roll! Reader 2

Bridge to Common Core

INTEGRATION OF KNOWLEDGE/IDEAS
This week children have integrated content presented in diverse formats and analyzed how different texts address similar topics. They have developed knowledge about how children work and play together at school to expand the unit topic of Cooperation.

Social Studies Knowledge Goals
Children have learned that working together with classmates

- helps them share tools and supplies
- helps them solve problems

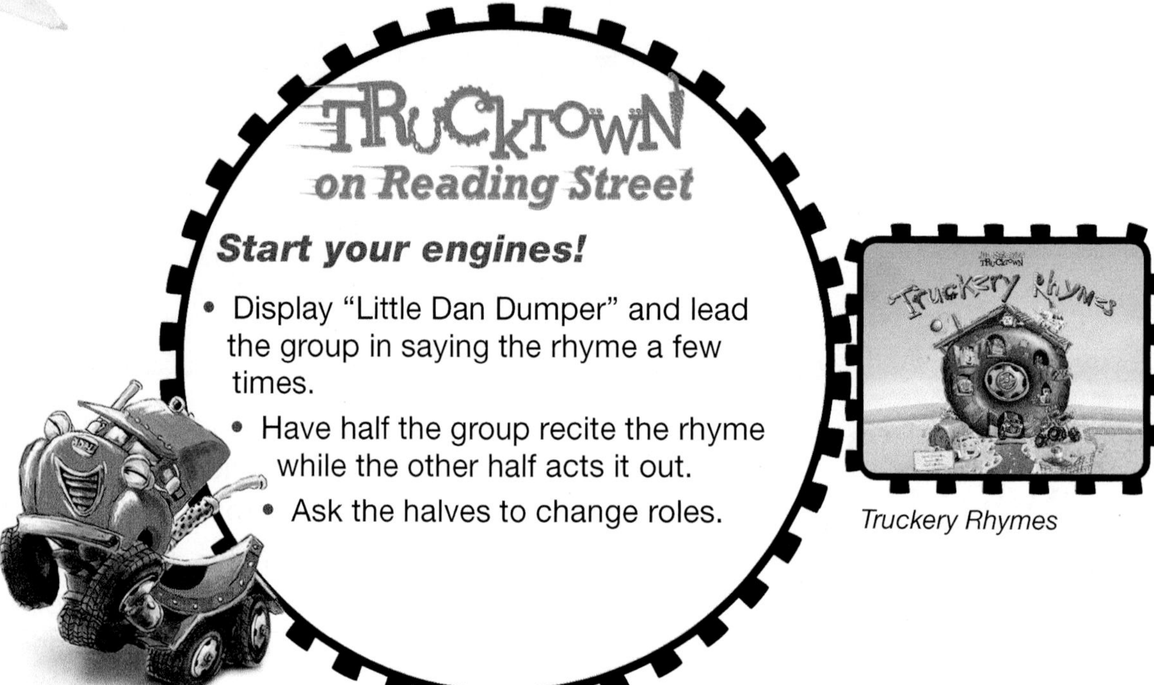
TRUCKTOWN
on Reading Street

Start your engines!

- Display "Little Dan Dumper" and lead the group in saying the rhyme a few times.
  - Have half the group recite the rhyme while the other half acts it out.
  - Ask the halves to change roles.

Truckery Rhymes

Content Knowledge

Zoom in on ©

Working and Playing Together at School

REVIEW THE CONCEPT Discuss with children what they have added to their knowledge about this unit of study, All Together Now. Encourage them to use the Amazing Words.

Build Oral Language

LISTEN FOR AMAZING WORDS Display Sing with Me Chart 2B. Let's sing "We're Proud of Our Nation." I want you to listen for the Amazing Words we learned this week. Remind children that the words *proud, preparation, cooperation, creation, float,* and *guide* are in the song. Sing the song several times to the tune of "B-I-N-G-O." Discuss how they work and play with other children. Remind children to speak one at a time.

We're Proud of Our Nation
Here's our teacher as our guide
With plans and preparation,
P-R-O-U-D,
P-R-O-U-D,
P-R-O-U-D,
We've built a new creation.
Talk with Me/Sing with Me Chart 2B

Talk with Me/Sing with Me Chart 2A

Build Oral Vocabulary

REVIEW AMAZING WORDS Display Talk with Me Chart 2A. We learned six new Amazing Words this week. Let's say the Amazing Words as I point to the pictures on the chart. Point to each picture and give children the chance to say the appropriate Amazing Word before offering it.

Have children supply the appropriate Amazing Word to complete each sentence.

Sally will ride on a _______ in the parade. (float)
It takes _______ to start a big project. (preparation)
Melissa is _______ of her dog's tricks. (proud)
They used paint and paper to make the _______. (creation)
Ms. Vogel is a _______ for the float. (guide)
The class knows it takes _______ to finish the float. (cooperation)

It's Friday

MONITOR PROGRESS Check Oral Vocabulary

FORMATIVE ASSESSMENT Demonstrate Word Knowledge Monitor the Amazing Words by asking the following questions. Have children use the Amazing Word in their answer.

- **What word means the act of getting something ready?** (preparation)
- **What word means the act of working together?** (cooperation)
- **What is a low, flat car in a parade?** (float)
- **What word means thinking well of people and things?** (proud)
- **Who or what can show the way?** (guide)
- **What is something new and original?** (creation)

If... children have difficulty using the Amazing Words,

then... reteach the words using the Robust Vocabulary Routine on the Routines Flip Chart.

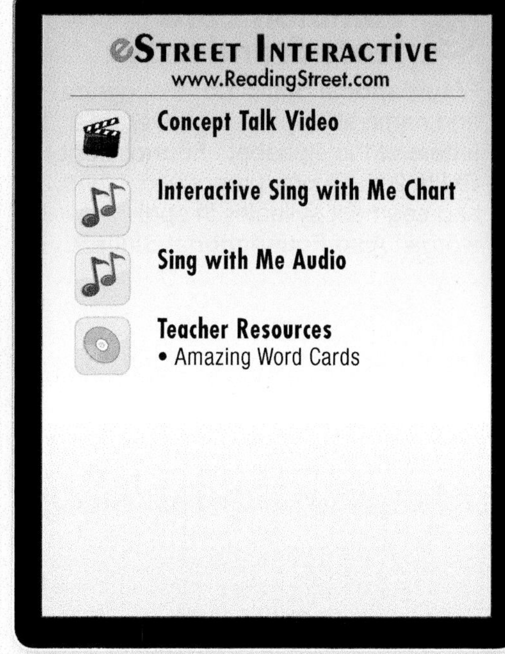

Amazing Words

proud	preparation
cooperation	creation
float	guide

Access for All

A Advanced

Amazing Words Have children tell what each Amazing Word means in their own words.

ELL

Check Concepts and Language Use the Day 5 instruction on ELL Poster 2 to monitor children's understanding of the lesson concept.

Common Core State Standards
Foundational Skills 1.d. Recognize and name all upper- and lowercase letters of the alphabet. **Foundational Skills 2.b.** Count, pronounce, blend, and segment syllables in spoken words. **Also Foundational Skills 2.**

Phonological Awareness

Review Syllables

COUNT SYLLABLES How many syllables are in the word *banana*? Let's clap once for each syllable to find out. There are three syllables: *ba-na-na.* Review clapping syllables with the following words: *flower, chair, house, salamander, monkey, television, butter, cup.*

REVIEW RHYMING WORDS Say this sentence aloud: *I am a fox that lives in a box.* Did you hear any rhyming words? Which words rhyme? *Fox* and *box* rhyme. Continue the activity using the following rhymes: *I am a little mouse who lives in a tiny house; My little pup drinks out of a cup; I know a frog who sleeps under a log.* Then say one of the words in the rhyme and have children count the syllables.

Letter Recognition

Teach/Model

Letters *Nn*

INTRODUCE/MODEL Display the *Nn* Alphabet Card. Point to the uppercase letter. This is uppercase *N.* What is the name of this letter? Repeat with lowercase *n.*

Alphabet Card

Guide Practice

GROUP PRACTICE Write the word *banana* on the board. Who can find lowercase *n* in this word? How many *n*'s are in the word *banana*? There are two *n*'s. Repeat with the words *cannon, Nancy,* and *noun.*

Continue the activity to review the letters *Ff, Gg, Hh, Ii, Jj, Kk, Ll,* and *Mm.* Use these words: *frog, hike, lemon, fish, goat, jingle, jolly, Kim, James, Mark, Fran.*

ON THEIR OWN Ask children to look around the room for the letters *Kk, Ll, Mm,* or *Nn.* As each letter is found, have children say the letter name. Then have children use *Reader's and Writer's Notebook,* p. 19, for more practice with letters *Nn.*

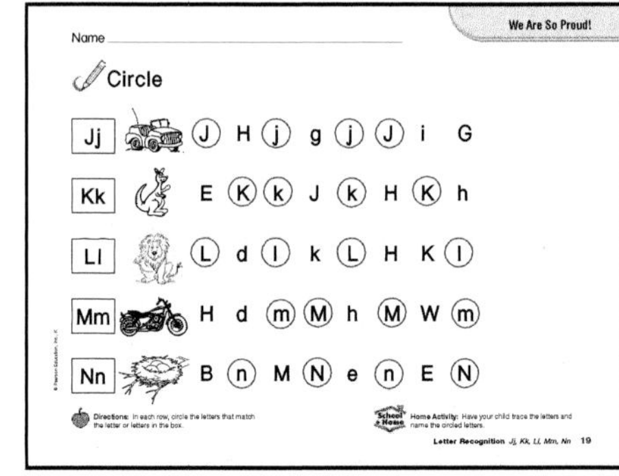
Name
We Are So Proud!
Circle
Jj J H j g j J i G
Kk E K k J k H K h
Ll L d l k L H K l
Mm H d m M h M W m
Nn B n M N e n E N

Reader's and Writer's Notebook, p. 19

Access for All

SI Strategic Intervention

Support Comprehension Pair children and have them discuss the pictures in Kindergarten Student Reader K.1.2 and Get Set, Roll! Reader 2. Ask them how the pictures in a story can tell a reader information in addition to what the words tell.

REVIEW HIGH-FREQUENCY WORDS Write the word *I* on the board. This is the word *I*. What is this word? Repeat the routine with *am.*

REREAD Have children reread one of the books specific to the target letters. You may wish to review the rebus words and high-frequency words that appear in each book prior to rereading.

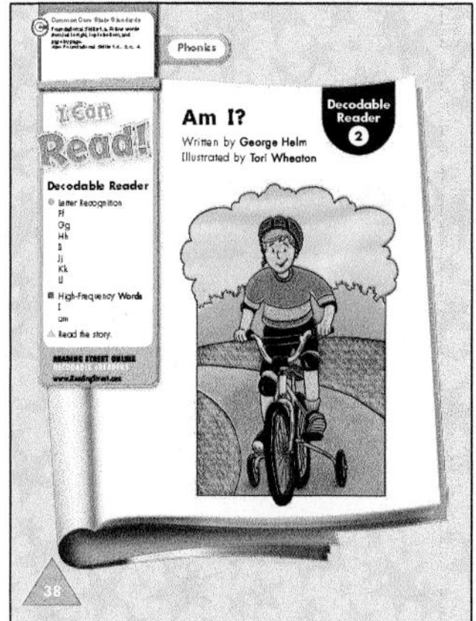

Decodable Reader 2
My Skills Buddy, p. 38

Kindergarten Student Reader K.1.2

Get Set, Roll! Reader 2

Day 5 SMALL GROUP TIME • Differentiate Close Reading, p. SG•19

OL On-Level	SI Strategic Intervention	A Advanced
• **Practice Letter Recognition** Recognize Letters *Jj, Kk, Ll, Mm, Nn* • **Read** "Gadget Is Gone!"	• **Reteach Letter Recognition** Recognize Letters *Jj, Kk, Ll, Mm, Nn* • **Read** "Gadget Is Gone!"	• **Extend Letter Recognition** Connect Letters to Sounds • **Read** "Gadget Is Gone!"

ELL

Place English Language Learners in the groups that correspond to their reading abilities in English.

If... children need more support with **Comprehension,**
then... use the ELL activities on pp. DI•30–DI•31 in the Teacher Resources section of the Digital Path.

Common Core State Standards

Foundational Skills 1.d. Recognize and name all upper- and lowercase letters of the alphabet. **Foundational Skills 3.c.** Read common high-frequency words by sight. (e.g., *the, of, to, you, she, my, is, are, do, does*).

Assess

- Identify letters *Ff, Gg, Hh, Ii, Jj, Kk, Ll, Mm,* and *Nn.*
- Read high-frequency words.

Assessment

Monitor Progress

Review Letter Recognition

WHOLE CLASS Draw a 3-square-by-3-square grid on a sheet of paper for each child. Randomly write the letters *Ff, Gg, Hh, Ii, Jj, Kk, Ll, Mm,* and *Nn* in the squares. Find the *g* and color that box red. Continue giving directions as you circulate around the room to check children's work.

MONITOR PROGRESS Check Letter and Word Reading

If... children cannot complete the whole-class assessment,
then... use the Reteach lesson in *First Stop.*

If... you are unsure of a child's grasp of this week's skills,
then... use the assessment below to obtain a clearer evaluation of the child's progress.

ONE-ON-ONE To facilitate individual progress monitoring, assess some children on Day 4 and the rest on Day 5. While individual children are being assessed, the rest of the class can practice writing the letters *Ff, Gg, Hh, Ii, Jj, Kk, Ll, Mm,* and *Nn,* or they can look for examples of those letters in this week's books.

LETTER READING Use the letter list on reproducible p. 195 to assess each child's ability to name the letters *Ff, Gg, Hh, Ii, Jj, Kk, Ll, Mm,* and *Nn.* We're going to name the letters in each row. I will do the first one. The first letter is uppercase *F.* For each child, record any problems.

WORD READING Use the word list on reproducible p. 195 to assess each child's ability to read high-frequency words. Have each child read the words aloud.

RECORD SCORES Monitor children's accuracy by recording their scores using the Letter and Word Reading Chart for this unit in *First Stop.*

Name ___________________________

Name the Letters

F	g	G	M	H	i
L	f	j	h	K	l
k	N	I	m	J	n

Read the Words

am ☐

I ☐

Copyright © Savvas Learning Company LLC. All Rights Reserved.

Note to Teacher: Children name each letter. Children read the words.

Scoring for Name the Letters/Read the Words: Score 1 point for each correct letter/word.

Letter Recognition (*Ff, Gg, Hh, Ii, Jj, Kk, Ll, Mm, Nn*) ______ /__18__

High-Frequency Words (*am, I*) ______ /__2__

MONITOR PROGRESS

- Letters *Ff, Gg, Hh, Ii, Jj, Kk, Ll, Mm, Nn*
- High-Frequency Words

Common Core State Standards

Speaking/Listening 2. Confirm understanding of a text read aloud or information presented orally or through other media by asking and answering questions about key details and requesting clarification if something is not understood. **Also Informational Text 1., 2., 3., 7.**

Let's Practice It!

Expository Text

- Listen to the selection.
- What is this selection about?
- How are the two flags alike? How are they different?
- Why does the U.S. flag have 13 stripes?
- What do the 50 stars on the U.S. flag stand for?

The United States Flag

First U.S. Flag

U.S. Flag Today

50

51

My Skills Buddy, pp. 50–51

Common Core State Standards

Informational Text 1. With prompting and support, ask and answer questions about key details in a text. **Speaking/Listening 2.** Confirm understanding of a text read aloud or information presented orally or through other media by asking and answering questions about key details and requesting clarification if something is not understood. **Also Informational Text 2., 3., 7.**

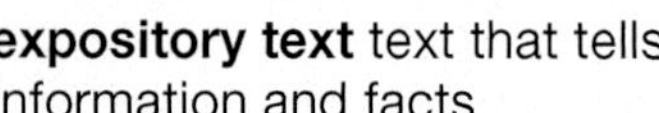

Academic Vocabulary

expository text text that tells information and facts

Let's Practice It!

Expository Text

TEACH Today you will listen to an expository text about the United States flag. An **expository text** tells information about a topic. Review the features of an expository text with children.

- An expository text gives information and facts about a topic.
- An expository text gives details about a topic.

Have children turn to pp. 50–51 of *My Skills Buddy.* I am going to read information about the United States flag. Look at the pictures. What details can you tell me about the flag? Look at the pictures as I read. Read the text of "The United States Flag." As you read, direct children to look at the appropriate picture.

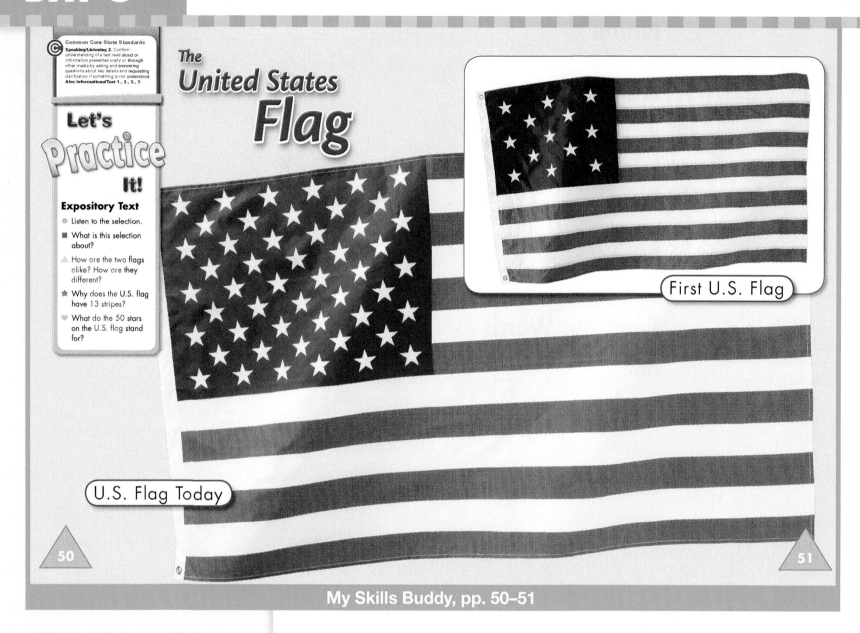

GUIDE PRACTICE Discuss the features of an expository text and the bulleted text on p. 50 of *My Skills Buddy* with children.

- An expository text gives information and facts about a topic. What is the topic of this expository text? (the United States flag)
- An expository text gives details about a topic. What details did you learn about the United States flag from what I read? (Leaders wanted to add a stripe and star for each state, but the flag would be too big.)
- Sometimes when we read an expository text, we think of more things we want to know. What questions do you have about the United States flag? (Why are the colors red, white, and blue?)

Teacher Read Aloud

The United States Flag

Every country has a flag. A flag is a piece of cloth usually shaped like a rectangle. A flag may be several colors. It often has a picture or design on it. A country's flag stands for the country. When people see the flag, they think about their country.

When the United States became a country, it needed a flag. Leaders decided the flag would have 13 stripes, seven red and six white. The flag would also have 13 white stars in a blue box. There would be one stripe and one star for each of the 13 states in the new country. Then a new stripe and a new star would be added each time a new state joined the country.

But a new stripe for each new state was not a good idea. Soon the flag would be too big! So leaders decided the U.S. flag would always have 13 stripes, one for each of the first 13 states. The flag would also have one star for each state.

Today the U.S. flag has 13 stripes and 50 stars.

Writing to Sources

Use Connect the Texts on pp. 12–13 to guide children in writing text-based responses using two sources.

Access for All

 Advanced

Practice Retelling Have children use the pictures on pp. 50–51 of *My Skills Buddy* to retell a new fact they learned about the United States flag.

Visual and Contextual Support To confirm their understanding, have children use evidence from the pictures and from what they heard in the Read Aloud to answer specific questions about the U.S. flag.

Common Core State Standards

Literature 3. With prompting and support, identify characters, settings, and major events in a story.

Assess

Identify setting.

Assessment

Monitor Progress

REVIEW SETTING When we read a story, we think about where the story happens and when the story happens. Where and when the story takes place is called the setting.

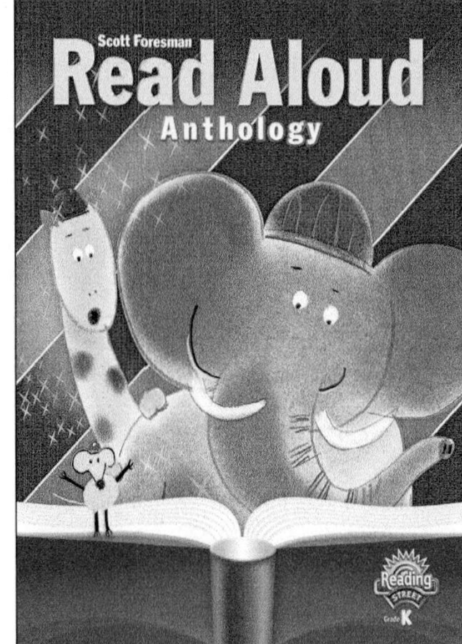

Read Aloud Anthology

READ "MR. SPUFFINGTON FIXES IT HIMSELF" Tell children that you are going to read a story called "Mr. Spuffington Fixes It Himself." Listen carefully while I read you a story. When I am done, I will ask you to tell me about the setting, or where and when the story takes place. Read "Mr. Spuffington Fixes It Himself" on p. 3 of *Read Aloud Anthology.*

CHECK SETTING After you read the story, ask children to tell where the story happens.

- Where does the story take place? (in Mr. Spuffington's bathroom)
- What clues in the story tell you this? (Mr. Spuffington is fixing his bathroom door. He breaks a faucet in the sink.)

Corrective feedback	**If...** a child cannot identify the setting of the story, **then...** reteach setting using the Reteach lesson in *First Stop.*

ASSESS SETTING Use the blackline master on p. 199. Make one copy for each child. Have children color the picture that shows the setting of "Mr. Spuffington Fixes It Himself."

Name ______________________________

Setting

Note to Teacher: Have children color the picture that shows where "Mr. Spuffington Fixes It Himself" takes place.

Copyright © Savvas Learning Company LLC. All Rights Reserved.

MONITOR PROGRESS

- Setting

Common Core State Standards

Writing 2. Use a combination of drawing, dictating, and writing to compose informative/explanatory texts in which they name what they are writing about and supply some information about the topic. **Language 1.a.** Print many upper- and lowercase letters. **Also Writing 7., 8., Speaking/Listening 1., Language 2.**

Access for All

Advanced

Conventions Have children say names for other children in the class. Then have them identify the letters in the names.

Daily Fix-It

i help sam rake leaves.

I help Sam rake leaves.

This week's practice sentences appear on *Teacher Resources DVD-ROM.*

Conventions

Review **Write Our Names**

REVIEW Remind children of what they learned about names. Every person has a name. When we write someone's name, we begin the name with an uppercase letter. What kind of letter do we write at the beginning of a person's name?

MODEL Melvin is a character in the story *Melvin.* I'm going to write Melvin's name on the board. Write *Melvin* on the board. What letter did I begin Melvin's name with? I know that names always begin with uppercase letters.

GUIDE PRACTICE Give each child a name tag. Ask children to write their name on their name tag and decorate it any way they like. Have children wear their name tags on their clothing.

ON THEIR OWN Have children walk around the class and introduce themselves to other children using this sentence frame: *Hi! My name is* _______. Then have each child point to his or her name tag and tell the letters in his or her name.

This Week We...

REVIEW Display *We Are So Proud!,* Sing with Me Chart 2B, Phonics Songs and Rhymes Chart 2, Decodable Reader 2 from *My Skills Buddy,* Kindergarten Student Reader K.1.2, and Get Set, Roll! Reader 2. This week we talked about how children work and play together. We read new books, and we sang new songs. Which book or song was your favorite? Let's share our ideas with each other.

Team Talk Pair children and have them take turns telling which book or song was their favorite and why.

MODEL Today we will make a list of things we can do when we work together. I know sharing ideas is important when children work together on a project. I will write *share ideas* on the list.

Working Together

1. share ideas

GUIDE PRACTICE Continue the list with children. Then read through the list.

Working Together

1. share ideas	**3. ask for help**
2. take turns	**4. be nice**

ON THEIR OWN Have children write or dictate a sentence about one of the ideas on the list. Display their sentences in the classroom as a reminder of ways they work together.

Daily Handwriting

Write uppercase *F* and *G* and lowercase *f* and *g* on the board. Review correct letter formation with children.

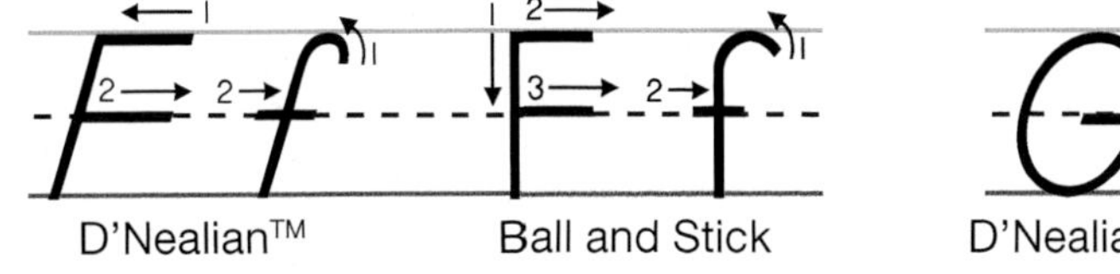

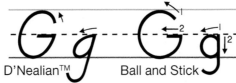

D'Nealian™ Ball and Stick

Have children write a row of uppercase *F* and *G* and a row of lowercase *f* and *g* on their Write-On Boards. Remind them to use proper left-to-right and top-to-bottom progression.

Bridge to Common Core

RESEARCH TO BUILD AND PRESENT KNOWLEDGE

When children work together to write a list of ideas, they are learning to participate in a shared writing project, recalling information from their experiences, and demonstrating their understanding of the subject.

Poster Preview Encourage children to look ahead to next week by previewing ELL Poster 3. Read the Poster Talk-Through to introduce the concept and vocabulary. Ask children to identify and describe objects and actions in the art.

Common Core State Standards

Literature 3. With prompting and support, identify characters, settings, and major events in a story.

Wrap Up Your Week!

Working and Playing Together at School

How do school children work and play together?

ILLUSTRATE SETTING This week we talked about how children can work and play together. We work and play together in this classroom. The classroom is our setting.

- Make a word web like the one shown and fill it with children's responses that describe the classroom.

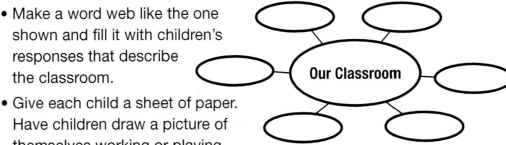

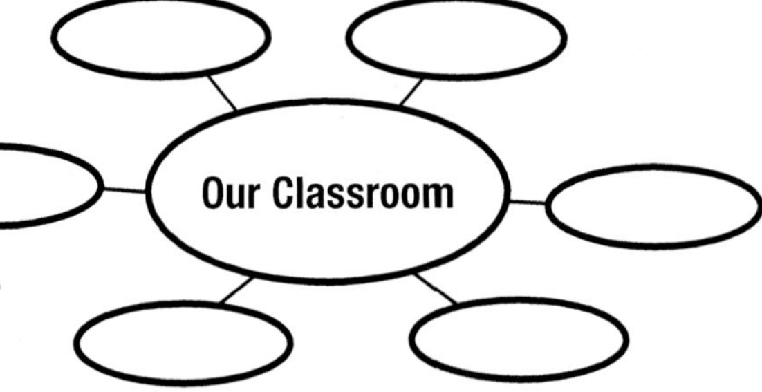

- Give each child a sheet of paper. Have children draw a picture of themselves working or playing together in the classroom. Remind them to include things that will help identify the setting as a classroom.
- Have children write or dictate a word or phrase about their picture.

Amazing Words

You've learned 006 words this week!

You've learned 012 words this year!

Next Week's Concept

Families Living, Working, and Playing Together

How do families cooperate?

Discuss next week's question. Help children make the connection between cooperating with friends and cooperating with family.

Tell children that next week they will read about a girl who has a very special toy.

Preview Next Week

Extend Your Day!

Science
Observe Effects of Weather

MATERIALS: pictures showing different types of weather conditions

IDENTIFY WEATHER CONDITIONS In the story *We Are So Proud!,* the children march in a parade. What kind of weather is good for a parade?

Display pictures that show a variety of weather conditions. Discuss the pictures with children. Name the type of weather and identify the clues in the picture that tell about the weather condition.

MAKE A COMPARISON CHART Make a four-column chart on chart paper. Label the four columns *Hot Weather, Cold Weather, Rainy Weather,* and *Snowy Weather.* In the appropriate column, write words or phrases that describe things associated with each type of weather. Have children use the information in the chart to draw a picture for each type of weather.

Weather Conditions

hot weather	cold weather	rainy weather	snowy weather
wearing bathing suit	wearing hat and gloves	using umbrellas	snow-covered trees and ground
swimming in a lake	skating outside	standing in a doorway	people skiing and sledding
sitting in the shade		wearing boots	people wearing hats, gloves, and snow pants
		lots of puddles	

Comprehension
Compare Settings

MATERIALS: Big Books *The Little School Bus* and *We Are So Proud!*

WHERE DO THE STORIES TAKE PLACE? Remind children that we think about when and where a story happens as we read. Have children compare the time, place, and weather in *The Little School Bus* and in *We Are So Proud!* Help them write sentences describing when and where the events in each story happen.

Vocabulary
Going Up or Down?

MATERIALS: colored game cards, game markers

USE DIRECTIONAL WORDS Make game cards by coloring each of 6 squares in a row a different color. Give each child a game card and a marker. Give directions such as these: Place your marker on the green square. Move your marker up 3 squares. Move your marker down 4 squares. What color are you on? Children who are on the correct color score a point.

Assessment Checkpoints for the Week

Weekly Assessment

Use the whole-class assessment on pages 194–195 and 198–199 in this Teacher's Edition to check:

- ✔ **Letters *Ff, Gg, Hh, Ii, Jj, Kk, Ll, Mm, Nn***
- ✔ **Comprehension** *Setting*
- ✔ **High-Frequency Words**

I	*am*

Managing Assessment

Use the Assessment Handbook for:

- ✔ **Observation Checklists**
- ✔ **Record-Keeping Forms**
- ✔ **Portfolio Assessment**

Assessment Handbook

TEACHER NOTES

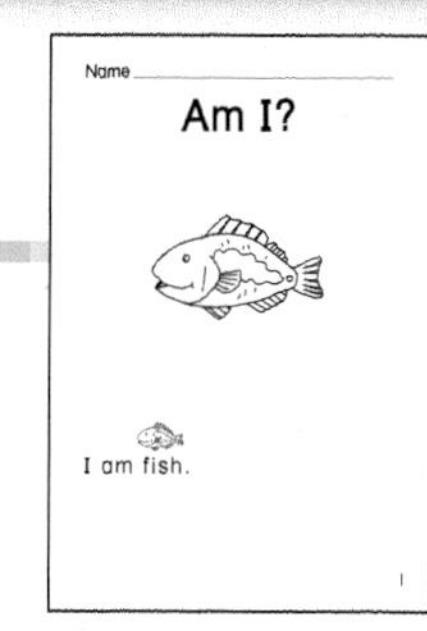

DAY 1 Differentiate Letter Recognition

- Letters *Ff* and *Gg*
  - Decodable Story
  - Advanced Selection "Let's Get a Pet"

DAY 2 Differentiate Letter Recognition

- Letters *Hh* and *Ii*
  - Decodable Reader

DAY 3 Differentiate Vocabulary

- Develop Vocabulary: Color Words
- Kindergarten Student Reader

DAY 4 Differentiate Language

- Develop Language
- Get Set, Roll! Reader

DAY 5 Differentiate Letter Recognition/ Close Reading

- Letters *Jj, Kk, Ll, Mm, Nn*
  - "Gadget Is Gone!"

Place English Language Learners in the groups that correspond to their reading abilities.
If... children need scaffolding and practice,
then... use the ELL notes on the page.

Independent Practice

Independent Practice Stations

See pp. 116 and 117 for Independent Stations.

Reading Street Digital Path

Independent Practice Activities available in the Digital Path.

Independent Reading

See p. 117 for independent reading suggestions.

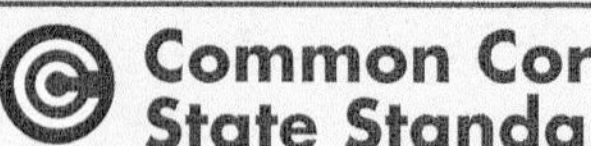

On-Level

Common Core State Standards

Literature 1. With prompting and support, ask and answer questions about key details in a text. **Literature 10.** Actively engage in group reading activities with purpose and understanding. **Foundational Skills 1.d.** Recognize and name all upper- and lowercase letters of the alphabet. **Foundational Skills 2.b.** Count, pronounce, blend, and segment syllables in spoken words. **Foundational Skills 3.c.** Read common high-frequency words by sight (e.g., *the, of, to, you, she, my, is, are, do, does*).

1 Build Word Knowledge

Practice Phonological Awareness

IDENTIFY SYLLABLES Display the *astronaut* Picture Card and ask a volunteer to name the picture. Then have children say the picture name as they clap the number of syllables in the word: *as-tro-naut.* Continue with these Picture Cards: *drum, fan, hippopotamus, jet, yard, umbrella, wagon, mitten, dog, bubble.*

Practice Letter Recognition

RECOGNIZE LETTERS *Ff* AND *Gg* Display the *Ff* and *Gg* Alphabet Cards. Have children identify the letters and pictures. Then write the letter *f* on chart paper. Have a child write the letter and say the letter name. Continue with the other letters until everyone has had a turn to identify a letter.

2 Read

Decodable Story 2 *Am I?*

READ Have children read the story. Then have them reread the text to develop automaticity.

HIGH-FREQUENCY WORDS Have children return to the text and identify the high-frequency words *I* and *am.* Help children demonstrate their understanding of these words by completing sentence frames such as these: _______ _______ *a student.* (I, am) _______ _______ *reading a story.* (I, am)

3 Reread for Fluency

Have children reread the Decodable Story *Am I?* individually to develop fluency.

Independent Reading Options

Trade Book Library

eStreet Interactive
www.ReadingStreet.com

Teacher's Guides available on the Leveled Reader Database.

On-Level

1 Build Word Knowledge

Practice Letter Recognition

RECOGNIZE LETTERS *Hh* AND *Ii* Show the *Hh* Alphabet Card. Point to each letter. This is uppercase *H.* This is lowercase *h.* Write the letters on chart paper. Call on volunteers to write the letters. Repeat for *Ii.* Then point to letters in random order and have children name them.

Practice High-Frequency Words

READ AND USE Write the high-frequency words *I* and *am* on several cards, one word on each card. Give the cards to children. Ask each child to read the word, show the card to the group, and use the word in a sentence. Gather the cards and hand them out again.

2 Read

Decodable Reader 2 *Am I?*

CONCEPTS OF PRINT Display Decodable Reader 2 in *My Skills Buddy.* Show children the illustrations and read aloud the title. What do you think the story is about?

READ Have children take turns reading the Decodable Reader. Pause at the end of each page to ask questions. Who is this? What is [child's name] doing?

3 Reread for Fluency

Have children reread the Decodable Reader *Am I?* individually to develop fluency.

STREET INTERACTIVE
www.ReadingStreet.com
Savvas eText
• Student Edition
Teacher Resources
• Reader's and Writer's Notebook

SMALL GROUP TIME

More Reading for Group Time

CONCEPT LITERACY

- Concept Words
- High-Frequency Words

Use these suggested readers or other text at children's instructional level.

STREET INTERACTIVE
www.ReadingStreet.com

Use the Leveled Reader Database for lesson plans and student pages for *I Help.*

If... children need more scaffolding and practice with phonological awareness and letter recognition,
then... use the activities on p. DI•29 in the Teacher Resources section of the Digital Path.

Common Core State Standards

Literature 1. With prompting and support, ask and answer questions about key details in a text. **Literature 10.** Actively engage in group reading activities with purpose and understanding. **Foundational Skills 3.c.** Read common high-frequency words by sight (e.g., *the, of, to, you, she, my, is, are, do, does*). **Language 5.a.** Sort common objects into categories (e.g., shapes, foods) to gain a sense of the concepts the categories represent. **Language 5.c.** Identify real-life connections between words and their use (e.g., note places at school that are *colorful*). **Language 6.** Use words and phrases acquired through conversations, reading and being read to, and responding to texts.

1 Build Word Knowledge

Develop Vocabulary

COLOR WORDS Have children return to p. 48 in *My Skills Buddy.* Review the color words *red, white,* and *blue.* Have children point to each color swatch and read the word. Ask them questions about the other pictures. What color is the fish? the star? the apple? Then have children take turns pointing to objects in the classroom or articles of clothing that are red, white, or blue. Ask them to tell about the object or clothing using the color word. For example, *Maya's shirt is red. The chart paper is white. My jeans are blue.*

Team Talk Have children work with a partner to use the color words in sentences.

2 Read

Kindergarten Student Reader *Cat and Dog Work*

REREAD Display the reader and have children tell the title of the story. Have them tell what they remember about the story. Then have children read the story chorally. After reading each page, ask children to tell what they see. Who is in the picture? Who is working? What kind of work are they doing? To check children's understanding, have them take turns reading the story to a partner and then retelling the story to the partner.

On-Level

1 Build Word Knowledge

Develop Language

Display the Big Book *We Are So Proud!* and read the text on pp. 2–3.

We've planned a grand parade,
a super celebration.
Our school and all our classes
will honor this great nation.
I am so proud!

- Ask children to read the text with you as you track the print.
- Point to the line, *We've planned a grand parade.*
- What does the word *grand* mean here? (big and fine-looking) What is another word that could be used in place of *grand?* Why do you think the author used the word *grand?*
- Let's try some other words in place of *grand* and see how they sound.
- Continue the routine with the words *super* and *great.* Point out that in these sentences, *super* and *great* have almost the same meaning and that children's suggested words can likely be used in place of either word.

2 Read

Get Set, Roll! Reader 2 *Melvin*

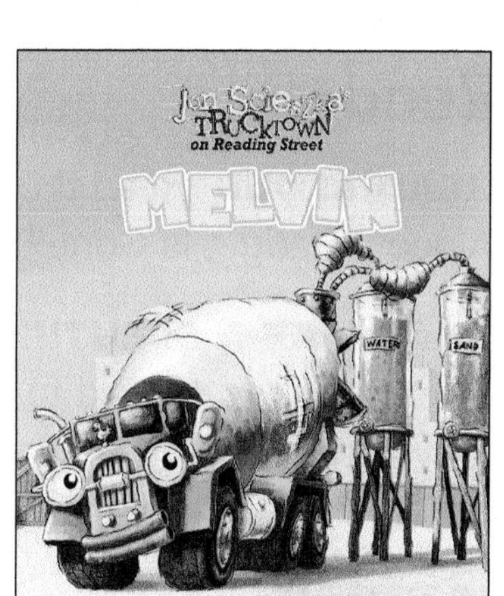

REVIEW HIGH-FREQUENCY WORDS Review the following high-frequency words with children: *I, am.* Ask them to use each word in a sentence.

REVIEW REBUS WORDS Distribute Letter Tiles to each child or use Letter Tile Drag and Drop in the Digital Path. Write the name *Melvin* on a card. This is the name *Melvin.* The letters in *Melvin* are *M, e, l, v, i, n.* Use your letters to build this word. What does this spell? Which character is Melvin? Continue the routine with the following words: *worried, glad.*

REREAD Have children whisper read *Melvin* as you listen to each child. Then have children take turns reading the story aloud.

SMALL GROUP TIME

ELL

If... children need more scaffolding and practice with vocabulary, **then...** use the ELL activities on p. DI•31 in the Teacher Resources section of the Digital Path.

On-Level

Common Core State Standards

Literature 1. With prompting and support, ask and answer questions about key details in a text. **Literature 10.** Actively engage in group reading activities with purpose and understanding. **Foundational Skills 1.d.** Recognize and name all upper- and lowercase letters of the alphabet.

1 Build Word Knowledge

Practice Letter Recognition

RECOGNIZE LETTERS *Jj, Kk, Ll, Mm, Nn* Display the *Jj, Kk, Ll, Mm,* and *Nn* Alphabet Cards. Have children identify the letters as you say the letter names. Write a mixture of these uppercase and lowercase letters on chart paper. Ask children to find the letter you name and circle it. Continue until all the letters have been circled.

REVIEW LETTERS *Ff–Nn* Draw the following letter grid on a sheet of paper and give each child a copy. First have children point to and name the letters. Then have them match uppercase and lowercase forms by coloring each letter pair a different color.

f	i	l	H	k	G
L	K	g	N	m	n
J	h	M	j	F	I

Corrective feedback	**If...** children have difficulty naming letters, **then...** review the letter names using the Alphabet Cards.

2 Text-Based Comprehension

Read

READ ALOUD Read the Reading Street Sleuth Read Aloud, "Gadget Is Gone!" on p. SG•25 to children.

READ LIKE A SLEUTH! Encourage children to cite evidence from the text to support their answers. You may wish to reread sections of the text to verify children's answers.

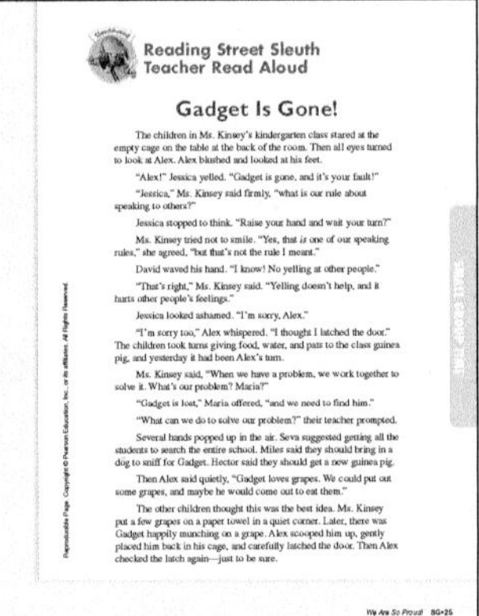

Reading Street Sleuth
Teacher Read Aloud

Gadget Is Gone!

The children in Ms. Kinsey's kindergarten class stared at the empty cage on the table at the back of the room. Then all eyes turned to look at Alex. Alex blushed and looked at his feet.

"Alex!" Jessica yelled. "Gadget is gone, and it's your fault!"

"Jessica," Ms. Kinsey said firmly, "what is our rule about speaking to others?"

Jessica stopped to think. "Raise your hand and wait your turn?"

Ms. Kinsey tried not to smile. "Yes, that *is* one of our speaking rules," she agreed, "but that's not the rule I meant."

David waved his hand. "I know! No yelling at other people."

"That's right," Ms. Kinsey said. "Yelling doesn't help, and it hurts other people's feelings."

Jessica looked ashamed. "I'm sorry, Alex."

"I'm sorry too," Alex whispered. "I thought I latched the door." The children took turns giving food, water, and pats to the class guinea pig, and yesterday it had been Alex's turn.

Ms. Kinsey said, "When we have a problem, we work together to solve it. What's our problem? Maria?"

"Gadget is lost," Maria offered, "and we need to find him."

"What can we do to solve our problem?" their teacher prompted.

Several hands popped up in the air. Seva suggested getting all the students to search the entire school. Miles said they should bring in a dog to sniff for Gadget. Hector said they should get a new guinea pig.

Then Alex said quietly, "Gadget loves grapes. We could put out some grapes, and maybe he would come out to eat them."

The other children thought this was the best idea. Ms. Kinsey put a few grapes on a paper towel in a quiet corner. Later, there was Gadget happily munching on a grape. Alex scooped him up, gently placed him back in his cage, and carefully latched the door. Then Alex checked the latch again—just to be sure.

Reproducible Page Copyright © Pearson Education, Inc., or its affiliates. All Rights Reserved.

We Are So Proud! SG•25

Look for Evidence How does Gadget get out of his cage? How do the children get Gadget back into his cage?

Ask Questions What questions about Gadget do you wish the author had answered?

Prove It! Performance Task Have children draw a picture of what the characters in the story do to get Gadget to come out of hiding. Ask children to label the picture with one or two key details from the text. Children may write or dictate a short phrase or sentence.

Gadget Is Gone!

The children in Ms. Kinsey's kindergarten class stared at the empty cage on the table at the back of the room. Then all eyes turned to look at Alex. Alex blushed and looked at his feet.

"Alex!" Jessica yelled. "Gadget is gone, and it's your fault!"

"Jessica," Ms. Kinsey said firmly, "what is our rule about speaking to others?"

Jessica stopped to think. "Raise your hand and wait your turn?"

Ms. Kinsey tried not to smile. "Yes, that *is* one of our speaking rules," she agreed, "but that's not the rule I meant."

David waved his hand. "I know! No yelling at other people."

"That's right," Ms. Kinsey said. "Yelling doesn't help, and it hurts other people's feelings."

Jessica looked ashamed. "I'm sorry, Alex."

"I'm sorry too," Alex whispered. "I thought I latched the door." The children took turns giving food, water, and pats to the class guinea pig, and yesterday it had been Alex's turn.

Ms. Kinsey said, "When we have a problem, we work together to solve it. What's our problem? Maria?"

"Gadget is lost," Maria offered, "and we need to find him."

"What can we do to solve our problem?" their teacher prompted.

Several hands popped up in the air. Seva suggested getting all the students to search the entire school. Miles said they should bring in a dog to sniff for Gadget. Hector said they should get a new guinea pig.

Then Alex said quietly, "Gadget loves grapes. We could put out some grapes, and maybe he would come out to eat them."

The other children thought this was the best idea. Ms. Kinsey put a few grapes on a paper towel in a quiet corner. Later, there was Gadget happily munching on a grape. Alex scooped him up, gently placed him back in his cage, and carefully latched the door. Then Alex checked the latch again—just to be sure.

Reproducible Page. Copyright © Pearson Education, Inc., or its affiliates. All Rights Reserved.

Strategic Intervention

Common Core State Standards

Literature 1. With prompting and support, ask and answer questions about key details in a text. **Literature 10.** Actively engage in group reading activities with purpose and understanding. **Foundational Skills 1.d.** Recognize and name all upper- and lowercase letters of the alphabet. **Foundational Skills 2.b.** Count, pronounce, blend, and segment syllables in spoken words. **Foundational Skills 3.c.** Read common high-frequency words by sight (e.g., *the, of, to, you, she, my, is, are, do, does*).

More Reading for Group Time

LISTEN TO ME READER

- Concepts of Print

Use these suggested readers or other text at children's instructional level.

eStreet Interactive
www.ReadingStreet.com

Use the Leveled Reader Database to access an online version of *Let's Count!*

If... children need more scaffolding and practice with phonological awareness and letter recognition, then... use the Phonics Transition lessons beginning on p. 447 in the *ELL Handbook.*

1 Build Word Knowledge

Reteach Phonological Awareness

LISTEN FOR SYLLABLES Explain to children that words have parts called *syllables.* When you say a word, you can listen for the number of parts, or syllables. You can count the syllables by clapping once for each syllable. I will say a word and clap once for each syllable. Say the word *cat* and clap one time. How many times did I clap? (one) How many syllables does the word *cat* have? (one) When I said *cat,* I clapped one time, so *cat* has one syllable. Repeat with the words *kitten, dog, and puppy.*

Reteach Letter Recognition

RECOGNIZE LETTERS *Ff* AND *Gg* Prepare several sets of letter cards with *F, f, G,* or *g* on each card. Place the cards in a box. Have a child take a card, say the letter name, and write the letter on chart paper. The other children can write the letter in the air. Continue the activity until all the cards are used.

2 Read

Decodable Story 2 *Am I?*

REVIEW HIGH-FREQUENCY WORDS Review the previously taught high-frequency words *am* and *I* by having children read each word as you point to it on the Word Wall. Then say one of the words and have children repeat the word with you.

Corrective feedback	**If...** children have difficulty reading the high-frequency words, **then...** say a word and have children point to the word. Repeat several times, giving assistance as needed.

READ Have children read the story.

3 Reread for Fluency

Have children reread the story *Am I?* chorally. Then have them reread the story several times individually to develop fluency.

1 Build Word Knowledge

Reteach Phonological Awareness

PRACTICE SYLLABLES Remind children that words have parts called *syllables.* We can hear the syllables of a word when we say the word. We can count the syllables by clapping once for each syllable we hear. Model clapping twice as you say *carrot: car-rot.* I clapped twice when I said *carrot,* so *carrot* has two syllables. Now I will say a word and I want you to tell me how many syllables you hear. Use these words: *apple, pear, broccoli, pizza, hamburger, grape.*

Reteach Letter Recognition

RECOGNIZE LETTERS *Hh* AND *Ii* Give each child two long paper strips, one short paper strip, and one paper dot. Display the *Hh* Alphabet Card. Point to *H.* What is the name of this letter? Have children make the letter *H* with their paper strips. Continue with the letters *h, I,* and *i.*

Reteach High-Frequency Words

REVIEW Write *am* on chart paper. This is the word *am.* Name the letters with me: *a, m, am.* Continue with *I.*

Corrective feedback	**If...** children have difficulty reading the words, **then...** say a word and have children point to the word. Repeat several times, giving assistance as needed.

2 Read

Decodable Reader 2 *Am I?*

CONCEPTS OF PRINT Display Decodable Reader 2 in *My Skills Buddy.* The title of this story is *Am I?* The author is George Helm. The illustrator is Tori Wheaton. Look at the picture on the cover. Look at the pictures inside. What do you think the story is about?

READ Let's read the story together. After reading chorally with children, have them reread the story several times with a partner and then independently.

SMALL GROUP TIME

Independent Reading Options

Trade Book Library

eStreet Interactive
www.ReadingStreet.com

Teacher's Guides available on the Leveled Reader Database.

If... children need more support with letter recognition,
then... use the ELL activities on p. DI•29 in the Teacher Resources section of the Digital Path.

Common Core State Standards

Literature 1. With prompting and support, ask and answer questions about key details in a text. **Literature 10.** Actively engage in group reading activities with purpose and understanding. **Foundational Skills 3.c.** Read common high-frequency words by sight (e.g., *the, of, to, you, she, my, is, are, do, does*). **Language 5.a.** Sort common objects into categories (e.g., shapes, foods) to gain a sense of the concepts the categories represent. **Language 5.c.** Identify real-life connections between words and their use (e.g., note places at school that are *colorful*). **Language 6.** Use words and phrases acquired through conversations, reading and being read to, and responding to texts.

1 Build Word Knowledge

Develop Vocabulary

RETEACH COLOR WORDS Have children return to p. 48 of *My Skills Buddy* to review the color words *red, white,* and *blue.*

- Is the dog red or white?
- Is the flower blue or red?
- Which is white—the star or the ball?
- Which is blue—the apple or the fish?

Write the words *red, white,* and *blue* on index cards. Ask children to use the cards to label objects in the classroom that are those colors.

2 Read

Kindergarten Student Reader *Cat and Dog Work*

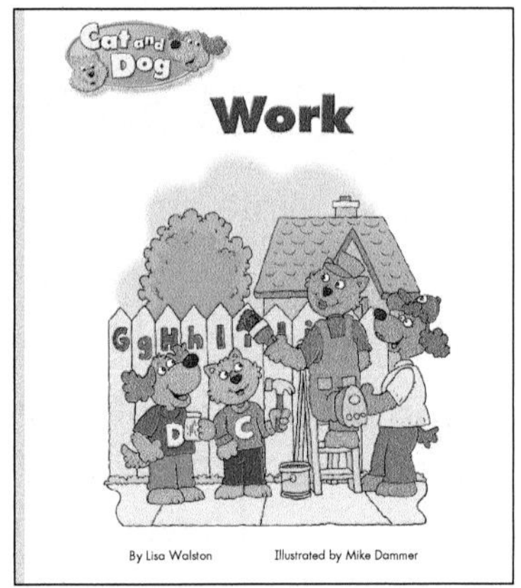

REVIEW REBUS WORDS Write *Cat* on chart paper. This is the word *Cat.* Name the letters with me: *C, a, t.* Repeat with the other rebus words *Dog, Mom, hammering, painting,* and *happy.*

REVIEW HIGH-FREQUENCY WORDS Write *I* on chart paper. Ask children to read the word with you. Have a volunteer read the word. Continue with the other high-frequency word *am.*

REREAD STORY Display the reader. The title of this book is *Cat and Dog Work.* What do you think the story is about? Read the story chorally with children. Pause at the end of each page to ask: Whom do you see? What are they doing? Who is talking? Have children reread the story several times to build fluency.

If... children need more scaffolding and practice with vocabulary, **then...** use the ELL activities on p. DI•31 in the Teacher Resources section of the Digital Path.

STREET INTERACTIVE
www.ReadingStreet.com

Savvas eText
- Student Edition
- Kindergarten Student Reader
- Get Set, Roll! Reader

1 Build Word Knowledge

Develop Language

Display the Big Book *We Are So Proud!* and read the text on pp. 2–3.

We've planned a grand parade,
a super celebration.
Our school and all our classes
will honor this great nation.
I am so proud!

- Ask children to read the text with you as you track the print.
- Point to the line, *We've planned a grand parade.*
- What does the word *grand* mean? What does *a grand parade* look like? What is another word that means almost the same thing as *grand?*
- I am going to say some words. I want you to tell me which word means almost the same thing as *grand: fast, sad, large, small, cheap.*
- Continue the routine with the word *proud.*

2 Read

Get Set, Roll! Reader 2 *Melvin*

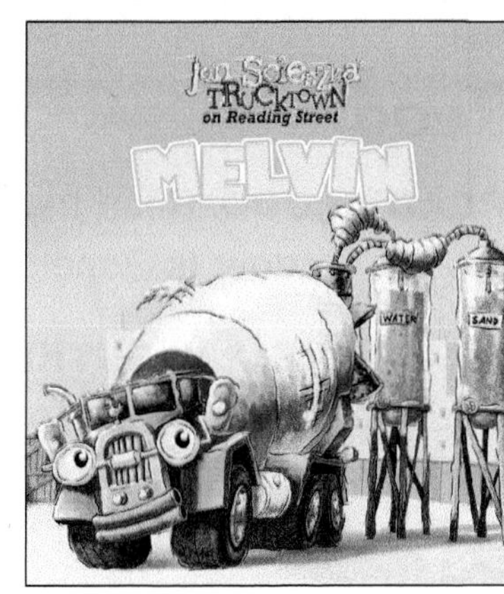

REVIEW HIGH-FREQUENCY AND REBUS WORDS Review the high-frequency and rebus words (*I, am, glad, worried, Melvin*) using the following routine.

1. Display and read the word.
2. Name the letters in the word.
3. Read the word. Use it in a sentence.

REREAD Have children chorally read aloud *Melvin* several times. Then ask them to take turns reading a page aloud.

SMALL GROUP TIME

Independent Reading Options

Trade Book Library

STREET INTERACTIVE
www.ReadingStreet.com

Teacher's Guides available on the Leveled Reader Database.

Common Core State Standards

Literature 1. With prompting and support, ask and answer questions about key details in a text. **Literature 10.** Actively engage in group reading activities with purpose and understanding. **Foundational Skills 1.d.** Recognize and name all upper- and lowercase letters of the alphabet.

1 Build Word Knowledge

Reteach Letter Recognition

RECOGNIZE LETTERS *Jj, Kk, Ll, Mm, Nn* Write an uppercase *J* on chart paper. Have children name the letter. This is uppercase *J.* What does lowercase *j* look like? Have a volunteer write a lowercase *j* next to the *J.* Continue the routine with *Kk, Ll, Mm,* and *Nn.* Then say letter names and have children point to the correct letters.

REVIEW LETTERS *Ff–Nn* Write the uppercase and lowercase letters *Ff* through *Nn* on index cards. Mix the cards and place them face up on a tabletop. First have children match the uppercase and lowercase forms of the letters. Then have children put the pairs of letters in alphabetical order.

Corrective feedback	**If...** children have difficulty with matching or alphabetical order, **then...** place the *Ff–Nn* Alphabet Cards in order on the chalk ledge for children to refer to.

2 Text-Based Comprehension

Read

READ ALOUD Read the Reading Street Sleuth Read Aloud, "Gadget Is Gone!" on p. SG•25 to children.

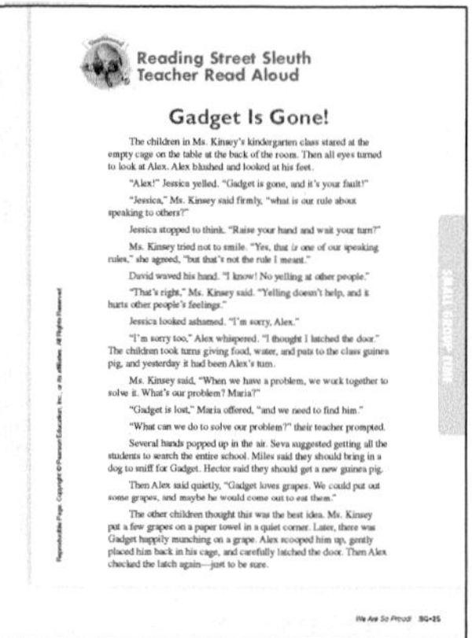
Reading Street Sleuth
Teacher Read Aloud

Gadget Is Gone!

The children in Ms. Kinsey's kindergarten class stared at the empty cage on the table at the back of the room. Then all eyes turned to look at Alex. Alex blushed and looked at his feet.

"Alex!" Jessica yelled. "Gadget is gone, and it's your fault!"

"Jessica," Ms. Kinsey said firmly, "what is our rule about speaking to others?"

Jessica stopped to think. "Raise your hand and wait your turn?"

Ms. Kinsey tried not to smile. "Yes, that *is* one of our speaking rules," she agreed, "but that's not the rule I meant."

David waved his hand. "I know! No yelling at other people."

"That's right," Ms. Kinsey said. "Yelling doesn't help, and it hurts other people's feelings."

Jessica looked ashamed. "I'm sorry, Alex."

"I'm sorry too," Alex whispered. "I thought I latched the door." The children took turns giving food, water, and pats to the class guinea pig, and yesterday it had been Alex's turn.

Ms. Kinsey said, "When we have a problem, we work together to solve it. What's our problem? Maria?"

"Gadget is lost," Maria offered, "and we need to find him."

"What can we do to solve our problem?" their teacher prompted.

Several hands popped up in the air. Seva suggested getting all the students to search the entire school. Miles said they should bring in a dog to sniff for Gadget. Hector said they should get a new guinea pig.

Then Alex said quietly, "Gadget loves grapes. We could put out some grapes, and maybe he would come out to eat them."

The other children thought this was the best idea. Ms. Kinsey put a few grapes on a paper towel in a quiet corner. Later, there was Gadget happily munching on a grape. Alex scooped him up, gently placed him back in his cage, and carefully latched the door. Then Alex checked the latch again—just to be sure.

We Are So Proud! SG•25

READ LIKE A SLEUTH! Encourage children to cite evidence from the text to support their answers. You may wish to reread sections of the text to verify children's answers.

Look for Evidence What problem do the children in Ms. Kinsey's class have? How do they solve the problem?

Ask Questions What questions would you ask the author about Gadget?

Prove It! Performance Task Have children draw a picture of what the characters in the story do to get Gadget to come out. Ask children to dictate a phrase or short sentence for the picture using one or two key details from the text. Read children's phrases or sentences to them as you track the print.

Advanced

1 Build Word Knowledge

Extend Letter Recognition

CONNECT *Ff* TO /f/ AND *Gg* TO /g/ Display the *Ff* Alphabet Card. Ask children to name the letters and identify the picture. Point to the letters *Ff* and say the picture name *fountain.* I am going to say a word. The word is *famous.* Do the words *fountain* and *famous* begin with the same sound? Say the words with me: *fountain, famous.* Because *fountain* and *famous* both begin with /f/, let's write the letter *f* in the air. Continue with these words: *feather, human, follow, funny, kitten, music, family, lemon.* Repeat the routine for *Gg* using these words: *goose, gallop, juicy, guitar, navy, good, gobble, metal, gather, ignore.*

2 Read

"Let's Get a Pet"

CONCEPTS OF PRINT Read aloud the title of the story, "Let's Get a Pet." Remember, the title of a story gives us clues to what the story is about. Ask children what the title tells them about the story. (The story is about one or more than one person getting a pet animal.)

Let's Get a Pet

I am Kim.
I am Kip.
We look for a pet.
See the tan cat, Kim.
We can get it.
See the little rat, Kip.
We can get it.
I like the cat!
I like the rat!
MOM!!
Kim, we can get the cat.
Kip, we can get the rat.

Advanced Phonics Selection 2

SG•32 All Together Now • Unit 1 • Week 2

TEACH STORY WORDS Present any story words that children may need help with, such as *see, look, tan, get, like,* and *for.* Use the words in sentences that give clues to their meanings. For example, I *see* a tree. I use my eyes to *see. Tan* is light brown. He wears *tan* pants.

READ Distribute copies of "Let's Get a Pet" from p. SG•32, and have children read it on their own. Then have them take turns reading the story aloud. After reading, have children tell whom the story is about and what happens.

SMALL GROUP TIME

More Reading for Group Time

INDEPENDENT READER

- More Challenging Text

Use the suggested Leveled Reader or other text at children's instructional level.

eStreet Interactive
www.ReadingStreet.com

Use the Leveled Reader Database for lesson plans and student pages for *Fun for Us.*

If... children need more practice with letter recognition,
then... use the Phonics Transition lessons beginning on p. 447 in the *ELL Handbook.*

Let's Get a Pet

I am Kim.
I am Kip.
We look for a pet.
See the tan cat, Kim.
We can get it.
See the little rat, Kip.
We can get it.
I like the cat!
I like the rat!
MOM!!
Kim, we can get the cat.
Kip, we can get the rat.

Reproducible Page. Copyright © Pearson Education, Inc., or its affiliates. All Rights Reserved.

Advanced Phonics Selection 2

Advanced

1 Build Word Knowledge

Extend Letter Recognition

 **CONNECT *Hh* TO /h/ AND *Ii* TO /i/** Display the *Hh* Alphabet Card. Ask children to name the letters and identify the picture. Point to the letters *Hh* and say the picture name *helicopter.* I am going to say a word. The word is *heavy.* Do the words *helicopter* and *heavy* begin with the same sound? Say the words with me: *helicopter, heavy.* Because *helicopter* and *heavy* both begin with /h/, let's write the letter *h* in the air. Continue with these words: *happy, fasten, hello, hurry, matter, lovely, hyena, gallon.* Repeat the routine for *Ii* using these words: *igloo, insect, jacket, image, ladder, inform, itchy, needle, iguana, kitchen.*

2 Read

Decodable Reader 2 *Am I?*

CONCEPTS OF PRINT Display Decodable Reader 2 in *My Skills Buddy.* Ask children to identify the author and illustrator.

READ Have children read the Decodable Reader quietly as you listen to them. Then have them take turns reading aloud one page at a time.

3 Reread for Fluency

Have children reread Decodable Reader 2 *Am I?* to develop fluency.

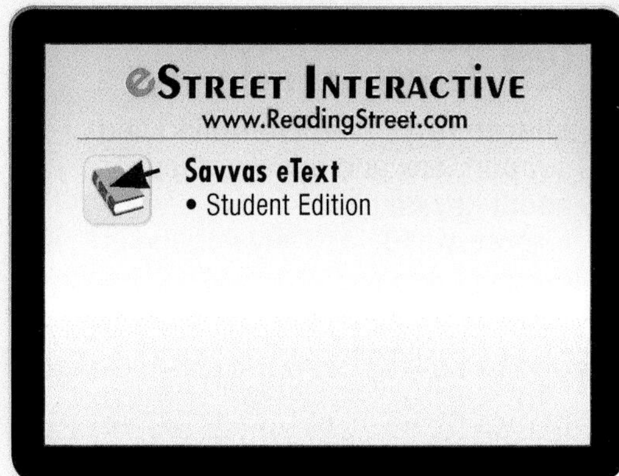

SMALL GROUP TIME

Independent Reading Options

Trade Book Library

Street Interactive
www.ReadingStreet.com

Teacher's Guides available on the Leveled Reader Database.

If... children need more support with letter recognition,
then... use the ELL activities on pp. DI•29, DI•32–DI•33 in the Teacher Resources section of the Digital Path.

Common Core State Standards

Literature 1. With prompting and support, ask and answer questions about key details in a text. **Literature 10.** Actively engage in group reading activities with purpose and understanding. **Foundational Skills 3.c.** Read common high-frequency words by sight (e.g., *the, of, to, you, she, my, is, are, do, does*). **Language 5.a.** Sort common objects into categories (e.g., shapes, foods) to gain a sense of the concepts the categories represent. **Language 5.c.** Identify real-life connections between words and their use (e.g., note places at school that are *colorful*). **Language 6.** Use words and phrases acquired through conversations, reading and being read to, and responding to texts.

1 Build Word Knowledge

Develop Vocabulary

COLOR WORDS Review the color words *red, white,* and *blue* with children. Have them use the words in sentences.

Let's learn more color words. Remember, we can use color words to describe what things look like. Have children identify the color words in these sentences.

- Sara named her *black* cat Midnight.
- We painted the kitchen walls *yellow.*
- The dancers wore shiny *green* outfits.

Team Talk Have children work in pairs to use *green, yellow,* and *black* in their own sentences. Ask them to draw a picture of something that is green, black, or yellow; color it; and write a phrase or sentence that includes the color word.

2 Read

Kindergarten Student Reader *Cat and Dog Work*

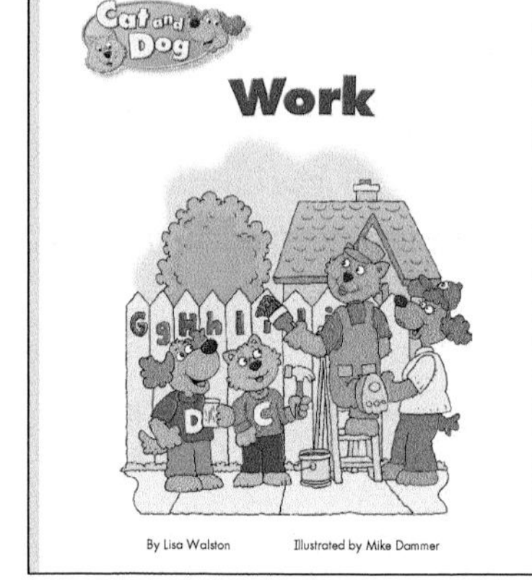

REREAD STORY Display the reader and have children read the title with you. Then have them read the story. Finally, have them reread the story aloud several times to build fluency.

EXTEND STORY Ask children to recall what the characters in the story are doing. What could happen next in the story? Encourage children to think of something Cat, Dog, and their moms might do to celebrate finishing the fence. Have children draw a picture and write a sentence to go with the picture.

ELL

If... children need more scaffolding and practice with vocabulary, **then...** use the ELL activities on p. DI•31 in the Teacher Resources section of the Digital Path.

Advanced

1 Build Word Knowledge

Develop Language

Display the Big Book *We Are So Proud!* and read the text on pp. 2–3.

We've planned a grand parade,
a super celebration.
Our school and all our classes
will honor this great nation.
I am so proud!

- Ask children to read the text with you as you track the print.
- Point to the line, *I am so proud!* Read this with me.
- What does the word *proud* mean? What is another word that has almost the same meaning as *proud*? Why did the author choose the word *proud*?
- Continue the routine with the words *grand, super,* and *great.*
- Team Talk Have children work with a partner to replace key words in a sentence with simpler words or synonyms without changing the meaning of the sentence. Use sentence frames, such as the following.

We've planned a ______ parade, a ______ celebration.

2 Read

Get Set, Roll! Reader 2 *Melvin*

REVIEW HIGH-FREQUENCY AND REBUS WORDS Review the high-frequency and rebus words by asking children to spell the words with Letter Tiles. (*I, am, glad, worried, Melvin*)

REREAD Have children whisper read *Melvin* as you listen to each child. Then have children take turns reading the story aloud.

3 Reread for Fluency

BUILD FLUENCY Have children read again with expression and accuracy. Encourage them to use self-correction techniques for any mistakes.

SMALL GROUP TIME

Independent Reading Options

Trade Book Library

eStreet Interactive
www.ReadingStreet.com
Teacher's Guides available on the Leveled Reader Database.

Advanced

Common Core State Standards

Literature 1. With prompting and support, ask and answer questions about key details in a text. **Literature 10.** Actively engage in group reading activities with purpose and understanding. **Foundational Skills 1.d.** Recognize and name all upper- and lowercase letters of the alphabet.

1 Build Word Knowledge

Extend Letter Recognition

CONNECT LETTERS TO SOUNDS Display the *Jj, Kk, Ll, Mm,* and *Nn* Alphabet Cards. Ask children to name the letters and identify the pictures. Point to each pair of letters in turn and say the picture names emphasizing each beginning sound. Now I am going to say two words. Tell me the sound at the beginning of both words and the letter that stands for that sound. Hold up the appropriate Alphabet Card and repeat the words together. Use these pairs of words: *kayak, kettle; label, listen; neighbor, notice; jolly, juggle; magnet, member.*

WRITE WORDS Distribute paper and pencils to children. Today we are going to use what we know about letters and the sounds they stand for to write words. I am going to say some words, and I want you to write them. Listen carefully.

1. Kim **2.** jig **3.** hill **4.** fin

2 Text-Based Comprehension

Read

READ ALOUD Read the Reading Street Sleuth Read Aloud, "Gadget Is Gone!" on p. SG•25 to children.

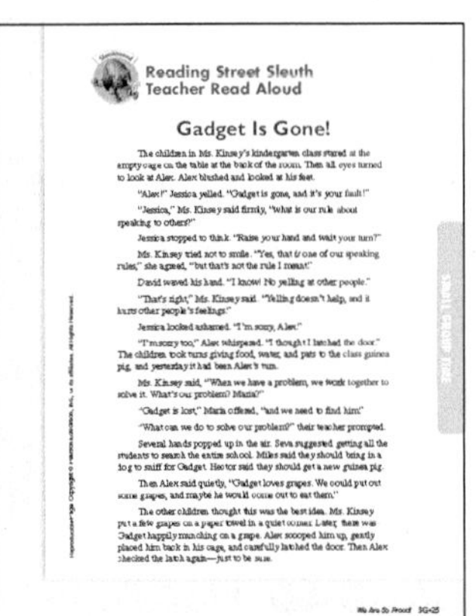
Reading Street Sleuth
Teacher Read Aloud

Gadget Is Gone!

The children in Ms. Kinsey's kindergarten class stared at the empty cage on the table at the back of the room. Then all eyes turned to look at Alex. Alex blushed and looked at his feet.

"Alex!" Jessica yelled. "Gadget is gone, and it's your fault!"

"Jessica," Ms. Kinsey said firmly, "what is our rule about speaking to others?"

Jessica stopped to think. "Raise your hand and wait your turn?"

Ms. Kinsey tried not to smile. "Yes, that *is* one of our speaking rules," she agreed, "but that's not the rule I meant."

David waved his hand. "I know! No yelling at other people."

"That's right," Ms. Kinsey said. "Yelling doesn't help, and it hurts other people's feelings."

Jessica looked ashamed. "I'm sorry, Alex."

"I'm sorry too," Alex whispered. "I thought I latched the door." The children took turns giving food, water, and pats to the class guinea pig, and yesterday it had been Alex's turn.

Ms. Kinsey said, "When we have a problem, we work together to solve it. What's our problem? Maria?"

"Gadget is lost," Maria offered, "and we need to find him!"

"What can we do to solve our problem?" their teacher prompted.

Several hands popped up in the air. Seva suggested getting all the students to search the entire school. Miles said they should bring in a dog to sniff for Gadget. Hector said they should get a new guinea pig.

Then Alex said quietly, "Gadget loves grapes. We could put out some grapes, and maybe he would come out to eat them."

The other children thought this was the best idea. Ms. Kinsey put a few grapes on a paper towel in a quiet corner. Later, there was Gadget happily munching on a grape. Alex scooped him up, gently placed him back in his cage, and carefully latched the door. Then Alex checked the latch again—just to be sure.

We Are So Proud SG•25

READ LIKE A SLEUTH! Encourage children to cite evidence from the text to support their answers. You may wish to reread sections of the text to verify children's answers.

Look for Evidence What event leads to Gadget getting out of his cage? What event leads to Gadget being put back into his cage?

Ask Questions What questions about Gadget do you wish the author had answered?

Prove It! Performance Task Have children draw a picture of what the characters in the story do to get Gadget to come out of hiding. Ask children to write a sentence or two using key details from the text. Have children read their sentences to you.

Teaching the Common Core State Standards This Week

The Common Core State Standards for English Language Arts are divided into strands for **Reading** (including **Foundational Skills**), **Writing**, **Speaking and Listening**, and **Language**. The chart below shows some of the content you will teach this week, strand by strand. Turn to this week's 5-Day Planner on pages 208–209 to see how this content is taught each day.

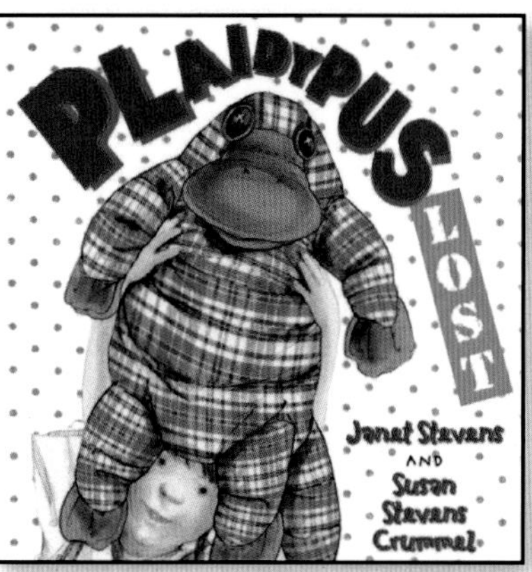

Common Core State Standards for English Language Arts

Reading Strand

- **Phonemic Awareness:** Initial Sounds and Sound Discrimination
- **Letter Recognition:** *Oo, Pp, Qq, Rr, Ss*
- **Text-Based Comprehension:** Sequence
- **High-Frequency Words:** *little, the*
- **Genre:** Realistic Fiction

Writing Strand

- **Wonderful, Marvelous Me**
- **Respond to Literature**
- **Genre:** Poem
- **Extend the Concept**
- **This Week We...**

Speaking and Listening Strand

- **Content Knowledge:** Build Oral Language
- **Listening and Speaking:** Listen for Rhyme and Rhythm

Language Strand

- **Oral Vocabulary: Amazing Words** *platypus, lost, found, around, market, groceries*
- **Vocabulary:** Words for Shapes
- **Academic Vocabulary:** *sequence, shape, poem, rhyme, rhythm, setting, fable*
- **Conventions:** What We Look Like

Text-Based Comprehension

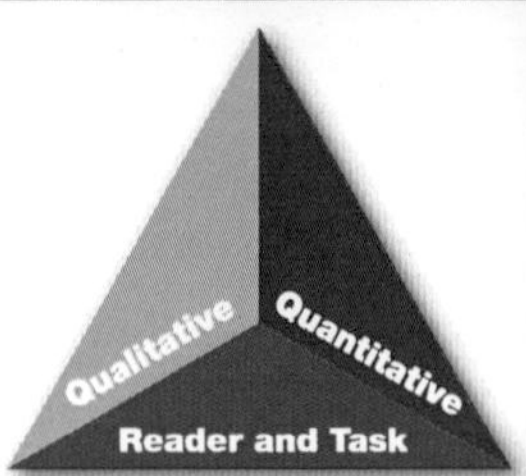

Text Complexity Measures

Use the rubric to familiarize yourself with the text complexity of ***Plaidypus Lost.***

Bridge to Complex Knowledge

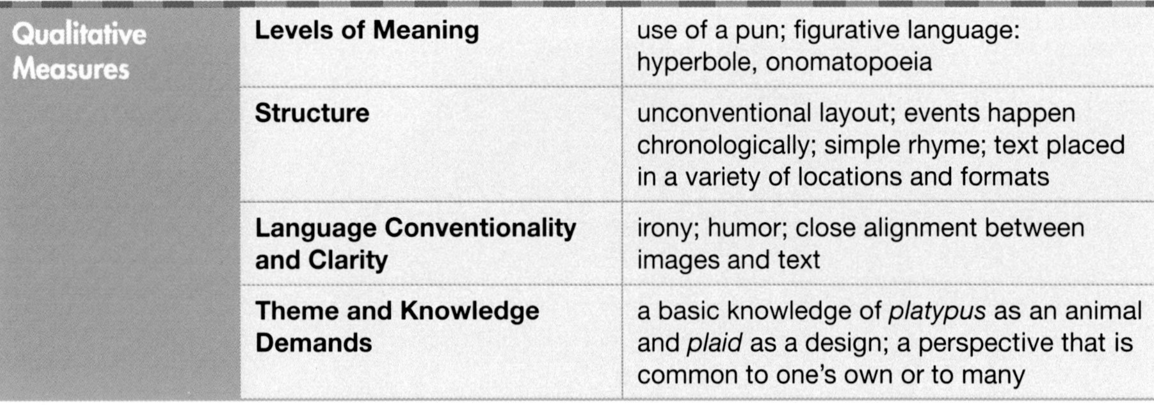

Qualitative Measures		
	Levels of Meaning	use of a pun; figurative language: hyperbole, onomatopoeia
	Structure	unconventional layout; events happen chronologically; simple rhyme; text placed in a variety of locations and formats
	Language Conventionality and Clarity	irony; humor; close alignment between images and text
	Theme and Knowledge Demands	a basic knowledge of *platypus* as an animal and *plaid* as a design; a perspective that is common to one's own or to many

Reader and Task Suggestions

FORMATIVE ASSESSMENT Based on assessment results, use the **Reader and Task Suggestions** in Access Main Selection to scaffold the selection or support independence for children as they read ***Plaidypus Lost.***

READER AND TASK SUGGESTIONS

Preparing to Read the Text	Leveled Tasks
• Review the Amazing Words and have children use them to talk about the selection. • Discuss the author's varied use of colors and sizes of texts.	• **Theme and Knowledge Demands** If children don't understand the name *Plaidypus,* have them use an illustration to explain what a platypus is and what *plaid* means. • **Structure** If children have difficulty with sequence, have them list the order of the places where Plaidypus was lost.

Recommended Placement This text is appropriate for placement as a read aloud at this level due to the qualitative elements of the selection.

Focus on Common Core State Standards ©

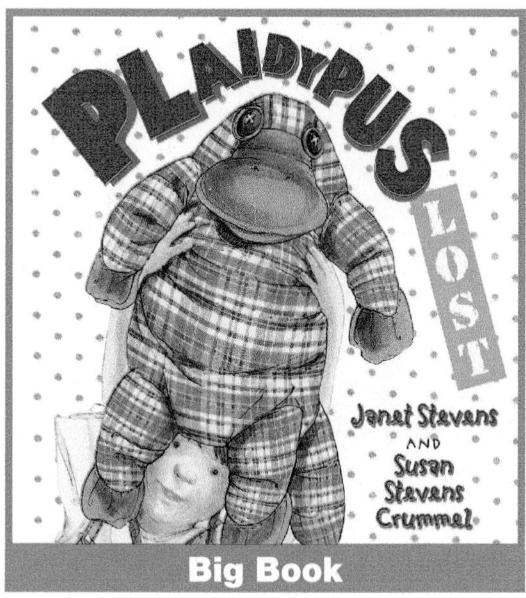

Text-Based Comprehension

 Sequence
CCSS Literature 2.,
CCSS Literature 3.

Letter Recognition

 *Oo, Pp, Qq, Rr, Ss*
CCSS Foundational Skills 1.a.,
CCSS Foundational Skills 1.d.

Writing and Conventions

Genre: Poem
CCSS Writing 2.,
CCSS Foundational Skills 2.a.

Conventions: What We Look Like
CCSS Language 5.c.,
CCSS Speaking/Listening 4.

Oral Vocabulary

Amazing Words

platypus	around
lost	found
market	groceries

CCSS Language 6.

Phonemic Awareness

Initial Sounds and Sound Discrimination
CCSS Foundational Skills 2.b.,
CCSS Foundational Skills 2.d.,
CCSS Foundational Skills 2.e.

High-Frequency Words

the little

CCSS Foundational Skills 3.c.

Listening and Speaking

Listen for Rhyme and Rhythm
CCSS Foundational Skills 2.a.

Preview Your Week

How do families cooperate?

Genre: Realistic Fiction

Letter Recognition: *Oo, Pp, Qq, Rr, Ss*

Text-Based Comprehension: Sequence

Build Content Knowledge

KNOWLEDGE GOALS
Children will understand that support from their families

- helps them take care of themselves
- helps them take care of their friends

BUILD ORAL VOCABULARY
This week, children will acquire the following academic vocabulary/ domain-specific words.

Amazing Words

platypus	around
lost	found
market	groceries

BUILD INDEPENDENT READERS
Children will enjoy becoming independent readers as they build decoding skills.

Get Set, Roll! Reader

Decodable Reader

OPTIONAL CONCEPT-BASED READING Use the Digital Path to access readers offering different levels of text complexity.

Concept Literacy

Listen to Me Reader

Student Reader

Independent Reader

This Week's Digital Resources

eStreet Interactive
www.ReadingStreet.com

Get Ready to Read

Big Question Video This video on the Digital Path introduces children to the unit question, *How do we live, work, and play together?*, and provides background for the reading children will do throughout the unit.

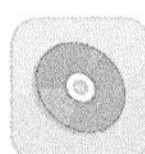
Background Building Audio CD This audio CD provides valuable background information about cooperating with family members to help children read and comprehend the weekly texts.

Concept Talk Video Use this video on the Digital Path to build momentum and introduce the weekly concept of cooperating with family members.

Interactive Sing with Me Chart and Audio "Purple Platypus," sung to the tune of "Baby Bumble Bee," introduces the Amazing Words with a catchy, concept-related song.

Phonics Songs and Rhymes Audio "Oh, My! Oh, No!," sung to the tune of "Rock-a-Bye Baby," helps children recognize *Oo, Pp, Qq, Rr,* and *Ss*.

Letter Tile Drag and Drop Using this interactive tool, children click and spell words to enhance their phonics skills.

Savvas eText For phonics and fluency support, use the eText of the Decodable Reader; the Student Reader; and the Get Set, Roll! Reader on the Leveled Reader Database.

Read and Comprehend

Envision It! Animations Use this colorful animation on the Digital Path to explain the target comprehension skill, Sequence.

Savvas eText Go to Savvas SuccessNet and use the eText of the many student edition pages in *My Skills Buddy* with audio support.

Story Sort Use the Story Sort Activity on the Digital Path after reading *Plaidypus Lost* to involve children in retelling.

Language Arts

Grammar Jammer Choose a whimsical animation on the Digital Path to provide an engaging lesson on What We Look Like that will capture children's attention.

Additional Resources

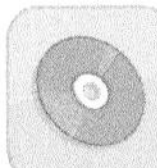
Teacher Resources DVD-ROM Use the following resources on the TR DVD or on Savvas SuccessNet throughout the week:

- Amazing Word Cards
- High-Frequency Word Cards
- Daily Fix-It Transparencies
- Reader's and Writer's Notebook
- Scoring Rubrics

This Week's Skills

Letter Recognition
Oo, Pp, Qq, Rr, Ss

Comprehension
Skill: Sequence

Language
Vocabulary: Words for Shapes
Conventions: What We Look Like

Writing
Wonderful, Marvelous Me!
Respond to Literature
Genre Writing
Extend the Concept
This Week We …

5-Day Planner

DAY 1

Get Ready to Read

Content Knowledge 214
Oral Vocabulary: *platypus, around, lost, found, market, groceries*

Phonemic Awareness 216
Initial Sounds

Monitor Progress
Check Phonemic Awareness

Letter Recognition 218
Oo

Handwriting 220
O and *o*

High-Frequency Words 221
the, little

READ Decodable Story 3 222
Little Me!

Read and Comprehend

Text-Based Comprehension 224
Sequence

Language Arts

Conventions 226
What We Look Like

Writing 227
Wonderful, Marvelous Me!
Daily Handwriting

Listening and Speaking 228
Listen for Rhyme and Rhythm

Extend Your Day! 229

DAY 2

Get Ready to Read

Content Knowledge 230
Oral Vocabulary: *platypus, around*

Phonemic Awareness 232
Initial Sounds

Letter Recognition 234
Pp

Monitor Progress
Check Letter Recognition

Handwriting 236
P and *p*

High-Frequency Words 237
the, little

READ Decodable Reader 3 238
The Little Toys

Read and Comprehend

Text-Based Comprehension 240
READ *Plaidypus Lost*—1st Read
Think, Talk, and Write

Monitor Progress Check Retelling

Language Arts

Conventions 243
What We Look Like

Writing 244
Respond to Literature
Daily Handwriting

Vocabulary 245
Words for Shapes

Extend Your Day! 247

DAY 3

Get Ready to Read

Content Knowledge 248
Oral Vocabulary: *lost, found*

Phonemic Awareness 250
Initial Sound Discrimination

Letter Recognition 252
Qq

Monitor Progress
Check Word Reading
High-Frequency Words

READ Kindergarten Student Reader 254
Cat and Dog Play

Read and Comprehend

Text-Based Comprehension 256
READ *Plaidypus Lost!*—2nd Read

Language Arts

Conventions 278
Write Our Names

Writing 279
Poem
Daily Handwriting

Listening and Speaking 280
Listen for Rhyme and Rhythm

Extend Your Day! 283

DAY 4

Get Ready to Read

Content Knowledge 284
Oral Vocabulary: *market, groceries*

Phonological Awareness 286
Review Syllables

Monitor Progress
Check Phonological Awareness

Letter Recognition 288
Rr

Get Set, Roll! Reader 3 289
READ *Pete*

Read and Comprehend

Text-Based Comprehension 290
Sequence
Review Setting
READ *Plaidypus Lost*—3rd Read

Language Arts

Conventions 292
What We Look Like

Writing 293
Extend the Concept
Daily Handwriting

Vocabulary 294
Words for Shapes

Extend Your Day! 295

DAY 5

Get Ready to Read

Content Knowledge 296
Review Oral Vocabulary

Monitor Progress
Check Oral Vocabulary

Phonemic Awareness 298
Review Initial Sounds

Letter Recognition 298
Ss

Assessment 300

Monitor Progress
Check Letter Recognition
Word Reading

Read and Comprehend

Let's Practice It! 302
Fable

Assessment 304
Review Sequence

Language Arts

Conventions 306
Review What We Look Like

Writing 307
This Week We …
Daily Handwriting

Wrap Up Your Week! 308

Extend Your Day! 309

Access for All

What do I do in group time?

It's as easy as 1-2-3!

1. TEACHER-LED SMALL GROUPS
2. INDEPENDENT PRACTICE STATIONS
3. INDEPENDENT READING

Small Group Time

Bridge to Common Core

SKILL DEVELOPMENT

- *Oo, Pp, Qq, Rr, Ss*
  Initial Sounds and Sound Discrimination
- Sequence

DEEP UNDERSTANDING

This Week's Knowledge Goals

Children will understand that support from their families

- helps them take care of themselves
- helps them take care of their friends

1 Small Group Lesson Plan

	DAY 1 Differentiate Letter Recognition	DAY 2 Differentiate Letter Recognition
OL On-Level pp. SG•38–SG•43	**Practice Letter Recognition** Recognize Letters *Oo* **Decodable Story** Read *Little Me!*	**Practice Letter Recognition** Recognize Letters *Pp* **Decodable Reader** Read *The Little Toys*
SI Strategic Intervention pp. SG•44–SG•48	**Reteach Letter Recognition** Recognize Letters *Oo* **Decodable Story** Read *Little Me!*	**Reteach Letter Recognition** Recognize Letters *Pp* **Decodable Reader** Read *The Little Toys*
A Advanced pp. SG•49–SG•54	**Extend Letter Recognition** Connect *Oo* to /o/ **Advanced Selection** Read "Pop! Pop!"	**Extend Letter Recognition** Connect *Pp* to /p/ **Decodable Reader** Read *The Little Toys*
ELL **If...** children need more scaffolding and practice...	**Phonemic Awareness and Letter Recognition** **then...** use the Letter Recognition activities beginning on p. 447 in the *ELL Handbook.*	**Phonemic Awareness and Letter Recognition** **then...** use the activities on p. DI•46 in the Teacher Resources section of the Digital Path.

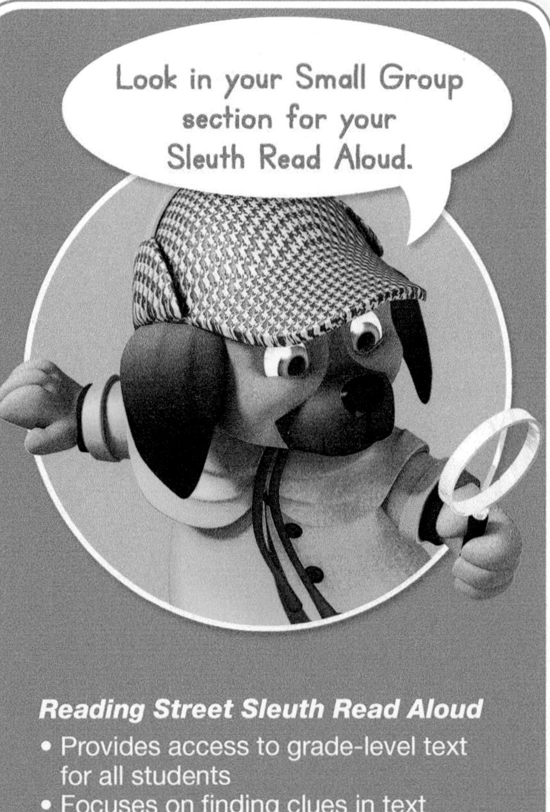

Reading Street Sleuth Read Aloud

- Provides access to grade-level text for all students
- Focuses on finding clues in text through close reading
- Builds capacity for complex text

Build Text-Based Comprehension

Plaidypus Lost

Optional Leveled Readers

Concept Literacy

Below Level

On Level

Advanced

Get Set, Roll! Reader

Decodable Reader

DAY 3 Differentiate Vocabulary	DAY 4 Differentiate Language	DAY 5 Differentiate Close Reading
Develop Vocabulary Practice Words for Shapes **Student Reader** Read *Cat and Dog Play*	**Build** Sentences and Words **Get Set, Roll! Reader** Read *Pete*	**Practice Letter Recognition** Recognize Letters *Qq, Rr, Ss* **Text-Based Comprehension** Read "Family Adventures"
Develop Vocabulary Reteach Words for Shapes **Student Reader** Read *Cat and Dog Play*	**Talk About** Sentences and Words **Get Set, Roll! Reader** Read *Pete*	**Reteach Letter Recognition** Recognize Letters *Qq, Rr, Ss* **Text-Based Comprehension** Read "Family Adventures"
Develop Vocabulary More Words for Shapes **Student Reader** Read *Cat and Dog Play*	**Extend** Sentences and Words **Get Set, Roll! Reader** Read *Pete*	**Extend Letter Recognition** Connect Letters to Sounds **Text-Based Comprehension** Read "Family Adventures"
Vocabulary **then...** use the ELL activities on p. DI•48 in the Teacher Resources section of the Digital Path.	**Developing Language** **then...** use the Language Workshops beginning on p. 306 in the *ELL Handbook.*	**Comprehension** **then...** use the ELL activities on pp. DI•47–DI•48 in the Teacher Resources section of the Digital Path.

 Independent Stations

Practice Last Week's Skills

Focus on these activities when time is limited.

ACCESS FOR ALL
- Below-Level Activities
- On-Level Activities
- Advanced Activities

LISTEN UP!

Listen for syllables.

OBJECTIVES
- Identify syllables in words.

MATERIALS
- *Listen Up!* Flip Chart Activity 3
- Picture Cards: *hammer, kite, nose, pig, rabbit, kitten*

 **Modeled Pronunciation Audio CD**

- Children name each Picture Card and clap for each syllable.
- Children name each Picture Card and clap for each syllable. Then they clap the syllables in their names.
- Children name each Picture Card and clap for each syllable. Then they clap the syllables in words they name.

WORD WORK

Identify letters *Ff, Gg, Hh, Ii, Jj, Kk, Ll, Mm, Nn.*

OBJECTIVES
- Identify letters *Ff, Gg, Hh, Ii, Jj, Kk, Ll, Mm, Nn.*

MATERIALS
- *Word Work* Flip Chart Activity 3
- Alphabet Cards: *Ff, Gg, Hh, Ii, Jj, Kk, Ll, Mm, Nn*
- Letter Tiles
- paper, pencils

 **Interactive Sound-Spelling Cards**  **Letter Tile Drag and Drop**

- Children find the *Ff, Gg, Hh, Ii, Jj, Kk, Ll, Mm*, and *Nn* Alphabet Cards.
- Children match the *Ff, Gg, Hh, Ii, Jj, Kk, Ll, Mm,* and *Nn* Alphabet Cards with Letter Tiles.
- Children match the *Ff, Gg, Hh, Ii, Jj, Kk, Ll, Mm,* and *Nn* Alphabet Cards with Letter Tiles and write each letter.

LET'S WRITE!

Write an invitation.

OBJECTIVES
- Write an invitation.

MATERIALS
- *Let's Write!* Flip Chart Activity 3
- paper, pencils, crayons

 **Grammar Jammer**

- Children draw a picture of an event and write the name of the person they will invite.
- Children draw a picture of an event. They write when and where the event will be.
- Children draw a picture of an event and write when and where the event will be. Then they write a sentence about it.

WORDS TO KNOW

Practice vocabulary.

OBJECTIVES
- Identify and use color words: *red, white, blue.*

MATERIALS
- *Words to Know* Flip Chart Activity 3
- classroom objects that are blue, black, green, red, and white
- Teacher-made word cards: *red, white, blue;* paper, crayons

 **Vocabulary Activities**  **Teacher Resources**
- High-Frequency Word Cards for Unit 1, Week 2

- Children find the red, white, and blue objects.
- Children match the red, white, and blue objects and the word cards for *red, white,* and *blue.*
- Children match the red, white, and blue objects and the word cards. Then they draw other things that are those colors.

Manage the Stations

Use these management tools to set up and organize your Practice Stations:

Practice Station Flip Charts

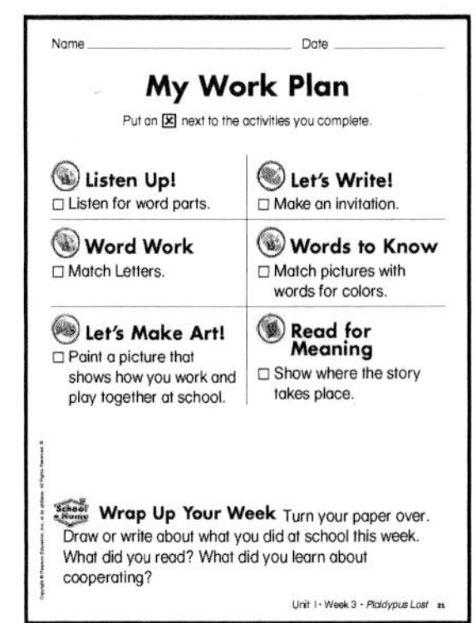

Classroom Management Handbook for Differentiated Instruction Practice Stations, p. 21

READ FOR MEANING

Use text-based comprehension tools.

OBJECTIVES

- Identify and describe story setting.

MATERIALS

- *Read for Meaning* Flip Chart Activity 3
- Little Book *We Are So Proud!*
- paper, pencils, crayons

 **Envision It! Animations**
- Leveled eReaders

● Children find a picture in a book that shows where the story takes place.

▲ Children draw a picture that shows where the story takes place.

■ Children draw a picture that shows where the story takes place. Then they write a sentence about the setting.

LET'S MAKE ART!

Use art to demonstrate understanding.

OBJECTIVES

- Paint a picture.

MATERIALS

- *Let's Make Art!* Flip Chart Activity 3
- paints, paper

● Children paint a picture that shows how they work and play with others at school.

▲ Children paint a picture that shows how they work and play with others at school. Then they write the names of classmates in their picture.

■ Children paint a picture that shows how they work and play with others at school. Then they write a title for their painting.

3 Independent Reading

Help children choose complex texts so that they can engage in paired and group reading and writing activities every day before, during, and after school.

Suggestions for this week's independent reading:
- Other stories by Janet Stevens
- *Who Lives Here?* by Tanya Roitman

BOOK TALK Have pairs or groups of children actively engage in reading activities through a discussion of their independent reading for the week. Focus their discussions with the following ideas:

Key Ideas and Details
- Retell the text to your partner or group.
- Identify the setting of the text.

Craft and Structure
- Name the title and author of the text.
- Talk about illustrations in the text.

Integration of Ideas
- With support, describe text/illustration relationships.
- Was this book like others I have read?

 **Savvas eText**
- Student Edition
- Decodable Readers
- Get Set, Roll! Readers
- Leveled Readers

 **Materials from School or Classroom Library**

DAY 1 at a Glance

Content Knowledge
Oral Vocabulary

Phonemic Awareness
Initial Sounds

Letter Recognition
Letters *Oo*

Handwriting
O and *o*

High-Frequency Words
the, little

Text-Based Comprehension
Sequence

Conventions
What We Look Like

Writing
Wonderful, Marvelous Me!

Listening and Speaking
Listen for Rhyme and Rhythm

Materials
- Student Edition
- Truckery Rhymes
- Talk with Me/Sing with Me Chart
- Reader's and Writer's Notebook
- Alphabet Cards
- Phonics Songs and Rhymes Chart

Bridge to Common Core

INTEGRATION OF KNOWLEDGE/IDEAS
This week children read, write, and talk about how families live, work, and play together.

Texts This Week
- "Purple Platypus"
- "Let's Go to the Park"
- *Plaidypus Lost*
- *Cat and Dog Play*
- "The Little Red Hen"

Social Studies Knowledge Goals
Children will understand that support from their families
- helps them take care of themselves
- helps them take care of their friends

Start your engines!
Display p. 7 of *Truckery Rhymes.*

- Read aloud "Three Loud Trucks" and track the print.
  - Reread the rhyme and have children chime in as they wish.
    - Ask children to identify the rhyming words. (*goo, blew, crew*)

Truckery Rhymes

Content Knowledge

Zoom in on ©

Families Living, Working, and Playing Together

CONCEPT TALK To explore the unit concept of All Together Now, tell children that this week they will listen, talk, sing, read, and write about how families cooperate. Write the Question of the Week on the board, *How do families cooperate?* Track each word as you read.

Build Oral Language

TALK ABOUT THE PLATYPUS Display Talk with Me Chart 3A. Point to the picture of the platypus. This animal is a platypus. We're going to read a story this week about a toy platypus. Look at the platypus. What do you notice about its bill, feet, and tail? Tell children to notice that the platypus has a bill like a duck's bill, webbed feet, and a broad, flat tail.

We are going to learn six new Amazing Words this week. Listen as I say each word: *platypus, around, lost, found, market, groceries.* Have children say each word as you point to the picture.

LISTEN FOR AMAZING WORDS Display Sing with Me Chart 3B. Tell children that they are going to sing a song about losing a toy. Read the title. Have children describe the pictures. Sing the song several times to the tune of "Baby Bumble Bee." Listen for the Amazing Words: *platypus, around, lost, found, market, groceries.* Have children stand up and sing with you.

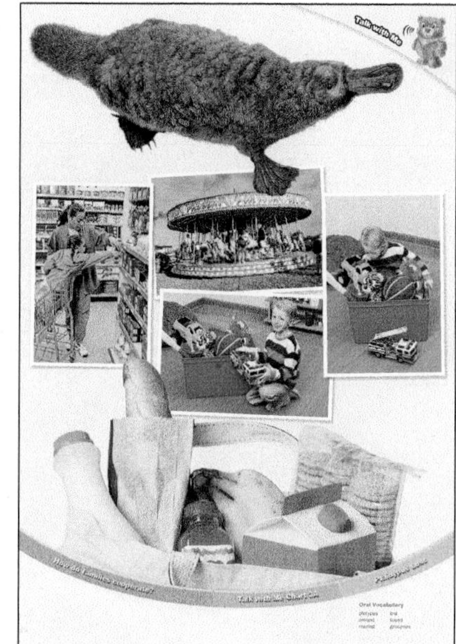

Talk with Me/Sing with Me Chart 3A

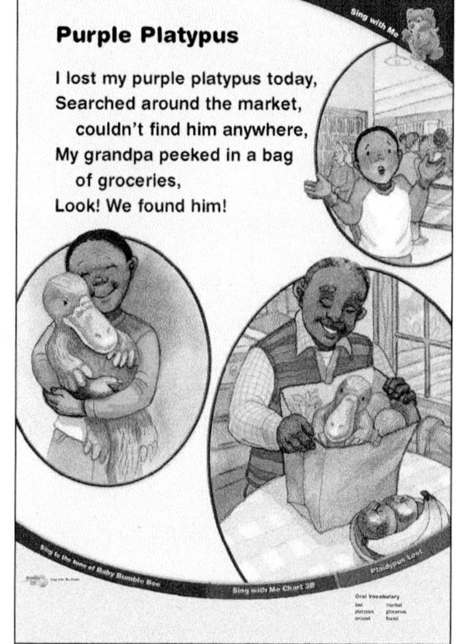
Purple Platypus
I lost my purple platypus today,
Searched around the market,
couldn't find him anywhere,
My grandpa peeked in a bag
of groceries,
Look! We found him!

Talk with Me/Sing with Me Chart 3B

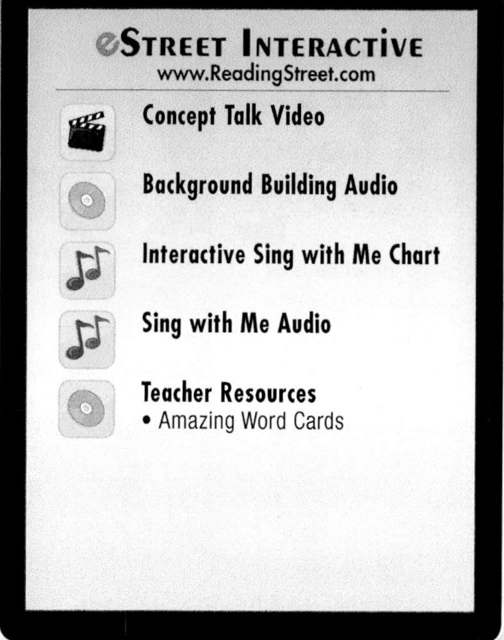
eStreet Interactive
www.ReadingStreet.com
Concept Talk Video
Background Building Audio
Interactive Sing with Me Chart
Sing with Me Audio
Teacher Resources
• Amazing Word Cards

Amazing Words

You've learned 0 1 2 words so far.

You'll learn 0 0 6 words this week!

platypus	around
lost	found
market	groceries

Access for All

A Advanced

Access Content Have children talk about their stuffed animal companions. What kind of animal is it? What do you like to do with your stuffed animal companion? Have children who do not have a stuffed animal companion talk about what kind of stuffed animal companion they would like to have.

Visual Support English learners will benefit from additional visual support to help them understand words in the song. For example, point to the *platypus* in the art to scaffold meaning.

Preteach Concepts Use the Day 1 instruction on ELL Poster 3 to assess and build background knowledge, develop concepts, and build oral vocabulary.

Common Core State Standards
Foundational Skills 2.d. Isolate and pronounce the initial, medial vowel, and final sounds (phonemes) in three-phoneme (consonant-vowel-consonant, or CVC) words.
Phonemic Awareness
Let's Listen for
Initial Sounds
Point to something that begins like pig. Say the word. Say the beginning sound.
Find other things in the picture that begin like pig. Say the words.
Say these words: pie, pumpkin, pepper. Do they begin the same? What about pears, cakes, apples?
Read Together
READING STREET ONLINE
BIG QUESTION VIDEO
www.ReadingStreet.com
52
53

My Skills Buddy, pp. 52–53

Common Core State Standards

Foundational Skills 2.d. Isolate and pronounce the initial, medial vowel, and final sounds (phonemes) in three-phoneme (consonant-vowel-consonant, or CVC) words.* (This does not include CVCs ending with /l/, /r/, or /x/.) **Also Foundational Skills 2., 2.a.**

Phonemic Awareness

Initial Sounds

INTRODUCE Today we will listen for words that begin with the same sound. Listen as I say some words: *pig, pan, pet.* Say the words with me: *pig, pan, pet.* These words begin with the same sound. Let's say the words again and listen to the beginning sound in each word: *pig, pan, pet.*

MODEL Have children look at the picture on pp. 52–53 of *My Skills Buddy.* Tell children they will be looking for things that begin with the same sound as *pig.* I see a boy pointing. *Pointing* and *pig* begin with the same sound. What other things do you see that begin with the same sound as *pig?*

GUIDE PRACTICE As children name pictures, guide them in saying what word has the same beginning sound. Discuss some of the bulleted items on p. 52 of *My Skills Buddy.* Save the other bulleted items for Day 2.

Corrective feedback	**If...** children have difficulty distinguishing words with the same initial sound, **then...** say *pig* again, isolating the initial sound—/p/ /p/ /p/, *pig.*

DISCRIMINATE INITIAL SOUNDS Display Picture Cards *pig, pen,* and *sun.* Two of these words begin with the same sound. Say: *pig, pen, sun. Pig* and *pen* begin with the same sound. Continue with the following sets of Picture Cards: *cap, man, cat; bed, mop, mug; fox, ten, fan.*

Let's play a game. I will say two words. If they begin with the same sound, stand up. If they do not begin with the same sound, sit down. Listen carefully: *pat, pen.* Do the words begin with the same sound? Yes, so stand up! Continue with *pig, can* (sit); *pay, pass* (stand); *fan, fun* (stand); *bat, win* (sit).

Corrective feedback	**If...** children cannot identify the same initial sounds, **then...** say the words again, isolating each initial sound.

RHYMING WORDS Remind children that rhyming words are words with the same middle and ending sounds. Listen as I say three words. Tell me which words are rhyming words. Display Picture Cards *sled, net, red.* Say: *sled, net, red.* Which of these words are rhyming words? Repeat the routine with the following sets of Picture Cards: *ant, can, van; block, clock, five.*

Access for All

 Advanced

Support Phonemic Awareness After they study the picture on pp. 52–53 of *My Skills Buddy,* have children choose and draw two things in the picture that begin with the same sound.

Teacher Tip

Be conscious of not blending the initial sound of the word with the next sound when emphasizing the initial sound children have to identify.

MONITOR PROGRESS

Check Phonemic Awareness Initial Sounds

FORMATIVE ASSESSMENT Say *ten, bed,* and *top.* Have children identify which words begin with the same sound. Continue with *bat, cake, cup; deer, dad, mom;* and *mice, penguin, moose.*

If... children cannot identify words with the same initial sound,

then... use the small-group Strategic Intervention lesson, p. SG•44, to reteach initial sounds.

Common Core State Standards

Foundational Skills 1.d. Recognize and name all upper- and lowercase letters of the alphabet.

Letter Recognition

Teach/Model

Letters *Oo*

Alphabet Card

INTRODUCE Display the *Oo* Alphabet Card. Point to the uppercase *O.* The name of this letter is uppercase *O.* What is the name of this letter? Point to the lowercase *o.* The name of this letter is lowercase *o.* What letter is this?

MODEL Write "Oh, My! Oh, No!" on the board. This is the title of the song we are going to sing today. Which letter is uppercase *O?* Have a child point to an uppercase *O.* I see another uppercase *O.* Have another child point to it. Then have children identify the lowercase *o.*

Guide Practice

GROUP PRACTICE Display Phonics Songs and Rhymes Chart 3. Teach children the song "Oh, My! Oh, No!" sung to the tune of "Rock-a-Bye Baby." Play the CD and sing the song several times. When children are familiar with the song, have them sing along with you, clapping their hands in time to the music. Then have them come up and point to uppercase *O* and lowercase *o* in the song lyrics. Encourage them to say the letter they identify.

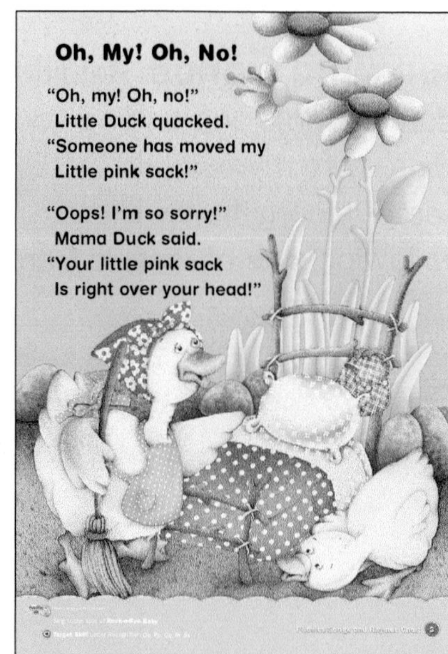

Oh, My! Oh, No!
"Oh, my! Oh, no!"
Little Duck quacked.
"Someone has moved my
Little pink sack!"
"Oops! I'm so sorry!"
Mama Duck said.
"Your little pink sack
Is right over your head!"

Phonics Songs and Rhymes Chart 3

ON THEIR OWN Have children make telescopes with their hands and look around the room for uppercase *O* and lowercase *o.* Ask them to identify the letters they find.

Blend Words

REVIEW To review letter names, use the *Aa, Bb, Cc, Dd,* and *Ee* Alphabet Cards to practice previously taught letters. Have children use their finger to write each letter on their hand as they say the name. Then use this process for blending syllables to have children blend new words.

CONNECT Say the word *robot.* *Robot* has two sound parts, or syllables: *ro-bot.* When we blend these syllables together, we say the word *robot.* Today we are going to learn how to blend syllables together to make words.

MODEL Tell children you are going to say a word with two syllables. The first syllable is *pud-.* Have children echo you. The next syllable is *-dle.* Have children echo you. Tell them you are going to blend the two syllables together to say the word. When I put the two syllables *pud-dle* together, I say *puddle.* We blend the syllables *pud-dle* together to make the word *puddle.*

GUIDE PRACTICE Continue the process with the words below. We are going to practice more words. Remember, I will say each syllable and you will repeat it. Then you will put the syllables together to say the word.

lit-tle	oc-to-pus	lad-der

Corrective feedback	**If...** children have trouble blending the syllables to make a word, **then...** model blending the syllables to say the word and then have children say it with you.

Access for All

Strategic Intervention

Anchor Vocabulary Explain to children the meaning of each word used in the blending routine.

Teacher Tip

For extra practice with blending syllables, use words children have seen in previous stories or books.

Letter Recognition Children may find it difficult to distinguish uppercase *O* and lowercase *o.* Write the letters on the board, emphasizing the difference in their sizes. Uppercase *O* is bigger than lowercase *o.* Have children write the letters on their Write-On Boards.

Common Core State Standards

Foundational Skills 3.c. Read common high-frequency words by sight. (e.g., *the, of, to, you, she, my, is, are, do, does*). **Language 1.a.** Print many upper- and lowercase letters. **Also Foundational Skills 1.b.**

Access for All

 Strategic Intervention

Handwriting Remind children that when they write the letters *Oo,* their pencil should not come off the paper. It takes only one line to write *Oo.*

Handwriting

INTRODUCE Write *Oo* on the board and point to *O.* This is uppercase *O.* We use uppercase letters at the beginning of sentences and names. Repeat with lowercase *o.*

MODEL UPPERCASE *O* Write *Oscar* on the board. Point to the uppercase *O.* This is uppercase *O.* Watch as I trace this uppercase *O* with my finger. Follow the stroke instructions pictured below.

GUIDE PRACTICE Have children write uppercase *O* in the air. Use your finger to make an uppercase *O* in the air. Now write it on your hand.

MODEL LOWERCASE *o* Write *ox* on the board. Point to *o.* This is lowercase *o.* Watch as I trace this lowercase *o* with my finger. Write another lowercase *o* on the board, following the stroke instructions. Again, have children write *o* in the air and on their hands.

GUIDE PRACTICE Have children use their Write-On Boards to write a row of uppercase *O* and a row of lowercase *o.*

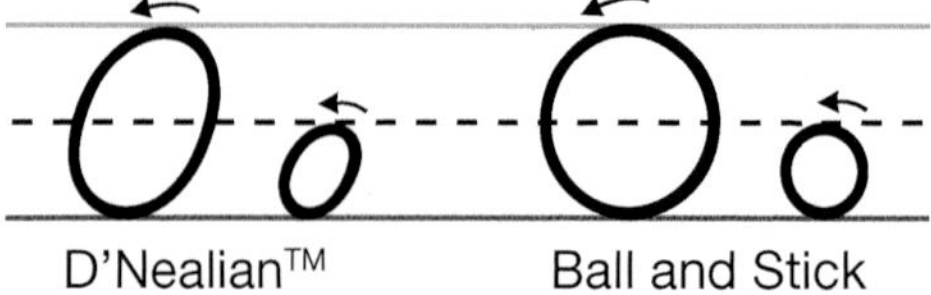

D'Nealian™ Ball and Stick

ON THEIR OWN Use *Reader's and Writer's Notebook,* pp. 25 and 26, for additional practice with *Oo.* Return to these pages on Days 2, 3, 4, and 5 to practice *Pp, Qq, Rr,* and *Ss.*

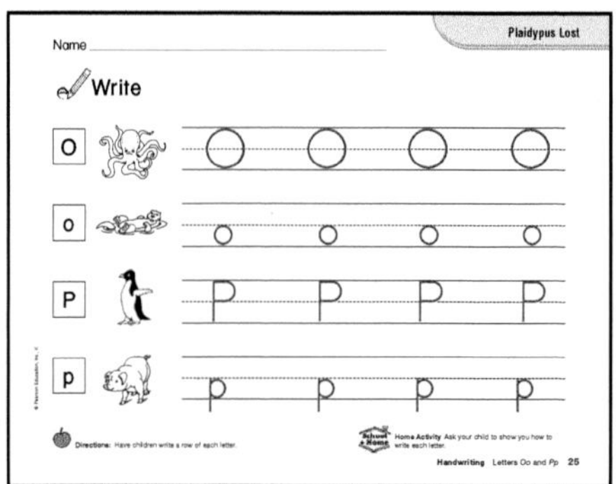

Reader's and Writer's Notebook, p. 25

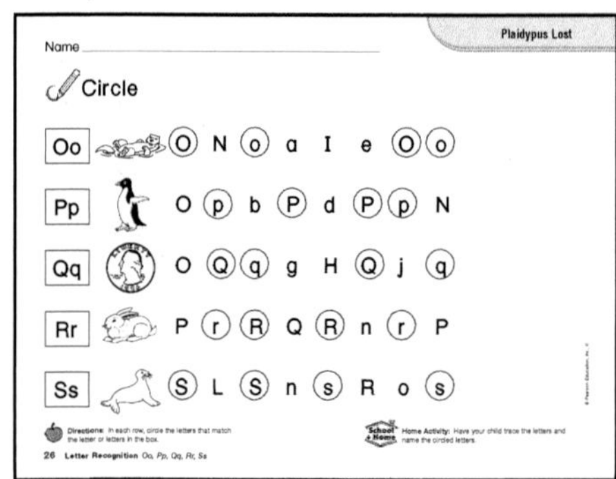

Reader's and Writer's Notebook, p. 26

High-Frequency Words

INTRODUCE Use the routine below to teach high-frequency words *the* and *little.*

Routine Nondecodable Words

1. **Say and Spell** Some words we must learn by remembering the letters rather than saying the sounds. We will say and spell the words to help learn them. Write *little* on the board. This is the word *little.* It has six letters. The letters in *little* are *l, i, t, t, l,* and *e.* Have children say and spell the word, first with you and then without you.
2. **Demonstrate Meaning** I can use the word *little* in lots of sentences. Here is one sentence: *A baby is little.* Now you use the word in a sentence.

Repeat the routine with the word *the.*

Add *the* and *little* to the Word Wall.

Routines Flip Chart

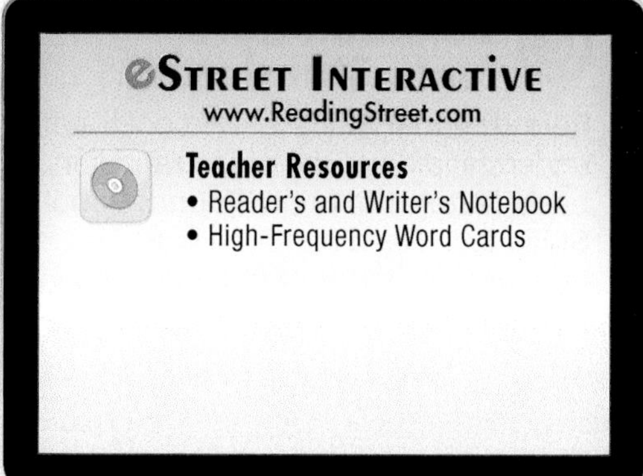

eStreet Interactive
www.ReadingStreet.com

Teacher Resources
- Reader's and Writer's Notebook
- High-Frequency Word Cards

High-Frequency Words Some languages, such as Chinese, do not have articles. Help children understand that in English the word *the* must be used before every definite noun. Provide examples of sentences with and without *the*, such as *I smell the flower* and *I smell flower,* so children can hear the difference.

Common Core State Standards

Foundational Skills 1. Demonstrate understanding of the organization and basic features of print. **Foundational Skills 3.c.** Read common high-frequency words by sight. (e.g., *the, of, to, you, she, my, is, are, do, does*).

Access for All

Strategic Intervention

Practice Rebus Words Have children point to the little animal on each page to reinforce the meaning of the rebus word.

Reader's and Writer's Notebook, pp. 27–28

Decodable Story 3

Read *Little Me!*

REVIEW Review the previously taught high-frequency words by having children read each word as you point to it on the Word Wall: *I, am, the, little.*

TEACH REBUS WORDS Write *otter* on the board. This is the word *otter.* Name the letters with me: *o, t, t, e, r, otter.* What word is this? Continue with *seal, rabbit, quail,* and *pig.* Look for these words in our story today. There will be a picture above the word to help you read it.

READ Tear out Decodable Story *Little Me!* on pp. 27–28 of *Reader's and Writer's Notebook.* Then fold the pages to form a book. Repeat this process with each child's *Reader's and Writer's Notebook.* Distribute the self-cover books to each child.

Today we will read a story about little animals. First let's look at our book. This is the right way to hold the book. Model how to hold the book. Point to the word *Little* on the cover. We know the book is right side up because the word looks right. Turn the book upside down. This is the wrong way to hold a book. The words and the pictures are upside down. We cannot read words if they are upside down! Turn the book right side up. Pick up your copy of the book and hold it right side up. Make sure the letters are right side up. Check to see that all children are holding their books correctly.

Point to the front cover. This is the front cover of our book. *Front* means the side that faces us. Open the book. These are the pages in our story. We turn the pages from right to left. Demonstrate how to turn the pages. Now you turn the pages from right to left. Observe and make sure all children are turning the pages correctly. This is the back cover. It is the part of the book we look at last. Point to the title of the story. What is the title of our book? The title of the story is *Little Me!* Where is the title of the story? Finally, explain to children that we read from top to bottom and model the process for them.

Have children read the story, holding the book right side up and turning the pages correctly. When they get to the final page, observe to ensure that children are reading from top to bottom. Have them track the print as they read.

Use the routine for reading decodable books to read Decodable Story 3.

eStreet Interactive
www.ReadingStreet.com

Teacher Resources
- Reader's and Writer's Notebook

Routine Reading Decodable Books

1. **Read Silently** Have children whisper read the story page by page as you listen in.
2. **Model Fluent Reading** Have children finger point as you read a page. Then have them reread the page without you.
3. **Read Chorally** Have children finger point as they chorally read the page. Continue reading page by page, repeating steps 1 and 2.
4. **Read Individually** Have children take turns reading aloud a page.
5. **Reread and Monitor Progress** As you listen to individual children reread, monitor progress and provide support.
6. **Reread with a Partner** Have children reread the story page by page with a partner.

Routines Flip Chart

Access Content After teaching the rebus words in Decodable Story 3, ask English language learners to share the words for *otter, seal, rabbit, quail,* and *pig* in their home languages.

Day 1 SMALL GROUP TIME • Differentiate Letter Recognition, p. SG•37

OL On-Level	SI Strategic Intervention	A Advanced
• **Practice Letter Recognition** Recognize Letters *Oo*	• **Reteach Letter Recognition** Recognize Letters *Oo*	• **Extend Letter Recognition** Connect *Oo* to /o/
• **Read** Decodable Story *Little Me!*	• **Read** Decodable Story *Little Me!*	• **Read** Advanced Selection "Pop! Pop!"

Place English Language Learners in the groups that correspond to their reading abilities in English.

If... children need more support with **Letter Recognition,**
then... use the Letter Recognition activities beginning on p. 447 in the *ELL Handbook.*

Comprehension

Envision It!

Sequence

READING STREET ONLINE
ENVISION IT! ANIMATIONS
www.ReadingStreet.com

Bye!
Bye!
Bye!

54 55

My Skills Buddy, pp. 54–55

Zoom in on

Common Core State Standards

Literature 2. With prompting and support, retell familiar stories, including key details. **Literature 3.** With prompting and support, identify characters, settings, and major events in a story. **Also Speaking/Listening 4.**

Skills Trace

Sequence
Introduce U1W3D1; U2W5D1; U4W1D1; U4W3D1
Practice U1W3D2; U1W3D3; U1W3D4; U2W5D2; U2W5D3; U2W5D4; U4W1D2; U4W1D3; U4W1D4; U4W3D2; U4W3D3; U4W3D4
Reteach/Review U1W3D5; U1W5D4; U2W2D4; U2W5D5; U2W6D4; U4W1D5; U4W3D5; U5W2D4
Assess/Test Benchmark Assessment U4
KEY: U=Unit W=Week D=Day

Text-Based Comprehension

Sequence

READ Remind children of the weekly concept—Families Living, Working, and Playing Together. Have children listen as you read aloud "Let's Go to the Park" on p. 225.

MODEL A CLOSE READ Model how to identify sequence as a tool to build comprehension.

Think Aloud When I read a story, I pay attention to the order in which things happen. First, Sam asks his dad, mom, and sister if they can go to the park, but they are all doing chores. Next, Sam says he will help them do their chores. Last, the chores are finished so the whole family can go to the park!

TEACH SEQUENCE In a story, things happen first, next, and last. The order in which things happen is called **sequence.** Good readers pay attention to the order, or sequence, of events to better understand the story.

Have children turn to pp. 54–55 in *My Skills Buddy* and look at the pictures. These pictures show a sequence of events.

- What happens first? (The mother bird sits on her eggs.)
- What happens next? (The mother bird feeds her babies.)
- What happens last? (The baby birds fly away.)

GUIDE PRACTICE Reread "Let's Go to the Park" and have children tell the order of the people Sam asks to go to the park.

- Who does Sam ask first to go to the park? (his dad)
- Who does he ask next? (his mom)
- Who does he ask last? (his sister)

Teacher Read Aloud

Let's Go to the Park

"Dad, may we have a picnic in the park?" Sam asked. Dad was doing laundry. Sam found Mom.

"Mom, may we play ball in the park?" Sam asked. Mom was working in the yard. Sam found his sister Jenny.

"Jenny, may we go swing in the park?" Sam asked. Jenny was cleaning her room.

Sam didn't give up. He helped Dad fold clothes. He helped Mom pull weeds. He put away toys in Jenny's room.

"Now can we go to the park?" Sam asked.

"Yes!" said Dad, Mom, and Jenny. They had a picnic. They played ball. Mom and Dad pushed Sam and Jenny on the swings.

Access for All

SI Strategic Intervention

Support Comprehension Display *The Little School Bus.* What animal gets on first? What animal gets on last? Page through the book to help children understand that the order in which the animals get on the bus is the sequence.

Academic Vocabulary 

sequence the order of events in a story, book, or play

Bridge to Common Core

KEY IDEAS AND DETAILS

When children identify the sequence of the major events in a story, they are analyzing how events develop over the course of the story. Answering questions about sequence of events helps children comprehend and summarize the text and gain familiarity with text structures.

Check Understanding Stop after reading each paragraph and discuss it with children. Clarify their understanding by asking questions such as these: *Who is Sam talking to? What is the person doing? What does Sam want to do?*

Conventions

What We Look Like

MAKE CONNECTIONS My hair is [color word]. My eyes are [color word]. What color is your hair? What color are your eyes? List children's responses. These words tell what we look like.

TEACH Talk with children about describing what we look like. When I smile, I look happy. The word *happy* tells you what I look like. Today we are going to practice using words that tell about, or describe, what a story character looks like.

MODEL Hold up the Big Book *The Little School Bus* and point to the pig. This is a pig. She is pink. Write the word *pink* on the board. The word *pink* tells what the pig looks like.

GUIDE PRACTICE Help children name other words that describe the animals on the cover of *The Little School Bus.* Look at the fox's ears. Are they big or little? Write *little* on the board. Look at the chick. Is the chick tall or short? Write *short* on the board. Look at the chick's glasses. Are they round or square? Write *round* on the board. Read the adjectives on the board, pointing to each word as you read it. These are words that tell what the characters look like.

Team Talk **APPLY** Pair children and have partners choose a book. Tell them to take turns using words to tell more about what the characters in the pictures look like.

Common Core State Standards

Writing 2. Use a combination of drawing, dictating, and writing to compose informative/explanatory texts in which they name what they are writing about and supply some information about the topic. **Speaking/Listening 4.** Describe familiar people, places, things, and events and, with prompting and support, provide additional detail. **Language 1.a.** Print many upper- and lowercase letters. **Also Writing 7., Speaking/Listening 1.**

Daily Fix-It

i am plaidypus.
I am Plaidypus.

This week's practice sentences appear on *Teacher Resources DVD-ROM.*

Wonderful, Marvelous Me! I Wonder About...

INTRODUCE Talk with children about curiosity. Have you ever wondered how something works or why something happens? When we wonder about something, we are *curious;* we want to learn about it. Why is it good to be curious? Encourage children to share their thoughts and ideas.

MODEL Today we're going to share our curiosity about something. I'm going to close my eyes and think of something I wonder about. My friend has a dog, and her dog pants a lot. Mimic a dog panting. I know dogs breathe by panting, but I have always wondered why dogs pant with their mouth instead of breathe through their nose like you and I do. Do any of you have a dog? Does your dog pant a lot? Draw a picture of a panting dog and write *Why do dogs pant?*

GUIDE PRACTICE Encourage children to help you come up with possible reasons why dogs pant. Write their ideas and draw pictures when appropriate. Then read from a reference source about why dogs pant. (By panting, a dog can cool its mouth and tongue, keeping its body temperature at a safe and normal level.)

INDEPENDENT WRITING Now you're going to share something you wonder about. Close your eyes and use your wonderful, marvelous curiosity. What do you wonder about? Why do you wonder about it? Have children write or dictate their ideas and then illustrate them.

Daily Handwriting

Write uppercase *O* and lowercase *o* on the board. Review correct letter formation with children.

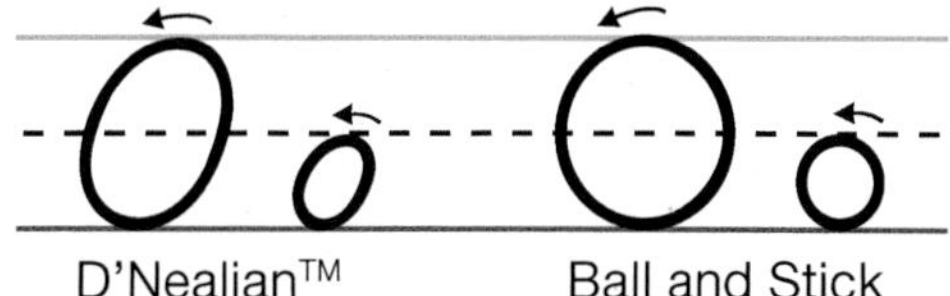

D'Nealian™ Ball and Stick

Have children write a row of uppercase *O* and a row of lowercase *o* on their Write-On Boards. Remind them to use proper left-to-right and top-to-bottom progression when writing *O* and *o*.

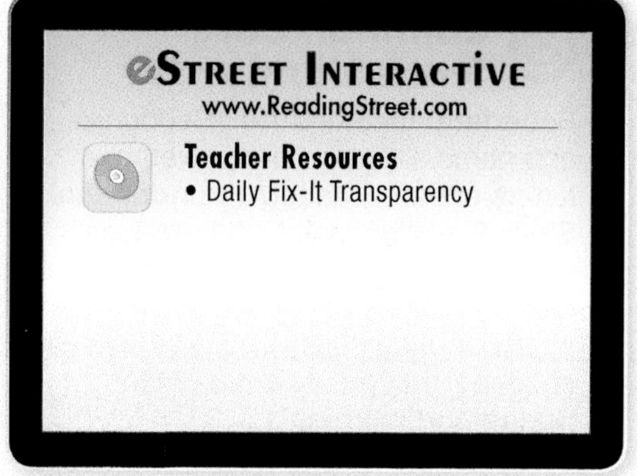

Write Guy *by Jeff Anderson*

Trait-by-Trait: Organization

Organization is a trait of good writing, but let's not be so concerned with form and forget about meaning. A child may develop a good way to communicate ideas that does not precisely follow the format we expect. There isn't only one way to reach the goal. And there isn't just one way to organize your writing. Reward creativity.

Bridge to Common Core

TEXT TYPES AND PURPOSES

Today children write and draw what they wonder about and why.

Expository/Informative/ Explanatory Writing

Children are learning to use writing to convey ideas and information clearly.

Throughout the week, children will have opportunities to write varied text types for different purposes.

5-Day Plan

DAY 1	Wonderful, Marvelous Me!
DAY 2	Respond to Literature
DAY 3	Genre Writing
DAY 4	Extend the Concept
DAY 5	This Week We...

Common Core State Standards

Foundational Skills 1.d. Recognize and name all upper- and lowercase letters of the alphabet. **Foundational Skills 2.a.** Recognize and produce rhyming words. **Language 5.c.** Identify real-life connections between words and their use (e.g., note places at school that are *colorful*). **Also Speaking/Listening 1.a.**

Listening and Speaking

Listen for Rhyme and Rhythm

TEACH Remind children that rhyming words have the same middle and ending sounds. Listen carefully: *bake, lake.* These words rhyme because they have the same middle and ending sounds. Explain that *rhythm* is the beat of a poem or a rhyme and demonstrate.

MODEL Listen for rhyming words as I sing a song. Remember, good listeners face the speaker, so face me while I sing.

Platypus, platypus, touch your nose.
Platypus, platypus, touch your toes.
Platypus, platypus, touch your head.
Platypus, platypus, go to bed.

What rhyming words do you hear? I hear the rhyming words *nose* and *toes.*

GUIDE PRACTICE Have children stand up and sing the song with you. Listen for rhyming words as we sing. Which words rhyme? (*nose, toes; head, bed*) Have children explain why the words rhyme. Refer children to the Rules for Listening and Speaking on pp. 1–2 of *Reader's and Writer's Notebook.* Repeat the song, clapping to the rhythm. Have children clap with you.

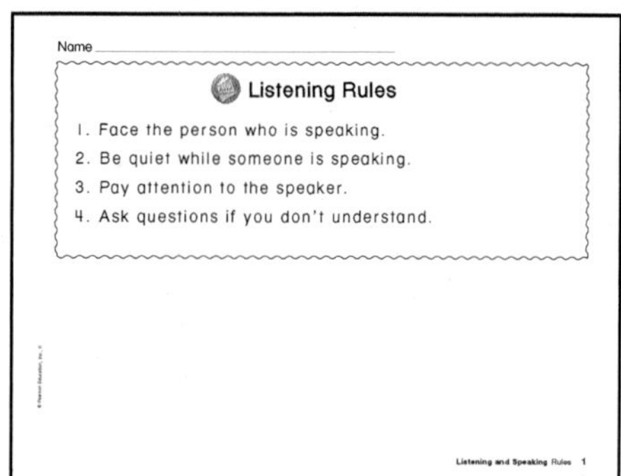
Name

Listening Rules

1. Face the person who is speaking.
2. Be quiet while someone is speaking.
3. Pay attention to the speaker.
4. Ask questions if you don't understand.

Reader's and Writer's Notebook, pp. 1–2

Wrap Up Your Day!

✓ **Oral Language** Today we talked about the Amazing Words we are going to learn. Let's name them: *platypus, around, lost, found, market, groceries.*

✓ **Conventions** Today we learned about words that describe people. Have children name words that tell what a favorite story character looks like.

✓ **Homework Idea** Send home the Family Times Newsletter from Let's Practice It! pp. 5–6 on the *Teacher Resources DVD-ROM.*

Tomorrow we will read about a stuffed animal companion.

Extend Your Day!

Social Studies
Following Rules

MATERIALS: crayons, paper

DISCUSS RULES Review with children how Sam helps his family so they all can go to the park. Tell children that the family has a rule that they must do their chores before they can play.

Tell children that people follow rules, such as sharing and taking turns, at home, in school, and in the community. Ask children to name some of these rules. Draw the following chart on the board. Read the headings. Write an example and then ask questions to help children name other rules to put on the chart.

- What are some school rules?
- What rules do you follow on the playground?
- What rules do you follow when you cross the street?
- What rules does your family have?

Rule	Where
obey the crossing guard	street corner

DRAW A PICTURE Read the chart to children. Have them choose a rule from the list and draw a picture showing it. Let them show their picture and tell about the rule and why it is important.

Conventions
What We Look Like

MATERIALS: paper, crayons

ILLUSTRATE A FAVORITE ANIMAL Discuss favorite animals, including pets and animals that live in your area.

- What is your favorite animal?
- Is the animal big or small? Does it fly or crawl?
- Does the animal have a hard shell or soft fur or feathers?

Have children draw a picture of a favorite animal. Then have them write or dictate words that tell what the animal looks like.

Letter Recognition
Letter Match

MATERIALS: cards with lowercase letters *a–o*

PICK A LETTER Write the following uppercase letters on the board.

B	D	A
M	L	C
J	H	I
K	F	E
O	N	G

Put the lowercase letter cards in a bag. Have a child draw a card, name the letter, and find the matching uppercase letter on the board. The game continues until all cards have been drawn. Mix the cards and put them back in the bag to begin a new game.

DAY 2 at a Glance

Content Knowledge
Oral Vocabulary

Phonemic Awareness
Initial Sounds

Letter Recognition
Letters *Pp*

Handwriting
P and *p*

Text-Based Comprehension
Sequence

Conventions
What We Look Like

Writing
Respond to Literature

Vocabulary
Words for Shapes

Materials

- Student Edition
- Truckery Rhymes
- Talk with Me/Sing with Me Chart
- Picture Cards
- Phonics Songs and Rhymes Chart
- Alphabet Cards
- Reader's and Writer's Notebook
- Big Book

Common Core State Standards

Speaking/Listening 1. Participate in collaborative conversations with diverse partners about *kindergarten topics and texts* with peers and adults in small and larger groups. **Language 6.** Use words and phrases acquired through conversations, reading and being read to, and responding to texts. **Also Language 4.**

Start your engines!
Display p. 7 of *Truckery Rhymes.* Point to "Three Loud Trucks." Which truck is reading the rhyme? That's Gabriella. Let's read the rhyme together. Now have a child point to the rhyming words as the class reads the rhyme again.

Truckery Rhymes

Content Knowledge

Zoom in on

Families Living, Working, and Playing Together

TALK ABOUT FAMILIES COOPERATING On the board, write the Question of the Week, *How do families cooperate?,* and track the print as you read it aloud. Have children answer the question in complete sentences. To reinforce the concept and focus children's attention, display Sing with Me Chart 3B. Tell children that they are going to sing about a lost toy.

Purple Platypus

I lost my purple platypus today,
Searched around the market,
couldn't find him anywhere,
My grandpa peeked in a bag
of groceries,
Look! We found him!

Talk with Me/Sing with Me Chart 3B

Build Oral Language

LISTEN FOR AMAZING WORDS The Amazing Words *platypus* and *around* are in the song "Purple Platypus." Have children describe the picture. Sing the song several times to the tune of "Baby Bumble Bee." Ask children to sing along with you. Have them clap when they hear *platypus* and *around.*

Build Oral Vocabulary

Amazing Words Robust Vocabulary Routine

1. **Introduce the Word** A *platypus* is an animal with a broad, flat tail; webbed feet; and a ducklike bill. What's our new Amazing Word for an animal with a broad, flat tail; webbed feet; and a ducklike bill? Say it with me: *platypus.*
2. **Demonstrate** Provide examples to show meaning. *The platypus has a flat tail.* What kind of feet does a *platypus* have?

   Repeat steps 1 and 2.

   Introduce the Word When you look in all directions, you look *around.* What's our new Amazing Word for when we look in all directions? Say it with me: *around.*

   Demonstrate *Grace looks all around for her shoes.* Act out how you can show someone how to look *around.*
3. **Apply** Tell children to use *platypus* and *around* in complete sentences. Have them draw a picture of a *platypus* looking all *around.*
4. **Display the Words** Have children point to and name letters in *platypus* and *around* that they recognize. Ask them to point to the letter *a* in both words.

Routines Flip Chart

USE AMAZING WORDS To reinforce the concept and the Amazing Words, have children supply the appropriate Amazing Word for each sentence.

A _______ has a flat tail, ducklike bill, and webbed feet. (platypus)
I looked _______ to see where I was. (around)

Amazing Words

platypus	around
lost	found
market	groceries

Access for All

SI Strategic Intervention

Physical Response Have children act out how they would look around the classroom.

Access Content Ask children to look at the picture of the platypus and have them tell about the animal, comparing it to animals they know.

Reinforce Vocabulary Use the Day 2 instruction on ELL Poster 3 to reinforce the meanings of high-frequency words.

Common Core State Standards Foundational Skills 2.d. Isolate and pronounce the initial, medial vowel, and final sounds (phonemes) in three-phoneme (consonant-vowel-consonant, or CVC) words.

Phonemic Awareness

Let's Listen for

Initial Sounds

- Point to something that begins like *pig*. Say the word. Say the beginning sound.
- Find other things in the picture that begin like *pig*. Say the words.
- Say these words: *pie, pumpkin, pepper.* Do they begin the same? What about *pears, cakes, apples?*

Read Together

READING STREET ONLINE
BIG QUESTION VIDEO
www.ReadingStreet.com

52 53

My Skills Buddy, pp. 52–53

Common Core State Standards

Foundational Skills 2.d. Isolate and pronounce the initial, medial vowel, and final sounds (phonemes) in three-phoneme (consonant-vowel-consonant, or CVC) words.* (This does not include CVCs ending with /l/, /r/, or /x/.) **Foundational Skills 2.e.** Add or substitute individual sounds (phonemes) in simple, one-syllable words to make new words.

Picture Card

Phonemic Awareness

Initial Sounds

IDENTIFY INITIAL SOUNDS Display the *pig* and *pen* Picture Cards. This is a pig. This is a pen. Listen to the beginning sounds in these words: *pig, pen.* Do they begin with the same sound? Yes, they do. Continue the routine with the *bag* and *bat* Picture Cards.

Picture Card

MODEL I am going to say three words. Two words have the same beginning sound, and one word has a different beginning sound. Listen carefully: *mop, duck, man*. Which words have the same beginning sound? *Mop* and *man* have the same beginning sound. Let's try some more. Continue with the following sets of words: *duck, dad, soap; sack, sorry, pink; little, lemon, head; pink, red, purple.*

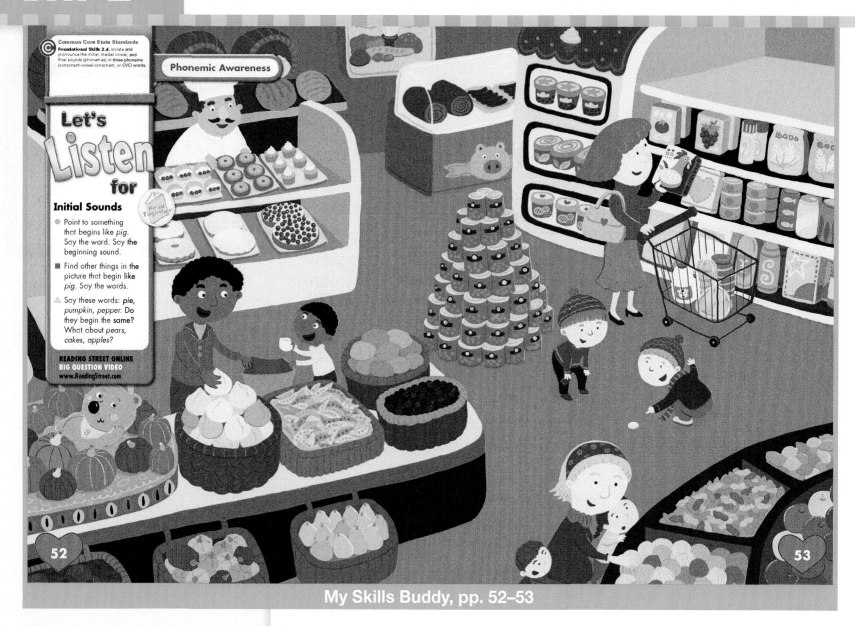

eStreet Interactive
www.ReadingStreet.com
Savvas eText
• Student Edition
Phonics Songs and Rhymes Audio

GUIDE PRACTICE Have children look at the picture on *My Skills Buddy,* pp. 52–53. Remember that we saw a boy pointing in the picture and that *pointing* and *pig* begin with the same sound. What other things in the picture begin with the same sound as *pig?* Discuss with children those bulleted items on p. 52 not discussed on Day 1.

Corrective feedback	**If...** children cannot identify words that begin with the same sound, **then...** say the words again, isolating the initial sounds. Have children echo you.

ON THEIR OWN Display Phonics Songs and Rhymes Chart 3. Remind children of the song "Oh, My! Oh, No!" sung to the tune of "Rock-a-Bye Baby." Sing the song several times. Have children join in. Then say pairs of words from the song. Ask children to say "Oh, yes!" if the words begin with the same sound and "Oh, no!" if they do not. Use these word pairs: *my, moved; pink, head; sack, sorry; little, right.*

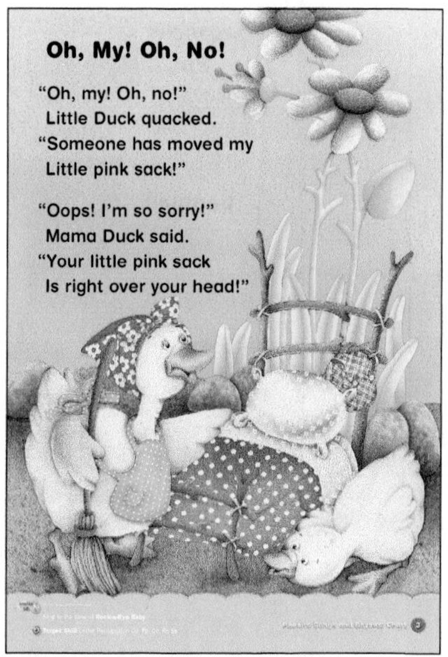
Oh, My! Oh, No!
"Oh, my! Oh, no!"
Little Duck quacked.
"Someone has moved my
Little pink sack!"
"Oops! I'm so sorry!"
Mama Duck said.
"Your little pink sack
Is right over your head!"
Phonics Songs and Rhymes Chart 3

Access for All

SI Strategic Intervention

Support Phonemic Awareness
Display the *doll* and *dog* Picture Cards. Say the words and have children repeat them. Then have them say just the beginning sound. Do these words begin with the same sound? Repeat the routine with the *fan, feather* and *map, mask* Picture Cards.

Common Core State Standards

Foundational Skills 1.d. Recognize and name all upper- and lowercase letters of the alphabet. **Foundational Skills 2.** Demonstrate understanding of spoken words, syllables, and sounds (phonemes). **Foundational Skills 2.b.** Count, pronounce, blend, and segment syllables in spoken words. **Also Foundational Skills 1., 1.a., 1.b., 1.c.**

Alphabet Card

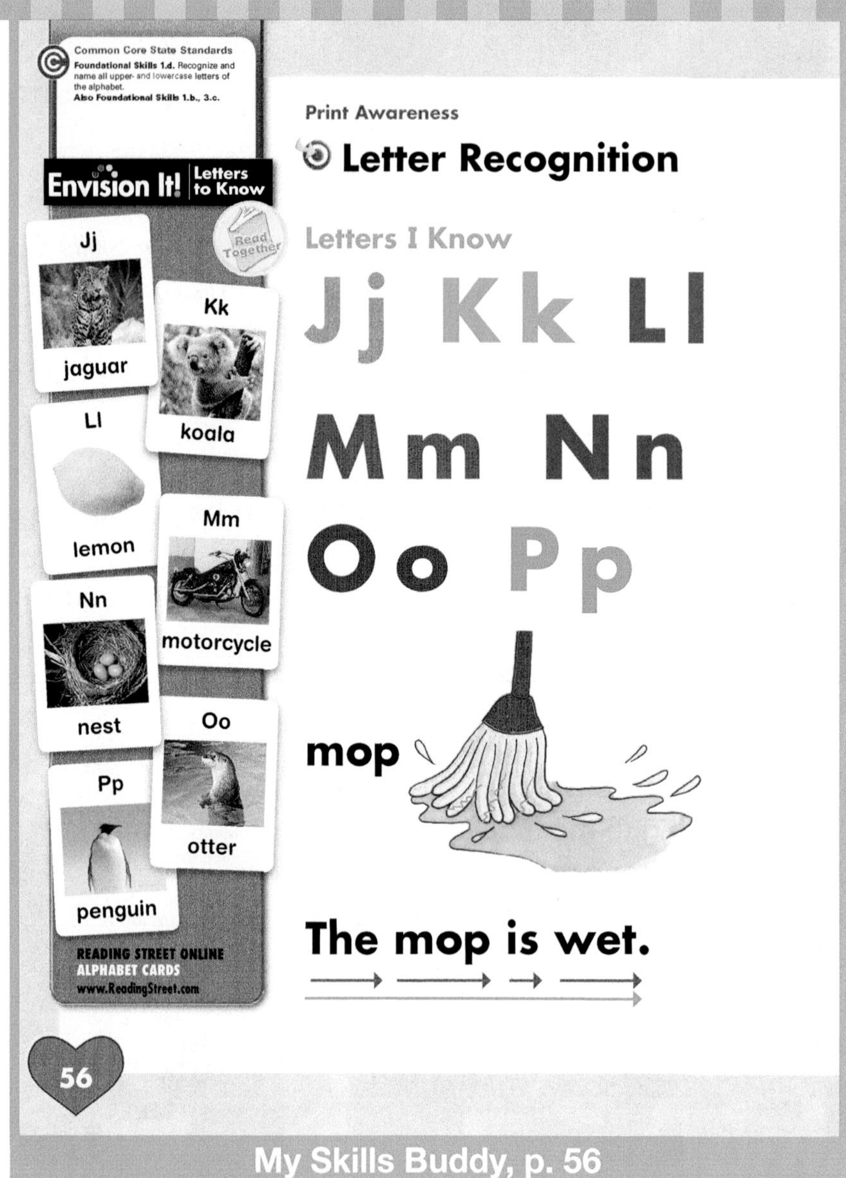

My Skills Buddy, p. 56

Letter Recognition

Teach/Model

Letters *Pp*

INTRODUCE/MODEL Display the *Pp* Alphabet Card. Point to uppercase *P*. This letter is uppercase *P*. What is the name of this letter? Repeat for lowercase *p*. Point to the penguin. This is a penguin. Write the word *penguin* on the board and point to the *p*. This letter is lowercase *p*. Display Phonics Songs and Rhymes Chart 3 “Oh, My! Oh, No!” Let’s find words with a *p*. (*pink, oops*)

Guide Practice

GROUP PRACTICE Have children identify the letters at the top of p. 56. Look at the mop. The letters *m, o, p* spell the word *mop.* When we put letters together, we can spell words. Read the sentence as children point to the red arrow under each word. The words I say match the words on the page. Now I will run my finger along the blue arrow as I read the whole sentence. Have children follow along.

CONNECT Say the word *window.* *Window* has two sound parts, or syllables. They are *win-* and *-dow.* When we blend the syllables together, we say the word *window.* Today we are going to practice blending syllables together to say words.

MODEL Tell children you are going to say a word with two syllables. The first syllable is *sur-.* Have children echo you. The next syllable is *-prise.* Have children echo you. Tell them you are going to blend the two syllables together to say the word. When I put the two syllables *sur-prise* together, I say *surprise.*

GUIDE PRACTICE Continue with the words below. I will say each syllable and you will repeat it. Then you will blend the syllables together to say the word.

but-tons	fish-er-man	patch-es

Check Letter Recognition Letter Names

FORMATIVE ASSESSMENT Write *Pat, pink, pen, Pam,* and *cap* on the board. Have children say a word with you and point to and name the letter *p* in the word.

If... children cannot recognize *Pp,*

then... use the small-group Strategic Intervention lesson, p. SG•45, to reteach letter names.

Continue to monitor children's progress during the week so that children can be successful with the Day 5 Assessment.

Access for All

 Advanced

Letter Recognition Have a group of children work together to lie down in the shape of the letter *p.*

Common Core State Standards

Foundational Skills 3.c. Read common high-frequency words by sight. (e.g., *the, of, to, you, she, my, is, are, do, does*). **Language 1.a.** Print many upper- and lowercase letters. **Also Foundational Skills 1., 1.c.**

Handwriting

INTRODUCE Write *Pp* on the board and point to *P.* This is uppercase *P.* We use uppercase letters at the beginning of sentences and names. Repeat with lowercase *p.*

MODEL UPPERCASE *P* Write *Pam* on the board. Point to the uppercase *P.* This is uppercase *P.* Watch as I trace this uppercase *P* with my finger. Follow the stroke instructions pictured below.

GUIDE PRACTICE Have children write uppercase *P* in the air. Use your finger to make an uppercase *P* in the air. Now write it on your hand.

MODEL LOWERCASE *p* Write *pal* on the board. Point to *p.* This is lowercase *p.* Watch as I trace this lowercase *p* with my finger. Write another lowercase *p* on the board, following the stroke instructions. Again, have children write *p* in the air and on their hands.

GUIDE PRACTICE Have children use their Write-On Boards to write a row of uppercase *P* and a row of lowercase *p.*

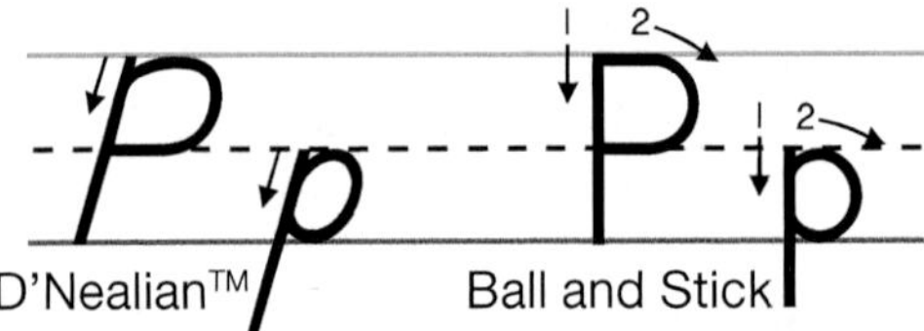

ON THEIR OWN Use *Reader's and Writer's Notebook,* pp. 25 and 26, for additional practice with *Pp*. Children will complete p. 26 later in the week.

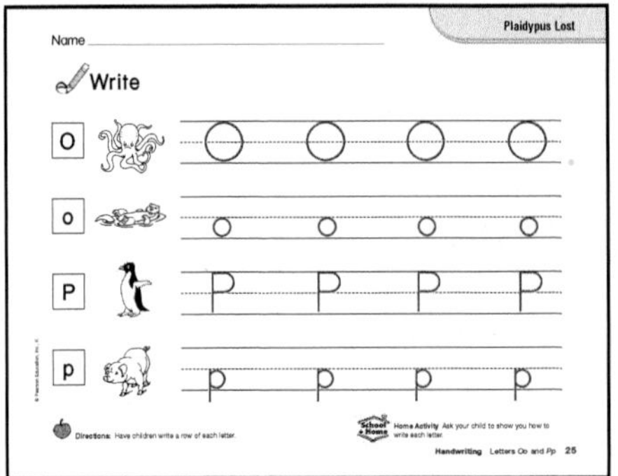

Reader's and Writer's Notebook, p. 25

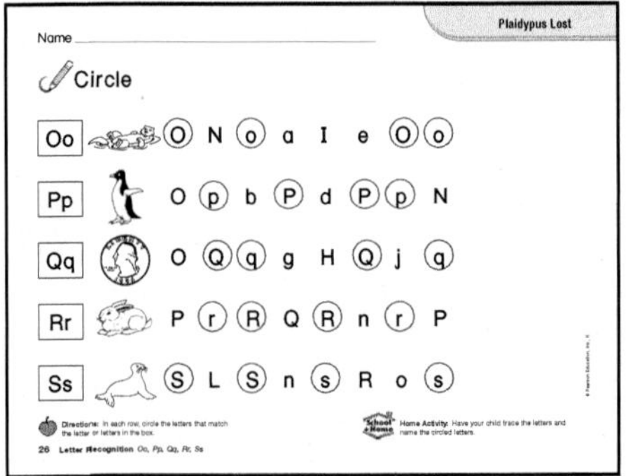

Reader's and Writer's Notebook, p. 26

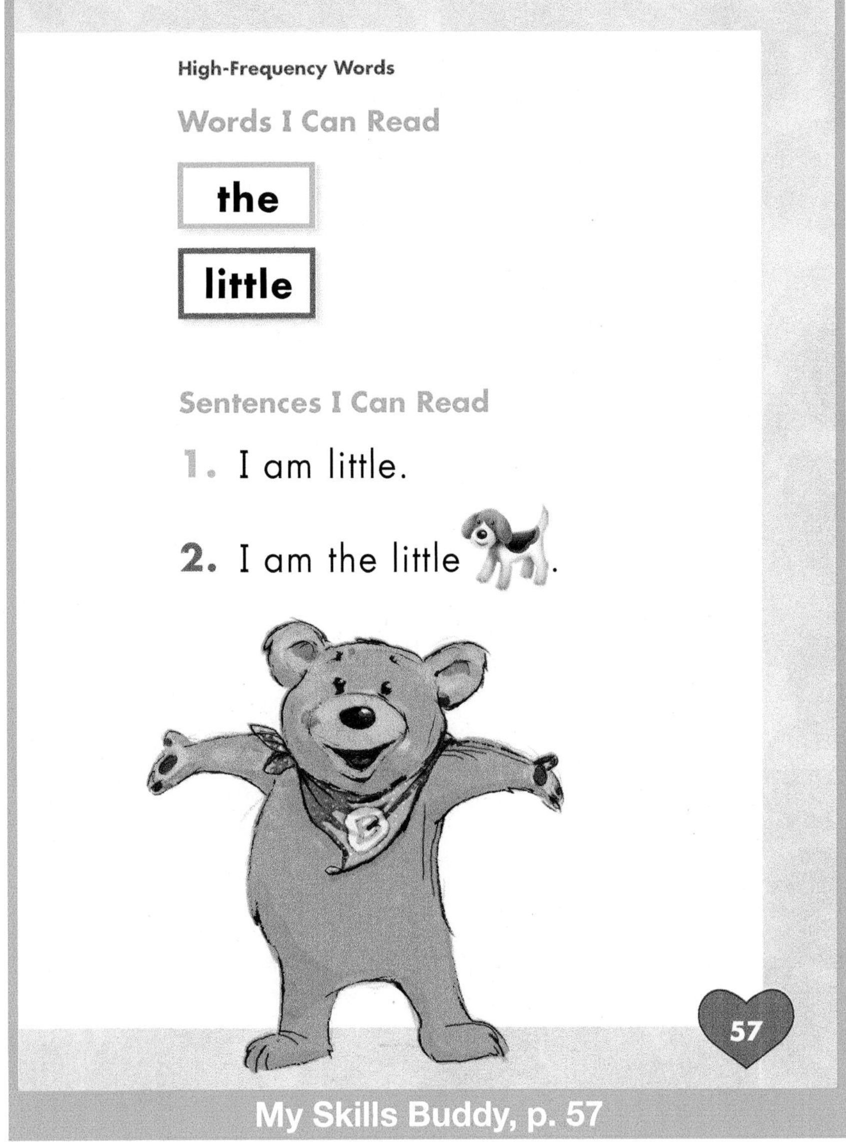
High-Frequency Words

Words I Can Read

the

little

Sentences I Can Read

1. I am little.

2. I am the little [dog].

57

My Skills Buddy, p. 57

High-Frequency Words

READ WORDS Have children turn to p. 57 of *My Skills Buddy.* Read the high-frequency words *the* and *little* together. Then have children point to each word and read it themselves.

READ SENTENCES Direct children to the blue numeral 1. This is a sentence. A sentence has spaces between words. Point to the words. This sentence has three words. Now point to the spaces. Have children point to the spaces in their books and read the sentence together. Repeat with sentence 2.

Team Talk Pair children and have partners take turns reading each of the sentences aloud.

ON THEIR OWN Use *Reader's and Writer's Notebook,* p. 29, for additional practice with this week's high-frequency words.

Access for All

SI Strategic Intervention

High-Frequency Words Explain to children that the word *little* refers to the size of something. Have children practice using the word *little* to describe things in the classroom. What in our classroom is *little?*

Plaidypus Lost

Name

Write Color

the little

The girl is little.

The dog is little.

The cat is little.

The pig is little.

High-Frequency Words 29

Reader's and Writer's Notebook, p. 29

High-Frequency Words After the Team Talk activity, have children continue to work in pairs to check understanding. Have one child read one of the sentences aloud while the other child makes a simple drawing to illustrate the sentence.

Common Core State Standards

Literature 6. With prompting and support, name the author and illustrator of a story and define the role of each in telling the story. **Foundational Skills 3.c.** Read common high-frequency words by sight. (e.g., *the, of, to, you, she, my, is, are, do, does*). **Foundational Skills 4.** Read emergent-reader texts with purpose and understanding. **Also Foundational Skills 1.a., 1.d.**

Decodable Reader 3

Read *The Little Toys*

REVIEW Review previously taught high-frequency words. Have children read each word as you point to it on the Word Wall: *I, am, the, little.*

TEACH REBUS WORDS Write *robot* on the board. This is the word *robot.* Say the letters with me: *r, o, b, o, t, robot.* Continue with *puzzle, queen, octopus, train, block,* and *spaceship.* Look for these words in our book today. There will be a picture above the word to help you read it.

CONCEPTS OF PRINT Have children turn to Decodable Reader 3, *The Little Toys,* on p. 58 of *My Skills Buddy.* Today we will read a story about toys. Point to the title. The title of this story is *The Little Toys.* What is the title? Point to the name of the author. The author's name is Roger Jons. The book *The Little Toys* was written by Roger Jons. The illustrator's name is Scot Salinski. What does the illustrator do?

READ Use the routine for reading decodable books to read Decodable Reader 3.

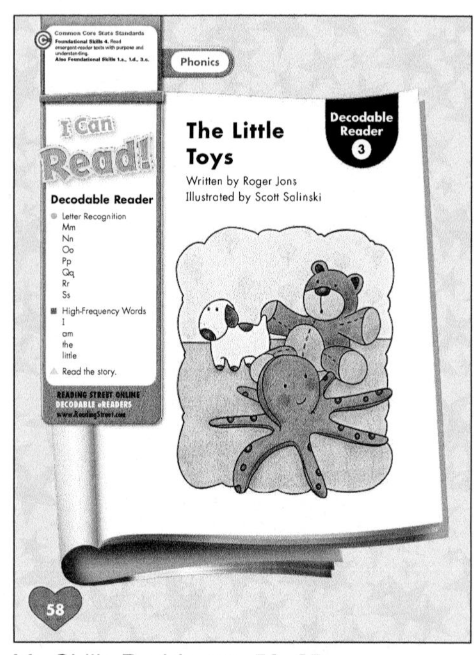

My Skills Buddy, pp. 58–65

Routine Reading Decodable Books

1. **Read Silently** Have children whisper read the book page by page as you listen in.
2. **Model Fluent Reading** Have children finger point as you read a page. Then have them reread the book without you.
3. **Read Chorally** Have children finger point as they chorally read the page. Continue reading page by page, repeating steps 1 and 2.
4. **Read Individually** Have children take turns reading aloud a page.
5. **Reread and Monitor Progress** As you listen to individual children reread, monitor progress and provide support.
6. **Reread with a Partner** Have children reread the book page by page with a partner.

Routines Flip Chart

Access for All

 Advanced

Make a Little Book Have children make their own book called *The Little Toys.* Have them fold a piece of paper in half. Tell them to draw a picture of a toy on each page. Then have them show their book and use this sentence frame to tell about each picture: *I am the little* ________.

Support Comprehension Before children read the Decodable Reader *The Little Toys,* use visuals to help them understand what a robot, puzzle, queen, and octopus are.

Day 2 SMALL GROUP TIME • Differentiate Letter Recognition, p. SG•37

OL On-Level	SI Strategic Intervention	A Advanced
• **Practice Letter Recognition** Recognize Letters *Pp* • **Read** Decodable Reader *The Little Toys*	• **Reteach Letter Recognition** Recognize Letters *Pp* • **Read** Decodable Reader *The Little Toys*	• **Extend Letter Recognition** Connect *Pp* to /p/ • **Read** Decodable Reader *The Little Toys*

Place English Language Learners in the groups that correspond to their reading abilities in English.

If... children need more support with **Letter Recognition,** **then...** use the activities on p. DI•46 in the Teacher Resources section of the Digital Path.

Text-Based Comprehension

Introduce Main Selection

CONCEPTS OF PRINT Display p. 8 of *Plaidypus Lost.* Use your finger to show the direction you would read the words. When we read a story, we start at the top and move to the bottom.

GENRE Realistic fiction is a made-up story that could happen in real life. Let's read about a girl and her toy.

PREVIEW AND PREDICT Display *Plaidypus Lost.* The title of this book is *Plaidypus Lost.* Tell me what you see on the cover. What do you think this book will be about? Take children on a walk through the book. Have them tell about what they see in each picture.

SET PURPOSE Remind children of the Question of the Week: *How do families cooperate?* Have children listen as you read.

MODEL Read *Plaidypus Lost* with expression to build interest in the text.

Routine Read for Understanding 

Deepen understanding by reading the selection multiple times.

1. **First Read**—Read the entire selection aloud to build interest in the text.
2. **Second Read**—Use the **Develop Vocabulary** notes on pages 258–277.
3. **Third Read**—Use the **Develop Comprehension** notes on pages 258–277.

Retell

CHECK RETELLING Have children turn to p. 66 of *My Skills Buddy.* Walk through the retelling boxes as children retell *Plaidypus Lost.* After they retell the story as a group, have children draw a picture to retell a favorite part. Have them write or dictate a word or sentence to go with their picture.

Check Retelling

If... children have difficulty retelling the story,

then... go through the story one page at a time, and ask children to tell what happens in their own words.

Common Core State Standards

Literature 2. With prompting and support, retell familiar stories, including key details. **Literature 10.** Actively engage in group reading activities with purpose and understanding. **Speaking/Listening 4.** Describe familiar people, places, things, and events and, with prompting and support, provide additional detail. **Also Literature 3., 5., Foundational Skills 1., 1.a.**

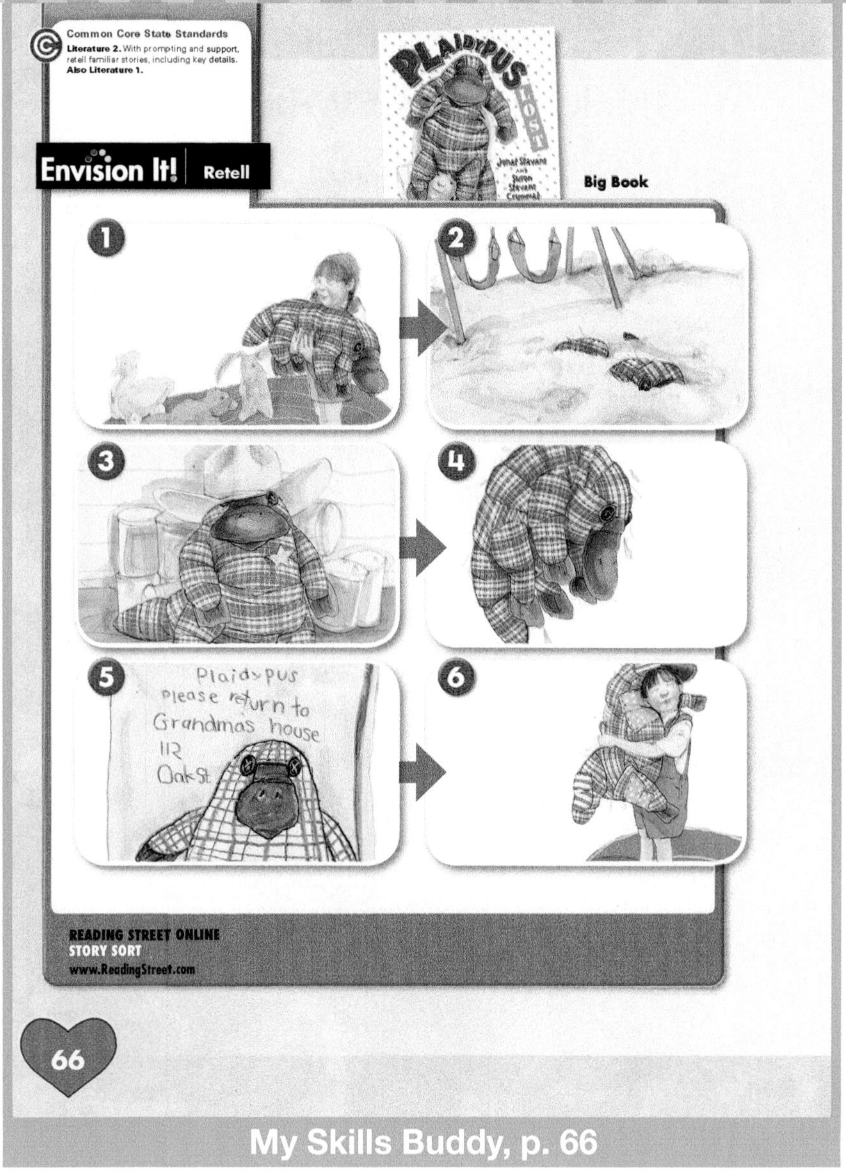

Common Core State Standards
Literature 2. With prompting and support, retell familiar stories, including key details. Also Literature 1.
Envision It! Retell
Big Book
Plaidypus please return to Grandmas house 112 Oak St
READING STREET ONLINE
STORY SORT
www.ReadingStreet.com
66

My Skills Buddy, p. 66

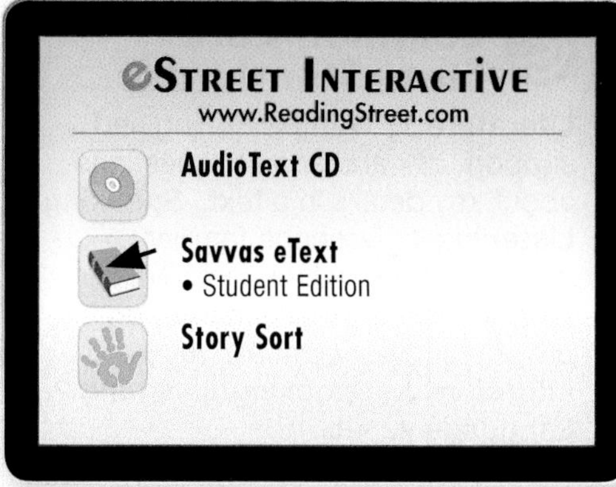

Access for All

 Advanced

Practice Sequence Encourage children to use the sequence words *first, next, then,* and *last* when they retell *Plaidypus Lost.*

Retelling Plan

- ☑ **Week 1** Assess Advanced students.
- ☑ **Week 2** Assess On-Level students.
- ☑ **This week assess Strategic Intervention students.**
- ☐ **Week 4** Assess Advanced students.
- ☐ **Week 5** Assess On-Level students.
- ☐ **Week 6** Assess Strategic Intervention students.

Scoring Rubric Narrative Retelling

	4	3	2	1
Connections	Makes connections and generalizes beyond the text	Makes connections to other events, stories, or experiences	Makes a limited connection to another event, story, or experience	Makes no connection to another event, story, or experience
Author's Purpose	Elaborates on author's purpose	Tells author's purpose with some clarity	Makes some connection to author's purpose	Makes no connection to author's purpose
Characters	Describes the main character(s) and any character development	Identifies the main character(s) and gives some information about them	Inaccurately identifies some characters or gives little information about them	Inaccurately identifies the characters or gives no information about them
Setting	Describes the time and location	Identifies the time and location	Omits details of time or location	Is unable to identify time or location
Plot	Describes the events in sequence using rich detail	Tells the plot with some errors in sequence that do not affect meaning	Tells parts of plot with gaps that affect meaning	Retelling has no sense of story

Survival Vocabulary Remind children that *lost* means "not knowing where you are." When you are lost, you can ask for help.

Literature 1. With prompting and support, ask and answer questions about key details in a text. **Speaking/ Listening 4.** Describe familiar people, places, things, and events and, with prompting and support, provide additional detail. **Also Literature 3., Speaking/Listening 2., Language 4., 4.b.**

Access for All

Sequence Use a sequence chart to identify the sequence in *Plaidypus Lost.* Once the entire sequence is mapped out, have children identify what happens first and what happens last. What does Plaidypus look like first? What does he look like last?

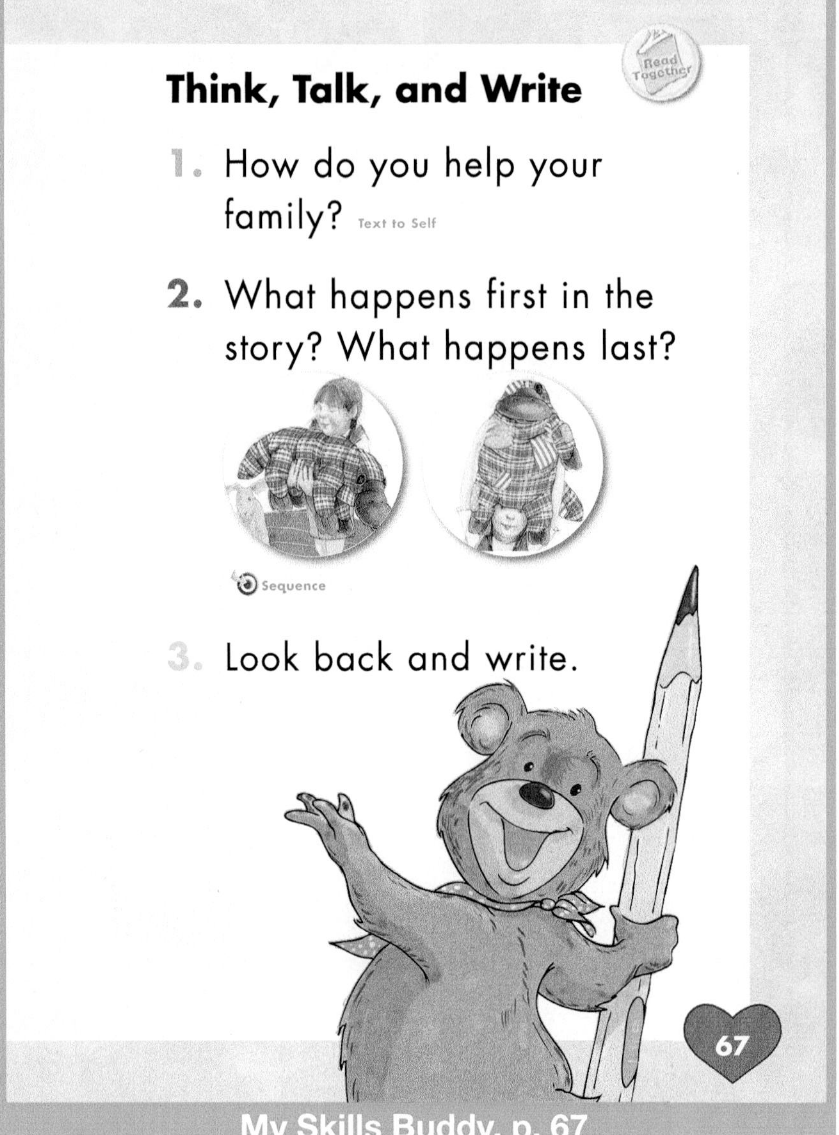

My Skills Buddy, p. 67

Think, Talk, and Write

DISCUSS CONCEPT We're learning about how families cooperate. Think about your family.

- What things do you do with your family?
- Why is it important to cooperate with family members?

CONFIRM PREDICTIONS Have children recall their predictions before you read *Plaidypus Lost.*

- What did you think the story would be about?
- Was your prediction correct?

Have children turn to p. 67 of *My Skills Buddy.* Read the questions and directives and have children respond.

1. **TEXT TO SELF** How do you help your family? Do you like helping out at home? What is your favorite thing to do?

2. **SEQUENCE** What happens first in the story? (The girl gets a new stuffed animal companion, a platypus.) What happens last? (The girl's stuffed animal companion gets fixed after it gets lost.)

3. **LOOK BACK AND WRITE • TEXT EVIDENCE** Let's look back at our story and write about it. We remember that the girl loses Plaidypus in the grocery store. Listen for where she looks for Plaidypus. Read pp. 20–21 of *Plaidypus Lost.* Now let's write our ideas. Discuss with children the directions the girl looks when she realizes Plaidypus is missing. Record their responses on chart paper. (She looks left and right. She looks high and low. She looks over and under.)

Conventions

What We Look Like

TEACH We talked about words we can use to tell what we look like. We can use these words to tell about, or describe, people, places, animals, and things.

GUIDE PRACTICE Let's look at Plaidypus on the cover of the book. What words can you use to tell what he looks like? I can use the word *colorful.* Write *colorful* on the board. Now let's tell whether Plaidypus looks happy or sad, tall or short, clean or dirty, big or little. Write the words on the board below *colorful.* Continue with other pictures of Plaidypus in the book.

Read the list with children. Write this sentence frame on the board:

Plaidypus looks ______.

Which word can we use to complete the sentence? Have children suggest words from the list. Write the word on the line. Repeat with other words on the list.

ON THEIR OWN Use *Reader's and Writer's Notebook,* p. 30, for more practice with what we look like.

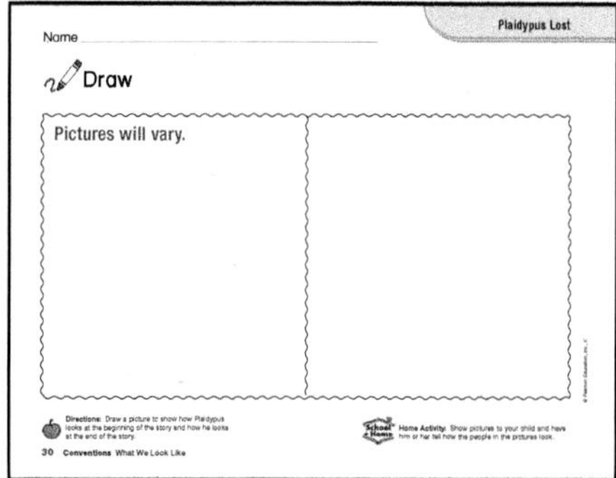

Reader's and Writer's Notebook, p. 30

AFFIXES AND MEANING Use the word *colorful* to introduce affixes and their role in word meaning. Circle *-ful* in *colorful.* The word part *-ful* means "full of." When *-ful* is added to *color,* it makes the word *colorful,* which means "full of color." We can use the word part *-ful* to help us figure out what a word means.

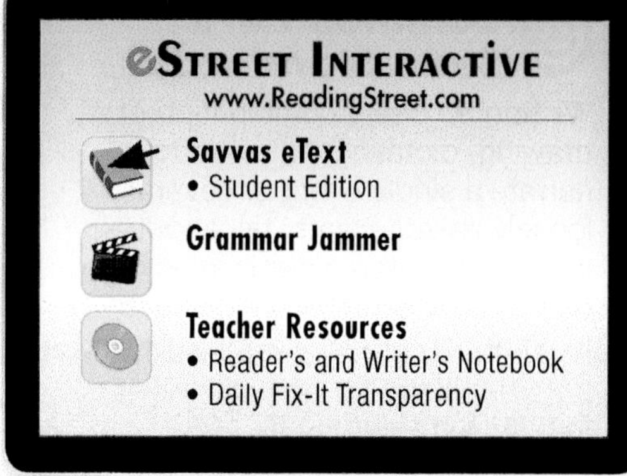

Writing to Sources
Use Write Like a Reporter on pp. 14–15 to guide children in writing text-based responses using one source.

Daily Fix-It
i found a platypus
I found a platypus.
This week's practice sentences appear on *Teacher Resources DVD-ROM.*

Bridge to Common Core

CONVENTIONS OF STANDARD ENGLISH
As children use words to describe people, places, animals, and things, they are starting to learn about adjectives and nouns, two important concepts in standard English grammar and usage.

Support Conventions Some children may provide words about Plaidypus's appearance, such as *cute* or *silly,* that others do not agree with. Point out that these are opinions, and each child has a right to his or her own thoughts and ideas.

Common Core State Standards

Writing 3. Use a combination of drawing, dictating, and writing to narrate a single event or several loosely linked events, tell about the events in the order in which they occurred, and provide a reaction to what happened. **Language 1.a.** Print many upper- and lowercase letters. **Language 5.a.** Sort common objects into categories (e.g., shapes, foods) to gain a sense of the concepts the categories represent. **Language 5.c.** Identify real-life connections between words and their use (e.g., note places at school that are *colorful*). **Also Literature 4., Language 5.**

Writing

Respond to Literature

DISCUSS Display *Plaidypus Lost.* Write the words *lost* and *found* on the board. Tell children to name the places where Plaidypus was lost and tell how he was found.

MODEL I remember that Plaidypus is lost at the market. He looks sad sitting on the shelf. I am going to write:

Plaidypus is lost in the market.

GUIDE PRACTICE Have children pick another place where Plaidypus is lost. Then help them write a sentence about it.

INDEPENDENT WRITING Have children choose one of the places where Plaidypus was lost or found and draw a picture. Have them write or dictate the word *lost* or *found* under their picture.

Daily Handwriting

Write uppercase *O* and *P* and *pop* on the board. Review correct letter formation with children.

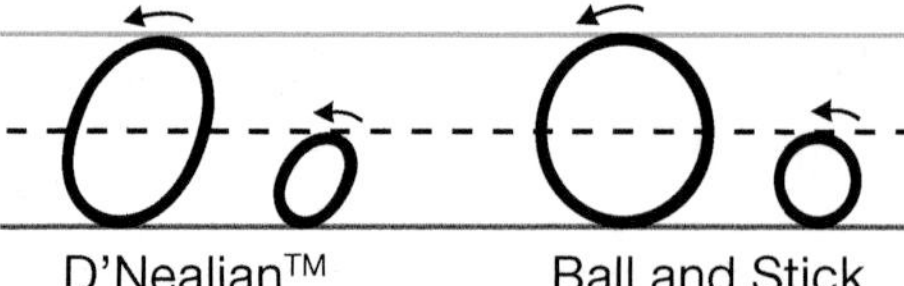

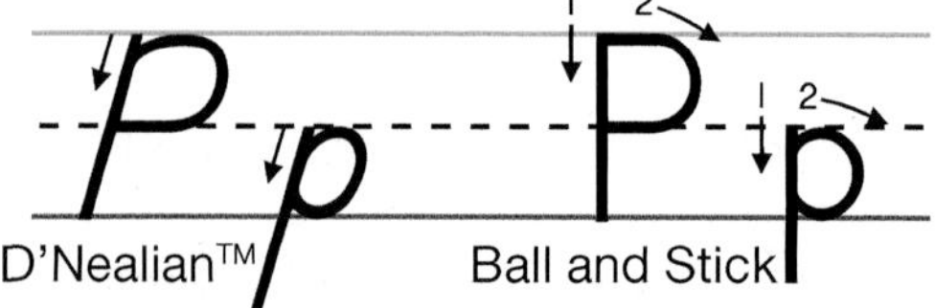

Have children write a row of uppercase *O* and *P* and *pop* on their Write-On Boards. Remind them to use proper left-to-right and top-to-bottom progression when writing *O, o, P,* and *p.*

Writing to Sources Use More Connect the Texts on pp. 222–293 to guide children in writing text-based responses within various forms and modes.

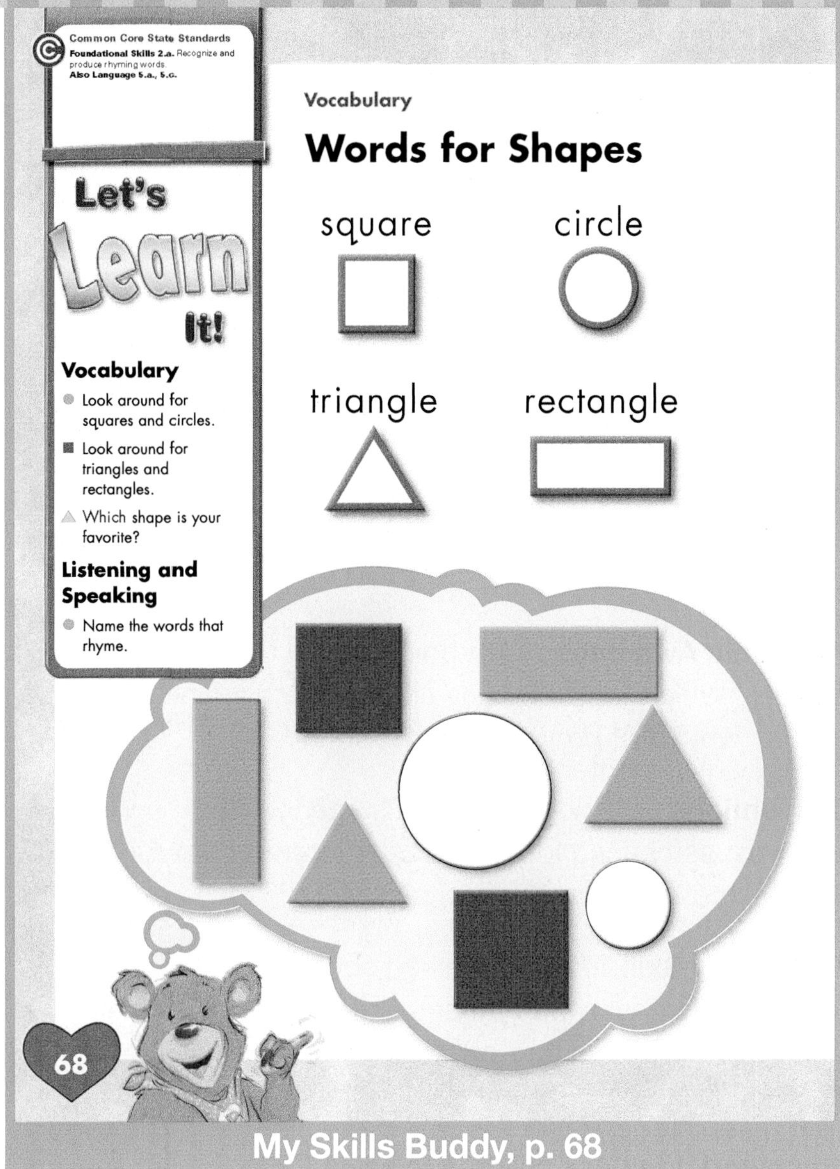

My Skills Buddy, p. 68

Vocabulary

Words for Shapes

TEACH Have children turn to p. 68 of *My Skills Buddy.* Use the first two Vocabulary bullets to guide the discussion about the shapes. Have children point to each shape and describe it.

GUIDE PRACTICE Write the words *square, triangle, circle,* and *rectangle* on the board. Point to each word as you read it and draw the shape.

Look at the shapes at the bottom of p. 68. What color are the squares? What color are the circles? Which shapes are blue?

ON THEIR OWN Have each child draw a picture of something that has a square, triangle, circle, or rectangle shape. Collect and mix the drawings. Have children sort them into shape categories and label each group.

Access for All

SI Strategic Intervention

Build Vocabulary Write the words for shapes on cards. Have children tell you what things in the classroom are that shape. Attach the cards to the objects.

Academic Vocabulary

shape the way something looks

Bridge to Common Core

VOCABULARY ACQUISITION AND USE

Learning about words that name shapes helps children understand the relationships among words in a specific category as well as acquire general academic words to use when reading or writing.

Support Writing Remind children that *lost* means "missing" and *found* means "located." Each time Plaidypus is lost and found, he is in a place. What places does the girl take Plaidypus? List the locations on the board and encourage children to use the list to write or dictate their sentence.

DAY 2

Common Core State Standards

Foundational Skills 2. Demonstrate understanding of spoken words, syllables, and sounds (phonemes). **Language 5.c.** Identify real-life connections between words and their use (e.g., note places at school that are *colorful*).

Wrap Up Your Day!

✔ **Content Knowledge** Today we read about a girl who keeps losing her stuffed animal, Plaidypus. What does a real platypus look like?

✔ **Phonemic Awareness** I am going to say three words: *band, fog, bell.* Which words begin with the same sound? Tell me another word that begins with that sound.

✔ **Conventions** I am going to say a sentence. Tell me which word tells what something looks like. *Juan drew a colorful picture.* Which word tells about Juan's picture?

✔ **Vocabulary Skill** Today we talked about words for shapes: *square, triangle, circle, rectangle.* Draw a picture of something that has a circle shape.

✔ **Homework Idea** Ask children to say a sentence that tells what they look like.

Preview DAY 3

Tomorrow we will reread the story *Plaidypus Lost.*

Extend Your Day!

Science
All About Platypuses

MATERIALS: Big Book *Plaidypus Lost,* paper, crayons, chart paper

MAKE A CHART Present the following information to children:

- Platypuses live in Australia. Use a globe to show the locations of Australia and the United States.
- A platypus has a long, flat bill like a duck. It is often called the duck-billed platypus. Show a picture of a platypus.
- A platypus is a good swimmer. It has webbed feet and a broad, flat tail.
- A platypus eats worms and shellfish. It also uses its bill to catch small animals in the water.
- A platypus is 16 to 22 inches long and weighs about 5 pounds.
- A platypus has a brown fur coat.
- A platypus lives in a burrow (a hole in the ground) near a stream.

Gather books about platypuses. Have children look at pictures of a real platypus. Then help them fill in a chart like the one shown here.

Platypus	
country	
home	
size	
color	
body part	
food	

Conventions
What We Look Like

MATERIALS: paper, crayons

ILLUSTRATE A FAMILY MEMBER Have children draw a picture of a family member. Encourage them to use many colors. Then have children write or dictate words that tell what their family member looks like in their picture.

Comprehension
Sequence

SEARCH FOR *PLAIDYPUS* Hide a stuffed "Plaidypus" toy in the room. Have children tell where they think they should look to find the toy. Write the steps on the board. Choose a child to look in each place. Add more areas until the toy is found. Review the list of places. Remind children that the list shows the order, or sequence, of places they looked to find the toy. Ask children to close their eyes and then hide the toy again.

Where to Look

1. in the closet
2. in the desk
3. under the sink
4. in the coat room
5. behind the bookcase

DAY 3 at a Glance

Content Knowledge
Oral Vocabulary

Phonemic Awareness
Initial Sound Discrimination

Letter Recognition
Letters *Qq*

Text-Based Comprehension
Sequence

Conventions
Review Write Our Names

Writing
Poem

Listening and Speaking
Listen for Rhyme and Rhythm

Materials

- Student Edition
- Truckery Rhymes
- Talk with Me/Sing with Me Chart
- Picture Cards
- Alphabet Cards
- Reader's and Writer's Notebook
- Student Reader K.1.3
- Big Book

Common Core State Standards

Speaking/Listening 1.a. Follow agreed-upon rules for discussions (e.g., listening to others and taking turns speaking about the topics and texts under discussion). **Language 5.b.** Demonstrate understanding of frequently occurring verbs and adjectives by relating them to their opposites (antonyms). **Language 6.** Use words and phrases acquired through conversations, reading and being read to, and responding to texts. **Also Language 4., 5.c.**

TRUCKTOWN
on Reading Street

Start your engines!
Display p. 7 of *Truckery Rhymes.* Do you know the song "Three Blind Mice"? Sing it first, and then have children sing it with you.

Three blind mice, three blind mice,
See how they run, see how they run!
They all ran after the farmer's wife.
Did you ever see such a sight in your life,
As three blind mice?

Truckery Rhymes

Content Knowledge

Zoom in on

Families Living, Working, and Playing Together

On the board, write the Question of the Week, *How do families cooperate?* Read it as you track the print. Talk with children about how families cooperate. Remind children to speak clearly and to take turns speaking.

Build Oral Language

LISTEN FOR AMAZING WORDS Display Sing with Me Chart 3B. Remind children that yesterday they sang "Purple Platypus" and listened for the words *platypus* and *around.* Today we are going to listen for the Amazing Words *lost* and *found.* Sing the song several times to the tune of "Baby Bumble Bee." Have children sing along with you, clapping their hands when they say the Amazing Words *lost* and *found.*

Purple Platypus
I lost my purple platypus today,
Searched around the market,
couldn't find him anywhere,
My grandpa peeked in a bag
of groceries,
Look! We found him!

Talk with Me/Sing with Me Chart 3B

Build Oral Vocabulary

Amazing Words Robust Vocabulary Routine

1. **Introduce the Word** Throughout the story, Plaidypus gets *lost. Lost* means that we can't find something. What's our new Amazing Word for when we can't find something? Say it with me: *lost.*

2. **Demonstrate** Provide examples to show meaning. *The little girl looks for Plaidypus when he is lost.* Have you ever *lost* something?

   Repeat steps 1 and 2.

   Introduce the Word In the story, Plaidypus is eventually *found.* Something that has been *found* has been located. What's our new Amazing Word for when something has been located? Say it with me: *found.*

   Demonstrate *As soon as Plaidypus is found, the little girl hugs him.* Where have you *found* something you lost?

3. **Apply** Have children use *lost* and *found* in complete sentences. Have them draw a picture of something they *lost* and then a picture of the place where they *found* it.

4. **Display the Words** Ask children what letters *lost* and *found* begin with. Ask them what letter they see in both words.

Routines Flip Chart

USE AMAZING WORDS To reinforce the concept and the Amazing Words, have children supply the appropriate Amazing Word for each sentence.

If something is missing, it is _______. (lost)
I _______ my missing shirt. (found)

OPPOSITES Explain to children that the words *lost* and *found* are opposites, or words with very different meanings. Help children use *lost/found* and the following pairs of opposites in sentences that show the meanings of the words: *sad/happy, hot/cold, stop/go, laugh/cry.*

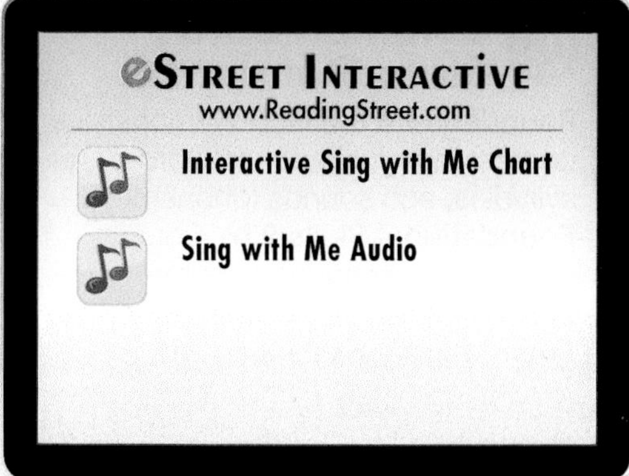

Amazing Words

platypus	around
lost	found
market	groceries

Access for All

 Advanced

Access Content Have children talk about what they would do if they found something that did not belong to them.

Access Content Have children share the words in their home languages for *lost* and *found.*

Expand Vocabulary Use the Day 3 instruction on ELL Poster 3 to help children expand their use of vocabulary to communicate about lesson concepts.

Common Core State Standards

Foundational Skills 2. Demonstrate understanding of spoken words, syllables, and sounds (phonemes). **Foundational Skills 2.b.** Count, pronounce, blend, and segment syllables in spoken words. **Also Foundational Skills 2.c., 2.d.**

Phonemic Awareness

Initial Sound Discrimination

ISOLATE INITIAL SOUNDS I will say two words. I want you to listen to the beginning sounds in the words and tell me whether the beginning sounds are the same or different. If the two words begin with the same sound, say "Same." If the two words begin with different sounds, say "Different." Listen carefully: *lost, left.* (same) *Lost* and *left* begin with the same sound. Let's listen again: *lost, left.* Continue the routine with these pairs of words: *buttons, back; new, lose; road, right; bush, rock; found, four; feet, ride.*

Display the *bubble* Picture Card. What is this? This is a bubble. Listen to the beginning sound in the word *bubble.* Now I will say two words. Listen to their beginning sounds and choose the word that begins like *bubble: big, little.* Say *bubble* and *big.* Now say *bubble* and *little.* Does *big* or *little* have the same beginning sound as *bubble?* (*big*) Yes, *big* and *bubble* begin with the same sound. Continue the routine with the *desk* Picture Card and the words *back, down.* Repeat with the *pail* Picture Card and the words *patch, dirt.*

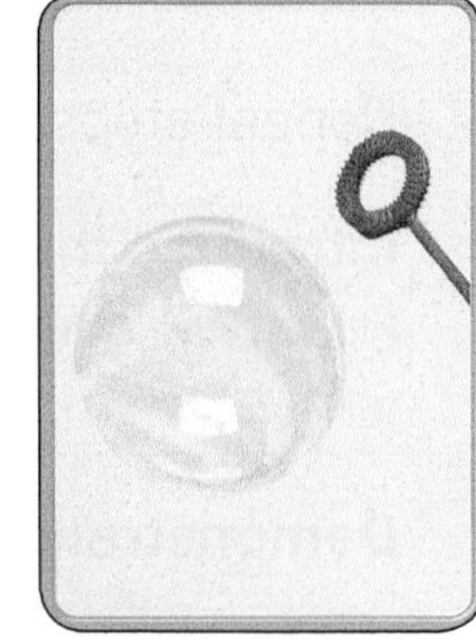

Picture Card

ON THEIR OWN Display the *feather, fan, ladybug,* and *leaf* Picture Cards. Have children choose two things that begin with the same sound and draw pictures of them.

BLEND SYLLABLES Remind children of the steps in blending syllables to say words. I am going to say a syllable, and you will repeat it: *snor-*. Now I am going to say another syllable, and you will repeat it: *-kel.* Now let's put the syllables together: *snor-kel, snorkel.* We blend syllables together to say the word *snorkel.* Repeat the routine with *teach-er* and *snip-pi-ty.*

Corrective feedback	**If...** children cannot blend the syllables together to say a word, **then...** model blending the syllables together to say the word and have children echo you.

CLAP SYLLABLES IN WORDS Listen to this word: *Plaidypus.* Have children repeat the word with you (*Plaid-y-pus*) and clap the parts, or syllables, as they say the word. Repeat the word again and have children clap and count the syllables. Continue with these words: *gro-cer-ies, mar-ket, lost, a-round, un-der, flip-pers, Grand-ma, Grand-moth-er.*

Access for All

 Strategic Intervention

Isolate Initial Sounds Children may have difficulty isolating only the initial sounds in words. Say the words like this: /l/ *-ost* and /l/ *-eft.* Then have children determine if the words begin with same initial sound.

Common Core State Standards

Foundational Skills 1.d. Recognize and name all upper- and lowercase letters of the alphabet.

Letter Recognition

Teach/Model

Letters *Qq*

INTRODUCE Display the *Qq* Alphabet Card. Point to the uppercase *Q*. This is uppercase *Q*. What is the name of this letter? Point to the lowercase *q*. This is lowercase *q*. What is the name of this letter?

Alphabet Card

MODEL Point to the queen on the Alphabet Card. This is a queen. Write the word *queen* on the board and point to *q*. This is lowercase *q*.

Guide Practice

GROUP PRACTICE Display Phonics Songs and Rhymes Chart 3, "Oh, My! Oh, No!" Let's look at the chart and find the word that begins with the letter *q*. Have children look for the word *quacked*. Read the word aloud and have children echo you. Then have them say all the letters in the word.

ON THEIR OWN Use *Reader's and Writer's Notebook,* pp. 26 and 31, for additional practice with letters *Qq*.

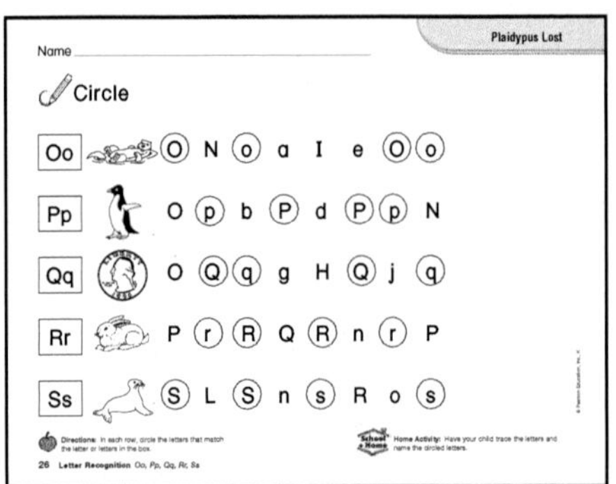
Name
Plaidypus Lost
Circle
Oo O N o a I e O o
Pp o p b P d P p N
Qq o Q q g H Q j q
Rr P r R Q R n r P
Ss S L S n s R o s
26 Letter Recognition Oo, Pp, Qq, Rr, Ss

Reader's and Writer's Notebook, p. 26

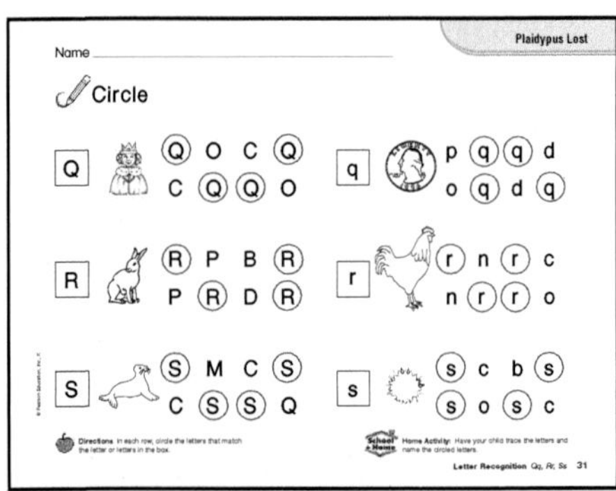
Name
Plaidypus Lost
Circle
Q Q O C Q C Q Q O
q p q q d o q d q
R R P B R P R D R
r r n r c n r r o
S S M C S C S S Q
s s c b s s o s c
Letter Recognition Qq, Rr, Ss 31

Reader's and Writer's Notebook, p. 31

REVIEW LETTER NAMES Display the *Pp* Alphabet Card. Point to the uppercase *P.* What is the name of this letter? Point to the lowercase *p.* What is the name of this letter? Continue the routine with the *Hh, Ii,* and *Jj* Alphabet Cards.

REVIEW HIGH-FREQUENCY WORDS Write *the* on the board. This is the word *the.* What is this word? Continue the routine with *little.*

Alphabet Card

Access for All

Advanced

Review Letter Names Show the Alphabet Cards for letters children have previously learned (*Aa–Qq*). Put the cards in random order. Have children work together to put the letters in alphabetical order. Ask children to identify each letter as they put it in order.

MONITOR PROGRESS Check Word Reading High-Frequency Words

FORMATIVE ASSESSMENT Write the following high-frequency words from Kindergarten Student Reader K.1.3, *Cat and Dog Play,* on the board. Have children take turns reading the words.

am	I	little	the

If... children cannot read the high-frequency words,
then... write the words on cards for them to practice at home.

If... children can successfully read the high-frequency words,
then... have them read Kindergarten Student Reader K.1.3, *Cat and Dog Play.*

 **Common Core State Standards**

Literature 10. Actively engage in group reading activities with purpose and understanding. **Foundational Skills 1.a.** Follow words from left to right, top to bottom, and page-by-page.

Access for All

SI Strategic Intervention

Use Illustrations Have children identify the animals in each of the pictures in *Cat and Dog Play.*

Student Reader

Read *Cat and Dog Play*

REVIEW Review the previously taught high-frequency words. Have children read each word as you point to it on the Word Wall: *I, am, the, little.*

TEACH REBUS WORDS Write *dad* on the board. This is the word *dad.* Name the letters with me: *d, a, d, dad.* Repeat the routine with *cat, dog, running, jumping,* and *happy.* Look for these words in the book we read today. There will be a picture above the word to help you read it.

READ Display Kindergarten Student Reader K.1.3. Today we are going to read a new book. Point to the front and back cover. Point to the title of the book. The title of this book is *Cat and Dog Play.* Remind children to hold their book right side up and to turn the pages one at a time. When we finish reading the words on the page, we turn the page. Let's practice turning the pages. Look at each picture as you turn the pages. What do you think will happen in this book?

Use the reading decodable books routine to read the Kindergarten Student Reader.

Routine Reading Decodable Books

1. **Read Silently** Have children whisper read the book page by page as you listen in.
2. **Model Fluent Reading** Have children finger point as you read a page. Then have them reread the page without you.
3. **Read Chorally** Have children finger point as they chorally read the page. Continue reading page by page, repeating steps 1 and 2.
4. **Read Individually** Have children take turns reading aloud a page.
5. **Reread and Monitor Progress** As you listen to individual children reread, monitor progress and provide support.
6. **Reread with a Partner** Have children reread the book page by page with a partner.

Routines Flip Chart

Kindergarten Student Reader K.1.3

eStreet Interactive
www.ReadingStreet.com

Savvas eText
- Kindergarten Student Reader

Day 3 SMALL GROUP TIME • Differentiate Vocabulary, p. SG•37

OL On-Level
- **Develop Vocabulary** Practice Words for Shapes
- **Read** Student Reader *Cat and Dog Play*

SI Strategic Intervention
- **Develop Vocabulary** Reteach Words for Shapes
- **Read** Student Reader *Cat and Dog Play*

A Advanced
- **Develop Vocabulary** More Words for Shapes
- **Read** Student Reader *Cat and Dog Play*

ELL

Place English Language Learners in the groups that correspond to their reading abilities in English.

If... children need more scaffolding and practice with **Vocabulary**, **then...** use the ELL activities on p. DI•48 in the Teacher Resources section of the Digital Path.

Text-Based Comprehension

Read Main Selection

RETELL THE SELECTION Have children turn to p. 66 of *My Skills Buddy* and use the retelling boxes to retell the story *Plaidypus Lost.*

Direct children to the first retelling box. This is when the girl gets her new stuffed companion, Plaidypus. Tell me what happens to him.

Continue reviewing the retelling boxes and having children retell the story.

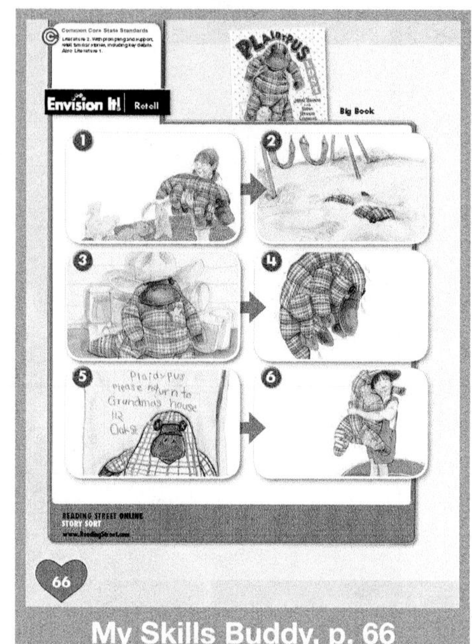

My Skills Buddy, p. 66

REVIEW SEQUENCE Display *Plaidypus Lost.* Let's review the sequence in this story.

- Where does Plaidypus get lost first? (the park)
- Where does Plaidypus get lost next? (the market)
- Where does Plaidypus get lost next? (the lake)
- Where does Plaidypus get lost last? (on a trip)

MORE PRACTICE Use *Reader's and Writer's Notebook,* p. 32, for additional practice with sequence.

Common Core State Standards

Literature 1. With prompting and support, ask and answer questions about key details in a text. **Literature 2.** With prompting and support, retell familiar stories, including key details. **Also Literature 3.**

Access for All

 Advanced

Practice Sequence Display the cover of *Plaidypus Lost.* Have children describe what they would need and how they would make a stuffed animal like Plaidypus.

Bridge to Common Core

CRAFT AND STRUCTURE

When children retell the story, they are analyzing the structure of a story, including the sequence of events. Use the Develop Vocabulary notes as you read the story to children a second time. Having them ask and answer questions about the story will enhance their comprehension.

Name
Plaidypus Lost
Number
3 2 1
1 3 2

Reader's and Writer's Notebook, p. 32

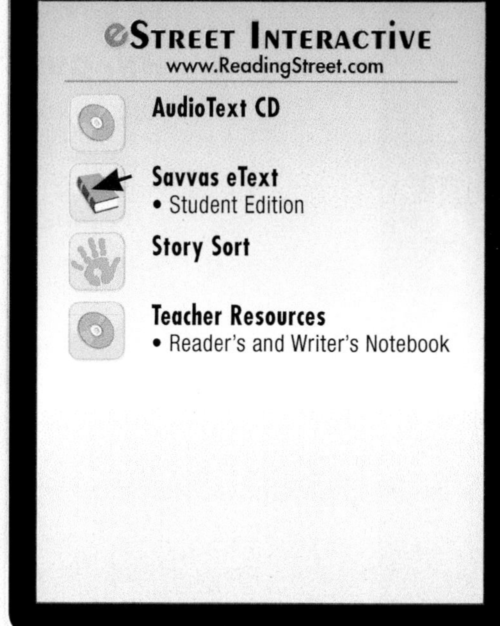

Access Main Selection

READER AND TASK SUGGESTIONS	
Preparing to Read the Text	**Leveled Tasks**
• Review the Amazing Words and have children use them to talk about the selection. • Discuss the author's varied use of colors and sizes of texts.	• **Theme and Knowledge Demands** If children don't understand the name *Plaidypus,* have them use an illustration to explain what a platypus is and what *plaid* means. • **Structure** If children have difficulty with sequence, have them list the order of the places where Plaidypus was lost.

See Text Complexity Measures for *Plaidypus Lost* on the tab at the beginning of this week.

READ Reread *Plaidypus Lost.* Follow the **2nd Read** beginning on p. 258, and use the **Develop Vocabulary** notes to prompt conversations about the story.

Routine Read for Understanding

Deepen understanding by reading the selection multiple times.

1. **First Read**—Read the entire selection aloud to build interest in the text.
2. **Second Read**—Use the **Develop Vocabulary** notes on pages 258–277.
3. **Third Read**—Use the **Develop Comprehension** notes on pages 258–277.

2ND READ

Develop Vocabulary

WH- QUESTION Point to the illustration on page 5. Something is cutting the plaid material. What is it? (scissors)

- The scissors are cutting the plaid material. What is cutting the plaid material?

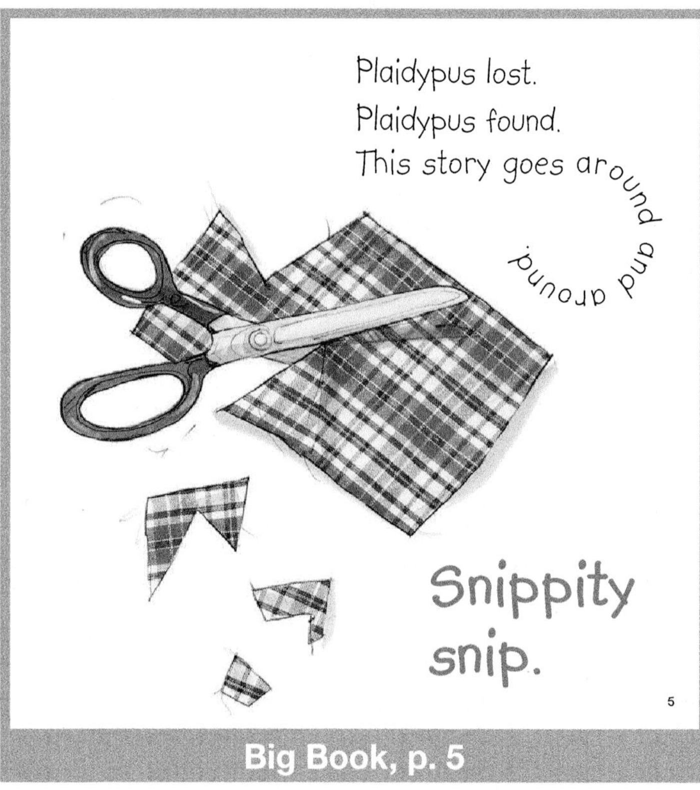

Plaidypus lost.
Plaidypus found.
This story goes around and around.
Snippity snip.
5

Big Book, p. 5

3RD READ

Develop Comprehension ©

MONITOR AND FIX UP What sound do the scissors make? If you don't remember what sound the scissors make, what can you do? (If I don't remember or understand something, I need to raise my hand and ask if we could reread the page.)

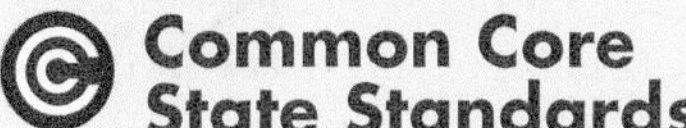

OPEN-ENDED What will the buttons be used for? (the animal's eyes)

- The buttons will be used for eyes. What do you think the plaid material and buttons will be used to make?

Common Core State Standards

Literature 1. With prompting and support, ask and answer questions about key details in a text. **Literature 2.** With prompting and support, retell familiar stories, including key details. **Literature 3.** With prompting and support, identify characters, settings, and major events in a story. **Literature 7.** With prompting and support, describe the relationship between illustrations and the story in which they appear (e.g., what moment in a story an illustration depicts).

Big Book, pp. 6–7

***WH*- QUESTION** Besides scissors and buttons, what other things are being used? (Other things being used include plaid material, a needle, thread, pins, and a pincushion.)

2ND READ

Develop Vocabulary

RECALL What does Grandma do with Grandpa's old plaid shirt? (makes a platypus)

- Grandma makes Plaidypus with Grandpa's old shirts. Who makes Plaidypus?

DEVELOP VOCABULARY shirt, Grandma

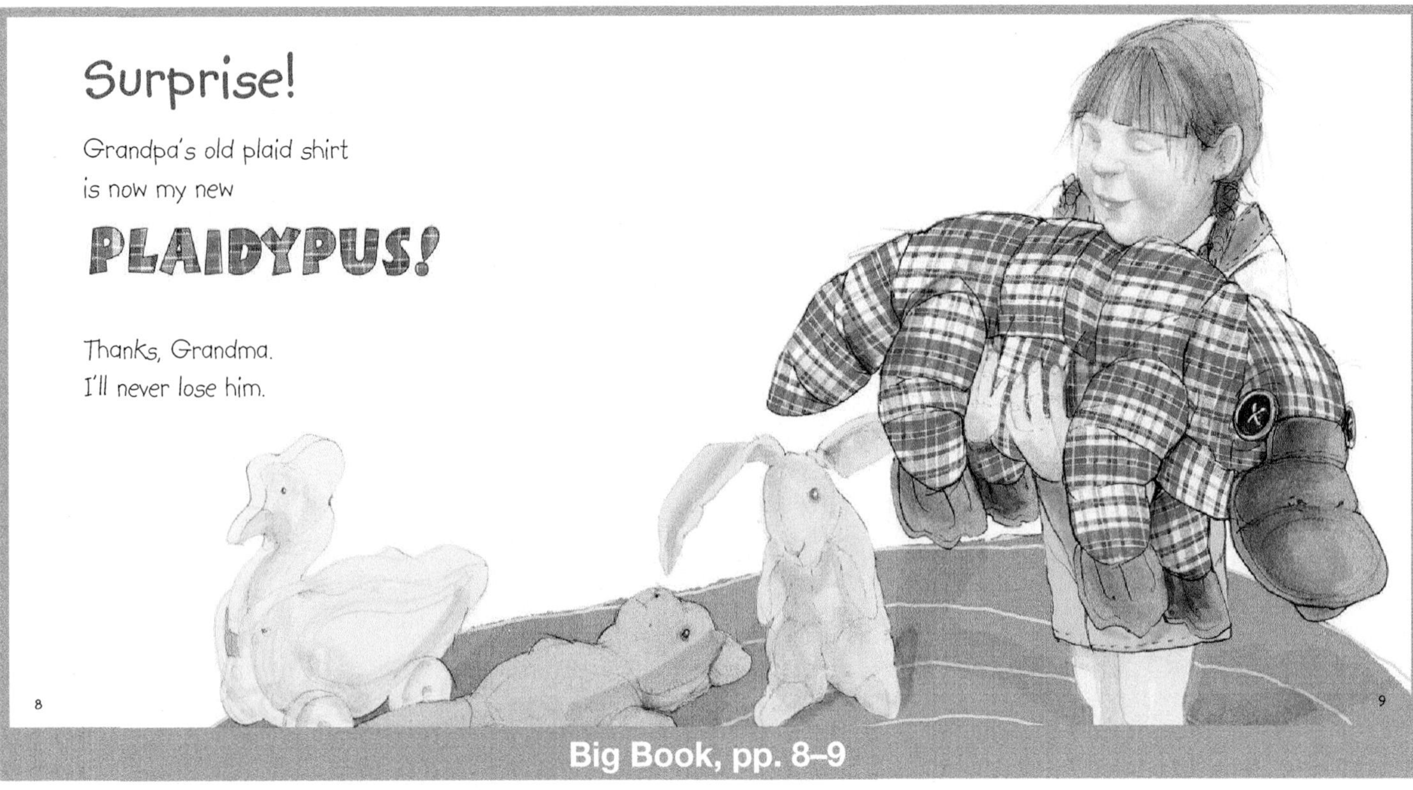
Surprise!
Grandpa's old plaid shirt
is now my new
PLAIDYPUS!
Thanks, Grandma.
I'll never lose him.
8
9

Big Book, pp. 8–9

3RD READ

Develop Comprehension ©

OPEN-ENDED How do Plaidypus and a real platypus look alike? How do they look different? (Plaidypus and a real platypus both have a flat tail and a ducklike bill. Plaidypus is different from a real platypus because he is made out of a plaid shirt.)

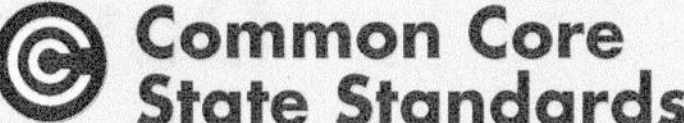

Common Core State Standards

Literature 1. With prompting and support, ask and answer questions about key details in a text. **Literature 2.** With prompting and support, retell familiar stories, including key details. **Literature 3.** With prompting and support, identify characters, settings, and major events in a story. **Literature 7.** With prompting and support, describe the relationship between illustrations and the story in which they appear (e.g., what moment in a story an illustration depicts).

***WH-* QUESTION** Who comes sliding down the slide? (Plaidypus)

- Plaidypus comes down the slide. What does Plaidypus come down?

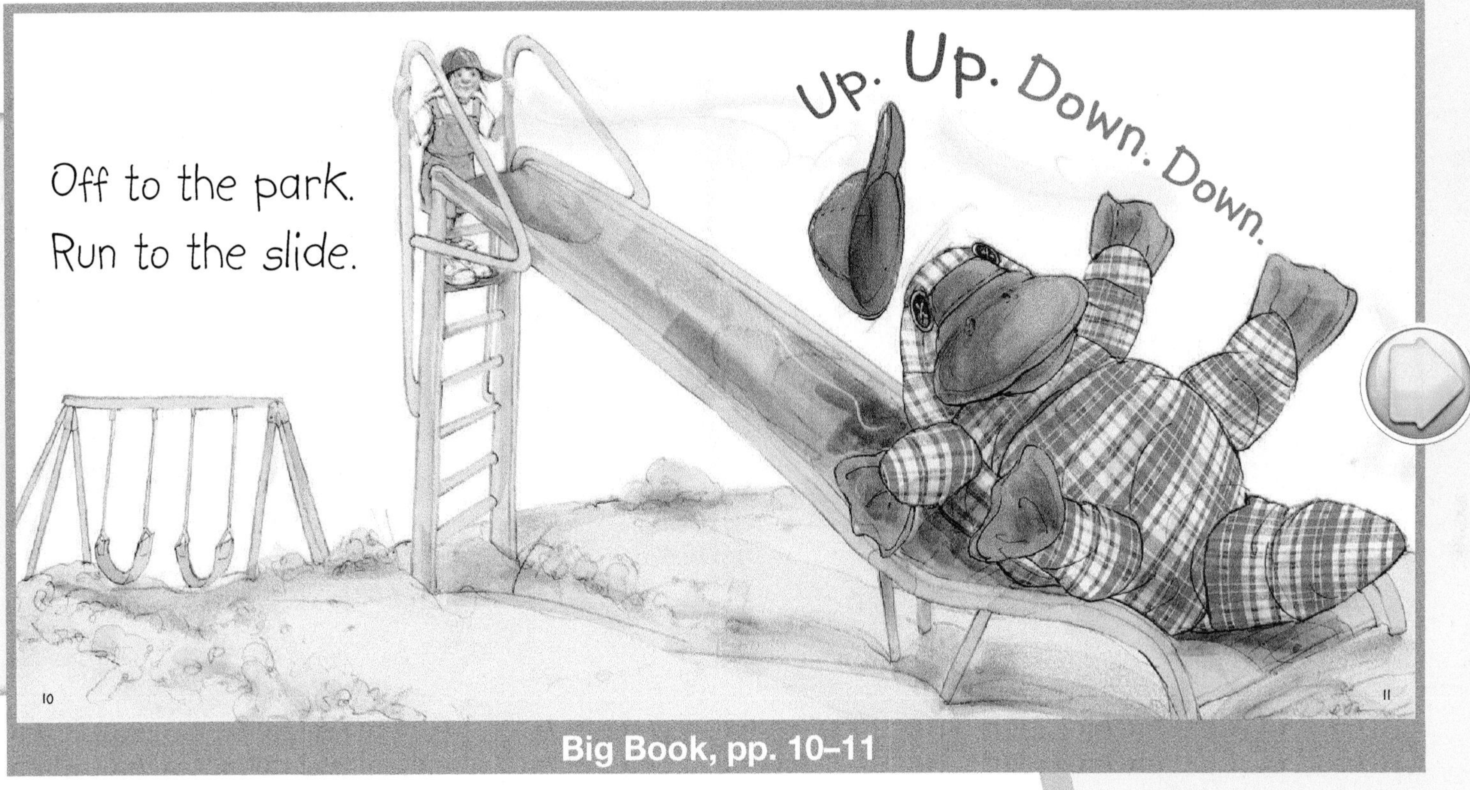
Off to the park.
Run to the slide.
Up. Up. Down. Down.
10
11

Big Book, pp. 10–11

OPEN-ENDED Why does the girl go to the park? (She wants to play on the slide and swings.)

2ND READ

Develop Vocabulary

DISTANCING What happens to the girl and Plaidypus? (They fall off the swing.)

- Plaidypus and the girl fall off the swing. Have you ever fallen off a swing? Tell me what happened.

DEVELOP VOCABULARY swing

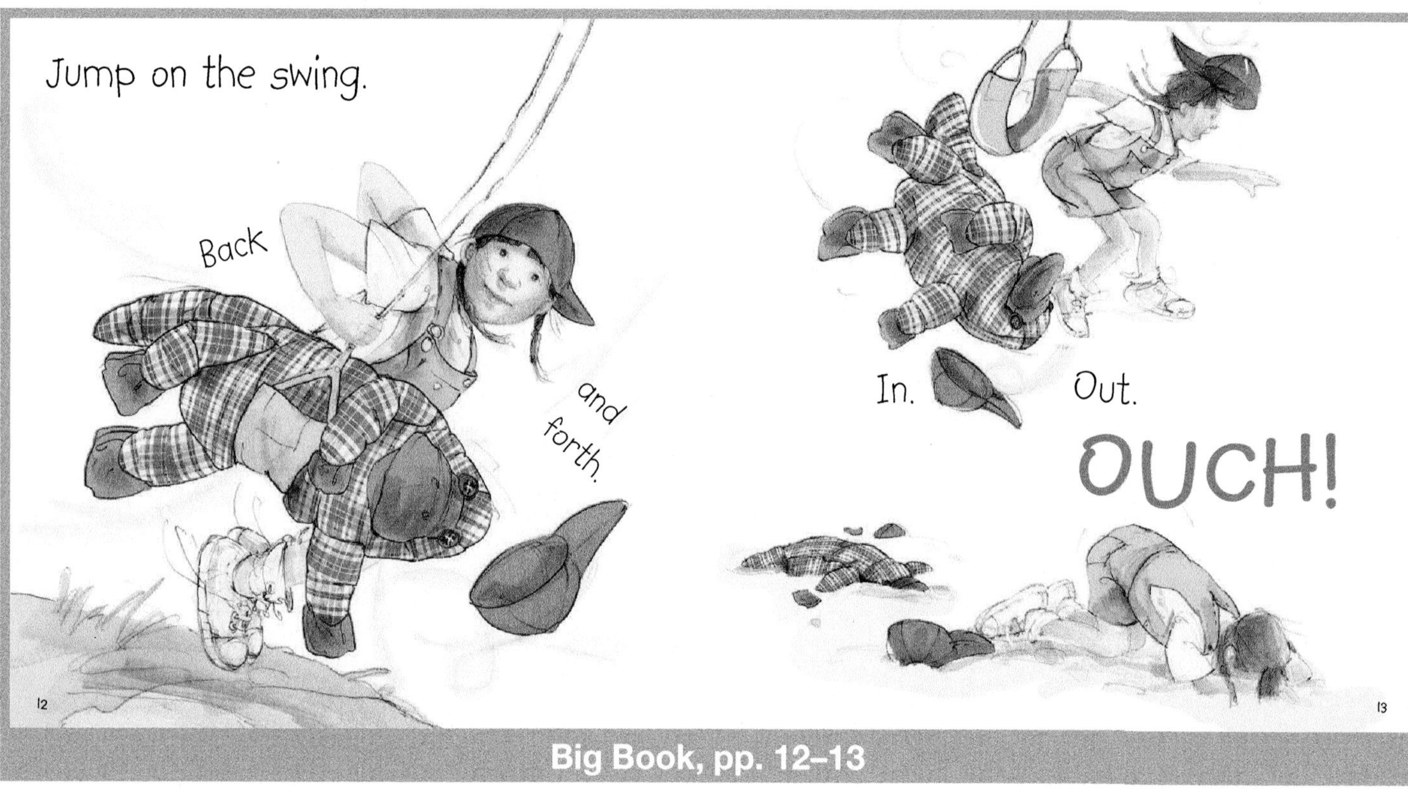

Big Book, pp. 12–13

3RD READ

Develop Comprehension ©

RECALL What does the girl say when she falls off the swing? (The girl says, "Ouch.")

RECALL The girl says, "Uh-oh." Why does she say "Uh-oh"? (She doesn't have Plaidypus.)

- The girl doesn't have Plaidypus with her. Where does she go to look for him?

Common Core State Standards

Literature 1. With prompting and support, ask and answer questions about key details in a text. **Literature 2.** With prompting and support, retell familiar stories, including key details. **Literature 3.** With prompting and support, identify characters, settings, and major events in a story. **Literature 7.** With prompting and support, describe the relationship between illustrations and the story in which they appear (e.g., what moment in a story an illustration depicts).

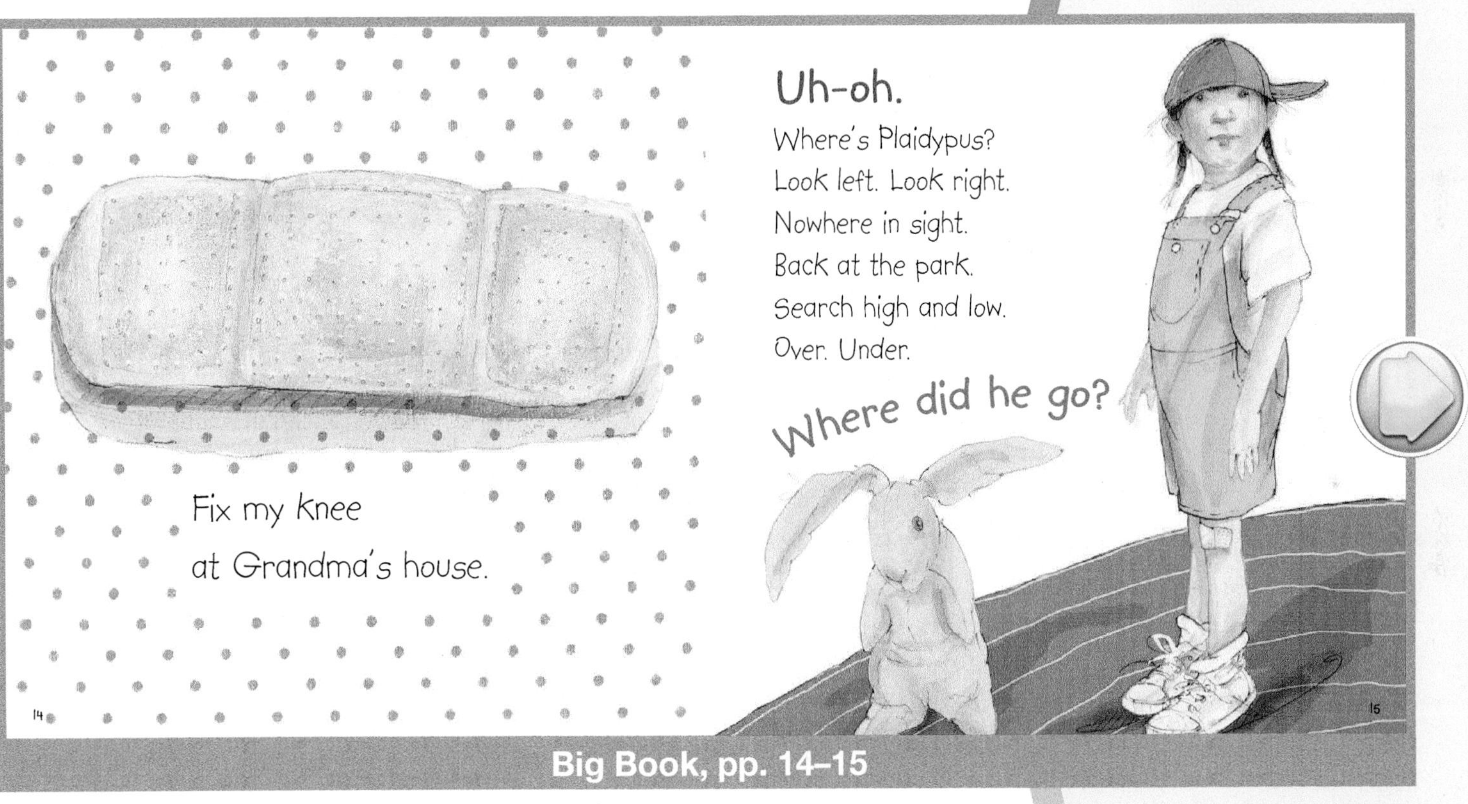
Fix my knee
at Grandma's house.
Uh-oh.
Where's Plaidypus?
Look left. Look right.
Nowhere in sight.
Back at the park.
Search high and low.
Over. Under.
Where did he go?
Big Book, pp. 14–15

***WH-* QUESTION** How does the girl look for Plaidypus at the park? (She looks high, low, over, and under.)

2ND READ

Develop Vocabulary

COMPLETION Where does the girl find Plaidypus? (in the sand)

- When the girl sees Plaidypus in the sand, she says, "I'm sorry, Plaidypus. I'll never, ever lose you again." Have children read the sentence with you.

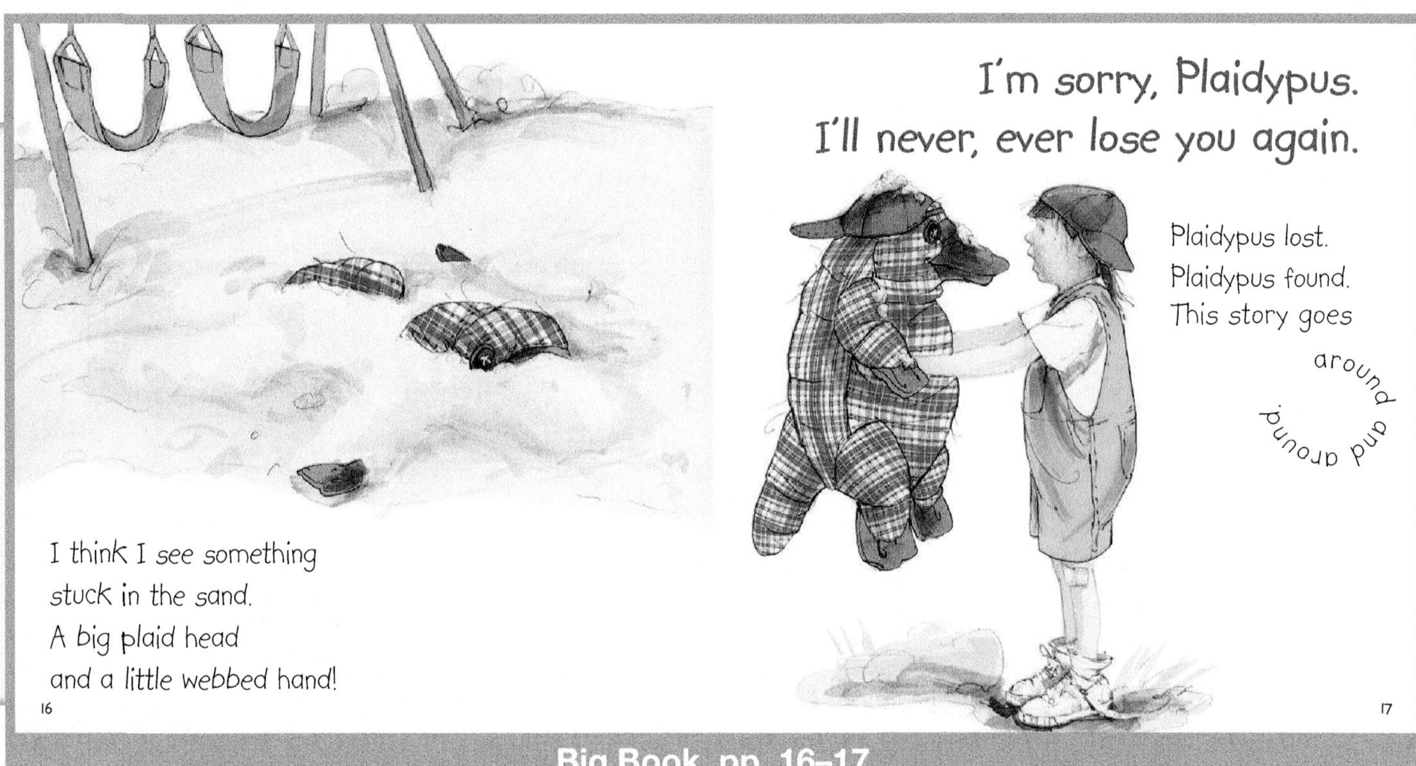

I think I see something
stuck in the sand.
A big plaid head
and a little webbed hand!
16
I'm sorry, Plaidypus.
I'll never, ever lose you again.
Plaidypus lost.
Plaidypus found.
This story goes
around
and around.
17

Big Book, pp. 16–17

3RD READ

Develop Comprehension ©

***WH-* QUESTION** Why is Plaidypus in the sand? (He fell off the swing.)

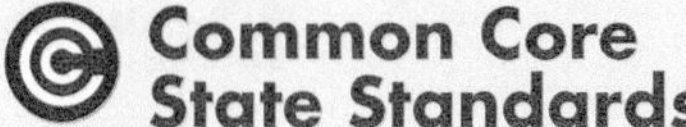

RECALL Where do the girl and Plaidypus go next? (to the market)

- They go to the market. What do they try to buy at the market?

Common Core State Standards

Literature 1. With prompting and support, ask and answer questions about key details in a text. **Literature 2.** With prompting and support, retell familiar stories, including key details. **Literature 3.** With prompting and support, identify characters, settings, and major events in a story. **Literature 7.** With prompting and support, describe the relationship between illustrations and the story in which they appear (e.g., what moment in a story an illustration depicts).

Off to the market.
Push the big cart.
Fast and slow.
Stop. Go.
18
Candy in.
Candy out.
19

Big Book, pp. 18–19

RECALL What kind of hat is Plaidypus wearing now? (He is wearing a cowboy hat.)

What kind of hat was he wearing before? (He was wearing a baseball cap.)

2ND READ

Develop Vocabulary

RECALL What does the girl discover after she helps put the groceries away? (Plaidypus is missing again.)

- Plaidypus is missing again. Where does the girl look for Plaidypus?

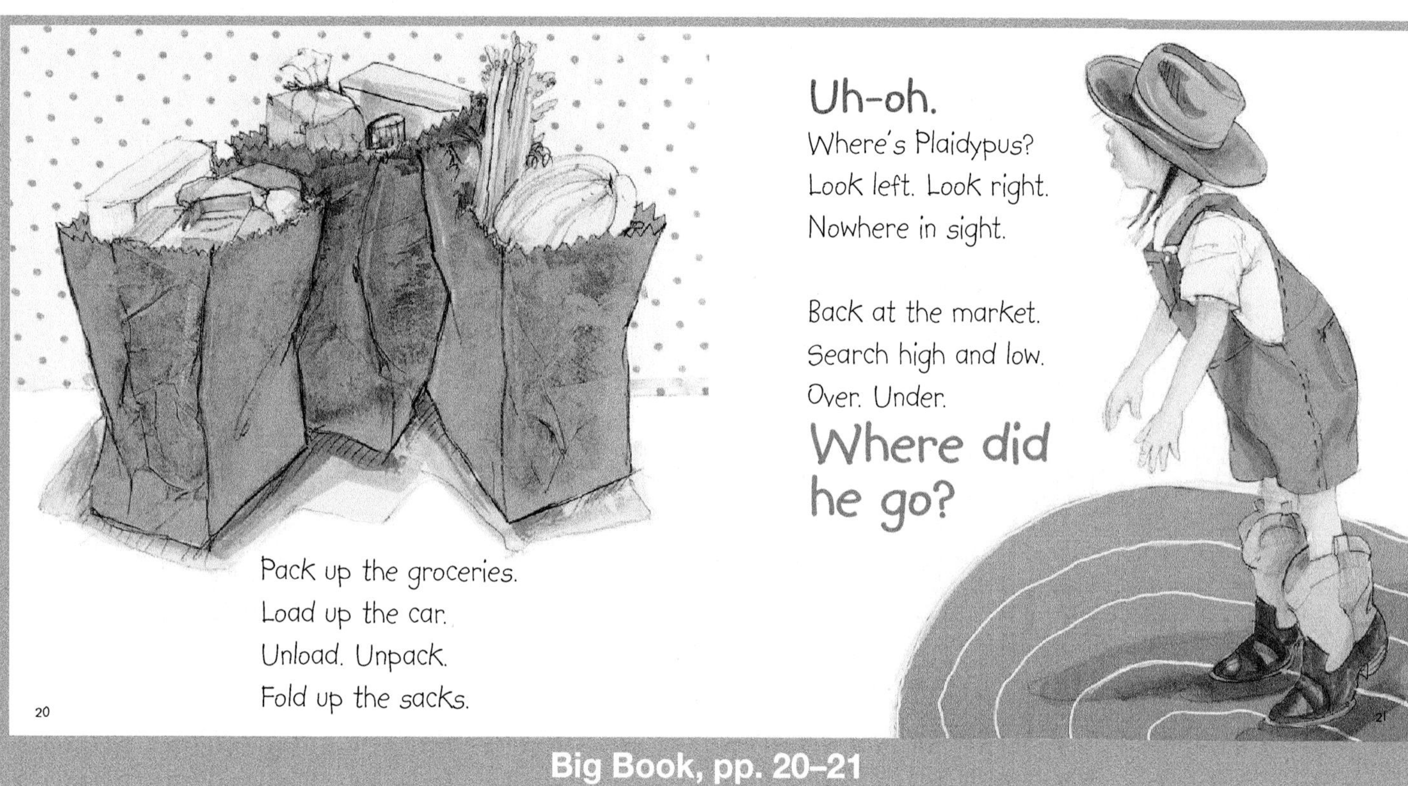

Pack up the groceries.
Load up the car.
Unload. Unpack.
Fold up the sacks.
20
Uh-oh.
Where's Plaidypus?
Look left. Look right.
Nowhere in sight.
Back at the market.
Search high and low.
Over. Under.
Where did he go?
21

Big Book, pp. 20–21

3RD READ

Develop Comprehension ©

INFERENCE Where do you think Plaidypus is? (I think he is in the grocery cart back at the market.)

WH- QUESTION What does the girl see on the shelf? (Plaidypus)

- What does she say to Plaidypus when she finds him on the shelf? ("I'm sorry, Plaidypus. I'll never, ever, ever lose you again.") Have children read the sentence with you.

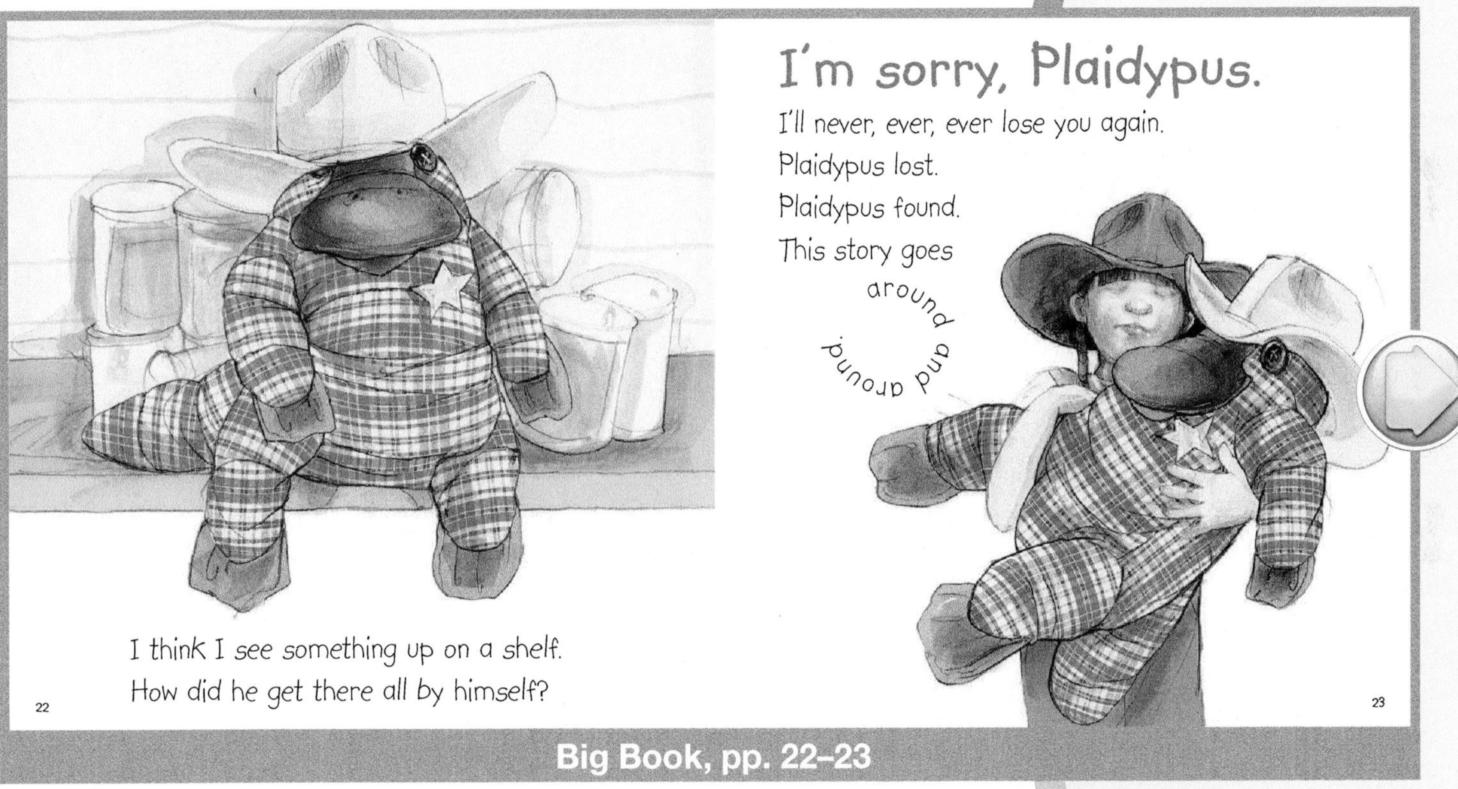

I think I see something up on a shelf.
How did he get there all by himself?
22
I'm sorry, Plaidypus.
I'll never, ever, ever lose you again.
Plaidypus lost.
Plaidypus found.
This story goes
around
and around.
23

Big Book, pp. 22–23

INFERENCE Plaidypus is on the shelf. How do you think Plaidypus got there? (I think when the girl was putting food back on the shelf, she put Plaidypus on the shelf instead.)

Common Core State Standards

Literature 1. With prompting and support, ask and answer questions about key details in a text. **Literature 2.** With prompting and support, retell familiar stories, including key details. **Literature 3.** With prompting and support, identify characters, settings, and major events in a story. **Literature 7.** With prompting and support, describe the relationship between illustrations and the story in which they appear (e.g., what moment in a story an illustration depicts).

2ND READ

Develop Vocabulary

***WH-* QUESTION** At the lake, does Plaidypus sink or float? (float)

- Plaidypus floats in the lake. What does Plaidypus do?

EXPAND VOCABULARY lake, sink, float

Off to the lake.
Go for a swim.
A snorkel for me.
A snorkel for him.
24
Into the water.
Out of the water.
Wet. Dry.
Sink. Float.
Hey!
There's my buddy
who lives down
the street.
Look at
these flippers.
Here on my feet!
Splashing
attack!
25

Big Book, pp. 24–25

3RD READ

Develop Comprehension ©

***WH-* QUESTION** What are both the girl and Plaidypus wearing? (They are both wearing masks and snorkels.)

What is the girl wearing and Plaidypus is not? (The girl is also wearing a swimsuit, an inner tube, and flippers.)

***WH-* QUESTION** How does the girl find out that Plaidypus is gone again? (She starts to offer him a cookie, but he's not there.)

- The girl has cookies for a snack and she wants to give Plaidypus a cookie too. What does she discover?

Common Core State Standards

Literature 1. With prompting and support, ask and answer questions about key details in a text. **Literature 2.** With prompting and support, retell familiar stories, including key details. **Literature 3.** With prompting and support, identify characters, settings, and major events in a story. **Literature 7.** With prompting and support, describe the relationship between illustrations and the story in which they appear (e.g., what moment in a story an illustration depicts).

A cookie for you,
a cookie for me, a cookie for . . .

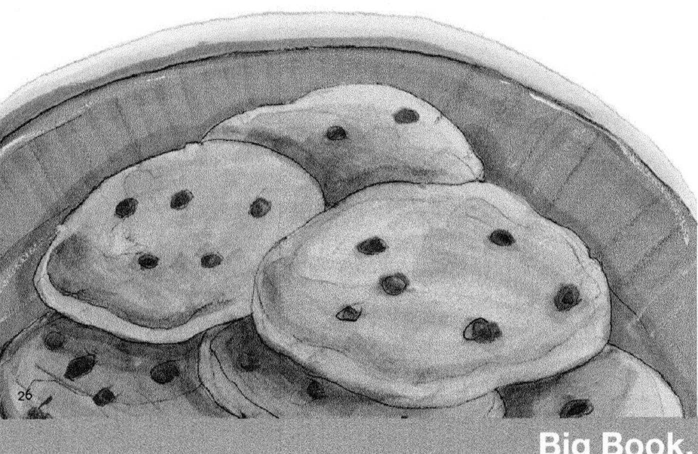

Uh-oh.

Where's Plaidypus?
Look left. Look right.
Nowhere in sight.
Back in the lake.
Search high and low.
Over. Under.

Where did he go?

26 27

Big Book, pp. 26–27

INFERENCE What do you think happened to Plaidypus? (I think he got really wet and heavy and sank into the lake.)

2ND READ

Develop Vocabulary

OPEN-ENDED What does the fisherman pull from the lake on his hook? (Plaidypus)

- Plaidypus is pulled from the lake on a fishing hook. What does the girl say? ("I'm sorry, Plaidypus. I'll never, ever, ever, ever lose you again.) Have children read the sentence with you.

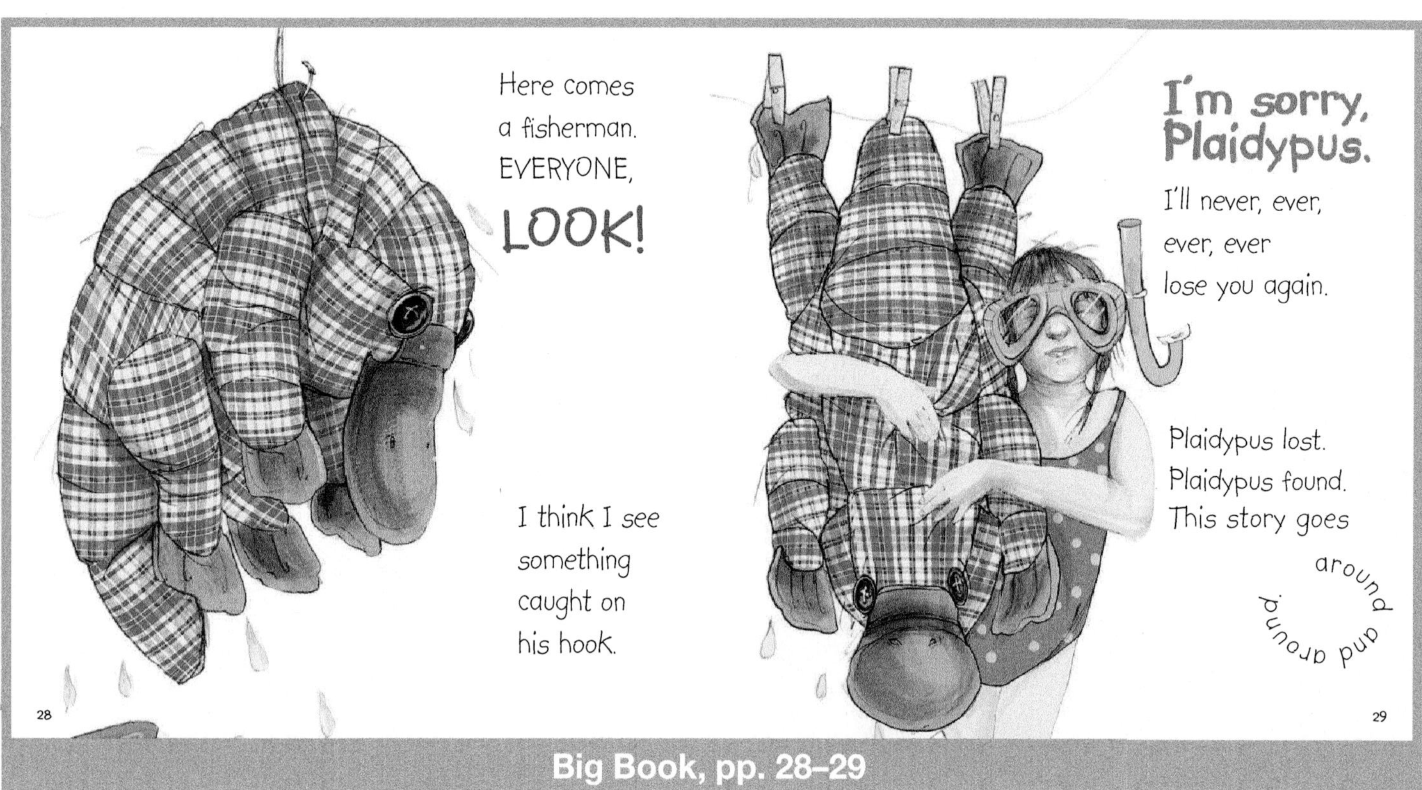
Here comes
a fisherman.
EVERYONE,
LOOK!
I think I see
something
caught on
his hook.
28
I'm sorry,
Plaidypus.
I'll never, ever,
ever, ever
lose you again.
Plaidypus lost.
Plaidypus found.
This story goes
around
and around
29

Big Book, pp. 28–29

3RD READ

Develop Comprehension ©

***WH*- QUESTION** What does Plaidypus look like when he is pulled from the lake? (Plaidypus looks wet.)

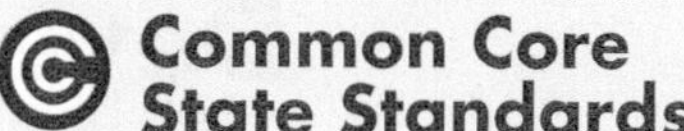

WH- QUESTION Where is the girl now? (in the car)

- The girl is in the car with Grandma. What is the girl doing with Plaidypus?

Common Core State Standards

Literature 1. With prompting and support, ask and answer questions about key details in a text. **Literature 2.** With prompting and support, retell familiar stories, including key details. **Literature 3.** With prompting and support, identify characters, settings, and major events in a story. **Literature 7.** With prompting and support, describe the relationship between illustrations and the story in which they appear (e.g., what moment in a story an illustration depicts).

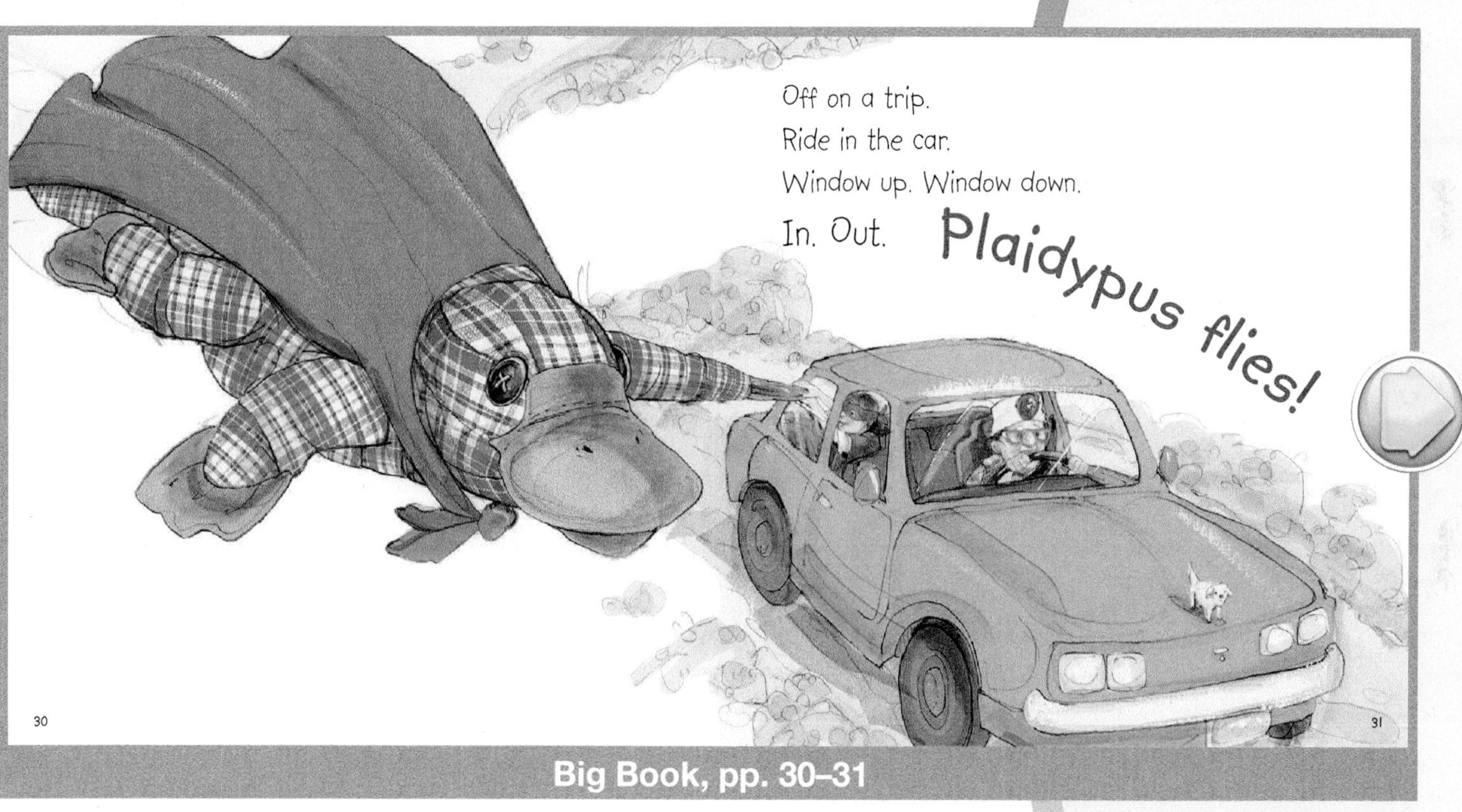

Off on a trip.
Ride in the car.
Window up. Window down.
In. Out.
Plaidypus flies!
30
31

Big Book, pp. 30–31

RECALL Where are Grandma, the girl, and Plaidypus going? (They are going on a trip.)

2ND READ

Develop Vocabulary

DISTANCING What does the car hit? (a bump)

- The car hits a bump in the road. What do you think happens to Plaidypus?

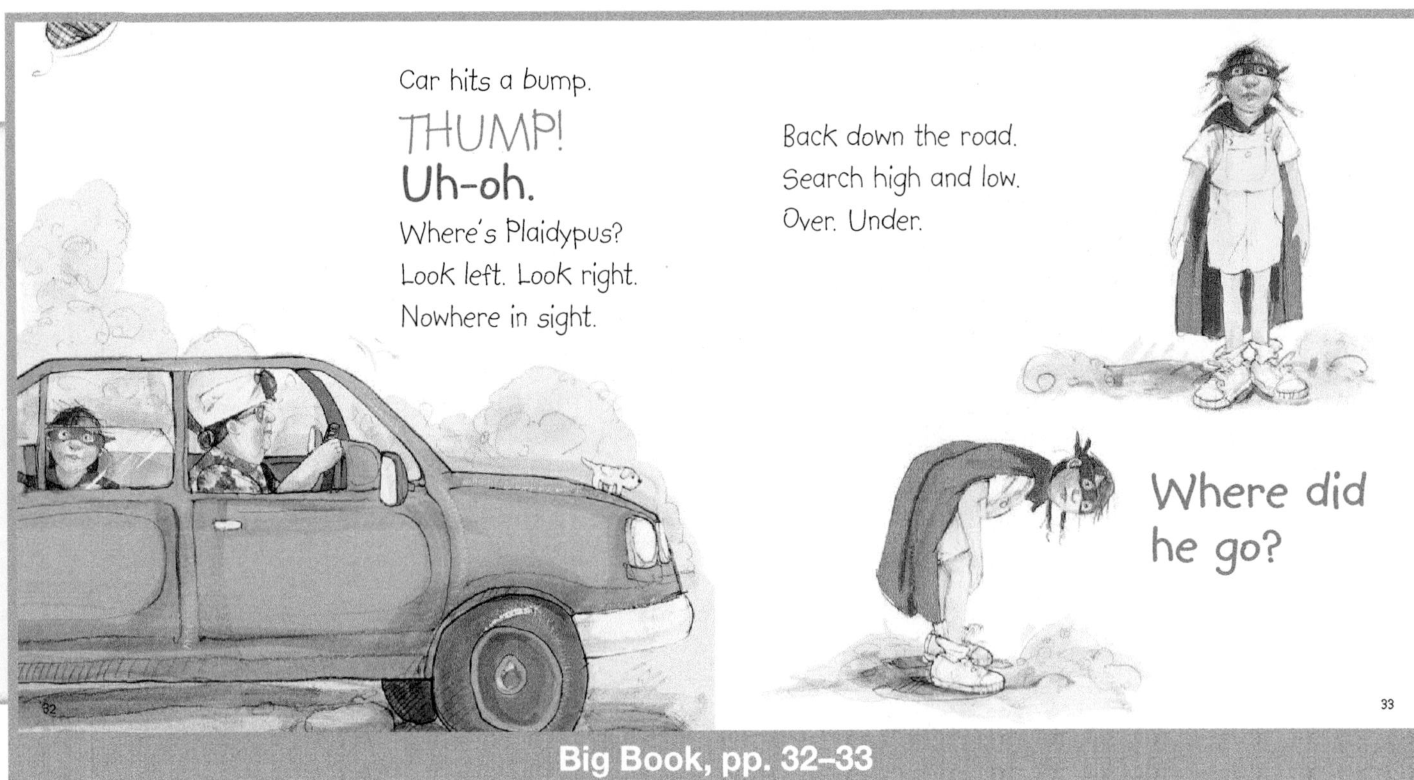

Car hits a bump.
THUMP!
Uh-oh.
Where's Plaidypus?
Look left. Look right.
Nowhere in sight.
Back down the road.
Search high and low.
Over. Under.
Where did he go?
32
33

Big Book, pp. 32–33

3RD READ

Develop Comprehension ©

RECALL What sound does the car make when it hits the bump? (The car makes a *thump* sound.)

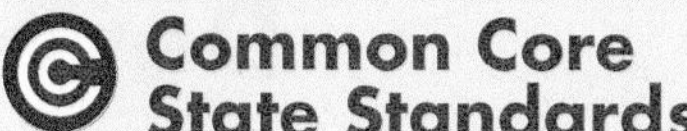

Common Core State Standards

Literature 1. With prompting and support, ask and answer questions about key details in a text. **Literature 2.** With prompting and support, retell familiar stories, including key details. **Literature 3.** With prompting and support, identify characters, settings, and major events in a story. **Literature 7.** With prompting and support, describe the relationship between illustrations and the story in which they appear (e.g., what moment in a story an illustration depicts).

RECALL What does the girl make to help her find Plaidypus? (a sign)

- The girl makes a sign. The sign tells people she is looking for Plaidypus. What does the girl put on the sign to show who Plaidypus is?

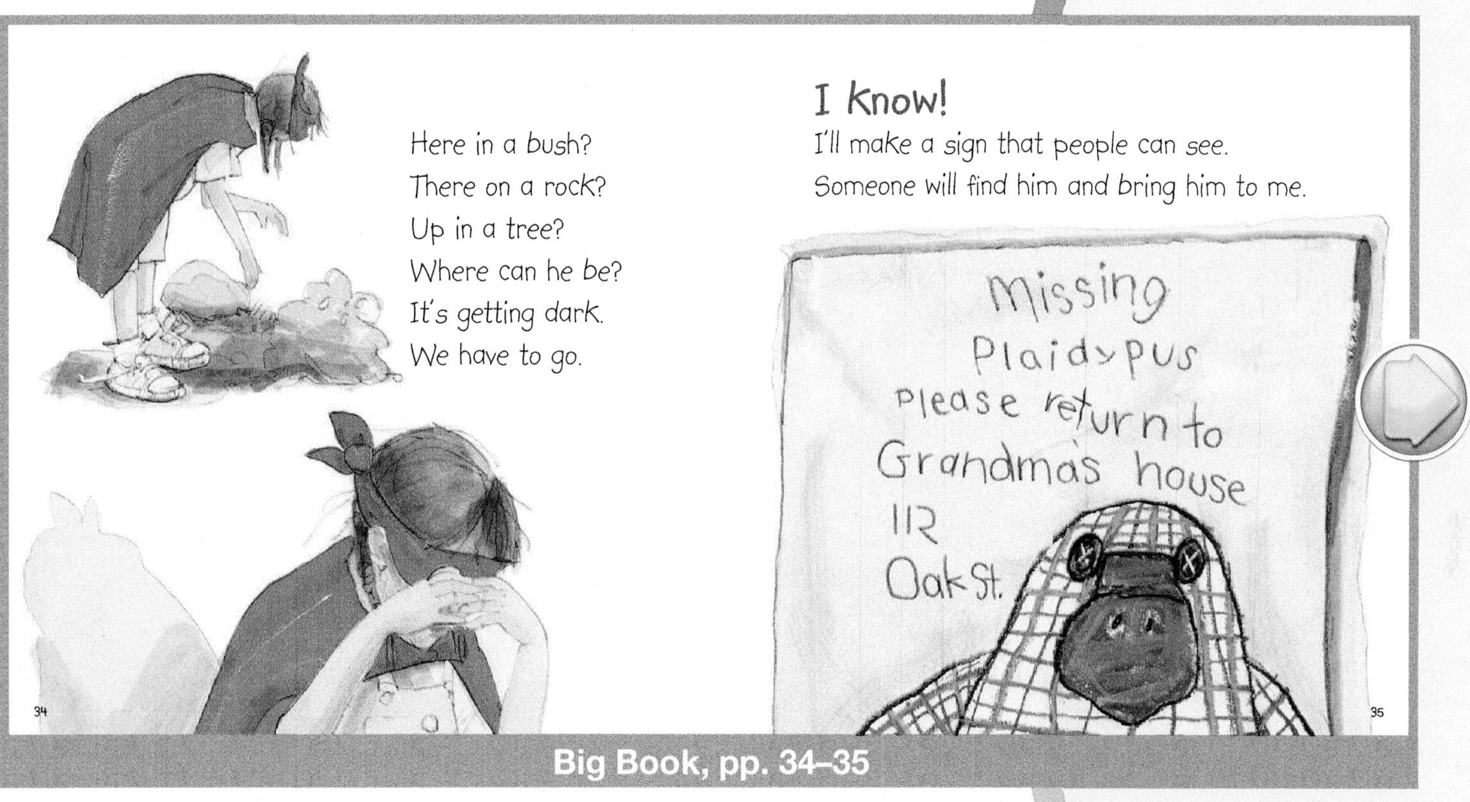

Here in a bush?
There on a rock?
Up in a tree?
Where can he be?
It's getting dark.
We have to go.
34
I Know!
I'll make a sign that people can see.
Someone will find him and bring him to me.
Missing
Plaidypus
Please return to
Grandma's house
112
Oak St.
35

Big Book, pp. 34–35

INFERENCE Why does the girl have to stop looking for Plaidypus when it gets dark? (It's getting dark, so soon she won't be able to see.)

2ND READ

Develop Vocabulary

OPEN-ENDED How many days does the girl wait? (four)

- The girl waits four days for Plaidypus to be returned. Do you think the girl will find Plaidypus this time?

One day. Two days.
Three days.
Four.
36
37
Big Book, pp. 36–37

3RD READ

Develop Comprehension ©

INFERENCE The girl waits four days for Plaidypus to be returned. How do you think the girl feels? Why? (I think she feels sad because she misses her toy and she is afraid she won't ever see him again.)

COMPLETION The girl hears a knock. She opens the door and finds a sack. What is in the sack? (Plaidypus)

- The girl finds Plaidypus in a sack at the door. What does the girl say to Plaidypus?

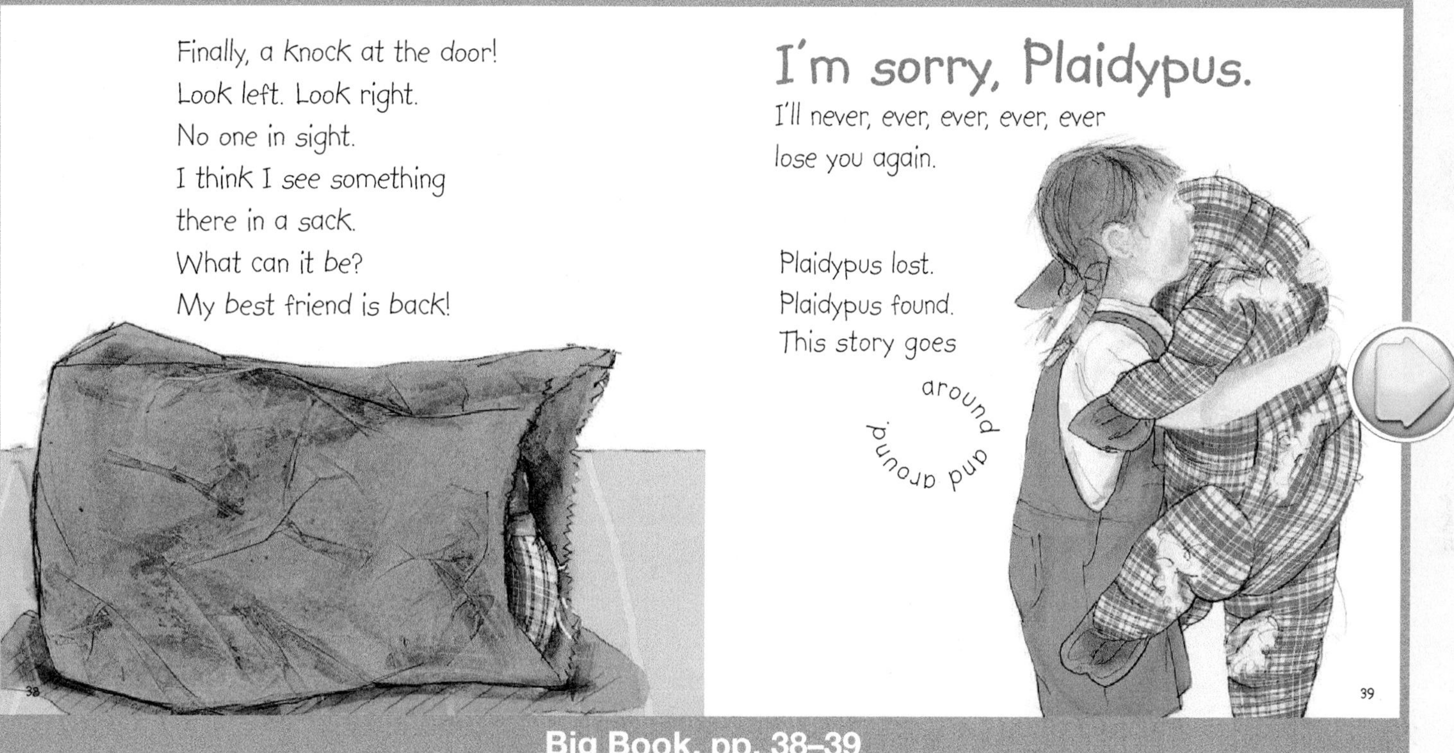

Finally, a knock at the door!
Look left. Look right.
No one in sight.
I think I see something
there in a sack.
What can it be?
My best friend is back!
I'm sorry, Plaidypus.
I'll never, ever, ever, ever, ever
lose you again.
Plaidypus lost.
Plaidypus found.
This story goes
around
and around
38
39

Big Book, pp. 38–39

DISTANCING Someone finds Plaidypus and returns him to the girl. What would you do if you found something that someone else lost? (I would try to find the person who was looking for it and give it back to him or her.)

Common Core State Standards

Literature 1. With prompting and support, ask and answer questions about key details in a text. **Literature 2.** With prompting and support, retell familiar stories, including key details. **Literature 3.** With prompting and support, identify characters, settings, and major events in a story. **Literature 7.** With prompting and support, describe the relationship between illustrations and the story in which they appear (e.g., what moment in a story an illustration depicts).

2ND READ

Develop Vocabulary

RECALL What is wrong with Plaidypus? (He's hurt.)

- Plaidypus is hurt. How is Plaidypus hurt?

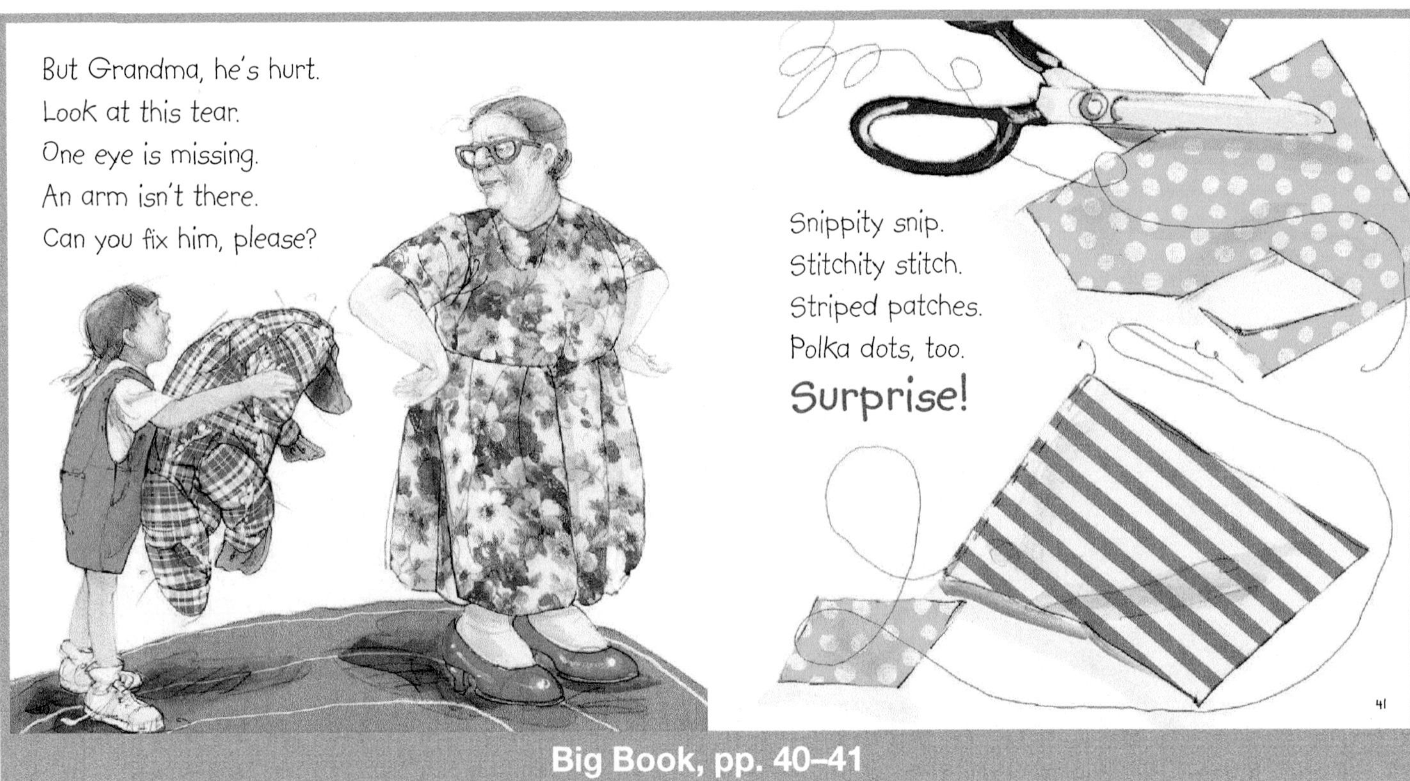

But Grandma, he's hurt.
Look at this tear.
One eye is missing.
An arm isn't there.
Can you fix him, please?
Snippity snip.
Stitchity stitch.
Striped patches.
Polka dots, too.
Surprise!
41

Big Book, pp. 40–41

3RD READ

Develop Comprehension ©

***WH-* QUESTION** Whom does the girl ask to fix Plaidypus? (The girl asks Grandma to fix him.)

COMPLETION What does Grandma do? (fixes Plaidypus)

- Grandma fixes Plaidypus. What does the girl promise she will never do? Let's read the sentence together.

Continue with DAY 3
Conventions
p. 278

Common Core State Standards

Literature 1. With prompting and support, ask and answer questions about key details in a text. **Literature 2.** With prompting and support, retell familiar stories, including key details. **Literature 3.** With prompting and support, identify characters, settings, and major events in a story. **Literature 7.** With prompting and support, describe the relationship between illustrations and the story in which they appear (e.g., what moment in a story an illustration depicts).

That old Plaidypus
is now my new one-eyed, one-armed
PLAIDA-
POLKA-
STRIPAPUS!
And I promise
I'll never, ever,
ever,
ever,
ever,
ever
lose you
again.
The
End
42
43

Big Book, pp. 42–43

RECALL Grandma fixes Plaidypus by sewing patches on him. What kinds of patches does she use? (Grandma uses striped and polka dot patches.)

Skip to DAY 4
Conventions
p. 292

Common Core State Standards

Foundational Skills 1.d. Recognize and name all upper- and lowercase letters of the alphabet. **Foundational Skills 2.a.** Recognize and produce rhyming words. **Writing 3.** Use a combination of drawing, dictating, and writing to narrate a single event or several loosely linked events, tell about the events in the order in which they occurred, and provide a reaction to what happened. **Language 1.a.** Print many upper- and lowercase letters. **Also Writing 7.**

Access for All

Strategic Intervention

Writing Names If children have difficulty writing their names, have them identify the letter or letters that cause the most trouble. Encourage them to practice writing just that letter, or letters, on their Write-On Boards.

Daily Fix-It

i am big sam.
I am big Sam.

This week's practice sentences appear on *Teacher Resources DVD-ROM.*

Conventions

Review Write Our Names

TEACH Remind children of what they learned about writing names. Everyone has a name. Names begin with an uppercase letter.

My name is (your name). Write your name on the board. Point to the uppercase letter. When I write my name, I use an uppercase letter for the first letter.

GUIDE PRACTICE Show the *man* Picture Card. I wonder what this man's name is. I think his name is Max. What names do you suggest? Write all the names on the board. Did I use an uppercase letter to begin each name? Repeat the routine with the *woman* Picture Card.

Have children write or dictate the name of a family member or friend on a sheet of paper. Then have them draw a picture to go with the name.

Team Talk Pair children and have partners take turns writing their own name on their Write-On Boards. Then have them identify some or all of the letters in their partner's name.

ON THEIR OWN Use *Reader's and Writer's Notebook,* p. 33, for more practice with writing names.

Reader's and Writer's Notebook, p. 33

Poem

TEACH Talk about poems with children. A **poem** is a type of writing that has short lines. Poems sometimes rhyme. We write poems to share experiences, feelings, or ideas. Poems can be about anything we want. What kinds of things can we write poems about? Write children's suggestions on the board.

MODEL This is a part from *Plaidypus Lost* that can be a poem. It is two lines. The two lines end with rhyming words. Write the following poem on the board:

> **Fast and slow.**
> **Stop. Go.**

Read the poem aloud, pointing to each word as you say it.

GUIDE PRACTICE Have children identify the rhyming words. Which words rhyme? Yes, *slow* and *go* rhyme. Display pp. 18–19 of *Plaidypus Lost*. What in the story goes fast and slow? What things do you know that go fast and slow? Write children's suggestions on the board.

INDEPENDENT WRITING Have children turn to p. 34 of *Reader's and Writer's Notebook*. Have children copy the poem adapted from *Plaidypus Lost*. Then have them draw a picture that tells about something they know that goes fast and slow.

Reader's and Writer's Notebook, p. 34

Daily Handwriting

Write *P, O,* and *pop* on the board. Review correct letter formation of uppercase *P* and *O* and lowercase *p* and *o*.

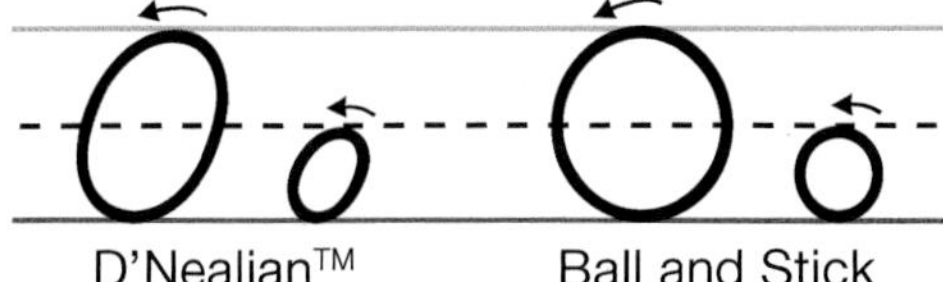

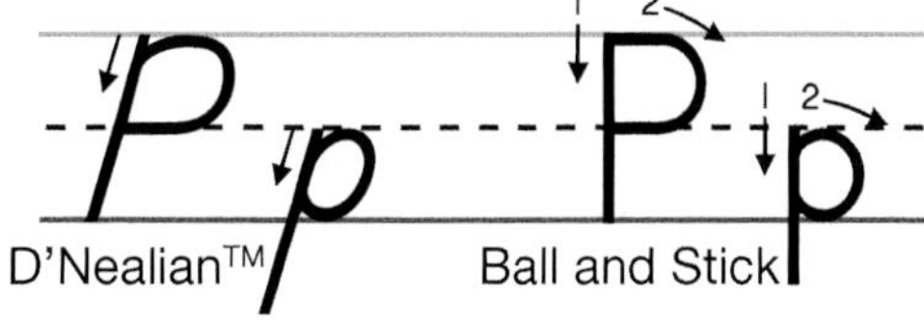

Have children write *P, O,* and *pop* on their Write-On Boards. Remind children to use proper left-to-right and top-to-bottom progression and proper spacing between letters when writing.

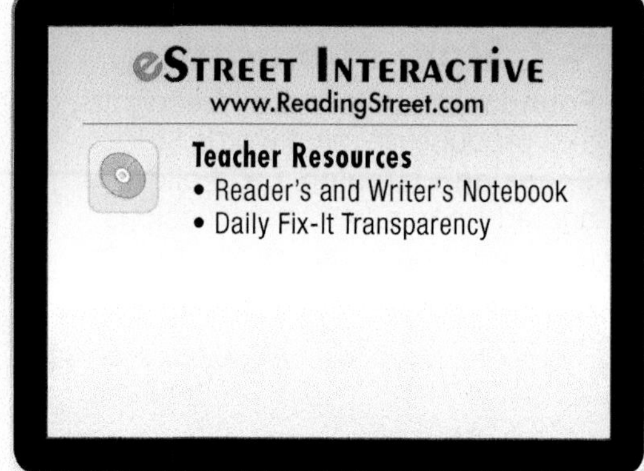

Academic Vocabulary

poem an expressive, imaginative piece of writing often arranged in lines having rhythm and rhyme

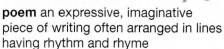

Professional Development: Learning Resources Teach children how to use a picture dictionary and encourage them to use it frequently to find words they don't know when reading, writing, or speaking. Suggest children keep a list of frequently used words as a reference. If possible, provide a bilingual dictionary in the classroom.

Common Core State Standards

Foundational Skills 2.a. Recognize and produce rhyming words. **Speaking/Listening 1.a.** Follow agreed-upon rules for discussions (e.g., listening to others and taking turns speaking about the topics and texts under discussion).

Academic Vocabulary

rhyme to have the same middle and ending sounds

rhythm a strong beat in a song or poem

Bridge to Common Core

COMPREHENSION AND COLLABORATION

As children identify the rhyming words and rhythm in a rhyme, they are learning to evaluate information presented orally, to follow agreed-upon rules, and to participate in a structured collaboration as part of a whole class.

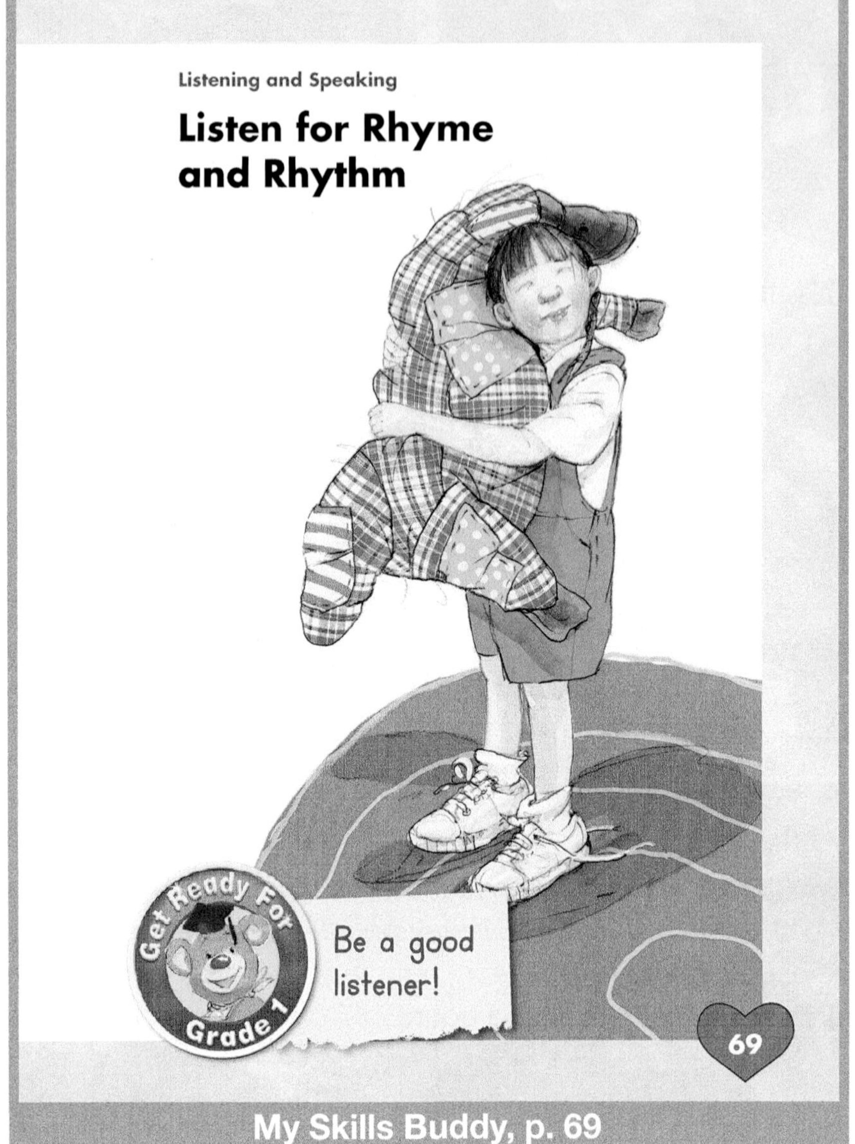

My Skills Buddy, p. 69

Listening and Speaking

Listen for Rhyme and Rhythm

TEACH Remind children that rhyming words have the same middle and ending sounds, and **rhythm** is the beat in a poem or rhyme. I can say *boy, joy,* and *toy* and know they are rhyming words because their middle and ending sounds are the same: *b-oy, j-oy, t-oy.*

MODEL Have children turn to p. 69 of *My Skills Buddy.* Use the Listening and Speaking bullet on p. 68 to guide the discussion. This is a picture from *Plaidypus Lost.* Think about how happy the girl is when Grandma fixes Plaidypus. Listen to the rhyme about Plaidypus and identify the rhyming words. Remember, good listeners face the speaker, so face me as I say the rhyme.

Plaidypus, Plaidypus went out to play.
Plaidypus, Plaidypus got lost one day.
Plaidypus, Plaidypus was found, they say.
Plaidypus, Plaidypus is here to stay.

Which words rhyme? I will say the rhyme again. Listen carefully. Repeat the rhyme, pausing at the end of each line. Have children identify the rhyming words. (*play, day, say, stay*)

INDEPENDENT PRACTICE Have children repeat the rhyme with you as they clap the rhythm of the words (one clap per syllable). Refer children to their Rules for Listening and Speaking from pp. 1–2 of *Reader's and Writer's Notebook.* Remind children to face the speaker when they are listening.

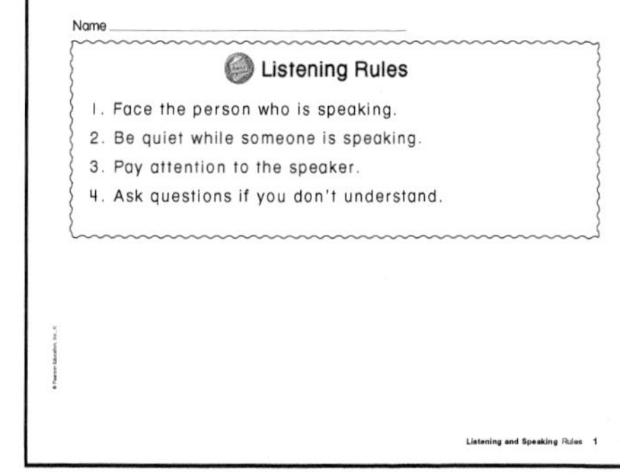
Name

Listening Rules

1. Face the person who is speaking.
2. Be quiet while someone is speaking.
3. Pay attention to the speaker.
4. Ask questions if you don't understand.

Listening and Speaking Rules 1

Reader's and Writer's Notebook, pp. 1–2

Be a Good Listener!

1. Face the person who is speaking.
2. Be quiet while someone is speaking.
3. Pay attention to the speaker.
4. Ask questions if you don't understand.

Support Rhyme After children identify the rhyming words, say the words one at a time: *play, day, say, stay.* Have children repeat the words. Remind them to listen to the ending sounds. These words end with *-ay.* Do you hear *-ay* in each word?

Common Core State Standards

Foundational Skills 1.d. Recognize and name all upper- and lowercase letters of the alphabet. **Speaking/ Listening 5.** Add drawings or other visual displays to descriptions as desired to provide additional detail. **Language 5.c.** Identify real-life connections between words and their use (e.g., note places at school that are *colorful*).

Wrap Up Your Day!

✔ **Content Knowledge** Today we talked about how you help family members. In what way does Grandma help her granddaughter in *Plaidypus Lost?*

✔ **Respond to Literature** Today we read about Cat and Dog. What do Cat and Dog do together in the story we read?

✔ **Conventions** Point to a child and have the child give a word to describe the girl in the book *Plaidypus Lost.* Have that child point to someone else to give another word about the girl, and so on. Write the words on the board and read the final list with children.

✔ **Homework Idea** Have children write the letters *O, o, P,* and *p.*

Preview DAY 4

Tomorrow we will read a story about a Trucktown friend, Payloader Pete.

Extend Your Day!

Social Studies
Plaidypus Travels

MATERIALS: paper, crayons

COMMUNITY PLACES Have children recall the story *Plaidypus Lost.* Remind them of the places in her community that the girl took Plaidypus. List the names of the places on a chart in a column labeled *Plaidypus's Story Travels.* Then have children think of places where they would take Plaidypus in their community. List their answers on the chart in a column labeled *Plaidypus's New Travels.*

Plaidypus's Story Travels	Plaidypus's New Travels
park	school
market	library
lake	store
	police station
	fire station
	bank
	friend's house

COMMUNITY TRAVEL Have children draw a picture of the place in their community where they would take Plaidypus to visit. Have them write or dictate the place's name. Display the pictures on a bulletin board titled *Community Places.*

Comprehension
Sequence Rhyme

MATERIALS: paper folded into three parts, crayons

FINDING SEQUENCE Read the following poem to children. Have them retell what happens first, next, and last in the poem. Ask them to draw pictures to show the order of events in the poem.

One little platypus lost in a shoe.
Another in a truck, now there are two.
Another little platypus lost by a tree.
With that one lost, now there are three.

Letter Recognition
Swim for Letters

MATERIALS: construction paper, craft sticks, scissors, crayons, glue

SWIMMING FOR LETTERS Cut out a brown paper platypus and add details. Attach the platypus to a craft stick. On the board, draw ten rows of waves, with a letter on each wave. Have a child take the stick platypus and move along the waves, saying the name of the letter on each wave. If needed, help the child name the letter. When the child has finished "swimming," another player takes a turn.

DAY 4 at a Glance

Content Knowledge
Oral Vocabulary

Phonological Awareness
Review Syllables

Letter Recognition
Letters *Rr*

Text-Based Comprehension
Sequence
Review Setting

Conventions
What We Look Like

Writing
Extend the Concept

Vocabulary
Words for Shapes

Materials

- Student Edition
- Truckery Rhymes
- Talk with Me/Sing with Me Chart
- Alphabet Cards
- Get Set, Roll! Reader 3
- Reader's and Writer's Notebook
- Big Book

Common Core State Standards

Speaking/Listening 2. Confirm understanding of a text read aloud or information presented orally or through other media by asking and answering questions about key details and requesting clarification if something is not understood. **Language 6.** Use words and phrases acquired through conversations, reading and being read to, and responding to texts. **Also Language 4., 5.c.**

TRUCKTOWN on Reading Street

Start your engines!

- Display "Three Loud Trucks" and lead the group in saying the rhyme a few times.
- Have the group clap the rhythm as they recite the rhyme.
- When children have mastered the rhythm, have them march around the room as they say the rhyme.

Truckery Rhymes

Content Knowledge

Zoom in on ©

Families Living, Working, and Playing Together

EXPAND THE CONCEPT On the board, write the Question of the Week, *How do families cooperate?* Read the question as you track the print. Tell children to respond in complete sentences. Display Sing with Me Chart 3B.

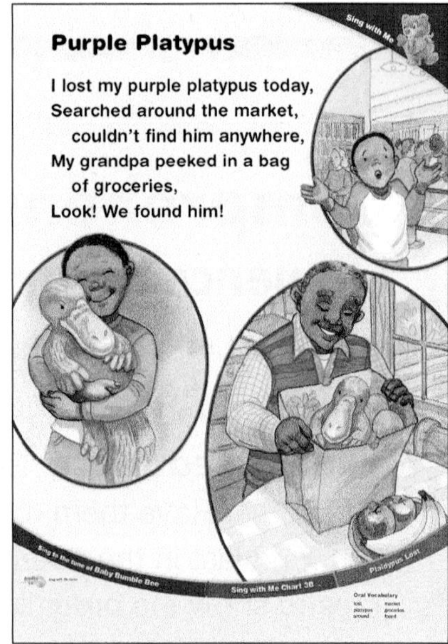

Purple Platypus
I lost my purple platypus today,
Searched around the market,
couldn't find him anywhere,
My grandpa peeked in a bag
of groceries,
Look! We found him!
Sing with Me Chart 3B

Talk with Me/Sing with Me Chart 3B

Build Oral Language

LISTEN FOR AMAZING WORDS We are going to sing this song again. Listen for the Amazing Words *market* and *groceries.* Sing the song several times with children to the tune of "Baby Bumble Bee." Have them stand up when they hear the Amazing Word *market* or *groceries.*

Build Oral Vocabulary

Amazing Words Robust Vocabulary Routine

1. **Introduce the Word** A store that sells food is called a *market.* What's our new Amazing Word for a store that sells food? Say it with me: *market.*
2. **Demonstrate** Provide examples to show meaning. *I bought apples, milk, and eggs when I went to the market.* Tell me some things you can find at the *market.*

   Repeat steps 1 and 2.

   Introduce the Word The food I buy at the market is also called *groceries.* What's our new Amazing Word for food bought at a market? Say it with me: *groceries.*

   Demonstrate *I carry my groceries in paper bags.* Pretend you are going to the market to buy *groceries.* What *groceries* would you buy?
3. **Apply** Have children use *market* and *groceries* to describe what the girl and Plaidypus do.
4. **Display the Words** Have children point to and name letters in *market* and *groceries* that they recognize. Ask them to find the letter *e* in both words.

Routines Flip Chart

USE AMAZING WORDS To reinforce the concept and the Amazing Words, have children supply the appropriate Amazing Word for each sentence.

I help unpack the ______ from the bags. (groceries)
I use a shopping cart at the ______. (market)

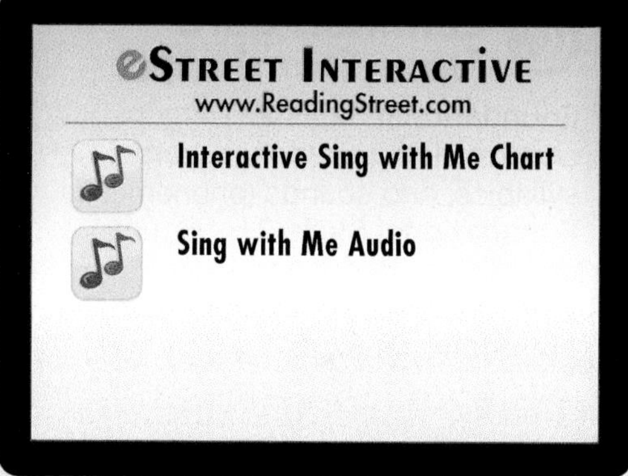

Amazing Words

platypus	around
lost	found
market	groceries

Access for All

SI Strategic Intervention

Access Content Have children tell what they know about a market. Point out that a market can also be called a grocery store.

Access Content Have children tell how they would say *market* and *groceries* in their home languages.

Produce Oral Language Use the Day 4 instruction on ELL Poster 3 to extend and enrich language.

Common Core State Standards

Foundational Skills 2. Demonstrate understanding of spoken words, syllables, and sounds (phonemes). **Foundational Skills 2.b.** Count, pronounce, blend, and segment syllables in spoken words. **Also Foundational Skills 2.a.**

Phonological Awareness

Review Syllables

PRACTICE Remember that words are made up of parts called syllables. To help us figure out how many syllables there are in a word, we clap once as we say each syllable in a word, and then we count how many times we clap. Let's count the syllables in *puzzle: puz-* (clap), *-zle* (clap). How many times did we clap? (two) How many syllables are in *puzzle?* (two) The word *puzzle* has two syllables: *puz-zle.*

Reread the first page in *Plaidypus Lost.* Have children read the sentences with you. Repeat each word in the sentences as children clap the syllables in each word.

Corrective feedback	**If...** children cannot clap syllables, **then...** say a two-syllable word slowly, emphasizing the syllables and clapping once for each syllable. Have children imitate you. Listen to this word: *market.* Clap the syllables with me: *mar-* (clap), *-ket* (clap). How many times did we clap?

BLEND SYLLABLES I will say word parts, or syllables. Then I want you to help me blend the syllables together to say a word. Listen carefully: *pro-mise.* Now blend the syllables together to say the word: *promise.* Repeat the routine with the words *bottom, Plaidypus, anywhere,* and *groceries.*

LISTEN FOR RHYMING WORDS Remember, when we listen for rhyming words, we listen to the middle and ending sounds in the words to see if they are the same. Listen to this sentence and name the rhyming words: *Jack and Jill went up the hill.* Which words rhyme? Repeat the routine with these sentences: *Hickory, dickory, dock, the mouse ran up the clock; Twinkle, twinkle, little star, how I wonder what you are.*

Check Phonological Awareness

FORMATIVE ASSESSMENT Say the following words and have children clap the syllables in each word: *together, happy, flippers.*

If... children cannot clap the syllables,

then... say the words slowly, pausing to clap once after each syllable. Have children clap with you.

Continue to monitor children's progress during the week so that they can be successful with the Day 5 Assessment.

Access for All

 Strategic Intervention

Blend Syllables Say each syllable and clap after you say it. Then clap while you say the syllable. Finally, blend the syllables to say the word.

Common Core State Standards

Literature 10. Actively engage in group reading activities with purpose and understanding. **Foundational Skills 1.d.** Recognize and name all upper- and lowercase letters of the alphabet. **Foundational Skills 3.c.** Read common high-frequency words by sight. (e.g., *the, of, to, you, she, my, is, are, do, does*).

Letter Recognition

Teach/Model

Letters *Rr*

INTRODUCE/MODEL Display the *Rr* Alphabet Card. Point to the uppercase *R.* This is uppercase *R.* What letter is this? Point to the lowercase *r.* This is lowercase *r.* What letter is this?

Rr
river
Alphabet Card

Guide Practice

GROUP PRACTICE Display Sing with Me Chart 3B, "Purple Platypus." Let's look at the chart and find a word that has lowercase *r* in it. Have children point out each lowercase *r* in the song and then help them say the words.

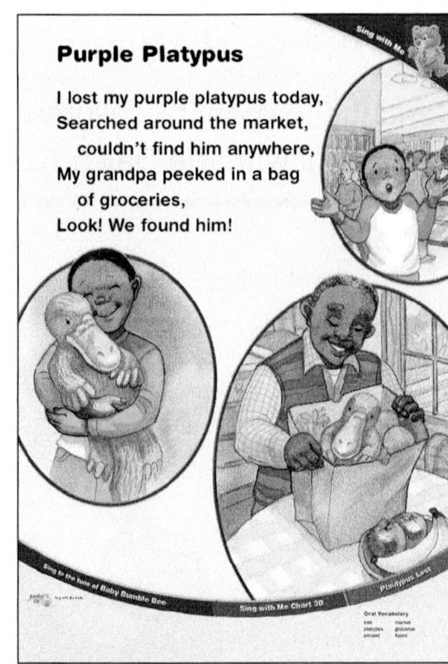
Purple Platypus
I lost my purple platypus today,
Searched around the market,
couldn't find him anywhere,
My grandpa peeked in a bag
of groceries,
Look! We found him!
Talk with Me/Sing with Me Chart 3B

Display pp. 10–11 of *Plaidypus Lost.* Have children identify uppercase *R* and lowercase *r.* Continue with other pages and have children continue identifying uppercase *R* and lowercase *r.*

ON THEIR OWN Have children make telescopes with their hands and look around the room for *Rr.* Then have children use *Reader's and Writer's Notebook,* pp. 26 and 31, for more practice with letters *Rr.*

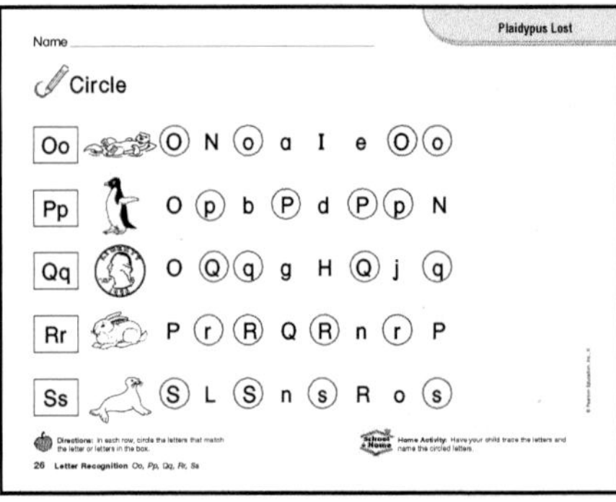
Name
Plaidypus Lost
Circle
Oo O N o a I e O o
Pp o p b P d P p N
Qq o Q q g H Q j q
Rr P r R Q R n r P
Ss S L S n s R o s

Reader's and Writer's Notebook, p. 26

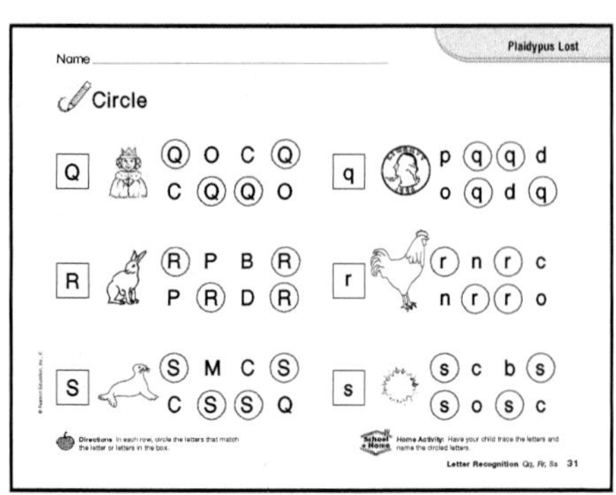
Name
Plaidypus Lost
Circle
Q Q o C Q C Q Q o
q p q q d o q d q
R R P B R P R D R
r r n r c n r r o
S S M C S C S S Q
s s c b s s o s c

Reader's and Writer's Notebook, p. 31

Get Set, Roll! Reader 3

Read *Pete*

REVIEW Review the high-frequency words *I, am, the,* and *little.* Have children find each word on the Word Wall.

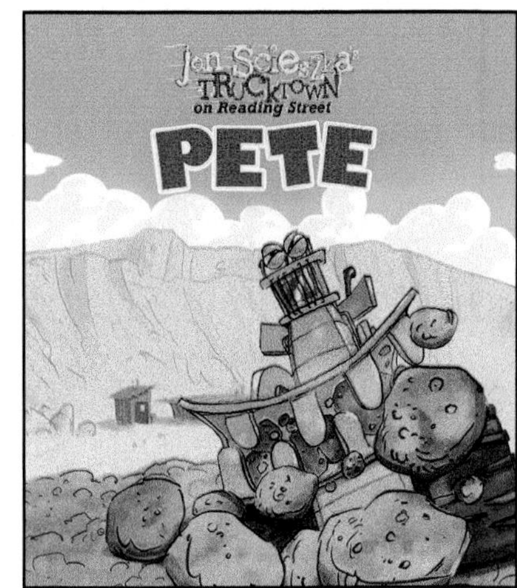

Get Set, Roll! Reader 3

TEACH REBUS WORDS Write *Pete* on the board. This is the name *Pete.* Name the letters with me: *P, e, t, e, Pete.* Repeat the procedure with *rocks* and *crunch.* Look for these words in the story today. A picture above the word will help you read it.

READ Today we will read a story about Payloader Pete. Point to the title of the book. What is the title of the book? (*Pete*) How does a title help us know what the book is about? It tells us we will read about Payloader Pete in this book.

Use the routine for reading decodable books in the Routines Flip Chart to read Get Set, Roll! Reader 3.

Day 4 SMALL GROUP TIME • Differentiate Language, p. SG•37

OL On-Level	SI Strategic Intervention	A Advanced
• **Build** Sentences and Words • **Read** Get Set, Roll! Reader *Pete*	• **Talk About** Sentences and Words • **Read** Get Set, Roll! Reader *Pete*	• **Extend** Sentences and Words • **Read** Get Set, Roll! Reader *Pete*

eSTREET INTERACTIVE
www.ReadingStreet.com

Savvas eText
• Get Set, Roll! Reader

Teacher Resources
• Reader's and Writer's Notebook

Access for All

 Strategic Intervention

Retell Have children use Get Set, Roll! Reader 3 to practice retelling a story.

Access Content Do a picture walk with children to preview the reader before starting the routine.

Place English Language Learners in the groups that correspond to their reading abilities in English.

If... children need more practice **Developing Language,**
then... use the Language Workshops in the *ELL Handbook* beginning on p. 306.

Zoom in on ©

Text-Based Comprehension

 **Common Core State Standards**

Literature 1. With prompting and support, ask and answer questions about key details in a text. **Literature 2.** With prompting and support, retell familiar stories, including key details. **Literature 3.** With prompting and support, identify characters, settings, and major events in a story.

Access for All

 Advanced

Draw Settings Have children choose their favorite setting from *Plaidypus Lost* and draw a picture of it.

Academic Vocabulary

setting where and when a story takes place

Sequence

PRACTICE Have children turn to the Sequence pictures on pp. 54–55 of *My Skills Buddy.* As you look at the pictures, remind children that in stories, something happens first, something happens next, and something happens last.

My Skills Buddy, pp. 54–55

Team Talk Pair children and have them take turns telling what they like to do when they play. What do you do first? What do you do next? What do you do last?

Review Setting

PRACTICE Direct children to the Literary Elements pictures on pp. 34–35 of *My Skills Buddy.*

The **setting** of a story is where and when the story takes place. Good readers pay attention to the setting of a story to help them understand the story. Look at the pictures. Tell children the story "The Tortoise and the Hare."

- Where are the tortoise and the hare? (outside at a park)
- When is the race taking place? (on a sunny day)

MORE PRACTICE For more practice with setting, use *Reader's and Writer's Notebook,* p. 35.

Reader's and Writer's Notebook, p. 35

Read Main Selection

GUIDE COMPREHENSION Display *Plaidypus Lost.* This story takes place in many different places.

- Where are the slides and the swings? (at the park)
- Where does the girl go to get her knee fixed? (to Grandma's house)
- Where is Plaidypus when he is sitting on a shelf? (at the market)
- Where is Plaidypus when he is caught on the hook? (in the lake)

READ Reread *Plaidypus Lost.* Return to p. 258. Follow the **3rd Read** and use the **Develop Comprehension** notes to give children the opportunity to gain a more complete understanding of the story.

Routine Read for Understanding

Deepen understanding by reading the selection multiple times.

1. **First Read**—Read the entire selection aloud to build interest in the text.
2. **Second Read**—Use the **Develop Vocabulary** notes on pages 258–277.
3. **Third Read**—Use the **Develop Comprehension** notes on pages 258–277.

Bridge to Common Core

RANGE OF READING AND LEVEL OF TEXT COMPLEXITY

Using the Develop Comprehension notes as you read the text a third time will help you assess how children are comprehending the authentic literary text in *Reading Street.* As the year progresses, children will improve as independent, proficient readers of complex text.

Common Core State Standards

Writing 3. Use a combination of drawing, dictating, and writing to narrate a single event or several loosely linked events, tell about the events in the order in which they occurred, and provide a reaction to what happened. **Speaking/Listening 4.** Describe familiar people, places, things, and events and, with prompting and support, provide additional detail. **Language 1.a.** Print many upper- and lowercase letters. **Also Writing 5., Speaking/Listening 1., Language 5.c.**

Access for All

Strategic Intervention

Support Conventions Have children draw a picture of how they would look if they got a new toy or lost their favorite toy. Then have them use the picture to think of a word that tells what they would look like.

Daily Fix-It

i am lost

I am lost.

This week's practice sentences appear on *Teacher Resources DVD-ROM.*

Conventions

What We Look Like

TEACH Remind children of what they learned about words that tell what we look like. We have been talking about words that tell what we look like, or that describe us. Some words that describe us tell about things such as our clothes or hair. Other words that describe us tell whether we look happy or sad. When something good happens, I look happy.

GUIDE PRACTICE Display *Plaidypus Lost.* Turn to the page with the girl holding her newly made Plaidypus. Have volunteers tell what the girl looks like. Have children tell how they would look if they had just been given a special toy they wanted. Make a list of the words they use.

Write these sentence frames on the board:

When I get a new toy, I look ______.

When I lose a toy, I look ______.

Have children think of words to use to complete each sentence. Write the word on the line. Then read the completed sentence, pointing to the descriptive word as you read it.

ON THEIR OWN Use *Reader's and Writer's Notebook,* p. 36, for more practice with words that tell what we look like.

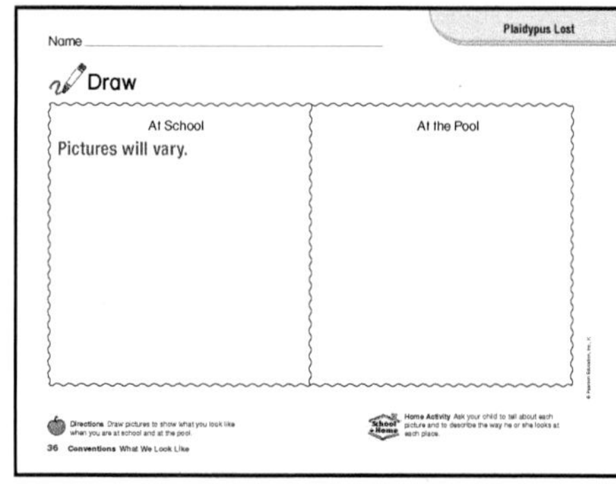
Name
Plaidypus Lost
Draw
At School
Pictures will vary.
At the Pool
36 Conventions What We Look Like

Reader's and Writer's Notebook, p. 36

Extend the Concept

DISCUSS This week we have been talking about how families cooperate, or work together to help one another. Each of us cooperates with the members of our own family and works together with them.

Ask children to think about why it is important to cooperate with family members. Talk with children about the things they do to help their family members.

GUIDE PRACTICE Use children's contributions to the discussion to write sentences.

I help my...	**dad make dinner.**
	sister clean up her toys.
	grandpa fold the laundry.

INDEPENDENT WRITING Have children write or dictate their own sentence about how they cooperate with their families, or they may copy a sentence from the board. Invite children to read their sentences to the class.

Daily Handwriting

Write uppercase *O* and *P* and lowercase *o* and *p* on the board. Review correct letter formation with children.

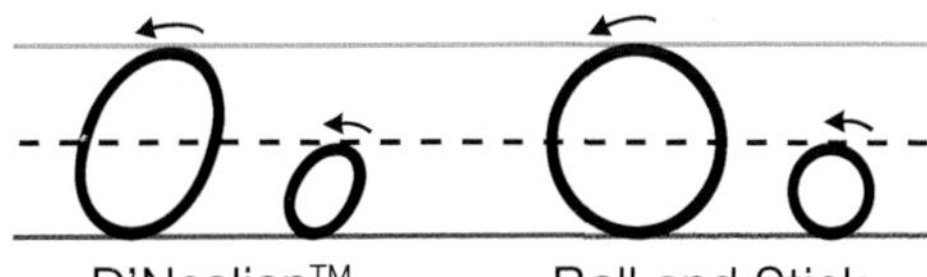

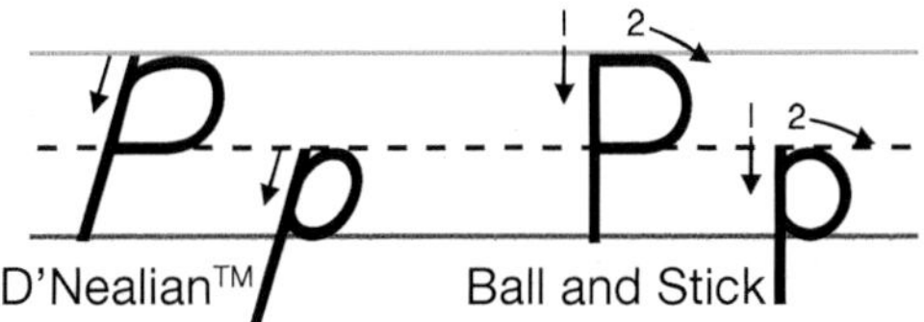

Have children write a row of uppercase *O* and *P* and a row of lowercase *o* and *p* on their Write-On Boards. Remind them to use proper left-to-right and top-to-bottom progression when writing *O, o, P,* and *p.*

eSTREET INTERACTIVE
www.ReadingStreet.com

Teacher Resources
- Reader's and Writer's Notebook
- Daily Fix-It Transparency

Bridge to Common Core

PRODUCTION AND DISTRIBUTION OF WRITING
With your guidance and support, children interact and collaborate with others to write sentences about real experiences and events.

Support Writing Before writing, have children dictate a list of family members. Then have children choose one person from the list and think of all the ways they help him or her. Repeat with the other family members. Have children choose one family member to write their sentence about.

Common Core State Standards

Language 5.a. Sort common objects into categories (e.g., shapes, foods) to gain a sense of the concepts the categories represent. **Language 5.c.** Identify real-life connections between words and their use (e.g., note places at school that are *colorful*). **Also Literature 4., Foundational Skills 1.d., 2.**

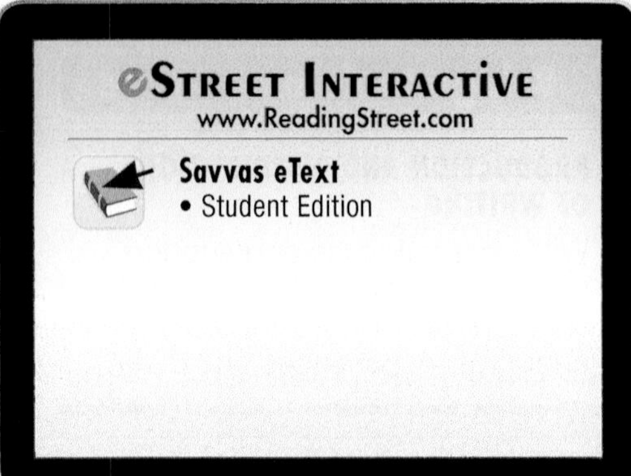

Vocabulary

Words for Shapes

TEACH Write the words *square, triangle, circle,* and *rectangle* on the board. Point to each word as you read it. These words tell the shape of something. Have children turn to p. 68 of *My Skills Buddy.* Use the last Vocabulary bullet in the discussion. Direct children to the shapes at the top of the page. Point to the square. What color are the squares at the bottom of the page? Repeat the routine with triangle, circle, and rectangle.

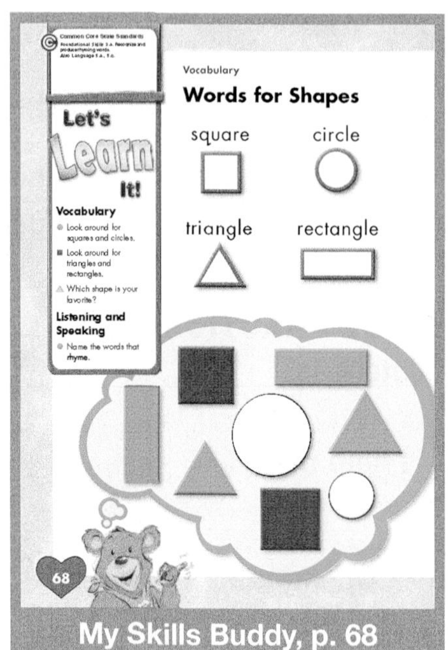

My Skills Buddy, p. 68

Team Talk Pair children and have them identify all of the red, blue, and white shapes and put them in categories.

Wrap Up Your Day!

✔ **Oral Language** Sing "Purple Platypus" with me. Clap your hands when you hear an Amazing Word—*platypus, around, lost, found, market,* or *groceries.*

✔ **Phonological Awareness** Today we worked with syllables. Have each child say his or her name, and as a class, clap the syllables in the name.

✔ **Homework Idea** Have children draw a "family photo" and write one word that describes what each person in their picture looks like.

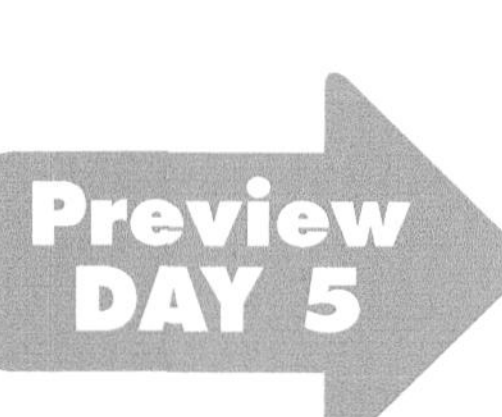

Tell children that tomorrow they will review some of the books and stories they have read this week.

Social Studies
Name and Address

MATERIALS: Big Book *Plaidypus Lost,* paper, markers or crayons, three-hole punch, yarn

WHERE GRANDMA LIVES Turn to p. 35 in *Plaidypus Lost.* Point out that the sign says Grandma lives at 112 Oak Street. Make a two-column chart. Label one column *Person* and the other column *Street.*

Person	Street
Grandma	112 Oak Street

Ask children to say their names and addresses. Add the information to the chart.

MAKE AN ADDRESS BOOK Have children draw a picture of their home and label it with their name and address. Have children show their picture and say their name and address.

Make a cover. Three-hole punch children's pages and use yarn to bind them together. Display the book in the classroom.

Comprehension
Plaidypus Plays Around

MATERIALS: paper, crayons or markers

MAKE PLAIDYPUS BOOKS Have children fold a sheet of paper in half to make a booklet. Ask them to think of places Plaidypus and the girl play.

Have children write a title for their "Plaidypus Plays Around" book. Ask them to draw pictures of the places the girl and Plaidypus go and what they do in each picture. At sharing time, have children show their booklets.

Letter Recognition
Letter Game

MATERIALS: cards with letters, buttons or beans

WRITE LETTERS Make cards as shown below on heavy paper. Arrange the letters in a different order on each card. Give each child a card and buttons or beans to cover up letters. Each child may cover up a "free" spot. Say a letter and have children find the letter and cover it with a button or bean. The first child to cover a row horizontally, vertically, or diagonally wins the game.

R	M	m	k
Q	free	K	P
L	o	r	l
J	p	q	O

DAY 5 at a Glance

Content Knowledge
Oral Vocabulary

Phonemic Awareness
Review Initial Sounds

Letter Recognition
Letters *Ss*

Assessment
Letter Recognition
High-Frequency Words
Comprehension

Text-Based Comprehension
Review Sequence

Conventions
Review What We Look Like

Writing
This Week We...

Materials

- Student Edition
- Truckery Rhymes
- Talk with Me/Sing with Me Chart
- Alphabet Cards
- Reader's and Writer's Notebook
- Read Aloud Anthology
- Student Reader K.1.3
- Get Set, Roll! Reader 3

Bridge to Common Core

INTEGRATION OF KNOWLEDGE/IDEAS
This week children have integrated content presented in diverse formats and analyzed how different texts address similar topics. They have developed knowledge about how families live, work, and play together to expand the unit topic of Cooperation.

Social Studies Knowledge Goals
Children have learned that support from their families

- helps them take care of themselves
- helps them take care of their friends

TRUCKTOWN on Reading Street

Start your engines!

- Display "Three Loud Trucks" and lead the group in saying the rhyme a few times.
  - Have half the group recite the rhyme while the other half acts it out.
    - Ask the halves to change roles.

Truckery Rhymes

Content Knowledge

Zoom in on

Families Living, Working, and Playing Together

REVIEW THE CONCEPT Discuss with children what they have added to their knowledge about this unit of study, All Together Now. Encourage them to use the Amazing Words.

Build Oral Language

LISTEN FOR AMAZING WORDS Display Sing with Me Chart 3B. Let's sing "Purple Platypus." I want you to listen for the Amazing Words we learned this week. Remind children that the words *platypus, around, lost, found, market,* and *groceries* are in the song. Sing the song several times to the tune of "Baby Bumble Bee." Discuss how children cooperate with their families. Remind children to speak one at a time.

Purple Platypus
I lost my purple platypus today,
Searched around the market,
couldn't find him anywhere,
My grandpa peeked in a bag
of groceries,
Look! We found him!
Talk with Me/Sing with Me Chart 3B

Build Oral Vocabulary

Talk with Me/Sing with Me Chart 3A

REVIEW AMAZING WORDS Display Talk with Me Chart 3A. We learned six new Amazing Words this week. Let's say the Amazing Words as I point to the pictures on the chart. Point to each picture and give children the chance to say the appropriate Amazing Word before offering it.

Have children supply the appropriate Amazing Word to complete each sentence.

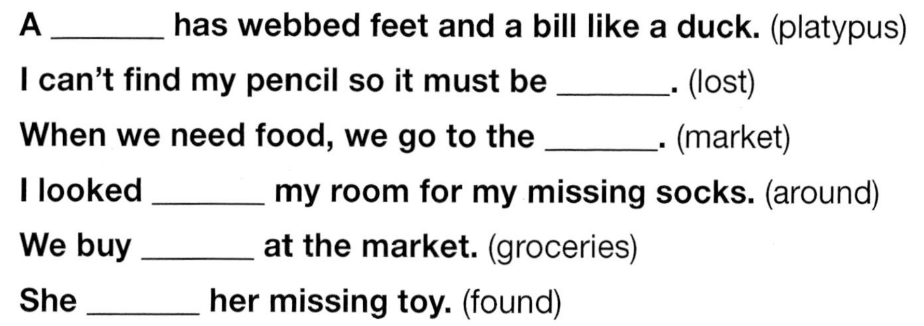

A _______ has webbed feet and a bill like a duck. (platypus)

I can't find my pencil so it must be _______. (lost)

When we need food, we go to the _______. (market)

I looked _______ my room for my missing socks. (around)

We buy _______ at the market. (groceries)

She _______ her missing toy. (found)

Check Oral Vocabulary

FORMATIVE ASSESSMENT Demonstrate Word Knowledge Monitor the Amazing Words by asking the following questions. Have children use the Amazing Word in their answer.

- **What is another word for food we buy at the market?** (groceries)
- **What animal has a flat tail, webbed feet, and a ducklike bill?** (platypus)
- **Where would you look if you looked in every direction?** (around)
- **What word means "missing"?** (lost)
- **Where can you go to buy food?** (market)
- **What word means "located"?** (found)

If... children have difficulty using the Amazing Words,

then... reteach the words using the Robust Vocabulary Routine on the Routines Flip Chart.

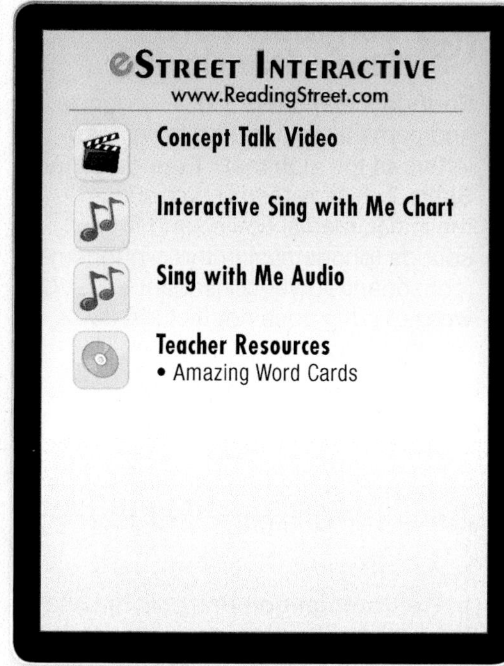

Amazing Words

platypus	around
lost	found
market	groceries

Access for All

 Strategic Intervention

Sentence Production If children answer a question using only a word or phrase, say the answer in a complete sentence and have children repeat the sentence.

Check Concepts and Language Use the Day 5 instruction on ELL Poster 3 to monitor children's understanding of the lesson concept.

Common Core State Standards

Foundational Skills 1.d. Recognize and name all upper- and lowercase letters of the alphabet. **Foundational Skills 2.d.** Isolate and pronounce the initial, medial vowel, and final sounds (phonemes) in three-phoneme (consonant-vowel-consonant, or CVC) words.* (This does not include CVCs ending with /l/, /r/, or /x/.)

Access for All

Strategic Intervention

Letter Recognition Pair children and have them take turns saying a letter (*Aa–Ss*) and finding it in a book or magazine.

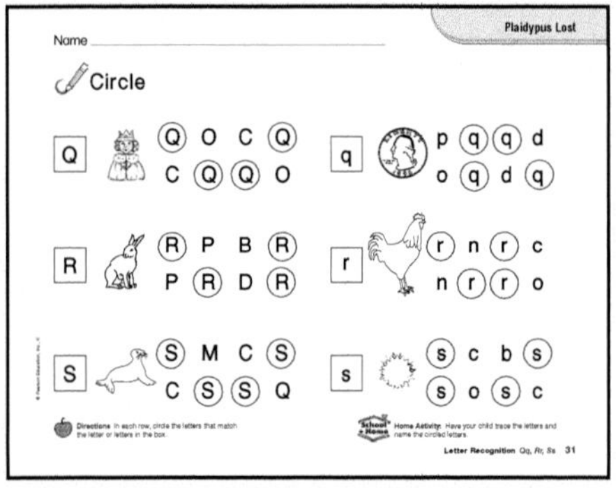

Name

Plaidypus Lost

Circle

Q Q O C Q C Q Q O

q p q q d o q d q

R R P B R P R D R

r r n r c n r r o

S S M C S C S S Q

s s c b s s o s c

Letter Recognition Qq, Rr, Ss 31

Reader's and Writer's Notebook, p. 31

Phonemic Awareness

Review Initial Sounds

ISOLATE INITIAL SOUNDS Say this sentence: Many happy monkeys make money for millions of people. Tell children to listen for words that begin alike. Have them repeat the sentence as they identify the words with the same beginning sound. Continue with these sentences: *Barry builds a beautiful red barn. Six sailors bit seaweed at the picnic.*

BLEND SYLLABLES Have children stand up. Listen carefully: *fish-er-man.* Blend these syllables together to say a word: *fisherman.* Repeat the routine with the syllables in *water* and *buddy.*

Letter Recognition

Teach/Model

Letters *Ss*

INTRODUCE Display the *Ss* Alphabet Card. Point to uppercase *S.* This is uppercase *S.* What is this letter? Repeat with lowercase *s.*

MODEL Display the *seal* Picture Card. This is a seal. Write the word *seal* on the board and point to the *s.* This letter is lowercase *s.*

Alphabet Card

Guide Practice

GROUP PRACTICE Display p. 5 of *Plaidypus Lost.* Ask children to name and point to the uppercase *S* on the page (*Snippity*). Then have them point to, name, and count each lowercase *s* on the page (7). Continue the routine with other pages in the story.

ON THEIR OWN Give pairs of children a storybook. Have one partner find and name uppercase *S* and the other partner find and name lowercase *s.* Then have children use *Reader's and Writer's Notebook,* p. 31, for more practice with letters *Ss.*

REVIEW HIGH-FREQUENCY WORDS Write the word *the* on the board. This is the word *the.* What is this word? Repeat the routine with *little.*

REREAD Have children reread one of the books specific to the target letters. You may wish to review the rebus words and high-frequency words that appear in each book prior to rereading.

Decodable Reader 3
My Skills Buddy, p. 58

Kindergarten Student Reader K.1.3

Get Set, Roll! Reader 3

Day 5 SMALL GROUP TIME • Differentiate Close Reading, p. SG•37

OL On-Level

- **Practice Letter Recognition** Recognize Letters *Qq, Rr, Ss*
- **Read** "Family Adventures"

SI Strategic Intervention

- **Reteach Letter Recognition** Recognize Letters *Qq, Rr, Ss*
- **Read** "Family Adventures"

A Advanced

- **Extend Letter Recognition** Connect Letters to Sounds
- **Read** "Family Adventures"

ELL

Place English Language Learners in the groups that correspond to their reading abilities in English.

If... children need more support with **Comprehension,**
then... use the ELL activities on pp. DI•47–DI•48 in the Teacher Resources section of the Digital Path.

Common Core State Standards

Foundational Skills 1.d. Recognize and name all upper- and lowercase letters of the alphabet.

Assess

- Identify uppercase and lowercase letters.
- Read high-frequency words.

Assessment

Monitor Progress

Review Letter Recognition

WHOLE CLASS Display the following Alphabet Cards in random order: *Oo, Pp, Qq, Rr, Ss.* Name a letter and have children select the appropriate card. Continue naming other letters.

MONITOR PROGRESS **Check Letter and Word Reading**

If... children cannot complete the whole-class assessment,

then... use the Reteach lesson in *First Stop.*

If... you are unsure of a child's grasp of this week's skills,

then... use the assessment below to obtain a clearer evaluation of the child's progress.

ONE-ON-ONE To facilitate individual progress monitoring, assess some children on Day 4 and the rest on Day 5. While individual children are being assessed, the rest of the class can look for examples of *Oo, Pp, Qq, Rr,* and *Ss* in this week's books.

LETTER READING Use the letter list on reproducible p. 301 to assess each child's ability to name the letters *Oo, Pp, Qq, Rr,* and *Ss.* We're going to name letters. I'll do the first one. This is uppercase *O.* For each child, record any problems.

WORD READING Use the words on reproducible p. 301 to assess each child's ability to read high-frequency words. Have each child read the words aloud.

RECORD SCORES Monitor children's accuracy by recording their scores using the Letter and Word Reading Chart for this unit in *First Stop.*

Name ___________________________________

Name the Letters

O	r	s	P	q
p	o	Q	S	R

Read the Words

the ☐
little ☐

Note to Teacher: Children name each letter. Children read the words.

Scoring for Name the Letters/Read the Words: Score 1 point for each correct letter/word.

Letter Recognition (*Oo, Pp, Qq, Rr, Ss*) _______ / 10
High-Frequency Words (*the, little*) _______ / 2

Copyright © Savvas Learning Company LLC. All Rights Reserved.

MONITOR PROGRESS
- Letters *Oo, Pp, Qq, Rr, Ss*
- High-Frequency Words

Common Core State Standards
Speaking/Listening 2. Confirm understanding of a text read aloud or information presented orally or through other media by asking and answering questions about key details and requesting clarification if something is not understood. **Also Literature 1., 3., 5.**

Let's Practice It!

Fable

- Listen to the fable.
- Why does the shepherd boy cry "Wolf!" the first two times?
- What lesson does the shepherd boy learn? Has anything like this ever happened to you? Tell about it.
- What do you think the shepherd boy might do next?
- A moral is a lesson learned. What new expression does this fable teach you?

The Boy Who Cried Wolf!

1 2 3 4

70 71

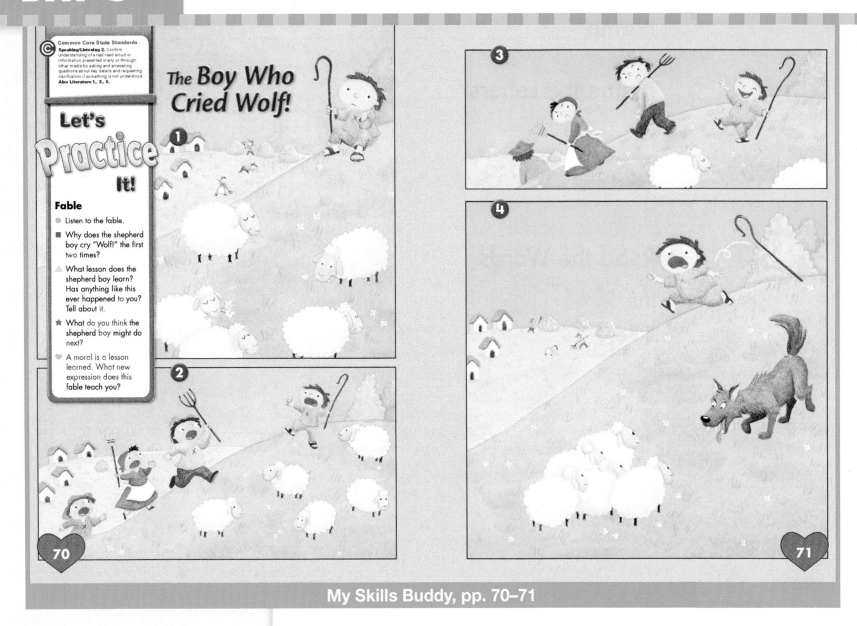

My Skills Buddy, pp. 70–71

Common Core State Standards

Literature 1. With prompting and support, ask and answer questions about key details in a text. **Literature 3.** With prompting and support, identify characters, settings, and major events in a story. **Literature 5.** Recognize common types of texts (e.g., storybooks, poems). **Speaking/Listening 2.** Confirm understanding of a text read aloud or information presented orally or through other media by asking and answering questions about key details and requesting clarification if something is not understood.

Academic Vocabulary

fable a story that teaches a moral, or lesson

Let's Practice It!

Fable

TEACH Today we are going to read a well-known fable. A **fable** is a type of story. Review the features of a fable with children.

- A fable tells a story.
- A fable has characters that learn lessons the hard way.
- A fable shares a lesson.

Have children turn to pp. 70–71 in *My Skills Buddy.* I am going to read you a fable called "The Boy Who Cried 'Wolf!'" Look at the pictures as I read. Read the text for "The Boy Who Cried 'Wolf!'" As you read, direct children to look at the appropriate picture.

GUIDE PRACTICE Discuss the features of fables and the bulleted text on p. 70 of *My Skills Buddy* with children.

- A fable tells a story. What happens in this story? (The boy calls "Wolf!" and the villagers come running, but there is no wolf. Next, the boy calls "Wolf!" again and the villagers come running, but there is no wolf. Last, a real wolf comes and the boy calls "Wolf!" but the villagers don't come because they think the boy is lying.)
- A fable has characters that learn lessons the hard way. Why does the boy call "wolf"? (He is bored watching the sheep.)
- Help children make inferences using plot by asking: Why would no wolves coming make the boy bored? (He got bored because with no wolves coming, he didn't have anything to do.)
- A fable shares a lesson. What does this fable teach you? (When you lie a lot, people will not believe you when you tell the truth.) Why is this a good lesson for you to learn? (Lying can get me into trouble and can cause problems.)

Writing to Sources

Use Connect the Texts on pp. 16–17 to guide children in writing text-based responses using two sources.

Access for All

A Advanced

Access Content Explain to children that "cry wolf" is an expression that people say. After listening to the story, have children tell what they think the expression means in their own words.

Teacher Read Aloud

The Boy Who Cried "Wolf"

Every day a shepherd boy took a flock of sheep to a pasture above the village. His job was to guard the sheep from wolves that might try to catch and eat them. But no wolves ever came, and the shepherd boy became bored. So just for fun he decided to play a trick.

"Wolf! Wolf!" the shepherd boy yelled.

All the villagers came running to help. The shepherd boy laughed at the sight. Angry and unhappy, the people went back to the village.

The next day, the shepherd boy played the trick again.

"Wolf! Wolf!" he yelled.

Again, the villagers came running to help. Again, the shepherd boy laughed at the sight. Again, the unhappy villagers went back to the village.

The next day, a wolf did come to the meadow and began chasing the sheep.

continued on p. 310a

Common Core State Standards

Literature 3. With prompting and support, identify characters, settings, and major events in a story. **Also Literature 1., 2.**

Assess

Identify the sequence of a story.

Assessment

Monitor Progress

REVIEW SEQUENCE In most stories, something happens first, something happens next, and something happens last. The order in which things happen in a story is called sequence. Good readers pay attention to the sequence of a story because it helps them understand the story.

READ "THE LITTLE RED HEN" Tell children that you are going to read them a story about a hen that bakes some bread. Ask them to think about the sequence of the events in the story. After I read the story, I am going to ask you to tell me about the sequence. Read "The Little Red Hen" on p. 5 of *Read Aloud Anthology.*

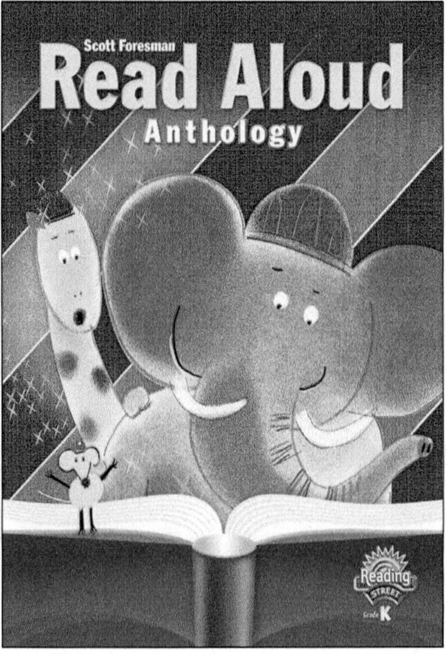

Read Aloud Anthology

CHECK SEQUENCE After you read the story, have children tell you the sequence of the events in the story.

- What does Little Red Hen do first when she finds grains of wheat? (She plants the wheat.)
- What does Little Red Hen do next? (She cuts the wheat.)
- What does she do after that? (She takes the wheat to the mill.)
- What does Little Red Hen do after that? (She mixes the flour into dough and bakes the bread.)
- What does she do last? (She eats the bread by herself.)

If... a child cannot identify the sequence of events in a story,
then... reteach sequence using the Reteach lesson in *First Stop.*

ASSESS SEQUENCE Use the blackline master on p. 305. Make one copy for each child. Have children cut out the pictures. Have them glue the pictures to another sheet of paper to show what happens first, next, and last in "The Little Red Hen."

Name ____________________

Sequence

Put the events from "The Little Red Hen" in order.

Note to Teacher: Have children cut out the pictures. Have them glue the pictures to another sheet of paper to show what happens first, next, and last in "The Little Red Hen."

Copyright © Savvas Learning Company LLC. All Rights Reserved.

MONITOR PROGRESS

- Sequence

Common Core State Standards

Writing 3. Use a combination of drawing, dictating, and writing to narrate a single event or several loosely linked events, tell about the events in the order in which they occurred, and provide a reaction to what happened. **Speaking/Listening 4.** Describe familiar people, places, things, and events and, with prompting and support, provide additional detail. **Language 1.a.** Print many upper- and lowercase letters. **Also Literature 3., Speaking/Listening 5.**

Daily Fix-It

the little cat got lost
The little cat got lost.

This week's practice sentences appear on *Teacher Resources DVD-ROM.*

Conventions

Review What We Look Like

REVIEW Remind children that a story usually has characters. The characters are the people or animals that the story is about. We can describe what the characters look like at different times in the story.

MODEL Make a two-column chart on the board. Write the column headings *Little Red Hen* and *Plaidypus* on the chart. Think about the part of "The Little Red Hen" when the hen is making bread. What words can we use to tell how she probably looks at this time? I think she probably looks busy. Write *busy* in the first column.

GUIDE PRACTICE Have children suggest other words to describe the hen. Add the words to the chart. What words can we use to tell how the hen probably looks when the dog, cat, and pig want to eat her bread? Write children's suggestions on the chart. Ask similar questions about Plaidypus at two different times in the story. When the chart is completed, read the words in each column and have children echo you.

ON THEIR OWN Have each child draw a picture of what Plaidypus looks like and a picture of what the little red hen looks like. Tell children to write or dictate words that describe their pictures.

This Week We...

REVIEW Display *Plaidypus Lost,* Sing with Me Chart 3B, Phonics Songs and Rhymes Chart 3, Decodable Reader 3 from *My Skills Buddy,* Kindergarten Student Reader K.1.3, and Get Set, Roll! Reader 3. This week we talked about how we cooperate with our families. We read new books, and we sang new songs. Which book or song was your favorite? Let's share our ideas with each other.

Team Talk Pair children and have them take turns telling which book or song was their favorite and why.

MODEL Today we will write about how we can help family members. We read about how Grandma helps the girl fix Plaidypus in *Plaidypus Lost.* I will write this sentence:

> **We can help fix things.**

GUIDE PRACTICE Continue writing sentences with children. Then read through the sentences.

> **We can set the table.**
> **We can share toys.**

ON THEIR OWN Have children write or dictate ideas about how they cooperate with their families.

Daily Handwriting

Write uppercase *O* and *P* and lowercase *o* and *p* on the board. Review correct letter formation with children.

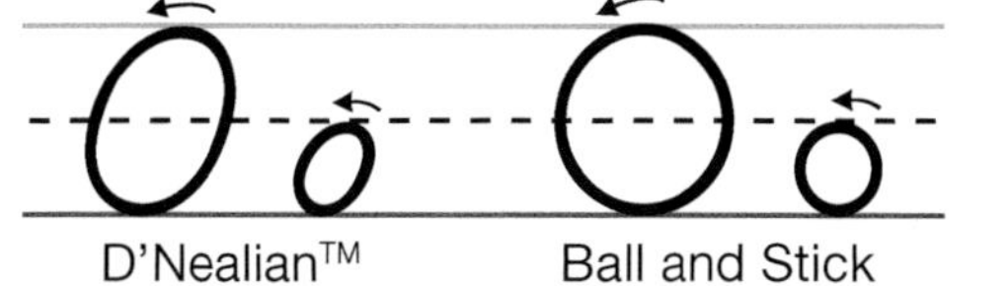

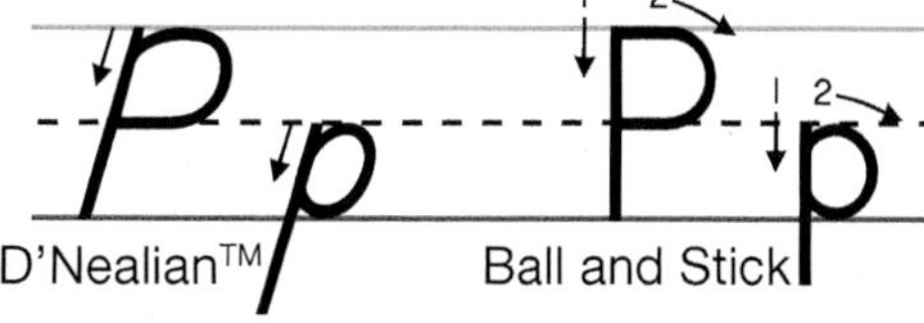

D'Nealian™ Ball and Stick D'Nealian™ Ball and Stick

Have children write a row of uppercase *O* and *P* and a row of lowercase *o* and *p* on their Write-On Boards. Remind them to use proper left-to-right and top-to-bottom progression.

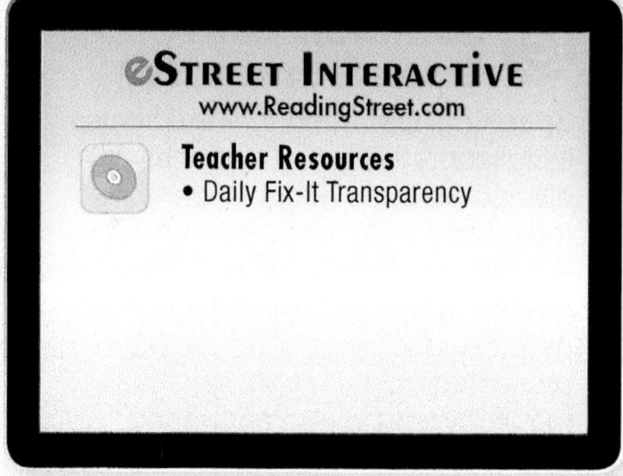

Access for All

SI Strategic Intervention

Support Writing Remind children that they already know the word *I*. Encourage children to begin their sentences with the word *I*.

Bridge to Common Core

PRODUCTION AND DISTRIBUTION OF WRITING

When children write sentences about ways they can help their families, they are learning to use writing to convey real experiences and events. They are also learning to produce writing in collaboration with others.

Poster Preview Encourage children to look ahead to next week by previewing ELL Poster 4. Read the Poster Talk-Through to introduce the concept and vocabulary. Ask children to identify and describe objects and actions in the art.

Common Core State Standards

Speaking/Listening 1. Participate in collaborative conversations with diverse partners about *kindergarten topics and texts* with peers and adults in small and larger groups. **Speaking/Listening 2.** Confirm understanding of a text read aloud or information presented orally or through other media by asking and answering questions about key details and requesting clarification if something is not understood. **Language 1.e.** Use the most frequently occurring prepositions (e.g., *to, from, in, out, on, off, for, of, by, with*).

Wrap Up Your Week!

Families Living, Working, and Playing Together

How do families cooperate?

ILLUSTRATE FAMILY COOPERATION This week we talked about how families cooperate. Families have to cooperate to live, work, and play together.

- Make a T-chart like the one shown.
- Write children's responses in the appropriate column.
- Give each child a sheet of paper.
- Have children draw a picture of a family member.
- Have children write or dictate a sentence or phrase about how they cooperate with that family member.

Family Member	How We Cooperate
sister	clean our room
brother	take care of our pet

Amazing Words

You've learned 006 words this week!

You've learned 018 words this year!

Next Week's Concept

People Working Together in a Community

How do people in a community cooperate?

Discuss next week's question. Guide children in making a connection between families cooperating and community members cooperating.

Tell children that next week they will read about a kindergarten class.

Preview Next Week

Extend Your Day!

Science
Our Senses

MATERIALS: chart paper, construction paper, crayons

FIND THE SENSES Write *see, hear, smell, touch,* and *taste* on chart paper. Read the first word and have children tell which part of their body they use to see. Draw a pair of eyes by the word *see.* Have children tell how they can find something if they use their eyes. Have volunteers demonstrate how to look for something you name. Continue with the other senses.

MAKE A SENSES BOOKLET Tell children to think about the story *Plaidypus Lost* and how the girl uses mainly her eyes to find Plaidypus. Have children draw a picture showing Plaidypus when he is lost and how they would use their five senses to find him. Children may wish to show themselves using one sense or more than one sense. Tell them to label the senses they would use.

Drama
Plaidypus Speaks

MATERIALS: Big Book *Plaidypus Lost*

LET'S PRETEND What would Plaidypus say if he could talk? What would his voice sound like? As a group, decide which voice sounds most like Plaidypus.

Begin a picture walk through the book *Plaidypus Lost.* Model speaking as Plaidypus, using a different voice for emphasis. I am so excited to have a girl to play with. She says she won't lose me.

Have children continue, using the "Plaidypus voice" in each situation.

Vocabulary
Where Is AlphaBuddy?

MATERIALS: AlphaBuddy, a box or bin

LOCATION AND POSITION This week we read about Plaidypus, who keeps getting lost! What if AlphaBuddy gets lost? What words could we use to describe where to find him?

Place AlphaBuddy on a desk. AlphaBuddy is on the desk. The word *on* tells me where to find AlphaBuddy. Continue modeling position words with AlphaBuddy: under the desk, over the desk, inside the box, outside the box.

Let children tell you where to find AlphaBuddy. Have them use the position words you modeled.

Assessment Checkpoints for the Week

Weekly Assessment

Use the whole-class assessment on pages 300–301 and 304–305 in this Teacher's Edition to check:

- ✓ **Letters *Oo, Pp, Qq, Rr, Ss***
- ✓ **Comprehension** *Sequence*
- ✓ **High-Frequency Words**

the	*little*

Managing Assessment

Use the Assessment Handbook for:

- ✓ **Observation Checklists**
- ✓ **Record-Keeping Forms**
- ✓ **Portfolio Assessment**

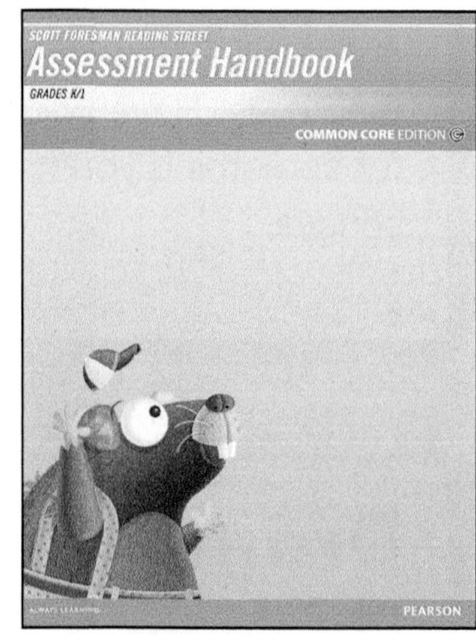

Assessment Handbook

Let's Practice It!

Teacher Read Aloud continued from p. 303

The Boy Who Cried "Wolf"

"Wolf! Wolf!" yelled the shepherd boy.

But the villagers did not come running this time. They thought the shepherd boy was trying to trick them again.

Moral: Liars won't be believed, even when they are telling the truth.

TEACHER NOTES

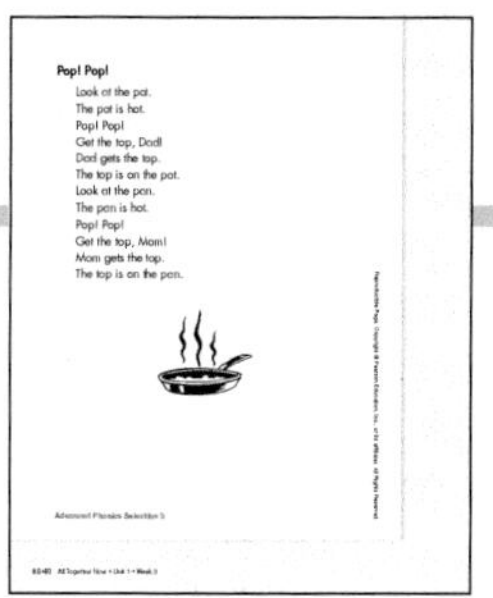

DAY 1 Differentiate Letter Recognition

- Letters *Oo*
- Decodable Story
- Advanced Selection "Pop! Pop!"

DAY 2 Differentiate Letter Recognition

- Letters *Pp*
- Decodable Reader

DAY 3 Differentiate Vocabulary

- Develop Vocabulary: Words for Shapes
- Kindergarten Student Reader

DAY 4 Differentiate Language

- Develop Language
- Get Set, Roll! Reader

DAY 5 Differentiate Letter Recognition/ Close Reading

- Letters *Qq, Rr, Ss*
- "Family Adventures"

Place English Language Learners in the groups that correspond to their reading abilities.
If... children need scaffolding and practice,
then... use the ELL notes on the page.

Independent Practice

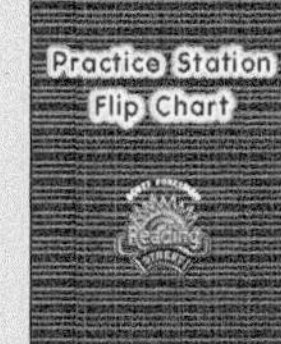

Independent Practice Stations

See pp. 212 and 213 for Independent Stations.

Reading Street Digital Path

Independent Practice Activities available in the Digital Path.

Independent Reading

See p. 213 for independent reading suggestions.

On-Level

Common Core State Standards

Literature 1. With prompting and support, ask and answer questions about key details in a text. **Literature 10.** Actively engage in group reading activities with purpose and understanding. **Foundational Skills 1.d.** Recognize and name all upper- and lowercase letters of the alphabet. **Foundational Skills 2.d.** Isolate and pronounce the initial, medial vowel, and final sounds (phonemes) in three-phoneme (consonant-vowel-consonant, or CVC) words.* (This does not include CVCs ending with /l/, /r/, or /x/.) **Foundational Skills 3.c.** Read common high-frequency words by sight (e.g., *the, of, to, you, she, my, is, are, do, does*).

Independent Reading Options

Trade Book Library

eStreet Interactive
www.ReadingStreet.com

Teacher's Guides available on the Leveled Reader Database.

1 Build Word Knowledge

Practice Phonemic Awareness

IDENTIFY INITIAL SOUNDS Tell children that you will say a sentence and they are to listen for and identify words that begin with the same sound. Say these sentences: *Sam saw the sun. Tim likes to talk to Tom. Cam will cook the corn. Marie mixes many things.*

Practice Letter Recognition

RECOGNIZE LETTERS *Oo* Display the *Oo* Alphabet Card. Have children name the letters with you. Have volunteers write uppercase *O* and lowercase *o* on chart paper. Ask children to explain how the two letters are different.

2 Read

Decodable Story 3 *Little Me!*

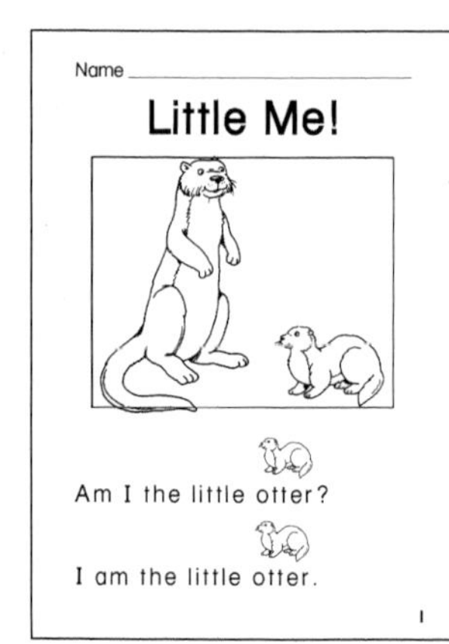

READ Have children read the story. Then have them reread the text to develop automaticity.

HIGH-FREQUENCY WORDS Have children return to the text and identify the high-frequency words *the* and *little.* Help children demonstrate their understanding of these words by completing sentence frames such as these: *We can read* _______ *story.* (the) *A bug is* _______. (little) Continue with the words *I* and *am*.

3 Reread for Fluency

Have children reread the Decodable Story *Little Me!* individually to develop fluency.

On-Level

1 Build Word Knowledge

Practice Letter Recognition

RECOGNIZE LETTERS *Pp* Show the *Pp* Alphabet Card. Point to each letter. This is uppercase *P*. This is lowercase *p*. Write the letters on chart paper. Call on volunteers to write the letters on the chart paper while the other children write them in the air.

Practice High-Frequency Words

CHOOSE AND USE Display the high-frequency word cards *the, little, I,* and *am.* Say the word *little* and choose a volunteer to point to the correct word card. Have children say the word and use it in a sentence. Continue with the other high-frequency words.

2 Read

Decodable Reader 3 *The Little Toys*

CONCEPTS OF PRINT Display Decodable Reader 3 in *My Skills Buddy.* Show children the illustrations and read aloud the title. What do you think the story is about?

READ Have children take turns reading the Decodable Reader. Pause at the end of each page to ask questions. What toy do you see? Is this toy big or little?

3 Reread for Fluency

Have children reread the Decodable Reader *The Little Toys* individually to develop fluency.

SMALL GROUP TIME

More Reading for Group Time

CONCEPT LITERACY

- Concept Words
- High-Frequency Words

Use these suggested readers or other text at children's instructional level.

eStreet Interactive
www.ReadingStreet.com

Use the Leveled Reader Database for lesson plans and student pages for *Families*.

If... children need more scaffolding and practice with phonemic awareness and letter recognition, **then...** use the activities on p. DI•46 in the Teacher Resources section of the Digital Path.

On-Level

Common Core State Standards

Literature 1. With prompting and support, ask and answer questions about key details in a text. **Literature 10.** Actively engage in group reading activities with purpose and understanding. **Foundational Skills 3.c.** Read common high-frequency words by sight (e.g., *the, of, to, you, she, my, is, are, do, does*). **Language 5.a.** Sort common objects into categories (e.g., shapes, foods) to gain a sense of the concepts the categories represent. **Language 5.c.** Identify real-life connections between words and their use (e.g., note places at school that are *colorful*). **Language 6.** Use words and phrases acquired through conversations, reading and being read to, and responding to texts.

1 Build Word Knowledge

Develop Vocabulary

WORDS FOR SHAPES Have children return to p. 68 in *My Skills Buddy.* Review the shape words *square, circle, triangle,* and *rectangle.* Have children point to each shape at the top of the page and read the word. AlphaBuddy is thinking of many shapes. Ask children the following questions about those shapes.

- Point to the squares. How many squares do you see? What color are the squares?
- Point to the circles. What color are the circles? Are the circles the same size?
- Point to the triangles. How many triangles do you see? What color are the triangles?
- Point to the rectangles. What color are the rectangles? How are the rectangles different?

Team Talk Have children work with a partner to use the words for shapes in sentences.

2 Read

Kindergarten Student Reader *Cat and Dog Play*

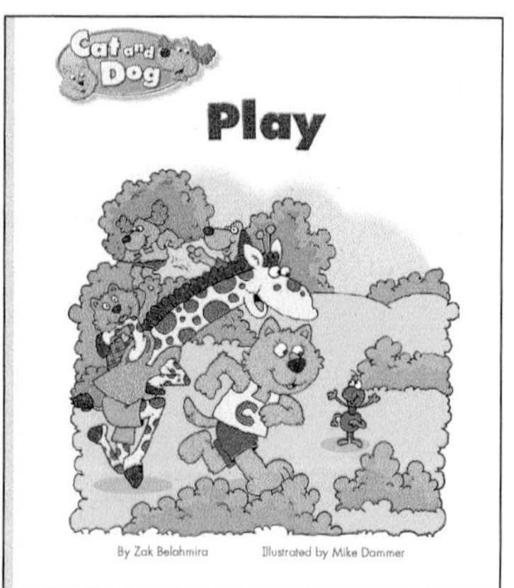

REREAD Display the reader and have children tell the title of the story. Have them tell what they remember about the story. Then have children read the story chorally. After reading each page, ask children to tell what they see. Where is the family? What are they going to do? How do the little cat and dog play? To check children's understanding, have them take turns reading the story to a partner and then retelling the story to the partner.

On-Level

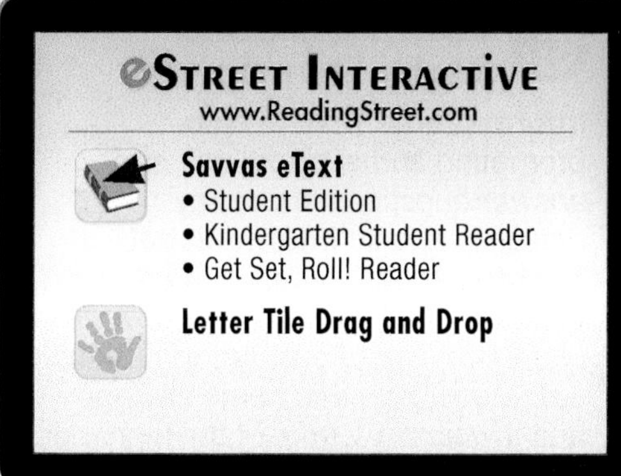

1 Build Word Knowledge

Develop Language

Display the Big Book *Plaidypus Lost* and read the text on p. 18.

Off to the market.
Push the big cart.
Fast and slow.
Stop. Go.

- Ask children to read the text with you as you track the print.
- Point to the line, *Push the big cart.*
- What does the word *big* mean? What is another word for *big?* Why do you think the author chose the word *big?*
- Team Talk Turn to your partner and try some other words in place of *big*.
- Continue the routine with the words *fast* and *slow.*

2 Read

Get Set, Roll! Reader 3 *Pete*

REVIEW HIGH-FREQUENCY WORDS Review the following high-frequency words with children: *I, am, the, little.* Ask them to use each word in a sentence.

REVIEW REBUS WORDS Distribute Letter Tiles to each child or use Letter Tile Drag and Drop in the Digital Path. Write the name *Pete* on a card. This is the name *Pete.* The letters in *Pete* are *P, e, t, e*. Use your letters to build this word. What does this spell? Which character is Pete? Continue the routine with the following words: *rocks, crunch.*

REREAD Have children whisper read *Pete* as you listen to each child. Then have children take turns reading the story aloud.

SMALL GROUP TIME

ELL

If... children need more scaffolding and practice with vocabulary, **then...** use the ELL activities on p. DI•48 in the Teacher Resources section of the Digital Path.

Common Core State Standards

Informational Text 1. With prompting and support, ask and answer questions about key details in a text. **Informational Text 10.** Actively engage in group reading activities with purpose and understanding. **Foundational Skills 1.d.** Recognize and name all upper- and lowercase letters of the alphabet.

1 Build Word Knowledge

Practice Letter Recognition

RECOGNIZE LETTERS *Qq, Rr, Ss* Display the *Qq, Rr,* and *Ss* Alphabet Cards. Have children identify the letters as you say the letter names. Write a mixture of these uppercase and lowercase letters on chart paper. Ask children to find the letter you name and circle it. Continue until all the letters have been circled.

REVIEW LETTERS *Oo–Ss* Display the *Oo, Pp, Qq, Rr,* and *Ss* Alphabet Cards. Ask a child to choose one of the letters and write it on chart paper. Have the child choose another child to identify the letter. That child then chooses and writes the next letter. Continue until many children have had turns.

Corrective feedback	**If...** children have difficulty naming letters, **then...** review the letter names using the Alphabet Cards.

2 Text-Based Comprehension

Read

READ ALOUD Read the Reading Street Sleuth Read Aloud, "Family Adventures," on p. SG•43 to children.

READ LIKE A SLEUTH! Encourage children to cite evidence from the text to support their answers. You may wish to reread sections of the text to verify children's answers.

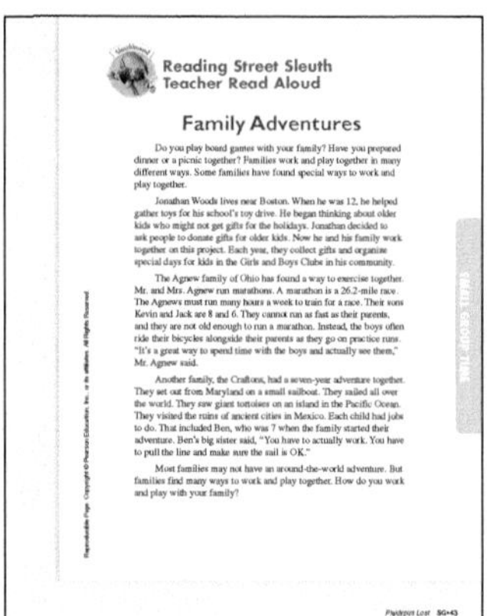
Reading Street Sleuth
Teacher Read Aloud

Family Adventures

Do you play board games with your family? Have you prepared dinner or a picnic together? Families work and play together in many different ways. Some families have found special ways to work and play together.

Jonathan Woods lives near Boston. When he was 12, he helped gather toys for his school's toy drive. He began thinking about older kids who might not get gifts for the holidays. Jonathan decided to ask people to donate gifts for older kids. Now he and his family work together on this project. Each year, they collect gifts and organize special days for kids in the Girls and Boys Clubs in his community.

The Agnew family of Ohio has found a way to exercise together. Mr. and Mrs. Agnew run marathons. A marathon is a 26.2-mile race. The Agnews must run many hours a week to train for a race. Their sons Kevin and Jack are 8 and 6. They cannot run as fast as their parents, and they are not old enough to run a marathon. Instead, the boys often ride their bicycles alongside their parents as they go on practice runs. "It's a great way to spend time with the boys and actually see them," Mr. Agnew said.

Another family, the Craftons, had a seven-year adventure together. They set out from Maryland on a small sailboat. They sailed all over the world. They saw giant tortoises on an island in the Pacific Ocean. They visited the ruins of ancient cities in Mexico. Each child had jobs to do. That included Ben, who was 7 when the family started their adventure. Ben's big sister said, "You have to actually work. You have to pull the line and make sure the sail is OK."

Most families may not have an around-the-world adventure. But families find many ways to work and play together. How do you work and play with your family?

Look for Evidence How do each of the three families work and play together?

Ask Questions If you could meet the children in one of these families, what questions would you want to ask them?

Prove It! Performance Task Have children draw a picture of the family adventure in the text that they think is most interesting. Ask them to label the picture with one or two key details from the text. Children may write or dictate a short phrase or sentence.

Family Adventures

Do you play board games with your family? Have you prepared dinner or a picnic together? Families work and play together in many different ways. Some families have found special ways to work and play together.

Jonathan Woods lives near Boston. When he was 12, he helped gather toys for his school's toy drive. He began thinking about older kids who might not get gifts for the holidays. Jonathan decided to ask people to donate gifts for older kids. Now he and his family work together on this project. Each year, they collect gifts and organize special days for kids in the Girls and Boys Clubs in his community.

The Agnew family of Ohio has found a way to exercise together. Mr. and Mrs. Agnew run marathons. A marathon is a 26.2-mile race. The Agnews must run many hours a week to train for a race. Their sons Kevin and Jack are 8 and 6. They cannot run as fast as their parents, and they are not old enough to run a marathon. Instead, the boys often ride their bicycles alongside their parents as they go on practice runs. "It's a great way to spend time with the boys and actually see them," Mr. Agnew said.

Another family, the Craftons, had a seven-year adventure together. They set out from Maryland on a small sailboat. They sailed all over the world. They saw giant tortoises on an island in the Pacific Ocean. They visited the ruins of ancient cities in Mexico. Each child had jobs to do. That included Ben, who was 7 when the family started their adventure. Ben's big sister said, "You have to actually work. You have to pull the line and make sure the sail is OK."

Most families may not have an around-the-world adventure. But families find many ways to work and play together. How do you work and play with your family?

Reproducible Page. Copyright © Pearson Education, Inc., or its affiliates. All Rights Reserved.

Strategic Intervention

Common Core State Standards

Literature 1. With prompting and support, ask and answer questions about key details in a text. **Literature 10.** Actively engage in group reading activities with purpose and understanding. **Foundational Skills 1.d.** Recognize and name all upper- and lowercase letters of the alphabet. **Foundational Skills 2.d.** Isolate and pronounce the initial, medial vowel, and final sounds (phonemes) in three-phoneme (consonant-vowel-consonant, or CVC) words.* (This does not include CVCs ending with /l/, /r/, or /x/.) **Foundational Skills 3.c.** Read common high-frequency words by sight (e.g., *the, of, to, you, she, my, is, are, do, does*).

More Reading for Group Time

LISTEN TO ME READER

- Concepts of Print

Use these suggested readers or other text at children's instructional level.

Street Interactive
www.ReadingStreet.com

Use the Leveled Reader Database to access an online version of *What Do You See?*

If... children need more scaffolding and practice with phonemic awareness and letter recognition, **then...** use the Phonics Transition lessons beginning on p. 447 in the *ELL Handbook.*

1 Build Word Knowledge

Reteach Phonemic Awareness

LISTEN FOR INITIAL SOUNDS Explain to children that words that begin the same have the same beginning sound. We can tell whether two words begin with the same sound by listening to the beginning sounds in the words. I will say two words and I want you to tell me whether they begin with the same sound. Use these word pairs: *book, ball; can, cook; day, wet; sun, soap; fish, fan; top, tire; pig, moon; pear, pencil.*

Reteach Letter Recognition

RECOGNIZE LETTERS *Oo* Write *Oo* on chart paper. Point out to children that the letters are shaped like a circle. This is uppercase *O*. This is lowercase *o*. Note that uppercase *O* is bigger than lowercase *o*. Write several uppercase *O*'s and lowercase *o*'s in random order on the chart paper. Point to each letter and ask children to identify it.

2 Read

Decodable Story 3 *Little Me!*

REVIEW HIGH-FREQUENCY WORDS Write *the* on chart paper. This is the word *the*. Say the word with me: *the*. Continue with the word *little*. Then review the words *I* and *am*.

Corrective feedback	**If...** children have difficulty reading the high-frequency words, **then...** say a word and have children point to the word. Repeat several times, giving assistance as needed.

READ Have children read the story.

3 Reread for Fluency

Have children reread the story *Little Me!* chorally. Then have them reread the story several times individually to develop fluency.

1 Build Word Knowledge

Reteach Phonemic Awareness

PRACTICE DISCRIMINATING INITIAL SOUNDS Remind children that words can begin with the same sound. Ask volunteers to give examples of words that begin with the same sound. I will say two words and I want you to tell me whether they begin with the same sound. Use these word pairs: *dog, duck; cub, cow; fan, hen; rope, rug; pig, horse; bird, bear.*

Reteach Letter Recognition

RECOGNIZE LETTERS *Pp* Display the *Pp* Alphabet Card. Point to each letter and say its name. Give each child a card with an uppercase *P* or lowercase *p* written on it. Have children find someone with the letter they need to make an uppercase and lowercase pair.

Reteach High-Frequency Words

REVIEW Write *little* on chart paper. This is the word *little.* Say the word with me: *little.* Continue with the words *the, I,* and *am.*

Corrective feedback	**If...** children have difficulty reading the words, **then...** say a word and have children point to the word. Repeat several times, giving assistance as needed.

2 Read

Decodable Reader 3
The Little Toys

CONCEPTS OF PRINT Display Decodable Reader 3 in *My Skills Buddy.* The title of this story is *The Little Toys.* The author is Roger Jons. The illustrator is Scott Salinski. Look at the picture on the cover. Look at the pictures inside. What do you think the story is about?

READ Let's read the story together. After reading chorally with children, have them reread the story several times with a partner and then independently.

SMALL GROUP TIME

Independent Reading Options

Trade Book Library

eStreet Interactive
www.ReadingStreet.com

Teacher's Guides available on the Leveled Reader Database.

If... children need more support with letter recognition,
then... use the ELL activities on p. DI•46 in the Teacher Resources section of the Digital Path.

Strategic Intervention

Common Core State Standards

Literature 1. With prompting and support, ask and answer questions about key details in a text. **Literature 10.** Actively engage in group reading activities with purpose and understanding. **Foundational Skills 3.c.** Read common high-frequency words by sight (e.g., *the, of, to, you, she, my, is, are, do, does*). **Language 5.a.** Sort common objects into categories (e.g., shapes, foods) to gain a sense of the concepts the categories represent. **Language 5.c.** Identify real-life connections between words and their use (e.g., note places at school that are *colorful*). **Language 6.** Use words and phrases acquired through conversations, reading and being read to, and responding to texts.

1 Build Word Knowledge

Develop Vocabulary

RETEACH WORDS FOR SHAPES Have children return to p. 58 of *My Skills Buddy* to review the shape words *square, circle, triangle*, and *rectangle.*

- Point to a square. How many sides does a square have?
- Point to a rectangle. How are a rectangle and a square alike? different?
- Point to a triangle. How many sides does a triangle have?
- Point to a circle. Does a circle have sides?

Write the words *square, circle, triangle,* and *rectangle* on index cards. Help children use the cards to label objects in the classroom that have those shapes.

2 Read

Kindergarten Student Reader *Cat and Dog Play*

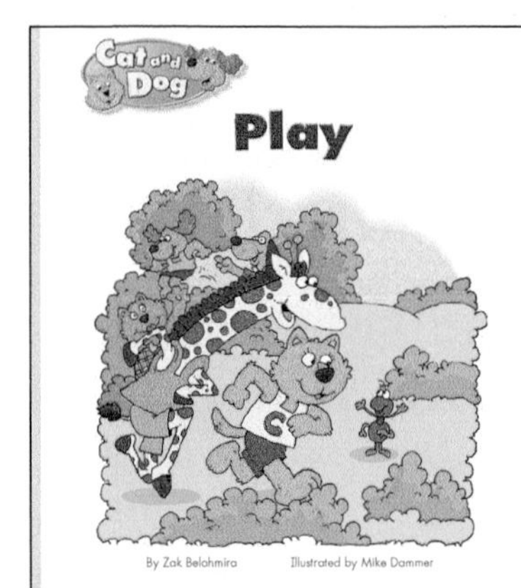

REVIEW REBUS WORDS Write *Cat* on chart paper. This is the word *Cat.* Name the letters with me: *C, a, t.* Repeat with the other rebus words *Dog, running, jumping,* and *happy.*

REVIEW HIGH-FREQUENCY WORDS Write *the* on chart paper. Ask children to read the word with you. Have a volunteer read the word. Continue with the other high-frequency words *little, I,* and *am.*

REREAD STORY Display the reader. The title of this book is *Cat and Dog Play.* What do you think the story is about? Read the story chorally with children. Pause at the end of each page to ask: Who is talking? What does the character say? What is the character doing? Have children reread the story several times to build fluency.

If... children need more scaffolding and practice with vocabulary, **then...** use the ELL activities on p. DI•48 in the Teacher Resources section of the Digital Path.

1 Build Word Knowledge

Develop Language

Display the Big Book *Plaidypus Lost* and read the text on p. 18.

Off to the market.
Push the big cart.
Fast and slow.
Stop. Go.

- Ask children to read the text with you as you track the print.
- Point to the line, *Push the big cart.*
- What does the word *big* mean? What is another word that means the same as *big?*
- I am going to say some words. I want you to tell me which words mean the same as *big: tiny, small, huge, large, little, enormous.*
- Why do you think the author used the word *big?*
- Continue the routine with the words *fast* and *slow.*

2 Read

Get Set, Roll! Reader 3 *Pete*

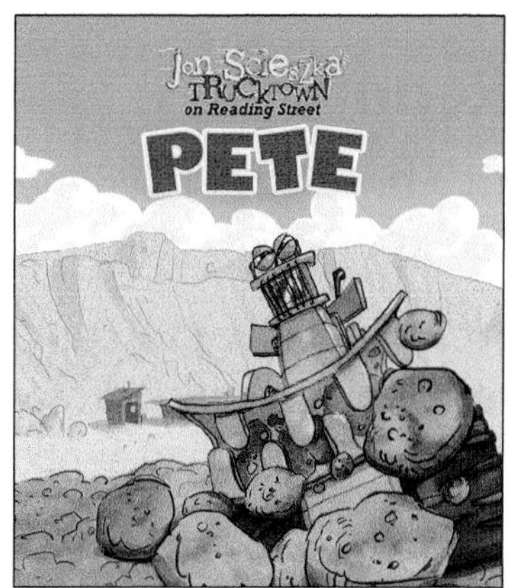

REVIEW HIGH-FREQUENCY AND REBUS WORDS Review the high-frequency and rebus words (*I, am, the, little, Pete, rocks, crunch*) using the following routine.

1. Display and read the word.
2. Name the letters in the word.
3. Read the word. Use it in a sentence.

REREAD Have children chorally read aloud *Pete* several times. Then ask them to take turns reading a page aloud.

eStreet Interactive
www.ReadingStreet.com

Savvas eText
- Student Edition
- Kindergarten Student Reader
- Get Set, Roll! Reader

SMALL GROUP TIME

Independent Reading Options

Trade Book Library

eStreet Interactive
www.ReadingStreet.com
Teacher's Guides available on the Leveled Reader Database.

Strategic Intervention

Common Core State Standards

Literature 1. With prompting and support, ask and answer questions about key details in a text. **Literature 10.** Actively engage in group reading activities with purpose and understanding. **Informational Text 1.** With prompting and support, ask and answer questions about key details in a text. **Informational Text 10.** Actively engage in group reading activities with purpose and understanding. **Foundational Skills 1.d.** Recognize and name all upper- and lowercase letters of the alphabet.

1 Build Word Knowledge

Reteach Letter Recognition

RECOGNIZE LETTERS *Qq, Rr, Ss* Display the *Qq, Rr,* and *Ss* Alphabet Cards. Have children point to and name the letters. Then write these words on chart paper: *Ralph, Queen, read, soup, quick, Sally.* Point to and read each word. Ask children to identify the letter that the word begins with.

REVIEW LETTERS *Oo–Ss* Write the uppercase and lowercase letters *Oo* through *Ss* on index cards. Mix the cards and place them face up on a tabletop. First have children sort the letters into a group of uppercase forms and a group of lowercase forms. Then have children put each group of letters in alphabetical order.

Corrective feedback	**If...** children have difficulty with sorting or alphabetical order, **then...** place the *Oo–Ss* Alphabet Cards in order on the chalk ledge for children to refer to.

2 Text-Based Comprehension

Read

READ ALOUD Read the Reading Street Sleuth Read Aloud, "Family Adventures," on p. SG•43 to children.

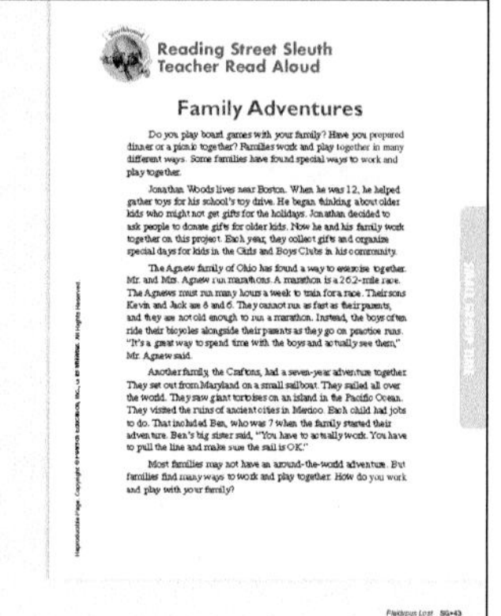

READ LIKE A SLEUTH! Encourage children to cite evidence from the text to support their answers. You may wish to reread sections of the text to verify children's answers.

Look for Evidence How does each family work and play together?

Ask Questions If you could talk to Jonathan, Kevin, or Ben, what questions would you ask him about his family's adventure?

Prove It! Performance Task Have children draw a picture of one of the families on their adventure. Ask children to dictate a phrase or short sentence for the picture using one or two key details from the text. Read children's phrases or sentences to them as you track the print.

Advanced

1 Build Word Knowledge

Extend Letter Recognition

CONNECT *Oo* TO /o/ Display the *Oo* Alphabet Card. Ask children to name the letters and identify the picture. Point to the letters *Oo* and say the picture name *otter.* I am going to say a word. The word is *olive.* Do the words *otter* and *olive* begin with the same sound? Say the words with me: *otter, olive.* Because *otter* and *olive* both begin with /o/, let's write the letter *o* in the air. Continue with these words: *octopus, rocket, option, ostrich, sandwich, question, oxen, puzzle.*

2 Read

"Pop! Pop!"

CONCEPTS OF PRINT Read aloud the title of the story, "Pop! Pop!" Remember, the title of a story usually gives us clues to what the story is about. Ask children what the title tells them about the story. (Something in the story makes the sound *pop! pop!* Maybe popcorn is popping or balloons are popping.)

Pop! Pop!

Look at the pot.
The pot is hot.
Pop! Pop!
Get the top, Dad!
Dad gets the top.
The top is on the pot.
Look at the pan.
The pan is hot.
Pop! Pop!
Get the top, Mom!
Mom gets the top.
The top is on the pan.

Advanced Phonics Selection 3

TEACH STORY WORDS Present any story words that children may need help with, such as *look, hot, get, pot,* and *pan.* Use the words in sentences that give clues to their meanings. For example, Ice is cold. Fire is *hot.* We heat soup in a *pot.* We fry eggs in a *pan.*

READ Distribute copies of "Pop! Pop!" from p. SG•50, and have children read it on their own. Then have them take turns reading the story aloud. After reading, have children tell whom the story is about and what happens.

SMALL GROUP TIME

More Reading for Group Time

INDEPENDENT READER

- More Challenging Text

Use the suggested Leveled Reader or other text at children's instructional level.

eStreet Interactive
www.ReadingStreet.com

Use the Leveled Reader Database for lesson plans and student pages for *Nick the Fix-It Man.*

If... children need more practice with letter recognition,
then... use the Phonics Transition lessons beginning on p. 447 in the *ELL Handbook.*

Pop! Pop!

Look at the pot.
The pot is hot.
Pop! Pop!
Get the top, Dad!
Dad gets the top.
The top is on the pot.
Look at the pan.
The pan is hot.
Pop! Pop!
Get the top, Mom!
Mom gets the top.
The top is on the pan.

Reproducible Page. Copyright © Pearson Education, Inc., or its affiliates. All Rights Reserved.

Advanced Phonics Selection 3

Advanced

1 Build Word Knowledge

Extend Letter Recognition

 **CONNECT *Pp* TO /p/** Display the *Pp* Alphabet Card. Ask children to name the letters and identify the picture. Point to the letters *Pp* and say the picture name *penguin.* I am going to say a word. The word is *purple.* Do the words *penguin* and *purple* begin with the same sound? Say the words with me: *penguin, purple.* Because *penguin* and *purple* both begin with /p/, let's write the letter *p* in the air. Continue with these words: *pattern, quarter, pencil, pocket, online, piglet, silver, raccoon.*

2 Read

Decodable Reader 3 *The Little Toys*

CONCEPTS OF PRINT Display Decodable Reader 3 in *My Skills Buddy.* Ask children to identify the author and illustrator.

READ Have children read the Decodable Reader quietly as you listen to them. Then have them take turns reading aloud one page at a time.

3 Reread for Fluency

Have children reread Decodable Reader 3 *The Little Toys* to develop fluency.

SMALL GROUP TIME

Independent Reading Options

Trade Book Library

eStreet Interactive
www.ReadingStreet.com
Teacher's Guides available on the Leveled Reader Database.

If... children need more support with letter recognition,
then... use the ELL activities on pp. DI•46, DI•49–DI•50 in the Teacher Resources section of the Digital Path.

Advanced

Common Core State Standards

Literature 1. With prompting and support, ask and answer questions about key details in a text. **Literature 10.** Actively engage in group reading activities with purpose and understanding. **Foundational Skills 3.c.** Read common high-frequency words by sight (e.g., *the, of, to, you, she, my, is, are, do, does*). **Language 5.a.** Sort common objects into categories (e.g., shapes, foods) to gain a sense of the concepts the categories represent. **Language 5.c.** Identify real-life connections between words and their use (e.g., note places at school that are *colorful*). **Language 6.** Use words and phrases acquired through conversations, reading and being read to, and responding to texts.

1 Build Word Knowledge

Develop Vocabulary

WORDS FOR SHAPES Review the shape words *square, circle, triangle,* and *rectangle* with children. Have them use the words in sentences.

Let's learn more words for shapes. Remember, we can use shape words to tell what things look like. Have children identify the words for shapes in these sentences.

- Home plate and the three bases form a baseball *diamond.*
- Tracy drew a large *heart* on the front of the card for her mom.
- The cars roared around the *oval* many times during the race.

Team Talk Have children work in pairs to use *diamond, heart,* and *oval* in their own sentences. Ask them to draw pictures of the three shapes and write a label for each picture that names the shape.

2 Read

Kindergarten Student Reader *Cat and Dog Play*

REREAD STORY Display the reader and have children read the title with you. Then have them read the story. Finally, have them reread the story aloud several times to build fluency.

EXTEND STORY Ask children to recall who the characters in the story are and what they are doing. What could happen next in the story? Encourage children to think of something the animals might do after their picnic. Have children draw a picture and write a sentence to go with the picture.

If... children need more scaffolding and practice with vocabulary, **then...** use the ELL activities on p. DI•48 in the Teacher Resources section of the Digital Path.

Advanced

1 Build Word Knowledge

Develop Language

Display the Big Book *Plaidypus Lost* and read the text on p. 18.

Off to the market.
Push the big cart.
Fast and slow.
Stop. Go.

- Ask children to read the text with you as you track the print.
- Point to the line, *Fast and slow.* Read this with me.
- What do the words *fast* and *slow* mean? What is another word that means the same as *fast?* as *slow?* Why did the author choose the words *fast* and *slow?*
- Continue the routine with the words *push* and *big.*
- Team Talk Have children work with a partner to replace key words in a sentence with simpler words or synonyms without changing the meaning of the sentence. Use sentence frames, such as the following.

  _____ the _____ cart.

2 Read

Get Set, Roll! Reader 3 *Pete*

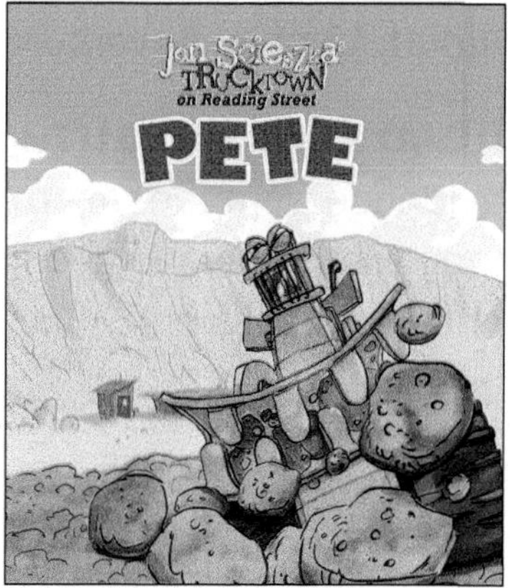

REVIEW HIGH-FREQUENCY AND REBUS WORDS Review the high-frequency and rebus words by asking children to spell the words with Letter Tiles. (*I, am, the, little, Pete, rocks, crunch*)

REREAD Have children whisper read *Pete* as you listen to each child. Then have children take turns reading the story aloud.

3 Reread for Fluency

BUILD FLUENCY Have children read again with expression and accuracy. Encourage them to use self-correction techniques for any mistakes.

SMALL GROUP TIME

Independent Reading Options

Trade Book Library

Street Interactive
www.ReadingStreet.com
Teacher's Guides available on the Leveled Reader Database.

Advanced

Common Core State Standards

Informational Text 1. With prompting and support, ask and answer questions about key details in a text. **Informational Text 10.** Actively engage in group reading activities with purpose and understanding. **Foundational Skills 1.d.** Recognize and name all upper- and lowercase letters of the alphabet.

1 Build Word Knowledge

Extend Letter Recognition

CONNECT LETTERS TO SOUNDS Display the *Qq, Rr,* and *Ss* Alphabet Cards. Ask children to name the letters and identify the pictures. Point to the letters and say the picture names emphasizing the beginning sounds. Note that *q* and *u* together spell the beginning sound /kw/ in most words that begin with *q*. Now I am going to say two words. Tell me the sound at the beginning of both words and the letter or letters that stand for that sound. Hold up the appropriate Alphabet Card and repeat the words together. Use these pairs of words: *saddle, super; quarrel, quiet; rubber, recall.*

WRITE WORDS Distribute paper and pencils to children. Today we are going to use what we know about letters and the sounds they stand for to write words. I am going to say some words, and I want you to write them. Listen carefully.

1. rod **2.** hop **3.** sip

2 Text-Based Comprehension

Read

READ ALOUD Read the Reading Street Sleuth Read Aloud, "Family Adventures," on p. SG•43 to children.

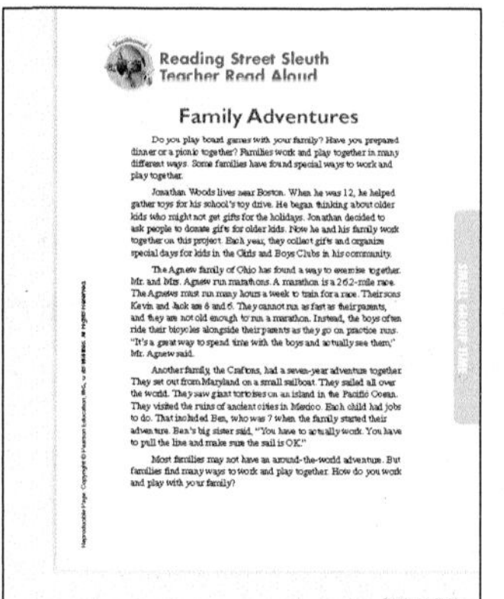

Reading Street Sleuth Teacher Read Aloud

Family Adventures

Do you play board games with your family? Have you prepared dinner or a picnic together? Families work and play together in many different ways. Some families have found special ways to work and play together.

Jonathan Woods lives near Boston. When he was 12, he helped gather toys for his school's toy drive. He began thinking about older kids who might not get gifts for the holidays. Jonathan decided to ask people to donate gifts for older kids. Now he and his family work together on this project. Each year, they collect gifts and organize special days for kids in the Girls and Boys Clubs in his community.

The Agnew family of Ohio has found a way to exercise together. Mr. and Mrs. Agnew run marathons. A marathon is a 26.2-mile race. The Agnews must run many hours a week to train for a race. Their sons Kevin and Jack are 8 and 6. They cannot run as fast as their parents, and they are not old enough to run a marathon. Instead, the boys often ride their bicycles alongside their parents as they go on practice runs. "It's a great way to spend time with the boys and actually see them," Mr. Agnew said.

Another family, the Craftons, had a seven-year adventure together. They set out from Maryland on a small sailboat. They sailed all over the world. They saw giant tortoises on an island in the Pacific Ocean. They visited the ruins of ancient cities in Mexico. Each child had jobs to do. That included Ben, who was 7 when the family started their adventure. Ben's big sister said, "You have to actually work. You have to pull the line and make sure the sail is OK."

Most families may not have an around-the-world adventure. But families find many ways to work and play together. How do you work and play with your family?

Platypus Lost SG•43

READ LIKE A SLEUTH! Encourage children to cite evidence from the text to support their answers. You may wish to reread sections of the text to verify children's answers.

Look for Evidence Summarize what each family does together. What do the families say about why they wanted to do these adventures?

Ask Questions Imagine you and your family are going to sail around the world. What questions would you want to ask the Craftons about their experiences?

Prove It! Performance Task Have children draw a picture of the family adventure in the text that they think is most interesting. Ask them to write a sentence or two using key details from the text. Have children read their sentences to you.

Teaching the Common Core State Standards This Week

The Common Core State Standards for English Language Arts are divided into strands for **Reading** (including **Foundational Skills**), **Writing**, **Speaking and Listening**, and **Language**. The chart below shows some of the content you will teach this week, strand by strand. Turn to this week's 5-Day Planner on pages 314–315 to see how this content is taught each day.

Reading Strand

- **Phonemic Awareness:** Initial Sounds
- **Letter Recognition:** *Tt, Uu, Vv, Ww, Xx, Yy, Zz*
- **Text-Based Comprehension:** Classify and Categorize
- **High-Frequency Words:** *little, the*
- **Genre:** Animal Fantasy

Common Core State Standards for English Language Arts

Writing Strand

- **Wonderful, Marvelous Me**
- **Respond to Literature**
- **Genre:** Instructions
- **Extend the Concept**
- **This Week We...**

Speaking and Listening Strand

- **Content Knowledge:** Build Oral Language
- **Listening and Speaking:** Tell About Me

Language Strand

- **Oral Vocabulary: Amazing Words** *bakery, fire station, park, post office, library, chaperone*
- **Vocabulary:** Location Words
- **Academic Vocabulary:** *classify and categorize, verb, instructions, setting, recipe*
- **Conventions:** What We Can Do

Text-Based Comprehension

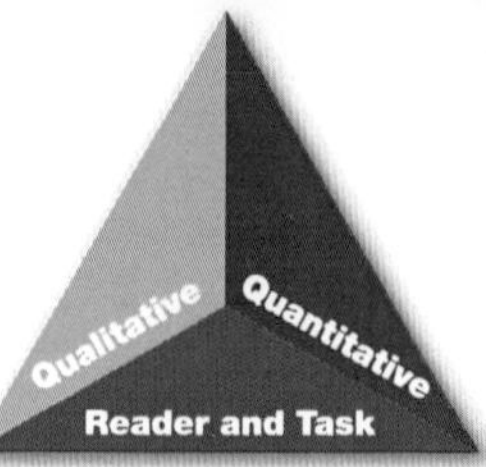

Text Complexity Measures

Use the rubric to familiarize yourself with the text complexity of ***Miss Bindergarten Takes a Field Trip with Kindergarten.***

Bridge to Complex Knowledge

Qualitative Measures	**Levels of Meaning**	only one level of meaning; understand that additional information can be gathered from the images
	Structure	simple rhyme; unpredictable layout
	Language Conventionality and Clarity	clear, natural, conversational language; close alignment of images and text
	Theme and Knowledge Demands	a basic knowledge of community workers

Reader and Task Suggestions

FORMATIVE ASSESSMENT Based on assessment results, use the **Reader and Task Suggestions** in Access Main Selection to scaffold the selection or support independence for children as they read ***Miss Bindergarten Takes a Field Trip with Kindergarten.***

READER AND TASK SUGGESTIONS	
Preparing to Read the Text	**Leveled Tasks**
• Review the Amazing Words and have children use them to talk about the selection. • Review the various shapes in the story and their names.	• **Theme and Knowledge Demands** If children need help with key details of the field trip, have them page through the book and tell what the community workers at the bakery, fire station, post office, and library do. • **Structure** If children will not have difficulty with the story format, have them read the names of the characters that begin with a colored letter. What pattern can they find?

Recommended Placement This text is appropriate for placement as a read aloud at this level due to the qualitative elements of the selection.

Focus on Common Core State Standards

Big Book

Text-Based Comprehension

Classify and Categorize
CCSS Literature 2.,
CCSS Literature 7.,
CCSS Language 5.a.

Letter Recognition

Tt, Uu, Vv, Ww, Xx, Yy, Zz
CCSS Foundational Skills 1.d.

Writing and Conventions

Genre: Instructions
CCSS Writing 2.

Conventions: What We Can Do
CCSS Speaking/Listening 4.

Oral Vocabulary

Amazing Words

bakery	fire station
park	post office
library	chaperone

CCSS Language 6.

Phonemic Awareness

Initial Sounds
CCSS Foundational Skills 2.d.,
CCSS Foundational Skills 2.e.

High-Frequency Words

the little

CCSS Foundational Skills 3.c.

Listening and Speaking

Talk About Me
CCSS Speaking/Listening 1.a.,
CCSS Speaking/Listening 4.

Preview Your Week

How do people in a community cooperate?

Big Book

Genre: Animal Fantasy

Letter Recognition: *Tt, Uu, Vv, Ww, Xx, Yy, Zz*

Text-Based Comprehension: Classify and Categorize

Build Content Knowledge

KNOWLEDGE GOALS
Children will understand that cooperating with others

- helps them have a fun time
- helps them learn new things

BUILD ORAL VOCABULARY
This week, children will acquire the following academic vocabulary/ domain-specific words.

Amazing Words

bakery	fire station
park	post office
library	chaperone

BUILD INDEPENDENT READERS
Children will enjoy becoming independent readers as they build decoding skills.

Get Set, Roll! Reader

Decodable Reader

OPTIONAL CONCEPT-BASED READING Use the Digital Path to access readers offering different levels of text complexity.

Concept Literacy

Listen to Me Reader

Student Reader

Independent Reader

This Week's Digital Resources

eStreet Interactive
www.ReadingStreet.com

Get Ready to Read

Big Question Video This video on the Digital Path introduces children to the unit question, *How do we live, work, and play together?*, and provides background for the reading children will do throughout the unit.

Background Building Audio CD This audio CD provides valuable background information about noises at a fire station to help children read and comprehend the weekly texts.

Concept Talk Video Use this video on the Digital Path to build momentum and introduce the weekly concept of people working together in a community.

Interactive Sing with Me Chart and Audio "On a Field Trip We Go," sung to the tune of "Oh, A-Hunting We Will Go," introduces the Amazing Words with a catchy, concept-related song.

Phonics Songs and Rhymes Audio "Yippee! Yahoo! Zippity-zip," sung to the tune of "Pop Goes the Weasel," helps children recognize *Tt, Uu, Vv, Ww, Xx, Yy,* and *Zz.*

Letter Tile Drag and Drop Using this interactive tool, children click and spell words to enhance their newly learned phonics skills.

Savvas eText For phonics and fluency support, use the eText of the Decodable Reader; the Student Reader; and the Get Set, Roll! Reader on the Leveled Reader Database.

Read and Comprehend

Envision It! Animations Use this colorful animation on the Digital Path to explain the target comprehension skill, Classify and Categorize.

Savvas eText Go to Savvas SuccessNet and use the eText of the many student edition pages in *My Skills Buddy* with audio support.

Story Sort Use the Story Sort Activity on the Digital Path after reading *Miss Bindergarten Takes a Field Trip* to involve children in retelling.

Language Arts

Grammar Jammer Choose a whimsical animation on the Digital Path to provide an engaging lesson on What We Can Do that will capture children's attention.

Additional Resources

Teacher Resources DVD-ROM Use the following resources on the TR DVD or on Savvas SuccessNet throughout the week:

- Amazing Word Cards
- High-Frequency Word Cards
- Daily Fix-It Transparencies
- Reader's and Writer's Notebook
- Scoring Rubrics

This Week's Skills

Letter Recognition
Tt, Uu, Vv, Ww, Xx, Yy, Zz

Comprehension
Skill: Classify and Categorize

Language
Vocabulary: Location Words
Conventions: What We Can Do

Writing
Wonderful, Marvelous Me!
Respond to Literature
Genre Writing
Extend the Concept
This Week We…

5-Day Planner

DAY 1

Get Ready to Read

Content Knowledge 320
Oral Vocabulary: *bakery, fire station, park, post office, library, chaperone*

Phonemic Awareness 322
Initial Sounds
Monitor Progress
Check Phonemic Awareness

Letter Recognition 324
Tt and *Uu*

Handwriting 326
T and *t*
U and *u*

High-Frequency Words 327
the, little

READ Decodable Story 4 328
Am I Little?

Read and Comprehend

Text-Based Comprehension 330
Classify and Categorize
Teacher Read Aloud

Language Arts

Conventions 332
What We Can Do

Writing 333
Wonderful, Marvelous Me!
Daily Handwriting

Listening and Speaking 334
Talk About Me

Extend Your Day! 335

DAY 2

Get Ready to Read

Content Knowledge 336
Oral Vocabulary: *bakery, fire station*

Phonemic Awareness 338
Initial Sounds

Letter Recognition 340
Vv
Monitor Progress
Check Letter Recognition

Handwriting 342
V and *v*

High-Frequency Words 343
the, little

READ Decodable Reader 4 344
At the Zoo

Read and Comprehend

Text-Based Comprehension 346
READ *Miss Bindergarten Takes a Field Trip*—1st Read
Think, Talk, and Write
Monitor Progress Check Retelling

Language Arts

Conventions 349
What We Can Do

Writing 350
Respond to Literature
Daily Handwriting

Vocabulary 351
Location Words

Extend Your Day! 353

DAY 3

Get Ready to Read

Content Knowledge 354
Oral Vocabulary: *park, post office*

Phonemic Awareness 356
Initial Sounds

Letter Recognition 358
Ww and *Xx*

Monitor Progress
Check Word Reading
High-Frequency Words

READ Kindergarten Student Reader 360
Cat and Dog Ride to Town

Read and Comprehend

Text-Based Comprehension 362
READ *Miss Bindergarten Takes a Field Trip*—2nd Read

Language Arts

Conventions 384
Review What We Look Like

Writing 385
Instructions
Daily Handwriting

Listening and Speaking 386
Talk About Me

Extend Your Day! 389

DAY 4

Get Ready to Read

Content Knowledge 390
Oral Vocabulary: *library, chaperone*

Phonemic Awareness 392
Review Initial Sounds

Monitor Progress
Check Phonemic Awareness

Letter Recognition 394
Yy and *Zz*

Get Set, Roll! Reader 4 395
READ *Pat*

Read and Comprehend

Text-Based Comprehension 396
Classify and Categorize
Review Setting
READ *Miss Bindergarten Takes a Field Trip*—3rd Read

Language Arts

Conventions 398
What We Can Do

Writing 399
Extend the Concept
Daily Handwriting

Vocabulary 400
Location Words

Extend Your Day! 401

DAY 5

Get Ready to Read

Content Knowledge 402
Review Oral Vocabulary

Monitor Progress
Check Oral Vocabulary

Phonemic Awareness 404
Review Initial Sounds

Letter Recognition 405
Review Letter Names

Assessment 406

Monitor Progress
Check Letter and Word Reading

Read and Comprehend

Let's Practice It! 408
Recipe

Assessment 410
Review Classify and Categorize

Language Arts

Conventions 412
Review What We Can Do

Writing 413
This Week We ...
Daily Handwriting

Wrap Up Your Week! 414

Extend Your Day! 415

Access for All

What do I do in group time?

It's as easy as 1-2-3!

1 TEACHER-LED SMALL GROUPS → 2 INDEPENDENT PRACTICE STATIONS → 3 INDEPENDENT READING

Small Group Time

Bridge to Common Core

SKILL DEVELOPMENT

- *Tt, Uu, Vv, Ww, Xx, Yy, Zz* Initial Sounds
- Classify and Categorize

DEEP UNDERSTANDING

This Week's Knowledge Goals

Children will understand that cooperating with others

- helps them have a fun time
- helps them learn new things

1 Small Group Lesson Plan

	DAY 1 Differentiate Letter Recognition	DAY 2 Differentiate Letter Recognition
OL On-Level pp. SG•56–SG•61	**Practice Letter Recognition** Recognize Letters *Tt, Uu* **Decodable Story** Read *Am I Little?*	**Practice Letter Recognition** Recognize Letters *Vv* **Decodable Reader** Read *At the Zoo*
SI Strategic Intervention pp. SG•62–SG•66	**Reteach Letter Recognition** Recognize Letters *Tt, Uu* **Decodable Story** Read *Am I Little?*	**Reteach Letter Recognition** Recognize Letters *Vv* **Decodable Reader** Read *At the Zoo*
A Advanced pp. SG•67–SG•72	**Extend Letter Recognition** Recognize Letters *Tt, Uu* **Decodable Story** Read *Am I Little?*	**Extend Letter Recognition** Connect *Vv* to /v/ **Decodable Reader** Read *At the Zoo*
ELL **If...** children need more scaffolding and practice...	**Phonemic Awareness and Letter Recognition** **then...** use the Letter Recognition activities beginning on p. 447 in the *ELL Handbook.*	**Phonemic Awareness and Letter Recognition** **then...** use the activities on p. DI•63 in the Teacher Resources section of the Digital Path.

Reading Street Sleuth Read Aloud
- Provides access to grade-level text for all students
- Focuses on finding clues in text through close reading
- Builds capacity for complex text

Build Text-Based Comprehension

Miss Bindergarten Takes a Field Trip

Optional Leveled Readers

Concept Literacy

Below Level

On Level

Advanced

Get Set, Roll! Reader

Decodable Reader

DAY 3 Differentiate Vocabulary	DAY 4 Differentiate Language	DAY 5 Differentiate Close Reading
Develop Vocabulary Practice Location Words **Student Reader** Read *Cat and Dog Ride To Town*	**Build** Sentences and Words **Get Set, Roll! Reader** Read *Pat*	**Practice Letter Recognition** Recognize Letters *Ww, Xx, Yy, Zz* **Text-Based Comprehension** Read "We Need a Park"
Develop Vocabulary Reteach Location Words **Student Reader** Read *Cat and Dog Ride To Town*	**Talk About** Sentences and Words **Get Set, Roll! Reader** Read *Pat*	**Reteach Letter Recognition** Recognize Letters *Ww, Xx, Yy, Zz* **Text-Based Comprehension** Read "We Need a Park"
Develop Vocabulary More Location Words **Student Reader** Read *Cat and Dog Ride To Town*	**Extend** Sentences and Words **Get Set, Roll! Reader** Read *Pat*	**Extend Letter Recognition** Connect Letters to Sounds **Text-Based Comprehension** Read "We Need a Park"
Vocabulary **then...** use the ELL activities on p. DI•65 in the Teacher Resources section of the Digital Path.	**Developing Language** **then...** use the Language Workshops beginning on p. 306 in the *ELL Handbook.*	**Comprehension** **then...** use the ELL activities on pp. DI•64–DI•65 in the Teacher Resources section of the Digital Path.

Independent Stations

Practice Last Week's Skills

Focus on these activities when time is limited.

ACCESS FOR ALL

- Below-Level Activities
- On-Level Activities
- Advanced Activities

LISTEN UP!

Match initial sounds and pictures.

OBJECTIVES

- Say and match initial sounds.

MATERIALS

- *Listen Up!* Flip Chart Activity 4
- Picture Cards: *gum, goat, goose, soap, seal, six, tent, taxi, top*
- paper, crayons

Modeled Pronunciation Audio CD

- Children choose four Picture Cards and say each name.
- Children name each Picture Card and name other words that begin with the same sound.
- Children name each Picture Card and match the cards that have the same beginning sound.

WORD WORK

Identify letters *Oo, Pp, Qq, Rr, Ss*.

OBJECTIVES

- Identify letters *Oo, Pp, Qq, Rr, Ss.*

MATERIALS

- *Word Work* Flip Chart Activity 4
- Alphabet Cards: *Oo, Pp, Qq, Rr, Ss* and cards for five previously taught letters
- Letter Tiles
- paper, pencils

Interactive Sound-Spelling Cards

Letter Tile Drag and Drop

- Children find Alphabet Cards *Oo, Pp, Qq, Rr,* and *Ss.*
- Children find Alphabet Cards *Oo, Pp, Qq, Rr,* and *Ss* and match them with Letter Tiles.
- Children find Alphabet Cards *Oo, Pp, Qq, Rr,* and *Ss,* match them with Letter Tiles, and write each letter.

LET'S WRITE!

Write a poem.

OBJECTIVES

- Write a poem.

MATERIALS

- *Let's Write!* Flip Chart Activity 4
- copies of poem starter:
  School is fun.
  We play and _________.
- paper, pencils, crayons

Grammar Jammer

- Children finish the poem with a partner and then draw a picture.
- Children finish the poem with a partner and think of another rhyming line. Then they draw a picture.
- Children finish the poem and write two more rhyming lines. Then they draw a picture.

WORDS TO KNOW

Practice vocabulary.

OBJECTIVES

- Identify and use words for shapes.

MATERIALS

- *Words to Know* Flip Chart Activity 4
- Teacher-made picture cards: *circle, square, triangle, rectangle*
- Teacher-made word cards: *circle, square, triangle, rectangle*
- paper, crayons

Vocabulary Activities

Teacher Resources
- High-Frequency Word Cards for Unit 1, Week 3

- Children find pictures that show a circle, a square, a triangle, and a rectangle and say the words.
- Children match each picture card with the word card.
- Children read each word card. Then they draw objects that have a circle, a square, a triangle, and a rectangle shape.

READ FOR MEANING

Use text-based comprehension tools.

OBJECTIVES

- Identify and describe the sequence of events.

MATERIALS

- *Read for Meaning* Flip Chart Activity 4
- Little Book *Plaidypus Lost*
- paper, pencils, crayons

Envision It! Animations
- Leveled eReaders

- ● Children tell what happened first, next, and last in a book.
- ▲ Children draw pictures to show what happened first, next, and last in a book.
- ■ Children draw pictures to show what happened first, next, and last in a book. Then they label the pictures *first, next,* and *last.*

LET'S MAKE ART!

Use art to demonstrate understanding.

OBJECTIVES

- Make a collage.

MATERIALS

- *Let's Make Art!* Flip Chart Activity 4
- old magazines
- paper, glue, scissors, pencils

- ● Children make a collage showing how people help each other.
- ▲ Children make a collage showing how people help each other. Then they tell about each picture.
- ■ Children make a collage showing how people help each other. Then they write a sentence to go with the collage.

Manage the Stations

Use these management tools to set up and organize your Practice Stations:

Practice Station Flip Charts

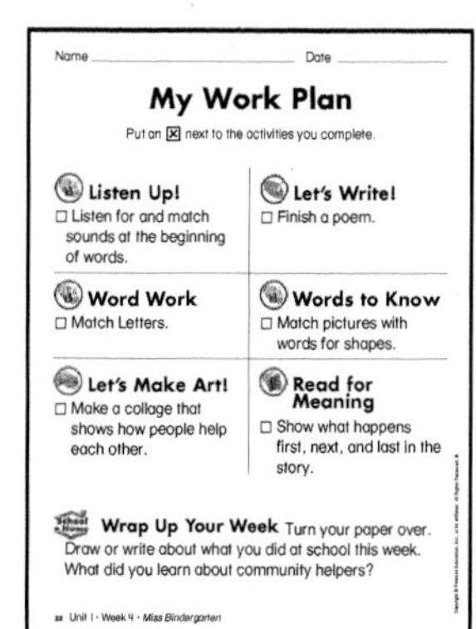

Name ________ Date ________

My Work Plan

Put an ☒ next to the activities you complete.

Listen Up!
☐ Listen for and match sounds at the beginning of words.

Let's Write!
☐ Finish a poem.

Word Work
☐ Match Letters.

Words to Know
☐ Match pictures with words for shapes.

Let's Make Art!
☐ Make a collage that shows how people help each other.

Read for Meaning
☐ Show what happens first, next, and last in the story.

Wrap Up Your Week Turn your paper over. Draw or write about what you did at school this week. What did you learn about community helpers?

Unit 1 • Week 4 • *Miss Bindergarten*

Classroom Management Handbook for Differentiated Instruction Practice Stations, p. 22

3 Independent Reading

Help children choose complex texts so that they can engage in paired and group reading and writing activities every day before, during, and after school.

Suggestions for this week's independent reading:
- Other stories by Joseph Slate
- *Firehouse Field Trip* by Danielle M. Denega

BOOK TALK Have pairs or groups of children actively engage in reading activities through a discussion of their independent reading for the week. Focus their discussions with the following ideas:

Key Ideas and Details
- Retell the text to your partner or group.
- Identify the main idea and one detail of the text.

Craft and Structure
- Name the title and author of the text.
- Talk about illustrations in the text.

Integration of Ideas
- With support, describe text/illustration relationships.
- Were the characters in this book like others I have read about?

Savvas eText
- Student Edition
- Decodable Readers
- Get Set, Roll! Readers
- Leveled Readers

Materials from School or Classroom Library

DAY 1 at a Glance

Content Knowledge
Oral Vocabulary

Phonemic Awareness
Initial Sounds

Letter Recognition
Letters *Tt* and *Uu*

Handwriting
T, t, U, and *u*

High-Frequency Words
the, little

Text-Based Comprehension
Classify and Categorize

Conventions
What We Can Do

Writing
Wonderful, Marvelous Me!

Listening and Speaking
Talk About Me

Materials

- Student Edition
- Truckery Rhymes
- Talk with Me/Sing with Me Chart
- Reader's and Writer's Notebook
- Alphabet Cards
- Picture Cards
- Phonics Songs and Rhymes Chart

Bridge to Common Core

INTEGRATION OF KNOWLEDGE/IDEAS
This week children read, write, and talk about how people in a community work together.

Texts This Week
- "On a Field Trip We Go"
- "Grandma's Garden"
- *Miss Bindergarten Takes a Field Trip with Kindergarten*
- *Cat and Dog Ride to Town*
- "Freshly Baked Bread"

Social Studies Knowledge Goals
Children will understand that cooperating with others
- helps them have a fun time
- helps them learn new things

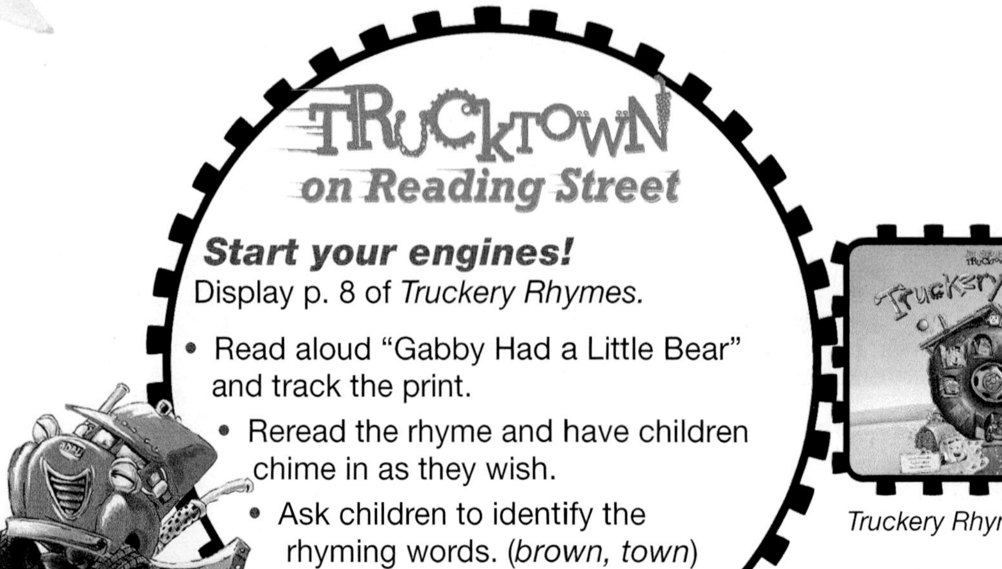

Start your engines!
Display p. 8 of *Truckery Rhymes.*

- Read aloud "Gabby Had a Little Bear" and track the print.
  - Reread the rhyme and have children chime in as they wish.
    - Ask children to identify the rhyming words. (*brown, town*)

Truckery Rhymes

Content Knowledge

Zoom in on

People Working Together in a Community

CONCEPT TALK To explore the unit concept of All Together Now, tell children that this week they will listen, talk, sing, read, and write about people working together in a community. Write the Question of the Week on the board, *How do people in a community cooperate?* Track each word as you read.

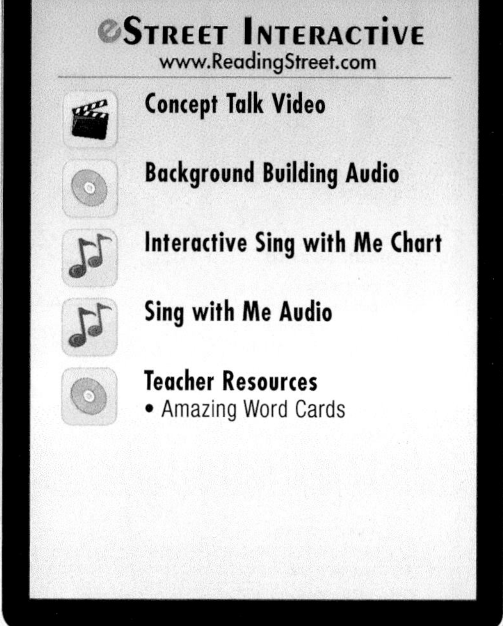
eStreet Interactive
www.ReadingStreet.com
Concept Talk Video
Background Building Audio
Interactive Sing with Me Chart
Sing with Me Audio
Teacher Resources
• Amazing Word Cards

Build Oral Language

TALK ABOUT COOPERATION IN A COMMUNITY Display Talk with Me Chart 4A. I see places that I know in these pictures. Point to the fire station. This is a fire station. I have visited a fire station with children many times. Let's talk about other places we see in these pictures. Encourage children to use complete sentences as they talk about the pictures.

This week we will be talking about how people in a community help one another. We are going to learn six new Amazing Words. Listen as I say the words. You may know some of them: *bakery, fire station, park, post office, library, chaperone.* Have children say each word as you point to the picture.

Talk with Me/Sing with Me Chart 4A

LISTEN FOR AMAZING WORDS Display Sing with Me Chart 4B. Tell children that they are going to sing a song about taking a class field trip. Read the title. Have children describe the illustration. Sing the song several times to the tune of "Oh, A-Hunting We Will Go." Listen for the Amazing Words: *bakery, fire station, park, post office, library, chaperone.* Have children stand up and sing with you.

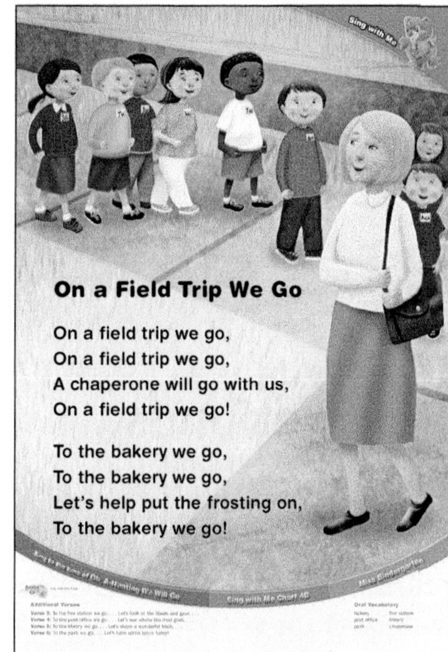
On a Field Trip We Go
On a field trip we go,
On a field trip we go,
A chaperone will go with us,
On a field trip we go!
To the bakery we go,
To the bakery we go,
Let's help put the frosting on,
To the bakery we go!
Talk with Me/Sing with Me Chart 4B

Amazing Words

You've learned 0 1 8 words this year.
You'll learn 0 0 6 words this week!

bakery	fire station
park	post office
library	chaperone

Access for All

SI Strategic Intervention

Amazing Words Display Talk with Me Chart 4A. Point to each picture and ask children to imagine what that Amazing Word is like. Have them tell about the place or person in complete sentences, such as *The bakery is warm. The park is sunny. The fire station is busy.*

Access Content Use the pictures on Talk with Me Chart 4A to help children understand words such as *post office* and *chaperone.*

ELL Support Additional ELL support and modified instruction is provided in the *ELL Handbook* and in the ELL Support lessons on the *Teacher Resources DVD-ROM.*

Preteach Concepts Use the Day 1 instruction on ELL Poster 4 to assess and build background knowledge, develop concepts, and build oral vocabulary.

Common Core State Standards
Foundational Skills 2.d. Isolate and pronounce the initial, medial vowel, and final sounds (phonemes) in three-phoneme (consonant-vowel-consonant, or CVC) words. **Also Foundational Skills 2.e.**

Phonemic Awareness

Let's Listen for Initial Sounds

Read Together

- ● Point to the pig in the puddle. Say "a pig in a puddle." What sound do you hear repeated?
- ■ Point to the man with the mouse. Say "a man with a mouse." What sound is repeated?
- ▲ Find things that begin with /b/, /d/, /k/, /p/, and /m/.
- ★ Name two things that begin like *ball, desk, key, pen,* and *met.*

READING STREET ONLINE
BIG QUESTION VIDEO
www.ReadingStreet.com

72

73

My Skills Buddy, pp. 72–73

Common Core State Standards

Foundational Skills 2.b. Count, pronounce, blend, and segment syllables in spoken words. **Foundational Skills 2.d.** Isolate and pronounce the initial, medial vowel, and final sounds (phonemes) in three-phoneme (consonant-vowel-consonant, or CVC) words.* (This does not include CVCs ending with /l/, /r/, or /x/.) **Also Foundational Skills 2., 2.e.**

Phonemic Awareness

Initial Sounds

INTRODUCE Today we are going to learn that some words start with the same sound and some words start with different sounds. Display *bed* and *bat* Picture Cards. This is a bed. This is a bat. *Bed* and *bat* start with /b/. Continue the routine with *dog* and *doll* Picture Cards.

Picture Card

MODEL Have children look at the picture on pp. 72–73 of *My Skills Buddy.* Let's listen for words that have the same beginning sound. I see a horse eating some hay. I hear the same sound at the beginning of the words *horse* and *hay.* The beginning, or first, sound is /h/. What other things do you see that begin with that same sound?

GUIDE PRACTICE As children name example words from the picture, guide them in stating that the words have the same beginning sound. Discuss some of the bulleted items on p. 72 of *My Skills Buddy.* Save the others for Day 2.

Corrective feedback	**If...** children have difficulty discriminating initial sounds, **then...** say *bed* and *bat* again, segmenting the initial sounds—/b/ *-ed,* /b/ *-at.*

DISCRIMINATE SOUNDS I will say three words. Two of the words begin with the same sound, and one word begins with a different sound. Tell me which word begins with a different sound. Listen: *mouse, mom, dad.* Which word begins with a different sound? *Mouse* and *mom* begin with /m/. *Dad* begins with /d/. *Dad* is different. Let's try some more. Continue with the following sets of words: *taxi, seven, ten; big, car, cow; milk, mitten, quiet; penguin, lamb, pig.*

Corrective feedback	**If...** children cannot identify the word that begins with a different sound, **then...** say the words again, isolating the initial sound in each word: /m/ /m/ /m/ *-ouse,* /m/ /m/ /m/ *-om,* /d/ /d/ /d/ *-ad.* Have children echo you. Then have them identify the two words that begin the same.

REVIEW SYLLABLES Let's listen to two words that begin with /u/. Listen carefully: *up, umbrella.* Let's clap our hands once as we say the word *up. Up* is a short word. It contains only one syllable. Now let's clap our hands as we say *um-brel-la. Umbrella* is a longer word. It contains three syllables. Listen for the three syllables and clap the syllables with me: *um-brel-la.*

Don't Wait Until Friday **MONITOR PROGRESS**

Check Phonemic Awareness Initial Sounds

FORMATIVE ASSESSMENT Say *fox, fan,* and *cat.* Have children identify the word that begins with a different initial sound. Continue with *paint, neck, purse; five, six, seven; bear, moose, boat.*

If... children cannot discriminate initial sounds,

then... have them say the words after you as you emphasize the initial sound of each word.

Access for All

 Advanced

Phonemic Awareness After studying the picture on pp. 72–73 of *My Skills Buddy,* have children draw their own picture. Ask them to include objects whose names begin with the same sound.

Teacher Tip

Be conscious of not blending the initial sound of the word with the next sound when emphasizing the sound that children have to identify.

Support Phonemic Awareness English learners may find it difficult to distinguish certain initial sounds, especially if the sounds do not exist in their home languages. If children make mistakes when identifying initial sounds, provide extra practice.

Common Core State Standards

Foundational Skills 1.d. Recognize and name all upper- and lowercase letters of the alphabet. **Foundational Skills 2.c.** Blend and segment onsets and rimes of single-syllable spoken words.

Access for All

 Advanced

Letter Recognition Have children look through appropriate newspapers, magazines, and ads for words with *Tt* and *Uu.* Have them cut out and glue the *Tt* words and the *Uu* words on separate sheets of paper.

Teacher Tip

If children have difficulty distinguishing uppercase *T* and *U* from lowercase *t* and *u,* have them trace the letters on the board and name them.

Letter Recognition

Teach/Model

Letters *Tt* and *Uu*

INTRODUCE Display the *Tt* Alphabet Card. Point to the turtle on the Alphabet Card. This is a turtle. *Turtle* begins with *t.* Point to the *Tt* at the top of the card. This is uppercase *T.* Can you make an uppercase *T* with your hands? This is lowercase *t.* Can you make a lowercase *t* with your fingers? Repeat the routine for *Uu.*

Tt
turtle
Alphabet Card

MODEL Display Sing with Me Chart 4B. I see a word that begins with an uppercase *T* in the title. It is the word *Trip.* Have children point to the word *Trip* and say it with you. I see a word that begins with lowercase *t.* It is the word *to.* Let's point to *to* and say the word. Continue the routine for *Uu,* writing *Uncle* and *up* on the board.

Guide Practice

GROUP PRACTICE Display Phonics Songs and Rhymes Chart 4. Teach children the song "Yippee! Yahoo! Zippity-zip!" sung to the tune "Pop Goes the Weasel." Play the CD and sing the song several times. When children are familiar with the song, have them sing it with you. Then have them come up and point to each *T, t,* and *u* on the chart.

ON THEIR OWN Have children make telescopes with their hands. Ask them to look around the room for *Tt* and *Uu.* Have them identify the letters they find.

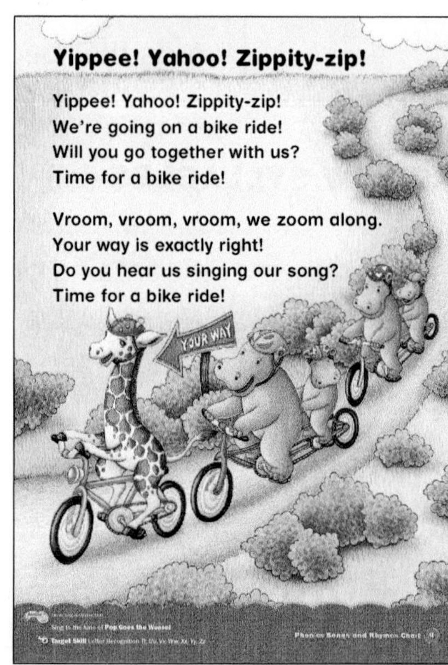
Yippee! Yahoo! Zippity-zip!
Yippee! Yahoo! Zippity-zip!
We're going on a bike ride!
Will you go together with us?
Time for a bike ride!
Vroom, vroom, vroom, we zoom along.
Your way is exactly right!
Do you hear us singing our song?
Time for a bike ride!
YOUR WAY
Phonics Songs and Rhymes Chart 4

Blend Words

REVIEW Display the *Pp* Alphabet Card. Point to uppercase *P.* What is the name of this letter? Repeat with lowercase *p.* Continue to review letter names with the following Alphabet Cards: *Qq, Rr, Ss.*

CONNECT Today we are going to learn how to put sounds together to make words. When I say *bat,* I am putting sounds together to make that word: /b/ and *-at.* Let's try one together. I'll say the beginning sound and then the middle and ending sounds and you put the sounds together to make a word: /m/ *-at,* /m/ *-at.* What is the word? (*mat*)

MODEL

- Say the beginning sound of a word and have children echo you. The beginning sound of the word is /s/.
- Say the ending part of a word and have children echo you. The ending part of the word is *-at.*
- Blend the sounds together to make the word and have children echo you. When I put the sounds together, it sounds like /s/ *-at,* /s/ *-at, sat.* We put sounds together to make the word *sat.*

GUIDE PRACTICE Continue the process with the words below. We are going to practice more words. Remember, first I will say the beginning sound and you will repeat it. Then I will say the ending part and you will repeat those sounds. Finally, you will put the sounds together to make a word.

man ran fan   **sit pit hit**   **hen pen den**

Corrective feedback **If...** children have trouble blending a word,
then... model blending the sounds to make the word. Have children say it with you.

Support Letter Recognition
English learners may have difficulty recognizing the difference between uppercase and lowercase *Tt* and *Uu.* Model the difference by writing each pair of letters on the board and stressing the size difference between the uppercase letter and the lowercase letter.

Common Core State Standards

Foundational Skills 3.c. Read common high-frequency words by sight. (e.g., *the, of, to, you, she, my, is, are, do, does*). **Language 1.a.** Print many upper- and lowercase letters. **Also Foundational Skills 1.b.**

Handwriting

INTRODUCE Write *Tt* on the board. Words that begin with *t* are written with either an uppercase *T* or a lowercase *t*. We use uppercase letters at the beginning of sentences or names.

MODEL UPPERCASE *T* Write the name *Trent* on the board. Point to the uppercase *T*. This is uppercase *T*. We use an uppercase letter for the first letter in a person's name. Watch as I trace the uppercase *T* with my finger. Follow the stroke instructions pictured below.

GUIDE PRACTICE Have children write the uppercase *T* in the air. Use your finger to make an uppercase *T* in the air. Now write it on the palm of your hand.

MODEL LOWERCASE *t* Point to the lowercase *t* in *Trent*. This is a lowercase *t*. Watch as I trace the lowercase *t* with my finger. Write another lowercase *t* on the board, following the stroke instructions. Again, have children write *t* in the air and on their hands.

GUIDE PRACTICE Have children use their Write-On Boards to write a row of uppercase *T* and a row of lowercase *t*.

Continue with *Uu* by writing *Ursula* on the board and repeating the routine.

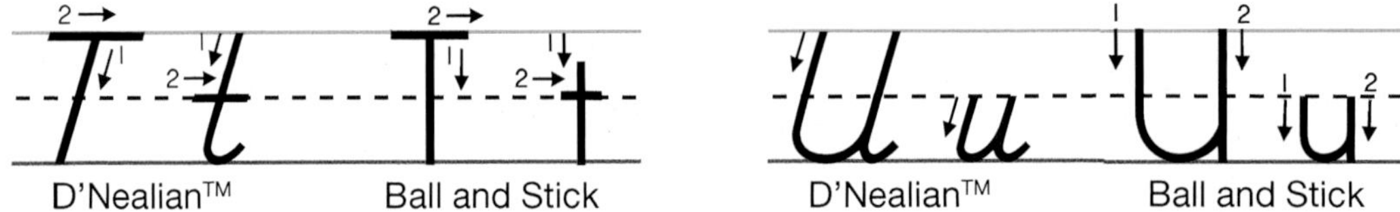

D'Nealian™ Ball and Stick D'Nealian™ Ball and Stick

ON THEIR OWN Use *Reader's and Writer's Notebook,* pp. 37 and 38, for additional practice with *Tt* and *Uu*. Return to these pages on Day 2 to practice *Vv*.

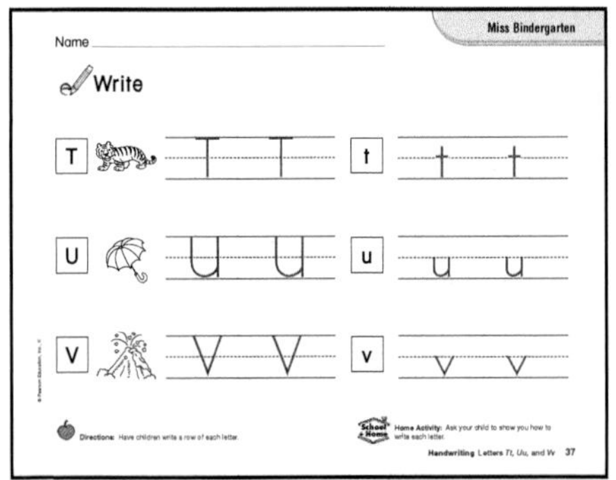

Reader's and Writer's Notebook, p. 37

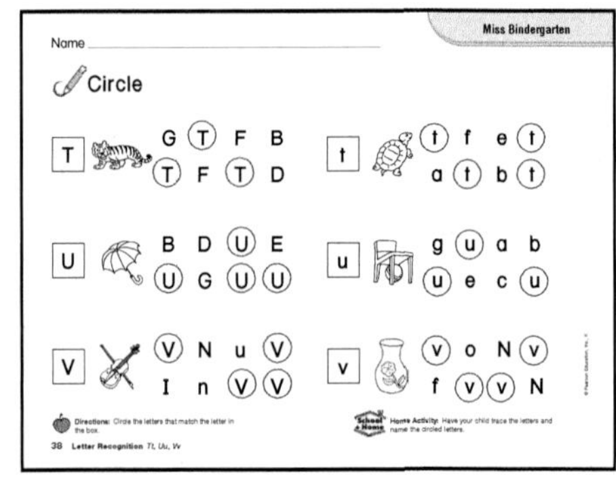

Reader's and Writer's Notebook, p. 38

High-Frequency Words

INTRODUCE Use the routine below to teach high-frequency words *the* and *little.*

Routine Nondecodable Words

1. **Say and Spell** Some words we must learn by remembering the letters rather than saying the sounds. We will say and spell the words to help learn them. Write *the* on the board. This is the word *the.* It has three letters. The letters in *the* are *t, h,* and *e.* Have children say and spell the word, first with you and then without you.

2. **Demonstrate Meaning** I can use the word *the* in lots of sentences. Listen: *The children ran outside.* Now you use the word in a sentence.

   Repeat the routine with the word *little.*

Routines Flip Chart

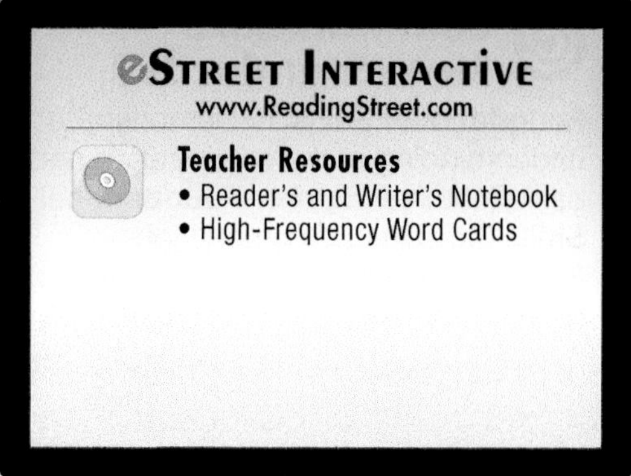

eStreet Interactive
www.ReadingStreet.com

Teacher Resources
- Reader's and Writer's Notebook
- High-Frequency Word Cards

Access for All

 Strategic Intervention

High-Frequency Words To help children who are having difficulty reading the high-frequency words, have them practice naming each letter in the words and then saying the words with you.

High-Frequency Words Some languages do not have articles. Provide extra practice if children omit the word *the* in their speech.

 **Common Core State Standards**

Foundational Skills 1. Demonstrate understanding of the organization and basic features of print. **Foundational Skills 3.c.** Read common high-frequency words by sight. (e.g., *the, of, to, you, she, my, is, are, do, does*).

Access for All

 Strategic Intervention

Access Decodable Story To help children understand the vocabulary in Decodable Story 4, have them discuss things that are little. Show pictures of a turtle, zebra, van, and watermelon. Help children name each picture and tell what they see.

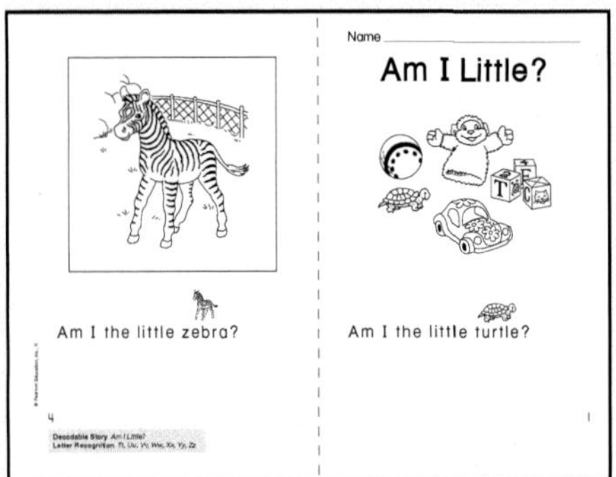

Reader's and Writer's Notebook, pp. 39–40

Decodable Story 4

Read *Am I Little?*

REVIEW Review the previously taught high-frequency words by having children read each word as you point to it on the Word Wall: *I, am, the, little.*

TEACH REBUS WORDS Write the word *turtle* on the board. This is the word *turtle.* Say the letters with me: *t, u, r, t, l, e, turtle.* Continue with *zebra*, *van*, and *watermelon.* Look for these words in our story today. There will be a picture above the word to help you read it.

READ Tear out Decodable Story *Am I Little?* on pp. 39–40 of each child's *Reader's and Writer's Notebook.* Then fold the pages to form a book. Distribute the self-cover books.

Today we will read a story about little things. First let's look at our story. This is the right way to hold the book. Model how to hold the book. Point to the words *Am I Little?* on the cover. We know the book is right side up because the words *Am I Little?* are right side up. Turn the book upside down. This is the wrong way to hold a book. The words and the pictures are upside down. We cannot read upside-down words! Turn the book right side up. Now hold your book right side up. Make sure the words are right side up. Check that all children are holding their books correctly.

Point to the front cover. This is the front cover. *Front* means the side that faces us. Open the book. These are the pages. We turn the pages from right to left. Demonstrate how to turn the pages. Now you turn the pages from right to left. Observe and make sure all children are turning the pages correctly. This is the back cover. It is the part of the book we look at last. Point to the title of the story. What is the title of the story? Where is the title? The title of the story is *Am I Little?* Finally, draw children's attention to the last page of the story. Explain that reading moves from top to bottom. They should read the question at the top of the page, then the question below it, and then the one below that.

Have children read the story, holding the book right side up and turning the pages correctly. When they get to the last page, observe to ensure that children are reading from top to bottom. Have children track the print with their fingers as they read.

Use the routine for reading decodable books to read Decodable Story 4.

Routine Reading Decodable Books

1. **Read Silently** Have children whisper read the story page by page as you listen in.
2. **Model Fluent Reading** Have children finger point as you read a page. Then have them reread the page without you.
3. **Read Chorally** Have children finger point as they chorally read the page. Continue reading page by page, repeating steps 1 and 2.
4. **Read Individually** Have children take turns reading aloud a page.
5. **Reread and Monitor Progress** As you listen to individual children reread, monitor progress and provide support.
6. **Reread with a Partner** Have children reread the story page by page with a partner.

Routines Flip Chart

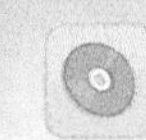

eStreet Interactive
www.ReadingStreet.com

Teacher Resources
- Reader's and Writer's Notebook

Day 1 SMALL GROUP TIME • Differentiate Letter Recognition, p. SG•55

OL On-Level	SI Strategic Intervention	A Advanced
• **Practice Letter Recognition** Recognize Letters *Tt, Uu*	• **Reteach Letter Recognition** Recognize Letters *Tt, Uu*	• **Extend Letter Recognition** Connect *Tt* to /t/, *Uu* to /u/
• **Read** Decodable Story *Am I Little?*	• **Read** Decodable Story *Am I Little?*	• **Read** Advanced Selection "Look at Me"

ELL

Access Decodable Story Before children read *Am I Little?,* practice using high-frequency words *I, am, the,* and *little* in complete sentences.

ELL

Place English Language Learners in the groups that correspond to their reading abilities in English.

If... children need more support with **Letter Recognition,** **then...** use the Letter Recognition activities beginning on p. 447 in the *ELL Handbook.*

My Skills Buddy, pp. 74–75

Zoom in on

Text-Based Comprehension

Classify and Categorize

READ Remind children of the weekly concept—People Working Together in a Community. Have children listen as you read aloud "Grandma's Garden" on p. 331.

MODEL A CLOSE READ Model how to classify and categorize as a tool to build comprehension.

As I read this story, I think about how the things Grandma and Tommy get are alike. I notice that most of the things can be used to make a garden. That is one way the things are alike.

TEACH CLASSIFY AND CATEGORIZE In a story, things may be alike in one way. *Alike* means the same. When we decide how things in a story are alike, we **classify and categorize** them. Good readers classify and categorize things in a story because it helps them understand the story.

Common Core State Standards

Literature 7. With prompting and support, describe the relationship between illustrations and the story in which they appear (e.g., what moment in a story an illustration depicts). **Language 5.a.** Sort common objects into categories (e.g., shapes, foods) to gain a sense of the concepts the categories represent. **Also Literature 9.**

Skills Trace

Classify and Categorize

Introduce U1W4D1; U1W6D1; U4W5D1

Practice U1W4D2; U1W4D3; U1W4D4; U1W6D2; U1W6D3; U1W6D4; U4W5D2; U4W5D3; U4W5D4

Reteach/Review U1W4D5; U1W6D5; U2W1D4; U2W5D4; U4W5D5

KEY: U=Unit W=Week D=Day

Have children turn to pp. 74–75 in *My Skills Buddy* and look at the pictures. Guide children as they describe what is happening in the pictures.

- What is in the boy's box in the first picture? (bears and blocks)
- Into what two groups does the boy put his toys? (bears and blocks)

GUIDE PRACTICE Reread "Grandma's Garden" and ask children what else Grandma and Tommy could get at the plant store. Help children list various plants. Guide children to see that the things on the list are alike because they can all be classified as plants.

MORE PRACTICE Display the Big Book *The Little School Bus.* Help children recall the animals in the story. Discuss ways in which the animals are alike, such as they are alike because they all ride the bus together.

Teacher Read Aloud

Grandma's Garden

Grandma asked Tommy to go shopping with her. First, they picked up a toothbrush for Grandma at the drugstore. Grandma asked the clerk if the store had shovels. The clerk said they must go to the hardware store. So they went to the hardware store and bought a shovel.

Grandma asked the clerk if the store had tomato plants. The clerk said they must go to the plant store. So they went to the plant store and bought tomato plants.

Grandma asked the clerk if the store had books about gardening. The clerk said they must go to the library. They went to the library and checked out a book about gardening.

At Grandma's house Tommy and Grandma read the book about gardening. They dug holes with the shovel. They planted the tomato plants.

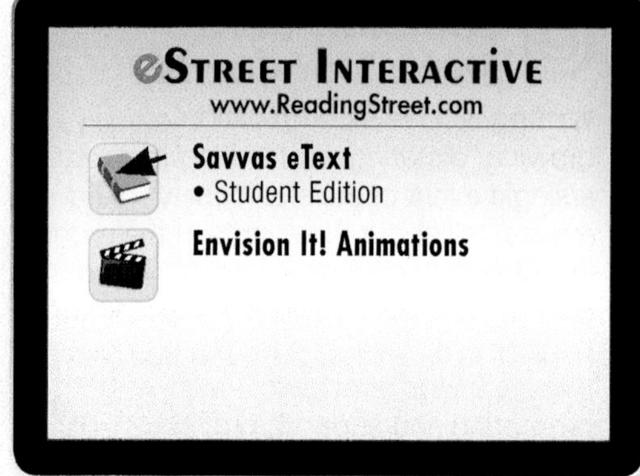

Access for All

SI Strategic Intervention

Support Comprehension If children have difficulty understanding how to classify and categorize, demonstrate the skill sorting green, red, and blue objects into three color groups and explaining what you did and why.

Academic Vocabulary 

classify and categorize to place things or ideas that are alike in at least one way into groups

Bridge to Common Core

KEY IDEAS AND DETAILS

When children classify and categorize key details in a story, they are analyzing how the details are alike. Answering classify and categorize questions about a story helps children learn to use evidence from the text and illustrations to support the conclusions they draw.

Support Listening Comprehension To support children's understanding of vocabulary they will hear in the Read Aloud, display and discuss visuals for words children may not know, such as *drugstore, hardware store, shovel, tomato plant,* and *library.*

Writing 3. Use a combination of drawing, dictating, and writing to narrate a single event or several loosely linked events, tell about the events in the order in which they occurred, and provide a reaction to what happened. **Speaking/ Listening 4.** Describe familiar people, places, things, and events and, with prompting and support, provide additional detail. **Language 1.a.** Print many upper- and lowercase letters. **Also Writing 7., 8.**

Academic Vocabulary 

verb a word that tells what we can do or be

Daily Fix-It

i like to walk fast
I like to walk fast.

This week's practice sentences appear on *Teacher Resources DVD-ROM.*

Conventions

What We Can Do

MAKE CONNECTIONS Today we listened to a story about Grandma and Tommy who dug holes and planted tomato plants in a garden. What are some things you like to do outside? List children's responses. These words name things we do. They are called *verbs.*

TEACH We can do many things. We can walk. Display the *playground* Picture Card. This place is a playground. We can walk to the playground. *Walk* is something we can do. We can also run on the playground. *Run* is something else we can do. What are other things we can do at the play-ground? Have children say other things they can do, such as *jump, slide, swing, skip,* and *play.*

Picture Card

MODEL Display the *hat* Picture Card. What can I do with a hat? I wear a hat. *Wear* tells what I can do. *Wear* is a verb. Continue with the *juice* (drink) and *bed* (sleep) Picture Cards.

GUIDE PRACTICE Display the following Picture Cards: *soap, tub, vacuum, waffle, yo-yo.* Have children say what they can do with the object in each picture. For example: *We wash with soap. We eat a waffle.*

Team Talk **APPLY** Pair children and have them take turns telling something they like to do at school. Have them dictate and illustrate their ideas.

Wonderful, Marvelous Me! I'll Tell You a Story...

INTRODUCE Talk with children about why people tell stories. Why do you think we tell stories? One reason we tell stories is to share our ideas and our imaginations. We all have such wonderful, marvelous imaginations! Have you ever imagined a story? Encourage children to share their thoughts and ideas about stories.

MODEL Today we're going to write a story about a community. I'm going to close my eyes and use my imagination. I have a story in my mind about animal helpers. A bunny named Bob can help at the bakery. Draw a picture of a bunny with a tray of bread. Write and say the caption: *Bob can help at the bakery.* Bob helps the baker by bringing bread to others in the community. He brings bread to his pal Dot at the fire station. Dot is a dog that helps at the fire station. Draw a picture of a Dalmatian with a firefighter's helmet. Write and say the caption: *Dot can help at the fire station.* What can Dot do to help at the fire station?

GUIDE PRACTICE Encourage children to help you come up with more ideas for your story. Write their ideas and draw pictures when appropriate.

INDEPENDENT WRITING Now you're going to tell a story about an animal helper in a community. Close your eyes and use your wonderful, marvelous imagination. What kind of animal do you see? What does the animal do to help the community? Have children dictate their ideas and then illustrate them.

Daily Handwriting

Write uppercase *T* and *U* and *tug* on the board. Review correct letter formation.

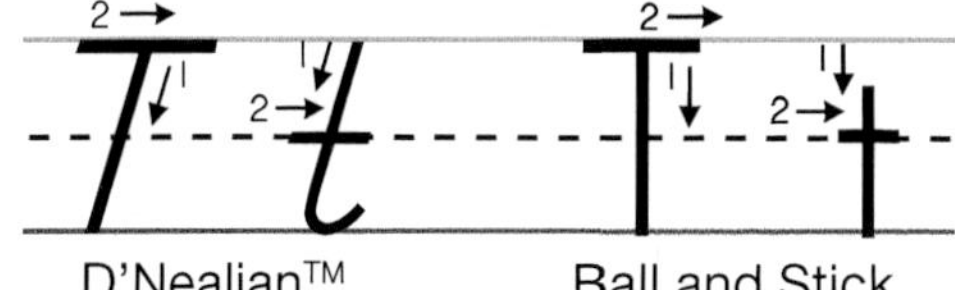
D'Nealian™ Ball and Stick

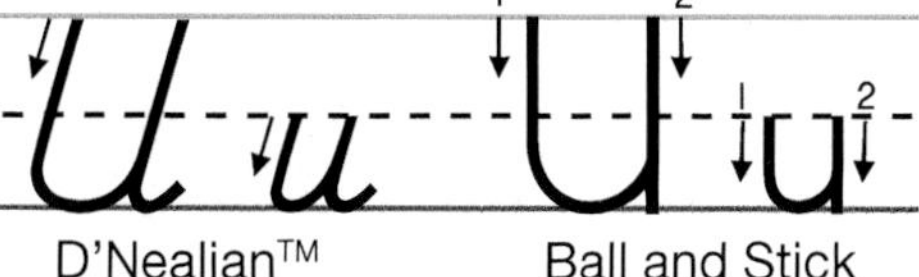
D'Nealian™ Ball and Stick

Have children write uppercase *T* and *U* and *tug* on their Write-On Boards. Remind them to use proper left-to-right and top-to-bottom progression and proper spacing between letters when writing.

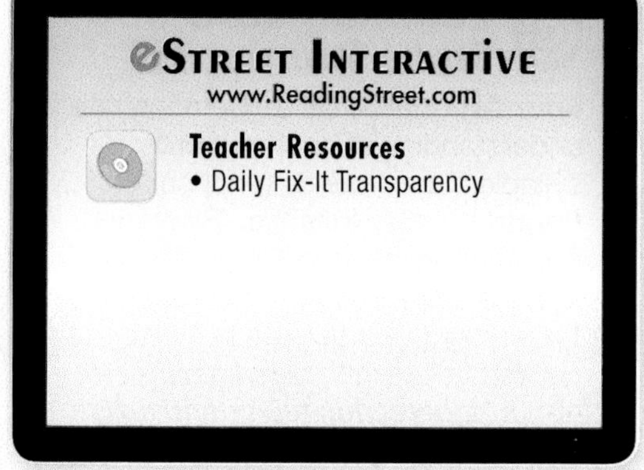

Write Guy *by Jeff Anderson*

Two Words: Subject, Verb!

Let's help children gain confidence in composing sentences. Guide partners as they make up fun two-word sentences: *Rex howled! Kathy giggled. Lions growl.* Then let children continue creating sentences, checking to make sure each includes a subject and a verb.

TEXT TYPES AND PURPOSES

Today children write and draw a story about a community.

Narrative Writing

Children are learning to narrate several real or imagined events using a structured sequence and well-chosen details.

Throughout the week, children will have opportunities to write varied text types for different purposes.

5-Day Plan

DAY 1	Wonderful, Marvelous Me!
DAY 2	Respond to Literature
DAY 3	Genre Writing
DAY 4	Extend the Concept
DAY 5	This Week We...

Conventions If children have difficulties naming a particular action in English, ask them to act it out and then provide them with the English word for the action.

Common Core State Standards

Foundational Skills 2. Demonstrate understanding of spoken words, syllables, and sounds (phonemes). **Foundational Skills 2.c.** Blend and segment onsets and rimes of single-syllable spoken words. **Speaking/Listening 1.** Participate in collaborative conversations with diverse partners about *kindergarten topics and texts* with peers and adults in small and larger groups. **Speaking/Listening 1.a.** Follow agreed-upon rules for discussions (e.g., listening to others and taking turns speaking about the topics and texts under discussion). **Also Speaking/Listening 6.**

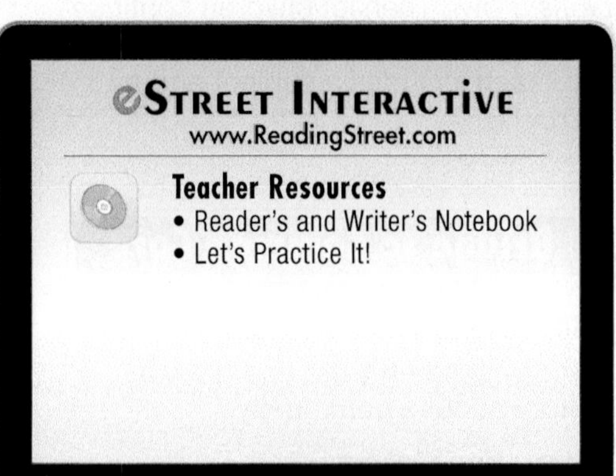

Listening and Speaking

Talk About Me

TEACH Today we are going to talk about ourselves. I talk about myself when I tell something about me, such as *My hair is brown.* Ask children to stand and tell the class something about themselves. Tell children that good speakers take turns and speak one at a time.

MODEL I am going to tell you something else about me. *I like to teach.* Now it is your turn to tell the class something you like to do.

GUIDE PRACTICE Have children use the following sentence frame in their responses: *I like to* _______. Ask them to respond one at a time. Refer children to the Rules for Listening and Speaking on pp. 1–2 of *Reader's and Writer's Notebook.* Tell them to share their ideas in loud, clear voices.

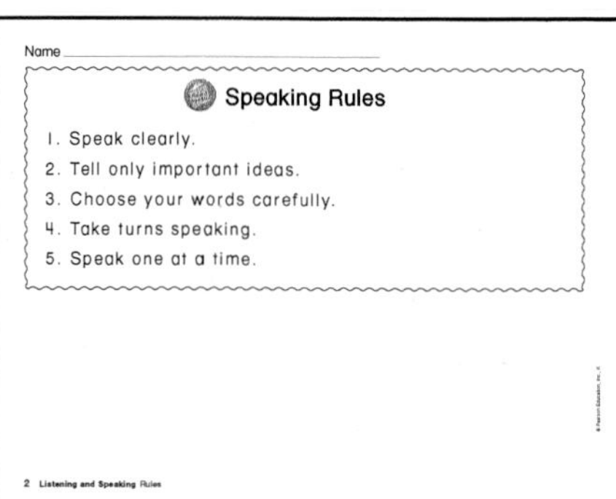
Name
Speaking Rules
1. Speak clearly.
2. Tell only important ideas.
3. Choose your words carefully.
4. Take turns speaking.
5. Speak one at a time.

Reader's and Writer's Notebook, pp. 1–2

Wrap Up Your Day!

- ✔ **Content Knowledge** Today we started talking about how people in a community cooperate, or help one another. Who are the helpers we have at school?
- ✔ **Oral Language** Today we talked about some places in a community. Let's name the Amazing Words: *bakery, fire station, park, post office, library, chaperone.*
- ✔ **Homework Idea** Send home the Family Times Newsletter from Let's Practice It! pp. 7–8 on *Teacher Resources DVD-ROM.*

Tomorrow we will read about a kindergarten class on a field trip.

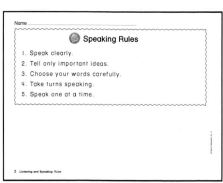

Extend Your Day!

Social Studies
What Is a Good Citizen?

MATERIALS: guest speaker or video about community helpers, white construction paper circles (4 inches in diameter), adhesive tape

DISCUSS BEING A GOOD CITIZEN Invite a community helper to speak to the class or show a video about the qualities of a good citizen. Before introducing the speaker or video, ask children to name as many community helpers as they can. If they need help, ask:

- Who helps take care of you when you are sick?
- Who keeps our parks and streets clean?

As a class, listen respectfully to the speaker or video. Give each child a circle made of white construction paper. Have children draw a picture of their favorite community helper and dictate a label for the helper.

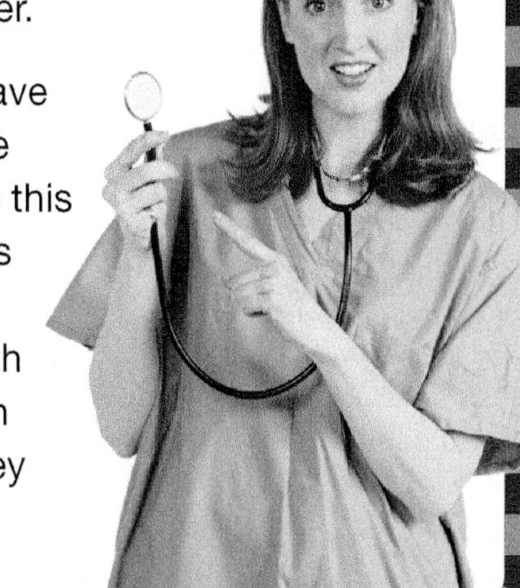

WRITE A SENTENCE Have children dictate a sentence explaining why they chose this helper. Write the sentences on the board. Then make the circles into stickers with adhesive tape. Let children wear the stickers when they go home.

Conventions
What We Can Do

MATERIALS: construction paper

ILLUSTRATE WHAT WE CAN DO Give each child a sheet of construction paper divided into two sections. Have children draw a picture of what they can do at home in one section and what they can do at school in the other section. Then have them dictate a label for each section.

Phonemic Awareness
Blending Onset and Rime

MATERIALS: Picture Cards: *cat, fan, bag, jet, man, mop, red, sun, web*

BLEND WORDS Display three picture cards. Say one word by emphasizing the initial sound and then the ending part. For example: /s/ *-un*, /s/ *-un.* Ask children to say the whole word and point to the picture for the word.

DAY 2 at a Glance

Content Knowledge
Oral Vocabulary

Phonemic Awareness
Initial Sounds

Letter Recognition
Letters *Vv*

Handwriting
V and *v*

Text-Based Comprehension
Classify and Categorize

Conventions
What We Can Do

Writing
Respond to Literature

Vocabulary
Location Words

Materials

- Student Edition
- Truckery Rhymes
- Talk with Me/Sing with Me Chart
- Picture Cards
- Phonics Songs and Rhymes Chart
- Alphabet Cards
- Reader's and Writer's Notebook
- Big Book

Common Core State Standards

Speaking/Listening 1. Participate in collaborative conversations with diverse partners about *kindergarten topics and texts* with peers and adults in small and larger groups. **Language 6.** Use words and phrases acquired through conversations, reading and being read to, and responding to texts.

TRUCKTOWN
on Reading Street

Start your engines!
Display p. 8 of *Truckery Rhymes.* Point to "Gabby Had a Little Bear."

Who remembers which truck this rhyme is about? Yes, it's about Gabby. Let's read the rhyme together. Now have a child point to the rhyming words as the class reads the rhyme again.

Truckery Rhymes

Content Knowledge

Zoom in on

People Working Together in a Community

TALK ABOUT COOPERATION IN A COMMUNITY On the board, write the Question of the Week, *How do people in a community cooperate?,* and track the print as you read it aloud. Have children answer the question in complete sentences. To reinforce the concept and focus children's attention, display Sing with Me Chart 4B. Tell children that they are going to sing about a class field trip.

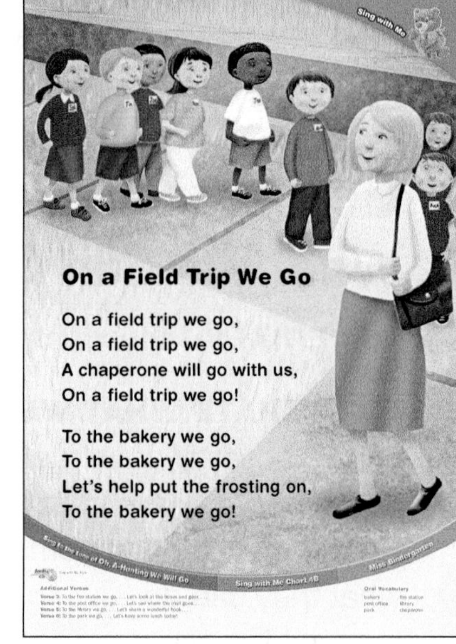
On a Field Trip We Go
On a field trip we go,
On a field trip we go,
A chaperone will go with us,
On a field trip we go!
To the bakery we go,
To the bakery we go,
Let's help put the frosting on,
To the bakery we go!

Talk with Me/Sing with Me Chart 4B

Build Oral Language

LISTEN FOR AMAZING WORDS The Amazing Words *bakery* and *fire station* are in the song "On a Field Trip We Go." Have children describe the picture. Sing the song several times to the tune of "Oh, A-Hunting We Will Go." Ask children to sing along with you. Have them raise their hands when they hear *bakery* and *fire station.*

Build Oral Vocabulary

Amazing Words Robust Vocabulary Routine

1. **Introduce the Word** A *bakery* is a place where bread, rolls, muffins, and other tasty things are baked and sold. What's our new Amazing Word for a place that makes and sells baked goods? Say it with me: *bakery.*

2. **Demonstrate** Provide examples to show meaning. *The bakery smells very good because bread is baked there.*

   Repeat steps 1 and 2.

   Introduce the Word A *fire station* is the building where fire engines are kept. What's our new Amazing Word for the building where fire engines are kept? Say it with me: *fire station.*

   Demonstrate *Firefighters work and rest at fire stations.*

3. **Apply** Tell children to use *bakery* and *fire station* in complete sentences. Have them use their imaginations to describe how they think these places sound and smell.

4. **Display the Words** Ask children what letters *bakery* and *fire station* begin with. Have them point to and name each beginning letter.

Routines Flip Chart

USE AMAZING WORDS To reinforce the concept and the Amazing Words, have children supply the appropriate Amazing Word for each sentence.

They buy bread at the _______ . (bakery)
We learn about fire safety at the _______ . (fire station)

Amazing Words

bakery	fire station
park	post office
library	chaperone

Access for All

 Strategic Intervention

Sentence Production If children have difficulty completing the sentences, say a sentence using each Amazing Word and ask children to choose the one that makes sense. Say the sentence together.

Amazing Words Invite children to share how they say *bakery* in their home languages. Ask children to name a favorite food that they can buy at a bakery.

Reinforce Vocabulary Use the Day 2 instruction on ELL Poster 4 to reinforce the meanings of high-frequency words.

Common Core State Standards
Foundational Skills 2.d. Isolate and pronounce the initial, medial vowel, and final sounds (phonemes) in three-phoneme (consonant-vowel-consonant, or CVC) words. **Also Foundational Skills 2.e.**

Phonemic Awareness

Let's Listen for Initial Sounds

Read Together

- Point to the pig in the puddle. Say "a pig in a puddle." What sound do you hear repeated?
- Point to the man with the mouse. Say "a man with a mouse." What sound is repeated?
- Find things that begin with /b/, /d/, /k/, /p/, and /m/.
- Name two things that begin like *ball, desk, key, pen,* and *met.*

READING STREET ONLINE
BIG QUESTION VIDEO
www.ReadingStreet.com

72 73

My Skills Buddy, pp. 72–73

Common Core State Standards

Foundational Skills 2.b. Count, pronounce, blend, and segment syllables in spoken words. **Foundational Skills 2.d.** Isolate and pronounce the initial, medial vowel, and final sounds (phonemes) in three-phoneme (consonant-vowel-consonant, or CVC) words.* (This does not include CVCs ending with /l/, /r/, or /x/.) **Also Foundational Skills 2., 2.e.**

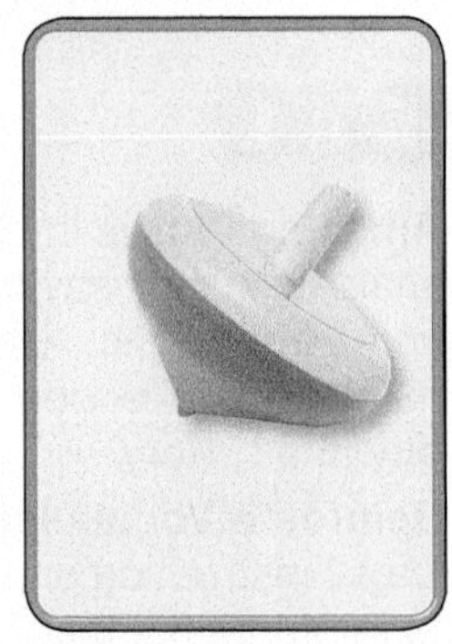

Picture Card

Phonemic Awareness

Initial Sounds

TEACH Display the *top* and *van* Picture Cards. Point to each picture. What is this? (a top) What is this? (a van) Listen to the beginning sounds in these words: *top, van.* Say the words with me: *top, van.* Do they begin with the same sound? (no) That's right. *Top* begins with /t/. *Van* begins with /v/. These are two different sounds.

Picture Card

MODEL Display the *tub* Picture Card. This is a tub. Which word has the same beginning sound as *tub: top* or *van? Tub* begins with /t/. *Top* begins with /t/. *Van* begins with /v/. *Tub* and *top* both begin with /t/. *Top* has the same beginning sound as *tub.* Repeat with the *vest, tent,* and *vase* Picture Cards.

GUIDE PRACTICE Have children look at the picture on *My Skills Buddy,* pp. 72–73. Remember we saw a horse eating hay in the picture. *Horse* and *hay* begin with the same sound: /h/. Let's look for other things in the picture that begin with the same sound. Discuss with children the bulleted items on p. 72 not discussed on Day 1.

Corrective feedback	**If...** children cannot identify words that begin with the same sound, **then...** say the words again, isolating the initial sound in each word. Listen to the beginning sounds in these words: /h/ *-orse,* /h/ *-ay.* What sound do you hear at the beginning of *horse* and *hay?* I hear /h/ at the beginning of *horse* and *hay.* Continue with these words: *boy, barn; kid, kite.*

ON THEIR OWN Display Phonics Songs and Rhymes Chart 4, "Yippee! Yahoo! Zippity-zip!" Remind children of the tune "Pop! Goes the Weasel." Have them sing the song with you several times. Then say pairs of words from the song. Have children say "Yes!" if the words begin with the same sound and "No!" if the words begin with different sounds. Use these word pairs: *bike, way; ride, right; hear, going; singing, song; time, with.*

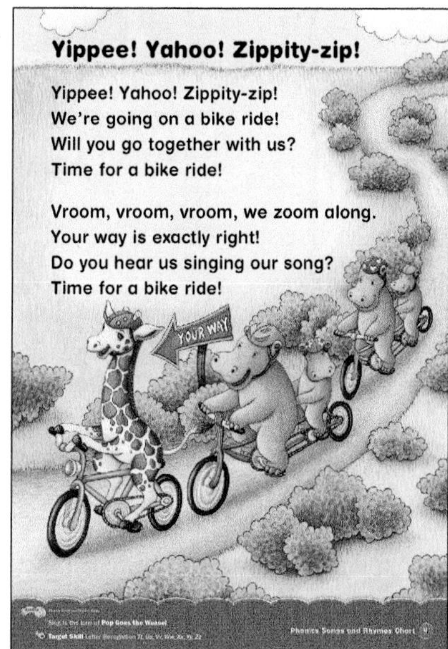

Yippee! Yahoo! Zippity-zip!
Yippee! Yahoo! Zippity-zip!
We're going on a bike ride!
Will you go together with us?
Time for a bike ride!
Vroom, vroom, vroom, we zoom along.
Your way is exactly right!
Do you hear us singing our song?
Time for a bike ride!
YOUR WAY

Phonics Songs and Rhymes Chart 4

REVIEW SYLLABLES Let's listen to two words that begin with /v/: *vest, volcano.* Let's clap our hands once as we say the word *vest. Vest* is a short word. It contains only one syllable. Now let's clap our hands as we say *vol-ca-no. Volcano* is a longer word. It contains three syllables. Listen for the three syllables and clap the syllables with me: *vol-ca-no.* Repeat the routine with the following pairs of words: *astronaut, apple; cap, caterpillar; hen, hippopotamus.*

Access for All

SI Strategic Intervention

Support Phonemic Awareness
Display the *cap, bat,* and *cat* Picture Cards. Say the words aloud with children. Have them draw pictures of the words that begin with the same sound.

Phonemic Awareness Children may find it difficult to distinguish certain beginning sounds, such as /v/ and /f/. You may need to provide additional practice with those sounds.

Common Core State Standards

Foundational Skills 1. Demonstrate understanding of the organization and basic features of print. **Foundational Skills 1.d.** Recognize and name all upper- and lowercase letters of the alphabet. **Foundational Skills 2.c.** Blend and segment onsets and rimes of single-syllable spoken words. **Also Foundational Skills 1.a., 1.b., 1.c.**

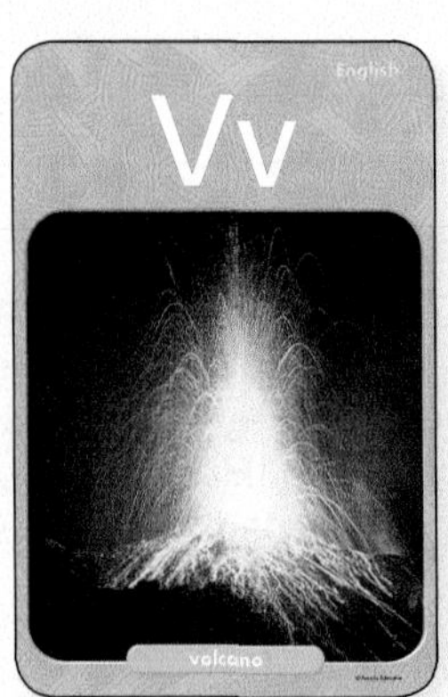

Alphabet Card

My Skills Buddy, p. 76

Letter Recognition

Teach/Model

Letters *Vv*

INTRODUCE Display the *Vv* Alphabet Card. Point to uppercase *V.* This is uppercase *V.* What is the name of this letter? Repeat for lowercase *v.*

MODEL Point to the volcano. This is a volcano. Write *volcano* on the board and point to the *v.* This is lowercase *v.* Write *Vesuvius* on the board. *Vesuvius* is the name of a volcano. Point to the *V.* This is uppercase *V.*

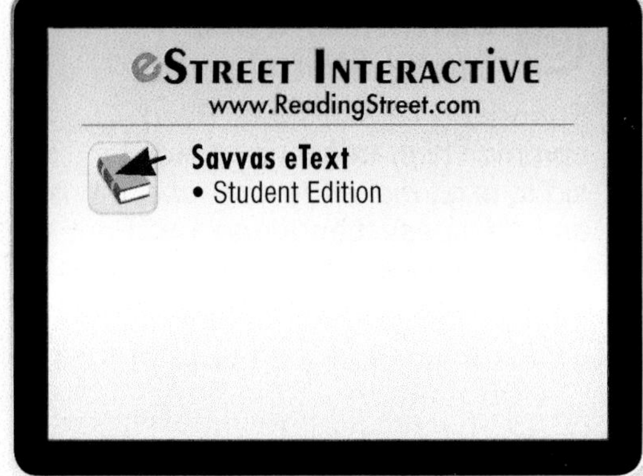

Guide Practice

GROUP PRACTICE Have children identify the letters at the top of p. 76 in *My Skills Buddy.* Look at the sun. This is the word *sun.* Words can be spoken, and they can be written or printed. Point to the sentence. This is a sentence. A sentence is a group of words. Spaces tell us where words begin and end. Have children follow along as you use the arrows to read the sentence.

Apply

CONNECT When I say *sit,* I put /s/ and *-it* together to make that word. Let's try one together. I'll say the beginning sound and the ending part, and you put them together to make the word: /p/ *-it,* /p/ *-it.* What is the word? (*pit*)

MODEL Say the beginning sound and ending part of a word and have children echo you. The beginning sound of the word is /h/. The ending part is *-it.* Blend the sounds together to make the word and have children echo you. We put the sounds together to make a word: /h/ *-it, hit.*

GUIDE PRACTICE Continue with the words below. Remember, first I will say the beginning sound and you will repeat it. Then I will say the ending part and you will repeat it. Then you will put the sounds together to make a word.

can tan pan fan lit fit bit ten den men

Don't Wait Until Friday

MONITOR PROGRESS Check Letter Recognition Letter Names

FORMATIVE ASSESSMENT Write the following rows on the board: *T U V T V; u v t v t.* Have children draw lines to match the uppercase and lowercase forms of the letters, naming each letter form as they match.

If... children cannot match and/or name letter forms,

then... use the small-group Strategic Intervention lessons, pp. SG•62–SG•63, to reteach *Vv, Tt,* and *Uu.*

Continue to monitor children's progress during the week so that children can be successful with the Day 5 Assessment.

Access for All

 Advanced

Letter Recognition Use letter tiles to spell the word *vent.* Have children name each letter in the word. Repeat the routine with the word *vast.*

Letter Recognition Children may confuse *Vv* with *Uu.* Define the words *point* and *curve,* and explain how these words can be used to describe *Vv* and *Uu* and to distinguish between them.

Foundational Skills 3.c. Read common high-frequency words by sight. (e.g., *the, of, to, you, she, my, is, are, do, does*). **Language 1.a.** Print many upper- and lowercase letters.

Access for All

 Strategic Intervention

Handwriting Write the letters *U* and *V* on the board. Point out that these letters can look similar if children are not careful when writing them. Have children practice writing a row of each letter to help them distinguish *U* from *V*.

Handwriting

Letters *Vv*

INTRODUCE Write *Vv* on the board. Words that begin with *v* are written with either an uppercase *V* or a lowercase *v*. Which letter is uppercase *V*? Which letter is lowercase *v*?

MODEL UPPERCASE *V* Write *Vivian* on the board. This is uppercase *V*. *Vivian* begins with uppercase *V*. We use an uppercase *V* to begin a sentence and for the first letter in a name. Watch as I trace the uppercase *V* with my finger. Write another *V* on the board, following the stroke instructions below.

GUIDE PRACTICE Have children write an uppercase *V* in the air. Use your finger to make an uppercase *V* in the air. Now write it on your hand.

MODEL LOWERCASE *v* Point to the lowercase *v* in *Vivian.* This is lowercase *v*. *Vivian* has a lowercase *v* in the middle. Watch as I trace the lowercase *v* with my finger. Write another lowercase *v* on the board, following the stroke instructions. Again, have children write *v* in the air and on their hands.

GUIDE PRACTICE Have children use their Write-On Boards to write a row of uppercase *V* and a row of lowercase *v*.

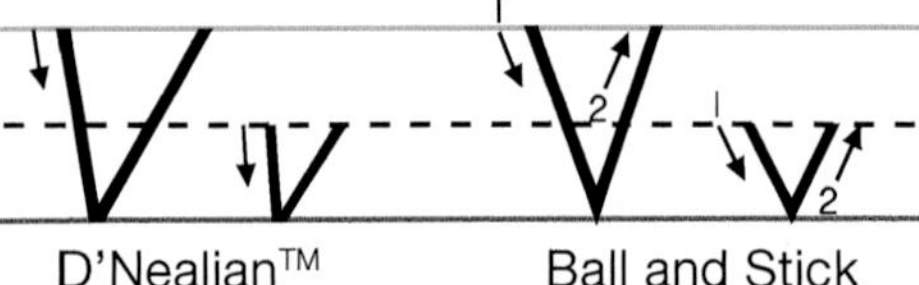

D'Nealian™ Ball and Stick

ON THEIR OWN Have children use their Write-On Boards to make a row of uppercase *V* and a row of lowercase *v*. Circulate around the room, assisting children as necessary. Then have children write the following words: *van, vet, vest.* Use *Reader's and Writer's Notebook,* pp. 37 and 38, to practice *Vv*.

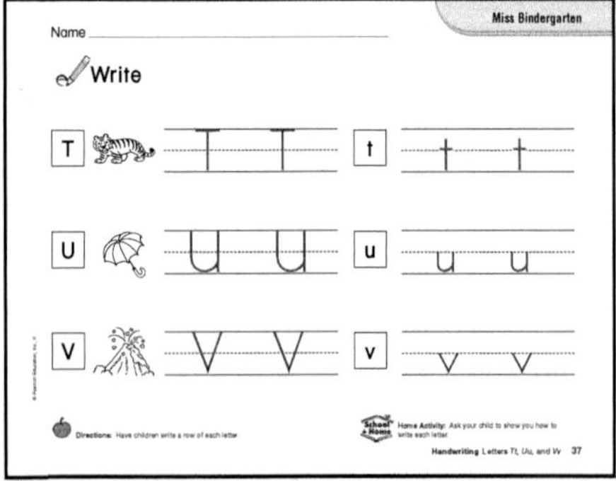

Reader's and Writer's Notebook, p. 37

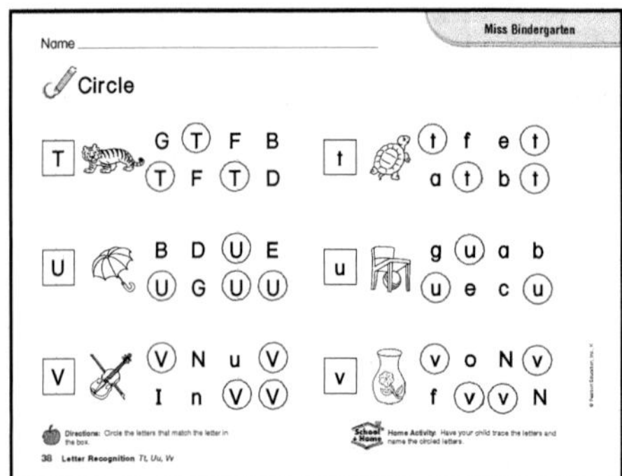

Reader's and Writer's Notebook, p. 38

High-Frequency Words

Words I Can Read

the

little

Sentences I Can Read

1. Am I little?

2. I am the little [cat].

77

My Skills Buddy, p. 77

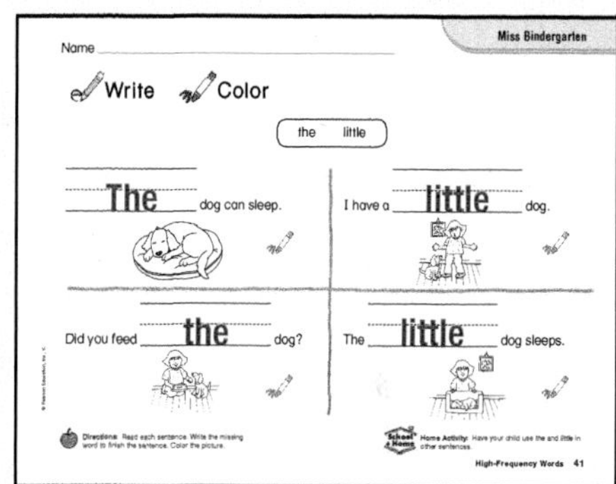

Reader's and Writer's Notebook, p. 41

High-Frequency Words

READ WORDS Have children turn to p. 77 of *My Skills Buddy.* Read the high-frequency words *the* and *little* together. Then have children point to each word and read it themselves.

READ SENTENCES Read the sentences on the *My Skills Buddy* page together to read the new high-frequency words in context.

 Pair children and have them take turns reading each of the sentences aloud.

ON THEIR OWN Use *Reader's and Writer's Notebook,* p. 41, for additional practice with this week's high-frequency words.

ELL

High-Frequency Words Ask children to make up phrases or sentences using this week's high-frequency words *the* and *little.* Have them illustrate their phrases or sentences and share them with a partner.

Common Core State Standards

Foundational Skills 1.d. Recognize and name all upper- and lowercase letters of the alphabet. **Foundational Skills 3.c.** Read common high-frequency words by sight. (e.g., *the, of, to, you, she, my, is, are, do, does*). **Foundational Skills 4.** Read emergent-reader texts with purpose and understanding. **Also Literature 6., 10., Foundational Skills 1.**

Access for All

SI Strategic Intervention

Support Reading Before children read *At the Zoo,* display pages from the book and introduce each rebus word. Write the words on the board and have children share what they know about each word.

Decodable Reader 4

Read *At the Zoo*

REVIEW Review the previously taught high-frequency words. Have children read each word as you point to it on the Word Wall: *I, am, the, little.*

TEACH REBUS WORDS Write the word *walrus* on the board. This is the word *walrus.* The letters are *w, a, l, r, u, s, walrus.* Say it with me. Repeat with *tiger, yak, ox, rhino, zebra,* and *umbrella bird.* Look for these words in the story we read today. There will be a picture above each word to help you read it.

CONCEPTS OF PRINT Have children turn to Decodable Reader 4, *At the Zoo,* on p. 78 of *My Skills Buddy.* Today we will read a story about little animals in a zoo. Point to the title. The title of this story is *At the Zoo.* What is the title? Point to the name of the author. The author's name is Nitty Jones. What does the author do? The illustrator's name is Amy Sparks. What does the illustrator do? Review the following parts of a book: front cover, back cover, pages.

READ Use the routine for reading decodable books to read Decodable Reader 4.

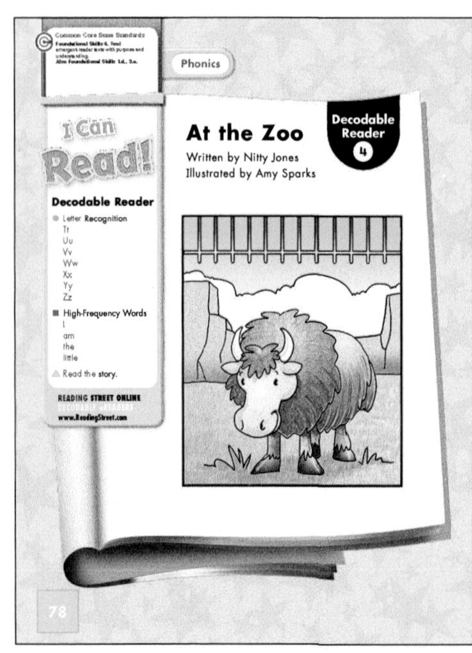

My Skills Buddy, pp. 78–85

Routine Reading Decodable Books

1. **Read Silently** Have children whisper read the book page by page as you listen in.
2. **Model Fluent Reading** Have children finger point as you read a page. Then have them reread the book without you.
3. **Read Chorally** Have children finger point as they chorally read the page. Continue reading page by page, repeating steps 1 and 2.
4. **Read Individually** Have children take turns reading aloud a page.
5. **Reread and Monitor Progress** As you listen to individual children reread, monitor progress and provide support.
6. **Reread with a Partner** Have children reread the book page by page with a partner.

Routines Flip Chart

Day 2 SMALL GROUP TIME • Differentiate Letter Recognition, p. SG•55

OL On-Level	SI Strategic Intervention	A Advanced
• **Practice Letter Recognition** Recognize Letters *Vv*	• **Reteach Letter Recognition** Recognize Letters *Vv*	• **Extend Letter Recognition** Connect *Vv* to /v/
• **Read** Decodable Reader *At the Zoo*	• **Read** Decodable Reader *At the Zoo*	• **Read** Decodable Reader *At the Zoo*

eSTREET INTERACTIVE
www.ReadingStreet.com

Savvas eText
• Student Edition

Access Decodable Reader Before children read *At the Zoo,* use visuals to help define the rebus words: *walrus, tiger, yak, ox, rhino, zebra, umbrella bird.*

Place English Language Learners in the groups that correspond to their reading abilities in English.

If... children need more support with **Letter Recognition,** **then...** use the activities on p. DI•63 in the Teacher Resources section of the Digital Path.

 **Common Core State Standards**

Literature 2. With prompting and support, retell familiar stories, including key details. **Literature 7.** With prompting and support, describe the relationship between illustrations and the story in which they appear (e.g., what moment in a story an illustration depicts). **Also Literature 5., Foundational Skills 1.a.**

Access for All

 Strategic Intervention

Access Content Help children understand the concept of community helpers by showing them pictures of community helpers in your town.

Text-Based Comprehension

Introduce Main Selection

CONCEPTS OF PRINT Display the cover of *Miss Bindergarten Takes a Field Trip.* Explain that reading moves from the top to the bottom of the page.

GENRE An animal fantasy is a story about animal characters that talk and act like people. Let's read about an animal class on a field trip.

PREVIEW AND PREDICT The title of this book is *Miss Bindergarten Takes a Field Trip.* Tell me what you see on the cover. Based on the title and the cover, what do you think this book will be about? Take children on a walk through the book. Have them tell what they see in each picture.

SET PURPOSE Remind children of the Question of the Week: *How do people in a community cooperate?* Have children listen as you read.

MODEL Read *Miss Bindergarten Takes a Field Trip* with expression to build interest in the text.

Routine Read for Understanding 

Deepen understanding by reading the selection multiple times.

1. **First Read**—Read the entire selection aloud to build interest in the text.
2. **Second Read**—Use the **Develop Vocabulary** notes on pages 364–383.
3. **Third Read**—Use the **Develop Comprehension** notes on pages 364–383.

Retell

CHECK RETELLING Have children turn to p. 86 of *My Skills Buddy.* Walk through the retelling boxes as children retell the story. After they retell the story as a group, have children draw a picture to retell a favorite part. Have them write or dictate a word or sentence to go with their picture.

Check Retelling

If... children have difficulty retelling the story,

then... go through the story one page at a time, and ask children to tell what happens in their own words.

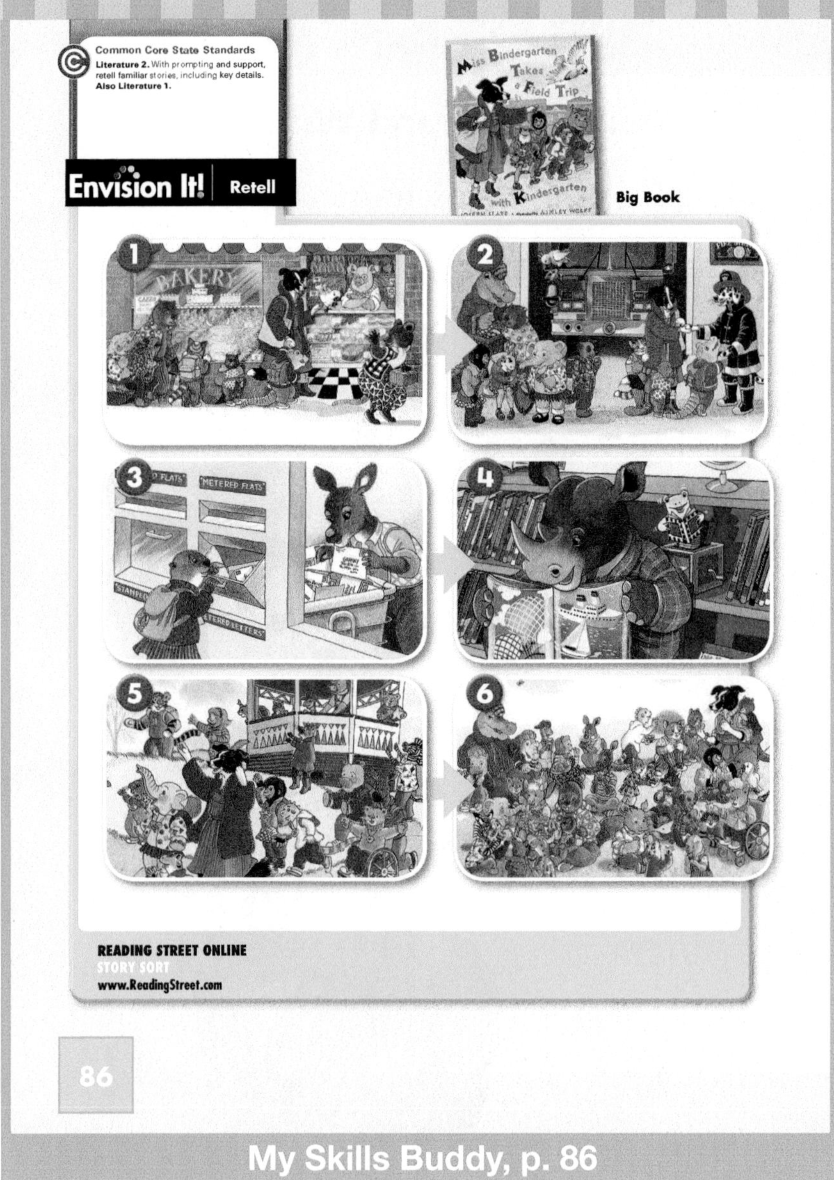

My Skills Buddy, p. 86

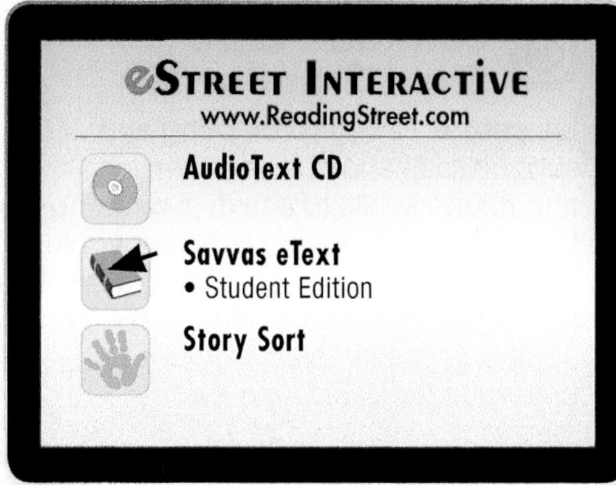

Retelling Plan

- ☑ **Week 1** Assess Advanced students.
- ☑ **Week 2** Assess On-Level students.
- ☑ **Week 3** Assess Strategic Intervention students.
- ☑ **This week assess Advanced students.**
- ☐ **Week 5** Assess On-Level students.
- ☐ **Week 6** Assess Strategic Intervention students.

Scoring Rubric Narrative Retelling

	4	3	2	1
Connections	Makes connections and generalizes beyond the text	Makes connections to other events, stories, or experiences	Makes a limited connection to another event, story, or experience	Makes no connection to another event, story, or experience
Author's Purpose	Elaborates on author's purpose	Tells author's purpose with some clarity	Makes some connection to author's purpose	Makes no connection to author's purpose
Characters	Describes the main character(s) and any character development	Identifies the main character(s) and gives some information about them	Inaccurately identifies some characters or gives little information about them	Inaccurately identifies the characters or gives no information about them
Setting	Describes the time and location	Identifies the time and location	Omits details of time or location	Is unable to identify time or location
Plot	Describes the events in sequence using rich detail	Tells the plot with some errors in sequence that do not affect meaning	Tells parts of plot with gaps that affect meaning	Retelling has no sense of story

Access Content If children do not know the English word for a place shown in the book, have them identify the place with a word they know, such as (Spanish) *correo* for post office. Supply the English word, and have children repeat it.

Common Core State Standards

Literature 1. With prompting and support, ask and answer questions about key details in a text. **Speaking/ Listening 4.** Describe familiar people, places, things, and events and, with prompting and support, provide additional detail. **Also Speaking/ Listening 2., Language 5.a.**

Access for All

Advanced

Writing Let children dictate and illustrate their own responses to the questions.

Think, Talk, and Write
Read Together
1. Who helps in our town?
Text to World
2. Which things belong together?
Classify and Categorize
3. Look back and write.
87

My Skills Buddy, p. 87

Think, Talk, and Write

DISCUSS CONCEPT We're learning about places and people in a community.

- Which place did you like best?
- Why did you like that place?
- What would you like to do at that place?

CONFIRM PREDICTIONS Have children recall their predictions before you read *Miss Bindergarten Takes a Field Trip.*

- What did you think the story would be about?
- Was your prediction correct?

Have children turn to p. 87 of *My Skills Buddy.* Read the questions and directives and have children respond.

1. **TEXT TO WORLD** Who helps in our town? Have you ever met a baker, firefighter, mail carrier, or librarian? What are some other helping jobs?

2. **CLASSIFY AND CATEGORIZE** Look at the pictures. Which things belong together? (the muffin and the loaf of bread) How are these things alike? (You can eat them. You can buy them at a bakery.)

3. **LOOK BACK AND WRITE • TEXT EVIDENCE** Let's look back at our story and write about it. The library is one place Miss Bindergarten's class visits. Look at the pictures to see what things we can do at a library. Read pp. 24–25 of *Miss Bindergarten Takes a Field Trip.* Now let's write our ideas. Record children's responses on chart paper. (We can sit. We can read. We can choose books. We can use computers.)

Conventions

What We Can Do

TEACH Remind children of what they learned about words for doing things. We can do many things. We can walk. We can talk. We can eat. We can sleep. The words *walk, talk, eat,* and *sleep* tell what we can do.

MODEL Display pp. 12–13 of *Miss Bindergarten Takes a Field Trip.* The children can do many things at the fire station. Gwen rings a bell, Henry holds a hose, and Ian laughs. *Rings, holds,* and *laughs* tell what the children are doing.

GUIDE PRACTICE Guide children to identify other things the children are doing in *Miss Bindergarten Takes a Field Trip.* Write the words in a list. When it is completed, read the words aloud with children.

ON THEIR OWN Use *Reader's and Writer's Notebook,* p. 42, for more practice with what we can do.

Name
Miss Bindergarten
Color Draw
Answers will vary.
42 Conventions What We Can Do

Reader's and Writer's Notebook, p. 42

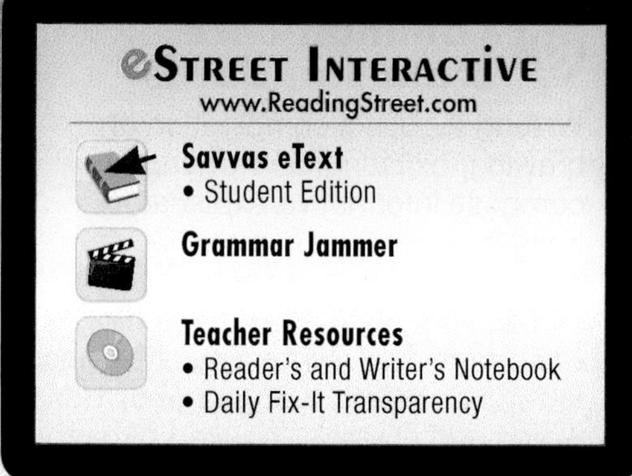

Writing to Sources

Use Write Like a Reporter on pp. 18–19 to guide children in writing text-based responses using one source.

Daily Fix-It

i can read a book

I can read a book.

This week's practice sentences appear on *Teacher Resources DVD-ROM.*

Bridge to Common Core

CONVENTIONS OF STANDARD ENGLISH

When children identify the words for doing things used in the story, they are starting to learn about verbs, an important concept in standard English grammar and usage.

Support Conventions To emphasize that all the words reviewed, modeled, and identified in the lesson tell about actions, act out each verb and ask children what you are doing. Encourage them to mimic your actions and say the words.

Common Core State Standards

Writing 2. Use a combination of drawing, dictating, and writing to compose informative/explanatory texts in which they name what they are writing about and supply some information about the topic. **Language 1.a.** Print many upper- and lowercase letters. **Language 6.** Use words and phrases acquired through conversations, reading and being read to, and responding to texts. **Also Literature 4., Language 5., 5.a., 5.c.**

Writing

Respond to Literature

DISCUSS Display *Miss Bindergarten Takes a Field Trip.* Ask children to name all of the community helpers they see in the story. Make a list of the helpers and how they help. Prompt with questions if necessary. Who helps you at the library?

MODEL Select a place Miss Bindergarten took her class. Tell children you are going to write a sentence about the community helper at that place and tell how he or she helps. We like to go to the library to pick out books. I will write a sentence about the librarian.

The librarian finds good books for us.

GUIDE PRACTICE Invite children to help you write more sentences about the community helpers from *Miss Bindergarten Takes a Field Trip.*

The baker makes good things to eat.

The mail carrier brings us letters.

INDEPENDENT WRITING Have children dictate ideas about community helpers or copy one of the sentences the class wrote together. Then have them illustrate their sentences.

Daily Handwriting

Write *V* and *v* on the board. Review correct letter formation of uppercase *V* and lowercase *v.*

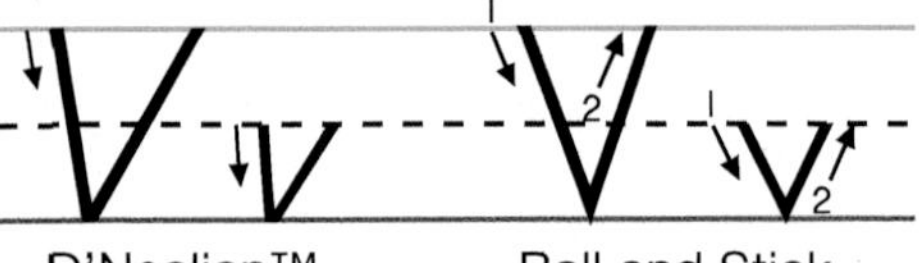

D'Nealian™ Ball and Stick

Have children write *V* and *v* on their Write-On Boards. Remind them to use proper left-to-right and top-to-bottom progression and proper spacing between letters when writing *V* and *v.*

Writing to Sources Use More Connect the Texts on pp. 222–293 to guide children in writing text-based responses within various forms and modes.

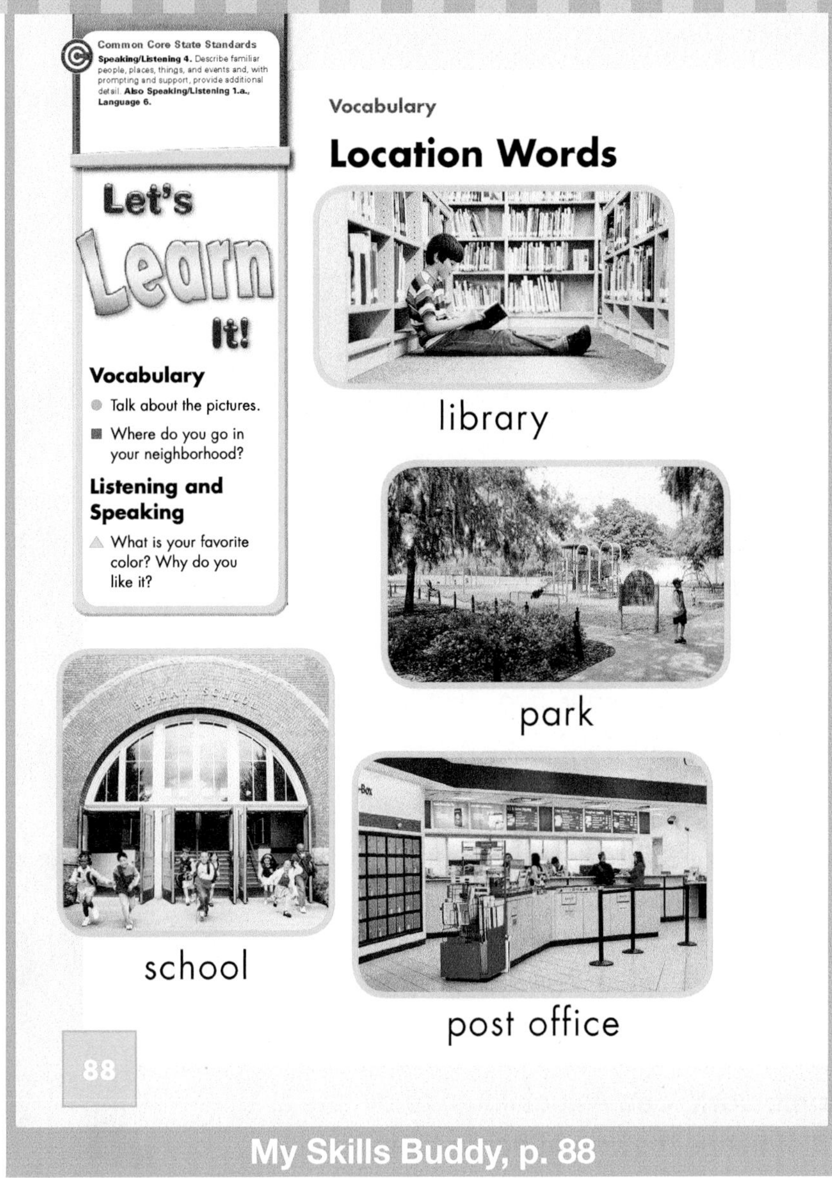

Common Core State Standards
Speaking/Listening 4. Describe familiar people, places, things, and events and, with prompting and support, provide additional detail. **Also Speaking/Listening 1.a., Language 6.**

Let's Learn It!

Vocabulary

- Talk about the pictures.
- Where do you go in your neighborhood?

Listening and Speaking

- What is your favorite color? Why do you like it?

Vocabulary

Location Words

library

park

school

post office

88

My Skills Buddy, p. 88

Vocabulary

Location Words

TEACH Have children turn to p. 88 of *My Skills Buddy.* Use the first Vocabulary bullet to guide discussion about location words, or words that tell about places. Point to each picture and tell children about the place.

GUIDE PRACTICE Write the words *library, park, school,* and *post office* on the board. Point to each word as you read it.

Draw a picture of a book on the board and give children this clue: We check out books here. Have them tell which location word matches the picture and clue. (*library*) Continue with other pictures and clues.

ON THEIR OWN Have children take turns describing what happens at one of the locations. Other children can guess which location is being described.

Access for All

SI Strategic Intervention

Build Vocabulary Take children on a picture walk through *Miss Bindergarten Takes a Field Trip.* Have them identify pictures of the location words *library, park, school,* and *post office.*

VOCABULARY ACQUISITION AND USE

Learning about location words, or names of places in a community, helps children understand the relationships among words in a category as well as expand their vocabulary by using frequently occurring nouns.

Access Vocabulary Ask children to tell the words for each of the locations in their home languages. Point out any cognates, such as *parque* (Spanish) and *park* or *escola* (Portuguese) and *school.*

Common Core State Standards

Speaking/Listening 2. Confirm understanding of a text read aloud or information presented orally or through other media by asking and answering questions about key details and requesting clarification if something is not understood. **Language 5.c.** Identify real-life connections between words and their use (e.g., note places at school that are *colorful*). **Also Speaking/Listening 1., 1.b., 5.**

Wrap Up Your Day!

✓ **Content Knowledge** Today we read about a field trip to different places around the community. Where does the class go? Help children list some answers to the question.

✓ **Phonemic Awareness** Tell children you will say three words. Say: *feather, hammer, five.* Do all of these words begin with the same sound? (no) Which words begin with the same sound? (*feather, five*)

✓ **Vocabulary Skill** Tell me about our location words. In which location can we buy stamps? In which location do we learn and play? Where can we check out books? Where can we play an outdoor game?

✓ **Homework Idea** Ask children to dictate a list of things they do at home tonight.

Preview DAY 3

Tomorrow we will read a story about Cat and Dog.

Extend Your Day!

Social Studies
Who Am I?

COMMUNITY HELPERS Review with children the different types of community helpers they read about in *Miss Bindergarten Takes a Field Trip.* Ask these questions:

- Who delivers all of our mail?
- Who keeps us safe in busy traffic?
- Who helps us learn new things?
- Who finds exciting books for us to read?
- What other kinds of community helpers are there?

Discuss examples of other community helpers, such as artists, musicians, politicians, custodians, police officers, transportation workers, and park rangers.

Have pairs of children choose a community helper and act out a short scene showing what he or she does. Children can make props to enhance the dramatization. Pairs can take turns presenting the scene to the class. Classmates can guess the name of the community helper.

Listening and Speaking
My Favorite Things

TELL ABOUT FAVORITE THINGS Ask children to think of several things they like best, such as their favorite color, food, animal, book, and game. Then have children take turns telling about themselves by describing two or three of their favorite things and telling why they like those things best. Model for children. My favorite color is blue. I like blue because it is the color of my eyes. My favorite food is cheese. I like to put cheese on almost everything. If necessary, prompt children to give more details by asking questions. Make sure all children get a chance to talk.

Comprehension
Classify and Categorize

LOUD AND SOFT SOUNDS Looking through *Miss Bindergarten Takes a Field Trip* with the class, have children dictate a list of sounds the kindergarten class might hear while they are on their field trip. Divide the list into two categories, *Loud* and *Soft.* Divide the class into two groups and have them act out the sounds. Talk about why some sounds need to be loud, such as a fire engine siren. Ask why some sounds need to be soft, such as asking a question at the library.

DAY 3 at a Glance

Content Knowledge
Oral Vocabulary

Phonemic Awareness
Initial Sounds

Letter Recognition
Letters *Ww* and *Xx*

Text-Based Comprehension
Classify and Categorize

Conventions
Review What We Look Like

Writing
Instructions

Listening and Speaking
Talk About Me

Materials

- Student Edition
- Truckery Rhymes
- Talk with Me/Sing with Me Chart
- Picture Cards
- Alphabet Cards
- Reader's and Writer's Notebook
- Student Reader K.1.4
- Big Book

Common Core State Standards

Speaking/Listening 1.a. Follow agreed-upon rules for discussions (e.g., listening to others and taking turns speaking about the topics and texts under discussion). **Language 6.** Use words and phrases acquired through conversations, reading and being read to, and responding to texts. **Also Language 4., 4.a.**

TRUCKTOWN on Reading Street

Start your engines!

Display p. 8 of *Truckery Rhymes.* Do you know the original "Mary Had a Little Lamb"? Recite it first, and then have children say it with you:

Mary had a little lamb,
Little lamb, little lamb.
Mary had a little lamb,
Its fleece was white as snow!

Truckery Rhymes

Content Knowledge

Zoom in on ©

People Working Together in a Community

On the board, write the Question of the Week, *How do people in a community cooperate?* Read the question as you track the print. Talk with children about how people help their communities. Remind children to speak clearly and to take turns speaking.

Build Oral Language

LISTEN FOR AMAZING WORDS Display Sing with Me Chart 4B. Remind children that yesterday they sang "On a Field Trip We Go" and listened for the words *bakery* and *fire station.* Today we are going to listen for the Amazing Words *park* and *post office.* Sing the song several times to the tune of "Oh, A-Hunting We Will Go." Have children sing along with you and clap when they say the Amazing Word *park* or *post office.*

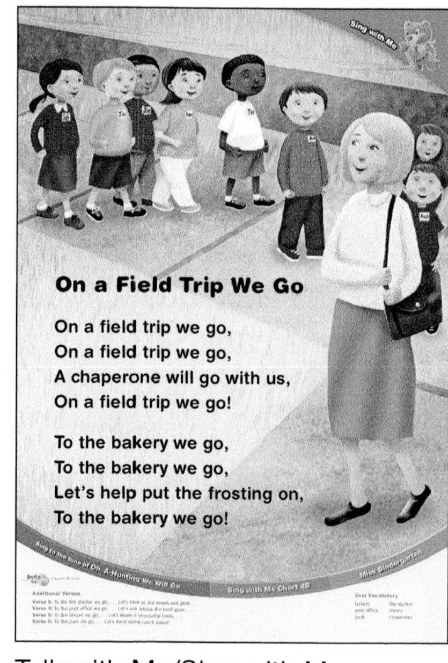
On a Field Trip We Go
On a field trip we go,
On a field trip we go,
A chaperone will go with us,
On a field trip we go!
To the bakery we go,
To the bakery we go,
Let's help put the frosting on,
To the bakery we go!

Talk with Me/Sing with Me Chart 4B

Build Oral Vocabulary

Amazing Words Robust Vocabulary Routine

1. **Introduce the Word** A *park* usually has trees, gardens, and open spaces where people can have picnics or play games. What's our new Amazing Word for an open space for people to have picnics or play games? Say it with me: *park.*

2. **Demonstrate** Provide examples to show meaning. *We can fly a kite at the park.*

   Repeat steps 1 and 2.

   Introduce the Word A *post office* is a place where people buy stamps and mail letters and packages. What's our new Amazing Word for a place that sells stamps and mails letters and packages? Say it with me: *post office.*

   Demonstrate *Rob is going to the post office to buy stamps.*

3. **Apply** Have children use *park* and *post office* in complete sentences. Have them illustrate their sentences.

4. **Display the Words** Have children point to and name letters in *park* and *post office* that they recognize. Ask them what they notice about the first letter in *park* and *post.*

Routines Flip Chart

USE AMAZING WORDS To reinforce the concept and the Amazing Words, have children supply the appropriate Amazing Word for each sentence.

> **We go to the ______ to play.** (park)
> **I mail my letter at the ______.** (post office)

MULTIPLE-MEANING WORDS Remind children that some words can mean more than one thing. You know that the word *park* means "an open space for people to have picnics or play games." *Park* can also mean "to put in a certain place," as in *park a car.* Use both meanings of the word in sentences and help children decide which meaning is being used.

Amazing Words

bakery	fire station
park	post office
library	chaperone

Access for All

 Strategic Intervention

Sentence Production If children have difficulty supplying an Amazing Word for a sentence frame, model saying the complete sentence and have children repeat it after you.

Visual Support Use the pictures on Talk with Me Chart 4A to help children complete the Amazing Word sentences.

Expand Vocabulary Use the Day 3 instruction on ELL Poster 4 to expand children's understanding of vocabulary connected to the lesson concepts.

Common Core State Standards

Foundational Skills 2.d. Isolate and pronounce the initial, medial vowel, and final sounds (phonemes) in three-phoneme (consonant-vowel-consonant, or CVC) words.* (This does not include CVCs ending with /l/, /r/, or /x/.) **Also Foundational Skills 2., 2.a., 2.b., 2.c., 2.e.**

Phonemic Awareness

Initial Sounds

REVIEW INITIAL SOUNDS Display the *wolf* Picture Card. This is a wolf. What sound does *wolf* start with? Repeat the routine with the *web* Picture Card.

Picture Card

MODEL What is the first sound in *watermelon?* Say it with me: /w/ /w/ /w/, *watermelon.* What is the first sound in *violet?* Listen carefully: /v/ /v/ /v/, *violet.* Does *violet* begin with the same sound as *watermelon?* Continue comparing initial sounds with the *wagon, vase, van,* and *waffle* Picture Cards.

Picture Card

GUIDE PRACTICE Place three Picture Cards in a row: *carrot, fan, five.* Say the picture names with me. Which one starts with a different sound? Which ones start with the same sound? What is that sound? Repeat the routine with the *rabbit, hat,* and *rock* Picture Cards.

REVIEW SYLLABLES How many syllables are in the word *watermelon?* Listen carefully: *wa-ter-me-lon.* Now clap with me: *wa-ter-me-lon.* Have children practice clapping to the syllables of *x-ray, wagon,* and *waffle.*

BLEND ONSET AND RIME Listen as I say the beginning sound and the ending part of a word: /w/ *-eb*, /w/ *-eb*. What is the word? The word is /w/ *-eb*, *web*. Continue blending onsets and rimes using the words *wet, six,* and *wax*.

Corrective feedback	**If...** children cannot blend sounds together to make a word, **then...** model blending the sounds together to make the word and have children echo you.

REVIEW RHYMING WORDS Remind children that rhyming words have the same middle and ending sounds. Listen to these words: *cat, mat, can.* Which of these words rhyme? Which of these words have the same middle and ending sounds? Listen again: *cat, mat, can. Cat* and *mat* have the same middle and ending sounds. Continue the routine with the following words: *fan, pin, pan; leg, log, dog.*

Access for All

 Advanced

Phonemic Awareness Say a word followed by a beginning sound, such as *tan,* /m/. Have children practice forming rhyming words by replacing the beginning sound of the word with the given new sound: /m/ *-an, man.*

Support Phonemic Awareness
Before beginning the Phonemic Awareness activities, make sure children understand the meanings of these Picture Card words: *wolf, web, wagon, vase, van, waffle.* Encourage children to say the words several times and listen to their pronunciations.

Common Core State Standards

Foundational Skills 1.d. Recognize and name all upper- and lowercase letters of the alphabet.

Letter Recognition

Teach/Model

Letters *Ww* and *Xx*

Alphabet Card

Alphabet Card

INTRODUCE Display the *Ww* Alphabet Card and point to the uppercase *W.* The name of this letter is uppercase *W.* What is the name of this letter? (uppercase *W*) Point to the lowercase *w.* This is the lowercase *w.* What is the name of this letter? (lowercase *w*) Point out that uppercase *W* and lowercase *w* look alike except for their difference in size. Display the *Xx* Alphabet Card and repeat the routine.

MODEL Point to the watermelon on the *Ww* Alphabet Card. This is a *watermelon.* Write the word *watermelon* on the board and point to the *w.* This letter is lowercase *w.* *Watermelon* begins with lowercase *w.* Repeat the routine with *x-ray* on the *Xx* Alphabet Card.

Guide Practice

GROUP PRACTICE Write these phrases in a list on the board: *Walt's watch, Wanda's wigs, Wendy's wagon.* Ask a child to find and circle an uppercase *W.* Continue until all forms of *Ww* have been circled.

ON THEIR OWN Use *Reader's and Writer's Notebook,* p. 43, for additional practice with letters *Ww* and *Xx.* Return to this page on Day 4 to practice *Yy* and *Zz.*

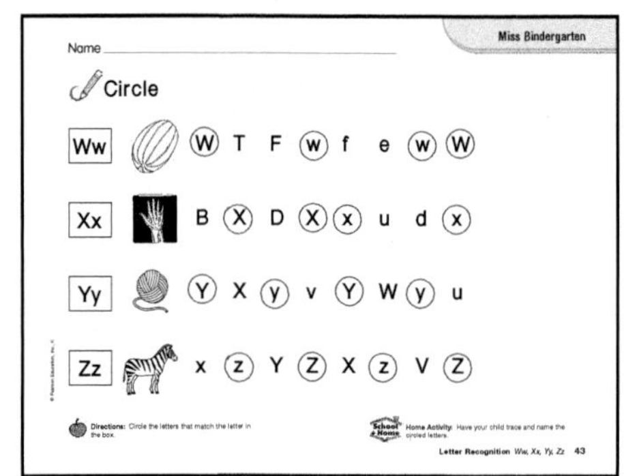

Name

Miss Bindergarten

Circle

Ww W T F w f e w W

Xx B X D X x u d x

Yy Y X y v Y W y u

Zz x z Y Z X z V Z

Reader's and Writer's Notebook, p. 43

REVIEW LETTER RECOGNITION Display the *Vv* Alphabet Card. The name of this letter is *v*. What is the name of this letter? Review the following Alphabet Cards: *Ww, Xx, Tt, Uu.*

Alphabet Card

REVIEW HIGH-FREQUENCY WORDS Write *the* on the board. This is the word *the.* What is this word? Continue the routine with *little, I,* and *am.*

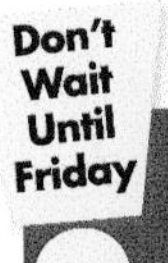

MONITOR PROGRESS Check Word Reading High-Frequency Words

FORMATIVE ASSESSMENT Write *I, am, the,* and *little* on the board. Have children take turns reading the words.

If... children cannot read the high-frequency words,
then... practice naming the letters and reading the words.

If... children can successfully read the high-frequency words,
then... have them read Kindergarten Student Reader K.1.4, *Cat and Dog Ride To Town.*

Access for All

Strategic Intervention

Letter Recognition Have children work in pairs to review the letters *Tt, Uu, Vv, Ww,* and *Xx.* Write the letters on flash cards. Have the first child display the flash card for his or her partner who then says the letter name aloud.

Access Vocabulary Point to the rebus words in Kindergarten Student Reader K.1.4, *Cat and Dog Ride To Town.* Define the words, and have children share those words in their home languages.

 **Common Core State Standards**

Literature 10. Actively engage in group reading activities with purpose and understanding. **Foundational Skills 3.c.** Read common high-frequency words by sight. (e.g., *the, of, to, you, she, my, is, are, do, does*).

Access for All

SI Strategic Intervention

High-Frequency Words Ask children to point out the person or thing that is called *I* in each picture.

Student Reader

Read *Cat and Dog Ride To Town*

REVIEW Review the previously taught high-frequency words. Have children read each word as you point to it on the Word Wall: *I, am, the, little.*

TEACH REBUS WORDS Write the word *bus* on the board. This is the word *bus.* Name the letters with me: *b, u, s, bus.* Repeat with *library, school, music store, firefighter, vet,* and *happy.* Look for these words in the story we read today. There will be a picture above the word to help you read it.

READ Display Kindergarten Student Reader K.1.4. Today we are going to read a new book. Point to the title of the book. The title of this book is *Cat and Dog Ride To Town.* The author is Najeeb Khan. Take children on a picture walk through the book. Look at the pictures. What do you think will happen in this story?

Use the reading decodable books routine to read the Kindergarten Student Reader.

Routine Reading Decodable Books

1. **Read Silently** Have children whisper read the book page by page as you listen in.
2. **Model Fluent Reading** Have children finger point as you read a page. Then have them reread the page without you.
3. **Read Chorally** Have children finger point as they chorally read the page. Continue reading page by page, repeating steps 1 and 2.
4. **Read Individually** Have children take turns reading aloud a page.
5. **Reread and Monitor Progress** As you listen to individual children reread, monitor progress and provide support.
6. **Reread with a Partner** Have children reread the book page by page with a partner.

Routines Flip Chart

Kindergarten Student Reader K.1.4

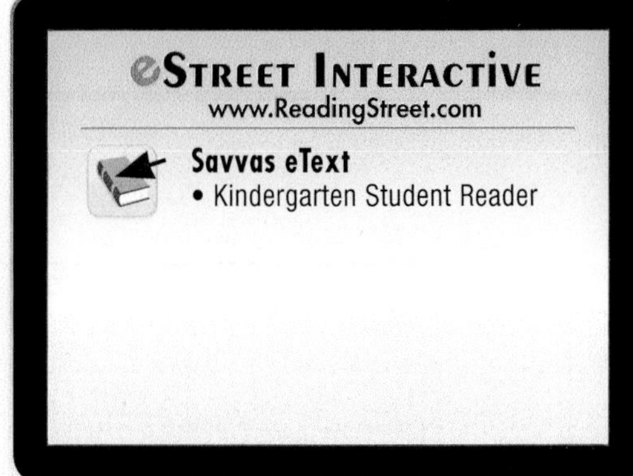

eStreet Interactive
www.ReadingStreet.com

Savvas eText
- Kindergarten Student Reader

Day 3 SMALL GROUP TIME • Differentiate Vocabulary, p. SG•55

OL On-Level
- **Develop Vocabulary** Practice Location Words
- **Read** Student Reader *Cat and Dog Ride To Town*

SI Strategic Intervention
- **Develop Vocabulary** Reteach Location Words
- **Read** Student Reader *Cat and Dog Ride To Town*

A Advanced
- **Develop Vocabulary** More Location Words
- **Read** Student Reader *Cat and Dog Ride To Town*

Place English Language Learners in the groups that correspond to their reading abilities in English.

If... children need more scaffolding and practice with **Vocabulary, then...** use the ELL activities on p. DI•65 in the Teacher Resources section of the Digital Path.

Text-Based Comprehension

Read Main Selection

RETELL THE SELECTION Have children turn to p. 86 of *My Skills Buddy* and use the retelling boxes to retell the story *Miss Bindergarten Takes a Field Trip.*

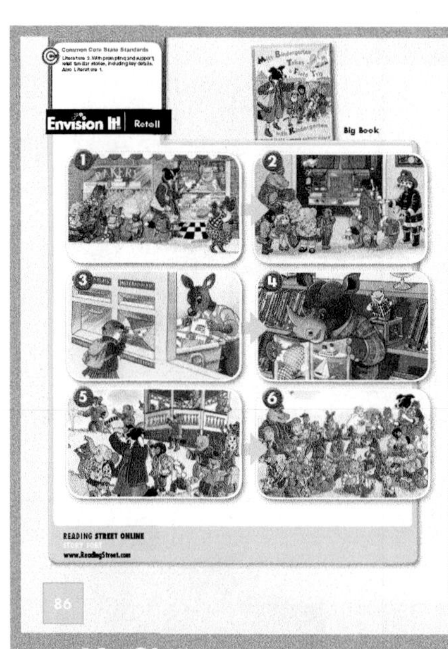
My Skills Buddy, p. 86

Direct children to the first retelling box. First, Miss Bindergarten's class goes to the bakery. Where do they go next?

Continue reviewing the retelling boxes and having children retell the story.

REVIEW CLASSIFY AND CATEGORIZE Display illustrations in *Miss Bindergarten Takes a Field Trip.* Let's group the places that the class visits in *Miss Bindergarten Takes a Field Trip.*

- Which places that the class visits sell things? (bakery, post office)
- Which places that the class visits provide services for the people in the community? (fire station, post office, library, park)
- Which of these places do we have in our community?

MORE PRACTICE Use *Reader's and Writer's Notebook,* p. 44, for additional practice with classify and categorize.

Common Core State Standards

Literature 2. With prompting and support, retell familiar stories, including key details. **Language 5.a.** Sort common objects into categories (e.g., shapes, foods) to gain a sense of the concepts the categories represent.

Access for All

SI Strategic Intervention

Review Genre Remind children that *Miss Bindergarten Takes a Field Trip* is an animal fantasy. Page through the book and have children discuss aspects of the story that make it an animal fantasy.

Bridge to Common Core

CRAFT AND STRUCTURE

When children retell the story, they are analyzing how the parts of the story relate to each other and to the whole. Reading the story to children a second time and using the Develop Vocabulary notes to ask them questions about text vocabulary will help children learn how to interpret words and phrases in a text.

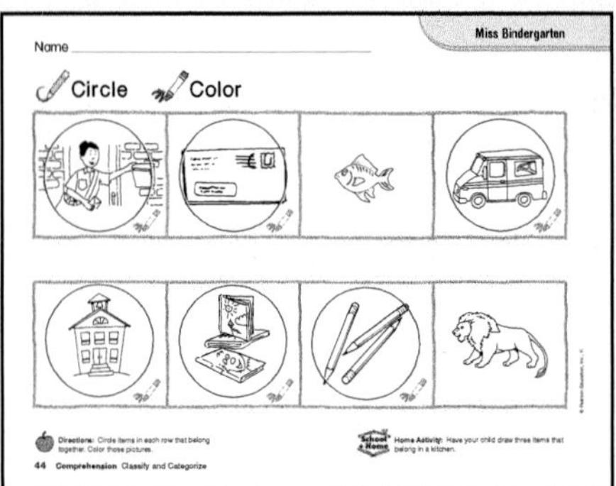

Reader's and Writer's Notebook, p. 44

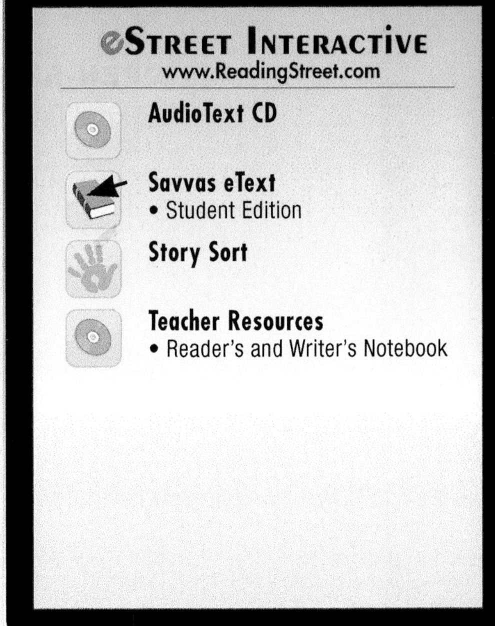

Access Main Selection

READER AND TASK SUGGESTIONS	
Preparing to Read the Text	**Leveled Tasks**
• Review the Amazing Words and have children use them to talk about the selection. • Review the various shapes in the story and their names.	• **Theme and Knowledge Demands** If children need help with key details of the field trip, have them page through the book and tell what the community workers at the bakery, fire station, post office, and library do. • **Structure** If children will not have difficulty with the story format, have them read the names of the characters that begin with a colored letter. What pattern can they find?

See Text Complexity Measures for *Miss Bindergarten Takes a Field Trip* on the tab at the beginning of this week.

READ Reread *Miss Bindergarten Takes a Field Trip.* Follow the **2nd Read** beginning on p. 364, and use the **Develop Vocabulary** notes to prompt conversations about the story.

Routine Read for Understanding

Deepen understanding by reading the selection multiple times.

1. **First Read**—Read the entire selection aloud to build interest in the text.
2. **Second Read**—Use the **Develop Vocabulary** notes on pages 364–383.
3. **Third Read**—Use the **Develop Comprehension** notes on pages 364–383.

Access Content Review the following terms with children: *classify and categorize*—to place things or ideas that are alike in at least one way into groups; *alike*—the same or similar.

2ND READ

Develop Vocabulary

OPEN-ENDED This is Miss Bindergarten's kindergarten class. What kind of animal is Miss Bindergarten? (a dog)

- Miss Bindergarten is a dog. What kinds of animals are the kindergarteners?

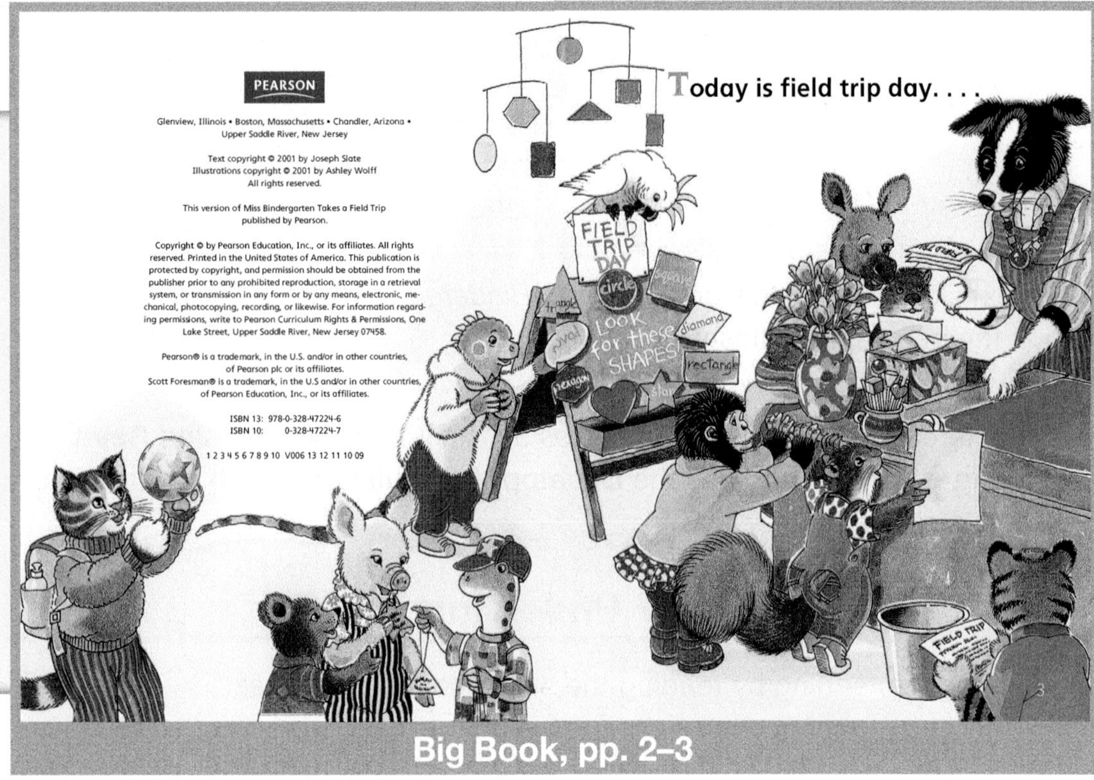

Glenview, Illinois • Boston, Massachusetts • Chandler, Arizona • Upper Saddle River, New Jersey

Text copyright © 2001 by Joseph Slate
Illustrations copyright © 2001 by Ashley Wolff
All rights reserved.

This version of Miss Bindergarten Takes a Field Trip published by Pearson.

Copyright © by Pearson Education, Inc., or its affiliates. All rights reserved. Printed in the United States of America. This publication is protected by copyright, and permission should be obtained from the publisher prior to any prohibited reproduction, storage in a retrieval system, or transmission in any form or by any means, electronic, mechanical, photocopying, recording, or likewise. For information regarding permissions, write to Pearson Curriculum Rights & Permissions, One Lake Street, Upper Saddle River, New Jersey 07458.

Pearson® is a trademark, in the U.S. and/or in other countries, of Pearson plc or its affiliates.
Scott Foresman® is a trademark, in the U.S and/or in other countries, of Pearson Education, Inc., or its affiliates.

ISBN 13: 978-0-328-47224-6
ISBN 10: 0-328-47224-7

1 2 3 4 5 6 7 8 9 10 V006 13 12 11 10 09

Big Book, pp. 2–3

3RD READ

Develop Comprehension ©

***WH-* QUESTION** What are the shapes Miss Bindergarten's class is supposed to look for? (triangles, circles, squares, diamonds, rectangles, stars, hearts, hexagons, and ovals)

WH- QUESTION How is Adam's parent helping Miss Bindergarten's class? (He is a chaperone.)

- Adam's dad and another parent are chaperones. Who is the other chaperone on this field trip?

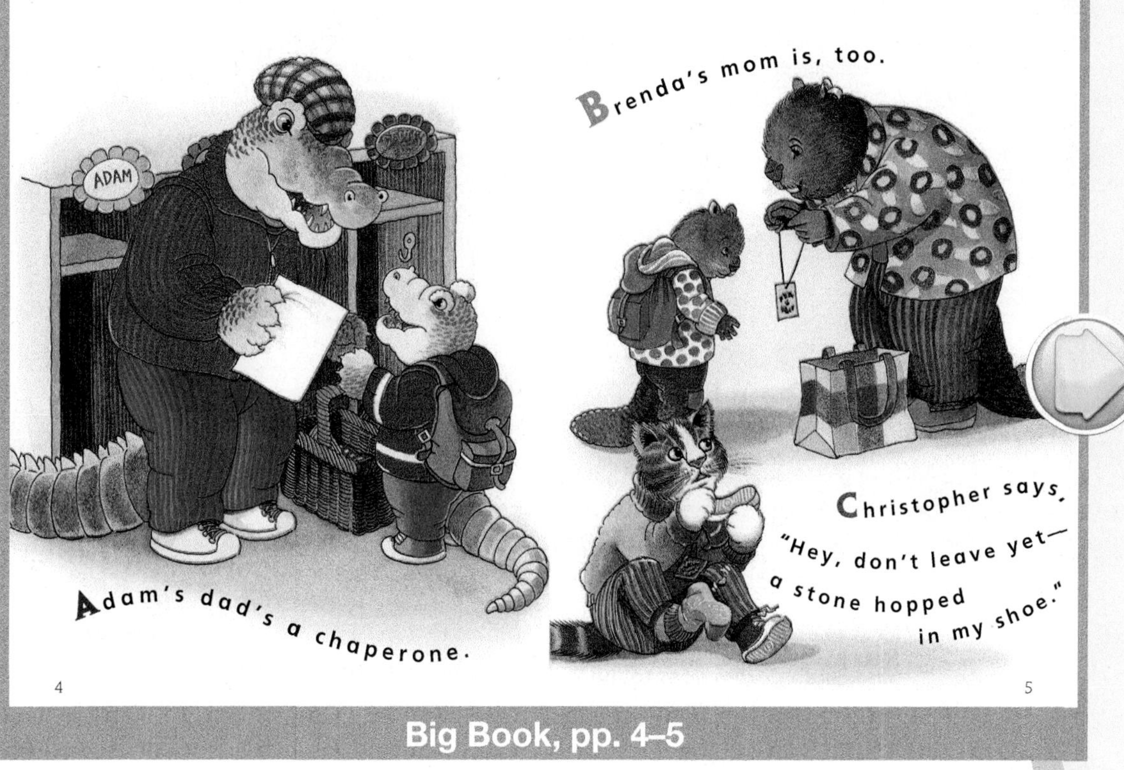

Big Book, pp. 4–5

INFERENCE Why do you think Miss Bindergarten needs chaperones to help her on the field trip? (I think she needs chaperones because she has many children to take care of on the field trip, more than she can take care of alone.)

Common Core State Standards

Literature 1. With prompting and support, ask and answer questions about key details in a text.
Literature 3. With prompting and support, identify characters, settings, and major events in a story.
Literature 7. With prompting and support, describe the relationship between illustrations and the story in which they appear (e.g., what moment in a story an illustration depicts).

2ND READ

Develop Vocabulary

***WH*- QUESTION** Where is the kindergarten class now? (at the bakery)

- The children are at the bakery. What kinds of food does the bakery sell?

DEVELOP VOCABULARY kindergarten

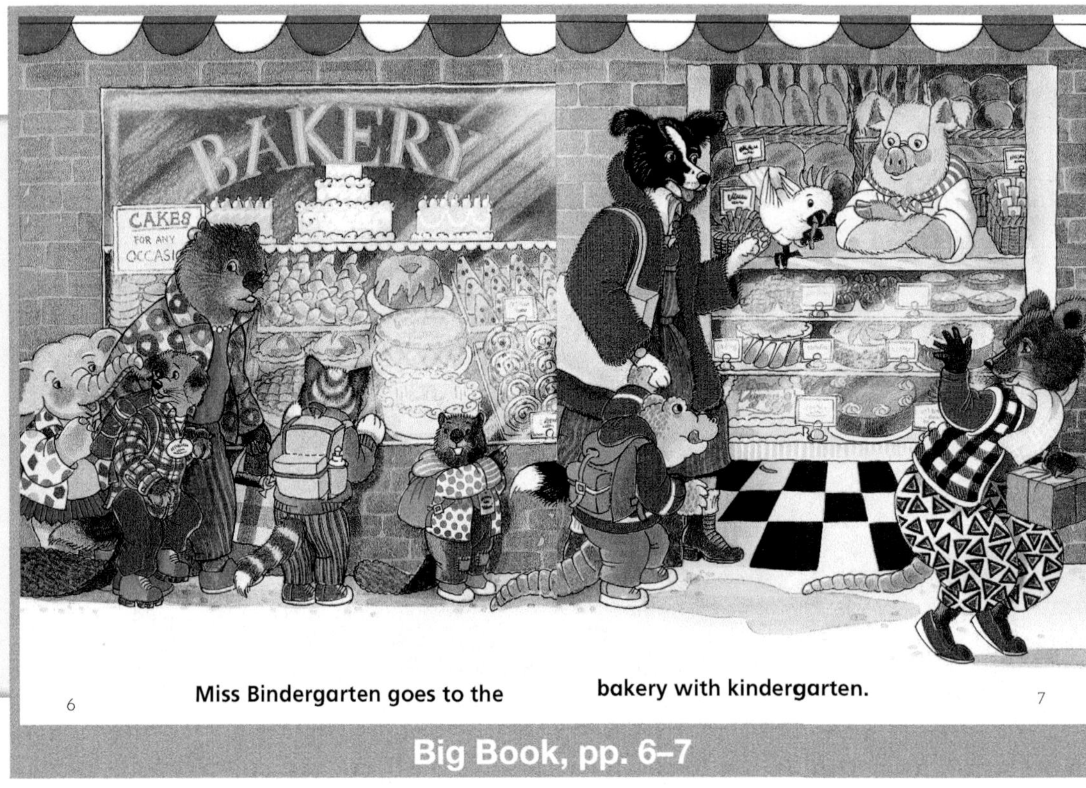

Big Book, pp. 6–7

3RD READ

Develop Comprehension ©

CLASSIFY AND CATEGORIZE How are the foods in these pictures alike? (They are all sold at the bakery. They are all made at the bakery.)

***WH*- QUESTION** The children are in the bakery. What are they making? (cookies and cakes)

- The children are making cookies and cakes. What different shapes do you see?

EXPAND VOCABULARY scrumptious

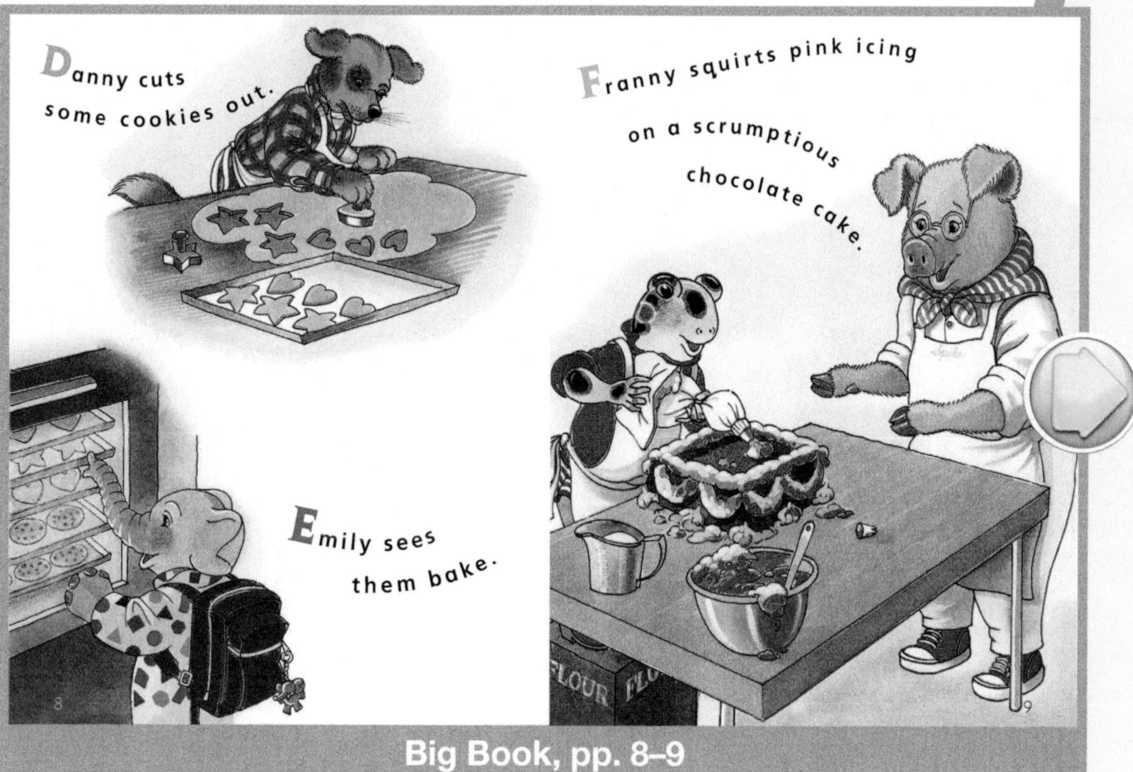

Big Book, pp. 8–9

INFERENCE How is Franny helping the baker? (She is decorating one of his cakes with icing.)

Common Core State Standards

Literature 1. With prompting and support, ask and answer questions about key details in a text.
Literature 3. With prompting and support, identify characters, settings, and major events in a story.
Literature 7. With prompting and support, describe the relationship between illustrations and the story in which they appear (e.g., what moment in a story an illustration depicts).

2ND READ

Develop Vocabulary

WH- QUESTION Where does Miss Bindergarten take the class next? (to the fire station)

- Miss Bindergarten takes the class to the fire station next. What special clothing is the firefighter wearing?

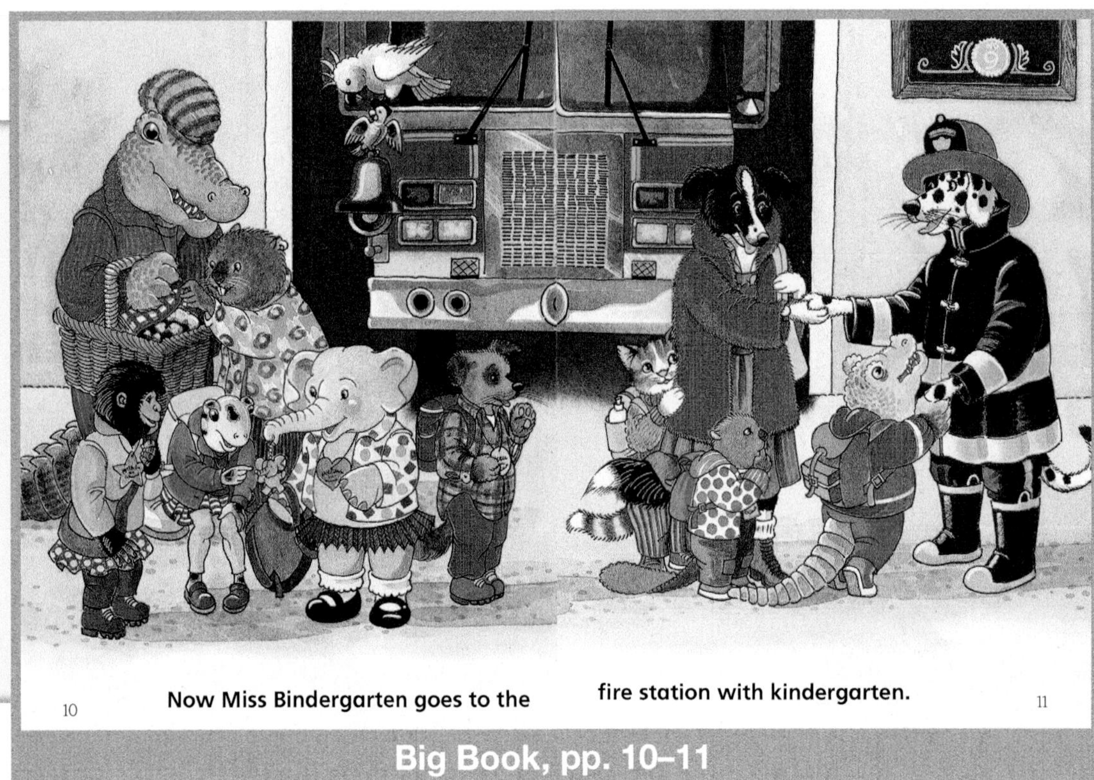

10
Now Miss Bindergarten goes to the
fire station with kindergarten.
11

Big Book, pp. 10–11

3RD READ

Develop Comprehension ©

OPEN-ENDED How can you tell that Miss Bindergarten's class is now at the fire station? (I see a fire engine inside the building and a firefighter talking to Miss Bindergarten and her class.)

RECALL The children are in the fire station. What are they doing? (playing)

- The children are playing with things at the fire station. What are Gwen, Henry, and Ian playing with?

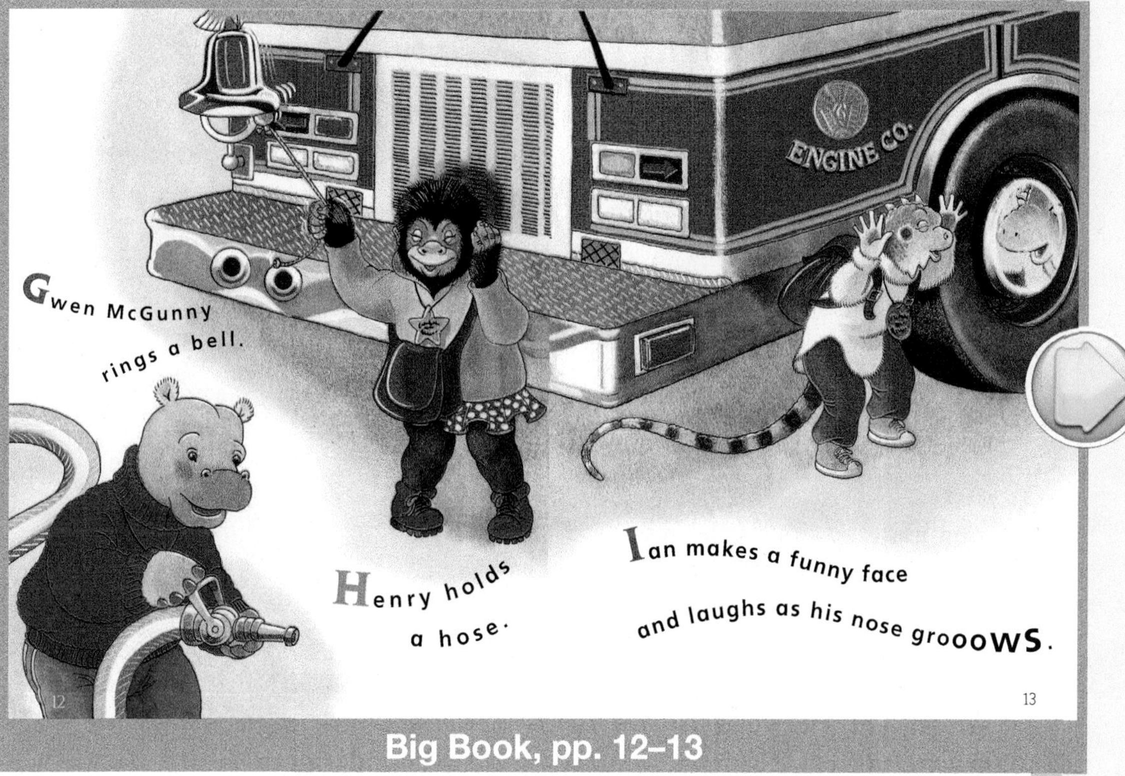

ENGINE CO.
Gwen McGunny rings a bell.
Henry holds a hose.
Ian makes a funny face and laughs as his nose grooows.
12
13

Big Book, pp. 12–13

INFERENCE Why does Ian laugh? (He makes a funny face at a shiny hubcap, and the shiny hubcap makes his nose look bigger and bigger.)

Common Core State Standards

Literature 1. With prompting and support, ask and answer questions about key details in a text.
Literature 3. With prompting and support, identify characters, settings, and major events in a story.
Literature 7. With prompting and support, describe the relationship between illustrations and the story in which they appear (e.g., what moment in a story an illustration depicts).

2ND READ

Develop Vocabulary

DISTANCING The children are learning about fire safety. What is Miss Bindergarten doing? (sliding down the pole)

- Firefighters wear special gear to protect themselves. What special gear do they wear? What are some things you wear to protect yourself?

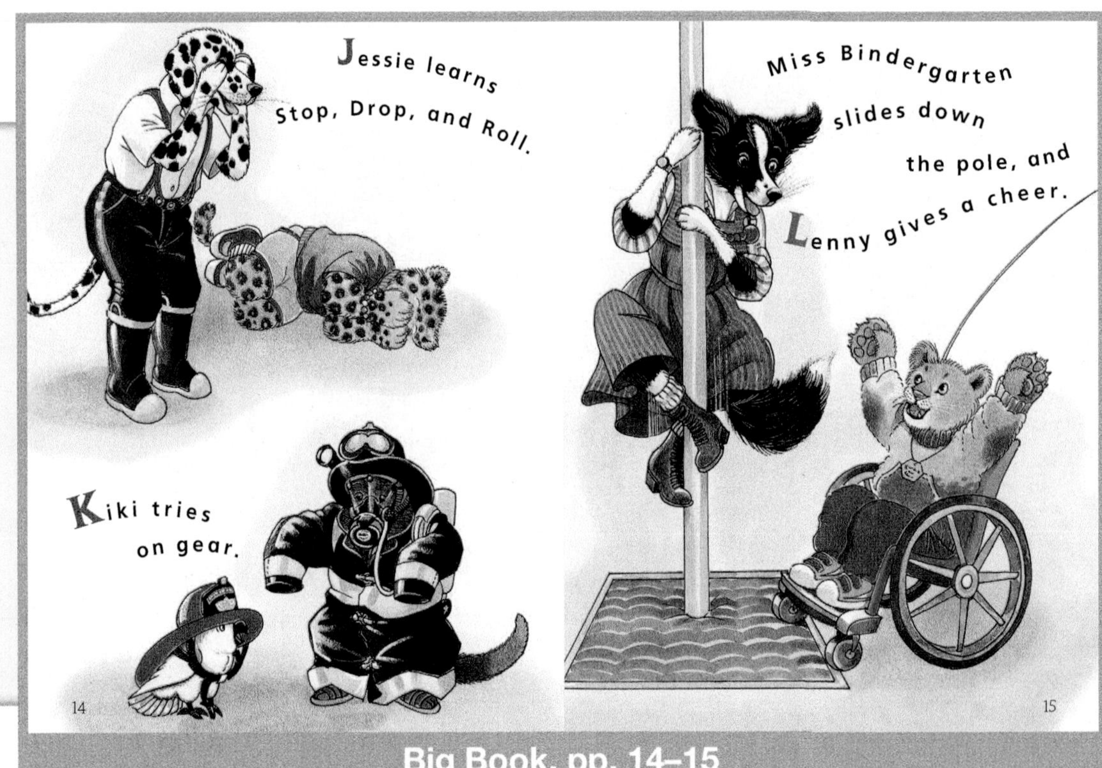

Big Book, pp. 14–15

3RD READ

Develop Comprehension ©

***WH-* QUESTION** What is Jessie learning how to do? (Jessie is learning how to Stop, Drop, and Roll.)

WH- QUESTION Where are the children going? (to the post office)

- The children are going to the post office. How many children are crossing the street?

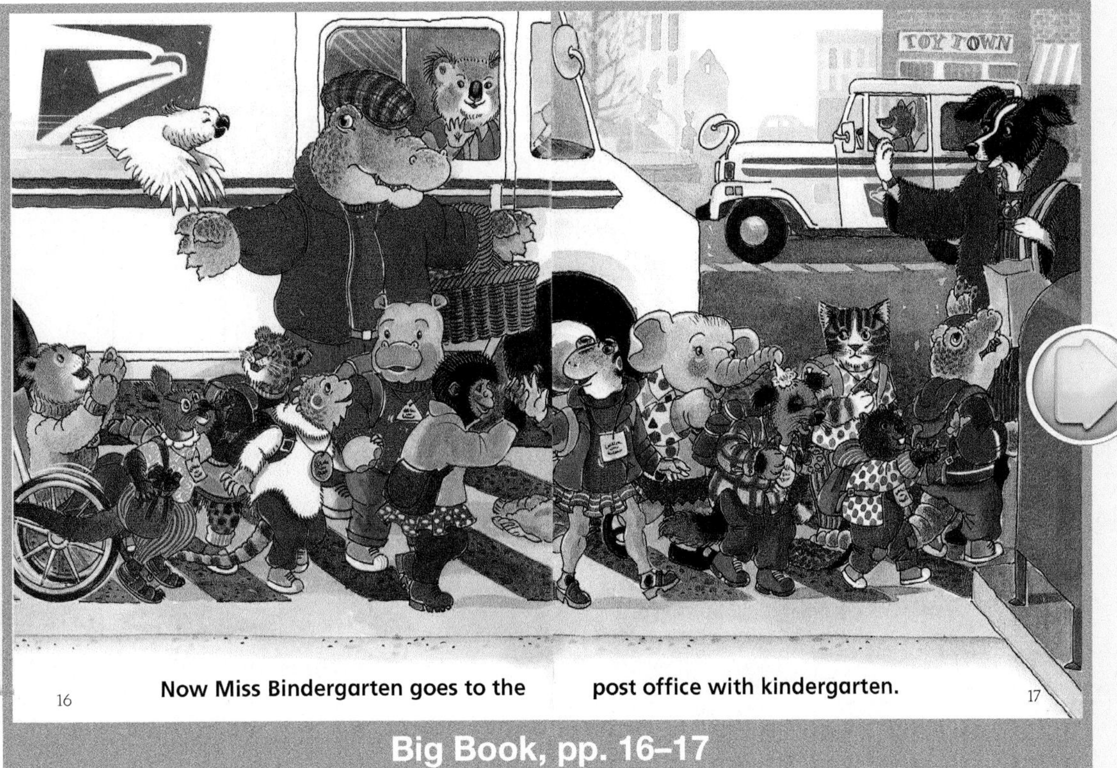

TOY TOWN
16
Now Miss Bindergarten goes to the
post office with kindergarten.
17

Big Book, pp. 16–17

OPEN-ENDED How is the chaperone helping Miss Bindergarten's class get to the post office? (The chaperone is helping the children cross the street safely.)

Common Core State Standards

Literature 1. With prompting and support, ask and answer questions about key details in a text.
Literature 3. With prompting and support, identify characters, settings, and major events in a story.
Literature 7. With prompting and support, describe the relationship between illustrations and the story in which they appear (e.g., what moment in a story an illustration depicts).

2ND READ

Develop Vocabulary

DISTANCING Point to Matty. What is Matty doing? (picking out stamps)

- Matty is picking out planet stamps. What other stamps do you see?

Big Book, pp. 18–19

3RD READ

Develop Comprehension ©

CLASSIFY AND CATEGORIZE How are Matty's, Noah's, and Ophelia's actions alike? (All three children are touching things. All three children are looking at things.)

OPEN-ENDED Point to Quentin. What is Quentin doing? (checking the scale)

- Quentin is using the scale to find out how much the big box weighs. What do you think will happen to the big box next?

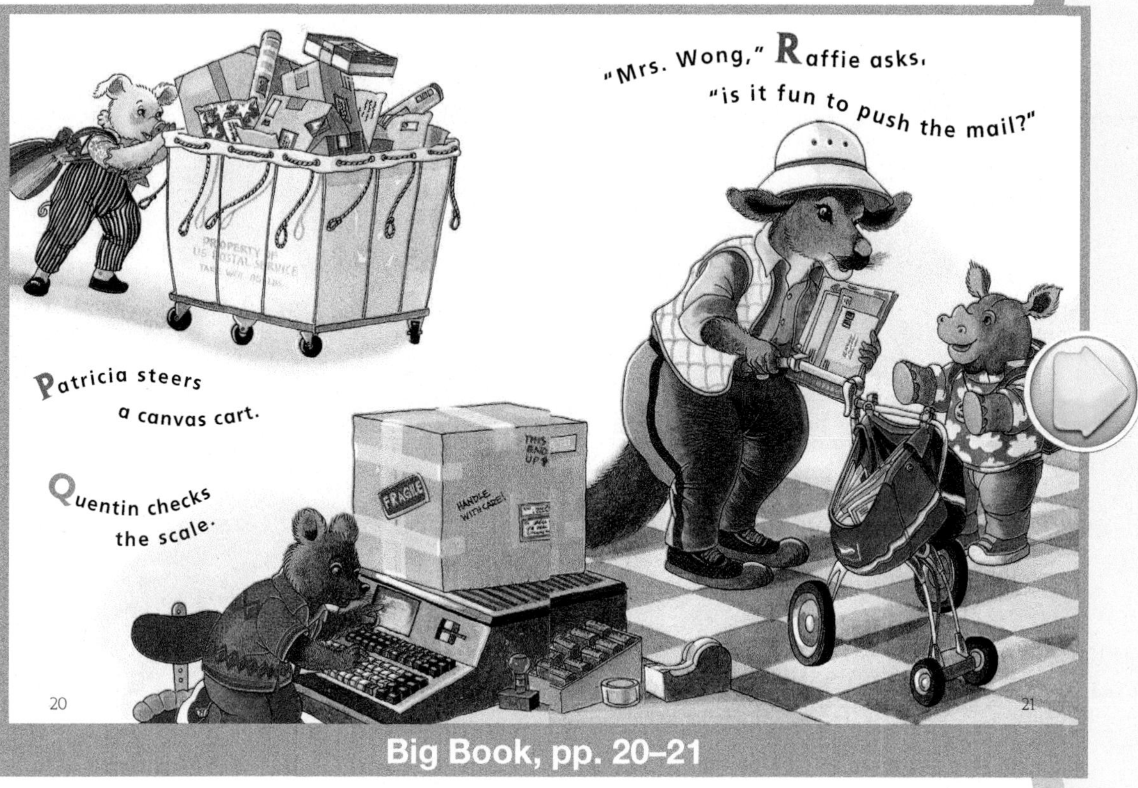

Big Book, pp. 20–21

INFERENCE How do you know that Mrs. Wong is a mail carrier? (Mrs. Wong is carrying mail, pushing mail in a cart, and wearing a mail carrier uniform.)

Common Core State Standards

Literature 1. With prompting and support, ask and answer questions about key details in a text. **Literature 3.** With prompting and support, identify characters, settings, and major events in a story. **Literature 7.** With prompting and support, describe the relationship between illustrations and the story in which they appear (e.g., what moment in a story an illustration depicts). **Also Literature 9.**

2ND READ

Develop Vocabulary

WH- QUESTION Where is Miss Bindergarten taking the kindergarteners? (to the library)

- Now the children are going to the library. There are many ways to get somewhere. What are some ways you see on these pages? What are other ways people get places?

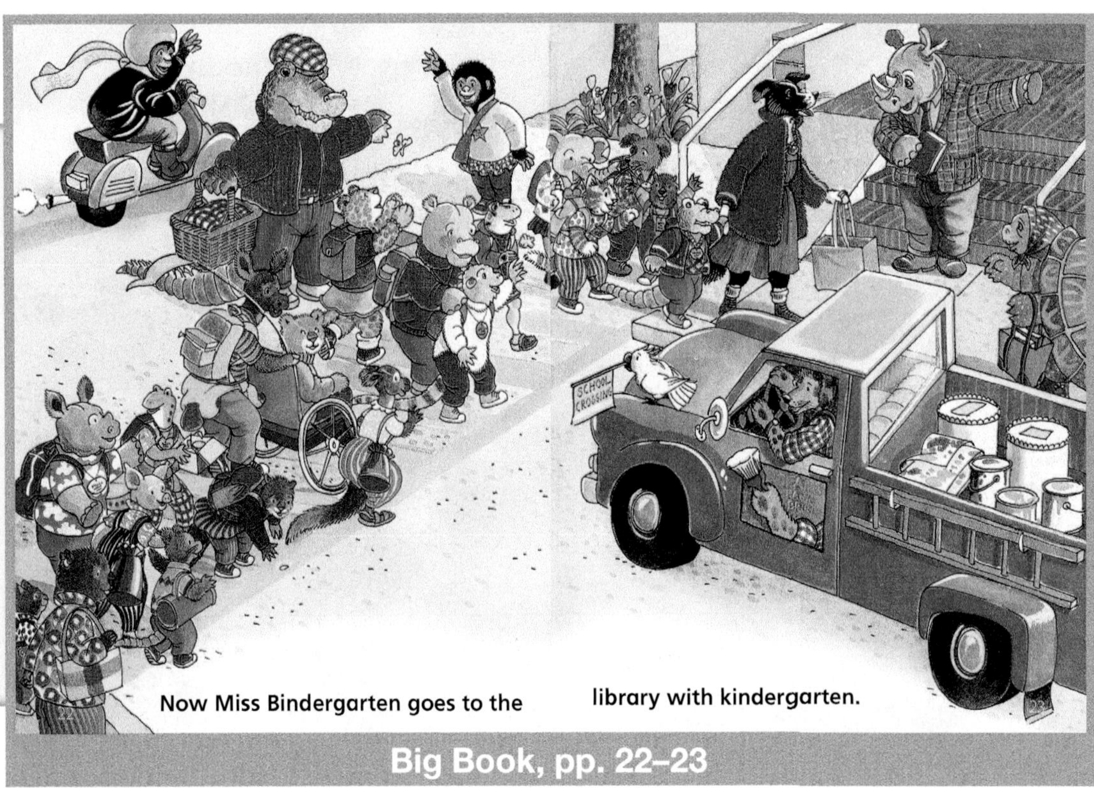

Now Miss Bindergarten goes to the
library with kindergarten.

Big Book, pp. 22–23

3RD READ

Develop Comprehension ©

WH- QUESTION How are the children getting to the library? (The children are walking across the street to get to the library.)

DISTANCING What do we find in libraries? (books)

- Libraries have books, magazines, DVDs, music CDs, and much more. This library has a computer to help people find things. What else can you do on a computer?

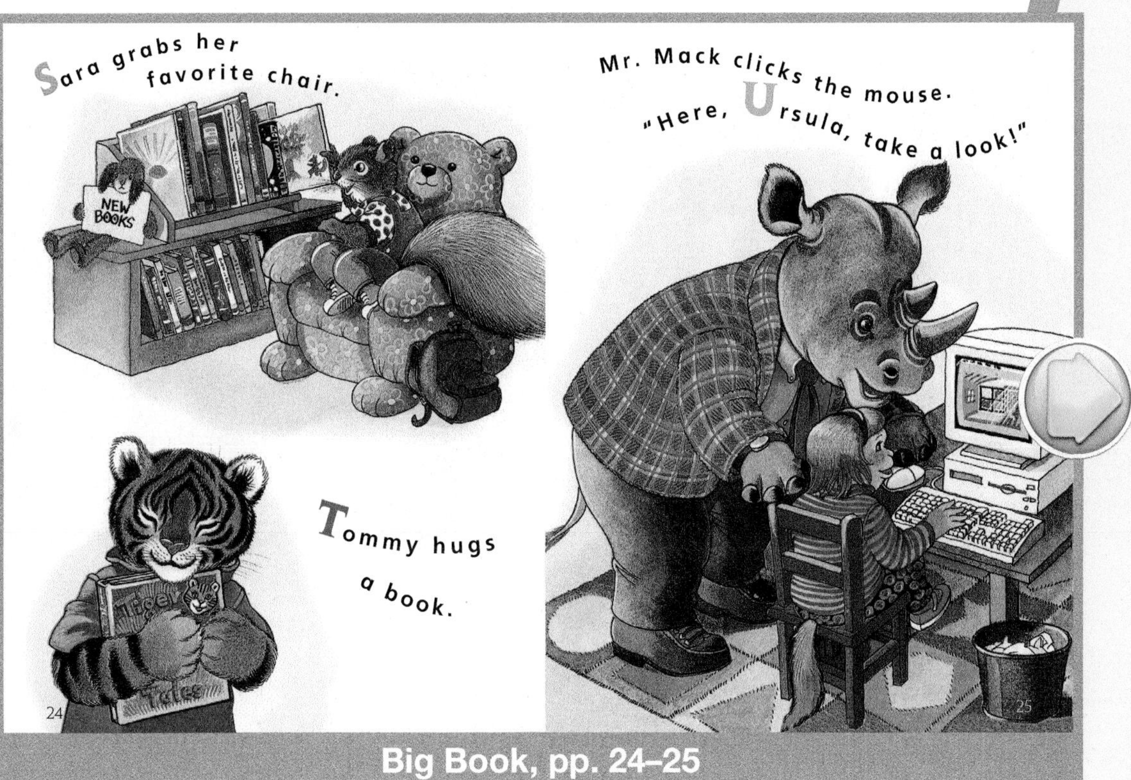

Big Book, pp. 24–25

INFERENCE Why do you think Tommy is hugging a book? (I think Tommy is hugging a book because he is happy about the book he found or because he just likes books.)

Common Core State Standards

Literature 1. With prompting and support, ask and answer questions about key details in a text. **Literature 3.** With prompting and support, identify characters, settings, and major events in a story. **Literature 7.** With prompting and support, describe the relationship between illustrations and the story in which they appear (e.g., what moment in a story an illustration depicts).

2ND READ

Develop Vocabulary

DISTANCING What shapes do you see on the rug? (hearts, triangles, circles, stars, diamonds, ovals, hexagons)

- There are hearts, triangles, and circles on the rug. What does our rug look like?

EXPAND VOCABULARY splendid

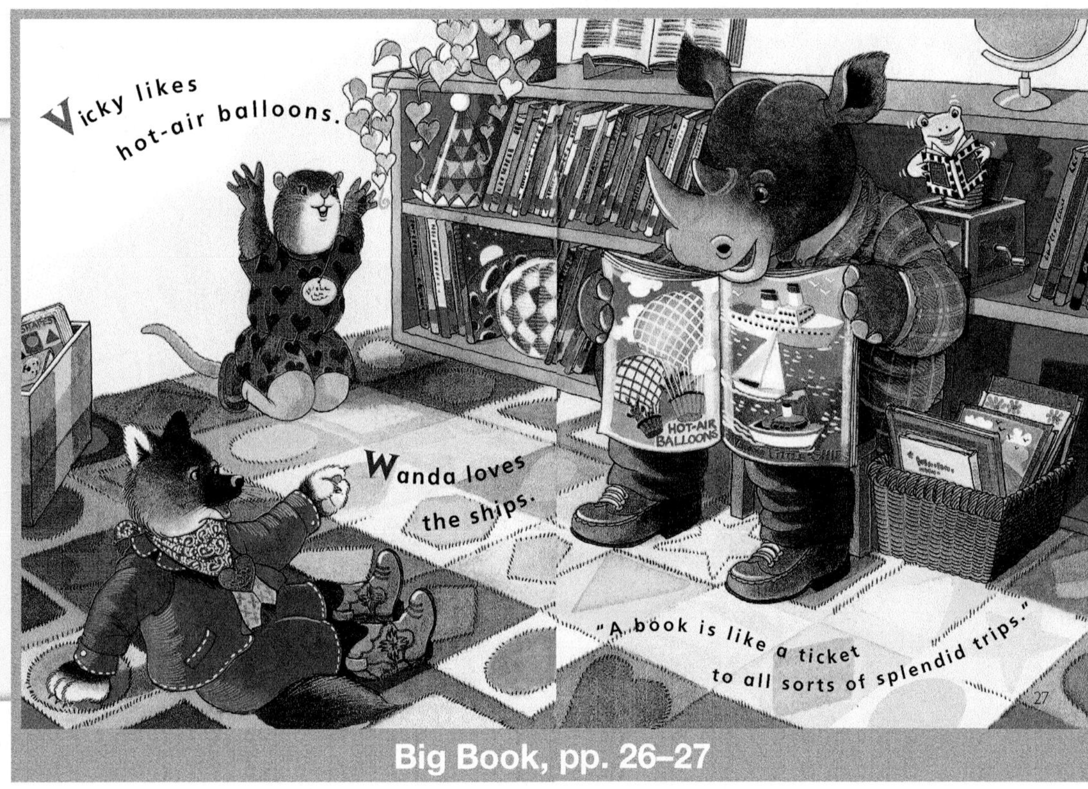

Big Book, pp. 26–27

3RD READ

Develop Comprehension ©

OPEN-ENDED What is the librarian doing in this picture? How can you tell? (The librarian is reading a book to the children. He is holding the book open so the children can see the pictures, and the children are reacting to what he is showing them.)

OPEN-ENDED Where is Miss Bindergarten taking the kindergarteners now? (to the park)

- Miss Bindergarten is taking the class to the park. Going to the park can be fun. What kinds of things can the children do there?

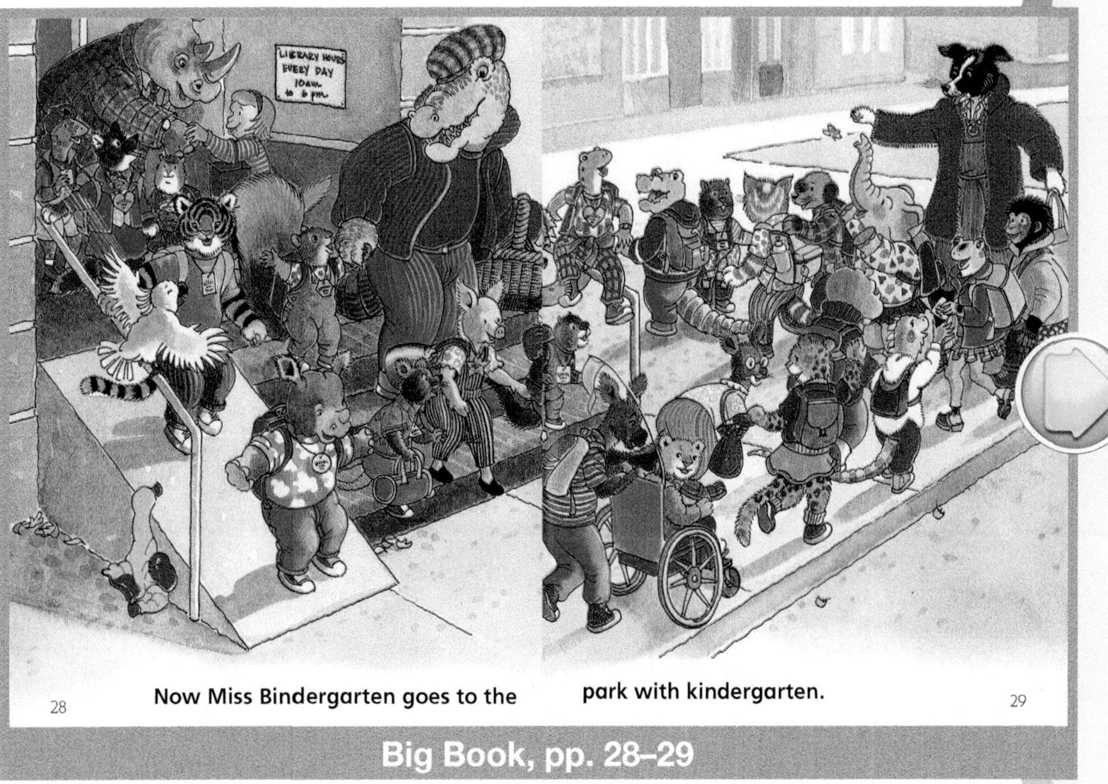

Big Book, pp. 28–29

CLASSIFY AND CATEGORIZE How are the park, the bakery, the library, the post office, and the fire station alike? (They are all places the kindergarteners go on their field trip. They are all places in a community.)

Common Core State Standards

Literature 1. With prompting and support, ask and answer questions about key details in a text. **Literature 3.** With prompting and support, identify characters, settings, and major events in a story. **Literature 7.** With prompting and support, describe the relationship between illustrations and the story in which they appear (e.g., what moment in a story an illustration depicts).

2ND READ

Develop Vocabulary

OPEN-ENDED What is the word for a parent who helps watch children on a field trip? (chaperone)

- Chaperones help the teacher and children on a field trip. What are some ways children can help the teacher on a field trip?

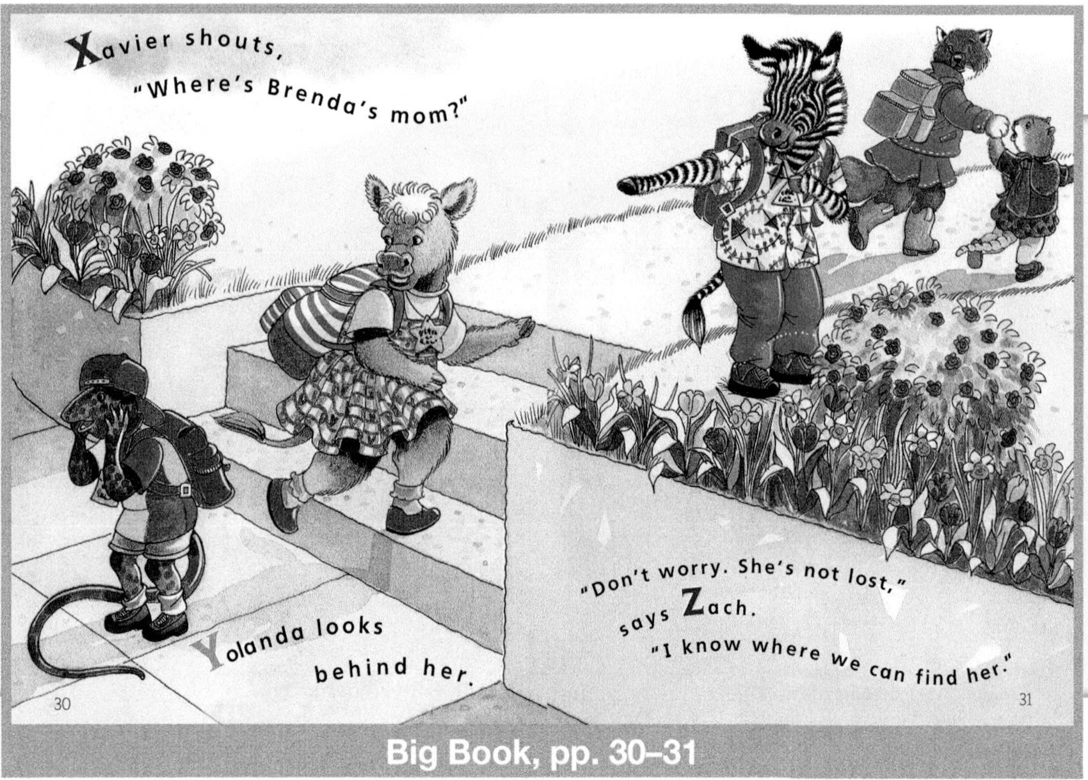
Xavier shouts,
"Where's Brenda's mom?"
Yolanda looks
behind her.
"Don't worry. She's not lost,"
says Zach.
"I know where we can find her."
30
31

Big Book, pp. 30–31

3RD READ

Develop Comprehension ©

***WH-* QUESTION** What does Zach say when Xavier can't find Brenda's mom? (Zach tells Xavier that he doesn't have to worry because he knows where they can find Brenda's mom.)

OPEN-ENDED What fun activities are the children doing in the park? (running and skipping)

- The children are running and skipping. Why do you think Miss Bindergarten stops the children?

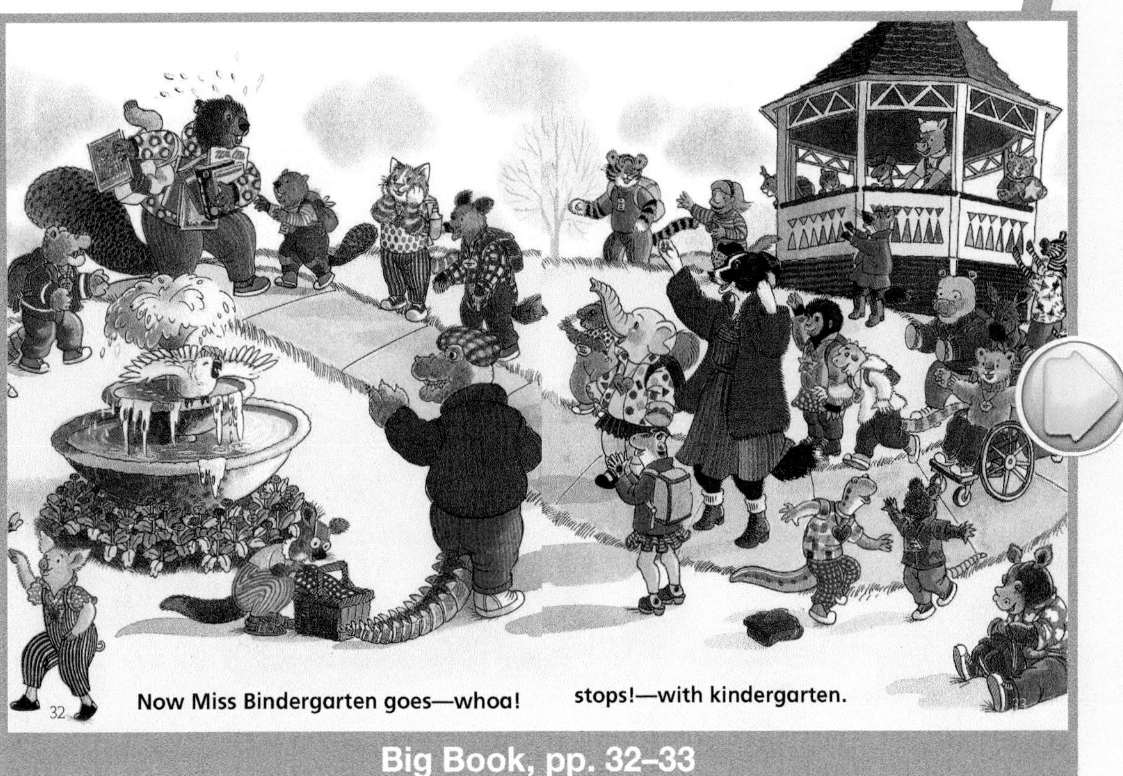

32
Now Miss Bindergarten goes—whoa!
stops!—with kindergarten.

Big Book, pp. 32–33

OPEN-ENDED How do you know Miss Bindergarten's class is at the park? (I see grass, a fountain, a bandstand, a sidewalk, and lots of space for walking and playing.)

Common Core State Standards

Literature 1. With prompting and support, ask and answer questions about key details in a text.
Literature 3. With prompting and support, identify characters, settings, and major events in a story.
Literature 7. With prompting and support, describe the relationship between illustrations and the story in which they appear (e.g., what moment in a story an illustration depicts). **Also Literature 4., Language 4.**

2ND READ

Develop Vocabulary

WH- QUESTION What are the parents and Miss Bindergarten doing? (getting food ready)

- Miss Bindergarten and the parents are getting the food ready for the children. What drink are the parents pouring for the children?

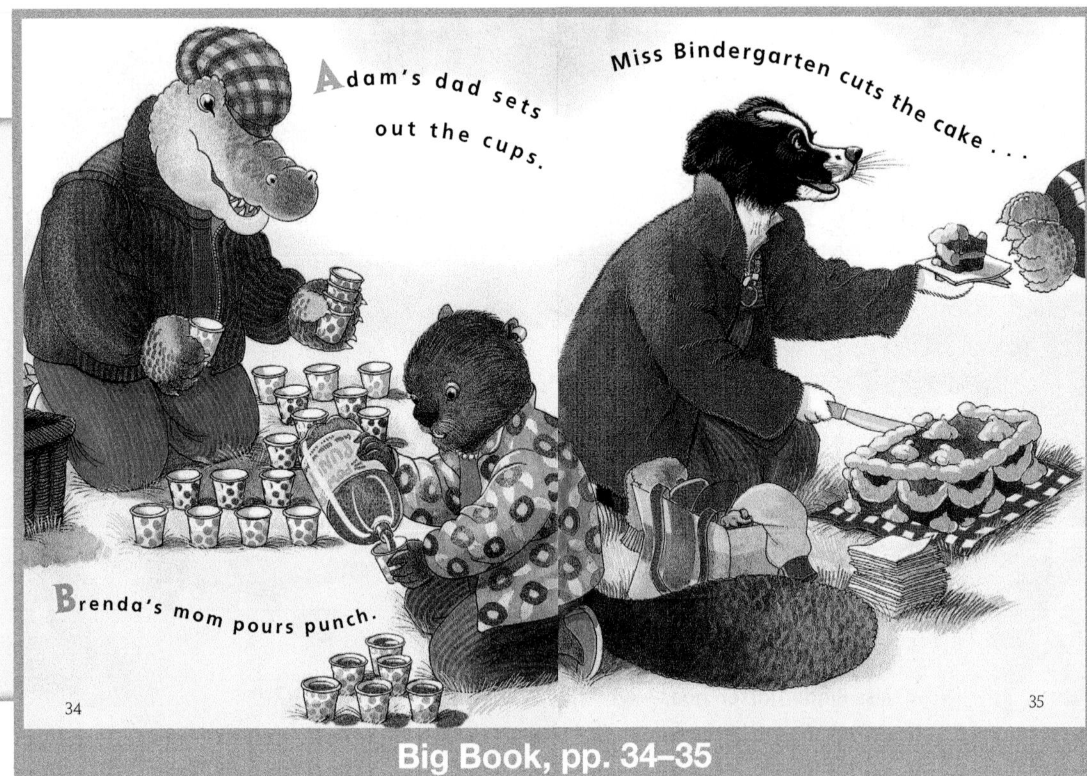
Adam's dad sets out the cups.
Miss Bindergarten cuts the cake . . .
Brenda's mom pours punch.
34
35
Big Book, pp. 34–35

3RD READ

Develop Comprehension ©

OPEN-ENDED What do you think the children are doing while Miss Bindergarten and the chaperones are getting the food ready? (I think the children are playing.)

OPEN-ENDED What are some foods that the children are munching? (grapes, bananas, and cake)

- The kindergarteners are eating grapes, bananas, and cake. What other kinds of food would be good to take on a field trip?

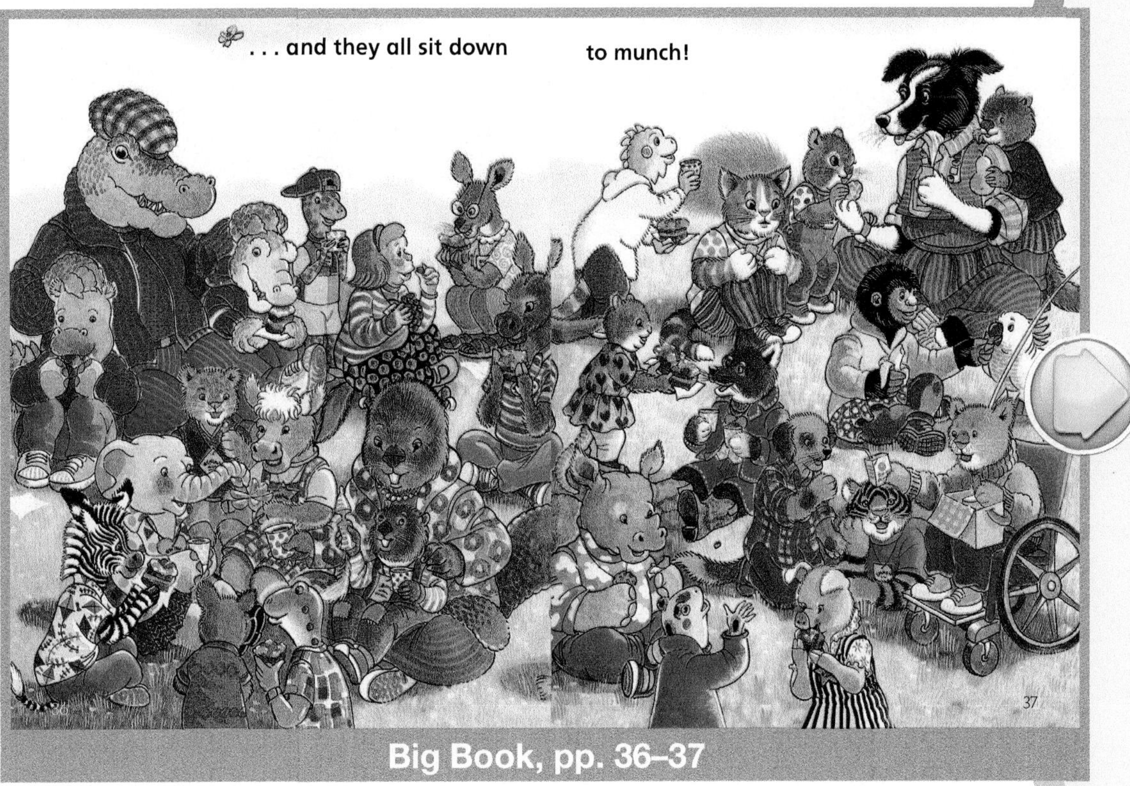

. . . and they all sit down
to munch!
37

Big Book, pp. 36–37

***WH-* QUESTION** What are the kindergarteners doing now? (They are eating cake and drinking punch in the park.)

Common Core State Standards

Literature 1. With prompting and support, ask and answer questions about key details in a text.
Literature 3. With prompting and support, identify characters, settings, and major events in a story.
Literature 7. With prompting and support, describe the relationship between illustrations and the story in which they appear (e.g., what moment in a story an illustration depicts).

2ND READ

Develop Vocabulary

RECALL What are some shapes the children found on their field trip? (squares, triangles, hearts, stars, rectangles)

- The children find many different shapes on their field trip. Point to each shape and say its name.

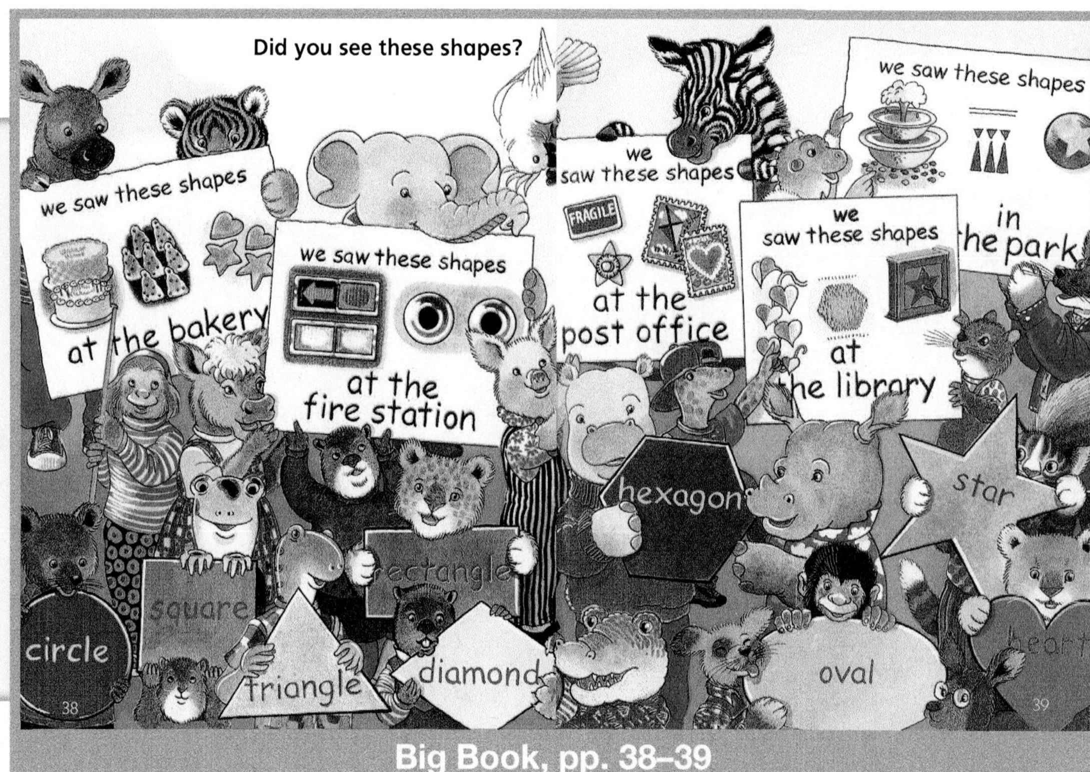

Big Book, pp. 38–39

3RD READ

Develop Comprehension ©

CLASSIFY AND CATEGORIZE How are a square, a triangle, and a rectangle alike? (They all have straight sides.) How are a circle, an oval, and a heart alike? (They do not have straight sides. They have rounded or curved sides.)

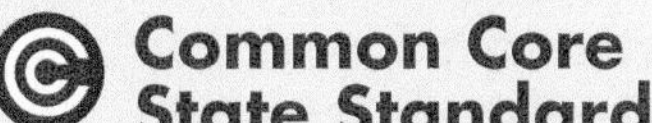

DISTANCING What is this box used for? (lost and found)

- This is a lost and found box. What do you use a lost and found box for?

Continue with DAY 3
Conventions
p. 384

Big Book, p. 40

***WH*- QUESTION** Where could the children have lost some of their things on this field trip? (The children could have lost their things at the bakery, the fire station, the post office, the park, or the library or while they were walking.)

Skip to DAY 4
Conventions
p. 398

Common Core State Standards

Literature 1. With prompting and support, ask and answer questions about key details in a text.
Literature 3. With prompting and support, identify characters, settings, and major events in a story.
Literature 7. With prompting and support, describe the relationship between illustrations and the story in which they appear (e.g., what moment in a story an illustration depicts).

Common Core State Standards

Writing 2. Use a combination of drawing, dictating, and writing to compose informative/explanatory texts in which they name what they are writing about and supply some information about the topic. **Speaking/Listening 4.** Describe familiar people, places, things, and events and, with prompting and support, provide additional detail. **Language 1.a.** Print many upper- and lowercase letters. **Also Speaking/Listening 5.**

Daily Fix-It

we helped fix her wagon
We helped fix her wagon.

This week's practice sentences appear on *Teacher Resources DVD-ROM.*

Conventions

Review What We Look Like

TEACH Remind children that we can use words to tell what we look like. Hold up AlphaBuddy. What does AlphaBuddy look like? AlphaBuddy is small. AlphaBuddy is furry.

Picture Card

GUIDE PRACTICE Display the *woman* Picture Card. This is a woman. What does the woman look like? Remind children to use complete sentences in their descriptions. Guide them by asking prompts such as the following: Are her eyes large or small? Is she tall or short? What color is her hair? As children describe what the woman looks like, write their describing words on the board. At the end of the discussion, read each word as you point to it. Then reread the list aloud with children.

Team Talk Pair children and have them take turns drawing and orally describing an animal character from *Miss Bindergarten Takes a Field Trip.* Have them dictate or copy describing words from the board to go with their pictures.

ON THEIR OWN Use *Reader's and Writer's Notebook,* p. 45, for more practice with what we look like.

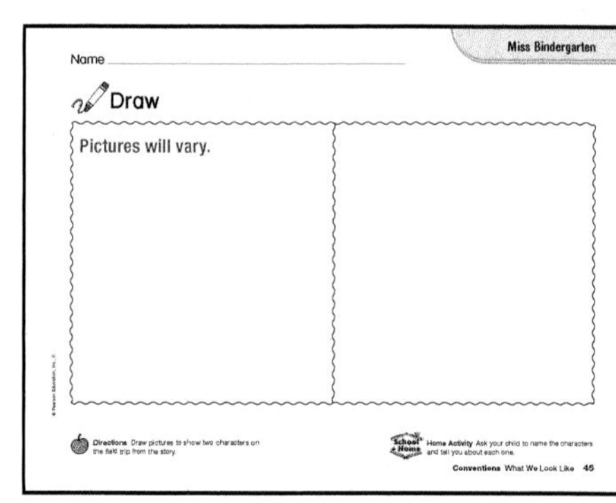

Name

Miss Bindergarten

Draw

Pictures will vary.

Conventions What We Look Like 45

Reader's and Writer's Notebook, p. 45

Instructions

TEACH Have you ever listened to instructions? **Instructions** are a group of words or sentences that tell how to do or make something. These words or sentences are often called *steps.* Good instructions have short, clear steps that are easy to understand.

MODEL Let's pretend we are teaching a younger brother or sister how to brush his or her teeth for the first time. We can help him or her by writing instructions. Draw a picture of toothpaste being squeezed onto a toothbrush. This picture shows the first step—the first thing to do. The first step is to squeeze toothpaste onto the toothbrush. I am going to write the word *squeeze* to tell the first step in our instructions. Write *squeeze* above the picture.

GUIDE PRACTICE Draw pictures of teeth being brushed and a glass of water for rinsing. Have children provide words to go with these steps.

INDEPENDENT WRITING Have children turn to p. 46 of *Reader's and Writer's Notebook.* Read the words at the top of the pictures. These instructions tell how to make a paper rabbit. Each word is a step. Have children copy the words on the lines.

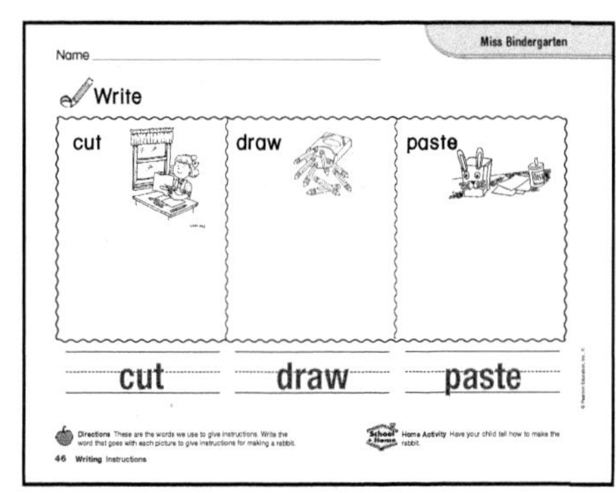

Reader's and Writer's Notebook, p. 46

Daily Handwriting

Write *Tt* and *Uu* on the board. Review correct letter formation of uppercase and lowercase *Tt* and *Uu.*

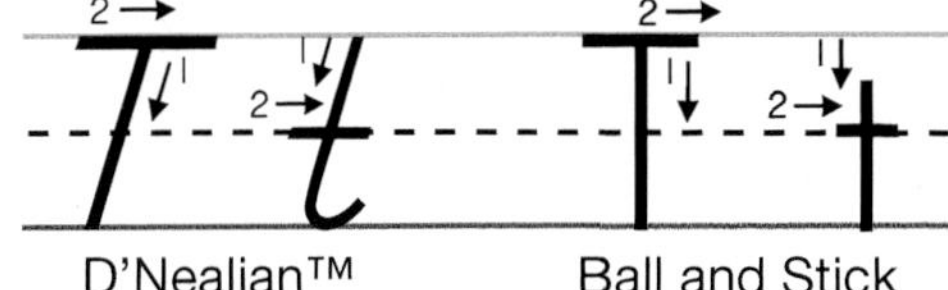
D'Nealian™ Ball and Stick

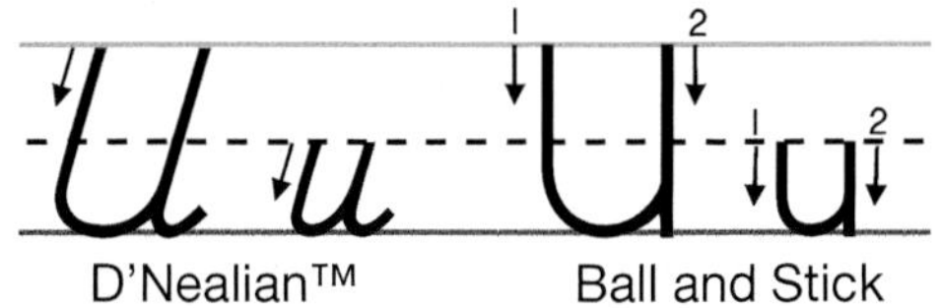
D'Nealian™ Ball and Stick

Have children write *Tt* and *Uu* on their Write-On Boards. Remind them to use proper left-to-right and top-to-bottom progression and proper spacing between letters when writing *Tt* and *Uu.*

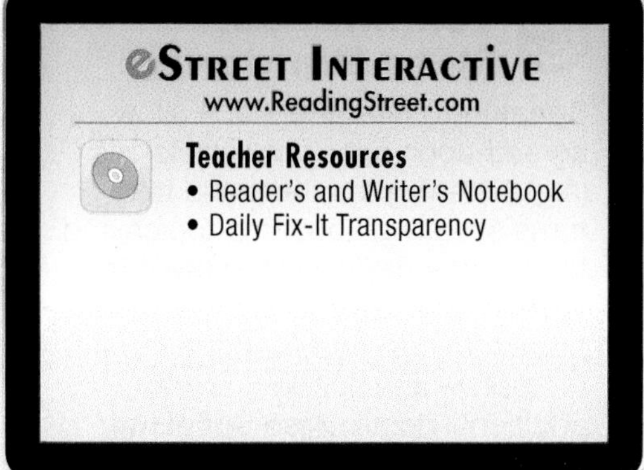

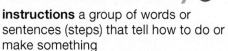

Academic Vocabulary 

instructions a group of words or sentences (steps) that tell how to do or make something

Support Writing Have English learners draw instructions for simple tasks. Encourage them to share their instructions orally. Provide English words when necessary.

Common Core State Standards

Speaking/Listening 1.a. Follow agreed-upon rules for discussions (e.g., listening to others and taking turns speaking about the topics and texts under discussion). **Speaking/Listening 4.** Describe familiar people, places, things, and events and, with prompting and support, provide additional detail. **Also Speaking/Listening 6.**

Bridge to Common Core

PRESENTATION OF KNOWLEDGE/IDEAS

As children share their favorite colors and foods with the class, they are learning to speak audibly; to express their thoughts, feelings, and ideas clearly; and to adapt their speech to a specific task, purpose, and audience.

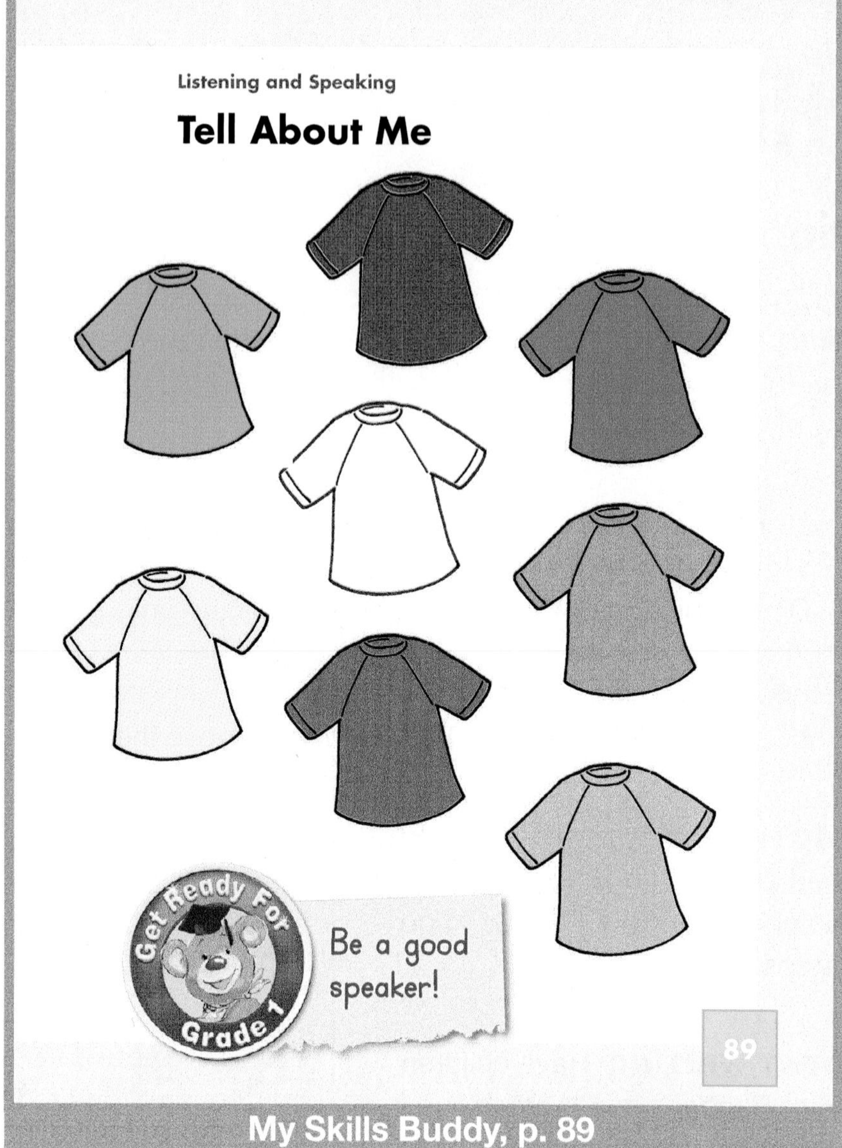

My Skills Buddy, p. 89

Listening and Speaking

Talk About Me

TEACH Remind children that good speakers show good manners by speaking one at a time. When they speak, they should speak loudly and clearly to make sure everyone can hear and understand them.

MODEL Have children turn to p. 89 of *My Skills Buddy.* Look at all of these colors! Point to each color as you say: I see green, red, blue, white, yellow, purple, orange, and pink. Discuss with children how a favorite color is something they can share about themselves. Use the Listening and Speaking bullet from p. 88 to guide discussion.

Using AlphaBuddy, have the class play "Somebody Special" based on identifiable distinctions, such as color of shirt or hair. AlphaBuddy will tell us about somebody special in the class and how that person is special. When AlphaBuddy talks about you, stand up and tell us your favorite color and why you like it. Everybody will get one turn.

Have AlphaBuddy say something about you: *I see somebody standing at the front of the room with a puppet.* Why, AlphaBuddy is talking about me! My favorite color is red because I think it is bright and cheerful.

INDEPENDENT PRACTICE Have AlphaBuddy say something about each child, such as one of the following statements:

- I see somebody special who is wearing a red shirt and blue shoes.
- I see somebody special who is wearing blue shorts and sneakers and is sitting in the back.

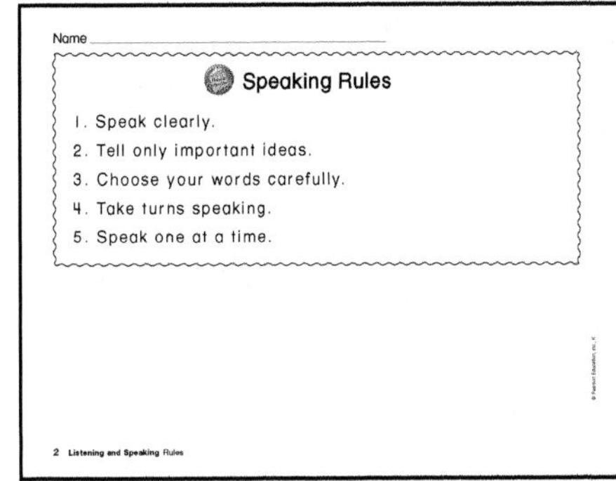
Name

Speaking Rules

1. Speak clearly.
2. Tell only important ideas.
3. Choose your words carefully.
4. Take turns speaking.
5. Speak one at a time.

2 Listening and Speaking Rules

Reader's and Writer's Notebook, pp. 1–2

Have children tell about their favorite food and why they like it. Refer children to their Rules for Listening and Speaking from pp. 1–2 of *Reader's and Writer's Notebook.* Tell children to speak loudly and clearly. Remind them to speak one at a time.

Be a Good Speaker!

1. Speak loudly and clearly.
2. Tell only important ideas.
3. Choose your words carefully.
4. Take turns speaking.
5. Speak one at a time.

Access for All

A Advanced

Extend Listening and Speaking Have children draw pictures of objects that are their favorite color. Suggest that they incorporate the illustrations into their Listening and Speaking activity responses.

Support Listening and Speaking Encourage English learners to join in after first observing other children. Help them participate by modeling the speaking skills with others before describing them.

Common Core State Standards

Language 5. With guidance and support from adults, explore word relationships and nuances in word meanings. **Also Speaking/ Listening 1.b, Language 5.a.**

Wrap Up Your Day!

- ✔ **Content Knowledge** Today we talked more about cooperation. In *Miss Bindergarten Takes a Field Trip,* how did the children, chaperones, and teacher cooperate with one another?
- ✔ **Respond to Literature** Today we read *Cat and Dog Ride To Town.* The animals visited different places. Where did they go? What did they see?
- ✔ **Conventions** Pair children and have them take turns using describing words to tell what their partners look like.
- ✔ **Homework Idea** Provide children with copies of the following sentence frame: *I wear (color).* Have children illustrate the sentence at home. Instruct them to draw a rebus word for the color they wear.

Preview DAY 4

Tomorrow we will read a story about our Trucktown friend, Pumper Pat.

Extend Your Day!

Social Studies
Jobs in the Community

MATERIALS: *Teacher Resources DVD-ROM: adult female, adult male;* scraps of various materials or colored papers; glue; drawing utensils

MAKE A HELPER Explain that many different helpers are needed to make a safe and healthy community. Show an example of a community helper. Think about a kind of job you might like when you grow up that could help a community. Make clothes to glue onto your paper people to dress them for work.

Then divide the class into four groups. Each group represents a different "community." Have children tell their group which job they chose and why. Ask the groups if they have all the kinds of community helpers they need to make their "community" safe and healthy. Give children time to determine what other helpers their community needs to make it a good place to live.

WRITE A WORD Have children write or dictate a word or sentence for the back of their paper that describes a job they might like when they grow up.

Comprehension
Classify and Categorize

MATERIALS: Big Book *Miss Bindergarten Takes a Field Trip*

PLACES AND HELPERS Take a picture walk through the illustrations of *Miss Bindergarten Takes a Field Trip.* Arrange children into two groups called *Places* and *Helpers.* The children in the *Places* group should each think of another place Miss Bindergarten's class could visit and share their ideas. The children in the *Helpers* group should each think of another helper they know about and then share their ideas. Let both groups use props from the classroom to represent their ideas.

Conventions
What Do We Look Like?

MATERIALS: construction paper, crayons

ILLUSTRATE WHAT WE LOOK LIKE Ask children to draw and color a picture of their own face. Before they do, ask them to think about their hair color and eye color and to be sure they include two eyes, a nose, a mouth, two ears, and hair. Point out that children can add other features if they wish, such as glasses or teeth.

DAY 4 at a Glance

Content Knowledge
Oral Vocabulary

Phonemic Awareness
Review Initial Sounds

Letter Recognition
Letters *Yy* and *Zz*

Text-Based Comprehension
Classify and Categorize
Review Setting

Conventions
What We Can Do

Writing
Extend the Concept

Vocabulary
Location Words

Materials

- Student Edition
- Truckery Rhymes
- Talk with Me/Sing with Me Chart
- Picture Cards
- Alphabet Cards
- Get Set, Roll! Reader 4
- Reader's and Writer's Notebook
- Big Book

Common Core State Standards

Speaking/Listening 2. Confirm understanding of a text read aloud or information presented orally or through other media by asking and answering questions about key details and requesting clarification if something is not understood. **Language 6.** Use words and phrases acquired through conversations, reading and being read to, and responding to texts.

TRUCKTOWN on Reading Street

Start your engines!

- Display "Gabby Had a Little Bear" and lead the group in saying the rhyme a few times.
- Have the group clap the rhythm as they recite the rhyme.
- When children have mastered the rhythm, have them march around the room as they say the rhyme.

Truckery Rhymes
Truckery Rhymes

Content Knowledge

Zoom in on ©

People Working Together in a Community

EXPAND THE CONCEPT On the board, write the Question of the Week, *How do people in a community cooperate?* Read it as you track the print. Tell children to respond in complete sentences. Display Sing with Me Chart 4B.

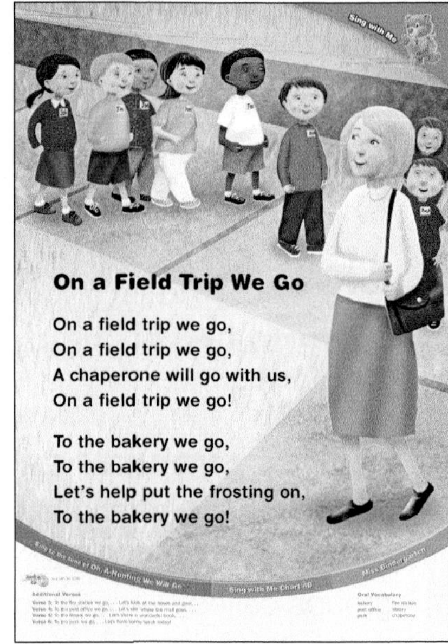
On a Field Trip We Go
On a field trip we go,
On a field trip we go,
A chaperone will go with us,
On a field trip we go!
To the bakery we go,
To the bakery we go,
Let's help put the frosting on,
To the bakery we go!
Talk with Me/Sing with Me Chart 4B

Build Oral Language

LISTEN FOR AMAZING WORDS We are going to sing this song again. Listen for the Amazing Words *library* and *chaperone.* Sing the song several times with children to the tune of "Oh, A-Hunting We Will Go." Have them stand up when they hear the Amazing Word *library* or *chaperone.*

Build Oral Vocabulary

Amazing Words Robust Vocabulary Routine

1. **Introduce the Word** A *library* has many books and other materials people can borrow. What's our new Amazing Word for a place people go to borrow books? Say it with me: *library.*
2. **Demonstrate** Provide examples to show meaning. *Our library has many exciting books to borrow!*

   Repeat steps 1 and 2.

   Introduce the Word A *chaperone* is an adult who helps the teacher watch children. What's our new Amazing Word for an adult who helps the teacher watch children? Say it with me: *chaperone.*

   Demonstrate *A chaperone helps the teacher get children onto the school bus.*
3. **Apply** Have children use *library* and *chaperone* in sentences. Then have them illustrate their sentences.
4. **Display the Words** Ask children what letters *library* and *chaperone* begin with. Have them point to and name each beginning letter.

Routines Flip Chart

USE AMAZING WORDS To reinforce the concept and the Amazing Words, have children supply the appropriate Amazing Word for each sentence.

The _______ has many books about firefighters. (library)
A parent can be a _______ on a class trip. (chaperone)

Amazing Words

bakery	fire station
park	post office
library	chaperone

Access for All

SI Strategic Intervention

Sentence Production If children's oral sentences lack subject-verb agreement, say each sentence correctly and have children repeat it.

Amazing Words If children need help completing the sentences, say a sentence using each Amazing Word and ask children to choose the sentence that makes sense.

Produce Oral Language Use the Day 4 instruction on ELL Poster 4 to extend and enrich language.

Common Core State Standards

Foundational Skills 2.d. Isolate and pronounce the initial, medial vowel, and final sounds (phonemes) in three-phoneme (consonant-vowel-consonant, or CVC) words.* (This does not include CVCs ending with /l/, /r/, or /x/.) **Also Foundational Skills 2., 2.b., 2.c.**

Phonemic Awareness

Review Initial Sounds

PRACTICE Display the *yak, yarn,* and *zoo* Picture Cards. Ask children to say the picture names. Listen to the beginning sounds in the words *yak, yarn,* and *zoo.* Which word begins with a different sound? Say the words with me: *yak, yarn, zoo.* Do *yak* and *yarn* begin the same? Yes, they do. Do *yarn* and *zoo* begin the same? No, they don't. *Zoo* does not begin with the same sound as *yak* and *yarn.* Continue the routine with these sets of words: *zebra, yellow, zipper; waffle, volcano, violet; tulip, walrus, window; tiger, vacuum, turtle.*

Picture Card

Picture Card

Picture Card

Corrective feedback

If... children cannot identify the word that begins with a different sound,
then... say each word slowly, separating the initial sound from the rest of the word: /y/ *-ak,* /y/ *-arn,* /z/ *-oo.* Have children echo you. Then repeat the activity.

PRACTICE Remind children how to blend sounds to make words. Tell them you are going to say the beginning sound and the ending part, and they are going to blend all the sounds together to make a word. Help me blend sounds to make a word. Listen as I say each part: /t/ *-op,* /t/ *-op.* Say it with me: /t/ *-op.* Now let's blend the sounds together to make a word: /t/ *-op, top.* What is the word? (*top*) Let's try one more. Repeat the routine with the word *mop.*

PRACTICE Display the *yo-yo* Picture Card. This is a yo-yo. There are two syllables, or parts, in this word: *yo-yo.* Say the word with me: *yo-yo.* Clap once for each syllable as you say the word: *yo-* (clap) *yo* (clap). How many times did we clap? (two) So we know that *yo-yo* has two syllables. Continue the routine with the words *zoo, yellow, zebra, yesterday, year, zipper,* and *zucchini.*

Picture Card

MONITOR PROGRESS Check Phonemic Awareness

FORMATIVE ASSESSMENT Say the word *kindergarten.* Ask children to clap and count the syllables as they say the word: *kin-der-gar-ten.* Continue with the words *chaperone, splendid, library,* and *munch.*

If... children cannot count the syllables in words,

then... ask them to hold up one finger for each syllable you say, and then have them count their fingers.

Continue to monitor children's progress during the week so that children can be successful with the Day 5 Assessment.

Access for All

 Advanced

Phonemic Awareness Have children compose primarily alliterative sentences, such as *Tom takes Tina to town* or *We wish for wiggly worms!* Then have them illustrate their sentences.

Support Phonemic Awareness If children's pronunciation impedes their ability to correctly count syllables, practice saying the words with them before the activity.

Common Core State Standards

Foundational Skills 1.b. Recognize that spoken words are represented in written language by specific sequences of letters. **Foundational Skills 1.d.** Recognize and name all upper- and lowercase letters of the alphabet. **Also Literature 10.**

Letter Recognition

Teach/Model

Letters *Yy* and *Zz*

INTRODUCE Display the *Yy* Alphabet Card and point to the uppercase *Y.* The name of this letter is uppercase *Y.* What is the name of this letter? Point to the lowercase *y.* The name of this letter is lowercase *y.* What is the name of this letter? Display the *Zz* Alphabet Card and repeat the routine.

Alphabet Card

MODEL Point to the yo-yo on the *Yy* Alphabet Card. This is a yo-yo. Write the word *yo-yo* on the board and point to each *y.* This letter is lowercase *y. Yo-yo* has two lowercase *y*'s. Repeat the routine with the zigzag on the *Zz* Alphabet Card.

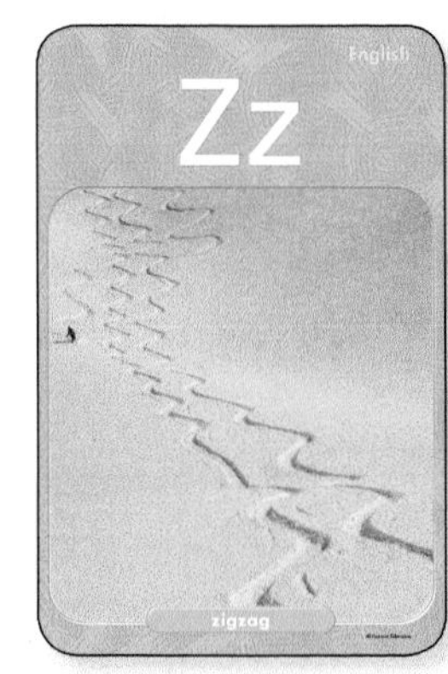

Alphabet Card

Guide Practice

GROUP PRACTICE Display Phonics Songs and Rhymes Chart 4. Let's sing the song about going on a bike ride. After singing the song several times, ask children to look for the words in the song that have *Y, y, Z,* or *z.* Have children take turns circling and naming those letters. Then sing the song again. This time, point to the words on the chart as they are sung and have children clap when they sing *Yy* or *Zz* words.

ON THEIR OWN Have children turn to p. 43 of *Reader's and Writer's Notebook* for more practice with letters *Yy* and *Zz.*

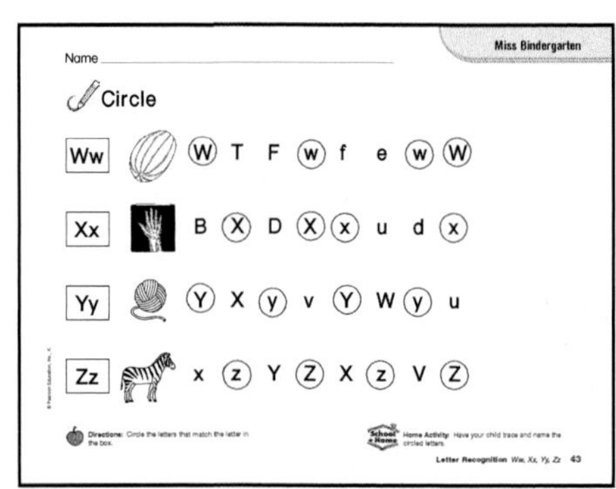
Miss Bindergarten

Name ____________

Circle

Ww W T F w f e w W

Xx B X D X x u d x

Yy Y X y v Y W y u

Zz x z Y Z X z V Z

Directions: Circle the letters that match the letter in the box.

School + Home Home Activity: Have your child trace and name the circled letters.

Letter Recognition *Ww, Xx, Yy, Zz* 43

Reader's and Writer's Notebook, p. 43

REVIEW Display the *Tt, Uu, Vv, Ww,* and *Xx* Alphabet Cards in random order. Ask children to point to the uppercase *W.* Continue to give letter names. Then rearrange the cards. Point to the lowercase *x.* What is the name of this letter? Continue to ask for letter names.

Get Set, Roll! Reader 4

Read *Pat*

REVIEW Review the high-frequency words *I, am, the,* and *little.* Have children find each word on the Word Wall.

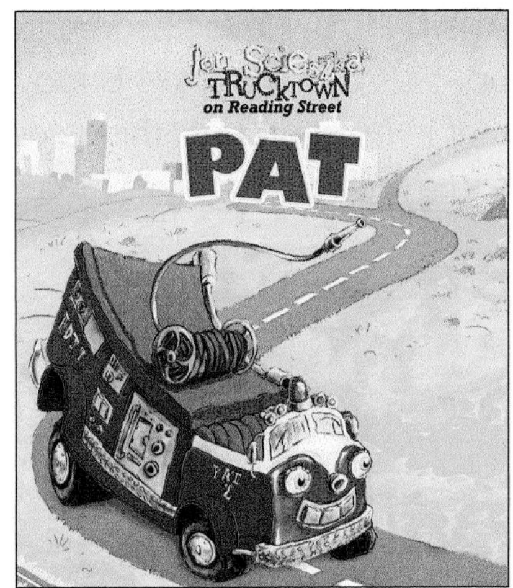

Get Set, Roll! Reader 4

TEACH REBUS WORDS Write the word *Pat* on the board. This is the name *Pat.* Name the letters with me: *P, a, t, Pat.* Continue with the other rebus words *fire, expressway, zig, zag,* and *splash.* Look for these words in the story today. A picture above each word will help you read it.

READ Today we will read a story about Pumper Pat, a fire truck and a Trucktown friend. Point to the title of the story. What is the title of the story? *Pat* is the title of the story. Look at the picture. What do you think the story will be about?

Use the routine for reading decodable books in the Routines Flip Chart to read Get Set, Roll! Reader 4.

Day 4 SMALL GROUP TIME • Differentiate Language, p. SG•55

OL On-Level	SI Strategic Intervention	A Advanced
• **Build** Sentences and Words • **Read** Get Set, Roll! Reader *Pat*	• **Talk About** Sentences and Words • **Read** Get Set, Roll! Reader *Pat*	• **Extend** Sentences and Words • **Read** Get Set, Roll! Reader *Pat*

eSTREET INTERACTIVE
www.ReadingStreet.com

Savvas eText
• Get Set, Roll! Reader

Phonics Songs and Rhymes Audio

Teacher Resources
• Reader's and Writer's Notebook

Access for All

Advanced

High-Frequency Words Hand out copies of the following sentence frame: *I am the little* ________. Have children draw rebus words to complete the sentence. Then have them read their sentences to the class.

Access Content Do a picture walk with children to preview the reader before starting the routine.

Place English Language Learners in the groups that correspond to their reading abilities in English.

If... children need more practice **Developing Language,**
then... use the Language Workshops in the *ELL Handbook* beginning on p. 306.

Text-Based Comprehension

Classify and Categorize

PRACTICE Have children turn to the Classify and Categorize pictures on pp. 74–75 of *My Skills Buddy.* As you look at the pictures, remind children that in most stories, things can be grouped together because they are alike in some way.

My Skills Buddy, pp. 74–75

Team Talk Have pairs of children find three objects in the classroom that are alike in some way. Have them identify a category in which to place the items, such as *Books* or *Writing Tools.*

Review Setting

PRACTICE Direct children to the Literary Elements pictures on pp. 14–15 of *My Skills Buddy.*

The **setting** of a story is when and where the story takes place. Good readers pay attention to the setting so that they can better understand the story. Let's review this story, "The Tortoise and the Hare." Review the story with children.

- When is this race taking place? (on a sunny day)
- Where is this race taking place? (on a path in a meadow)

MORE PRACTICE For more practice with setting, use *Reader's and Writer's Notebook,* p. 47.

Common Core State Standards

Literature 1. With prompting and support, ask and answer questions about key details in a text. **Literature 3.** With prompting and support, identify characters, settings, and major events in a story. **Language 5.a.** Sort common objects into categories (e.g., shapes, foods) to gain a sense of the concepts the categories represent.

Access for All

SI Strategic Intervention

Practice Setting Display Decodable Reader 4, Kindergarten Student Reader K.1.4, and Get Set, Roll! Reader 4. Have children practice identifying the settings in these stories.

Academic Vocabulary

setting the time (when) and place (where) of a story

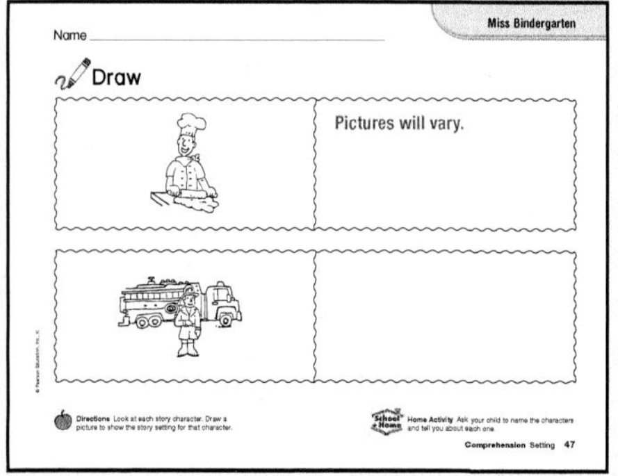

Reader's and Writer's Notebook, p. 47

Read Main Selection

GUIDE COMPREHENSION Display *Miss Bindergarten Takes a Field Trip.* Miss Bindergarten's class goes to many different places! Let's think about the details of this story's setting.

- Where does this story take place? (school, bakery, fire station, post office, library, and park; on several streets)
- When does this story take place? (on a school day)

READ Reread *Miss Bindergarten Takes a Field Trip.* Return to p. 364. Follow the **3rd Read** and use the **Develop Comprehension** notes to give children the opportunity to gain a more complete understanding of the story.

Routine Read for Understanding

Deepen understanding by reading the selection multiple times.

1. **First Read**—Read the entire selection aloud to build interest in the text.
2. **Second Read**—Use the **Develop Vocabulary** notes on pages 364–383.
3. **Third Read**—Use the **Develop Comprehension** notes on pages 364–383.

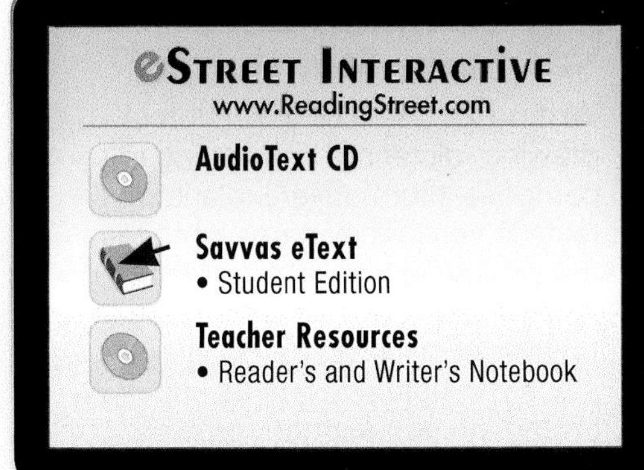

Bridge to Common Core

RANGE OF READING AND LEVEL OF TEXT COMPLEXITY
Using the Develop Comprehension notes as you read the text a third time will help you assess how well children are comprehending the authentic literary text in *Reading Street.* As the year progresses, children will improve as independent, proficient readers of complex text.

Professional Development: Support Discussions "Once children have gained enough familiarity with English to participate even at a rudimentary level in discussions about reading selections and content, they begin to learn that the materials they are reading have something to say to them, and that hearing what they have to say is the real purpose of learning to read."—Dr. Lilly Wong Fillmore, University of California at Berkeley

Common Core State Standards

Writing 2. Use a combination of drawing, dictating, and writing to compose informative/explanatory texts in which they name what they are writing about and supply some information about the topic. **Speaking/ Listening 4.** Describe familiar people, places, things, and events and, with prompting and support, provide additional detail. **Language 1.a.** Print many upper- and lowercase letters. **Also Writing 5.**

Daily Fix-It

the class went to the fire station
The class went to the fire station.

This week's practice sentences appear on *Teacher Resources DVD-ROM.*

Conventions

What We Can Do

TEACH Remind children that we can use words to tell what we can do.

MODEL I can do many things. Jump up and down. What can I do? I can jump. Laugh out loud. What else can I do? I can laugh. *Jump* and *laugh* are words that tell what I can do.

GUIDE PRACTICE What are some things you can do? Have children stand up and act out something they can do. As each child demonstrates something he or she can do, have children identify the action and then write the word on the board. After children have finished giving their examples, read the list aloud, pointing to each word as you say it.

ON THEIR OWN Use *Reader's and Writer's Notebook,* p. 48, for more practice with what we can do.

Name
Miss Bindergarten
Draw
Pictures will vary.

Reader's and Writer's Notebook, p. 48

Extend the Concept

DISCUSS Display *Miss Bindergarten Takes a Field Trip.* We just read a story about children exploring their community and learning from community helpers. Who are some of the community helpers the children visit on their trip? What do these people do? How are they like the community helpers we know?

GUIDE PRACTICE A baker is a community helper. What does a baker do to help us? A baker makes bread for us. Write the sentence on the board.

A baker makes bread for us.

Encourage children to help you think of other community helpers and what they do. With the class, complete a sentence frame similar to the one below for each type of community helper:

A postal worker _______.

INDEPENDENT WRITING Have children write or dictate their own ideas about community workers. Have them illustrate and share their ideas with the class.

Daily Handwriting

Write *V* and *v* on the board. Review correct letter formation of uppercase *V* and lowercase *v*.

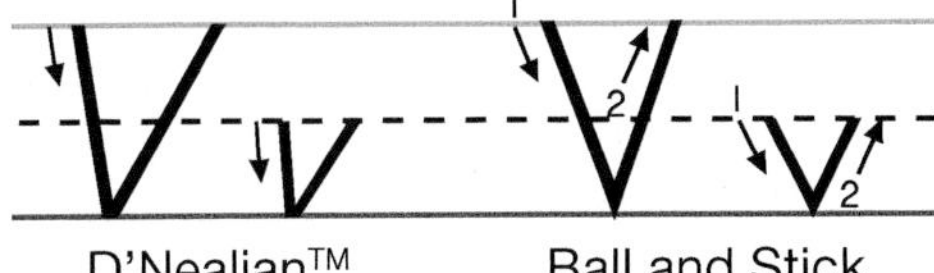

D'Nealian™ Ball and Stick

Have children write *V* and *v* on their Write-On Boards. Remind them to use proper left-to-right and top-to-bottom progression and proper spacing between letters when writing *V* and *v*.

Access for All

 Advanced

Writing Have children find a picture of a community helper in a children's magazine or a book. Help children cut out or make a copy of the picture and glue it to construction paper. Then have them dictate a label for the picture that includes the name of the helper and where he or she works.

PRODUCTION AND DISTRIBUTION OF WRITING

With your guidance and support, children interact and collaborate with others to write sentences that demonstrate understanding of community workers and their jobs.

Support Writing As children dictate, supply English words, if needed, to help them express their ideas.

Common Core State Standards

Language 5. With guidance and support from adults, explore word relationships and nuances in word meanings. **Language 5.c.** Identify real-life connections between words and their use (e.g., note places at school that are *colorful*). **Language 6.** Use words and phrases acquired through conversations, reading and being read to, and responding to texts. **Also Literature 4., Speaking/ Listening 5.**

Vocabulary

Location Words

TEACH Write the words *school, library, post office,* and *park* on the board. Point to each word as you read it. These words tell about some places in a community. Have children turn to p. 88 of *My Skills Buddy.* Point to the picture of the library. What is this place? What can people do here? Repeat for the other three pictures. Then use the second Vocabulary bullet on the page to guide a discussion about places in your community.

Team Talk Pair children. One partner describes one of the locations on p. 88. The other partner guesses the location. Then have children switch roles and repeat the routine.

My Skills Buddy, p. 88

Wrap Up Your Day!

✔ **Oral Language** Display p. 4 of *Miss Bindergarten Takes a Field Trip.* Read the page and review the Amazing Word *chaperone.* Continue with other pages to review *bakery, post office, fire station, library,* and *park.*

✔ **Conventions and Vocabulary** I am going to say a location word. I want you to tell me something we can do there. Listen carefully: *school.*

✔ **Homework Idea** Have children bring in a photograph or drawing of themselves doing something they like. Have them show and talk about the picture to the class.

Tell children that tomorrow they will review some of the books and stories they have read this week.

Extend Your Day!

Social Studies
What Is a Community Helper?

MATERIALS: construction paper, crayons, jar

COMMUNITY HELPERS Choose five or six community helpers, such as doctor, police officer, store owner, firefighter, bus driver, and postal worker. For each child in the class, write one community helper on a slip of paper and place it in a jar. Have children pick a helper out of the jar. Children with the same helper sit together in a group. Members of a group will each draw and color something that represents their helper.

Help children generate ideas for their drawings. For example, the postal workers can draw a mailbox and mail; the doctors can draw bandages and crutches. The groups will then present their pictures and describe to the class what their community helper does.

If children have trouble thinking of things to say, prompt them with questions. What does your community helper do? What tools does the helper need to do the job? Have you ever met this kind of community helper?

Conventions
What We Can Do

MATERIALS: construction paper, crayons

ILLUSTRATE WHAT WE CAN DO Write a list of activity words that include the letters of the week: *Tt, Uu, Vv, Ww, Xx, Yy, Zz.* Have children pick one of the activities and copy or dictate the word(s) on a sheet of construction paper. Have them draw a picture of themselves doing the activity below the word(s). The list may include the following: *win prizes, take a walk, exercise, yawn, use a yo-yo.*

Comprehension
Compare and Contrast

MATERIALS: Big Book *Miss Bindergarten Takes a Field Trip,* paper, crayons

PLACES IN TOWN Divide a sheet of paper into quarters. Have children copy or dictate the name of one of the places in *Miss Bindergarten Takes a Field Trip* on each section. Some places could include a bakery, a park, a school, a fire station, a post office, or a library. In each section, children will draw or write things they could find in each place. Allow time for children to show the class what places they chose and what they drew.

DAY 5 at a Glance

Content Knowledge
Oral Vocabulary

Phonemic Awareness
Review Initial Sounds

Letter Recognition
Review Letter Names

Assessment
Letter Recognition
High-Frequency Words
Comprehension

Text-Based Comprehension
Review Classify and Categorize

Conventions
Review What We Can Do

Writing
This Week We…

Materials

- Student Edition
- Truckery Rhymes
- Talk with Me/Sing with Me Chart
- Read Aloud Anthology
- Student Reader K.1.4
- Get Set, Roll! Reader 4

Bridge to Common Core

INTEGRATION OF KNOWLEDGE/IDEAS

This week children have integrated content presented in diverse formats and analyzed how different texts address similar topics. They have developed knowledge about how people in a community work together to expand the unit topic of Cooperation.

Social Studies Knowledge Goals

Children have learned that cooperating with others

- helps them have a fun time
- helps them learn new things

TRUCKTOWN
on Reading Street

Start your engines!

- Display "Gabby Had a Little Bear" and lead the group in saying the rhyme a few times.
  - Have half the group recite the rhyme while the other half acts it out.
    - Ask the halves to change roles.

Truckery Rhymes
Truckery Rhymes

Content Knowledge

Zoom in on

People Working Together in a Community

REVIEW THE CONCEPT Discuss with children what they have added to their knowledge about this unit of study, All Together Now. Encourage them to use the Amazing Words.

Build Oral Language

LISTEN FOR AMAZING WORDS Display Sing with Me Chart 4B. Let's sing "On a Field Trip We Go." I want you to listen for the Amazing Words we learned this week. Remind children that the words *bakery, fire station, park, post office, library,* and *chaperone* are in the song. Sing the song several times to the tune of "Oh, A-Hunting We Will Go." Have children skip each time they hear an Amazing Word. Then discuss why all the places in the song are important to a community. Remind children to share their responses one at a time.

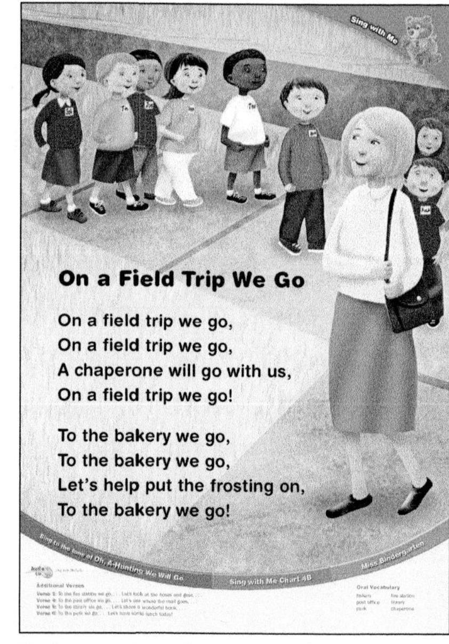
On a Field Trip We Go
On a field trip we go,
On a field trip we go,
A chaperone will go with us,
On a field trip we go!
To the bakery we go,
To the bakery we go,
Let's help put the frosting on,
To the bakery we go!
Talk with Me/Sing with Me Chart 4B

Build Oral Vocabulary

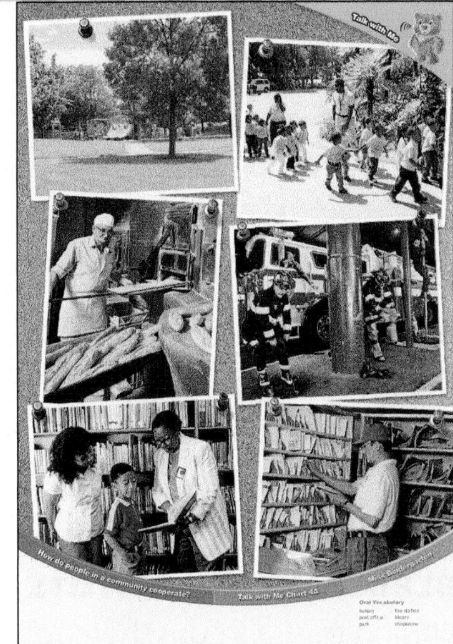
Talk with Me/Sing with Me Chart 4A

REVIEW AMAZING WORDS Display Talk with Me Chart 4A. We learned six new Amazing Words this week. Let's say the Amazing Words as I point to the pictures on the chart. Point to each picture and give children the chance to say the appropriate Amazing Word before offering it.

Have children supply the appropriate Amazing Word to complete each sentence.

I cannot wait to slide down the pole at the _______. (fire station)
My teacher needs a _______ to help her on our trip. (chaperone)
We can smell fresh bread at the _______. (bakery)
The _______ was filled with children playing games. (park)
I use a computer to find a book at the _______. (library)
Mom buys some stamps at the _______. (post office)

It's Friday

MONITOR PROGRESS Check Oral Vocabulary

FORMATIVE ASSESSMENT Demonstrate Word Knowledge Monitor the Amazing Words by asking the following questions. Have children use the Amazing Word in their answer.

- **Where are muffins and bread baked?** (bakery)
- **Where would a person go to mail a package?** (post office)
- **Where are fire trucks kept?** (fire station)
- **Where can you go to borrow books?** (library)
- **Where would you find a place with swings and a slide?** (park)
- **Who helps a teacher on a field trip?** (chaperone)

If... children have difficulty using the Amazing Words,
then... reteach the words using the Robust Vocabulary Routine on the Routines Flip Chart.

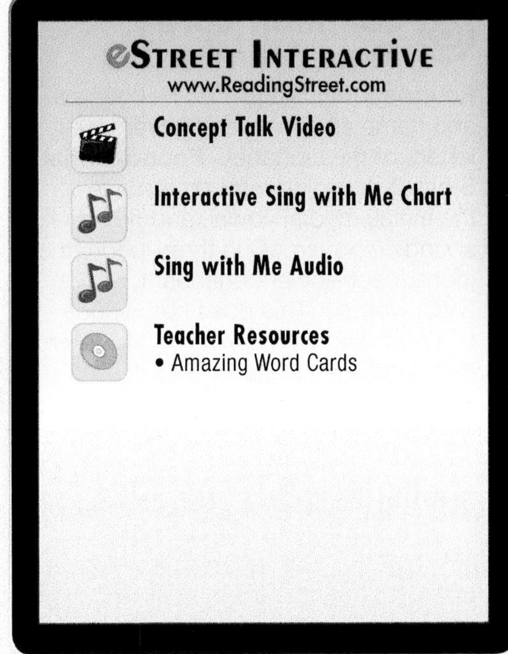

Amazing Words

bakery	fire station
park	post office
library	chaperone

Access for All

Advanced

Sentence Production Have children choose one Amazing Word. Ask them to say a complete sentence using that word.

ELL

Check Concepts and Language Use the Day 5 instruction on ELL Poster 4 to monitor children's understanding of the lesson concept.

Common Core State Standards

Foundational Skills 1.d. Recognize and name all upper- and lowercase letters of the alphabet. **Foundational Skills 2.d.** Isolate and pronounce the initial, medial vowel, and final sounds (phonemes) in three-phoneme (consonant-vowel-consonant, or CVC) words.* (This does not include CVCs ending with /l/, /r/, or /x/.) **Also Foundational Skills 2., 2.e.**

Phonemic Awareness

Review Initial Sounds

INITIAL SOUNDS Listen to these three words: *bake, park, pole.* Which word begins with a different sound? *Bake* begins with a sound that is different from the beginning sound in *park* and *pole.* Continue with the following words: *holds, hugs, push; mail, look, mom; dad, dog, cap; fun, face, gear.*

BLEND AND SUBSTITUTE SOUNDS Listen to this beginning sound and ending part and put them together to make a word: /b/ *-it,* /b/ *-it.* What word is that? (*bit*) When I change the first sound to /h/, /h/ *-it,* what word is that? (*hit*) Continue with the following words: *fit, pit, sit.*

COUNT SYLLABLES How many syllables are in the name *Bindergarten?* Let's clap once for each syllable to find out: *Bin-der-gar-ten.* There are four syllables in *Bindergarten.* Continue the routine with these names: *Christopher, Wanda, Emily, Noah, Jessie, Yolanda.*

Letter Recognition

Review Letter Names

TEACH Display the *Yy* Alphabet Card. What is the name of this letter? Repeat the routine with the *Zz* Alphabet Card. Display all of the Alphabet Cards. Point to a card and ask a child to name both letter forms.

REVIEW HIGH-FREQUENCY WORDS Write the word *the* on the board. This is the word *the*. What is this word? Repeat the routine with *little.*

REREAD Have children reread one of the books specific to the target letters. You may wish to review the high-frequency and rebus words that appear in each book prior to rereading.

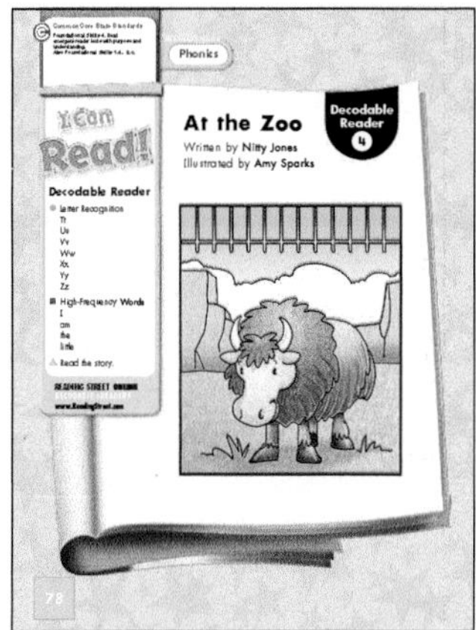

Decodable Reader 4
My Skills Buddy, p. 78

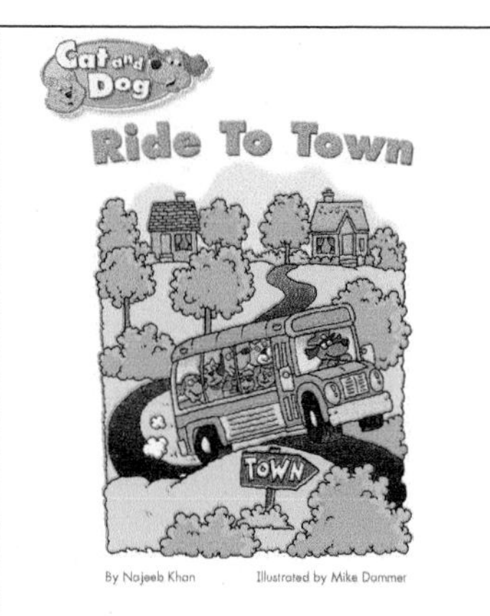

Kindergarten Student Reader K.1.4

Get Set, Roll! Reader 4

Access for All

A Advanced

Letter Recognition and Handwriting Have children look for words with *Tt, Uu, Vv, Xx, Yy,* and *Zz* in Decodable Reader 4, Kindergarten Student Reader K.1.4, or Get Set, Roll! Reader 4. Ask children to copy the letters on a sheet of paper or on their Write-On Boards.

Day 5 SMALL GROUP TIME • Differentiate Close Reading, p. SG•55

OL On-Level

- **Practice Letter Recognition** Recognize Letters *Ww, Xx, Yy, Zz*
- **Read** "We Need a Park"

SI Strategic Intervention

- **Reteach Letter Recognition** Recognize Letters *Ww, Xx, Yy, Zz*
- **Read** "We Need a Park"

A Advanced

- **Extend Letter Recognition** Connect Letters to Sounds
- **Read** "We Need a Park"

Place English Language Learners in the groups that correspond to their reading abilities in English.

If... children need more support with **Comprehension,**
then... use the ELL activities on pp. DI•64–DI•65 in the Teacher Resources section of the Digital Path.

Common Core State Standards

Foundational Skills 1.d. Recognize and name all upper- and lowercase letters of the alphabet. **Foundational Skills 3.c.** Read common high-frequency words by sight. (e.g., *the, of, to, you, she, my, is, are, do, does*).

Assess

- Identify letters *Tt, Uu, Vv, Ww, Xx, Yy,* and *Zz.*
- Read high-frequency words.

Assessment

Monitor Progress

Review Letter Names

WHOLE CLASS Display the following Alphabet Cards: *Tt, Uu, Vv, Ww, Xx, Yy, Zz.* Randomly name a letter on one of the cards. Have children write the letter. Continue by naming the other letters on the cards.

MONITOR PROGRESS **Check Letter and Word Reading**

If... children cannot complete the whole-class assessment,
then... use the Reteach lesson in *First Stop.*

If... you are unsure of a child's grasp of this week's skills,
then... use the assessment below to obtain a clearer evaluation of the child's progress.

ONE-ON-ONE To facilitate individual progress monitoring, assess some children on Day 4 and the rest on Day 5. While individual children are being assessed, the rest of the class can reread this week's books and look for target letters.

LETTER READING Use the list of letters on reproducible p. 407 to assess each child's ability to name letters *Tt, Uu, Vv, Ww, Xx, Yy,* and *Zz.* Have the child name the letters in each row. For each child, record any problems with letter recognition.

WORD READING Use the word list on reproducible p. 407 to assess a child's ability to read high-frequency words. Have each child read the words aloud.

RECORD SCORES Monitor children's accuracy by recording their scores using the Letter Recognition Chart for this unit in *First Stop.*

Name ______________________________

Name the Letters

T	v	W	y	u
U	Y	x	z	t
Z	w	V	y	X

Read the Words

little ☐

the ☐

Copyright © Savvas Learning Company LLC. All Rights Reserved.

Note to Teacher: Children name each letter. Children read words.

Scoring for Name the Letters/Read the Words: Score 1 point for each correct letter/word.

Letter Recognition (*Tt, Uu, Vv, Ww, Xx, Yy, Zz*) _______ /__15__
High-Frequency Words (*little, the*) _______ /__2__

MONITOR PROGRESS

- Letters *Tt, Uu, Vv, Ww, Xx, Yy, Zz*
- High-Frequency Words

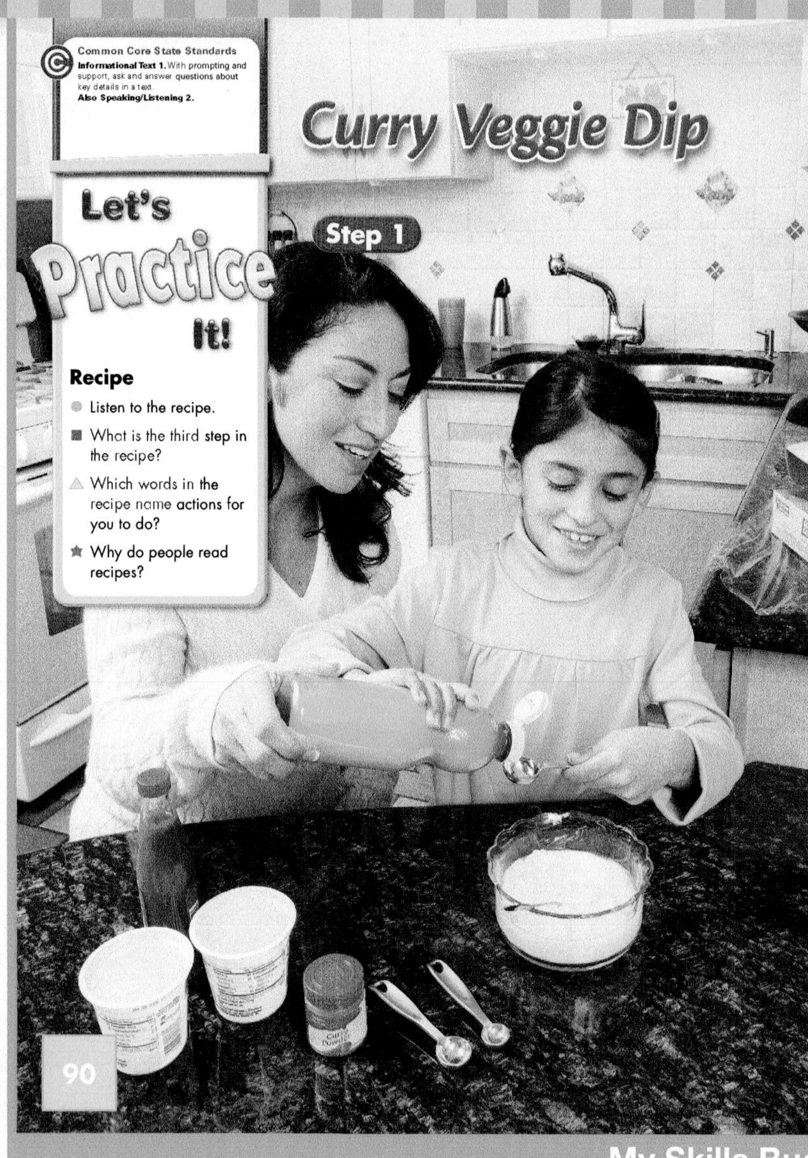

Curry Veggie Dip
Let's Practice It!
Recipe
Listen to the recipe.
What is the third step in the recipe?
Which words in the recipe name actions for you to do?
Why do people read recipes?
Step 1
90

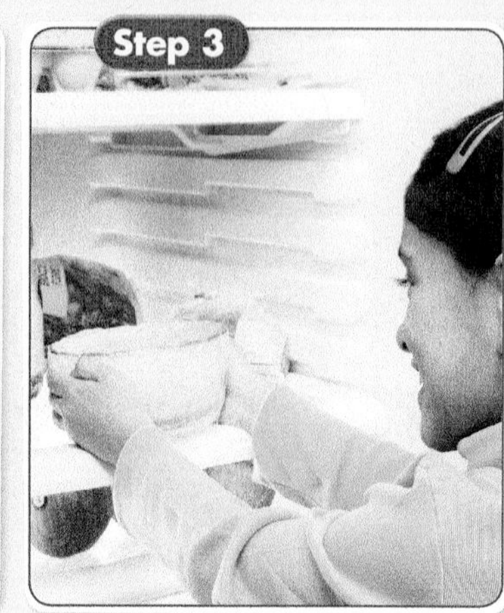

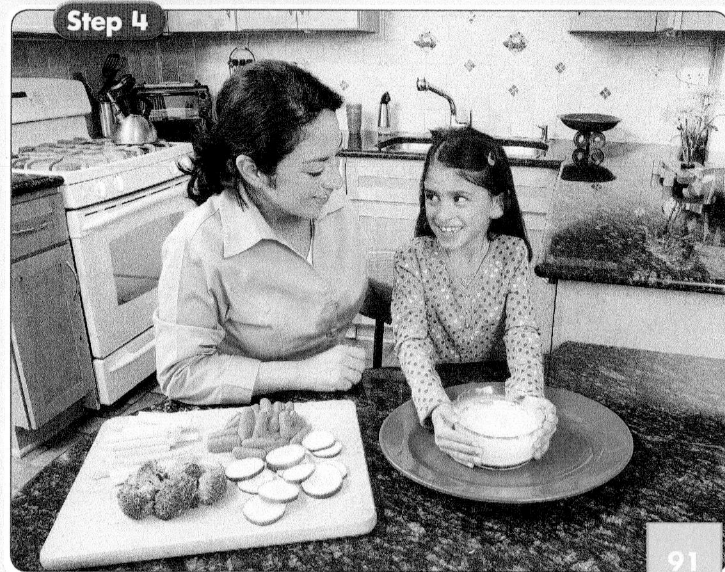

My Skills Buddy, pp. 90–91

Common Core State Standards

Informational Text 1. With prompting and support, ask and answer questions about key details in a text. **Speaking/Listening 2.** Confirm understanding of a text read aloud or information presented orally or through other media by asking and answering questions about key details and requesting clarification if something is not understood. **Speaking/Listening 4.** Describe familiar people, places, things, and events and, with prompting and support, provide additional detail. **Also Informational Text 2., 7.**

Academic Vocabulary

recipe a set of instructions that tells how to prepare or cook food

Let's Practice It!

Recipe

TEACH Today you will listen to a recipe for a delicious snack. A **recipe** is a set of instructions that tells us how to make food. Review the features of recipes with children.

- A recipe tells how to make food.
- A recipe includes a list of things you will need.
- A recipe is organized in steps.

Have children turn to pp. 90–91 of *My Skills Buddy.* I am going to read a recipe for a yummy food we can make. Look at the pictures as you listen to the steps. Read the text of "Curry Veggie Dip." As you read, direct children to look at the appropriate picture and step numbers.

GUIDE PRACTICE Discuss the recipe and the bulleted text on p. 90 of *My Skills Buddy* with children.

- A recipe tells how to make food. What food does this recipe tell how to make? (curry veggie dip) What action words are used in the recipe to tell how to make curry veggie dip? (spoon, add, stir, mix, cover, serve)
- A recipe includes a list of things you will need. What do you need to make curry veggie dip? (plain yogurt, lemon juice, curry powder, hot sauce)
- A recipe is organized in steps. How many steps are there in this recipe? (four) Do you add lemon juice before or after curry powder? (before)
- People use recipes every day. Why do people listen to or read recipes? (to learn how to make something)

Teacher Read Aloud

Curry Veggie Dip

Here is a recipe for a tasty snack you can make to eat after school or to take on a picnic.

This is what you need:

1½ cups plain yogurt

1 teaspoon lemon juice

1 teaspoon curry powder

¼ teaspoon hot sauce

This is what you do:

1. Spoon the yogurt into a small bowl. Add the lemon juice and stir.
2. Add the curry powder and hot sauce a little at a time. Stir and taste the dip before adding more. Then mix until well blended.
3. Cover the top of the bowl with a lid or plastic wrap. Put the bowl in the refrigerator.
4. When you're ready, serve the dip with raw vegetables, such as carrots, celery sticks, cucumber slices, or broccoli pieces.

Writing to Sources

Use Connect the Texts on pp. 20–21 to guide children in writing text-based responses using two sources.

Access for All

Access Content Have children draw the steps they would take to prepare a simple snack, such as peanut butter and crackers.

Access Content Have children discuss foods or a simple recipe from another culture that they know well.

Common Core State Standards

Language 5.a. Sort common objects into categories (e.g., shapes, foods) to gain a sense of the concepts the categories represent.

Assess

Classify and categorize elements of the story.

Assessment

Monitor Progress

REVIEW CLASSIFY AND CATEGORIZE In many stories, things can be grouped together because they are alike in some way. When we group things, we say we classify and categorize them. What do we do when we put things in a group because they are alike in some way? (classify and categorize)

READ "FRESHLY BAKED BREAD" Tell children you are going to read a story about a baker making bread. Ask them to listen for things they can group together. Listen carefully. I am going to ask you to group things from the story based on how these things are alike in some way. Read "Freshly Baked Bread" on p. 7 of *Read Aloud Anthology.*

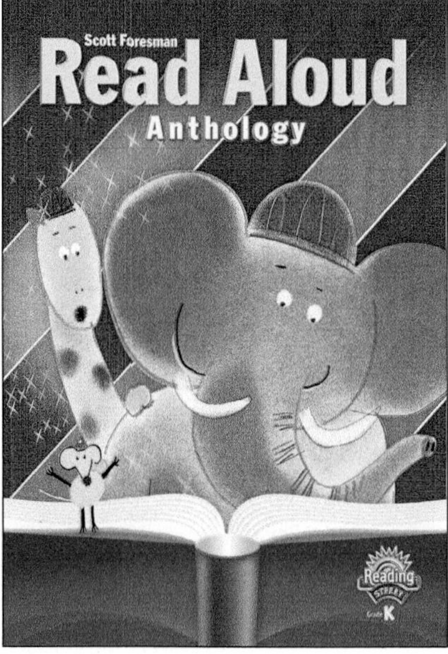

Read Aloud Anthology

CHECK CLASSIFY AND CATEGORIZE After you read the story, ask children to group things from the story into categories.

- Who are the workers at the bakery? (Frank, Leena, Juan, Keisha, Amanda)
- Ingredients are foods that we mix to make a different kind of food. What ingredients do they use at the bakery? (flour, salt, sugar, shortening, yeast, milk)
- How are the loaves, rolls, breadsticks, cookies, pies, doughnuts, bagels, and cakes alike? (They are all made at Frank's bakery. They are all made by a team of bakers. They are all made from flour.)

Corrective feedback	**If...** children cannot classify and categorize, **then...** reteach classify and categorize using the Reteach lesson in *First Stop.*

ASSESS CLASSIFY AND CATEGORIZE Use the blackline master on p. 411. Make one copy for each child. Have children cut out the pictures and sort them into two groups: "Tools for Baking" and "Ingredients for Baking." Have them glue the groups on a separate sheet of paper.

Name ____________________

Classify and Categorize

Sort these items into "tools" and "ingredients."

Note to Teacher: Have children cut out the pictures and sort them into two groups: "Tools for Baking" and "Ingredients for Baking." Children should glue the groups of pictures on another sheet of paper.

Copyright © Savvas Learning Company LLC. All Rights Reserved.

MONITOR PROGRESS

- **Classify and Categorize**

Common Core State Standards

Writing 1. Use a combination of drawing, dictating, and writing to compose opinion pieces in which they tell a reader the topic or the name of the book they are writing about and state an opinion or preference about the topic or book (e.g., *My favorite book is* . . .). **Speaking/Listening 4.** Describe familiar people, places, things, and events and, with prompting and support, provide additional detail. **Language 1.a.** Print many upper- and lowercase letters. **Also Writing 7.**

Daily Fix-It

i am little

I am little.

This week's practice sentences appear on *Teacher Resources DVD-ROM.*

Conventions

Review What We Can Do

REVIEW Remind children that we can use words to tell what we can do.

MODEL Show p. 12 from *Miss Bindergarten Takes a Field Trip.* What can Gwen do? Gwen can ring a bell. I can do that too. Write this sentence frame on the board and complete it.

I can ______.

GUIDE PRACTICE Show other pages from the book. Reread the text. What can (character's name) do? Have children answer the question and then use the verb to complete the sentence frame.

ON THEIR OWN Ask each child to cut out and glue a magazine picture or to draw a picture that shows something he or she can do. Have children dictate or write a word or words to complete the sentence frame as a caption for the picture.

This Week We...

REVIEW Display *Miss Bindergarten Takes a Field Trip,* Sing with Me Chart 4B, Phonics Songs and Rhymes Chart 4, *Cat and Dog Ride To Town,* and *At the Zoo.* We read some new books this week, and we sang some new songs. Which book or song is your favorite? My favorite is the story about the children going on a field trip to different places.

MODEL WRITING A SENTENCE One of the places the kindergarteners visit is the library. The library is my favorite place. I will write a sentence about that. Write the following sentence on the board and read it to children. (*Your name*) *likes the library.*

GUIDE PRACTICE Ask a child to name his or her favorite place from the stories. Write a sentence using the child's name, the verb *likes,* and the name of the place. Continue until every child has contributed a sentence to the list. Then have children echo the list.

Saad likes the bakery.
Maria likes the fire station.
Nick likes the park.

ON THEIR OWN Have children copy or dictate the sentence about their favorite place and draw a picture that shows the place. Have them share their illustration and writing with the class. Post the pictures on a bulletin board titled "Our Favorite Places."

Daily Handwriting

Write uppercase and lowercase letters *Tt, Uu,* and *Vv* on the board. Review correct letter formation with children.

Have children write a row each of uppercase and lowercase letters *Tt, Uu,* and *Vv* on their Write-On Boards. Remind them to use proper left-to-right and top-to-bottom progression.

Bridge to Common Core

RESEARCH TO BUILD AND PRESENT KNOWLEDGE
When children draw and write about their favorite place in the texts they read this week, they are learning to express their opinion. Learning how to write opinion sentences will help children when they write more complex opinion pieces.

Poster Preview Encourage children to look ahead to next week by previewing ELL Poster 5. Read the Poster Talk-Through to introduce the concept and vocabulary. Ask children to identify and describe objects and actions in the art.

Common Core State Standards

Language 1.a. Print many upper- and lowercase letters. **Language 5.a.** Sort common objects into categories (e.g., shapes, foods) to gain a sense of the concepts the categories represent. **Language 5.c.** Identify real-life connections between words and their use (e.g., note places at school that are *colorful*).

Wrap Up Your Week!

People Working Together in a Community

How do people in a community cooperate?

ILLUSTRATE CLASSIFY AND CATEGORIZE This week we talked about how people in a community cooperate. A community has many kinds of workers.

- Make a T-chart like the one shown. Have children identify community workers they read about.
- Ask children which community workers help others. Write their responses in the first column.
- Ask children which community workers provide things that people need. Write their responses in the second column.
- Discuss with children how the workers in each group are alike.

They Help Others	They Provide Things
librarian	baker
firefighter	postal worker

Amazing Words

You've learned 006 words this week!

You've learned 024 words this year!

Next Week's Concept

What Friends Do Together

What do you like to do with your friends?

Discuss next week's question. Talk with children about what they like to do with friends.

Tell children that next week they will read about what Trucktown friends like to do together.

Preview Next Week

Extend Your Day!

Social Studies

What Do Community Helpers Do?

MATERIALS: chart paper

We have looked at different community helpers and what they do to make a community safe and healthy. If you talked with these helpers, what are some things they would tell you to do?

Think back to your own experiences with community helpers. For example, when you visited the dentist, what is one thing he or she may have told you? (It is important to brush your teeth three times a day or do not eat too many sweet things.)

Have children think of several community helpers and tell the types of things the community helpers might say to them.

Record children's answers on a web like the one shown. Write the name of the community helper in the oval and the things he or she might say in the boxes. Make a web for each community helper children discuss.

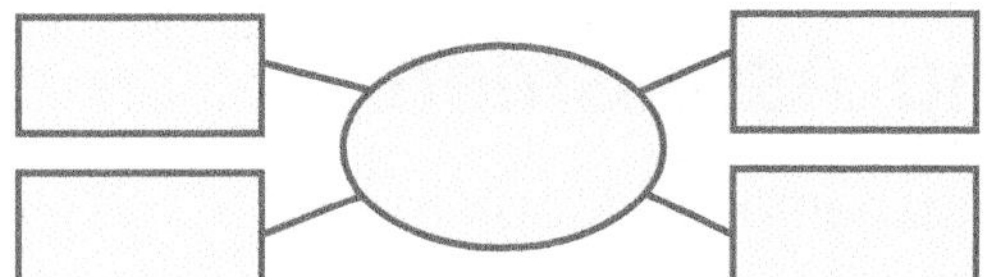

Letter Recognition

Connect to Phonics

MATERIALS: construction paper 4" × 4" squares, crayons, pictures, tape

LET'S WORK TOGETHER Give each child a square of construction paper. Have each child write a different uppercase and lowercase form of a letter on the square and decorate it with pictures of items whose names begin with the letter. Tape the completed squares together to form a quilt. Add plain colored squares as needed. Display the quilt on the classroom wall.

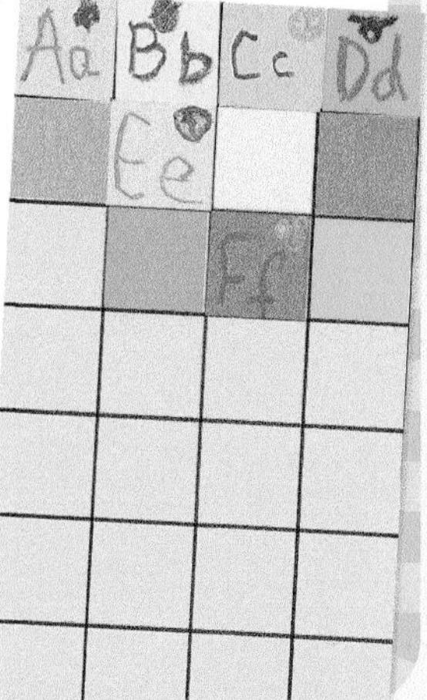

Math

Classify and Categorize

MATERIALS: Big Book *Miss Bindergarten Takes a Field Trip,* shape patterns, construction paper, scissors, glue

PLACE/SHAPE CHART Take a picture walk through the Big Book and find pictures of circles and rectangles. Record the information on a chart like the one shown. Have children use the shape patterns to cut out shapes and then glue them to the chart.

Place	Circle shape	Rectangle shape
bakery	bagels	loaf of bread

Assessment Checkpoints for the Week

Weekly Assessment

Use the whole-class assessment on pages 406–407 and 410–411 in this Teacher's Edition to check:

✓ **Letters *Tt, Uu, Vv, Ww, Xx, Yy, Zz***

✓ **Comprehension** *Classify and Categorize*

✓ **High-Frequency Words** *the* *little*

Managing Assessment

Use the Assessment Handbook for:

✓ **Observation Checklists**

✓ **Record-Keeping Forms**

✓ **Portfolio Assessment**

Assessment Handbook

TEACHER NOTES

TEACHER NOTES

DAY 1 Differentiate Letter Recognition

- Letters *Tt* and *Uu*
  - Decodable Story
  - Advanced Selection "Look at Me"

DAY 2 Differentiate Letter Recognition

- Letters *Vv*
  - Decodable Reader

DAY 3 Differentiate Vocabulary

- Develop Vocabulary: Location Words
- Kindergarten Student Reader

DAY 4 Differentiate Language

- Develop Language
- Get Set, Roll! Reader

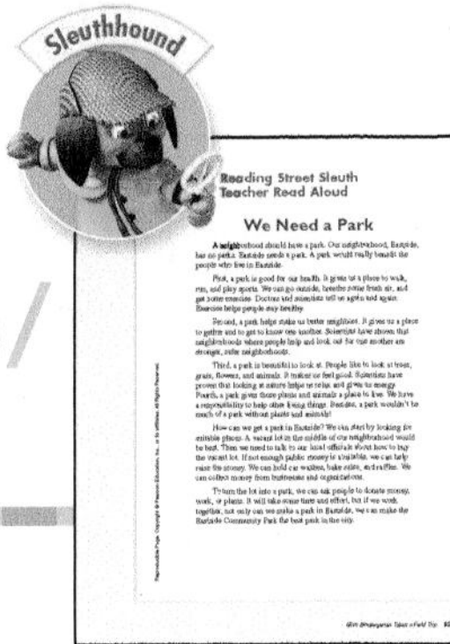

DAY 5 Differentiate Letter Recognition/ Close Reading

- Letters *Ww, Xx, Yy, Zz*
  - "We Need a Park"

Place English Language Learners in the groups that correspond to their reading abilities.
If... children need scaffolding and practice,
then... use the ELL notes on the page.

Independent Practice

Independent Practice Stations

See pp. 318 and 319 for Independent Stations.

Reading Street Digital Path

Independent Practice Activities available in the Digital Path.

Independent Reading

See p. 319 for independent reading suggestions.

On-Level

Common Core State Standards

Literature 1. With prompting and support, ask and answer questions about key details in a text. **Literature 10.** Actively engage in group reading activities with purpose and understanding. **Foundational Skills 1.d.** Recognize and name all upper- and lowercase letters of the alphabet. **Foundational Skills 2.d.** Isolate and pronounce the initial, medial vowel, and final sounds (phonemes) in three-phoneme (consonant-vowel-consonant, or CVC) words.* (This does not include CVCs ending with /l/, /r/, or /x/.) **Foundational Skills 3.c.** Read common high-frequency words by sight (e.g., *the, of, to, you, she, my, is, are, do, does*).

1 Build Word Knowledge

Practice Phonemic Awareness

LISTEN FOR INITIAL SOUNDS Two words that begin with the same sound have the same initial sound. *Initial* means "first" or "beginning." Say these words: *bat, big, ball.* Have children repeat the words with you. How are these words alike? Yes, they all begin with the same sound. Have children say the following sets of words and tell which words in each set begin with the same sound: *mat, mouse, top; rock, soap, sign; desk, girl, door; paint, paper, table.*

Practice Letter Recognition

RECOGNIZE LETTERS *Tt* AND *Uu* Display the *Tt* and *Uu* Alphabet Cards. Have children identify the letters and pictures. Then write the letter *U* on chart paper. Have a child write the letter and say the letter name. Continue with the other letters until everyone has had a turn to identify a letter.

2 Read

Decodable Story 4 *Am I Little?*

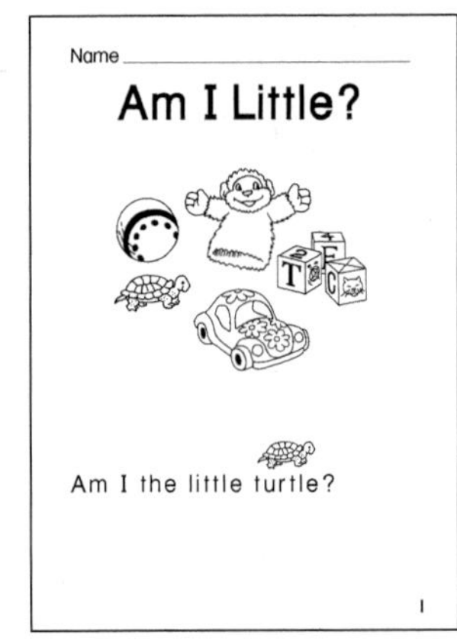

READ Have children read the story. Then have them reread the text to develop automaticity.

HIGH-FREQUENCY WORDS Have children return to the text and identify the high-frequency words *the* and *little.* Help children demonstrate their understanding of these words by completing sentence frames such as these: _______ *clock is on* _______ *wall.* (The, the) *A kitten is* _______. (little) Continue with the words *I* and *am.*

3 Reread for Fluency

Have children reread the Decodable Story *Am I Little?* individually to develop fluency.

Independent Reading Options

Trade Book Library

eSTREET INTERACTIVE
www.ReadingStreet.com

Teacher's Guides available on the Leveled Reader Database.

On-Level

1 Build Word Knowledge

Practice Letter Recognition

RECOGNIZE LETTERS *Vv* Display the *Vv* Alphabet Card. Have children name the letters with you. Have volunteers write uppercase *V* and lowercase *v* on chart paper. Ask children to explain how the two letters are different.

Practice High-Frequency Words

CHOOSE AND USE Display the high-frequency word cards *the, little, I,* and *am.* Say the word *the* and choose a volunteer to point to the correct word card. Have children say the word and use it in a sentence. Continue with the other high-frequency words.

2 Read

Decodable Reader 4 *At the Zoo*

CONCEPTS OF PRINT Display Decodable Reader 4 in *My Skills Buddy.* Show children the illustrations and read aloud the title. What do you think the story is about?

READ Have children take turns reading the Decodable Reader. Pause at the end of each page to ask questions. What animal do you see? Is this animal big or little?

3 Reread for Fluency

Have children reread the Decodable Reader *At the Zoo* individually to develop fluency.

SMALL GROUP TIME

More Reading for Group Time

CONCEPT LITERACY

- Concept Words
- High-Frequency Words

Use these suggested readers or other text at children's instructional level.

eStreet Interactive
www.ReadingStreet.com

Use the Leveled Reader Database for lesson plans and student pages for *Who Helps?*

If... children need more scaffolding and practice with phonemic awareness and letter recognition, **then...** use the activities on p. DI•63 in the Teacher Resources section of the Digital Path.

Common Core State Standards

Literature 1. With prompting and support, ask and answer questions about key details in a text. **Literature 10.** Actively engage in group reading activities with purpose and understanding. **Foundational Skills 3.c.** Read common high-frequency words by sight (e.g., *the, of, to, you, she, my, is, are, do, does*). **Language 5.a.** Sort common objects into categories (e.g., shapes, foods) to gain a sense of the concepts the categories represent. **Language 5.c.** Identify real-life connections between words and their use (e.g., note places at school that are *colorful*). **Language 6.** Use words and phrases acquired through conversations, reading and being read to, and responding to texts.

1 Build Word Knowledge

Develop Vocabulary

LOCATION WORDS Have children return to p. 88 in *My Skills Buddy.* Review the location words *library, park, school,* and *post office.* Point to each picture and ask children to name the place shown in the picture. Then ask children the following questions.

- Where can we go to learn how to read, write, and think?
- Where can we go to borrow a book or a movie?
- Where can we go to mail a package or buy stamps?
- Where can we go to take a walk or play a game outside?

Team Talk Have children work with a partner to use the location words in sentences.

2 Read

Kindergarten Student Reader *Cat and Dog Ride to Town*

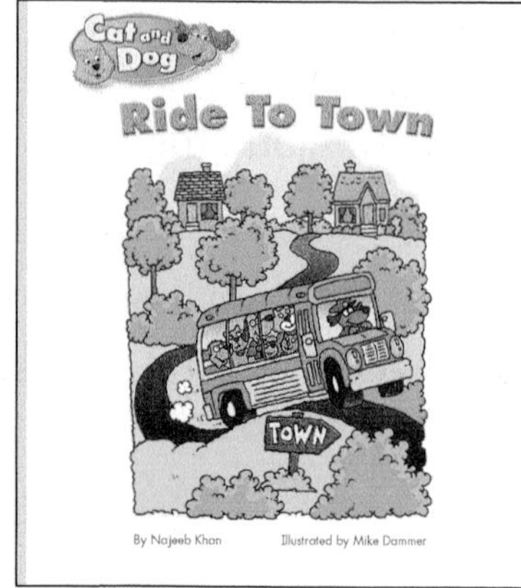

REREAD Display the reader and have children tell the title of the story. Have them tell what they remember about the story. Then have children read the story chorally. After reading each page, ask children to tell what they see. How do Cat and Dog get to town? Where do they go? What do they do or see there? To check children's understanding, have them take turns reading the story to a partner and then retelling the story to the partner.

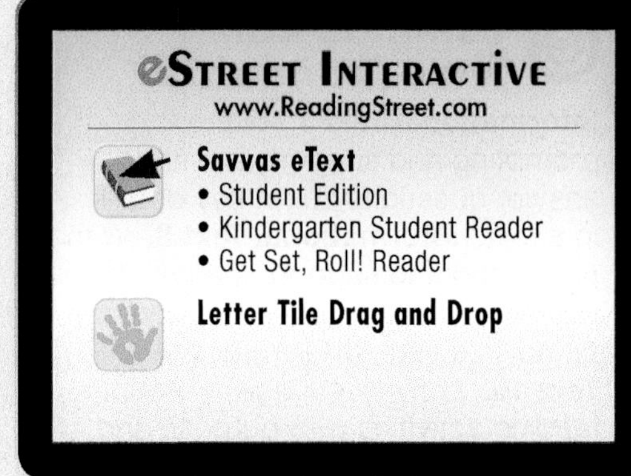

1 Build Word Knowledge

Develop Language

Display the Big Book *Miss Bindergarten Takes a Field Trip* and read the text on pp. 12–13.

Gwen McGunny rings a bell.
Henry holds a hose.
Ian makes a funny face
and laughs as his nose grooows.

- Ask children to read the text with you as you track the print.
- Point to the line, *Henry holds a hose.*
- What does the word *holds* mean here? What is another word that means the same as *holds?* Why do you think the author chose the word *holds?*
- **Team Talk** Turn to your partner and try some other words in place of *holds.*
- Continue the routine with the words *rings* and *laughs.*

2 Read

Get Set, Roll! Reader 4 *Pat*

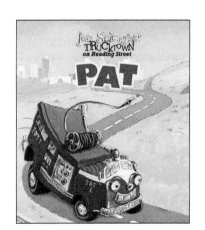

REVIEW HIGH-FREQUENCY WORDS Review the following high-frequency words with children: *I, am, the, little.* Ask them to use each word in a sentence.

REVIEW REBUS WORDS Distribute Letter Tiles to each child or use Letter Tile Drag and Drop in the Digital Path. Write the name *Pat* on a card. Use your letters to build this word. This spells the name of one of our Trucktown friends. What does this spell? Which character is Pat? Continue the routine with these words: *fire, expressway, zig, zag, splash.*

REREAD Have children whisper read *Pat* as you listen to each child. Then have children take turns reading the story aloud.

If... children need more scaffolding and practice with vocabulary, **then...** use the ELL activities on p. DI•65 in the Teacher Resources section of the Digital Path.

On-Level

Common Core State Standards

Informational Text 1. With prompting and support, ask and answer questions about key details in a text. **Informational Text 8.** With prompting and support, identify the reasons an author gives to support points in a text. **Informational Text 10.** Actively engage in group reading activities with purpose and understanding. **Foundational Skills 1.d.** Recognize and name all upper- and lowercase letters of the alphabet.

1 Build Word Knowledge

Practice Letter Recognition

RECOGNIZE LETTERS *Ww, Xx, Yy, Zz* Display the *Ww, Xx, Yy,* and *Zz* Alphabet Cards. Say the letter names and have children point to the correct letters. Write the eight letters in random order on chart paper. Say a letter name and have children find that letter and circle it. Continue until all the letters have been circled.

REVIEW LETTERS *Tt–Zz* Draw the following letter grid on a sheet of paper and give each child a copy. First have children point to and name the letters. Then have them match uppercase and lowercase forms by coloring each letter pair a different color.

X	U	y	v	T
V	t	♥	W	x
z	w	Y	u	Z

Corrective feedback

If... children have difficulty naming letters or matching letter forms,
then... review the letter names and forms using the Alphabet Cards.

2 Text-Based Comprehension

Read

READ ALOUD Read the Reading Street Sleuth Read Aloud, “We Need a Park,” on p. SG•61 to children.

READ LIKE A SLEUTH! Encourage children to cite evidence from the text to support their answers. You may wish to reread sections of the text to verify children’s answers.

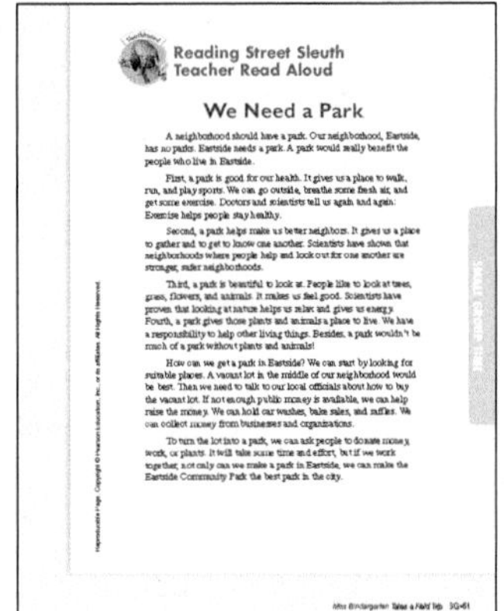
Reading Street Sleuth
Teacher Read Aloud

We Need a Park

A neighborhood should have a park. Our neighborhood, Eastside, has no parks. Eastside needs a park. A park would really benefit the people who live in Eastside.

First, a park is good for our health. It gives us a place to walk, run, and play sports. We can go outside, breathe some fresh air, and get some exercise. Doctors and scientists tell us again and again: Exercise helps people stay healthy.

Second, a park helps make us better neighbors. It gives us a place to gather and to get to know one another. Scientists have shown that neighborhoods where people help and look out for one another are stronger, safer neighborhoods.

Third, a park is beautiful to look at. People like to look at trees, grass, flowers, and animals. It makes us feel good. Scientists have proven that looking at nature helps us relax and gives us energy. Fourth, a park gives those plants and animals a place to live. We have a responsibility to help other living things. Besides, a park wouldn't be much of a park without plants and animals!

How can we get a park in Eastside? We can start by looking for suitable places. A vacant lot in the middle of our neighborhood would be best. Then we need to talk to our local officials about how to buy the vacant lot. If not enough public money is available, we can help raise the money. We can hold car washes, bake sales, and raffles. We can collect money from businesses and organizations.

To turn the lot into a park, we can ask people to donate money, work, or plants. It will take some time and effort, but if we work together, not only can we make a park in Eastside, we can make the Eastside Community Park the best park in the city.

Look for Evidence What reasons does the author give to support the idea that Eastside needs a park?

Ask Questions How can the author make this opinion piece stronger? What other questions should the author answer?

Prove It! Performance Task Have children draw a picture of a neighborhood park. Ask them to label the picture with one or two key details from the text. Children may write or dictate a short phrase or sentence.

We Need a Park

A neighborhood should have a park. Our neighborhood, Eastside, has no parks. Eastside needs a park. A park would really benefit the people who live in Eastside.

First, a park is good for our health. It gives us a place to walk, run, and play sports. We can go outside, breathe some fresh air, and get some exercise. Doctors and scientists tell us again and again: Exercise helps people stay healthy.

Second, a park helps make us better neighbors. It gives us a place to gather and to get to know one another. Scientists have shown that neighborhoods where people help and look out for one another are stronger, safer neighborhoods.

Third, a park is beautiful to look at. People like to look at trees, grass, flowers, and animals. It makes us feel good. Scientists have proven that looking at nature helps us relax and gives us energy. Fourth, a park gives those plants and animals a place to live. We have a responsibility to help other living things. Besides, a park wouldn't be much of a park without plants and animals!

How can we get a park in Eastside? We can start by looking for suitable places. A vacant lot in the middle of our neighborhood would be best. Then we need to talk to our local officials about how to buy the vacant lot. If not enough public money is available, we can help raise the money. We can hold car washes, bake sales, and raffles. We can collect money from businesses and organizations.

To turn the lot into a park, we can ask people to donate money, work, or plants. It will take some time and effort, but if we work together, not only can we make a park in Eastside, we can make the Eastside Community Park the best park in the city.

Reproducible Page. Copyright © Pearson Education, Inc., or its affiliates. All Rights Reserved.

Strategic Intervention

Common Core State Standards

Literature 1. With prompting and support, ask and answer questions about key details in a text. **Literature 10.** Actively engage in group reading activities with purpose and understanding. **Foundational Skills 1.d.** Recognize and name all upper- and lowercase letters of the alphabet. **Foundational Skills 2.d.** Isolate and pronounce the initial, medial vowel, and final sounds (phonemes) in three-phoneme (consonant-vowel-consonant, or CVC) words.* (This does not include CVCs ending with /l/, /r/, or /x/.) **Foundational Skills 3.c.** Read common high-frequency words by sight (e.g., *the, of, to, you, she, my, is, are, do, does*).

More Reading for Group Time

LISTEN TO ME READER

- Concepts of Print

Use these suggested readers or other text at children's instructional level.

eStreet Interactive
www.ReadingStreet.com

Use the Leveled Reader Database to access an online version of *Can You Find It?*

If... children need more scaffolding and practice with phonemic awareness and letter recognition, **then...** use the Phonics Transition lessons beginning on p. 447 in the *ELL Handbook.*

1 Build Word Knowledge

Reteach Phonemic Awareness

LISTEN FOR INITIAL SOUNDS Remind children that words that begin the same have the same beginning, or initial, sound. We can tell whether two words begin with the same sound by listening to the initial sounds in the words. *Initial* means "first" or "beginning." I will say two words and I want you to tell me whether they begin with the same sound. Use these word pairs: *pig, pen; can, mop; book, bat; ball, wall; hat, hug.*

Reteach Letter Recognition

RECOGNIZE LETTERS *Tt* AND *Uu* Write *Uu* on chart paper. This is uppercase *U*. This is lowercase *u*. Point out that *U* and *u* look alike except that *U* is bigger than *u*. Write *T* and *t* on the chart paper. This is uppercase *T*. This is lowercase *t*. Ask children how these letters are alike and different. Then point to the letters in random order and have children say the letter names.

2 Read

Decodable Story 4 *Am I Little?*

REVIEW HIGH-FREQUENCY WORDS Write *the* on chart paper. This is the word *the*. Say the letters with me: *t, h, e*. Continue with the word *little*. Then review the words *I* and *am*.

Corrective feedback	**If...** children have difficulty reading the high-frequency words, **then...** say a word and have children point to the word. Repeat several times, giving assistance as needed.

READ Have children read the story.

3 Reread for Fluency

Have children reread the story *Am I Little?* chorally. Then have them reread the story several times individually to develop fluency.

1 Build Word Knowledge

Reteach Phonemic Awareness

PRACTICE DISCRIMINATING INITIAL SOUNDS Display the *top* and *tent* Picture Cards. Say the picture names and have children repeat the picture names with you. Do these words begin the same? Do they have the same initial sound? Yes, *top* and *tent* begin with the same sound. Continue with these pairs of Picture Cards: *box, can; seal, sock; pan, red; nut, nest; mop, man; jam, hat; desk, dog.*

Reteach Letter Recognition

RECOGNIZE LETTERS *Vv* Display the *Vv* Alphabet Card. Point to and name each letter. Then point to lowercase *v.* What letter is this? Point to uppercase *V.* What letter is this? Write the name *Vivian* on chart paper. Have children find uppercase *V* and lowercase *v* in the word.

Reteach High-Frequency Words

REVIEW Have children read each previously taught high-frequency word as you point to it on the Word Wall.

the	little	I	am

Corrective feedback	**If...** children have difficulty reading the words, **then...** say a word and have children point to the word. Repeat several times, giving assistance as needed.

2 Read

Decodable Reader 4 *At the Zoo*

CONCEPTS OF PRINT Display Decodable Reader 4 in *My Skills Buddy.* The title of this story is *At the Zoo.* The author is Nitty Jones. The illustrator is Amy Sparks. Look at the picture on the cover. Look at the pictures inside. What do you think the story is about?

READ Let's read the story together. After reading chorally with children, have them reread the story several times with a partner and then independently.

SMALL GROUP TIME

Independent Reading Options

Trade Book Library

eStreet Interactive
www.ReadingStreet.com

Teacher's Guides available on the Leveled Reader Database.

If... children need more support with letter recognition,
then... use the ELL activities on p. DI•63 in the Teacher Resources section of the Digital Path.

Strategic Intervention

Common Core State Standards

Literature 1. With prompting and support, ask and answer questions about key details in a text. **Literature 10.** Actively engage in group reading activities with purpose and understanding. **Foundational Skills 3.c.** Read common high-frequency words by sight (e.g., *the, of, to, you, she, my, is, are, do, does*). **Language 5.a.** Sort common objects into categories (e.g., shapes, foods) to gain a sense of the concepts the categories represent. **Language 5.c.** Identify real-life connections between words and their use (e.g., note places at school that are *colorful*). **Language 6.** Use words and phrases acquired through conversations, reading and being read to, and responding to texts.

1 Build Word Knowledge

Develop Vocabulary

RETEACH LOCATION WORDS Have children return to p. 88 of *My Skills Buddy* to review the location words *library, park, school,* and *post office.*

- Which picture shows a park? What can we do in a park?
- Which picture shows a school? What do we do at school?
- Which picture shows a library? What can we do in a library?
- Which picture shows a post office? What can we do in a post office?

Display other pictures of a library, park, school, and post office. Write the words on index cards. Ask children to label the pictures with the cards.

2 Read

Kindergarten Student Reader *Cat and Dog Ride to Town*

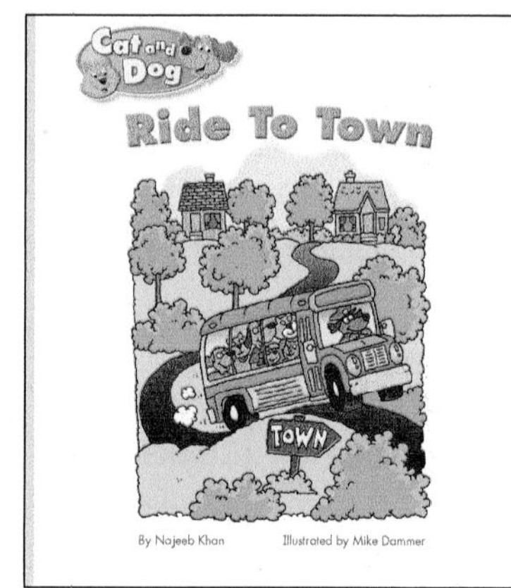

REVIEW REBUS WORDS Write *bus* on chart paper. This is the word *bus.* Name the letters with me: *b, u, s.* Repeat with the other rebus words *library, school, music store, firefighter, vet,* and *happy.*

REVIEW HIGH-FREQUENCY WORDS Write *little* on chart paper. Ask children to read the word with you. Have a volunteer read the word. Continue with the other high-frequency words *the, I,* and *am.*

REREAD STORY Display the reader. The title of this book is *Cat and Dog Ride to Town.* What do you think the story is about? Read the story chorally with children. Pause at the end of each page to ask: Whom do you see? Where are they? What are they doing? Have children reread the story several times to build fluency.

ELL

If... children need more scaffolding and practice with vocabulary,
then... use the ELL activities on p. DI•65 in the Teacher Resources section of the Digital Path.

1 Build Word Knowledge

Develop Language

Display the Big Book *Miss Bindergarten Takes a Field Trip* and read the text on pp. 12–13.

Gwen McGunny rings a bell.
Henry holds a hose.
Ian makes a funny face
and laughs as his nose grooows.

- Ask children to read the text with you as you track the print.
- Point to the line, *Henry holds a hose.*
- What does the word *holds* mean? What is another word that means the same as *holds?*
- I am going to say three words. I want you to tell me which word means the same as *holds: grips, cuts, drops; stores, grabs, waves; drags, sees, grasps.*
- Why do you think the author used the word *holds?*
- Continue the routine with the words *rings* and *laughs.*

2 Read

Get Set, Roll! Reader 4 *Pat*

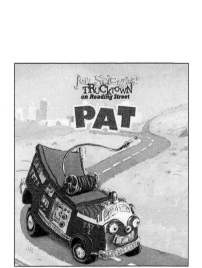

REVIEW HIGH-FREQUENCY AND REBUS WORDS Review the high-frequency and rebus words (*I, am, the, little, Pat, fire, expressway, zig, zag, splash*) using the following routine.

1. Display and read the word.
2. Name the letters in the word.
3. Read the word. Use it in a sentence.

REREAD Have children chorally read aloud *Pat* several times. Then ask them to take turns reading a page aloud.

Independent Reading Options

Trade Book Library

eSTREET INTERACTIVE
www.ReadingStreet.com

Teacher's Guides available on the Leveled Reader Database.

Common Core State Standards

Literature 1. With prompting and support, ask and answer questions about key details in a text. **Literature 10.** Actively engage in group reading activities with purpose and understanding. **Informational Text 1.** With prompting and support, ask and answer questions about key details in a text. **Informational Text 8.** With prompting and support, identify the reasons an author gives to support points in a text. **Informational Text 10.** Actively engage in group reading activities with purpose and understanding. **Foundational Skills 1.d.** Recognize and name all upper- and lowercase letters of the alphabet.

1 Build Word Knowledge

Reteach Letter Recognition

RECOGNIZE LETTERS *Ww, Xx, Yy, Zz* Write the letters *W, w, X, x, Y, y, Z,* and *z* on index cards. Place the cards in a box. Have a child take a card, name the letter, and write the letter on chart paper. The other children can write the letter in the air. Continue until all cards have been used. Repeat until everyone gets a chance to write a letter on the chart paper.

REVIEW LETTERS *Tt–Zz* Write the letters *T, t, U, u, V,* and *v* on index cards. Add these cards to the cards from the activity above. Mix the cards and place them face up on a tabletop. First have children match the uppercase and lowercase forms of the letters. Then have children put the pairs of letters in alphabetical order.

Corrective feedback

If... children have difficulty with matching or alphabetical order,
then... place the *Tt–Zz* Alphabet Cards in order on the chalk ledge for children to refer to.

2 Text-Based Comprehension

Read

READ ALOUD Read the Reading Street Sleuth Read Aloud, "We Need a Park," on p. SG•61 to children.

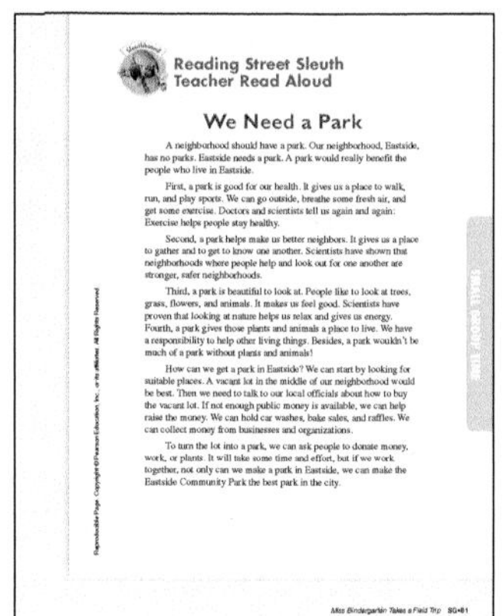
Reading Street Sleuth
Teacher Read Aloud

We Need a Park

A neighborhood should have a park. Our neighborhood, Eastside, has no parks. Eastside needs a park. A park would really benefit the people who live in Eastside.

First, a park is good for our health. It gives us a place to walk, run, and play sports. We can go outside, breathe some fresh air, and get some exercise. Doctors and scientists tell us again and again: Exercise helps people stay healthy.

Second, a park helps make us better neighbors. It gives us a place to gather and to get to know one another. Scientists have shown that neighborhoods where people help and look out for one another are stronger, safer neighborhoods.

Third, a park is beautiful to look at. People like to look at trees, grass, flowers, and animals. It makes us feel good. Scientists have proven that looking at nature helps us relax and gives us energy. Fourth, a park gives those plants and animals a place to live. We have a responsibility to help other living things. Besides, a park wouldn't be much of a park without plants and animals!

How can we get a park in Eastside? We can start by looking for suitable places. A vacant lot in the middle of our neighborhood would be best. Then we need to talk to our local officials about how to buy the vacant lot. If not enough public money is available, we can help raise the money. We can hold car washes, bake sales, and raffles. We can collect money from businesses and organizations.

To turn the lot into a park, we can ask people to donate money, work, or plants. It will take some time and effort, but if we work together, not only can we make a park in Eastside, we can make the Eastside Community Park the best park in the city.

Reproducible Page. Copyright © Pearson Education, Inc., or its affiliates. All Rights Reserved.

Miss Bindergarten Takes a Field Trip SG•61

READ LIKE A SLEUTH! Encourage children to cite evidence from the text to support their answers. You may wish to reread sections of the text to verify children's answers.

Look for Evidence What is the author's opinion? (Eastside needs a park.) What reasons does the author give to support this opinion?

Ask Questions What else do you need to know about the park? What other questions should the author answer?

Prove It! Performance Task Have children draw a picture of a neighborhood park. Ask them to dictate a phrase or short sentence for the picture using one or two key details from the text. Read children's phrases or sentences to them as you track the print.

Advanced

1 Build Word Knowledge

Extend Letter Recognition

CONNECT *Tt* TO /t/ AND *Uu* TO /u/ Display the *Tt* Alphabet Card. Ask children to name the letters and identify the picture. Point to the letters *Tt* and say the picture name *turtle.* I am going to say a word. The word is *target.* Do the words *turtle* and *target* begin with the same sound? Say the words with me: *turtle, target.* Because *turtle* and *target* both begin with /t/, let's write the letter *t* in the air. Continue with these words: *tissue, yellow, temper, topic, weather, valley, tasty, zero.* Repeat the routine for *Uu* using these words: *umbrella, upset, water, uncle, tumble, ultimate, under, zipper, umpire, very.*

2 Read

"Look at Me"

CONCEPTS OF PRINT Read aloud the title of the story, "Look at Me." Remember, the title of a story usually gives us clues to what the story is about. Ask children what the title tells them about the story. (Someone in the story wants someone else to watch what he or she is doing.)

TEACH STORY WORDS Present any story words that children may need help with, such as *looks, taps, nods, pats, hops, like* (meaning "in the same way as"), *and*, and *rest.* Use the words in sentences that give clues to their meanings. For example, I look *like* my mom. My mom and I look alike. First I run. Then I stop and *rest.*

READ Distribute copies of "Look at Me" from p. SG•68, and have children read it on their own. Then have them take turns reading the story aloud. After reading, have children tell whom the story is about and what happens.

More Reading for Group Time

INDEPENDENT READER

- More Challenging Text

Use the suggested Leveled Reader or other text at children's instructional level.

eStreet Interactive
www.ReadingStreet.com

Use the Leveled Reader Database for lesson plans and student pages for *Red and Blue.*

If... children need more practice with letter recognition,
then... use the Phonics Transition lessons beginning on p. 447 in the *ELL Handbook.*

Look at Me

Pam looks at me.
I tap.
Pam taps like me.
I nod.
Pam nods like me.
I look at Pam.
Pam pats.
I pat like Pam.
Pam hops.
I hop like Pam.
Pam and I sit.
We have to rest!
I look at Pam.
I rap.

Reproducible Page. Copyright © Pearson Education, Inc., or its affiliates. All Rights Reserved.

Advanced Phonics Selection 4

Advanced

1 Build Word Knowledge

Extend Letter Recognition

 **CONNECT *Vv* TO /v/** Display the *Vv* Alphabet Card. Ask children to name the letters and identify the picture. Point to the letters *Vv* and say the picture name *volcano.* I am going to say a word. The word is *violin.* Do the words *volcano* and *violin* begin with the same sound? Say the words with me: *volcano, violin.* Because *volcano* and *violin* both begin with /v/, let's write the letter *v* in the air. Continue with these words: *vanilla, yesterday, vegetable, volunteer, tambourine, vacation, wilderness, uppercase.*

2 Read

Decodable Reader 4 *At the Zoo*

CONCEPTS OF PRINT Display Decodable Reader 4 in *My Skills Buddy.* Ask children to identify the author and illustrator.

READ Have children read the Decodable Reader quietly as you listen to them. Then have them take turns reading aloud one page at a time.

3 Reread for Fluency

Have children reread Decodable Reader 4 *At the Zoo* to develop fluency.

SMALL GROUP TIME

Independent Reading Options

Trade Book Library

eStreet Interactive
www.ReadingStreet.com

Teacher's Guides available on the Leveled Reader Database.

ELL

If... children need more support with letter recognition,
then... use the ELL activities on pp. DI•63, DI•66–DI•67 in the Teacher Resources section of the Digital Path.

Advanced

Common Core State Standards

Literature 1. With prompting and support, ask and answer questions about key details in a text. **Literature 10.** Actively engage in group reading activities with purpose and understanding. **Foundational Skills 3.c.** Read common high-frequency words by sight (e.g., *the, of, to, you, she, my, is, are, do, does*). **Language 5.a.** Sort common objects into categories (e.g., shapes, foods) to gain a sense of the concepts the categories represent. **Language 5.c.** Identify real-life connections between words and their use (e.g., note places at school that are *colorful*). **Language 6.** Use words and phrases acquired through conversations, reading and being read to, and responding to texts.

1 Build Word Knowledge

Develop Vocabulary

LOCATION WORDS Review the location words *library, park, school,* and *post office* with children. Have them use the words in sentences.

Let's learn more location words. Remember, location words name places. Have children identify the location words in these sentences.

- The police car parked in front of the *police station.*
- The ambulance rushed to the *hospital.*
- We bought milk and bread at the *grocery store.*

Team Talk Have children work in pairs to use *police station, hospital,* and *grocery store* in their own sentences. Ask them to illustrate one of the new location words and write a phrase or sentence to describe their picture.

2 Read

Kindergarten Student Reader *Cat and Dog Ride to Town*

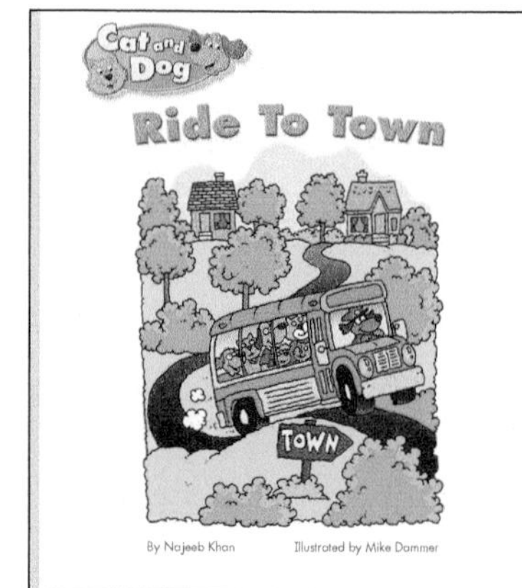

REREAD STORY Display the reader and have children read the title with you. Then have them read the story. Finally, have them reread the story aloud several times to build fluency.

EXTEND STORY Ask children to recall who the characters in the story are and what places they are visiting. What could happen next in the story? Encourage children to think of another place that the characters go while they are in the town. Have children draw a picture and write a sentence to go with the picture.

If... children need more scaffolding and practice with vocabulary, **then...** use the ELL activities on p. DI•65 in the Teacher Resources section of the Digital Path.

Advanced

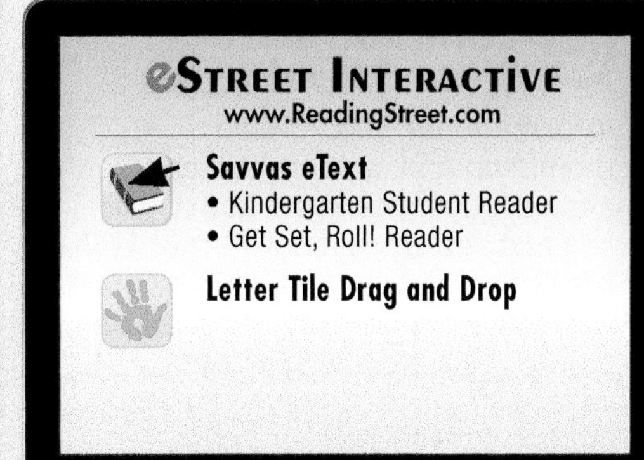

1 Build Word Knowledge

Develop Language

Display the Big Book *Miss Bindergarten Takes a Field Trip* and read the text on pp. 12–13.

Gwen McGunny rings a bell.
Henry holds a hose.
Ian makes a funny face
and laughs as his nose grooows.

- Ask children to read the text with you as you track the print.
- Point to the line, *Ian makes a funny face.* Read this with me.
- What does the word *funny* mean here? What is another word that has almost the same meaning as *funny*? Why did the author choose the word *funny*?
- Continue the routine with the words *laughs, rings,* and *holds.*
- Team Talk Have children work with a partner to replace key words in a sentence with simpler words or synonyms without changing the meaning of the sentence. Use sentence frames, such as the following.

  Gwen McGunny _______ a bell.

  Henry _______ a hose.

2 Read

Get Set, Roll! Reader 4 *Pat*

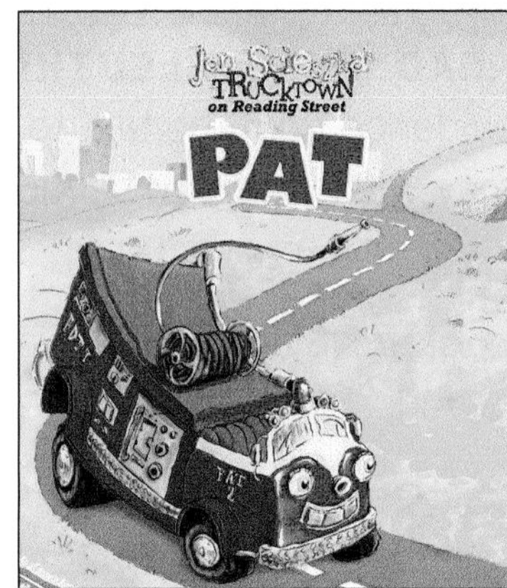

REVIEW HIGH-FREQUENCY AND REBUS WORDS Review the high-frequency and rebus words by asking children to spell the words with Letter Tiles. (*I, am, the, little, Pat, fire, expressway, zig, zag, splash*)

REREAD Have children whisper read *Pat* as you listen to each child. Then have children take turns reading the story aloud.

3 Reread for Fluency

BUILD FLUENCY Have children read again with expression and accuracy. Encourage them to use self-correction techniques for any mistakes.

SMALL GROUP TIME

Independent Reading Options

Trade Book Library

eStreet Interactive
www.ReadingStreet.com

Teacher's Guides available on the Leveled Reader Database.

Advanced

Common Core State Standards

Informational Text 1. With prompting and support, ask and answer questions about key details in a text. **Informational Text 8.** With prompting and support, identify the reasons an author gives to support points in a text. **Informational Text 10.** Actively engage in group reading activities with purpose and understanding. **Foundational Skills 1.d.** Recognize and name all upper- and lowercase letters of the alphabet.

1 Build Word Knowledge

Extend Letter Recognition

CONNECT LETTERS TO SOUNDS Display the *Ww, Xx, Yy,* and *Zz* Alphabet Cards. Ask children to name the letters and identify the pictures. Point to the letters and say the picture names emphasizing the beginning sounds. Explain that the /eks/ sound spelled *x* is usually found at the end, not the beginning, of words. Now I am going to say two words. Tell me the sound at the beginning of both words and the letter that stands for that sound. Hold up the appropriate Alphabet Card and repeat the words together. Use these pairs of words: *yogurt, yummy; waffle, willow; zebra, zany.*

WRITE WORDS Distribute paper and pencils to children. Today we are going to use what we know about letters and the sounds they stand for to write words. I am going to say some words, and I want you to write them. Listen carefully.

1. yet **2.** cub **3.** van **4.** fox **5.** zip **6.** wag

2 Text-Based Comprehension

Read

READ ALOUD Read the Reading Street Sleuth Read Aloud, "We Need a Park," on p. SG•61 to children.

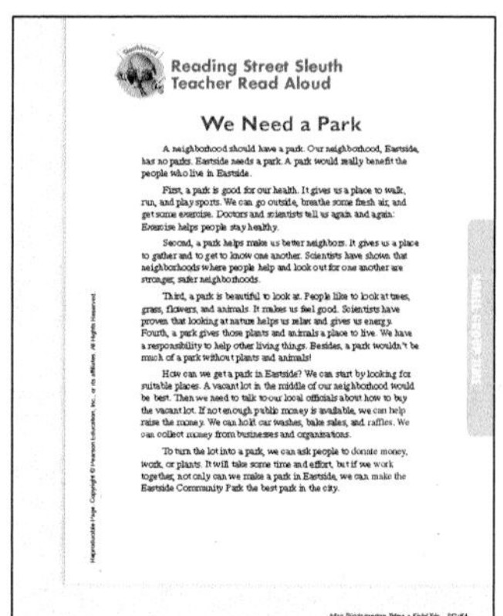

Reading Street Sleuth Teacher Read Aloud

We Need a Park

A neighborhood should have a park. Our neighborhood, Eastside, has no parks. Eastside needs a park. A park would really benefit the people who live in Eastside.

First, a park is good for our health. It gives us a place to walk, run, and play sports. We can go outside, breathe some fresh air, and get some exercise. Doctors and scientists tell us again and again: Exercise helps people stay healthy.

Second, a park helps make us better neighbors. It gives us a place to gather and to get to know one another. Scientists have shown that neighborhoods where people help and look out for one another are stronger, safer neighborhoods.

Third, a park is beautiful to look at. People like to look at trees, grass, flowers, and animals. It makes us feel good. Scientists have proven that looking at nature helps us relax and gives us energy. Fourth, a park gives those plants and animals a place to live. We have a responsibility to help other living things. Besides, a park wouldn't be much of a park without plants and animals!

How can we get a park in Eastside? We can start by looking for suitable places. A vacant lot in the middle of our neighborhood would be best. Then we need to talk to our local officials about how to buy the vacant lot. If not enough public money is available, we can help raise the money. We can hold car washes, bake sales, and raffles. We can collect money from businesses and organizations.

To turn the lot into a park, we can ask people to donate money, work, or plants. It will take some time and effort, but if we work together, not only can we make a park in Eastside, we can make the Eastside Community Park the best park in the city.

READ LIKE A SLEUTH! Encourage children to cite evidence from the text to support their answers. You may wish to reread sections of the text to verify children's answers.

Look for Evidence What reasons does the author give to support his or her opinion?

Ask Questions What other questions do you think the author should answer to make his or her opinion piece stronger?

Prove It! Performance Task Have children draw pictures of a vacant lot and a neighborhood park. Ask them to write a sentence or two for each picture using key details from the text. Have children read their sentences to you.

Teaching the Common Core State Standards This Week

The Common Core State Standards for English Language Arts are divided into strands for **Reading** (including **Foundational Skills**), **Writing**, **Speaking and Listening**, and **Language**. The chart below shows some of the content you will teach this week, strand by strand. Turn to this week's 5-Day Planner on pages 420–421 to see how this content is taught each day.

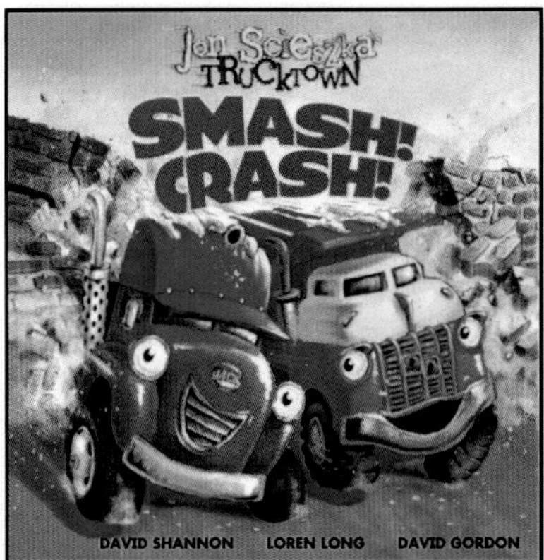

Reading Strand

- **Phonemic Awareness:** Initial and Final /m/
- **Phonics:** /m/ Spelled *Mm*
- **Text-Based Comprehension:** Character
- **High-Frequency Words:** *a, to*
- **Genre:** Fantasy

Writing Strand

- **Wonderful, Marvelous Me**
- **Respond to Literature**
- **Genre:** Caption
- **Extend the Concept**
- **This Week We...**

Common Core State Standards for English Language Arts

Speaking and Listening Strand

- **Content Knowledge:** Build Oral Language
- **Listening and Speaking:** Announcements/Messages

Language Strand

- **Oral Vocabulary: Amazing Words** *signals, dud, proper, pirates, perfect, fabulous*
- **Vocabulary:** Position Words
- **Academic Vocabulary:** *blend, character, noun, fantasy, caption, announcement, sequence, signs, consonant*
- **Conventions:** Nouns for People and Animals

Text-Based Comprehension

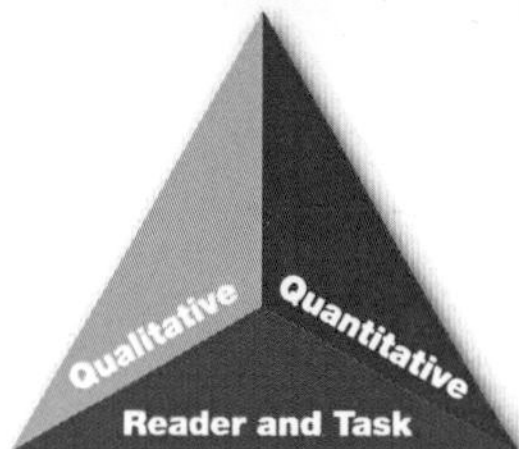

Text Complexity Measures

Use the rubric to familiarize yourself with the text complexity of ***Smash! Crash!***

Bridge to Complex Knowledge

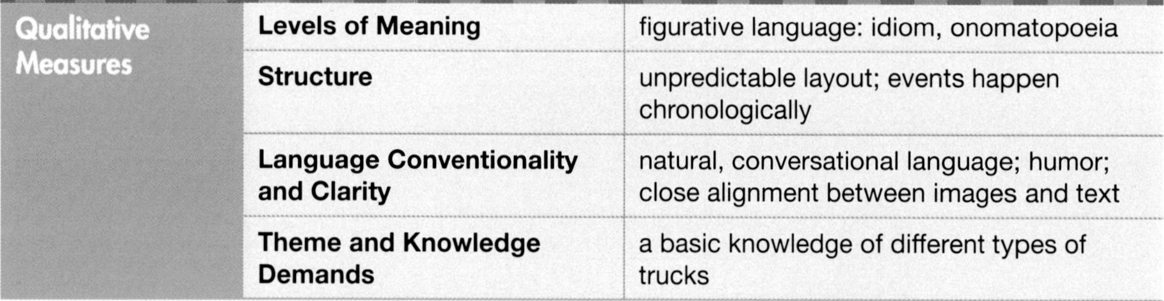

Qualitative Measures		
	Levels of Meaning	figurative language: idiom, onomatopoeia
	Structure	unpredictable layout; events happen chronologically
	Language Conventionality and Clarity	natural, conversational language; humor; close alignment between images and text
	Theme and Knowledge Demands	a basic knowledge of different types of trucks

Reader and Task Suggestions

FORMATIVE ASSESSMENT Based on assessment results, use the **Reader and Task Suggestions** in Access Main Selection to scaffold the selection or support independence for children as they read ***Smash! Crash!***

READER AND TASK SUGGESTIONS	
Preparing to Read the Text	**Leveled Tasks**
• Review the Amazing Words and have children use them to talk about the selection. • Discuss the use of quotation marks to show words that the characters say in a story.	• **Theme and Knowledge Demands** If children have trouble remembering key details, have them look at the illustrations carefully, name each character, and tell what kind of truck it is.

Recommended Placement This text is appropriate for placement as a read aloud at this level due to the qualitative elements of the selection.

Focus on Common Core State Standards

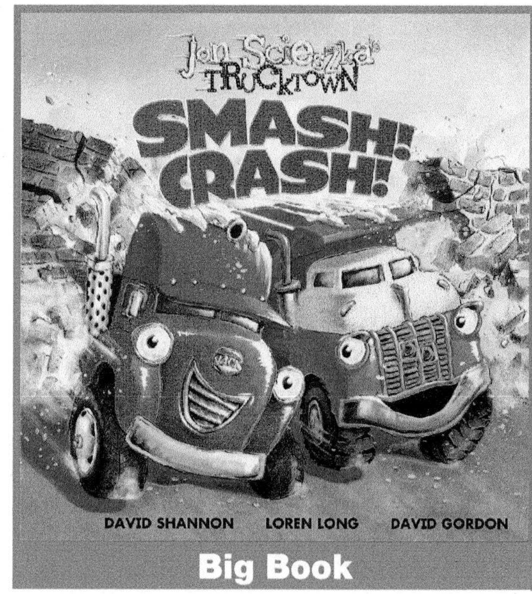

Jon Scieszka's
TRUCKTOWN
SMASH! CRASH!
DAVID SHANNON LOREN LONG DAVID GORDON

Big Book

Text-Based Comprehension

 **Character**
CCSS Literature 2.,
CCSS Literature 3.

Phonics

 **/m/ Spelled *Mm***
CCSS Foundational Skills 1.d.,
CCSS Foundational Skills 2.,
CCSS Foundational Skills 2.d.

Writing and Conventions

Genre: Caption
CCSS Writing 2.

Conventions: Nouns for People and Animals
CCSS Speaking/Listening 4.,
CCSS Language 1.b.

Oral Vocabulary

Amazing Words

signals	dud
proper	pirates
perfect	fabulous

CCSS Language 6.

Phonemic Awareness

Initial and Final /m/
CCSS Foundational Skills 2.d.,
CCSS Foundational Skills 2.e.

High-Frequency Words

a to

CCSS Foundational Skills 3.c.

Listening and Speaking

Announcements/Messages
CCSS Speaking/Listening 1.a.

Preview Your Week

What do you like to do with your friends?

Big Book

Genre: Fantasy

Phonics: /m/ Spelled *Mm*

Text-Based Comprehension: Character

Build Content Knowledge

KNOWLEDGE GOALS
Children will understand that playing with others

- helps them share fun experiences
- helps them share a common goal

BUILD ORAL VOCABULARY
This week, children will acquire the following academic vocabulary/ domain-specific words.

Amazing Words

signals	dud
proper	pirates
perfect	fabulous

BUILD INDEPENDENT READERS
Children will enjoy becoming independent readers as they build decoding skills.

Get Set, Roll! Reader

Decodable Reader

OPTIONAL CONCEPT-BASED READING Use the Digital Path to access readers offering different levels of text complexity.

Concept Literacy

Listen to Me Reader

Student Reader

Independent Reader

This Week's Digital Resources

eStreet Interactive

www.ReadingStreet.com

Get Ready to Read

Big Question Video This video on the Digital Path introduces children to the unit question, *How do we live, work, and play together?,* and provides background for the reading children will do throughout the unit.

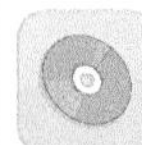

Background Building Audio CD This audio CD provides valuable background information about what friends like to do together to help children read and comprehend the weekly texts.

Concept Talk Video Use this video on the Digital Path to build momentum and introduce the weekly concept of friends doing things together.

Interactive Sing with Me Chart and Audio "Won't You Play With Me?," sung to the tune of "Zip a Dee Doo Dah," introduces the Amazing Words with a catchy, concept-related song.

Phonics Songs and Rhymes Audio "Mr. Malcolm Monkey," sung to the tune of "I'm a Little Teapot," helps teach the phonics skill consonant *Mm*/m/.

Letter Tile Drag and Drop Using this interactive tool, children click and spell words to enhance their newly learned phonics skills.

Savvas eText For phonics and fluency support, use the eText of the Decodable Reader; the Student Reader; and the Get Set, Roll! Reader on the Leveled Reader Database.

Read and Comprehend

Envision It! Animations Use this colorful animation on the Digital Path to explain the target comprehension skill, Character.

Savvas eText Go to Savvas SuccessNet and use the eText of the many student edition pages in *My Skills Buddy* with audio support.

Story Sort Use the Story Sort Activity on the Digital Path after reading *Smash! Crash!* to involve children in retelling.

Language Arts

Grammar Jammer Choose a whimsical animation on the Digital Path to provide an engaging lesson on Nouns for People and Animals that will capture children's attention.

Additional Resources

Teacher Resources DVD-ROM Use the following resources on the TR DVD or on Savvas SuccessNet throughout the week:

- Amazing Word Cards
- High-Frequency Word Cards
- Daily Fix-It Transparencies
- Reader's and Writer's Notebook
- Scoring Rubrics

This Week's Skills

Phonics
/m/ Spelled *Mm*

Comprehension
Skill: Character

Language
Vocabulary: Position Words
Conventions: Nouns for People and Animals

Writing
Wonderful, Marvelous Me!
Respond to Literature
Genre Writing
Extend the Concept
This Week We …

5-Day Planner

DAY 1

Get Ready to Read

Content Knowledge 426
Oral Vocabulary: *signals, dud, proper, pirates, perfect, fabulous*

Phonemic Awareness 428
Initial /m/
Monitor Progress
Check Phonemic Awareness

Phonics 430
/m/ Spelled *Mm*

Handwriting 432
Mm

High-Frequency Words 433
a, to

READ Decodable Story 5 434
Little Mouse

Read and Comprehend

Text-Based Comprehension 436
Character

Language Arts

Conventions 438
Nouns for People and Animals

Writing 439
Wonderful, Marvelous Me!
Daily Handwriting

Listening and Speaking 440
Announcements/Messages

Extend Your Day! 441

DAY 2

Get Ready to Read

Content Knowledge 442
Oral Vocabulary: *signals, dud*

Phonemic Awareness 444
Initial /m/

Phonics 446
/m/ Spelled *Mm*
Monitor Progress
Check Sound-Spelling

Handwriting 448
Write Words with *Mm*

High-Frequency Words 449
a, to

READ Decodable Reader 5 450
Animal Friends

Read and Comprehend

Text-Based Comprehension 452
READ *Smash! Crash!*—1st Read
Think, Talk, and Write
Monitor Progress Check Retelling

Language Arts

Conventions 455
Names for People and Animals

Writing 456
Respond to Literature
Daily Handwriting

Vocabulary 457
Position Words

Extend Your Day! 459

DAY 3

Get Ready to Read

Content Knowledge 460
Oral Vocabulary: *proper, pirates*

Phonemic Awareness 462
Initial and Final /m/

Phonics 464
/m/ Spelled *Mm*

Monitor Progress
Check Word Reading
High-Frequency Words

READ Kindergarten Student Reader 466
Cat and Dog Eat Together

Read and Comprehend

Text-Based Comprehension 468
READ *Smash! Crash!*—2nd Read

Language Arts

Conventions 486
Review What We Can Do

Writing 487
Caption
Daily Handwriting

Listening and Speaking 488
Announcements/Messages

Extend Your Day! 491

DAY 4

Get Ready to Read

Content Knowledge 492
Oral Vocabulary: *perfect, fabulous*

Phonemic Awareness 494
Review Initial Sound Discrimination

Letter Recognition 495
Review Letter Names

Monitor Progress
Check Letter Recognition

Spelling 496
/m/ Spelled *Mm*

Get Set, Roll! Reader 5 497
READ *Zoom!*

Read and Comprehend

Text-Based Comprehension 498
Character
Review Sequence
READ *Smash! Crash!*—3rd Read

Language Arts

Conventions 500
Nouns for People and Animals

Writing 501
Extend the Concept
Daily Handwriting

Vocabulary 502
Position Words

Extend Your Day! 503

DAY 5

Get Ready to Read

Content Knowledge 504
Review Oral Vocabulary

Monitor Progress
Check Oral Vocabulary

Phonemic Awareness 506
Review /m/

Phonics 507
Review /m/ Spelled *Mm*

Assessment 508

Monitor Progress
Check Sound Discrimination and Word Reading

Read and Comprehend

Let's Practice It! 510
Signs

Assessment 512
Review Character

Language Arts

Conventions 514
Review Nouns for People and Animals

Writing 515
This Week We ...
Daily Handwriting

Wrap Up Your Week! 516

Extend Your Day! 517

Access for All

What do I do in group time?
It's as easy as 1-2-3!

1 TEACHER-LED SMALL GROUPS → 2 INDEPENDENT PRACTICE STATIONS → 3 INDEPENDENT READING

Small Group Time

Bridge to Common Core

SKILL DEVELOPMENT
- /m/ Spelled *Mm*
- Initial and Final /m/
- Character

DEEP UNDERSTANDING

This Week's Knowledge Goals

Children will understand that playing with others
- helps them share fun experiences
- helps them share a common goal

1 Small Group Lesson Plan

	DAY 1	DAY 2
	Differentiate Phonics	Differentiate Phonics
OL On-Level pp. SG•74–SG•79	**Practice Phonics** Identify *m* Words **Decodable Story** Read *Little Mouse*	**Practice Phonics** More *m* Words **Decodable Reader** Read *Animal Friends*
SI Strategic Intervention pp. SG•80–SG•84	**Reteach Phonics** Connect /m/ to *m* **Decodable Story** Read *Little Mouse*	**Reteach Phonics** Recognize *m* **Decodable Reader** Read *Animal Friends*
A Advanced pp. SG•85–SG•90	**Extend Phonics** More *m* Words **Advanced Selection** Read "Mim's Cat Sam"	**Extend Phonics** Blend *m* Words **Decodable Reader** Read *Animal Friends*
ELL **If...** children need more scaffolding and practice...	**Phonemic Awareness and Phonics** **then...** use the Phonics activities beginning on p. 447 in the *ELL Handbook.*	**Phonemic Awareness and Phonics** **then...** use the activities on p. DI•80 in the Teacher Resources section of the Digital Path.

Reading Street Sleuth Read Aloud

- Provides access to grade-level text for all students
- Focuses on finding clues in text through close reading
- Builds capacity for complex text

Build Text-Based Comprehension

Smash! Crash!

Optional Leveled Readers

Concept Literacy

Below Level

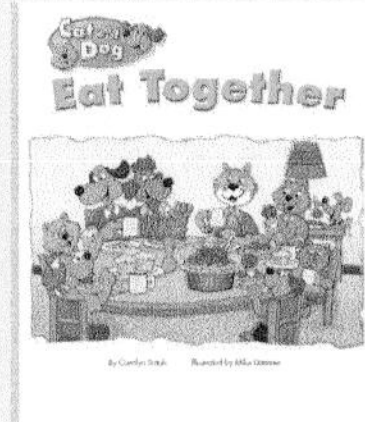

On Level

Advanced

Get Set, Roll! Reader

Decodable Reader

DAY 3	DAY 4	DAY 5
Differentiate Vocabulary	**Differentiate Language**	**Differentiate Close Reading**
Develop Vocabulary Practice Position Words **Student Reader** Read *Cat and Dog Eat Together*	**Build** Sentences and Words **Get Set, Roll! Reader** Read *Zoom!*	**Phonics** Spell *m* Words **Text-Based Comprehension** Read "Fun with Marbles"
Develop Vocabulary Reteach Position Words **Student Reader** Read *Cat and Dog Eat Together*	**Talk About** Sentences and Words **Get Set, Roll! Reader** Read *Zoom!*	**Phonics** Blend *m* Words **Text-Based Comprehension** Read "Fun with Marbles"
Develop Vocabulary More Position Words **Student Reader** Read *Cat and Dog Eat Together*	**Extend** Sentences and Words **Get Set, Roll! Reader** Read *Zoom!*	**Phonics** Write Sentences with *m* Words **Text-Based Comprehension** Read "Fun with Marbles"
Vocabulary **then...** use the ELL activities on p. DI•82 in the Teacher Resources section of the Digital Path.	**Developing Language** **then...** use the Language Workshops beginning on p. 306 in the *ELL Handbook.*	**Comprehension** **then...** use the ELL activities on pp. DI•81–DI•82 in the Teacher Resources section of the Digital Path.

Independent Stations

Practice Last Week's Skills

Focus on these activities when time is limited.

ACCESS FOR ALL
- Below-Level Activities
- On-Level Activities
- Advanced Activities

LISTEN UP!

Match initial sounds and pictures.

OBJECTIVES
- Listen and match initial sounds.

MATERIALS
- *Listen Up!* Flip Chart Activity 5
- Picture Cards: *desk, doll, duck, lake, lamp, leaf, pail, pan, yarn, yo-yo*
- paper, crayons

Modeled Pronunciation Audio CD

- Children choose four Picture Cards and say each name.
- Children name each Picture Card and name other words that begin with the same sound.
- Children name each Picture Card and match the cards that have the same beginning sound.

WORD WORK

Identify letters *Tt, Uu, Vv, Ww, Xx, Yy, Zz.*

OBJECTIVES
- Identify letters *Tt, Uu, Vv, Ww, Xx, Yy, Zz.*

MATERIALS
- *Word Work* Flip Chart Activity 5
- Alphabet Cards: *Tt, Uu, Vv, Ww, Xx, Yy, Zz*
- Letter Tiles
- paper, pencils

Interactive Sound-Spelling Cards

Letter Tile Drag and Drop

- Children find Alphabet Cards for letters *Tt, Uu, Vv, Ww, Xx, Yy,* and *Zz* and name each letter.
- Children match Alphabet Cards *Tt, Uu, Vv, Ww, Xx, Yy,* and *Zz* with Letter Tiles.
- Children match Alphabet Cards *Tt, Uu, Vv, Ww, Xx, Yy,* and *Zz* with Letter Tiles and write each letter.

LET'S WRITE!

Write instructions.

OBJECTIVES
- Write instructions.

MATERIALS
- *Let's Write!* Flip Chart Activity 5
- paper, pencils, crayons

Grammar Jammer

- Children draw pictures to show the steps for watering a plant.
- Children draw pictures to show the steps for watering a plant and number each step.
- Children draw pictures to show the steps for watering a plant and write a sentence for each step.

WORDS TO KNOW

Practice vocabulary.

OBJECTIVES
- Identify and use words for locations.

MATERIALS
- *Words to Know* Flip Chart Activity 5
- paper, pencils, crayons

Vocabulary Activities

Teacher Resources
- High-Frequency Word Cards for Unit 1, Week 4

- Children draw a picture of a school and label it *school.*
- Children draw a picture of themselves at school, the library, the post office, or a park. Then they label the picture.
- Children draw a picture of themselves at school, the library, the post office, or a park. Then they write a sentence about the picture.

READ FOR MEANING

Use text-based comprehension tools.

OBJECTIVES

- Classify and categorize items into groups.

MATERIALS

- *Read for Meaning* Flip Chart Activity 5
- Little Book *Miss Bindergarten Takes a Field Trip*
- paper, pencils, crayons

Envision It! Animations
- Leveled eReaders

- ● Children name things in a book that belong in a library and things that belong in a post office.
- ▲ Children point to things in a book that belong in a bakery and draw pictures to show things that belong in a park.
- ■ Children draw one picture that shows things that belong in a library and another that shows things that belong in a school.

LET'S MAKE ART!

Use art to demonstrate understanding.

OBJECTIVES

- Paint a picture.

MATERIALS

- *Let's Make Art!* Flip Chart Activity 5
- paint, paper, pencils

- ● Children paint a picture of someone in school who helps them.
- ▲ Children paint a picture of someone in school who helps them and labels the picture with that person's name.
- ■ Children paint a picture of someone in school who helps them. On another paper, they write who it is and how he or she helps.

Manage the Stations

Use these management tools to set up and organize your Practice Stations:

Practice Station Flip Charts

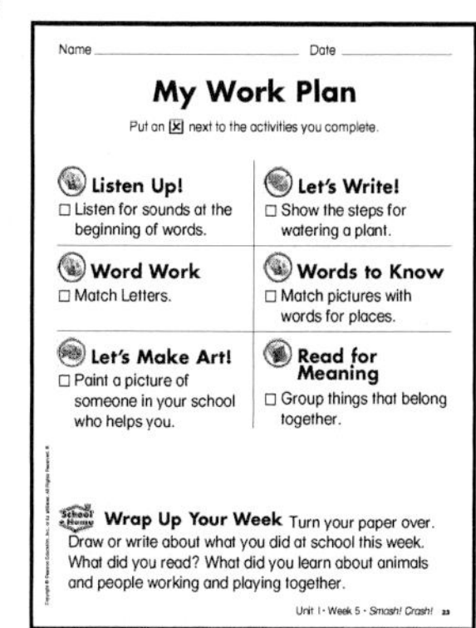

Name ____________ Date ________

My Work Plan

Put an ☒ next to the activities you complete.

Listen Up!
☐ Listen for sounds at the beginning of words.

Let's Write!
☐ Show the steps for watering a plant.

Word Work
☐ Match Letters.

Words to Know
☐ Match pictures with words for places.

Let's Make Art!
☐ Paint a picture of someone in your school who helps you.

Read for Meaning
☐ Group things that belong together.

Wrap Up Your Week Turn your paper over. Draw or write about what you did at school this week. What did you read? What did you learn about animals and people working and playing together.

Unit 1 • Week 5 • *Smash! Crash!* 23

Classroom Management Handbook for Differentiated Instruction Practice Stations, p. 23

3 Independent Reading

Help children choose complex texts so that they can engage in paired and group reading and writing activities every day before, during, and after school.

Suggestions for this week's independent reading:

- *How Do Dinosaurs Play With Their Friends?* by Jane Yolen
- *Puppy Mudge Wants to Play* by Cynthia Rylant

BOOK TALK Have pairs or groups of children actively engage in reading activities through a discussion of their independent reading for the week. Focus their discussions with the following ideas:

Key Ideas and Details

- Retell the text to your partner or group.
- Ask and answer questions about one detail of the text.

Craft and Structure

- Name the author and illustrator of the text.
- Talk about illustrations in the text.

Integration of Ideas

- With support, compare experiences of characters with those in other stories.
- Was this book like others I have read?

Savvas eText
- Student Edition
- Decodable Readers
- Get Set, Roll! Readers
- Leveled Readers

Materials from School or Classroom Library

DAY 1 at a Glance

Content Knowledge
Oral Vocabulary

Phonemic Awareness
Initial /m/

Phonics
/m/ Spelled *Mm*

Handwriting
M and *m*

High-Frequency Words
a, to

Text-Based Comprehension
Character

Conventions
Nouns for People and Animals

Writing
Wonderful, Marvelous Me!

Listening and Speaking
Announcements/Messages

Materials

- Student Edition
- Truckery Rhymes
- Talk with Me/Sing with Me Chart
- Reader's and Writer's Notebook
- Alphabet Cards
- Picture Cards
- Phonics Songs and Rhymes Chart

Bridge to Common Core

INTEGRATION OF KNOWLEDGE/IDEAS
This week children read, write, and talk about what friends do together.

Texts This Week

- "Won't You Play with Me?"
- "Dancing Together"
- *Smash! Crash!*
- *Cat and Dog Eat Together*
- "Sam Sings"

Social Studies Knowledge Goals
Children will understand that playing with others

- helps them share fun experiences
- helps them share a common goal

TRUCKTOWN on Reading Street

Start your engines!
Display p. 9 of *Truckery Rhymes.*

- Read aloud "Peter, Peter, Payload Eater" and track the print.
  - Reread the rhyme and have children chime in as they wish.
    - Ask children to identify the rhyming words. (*eater, heater; fell, well*)

Truckery Rhymes

Content Knowledge

What Friends Do Together

CONCEPT TALK To explore the unit concept of All Together Now, tell children that this week they will listen, talk, sing, read, and write about friendship. Write the Question of the Week on the board, *What do you like to do with your friends?* Track each word as you read.

Build Oral Language

TALK ABOUT WHAT FRIENDS DO TOGETHER Display Talk with Me Chart 5A. What do you see in these pictures? Look at the girl holding the sign. What does that sign mean? The sign tells us to stop. Look at the children dressed up. Tell me what they are wearing. What do you see in the other pictures?

We are going to learn six new Amazing Words this week. Listen as I say each word: *signals, dud, proper, pirates, perfect, fabulous.* Have children say each word as you point to the picture.

STOP
Talk with Me/Sing with Me Chart 5A

LISTEN FOR AMAZING WORDS Display Sing with Me Chart 5B. Tell children they are going to sing a song about playing with friends. Read the title. Have children describe the picture. Sing the song several times to the tune of "Zip a Dee Doo Dah." Listen for the Amazing Words: *signals, dud, proper, pirates, perfect, fabulous.* Have children stand up and sing with you.

Won't You Play With Me?
It's a fabulous day out, can't you see?
My, oh my, won't you play with me?
A perfect day for whatever will be,
A fabulous day out, can't you see?
We can stay out on the high seas.
We'll be pirates,
Or sailors,
Or whatever we want to be.
Change your day from a dud to a great jamboree.
A perfect day for whatever will be!
Talk with Me/Sing with Me Chart 5B

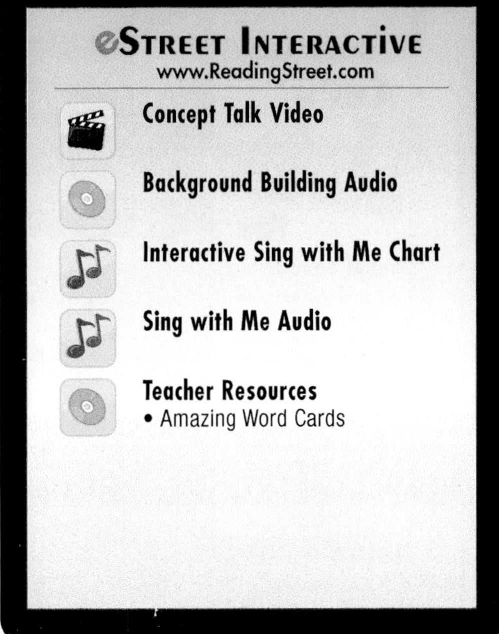
eStreet Interactive
www.ReadingStreet.com
Concept Talk Video
Background Building Audio
Interactive Sing with Me Chart
Sing with Me Audio
Teacher Resources
• Amazing Word Cards

Amazing Words

You've learned 0 2 4 words so far.

You'll learn 0 0 6 words this week!

signals	dud
proper	pirates
perfect	fabulous

Access for All

A Advanced

Extend Discussion Have children explain a game they like to play with their friends. Ask them to tell about the rules of the game and why they like to play the game.

Visual Support English learners will benefit from additional visual support to help them understand words in the song. For example, point to the pirates in the art to scaffold meaning. Have children describe how they know the children in the picture are pirates.

ELL Support Additional ELL support and modified instruction is provided in the *ELL Handbook* and in the ELL Support lessons on *Teacher Resources DVD-ROM.*

Preteach Concepts Use the Day 1 instruction on ELL Poster 5 to assess and build background knowledge, develop concepts, and build oral vocabulary.

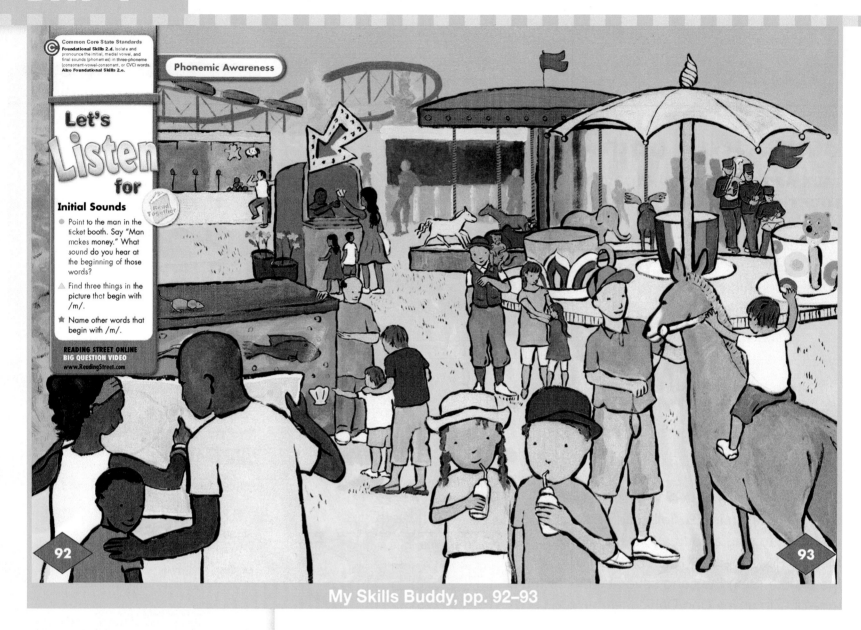

Common Core State Standards
Foundational Skills 2.d. Isolate and pronounce the initial, medial vowel, and final sounds (phonemes) in three-phoneme (consonant-vowel-consonant, or CVC) words. **Also Foundational Skills 2.e.**

Phonemic Awareness

Let's Listen for

Initial Sounds

Read Together

- Point to the man in the ticket booth. Say "Man makes money." What sound do you hear at the beginning of those words?
- Find three things in the picture that begin with /m/.
- Name other words that begin with /m/.

READING STREET ONLINE
BIG QUESTION VIDEO
www.ReadingStreet.com

92 93

My Skills Buddy, pp. 92–93

Common Core State Standards

Foundational Skills 2.b. Count, pronounce, blend, and segment syllables in spoken words. **Foundational Skills 2.d.** Isolate and pronounce the initial, medial vowel, and final sounds (phonemes) in three-phoneme (consonant-vowel-consonant, or CVC) words.* (This does not include CVCs ending with /l/, /r/, or /x/.) **Also Foundational Skills 2., 2.e.**

Phonemic Awareness

Initial /m/

INTRODUCE Today we will learn a new sound. Listen carefully: /m/ /m/ /m/. Say it with me: /m/ /m/ /m/. Display the *moon* Picture Card. *Moon* begins with /m/ /m/ /m/, *moon.* What sound does *moon* begin with? Repeat the routine using the *mitten, moose, man,* and *mug* Picture Cards.

Picture Card

MODEL Have children look at the picture on pp. 92–93 of *My Skills Buddy.* Tell them that they will be listening for a new sound—/m/. I see a marching band. What sound do you hear at the beginning of *marching?* I hear /m/ at the beginning of *marching.* The first sound in *marching* is /m/. What other things do you see that begin with that sound?

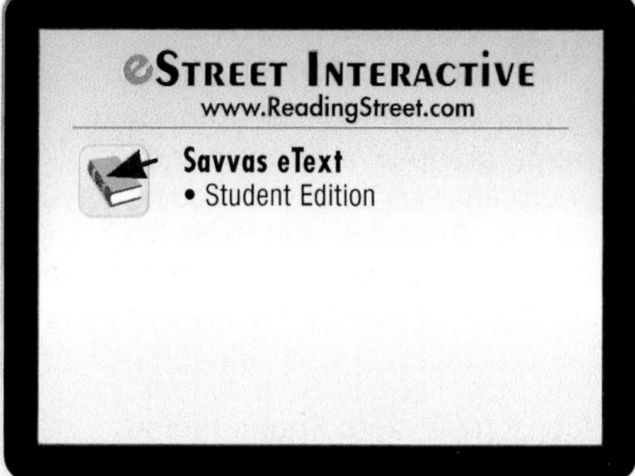

GUIDE PRACTICE As children name example words from the picture, guide them in stating that /m/ is the beginning sound. Discuss with children some of the bulleted items on p. 92 of *My Skills Buddy.* Save the other bulleted items for discussion on Day 2.

Corrective feedback	**If...** children have difficulty naming words with /m/, **then...** say *marching* again, stretching the beginning sound: /m/ /m/ /m/, *marching.*

DISCRIMINATE SOUNDS Display the *moon* and *cat* Picture Cards. This is the moon. This is a cat. *Moon* begins with /m/. *Cat* begins with /k/. Does *cat* begin with the same sound as *moon?* Say the words and sounds with me: *moon,* /m/; *cat,* /k/. No, *moon* and *cat* do not begin with the same sound. Continue the activity with the following pairs of Picture Cards: *moose, pan; man, map; fox, mask; mitten, goose; mug, mop.*

Corrective feedback	**If...** children cannot discriminate initial /m/, **then...** have them enunciate /m/ as they say *moon.* When you say the first sound in *moon,* you press your lips together. Say /m/ with me: /m/ /m/ /m/. Are your lips together? Say *moon* with me: *moon.* Repeat the activity with *make, mat,* and *mug.*

SEGMENT Say the word *moon* as you clap one time. How many parts, or syllables, does the word *moon* have? How many claps do you hear? Say the word *mountain* as you clap two times. Repeat the questions. Then have children say each word and clap the number of syllables with you. Continue with the words *mug, music, mother, man, museum,* and *mop.*

Don't Wait Until Friday

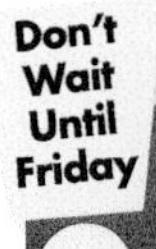

MONITOR PROGRESS

Check Phonemic Awareness Words with Initial /m/

FORMATIVE ASSESSMENT Say *bear* and *mouse.* Have children identify the word that begins with /m/. Continue with *seal, mug; mother, top; monster, pillow;* and *house, map.*

If... children cannot discriminate /m/ words,

then... use the small-group Strategic Intervention lesson, p. SG•80, to reteach /m/.

Access for All

SI Strategic Intervention

Identify /m/ Words Have children draw a picture of something that begins with /m/. Then have them use this sentence frame to identify the initial sound: ________ *begins with /m/.*

Support Phonemic Awareness Point to parts of the picture on pp. 92–93 of *My Skills Buddy* as you say the corresponding words. Then say each word and have children point to the correct part of the picture.

Common Core State Standards

Foundational Skills 3. Know and apply grade-level phonics and word analysis skills in decoding words. **Foundational Skills 3.a.** Demonstrate basic knowledge of one-to-one letter-sound correspondences by producing the primary or many of the most frequent sounds for each consonant. **Also Foundational Skills 2., 2.c.**

Skills Trace

/m/ Spelled *Mm*

Introduce U1W5D1

Practice U1W5D2; U1W5D3

Reteach/Review U1W5D5; U1W6D4; U2W6D4

Assess/Test Benchmark Assessment U1

KEY: U=Unit W=Week D=Day

Academic Vocabulary

consonant every letter of the alphabet except *a, e, i, o,* and *u*

Phonics

Teach/Model

/m/ Spelled *Mm*

INTRODUCE Display the *Mm* Alphabet Card. Point to the motorcycle on the Alphabet Card. *Motorcycle* begins with /m/. Say the word with me: *motorcycle.* Write *motorcycle* on the board and point to *m. Motorcycle* begins with /m/ spelled *m.* Now point to the letters *Mm* on the card. The sound for this letter is /m/. The names of these letters are uppercase *M* and lowercase *m.* What is the sound for this letter? What are the names of these letters? Explain that the letter *m* is a consonant.

Mm
motorcycle
Alphabet Card

MODEL Write *Mr. Malcolm Monkey* on the board. Point to the first *M.* When I see this letter, I think of the sound /m/. The first word is *Mr.*—/m/, *Mr.* Point to *Malcolm.* The next word begins with *M* too. I know that when I see an *m,* the sound will be /m/. The second word is *Malcolm.* Repeat with the word *Monkey.* The song we will sing is "Mr. Malcolm Monkey."

Guide Practice

GROUP PRACTICE Display Phonics Songs and Rhymes Chart 5. Teach children the song "Mr. Malcolm Monkey" sung to the tune of "I'm a Little Teapot." Play the CD and sing the song several times. I hear many words that begin with /m/. When you hear a word that begins with /m/, clap your hands. As you sing the song, point to words that begin with *m.*

Mr. Malcolm Monkey
Mr. Malcolm Monkey makes me smile.
I meet him on Mondays,
We play for a while.
We dream of making muffins, any style!
Munch on one, Mrs. Mary Moose!
Phonics Songs and Rhymes Chart 5

ON THEIR OWN Play "I Spy." Model the game for children. I spy an uppercase *M* on the calendar. I say /m/. Point to the *M.* Have children take turns spying and pointing out examples of uppercase *M* and lowercase *m* that they find in the classroom. When they point to *M* or *m,* have them say /m/.

Apply

Blend Words

REVIEW To review letter names, use the *Bb, Dd, Gg, Pp,* and *Tt* Alphabet Cards. Point to a letter on a card and ask children to name the letter. When all the letters have been named, repeat the activity with a different set of Alphabet Cards. Then use this process to blend onset /m/ and rimes.

CONNECT Write the letter *m.* What is the sound for this letter? The sound is /m/. Say it with me: /m/ /m/ /m/. When you see this letter in a word, what sound will you say?

MODEL Write *map* on the board.

- Point to *m* and ask: What is the sound for this letter? Say it with me: /m/ /m/ /m/.
- The beginning sound in *map* is /m/. *Map* ends with *-ap.* When I blend the beginning sound /m/ and the ending *-ap,* I make the word *map:* /m/ *-ap, map.*
- Say the sounds with me: /m/ *-ap.* Now let's blend the sounds together. Listen as I do it: /m/ *-ap, map.* Say it with me: /m/ *-ap, map.* Now you say it without me.
- Listen as I use the word *map* in a sentence: *The map is on the wall.* Say it with me. Have children use *map* in a sentence.

GROUP PRACTICE Continue the process with the words below:

mat **men** **mix** **mop** **mug**

Corrective feedback	**If...** children have trouble blending a word, **then...** model blending the onset and rime to read each word. Have children say it with you.

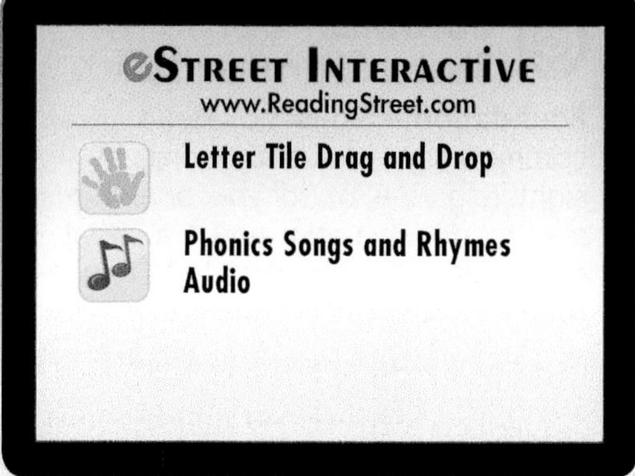

eStreet Interactive
www.ReadingStreet.com
Letter Tile Drag and Drop
Phonics Songs and Rhymes Audio

Access for All

SI Strategic Intervention

Identify /m/ Ask children to point to and name things on the Phonics Songs and Rhymes Chart that illustrate /m/ words in the song.

Academic Vocabulary 

blend to say the sounds for the letters in a word quickly and smoothly enough that the sounds merge to form the entire word

Support Blending If children need more practice blending onset /m/ and rimes, use the following words in addition to those in the lesson: *Mac, mad, man, Meg, met, mob, mom, mud.*

DAY 1

Common Core State Standards

Foundational Skills 3.c. Read common high-frequency words by sight. (e.g., *the, of, to, you, she, my, is, are, do, does*). **Language 1.a.** Print many upper- and lowercase letters. **Also Foundational Skills 1.b.**

Handwriting

INTRODUCE Write *Mm* on the board. Words that begin with /m/ are written with an uppercase *M* or a lowercase *m.* Which letter is uppercase *M?* Which letter is lowercase *m?*

MODEL UPPERCASE *M* Write *Maria* on the board. Point to the uppercase *M.* This is uppercase *M.* We use uppercase letters to begin sentences and names. Watch as I trace this uppercase *M* with my finger. Follow the stroke instructions pictured below.

GUIDE PRACTICE Have children write uppercase *M* in the air. Use your finger to make an uppercase *M* in the air. Now write it on your hand.

MODEL LOWERCASE *m* Write *moon* on the board. Point to the lowercase *m.* This is lowercase *m.* Watch as I trace this lowercase *m* with my finger. Write another lowercase *m* on the board, following the stroke instructions. Again, have children write *m* in the air and on their hands.

GUIDE PRACTICE Have children use their Write-On Boards to write a row of uppercase *M* and a row of lowercase *m.*

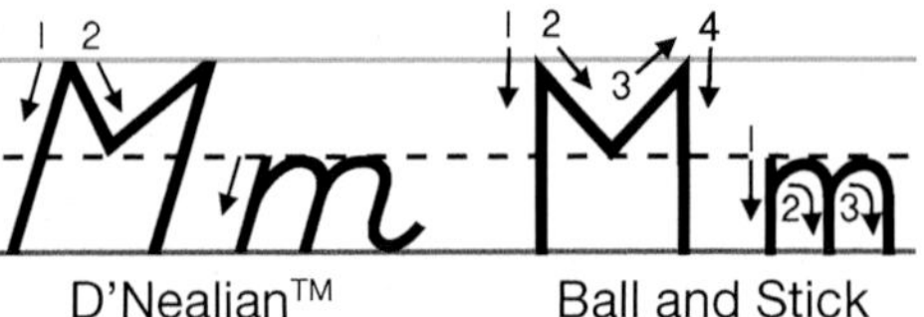

D'Nealian™ Ball and Stick

ON THEIR OWN Use *Reader's and Writer's Notebook,* pp. 49 and 50, for additional practice with initial *m.*

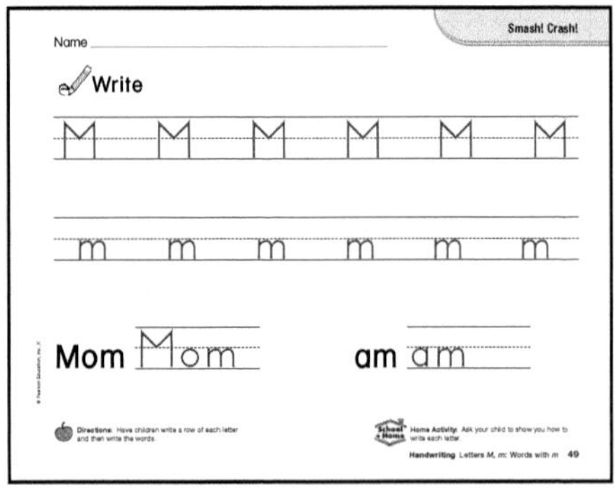

Name
Smash! Crash!
Write
M M M M M M
m m m m m m
Mom Mom
am am

Reader's and Writer's Notebook, p. 49

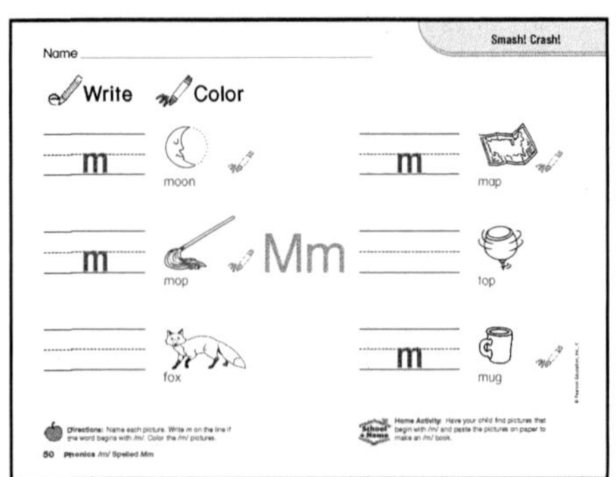

Name
Smash! Crash!
Write Color
m moon
m map
m mop
Mm
top
fox
m mug

Reader's and Writer's Notebook, p. 50

High-Frequency Words

INTRODUCE Use the routine below to teach high-frequency words *a* and *to.*

Routine Nondecodable Words

1. **Say and Spell** Some words we have to learn by remembering the letters rather than saying the sounds. We will say and spell the words to help learn them. Write *a* on the board. This is the word *a.* It has one letter. The letter in the word *a* is *a.* Have children say and spell the word, first with you and then without you.
2. **Demonstrate Meaning** I can use the word *a* in lots of sentences. Here is one sentence: *I have a pen.* Now you use the word in a sentence.

Repeat the routine with the word *to.*

Add *a* and *to* to the Word Wall.

Routines Flip Chart

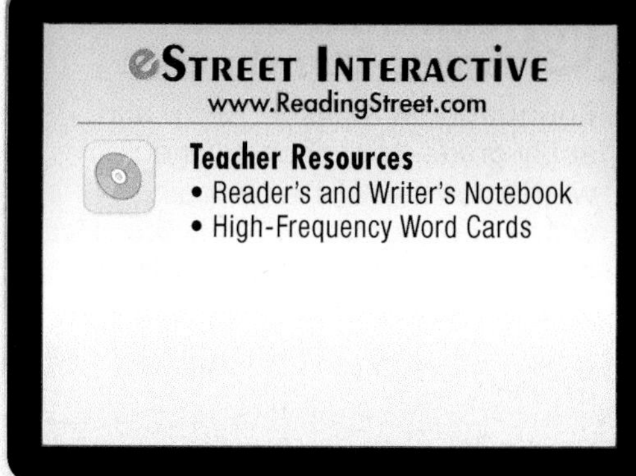

eSTREET INTERACTIVE
www.ReadingStreet.com
Teacher Resources
• Reader's and Writer's Notebook
• High-Frequency Word Cards

Access for All

 Strategic Intervention

Support High-Frequency Words
Explain to children that *a* refers to one thing or person. Have children practice using the word by pointing to one thing in the classroom and saying a phrase, such as *a book, a teacher, a boy,* or *a pencil.*

Support High-Frequency Words
Explain that the word *a* is like the word *one* and is used before a noun. For Spanish speakers, point out that *a* is like *un* and *una.* Write and read examples of when to use and not use *a: I see dogs. I see a dog. I see a small dog.*

Common Core State Standards

Foundational Skills 3. Know and apply grade-level phonics and word analysis skills in decoding words. **Foundational Skills 3.c.** Read common high-frequency words by sight. (e.g., *the, of, to, you, she, my, is, are, do, does*). **Also Foundational Skills 1., 4.**

Access for All

Strategic Intervention

Practice High-Frequency Words Write one of the previously taught high-frequency words on the board. Read the word with children. Ask them to find examples of the word in the story. Repeat the routine with other high-frequency words.

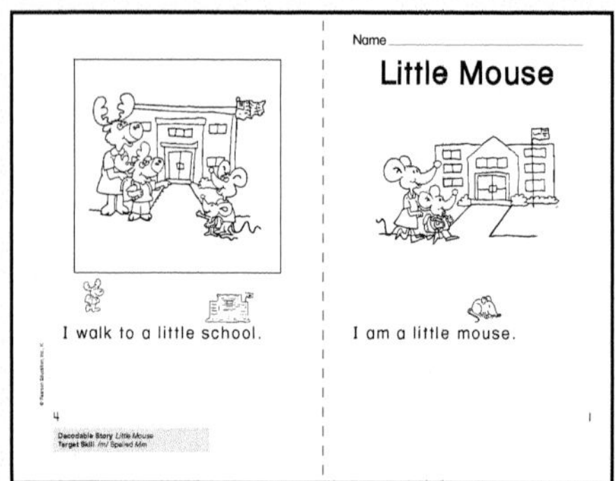

Reader's and Writer's Notebook, pp. 51–52

Decodable Story 5

Read *Little Mouse*

REVIEW Review the following high-frequency words by having children read each word as you point to it on the Word Wall: *I, am, little, a, to.*

TEACH REBUS WORDS Write the word *mouse* on the board. This is the word *mouse.* Name the letters with me: *m, o, u, s, e, mouse.* Repeat with the words *walk, school,* and *moose.* Look for these words in the story we read today. There will be a picture above the word to help you read it.

READ Tear out Decodable Story *Little Mouse* on pp. 51–52 of *Reader's and Writer's Notebook.* Then fold the pages to form a book. Repeat this process with each child's *Reader's and Writer's Notebook.* Distribute the self-cover books to children.

Today we will read a story about a mouse. First let's look at our story. This is the right way to hold the book. Model how to hold the book. Point to the word *Mouse* on the cover. We know it is right side up because the word *Mouse* looks right. Turn the book upside down. This is the wrong way to hold a book. The words and the pictures are upside down. We cannot read words if they are upside down! Turn the book right side up. Pick up your copy of the book and hold it right side up. Make sure you are holding it correctly. Is the word *Mouse* right side up? Check to see that all children are holding their books correctly.

Point to the front cover. This is the front cover of our book. *Front* means the side that faces us. Open the book. These are the pages in our story. We turn the pages from right to left. Demonstrate how to turn the pages. Now you turn the pages from right to left. Observe and make sure all children are turning the pages correctly. This is the back cover. It is the part of the book we look at last. Point to the title of the story. What is the title of our book? The title of the story is *Little Mouse.* Where is the title of the story? Point to where the title appears on the page. Have children read the story, holding the book right side up and turning the pages correctly.

Use the routine for reading decodable books to read Decodable Story 5.

eStreet Interactive
www.ReadingStreet.com

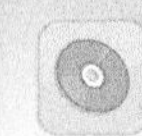

Teacher Resources
- Reader's and Writer's Notebook

Routine Reading Decodable Books

1. **Read Silently** Have children whisper read the story page by page as you listen in.
2. **Model Fluent Reading** Have children finger point as you read a page. Then have them reread the page without you.
3. **Read Chorally** Have children finger point as they chorally read the page. Continue reading page by page, repeating steps 1 and 2.
4. **Read Individually** Have children take turns reading aloud a page.
5. **Reread and Monitor Progress** As you listen to individual children reread, monitor progress and provide support.
6. **Reread with a Partner** Have children reread the story page by page with a partner.

Routines Flip Chart

Day 1 SMALL GROUP TIME • Differentiate Phonics, p. SG•73

OL On-Level
- **Practice Phonics** Identify *m* Words
- **Read** Decodable Story *Little Mouse*

SI Strategic Intervention
- **Reteach Phonics** Connect /m/ to *m*
- **Read** Decodable Story *Little Mouse*

A Advanced
- **Extend Phonics** More *m* Words
- **Read** Advanced Selection "Mim's Cat Sam"

Place English Language Learners in the groups that correspond to their reading abilities in English.

If... children need more support with **Phonics,**
then... use the Phonics activities beginning on p. 447 in the *ELL Handbook.*

Common Core State Standards
Literature 3. With prompting and support, identify characters, settings, and major events in a story.

Comprehension

Envision It!

Literary Elements

READING STREET ONLINE
ENVISION IT! ANIMATION
www.ReadingStreet.com

Characters

Setting

Plot

START

FINISH

94

95

My Skills Buddy, pp. 94–95

Zoom in on

Literature 3. With prompting and support, identify characters, settings, and major events in a story.

Skills Trace

Character

Introduce U1W1D1; U1W5D1; U4W4D1; U6W2D1

Practice U1W1D2; U1W1D3; U1W1D4; U1W5D2; U1W5D3; U1W5D4; U4W4D2; U4W4D3; U4W4D4; U6W2D2; U6W2D3; U6W2D4

Reteach/Review U1W1D5; U1W2D4; U1W5D5; U3W4D4; U4W4D5; U5W4D4; U6W2D5

Assess/Test Benchmark Assessment U1; U6

KEY: U=Unit W=Week D=Day

Text-Based Comprehension

Character

READ Remind children of the weekly concept—What Friends Do Together. Have children listen as you read aloud "Dancing Together" on p. 437.

MODEL A CLOSE READ Model how to identify characters as a tool to build comprehension.

When I read a story, I pay attention to the people or animals in the story. The people in "Dancing Together" are the three children, Amy, Will, and Kim.

TEACH CHARACTER A story may be about one or more than one person or animal. The people or animals that a story is about are called **characters.** Good readers pay attention to the characters in a story because it helps them understand whom the story is about.

Have children turn to pp. 94–95 in *My Skills Buddy* and look at the pictures.

Tell children the story of "The Tortoise and the Hare."

- Who are the characters in this story? (the tortoise and the hare)
- Are the characters people or animals? (They are animals.)

GUIDE PRACTICE Reread "Dancing Together" and ask children who the characters in the story are. Amy, Will, and Kim are the characters. How do we know that these characters are good friends? (The story tells us that they like to spend time together and that they share what they learn in their dance classes.)

MORE PRACTICE Display Big Book *Plaidypus Lost.* Page through the story. Help children recall and describe the characters in the story. For example, after they identify the girl, ask them to describe her. She loves to take Plaidypus everywhere, but she is forgetful.

Teacher Read Aloud

Dancing Together

Amy's house has a big back porch. Amy and her friends Will and Kim like to dance on the porch. As the music plays, Amy leaps, Will twirls, and Kim jigs. They pretend they are dancing on a stage.

One day Amy says, "Guess what! My mom says I can go to dance class."

Will and Kim are happy for Amy. They want to take dance classes too. They talk to their parents. The next day they have news.

"I'm going to dance class!" says Will.

"I'm going to dance class!" says Kim.

Now when the friends listen to music together, they show one another what they have learned in their dance classes. Amy jigs, Will leaps, and Kim twirls.

Access for All

 Advanced

Access Prior Knowledge Ask children who know the story "The Tortoise and the Hare" well to tell the story to their classmates.

Academic Vocabulary 

character a person or animal in a story, book, poem, or play

Bridge to Common Core

KEY IDEAS AND DETAILS

When children identify and describe the characters in a story, they are determining key details in the story. Answering questions about characters helps children use evidence from the text and illustrations to support conclusions they draw about the story.

Support Listening Comprehension Use the modified Read Aloud from the ELL Support lessons (p. DI•81) on *Teacher Resources DVD-ROM* to build background knowledge. Preview new vocabulary and support understanding of complex text with visuals from *My Skills Buddy* and online sources.

Writing 2. Use a combination of drawing, dictating, and writing to compose informative/explanatory texts in which they name what they are writing about and supply some information about the topic. **Language 1.a.** Print many upper- and lowercase letters. **Language 1.b.** Use frequently occurring nouns and verbs. **Also Speaking/Listening 4., Language 4., 4.b.**

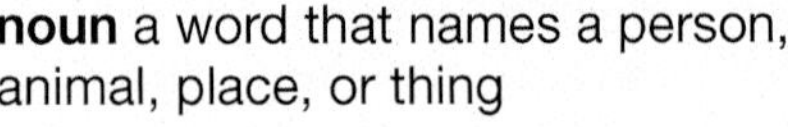

noun a word that names a person, animal, place, or thing

Daily Fix-It

my mom is a nurse
My mom is a nurse.

This week's practice sentences appear on *Teacher Resources DVD-ROM.*

Conventions

Nouns for People and Animals

MAKE CONNECTIONS Today we listened to a story about three children. The word *children* is a naming word. It names the people in the story. What are some other naming words for people? List children's responses. *Girl, boy, man,* and *woman* are words that name people. These words are called *nouns.*

TEACH Explain to children that a **noun** is a word that names a person, animal, place, or thing. I am a teacher. Write *teacher* on the board. The word *teacher* is a naming word. *Teacher* is a noun for a person. Display the *cat* Picture Card. This is a cat. Write *cat* on the board. The word *cat* is a noun for an animal.

MODEL Display the *queen* and *elephant* Picture Cards. Point to the queen. What noun can I use to name this person? I know she is a queen. The word *queen* is a noun. It names this person. Write *queen* on the board. Then point to the elephant. This is an elephant. The word *elephant* names an animal. Write *elephant* on the board.

GUIDE PRACTICE Write the following sentence frames on the board:

I work on a farm. I am a _______. (farmer)
I take care of you when you are sick. I am a _______. (doctor)
I have long ears and like to hop. I am a _______. (rabbit)
I buzz around flowers. I am a _______. (bee)

Tell children to listen to the clue you give them. Ask them what noun they could use to name the person or animal. Write the noun for a person or animal on the line. Read each clue again, pointing to the noun as you say it. Echo read the sentences with children. Then have them use the nouns in their own sentences.

Team Talk **APPLY** Pair children and have them take turns telling nouns that name people and animals. Then have them draw a picture for one of the nouns.

AFFIXES AND MEANING Write the words *teacher* and *farmer* on the board and circle *-er* in each. The word part *-er* can mean "a person who." When *-er* is added to *teach,* it makes the word *teacher,* "a person who teaches." When *-er* is added to *farm,* it makes the word *farmer,* "a person who farms." We can use the word part *-er* to help us figure out what a word means.

Wonderful, Marvelous Me! I Just Learned...

INTRODUCE Talk with children about learning. Every day when we come to school, we learn new things. What kinds of things do we learn at school? We also learn things at home. What kinds of things do we learn at home? Encourage children to share their thoughts and ideas about what they learn at school and at home.

MODEL Today we're going to tell about something wonderful and marvelous that we've learned. I'm going to close my eyes and think about the things I've learned lately. I really like pancakes, but I didn't know how to make them. Last week I found a cookbook in the library and followed a recipe. The first time I made the pancakes, they were not very good! They were lumpy, and I burned them. Draw a picture of lumpy, burnt pancakes. But I tried again because it often takes many tries to learn something new, doesn't it? The next time I made the pancakes, they were a little better. I didn't burn them, but they were still lumpy. Draw a picture of lumpy pancakes. I tried again, and this time they were just right! Draw a picture of delicious pancakes.

INDEPENDENT WRITING Now you're going to tell about something you just learned. Maybe it's something you know, such as your address. Maybe it's something you know how to do, such as tying your shoes. Close your eyes and think about something wonderful and marvelous that you've learned. Have children write or dictate their ideas and then illustrate them.

Daily Handwriting

Write *Matt* and *mop* on the board. Review correct letter formation of uppercase *M* and lowercase *m.*

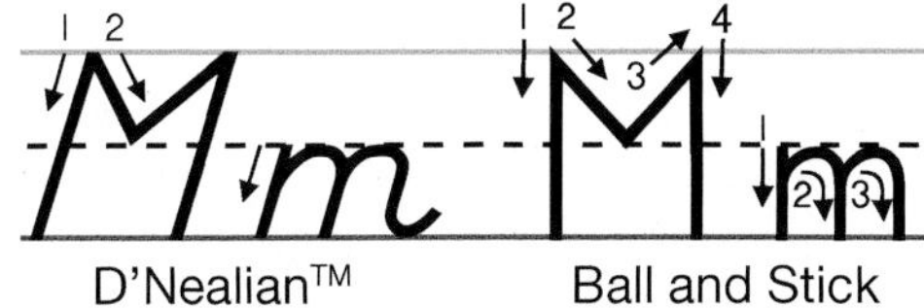

D'Nealian™ Ball and Stick

Have children write *Matt* and *mop* on their Write-On Boards. Remind them to use proper left-to-right and top-to-bottom progression and proper spacing between letters when writing *M* and *m.*

Write Guy *by Jeff Anderson*

Writers Write

Children writers succeed in classrooms where they write. Simple, isn't it? Don't forget daily writing. Children need to read and write every day. Teachers do not need to read and assess everything that children write.

Bridge to Common Core

TEXT TYPES AND PURPOSES

Today children write about and draw something new they have learned.

Expository/Informative/Explanatory Writing

Children are using writing to convey ideas and information clearly.

Throughout the week, children will have opportunities to write varied text types for different purposes.

5-Day Plan

DAY 1	Wonderful, Marvelous Me!
DAY 2	Respond to Literature
DAY 3	Genre Writing
DAY 4	Extend the Concept
DAY 5	This Week We...

Common Core State Standards

Literature 3. With prompting and support, identify characters, settings, and major events in a story. **Speaking/Listening 1.a.** Follow agreed-upon rules for discussions (e.g., listening to others and taking turns speaking about the topics and texts under discussion). **Speaking/Listening 6.** Speak audibly and express thoughts, feelings, and ideas clearly. **Language 1.b.** Use frequently occurring nouns and verbs.

Listening and Speaking

Announcements/Messages

TEACH When we make an announcement or leave a message, we usually want to tell about something important. The announcement or message should be as short as possible so that it is easy for people to understand and remember. An announcement or message should also include all the important information. What do people need to know?

MODEL I am going to call a friend and leave a message. Listen closely to what I say and how I say it. Pretend to talk into a phone and leave a message inviting a friend to go out to dinner. Did I speak clearly? Did I include important information?

GUIDE PRACTICE Have children make an announcement about an upcoming trip or leave a message inviting a friend to come over to play. Remind them to include all the important information, such as the date and time of the event or their name. Refer children to the Rules for Listening and Speaking on pp. 1–2 of *Reader's and Writer's Notebook.* Remind them to take turns speaking and to speak clearly.

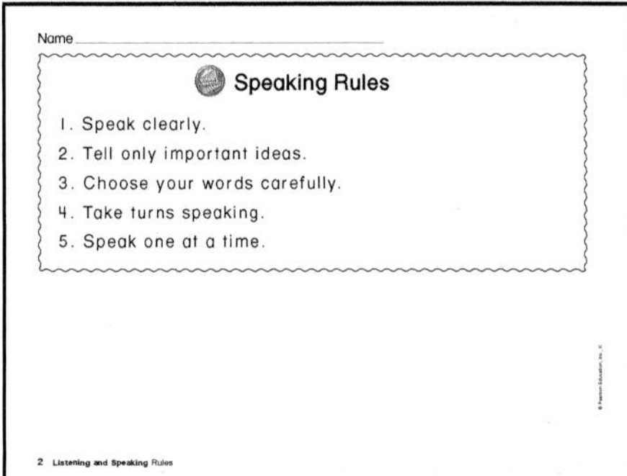
Name

Speaking Rules

1. Speak clearly.
2. Tell only important ideas.
3. Choose your words carefully.
4. Take turns speaking.
5. Speak one at a time.

Reader's and Writer's Notebook, pp. 1–2

Wrap Up Your Day!

✔ **Oral Language** Today we talked about playing with friends. Let's say the Amazing Words again: *signals, dud, proper, pirates, perfect, fabulous.*

✔ **Conventions** Today we learned about nouns for people and animals. Let's think of a noun for a person and a noun for an animal.

✔ **Homework Idea** Send home the Family Times Newsletter from Let's Practice It! pp. 9–10 on *Teacher Resources DVD-ROM.*

Tomorrow we will read about trucks that are friends.

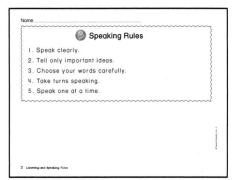

Extend Your Day!

Social Studies

Family Responsibility

MATERIALS: paper, crayons, chart paper

DISCUSS FAMILY RESPONSIBILITY Ask children to name jobs, chores, or other responsibilities they have at home. Prompt children's thinking by asking questions to help them think of possible jobs and duties. When you get up in the morning, what jobs do you do on your own before you go to school? When you get home from school in the afternoon, what do you do to help your mom and dad? List children's responses on the board.

- pick up toys
- make bed
- put away clothes
- set table
- hang up backpack

Discuss with children why it is important for all family members to help at home. Why is it a good idea to divide up the work among everyone? What would happen if no one in a family did his or her jobs?

DRAW AND LABEL PICTURES Have children draw pictures of themselves doing jobs at home. Then have them write or dictate captions for their pictures. Compile the pictures to make a class book titled *How We Help Our Families.*

Conventions

Who Are They?

MATERIALS: magazine pictures of people, paste, paper, crayons, pencils

NOUNS TO NAME PEOPLE Have children look through the pictures and choose one. Have them paste their person at the top of a sheet of paper. Remember, we can use nouns to name people. Look at your person. Think of a noun you can use to name this person. Have children write or dictate a noun in the space below their picture. They can think of as many nouns as they wish. After children share their pictures with the class, post them on a bulletin board labeled *Nouns That Name People.*

Comprehension

We Like to Dance

REVIEW THE READ ALOUD Reread *Dancing Together.* Who are the characters in this story? What do they like to do together? What happens first in the story? next? last? Make sure children are familiar with the characters, setting, and plot and the meanings of *leaps, twirls,* and *jigs.*

ACT OUT THE STORY Have three children pretend to be Amy, Will, and Kim and act out the story, including the dancing and dialogue. Repeat with other groups of children. As a challenge, children can create additional actions and dialogue for their characters.

DAY 2 at a Glance

Content Knowledge
Oral Vocabulary

Phonemic Awareness
Initial /m/

Phonics
/m/ Spelled *Mm*

Handwriting
Words with *Mm*

Text-Based Comprehension
Character

Conventions
Nouns for People and Animals

Writing
Respond to Literature

Vocabulary
Position Words

Materials

- Student Edition
- Truckery Rhymes
- Talk with Me/Sing with Me Chart
- Picture Cards
- Phonics Songs and Rhymes Chart
- Alphabet Cards
- Reader's and Writer's Notebook
- Big Book

Common Core State Standards

Speaking/Listening 1.a. Follow agreed-upon rules for discussions (e.g., listening to others and taking turns speaking about the topics and texts under discussion). **Language 6.** Use words and phrases acquired through conversations, reading and being read to, and responding to texts. **Also Language 5.c.**

TRUCKTOWN on Reading Street

Start your engines!
Display p. 9 of *Truckery Rhymes.* Point to "Peter, Peter, Payload Eater." Who remembers which truck this rhyme is about? Yes, it's about Pete. Let's read the rhyme together. Have a child point to the rhyming words as the class reads the rhyme again. Give additional children the opportunity to say the rhyme aloud and track the print.

Truckery Rhymes

Content Knowledge

What Friends Do Together

TALK ABOUT WHAT FRIENDS DO TOGETHER On the board, write the Question of the Week, *What do you like to do with your friends?,* and track the print as you read it aloud. Have children answer the question in complete sentences. To reinforce the concept and focus children's attention, display Sing with Me Chart 5B. Tell children that they are going to sing a song about playing with friends.

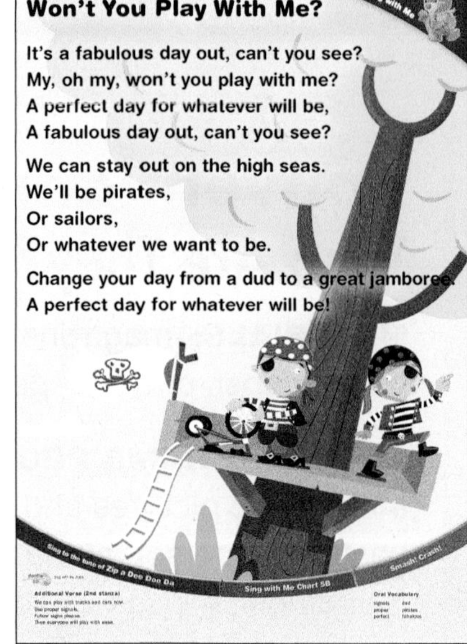

Won't You Play With Me?
It's a fabulous day out, can't you see?
My, oh my, won't you play with me?
A perfect day for whatever will be,
A fabulous day out, can't you see?
We can stay out on the high seas.
We'll be pirates,
Or sailors,
Or whatever we want to be.
Change your day from a dud to a great jamboree.
A perfect day for whatever will be!
Sing with Me Chart 5B

Talk with Me/Sing with Me Chart 5B

Build Oral Language

LISTEN FOR AMAZING WORDS The Amazing Words *signals* and *dud* are in the song "Won't You Play With Me?" Read the title and have children describe the children in the picture. Sing the song several times to the tune of "Zip a Dee Doo Dah," until children become familiar with the words and can sing along. Have them clap when they hear *signals* and *dud.*

Build Oral Vocabulary

Amazing Words Robust Vocabulary Routine

1. **Introduce the Word** When you raise your hand, you *signal* for me to call on you. *Signals* means makes a gesture, action, or sound that draws attention. When someone *signals,* we usually know what he or she means. What's our new Amazing Word for uses actions or sounds to get someone's attention? Say it with me: *signals.*

2. **Demonstrate** Provide examples to show meaning. *A bell signals the end of school.* What else can a bell *signal?*

   Repeat steps 1 and 2.

   Introduce the Word A *dud* is something that doesn't work properly or doesn't do what it was meant to do. What's our new Amazing Word for something that doesn't work properly? Say it with me: *dud.*

   Demonstrate *Our TV is not working. It's a dud.*

3. **Apply** Tell children to use *signals* and *dud* in complete sentences. Have children draw a picture to illustrate one of their sentences.

4. **Display the Words** Ask children what letters *signals* and *dud* begin with. Have them point to and name each beginning letter.

Routines Flip Chart

USE AMAZING WORDS To reinforce the concept and the Amazing Words, have children supply the appropriate Amazing Word for each sentence.

The coach _______ to the player by raising his hand. (signals)
Shop carefully for a new car and don't buy a _______. (dud)

Amazing Words

signals	dud
proper	pirates
perfect	fabulous

Access for All

 Advanced

Expand Vocabulary Have children show how they would signal to someone to follow them and to be quiet.

Visual Support To make sure children understand that to signal usually involves making a motion, demonstrate ways to signal for children to imitate, such as waving to say good-bye or nodding to show you agree.

Reinforce Vocabulary Use the Day 2 instruction on ELL Poster 5 to reinforce the meanings of high-frequency words.

Common Core State Standards
Foundational Skills 2.d. Isolate and pronounce the initial, medial vowel, and final sounds (phonemes) in three-phoneme (consonant-vowel-consonant, or CVC) words. **Also Foundational Skills 2.e.**

Phonemic Awareness

Let's Listen for

Initial Sounds

- Point to the man in the ticket booth. Say "Man makes money." What sound do you hear at the beginning of those words?
- Find three things in the picture that begin with /m/.
- Name other words that begin with /m/.

Read Together

READING STREET ONLINE
BIG QUESTION VIDEO
www.ReadingStreet.com

92 93

My Skills Buddy, pp. 92–93

Foundational Skills 2.d. Isolate and pronounce the initial, medial vowel, and final sounds (phonemes) in three-phoneme (consonant-vowel-consonant, or CVC) words.* (This does not include CVCs ending with /l/, /r/, or /x/.) **Also Foundational Skills 2., 2.e.**

Phonemic Awareness

Initial /m/

ISOLATE INITIAL /m/ Display the *moose* Picture Card. This is a moose. *Moose* begins with /m/. What is this? What sound does it begin with? Continue the routine with the *map, mitten, mop,* and *mug* Picture Cards.

Picture Card

GUIDE PRACTICE Have children look at the picture on *My Skills Buddy,* pp. 92–93. Remember that we saw a marching band in the picture. *Marching* begins with /m/. What other things that begin with /m/ did we find in the picture? Name other things that begin like *marching.* Discuss with children those bulleted items on p. 92 not discussed on Day 1.

ISOLATE FINAL /m/ Display the *jam* Picture Card. This is jam. Listen as I say the sounds in *jam:* /j/ /a/ /m/. I hear /m/ at the end: /j/ /a/ /m/. Say the sounds with me: /j/ /a/ /m/. The last sound is /m/. Continue with the following words: *hem, gum, Tim, game, dime, home.*

Now I'm going to say two words. One word ends with /m/; the other word does not. Listen carefully: *sit, Sam. Sam* ends with /m/. The sounds in *Sam* are /s/ /a/ /m/. Where do you hear /m/? I hear /m/ at the end. Continue with the following pairs of words: *dim, bed; hip, hum; bag, gem; Tom, pen.*

Corrective feedback	**If...** children cannot discriminate final /m/, **then...** have them enunciate /m/ as they segment final /m/ words. Listen as I segment a word: /h/ /a/ /m/, *ham.* Say the sounds with me: /h/ /a/ /m/. What sound do you hear at the end? I hear /m/ at the end. Continue with the following words: *Sam, hum, Jim, came, time, dome.*

ON THEIR OWN Display Phonics Songs and Rhymes Chart 5, "Mr. Malcolm Monkey." Remind children of the tune "I'm a Little Teapot." Have them sing the song with you several times. This time I want you to clap when you hear /m/ at the end of a word. We can do it together the first time.

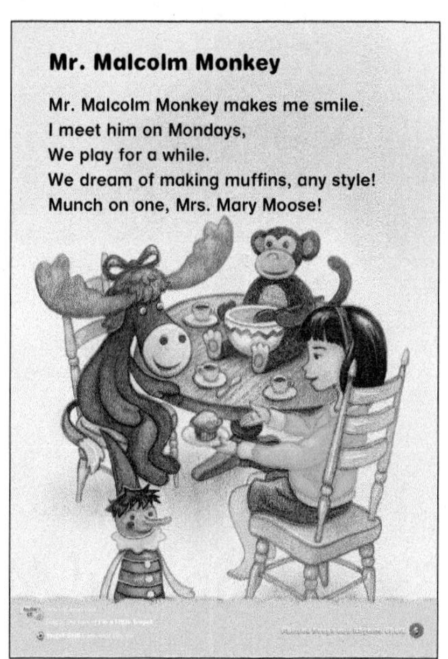

Mr. Malcolm Monkey
Mr. Malcolm Monkey makes me smile.
I meet him on Mondays,
We play for a while.
We dream of making muffins, any style!
Munch on one, Mrs. Mary Moose!

Phonics Songs and Rhymes Chart 5

REVIEW BLENDING Listen to the sounds in this word: /h/ /i/ /m/. Say them with me: /h/ /i/ /m/. Now I'm going to blend the sounds together to say the word: /h/ /i/ /m/, *him.* Now you try it with me: /h/ /i/ /m/, *him.* Continue the blending routine with the following words: *gum, Sam, Tim.*

Language Transfer The /m/ sound transfers completely from Spanish to English. For Spanish speakers, you can provide examples of Spanish words with /m/: *mamá, manzana* (apple), *mesa* (table).

ELL Support For additional support for language transfer, see Linguistic Contrastive Analysis in the *ELL Handbook.*

Common Core State Standards

Foundational Skills 2.c. Blend and segment onsets and rimes of single-syllable spoken words. **Foundational Skills 3.a.** Demonstrate basic knowledge of one-to-one letter-sound correspondences by producing the primary or many of the most frequent sounds for each consonant. **Also Foundational Skills 1., 1.b., 1.d., 2.d.**

Alphabet Card

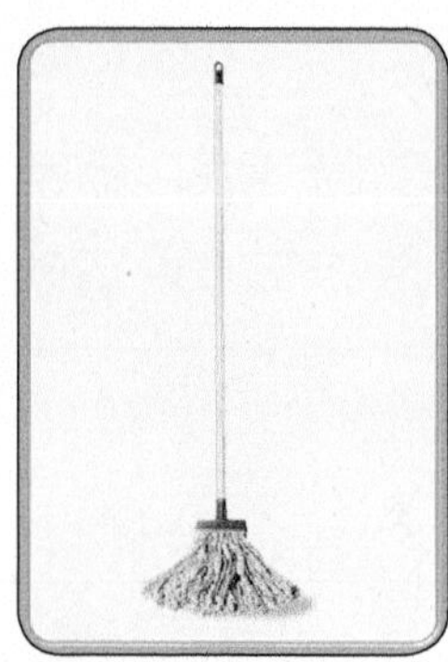
Picture Card

My Skills Buddy, p. 96

Phonics

Teach/Model

/m/ Spelled *Mm*

TEACH /m/*Mm* Point to the motorcycle on the *Mm* Alphabet Card. What is this? What sound does *motorcycle* begin with? *Motorcycle* begins with /m/. Write *motorcycle* on the board and point to the letter *m.* The letter for /m/ is *m.*

MODEL Display the *mop* Picture Card. What is this? Where do you hear /m/ in *mop?* (at the beginning) Write *mop* on the board. Point to *m.* When you see this letter, what sound will you say? Have children blend /m/ *-op* to say *mop.*

Guide Practice

REVIEW Have children open *My Skills Buddy* to p. 96 and review *Ww* through *Zz.* Point to the fox. This is a fox. These letters make the word *fox.* Words can be spoken and written or printed. Read the sentence aloud. This is a sentence. A sentence has spaces between words. Point to the words and then the spaces. Reread the sentence. Each word I say matches a word in this sentence.

Apply

CONNECT Write the letter *m.* What is the sound for this letter? The sound is /m/. Say it with me: /m/ /m/ /m/. When you see this letter in a word, what sound will you say?

MODEL Write the word *men* on the board.

- Point to *m* and ask: What is the sound for this letter? Say it with me: /m/ /m/ /m/. The beginning sound in *men* is /m/. *Men* ends with *-en.*
- Say the sounds with me: /m/ *-en.* Now let's blend the sounds together. Listen as I do it: /m/ *-en, men.* Say it with me: /m/ *-en, men.* Now you say it without me.
- Listen as I use *men* in a sentence: *The men get on the bus.* Say it with me. Have children use *men* in a sentence.

GROUP PRACTICE Continue with these words:

mad	met	mix	mop	mug

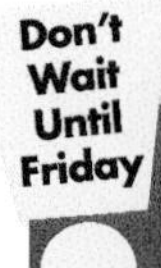

Don't Wait Until Friday MONITOR PROGRESS Check Sound-Spelling /m/ Spelled *Mm*

FORMATIVE ASSESSMENT Have children write *Mm* on a card. I am going to read some sentences. When you hear a word that has /m/ in it, hold your card up. *Tom and Mary go to music on Monday. Miguel and his mom march in mud. Michelle likes to munch on ham.*

If... children cannot discriminate /m/ words,

then... use the small-group Strategic Intervention lesson, p. SG•81, to reteach /m/ spelled *Mm.*

Continue to monitor children's progress during the week so that children can be successful with the Day 5 Assessment.

Access for All

Strategic Intervention

Concepts of Print Have children look for sentences in books. Tell them to count the words in the sentences. Then have them point out the spaces between the words.

Common Core State Standards

Foundational Skills 3.c. Read common high-frequency words by sight. (e.g., *the, of, to, you, she, my, is, are, do, does*). **Language 1.a.** Print many upper- and lowercase letters.

Handwriting

Write Words with *Mm*

REVIEW Write *Mom* on the board. This is the name *Mom.* I use an uppercase *M* for the first letter in *Mom.* Watch me make an uppercase *M.* Write another uppercase *M* on the board using the strokes indicated in the model. There is another *m* in the name *Mom.* It is at the end. It is lowercase *m.* Watch me make a lowercase *m.* Write another lowercase *m* on the board using the proper strokes.

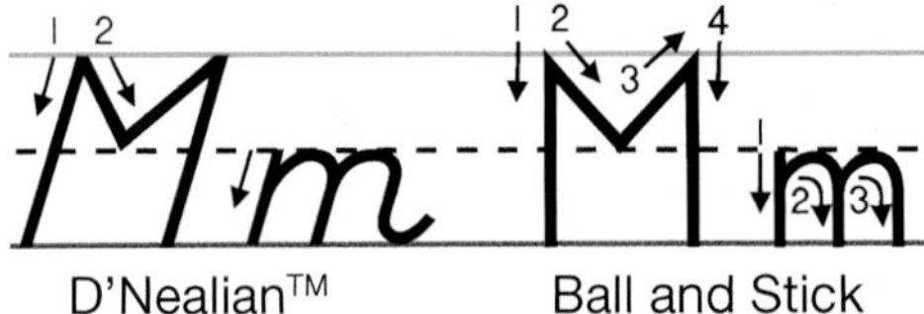

D'Nealian™ Ball and Stick

GUIDE PRACTICE Have children use their Write-On Boards to make a row of uppercase *M* and a row of lowercase *m.* Circulate around the room, assisting children as necessary. Then have children write the following words: *map, gum, Matt.*

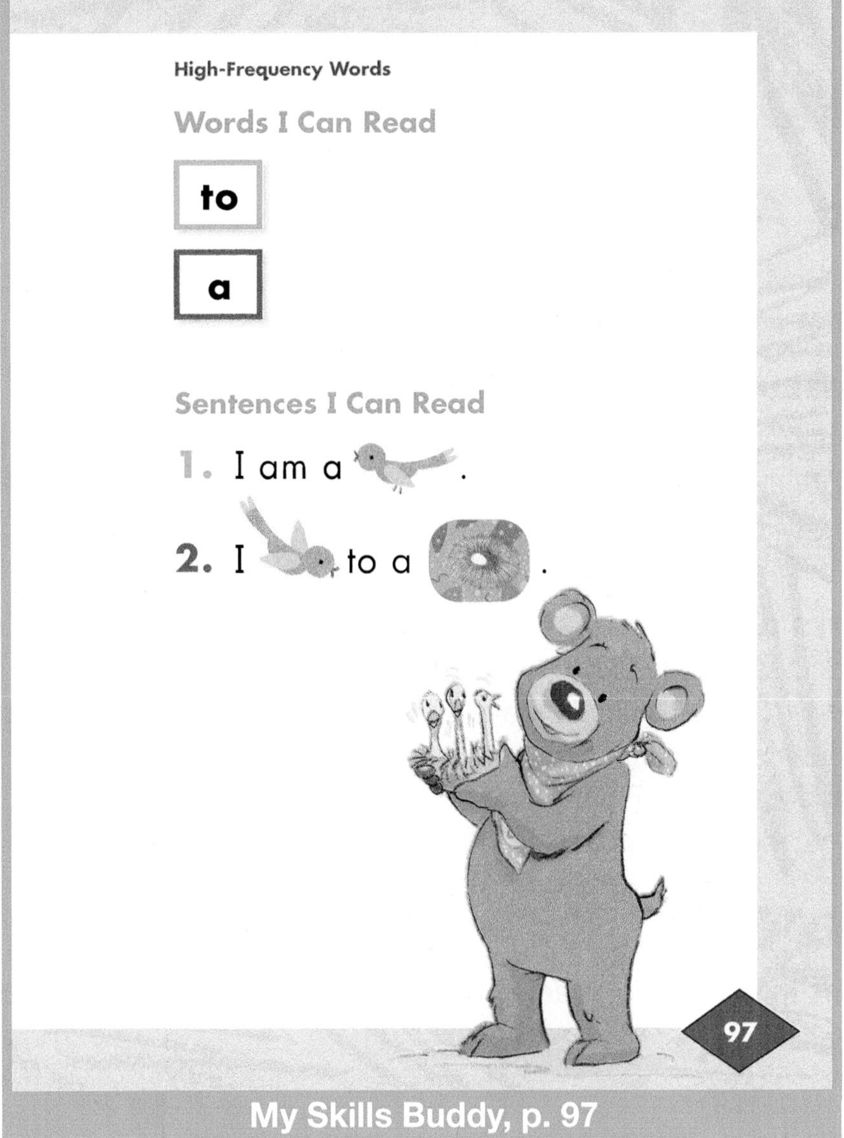

High-Frequency Words
Words I Can Read
to
a
Sentences I Can Read
1. I am a .
2. I to a .
97

My Skills Buddy, p. 97

High-Frequency Words

READ WORDS Have children turn to p. 97 of *My Skills Buddy.* Read the high-frequency words *to* and *a* together. Then have children point to each word and read it themselves.

READ SENTENCES Read the sentences on the *My Skills Buddy* page together to read the new high-frequency words in context.

 Team Talk Pair children and have them take turns reading each of the sentences aloud.

ON THEIR OWN Use *Reader's and Writer's Notebook,* p. 53, for additional practice with this week's high-frequency words.

Access for All

Ⓐ Advanced

High-Frequency Word Sentences
Encourage children to use other animals in the sentences on p. 97 of *My Skills Buddy.* Then have them say the completed sentences.

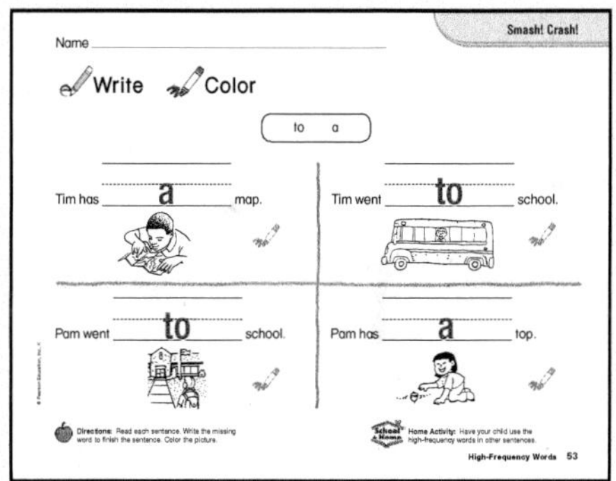

Reader's and Writer's Notebook, p. 53

 **Common Core State Standards**

Foundational Skills 3. Know and apply grade-level phonics and word analysis skills in decoding words. **Foundational Skills 3.c.** Read common high-frequency words by sight. (e.g., *the, of, to, you, she, my, is, are, do, does*). **Foundational Skills 4.** Read emergent-reader texts with purpose and understanding. **Also Foundational Skills 1.d., 3.a.**

Access for All

SI Strategic Intervention

Recognize /m/*Mm* Before children read *Animal Friends,* review /m/ with the *man, map, mop,* and *mug* Picture Cards.

Decodable Reader 5

Read *Animal Friends*

REVIEW Review the previously taught high-frequency words. Have children read each word as you point to it on the Word Wall: *I, am, a, little.*

TEACH REBUS WORDS Write the word *monkey* on the board. This is the word *monkey.* Name the letters with me: *m, o, n, k, e, y, monkey.* Repeat the routine with the words *mule, mouse, minnow, moth, mole,* and *moose.* Look for these words in our story today. There will be a picture above the word to help you read it.

CONCEPTS OF PRINT Have children turn to Decodable Reader 5, *Animal Friends,* on p. 98 of *My Skills Buddy.* Point to the title. The title of the story is *Animal Friends.* Have children make inferences based on the title and illustrations in the story. For example, children should infer that this story will be about friendly animals. Point to the name of the author. The author's name is Phil Morton. *Animal Friends* was written by Phil Morton. What sound do you hear at the beginning of *Morton?* We will read lots of words that begin with /m/ in this book.

READ Use the routine for reading decodable books to read Decodable Reader 5.

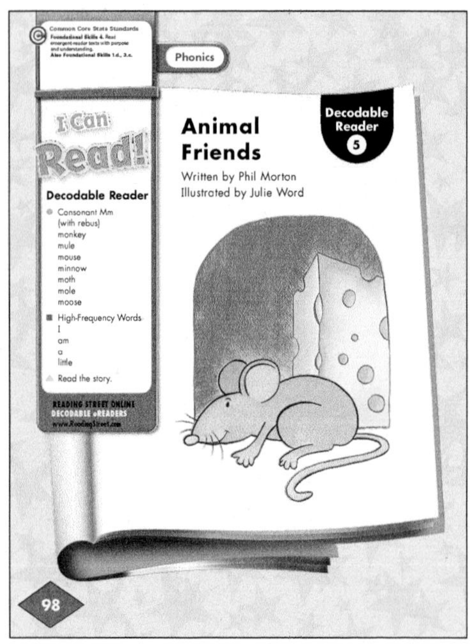

My Skills Buddy, pp. 98–105

I am a little monkey.
99

I am a little mule.
100
I am a little mouse.
101

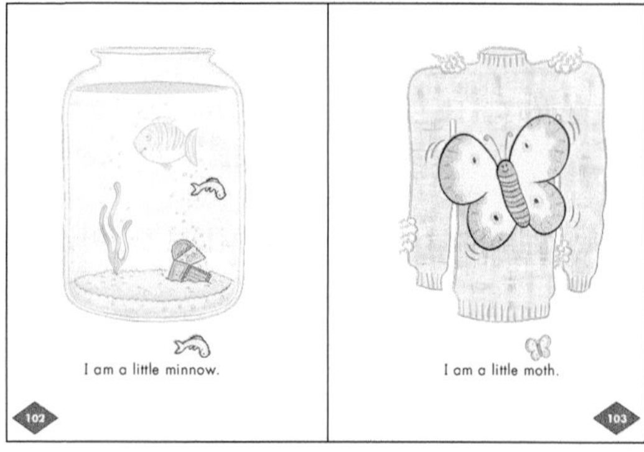

I am a little minnow.
102
I am a little moth.
103

I am a little mole.
104
I am a little moose.
Am I little?
105

Routine Reading Decodable Books

1. **Read Silently** Have children whisper read the book page by page as you listen in.
2. **Model Fluent Reading** Have children finger point as you read a page. Then have them reread the book without you.
3. **Read Chorally** Have children finger point as they chorally read the page. Continue reading page by page, repeating steps 1 and 2.
4. **Read Individually** Have children take turns reading aloud a page.
5. **Reread and Monitor Progress** As you listen to individual children reread, monitor progress and provide support.
6. **Reread with a Partner** Have children reread the book page by page with a partner.

Routines Flip Chart

eStreet Interactive
www.ReadingStreet.com

Savvas eText
- Student Edition

Access for All

Strategic Intervention

Support Comprehension Have children point to the animal in the picture that the sentence on the page is referring to.

Day 2 SMALL GROUP TIME • Differentiate Phonics, p. SG•73

OL On-Level	SI Strategic Intervention	A Advanced
• **Practice Phonics** More *m* Words • **Read** Decodable Reader *Animal Friends*	• **Reteach Phonics** Recognize *m* • **Read** Decodable Reader *Animal Friends*	• **Extend Phonics** Blend *m* Words • **Read** Decodable Reader *Animal Friends*

Place English Language Learners in the groups that correspond to their reading abilities in English.

If... children need more support with **Phonics,**
then... use the activities on p. DI•80 in the Teacher Resources section of the Digital Path.

 Common Core State Standards

Literature 2. With prompting and support, retell familiar stories, including key details. **Literature 7.** With prompting and support, describe the relationship between illustrations and the story in which they appear (e.g., what moment in a story an illustration depicts). **Also Literature 5.**

Access for All

 Strategic Intervention

Predict After children make their predictions about *Smash! Crash!* based on the title and the cover, have them explain why they think that. Tell children that sometimes we use what we already know to better understand what we read.

Academic Vocabulary

fantasy a story that could not happen

Text-Based Comprehension

Introduce Main Selection

CONCEPTS OF PRINT Display *Smash! Crash!* This is the front cover of the book. This is the back cover. What do these pictures show? (trucks)

GENRE A **fantasy** is a story that could not really happen. Let's read about trucks that play together.

PREVIEW AND PREDICT Display *Smash! Crash!* The title is *Smash! Crash!* What do you see on the front cover? Think about the cover and the title. What do you think this book will be about? Take children on a walk through the book. Have them tell about what they see in each picture.

SET PURPOSE Remind children of the Question of the Week: *What do you like to do with your friends?* Have children listen as you read.

MODEL Read *Smash! Crash!* with expression to build interest in the text.

Routine: Read for Understanding 

Deepen understanding by reading the selection multiple times.

1. **First Read**—Read the entire selection aloud to build interest in the text.
2. **Second Read**—Use the **Develop Vocabulary** notes on pages 469–485.
3. **Third Read**—Use the **Develop Comprehension** notes on pages 469–485.

Retell

CHECK RETELLING Have children turn to p. 106 of *My Skills Buddy.* Walk through the retelling boxes as children retell *Smash! Crash!* After they retell the story as a group, have children draw a picture to retell a favorite part. Have them write or dictate a word or sentence to go with their picture.

Check Retelling

If... children have difficulty retelling the story,

then... go through the story one page at a time, and ask children to tell what happens in their own words.

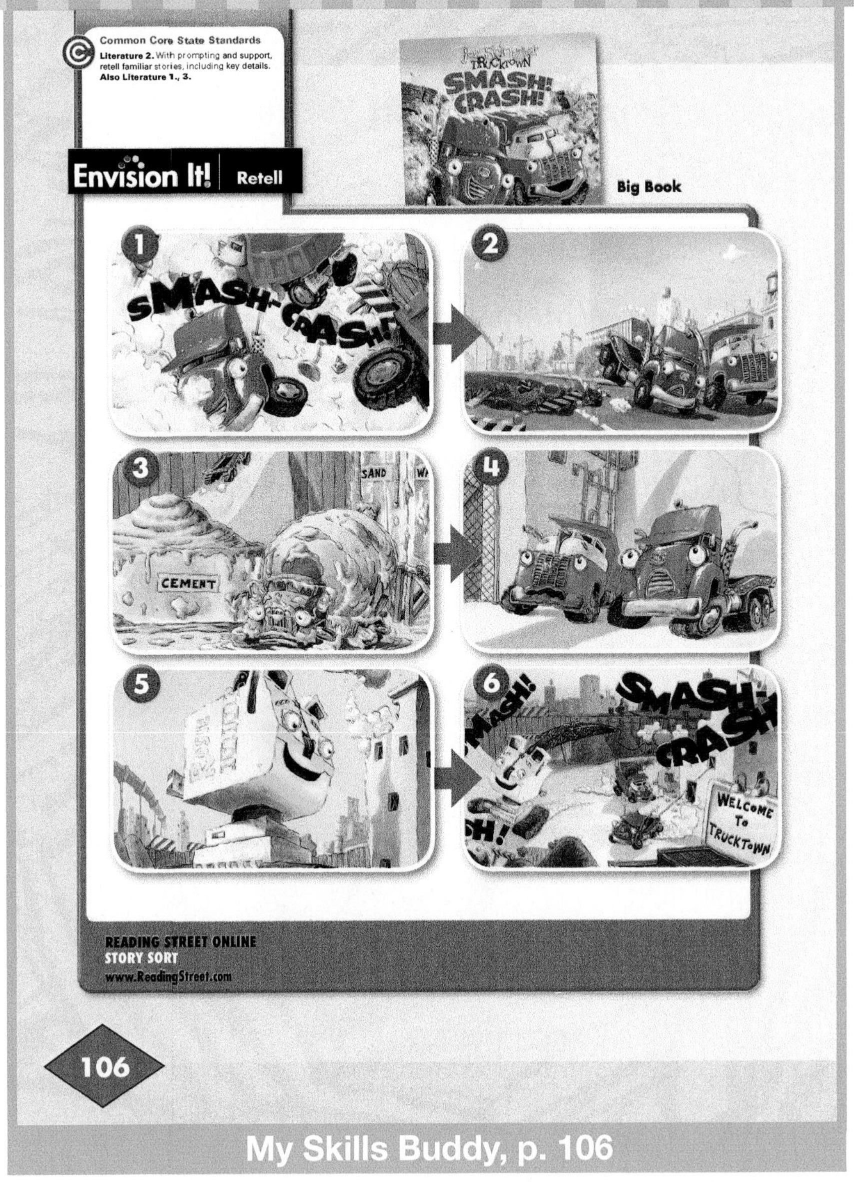

My Skills Buddy, p. 106

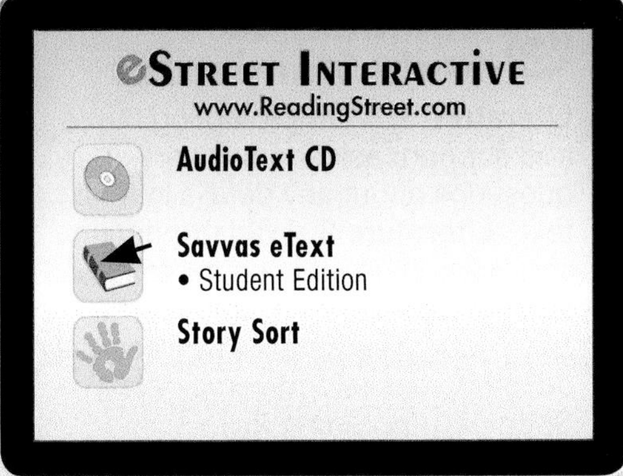

Retelling Plan

- ☑ **Week 1** Assess Advanced students.
- ☑ **Week 2** Assess On-Level students.
- ☑ **Week 3** Assess Strategic Intervention students.
- ☑ **Week 4** Assess Advanced students.
- ☑ **This week assess On-Level students.**
- ☐ **Week 6** Assess Strategic Intervention students.

Scoring Rubric Narrative Retelling

	4	3	2	1
Connections	Makes connections and generalizes beyond the text	Makes connections to other events, stories, or experiences	Makes a limited connection to another event, story, or experience	Makes no connection to another event, story, or experience
Author's Purpose	Elaborates on author's purpose	Tells author's purpose with some clarity	Makes some connection to author's purpose	Makes no connection to author's purpose
Characters	Describes the main character(s) and any character development	Identifies the main character(s) and gives some information about them	Inaccurately identifies some characters or gives little information about them	Inaccurately identifies the characters or gives no information about them
Setting	Describes the time and location	Identifies the time and location	Omits details of time or location	Is unable to identify time or location
Plot	Describes the events in sequence using rich detail	Tells the plot with some errors in sequence that do not affect meaning	Tells parts of plot with gaps that affect meaning	Retelling has no sense of story

Common Core State Standards

Literature 1. With prompting and support, ask and answer questions about key details in a text. **Literature 3.** With prompting and support, identify characters, settings, and major events in a story. **Language 1.b.** Use frequently occurring nouns and verbs. **Also Speaking/Listening 2.**

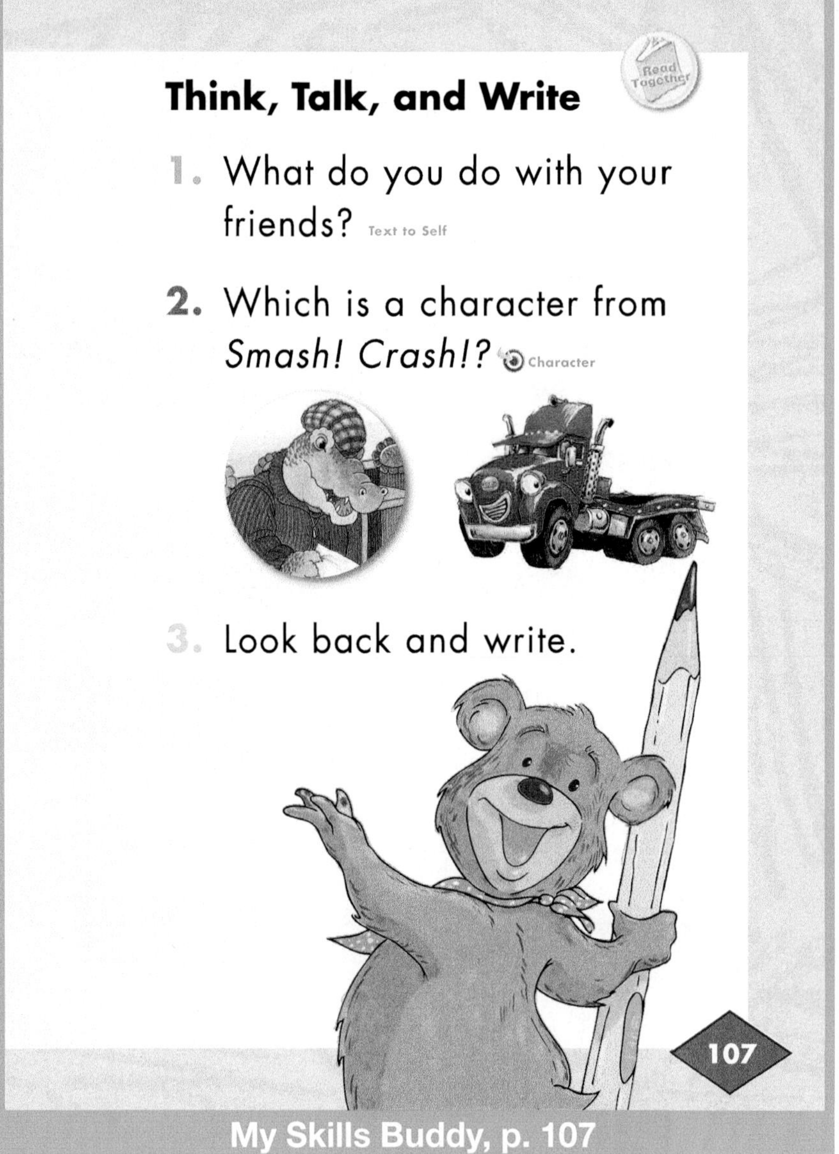

Think, Talk, and Write
Read Together
1. What do you do with your friends? Text to Self
2. Which is a character from Smash! Crash!? Character
3. Look back and write.
107

My Skills Buddy, p. 107

Think, Talk, and Write

DISCUSS CONCEPT We've been learning about things to do with friends. Think about what you do with your friends.

- What is your favorite thing to do with your friends?
- When do you play with your friends?
- How are you and your friends like Jack Truck and his friends?

CONFIRM PREDICTIONS Have children recall their predictions before you read *Smash! Crash!*

- What did you think the story would be about?
- Was your prediction correct?

Have children turn to p. 107 of *My Skills Buddy.* Read the questions and directives and have children respond.

1. **TEXT TO SELF** What do you do with your friends? Where is your favorite place to play with your friends?

2. **CHARACTER** Which is a character from *Smash! Crash!?* What things does the character do in *Smash! Crash!?*

3. **LOOK BACK AND WRITE • TEXT EVIDENCE** Let's look back at our story and write about it. We remember that Jack and Dan want Monster Truck Max to help them smash and crash, but he is busy. Listen for what Max has to do. Read pp. 16–20 of *Smash! Crash!* Now let's write our ideas. Discuss with children why Max can't play and how Jack and Dan help him. Record children's responses on chart paper. (Max must stack barrels by two. Jack and Dan smash and crash. The barrels are smacked, whacked, and stacked.)

Conventions

Nouns for People and Animals

TEACH Remind children that a noun is a word that names a person, animal, place, or thing.

GUIDE PRACTICE Display the *dog* and *man* Picture Cards. Point to each picture. What are these pictures? This is a dog. This is a man. Write the words *dog* and *man* on the board. Which word names an animal? *Dog* names an animal. The word *dog* is a noun for an animal. Which word names a person? *Man* names a person. The word *man* is a noun for a person.

Write the following sentence frames on the board:

I want to be a _______ when I grow up.

I would like to have a pet _______.

Have children complete the first sentence with a noun for a person and the second sentence with a noun for an animal. Write their responses in the blanks. Read the completed sentences with children, pointing to the nouns.

ON THEIR OWN Use *Reader's and Writer's Notebook,* p. 54, for more practice reading, writing, and saying nouns for people and animals.

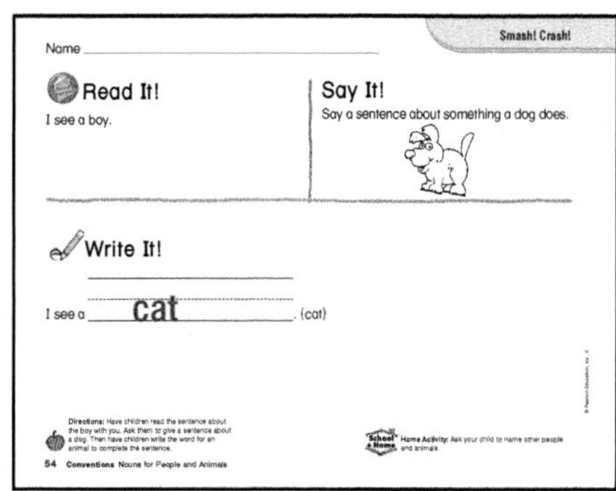

Reader's and Writer's Notebook, p. 54

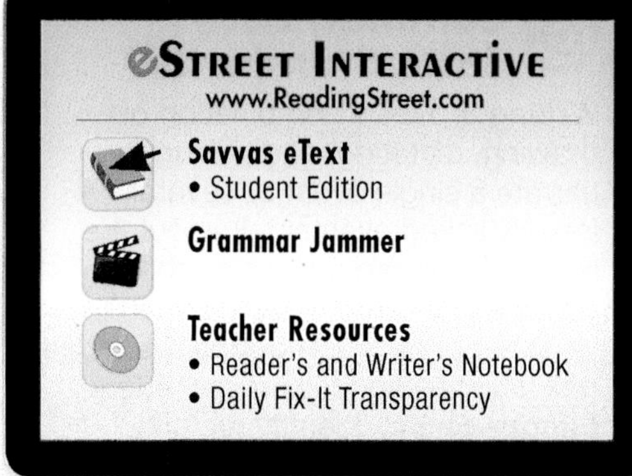

Writing to Sources

Use Write Like a Reporter on pp. 22–23 to guide children in writing text-based responses using one source.

Daily Fix-It

we can have fun with animals

We can have fun with animals.

This week's practice sentences appear on *Teacher Resources DVD-ROM.*

Bridge to Common Core

CONVENTIONS OF STANDARD ENGLISH

As children identify nouns that name people and animals and choose appropriate nouns to complete sentences, they are demonstrating their command of standard English grammar and usage.

Common Core State Standards

Writing 3. Use a combination of drawing, dictating, and writing to narrate a single event or several loosely linked events, tell about the events in the order in which they occurred, and provide a reaction to what happened. **Language 1.a.** Print many upper- and lowercase letters. **Language 5.c.** Identify real-life connections between words and their use (e.g., note places at school that are *colorful*). **Language 6.** Use words and phrases acquired through conversations, reading and being read to, and responding to texts.

Writing to Sources

Use More Connect the Texts on pp. 222–293 to guide children in writing text-based responses within various forms and modes.

Writing

Respond to Literature

DISCUSS Display *Smash! Crash!* Discuss with children the different trucks Jack Truck and Dump Truck Dan see when they are smashing and crashing.

MODEL In the story, Jack and Dan want to smash and crash all over Trucktown. They try to get other trucks to play with them. I am going to write:

Jack and Dan want Cement Mixer Melvin to play.
They want Monster Truck Max to smash and crash.

GUIDE PRACTICE In a row on the board, write three short sentences or draw three simple illustrations that tell about the story events. Label them *Beginning, Middle,* and *End.*

Invite children to help you write more sentences about the other trucks Jack and Dan want to play with and what they help those trucks do.

Jack and Dan mix the cement.
They stack the barrels.

INDEPENDENT WRITING Have children write or dictate about Jack and Dan. Some children may wish to use this sentence frame:

Jack and Dan ______.

Then have children illustrate their sentences.

Daily Handwriting

Write *Matt* and *mug* on the board. Review correct letter formation of uppercase *M* and lowercase *m.*

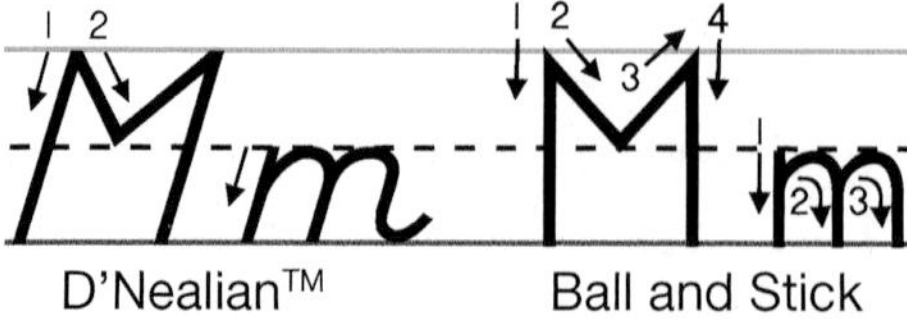

Have children write *Matt* and *mug* on their Write-On Boards. Remind them to use proper left-to-right and top-to-bottom progression when writing *M* and *m.*

Common Core State Standards

Speaking/Listening 1.a. Follow agreed-upon rules for discussions (e.g., listening to others and taking turns speaking about the topics and texts under discussion). **Also Speaking/Listening 6., Language 6.**

Let's Learn It!

Vocabulary

- Talk about the pictures.
- Put your hand up . . . now down.
- Put your hand in your pocket. Now take it out.

Listening and Speaking

- Make an announcement.
- Listen to a classmate's message or announcement.
- Retell or summarize your classmate's message or announcement.

Vocabulary

Position Words

in

out

up

down

108

My Skills Buddy, p. 108

Vocabulary

Position Words

TEACH Have children turn to p. 108 of *My Skills Buddy.* Use the first Vocabulary bullet to guide discussion about the position words *up, down, in,* and *out.* Act out each word and have children tell which word you are showing.

GUIDE PRACTICE Write the words *up, down, in,* and *out* on the board. Point to each word as you read it.

Have children look again at the pictures on p. 108 of *My Skills Buddy.* Point to each picture and have children say the position word that goes with it.

ON THEIR OWN Have children stand in a circle. Give them directions, such as crouch down, jump up, put your hands in the circle, and take your hands out of the circle. Call on children to tell what they are doing, using the position word.

Access for All

Advanced

Extend Vocabulary Explain to children that *up/down* and *in/out* are opposites. Have children choose a pair of opposites and draw a picture to illustrate them.

Bridge to Common Core

VOCABULARY ACQUISITION AND USE

When children use position words correctly, they are demonstrating their comprehension of the relationships among words in a category and of the connections between words and their use in describing with precision.

Access Vocabulary Use physical response to clarify the meanings of the words *up, down, in,* and *out.* For example, use one hand to point to the floor and *say down.* Then use the other hand to point to the ceiling and say *up.* What things are down? What things are up?

Common Core State Standards

Foundational Skills 3.a. Demonstrate basic knowledge of one-to-one letter-sound correspondences by producing the primary or many of the most frequent sounds for each consonant. **Speaking/Listening 5.** Add drawings or other visual displays to descriptions as desired to provide additional detail. **Language 1.b.** Use frequently occurring nouns and verbs.

Wrap Up Your Day!

✔ **Content Knowledge** Today we read about Jack Truck and Dump Truck Dan. They are best friends. What do they like to do together?

✔ **Phonemic Awareness** I am going to recite a chant. Clap when you hear words that begin or end with /m/: *Tom Mouse ate muffins with jam. Oh, my!*

✔ **Vocabulary Skill** Today we talked about words that tell about positions: *up, down, in, out*. Point your finger up. Now point your finger down.

✔ **Homework Idea** Have children write or dictate a noun for a person or an animal they see at their home.

Preview DAY 3

Tomorrow we will read more about Jack Truck and Dump Truck Dan.

Extend Your Day!

Science
Make-Believe or Real?

MATERIALS: Decodable Story 5, *Little Mouse;* paper; crayons; chart paper

DISCUSS MAKE-BELIEVE AND REAL ANIMALS Review Decodable Story 5, *Little Mouse,* with children. Ask them to look at the things the little mouse does. Do you think real mice do these things?

Little Mouse	Real Mice
wears clothes	live in fields
carries backpack	eat seeds
walks on two feet	walk on four feet
talks	squeak
goes to school	

Make a two-column chart on chart paper listing children's descriptions of things the little mouse does and of things real mice do. Have children compare and contrast the lists.

WRITE ABOUT MAKE-BELIEVE AND REAL MICE Divide a sheet of paper in half for each child. On one half of the paper, have children draw and label something the little mouse in the story does. On the other half, have them draw and label something a real mouse would do.

Phonics
/m/ Spelled *Mm*

MATERIALS: Picture Cards: *mop, cat, dog, moon, mask, pig, mug;* paper; crayons

/m/ WORDS Display the *mop* Picture Card. What is the first sound in *mop?* What is the letter for /m/? Display the *cat* Picture Card. What is this? Does *cat* begin with the same sound as *mop?* Continue with the remaining Picture Cards until children have identified the words that begin with /m/*Mm.*

DRAW AND LABEL /m/ WORDS On a sheet of paper, have children draw the four objects that begin with /m/*Mm* and write the letter *m* under each picture.

Conventions
Nouns for Animals

MATERIALS: Picture Cards: *pig, kangaroo, dog, elephant, frog, robin, tiger, wolf*

IDENTIFY NOUNS Display the Picture Cards. Give clues and encourage children to choose the card for the unknown animal and use the noun to name that animal. I am an animal you see at the zoo. I am orange and black. What am I? Continue with the remaining cards.

Picture Card

DAY 3 at a Glance

Content Knowledge
Oral Vocabulary

Phonemic Awareness
Initial and Final /m/

Phonics
/m/ Spelled *Mm*

Text-Based Comprehension
Character

Conventions
Review What We Can Do

Writing
Caption

Listening and Speaking
Announcements/Messages

Materials

- Student Edition
- Truckery Rhymes
- Talk with Me/Sing with Me Chart
- Picture Cards
- Reader's and Writer's Notebook
- Student Reader K.1.5
- Big Book

Common Core State Standards

Speaking/Listening 1.a. Follow agreed-upon rules for discussions (e.g., listening to others and taking turns speaking about the topics and texts under discussion). **Language 6.** Use words and phrases acquired through conversations, reading and being read to, and responding to texts. **Also Language 5.c.**

TRUCKTOWN on Reading Street

Start your engines!

Display p. 9 of *Truckery Rhymes.* Do you know the original "Peter, Peter, Pumpkin Eater"? Recite it first, and then have children repeat it with you:

Peter, Peter, pumpkin eater,
Had a wife and couldn't keep her.
Put her in a pumpkin shell
And there he kept her very well.

Truckery Rhymes

Content Knowledge

Zoom in on

What Friends Do Together

On the board, write the Question of the Week, *What do you like to do with your friends?* Read the question as you track the print. Talk with children about what they do with their friends. Remind children to speak clearly and to take turns speaking.

Build Oral Language

LISTEN FOR AMAZING WORDS Display Sing with Me Chart 5B. Remind children that yesterday they sang "Won't You Play With Me?" and listened for the words *signals* and *dud.* Today we are going to listen for the Amazing Words *proper* and *pirates.* Sing the song several times to the tune of "Zip a Dee Doo Dah." Have children sing along with you, clapping their hands when they say the Amazing Words *proper* and *pirates.*

Won't You Play With Me?
It's a fabulous day out, can't you see?
My, oh my, won't you play with me?
A perfect day for whatever will be,
A fabulous day out, can't you see?
We can stay out on the high seas.
We'll be pirates,
Or sailors,
Or whatever we want to be.
Change your day from a dud to a great jamboree.
A perfect day for whatever will be!

Talk with Me/Sing with Me Chart 5B

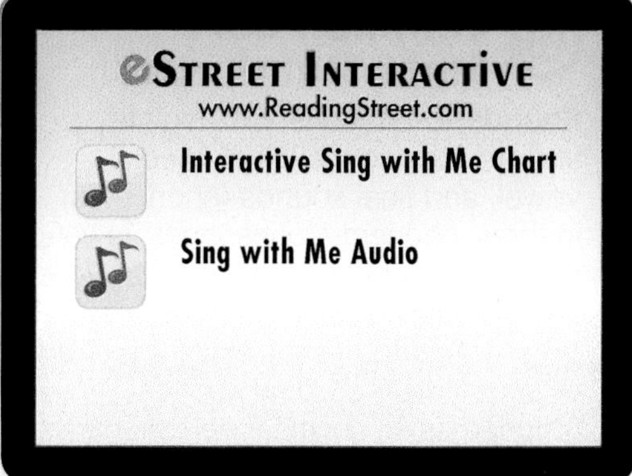

Build Oral Vocabulary

Amazing Words Robust Vocabulary Routine

1. **Introduce the Word** When we say something is *proper,* we mean it is right or correct. We can wear *proper* clothes, say *proper* things, and do *proper* things. What's our new Amazing Word for right or correct? Say it with me: *proper.*
2. **Demonstrate** Provide examples to show meaning. *She wore the proper dress to the dance.* What are *proper* things to wear to school? What is the *proper* way to act toward adults?

   Repeat steps 1 and 2.

   Introduce the Word In the story *Smash! Crash!,* some of the trucks pretend to be *pirates. Pirates* are people who rob ships at sea. What's our new Amazing Word for people who steal things from ships at sea? Say it with me: *pirates.*

   Demonstrate *Some pirates wear eye patches.* What other things do you think *pirates* wear?
3. **Apply** Have children use *proper* and *pirates* in complete sentences. Have them show how they would act like a *pirate.*
4. **Display the Words** Have children point to and name letters in *proper* and *pirates* that they recognize. Ask them what they notice about the first letter in each word.

Routines Flip Chart

USE AMAZING WORDS To reinforce the concept and the Amazing Words, have children supply the appropriate Amazing Word for each sentence.

The ______ sail the seas looking for ships to rob. (pirates)
Sharing toys is the ______ thing to do. (proper)

Amazing Words

signals	dud
proper	pirates
perfect	fabulous

Access for All

Advanced

Build Vocabulary Have children draw a picture of pirates. Encourage them to use their imaginations as they draw their pirates. Have children use the picture on Sing with Me Chart 5B as an example.

Visual Support Use the pictures on Talk with Me Chart 5A to help children complete the Amazing Word sentences.

Expand Vocabulary Use the Day 3 instruction on ELL Poster 5 to expand children's use of vocabulary about the lesson concept.

Common Core State Standards

Foundational Skills 2.d. Isolate and pronounce the initial, medial vowel, and final sounds (phonemes) in three-phoneme (consonant-vowel-consonant, or CVC) words.* (This does not include CVCs ending with /l/, /r/, or /x/.) **Foundational Skills 2.e.** Add or substitute individual sounds (phonemes) in simple, one-syllable words to make new words.

Phonemic Awareness

Initial and Final /m/

REVIEW INITIAL /m/ Display the *mop* Picture Card. This is a mop. *Mop* begins with /m/ /m/ /m/, *mop.* What sound do you hear at the beginning of *mop?* Continue with the *man, map,* and *moose* Picture Cards.

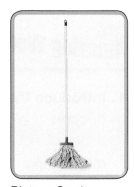

Picture Card

PRACTICE FINAL /m/ Display the *gum* Picture Card. This is gum. Listen to the sounds in *gum:* /g/ /u/ /m/. How many sounds do you hear? (three) Is /m/ the first sound in *gum:* /g/ /u/ /m/? (no) Is /m/ the second sound in *gum:* /g/ /u/ /m/? (no) The /m/ in *gum* is the last sound. Continue the routine with the following words: *ham, Jim, Tom, him, sum.*

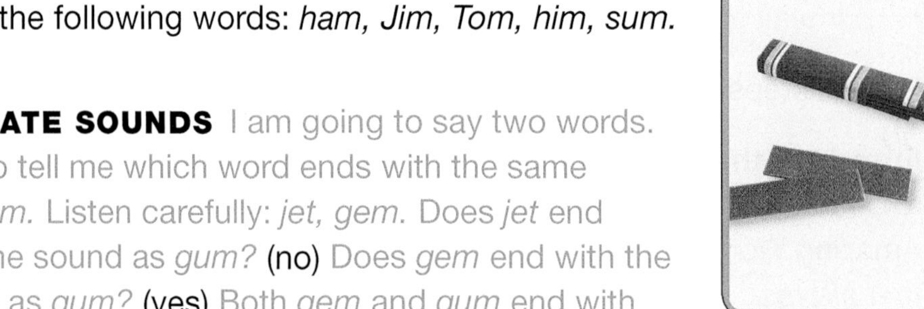

Picture Card

DISCRIMINATE SOUNDS I am going to say two words. I want you to tell me which word ends with the same sound as *gum.* Listen carefully: *jet, gem.* Does *jet* end with the same sound as *gum?* (no) Does *gem* end with the same sound as *gum?* (yes) Both *gem* and *gum* end with /m/. Let's say the sounds together: /j/ /e/ /m/, /g/ /u/ /m/. Continue the routine with these word pairs: *bed, Sam; dim, hop; rob, jam.*

ON THEIR OWN Display the *mask, drum, jam,* and *hat* Picture Cards. Have children choose one of the pictures to draw. Tell children to write an *m* on their paper if the picture name ends with /m/.

DISCRIMINATE INITIAL SOUNDS I am going to say three words. I want you to tell me which two words begin with /m/. Listen carefully: *mud, pet, men.* Does *mud* begin with /m/? (yes) Does *pet* begin with /m/? (no) Does *men* begin with /m/? (yes) *Mud* and *men* both begin with /m/. Continue the routine with these sets of words: *top, met, mad; mug, Mac, dig; Meg, box, mat.*

Corrective feedback	**If...** children cannot discriminate initial sounds, **then...** have them say the sounds in each word, repeating the initial sound several times.

Access for All

 Advanced

Isolate Initial Sounds Say the words *mat* and *cat.* Which sound is different, the beginning or the end? Which word begins with /m/? Repeat the routine with *mop, top* and *met, set.*

Teacher Tip

Use sound discrimination activities that focus on a consonant sound in the initial and final positions in words to check children's understanding of the sound.

Common Core State Standards

Foundational Skills 1.d. Recognize and name all upper- and lowercase letters of the alphabet. **Foundational Skills 3.a.** Demonstrate basic knowledge of one-to-one letter-sound correspondences by producing the primary or many of the most frequent sounds for each consonant. **Also Foundational Skills 2.d., 3.c.**

Phonics

Blend Sounds

/m/ Spelled *Mm*

REVIEW /m/*Mm* Display the *Mm* Alphabet Card and point to the motorcycle. What sound do you hear at the beginning of *motorcycle?* What letter spells that sound? Point to the letters *Mm.* What is the sound for this letter? What are the names of these letters?

REVIEW LETTER NAMES Use Alphabet Cards to review the following letter names: *Aa, Ee, Gg, Ii, Mm, Oo, Tt, Uu.* Have children identify the uppercase letters and lowercase letters.

BLEND Write the word *map* on the board and point to *m.* What is the sound for this letter? *Map* ends with *-ap.* Let's blend /m/ and *-ap* to make the word *map:* /m/ *-ap, map.* Continue with the words *man, met,* and *mug.*

Write the word *ham* on the board and point to *m.* What is the sound for this letter? *Ham* begins with *ha-.* Let's blend *ha-* and /m/ to make the word *ham: ha-* /m/, *ham.* Continue with the words *yum, Jim,* and *Tom.*

MORE PRACTICE Use *Reader's and Writer's Notebook,* p. 55, for additional practice with /m/.

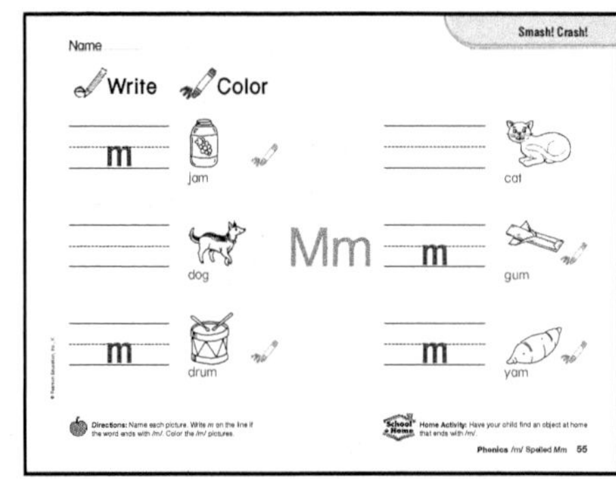

Reader's and Writer's Notebook, p. 55

REVIEW LETTER NAMES Display the *Bb, Ff, Ss,* and *Vv* Alphabet Cards. Point to the uppercase and lowercase letters on the cards in random order. Ask children to identify each letter as you point to it. When children have identified all eight letters, display four different Alphabet Cards and continue in the same way.

REVIEW HIGH-FREQUENCY WORDS Write *to* on the board. This is the word *to.* What is this word? Continue the routine with *a, the, I,* and *am.*

Access for All

Support Phonics Mix the /m/ Picture Cards with other Picture Cards. Show each Picture Card and have children say the picture name. Ask them if it begins with /m/. When children have identified the /m/ Picture Cards, write the picture names on the board. Have volunteers circle each *m* as they say the word.

Check Word Reading High-Frequency Words

FORMATIVE ASSESSMENT Write the following high-frequency words from Kindergarten Student Reader K.1.5, *Cat and Dog Eat Together,* on the board. Have children take turns reading the words.

I	the	a	am	to

If... children cannot read the high-frequency words,
then... write the words on cards for them to practice at home.

If... children can successfully read the high-frequency words,
then... have them read Kindergarten Student Reader K.1.5, *Cat and Dog Eat Together.*

Student Reader

Read *Cat and Dog Eat Together*

REVIEW Review the previously taught high-frequency words. Have children read each word as you point to it on the Word Wall: *I, am, to, the, a.*

TEACH REBUS WORDS Write *Mom* on the board. This is the word *Mom.* Name the letters with me: *M, o, m, Mom.* Repeat with *talking, mixing, muffins, reading, mouse, eating, meatball, mopping,* and *mess.* Look for these words in the book we read today. There will be a picture above the word to help you read it.

READ Display Kindergarten Student Reader K.1.5. Today we are going to read a new book. Point to and identify the front and back cover. Hold your book right side up. This is how you hold a book when you read. Point to the title. The title of this book is *Cat and Dog Eat Together.* The author's name is Carolyn Satoh. Remind children to turn the pages one at a time. When we finish reading the words on the page, we turn the page. Demonstrate how to correctly turn the pages in the book. As you turn the pages, have children predict what might happen in the book based on the illustrations.

Use the reading decodable books routine to read the Kindergarten Student Reader.

Routine Reading Decodable Books

1. **Read Silently** Have children whisper read the book page by page as you listen in.
2. **Model Fluent Reading** Have children finger point as you read a page. Then have them reread the page without you.
3. **Read Chorally** Have children finger point as they chorally read the page. Continue reading page by page, repeating steps 1 and 2.
4. **Read Individually** Have children take turns reading aloud a page.
5. **Reread and Monitor Progress** As you listen to individual children reread, monitor progress and provide support.
6. **Reread with a Partner** Have children reread the book page by page with a partner.

Routines Flip Chart

Common Core State Standards

Literature 10. Actively engage in group reading activities with purpose and understanding. **Foundational Skills 4.** Read emergent-reader texts with purpose and understanding. **Also Foundational Skills 1.**

Access for All

 Strategic Intervention

Support Rebus Words The words *talking, mixing, reading, eating,* and *mopping* are in this book. These words are action words. They tell things we can do. Have children practice acting out each word.

Kindergarten Student Reader K.1.5

eStreet Interactive
www.ReadingStreet.com

Savvas eText
- Kindergarten Student Reader

Day 3 SMALL GROUP TIME • Differentiate Vocabulary, p. SG•73

OL On-Level
- **Develop Vocabulary** Practice Position Words
- **Read** Student Reader *Cat and Dog Eat Together*

SI Strategic Intervention
- **Develop Vocabulary** Reteach Position Words
- **Read** Student Reader *Cat and Dog Eat Together*

A Advanced
- **Develop Vocabulary** More Position Words
- **Read** Student Reader *Cat and Dog Eat Together*

ELL

Place English Language Learners in the groups that correspond to their reading abilities in English.

If... children need more scaffolding and practice with **Vocabulary, then...** use the ELL activities on p. DI•82 in the Teacher Resources section of the Digital Path.

Common Core State Standards

Literature 2. With prompting and support, retell familiar stories, including key details. **Literature 3.** With prompting and support, identify characters, settings, and major events in a story. **Also Literature 9.**

Bridge to Common Core

CRAFT AND STRUCTURE

When children retell the story, they are analyzing how story elements, such as characters, relate to the whole story structure. Using the Develop Vocabulary notes as you read the text a second time focuses children's attention on comprehending unknown words and word choices.

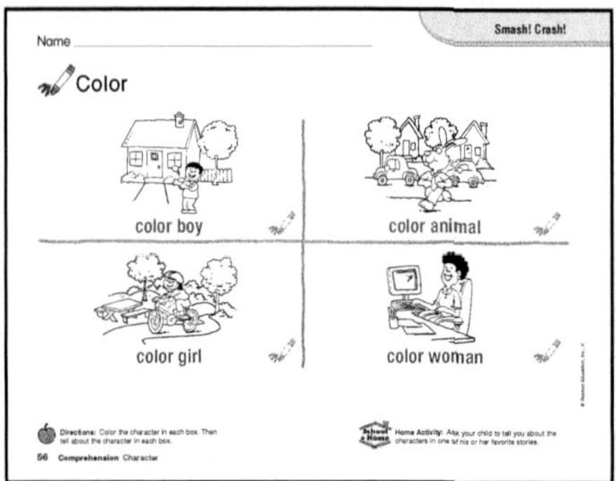

Reader's and Writer's Notebook, p. 56

Text-Based Comprehension

Read Main Selection

RETELL THE SELECTION Have children turn to p. 106 of *My Skills Buddy* and use the retelling boxes to retell the story. Direct children to the first retelling box. Continue reviewing the retelling boxes and having children retell the story.

REVIEW CHARACTER Display illustrations in *Smash! Crash!* Let's review the characters in the story.

MORE PRACTICE Use *Reader's and Writer's Notebook,* p. 56, for more practice with character.

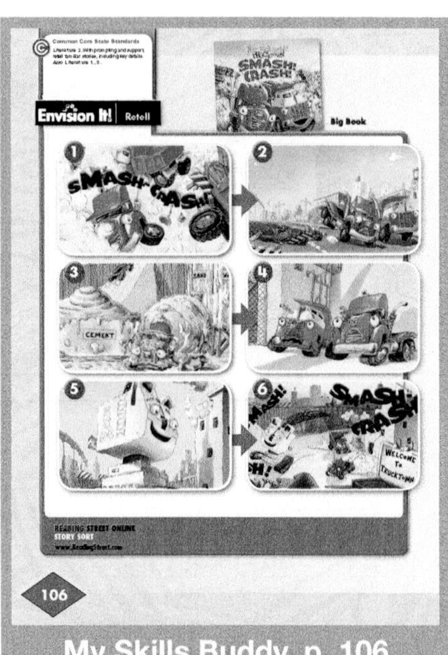

My Skills Buddy, p. 106

Access Main Selection

READER AND TASK SUGGESTIONS	
Preparing to Read the Text	**Leveled Tasks**
• Review the Amazing Words and have children use them to talk about the selection. • Discuss the use of quotation marks to show words that the characters say in a story.	• **Theme and Knowledge Demands** If children have trouble remembering key details, have them look at the illustrations carefully, name each character, and tell what kind of truck it is.

See Text Complexity Measures for *Smash! Crash!* on the weekly tab.

READ Reread *Smash! Crash!* Follow the **2nd Read** beginning on p. 469, and use the **Develop Vocabulary** notes to prompt conversations about the story.

Routine Read for Understanding

Deepen understanding by reading the selection multiple times.

1. **First Read**—Read the entire selection aloud to build interest in the text.
2. **Second Read**—Use the **Develop Vocabulary** notes on pages 469–485.
3. **Third Read**—Use the **Develop Comprehension** notes on pages 469–485.

2ND READ

Develop Vocabulary

***WH*- QUESTION** This is Jack and Dan. What kind of truck is Dan? (He is a dump truck.)

- Dan is a dump truck. Where are Jack and Dan?

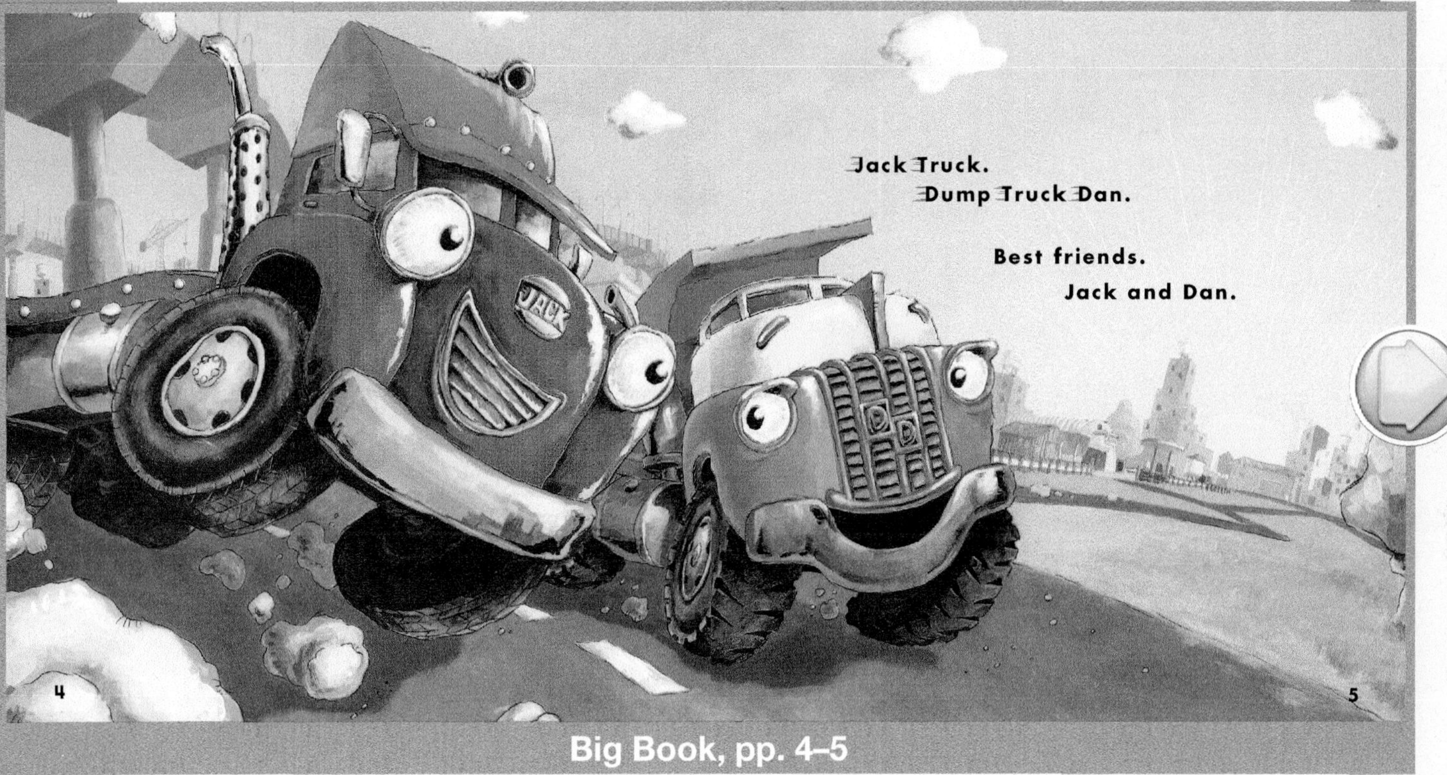
Jack Truck.
Dump Truck Dan.
Best friends.
Jack and Dan.
JACK
4
5

Big Book, pp. 4–5

3RD READ

Develop Comprehension ©

OPEN-ENDED How are Jack Truck and Dump Truck Dan alike? (They are both trucks. They both have wheels. They both carry things.) How are they different? (They are different colors. Dan can dump things.)

2ND READ

Develop Vocabulary

***WH*- QUESTION** Look at the picture on page 6. Why does Dan ask Jack what they should do? (There is a big hole in the road, and they can't get around it.)

- Jack and Dan stop at the big hole in the road. What do you think they will do to get around the hole?

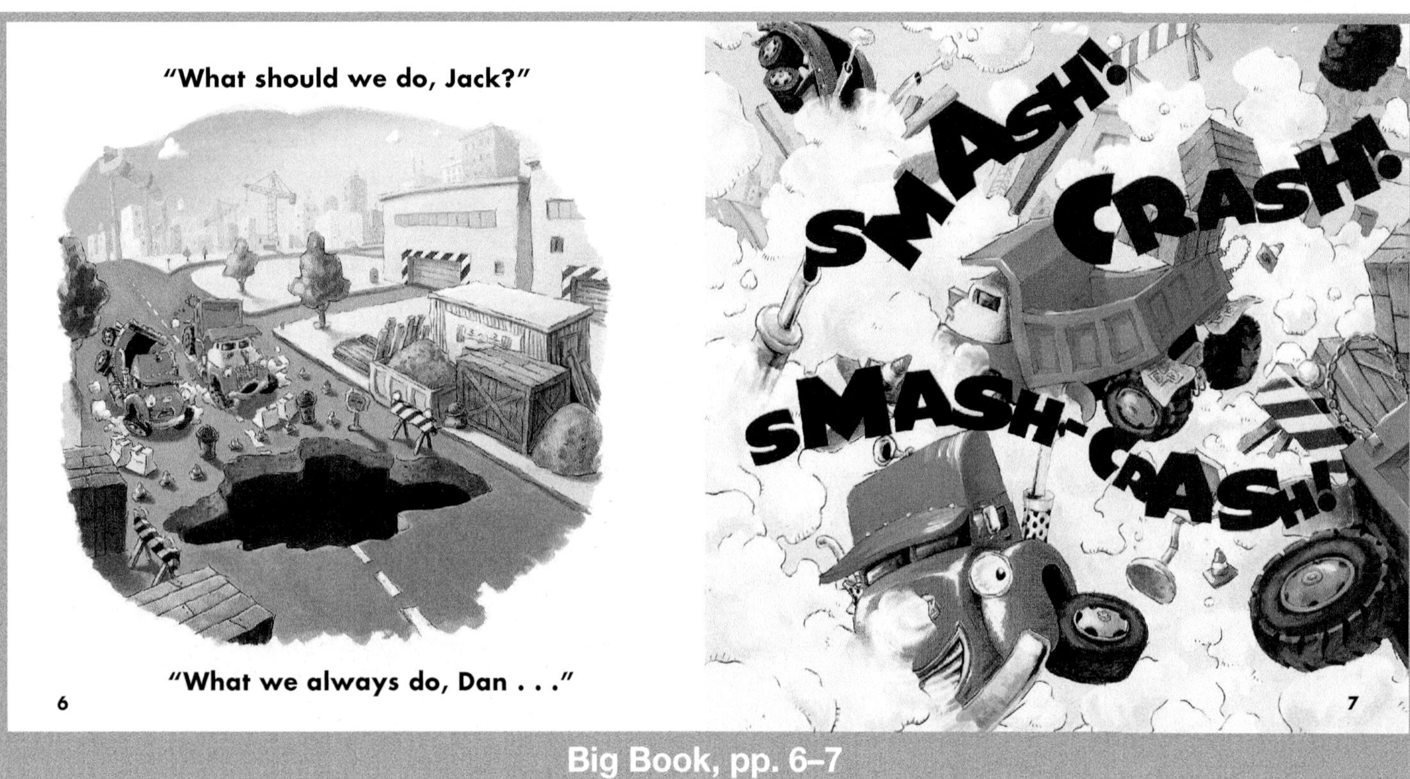

"What should we do, Jack?"
"What we always do, Dan . . ."
6
SMASH!
CRASH!
SMASH-CRASH!
7

Big Book, pp. 6–7

3RD READ

Develop Comprehension ©

OPEN-ENDED Jack and Dan make a mess when they smash and crash. Do you think people like it when Jack and Dan smash and crash? (No, because someone will have to clean up the mess.)

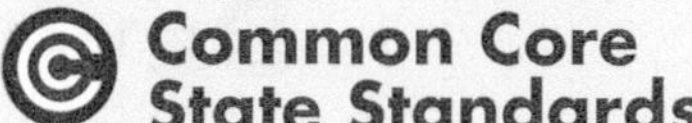

WH- QUESTION What happens after Jack and Dan smash and crash? (A shadow falls and a big voice calls.)

- Something blocks the sun and makes a shadow on the ground. What does a shadow look like?

DEVELOP VOCABULARY shadow

Common Core State Standards

Literature 1. With prompting and support, ask and answer questions about key details in a text.
Literature 3. With prompting and support, identify characters, settings, and major events in a story.
Literature 7. With prompting and support, describe the relationship between illustrations and the story in which they appear (e.g., what moment in a story an illustration depicts).

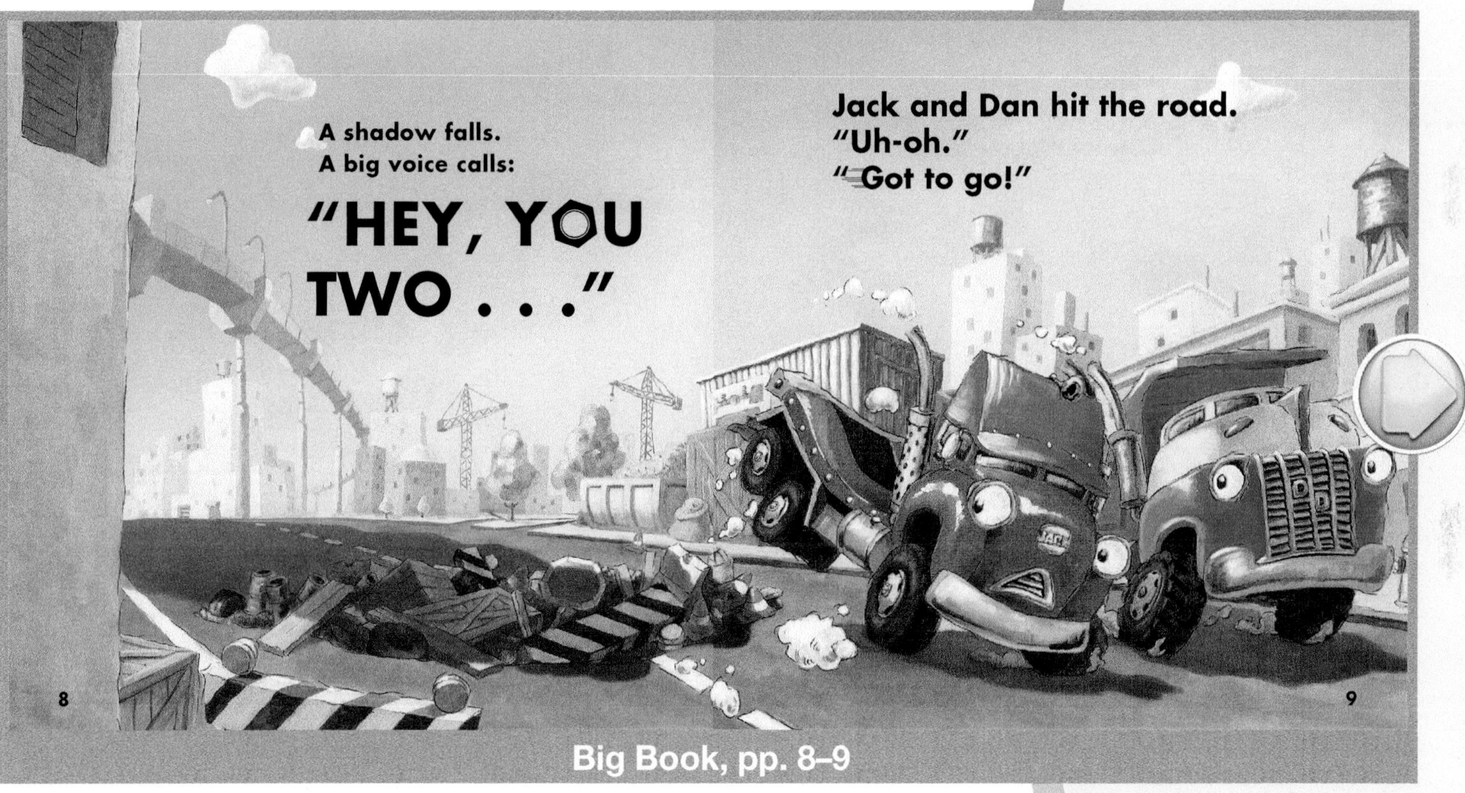

Big Book, pp. 8–9

INFERENCE Jack and Dan look worried and scared. Why? (Someone with a big voice is trying to talk to them. The voice probably sounds scary. They probably think they are in trouble.)

2ND READ

Develop Vocabulary

OPEN-ENDED What kind of truck is Melvin? (a cement mixer)

- Melvin mixes cement. How can he get messy from mixing cement?

DEVELOP VOCABULARY messy

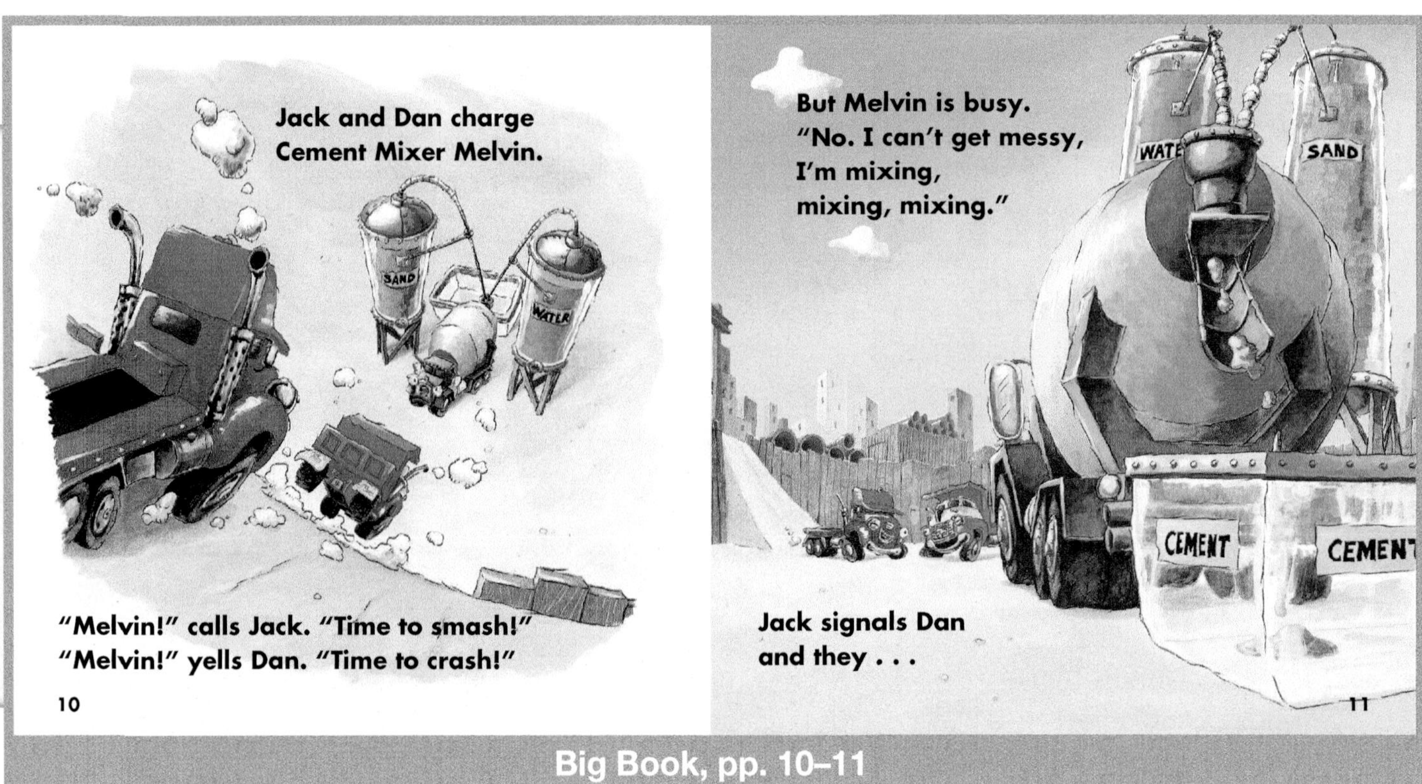

Jack and Dan charge
Cement Mixer Melvin.
SAND
WATER
"Melvin!" calls Jack. "Time to smash!"
"Melvin!" yells Dan. "Time to crash!"
10
But Melvin is busy.
"No. I can't get messy,
I'm mixing,
mixing, mixing."
WATE
SAND
CEMENT
CEMENT
Jack signals Dan
and they . . .
11

Big Book, pp. 10–11

3RD READ

Develop Comprehension ©

INFERENCE How do you think Jack signals Dan? (Jack winks at Dan.) What do you think the winking means? (I think the winking means they are going to smash and crash.)

RECALL What do Jack and Dan smash and crash into? (the two towers of sand and water that Melvin is mixing)

- Jack and Dan smash and crash into the towers of sand and water. Do you think Melvin is happy that Jack and Dan smash and crash?

Common Core State Standards

Literature 1. With prompting and support, ask and answer questions about key details in a text.
Literature 3. With prompting and support, identify characters, settings, and major events in a story.
Literature 7. With prompting and support, describe the relationship between illustrations and the story in which they appear (e.g., what moment in a story an illustration depicts).

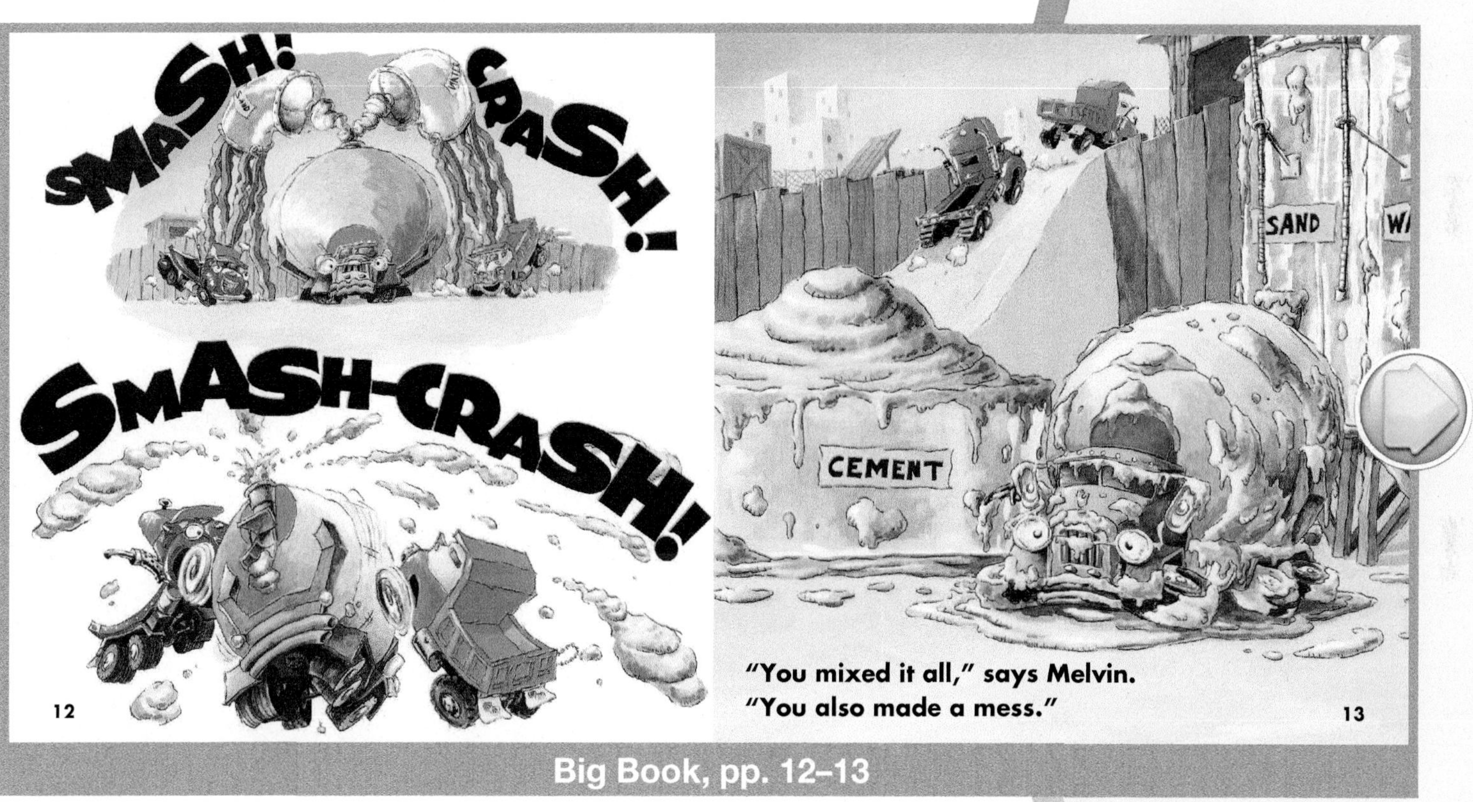
SMASH!
CRASH!
SMASH-CRASH!
12
SAND
CEMENT
"You mixed it all," says Melvin.
"You also made a mess."
13
Big Book, pp. 12–13

RECALL How do Jack and Dan help Melvin? (They mix all the cement for him.) How do Jack and Dan not help Melvin? (They make a mess.)

2ND READ

Develop Vocabulary

COMPLETION Why do Jack and Dan step on the gas and go? (The shadow is back and calls out to them.)

- The shadow is back, so Jack and Dan leave. Tell me what the shadow says.

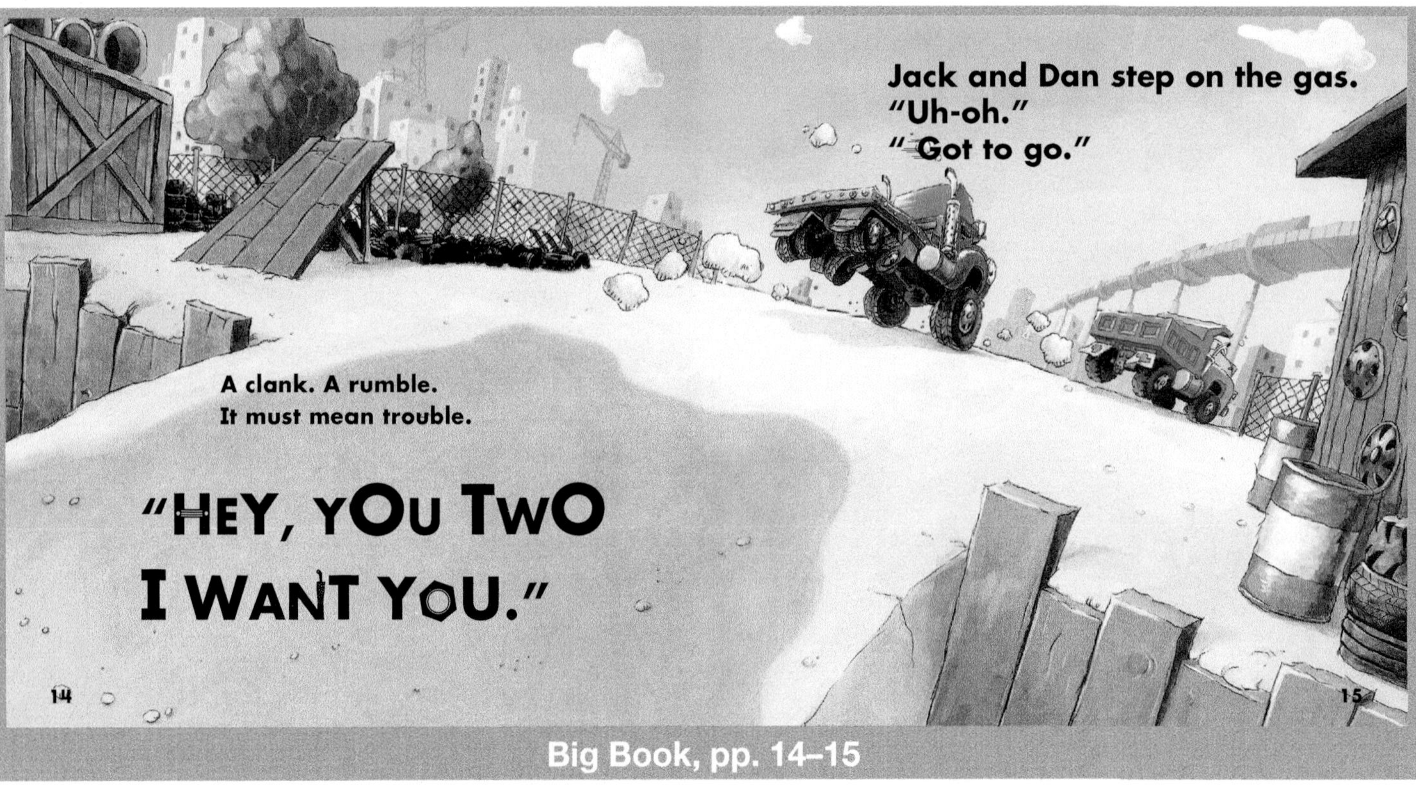

Big Book, pp. 14–15

3RD READ

Develop Comprehension ©

INFERENCE How do you know the shadow is back? (The picture shows a shadow, and the shadow says, "Hey, you two. I want you.")

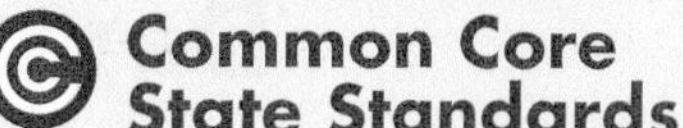

RECALL What truck do Jack and Dan meet next? (Monster Truck Max)

- Jack and Dan want to smash and crash with Monster Truck Max, but he is stacking barrels. What must Max do with the barrels?

DEVELOP VOCABULARY barrels

Common Core State Standards

Literature 1. With prompting and support, ask and answer questions about key details in a text.
Literature 3. With prompting and support, identify characters, settings, and major events in a story.
Literature 7. With prompting and support, describe the relationship between illustrations and the story in which they appear (e.g., what moment in a story an illustration depicts).

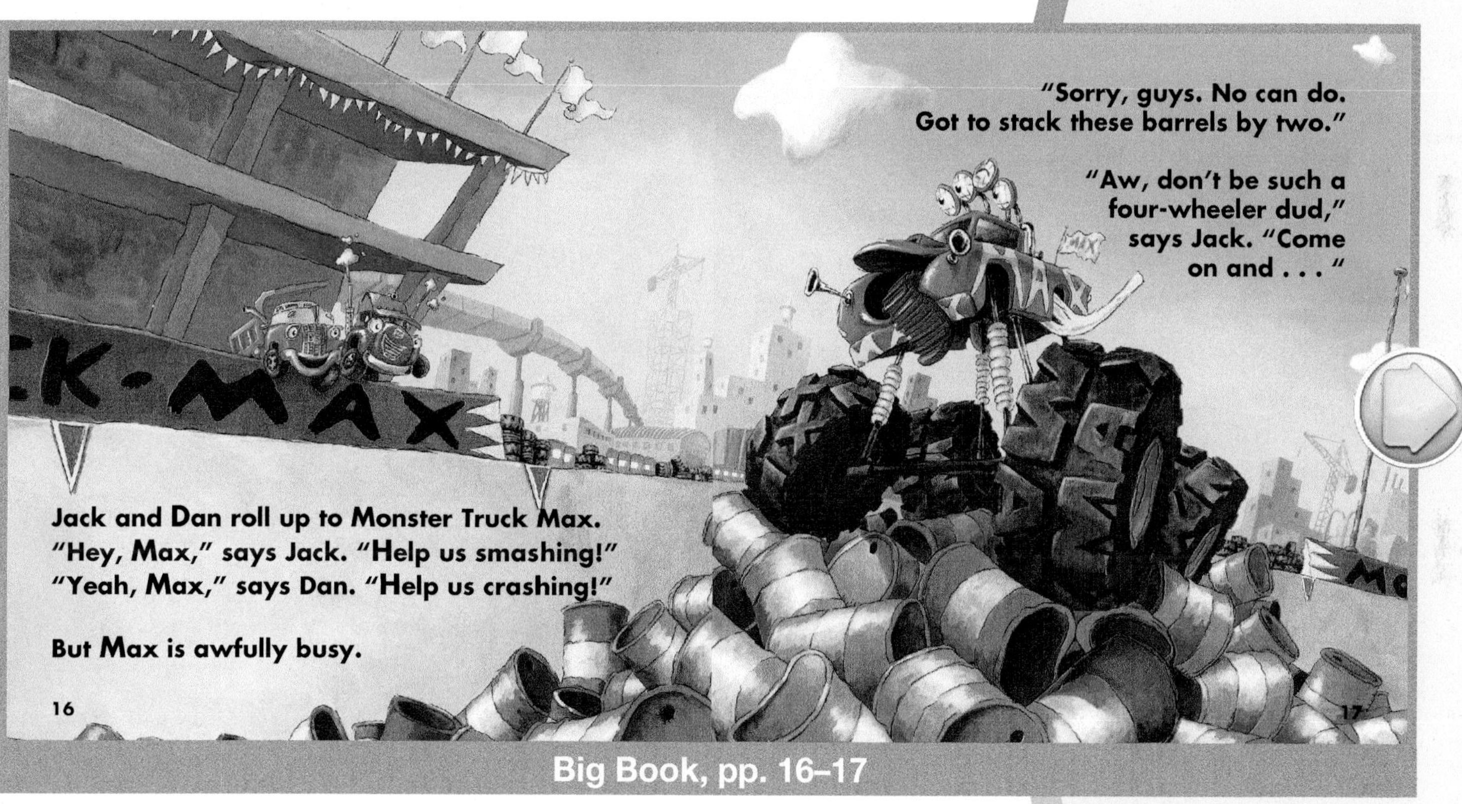

"Sorry, guys. No can do.
Got to stack these barrels by two."
"Aw, don't be such a
four-wheeler dud,"
says Jack. "Come
on and . . . "
Jack and Dan roll up to Monster Truck Max.
"Hey, Max," says Jack. "Help us smashing!"
"Yeah, Max," says Dan. "Help us crashing!"
But Max is awfully busy.
16
17

Big Book, pp. 16–17

CHARACTER Max is a monster truck. Tell me what Max looks like. (Max has four very big wheels. He can drive over barrels.)

2ND READ

Develop Vocabulary

DISTANCING What do Jack and Dan do with the barrels? (They smash and crash.)

- Jack and Dan are best friends who love to smash and crash together. What do you and your best friends like to do together?

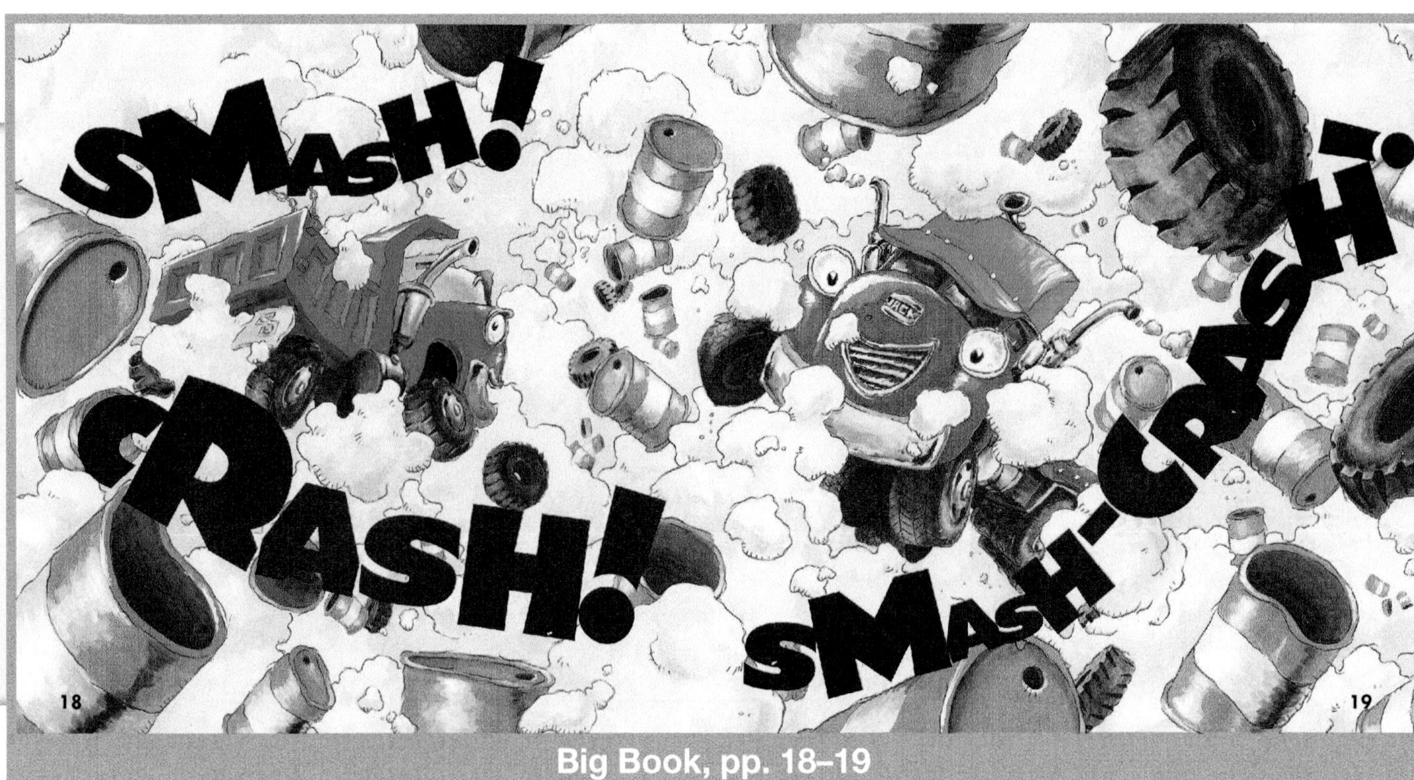
SMASH!
CRASH!
SMASH-CRASH!
18
19

Big Book, pp. 18–19

3RD READ

Develop Comprehension ©

OPEN-ENDED Why do you think Jack and Dan like to smash and crash? (They like to smash and crash because they think it is fun. Jack looks like he is smiling.)

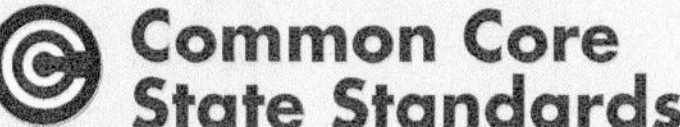

RECALL What do Jack and Dan do to the barrels? (The barrels are smacked, whacked, and stacked to the max.)

- Jack and Dan stack the barrels when they smash and crash. Do you think Max is happy the barrels are stacked like that?

EXPAND VOCABULARY to the max, weird

Common Core State Standards

Literature 1. With prompting and support, ask and answer questions about key details in a text.
Literature 3. With prompting and support, identify characters, settings, and major events in a story.
Literature 7. With prompting and support, describe the relationship between illustrations and the story in which they appear (e.g., what moment in a story an illustration depicts).

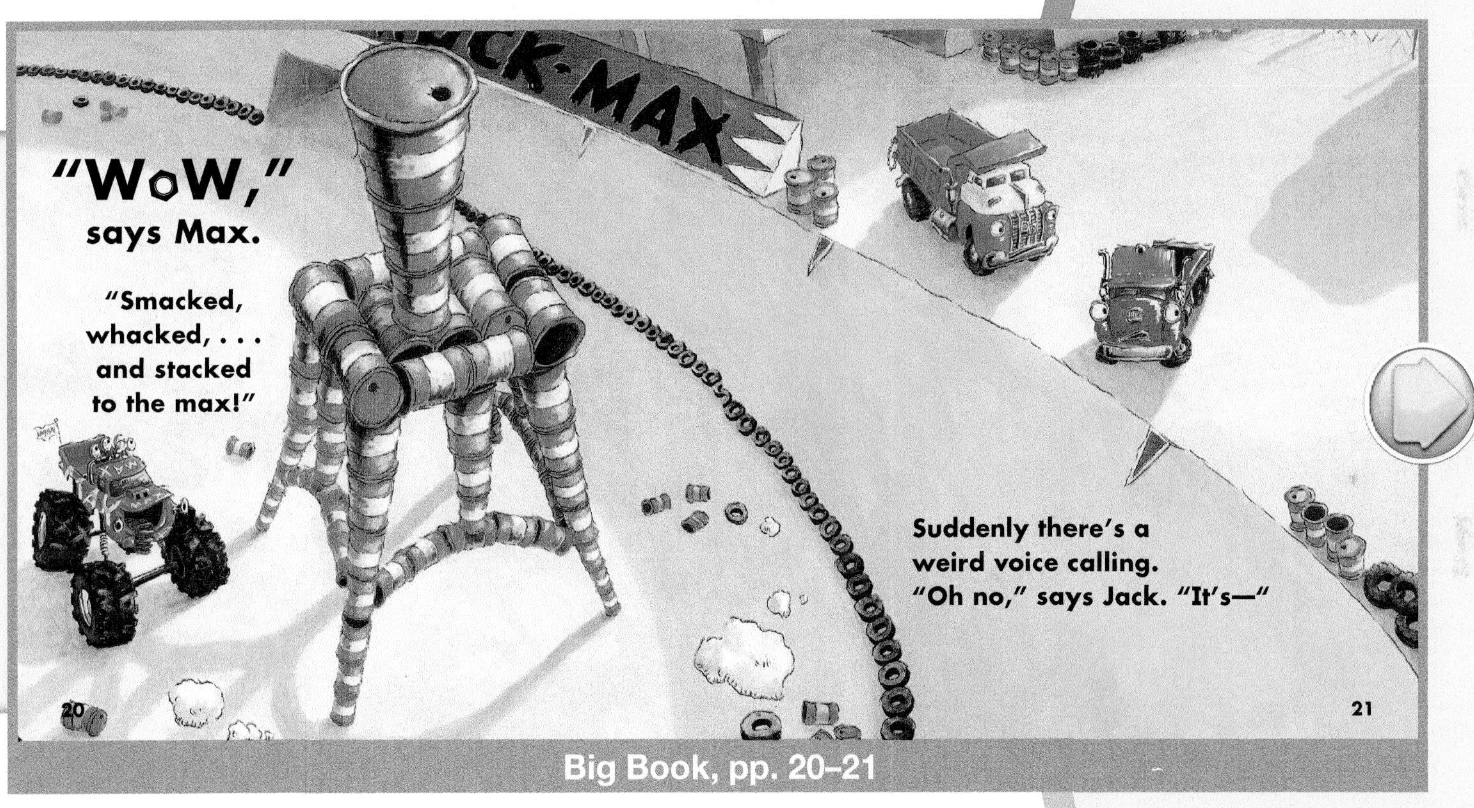

Big Book, pp. 20–21

INFERENCE Jack and Dan hear a weird voice. Do you think Jack likes the person who has the voice? (No, because he says, "Oh no.")

2ND READ

Develop Vocabulary

CHARACTER This is Izzy. What kind of truck is Izzy? (an ice cream truck)

- Izzy is an ice cream truck. Tell me about Izzy. Does Izzy look and act like a real ice cream truck?

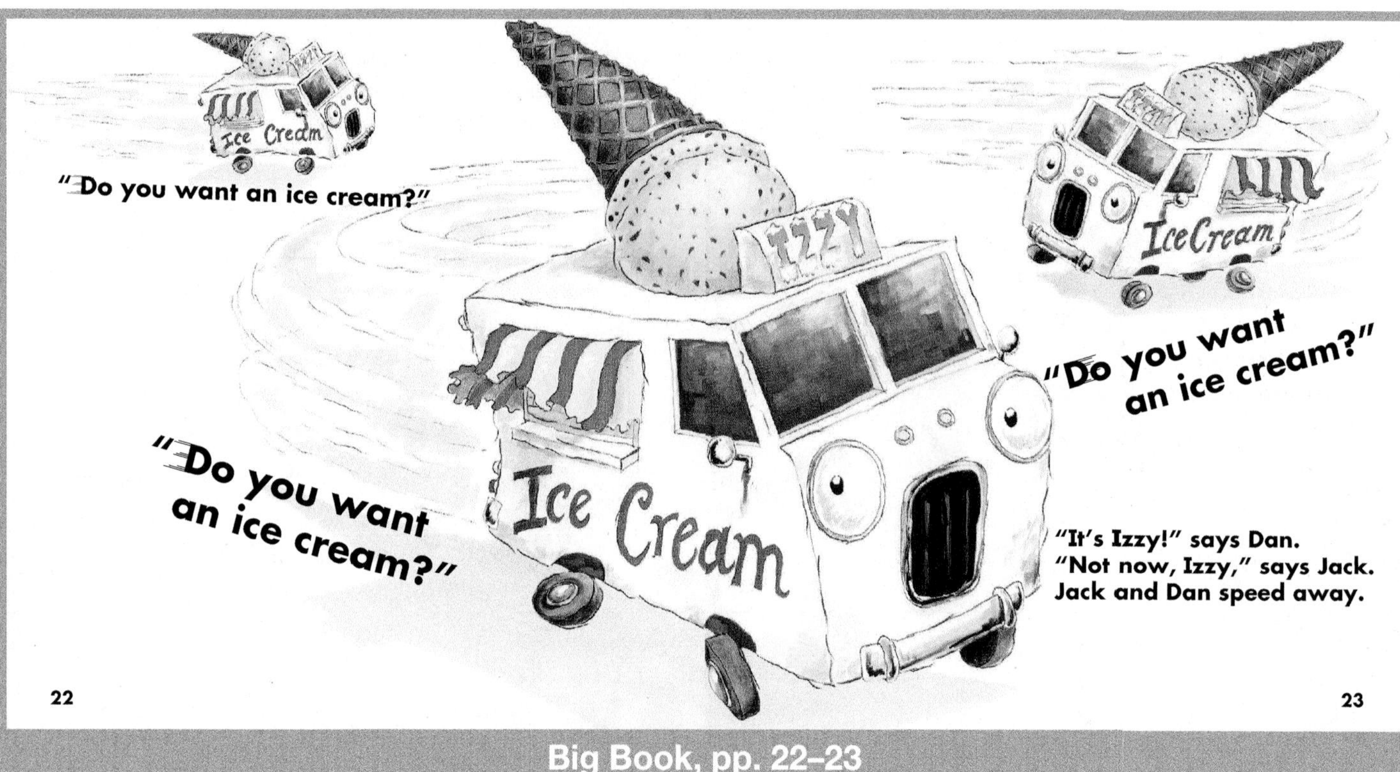

Ice Cream
"Do you want an ice cream?"
Izzy
Ice Cream
"Do you want an ice cream?"
Ice Cream
"Do you want an ice cream?"
"It's Izzy!" says Dan.
"Not now, Izzy," says Jack.
Jack and Dan speed away.
22
23

Big Book, pp. 22–23

3RD READ

Develop Comprehension ©

RECALL What do Jack and Dan do when Izzy comes by? (They tell him they don't want any ice cream, and they speed away.)

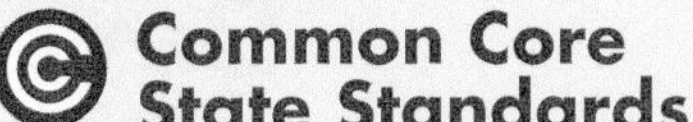

***WH-* QUESTION** Which trucks do Jack and Dan see next? (Gabriella Garbage Truck and Grader Kat)

- Gabriella Garbage Truck and Grader Kat are busy. What are they playing?

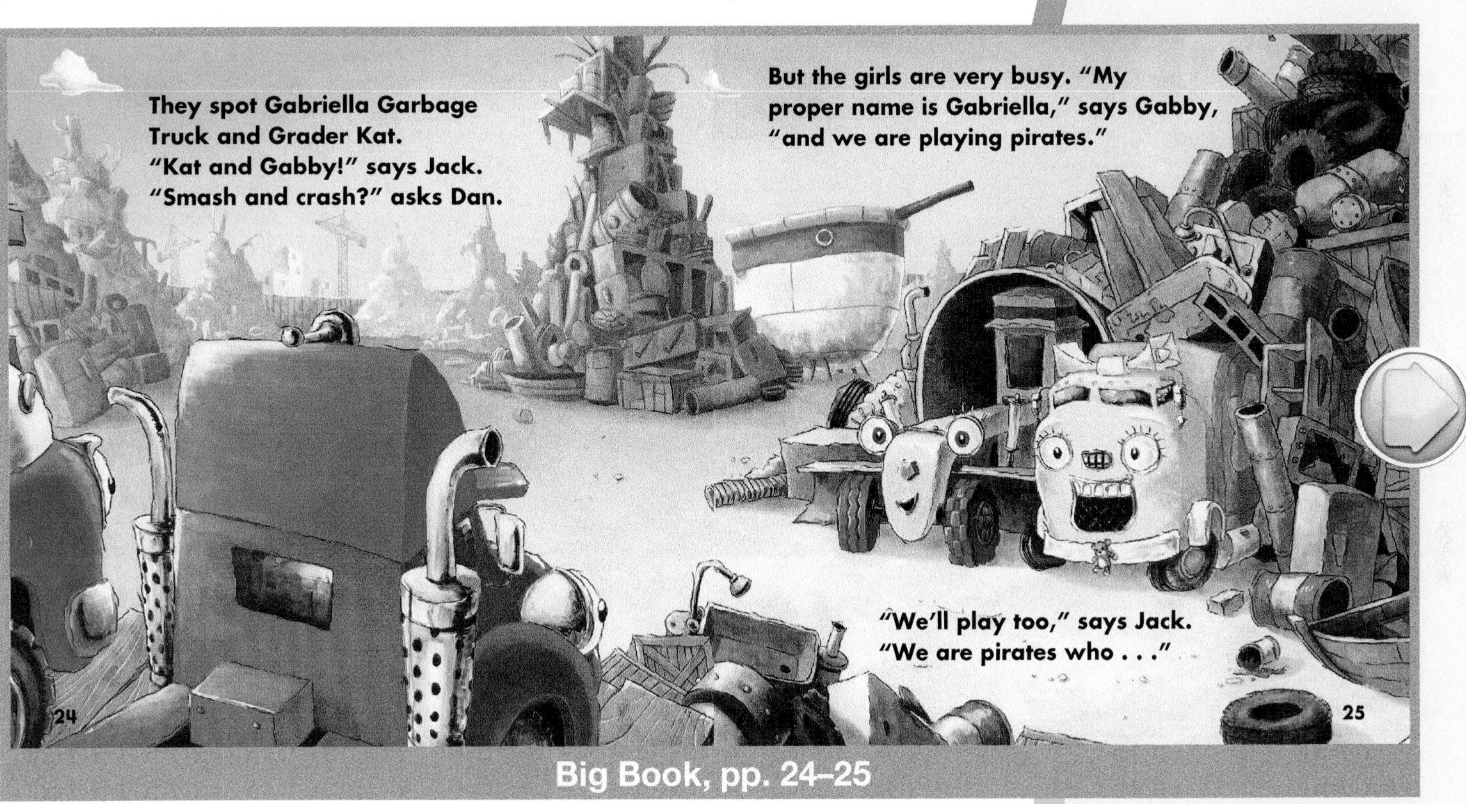

Big Book, pp. 24–25

***WH-* QUESTION** Why does Jack call Gabriella "Gabby"? (Gabby is Gabriella's nickname. It is a shorter version of her name, Gabriella.)

Common Core State Standards

Literature 1. With prompting and support, ask and answer questions about key details in a text.
Literature 3. With prompting and support, identify characters, settings, and major events in a story.
Literature 7. With prompting and support, describe the relationship between illustrations and the story in which they appear (e.g., what moment in a story an illustration depicts).

2ND READ

Develop Vocabulary

WH- QUESTION Where are Gabby and Kat playing? (on a pirate fort)

• Gabby and Kat play pirates on a pirate fort. Tell me about the fort.

DEVELOP VOCABULARY fort

SMASH!
CRASH!
SMASH!
CRASH!
"A perfect pirate fort," says Kat.
"Fabulous," says Gabby.
26
27

Big Book, pp. 26–27

3RD READ

Develop Comprehension ©

OPEN-ENDED How do you think Gabby and Kat play pirates? (I think they get on the ship and pretend they are sailing on the sea. Gabby wears an eye patch, and Kat wears a scarf on her head.)

WH- QUESTION What does the shadow say to Jack and Dan? ("Hey, you two. I want you. I want you to...")

- The shadow wants Jack and Dan to do something. What do you think it wants Jack and Dan to do?

Common Core State Standards

Literature 1. With prompting and support, ask and answer questions about key details in a text.
Literature 3. With prompting and support, identify characters, settings, and major events in a story.
Literature 7. With prompting and support, describe the relationship between illustrations and the story in which they appear (e.g., what moment in a story an illustration depicts).

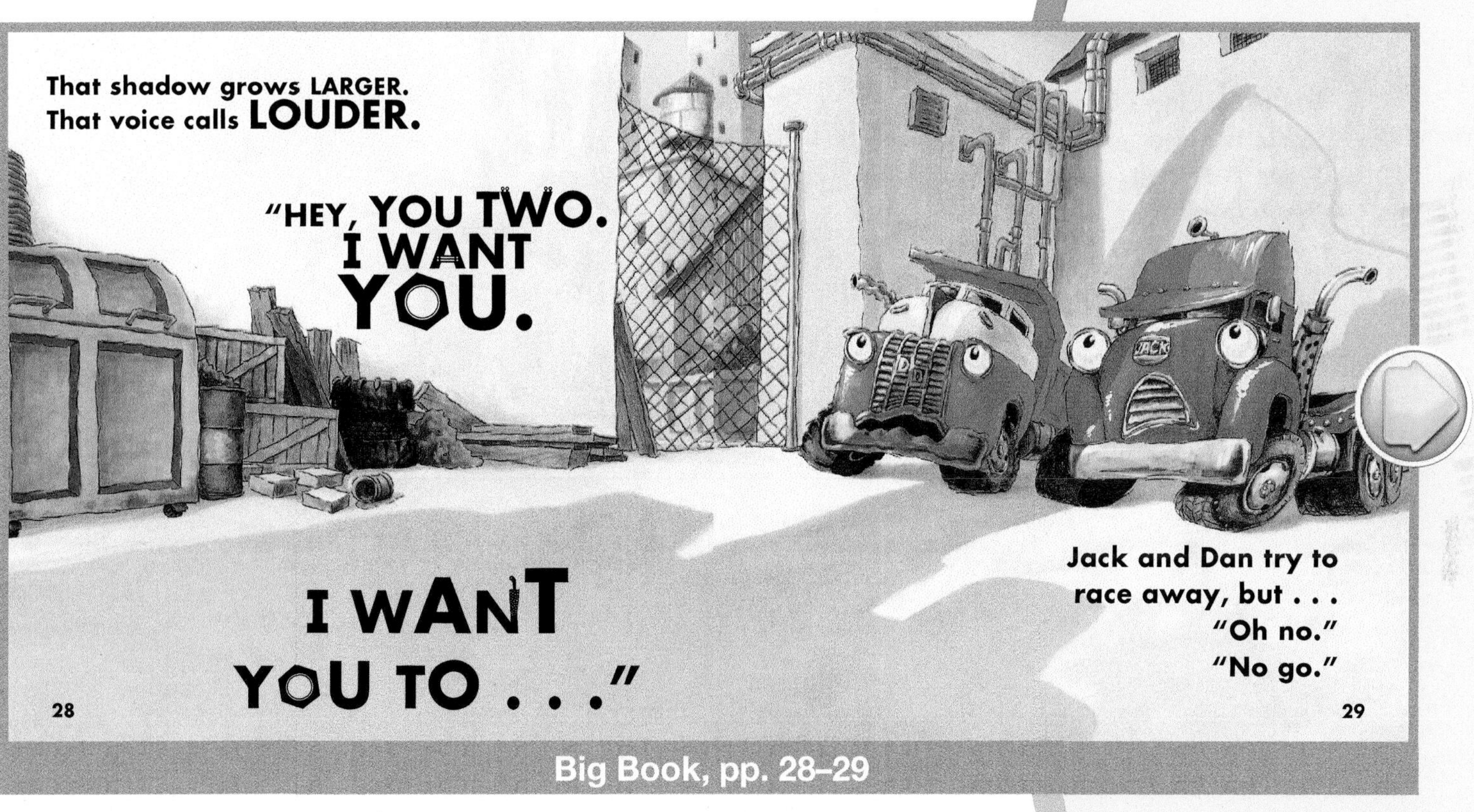
That shadow grows LARGER.
That voice calls LOUDER.
"HEY, YOU TWO.
I WANT
YOU.
I WANT
YOU TO . . ."
Jack and Dan try to
race away, but . . .
"Oh no."
"No go."
28
29
Big Book, pp. 28–29

INFERENCE How do you think Jack and Dan feel when the shadow comes back? (I think they are scared because they don't know who the shadow is or what the shadow wants. The shadow grows bigger and the voice calls louder.)

2ND READ

Develop Vocabulary

***WH*- QUESTION** Who is the shadow? (Wrecking Crane Rosie)

- Wrecking Crane Rosie is the shadow that has been following Jack and Dan. Where do you think Rosie is taking Jack and Dan?

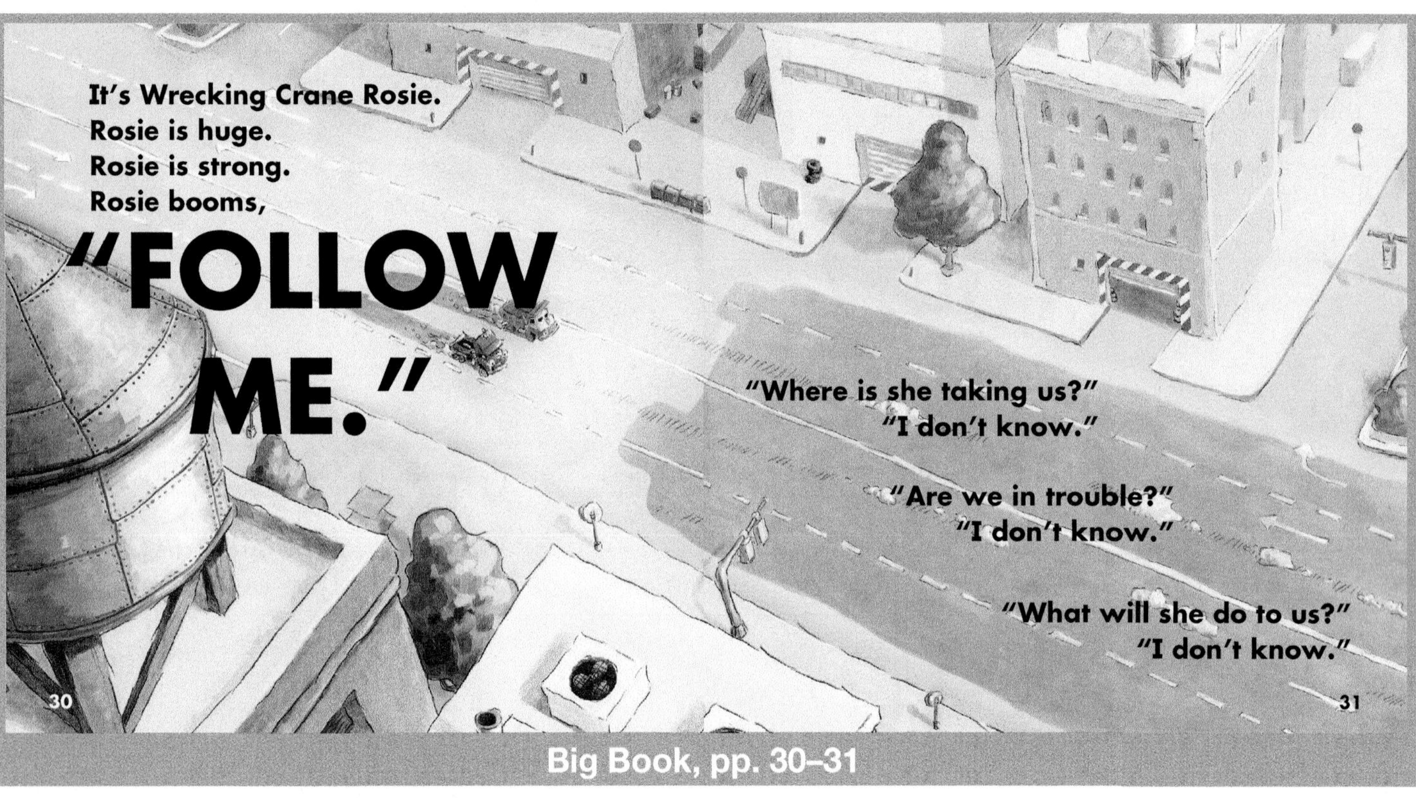

It's Wrecking Crane Rosie.
Rosie is huge.
Rosie is strong.
Rosie booms,
"FOLLOW
ME."
"Where is she taking us?"
"I don't know."
"Are we in trouble?"
"I don't know."
"What will she do to us?"
"I don't know."
30
31

Big Book, pp. 30–31

3RD READ

Develop Comprehension ©

INFERENCE Why do you think Jack and Dan think they are in trouble with Rosie? (They have been smashing and crashing all over Trucktown. Maybe Rosie is mad that they have been making a mess or that they did not ask her to smash and crash with them.)

WH- QUESTION What are Jack and Dan doing? (They are staring at Rosie. They are listening to Rosie.)

- Jack and Dan are staring at and listening to Rosie. Why do you think the words Rosie says are so big on the page?

"HEY, YOU TWO. I WANT YOU. I WANT YOU TO..."
32
33

Big Book, pp. 32–33

MONITOR AND FIX UP Why do Jack and Dan just stare at Rosie? This might be a difficult question for children. When you don't understand why characters do something, you can go back and reread to find out. Then you can think about how you would react in the same situation. When you reread, you learn that Rosie is huge and strong and that Jack and Dan think they may be in trouble for smashing and crashing. They are probably scared. How would you act if you were Jack or Dan?

Common Core State Standards

Literature 1. With prompting and support, ask and answer questions about key details in a text.
Literature 3. With prompting and support, identify characters, settings, and major events in a story.
Literature 7. With prompting and support, describe the relationship between illustrations and the story in which they appear (e.g., what moment in a story an illustration depicts).

2ND READ

Develop Vocabulary

WH- QUESTION Who is this big truck? (Wrecking Crane Rosie)

- Wrecking Crane Rosie is a big truck. What does she do with her red wrecking ball?

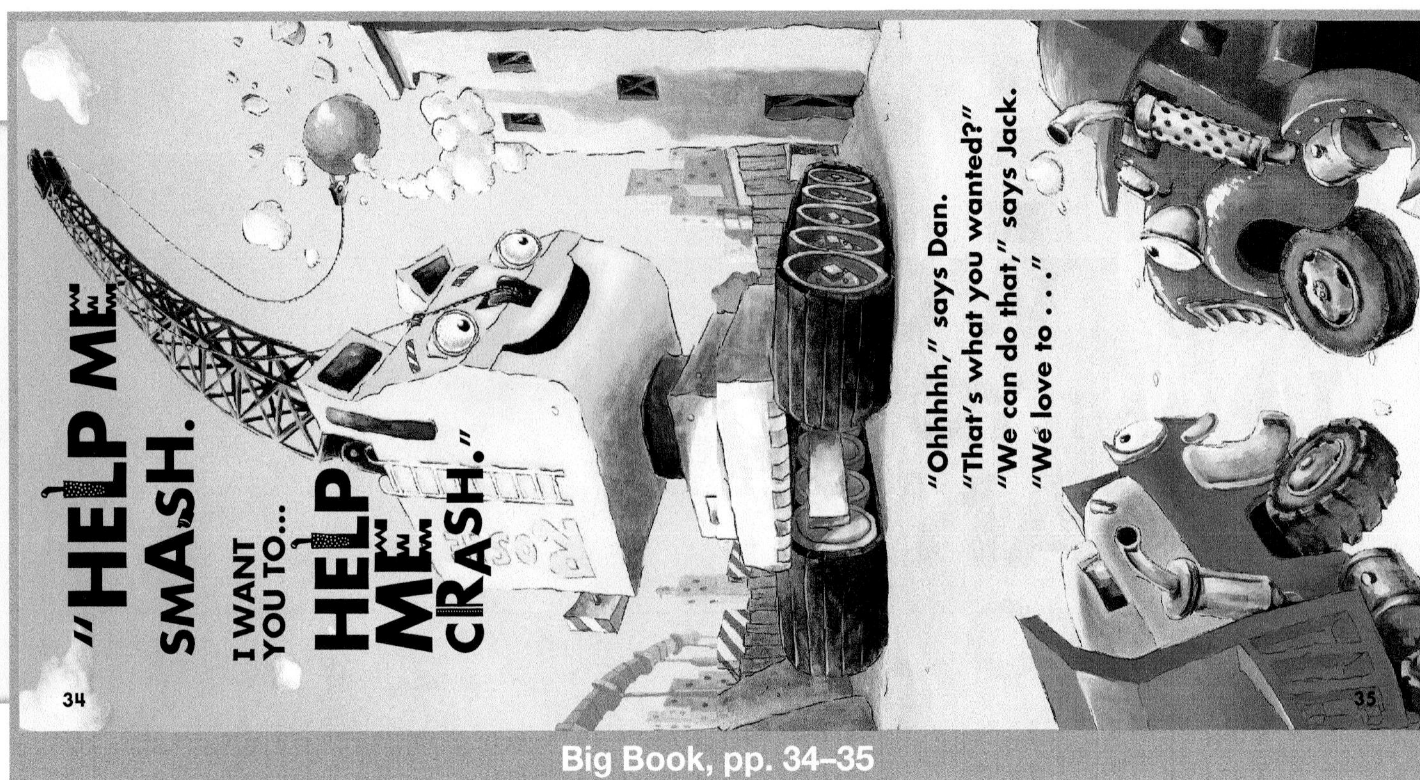

Big Book, pp. 34–35

3RD READ

Develop Comprehension ©

OPEN-ENDED How do you think Jack and Dan feel now that they know Rosie only wants them to help her smash and crash? (I think they are relieved because they are not in trouble. I think they are happy because they love to smash and crash.)

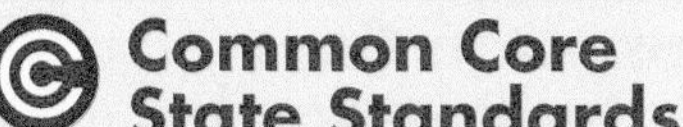

WH- QUESTION What are Jack, Dan, and Rosie smashing and crashing? (They are smashing and crashing a building.)

- Jack, Dan, and Rosie work together to smash and crash a building. What other things did Jack and Dan smash and crash in the book?

Continue with DAY 3
Conventions
p. 486

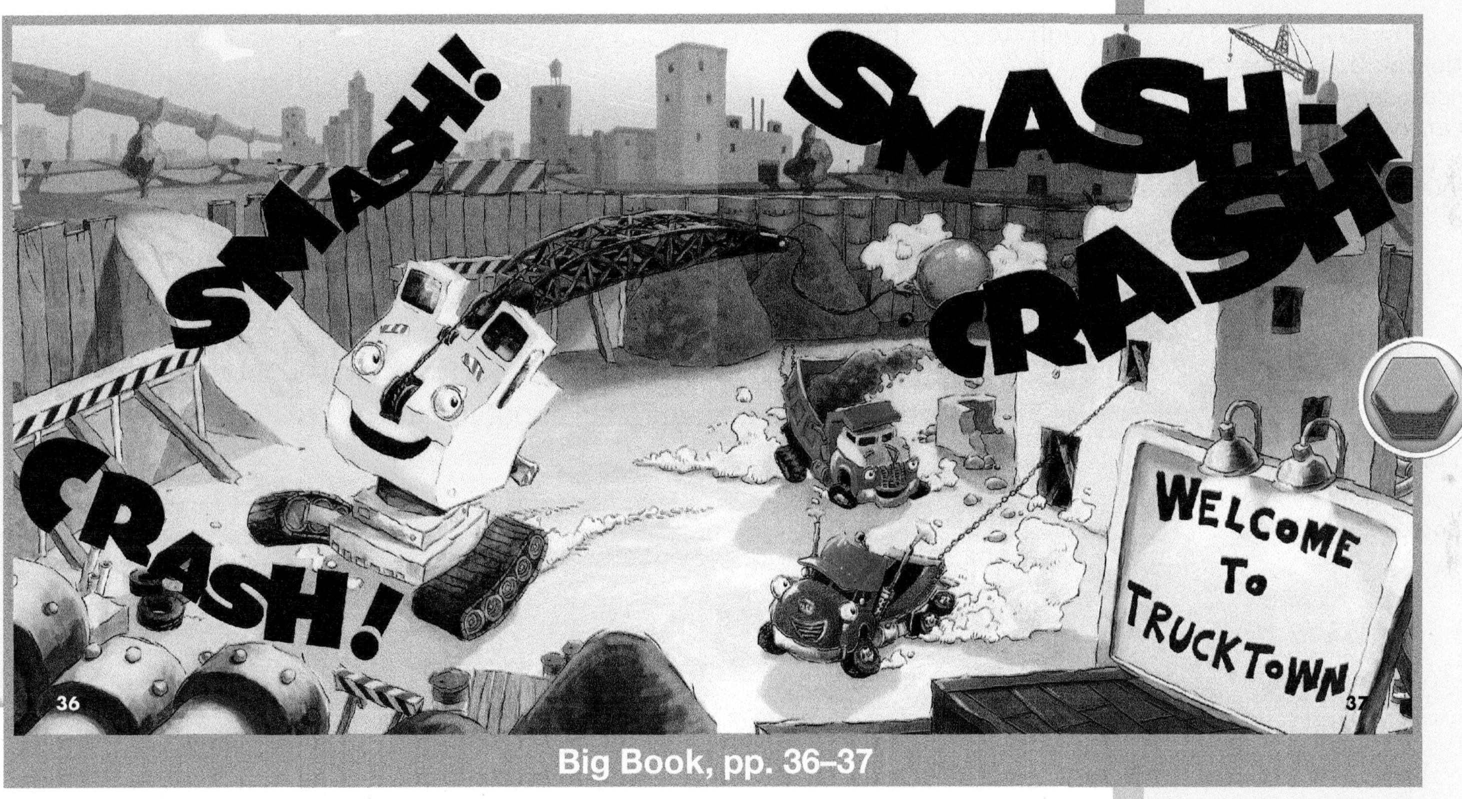
SMASH!
CRASH!
SMASH-CRASH!
WELCOME To TRUCKTOWN
36
37
Big Book, pp. 36–37

DISTANCING Jack and Dan help Rosie smash and crash. How do you help your friends? (I help my friends read and pick up their toys.)

Skip to DAY 4
Conventions
p. 500

Common Core State Standards

Literature 1. With prompting and support, ask and answer questions about key details in a text.
Literature 3. With prompting and support, identify characters, settings, and major events in a story.
Literature 7. With prompting and support, describe the relationship between illustrations and the story in which they appear (e.g., what moment in a story an illustration depicts).

Common Core State Standards

Writing 2. Use a combination of drawing, dictating, and writing to compose informative/explanatory texts in which they name what they are writing about and supply some information about the topic. **Language 1.a.** Print many upper- and lowercase letters. **Language 1.b.** Use frequently occurring nouns and verbs.

Access for All

 Advanced

Identify What We Can Do Say the following sentences: *Jenny jumps rope. Rob skips to school. Max runs in the yard.* Have children identify the word in each sentence that tells what we can do.

Daily Fix-It

matt jumps with mary.
Matt jumps with Mary.

This week's practice sentences appear on *Teacher Resources DVD-ROM.*

Conventions

Review What We Can Do

TEACH Write these verbs on the board in two columns:

run	sing
dance	skip
play	read

Remind children of what they learned about what we can do. We learned about words that tell what we can do. These words are called *verbs.* Read each word on the list. Have children say each word after you. These verbs are words that tell what we can do. Demonstrate each verb on the list.

GUIDE PRACTICE What can you do? Have children stand up and pantomime things they can do. Prompt them with questions such as these: Can you jump? Can you spin? Can you write? They can use verbs from the list or they can make up actions of their own.

Team Talk Pair children and have them take turns acting out things they can do. Then have them use a word to tell about the thing they can do.

ON THEIR OWN Use *Reader's and Writer's Notebook,* p. 57, for more practice with what we can do.

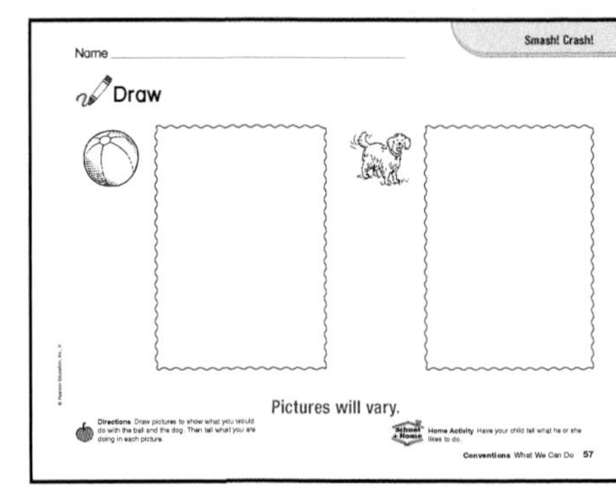

Reader's and Writer's Notebook, p. 57

Caption

TEACH Display simple pictures you have drawn of a bus, a car, a motorcycle, and a bicycle. Look at these pictures. What can we learn from a picture? (We can learn what something looks like.) Pictures show us the shapes, colors, or sizes of things. What can you tell about each one of these pictures? Encourage children to tell something about each picture you drew.

MODEL Display the *apple* Picture Card on the board. This is a picture of a fruit. The picture shows me it is hanging from a branch. The picture shows me it is red and round.

I am going to write a caption for this picture. A **caption** is a word next to a picture that tells about the picture. Write the word *apple* under the picture. Read the caption. This caption tells me that this is an apple. Draw a picture of an apple next to the Picture Card and write the caption *apple* under it. We can use captions for pictures we draw too.

GUIDE PRACTICE Have children provide captions for other pictures you draw. Write their captions under the pictures.

INDEPENDENT WRITING Have children turn to p. 58 of *Reader's and Writer's Notebook*. Have children write or dictate a caption for each picture. Then have them color the picture.

Reader's and Writer's Notebook, p. 58

Daily Handwriting

Write *Mom* and *am* on the board. Review correct letter formation of uppercase *M* and lowercase *m*.

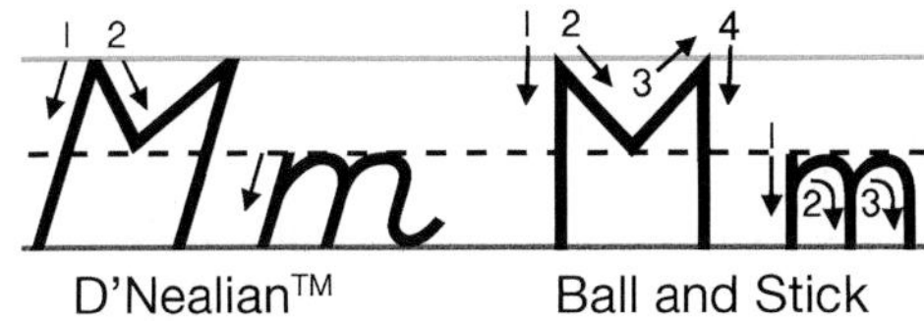

D'Nealian™ Ball and Stick

Have children write *Mom* and *am* on their Write-On Boards. Remind children to use proper left-to-right and top-to-bottom progression and proper spacing between letters when writing *M* and *m*.

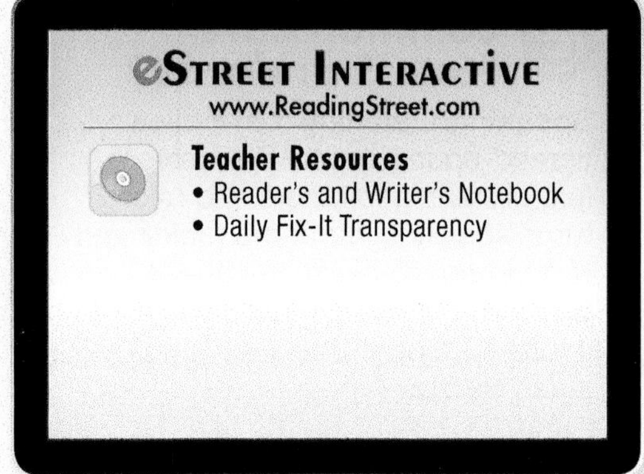

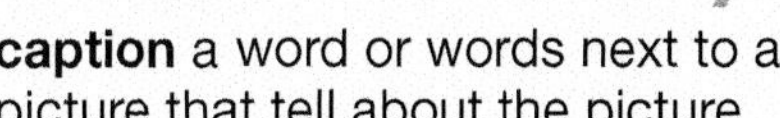

caption a word or words next to a picture that tell about the picture

Support Writing Before children write captions on their *Reader's and Writer's Notebook* page, discuss with them what the pictures show. Then have them choose a word from the discussion they think is the best word for their caption. Let children write the word in their home languages as well as in English.

Common Core State Standards

Speaking/Listening 1.a. Follow agreed-upon rules for discussions (e.g., listening to others and taking turns speaking about the topics and texts under discussion). **Speaking/Listening 6.** Speak audibly and express thoughts, feelings, and ideas clearly.

Academic Vocabulary

announcement a short statement that tells important information

Bridge to Common Core

PRESENTATION OF KNOWLEDGE/IDEAS

As children take turns making announcements, they are learning to speak audibly; to present information orally using an organization listeners can follow; and to adapt their speech to a specific task and purpose.

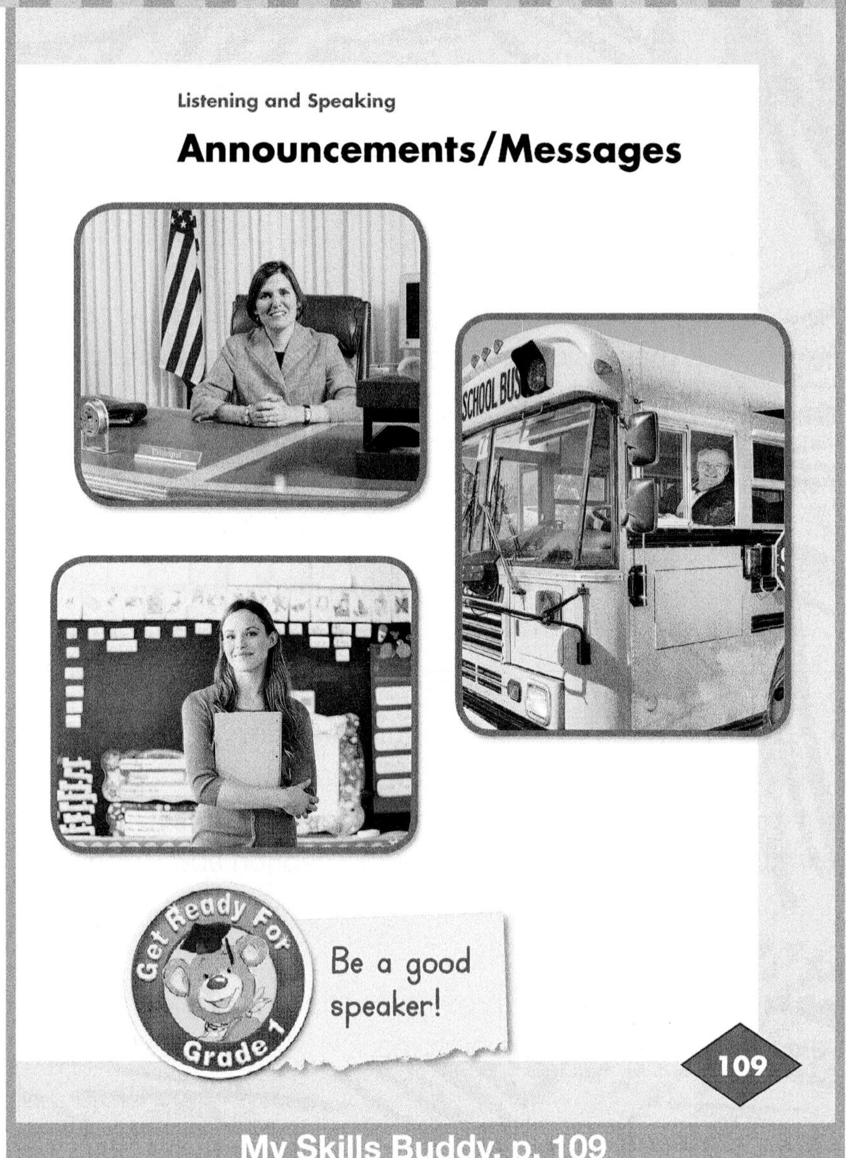

My Skills Buddy, p. 109

Listening and Speaking

Announcements/Messages

TEACH Remind children that we use announcements and messages when we want to tell others something important, so it is important to speak loudly and clearly and to take turns speaking so everyone can hear what he or she needs to know. Announcements and messages should be short and include only necessary information.

MODEL Have children turn to p. 109 of *My Skills Buddy.* Direct children to the picture of the principal. AlphaBuddy is going to make an announcement. Listen carefully:

- Attention, all teachers! We will have indoor recess today due to rain.

This is an announcement a principal could make to the school. It is short and includes important information for teachers.

GUIDE PRACTICE Have AlphaBuddy make other announcements that go with the pictures on the page.

- I will not be here tomorrow, so there will be a substitute teacher.
- Please keep your hands inside the bus at all times.

Use the Listening and Speaking bullets on p. 108 of *My Skills Buddy.* Have children think of other announcements that can be made by the person in each picture on the page.

INDEPENDENT PRACTICE In *Miss Bindergarten Takes a Field Trip,* the kindergarten class goes on a field trip around the town. Let's pretend Miss Bindergarten wants to make an announcement about the places the class will go and the things the class will do. What do you think she should say in her announcement? Remember, an announcement should be short and tell only what is necessary. Have children take turns making an announcement, pretending to be Miss Bindergarten. Refer them to their Rules for Listening and Speaking from pp. 1–2 of *Reader's and Writer's Notebook.* Remind children to take turns, to speak one at a time, and to speak loudly and clearly.

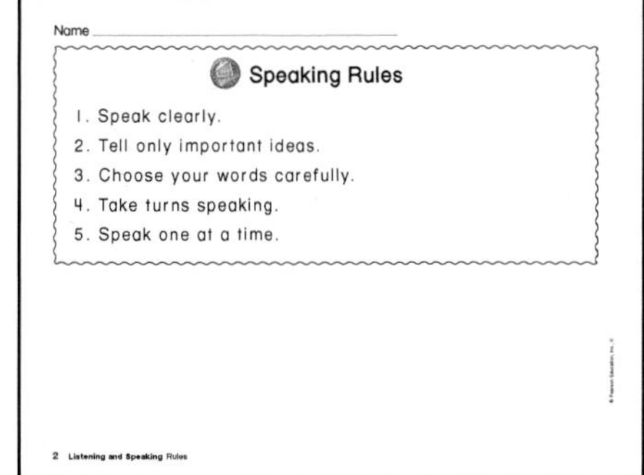
Name

Speaking Rules

1. Speak clearly.
2. Tell only important ideas.
3. Choose your words carefully.
4. Take turns speaking.
5. Speak one at a time.

2 Listening and Speaking Rules

Reader's and Writer's Notebook, pp. 1–2

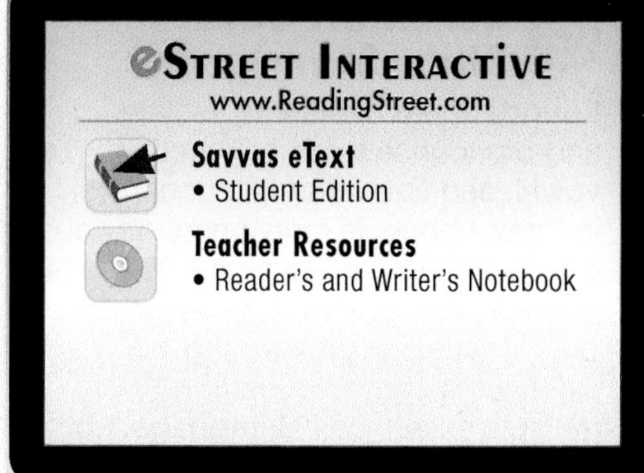

Be a Good Speaker!

1. Speak loudly and clearly.
2. Tell only important ideas.
3. Choose your words carefully.
4. Take turns speaking.
5. Speak one at a time.

Access for All

SI Strategic Intervention

Alternate Audience Children may feel more comfortable making their announcements to a small group or a partner.

Support Listening and Speaking Pair English learners with more proficient speakers so that they can learn from each other's strengths. Encourage partners to review *Miss Bindergarten Takes a Field Trip* to look for ideas they can use in their announcements.

Common Core State Standards

Foundational Skills 2.d. Isolate and pronounce the initial, medial vowel, and final sounds (phonemes) in three-phoneme (consonant-vowel-consonant, or CVC) words.* (This does not include CVCs ending with /l/, /r/, or /x/.) **Speaking/Listening 1.b.** Continue a conversation through multiple exchanges. **Language 1.b.** Use frequently occurring nouns and verbs.

Wrap Up Your Day!

- ✔ **Content Knowledge** Today we reread the story of Jack and Dan. What do these friends like to do together?
- ✔ **Respond to Literature** Today we read about Cat and Dog. They like to eat muffins and meatballs. Why do you think they like to eat muffins and meatballs? What else might they like to eat?
- ✔ **Conventions** Ask a child to act out something he or she can do. Have classmates guess what the child is doing.
- ✔ **Homework Idea** Have children draw pictures of foods whose names begin with /m/.

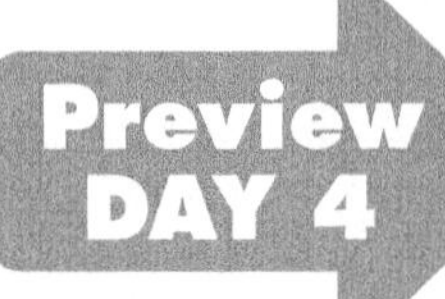

Tomorrow we will read a story about two of our other Trucktown friends, Melvin and Max.

Social Studies
Community Trucks

MATERIALS: Big Book *Smash! Crash!*, paper, crayons or markers

DISCUSS TRUCKS Have children think about the different trucks they read about in *Smash! Crash!* or in other books. List the trucks on the board.

dump truck	**garbage truck**	**cement mixer**
ice cream truck	**grader**	**monster truck**
tow truck	**big rig**	**wrecking crane**

Have children think of other trucks in their community, such as a tractor, a fire truck, or an ambulance. Encourage children to talk about what each truck does.

Discuss with children how each truck helps the community. For example, a tow truck brings cars that don't work to get fixed or a fire truck races to help put out a fire.

- Have you ever seen these trucks in your community?
- Who drives these trucks? How do these trucks help in your community?

DRAW PICTURES Have children choose a truck and draw a picture of it helping in the community. Remind them to add a driver to the picture.

Phonics
/m/ in the Center

MATERIALS: Picture Cards: *map, man, mitten, moon, mop, mug, hat, fox, dog, bed, cat*

/m/ PICTURES Have children sit in a circle. Mix the Picture Cards and give them to one child. Have that child show a card and name the picture. If the picture name begins with /m/, the child places the card in the center of the circle and gives the cards to the next person. If the picture name does not begin with /m/, the child places the card outside the circle and passes the cards. Continue until all /m/ cards are in the center.

Conventions
What Am I Doing?

MATERIALS: small objects that children can use to perform an action, such as a pencil, a jump rope, a comb, a book, a cell phone, a spoon

PLAY CHARADES Place the objects in a paper bag. Have a child come to the front of the class, take an object from the bag, and then act out a verb that goes with the object. The other children try to guess what the verb is. The child who correctly guesses the action is next to pick an object and act out a verb.

DAY 4 at a Glance

Content Knowledge
Oral Vocabulary

Phonemic Awareness
Review Initial Sound Discrimination

Letter Recognition
Review Letter Names
Blending

Text-Based Comprehension
Character
Review Sequence

Conventions
Nouns for People and Animals

Writing
Extend the Concept

Vocabulary
Position Words

Materials

- Student Edition
- Truckery Rhymes
- Talk with Me/Sing with Me Chart
- Picture Cards
- Alphabet Cards
- Get Set, Roll! Reader 5
- Reader's and Writer's Notebook
- Big Book

Common Core State Standards

Speaking/Listening 1. Participate in collaborative conversations with diverse partners about *kindergarten topics and texts* with peers and adults in small and larger groups. **Language 6.** Use words and phrases acquired through conversations, reading and being read to, and responding to texts. **Also Language 5.c.**

TRUCKTOWN
on Reading Street

Start your engines!

- Display "Peter, Peter, Payload Eater" and lead the group in saying the rhyme a few times.
- Have the group clap the rhythm as they recite the rhyme.
- When children have mastered the rhythm, have them march around the room as they say the rhyme.

Truckery Rhymes
Truckery Rhymes

Content Knowledge

Zoom in on

What Friends Do Together

EXPAND THE CONCEPT On the board, write the Question of the Week, *What do you like to do with your friends?* Read the question as you track the print. Tell children to respond in complete sentences. Display Sing with Me Chart 5B.

Won't You Play With Me?
It's a fabulous day out, can't you see?
My, oh my, won't you play with me?
A perfect day for whatever will be,
A fabulous day out, can't you see?
We can stay out on the high seas.
We'll be pirates,
Or sailors,
Or whatever we want to be.
Change your day from a dud to a great jamboree.
A perfect day for whatever will be!
Sing to the tune of "Zip a Dee Doo Dah"
Sing with Me Chart 5B
Talk with Me/Sing with Me Chart 5B

Build Oral Language

LISTEN FOR AMAZING WORDS We are going to sing this song again. Listen for the Amazing Words *perfect* and *fabulous.* Sing the song several times with children to the tune of "Zip a Dee Doo Dah." Have them stand up when they hear the word *perfect* or *fabulous.*

Build Oral Vocabulary

Amazing Words Robust Vocabulary Routine

1. **Introduce the Word** Something that has no mistakes is *perfect.* What's our new Amazing Word to describe something as being the best it can be? Say it with me: *perfect.*
2. **Demonstrate** Provide examples to show meaning. *It is a perfect day for flying a kite.* What kind of day is *perfect* for flying a kite?

   Repeat steps 1 and 2.

   Introduce the Word When something is wonderful or really good, we can say it is *fabulous.* What's our new Amazing Word to describe something as wonderful? Say it with me: *fabulous.*

   Demonstrate *That play we saw was fabulous!*
3. **Apply** Have children use *perfect* and *fabulous* to describe something they have seen or done.
4. **Display the Words** Ask children what letters *perfect* and *fabulous* begin with. Have them point to and name each beginning letter.

Routines Flip Chart

USE AMAZING WORDS To reinforce the concept and the Amazing Words, have children supply the appropriate Amazing Word for each sentence.

Mike made no mistakes and got a _______ score. (perfect)
Jess did a _______ dance in the talent show. (fabulous)

Amazing Words

signals	dud
proper	pirates
perfect	fabulous

Access for All

 Advanced

Expand Vocabulary Have children discuss other words for *fabulous.* Can something be really good and *fabulous?* Tell children that the word *fabulous* is a vivid word that can make their writing and language more interesting.

Cognates Spanish speakers may recognize that *perfecto* is a cognate for *perfect,* one of today's Amazing Words.

Produce Oral Language Use the Day 4 instruction on ELL Poster 5 to extend and enrich language.

Common Core State Standards

Foundational Skills 1.d. Recognize and name all upper- and lowercase letters of the alphabet. **Foundational Skills 2.d.** Isolate and pronounce the initial, medial vowel, and final sounds (phonemes) in three-phoneme (consonant-vowel-consonant, or CVC) words.* (This does not include CVCs ending with /l/, /r/, or /x/.)

Phonemic Awareness

Review Initial Sound Discrimination

PRACTICE I will say three words. Two of the words begin with the same sound, and one word begins with a different sound. I want you to tell me which word begins with a different sound. Listen to the beginning sounds in these words: *bug, dog, bed.* Which word begins with a different sound? (*dog*) Continue with these sets of words: *fat, fig, jet; top, sit, tan; met, pin, pot.*

Picture Card

Display the *hat* Picture Card. What is this? (*hat*) Listen to the sound at the beginning of *hat.* Display the *rug* Picture Card. What is this? (*rug*) Listen to the sound at the beginning of *rug.* Does *rug* begin with the same sound as *hat?* (no) Continue with these pairs of Picture Cards: *wig, web; net, gum; cap, can.*

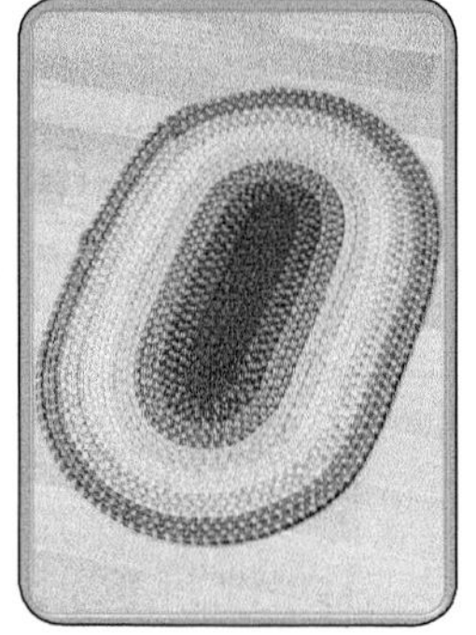

Picture Card

Corrective feedback

If... children cannot discriminate initial sounds in words,
then... separate each word into its onset and rime and repeat the word, emphasizing the onset. Listen to this word: /h/ *-at.* The beginning sound is /h/. Listen to this word: /h/ *-ot.* Does /h/ *-ot* begin the same as /h/ *-at?* Repeat the routine with *pin* and *pat.*

Letter Recognition

Review Letter Names

PRACTICE Display the *Aa* Alphabet Card. Point to the uppercase *A.* What is the name of this letter? Point to the lowercase *a.* What is the name of this letter? Continue with the *Dd, Gg, Ii, Ll,* and *Pp* Alphabet Cards.

Display the *Bb, Ee, Hh, Kk,* and *Oo* Alphabet Cards in a row on the chalk ledge. Ask a child to point to the uppercase *K,* ask another child to point to the lowercase *e,* and so on. When children have identified all the letters, replace the cards with the *Cc, Ff, Jj, Qq,* and *Ss* Alphabet Cards and then the *Nn, Rr,* and *Tt* Alphabet Cards.

Alphabet Card

Access for All

Strategic Intervention

Letter Review Before doing the Letter Recognition activity, place the Alphabet Cards in order on the chalk ledge and name the letters with children.

Don't Wait Until Friday **MONITOR PROGRESS** **Check Letter Recognition**

FORMATIVE ASSESSMENT Gather the following Alphabet Cards: *Mm, Uu, Vv, Ww, Xx, Yy, Zz.* Display one Alphabet Card at a time. Ask children to name the letters on the card.

If... children cannot name the letters,

then... name the letters on each Alphabet Card and have children repeat after you.

Continue to monitor children's progress during the week so that children can be successful with the Day 5 Assessment.

Common Core State Standards

Literature 10. Actively engage in group reading activities with purpose and understanding. **Foundational Skills 2.d.** Isolate and pronounce the initial, medial vowel, and final sounds (phonemes) in three-phoneme (consonant-vowel-consonant, or CVC) words.* (This does not include CVCs ending with /l/, /r/, or /x/.) **Foundational Skills 3.a.** Demonstrate basic knowledge of one-to-one letter-sound correspondences by producing the primary or many of the most frequent sounds for each consonant.

Blending

/m/ Spelled *Mm*

Routine Blend Words

1. **Review Sound-Spellings** Display the *Mm* Alphabet Card. This is a motorcycle. *Motorcycle* begins with /m/. What is the letter for /m/? (*m*)

2. **Model** Write the word *mop* on the board. Point to *m.* What is the sound for this letter? Say it with me: /m/ /m/ /m/.
   - The beginning sound in *mop* is /m/. *Mop* ends with *-op.* When I blend the beginning sound /m/ and the ending *-op,* I make the word *mop: /m/ -op, mop.*
   - Say the sounds with me: /m/ *-op.* Now let's blend the sounds together. Listen as I do it: /m/ *-op, mop.* Say it with me: /m/ *-op, mop.* Now you say it without me.
   - Listen as I use the word *mop* in a sentence: *The mop is in the bucket.* Say the sentence with me. Ask children to use *mop* in a sentence.

   Write the word *jam* on the board. Point to *m.* What is the sound for this letter? Say it with me: /m/ /m/ /m/.
   - The ending sound in *jam* is /m/. *Jam* begins with *ja-.* When I blend the beginning *ja-* and the ending sound /m/, I make the word *jam: ja-* /m/, *jam.*
   - Say the sounds with me: *ja-* /m/. Now let's blend the sounds together. Listen as I do it: *ja-* /m/, *jam.* Say it with me: *ja-* /m/, *jam.* Now you say it without me.
   - Listen as I use the word *jam* in a sentence: *I like jam on toast.* Say the sentence with me. Ask children to use *jam* in a sentence.

3. **Guide Practice** Continue the routine with the words below. We are going to blend some more words. Remember, first we look for /m/ in the word. Next, we name the beginning or ending. Then we blend the two together to make the word. Use these words: *mad, mug, met, yam, rim, sum.*

4. **On Your Own** Write the following sentence on the board: *Meg met Pam.* Read it aloud. Ask children to draw a picture to illustrate the sentence. Then have them copy the sentence as a caption for their picture.

Routines Flip Chart

Get Set, Roll! Reader 5

Read *Zoom!*

REVIEW Review the high-frequency words *I, am, to,* and *a.* Have children find each word on the Word Wall.

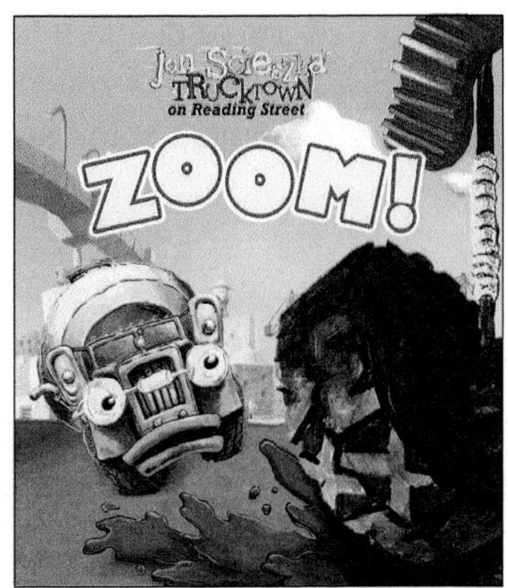

Get Set, Roll! Reader 5

TEACH REBUS WORDS Write the word *Melvin* on the board. This is the name *Melvin.* Name the letters with me: *M, e, l, v, i, n, Melvin.* Repeat the routine with *pour, Max, zoom, mall,* and *splash.* Look for these words in the story today. A picture above the word will help you read it.

READ Today we will read a story about our friends Melvin and Max. Point to the title of the book. What is the title of the book? (*Zoom!*) We will read some words with /m/ in this book.

Use the routine for reading decodable books in the Routines Flip Chart to read Get Set, Roll! Reader 5.

Day 4 SMALL GROUP TIME • Differentiate Language, p. SG•73

OL On-Level	SI Strategic Intervention	A Advanced
• **Build** Sentences and Words • **Read** Get Set, Roll! Reader *Zoom!*	• **Talk About** Sentences and Words • **Read** Get Set, Roll! Reader *Zoom!*	• **Extend** Sentences and Words • **Read** Get Set, Roll! Reader *Zoom!*

eSTREET INTERACTIVE
www.ReadingStreet.com

Savvas eText
• Get Set, Roll! Reader

Access for All

SI Strategic Intervention

Support Concepts of Print Remind children to hold their book right side up and to turn the page once they finish reading the words on the page. Encourage them to use their finger to follow the words left to right.

ELL

Access Content Do a picture walk with children to preview the reader before starting the routine.

ELL

Place English Language Learners in the groups that correspond to their reading abilities in English.

If... children need more practice **Developing Language,**
then... use the Language Workshops in the *ELL Handbook* beginning on p. 306.

 Common Core State Standards

Literature 1. With prompting and support, ask and answer questions about key details in a text. **Literature 3.** With prompting and support, identify characters, settings, and major events in a story.

Access for All

 Advanced

Practice Sequence Have children discuss whether *Smash! Crash!* will still make sense if the order of the events is changed. What if Jack and Dan help Rosie smash and crash at the beginning of the story? How will that change the story?

Academic Vocabulary

sequence the order of events in a selection or story

Text-Based Comprehension

Character

PRACTICE Have children turn to the Literary Elements pictures on pp. 94–95 of *My Skills Buddy.* As you look at the pictures, remind children that the people and animals in the story are called characters.

My Skills Buddy, pp. 94–95

Team Talk Pair children and have them take turns telling a short story. Then have them identify the characters in their stories.

Review Sequence

PRACTICE Direct children to the Sequence pictures on pp. 54–55 of *My Skills Buddy.*

In most stories, something happens first, something happens next, and something happens last. The order in which things happen in a story is called **sequence.** Good readers pay attention to the sequence to follow the events in the story.

- What happens first? (The mama bird sits on eggs in a nest.)
- What happens next? (The mama bird feeds the baby birds.)
- What happens last? (The baby birds grow up and fly away.)

MORE PRACTICE For more practice with sequence, use *Reader's and Writer's Notebook,* p. 59.

Reader's and Writer's Notebook, p. 59

Read Main Selection

GUIDE COMPREHENSION Display *Smash! Crash!* In this story, something happens first, something happens next, and something happens last.

- What happens first in *Smash! Crash!*? (Jack and Dan smash and crash around Trucktown.)
- Which trucks do Jack and Dan ask to smash and crash with them? (Cement Mixer Melvin, Monster Truck Max, Gabriella Garbage Truck, and Grader Kat)
- What happens at the end of the story? (Jack and Dan help Wrecking Crane Rosie smash and crash.)

READ Reread *Smash! Crash!* Return to p. 469. Follow the **3rd Read** and use the **Develop Comprehension** notes to give children the opportunity to gain a more complete understanding of the story.

Routine Read for Understanding

Deepen understanding by reading the selection multiple times.

1. **First Read**—Read the entire selection aloud to build interest in the text.
2. **Second Read**—Use the **Develop Vocabulary** notes on pages 469–485.
3. **Third Read**—Use the **Develop Comprehension** notes on pages 469–485.

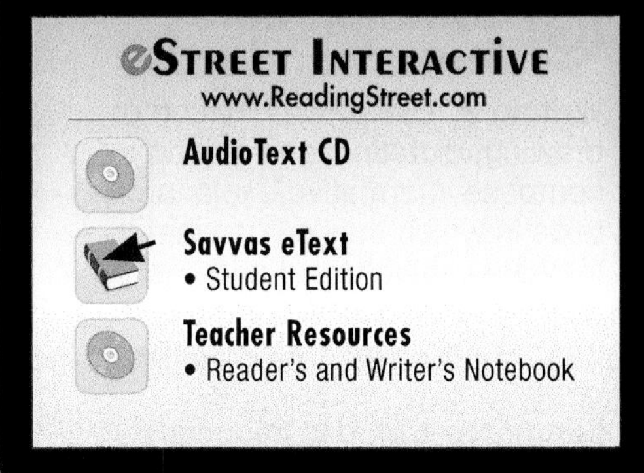

Bridge to Common Core

RANGE OF READING AND LEVEL OF TEXT COMPLEXITY
Using the Develop Comprehension notes as you read the text a third time will help you assess how well children are comprehending the authentic literary text in *Reading Street.* As the year progresses, children will improve as independent, proficient readers of complex text.

Common Core State Standards

Writing 2. Use a combination of drawing, dictating, and writing to compose informative/explanatory texts in which they name what they are writing about and supply some information about the topic. **Language 1.a.** Print many upper- and lowercase letters. **Language 1.b.** Use frequently occurring nouns and verbs. **Also Writing 5., 8., Speaking/Listening 4.**

Access for All

Strategic Intervention

Support Conventions Pair children and have them take turns describing a person or an animal. When they think they know what animal or person their partner is describing, have them name the noun and use it in a complete sentence.

Daily Fix-It

i went to A store.

I went to a store.

This week's practice sentences appear on *Teacher Resources DVD-ROM.*

Conventions

Nouns for People and Animals

TEACH Remind children of what they learned about nouns. A noun is a word that names a person, animal, place, or thing.

Point to yourself. I am a teacher. I am a woman (man). I am a mother (father). I have a dog. I have a fish. *Teacher, woman,* and *mother* are words that name me, a person. They are nouns. *Dog* and *fish* are words that name animals. They are nouns.

GUIDE PRACTICE Write these sentences on the board:

The woman drives the truck.
Catch that fast dog!
The librarian helps me find books.
A bird lives in a nest.

I am going to read these sentences. When I read them, I will point to each word as I say it. When you hear a noun for a person or an animal, I want you to raise your hand. Raise your hand to demonstrate. Then I want you to tell me the noun. Have children identify the nouns *woman, dog, librarian,* and *bird.* Underline the noun for a person or an animal in each sentence as you say it.

ON THEIR OWN Use *Reader's and Writer's Notebook,* p. 60, for more practice reading, writing, and saying nouns for people and animals.

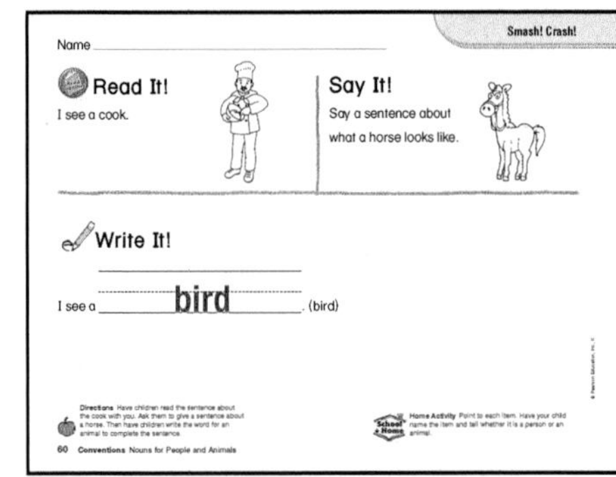

Name

Smash! Crash!

Read It!

I see a cook.

Say It!

Say a sentence about what a horse looks like.

Write It!

I see a bird (bird)

Reader's and Writer's Notebook, p. 60

Extend the Concept

DISCUSS We just read a story about two best friends. Jack's and Dan's favorite thing to do together is smash and crash. They may make a mess, but they have fun. Like Jack and Dan, we have fun when we play with our friends.

Ask children to think about what they do when they play to make sure everyone is having fun. Talk with children about the games and activities they play with their friends.

GUIDE PRACTICE Use children's contributions to the discussion to write sentences.

When we play...	we share our toys.
	we are nice.
	we pretend to be animals.

INDEPENDENT WRITING Have children write or dictate their own sentence about how they play with their friends, or they may copy a sentence from the board. Show children the picture dictionary on pp. 132–143 of *My Skills Buddy.* This is a picture dictionary. It has pictures to show you what words mean. You can use this to help you spell words when you write. You can also use it to help you find out what a word means. Encourage children to use the picture dictionary when they write about how they play with their friends. Invite children to read their sentences to the class.

Daily Handwriting

Write uppercase *M* and lowercase *m* on the board. Review correct letter formation with children.

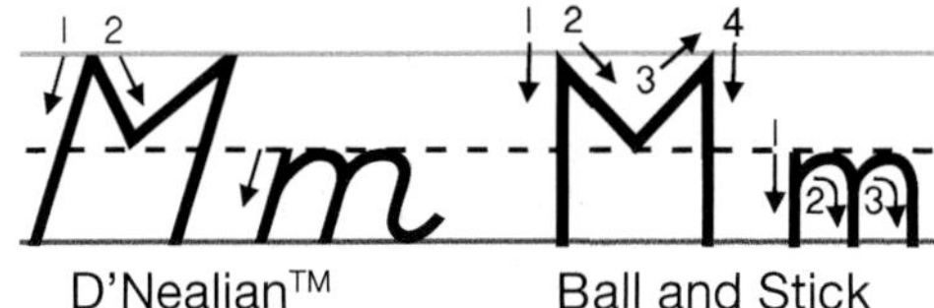

D'Nealian™ Ball and Stick

Have children write a row of uppercase *M* and a row of lowercase *m* on their Write-On Boards. Remind them to use proper left-to-right and top-to-bottom progression when writing *M* and *m.*

Bridge to Common Core

PRODUCTION AND DISTRIBUTION OF WRITING
With your guidance and support, children interact and collaborate with others to write sentences about real experiences and events.

Professional Development: Support Writing Skills English learners who already have some writing skills in their home languages may develop these skills by occasionally writing in both languages. Labels for pictures written in a home language and in English can help children with writing and learning English.

Common Core State Standards

Literature 2. With prompting and support, retell familiar stories, including key details. **Foundational Skills 2.** Demonstrate understanding of spoken words, syllables, and sounds (phonemes). **Speaking/ Listening 1.** Participate in collaborative conversations with diverse partners about *kindergarten topics and texts* with peers and adults in small and larger groups. **Language 5.c.** Identify real-life connections between words and their use (e.g., note places at school that are *colorful*).

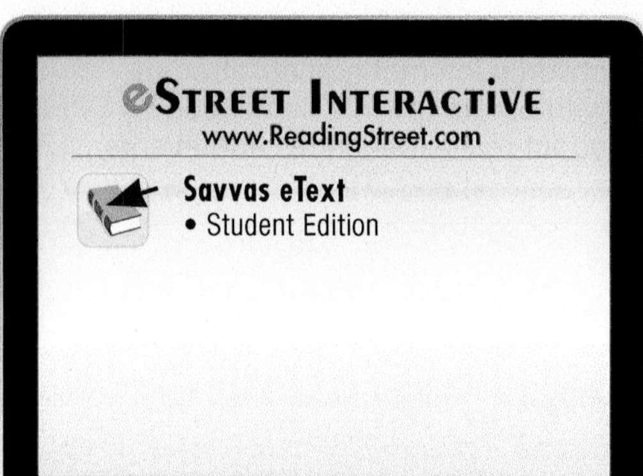

Vocabulary

Position Words

TEACH Write the words *up, down, in,* and *out.* Point to each word as you read it. These words tell about the position of something, or where it is. Have children turn to p. 108 of *My Skills Buddy.* Use the last two Vocabulary bullets in the discussion. Direct children to the pictures of the girl pointing up and down. Which girl is pointing up? Which girl is pointing down? Have children point to the picture of the dog in the doghouse and then to the picture of the dog out of the doghouse.

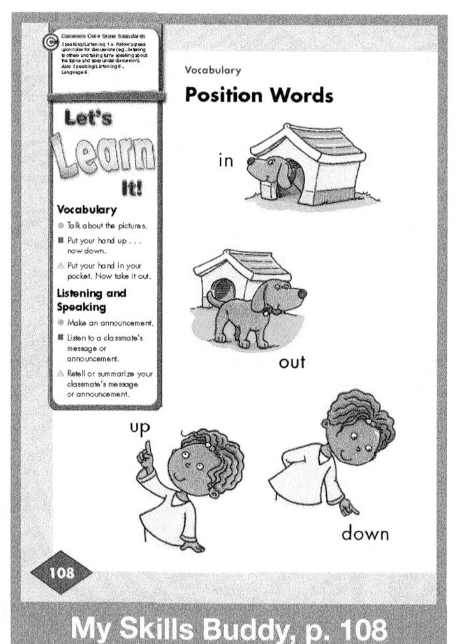

My Skills Buddy, p. 108

Team Talk Pair children and have them take turns using the position words *up, down, in,* and *out* in complete sentences.

Wrap Up Your Day!

- ✔ **Oral Language** Sing "Won't You Play with Me?" with me. Clap your hands when you hear an Amazing Word—*signals, dud, proper, pirates, perfect,* or *fabulous.*
- ✔ **Phonemic Awareness** I am going to say two sentences. Clap when you hear a word that has /m/ in it: *Tom made a map of his home. May Jim and I make you some muffins?*
- ✔ **Homework Idea** Ask children to draw a self-portrait and use as many nouns as they can think of to label their pictures.

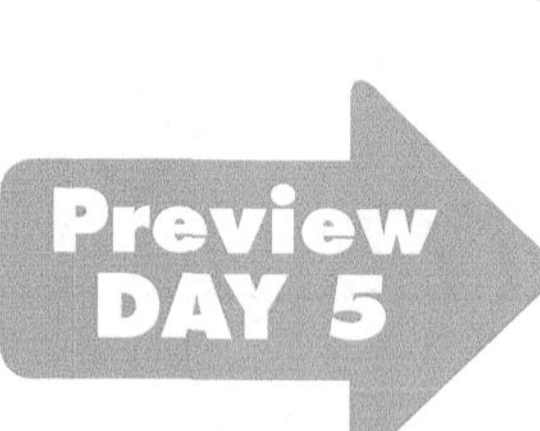

Tell children that tomorrow they will review some of the books and stories they have read this week.

Extend Your Day!

Social Studies
Working Together

MATERIALS: poster board, crayons, scissors, glue, patterns on *Teacher Resources DVD-ROM: community helpers*

DISCUSS SITUATIONS INVOLVING RESPONSIBILITY Talk to children about responsibility. Tell them about your responsibilities as a teacher. Give examples of responsibilities people have when they work together as a team. Help children identify their responsibilities as members of the class. Discuss classroom duties they are responsible for and the behavior they are expected to show.

WORK TOGETHER TO CREATE A POSTER Divide the class into small groups. Tell each group to create a poster titled "Nouns for People." Summarize the process as follows:

- Write a title at the top of the poster.
- Color and cut out pictures of people from the patterns.
- Glue the pictures on the poster.
- Label each picture with a noun.

Remind group members to work together and share the responsibilities for creating the poster. Invite groups to share their posters with the class and to tell about each member's role in completing the task.

Phonemic Awareness
The /m/ Game

MATERIALS: bean bag

THINK OF /m/ WORDS Ask children to sit in a circle on the floor. Have them start passing a bean bag around the circle. Tell children you will say a word that begins with /m/, and the child who is holding the bean bag at that moment is to say your word and another word that begins with /m/ and then pass the bean bag on. The next child must repeat the first two /m/ words and add another /m/ word, and so on. Start with the word *mouse,* emphasizing the beginning /m/. As a challenge, play the game again, this time using words that end with /m/.

Drama
Dramatize the Story

MATERIALS: Big Book *Smash! Crash!*

ACT OUT THE STORY Have children help you retell *Smash! Crash!* Display the book and have children retell the events as you show each page. Then have volunteers take turns acting out scenes from the story. After the presentations, have children draw a picture of their favorite part of the story.

DAY 5 at a Glance

Content Knowledge
Oral Vocabulary

Phonemic Awareness
Review /m/

Phonics
Review /m/ Spelled *Mm*

Assessment
Phonics
High-Frequency Words
Comprehension

Text-Based Comprehension
Review Character

Conventions
Review Nouns for People and Animals

Writing
This Week We...

Materials

- Student Edition
- Truckery Rhymes
- Talk with Me/Sing with Me Chart
- Picture Cards
- Alphabet Cards
- Read Aloud Anthology
- Student Reader K.1.5
- Get Set, Roll! Reader 5

Bridge to Common Core

INTEGRATION OF KNOWLEDGE/IDEAS
This week children have integrated content presented in diverse formats and analyzed how different texts address similar topics. They have developed knowledge about what friends do together to expand the unit topic of Cooperation.

Social Studies Knowledge Goals
Children have learned that playing with others

- helps them share fun experiences
- helps them share a common goal

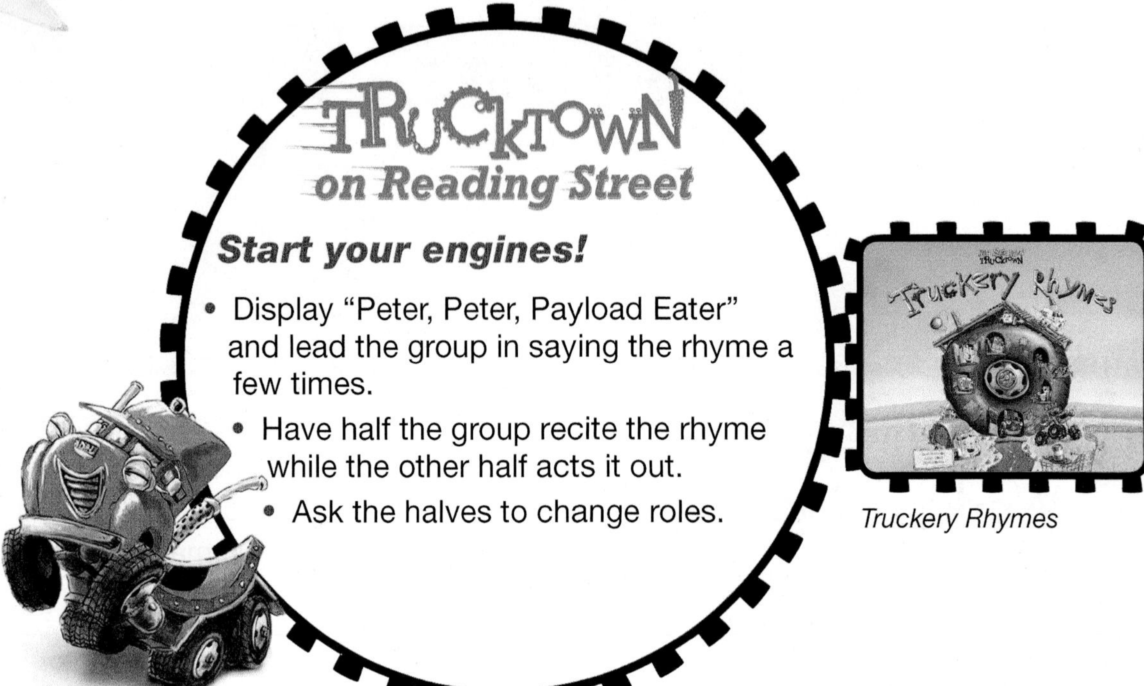
TRUCKTOWN
on Reading Street

Start your engines!

- Display "Peter, Peter, Payload Eater" and lead the group in saying the rhyme a few times.
- Have half the group recite the rhyme while the other half acts it out.
- Ask the halves to change roles.

Truckery Rhymes

Truckery Rhymes

Content Knowledge

Zoom in on

What Friends Do Together

REVIEW THE CONCEPT Discuss with children what they have added to their knowledge about this unit of study, All Together Now. Encourage them to use the Amazing Words.

Build Oral Language

LISTEN FOR AMAZING WORDS Display Sing with Me Chart 5B. Let's sing "Won't You Play with Me?" I want you to listen for the Amazing Words we learned this week. Remind children that the words *signals, dud, proper, pirates, perfect,* and *fabulous* are in the song. Sing the song several times to the tune of "Zip a Dee Doo Dah." Have children clap their hands when they hear an Amazing Word. Then discuss their favorite games to play with their friends. Remind children to speak one at a time.

Won't You Play With Me?
It's a fabulous day out, can't you see?
My, oh my, won't you play with me?
A perfect day for whatever will be,
A fabulous day out, can't you see?
We can stay out on the high seas.
We'll be pirates,
Or sailors,
Or whatever we want to be.
Change your day from a dud to a great jamboree.
A perfect day for whatever will be!

Talk with Me/Sing with Me Chart 5B

Build Oral Vocabulary

Talk with Me/Sing with Me Chart 5A

REVIEW AMAZING WORDS Display Talk with Me Chart 5A. We learned six new Amazing Words this week. Let's say the Amazing Words as I point to the pictures on the chart. Point to each picture and give children the chance to say the appropriate Amazing Word before offering it.

Have children supply the appropriate Amazing Word.

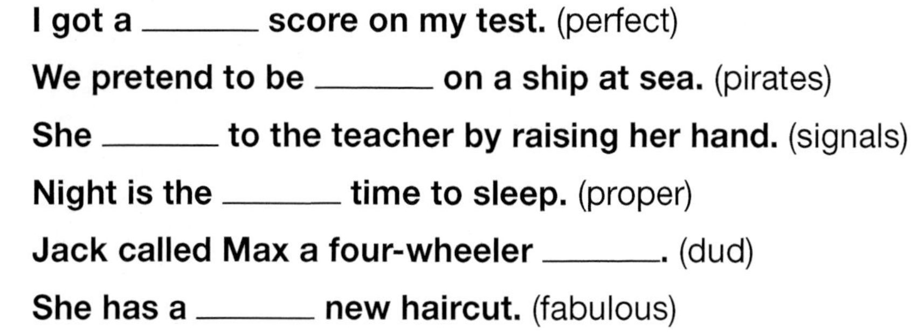

I got a ______ score on my test. (perfect)
We pretend to be ______ on a ship at sea. (pirates)
She ______ to the teacher by raising her hand. (signals)
Night is the ______ time to sleep. (proper)
Jack called Max a four-wheeler ______. (dud)
She has a ______ new haircut. (fabulous)

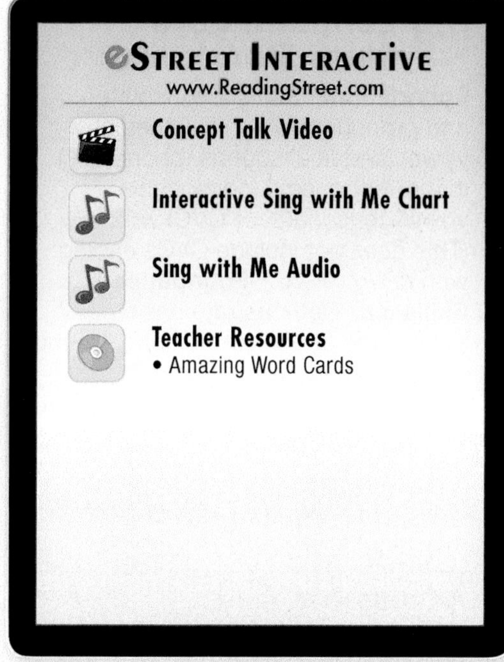

Amazing Words

signals	dud
proper	pirates
perfect	fabulous

It's Friday MONITOR PROGRESS Check Oral Vocabulary

FORMATIVE ASSESSMENT Demonstrate Word Knowledge Monitor the Amazing Words by asking the following questions. Have children use the Amazing Word in their answer.

- **What are motions or sounds that draw attention?** (signals)
- **How do we describe something that has no mistakes?** (perfect)
- **What is a word for something that doesn't work properly?** (dud)
- **What is another word for *wonderful?*** (fabulous)
- **How do we describe the way that is right or correct?** (proper)
- **Who are people who rob ships at sea?** (pirates)

If... children have difficulty using the Amazing Words,

then... reteach the words using the Robust Vocabulary Routine on the Routines Flip Chart.

Access for All

A Advanced

Words in Context Have children choose one Amazing Word and tell how it is used in *Smash! Crash!*

ELL

Check Concepts and Language Use the Day 5 instruction on ELL Poster 5 to monitor children's understanding of the lesson concept.

Common Core State Standards

Foundational Skills 2.d. Isolate and pronounce the initial, medial vowel, and final sounds (phonemes) in three-phoneme (consonant-vowel-consonant, or CVC) words.* (This does not include CVCs ending with /l/, /r/, or /x/.) **Foundational Skills 3.a.** Demonstrate basic knowledge of one-to-one letter-sound correspondences by producing the primary or many of the most frequent sounds for each consonant.

Access for All

Strategic Intervention

Support Phonemic Awareness Have children identify things in the classroom whose names begin or end with /m/. Ask children what letter the word begins or ends with. Write the words on the board.

Phonemic Awareness

Review /m/

ISOLATE INITIAL AND FINAL /m/ Display the *moose* Picture Card. What is the beginning sound in *moose?* Say the word with me: /m/ /m/ /m/, *moose.* Continue to review initial /m/ with the *map, mask, mop,* and *mug* Picture Cards.

Picture Card

Display the *jam* Picture Card. What is the last sound in *jam?* Say it again: *jam,* /m/ /m/ /m/. The last sound in *jam* is /m/. Continue to review final /m/ with these words: *ham, Tim, slam.*

DISCRIMINATE INITIAL AND FINAL SOUNDS I am going to say some /m/ words. When you hear /m/ at the beginning of the word, put both hands on your head. When you hear /m/ at the end of the word, put both hands in your lap. Listen carefully: *mud.* Do you hear /m/ at the beginning or at the end of *mud?* I hear /m/ at the beginning, so I will put both hands on my head. Continue with the following words: *mitt, hum, men, hem, Matt, Kim.*

Picture Card

Phonics

Review /m/ Spelled *Mm*

TEACH /m/*Mm* Display the *Mm* Alphabet Card. This is a motorcycle. What sound do you hear at the beginning of *motorcycle?* What letter spells that sound?

Alphabet Card

REVIEW HIGH-FREQUENCY WORDS Write the word *a* on the board. This is the word *a.* What is this word? Repeat the routine with *to.*

APPLY PHONICS Have children reread one of the books specific to the target letter sound. You may wish to review the rebus words and high-frequency words that appear in each book prior to rereading.

Decodable Reader 5
My Skills Buddy, p. 98

Kindergarten Student Reader K.1.5

Get Set, Roll! Reader 5

Day 5 SMALL GROUP TIME • Differentiate Close Reading, p. SG•73

OL On-Level
- **Phonics** Spell *m* Words
- **Read** "Fun with Marbles"

SI Strategic Intervention
- **Phonics** Blend *m* Words
- **Read** "Fun with Marbles"

A Advanced
- **Phonics** Write Sentences with *m* Words
- **Read** "Fun with Marbles"

ELL

Place English Language Learners in the groups that correspond to their reading abilities in English.

If... children need more support with **Comprehension,**
then... use the ELL activities on pp. DI•81–DI•82 in the Teacher Resources section of the Digital Path.

Common Core State Standards

Foundational Skills 2.d. Isolate and pronounce the initial, medial vowel, and final sounds (phonemes) in three-phoneme (consonant-vowel-consonant, or CVC) words.* (This does not include CVCs ending with /l/, /r/, or /x/.) **Foundational Skills 3.a.** Demonstrate basic knowledge of one-to-one letter-sound correspondences by producing the primary or many of the most frequent sounds for each consonant. **Foundational Skills 3.c.** Read common high-frequency words by sight. (e.g., *the, of, to, you, she, my, is, are, do, does*).

Assess

- Identify words that begin with /m/.
- Read high-frequency words.

Assessment

Monitor Progress

Review /m/ Spelled *Mm*

WHOLE CLASS Have children number a sheet of paper from 1 to 6. Read the list of words below. For each word, have children write an *m* next to the corresponding number if the word begins with /m/ or an *X* if it does not.

1. duck	**2. middle**	**3. car**
4. moon	**5. lizard**	**6. melon**

MONITOR PROGRESS Check Sound Discrimination and Word Reading

If... children cannot complete the whole-class assessment,
then... use the Reteach lesson in *First Stop.*

If... you are unsure of a child's grasp of this week's skills,
then... use the assessment below to obtain a clearer evaluation of the child's progress.

ONE-ON-ONE To facilitate individual progress monitoring, assess some children on Day 4 and the rest on Day 5. While individual children are being assessed, the rest of the class can reread this week's books and look for words with /m/ and high-frequency words.

SOUND DISCRIMINATION Use the pictures on reproducible p. 509 to assess each child's ability to identify initial /m/ words. We're going to identify pictures whose names begin with /m/. I'll do the first one. This is a mop. *Mop* begins with /m/. For each child, record any problems.

WORD READING Use the words on reproducible p. 509 to assess each child's ability to read high-frequency words. Have children read the words aloud.

RECORD SCORES Monitor children's accuracy by recording their scores using the Sound Discrimination and Word Reading Chart for this unit in *First Stop.*

Name ____________________

Name the Sound

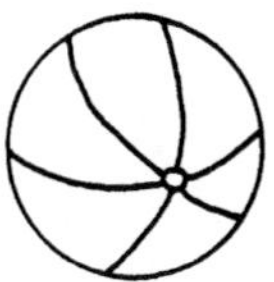

Read the Words

a ☐

to ☐

Copyright © Savvas Learning Company LLC. All Rights Reserved.

Note to Teacher: Children listen for and identify initial /m/. Children read the words.

Scoring for Name the Sound/Read the Words: Score 1 point for each correct sound/word.

Name the Sound (*mop, mouse, map, man, mitten*) _______ / 5

High-Frequency Words (*a, to*) _______ / 2

MONITOR PROGRESS

- /m/ Spelled *Mm*
- High-Frequency Words

Common Core State Standards **Literature 1.** With prompting and support, ask and answer questions about key details in a text. **Also Literature 3., 7.**

Let's Practice It!

Signs

- Listen to the selection.
- What is the selection about?
- Point to each sign. Tell what it means.
- Why does each stand at the market have a sign? Who will read the signs?
- How do the signs help Sandra with her plans?

At a Farmer's Market

Apples 10 for $1

Corn 6 for $2

Pumpkins $3 each

Green Beans $2 a bag

Carrots $1 a bunch

Farmer's market

110

111

My Skills Buddy, pp. 110–111

Common Core State Standards

Literature 1. With prompting and support, ask and answer questions about key details in a text. **Literature 7.** With prompting and support, describe the relationship between illustrations and the story in which they appear (e.g., what moment in a story an illustration depicts). **Also Literature 3.**

Academic Vocabulary

signs groups of words and/or pictures that give information

Let's Practice It!

Signs

TEACH Today you will listen to a story about a woman's trip to a farmer's market. The woman uses signs to help her get what she needs. A **sign** tells information. Review the features of signs with children.

- Signs have words, numbers, or pictures.
- Signs tell only important information.
- Signs often have specific meanings.

Have children turn to pp. 110–111 of *My Skills Buddy.* I am going to read a story about a trip to the farmer's market. Look at the pictures. Continue to look at the pictures as I read. Read the text of "At a Farmer's Market." As you read, direct children to follow the woman's route on the picture.

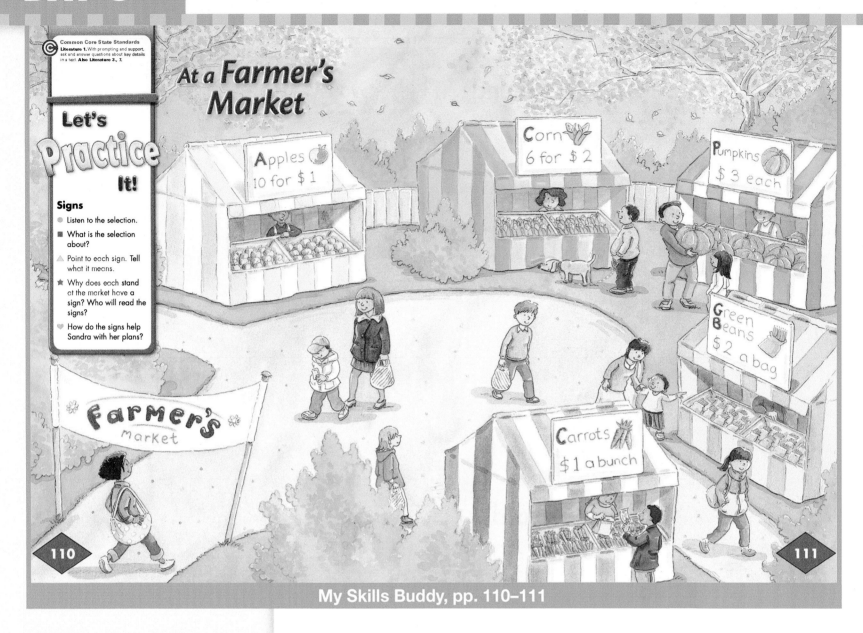

GUIDE PRACTICE Discuss the features of signs and the bulleted text on p. 110 of *My Skills Buddy* with children.

- Signs have words, numbers, or pictures. What do you think the pictures are for? (The pictures show what the signs are about.)
- Signs tell only important information. What important information needs to go on a sign at a farmer's market? (what kind of food and what it costs)
- Signs often have specific meanings. What do the numbers on these signs mean? (how much the food costs)
- Why do you think a famer's market needs signs? (so that people can see the information they need instead of asking; so that the people who sell food don't have to keep saying what they are selling and how much it costs)

Writing to Sources

Use Connect the Texts on pp. 24–25 to guide children in writing text-based responses using two sources.

Teacher Read Aloud

At a Farmer's Market

It is a crisp fall Saturday morning. Sandra is at a farmer's market. She knows exactly what she wants to get there. She has many plans.

First, Sandra plans to decorate her front porch with pumpkins. She wants three pumpkins. *Can she get pumpkins at the market? How much will she pay for each pumpkin?*

Next, Sandra plans to decorate her front door with corn. She wants six ears of corn. *Where can she get corn at the market? How much will she pay for the corn?*

Then Sandra plans to make vegetable soup. She wants some green beans and carrots. *How much will she pay for a bag of beans? How many bunches of carrots can she get for one dollar?*

Last, Sandra plans to bake an apple pie. She wants ten apples. *Are there apples at the market? How much will she pay for ten apples?*

Sandra will put all the food in her bag. Then she will hurry home. She has many things to do!

Access for All

 Advanced

Access Content Have children think about other signs they have seen. What is the reason for the sign?

Common Core State Standards

Literature 3. With prompting and support, identify characters, settings, and major events in a story.

Assess

Identify character.

Assessment

Monitor Progress

REVIEW CHARACTER The people or animals that a story is about are called characters. Good readers pay attention to the characters because it helps them understand the story.

READ "SAM SINGS" Tell children that you are going to read them a story about a boy who likes to sing but not in front of an audience. Ask them to think about the characters as they listen to the story. After I read the story, I am going to ask you to tell me about the characters in the story. Read "Sam Sings" on p. 9 of *Read Aloud Anthology.*

Read Aloud Anthology

CHECK CHARACTER After you read the story, have children tell you about the characters.

- Who are the characters in the story? (Sam, Mrs. Norris, Alex, Laura)
- How are Sam, Alex, and Laura alike? (They are second graders. They are in Mrs. Norris's class. They are friends.)
- At the beginning of the story, how does Sam feel about singing in the spring musical? (He is afraid to do it.) How does he feel about it at the end of the story? (He enjoys doing it.)

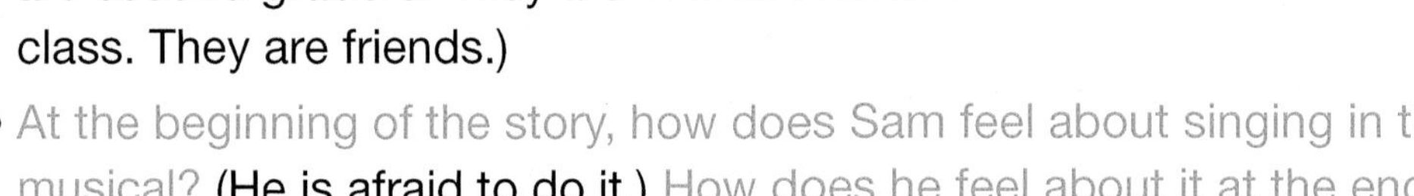

Corrective feedback	**If...** a child cannot identify the characters, **then...** reteach character using the Reteach lesson in *First Stop.*

ASSESS CHARACTER Use the blackline master on p. 513. Make one copy for each child. Have children identify and then cut out the characters from "Sam Sings." Have children glue the characters to another sheet of paper and color them.

Name ___

Character

Cut out the characters from "Sam Sings."

Copyright © Savvas Learning Company LLC. All Rights Reserved.

Note to Teacher: Have children cut out the characters from the story and glue them to another sheet of paper. Have them color the pictures.

MONITOR PROGRESS

- Character

Common Core State Standards

Writing 2. Use a combination of drawing, dictating, and writing to compose informative/explanatory texts in which they name what they are writing about and supply some information about the topic. **Language 1.a.** Print many upper- and lowercase letters. **Language 1.b.** Use frequently occurring nouns and verbs. **Also Writing 7., Language 5.a.**

Daily Fix-It

the pigs were safe
The pigs were safe.

This week's practice sentences appear on *Teacher Resources DVD-ROM.*

Conventions

Review Nouns for People and Animals

REVIEW Remind children of what they learned about nouns. A noun is a word that names a person, animal, place, or thing.

MODEL Draw a three-column chart on the board. Label the first column *Nouns,* the second column *People,* and the third column *Animals.*

Write these words in the *Nouns* column: *boy, girl, dog, cat, dad, sister, pig, sheep, goat.* Point to the first noun and read it aloud. This word is *boy.* It is a noun that names a person. I will put a check mark in the *People* column because *boy* is a noun that names a person.

GUIDE PRACTICE Continue pointing to and reading the other nouns on the chart. Have children repeat the noun after you and decide in which column to put the check mark. After children have completed the chart, have them suggest other nouns for the *Nouns* column. Write the nouns and have the class decide whether to put the check mark in the *People* column or the *Animals* column.

ON THEIR OWN After all of the nouns have been classified as people or animals, have children choose one noun and use it in a complete sentence.

This Week We...

REVIEW Display *Smash! Crash!,* Sing with Me Chart 5B, Phonics Songs and Rhymes Chart 5, Decodable Reader 5 from *My Skills Buddy,* Kindergarten Student Reader K.1.5, and Get Set, Roll! Reader 5. This week we talked about what we do with our friends. We read new books, and we sang new songs. Which book or song was your favorite? Let's share our ideas with each other.

Team Talk Pair children and have them take turns telling which book or song was their favorite and why.

MODEL WRITING A LIST Today we will write a list of things we like to do with our friends. I will write *draw pictures* and *write stories* on the list:

Things to Do with Friends

1. draw pictures **2. write stories**

GUIDE PRACTICE Continue the list with children. Then read through the list.

Things to Do with Friends

1. draw pictures	**2. write stories**
3. sing silly songs	**4. play games**
5. play tag	**6. read books**

ON THEIR OWN Have children write or dictate a sentence about their favorite activity to do with friends.

Daily Handwriting

Write uppercase *M* and lowercase *m* on the board. Review correct letter formation with children.

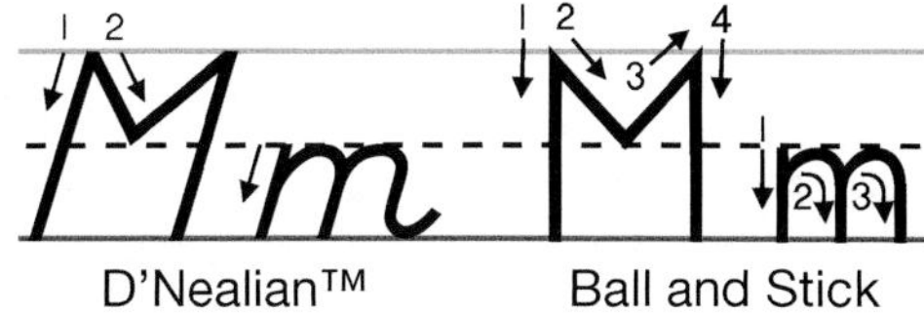

Have children write a row of uppercase *M* and a row of lowercase *m* on their Write-On Boards. Remind them to use proper left-to-right and top-to-bottom progression.

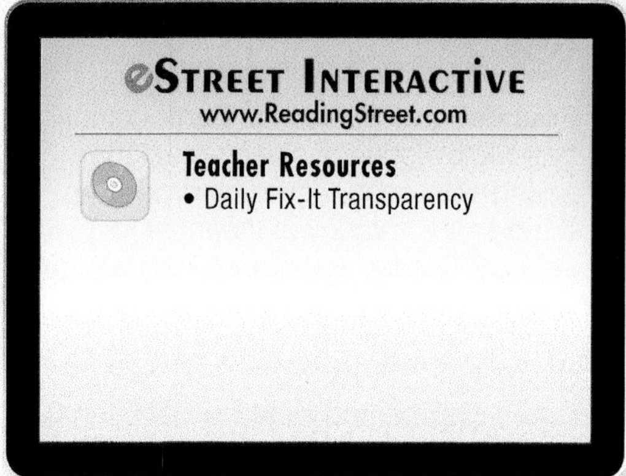

Access for All

SI Strategic Intervention

Support Writing Before writing, have children draw pictures of what they like to do with their friends. Then they can dictate a sentence about their drawing.

Bridge to Common Core

RESEARCH TO BUILD AND PRESENT KNOWLEDGE

When children work together to write a list of ideas, they are learning to participate in a shared writing project, recalling information from their experiences, and demonstrating their understanding of the subject.

Poster Preview Encourage children to look ahead to next week by previewing ELL Poster 6. Read the Poster Talk-Through to introduce the concept and vocabulary. Ask children to identify and describe objects and actions in the art.

Common Core State Standards

Foundational Skills 3.a. Demonstrate basic knowledge of one-to-one letter-sound correspondences by producing the primary or many of the most frequent sounds for each consonant. **Speaking/ Listening 1.** Participate in collaborative conversations with diverse partners about *kindergarten topics and texts* with peers and adults in small and larger groups. **Speaking/ Listening 4.** Describe familiar people, places, things, and events and, with prompting and support, provide additional detail. **Speaking/ Listening 5.** Add drawings or other visual displays to descriptions as desired to provide additional detail. **Language 1.b.** Use frequently occurring nouns and verbs.

Wrap Up Your Week!

What Friends Do Together

What do you like to do with your friends?

ILLUSTRATE CHARACTER This week we talked about things we like to do with our friends. We read about what best friends Jack Truck and Dump Truck Dan do together.

- Make a word web like the one shown and have children fill it with characters from *Smash! Crash!*
- These trucks are the characters in the story. Which truck is your favorite?
- Have children draw a picture of their favorite truck and something that truck does with his or her friends in the story. Then have children draw a picture of themselves and a friend doing something together.

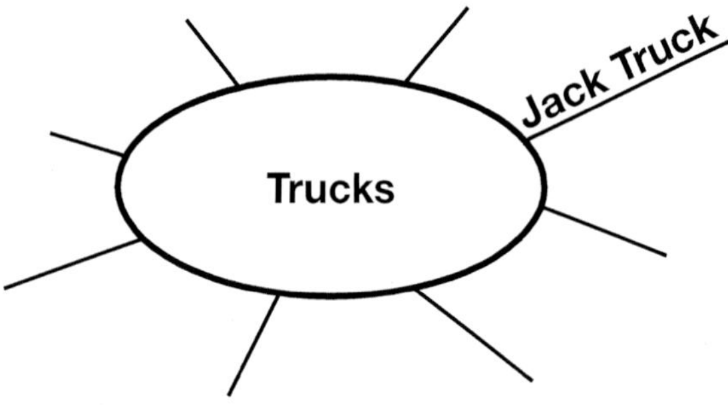

Amazing Words

You've learned 006 words this week!

You've learned 030 words this year!

Next Week's Concept

People and Machines Working Together

How do machines help people work?

Discuss next week's question. Talk with children about how people use machines to help them do work.

Tell children that next week they will read about some helpful machines.

Preview Next Week

Extend Your Day!

Social Studies
Good Friends

MATERIALS: chart paper, markers

DISCUSS QUALITIES OF A GOOD FRIEND Talk with children about what makes someone a good friend. Explain that we choose friends because of what they are like.

- What are your friends like?
- What makes them good friends?
- Why do you like to play with them?
- What makes you a good friend?
- How do you learn how to be a good friend?

Make a list of the qualities that children suggest.

Good Friends	
good listeners	nice
share toys	play with me
make me laugh	help me do things

DRAW A PICTURE Have children draw a picture of themselves playing with friends. Tell them to write or dictate a word or phrase that tells about a good quality in a friend.

Phonics
Match *m* to /m/

MATERIALS: Picture Cards: *kite, map, mitten, moon, mop, pig, rock, seal;* four index cards with *m* written on them

IDENTIFY /m/ WORDS Mix the Picture Cards and place them face up in a row. Have a child take an index card and place it on a picture whose name begins with /m/. Continue until all the index cards are matched with /m/ Picture Cards. Collect the cards and begin a new game.

Conventions
Name My Job

GUESS NOUNS FOR PEOPLE Review with children that we use nouns to name people. Together generate a list of nouns that name people's jobs, such as *teacher, doctor, carpenter, actor, truck driver,* and *store clerk,* and write them on the board. Have a child secretly choose a job from the list and either pantomime doing the job or give clues about it while classmates try to guess the person's job.

Assessment Checkpoints for the Week

Weekly Assessment

Use the whole-class assessment on pages 508–509 and 512–513 in this Teacher's Edition to check:

- ✓ **/m/ Spelled *Mm***
- ✓ **Comprehension** *Character*
- ✓ **High-Frequency Words**

a	*to*

You will find the Weekly Assessments on Day 5 of this week's lesson.

Managing Assessment

Use the Assessment Handbook for:

- ✓ **Observation Checklists**
- ✓ **Record-Keeping Forms**
- ✓ **Portfolio Assessment**

Assessment Handbook
COMMON CORE EDITION
PEARSON
Assessment Handbook

TEACHER NOTES

TEACHER NOTES

DAY 1 Differentiate Phonics

- Consonant *m*/m/
  - Decodable Story
  - Advanced Selection "Mim's Cat Sam"

DAY 2 Differentiate Phonics

- Consonant *m*/m/
  - Decodable Reader

DAY 3 Differentiate Vocabulary

- Develop Vocabulary: Position Words
- Kindergarten Student Reader

DAY 4 Differentiate Language

- Develop Language
- Get Set, Roll! Reader

DAY 5 Differentiate Close Reading

- Phonics
- "Fun with Marbles"

Place English Language Learners in the groups that correspond to their reading abilities.
If... children need scaffolding and practice,
then... use the ELL notes on the page.

Independent Practice

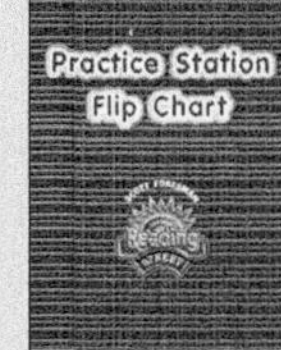

Independent Practice Stations

See pp. 424 and 425 for Independent Stations.

Reading Street Digital Path

Independent Practice Activities available in the Digital Path.

Independent Reading

See p. 425 for independent reading suggestions.

OL
On-Level

Common Core State Standards

Literature 1. With prompting and support, ask and answer questions about key details in a text. **Literature 10.** Actively engage in group reading activities with purpose and understanding. **Foundational Skills 2.d.** Isolate and pronounce the initial, medial vowel, and final sounds (phonemes) in three-phoneme (consonant-vowel-consonant, or CVC) words.* (This does not include CVCs ending with /l/, /r/, or /x/.) **Foundational Skills 3.a.** Demonstrate basic knowledge of one-to-one letter-sound correspondences by producing the primary or many of the most frequent sounds for each consonant. **Foundational Skills 3.c.** Read common high-frequency words by sight (e.g., *the, of, to, you, she, my, is, are, do, does*).

1 Build Word Knowledge

Practice Phonemic Awareness

CLAP FOR /m/ I am going to tell you a story. When you hear a word that begins with /m/, clap your hands and say the word. Tell the following story, emphasizing and pausing after each /m/ word:

I like *my* friend *Monkey. My* friend *Monkey* is *magnificent.* He reads books about *mysteries, munches* on pancakes with *maple* syrup, and *makes muffins* in the kitchen.

Practice Phonics

MATCH /m/ TO *Mm* Give children each a note card and ask them to write the letter *m* on it. Retell the story and have children raise their *m* card when they hear a word that begins with /m/.

2 Read

Decodable Story 5 *Little Mouse*

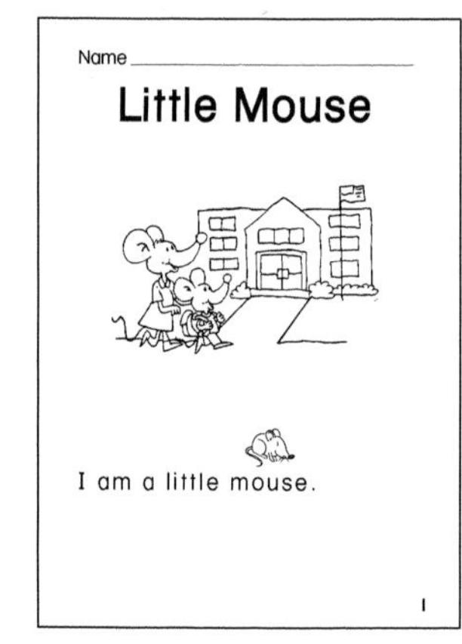
Name
Little Mouse
I am a little mouse.
1

READ Have children read the story. Then have them reread the text to develop automaticity.

HIGH-FREQUENCY WORDS Have children return to the text and identify the high-frequency words *to, am, I, little,* and *a.* Help children demonstrate their understanding of these words by providing sentence frames such as these: *An elephant is big, and a mouse is* ______. (little) *Watch me walk* ______ *the board.* (to)

3 Reread for Fluency

Have children reread the Decodable Story *Little Mouse* individually to develop fluency.

Independent Reading Options

Trade Book Library

eStreet Interactive
www.ReadingStreet.com

Teacher's Guides available on the Leveled Reader Database.

On-Level

1 Build Word Knowledge

Practice Phonics

MORE *m* WORDS Distribute paper and crayons to children. Then display the *man, map, garden, bed, mitten, moon, ten,* and *mop* Picture Cards one at a time. Have one child identify the picture you are displaying. Then have all children write the letter *m* on their paper if the picture name begins with /m/.

Practice High-Frequency Words

CHOOSE AND USE Display the following high-frequency word cards: *I, a, the, is, little, to.* Say the word *little.* Choose a child to point to the word. Have children say the word and use it in a sentence. Continue with the other words.

2 Read

Decodable Reader 5 *Animal Friends*

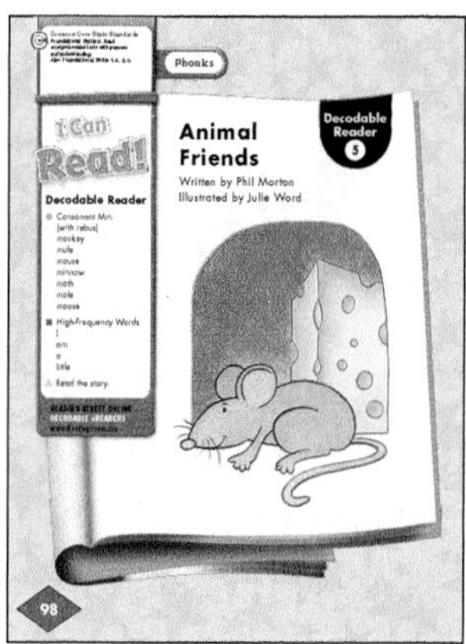

CONCEPTS OF PRINT Display Decodable Reader 5 in *My Skills Buddy.* Show children the illustrations and read aloud the title. What do you think the story is about?

READ Have children take turns reading the Decodable Reader. Pause at the end of each page to ask questions. What animal do you see? Is it big or little?

3 Reread for Fluency

Have children reread the Decodable Reader *Animal Friends* individually to develop fluency.

SMALL GROUP TIME

More Reading for Group Time

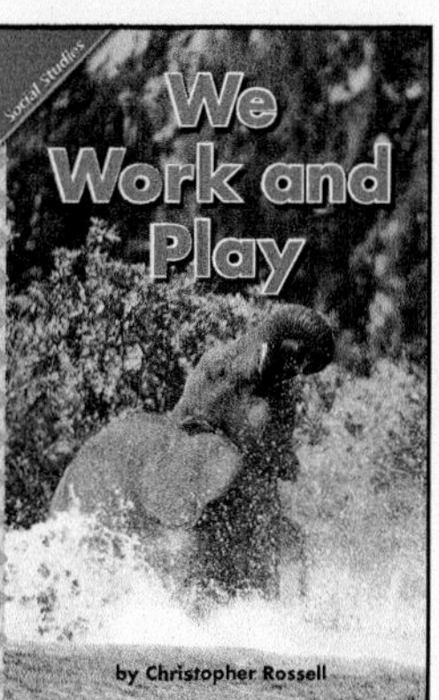

CONCEPT LITERACY

- Concept Words
- High-Frequency Words

Use these suggested readers or other text at children's instructional level.

eStreet Interactive
www.ReadingStreet.com

Use the Leveled Reader Database for lesson plans and student pages for *We Work and Play.*

If... children need more scaffolding and practice with phonemic awareness and phonics,
then... use the activities on p. DI•80 in the Teacher Resources section of the Digital Path.

Common Core State Standards

Literature 1. With prompting and support, ask and answer questions about key details in a text. **Literature 10.** Actively engage in group reading activities with purpose and understanding. **Foundational Skills 3.c.** Read common high-frequency words by sight (e.g., *the, of, to, you, she, my, is, are, do, does*). **Language 5.a.** Sort common objects into categories (e.g., shapes, foods) to gain a sense of the concepts the categories represent. **Language 5.c.** Identify real-life connections between words and their use (e.g., note places at school that are *colorful*). **Language 6.** Use words and phrases acquired through conversations, reading and being read to, and responding to texts.

1 Build Word Knowledge

Develop Vocabulary

POSITION WORDS Have children return to p. 108 in *My Skills Buddy.* Review the position words *in, out, up,* and *down.* Point to each picture of the dog. Is the dog in or out? Point to each picture of the girl. Is the girl pointing up or down? Give the following directions to children.

- Point to the word *up.* Now point up.
- Point to the word *down.* Now point down.
- Point to the word *in.* Now put your hands in your lap.
- Take your hands out of your lap. Now point to the word *out.*

Team Talk Have children work with a partner to use the position words in sentences.

2 Read

Kindergarten Student Reader *Cat and Dog Eat Together*

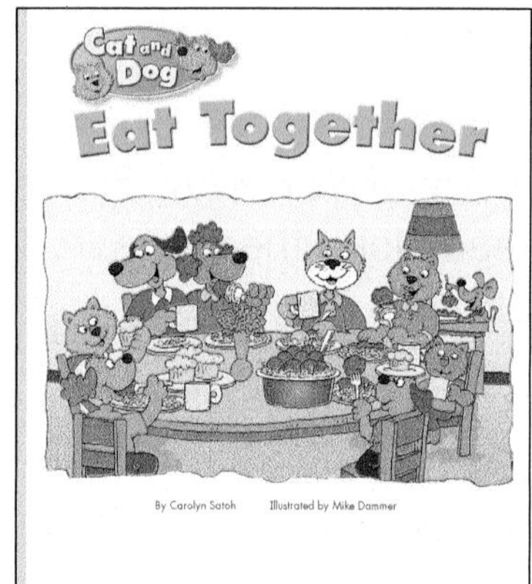

REREAD Display the reader and have children tell the title of the book. Have them tell what they remember about the story. Then have children read the story chorally. After reading each page, ask children to tell what they see. What do Cat and Dog do? To check children's understanding, have them take turns reading the story to a partner and then retelling the story to the partner.

On-Level

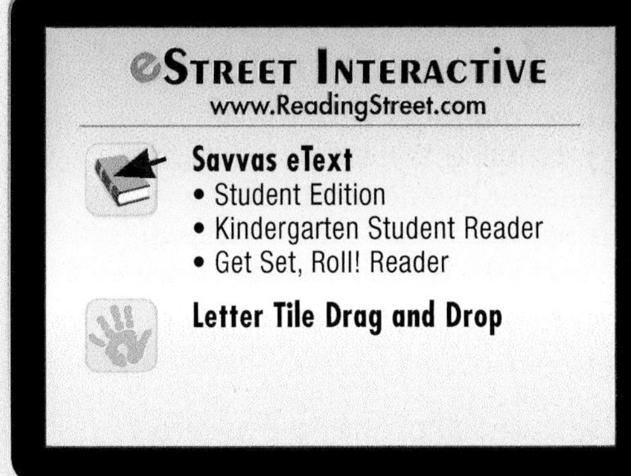

1 Build Word Knowledge

Develop Language

Display the Big Book *Smash! Crash!* and read the text on p. 30.

It's Wrecking Crane Rosie.
Rosie is huge.
Rosie is strong.
Rosie booms,
"FOLLOW ME."

- Ask children to read the text with you as you track the print.
- Point to the line, *Rosie is huge.*
- What does the word *huge* mean? What is another word for *huge?* Why do you think the author chose the word *huge?*
- Team Talk Turn to your partner and try some other words in place of *huge.*
- Continue the routine with the words *strong* and *booms.*

2 Read

Get Set, Roll! Reader 5 *Zoom!*

REVIEW HIGH-FREQUENCY WORDS Review the following high-frequency words with children: *I, am, to, a.* Ask children to use each word in a sentence.

REVIEW REBUS WORDS Distribute Letter Tiles to each child or use Letter Tile Drag and Drop in the Digital Path. Write the name *Melvin* on a card. Use your letters to build this word. This spells the name of one of our Trucktown friends. What does this spell? Which character is Melvin? Continue the routine with the following words: *pour, Max, zoom, mall, splash.*

REREAD Have children whisper read *Zoom!* as you listen to each child. Then have children take turns reading the story aloud.

SMALL GROUP TIME

If... children need more scaffolding and practice with vocabulary, **then...** use the ELL activities on p. DI•82 in the Teacher Resources section of the Digital Path.

On-Level

Common Core State Standards

Informational Text 1. With prompting and support, ask and answer questions about key details in a text. **Informational Text 10.** Actively engage in group reading activities with purpose and understanding. **Foundational Skills 3.a.** Demonstrate basic knowledge of one-to-one letter-sound correspondences by producing the primary or many of the most frequent sounds for each consonant. **Language 2.d.** Spell simple words phonetically, drawing on knowledge of sound-letter relationships.

1 Build Word Knowledge

Practice Phonics

SPELL WORDS Distribute Letter Tiles to children. Spell the word *mat* with your tiles and point to the *m.* What is the name of this letter? What is the sound for this letter? Point to *-at* and ask children to name the letters. When these two letters are together, they stand for the sounds /at/. We call them a word family because we can add different letters at the beginning and change the beginning sound, but the middle and ending sounds will stay the same. Let's spell some words with our Letter Tiles. Spell the word *mat.* Watch as children build the word. Have them name the letters in the word and then blend the initial sound and word family to read the word. Continue the routine with these words: *cat, hat, sat, pat, rat.*

Corrective feedback	**If...** children have trouble spelling words, **then...** break the word into individual phonemes and ask children to connect each sound to a letter name.

2 Text-Based Comprehension

Read

READ ALOUD Read the Reading Street Sleuth Read Aloud, "Fun with Marbles," on p. SG•79 to children.

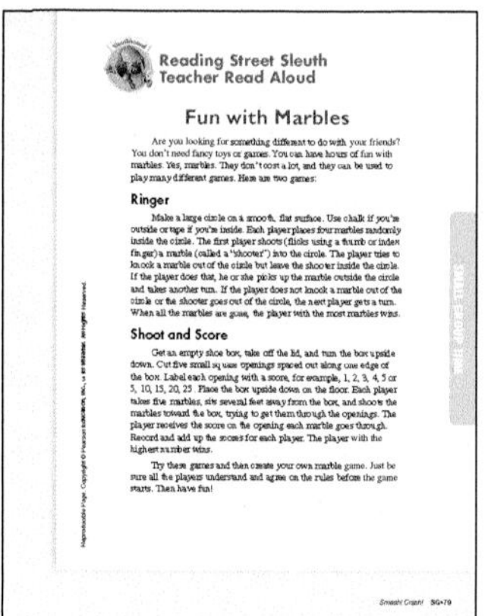
Reading Street Sleuth Teacher Read Aloud

Fun with Marbles

Are you looking for something different to do with your friends? You don't need fancy toys or games. You can have hours of fun with marbles. Yes, marbles. They don't cost a lot, and they can be used to play many different games. Here are two games:

Ringer

Make a large circle on a smooth, flat surface. Use chalk if you're outside or tape if you're inside. Each player places four marbles randomly inside the circle. The first player shoots (flicks using a thumb or index finger) a marble (called a "shooter") into the circle. The player tries to knock a marble out of the circle but leave the shooter inside the circle. If the player does that, he or she picks up the marble outside the circle and takes another turn. If the player does not knock a marble out of the circle or the shooter goes out of the circle, the next player gets a turn. When all the marbles are gone, the player with the most marbles wins.

Shoot and Score

Get an empty shoe box, take off the lid, and turn the box upside down. Cut five small square openings spaced out along one edge of the box. Label each opening with a score, for example, 1, 2, 3, 4, 5 or 5, 10, 15, 20, 25. Place the box upside down on the floor. Each player takes five marbles, sits several feet away from the box, and shoots the marbles toward the box, trying to get them through the openings. The player receives the score on the opening each marble goes through. Record and add up the scores for each player. The player with the highest number wins.

Try these games and then create your own marble game. Just be sure all the players understand and agree on the rules before the game starts. Then have fun!

Smash! Crash! SG•79

READ LIKE A SLEUTH! Encourage children to cite evidence from the text to support their answers. You may wish to reread sections of the text to verify children's answers.

Look for Evidence What is the goal of Ringer? What must the players do to win the game?

Ask Questions What questions do you have about Shoot and Score that the text doesn't answer?

Prove It! Performance Task Have children draw a picture that shows the setup for one of the marble games. Ask them to label parts of the picture using key details from the text. Children may write or dictate a short phrase or sentence.

Fun with Marbles

Are you looking for something different to do with your friends? You don't need fancy toys or games. You can have hours of fun with marbles. Yes, marbles. They don't cost a lot, and they can be used to play many different games. Here are two games:

Ringer

Make a large circle on a smooth, flat surface. Use chalk if you're outside or tape if you're inside. Each player places four marbles randomly inside the circle. The first player shoots (flicks using a thumb or index finger) a marble (called a "shooter") into the circle. The player tries to knock a marble out of the circle but leave the shooter inside the circle. If the player does that, he or she picks up the marble outside the circle and takes another turn. If the player does not knock a marble out of the circle or the shooter goes out of the circle, the next player gets a turn. When all the marbles are gone, the player with the most marbles wins.

Shoot and Score

Get an empty shoe box, take off the lid, and turn the box upside down. Cut five small square openings spaced out along one edge of the box. Label each opening with a score, for example, 1, 2, 3, 4, 5 or 5, 10, 15, 20, 25. Place the box upside down on the floor. Each player takes five marbles, sits several feet away from the box, and shoots the marbles toward the box, trying to get them through the openings. The player receives the score on the opening each marble goes through. Record and add up the scores for each player. The player with the highest number wins.

Try these games and then create your own marble game. Just be sure all the players understand and agree on the rules before the game starts. Then have fun!

SMALL GROUP TIME

Reproducible Page. Copyright © Pearson Education, Inc., or its affiliates. All Rights Reserved.

Common Core State Standards

Literature 1. With prompting and support, ask and answer questions about key details in a text. **Literature 10.** Actively engage in group reading activities with purpose and understanding. **Foundational Skills 2.d.** Isolate and pronounce the initial, medial vowel, and final sounds (phonemes) in three-phoneme (consonant-vowel-consonant, or CVC) words.* (This does not include CVCs ending with /l/, /r/, or /x/.) **Foundational Skills 3.a.** Demonstrate basic knowledge of one-to-one letter-sound correspondences by producing the primary or many of the most frequent sounds for each consonant. **Foundational Skills 3.c.** Read common high-frequency words by sight (e.g., *the, of, to, you, she, my, is, are, do, does*).

More Reading for Group Time

LISTEN TO ME READER

- Concepts of Print

Use these suggested readers or other text at children's instructional level.

eSTREET INTERACTIVE
www.ReadingStreet.com

Use the Leveled Reader Database to access an online version of *Meet Mouse and Moose.*

If... children need more scaffolding and practice with phonemic awareness and phonics,
then... use the Phonics Transition lessons beginning on p. 447 in the *ELL Handbook.*

1 Build Word Knowledge

Reteach Phonemic Awareness

ISOLATE /m/ Display the *moon* Picture Card. This is the moon. *Moon* begins with /m/. Say it with me: /m/ /m/ /m/, *moon.* Repeat with the *mop, mug, man,* and *mask* Picture Cards.

Reteach Phonics

CONNECT /m/ TO *Mm* I am going to say three words. I want you to tell me which word begins with /m/. Listen carefully: *rake, pen, mat.* Say the words with me: *rake, pen, mat.* Which word begins with /m/? *Mat* begins with /m/. *Rake* and *pen* do not begin with /m/. Display the *Mm* Alphabet Card. The letter *m* stands for /m/. The word *mat* begins with the letter *m.* Continue with these sets of words: *pail, water, mop; dirt, mud, sand; mouse, cow, deer; man, girl, boy.*

2 Read

Decodable Story 5 *Little Mouse*

REVIEW HIGH-FREQUENCY WORDS Write *to* on chart paper. This is the word *to.* What word is this? Say the word with me. Listen for the word in the sentence I say. Clap when you hear the word. *I went to school.* Continue with the high-frequency words *am, I, little,* and *a.*

Corrective feedback	**If...** children have difficulty reading the high-frequency words, **then...** say a word and have children point to the word. Repeat several times, giving assistance as needed.

READ Have children read the story.

3 Reread for Fluency

Have children reread the story *Little Mouse* chorally. Then have them reread the story several times individually to develop fluency.

1 Build Word Knowledge

Reteach Phonemic Awareness

DISCRIMINATE /m/ Display Phonics Songs and Rhymes Chart 5. Sing "Mr. Malcolm Monkey" to the tune of "I'm a Little Teapot" several times with children. Ask them to clap when they hear an /m/ word in the song.

Reteach Phonics

RECOGNIZE *Mm* Ask children to name words that begin with /m/. List the words as children say them. Have children echo read the list of words with you. Then ask them to take turns circling the *m*'s on the list.

Reteach High-Frequency Words

REVIEW Have children read each previously taught high-frequency word as you point to it on the Word Wall.

I	am	a	to	little	the

Corrective feedback	If... children have difficulty reading the words, then... say a word and have children point to the word. Repeat several times, giving assistance as needed.

2 Read

Decodable Reader 5 *Animal Friends*

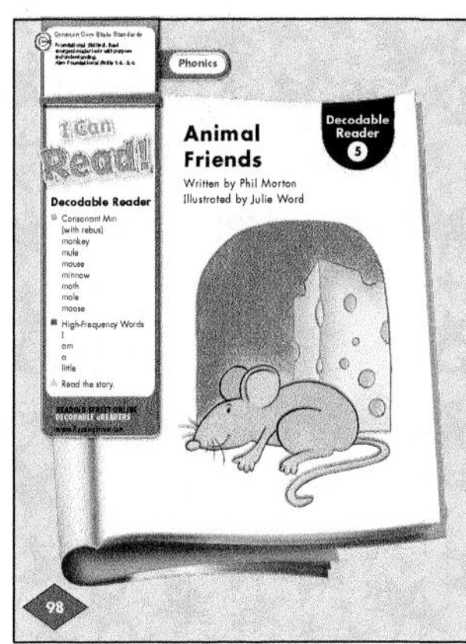

CONCEPTS OF PRINT Display Decodable Reader 5 in *My Skills Buddy.* The title of this story is *Animal Friends*. The author is Phil Morton. The illustrator is Julie Word. Look at the picture on the cover. Look at the pictures inside. What do you think the story is about?

READ Let's read the story together. After reading chorally with children, have them reread the story several times with a partner and then independently.

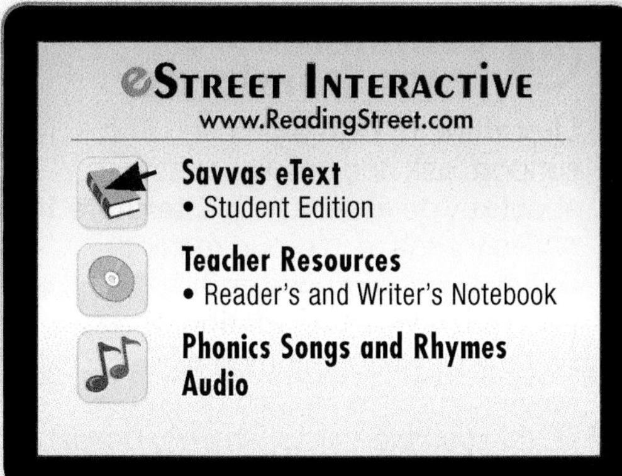

eSTREET INTERACTIVE
www.ReadingStreet.com
Savvas eText
• Student Edition
Teacher Resources
• Reader's and Writer's Notebook
Phonics Songs and Rhymes Audio

SMALL GROUP TIME

Independent Reading Options

Trade Book Library

eSTREET INTERACTIVE
www.ReadingStreet.com

Teacher's Guides available on the Leveled Reader Database.

If... children need more support with phonics,
then... use the ELL activities on p. DI•80 in the Teacher Resources section of the Digital Path.

Common Core State Standards

Literature 1. With prompting and support, ask and answer questions about key details in a text. **Literature 10.** Actively engage in group reading activities with purpose and understanding. **Foundational Skills 3.c.** Read common high-frequency words by sight (e.g., *the, of, to, you, she, my, is, are, do, does*). **Language 5.a.** Sort common objects into categories (e.g., shapes, foods) to gain a sense of the concepts the categories represent. **Language 5.c.** Identify real-life connections between words and their use (e.g., note places at school that are *colorful*). **Language 6.** Use words and phrases acquired through conversations, reading and being read to, and responding to texts.

1 Build Word Knowledge

Develop Vocabulary

RETEACH POSITION WORDS Have children return to p. 108 of *My Skills Buddy* to review the position words *in, out, up,* and *down.*

- Which picture shows the dog in the doghouse? out of the doghouse?
- Which picture shows the girl pointing up? pointing down?

Act out each position word, telling what you are doing. For example, put paper in the wastebasket and say: *I put paper in the wastebasket.* Have children tell you which position word you acted out.

2 Read

Kindergarten Student Reader *Cat and Dog Eat Together*

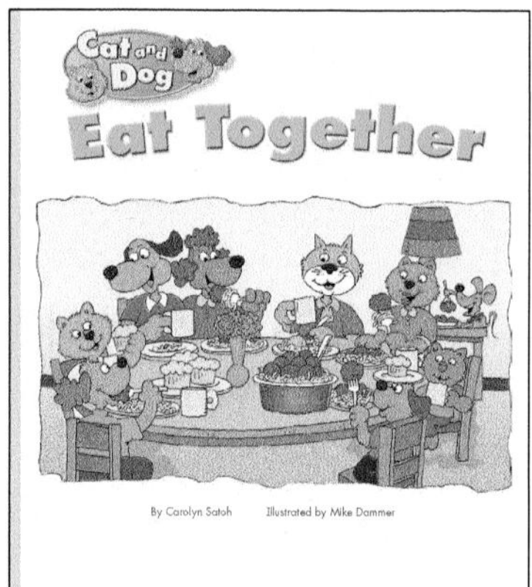

REVIEW REBUS WORDS Write *mouse* on chart paper. This is the word *mouse.* Name the letters with me: *m, o, u, s, e.* Repeat with the other rebus words *talking, mixing, muffins, reading, Mom, eating, meatball, mopping,* and *mess.*

REVIEW HIGH-FREQUENCY WORDS Write *I* on chart paper. Ask children to read the word with you. Have a volunteer read the word. Continue with the other high-frequency words *am, to, the, little,* and *a.*

REREAD STORY Display the reader. The title of this book is *Cat and Dog Eat Together.* What do you think the story is about? Read the story chorally with children. Pause at the end of each page to ask: Where is Cat? What is Cat doing? Where is Dog? What is Dog doing? Remind children that Cat and Dog are the two main characters in the story. This story is about Cat and Dog. Have children reread the story several times to build fluency.

ELL

If... children need more scaffolding and practice with vocabulary,
then... use the ELL activities on p. DI•82 in the Teacher Resources section of the Digital Path.

1 Build Word Knowledge

Develop Language

Display the Big Book *Smash! Crash!* and read the text on p. 30.

It's Wrecking Crane Rosie.
Rosie is huge.
Rosie is strong.
Rosie booms,
"FOLLOW ME."

- Ask children to read the text with you as you track the print.
- Point to the line, *Rosie is huge.*
- What does the word *huge* mean? What is another word that means the same as *huge?*
- I am going to say three words. I want you to tell me which word means the same as *huge: big, small, tiny; little, large, miniature.*
- Why do you think the author used the word *huge?*
- Continue the routine with the words *strong* and *booms.*

2 Read

Get Set, Roll! Reader 5 *Zoom!*

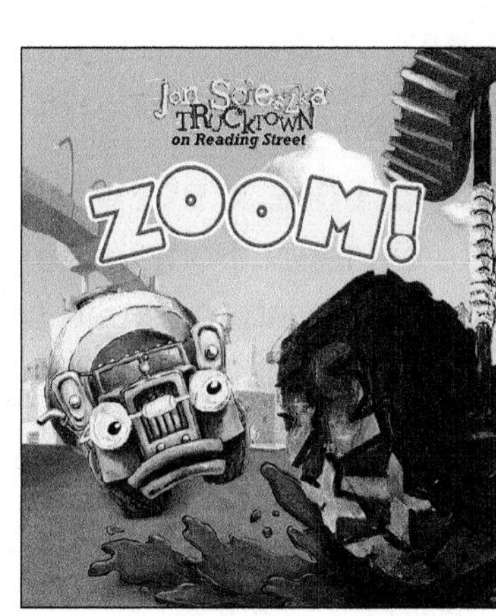

REVIEW HIGH-FREQUENCY AND REBUS WORDS Review the high-frequency and rebus words (*I, am, to, a, Melvin, Max, pour, zoom, mall, splash*) using the following routine.

1. Display and read the word.
2. Name the letters in the word.
3. Read the word. Use it in a sentence.

REREAD Have children chorally read aloud *Zoom!* several times. Then ask them to take turns reading a page aloud.

eSTREET INTERACTIVE
www.ReadingStreet.com

Savvas eText
- Student Edition
- Kindergarten Student Reader
- Get Set, Roll! Reader

SMALL GROUP TIME

Independent Reading Options

Trade Book Library

eSTREET INTERACTIVE
www.ReadingStreet.com

Teacher's Guides available on the Leveled Reader Database.

Common Core State Standards

Literature 1. With prompting and support, ask and answer questions about key details in a text. **Literature 10.** Actively engage in group reading activities with purpose and understanding. **Informational Text 1.** With prompting and support, ask and answer questions about key details in a text. **Informational Text 10.** Actively engage in group reading activities with purpose and understanding. **Foundational Skills 3.a.** Demonstrate basic knowledge of one-to-one letter-sound correspondences by producing the primary or many of the most frequent sounds for each consonant. **Language 2.d.** Spell simple words phonetically, drawing on knowledge of sound-letter relationships.

1 Build Word Knowledge

Reteach Phonics

BLEND WORDS Distribute Letter Tiles to children. Spell the word *mat* with your tiles and point to the *m*. What is the name of this letter? What is the sound for this letter? Point to *-at* and ask children to name the letters. When these two letters are together, they stand for the sounds /at/. We call them a word family because we can add different letters at the beginning and change the beginning sound, but the middle and ending sounds will stay the same. Find your *m, a, t* Letter Tiles and then spell the word. Let's name the letters and then read the word. Continue the routine with these words: *cat, hat, sat, pat, rat.*

Corrective feedback	If... children have trouble blending sounds to read, then... have them name the letters in each word.

2 Text-Based Comprehension

Read

READ ALOUD Read the Reading Street Sleuth Read Aloud, "Fun with Marbles," on p. SG•79 to children.

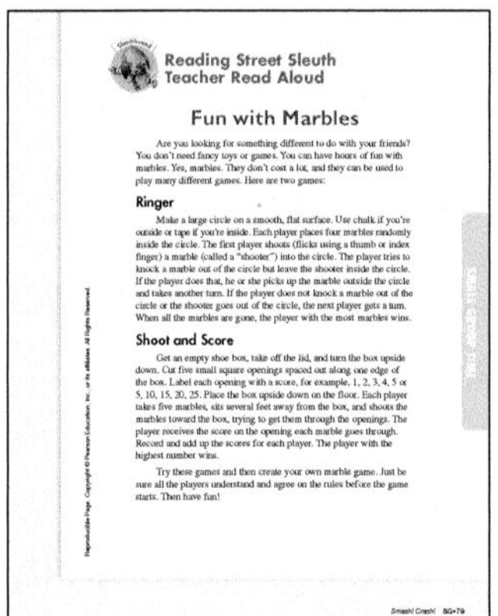

Reading Street Sleuth
Teacher Read Aloud

Fun with Marbles

Are you looking for something different to do with your friends? You don't need fancy toys or games. You can have hours of fun with marbles. Yes, marbles. They don't cost a lot, and they can be used to play many different games. Here are two games:

Ringer

Make a large circle on a smooth, flat surface. Use chalk if you're outside or tape if you're inside. Each player places four marbles randomly inside the circle. The first player shoots (flicks using a thumb or index finger) a marble (called a "shooter") into the circle. The player tries to knock a marble out of the circle but leave the shooter inside the circle. If the player does that, he or she picks up the marble outside the circle and takes another turn. If the player does not knock a marble out of the circle or the shooter goes out of the circle, the next player gets a turn. When all the marbles are gone, the player with the most marbles wins.

Shoot and Score

Get an empty shoe box, take off the lid, and turn the box upside down. Cut five small square openings spaced out along one edge of the box. Label each opening with a score, for example, 1, 2, 3, 4, 5 or 5, 10, 15, 20, 25. Place the box upside down on the floor. Each player takes five marbles, sits several feet away from the box, and shoots the marbles toward the box, trying to get them through the openings. The player receives the score on the opening each marble goes through. Record and add up the scores for each player. The player with the highest number wins.

Try these games and then create your own marble game. Just be sure all the players understand and agree on the rules before the game starts. Then have fun!

Reproducible Page Copyright © Pearson Education, Inc., or its affiliates. All Rights Reserved.

Smash! Crash! SG•79

READ LIKE A SLEUTH! Encourage children to cite evidence from the text to support their answers. You may wish to reread sections of the text to verify children's answers.

Look for Evidence How do you win Shoot and Score?

Ask Questions What questions do you have about Ringer that the text doesn't answer?

Prove It! Performance Task Have children draw a picture of the box used in Shoot and Score. Ask them to dictate a phrase or short sentence for the picture using one or two key details from the text. Read children's phrases or sentences to them as you track the print.

Advanced

1 Build Word Knowledge

Extend Phonics

/m/ SPELLED *Mm* Have children write *Mm* on an index card. Ask them to hold up their *Mm* card when they hear a word that begins with /m/. Say longer or more complex words such as these:

marble	**turtle**	**motor**	**dollar**	**money**
pillow	**many**	**basket**	**mirror**	**muffins**
mittens	**morning**	**machine**	**metal**	**napkin**

2 Read

"Mim's Cat Sam"

Mim's Cat Sam
I am Mim.
I have a cat.
My cat is Sam.
I sit on my mat.
Sam sits on me.
I nap on my mat.
Sam naps on me.
Sam is not little.
Sam is BIG.
Look, Sam.
It is a mat for you.
Sam likes *my* mat.

CONCEPTS OF PRINT Read aloud the title of the story, "Mim's Cat Sam." Remember, the title of a story gives us clues to what the story is about. Ask children what the title tells them about the story. (There is a character named Mim. Mim has a cat named Sam.)

TEACH STORY WORDS Present any story words that children may need help with, such as *my, big, look,* and *likes.* Use the words in sentences that give clues to their meanings. For example, This is *my* desk. This desk belongs to me. A bug is little, but a bear is *big.*

READ Distribute copies of "Mim's Cat Sam" from p. SG•86, and have children read it on their own. Then have them take turns reading the story aloud. After reading, have children tell whom the story is about and what happens.

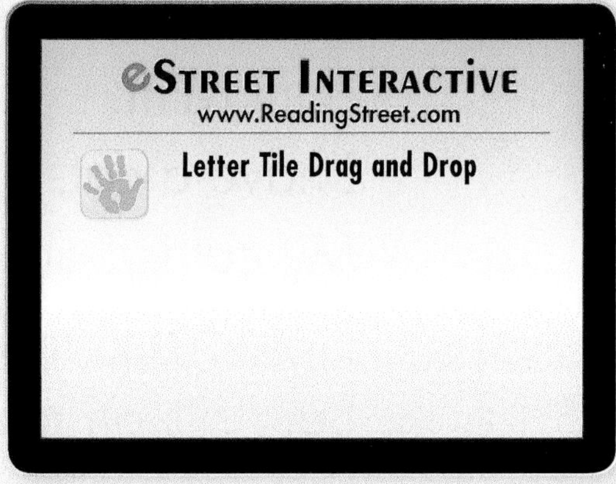

More Reading for Group Time

INDEPENDENT READER

- More Challenging Text

Use the suggested Leveled Reader or other text at children's instructional level.

STREET INTERACTIVE
www.ReadingStreet.com

Use the Leveled Reader Database for lesson plans and student pages for *We Have Fun Together.*

If... children need more practice with phonics,
then... use the Phonics Transition lessons beginning on p. 447 in the *ELL Handbook.*

Mim's Cat Sam

I am Mim.
I have a cat.
My cat is Sam.
I sit on my mat.
Sam sits on me.
I nap on my mat.
Sam naps on me.
Sam is not little.
Sam is BIG.
Look, Sam.
It is a mat for you.
Sam likes *my* mat.

Advanced Phonics Selection 5

Reproducible Page. Copyright © Pearson Education, Inc., or its affiliates. All Rights Reserved.

Advanced

1 Build Word Knowledge

Extend Phonics

BLEND *m* WORDS Write the word *mop* on an index card. Display the card and say the word. Point to the *m.* What is the sound for this letter? Yes, the sound for this letter is /m/. Say it with me: /m/ /m/ /m/. The beginning sound in *mop* is /m/. *Mop* ends with *-op.* Run your finger under the letters *op.* Say the sounds with me: /m/ *-op.* Now let's blend the sounds together: /m/ *-op, mop.* Say it with me: /m/ *-op, mop.* Now you say it without me.

Listen as I use *mop* in a sentence. *Mom used a mop to clean the floor.* Have children use *mop* in a sentence.

Continue with the words *map, mug, mix,* and *mud.*

2 Read

Decodable Reader 5 *Animal Friends*

CONCEPTS OF PRINT Display Decodable Reader 5 in *My Skills Buddy.* Ask children to identify the author and illustrator.

READ Have children read the Decodable Reader quietly as you listen to them. Then have them take turns reading aloud one page at a time.

3 Reread for Fluency

Have children reread Decodable Reader 5 *Animal Friends* to develop fluency.

SMALL GROUP TIME

Independent Reading Options

Trade Book Library

eStreet Interactive
www.ReadingStreet.com

Teacher's Guides available on the Leveled Reader Database.

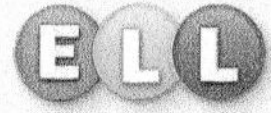

If... children need more support with phonics,
then... use the ELL activities on pp. DI•80 and DI•83 in the Teacher Resources section of the Digital Path.

Common Core State Standards

Literature 1. With prompting and support, ask and answer questions about key details in a text. **Literature 10.** Actively engage in group reading activities with purpose and understanding. **Foundational Skills 3.c.** Read common high-frequency words by sight (e.g., *the, of, to, you, she, my, is, are, do, does*). **Language 5.a.** Sort common objects into categories (e.g., shapes, foods) to gain a sense of the concepts the categories represent. **Language 5.c.** Identify real-life connections between words and their use (e.g., note places at school that are *colorful*). **Language 6.** Use words and phrases acquired through conversations, reading and being read to, and responding to texts.

If... children need more scaffolding and practice with vocabulary, **then...** use the ELL activities on p. DI•82 in the Teacher Resources section of the Digital Path.

1 Build Word Knowledge

Develop Vocabulary

POSITION WORDS Review the position words *in, out, up,* and *down* with children. Have them use the words in sentences.

Let's learn more position words. Remember, position words tell where things are located. Have children identify the position words in these sentences.

- The cat hid *under* the chair.
- The birds flew *over* the trees.
- He put the vase *on* the table.

Team Talk Have children work in pairs to use *under, over,* and *on* in their own sentences. They may then illustrate a position word and write a phrase or sentence to describe it.

2 Read

Kindergarten Student Reader *Cat and Dog Eat Together*

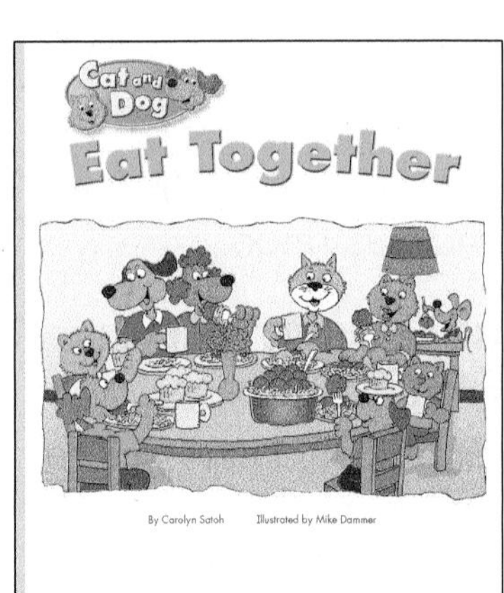

REREAD STORY Display the reader and have children read the title with you. Then have them read the story. Finally, have them reread the story aloud several times to build fluency.

EXTEND STORY Ask children to recall things Cat and Dog do in the story. What is something else Cat and Dog might do? Remind children to include at least one *Mm* word. Have them draw a picture and write a phrase or short sentence to go with the picture.

Advanced

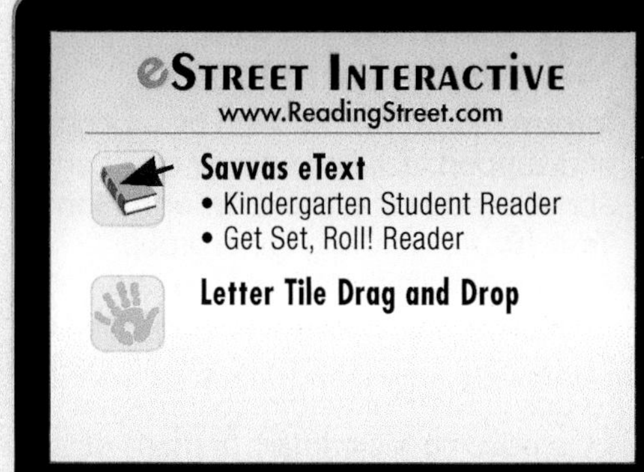

1 Build Word Knowledge

Develop Language

Display the Big Book *Smash! Crash!* and read the text on p. 30.

It's Wrecking Crane Rosie.
Rosie is huge.
Rosie is strong.
Rosie booms,
"FOLLOW ME."

- Ask children to read the text with you as you track the print.
- Point to the line, *Rosie booms.* Read this with me.
- What does the word *booms* mean? What is another word that means the same as *booms?* Why did the author choose the word *booms?*
- Continue the routine with the words *huge* and *strong.*
- Team Talk Have children work with a partner to replace key words in a sentence with simpler words or synonyms without changing the meaning of the sentence. Use sentence frames, such as the following.

  Rosie is _______.

2 Read

Get Set, Roll! Reader 5 *Zoom!*

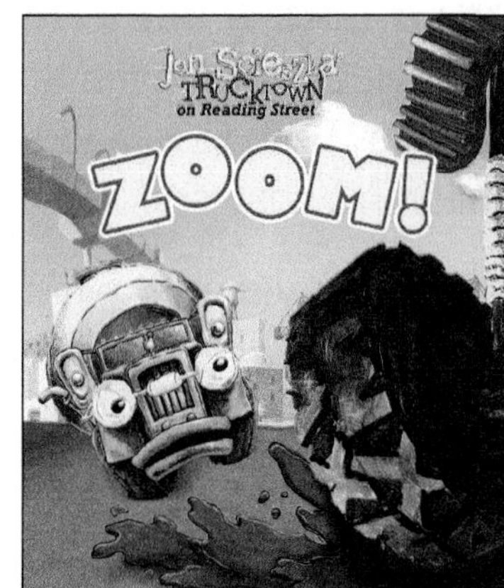

REVIEW HIGH-FREQUENCY AND REBUS WORDS Review the high-frequency and rebus words by asking children to spell the words with Letter Tiles. (*I, am, to, a, Melvin, Max, pour, zoom, mall, splash*)

REREAD Have children whisper read *Zoom!* as you listen to each child. Then have children take turns reading the story aloud.

3 Reread for Fluency

BUILD FLUENCY Have children read again with expression and accuracy. Encourage them to use self-correction techniques for any mistakes.

SMALL GROUP TIME

Independent Reading Options

Trade Book Library

eStreet Interactive
www.ReadingStreet.com
Teacher's Guides available on the Leveled Reader Database.

Common Core State Standards

Informational Text 1. With prompting and support, ask and answer questions about key details in a text. **Informational Text 10.** Actively engage in group reading activities with purpose and understanding. **Foundational Skills 3.a.** Demonstrate basic knowledge of one-to-one letter-sound correspondences by producing the primary or many of the most frequent sounds for each consonant. **Language 1.** Demonstrate command of the conventions of standard English grammar and usage when writing or speaking. **Language 2.** Demonstrate command of the conventions of standard English capitalization, punctuation, and spelling when writing. **Language 2.d.** Spell simple words phonetically, drawing on knowledge of sound-letter relationships.

1 Build Word Knowledge

Extend Phonics

FINISH *m* WORDS Say the word *mix.* Do you hear /m/ in *mix?* Listen carefully: /m/ *-ix.* Use Letter Tiles to spell the middle and ending sounds in *mix.* Have children tell you where to add the *m* Letter Tile to finish the word, or ask a volunteer to add the letter in the correct place. Then say the word together: /m/ *-ix.* Continue with these words: *mud, hem, mitt, dim, mat, ham, men, yum, mad, mom.*

WRITE SENTENCES Distribute paper and pencils to children. Today we are going to use what we know about letters and the sounds they stand for to write short sentences. I am going to say a sentence, and I want you to write the sentence. Listen carefully.

1. I am a little cat. **2.** I sit on a little mat. **3.** I am in a hat.

2 Text-Based Comprehension

Read

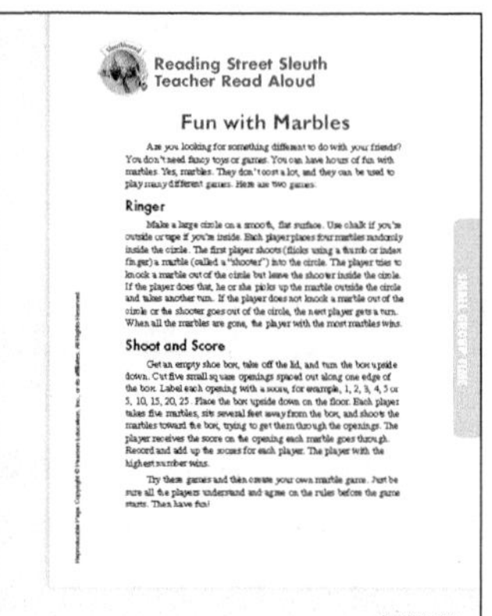
Reading Street Sleuth Teacher Read Aloud

Fun with Marbles

Ringer

Shoot and Score

READ ALOUD Read the Reading Street Sleuth Read Aloud, "Fun with Marbles," on p. SG•79 to children.

READ LIKE A SLEUTH! Encourage children to cite evidence from the text to support their answers. You may wish to reread sections of the text to verify children's answers.

Look for Evidence What is the goal of Ringer? What must the players do to win the game?

Ask Questions What questions do you have about Shoot and Score that the text doesn't answer?

Prove It! Performance Task Have children draw a picture that shows the setup for one of the marble games. Ask them to write one or two sentences that explain the picture using key details from the text. Have children read their sentences to you.

Teaching the Common Core State Standards This Week

The Common Core State Standards for English Language Arts are divided into strands for **Reading** (including **Foundational Skills**), **Writing**, **Speaking and Listening**, and **Language**. The chart below shows some of the content you will teach this week, strand by strand. Turn to this week's 5-Day Planner on pages 522–523 to see how this content is taught each day.

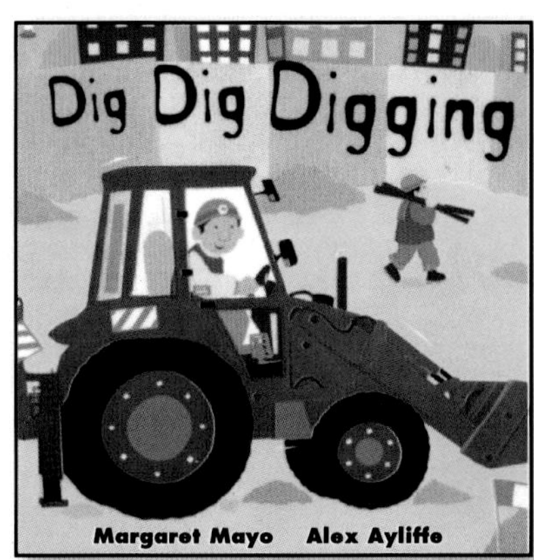

Common Core State Standards for English Language Arts

Reading Strand

- **Phonemic Awareness:** Initial and Final /t/
- **Phonics:** /t/ Spelled *Tt*
- **Text-Based Comprehension:** Classify and Categorize
- **High-Frequency Words:** *a, to*
- **Genre:** Nonfiction

Writing Strand

- **Writing Process:** Story
- **Plan**
- **Draft**
- **Revise**
- **Edit**
- **Share**

Speaking and Listening Strand

- **Content Knowledge:** Build Oral Language
- **Listening and Speaking:** Drama–Respond to Literature

Language Strand

- **Oral Vocabulary: Amazing Words** *scooping, swooshing, squelching, gobbling, spinning, rumbling*
- **Vocabulary:** Words for Sizes
- **Academic Vocabulary:** *classify and categorize, noun, draft, revise, drama, edit*
- **Conventions:** Nouns for Places and Things

Text-Based Comprehension

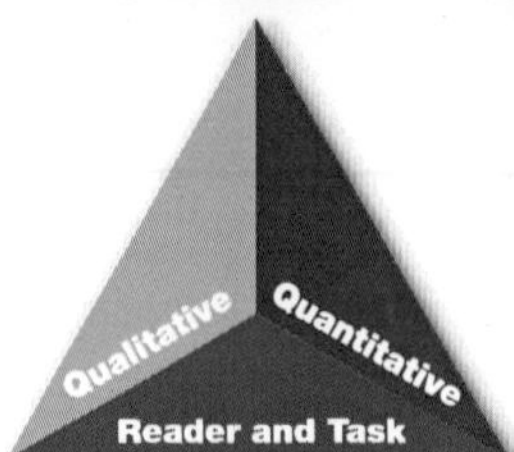

Text Complexity Measures

Use the rubric to familiarize yourself with the text complexity of ***Dig Dig Digging.***

Bridge to Complex Knowledge

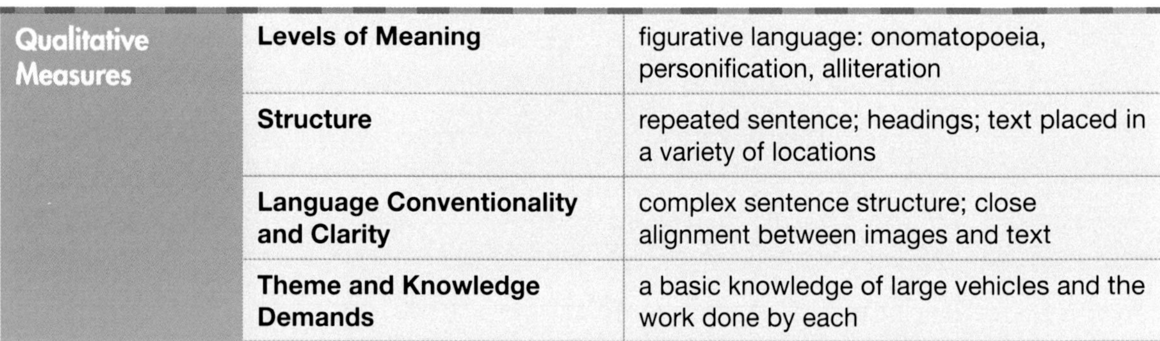

Qualitative Measures		
	Levels of Meaning	figurative language: onomatopoeia, personification, alliteration
	Structure	repeated sentence; headings; text placed in a variety of locations
	Language Conventionality and Clarity	complex sentence structure; close alignment between images and text
	Theme and Knowledge Demands	a basic knowledge of large vehicles and the work done by each

Reader and Task Suggestions

FORMATIVE ASSESSMENT Based on assessment results, use the **Reader and Task Suggestions** in Access Main Selection to scaffold the selection or support independence for children as they read ***Dig Dig Digging.***

READER AND TASK SUGGESTIONS

Preparing to Read the Text	Leveled Tasks
• Review the Amazing Words and have children use them to talk about the selection. • Review the use of headings and illustrations to introduce topics.	• **Theme Knowledge and Demands** For children ready to develop text-to-text connections, have them decide which trucks from *Smash! Crash!* belong on pages 10–11, 12–13, and 16–17 of the selection. • **Language Conventionality and Clarity** If children need support with the complex sentence structure, point out some of the repeated action words. Have children find and read other examples of repeated action words.

Recommended Placement This text is appropriate for placement as a read aloud at this level due to the qualitative elements of the selection.

Focus on Common Core State Standards ©

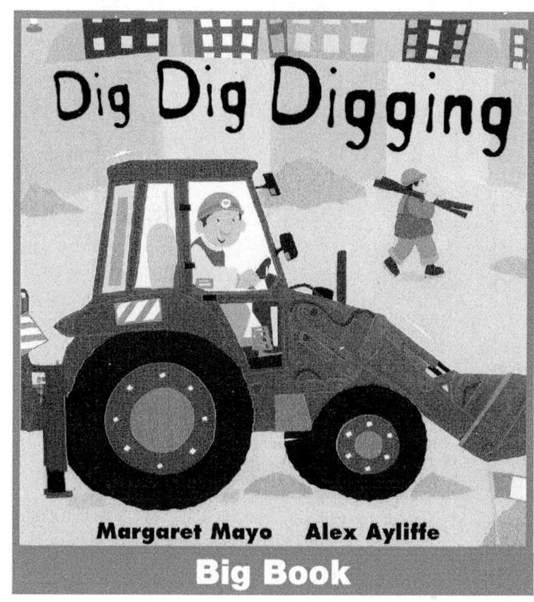

Text-Based Comprehension

 **Classify and Categorize**
CCSS Informational Text 7.,
CCSS Language 5.a.

Phonics

/t/ Spelled *Tt*
CCSS Foundational Skills 2.c.,
CCSS Foundational Skills 3.a.

Writing and Conventions

Genre: Story
CCSS Writing 3.,
CCSS Writing 5.

Conventions: Nouns for Places and Things
CCSS Language 1.,
CCSS Language 1.b.

Oral Vocabulary

Amazing Words

scooping	swooshing
squelching	gobbling
spinning	rumbling

CCSS Language 6.

Phonemic Awareness

Initial and Final /t/
CCSS Foundational Skills 2.d.,
CCSS Foundational Skills 2.e.

High-Frequency Words

a to

CCSS Foundational Skills 3.c.

Listening and Speaking

Drama—Respond to Literature
CCSS Speaking/Listening 1.a.,
CCSS Speaking/Listening 4.

Preview Your Week

How do machines help people work?

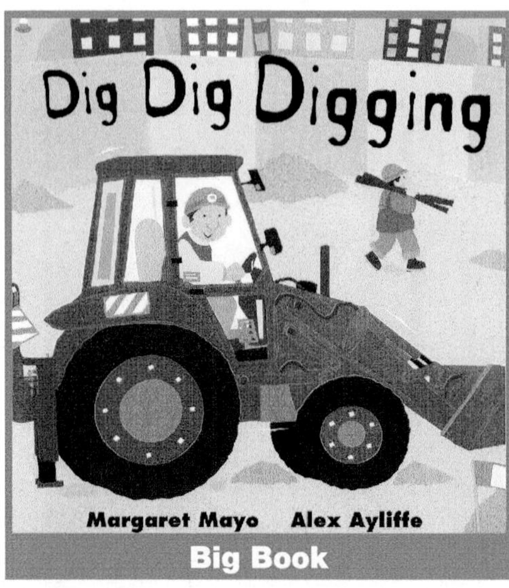

Genre: Concept Book

Phonics: /t/ Spelled *Tt*

Text-Based Comprehension: Classify and Categorize

Build Content Knowledge

KNOWLEDGE GOALS
Children will understand that working with machines

- helps get a lot of work done
- helps with many different jobs

BUILD ORAL VOCABULARY
This week, children will acquire the following academic vocabulary/ domain-specific words.

Amazing Words

scooping	swooshing
squelching	gobbling
spinning	rumbling

BUILD INDEPENDENT READERS
Children will enjoy becoming independent readers as they build decoding skills.

Get Set, Roll! Reader

Decodable Reader

OPTIONAL CONCEPT-BASED READING Use the Digital Path to access readers offering different levels of text complexity.

Concept Literacy

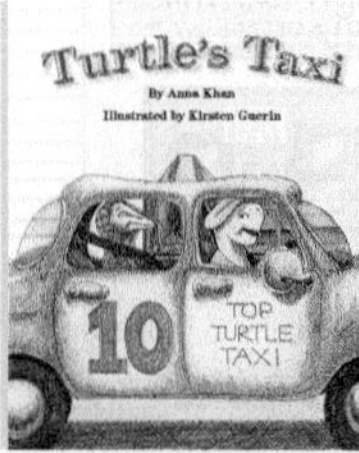

Listen to Me Reader

Student Reader

Independent Reader

This Week's Digital Resources

eStreet Interactive
www.ReadingStreet.com

Get Ready to Read

Big Question Video This video on the Digital Path introduces children to the unit question, *How do we live, work, and play together?*, and provides background for the reading children will do throughout the unit.

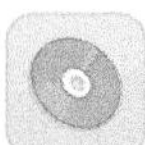
Background Building Audio CD This audio CD provides valuable background information about sounds from a construction site to help children read and comprehend the weekly texts.

Concept Talk Video Use this video on the Digital Path to build momentum and introduce the weekly concept of machines helping people.

Interactive Sing with Me Chart and Audio "Look at Them Go!," sung to the tune of "The Wheels on the Bus," introduces the Amazing Words with a catchy, concept-related song.

Phonics Songs and Rhymes Audio "Tick, Tick, Tock," sung to the tune of "Three Blind Mice," helps teach the phonics skill of consonant *Tt*/t/.

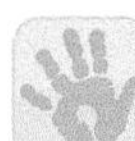
Letter Tile Drag and Drop Using this interactive tool, children click and spell words to enhance their newly learned phonics skills.

Savvas eText For phonics and fluency support, use the eText of the Decodable Reader; the Student Reader; and the Get Set, Roll! Reader on the Leveled Reader Database.

Read and Comprehend

Envision It! Animations Use this colorful animation on the Digital Path to explain the target comprehension skill, Classify and Categorize.

Savvas eText Go to Savvas SuccessNet and use the eText of the many student edition pages in *My Skills Buddy* with audio support.

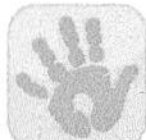
Story Sort Use the Story Sort Activity on the Digital Path after reading *Dig Dig Digging* to involve children in retelling.

Language Arts

Grammar Jammer Choose a whimsical animation on the Digital Path to provide an engaging lesson on Nouns for Places and Things that will capture children's attention.

Additional Resources

Teacher Resources DVD-ROM Use the following resources on the TR DVD or on Savvas SuccessNet throughout the week:

- Amazing Word Cards
- High-Frequency Word Cards
- Daily Fix-It Transparencies
- Reader's and Writer's Notebook
- Scoring Rubrics

This Week's Skills

Phonics
/t/ Spelled *Tt*

Comprehension
Skill: Classify and Categorize

Language
Vocabulary: Words for Sizes
Conventions: Nouns for Places and Things

Writing
Plan a Story
Draft a Story
Revise a Story
Edit a Story
Share a Story

5-Day Planner

DAY 1

Get Ready to Read

Content Knowledge 528
Oral Vocabulary: *scooping, swooshing, squelching, gobbling, spinning, rumbling*

Phonemic Awareness 530
Initial /t/
Monitor Progress
Check Phonemic Awareness

Phonics 532
/t/ Spelled *Tt*

Handwriting 534
Tt

High-Frequency Words 535
a, to

READ Decodable Story 6 536
Tam!

Read and Comprehend

Text-Based Comprehension 538
Classify and Categorize

Language Arts

Conventions 540
Nouns for Places and Things

Writing 541
Plan a Story

Listening and Speaking 542
Respond to Literature: Drama

Extend Your Day! 543

DAY 2

Get Ready to Read

Content Knowledge 544
Oral Vocabulary: *scooping, swooshing*

Phonemic Awareness 546
Initial /t/

Phonics 548
/t/ Spelled *Tt*
Monitor Progress
Check Sound-Spelling

Handwriting 550
Write Words with *Tt*

High-Frequency Words 551
a, to

READ Decodable Reader 6 552
Let's Go

Read and Comprehend

Text-Based Comprehension 554
READ *Dig Dig Digging*—1st Read
Think, Talk, and Write
Monitor Progress Check Retelling

Language Arts

Conventions 557
Names for Places and Things

Writing 558
Draft a Story

Vocabulary 559
Words for Sizes

Extend Your Day! 561

DAY 3

Get Ready to Read

Content Knowledge 562
Oral Vocabulary: *squelching, gobbling*

Phonemic Awareness 564
Final /t/

Phonics 566
/t/ Spelled *Tt*

Monitor Progress
Check Word Reading
High-Frequency Words

READ Kindergarten Student Reader 568
At the Toy Store

Read and Comprehend

Text-Based Comprehension 570
READ *Dig Dig Digging!*—2nd Read

Language Arts

Conventions 584
Review Nouns for People and Animals

Writing 585
Revise a Story

Listening and Speaking 586
Respond to Literature: Drama

Extend Your Day! 589

DAY 4

Get Ready to Read

Content Knowledge 590
Oral Vocabulary: *spinning, rumbling*

Phonemic Awareness 592
Review Initial and Final /m/

Phonics 593
Review /m/ Spelled *Mm*

Monitor Progress
Check Letter Recognition

Spelling 594
/t/ Spelled Tt

Get Set, Roll! Reader 6 595
READ *Ted*

Read and Comprehend

Text-Based Comprehension 596
Classify and Categorize
Review Setting
READ *Dig Dig Digging*—3rd Read

Language Arts

Conventions 598
Nouns for Places and Things

Writing 599
Edit a Story

Vocabulary 600
Words for Sizes

Extend Your Day! 601

DAY 5

Get Ready to Read

Content Knowledge 602
Review Oral Vocabulary

Monitor Progress
Check Oral Vocabulary

Phonemic Awareness 604
Review /t/

Phonics 605
Review /t/ Spelled *Tt*

Assessment 606

Monitor Progress
Check Word and Sentence Reading

Read and Comprehend

Let's Practice It! 608
Folk Tale

Assessment 610
Review Classify and Categorize

Language Arts

Conventions 612
Review Nouns for Places and Things

Writing 613
Share a Story

Wrap Up Your Week! 614

Extend Your Day! 615

Access for All

What do I do in group time?
It's as easy as 1-2-3!

1 TEACHER-LED SMALL GROUPS → 2 INDEPENDENT PRACTICE STATIONS → 3 INDEPENDENT READING

Small Group Time

Bridge to Common Core

SKILL DEVELOPMENT
- /t/ Spelled *Tt*
- Initial and Final /t/
- Classify and Categorize

DEEP UNDERSTANDING

This Week's Knowledge Goals

Children will understand that working with machines
- helps get a lot of work done
- helps with many different jobs

1 Small Group Lesson Plan

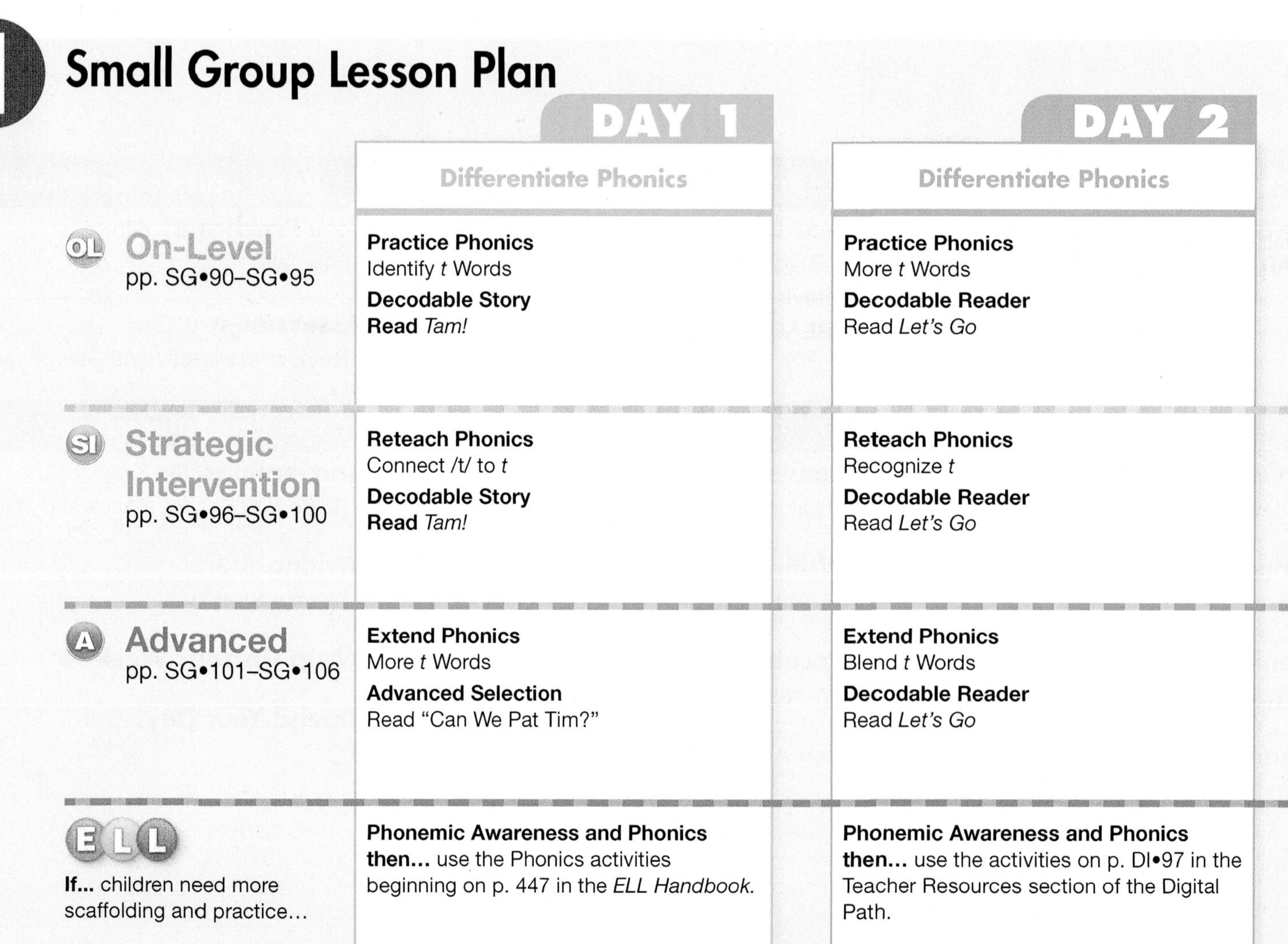

	DAY 1 Differentiate Phonics	DAY 2 Differentiate Phonics
OL On-Level pp. SG•90–SG•95	**Practice Phonics** Identify *t* Words **Decodable Story** **Read** *Tam!*	**Practice Phonics** More *t* Words **Decodable Reader** Read *Let's Go*
SI Strategic Intervention pp. SG•96–SG•100	**Reteach Phonics** Connect /t/ to *t* **Decodable Story** **Read** *Tam!*	**Reteach Phonics** Recognize *t* **Decodable Reader** Read *Let's Go*
A Advanced pp. SG•101–SG•106	**Extend Phonics** More *t* Words **Advanced Selection** Read "Can We Pat Tim?"	**Extend Phonics** Blend *t* Words **Decodable Reader** Read *Let's Go*
ELL **If...** children need more scaffolding and practice...	**Phonemic Awareness and Phonics** **then...** use the Phonics activities beginning on p. 447 in the *ELL Handbook.*	**Phonemic Awareness and Phonics** **then...** use the activities on p. DI•97 in the Teacher Resources section of the Digital Path.

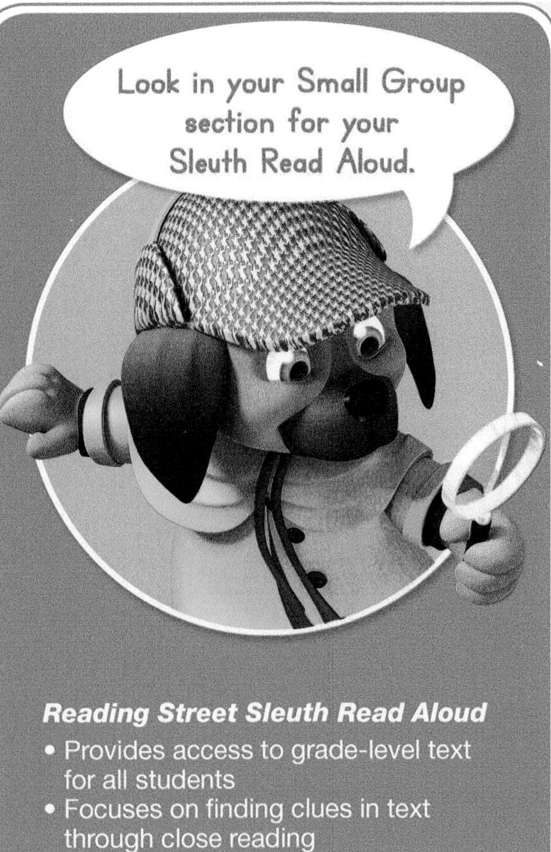

Reading Street Sleuth Read Aloud

- Provides access to grade-level text for all students
- Focuses on finding clues in text through close reading
- Builds capacity for complex text

Build Text-Based Comprehension

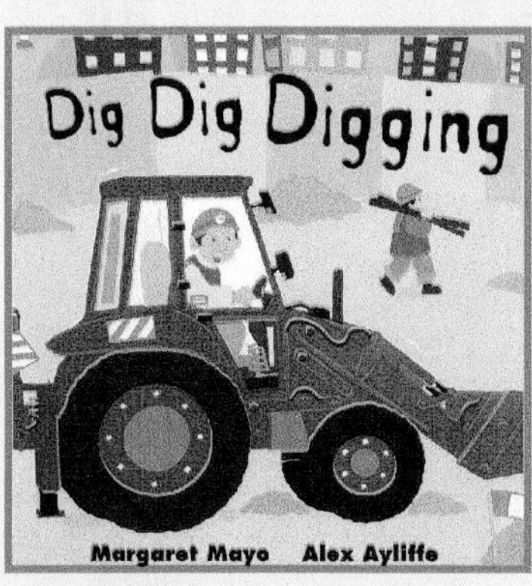

Dig Dig Digging

Optional Leveled Readers

Concept Literacy

Below Level

On Level

Advanced

Get Set, Roll! Reader

Decodable Reader

DAY 3	DAY 4	DAY 5
Differentiate Vocabulary	Differentiate Language	Differentiate Close Reading
Develop Vocabulary Practice Words for Sizes **Student Reader** Read *At the Toy Store*	**Build** Sentences and Words **Get Set, Roll! Reader** Read *Ted*	**Phonics** Spell *t* Words **Text-Based Comprehension** Read "Simple Machines"
Develop Vocabulary Reteach Words for Sizes **Student Reader** Read *At the Toy Store*	**Talk About** Sentences and Words **Get Set, Roll! Reader** Read *Ted*	**Phonics** Blend *t* Words **Text-Based Comprehension** Read "Simple Machines"
Develop Vocabulary More Words for Sizes **Student Reader** Read *At the Toy Store*	**Extend** Sentences and Words **Get Set, Roll! Reader** Read *Ted*	**Phonics** Write Sentences with *t* Words **Text-Based Comprehension** Read "Simple Machines"
Vocabulary **then...** use the ELL activities on p. DI•99 in the Teacher Resources section of the Digital Path.	**Developing Language** **then...** use the Language Workshops beginning on p. 306 in the *ELL Handbook.*	**Comprehension** **then...** use the ELL activities on pp. DI•98–DI•99 in the Teacher Resources section of the Digital Path.

2 Independent Stations

Practice Last Week's Skills

Focus on these activities when time is limited.

ACCESS FOR ALL
- Below-Level Activities
- On-Level Activities
- Advanced Activities

LISTEN UP!

Match initial sounds and pictures.

OBJECTIVES
- Identify words with initial /m/.

MATERIALS
- *Listen Up!* Flip Chart Activity 6
- Picture Cards: *drum, juice, man, moon, mop, mug, puzzle, tiger*

Modeled Pronunciation Audio CD

- ● Children find one /m/ Picture Card and say the word.
- ▲ Children find the /m/ Picture Cards and say the words.
- ■ Children tell objects whose names begin with /m/.

WORD WORK

Identify words with /m/ spelled *Mm*.

OBJECTIVES
- Identify words with /m/ spelled *Mm.*

MATERIALS
- *Word Work* Flip Chart Activity 6
- Alphabet Cards: *Mm, Pp, Tt, Ss*
- Picture Cards: *hen, mask, mitten, moose, top*
- Letter Tiles; paper, pencils

Interactive Sound-Spelling Cards

Letter Tile Drag and Drop

- ● Children find the *Mm* Alphabet Card and Picture Cards whose names begin with *Mm.*
- ▲ Children find the *Mm* Alphabet Card and Picture Cards and classroom objects whose names begin with *Mm.*
- ■ Children name an *Mm* Picture Card. Then they name other *Mm* words and use the Letter Tiles to spell the words.

LET'S WRITE!

Write a caption.

OBJECTIVES
- Write a caption.

MATERIALS
- *Let's Write!* Flip Chart Activity 6
- paper, pencils

Grammar Jammer

- ● Children choose a picture and write a word to go with the picture.
- ▲ Children choose a picture and write a short caption to go with the picture.
- ■ Children choose a picture and write a sentence about the picture. Then they tell a partner about the picture.

WORDS TO KNOW

Practice vocabulary.

OBJECTIVES
- Identify and use words for position.

MATERIALS
- *Words to Know* Flip Chart Activity 6
- Teacher-made word cards: *up, down, in, out*
- old magazines, paper, pencils, scissors, glue

Vocabulary Activities

Teacher Resources
- High-Frequency Word Cards for Unit 1, Week 5

- ● Children cut out a picture of something that is *in* and something that is *out.* Then they find the word cards that match the picture.
- ▲ Children cut out pictures of things that are *in, out, up,* and *down.* Then they write a label to tell the position each picture shows.
- ■ Children cut out pictures of things that are *in, out, up,* and *down.* Then they write sentences using the position words.

READ FOR MEANING

Use text-based comprehension tools.

OBJECTIVES

- Identify and describe a story character.

MATERIALS

- *Read for Meaning* Flip Chart Activity 6
- Little Book *Smash! Crash!*
- paper, pencils, crayons

Envision It! Animations
- Leveled eReaders

- ● Children choose a character in the Little Book. Then they draw a picture of the character.
- ▲ Children name a character in the Little Book. Then they draw a picture that shows what the character can do and label it.
- ■ Children name a character in the Little Book. Then they draw a picture of the character and write a sentence about the character.

LET'S MAKE ART!

Use art to demonstrate understanding.

OBJECTIVES

- Draw a picture.

MATERIALS

- *Let's Make Art!* Flip Chart Activity 6
- Retelling Cards for *Dig Dig Digging*
- construction paper squares, circles, and triangles of different colors
- paper, pencils, crayons, glue

- ● Children look at the Retelling Cards and use the shapes to make a machine that helps people.
- ▲ Children look at the Retelling Cards and use the shapes to make a machine that helps people. Then they write one or two words that describe the machine.
- ■ Children look at the Retelling Cards and use the shapes to make a machine that helps people. Then they write about the machine and tell what it does.

Manage the Stations

Use these management tools to set up and organize your Practice Stations:

Practice Station Flip Charts

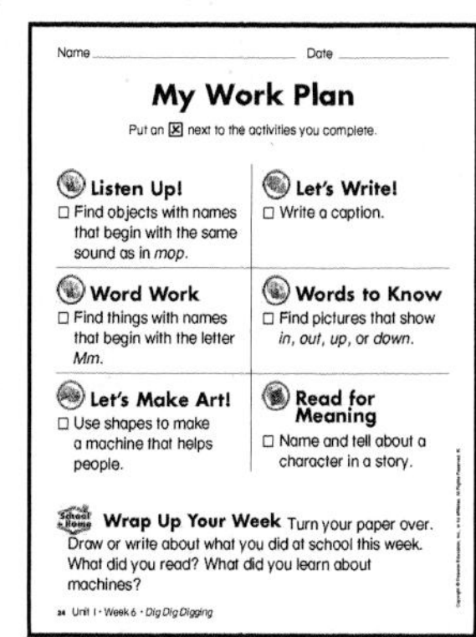

Name ______ Date ______

My Work Plan

Put an ☒ next to the activities you complete.

Listen Up!
☐ Find objects with names that begin with the same sound as in *mop*.

Let's Write!
☐ Write a caption.

Word Work
☐ Find things with names that begin with the letter *Mm*.

Words to Know
☐ Find pictures that show *in*, *out*, *up*, or *down*.

Let's Make Art!
☐ Use shapes to make a machine that helps people.

Read for Meaning
☐ Name and tell about a character in a story.

Wrap Up Your Week Turn your paper over. Draw or write about what you did at school this week. What did you read? What did you learn about machines?

24 Unit 1 • Week 6 • *Dig Dig Digging*

Classroom Management Handbook for Differentiated Instruction Practice Stations, p. 24

3 Independent Reading

Help children choose complex texts so that they can engage in paired and group reading and writing activities every day before, during, and after school.

Suggestions for this week's independent reading:

- *Trashy Town* by Andrea Zimmerman
- *A Truck Can Help* by Judy Kentor Schmauss

BOOK TALK Have pairs or groups of children actively engage in reading activities through a discussion of their independent reading for the week. Focus their discussions with the following ideas:

Key Ideas and Details

- Retell the text to your partner or group.
- Ask and answer questions about one detail of the text.

Craft and Structure

- Name the author and illustrator of the text.
- Talk about illustrations in the text.

Integration of Ideas

- With support, compare experiences of characters with those in other stories.
- Was this book like others I have read?

Savvas eText
- Student Edition
- Decodable Readers
- Get Set, Roll! Readers
- Leveled Readers

Materials from School or Classroom Library

DAY 1 at a Glance

Content Knowledge
Oral Vocabulary

Phonemic Awareness
Initial /t/

Phonics
/t/ Spelled *Tt*

Handwriting
T and *t*

High-Frequency Words
a, to

Text-Based Comprehension
Classify and Categorize

Conventions
Nouns for Places and Things

Writing
Plan a Story

Listening and Speaking
Respond to Literature: Drama

Materials

- Student Edition
- Truckery Rhymes
- Talk with Me/Sing with Me Chart
- Reader's and Writer's Notebook
- Alphabet Cards
- Picture Cards
- Phonics Songs and Rhymes Chart

Bridge to Common Core

INTEGRATION OF KNOWLEDGE/IDEAS
This week children read, write, and talk about how people and machines work together.

Texts This Week

- "Look at Them Go!"
- "Working in the Kitchen"
- *Dig Dig Digging*
- *At the Toy Store*
- "The Color Song"

Science Knowledge Goals
Children will understand that working with machines

- helps get a lot of work done
- helps with many different jobs

Start your engines!
Display p. 10 of *Truckery Rhymes.*

- Read aloud "This Is the Way" and track the print.
- Reread the rhyme and have children chime in as they wish.
- Ask children to identify the repeating words. (*dirt, scoop, dump, smooth*)

Truckery Rhymes

Content Knowledge

Zoom in on ©

People and Machines Working Together

CONCEPT TALK To explore the unit concept of All Together Now, tell children that this week they will listen, talk, sing, read, and write about machines helping people. Write the Question of the Week on the board, *How do machines help people work?* Track each word as you read.

Build Oral Language

TALK ABOUT PEOPLE AND MACHINES WORKING TOGETHER Display Talk with Me Chart 6A. This week we will be talking about how people and machines work together. The pictures show machines that help people every day. What machines do you see in these pictures? Have children respond in complete sentences.

We are going to learn six Amazing Words this week. Listen as I say the words: *scooping, swooshing, squelching, gobbling, spinning, rumbling.* Have children say each word as you point to the picture.

Talk with Me/Sing with Me Chart 6A

LISTEN FOR AMAZING WORDS Display Sing with Me Chart 6B. Tell children they are going to sing a song about the work that machines do. Read the title. Have children describe the picture. Sing the song several times to the tune of "The Wheels on the Bus." Listen for the Amazing Words: *scooping, swooshing, squelching, gobbling, spinning, rumbling.* Have children stand up and sing with you.

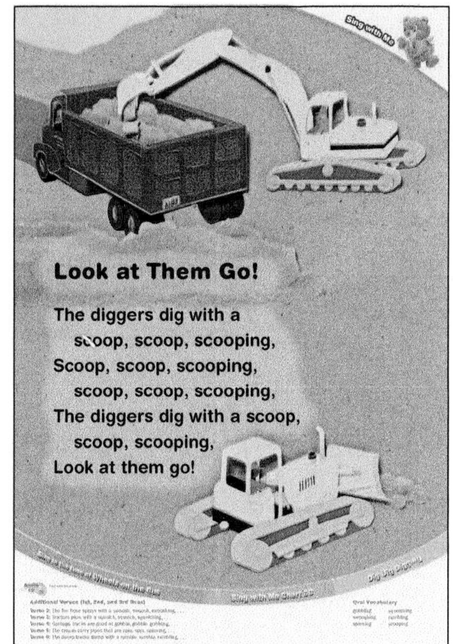
Look at Them Go!
The diggers dig with a
scoop, scoop, scooping,
Scoop, scoop, scooping,
scoop, scoop, scooping,
The diggers dig with a scoop,
scoop, scooping,
Look at them go!
Talk with Me/Sing with Me Chart 6B

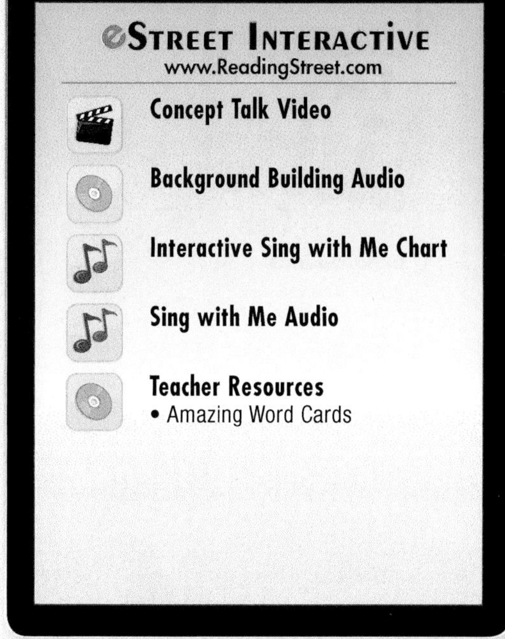
eStreet Interactive
www.ReadingStreet.com
Concept Talk Video
Background Building Audio
Interactive Sing with Me Chart
Sing with Me Audio
Teacher Resources
• Amazing Word Cards

Amazing Words

You've learned 030 words so far.

You'll learn 006 words this week!

scooping	swooshing
squelching	gobbling
spinning	rumbling

Access for All

SI Strategic Intervention

Support Vocabulary To help children understand the words *squelching* and *swooshing* in the song, explain that the words *squelch* and *swoosh* are meant to sound like the sounds that machines make as they do work.

ELL Support Additional ELL support and modified instruction is provided in the *ELL Handbook* and in the ELL Support lessons on *Teacher Resources DVD-ROM.*

Preteach Concepts Use the Day 1 Instruction on ELL Poster 6 to assess and build background knowledge, develop concepts, and build oral vocabulary.

Common Core State Standards
Foundational Skills 2.d. Isolate and pronounce the initial, medial vowel, and final sounds (phonemes) in three-phoneme (consonant-vowel-consonant, or CVC) words. **Also Foundational Skills 2.e.**

Phonemic Awareness

Let's Listen for

Initial Sounds

Read Together

- Point to the table. Say, "two tan tables." What sound do you hear at the beginning of those words?
- Find three things in the picture that begin with /t/.
- Name other words that begin with /t/.

READING STREET ONLINE
BIG QUESTION VIDEO
www.ReadingStreet.com

112 113

My Skills Buddy, pp. 112–113

Common Core State Standards

Foundational Skills 2.d. Isolate and pronounce the initial, medial vowel, and final sounds (phonemes) in three-phoneme (consonant-vowel-consonant, or CVC) words.* (This does not include CVCs ending with /l/, /r/, or /x/.) **Foundational Skills 2.e.** Add or substitute individual sounds (phonemes) in simple, one-syllable words to make new words.

Phonemic Awareness

Initial /t/

INTRODUCE Today we are going to learn a new sound. Listen carefully: /t/ /t/ /t/. Say it with me: /t/ /t/ /t/. Display the *taxi* Picture Card. *Taxi* begins with /t/ /t/ /t/, *taxi*. What sound does *taxi* begin with? Continue the routine with the *tent, tiger, toes,* and *tub* Picture Cards.

Picture Card

MODEL Have children look at the picture on pp. 112–113 of *My Skills Buddy.* Tell them they will be listening for a new sound—/t/. I see a target in the picture. What sound do you hear at the beginning of *target?* I hear /t/ at the beginning of *target.* The first sound in *target* is /t/. What other things do you see that begin with /t/?

GUIDE PRACTICE As children name example words from the picture, guide them in stating that /t/ is the beginning sound. Discuss some of the bulleted items on p. 112 of *My Skills Buddy.* Save the other bulleted items for discussion on Day 2.

Corrective feedback | **If...** children have difficulty naming words with /t/, **then...** say *target* again, emphasizing the beginning sound: /t/ /t/ /t/, *target.*

DISCRIMINATE INITIAL SOUNDS Have children stand by a desk or table. I will say a word. If the word begins with /t/, I want you to tap the table. If the word does not begin with /t/, hop on one foot. Listen carefully: *tape* (tap); *mug* (hop); *target* (tap); *four* (hop); *tag* (tap); *toast* (tap); *book* (hop); *today* (tap).

Corrective feedback | **If...** children cannot discriminate initial /t/, **then...** have them say /t/ /t/ /t/, *top.* When you say *top,* your tongue touches the top of your mouth behind your teeth. Say *top* with me: *top.* Repeat the activity with *time, tone, tap, Ted,* and *ton.*

SEGMENT Review segmenting sounds. Listen to the sounds in the word *top.* Say *top* with me: /t/ /o/ /p/. There are three sounds in *top.* Say the sounds with me again: /t/ /o/ /p/. What is the first sound in *top?* The first sound in *top* is /t/. Continue with *tip, tap, ten, Tom,* and *tub.*

MONITOR PROGRESS — Check Phonemic Awareness Words with Initial /t/

FORMATIVE ASSESSMENT Say *taxi* and *bed.* Have children identify which word begins with /t/. Continue with *tent, dog; toes, fan; tub, pig;* and *make, tell.*

If... children cannot discriminate initial /t/,

then... use the small-group Strategic Intervention lesson, p. SG•98, to reteach /t/.

Access for All

 Strategic Intervention

Support Pronunciation Be conscious of using the correct pronunciation of /t/. Many children will mistakenly use /d/ in place of /t/.

Support Phonemic Awareness Variations of the English /t/ exist in many languages. Work with children to help them produce the sharp /t/ when the letter *t* is at the beginning of the word. Show them how when you make the sound /t/, air comes out of your mouth.

Common Core State Standards

Foundational Skills 2.c. Blend and segment onsets and rimes of single-syllable spoken words. **Foundational Skills 3.a.** Demonstrate basic knowledge of one-to-one letter-sound correspondences by producing the primary or many of the most frequent sounds for each consonant.

Skills Trace

/t/ Spelled *Tt*

Introduce U1W6D1

Practice U1W6D2; U1W6D3

Reteach/Review U1W6D5; U2W1D4; U2W6D4

Assess/Test Benchmark Assessment U1

KEY: U=Unit W=Week D=Day

Teacher Tip

If children have difficulty distinguishing uppercase *T* from lowercase *t,* have them write the letters on separate index cards to keep on their desks for reference.

Phonics

Teach/Model

/t/ Spelled *Tt*

INTRODUCE Display the *Tt* Alphabet Card. Point to the turtle on the Alphabet Card. *Turtle* begins with /t/. Say the word with me: *turtle.* Write *turtle* on the board and point to the *t.* *Turtle* begins with /t/ spelled *t.* Now point to the letters *Tt* on the card. The sound for this letter is /t/. The names of these letters are uppercase *T* and lowercase *t.* What is the sound for this letter? What are the names of these letters?

Tt
turtle

Alphabet Card

MODEL Write "Tick, Tick, Tock" on the board. Point to the first *T.* When I see this letter, I think of the sound /t/. The first word is *Tick*—/t/, *Tick.* Point to *Tock.* This word begins with /t/ too. I know that when I see a *T,* the sound will usually be /t/. This word is *Tock.* The song we will sing is "Tick, Tick, Tock."

Guide Practice

GROUP PRACTICE Display Phonics Songs and Rhymes Chart 6. Teach children the song "Tick, Tick, Tock" sung to the tune of "Three Blind Mice." Play the CD and sing the song several times. I hear words that begin with /t/. When you hear a word that begins with /t/, clap your hands. Have volunteers come up and point to words that begin with *t.*

Tick, Tick, Tock
Tick, tick, tock; tick, tick, tock.
Grandfather Clock, Grandfather Clock.
He ticks and tocks every day and night.
He tells Pat the time
Any time he likes.
He ticks when it's dark
And he tocks when it's light.
Oh, tick, tick, tock.

Phonics Songs and Rhymes Chart 6

ON THEIR OWN Organize children into small groups. Have children in each group walk around the room together to find an example of an uppercase *T* and a lowercase *t.* Have them say /t/ when they see a *T* or *t.*

Blend Words

REVIEW To review the sound-spelling of /m/*Mm,* use the *Mm* Alphabet Card and the *map* Picture Card. What are the names of these letters? What is the sound for this letter? Then use this process to have children blend onset and rime.

CONNECT Write the letter *t.* What is the sound for this letter? The sound is /t/. Say it with me: /t/ /t/ /t/. When you see this letter in a word, what sound will you say?

MODEL Write the word *Tim* on the board.

- Touch under the letter *T.* What is the sound for this letter? Say it with me: /t/ /t/ /t/.
- The beginning sound in *Tim* is /t/. *Tim* ends with *-im.* When I blend the beginning sound /t/ and the ending *-im,* I make the word *Tim: /t/ -im, Tim.*
- Say the sounds with me: /t/ *-im.* Now let's blend the sounds together. Listen as I do it: /t/ *-im, Tim.* Say it with me: /t/ *-im, Tim.* Now you say it without me.
- Listen as I use *Tim* in a sentence: *Tim rides his bike.* Say it with me. Then have children use *Tim* in their own sentences.

GROUP PRACTICE Continue the process with the words below. We are going to practice some more words. Remember, first we say the beginning sound. Next, we say the ending. Then we blend the beginning sound and the ending to make the word.

Tam	Tom	tub	top	tip	tell

Corrective feedback	**If...** children have trouble reading a word, **then...** model blending onset and rime to read each word. Have children say it with you.

Support Phonics Children from various language backgrounds may pronounce /t/ as /d/. Model correct pronunciation by saying a short phrase or sentence with both /d/ and /t/, such as *Do take one.* Have children repeat the sentence, and then call their attention to the beginning sounds of the words *Do* and *take.*

Common Core State Standards

Foundational Skills 3.c. Read common high-frequency words by sight. (e.g., *the, of, to, you, she, my, is, are, do, does*). **Language 1.a.** Print many upper- and lowercase letters. **Also Foundational Skills 1.b.**

Access for All

Advanced

Practice Handwriting Have children draw pictures for words they know that begin with uppercase *T* or lowercase *t*. Then have them write or dictate labels for their drawings.

Handwriting

INTRODUCE Write *Tt* on the board. Words that begin with /t/ are written with an uppercase *T* or a lowercase *t*. Which letter is uppercase *T*? Which letter is lowercase *t*?

MODEL UPPERCASE *T* Write *Tom* on the board. Point to the uppercase *T*. This is the uppercase *T*. We use uppercase letters to begin sentences and names. Watch as I trace this uppercase *T* with my finger. Follow the stroke instructions pictured below.

GUIDE PRACTICE Have children write the uppercase *T* in the air. Use your finger to make an uppercase *T* in the air. Now write it on your hand.

MODEL LOWERCASE *t* Write *tip* on the board. Point to the lowercase *t*. This is lowercase *t*. Watch as I trace this lowercase *t* with my finger. Write another lowercase *t* on the board, following the stroke instructions. Again, have children write *t* in the air and on their hands.

GUIDE PRACTICE Have children use their Write-On Boards to write a row of uppercase *T* and a row of lowercase *t*.

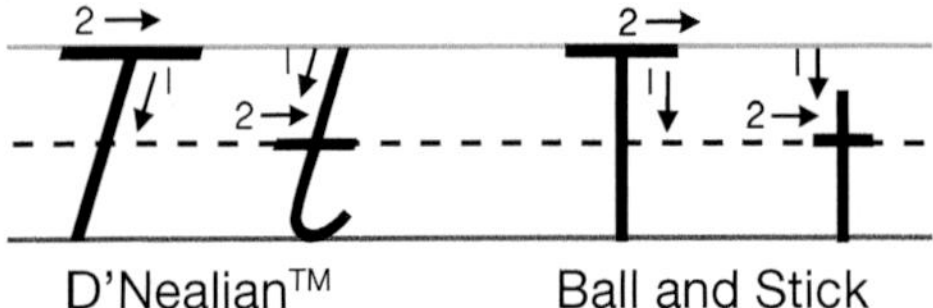

D'Nealian™ Ball and Stick

ON THEIR OWN Use *Reader's and Writer's Notebook,* pp. 61 and 62, for additional practice with *Tt*.

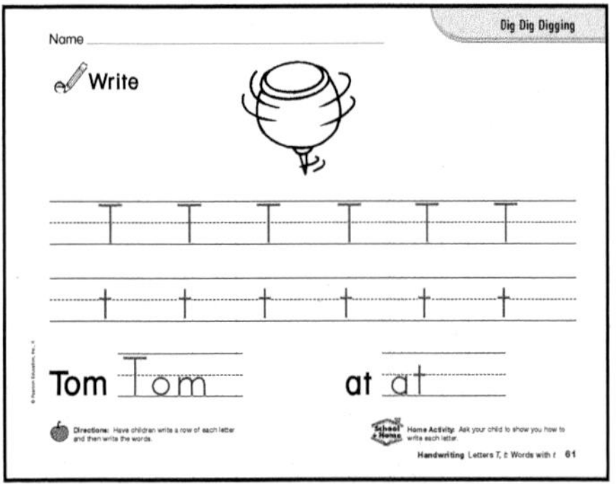

Reader's and Writer's Notebook, p. 61

Reader's and Writer's Notebook, p. 62

High-Frequency Words

INTRODUCE Use the routine below to teach high-frequency words *a* and *to.*

Routine Nondecodable Words

1. **Say and Spell** Some words we have to learn by remembering the letters rather than saying the sounds. We will say and spell the words to help learn them. Write *a* on the board. This is the word *a.* It has one letter. The letter in the word is *a.* Have children say and spell the word, first with you and then without you.
2. **Demonstrate Meaning** I can use the word *a* in lots of sentences. Here is one sentence: *I have a pencil.* Now you use the word in a sentence.

Repeat the routine with the word *to.*

Routines Flip Chart

eStreet Interactive
www.ReadingStreet.com

Teacher Resources
- Reader's and Writer's Notebook
- High-Frequency Word Cards

Common Core State Standards

Foundational Skills 3.a. Demonstrate basic knowledge of one-to-one letter-sound correspondences by producing the primary or many of the most frequent sounds for each consonant. **Foundational Skills 3.c.** Read common high-frequency words by sight. (e.g., *the, of, to, you, she, my, is, are, do, does*). **Foundational Skills 4.** Read emergent-reader texts with purpose and understanding.

Access for All

Strategic Intervention

Access Decodable Story Before reading, review /t/ words with children using the *taxi, ten, top,* and *tub* Picture Cards. After reading, ask children to point to and read the /t/ words in the story.

Decodable Story 6

Read *Tam!*

REVIEW Review the following high-frequency words by having children read each word as you point to it on the Word Wall.

I	am	to	a

TEACH REBUS WORDS Write *Tam* on the board. This is the word *Tam.* Name the letters with me: *T, a, m, Tam.* Continue with *turtle, walk, tent, turkey,* and *table.* Look for these words in our story today. There will be a picture above the word to help you read it.

READ Display Decodable Story 6, *Tam!* Today we will read a story about a turtle named Tam. What is the title of the story? Point to the title of the story. *Tam!* is the title of the story. What sound do you hear at the beginning of *Tam?* We will read many words that begin with /t/ in this story. Have children read Decodable Story 6 on pp. 63–64 in *Reader's and Writer's Notebook.*

Reader's and Writer's Notebook, pp. 63–64

Use the routine for reading decodable books to read Decodable Story 6.

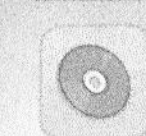

Teacher Resources
- Reader's and Writer's Notebook

Routine Reading Decodable Books

1. **Read Silently** Have children whisper read the story page by page as you listen in.
2. **Model Fluent Reading** Have children finger point as you read a page. Then have them reread the page without you.
3. **Read Chorally** Have children finger point as they chorally read the page. Continue reading page by page, repeating steps 1 and 2.
4. **Read Individually** Have children take turns reading aloud a page.
5. **Reread and Monitor Progress** As you listen to individual children reread, monitor progress and provide support.
6. **Reread with a Partner** Have children reread the story page by page with a partner.

Routines Flip Chart

Day 1 SMALL GROUP TIME • Differentiate Phonics, p. SG•89

OL On-Level
- **Practice Phonics** Identify *t* Words
- **Read** Decodable Story *Tam!*

SI Strategic Intervention
- **Reteach Phonics** Connect /t/ to *t*
- **Read** Decodable Story *Tam!*

A Advanced
- **Extend Phonics** More *t* Words
- **Read** Advanced Selection "Can We Pat Tim?"

Place English Language Learners in the groups that correspond to their reading abilities in English.

If... children need more support with **Phonics,**
then... use the Phonics activities beginning on p. 447 in the *ELL Handbook.*

Common Core State Standards
Language 5.a. Sort common objects into categories (e.g., shapes, foods) to gain a sense of the concepts the categories represent.

Comprehension

Envision It!
Classify and Categorize

READING STREET ONLINE
ENVISION IT! ANIMATIONS
www.ReadingStreet.com

114

115

My Skills Buddy, pp. 114–115

Zoom in on

Common Core State Standards

Language 5.a. Sort common objects into categories (e.g., shapes, foods) to gain a sense of the concepts the categories represent.

Skills Trace

Classify and Categorize

Introduce U1W4D1; U1W6D1; U4W5D1

Practice U1W4D2; U1W4D3; U1W4D4; U1W6D2; U1W6D3; U1W6D4; U4W5D2; U4W5D3; U4W5D4

Reteach/Review U1W4D5; U1W6D5; U2W1D4; U2W5D4; U4W5D5

KEY: U=Unit W=Week D=Day

Text-Based Comprehension

Classify and Categorize

READ Remind children of the weekly concept—People and Machines Working Together. Have children listen as you read aloud "Working in the Kitchen" on p. 539.

MODEL A CLOSE READ Model how to classify and categorize as a tool to build comprehension.

As I read this story, I think about how the things Jackie and Mom use are alike. They are all things that can be used to make blueberry muffins. That is one way the things are alike.

TEACH CLASSIFY AND CATEGORIZE When we **classify and categorize,** we put things into a group because the things are alike in some way. Good readers pay attention to ways in which things are alike in a story. This helps them understand the story.

Have children turn to pp. 114–115 in *My Skills Buddy.* Help me tell what kinds of toys the boy has. Guide children as they describe the first picture. Now look at the second picture. How are the toys in the first row alike? How are the toys in the second row alike?

GUIDE PRACTICE Reread "Working in the Kitchen." Have children tell why we can put flour, sugar, eggs, milk, and blueberries in a group.

- How are they alike? (They are what we use to make blueberry muffins.)
- How are a mixing bowl, a mixer, a blender, a muffin pan, and an oven alike? (They are all tools we need to make muffins.)

Teacher Read Aloud

Working in the Kitchen

The kids on Jackie's street are cleaning up the park on Saturday. Afterwards, they will have a snack at Jackie's house.

On Friday, Jackie and Mom work in the kitchen. Jackie measures flour and sugar into a mixing bowl. Mom mixes them with the mixer. Jackie puts eggs and milk in the blender. She presses the On button. Mom mixes everything together with blueberries. Jackie pours the batter into the muffin pan and puts the pan into the oven. The blueberry muffins smell good. Jackie and Mom put the bowls and pans in the dishwasher. Soon they are clean.

The next day the kids work hard in the park. Then they come back to Jackie's house. They are ready for those blueberry muffins!

Access for All

SI Strategic Intervention

Access Content Demonstrate how children can classify and categorize using a graphic organizer. Draw a two-column chart on the board. Label the columns *Things We Do at Home* and *Things We Do at School.* Have children draw pictures of activities and tape them in the proper column.

Academic Vocabulary

classify and categorize to place things that are alike in at least one way into a group

Bridge to Common Core

KEY IDEAS AND DETAILS

When children classify and categorize key ideas or details in a selection, they are analyzing how the ideas or details are alike. Answering classify and categorize questions about a selection helps children learn to use evidence from the text and illustrations to support the connections they describe.

Support Listening Comprehension Before listening, ask children to share experiences they have had working in the kitchen to make things to eat. After listening, have children compare their experiences to what they heard in the Read Aloud.

Conventions

Nouns for Places and Things

MAKE CONNECTIONS Today we listened to a story about Jackie and Mom making a snack at their home. The word *home* names a place. What are some places near your home? The word *snack* names a thing. What things do you like to eat for a snack? List children's responses. These words are called *nouns.*

TEACH Remind children that **nouns** name people, animals, places, and things. Today we are going to practice using nouns for places and things.

MODEL The word *school* is a noun because it names one place. *I go home after school. School* and *home* are nouns for places.

A crayon is one thing we use to draw pictures. The word *crayon* is a noun because it names one thing. A marker is another thing we can use to draw a picture. *Crayon* and *marker* are nouns for things.

GUIDE PRACTICE Show children the picture of the bakery from *Miss Bindergarten Takes a Field Trip,* pp. 6–7. I know this is a bakery, and I know a bakery is a place. So the word *bakery* is a noun for a place. Point to the cake on p. 9 of the Big Book. I know this is a cake, and I know a cake is a thing. So the word *cake* is a noun for a thing. Show children pictures of other places and things in the book. Have children name each noun as you show them the picture. Write the nouns on the board and echo read them with children. Have children choose a noun and copy it onto their Write-On Boards.

Team Talk **APPLY** Pair children and have them take turns telling a noun for a place they like to go. Have children illustrate their nouns and write or dictate labels.

Common Core State Standards

Writing 3. Use a combination of drawing, dictating, and writing to narrate a single event or several loosely linked events, tell about the events in the order in which they occurred, and provide a reaction to what happened. **Language 1.b.** Use frequently occurring nouns and verbs. **Also Writing 1., 7., 8.**

Access for All

Strategic Intervention

Support Conventions Have children connect the different kinds of nouns—person, animal, place, or thing—by asking them to stand when they hear a *thing* or *place* noun and clap when they hear a *person* or *animal* noun. Use the following list: *tiger, apple, teacher, home, lamp, pup, store, queen, park, car, mouse, girl.*

Academic Vocabulary 

noun a word that names a person, animal, place, or thing

Daily Fix-It

trucks are big

Trucks are big.

This week's practice sentences appear on *Teacher Resources DVD-ROM.*

Writing Process: Plan a Story

TEACH: GENERATE IDEAS Talk with children about narrative writing. Some writing tells stories, and sometimes writers tell stories about themselves. They may tell stories about things that have happened to them. They may tell stories about things they have done. They may write about things they like and tell us their opinion about the things.

We have talked about ways people live, work, and play together. As a class, we work and play together. Every day we do many different activities together. This week we are going to write a story about our favorite class activity.

MODEL: GENERATE IDEAS When we write a story about ourselves, the first thing we do is decide what our story will be about. What are some things we do together? Which of these activities do you like best? Write *Class Activities* on the board. Every morning we sing our "Hello!" song, and we fill in our weather chart. I like our morning activities! Write *sing "Hello!" song* and *fill in weather chart* under *Class Activities.*

GUIDE PRACTICE: GENERATE IDEAS Encourage children to generate other story ideas for the list. If necessary, prompt with questions such as these: What do we do when we sit in our Reading Circle? What do we do during Snack Time? What do we do when we take turns in Sharing Time?

Have children turn to p. 65 in *Reader's and Writer's Notebook* and draw pictures of class activities. When they are finished, add their activities to the list on the board. As a class, vote to find out which activity is the class favorite (for example, *go to music class*). Write the story idea *go to music class* on the board.

INDEPENDENT WRITING Have children draw a picture for the chosen story idea on p. 66 in *Reader's and Writer's Notebook.* Encourage them to make their picture as detailed as possible.

Name
Dig Dig Digging
Draw
Idea 1 | Idea 2 | Idea 3
Pictures will vary.
Writing Process Planning 65

Reader's and Writer's Notebook, pp. 65–66

Bridge to Common Core

TEXT TYPES AND PURPOSES

Today children plan a story.

Narrative Writing

Children are learning about the first step in the writing process. Generating a list of story ideas helps them see that they have many options for their narrative writing.

Throughout the week, children will learn about the steps in the writing process as they write a class narrative.

5-Day Plan

DAY 1	Plan a Story
DAY 2	Draft a Story
DAY 3	Revise a Story
DAY 4	Edit a Story
DAY 5	Share a Story

Common Core State Standards

Speaking/Listening 1. Participate in collaborative conversations with diverse partners about *kindergarten topics and texts* with peers and adults in small and larger groups. **Speaking/Listening 1.a.** Follow agreed-upon rules for discussions (e.g., listening to others and taking turns speaking about the topics and texts under discussion). **Speaking/Listening 1.b.** Continue a conversation through multiple exchanges. **Also Foundational Skills 3.a., Language 5.a.**

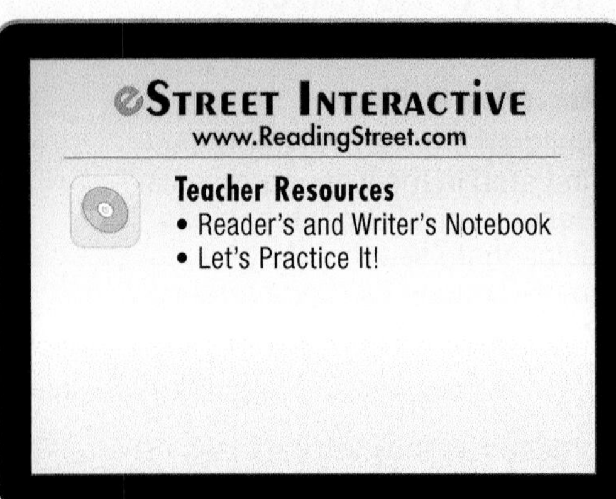

Listening and Speaking

Respond to Literature: Drama

TEACH In the book *Miss Bindergarten Takes a Field Trip,* we learned about places and the people who work in those places. Today we're going to act out some of the things we learned from Miss Bindergarten's field trip. We'll use our imaginations to pretend to be the workers in those places.

MODEL Open *Miss Bindergarten Takes a Field Trip* to pp. 6–7. I am going to pretend to work in a bakery. What shall I make? Pretend to put on oven mitts before putting dough in the oven. Now you make something for the bakery. Have children work in pairs to brainstorm ideas about something they would like to bake. Allow children to pantomime baking. Have them narrate their actions. Remind children to be good listeners by facing the speaker.

GUIDE PRACTICE Have children practice dramatizing other jobs in the following places from *Miss Bindergarten Takes a Field Trip:* fire station, post office, library. Refer children to the Rules for Listening and Speaking on pp. 1–2 of *Reader's and Writer's Notebook.* Remind them to face the speaker (actor) when they are listening to him or her.

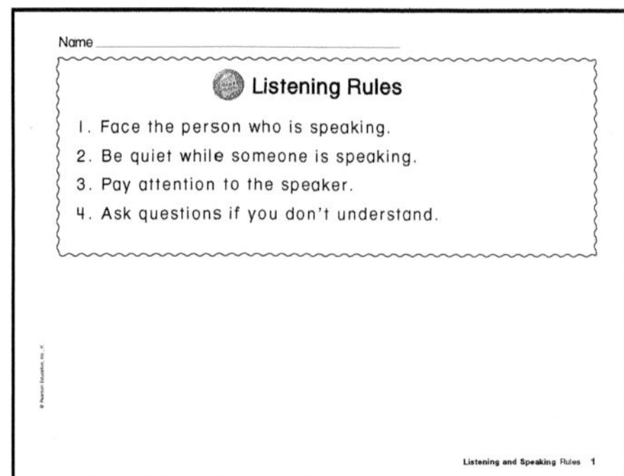
Name

Listening Rules

1. Face the person who is speaking.
2. Be quiet while someone is speaking.
3. Pay attention to the speaker.
4. Ask questions if you don't understand.

Listening and Speaking Rules 1

Reader's and Writer's Notebook, pp. 1–2

Wrap Up Your Day!

- ✔ **Content Knowledge** Today we talked about machines that help people do work. What kinds of machines have you seen before? How did they help people?
- ✔ **Homework Idea** Have children take home the Family Times Newsletter from Let's Practice It! pp. 11–12 on the *Teacher Resources DVD-ROM.*

Tomorrow we will read about machines that work all day.

Extend Your Day!

Science
Properties of Rocks, Soil, and Water

MATERIALS: four small rocks, four paper cups filled with soil, four paper cups filled with water, a small table covered with newspapers, three-column chart on chart paper or Graphic Organizer 5

DESCRIBE ROCKS, SOIL, AND WATER Have children sit in four groups in front of the table. As children pass one rock around their group, ask them to tell about the rock.

- What colors does the rock have?
- Is the rock heavy or light? smooth or rough?

Write children's responses on the chart under the word *Rock.* Have each group line up in front of a cup of soil. Tell each child in turn to look at and feel the soil. Have children offer responses for the chart. Record the responses in the *Soil* column. Repeat the process for the cups of water.

Rock	Soil	Water

Illustrate Locations

MATERIALS: paper, crayons

Ask children to think about where they can find rocks, soil, and water. Have them draw a picture of one of those places and write or dictate the name of that place on their illustration.

Comprehension
Classify and Categorize

MATERIALS: animal Picture Cards

GROUP ANIMALS Show children the animal Picture Cards. Ask them to help you separate the animals into groups (such as big and small animals or animals on land and in water). Hold up a card and have children tell you which group the animal belongs in. Place the animal Picture Card in the appropriate group. Repeat using two or more new categories.

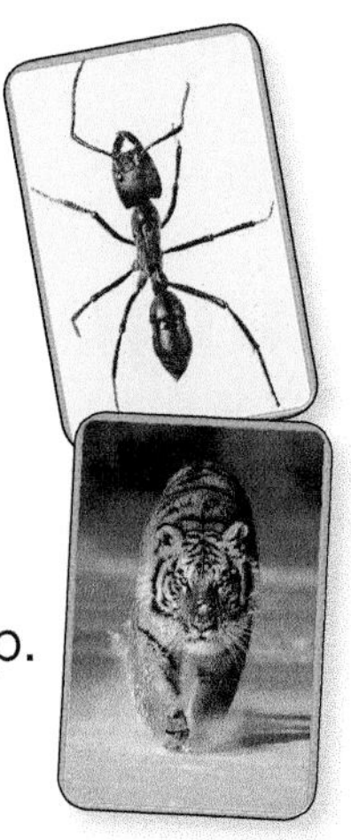

Phonics
/t/ *Tt* Words

MATERIALS: construction paper, crayons

MAKE /t/*Tt* SENTENCES Help children make up sentences with as many words that begin with /t/ as they can. Be creative. Write the sentences on the board and have children repeat the sentences with you. Then have them copy and illustrate the sentences.

Tina's toy takes its time.

DAY 2 at a Glance

Content Knowledge
Oral Vocabulary

Phonemic Awareness
Initial /t/

Phonics
/t/ Spelled *Tt*

Handwriting
Words with *Tt*

Text-Based Comprehension
Classify and Categorize

Conventions
Nouns for Places and Things

Writing
Draft a Story

Vocabulary
Words for Sizes

Materials

- Student Edition
- Truckery Rhymes
- Talk with Me/Sing with Me Chart
- Picture Cards
- Phonics Songs and Rhymes Chart
- Alphabet Cards
- Reader's and Writer's Notebook
- Big Book

Common Core State Standards

Speaking/Listening 1.a. Follow agreed-upon rules for discussions (e.g., listening to others and taking turns speaking about the topics and texts under discussion). **Language 6.** Use words and phrases acquired through conversations, reading and being read to, and responding to texts.

TRUCKTOWN on Reading Street

Start your engines!

Display p. 10 of *Truckery Rhymes.* Point to "This Is the Way." Who remembers what the trucks do in this rhyme? Yes, they scoop, dump, and smooth dirt. They also zoom and play! Let's read the rhyme together. Now have children act out the repeating words as the class reads the rhyme again. Give children the opportunity to say verses aloud and track the print.

Truckery Rhymes
Truckery Rhymes

Content Knowledge

Zoom in on

People and Machines Working Together

TALK ABOUT PEOPLE AND MACHINES WORKING TOGETHER On the board, write the Question of the Week, *How do machines help people work?,* and track the print as you read it aloud. Have children answer the question audibly and clearly and in complete sentences. To reinforce the concept and focus their attention, display Sing with Me Chart 6B. Tell children that they are going to sing a song about machines.

Look at Them Go!
The diggers dig with a
scoop, scoop, scooping,
Scoop, scoop, scooping,
scoop, scoop, scooping,
The diggers dig with a scoop,
scoop, scooping,
Look at them go!
Talk with Me/Sing with Me Chart 6B

Build Oral Language

LISTEN FOR AMAZING WORDS Listen for the Amazing Words *scooping* and *swooshing.* Read the title and have children describe the picture. Sing the song several times to the tune of "The Wheels on the Bus." Tell children to clap when they hear the Amazing Words *scooping* and *swooshing.*

Build Oral Vocabulary

Amazing Words Robust Vocabulary Routine

1. **Introduce the Word** Digger trucks are busy *scooping* up dirt. *Scooping* means digging something up to make a hole. What is our new Amazing Word for digging something up to make a hole? Say it with me: *scooping.*

2. **Demonstrate** Provide examples to show meaning. *The diggers are scooping up dirt.*

   Repeat steps 1 and 2.

   Introduce the Word You can hear water *swooshing* when it comes out of a hose. *Swooshing* means the sound of water or air rushing by. What is our new Amazing Word for the sound of water or air rushing by? Say it with me: *swooshing.*

   Demonstrate *A train makes a swooshing sound when it rushes by.*

3. **Apply** Have children use *scooping* and *swooshing* in complete sentences. Have them act out the words.

4. **Display the Words** Have children point to and name letters in *scooping* and *swooshing* that they recognize. Ask them what letters they see in both words.

Routines Flip Chart

USE AMAZING WORDS To reinforce the concept and the Amazing Words, have children supply the appropriate Amazing Word for each sentence.

She is ______ up dirt in the garden. (scooping)
Running water makes a ______ sound. (swooshing)

Amazing Words

scooping	swooshing
squelching	gobbling
spinning	rumbling

Access for All

 Strategic Intervention

Sentence Production If children have difficulty completing the sentences, model saying the complete sentence with the Amazing Word and then have them repeat it after you.

Support Vocabulary Demonstrate the Amazing Words with physical examples of scooping and swooshing. Use a toy shovel to scoop blocks out of a bin. Fill a small tub with water. Rapidly stir the water to make a swooshing sound. Let children participate in the demonstrations to reinforce their understanding.

Reinforce Vocabulary Use the Day 2 instruction on ELL Poster 6 to reinforce the meanings of high-frequency words.

Common Core State Standards

Foundational Skills 2.d. Isolate and pronounce the initial, medial vowel, and final sounds (phonemes) in three-phoneme (consonant-vowel-consonant, or CVC) words. **Also Foundational Skills 2.e.**

Phonemic Awareness

Let's Listen for Initial Sounds

- Point to the table. Say, "two tan tables." What sound do you hear at the beginning of those words?
- Find three things in the picture that begin with /t/.
- Name other words that begin with /t/.

Read Together

READING STREET ONLINE
BIG QUESTION VIDEO
www.ReadingStreet.com

112 113

My Skills Buddy, pp. 112–113

Common Core State Standards

Foundational Skills 2.d. Isolate and pronounce the initial, medial vowel, and final sounds (phonemes) in three-phoneme (consonant-vowel-consonant, or CVC) words.* (This does not include CVCs ending with /l/, /r/, or /x/.) **Also Foundational Skills 2.a.**

Phonemic Awareness

Initial /t/

TEACH Display the *taxi* Picture Card. This is a taxi. *Taxi* begins with /t/. What is this? What sound does it begin with?

Picture Card

MODEL Display the *top* Picture Card. This is a top. Listen carefully to the sounds: /t/ *-op.* I hear /t/ at the beginning of *top.* What is the beginning sound you hear in *top?* Say it with me: /t/ /t/ /t/, *top.* Continue the routine with the *tiger* and *tent* Picture Cards.

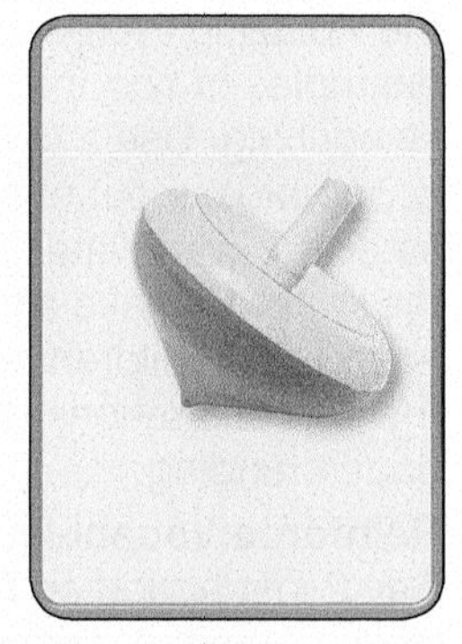
Picture Card

GUIDE PRACTICE Have children look at the picture on *My Skills Buddy,* pp. 112–113. Remember that we can see many things that begin with /t/. We found a target. What other things that begin with /t/ did we find in this picture? Name other things that begin like *target.* Discuss the bulleted points on p. 112 that were not discussed on Day 1.

Corrective feedback **If...** children cannot discriminate initial /t/, **then...** have them enunciate /t/ as they segment words that begin with /t/. Listen as I segment a word: /t/ /a/ /p/, *tap.* What sound do you hear at the beginning of *tap?* I hear /t/ at the beginning of *tap.* Continue with the following words: *Tim, tag, Ted, tip.*

ON THEIR OWN Display Phonics Songs and Rhymes Chart 6, "Tick, Tick, Tock." Remind children of the tune "Three Blind Mice." Sing the song several times. Have children join in. This time I want you to clap your hands each time you hear a word that begins with /t/.

Tick, Tick, Tock
Tick, tick, tock; tick, tick, tock.
Grandfather Clock, Grandfather Clock.
He ticks and tocks every day and night.
He tells Pat the time
Any time he likes.
He ticks when it's dark
And he tocks when it's light.
Oh, tick, tick, tock.

Phonics Songs and Rhymes Chart 6

REVIEW RHYMING WORDS Let's listen to some words that begin with different sounds but have the same middle and ending sounds. Remember, words that have the same middle and ending sounds are rhyming words. Listen to the sounds in this word: /m/ /a/ /t/, *mat.* Say it with me: /m/ /a/ /t/, *mat.* Now listen to these words: /k/ /a/ /t/, *cat;* /t/ /o/ /p/, *top.* Which word rhymes with *mat: cat* or *top?* (*cat*) Yes, *cat* rhymes with *mat.* Let's do some more. Continue the activity with the following words: *map, cap, tub; hot, lap, pot; jet, men, ten.*

Extend Language Mechanical sounds are verbalized in different ways in different languages. In English, we use the words *tick* and *tock* to represent the sounds that a clock makes. Have children practice saying these words, emphasizing the initial /t/.

Common Core State Standards

Foundational Skills 2.c. Blend and segment onsets and rimes of single-syllable spoken words. **Foundational Skills 3.a.** Demonstrate basic knowledge of one-to-one letter-sound correspondences by producing the primary or many of the most frequent sounds for each consonant.

Alphabet Card

Picture Card

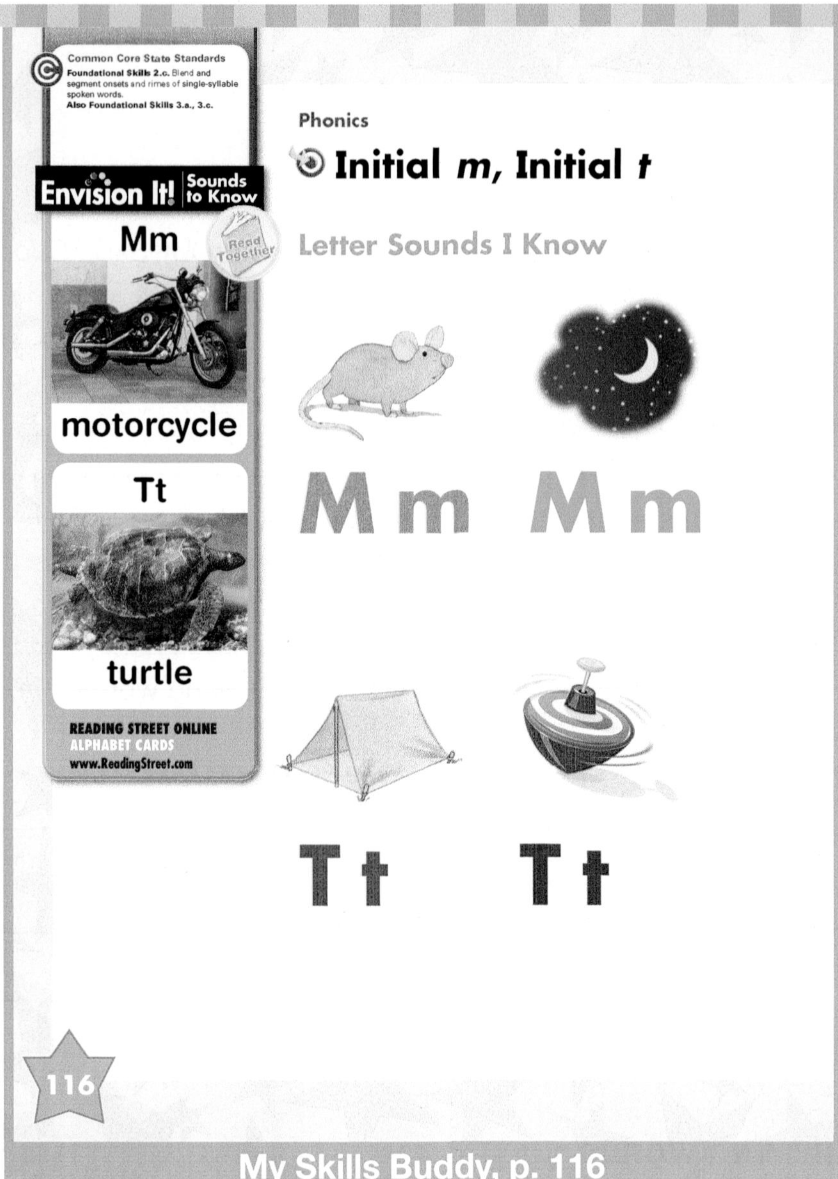

My Skills Buddy, p. 116

Phonics

Teach/Model

/t/ Spelled *Tt*

TEACH /t/*Tt* Point to the turtle on the *Tt* Alphabet Card. What is this? What sound does *turtle* begin with? *Turtle* begins with /t/. Write *turtle* on the board and point to the letter *t.* The letter for /t/ is *t.* What letter does *turtle* begin with?

MODEL Display the *ten* Picture Card. What is this? Say the sounds in *ten* with me: /t/ /e/ /n/, *ten.* Where do you hear /t/ in *ten?* (at the beginning) Write *ten* on the board. Point to *t* as you say /t/ *-en.* Continue with the words *tub, tab,* and *Ted.*

Guide Practice

GROUP PRACTICE Have children open *My Skills Buddy* to p. 116. Review the letters *Mm* and *Tt.* Then point to the tent. What is this? (*tent*) What sound does *tent* begin with? Say it with me: /t/ /t/ /t/, *tent.* Point to the top. This is a top. What sound does *top* begin with? (/t/) What letter stands for /t/ in *tent* and *top?* (*Tt*) Repeat the routine for /m/*Mm* with the *mouse* and *moon* pictures.

Apply

CONNECT Write the letter *t.* What is the sound for this letter? The sound is /t/. Say it with me: /t/ /t/ /t/. When you see this letter in a word, what sound will you say?

MODEL Write the word *top* on the board.

- Point to *t* and ask: What is the sound for this letter? Say it with me: /t/ /t/ /t/. The beginning sound in *top* is /t/.
- *Top* ends with *-op.* When I blend the beginning sound /t/ and the ending *-op,* I make the word *top:* /t/ *-op, top.*
- Say the sounds with me: /t/ *-op.* Now let's blend the sounds together. Say it with me: /t/ *-op, top.* Now you say it without me.
- Listen as I use *top* in a sentence: *Tim spins a top.* Say it with me. Then have children use *top* in their own sentences.

GROUP PRACTICE Continue with these words:

tug	tap	Tom	tip	tell	Tim

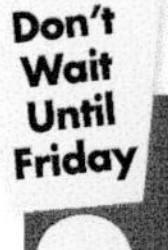

Don't Wait Until Friday **MONITOR PROGRESS**

Check Sound-Spelling /t/ Spelled *Tt*

FORMATIVE ASSESSMENT Have each child write the letters *Tt* on a card. I am going to read some words. When you hear a word with /t/, hold up your *Tt* card. Say: *table, like, team, mall, beat, flat, let, real, tool, back, lot.*

If... children cannot discriminate /t/ words,

then... use the small-group Strategic Intervention lesson, p. SG•99, to reteach /t/.

Continue to monitor children's progress during the week so that children can be successful with the Day 5 Assessment.

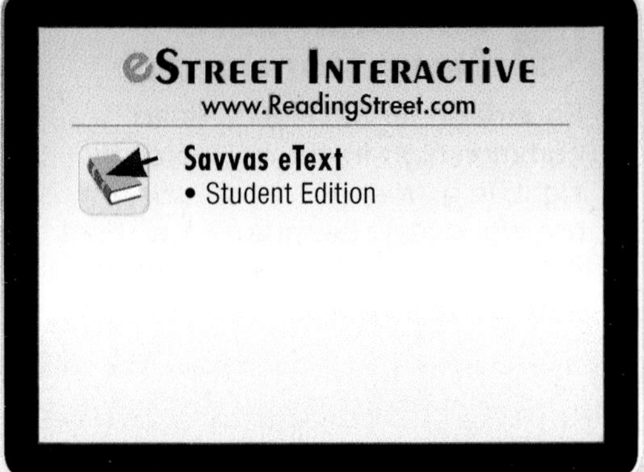

Access for All

SI Strategic Intervention

Support Phonics For more practice with *Mm* and *Tt,* continue the Group Practice activity using these Picture Cards: *map, mop, mug, tiger, toes, tub.*

Access Content Some children's home languages may share with English /t/ spelled *Tt* or /m/ spelled *Mm.* Find examples from their home languages to practice /t/*Tt* and /m/*Mm,* such as the following: *madre* (Spanish, *mother*); *mapa* (Polish, *map*); *tabela* (Polish, *table*); *teatro* (Spanish, *theater*). To extend vocabulary, choose examples that have the same initial sound in the English translation.

Common Core State Standards

Foundational Skills 3.c. Read common high-frequency words by sight. (e.g., *the, of, to, you, she, my, is, are, do, does*). **Language 1.a.** Print many upper- and lowercase letters. **Also Language 1.b.**

Handwriting

Write Words with *Tt*

REVIEW Write *Tom* on the board. This is the word *Tom.* I use an uppercase *T* for the first letter in *Tom* because it is a name. Watch me make an uppercase *T.* Write another uppercase *T* on the board using the instructional strokes indicated in the model.

Write *tin* on the board. This is the word *tin.* I use a lowercase *t* for the first letter in *tin.* Watch me make a lowercase *t.* Write another lowercase *t* on the board using the proper instructional strokes.

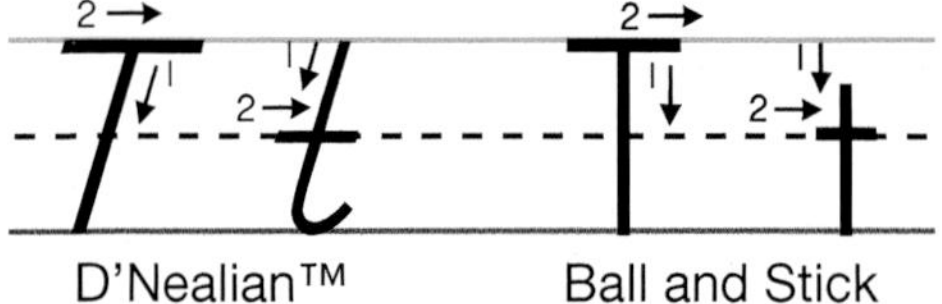

D'Nealian™ Ball and Stick

GUIDE PRACTICE Have children use their Write-On Boards to make a row of uppercase *T* and a row of lowercase *t.* Circulate around the room, assisting children as necessary. Write the following words on the board and have children copy them: *top, at, tub.*

High-Frequency Words

Words I Can Read

to

a

Sentences I Can Read

1. I am a little .

2. I to .

117

My Skills Buddy, p. 117

High-Frequency Words

READ WORDS Have children turn to p. 117 of *My Skills Buddy.* Read the high-frequency words *to* and *a* together. Then have children point to each word and read it themselves.

Remind children that words can be spoken (say the word *to*) and written or printed (point to the word *to* on the page).

READ SENTENCES Read the sentences on *My Skills Buddy,* p. 117, together to read the new high-frequency words in context.

Team Talk Pair children and have them take turns reading each of the sentences aloud.

ON THEIR OWN Use *Reader's and Writer's Notebook,* p. 67, for additional practice with this week's high-frequency words.

Access for All

SI Strategic Intervention

Support High-Frequency Words Connect the high-frequency word *to* to children's work with initial *t.* What sound does *to* begin with? (/t/) *To* begins with /t/. What is the letter for /t/? (*Tt*) Have children copy a row of *to* on their Write-On Boards, using the Word Wall as a reference.

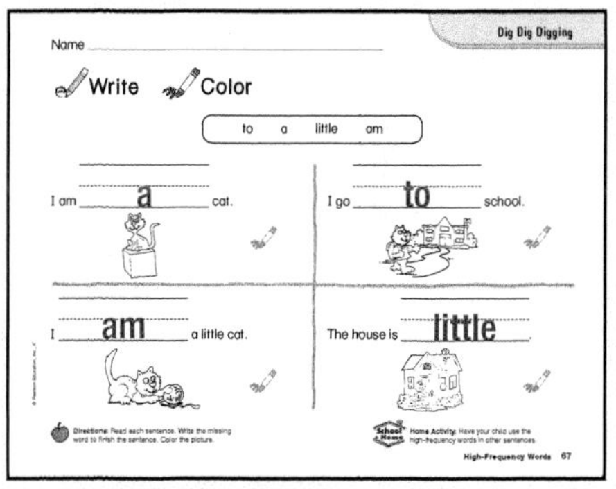
Name

Dig Dig Digging

Write Color

to a little am

I am a cat.

I go to school.

I am a little cat.

The house is little.

Reader's and Writer's Notebook, p. 67

High-Frequency Words Have children practice the high-frequency word *to* by sharing places they like to go. Have them use the following sentence frame: *I like to go to* ________.

Common Core State Standards
Literature 6. With prompting and support, name the author and illustrator of a story and define the role of each in telling the story. **Foundational Skills 3.a.** Demonstrate basic knowledge of one-to-one letter-sound correspondences by producing the primary or many of the most frequent sounds for each consonant. **Foundational Skills 3.c.** Read common high-frequency words by sight. (e.g., *the, of, to, you, she, my, is, are, do, does*). **Foundational Skills 4.** Read emergent-reader texts with purpose and understanding.

Access for All

SI Strategic Intervention

Support Phonemic Awareness
Before children read *Let's Go,* review /t/ words with the following Picture Cards: *taxi, tent, tiger, toes.*

Decodable Reader 6

Read *Let's Go*

REVIEW Review the previously taught high-frequency words. Have children read each word as you point to it on the Word Wall.

I	to	a

CONCEPTS OF PRINT Have children turn to Decodable Reader 6, *Let's Go,* on p. 118 of *My Skills Buddy.* Today we will read about a boy who goes to the Wild Animal Park. Point to the title of the story. The title of the story is *Let's Go.* What is the title of the story? Point to the name of the author. The author's name is Liz Cristie. *Let's Go* was written by Liz Cristie. What does an author do? The illustrator's name is Larry Jordon. What does an illustrator do?

READ Use the routine for reading decodable books to read Decodable Reader 6.

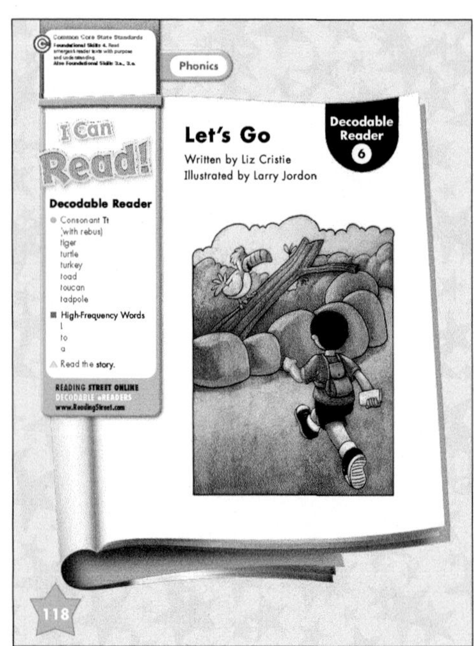

My Skills Buddy, pp. 118–125

I walk to a tiger.

I walk to a turtle.

I walk to a turkey.

I walk to a toad.
I walk to a toucan.

I walk to a tadpole.

I walk home.

eStreet Interactive
www.ReadingStreet.com

Savvas eText
• Student Edition

Routine Reading Decodable Books

1. **Read Silently** Have children whisper read the book page by page as you listen in.
2. **Model Fluent Reading** Have children finger point as you read a page. Then have them reread the page without you.
3. **Read Chorally** Have children finger point as they chorally read the page. Continue reading page by page, repeating steps 1 and 2.
4. **Read Individually** Have children take turns reading aloud a page.
5. **Reread and Monitor Progress** As you listen to individual children reread, monitor progress and provide support.
6. **Reread with a Partner** Have children reread the book page by page with a partner.

Routines Flip Chart

Access for All

Advanced

Practice Phonics Display the *Tt* Alphabet Card. Have children name the sound and then the letter name.

Day 2 SMALL GROUP TIME • Differentiate Phonics, p. SG•89

OL On-Level	SI Strategic Intervention	A Advanced
• **Practice Phonics** More *t* Words • **Read** Decodable Reader *Let's Go*	• **Reteach Phonics** Recognize *t* • **Read** Decodable Reader *Let's Go*	• **Extend Phonics** Blend *t* Words • **Read** Decodable Reader *Let's Go*

Place English Language Learners in the groups that correspond to their reading abilities in English.

If... children need more support with **Phonics**,
then... use the activities on p. DI•97 in the Teacher Resources section of the Digital Path.

Common Core State Standards

Informational Text 2. With prompting and support, identify the main topic and retell key details of a text. **Informational Text 7.** With prompting and support, describe the relationship between illustrations and the text in which they appear (e.g., what person, place, thing, or idea in the text an illustration depicts). **Also Informational Text 5., 6., 10.**

Text-Based Comprehension

Introduce Main Selection

CONCEPTS OF PRINT Display the cover of *Dig Dig Digging.* Margaret Mayo and Alex Ayliffe are the authors. What do authors do? (write the book)

GENRE A concept book teaches readers about a concept using illustrations and text. Let's read the selection to learn about machines.

PREVIEW AND PREDICT Display *Dig Dig Digging.* What do you see on the cover? I see a bulldozer and a man with boards. The title is *Dig Dig Digging.* What do you think this book will be about? Take children on a walk through the book. Have them describe the illustrations.

SET PURPOSE Remind children of the Question of the Week: *How do machines help people work?* Have children listen as you read.

MODEL Read *Dig Dig Digging* with expression to build interest in the text.

Routine Read for Understanding 

Deepen understanding by reading the selection multiple times.

1. **First Read**—Read the entire selection aloud to build interest in the text.
2. **Second Read**—Use the **Develop Vocabulary** notes on pages 572–583.
3. **Third Read**—Use the **Develop Comprehension** notes on pages 572–583.

Retell

CHECK RETELLING Have children turn to p. 126 of *My Skills Buddy.* Walk through the retelling boxes as children retell *Dig Dig Digging.* After they retell the selection as a group, have children draw a picture to retell their favorite part. Have them write or dictate a word or sentence to go with the picture.

Check Retelling

If... children have difficulty retelling the selection,

then... go through the selection one page at a time, and ask children to tell what they learned in their own words.

My Skills Buddy, p. 126

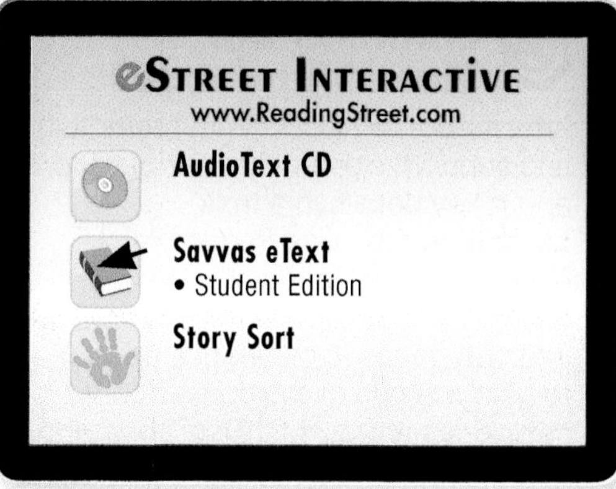

Access for All

SI Strategic Intervention

Access Content Have children practice retelling the selection by first working with a partner.

Retelling Plan

- ☑ **Week 1** Assess Advanced students.
- ☑ **Week 2** Assess On-Level students.
- ☑ **Week 3** Assess Strategic Intervention students.
- ☑ **Week 4** Assess Advanced students.
- ☑ **Week 5** Assess On-Level students.
- ☑ **This week assess Strategic Intervention students.**

Scoring Rubric Expository Retelling

	4	3	2	1
Connections	Makes connections and generalizes beyond the text	Makes connections to other events, texts, or experiences	Makes a limited connection to another event, text, or experience	Makes no connection to another event, text, or experience
Author's Purpose	Elaborates on author's purpose	Tells author's purpose with some clarity	Makes some connection to author's purpose	Makes no connection to author's purpose
Topic	Describes the main topic	Identifies the main topic with some details early in retelling	Identifies the main topic	Retelling has no sense of topic
Important Ideas	Gives accurate information about ideas using key vocabulary	Gives accurate information about ideas with some key vocabulary	Gives limited or inaccurate information about ideas	Gives no information about ideas
Conclusions	Draws conclusions and makes inferences to generalize beyond the text	Draws conclusions about the text	Is able to tell some learnings about the text	Is unable to draw conclusions or make inferences about the text

Cognates Help children understand that other languages have words for *machine,* such as *macchina* (Italian), *machine* (French), *makina* (Filipino), *máquina* (Spanish, Portuguese), and *maschine* (German), that are similar to the English word.

Common Core State Standards

Informational Text 1. With prompting and support, ask and answer questions about key details in a text. **Language 1.b.** Use frequently occurring nouns and verbs. **Language 5.a.** Sort common objects into categories (e.g., shapes, foods) to gain a sense of the concepts the categories represent. **Also Speaking/ Listening 2.**

Access for All

Advanced

Look Back and Write Let children write, dictate, or draw their own responses to the questions.

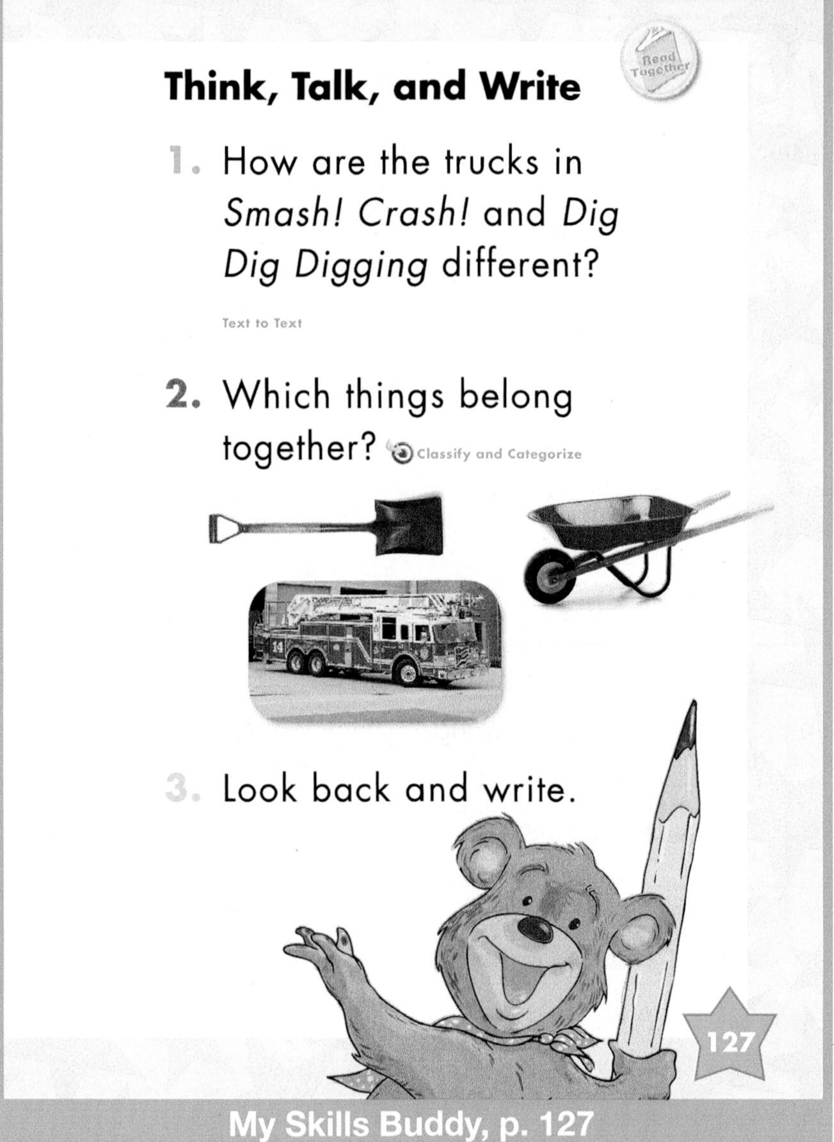
Think, Talk, and Write
Read Together
1. How are the trucks in *Smash! Crash!* and *Dig Dig Digging* different?
Text to Text
2. Which things belong together?
Classify and Categorize
3. Look back and write.
127

My Skills Buddy, p. 127

Think, Talk, and Write

DISCUSS CONCEPT We're learning about how machines help people do work. Think about what it would be like to control one of these big machines.

- How would you like to work all day digging and scooping?
- Would you like to be a firefighter and drive a fire engine? Why?
- Which of the machines do you like best? Why?

CONFIRM PREDICTIONS Have children recall their predictions before you read *Dig Dig Digging.*

- What did you think the selection would be about?
- Was your prediction correct?

Have children turn to p. 127 of *My Skills Buddy.* Read the questions and directives and have children respond. Remind them that good speakers speak loudly and clearly and speak one a time.

1. **TEXT TO TEXT** How are the trucks in *Smash! Crash!* and *Dig Dig Digging* different? Which trucks are like the trucks you see in real life? Which trucks do things real trucks cannot do?

2. **CLASSIFY AND CATEGORIZE** Which things belong together? Which of these things can only be used by grown-ups? (fire truck) Which of these things can both children and grown-ups use? (shovel, wheelbarrow) What categories, or groups, can we make for these things? (*Things Grown-ups Use; Things Children and Grown-ups Use*)

3. **LOOK BACK AND WRITE • TEXT EVIDENCE** Let's look back at our story and write about it. We remember that different machines do different things. They help people in different ways. Listen for how trucks can help. Read pp. 24–25 of *Dig Dig Digging.* Now let's write our ideas. Discuss with children what trucks can do to help people and record children's responses on chart paper. (Trucks carry things. Trucks travel far. They can carry big loads and small loads.)

Conventions

Nouns for Places and Things

TEACH Remind children that nouns are words that name people, animals, places, or things. Today we are going to practice using nouns for places and things.

GUIDE PRACTICE Display pp. 6–7 of *Dig Dig Digging.* I will name one thing I see on these pages: *hose.* What things do you see? (*hill, house, hat, water, fire engine*) These words are nouns for things. Write the words on the board and point to each word as you read it. Point to the neighborhood on the page. This is a neighborhood. *Neighborhood* is a noun that names a place. What other nouns for places do you know? Write the words on the board, pointing to each word as you read it.

ON THEIR OWN Use *Reader's and Writer's Notebook,* p. 68, for more practice reading, writing, and saying nouns for places and things.

Name
Dig Dig Digging
Read It!
I see a book.
Say It!
Say a sentence that tells about your favorite book.
Write It!
I see a park. (park)

Reader's and Writer's Notebook, p. 68

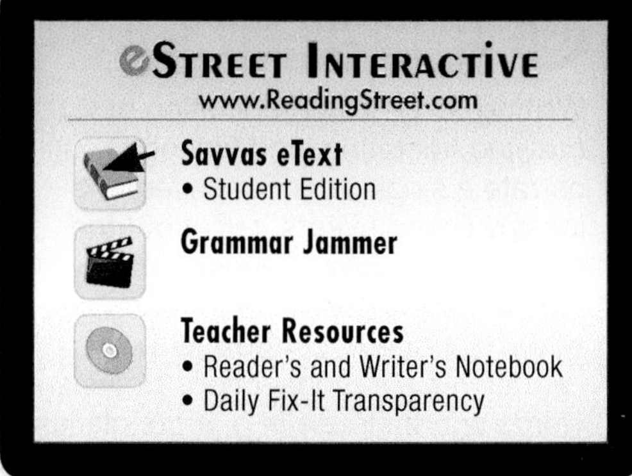

Writing to Sources

Use Write Like a Reporter on pp. 26–27 to guide children in writing text-based responses using one source.

Daily Fix-It

a truck can work all day

A truck can work all day.

This week's practice sentences appear on *Teacher Resources DVD-ROM.*

CONVENTIONS OF STANDARD ENGLISH

As children recognize and offer nouns that name places and things, they are demonstrating their command of standard English grammar and usage.

Support Conventions Have children go on a "noun hunt." Ask them to look for objects in the classroom, such as pencils, paper, crayons, or blocks. Have children name the objects they find. Explain that each name is a noun for a thing.

Common Core State Standards

Writing 3. Use a combination of drawing, dictating, and writing to narrate a single event or several loosely linked events, tell about the events in the order in which they occurred, and provide a reaction to what happened. **Language 5.c.** Identify real-life connections between words and their use (e.g., note places at school that are *colorful*). **Language 6.** Use words and phrases acquired through conversations, reading and being read to, and responding to texts. **Also Writing 1., 6., 7., Language 5.b.**

Writing to Sources

Use More Connect the Texts on pp. 222–293 to guide children in writing text-based responses within various forms and modes.

Academic Vocabulary

draft a first version of a piece of writing

Writing

Zoom in on

Writing Process: Draft a Story

TEACH Today we're going to decide what will happen in our story about our music class. Then we're going to write a draft of our story. A **draft** is a first try at writing. We'll come back to our draft later and make it better. Right now we want to figure out how to get our words down on paper in the right order.

MODEL Explain that a story has a beginning, a middle, and an end. In a story, something that happens first is at the beginning, something that happens next is in the middle, and something that happens last is at the end. Listen as I tell you a story about myself: I didn't put on my boots before I left my house. My feet got wet and cold when I walked to school. Next time I will wear my boots! In a row on the board, write the three sentences in your story. Label them *Beginning, Middle,* and *End.*

GUIDE PRACTICE Write *Beginning, Middle,* and *End* in a row on the board. What happens at the beginning of our story? What happens first in our music class? (Possible event: The music teacher plays the piano.) Write or illustrate children's suggestions under *Beginning.* What happens in the middle of our story? What happens next in our music class? (Possible event: We learn new songs.) Write or illustrate children's suggestions under *Middle.* What happens at the end of our story? What happens last in our music class? (Possible event: We sing the songs together.) Write or illustrate children's suggestions under *End.*

Reread and discuss the events you wrote on the board. As a class, choose a beginning event, a middle event, and an ending event for the story. Then ask children to include their opinion about one event. (Possible response for End event: We sound good.) Add the sentence to the story.

INDEPENDENT WRITING On p. 69 in *Reader's and Writer's Notebook,* have children draw pictures of the events at the beginning, in the middle, and at the end of the class story. Then have them write or dictate words and sentences about the events or copy your sentences from the board on p. 70 in *Reader's and Writer's Notebook.* If computers are available, and children have the necessary skills, let them use the computers to draft the class story.

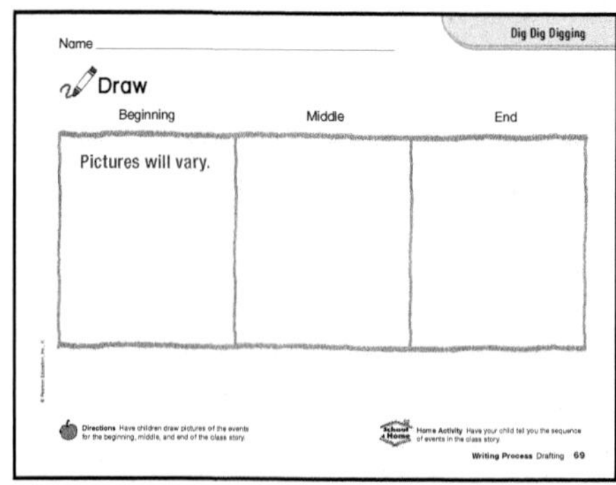

Reader's and Writer's Notebook, pp. 69–70

Common Core State Standards

Speaking/Listening 4. Describe familiar people, places, things, and events and, with prompting and support, provide additional detail. **Also Speaking/Listening 1.a., Language 5.a., 5.c., 6.**

Let's Learn It!

Vocabulary

- Talk about the pictures.
- What do you see that is big? What is little?
- Who is tall and who is short?

Listening and Speaking

- Where do AlphaBuddy's stories take place?

Vocabulary

Words for Sizes

big

little

tall

short

128

My Skills Buddy, p. 128

Vocabulary

Words for Sizes

TEACH Have children turn to p. 128 of *My Skills Buddy.* Use the first Vocabulary bullet to guide discussion about the size words *big, little, tall,* and *short.* Have children point to each picture and tell about it using a size word.

GUIDE PRACTICE Write the words *big, little, tall,* and *short* on the board. Point to each word as you read it.

Point out that *big/little* and *tall/short* are opposites. Write the words on separate index cards. Have children show they understand the words by using the cards to label appropriate objects in the classroom.

ON THEIR OWN Have children use books or blocks to make a tall stack and a short stack. Then have children draw a big circle and a little circle on the board.

Access for All

Support Vocabulary Use Picture Cards to help children practice using size words. Display one pair of pictures, and ask children to describe the pictures using *big, little, tall,* or *short.* Use these pairs of Picture Cards: *ant, elephant; frog, zebra; mop, slide.*

VOCABULARY ACQUISITION AND USE

Learning about words that describe sizes helps children understand the relationships among words in a specific category and the connections between words and their use in describing.

Access Vocabulary Have children share how they would say the size words *big, little, tall,* and *short* in their home languages.

Common Core State Standards

Foundational Skills 3.a. Demonstrate basic knowledge of one-to-one letter-sound correspondences by producing the primary or many of the most frequent sounds for each consonant. **Speaking/Listening 2.** Confirm understanding of a text read aloud or information presented orally or through other media by asking and answering questions about key details and requesting clarification if something is not understood. **Language 5.a.** Sort common objects into categories (e.g., shapes, foods) to gain a sense of the concepts the categories represent. **Also Foundational Skills 2., Speaking/Listening 1.b.**

Wrap Up Your Day!

✔ **Content Knowledge** Today we read about the machines in *Dig Dig Digging.* They are busy helping people. What do some of the machines do?

✔ **Phonemic Awareness** I am going to read some silly sentences. Clap when you hear /t/ words: *The tiny terrier likes tacos. Tom tastes toast and cheese. Tim bought tuna and turnips.*

✔ **Vocabulary Skill** Have children use body movements to make themselves tall (stretching up), short (stooping), large (stretching out arms, puffing cheeks), and small (scrunching into a ball).

✔ **Homework Idea** Have children take the take-home versions of Decodable Reader 6 to share with their families.

Preview DAY 3

Tomorrow we will read a story about going to a toy store.

Extend Your Day!

Science
Machines and People

MATERIALS: hand-held or full-size vacuum cleaner, paper, drawing and writing tools, three-column chart on chart paper or Graphic Organizer 5

HOW DO MACHINES HELP PEOPLE? Have children think about how machines help people do work around the house. If they need help, ask these questions:

- What machines does your family use at home to make things clean?
- How does your family use machines to help prepare food?

Discuss with children how machines help us and make our work easier. Record chores in the first column of the chart. Next to each chore, write how to do that chore with no machines and with machines.

chore	no machines	with machines
cook	wood, fire	stove
wash clothes	one piece at a time, with hands in water	washing machine

WRITE ABOUT MACHINES Have children make up sentences about machines and how they help us. Write their sentences on the board. Have children copy one sentence and illustrate it.

Comprehension
Classify and Categorize

MATERIALS: mural paper, crayons, markers

HUNTING FOR MACHINES Take a walk through the school, looking for people using machines. Back in the classroom, discuss the machines children saw helping people around the school.

Attach mural paper to a wall. Have children make a mural of machines they saw on their walk. Divide the paper into sections and label each section for a different part of the school. Assign one part of the school to each group of three or four children and have them focus on the machines in that part.

Phonics
Initial Sounds

MATERIALS: plastic letter or letter tile *t,* Phonics Songs and Rhymes Audio CD

WHAT BEGINS WITH *T?* Have children sit in a circle. Pass the letter *t* around the circle while you play "Tick, Tick, Tock" from the CD, pausing randomly. When the song stops, whoever is holding the letter says a word beginning with *t.* Repeat until many children have had a turn.

DAY 3 at a Glance

Content Knowledge
Oral Vocabulary

Phonemic Awareness
Final /t/

Phonics
/t/ Spelled *Tt*

Text-Based Comprehension
Classify and Categorize

Conventions
Review Nouns for People and Animals

Writing
Revise a Story

Listening and Speaking
Respond to Literature: Drama

Materials

- Student Edition
- Truckery Rhymes
- Talk with Me/Sing with Me Chart
- Picture Cards
- Alphabet Cards
- Reader's and Writer's Notebook
- Student Reader K.1.6
- Big Book

Common Core State Standards

Speaking/Listening 2. Confirm understanding of a text read aloud or information presented orally or through other media by asking and answering questions about key details and requesting clarification if something is not understood. **Language 6.** Use words and phrases acquired through conversations, reading and being read to, and responding to texts.

TRUCKTOWN
on Reading Street

Start your engines!

Display p. 10 of *Truckery Rhymes.* Do you know the original "This Is the Way (We Go to School)"? Recite it first, and then have children repeat it with you:

This is the way we go to school
Go to school, go to school.
This is the way we go to school
Early in the morning.

Truckery Rhymes

Content Knowledge

Zoom in on

People and Machines Working Together

On the board, write the Question of the Week, *How do machines help people work?* Read the question as you track the print. Talk with children about how machines help people work. Have children respond in complete sentences. Remind them to speak one at a time.

Build Oral Language

LISTEN FOR AMAZING WORDS Display Sing with Me Chart 6B. Recall with children that yesterday they sang two verses of "Look at Them Go!" and learned the Amazing Words *scooping* and *swooshing.* Tell them that they are going to sing the song again. Today we will listen for the Amazing Words *squelching* and *gobbling.* Sing the song several times to the tune of "The Wheels on the Bus." Have children imitate the machines that make the *squelching* and *gobbling* sounds when they hear those Amazing Words.

Look at Them Go!
The diggers dig with a
scoop, scoop, scooping,
Scoop, scoop, scooping,
scoop, scoop, scooping,
The diggers dig with a scoop,
scoop, scooping,
Look at them go!

Talk with Me/Sing with Me Chart 6B

Build Oral Vocabulary

Amazing Words Robust Vocabulary Routine

1. **Introduce the Word** *Squelching* is a sound mud makes as it is pulled up or stepped on. What is our new Amazing Word for a sound mud makes? Say it with me: *squelching.*
2. **Demonstrate** Provide examples to show meaning. *We made squelching sounds walking in the muddy field.*

   Repeat steps 1 and 2.

   Introduce the Word The word *gobbling* means eating very quickly. What is our new Amazing Word for eating very quickly? Say it with me: *gobbling.*

   Demonstrate *The dog is gobbling food from his dish.*
3. **Apply** Have children use *squelching* and *gobbling* to describe what tractors and garbage trucks do.
4. **Display the Words** Have children name the letters that *squelching* and *gobbling* begin with. Then ask them what they notice about the last three letters in both words.

Routines Flip Chart

USE AMAZING WORDS To reinforce the concept and the Amazing Words, have children supply the appropriate Amazing Word for each sentence.

I am so hungry I am ______ my lunch. (gobbling)
The pig is ______ through the mud. (squelching)

Amazing Words

scooping
squelching
spinning
swooshing
gobbling
rumbling

Access for All

Strategic Intervention

Physical Response Have children use clay to act out the motions and sounds of *squelching.* Have them demonstrate *gobbling* by pretending to be garbage trucks, picking up pieces of paper from the floor.

Common Core State Standards

Foundational Skills 2.d. Isolate and pronounce the initial, medial vowel, and final sounds (phonemes) in three-phoneme (consonant-vowel-consonant, or CVC) words.* (This does not include CVCs ending with /l/, /r/, or /x/.) **Foundational Skills 2.e.** Add or substitute individual sounds (phonemes) in simple, one-syllable words to make new words.

Access for All

Advanced

Initial /t/ Have children page through this week's stories. Tell them to find and copy two words that begin with /t/ on their Write-On Boards.

Phonemic Awareness

Final /t/

REVIEW INITIAL /t/ Display the *taxi* Picture Card. What is the first sound in *taxi?* Say the word with me: /t/ /t/ /t/, *taxi.* The first sound in *taxi* is /t/. Continue the review with the *tiger, ten,* and *toes* Picture Cards.

Picture Card

TEACH FINAL /t/ Display the *bat* Picture Card. This is a bat. Listen as I say the sounds: /b/ /a/ /t/. I hear /t/ at the end of the word: /b/ /a/ /t/. Say it with me: /b/ /a/ /t/; /t/ is at the end. Let's try some more. Continue with the following Picture Cards: *boat, cat, goat, hat, kite, net.*

Picture Card

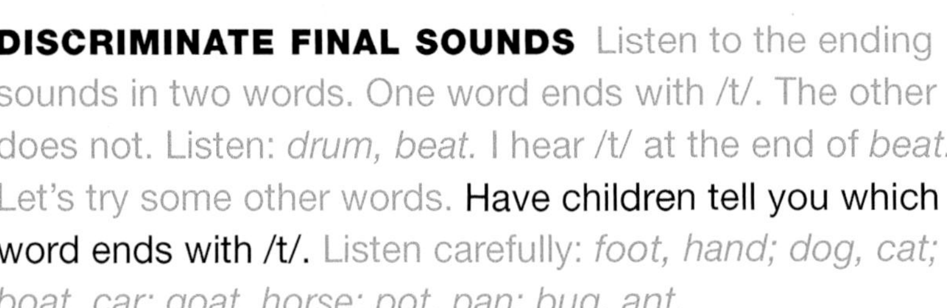

DISCRIMINATE FINAL SOUNDS Listen to the ending sounds in two words. One word ends with /t/. The other does not. Listen: *drum, beat.* I hear /t/ at the end of *beat.* Let's try some other words. Have children tell you which word ends with /t/. Listen carefully: *foot, hand; dog, cat; boat, car; goat, horse; pot, pan; bug, ant.*

ON THEIR OWN Display the *apple, cat, rabbit*, and *nut* Picture Cards. Have children choose a Picture Card that ends with /t/, draw their own picture, and write a *t* on their paper.

SEGMENT Listen to the sounds in the word *fit:* /f/ /i/ /t/. Say them with me: /f/ /i/ /t/. How many sounds do you hear? There are three sounds in *fit.* Let's try some more words. Continue the routine with the following words: *fat, tip, top, him, it, cat, kit, dot.*

Corrective feedback	**If...** children cannot segment the words, **then...** provide practice segmenting the words in chunks: /f/ *-it.*

SUBSTITUTE FINAL SOUNDS Listen to the sounds in this word: *can,* /k/ /a/ /n/, *can.* Say it with me: /k/ /a/ /n/, *can.* I can make a new word by changing the last sound in *can* to /t/. Listen: /k/ /a/ /t/, *cat.* Say it with me as I blend the new sounds: /k/ /a/ /t/, *cat.* Continue substituting final sounds with the following words: *fin, fit; man, mat.*

Support Phonemic Awareness In Spanish, the letter *t* represents a sound that is similar to the sound in English. It may transfer readily to English reading for many children, so they may need minimal instruction for this consonant. Have Spanish-speaking children work with other English learners to practice /t/.

Common Core State Standards

Foundational Skills 3.a. Demonstrate basic knowledge of one-to-one letter-sound correspondences by producing the primary or many of the most frequent sounds for each consonant.

Phonics

Blend Sounds

/t/ Spelled *Tt*

REVIEW *T* Display the *Tt* Alphabet Card. This is a turtle. What sound do you hear at the beginning of *turtle?* What letter spells that sound? Point to the letters *Tt.* What is the sound for this letter? What are the names of these letters?

Alphabet Card

BLEND Write the word *tug* on the board and point to *t.* What is the sound for this letter? (/t/) *Tug* ends with *-ug.* Let's blend /t/ and *-ug* to make the word *tug: /t/ -ug, tug.* Continue with the words *Tom, tip,* and *tell.*

Write the word *sat* on the board and point to *t.* What is the sound for this letter? (/t/) *Sat* begins with *sa-.* Let's blend *sa-* and /t/ to make the word *sat: sa- /t/, sat.* Continue with the words *hit, not,* and *cut.*

MORE PRACTICE Use *Reader's and Writer's Notebook,* p. 71, for additional practice with /t/.

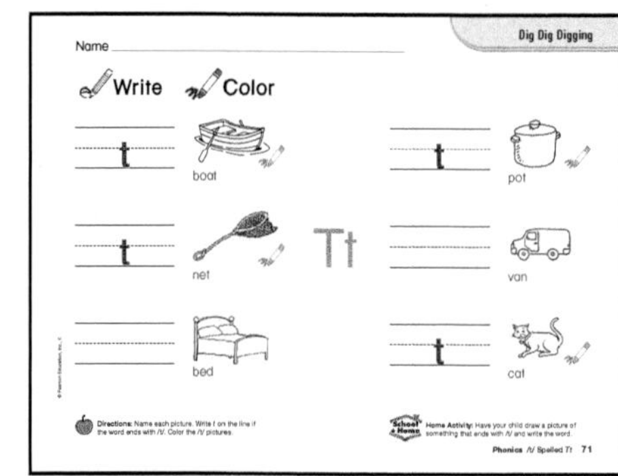

Reader's and Writer's Notebook, p. 71

REVIEW SOUND-SPELLING Display the *Mm* Alphabet Card. Point to the motorcycle. What sound do you hear at the beginning of *motorcycle?* What is the letter that spells that sound?

REVIEW HIGH-FREQUENCY WORDS Write *to* on the board. This is the word *to.* What is this word? Continue the routine with *I, am, the, little,* and *a.*

Alphabet Card

MONITOR PROGRESS Check Word Reading High-Frequency Words

FORMATIVE ASSESSMENT Write *I, am, the, little, to,* and *a* on the board. Have children take turns reading the words.

If... children cannot read the high-frequency words,
then... have them first say the letters in the words and then read the words.

If... children can successfully read the high-frequency words,
then... have them read Kindergarten Student Reader K.1.6, *At the Toy Store.*

Access for All

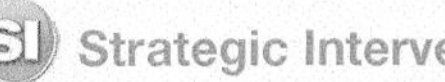

Connect Sound-Spelling For more practice, have children work with the *Tt* Alphabet Card.

Support High-Frequency Words Review how to pronounce high-frequency words *am, I, little,* and *the.* Coach children when necessary.

Literature 10. Actively engage in group reading activities with purpose and understanding. **Foundational Skills 3.a.** Demonstrate basic knowledge of one-to-one letter-sound correspondences by producing the primary or many of the most frequent sounds for each consonant. **Foundational Skills 3.c.** Read common high-frequency words by sight. (e.g., *the, of, to, you, she, my, is, are, do, does*).

Access for All

Access Content You may want to explain to children that the name of the toy in the picture is the /t/*Tt* word on the page.

Student Reader

Read *At the Toy Store*

REVIEW Review the previously taught high-frequency words. Have children read each word as you point to it on the Word Wall.

I	am	the	little	to	a

INITIAL /t/*Tt* Write the word *tiger* on the board. This word is *tiger.* The word *tiger* is in the story we are going to read. What sound does *tiger* begin with? (/t/) What letter stands for the sound /t/ in *tiger?* (*Tt*) We will read many words that begin with /t/ like *tiger* in our story. As we read, point to words that begin with /t/*Tt.*

READ Display Kindergarten Student Reader K.1.6, *At the Toy Store.* Today we are going to read a new book. Point to the title. What is the title of this book? The title of this book is *At the Toy Store.* The author's name is Lindsey Domke.

Use the reading decodable books routine to read the Kindergarten Student Reader.

Routine Reading Decodable Books

1. **Read Silently** Have children whisper read the book page by page as you listen in.
2. **Model Fluent Reading** Have children finger point as you read a page. Then have them reread the page without you.
3. **Read Chorally** Have children finger point as they chorally read the page. Continue reading page by page, repeating steps 1 and 2.
4. **Read Individually** Have children take turns reading aloud a page.
5. **Reread and Monitor Progress** As you listen to individual children reread, monitor progress and provide support.
6. **Reread with a Partner** Have children reread the book page by page with a partner.

Routines Flip Chart

I am a little top.

3

I am a little turkey.

4

Kindergarten Student Reader K.1.6

Day 3

SMALL GROUP TIME • Differentiate Vocabulary, p. SG•89

OL On-Level	SI Strategic Intervention	A Advanced
• **Develop Vocabulary** Practice Words for Sizes • **Read** Student Reader *At the Toy Store*	• **Develop Vocabulary** Reteach Words for Sizes • **Read** Student Reader *At the Toy Store*	• **Develop Vocabulary** More Words for Sizes • **Read** Student Reader *At the Toy Store*

ELL

Place English Language Learners in the groups that correspond to their reading abilities in English.

If... children need more scaffolding and practice with **Vocabulary,** **then...** use the ELL activities on p. DI•99 in the Teacher Resources section of the Digital Path.

Text-Based Comprehension

Read Main Selection

RETELL THE SELECTION Have children turn to p. 126 of *My Skills Buddy* and use the retelling boxes to retell the selection *Dig Dig Digging.*

Direct children to the first retelling box. This is a digger. Tell me what a digger can do.

Continue reviewing the retelling boxes and having children retell the selection.

My Skills Buddy, p. 126

REVIEW CLASSIFY AND CATEGORIZE Display illustrations in *Dig Dig Digging.* Let's classify and categorize the machines.

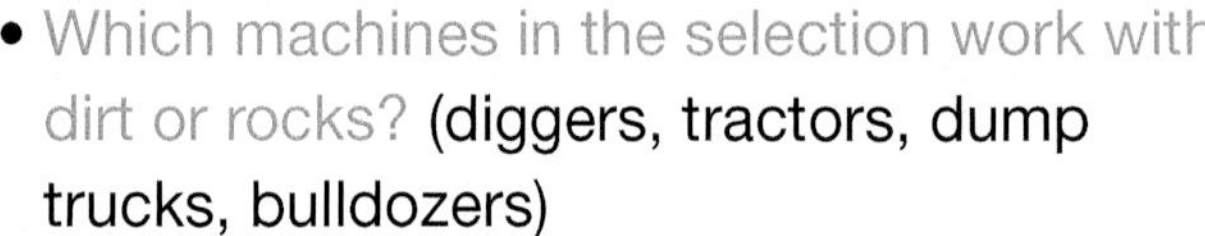

- Which machines in the selection work with dirt or rocks? (diggers, tractors, dump trucks, bulldozers)
- In the selection, which machines are used to save people? (fire engines, rescue helicopters)

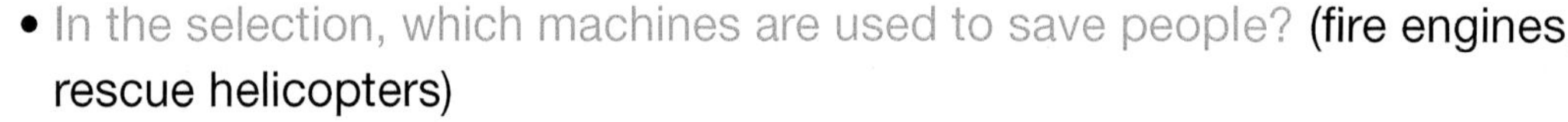

- Which of the machines in the selection work outdoors? (all of them)

MORE PRACTICE Use *Reader's and Writer's Notebook,* p. 72, for additional practice with classify and categorize.

Common Core State Standards

Informational Text 2. With prompting and support, identify the main topic and retell key details of a text. **Informational Text 7.** With prompting and support, describe the relationship between illustrations and the text in which they appear (e.g., what person, place, thing, or idea in the text an illustration depicts). **Language 5.a.** Sort common objects into categories (e.g., shapes, foods) to gain a sense of the concepts the categories represent. **Also Informational Text 10.**

Bridge to Common Core

CRAFT AND STRUCTURE

As children retell the selection, they are learning how the purpose of the selection—to teach readers about machines—shapes its content: Each spread tells about a different kind of machine. Reading the selection to children a second time and using the Develop Vocabulary notes will help children determine the technical and figurative meanings of words used in the text.

Name

Dig Dig Digging

Color

72 Comprehension Classify and Categorize

Reader's and Writer's Notebook, p. 72

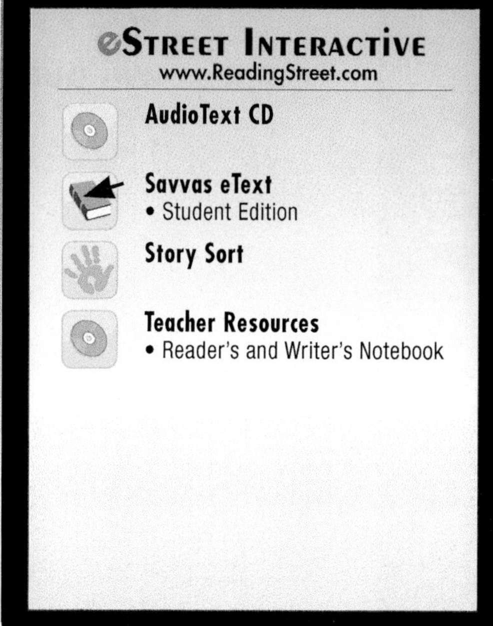

Access Main Selection

READER AND TASK SUGGESTIONS	
Preparing to Read the Text	**Leveled Tasks**
• Review the Amazing Words and have children use them to talk about the selection. • Review the use of headings and illustrations to introduce topics.	• **Theme Knowledge and Demands** For children ready to develop text-to-text connections, have them decide which trucks from *Smash! Crash!* belong on pages 10–11, 12–13, and 16–17 of the selection. • **Language Conventionality and Clarity** If children need support with the complex sentence structure, point out some of the repeated action words. Have children find and read other examples of repeated action words.

See Text Complexity Measures for *Dig Dig Digging* on the tab at the beginning of this week.

READ Reread *Dig Dig Digging.* Follow the **2nd Read** beginning on p. 572, and use the **Develop Vocabulary** notes to prompt conversations about the selection.

Routine Read for Understanding

Deepen understanding by reading the selection multiple times.

1. **First Read**—Read the entire selection aloud to build interest in the text.
2. **Second Read**—Use the **Develop Vocabulary** notes on pages 572–583.
3. **Third Read**—Use the **Develop Comprehension** notes on pages 572–583.

2ND READ

Develop Vocabulary

WH- QUESTION Why do the workers use diggers? (to dig holes)

- Diggers scoop up the dirt. What are the diggers doing in the picture?

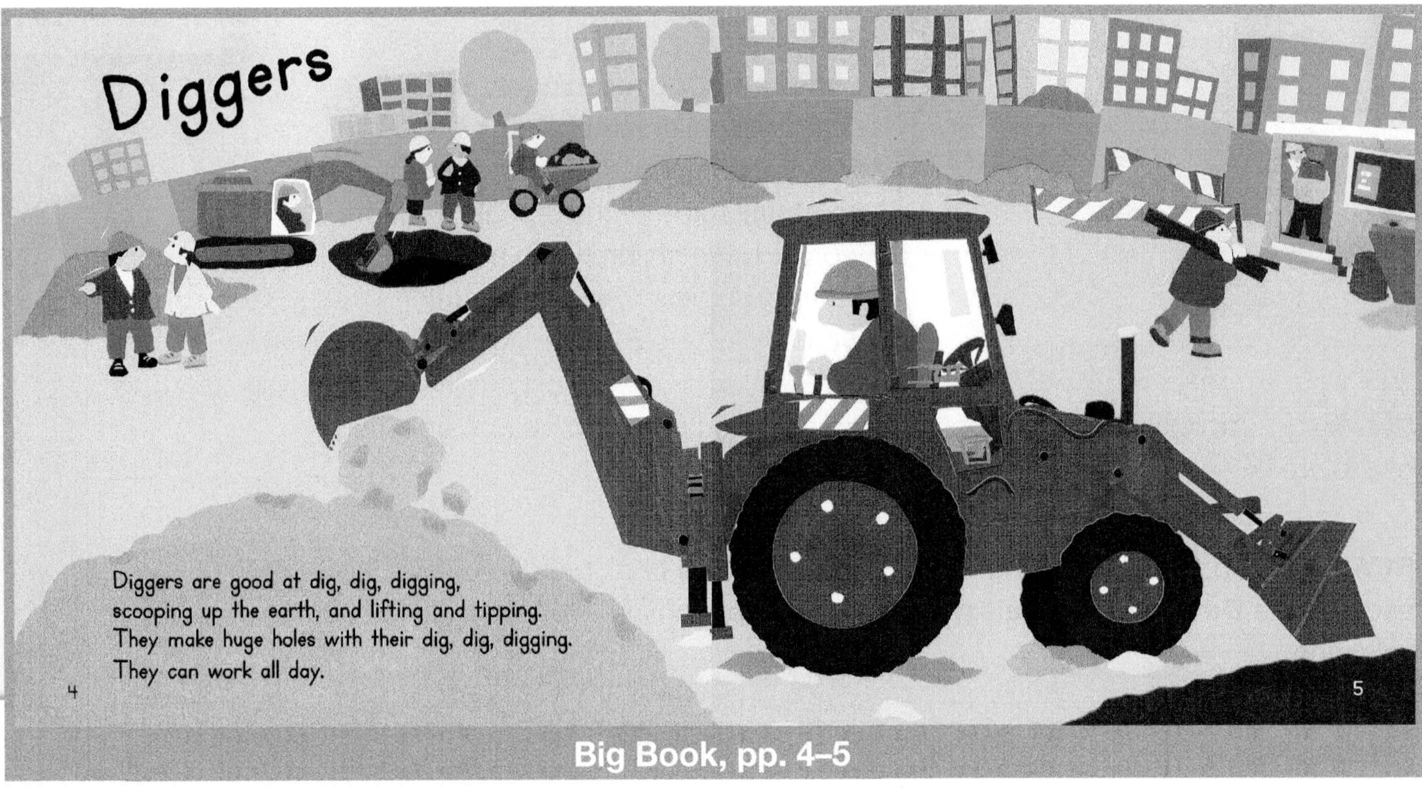

Diggers
Diggers are good at dig, dig, digging,
scooping up the earth, and lifting and tipping.
They make huge holes with their dig, dig, digging.
They can work all day.
4
5

Big Book, pp. 4–5

3RD READ

Develop Comprehension ©

RETELL What are diggers good at? (They are good at digging, scooping up the earth, and lifting and tipping.)

WH- QUESTION Why might fire engines have to race, or go fast? (to get to a fire quickly)

- The firefighters are racing to get to the fire. Point to each firefighter in the picture and ask: What is this firefighter doing?

DEVELOP VOCABULARY fire engines

Common Core State Standards

Informational Text 1. With prompting and support, ask and answer questions about key details in a text. **Informational Text 2.** With prompting and support, identify the main topic and retell key details of a text. **Informational Text 7.** With prompting and support, describe the relationship between illustrations and the text in which they appear (e.g., what person, place, thing, or idea in the text an illustration depicts).

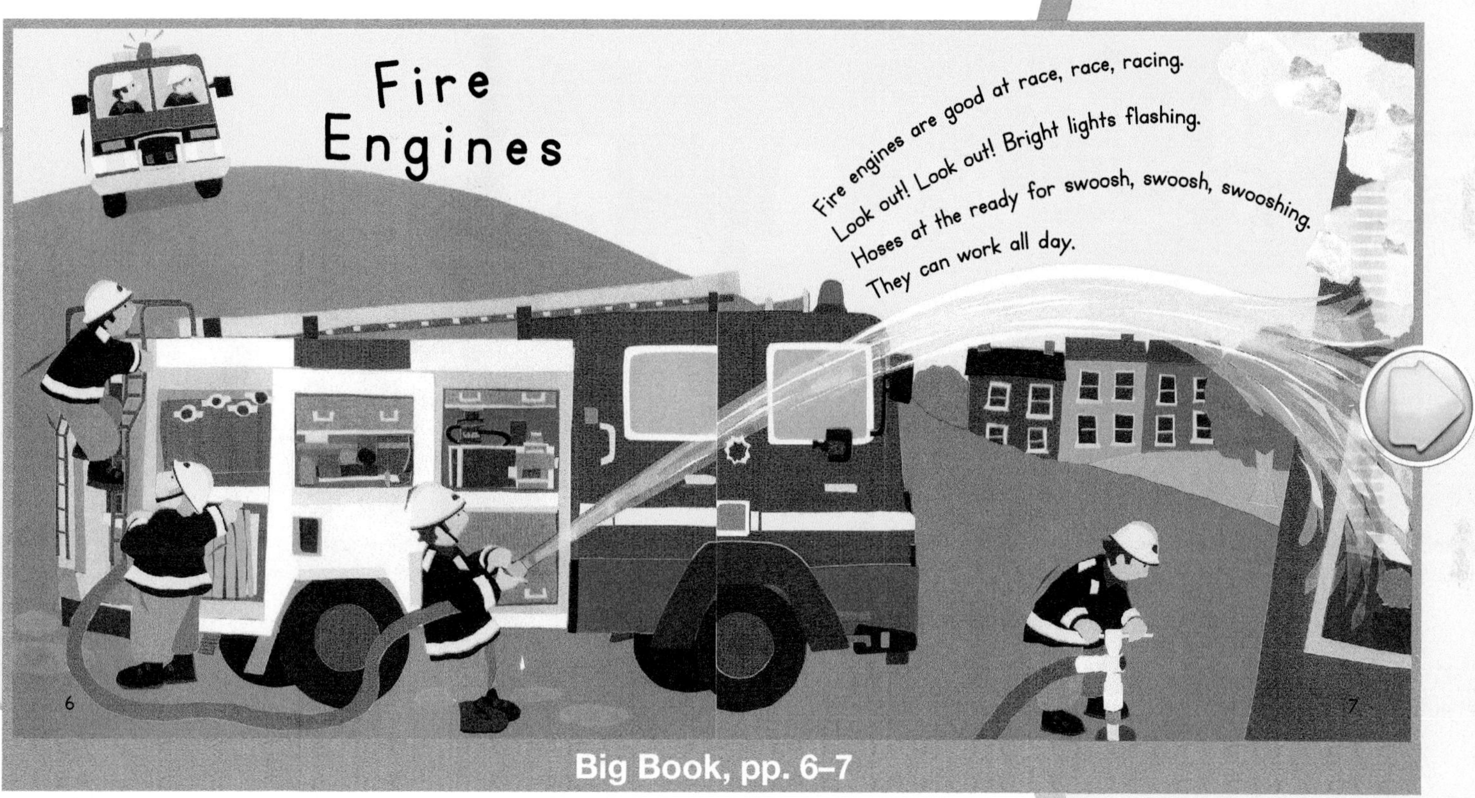

Big Book, pp. 6–7

MONITOR AND FIX UP What do firefighters do with hoses? (They use hoses to put out fires.) If you didn't understand what firefighters do with hoses, what could you do? (If I don't understand what is read, I need to raise my hand and ask if we could reread the page or talk about the picture.)

2ND READ

Develop Vocabulary

***WH-* QUESTION** Look at the picture. What kind of worker uses a tractor? (farmer)

- The farmers are driving the tractors. What are the tractors doing?

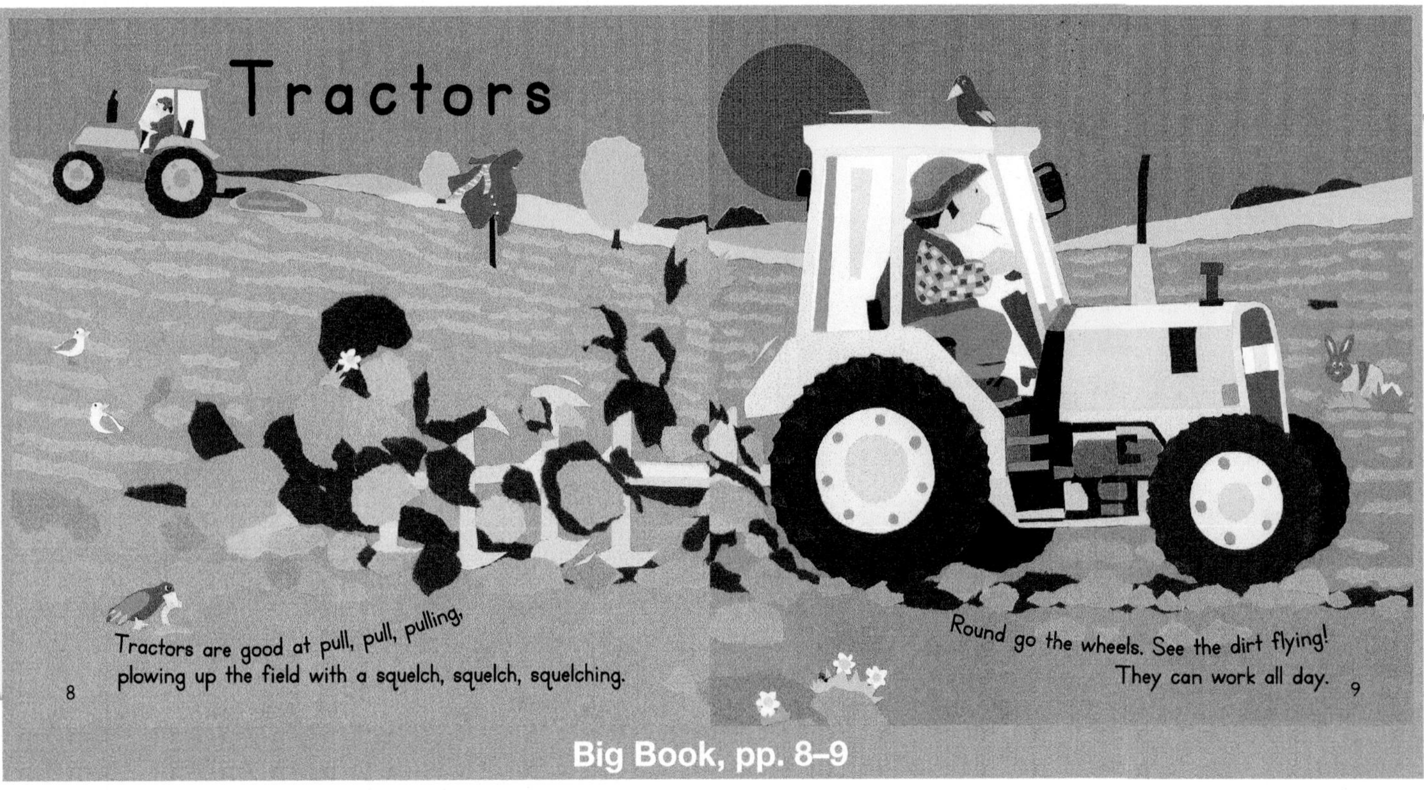

Tractors
Tractors are good at pull, pull, pulling,
plowing up the field with a squelch, squelch, squelching.
8
Round go the wheels. See the dirt flying!
They can work all day.
9

Big Book, pp. 8–9

3RD READ

Develop Comprehension ©

OPEN-ENDED Why do farmers use tractors to plow up fields? (They use tractors to plow up the fields to get them ready for planting seeds.)

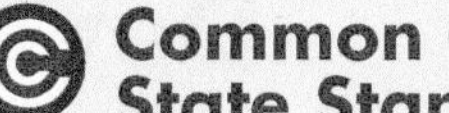

Common Core State Standards

Informational Text 1. With prompting and support, ask and answer questions about key details in a text.
Informational Text 2. With prompting and support, identify the main topic and retell key details of a text.
Informational Text 7. With prompting and support, describe the relationship between illustrations and the text in which they appear (e.g., what person, place, thing, or idea in the text an illustration depicts).

***WH-* QUESTION** What do the garbage trucks do with the garbage? (gobble, crunch, squeeze, and squash)

- The garbage trucks gobble, crunch, squeeze, and squash the garbage. Why do they do that to the garbage?

Big Book, pp. 10–11

OPEN-ENDED Where do garbage trucks get the garbage they gobble and crunch? (They get the garbage from where we put it outside our homes and from big buildings.)

2ND READ

Develop Vocabulary

RECALL What are the cranes lifting to the top of the building? (bricks)

- The crane is lifting bricks up. What else do cranes do at the construction site?

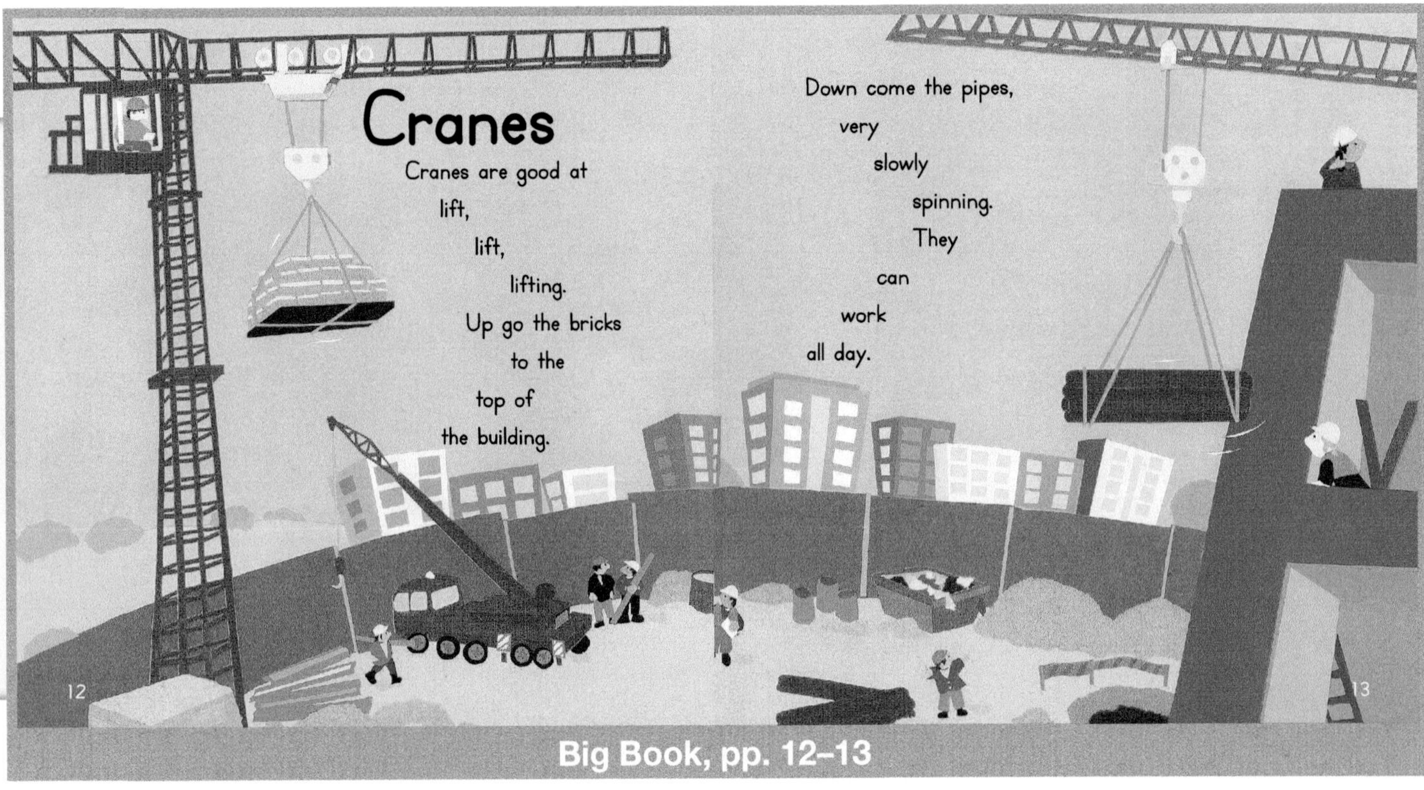
Cranes
Cranes are good at
lift,
lift,
lifting.
Up go the bricks
to the
top of
the building.
12
Down come the pipes,
very
slowly
spinning.
They
can
work
all day.
13
Big Book, pp. 12–13

3RD READ

Develop Comprehension ©

CLASSIFY AND CATEGORIZE How are diggers, fire engines, tractors, and garbage trucks alike? (They all do work. They all have wheels. They are all big machines.)

WH- QUESTION What do transporters do? (move cars)

- The transporters are moving cars from place to place. How many cars are on this transporter?

EXPAND VOCABULARY transporters

Common Core State Standards

Informational Text 1. With prompting and support, ask and answer questions about key details in a text. **Informational Text 2.** With prompting and support, identify the main topic and retell key details of a text. **Informational Text 7.** With prompting and support, describe the relationship between illustrations and the text in which they appear (e.g., what person, place, thing, or idea in the text an illustration depicts).

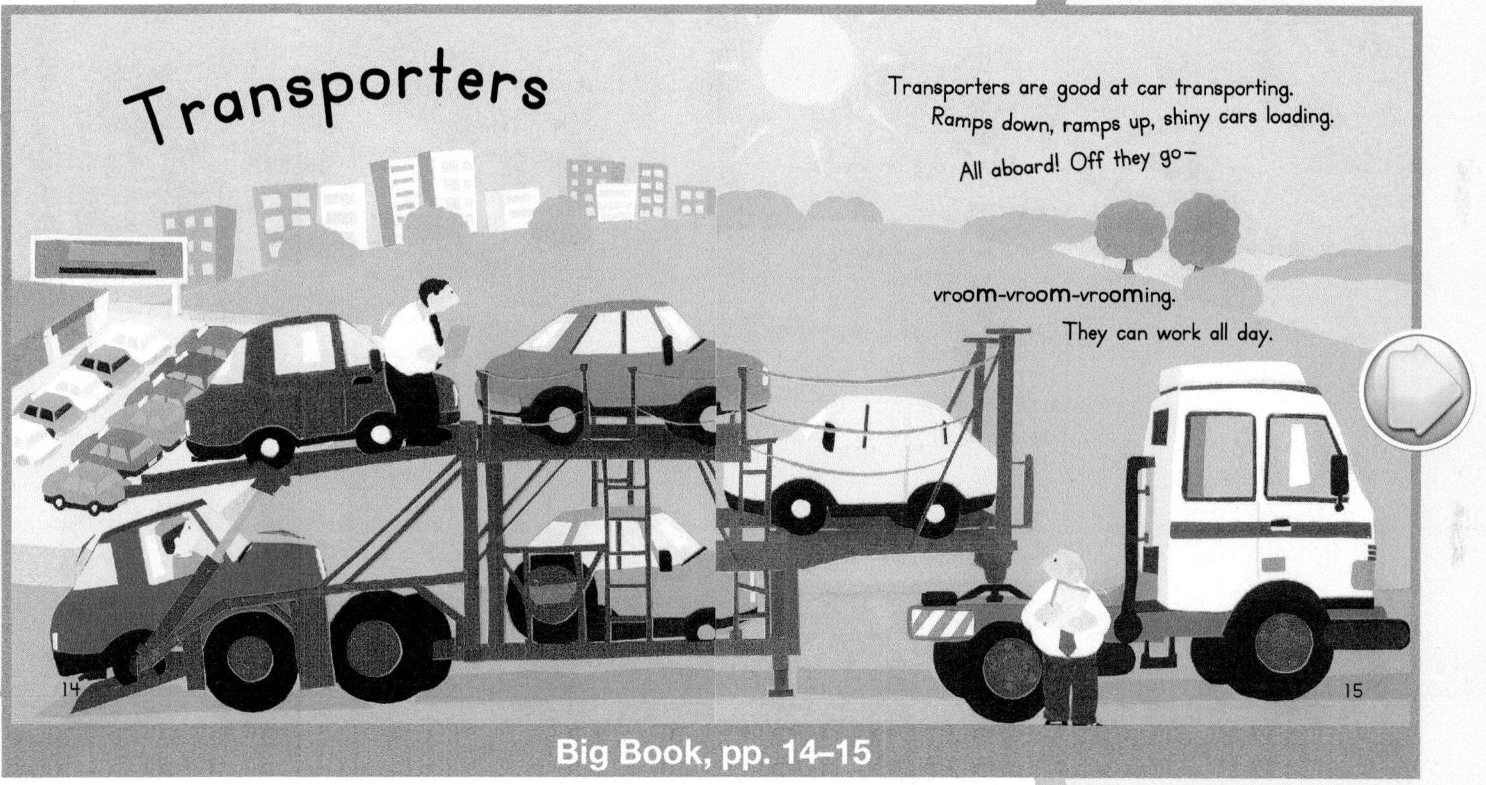

Big Book, pp. 14–15

OPEN-ENDED • INFERENCE Where do you think the transporters get the cars they carry? (They probably get them from the factories where the cars are made.) Where do you think the transporters take the cars? (They probably take them to places where people can buy the cars.)

2ND READ

Develop Vocabulary

OPEN-ENDED What are dump trucks good at? (dumping, carrying heavy loads, tipping)

- Dump trucks carry and dump heavy loads. Where do you think they dump their loads?

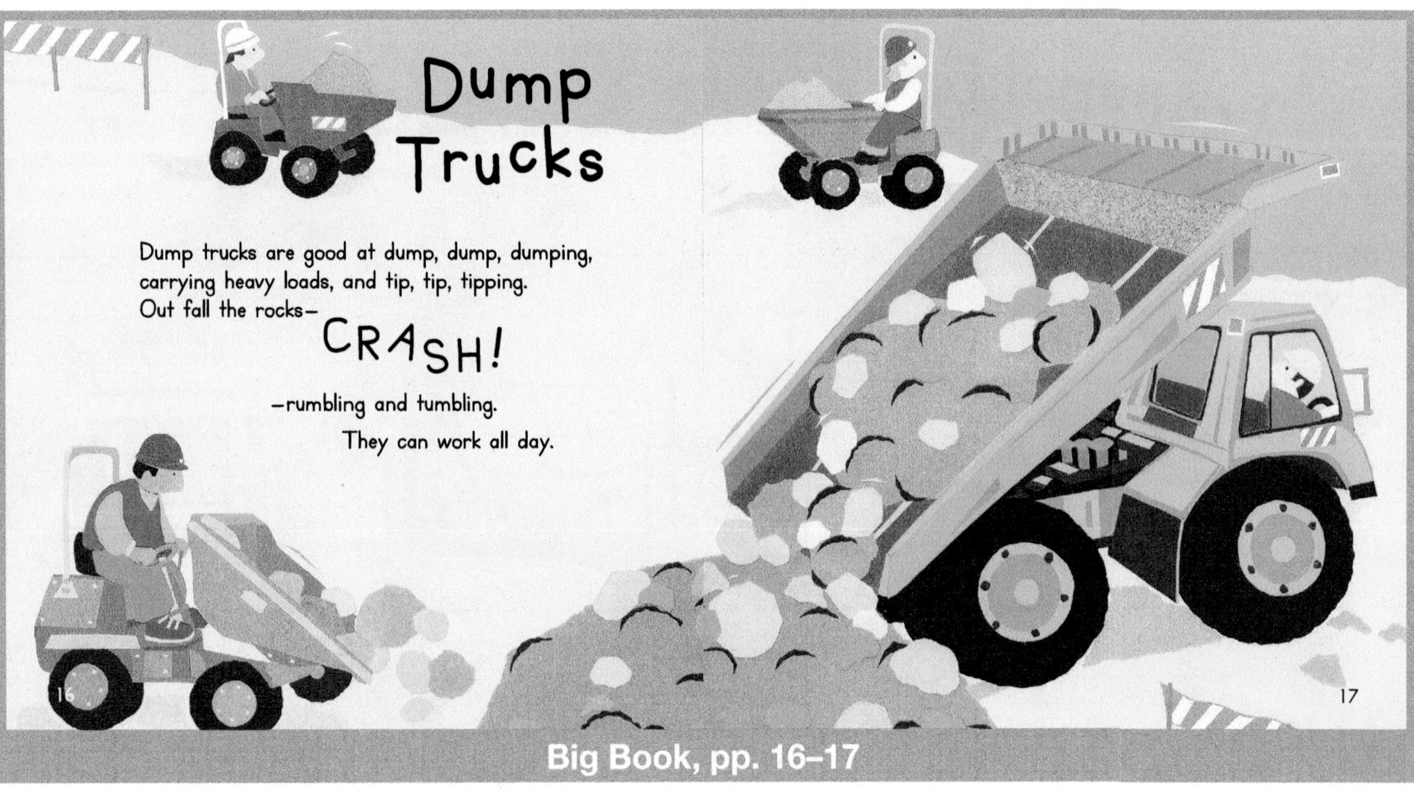

Big Book, pp. 16–17

3RD READ

Develop Comprehension ©

CLASSIFY AND CATEGORIZE I see different kinds of dump trucks. How are they alike? (They all can carry loads and dump them.) How are they different? (One is big and the others are little.)

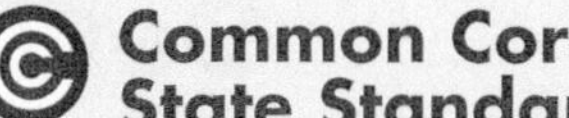

OPEN-ENDED What do the helicopters do? (They rescue people who need help.)

- The helicopters use a rope to rescue people. Why do you think the helicopters use a rope?

DEVELOP VOCABULARY helicopters

Common Core State Standards

Informational Text 1. With prompting and support, ask and answer questions about key details in a text. **Informational Text 2.** With prompting and support, identify the main topic and retell key details of a text. **Informational Text 4.** With prompting and support, ask and answer questions about unknown words in a text. **Informational Text 7.** With prompting and support, describe the relationship between illustrations and the text in which they appear (e.g., what person, place, thing, or idea in the text an illustration depicts).

Big Book, pp. 18–19

***WH-* QUESTION • INFERENCE** What are the rotor blades on a helicopter? (The rotor blades are the metal pieces that spin on the top and tail of a helicopter.) What do the rotor blades do? (They help lift and move the helicopter.)

2ND READ

Develop Vocabulary

OPEN-ENDED What is the road roller doing? (rolling, pressing hot tar to make a new road)

- The workers are making a new road. Why do the workers use a road roller?

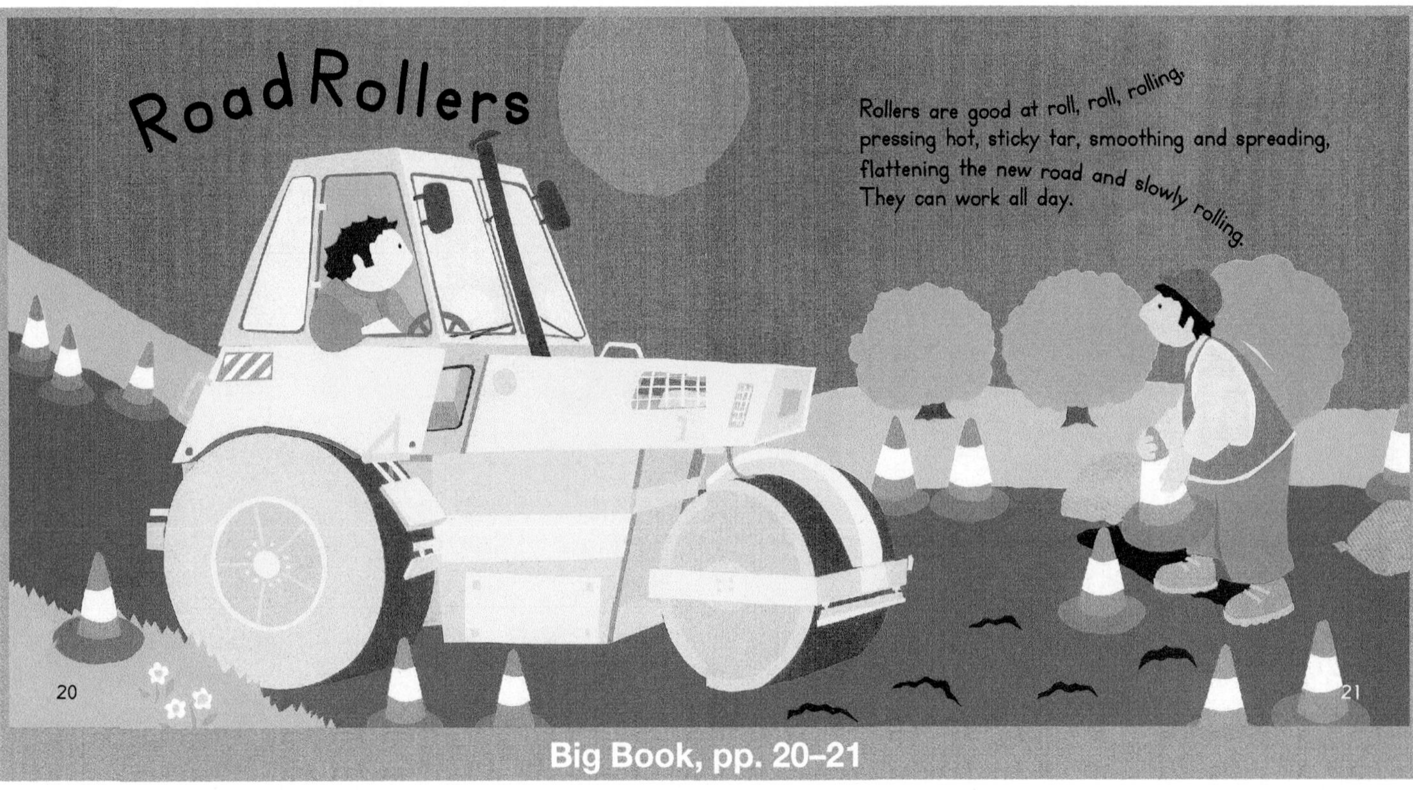

Road Rollers
Rollers are good at roll, roll, rolling,
pressing hot, sticky tar, smoothing and spreading,
flattening the new road and slowly rolling.
They can work all day.
20
21

Big Book, pp. 20–21

3RD READ

Develop Comprehension ©

INFERENCE Do you think the road roller is heavy? Why? (The road roller must be very heavy because it needs to press down the hot tar to make the new road flat and smooth.)

COMPLETION What are the bulldozers good at? (pushing, scraping, shoving)

- Bulldozers push, scrape, and shove. Let's read this page together. Have children join in as you reread the page several times.

EXPAND VOCABULARY bulldozers

Common Core State Standards

Informational Text 1. With prompting and support, ask and answer questions about key details in a text. **Informational Text 2.** With prompting and support, identify the main topic and retell key details of a text. **Informational Text 4.** With prompting and support, ask and answer questions about unknown words in a text. **Informational Text 7.** With prompting and support, describe the relationship between illustrations and the text in which they appear (e.g., what person, place, thing, or idea in the text an illustration depicts).

Big Book, pp. 22–23

INFERENCE What are the caterpillar treads on the bulldozer? (They are the ridges on the belt that goes around the wheels.) How do you think the caterpillar treads help the bulldozer work? (They help it grip the rough, bumpy ground.)

2ND READ

Develop Vocabulary

OPEN-ENDED What are the trucks doing? (traveling, carrying loads, blowing their horns)

- The trucks are carrying different loads. What do you think the trucks are carrying?

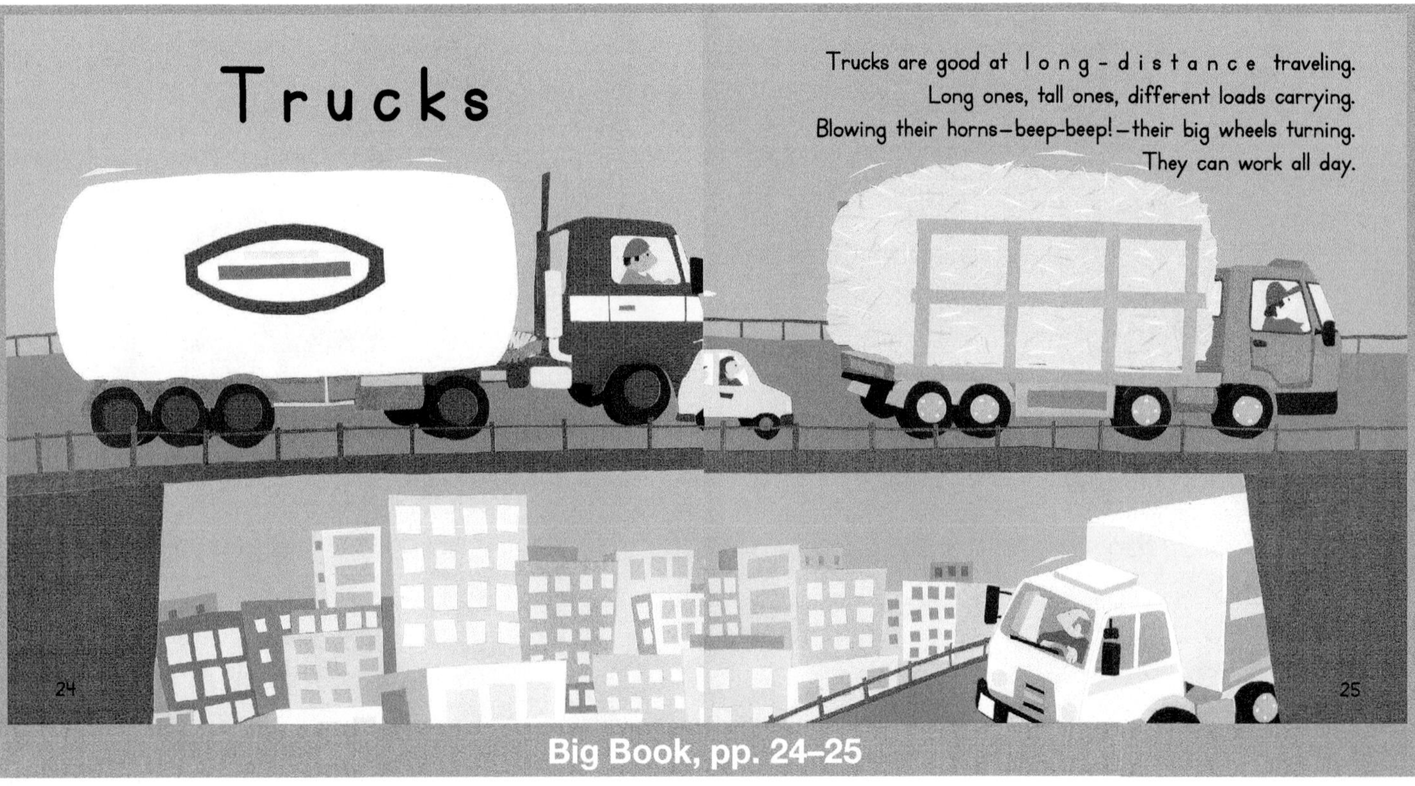

Trucks
Trucks are good at l o n g - d i s t a n c e traveling.
Long ones, tall ones, different loads carrying.
Blowing their horns—beep-beep!—their big wheels turning.
They can work all day.
24
25

Big Book, pp. 24–25

3RD READ

Develop Comprehension ©

CLASSIFY AND CATEGORIZE Look at the picture. How can we put the trucks into groups? (Some carry their loads uncovered. Some carry their loads covered up in containers. All of them are big, have many wheels, and carry loads.)

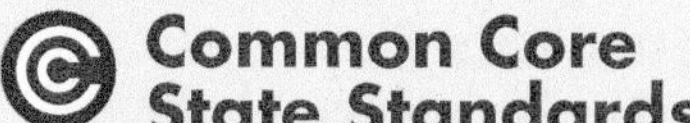

OPEN-ENDED What do the machines do after a busy day? (rest)

- The machines are resting after a busy day. How can you tell they are resting?

DEVELOP VOCABULARY machines

Continue with DAY 3
Conventions
p. 584

Common Core State Standards

Informational Text 1. With prompting and support, ask and answer questions about key details in a text. **Informational Text 2.** With prompting and support, identify the main topic and retell key details of a text. **Informational Text 7.** With prompting and support, describe the relationship between illustrations and the text in which they appear (e.g., what person, place, thing, or idea in the text an illustration depicts).

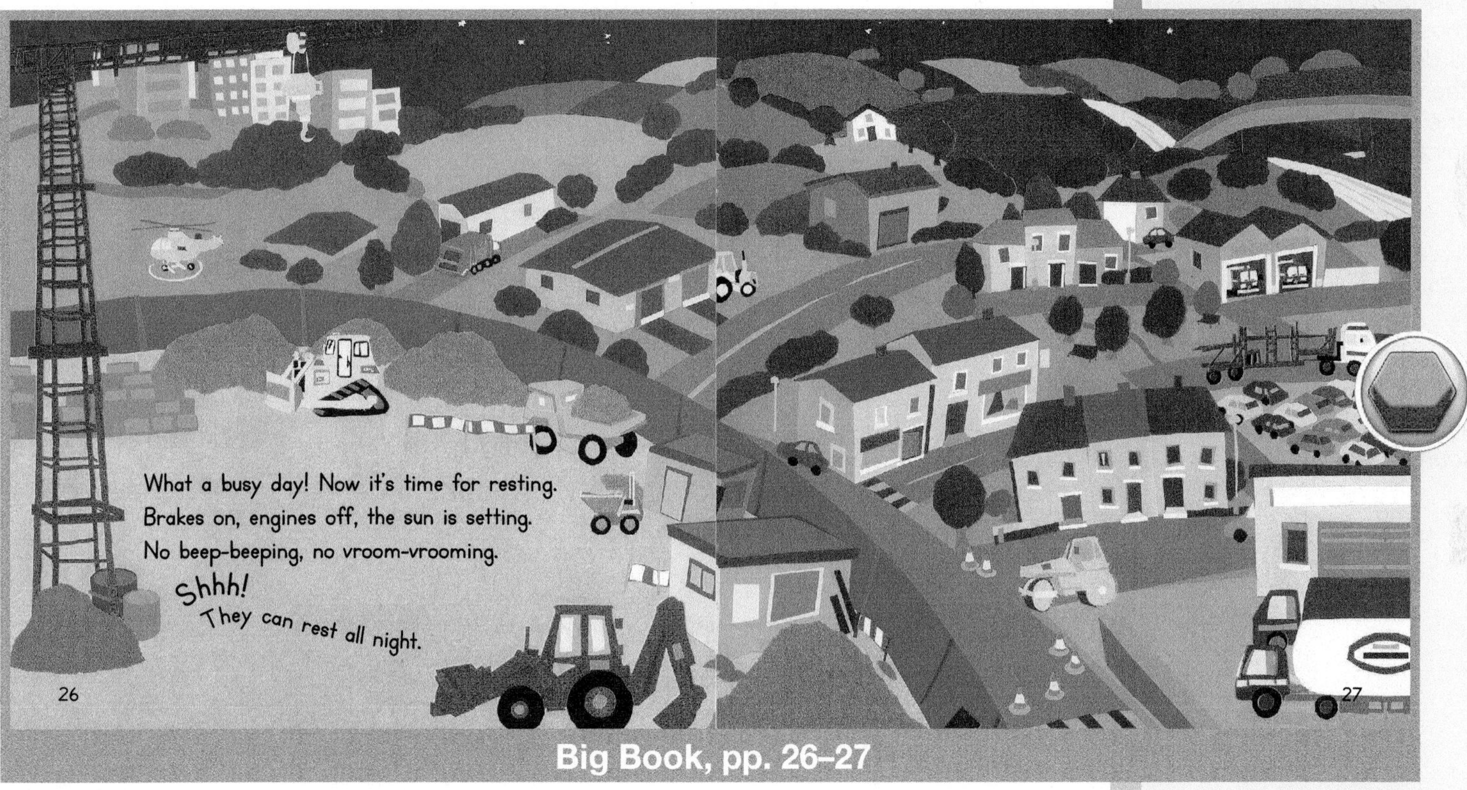

What a busy day! Now it's time for resting.
Brakes on, engines off, the sun is setting.
No beep-beeping, no vroom-vrooming.
Shhh!
They can rest all night.
26
27

Big Book, pp. 26–27

INFERENCE Why do you think the machines rest all night? (They probably rest all night because the workers and drivers are tired and need to rest.)

Skip to DAY 4
Conventions
p. 598

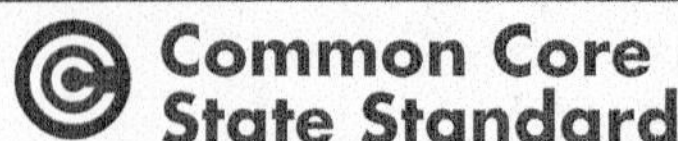

Common Core State Standards

Writing 5. With guidance and support from adults, respond to questions and suggestions from peers and add details to strengthen writing as needed. **Language 1.b.** Use frequently occurring nouns and verbs. **Also Writing 1., 6., 7.**

Access for All

 Advanced

Extend Conventions Connect the review of nouns for people and animals with nouns for places and things. Have children add to their drawings from the Team Talk activity to include a thing the person might use or a place the animal might live.

Daily Fix-It

the truck brings food
The truck brings food.

This week's practice sentences appear on *Teacher Resources DVD-ROM.*

Conventions

Review Nouns for People and Animals

TEACH Write these sentences on the board:

I am a teacher.

We have a pet hamster.

Remind children of what they have learned about nouns for people and animals. Nouns are naming words. Some nouns name people. Some nouns name animals. Point to *teacher* as you read the first sentence. *Teacher* is a noun that names a person. Point to *hamster* as you read the second sentence. *Hamster* is a noun that names an animal.

GUIDE PRACTICE Hold up AlphaBuddy. What kind of animal is AlphaBuddy? AlphaBuddy is a bear. *Bear* is a noun that names an animal. Display the *man* Picture Card. This is a man. Is the word *man* a noun? Yes, it names a person, so it is a noun. Continue with these Picture Cards: *cat, duck, pig, queen, woman.*

Picture Card

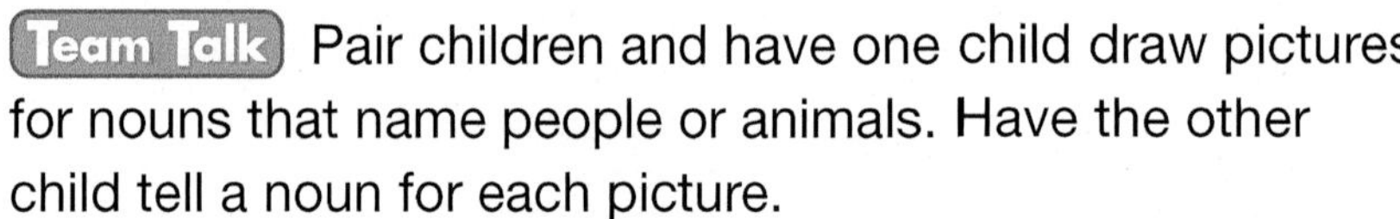

Team Talk Pair children and have one child draw pictures for nouns that name people or animals. Have the other child tell a noun for each picture.

ON THEIR OWN Use *Reader's and Writer's Notebook,* p. 73, for more practice with nouns for people and animals.

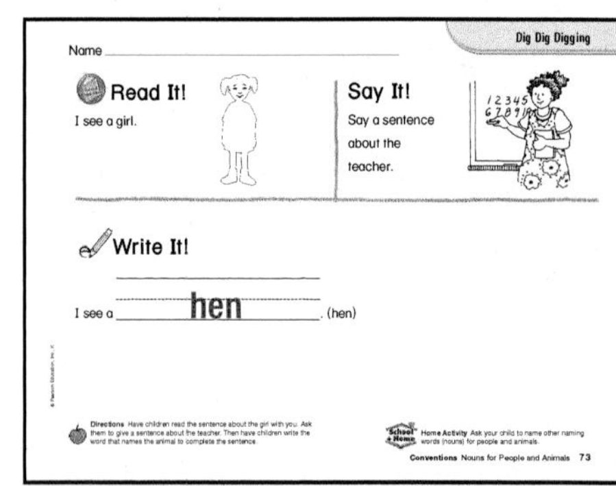

Name

Dig Dig Digging

Read It!

I see a girl.

Say It!

Say a sentence about the teacher.

Write It!

I see a hen. (hen)

Conventions Nouns for People and Animals 73

Reader's and Writer's Notebook, p. 73

Writing Process: Revise a Story

TEACH Yesterday we wrote a draft of our story about our music class. We wrote sentences for the beginning, middle, and end. Today we're going to revise our story. When we **revise** our writing, we make it better. One way to make our story better is to add more details or sentences. How can adding more details make our story better? Encourage children to share their thoughts. (Adding more details can make our story more interesting and fun for readers.)

MODEL Let's look at the writing we did yesterday. We wrote three sentences about our music class. Review the story with children. Our first sentence is *The music teacher plays the piano.* I think we need a better beginning for our story. We need to add a sentence that says clearly what our story is about so readers will know. Let's add this beginning sentence: *We go to music class every Friday.*

GUIDE PRACTICE We wrote about what we do in our music class—learn and sing songs—but we didn't say how we feel about our music class. That would make a better ending for our story because it tells readers more details about us. How do we feel, or what is our opinion, about our music class? Let children suggest a sentence. *Music class is fun!* That's good! That sentence helps readers know why we decided to write about our music class. Let's add the sentence at the end of our story. Review the revised story together. (*We go to music class every Friday. The music teacher plays the piano. We learn new songs. We sing the songs together. We sound good. Music class is fun!*)

INDEPENDENT WRITING On p. 74 in *Reader's and Writer's Notebook,* have children draw more pictures and/or write or dictate more words or sentences that can be added to the story. If computers are available, and children have the necessary skills, let them use the computers to revise the class story.

Dig Dig Digging

Name ____________

Draw Write

Details to Add

Pictures and answers will vary.

Directions Have children draw pictures or write words or sentences with details about the class story.

Home Activity Ask your child to explain how the details can be added to the class story.

74 Writing Process Revising

Reader's and Writer's Notebook, p. 74

Academic Vocabulary 

revise look over and improve

Express Feelings in Writing
Remind children that telling about their feelings can make their writing more interesting. Encourage them to tell about their feelings in a few words or short phrases. Rephrase what they say in complete sentences and have children repeat the sentences after you.

Common Core State Standards

Speaking/Listening 1.a. Follow agreed-upon rules for discussions (e.g., listening to others and taking turns speaking about the topics and texts under discussion). **Speaking/ Listening 4.** Describe familiar people, places, things, and events and, with prompting and support, provide additional detail.

Academic Vocabulary

drama a form of story told through motions and spoken words

Bridge to Common Core

COMPREHENSION AND COLLABORATION

When children act out machines from the selection, they are participating in a collaboration with classmates, expressing their own ideas, and demonstrating their understanding of information presented in the text.

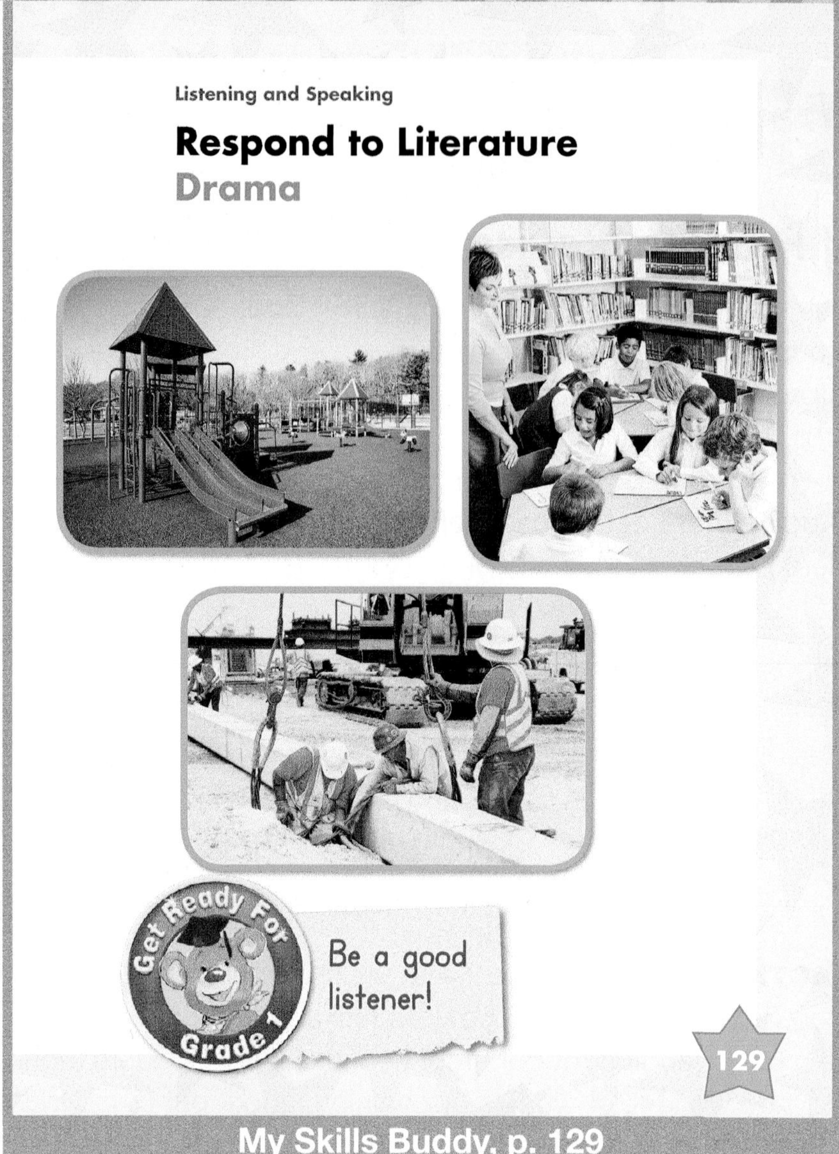

My Skills Buddy, p. 129

Listening and Speaking

Respond to Literature: Drama

TEACH Remind children that when they respond to a story through drama, they use their imaginations. They can act out what happens in a story.

MODEL Today I'm going to show you how I would act like a truck. If I were going to make a noise like a dump truck at a work site, I'd rrrrrrrumble! If I were going to act like a dump truck, I'd drop a load of rocks like this. Model for children how a dump truck would dump a load of rocks.

GUIDE PRACTICE Have children turn to p. 129 of *My Skills Buddy.* Discuss with them the Listening and Speaking bullet on p. 128. Have children play "Where does the story happen?" based on clues given by AlphaBuddy. AlphaBuddy will give some clues about a setting. Remember, the setting is the place and time in which a story happens. Listen carefully so that you can name the setting he is talking about. Use the photographs to help you. Have AlphaBuddy give the following clues:

- This story happens inside a place. This place has children, books, and a teacher. This place is a ______. (school)
- This story happens outside. Children are playing on a slide, and there are trees and a ball field. This place is a ______. (park)
- This is an area full of trucks. Workers and machines are fixing a road that is broken. This story takes place at a ______. (worksite)

Have children make up actions and words for what these children would say while playing at the park.

INDEPENDENT PRACTICE Assign a machine noise or motion to each child. Now let's pretend we are at the worksite setting. Each of you will act out the motion and noise of a different machine. Refer to the Rules for Listening and Speaking from pp. 1–2 of *Reader's and Writer's Notebook.* Remind children to face the speaker to show they are listening attentively.

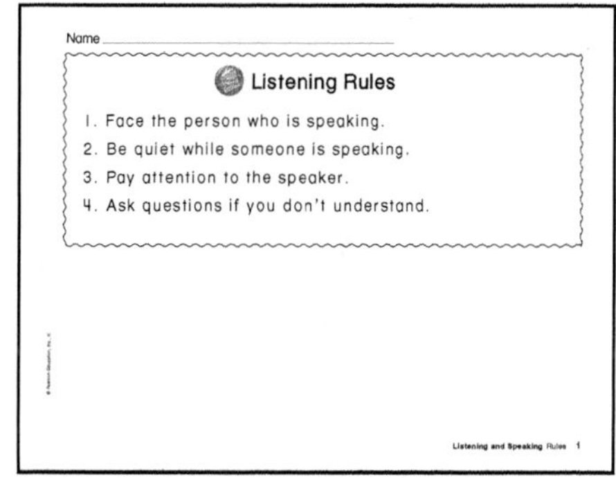
Name

Listening Rules

1. Face the person who is speaking.
2. Be quiet while someone is speaking.
3. Pay attention to the speaker.
4. Ask questions if you don't understand.

Listening and Speaking Rules 1

Reader's and Writer's Notebook, pp. 1–2

Be a Good Listener!

1. Face the person who is speaking.
2. Be quiet while someone is speaking.
3. Pay attention to the speaker.
4. Ask questions if you don't understand.

Access for All

SI Strategic Intervention

Access Content Have children join in the activity after first observing how the other children are participating.

Professional Development "For beginning English Learners, *Total Physical Response,* in which they follow commands such as 'Turn around,' can be highly effective. The meanings of words can be demonstrated through *gestures* and *pantomime.*" —Dr. Jim Cummins, University of Toronto

Common Core State Standards

Speaking/Listening 2. Confirm understanding of a text read aloud or information presented orally or through other media by asking and answering questions about key details and requesting clarification if something is not understood. **Language 5.c.** Identify real-life connections between words and their use (e.g., note places at school that are *colorful*).

Wrap Up Your Day!

- ✔ **Content Knowledge** Today we read about busy machines again. What machines take cars from factories to car dealers? (transporters)
- ✔ **Respond to Literature** Today we read a story about a toy store. What did you like about this story? Which toy did you like best? Why?
- ✔ **Conventions** Have children take turns thinking of and saying a noun they can use to name themselves and a noun they can use to name an animal.
- ✔ **Homework Idea** Ask children to look around at home for a machine whose name begins or ends with /t/. Have them draw a picture of it to bring to school the following day.

Preview DAY 4

Tomorrow we will read a story about three of our Trucktown friends.

Extend Your Day!

Science
How Do Things Move?

MATERIALS: six large blocks, one small block, toy truck, toy wagon, large piece of heavy cardboard

USING RAMPS Make stairs out of six stacked blocks. Imagine that you are small enough to use these as real stairs.

- How will you get this block to the top of the stairs? (carry it)
- Will the truck or wagon help you? (No, the wheels can't go up stairs.)

Place the cardboard to make a ramp. Point to the floor at the base of the ramp and then to the top of the ramp.

- Now which is easier, carrying the block or rolling it in the truck or wagon? (rolling it in the truck or wagon)

Have children volunteer one at a time to use the toys to move the block to the top of the stairs. Point out that the ramp and other machines make it easier to get the block up to the top.

Health
Machine Stretches

PRETEND WHILE WE STRETCH Repeat each of these stretches three times.

Crane: Move like a crane. Put your hands together and stretch your arms high. Pretend to pick something up. Bend at your waist and swing your arms down slowly.

Digger: Let's be a digger. Bend your knees and arms and scoop up some dirt. Twist slowly to one side and then the other.

Garbage Truck: Stand up to be a garbage truck. Bend a little at the waist and hold your arms out in front of you. Open and close your arms to gobble garbage.

Art
Brick by Brick

MATERIALS: Big Book *Dig Dig Digging,* colored paper cut in small rectangles, large dark blue or brown construction paper, chalk, glue

MOSAIC CONSTRUCTION Show children the cover of *Dig Dig Digging* and point out the buildings. We are going to design buildings like these. Using the chalk, draw a few rectangles on your paper. Draw some smaller squares or rectangles inside to look like windows and doors. Build your buildings by gluing small pieces of paper, like bricks, inside the chalk lines. Use different colors to make the windows and doors. Remember, a dot of glue is enough for each "brick."

DAY 4 at a Glance

Content Knowledge
Oral Vocabulary

Phonemic Awareness
Review Initial and Final /m/

Phonics
Review /m/ Spelled *Mm*
Blending

Text-Based Comprehension
Classify and Categorize
Review Setting

Conventions
Nouns for Places and Things

Writing
Edit a Story

Vocabulary
Words for Sizes

Materials

- Student Edition
- Truckery Rhymes
- Talk with Me/Sing with Me Chart
- Picture Cards
- Alphabet Cards
- Get Set, Roll! Reader 6
- Reader's and Writer's Notebook
- Big Book

Common Core State Standards

Speaking/Listening 2. Confirm understanding of a text read aloud or information presented orally or through other media by asking and answering questions about key details and requesting clarification if something is not understood. **Language 6.** Use words and phrases acquired through conversations, reading and being read to, and responding to texts. **Also Language 5.c.**

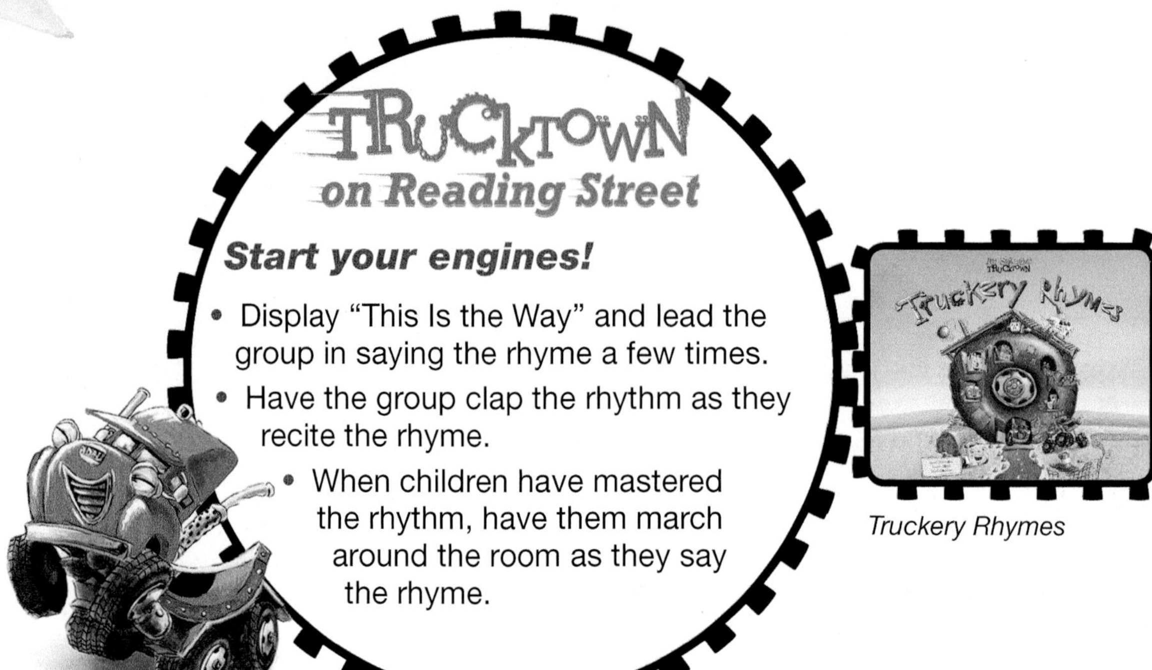
TRUCKTOWN
on Reading Street
Truckery Rhymes

Start your engines!

- Display "This Is the Way" and lead the group in saying the rhyme a few times.
- Have the group clap the rhythm as they recite the rhyme.
- When children have mastered the rhythm, have them march around the room as they say the rhyme.

Truckery Rhymes

Content Knowledge

Zoom in on

People and Machines Working Together

EXPAND THE CONCEPT On the board, write the Question of the Week, *How do machines help people work?* Read the question as you track the print. Tell children to respond audibly and clearly in complete sentences. Display Sing with Me Chart 6B.

Look at Them Go!
The diggers dig with a
scoop, scoop, scooping,
Scoop, scoop, scooping,
scoop, scoop, scooping,
The diggers dig with a scoop,
scoop, scooping,
Look at them go!

Talk with Me/Sing with Me Chart 6B

Build Oral Language

LISTEN FOR AMAZING WORDS We are going to sing this song again. Listen for the Amazing Words *spinning* and *rumbling.* Sing the song several times with children to the tune of "The Wheels on the Bus." Have children clap when they hear the Amazing Words *spinning* and *rumbling.*

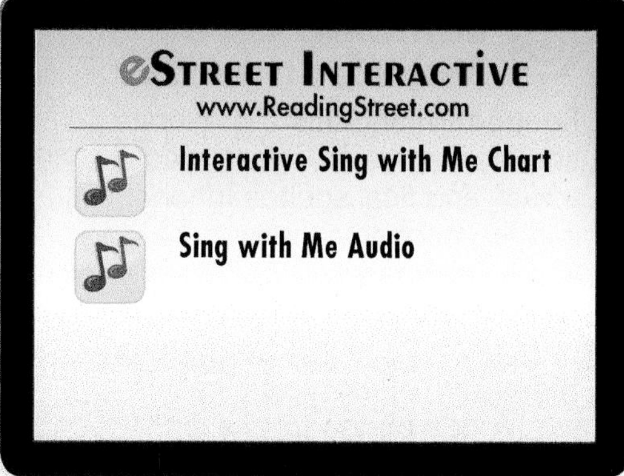

Build Oral Vocabulary

Amazing Words Robust Vocabulary Routine

1. **Introduce the Word** When a top is moving, it is *spinning. Spinning* is when something turns around and around. What is our new Amazing Word for turning around and around? Say it with me: *spinning.*

2. **Demonstrate** Provide examples to show meaning. *When a helicopter flies, its rotor blades are spinning.* What other *spinning* things can you think of?

   Repeat steps 1 and 2.

   Introduce the Word Rocks being dumped make a *rumbling* sound. *Rumbling* is a noise like thunder. What is our new Amazing Word for a noise like thunder? Say it with me: *rumbling.*

   Demonstrate *When we dump blocks out of a box, they make a rumbling sound.* What else makes a *rumbling* sound?

3. **Apply** Have children use *spinning* and *rumbling* in complete sentences. Have them draw a picture to illustrate their sentences.

4. **Display the Words** Have children point to and name letters in *spinning* and *rumbling* that they recognize. Ask them what letters they see in both words.

Routines Flip Chart

USE AMAZING WORDS To reinforce the concept and the Amazing Words, have children supply the appropriate Amazing Word for each sentence.

The yo-yo was _______ on the string. (spinning)
I like to hear thunder _______ during a storm. (rumbling)

Amazing Words

scooping	swooshing
squelching	gobbling
spinning	rumbling

Access Vocabulary Ask children to share how they would say *spinning* and *rumbling* in their home languages. Have a volunteer make a rumbling sound and then use *rumbling* in a sentence in his or her home language.
Produce Oral Language Use the Day 4 instruction on ELL Poster 6 to extend and enrich language.

Common Core State Standards
Foundational Skills 2.d. Isolate and pronounce the initial, medial vowel, and final sounds (phonemes) in three-phoneme (consonant-vowel-consonant, or CVC) words.* (This does not include CVCs ending with /l/, /r/, or /x/.) **Foundational Skills 3.a.** Demonstrate basic knowledge of one-to-one letter-sound correspondences by producing the primary or many of the most frequent sounds for each consonant. **Also Foundational Skills 1.d.**

Phonemic Awareness

Review Initial and Final /m/

PRACTICE Display the *map* Picture Card. This is a map. *Map* begins with /m/. What sound does *map* begin with? (/m/) Continue the routine with the *mitten, moon,* and *mop* Picture Cards.

Picture Card

Display the *drum* Picture Card. This is a drum. Where do you hear /m/ in the word *drum? Drum* ends with /m/. What sound does *drum* end with? (/m/) Continue the routine with the words *ham, slam,* and *Pam.*

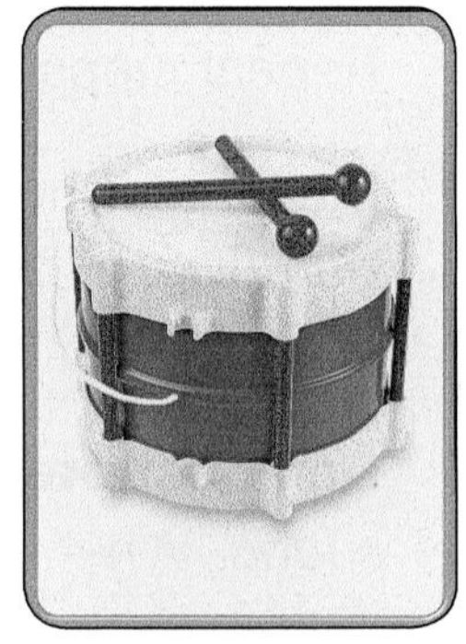
Picture Card

Corrective feedback **If...** children cannot discriminate /m/,
then... have them say /m/ several times. When you say /m/, you press your lips together. Have children practice saying /m/ and then repeat the discrimination activity.

Phonics

Review /m/ Spelled *Mm*

PRACTICE Display the *Mm* Alphabet Card. This is a motorcycle. *Motorcycle* begins with /m/. What letter spells the sound /m/? Yes, the letter *m.*

Alphabet Card

Display the *man* Picture Card. What is this? This is a man. What sound do you hear at the beginning of the word *man?* (/m/) What is the letter for /m/? (*Mm*) Write the word *man* on the board and have a volunteer underline the *m.* The letter for /m/ is *m.* Continue the routine with the *mop* and *mug* Picture Cards for initial /m/ and the *drum, gum,* and *jam* Picture Cards for final /m/.

Picture Card

MONITOR PROGRESS Check Letter Recognition

FORMATIVE ASSESSMENT Display all of the Alphabet Cards in random order. Point to any card and ask children to name the letter.

If... children cannot identify the letter names,

then... display three or four Alphabet Cards at a time and identify the letters before asking children to name them. Continue with other sets of cards.

Continue to monitor children's progress during the week so that children can be successful with the Day 5 Assessment. See the Skills Trace on p. 532.

Access for All

SI Strategic Intervention

Write *Mm* Display Picture Cards with pictures that begin with *m.* Have children choose a Picture Card to draw. Have them write a row of uppercase *M* and a row of lowercase *m* below their drawings.

Teacher Tip

Have the entire set of Alphabet Cards available for the letter recognition activity.

Support Phonemic Awareness The /m/ sound exists in many languages, so English language learners may be readily able to hear and pronounce this sound.

Common Core State Standards

Literature 10. Actively engage in group reading activities with purpose and understanding. **Foundational Skills 2.d.** Isolate and pronounce the initial, medial vowel, and final sounds (phonemes) in three-phoneme (consonant-vowel-consonant, or CVC) words.* (This does not include CVCs ending with /l/, /r/, or /x/.) **Foundational Skills 3.a.** Demonstrate basic knowledge of one-to-one letter-sound correspondences by producing the primary or many of the most frequent sounds for each consonant. **Also Foundational Skills 1., 2., 3., 3.c.**

Blending

/t/ Spelled *Tt*

Routine Blend Words

1. **Review *Tt*** Display the *Tt* Alphabet Card. This is a turtle. *Turtle* begins with /t/. What letter spells this sound? (*Tt*) Continue the routine with the *Mm* Alphabet Card.

2. **Model** Write the word *tap* on the board. Point to *t*. What is the sound for this letter? Say it with me: /t/ /t/ /t/.
   - The beginning sound in *tap* is /t/. *Tap* ends with *-ap*. When I blend the beginning sound /t/ and the ending *-ap,* I make the word *tap: /t/ -ap, tap.*
   - Say the sounds with me: /t/ *-ap.* Now let's blend the sounds together. Listen as I do it: /t/ *-ap, tap.* Say it with me: /t/ *-ap, tap.* Now you say it without me.
   - Listen as I use the word *tap* in a sentence: *He will tap on the window.* Say the sentence with me. Have children use *tap* in a sentence.

Write the word *hat* on the board. Point to *t*. What is the sound for this letter? Say it with me: /t/ /t/ /t/.

- The ending sound in *hat* is /t/. *Hat* begins with *ha-*. When I blend the beginning *ha-* and the ending sound /t/, I make the word *hat: ha-* /t/, *hat.*
- Say the sounds with me: *ha-* /t/. Now let's blend the sounds together. Listen as I do it: *ha-* /t/, *hat.* Say it with me: *ha-* /t/, *hat.* Now you say it without me.
- Listen as I use the word *hat* in a sentence: *Ann lost her hat.* Say the sentence with me. Ask children to use *hat* in a sentence.

3. **Guide Practice** Continue the routine with the words below. We are going to blend some more words. Remember, first we look for the /t/ in the word. Next, we say the beginning or ending. Then we blend the sounds to make the word.

tell	Tom	tug	get	sit	not

4. **On Your Own** Write the following sentence on the board: *Pat got ten tops.* Read it aloud. Have children draw a picture for the sentence. Then have them copy the sentence as a caption for their picture.

Routines Flip Chart

Get Set, Roll! Reader 6

Read *Ted*

REVIEW Review the high-frequency words *the, to, I,* and *am.* Have children find each word on the Word Wall.

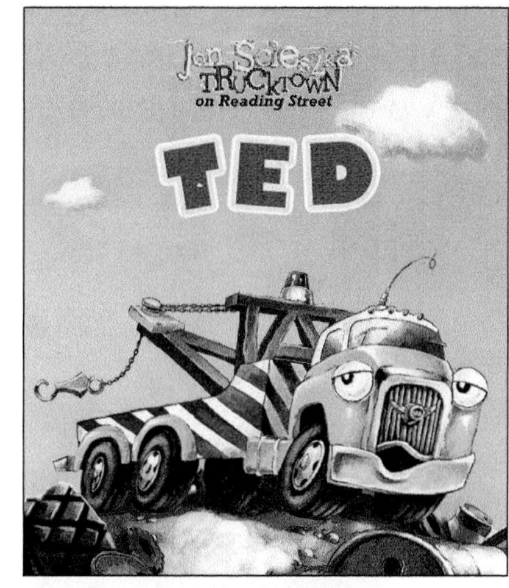

Get Set, Roll! Reader 6

TEACH REBUS WORDS Write *Ted* on the board. This word is *Ted.* Name the letters with me: *T, e, d.* Continue with *Jack, Rita, tows,* and *garage.* A picture above each of these words will help you read it.

READ Today we will read a book about Ted. Point to the title of the book. *Ted* is the title of the book. The title is on the cover. Where is the title? (on the cover) Open Get Set, Roll! Reader 6. The inside of the book has the story written on its pages. What is on the inside of a book? (the story, the pages) We will read /t/ words in this book.

Use the routine for reading decodable books in the Routines Flip Chart to read Get Set, Roll! Reader 6.

Access for All

Advanced

Access Content After reading the story together, have groups of three act out what happened in the story and what they think will happen next.

Access Content Do a picture walk with children to preview the reader before starting the routine.

Day 4 SMALL GROUP TIME • Differentiate Language, p. SG•89

OL On-Level	SI Strategic Intervention	A Advanced
• **Build** Sentences and Words • **Read** Get Set, Roll! Reader *Ted*	• **Talk About** Sentences and Words • **Read** Get Set, Roll! Reader *Ted*	• **Extend** Sentences and Words • **Read** Get Set, Roll! Reader *Ted*

Place English Language Learners in the groups that correspond to their reading abilities in English.

If... children need more practice **Developing Language,**
then... use the Language Workshops in the *ELL Handbook* beginning on p. 306.

Text-Based Comprehension

Classify and Categorize

PRACTICE Have children turn to the Classify and Categorize pictures on pp. 114–115 of *My Skills Buddy.* As you look at the pictures, remind children that we can put things in a group if they are alike in some way.

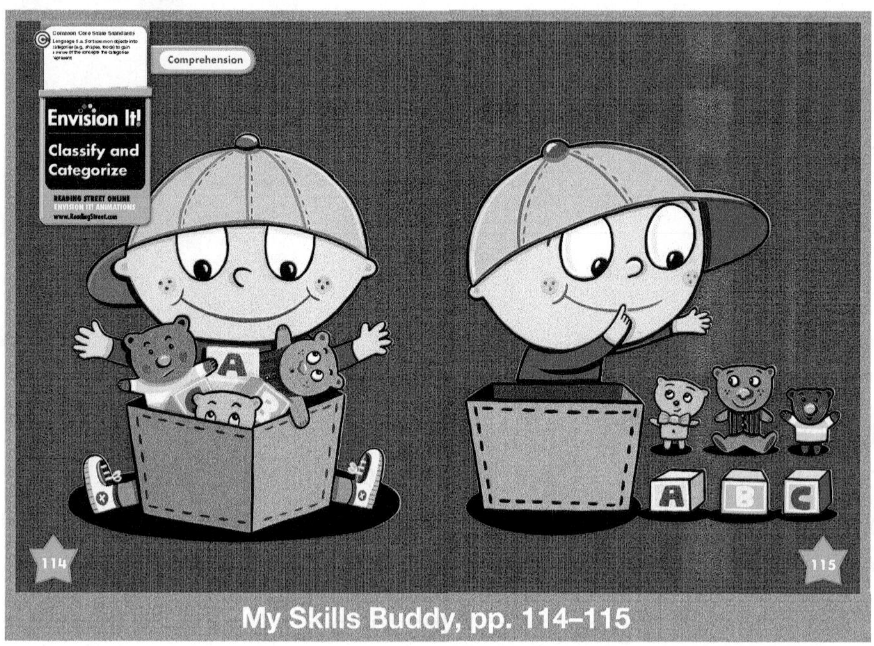

My Skills Buddy, pp. 114–115

Team Talk Pair children and have them classify and categorize things they do with friends and things they do with their families.

Review Setting

PRACTICE Direct children to the Literary Elements pictures on pp. 34–35 of *My Skills Buddy.*

The setting of a story is where and when the story takes place. Good readers always think about the setting when they read a story because it helps them understand the story.

- Look at the first picture. What does it show? (the starting line of a race)
- What is the setting of the story? (a race on a path)

MORE PRACTICE For more practice with setting, use *Reader's and Writer's Notebook,* p. 75.

Reader's and Writer's Notebook, p. 75

Common Core State Standards

Literature 3. With prompting and support, identify characters, settings, and major events in a story. **Informational Text 1.** With prompting and support, ask and answer questions about key details in a text. **Language 5.a.** Sort common objects into categories (e.g., shapes, foods) to gain a sense of the concepts the categories represent. **Also Informational Text 10.**

Access for All

Setting Remind children that both the words and the pictures in a story can tell when and where a story takes place.

Read Main Selection

GUIDE COMPREHENSION Display *Dig Dig Digging.* This selection is about machines that help people do work.

- Where do the machines work? (outside)
- When do the machines work? (during the day)
- What can we say is the setting for this selection? (outside during the day)

READ Reread *Dig Dig Digging.* Return to p. 572. Follow the **3rd Read** and use the **Develop Comprehension** notes to give children the opportunity to gain a more complete understanding of the selection.

Routine Read for Understanding 

Deepen understanding by reading the selection multiple times.

1. **First Read**—Read the entire selection aloud to build interest in the text.
2. **Second Read**—Use the **Develop Vocabulary** notes on pages 572–583.
3. **Third Read**—Use the **Develop Comprehension** notes on pages 572–583.

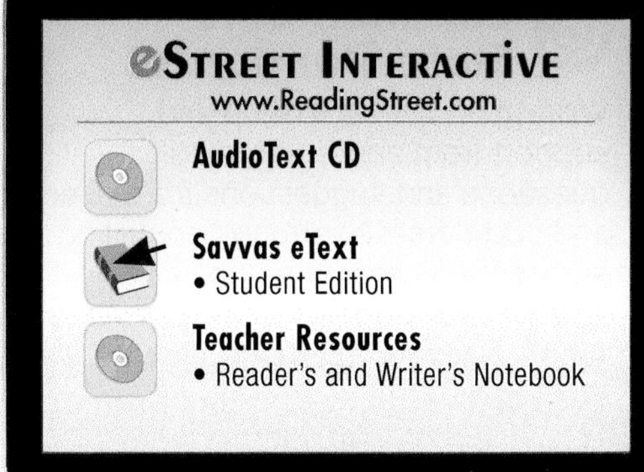

Bridge to Common Core

RANGE OF READING AND LEVEL OF TEXT COMPLEXITY
Using the Develop Comprehension notes as you read the text a third time will help you assess how well children are comprehending the authentic informational text in *Reading Street.* As the year progresses, children will improve as independent, proficient readers of complex text.

Access Content Make simple drawings of some of the vehicles and machines. Point out to children that vehicles are wheeled, or moving machines.

Common Core State Standards

Writing 5. With guidance and support from adults, respond to questions and suggestions from peers and add details to strengthen writing as needed. **Language 1.b.** Use frequently occurring nouns and verbs. **Also Foundational Skills 1.c., Writing 6., 7.**

Daily Fix-It

miss Bindergarten took the class to the library

Miss Bindergarten took the class to the library.

This week's practice sentences appear on *Teacher Resources DVD-ROM.*

Conventions

Nouns for Places and Things

TEACH Remind children of what they learned about nouns. We have been talking about nouns, or words that name places, things, people, and animals. This week we are learning about nouns for places and things.

Some nouns name places. *School* is a noun that names a place. Other words that name places are *house* and *street.* Listen to this sentence: *We went to the zoo.* The word *zoo* is a noun that names a place.

Some nouns name things. *Chair* and *table* name things we find in school. Listen to this sentence: *The apple is red.* The word *apple* is a noun that names a thing.

GUIDE PRACTICE Write *bakery* on the board. Point to the word as you read it. Is *bakery* the name of a place or a thing? Continue with *fire station, truck, library, book, city, tree,* and *park.* After children identify the nouns as naming places or things, reread the words on the board with them, pointing to each word as you say it. With children, think of sentences using the nouns and write them on the board.

ON THEIR OWN Use *Reader's and Writer's Notebook,* p. 76, for more practice reading, writing, and saying nouns for places and things.

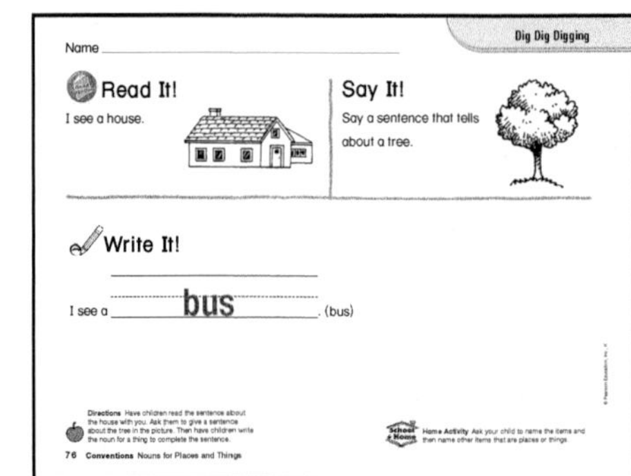

Reader's and Writer's Notebook, p. 76

Writing Process: Edit a Story

TEACH Remind children of the work they have done on their story so far. What steps in the writing process have we done so far in writing our story? (We chose an idea when we planned our story; we wrote sentences for the beginning, middle, and end when we drafted our story; we added more details and sentences when we revised our story.) Today we will edit our story. When we **edit** our writing, we check to make sure we've written everything correctly. Did we use correct spacing between letters and words? Remind children that we leave small spaces between the letters in a word and bigger spaces between the words in a sentence. Correct letter and word spaces help make our words and sentences clear and easy for others to read.

MODEL Reread the story you wrote. Point out the correct spacing between letters and words. Have children point out anything they think needs to be fixed. Show them how you would mark these corrections.

GUIDE PRACTICE Help children complete the editing activity on p. 77 in *Reader's and Writer's Notebook.* Ask them what needs to be fixed in each sentence. After children circle the errors, you may wish to have them write the words or sentences correctly on the lines.

INDEPENDENT WRITING Children can practice proper letter and word spacing by copying on p. 78 in *Reader's and Writer's Notebook* some or all of the sentences from the class story. Remind them to use small spaces between the letters in a word and bigger spaces between the words in a sentence. Point out that children can use your sentences on the board as a model. If computers are available, and children have the necessary skills, let them use the computers to edit the class story.

Name
Dig Dig Digging
Circle Write
1. We like m u s i c.
2. Thisis a new song.
3. She plays forus.

Reader's and Writer's Notebook, pp. 77–78

Academic Vocabulary

edit correct errors

Bridge to Common Core

PRODUCTION AND DISTRIBUTION OF WRITING

With your guidance and support, children are developing a class narrative using the writing process. They have planned, drafted, and revised the writing, and now they are editing it for clarity and accuracy before the last step, sharing their work with others.

Support Writing As children write or dictate, supply English words if needed to help them express their ideas.

Common Core State Standards

Foundational Skills 2. Demonstrate understanding of spoken words, syllables, and sounds (phonemes). **Foundational Skills 3.a.** Demonstrate basic knowledge of one-to-one letter-sound correspondences by producing the primary or many of the most frequent sounds for each consonant. **Language 5.a.** Sort common objects into categories (e.g., shapes, foods) to gain a sense of the concepts the categories represent. **Language 5.c.** Identify real-life connections between words and their use (e.g., note places at school that are *colorful*).

Vocabulary

Words for Sizes

TEACH Write the words *big, little, tall,* and *short* on the board. Point to each word as you read it. These words tell the sizes of things. Have children turn to p. 128 of *My Skills Buddy.* Use the remaining Vocabulary bullets in the discussion. Direct children to the picture of the large truck. Is this truck big or little? Then direct them to the small toy truck. Is this truck big or little? Have children point to the picture of two women and tell which woman is tall and which woman is short.

My Skills Buddy, p. 128

Team Talk Pair children and have each child find an object in the classroom to identify as big, little, tall, or short.

Wrap Up Your Day!

✔ **Oral Language** Sing "Look at Them Go!" with me. Clap when you hear an Amazing Word—*scooping, swooshing, squelching, gobbling, spinning, rumbling.*

✔ **Phonemic Awareness** I'm going to say some sentences. Clap when you hear /t/ words: *Ted is going to town today. Tanya has ten tiny toes.*

✔ **Homework Idea** Have children think of nouns for places in their neighborhoods.

Preview DAY 5

Tell children that tomorrow they will review some of the books and stories they have read this week.

Extend Your Day!

Science
Pipeline

MATERIALS: construction paper, small marble, tape, drawing paper

MOVEMENT Give each child a sheet of construction paper. I want to move this marble from my desk all the way back to the table. What ideas do you have about how we can move the ball across the room? Have children say if there are any ways they might use the sheet of paper to move the marble, and test any hypotheses you think have merit, such as carrying the marble by using the sheet of paper as a hammock.

Then tell children to roll their paper into tubes the long way. Make sure the tubes are wide enough to hold the marble. Secure each tube with tape. How do you think we could use these tubes to move the marble from my desk to the table?

Have children form a pipeline by holding their tubes end to end. Our paper tubes are shaped like pipes. What kinds of things do people use pipes to move? (liquids such as water and gasoline)

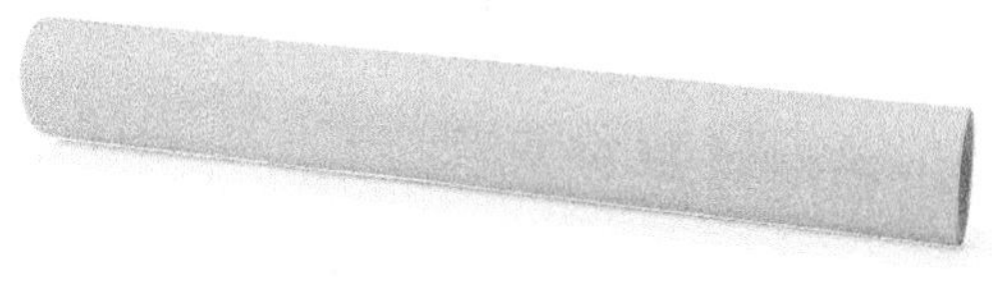

Phonics
Initial Consonants

MATERIALS: paper, crayons

CONNECT SOUND TO LETTER Give each child a sheet of paper divided into eight sections, numbered 1 to 8. Tell children to listen for the beginning sound in each word you say. Say a word. Have children write the letter for the initial sound. Use this list: *mom, mirror, ten, me, table, teeth, magic, tiny.*

Comprehension
Sorting Blocks

MATERIALS: variety of blocks

CLASSIFY AND CATEGORIZE
Provide a pile of mixed blocks. Discuss how the blocks are alike (material, color, size) and different. Have children work together to classify and categorize the blocks. For example, they can put all the red blocks in one pile. Mix the blocks up again, and then have children put all the square blocks in a pile. Continue to have children sort the blocks into groups according to one shared characteristic.

DAY 5 at a Glance

Content Knowledge
Oral Vocabulary

Phonemic Awareness
Review /t/

Phonics
Review /t/ Spelled *Tt*

Assessment
Phonics
High-Frequency Words
Comprehension

Text-Based Comprehension
Review Classify and Categorize

Conventions
Review Nouns for Places and Things

Writing
Share a Story

Materials

- Student Edition
- Truckery Rhymes
- Talk with Me/Sing with Me Chart
- Picture Cards
- Alphabet Cards
- Reader's and Writer's Notebook
- Read Aloud Anthology
- Student Reader K.1.6
- Get Set, Roll! Reader 6

Bridge to Common Core

INTEGRATION OF KNOWLEDGE/IDEAS
This week children have integrated content presented in diverse formats and analyzed how different texts address similar topics. They have developed knowledge about how people and machines work together to expand the unit topic of Cooperation.

Science Knowledge Goals
Children have learned that working with machines

- helps get a lot of work done
- helps with many different jobs

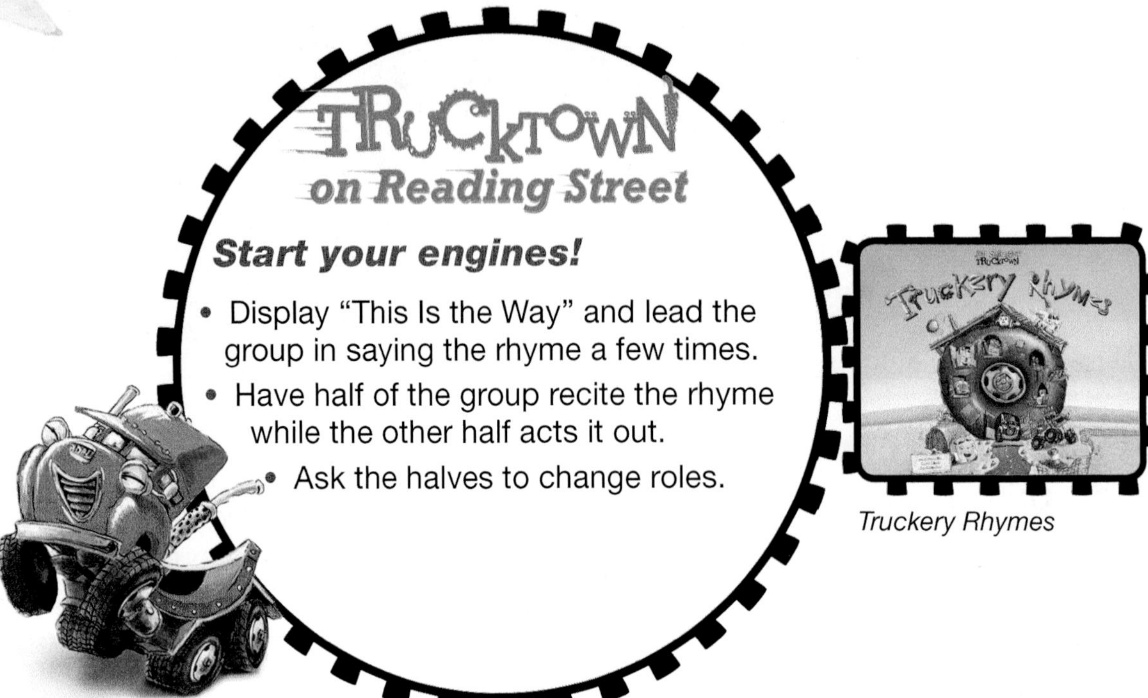

TRUCKTOWN
on Reading Street

Start your engines!

- Display "This Is the Way" and lead the group in saying the rhyme a few times.
- Have half of the group recite the rhyme while the other half acts it out.
- Ask the halves to change roles.

Truckery Rhymes

Truckery Rhymes

Content Knowledge

Zoom in on Ⓒ

People and Machines Working Together

REVIEW THE CONCEPT Discuss with children what they have added to their knowledge about this unit of study, All Together Now. Encourage them to use the Amazing Words.

Build Oral Language

LISTEN FOR AMAZING WORDS Display Sing with Me Chart 6B. Let's sing "Look at Them Go!" again. I want you to listen for the Amazing Words we learned this week. Say them with me: *scooping, swooshing, squelching, gobbling, spinning, rumbling.* Sing the song several times to the tune of "The Wheels on the Bus." Have children imitate a machine every time they hear an Amazing Word. Then discuss how each machine helps people do work. Remind children to take turns sharing their responses.

Look at Them Go!
The diggers dig with a
scoop, scoop, scooping,
Scoop, scoop, scooping,
scoop, scoop, scooping,
The diggers dig with a scoop,
scoop, scooping,
Look at them go!

Talk with Me/Sing with Me Chart 6B

Build Oral Vocabulary

Talk with Me/Sing with Me Chart 6A

REVIEW AMAZING WORDS Display Talk with Me Chart 6A. We learned six new Amazing Words this week. Let's say the Amazing Words as I point to the pictures on the chart. Point to each picture and give children the chance to say the appropriate Amazing Word before offering it.

Have children supply the appropriate Amazing Word to complete each sentence.

The digger is _______ up dirt and moving it. (scooping)
The hose is _______ water across the sidewalk. (swooshing)
The hikers are _______ through the mud. (squelching)
The hungry puppy is _______ his dinner. (gobbling)
The toy top is _______ on the floor. (spinning)
The big bus is _______ down the street. (rumbling)

MONITOR PROGRESS Check Oral Vocabulary

FORMATIVE ASSESSMENT Demonstrate Word Knowledge Monitor the Amazing Words by saying the following definitions. Tell children to use the Amazing Word in their answer.

- **what diggers are doing when they dig** (scooping)
- **the sound rushing water or air makes** (swooshing)
- **the sound mud makes as it is stepped on** (squelching)
- **what garbage trucks are doing when they pick up garbage** (gobbling)
- **what wheels are doing when they are moving** (spinning)
- **the sound you hear when rocks are dumped** (rumbling)

If... children have difficulty using the Amazing Words,
then... reteach the words using the Robust Vocabulary Routine on the Routines Flip Chart.

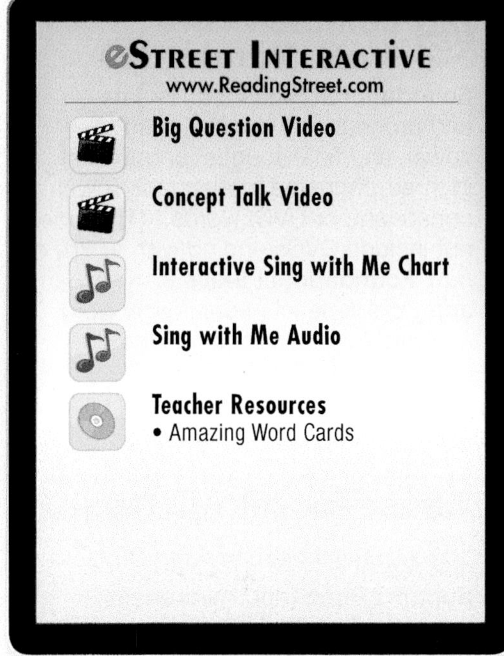

Amazing Words

scooping	swooshing
squelching	gobbling
spinning	rumbling

Access for All

 Strategic Intervention

Word Choice Some children may have difficulty remembering the six Amazing Words. After you read each question, offer two or three Amazing Words for children to choose from.

Sentence Production Have children choose one Amazing Word. Ask them to say a complete sentence using that word. Have children illustrate their sentence.

Check Concepts and Language Use the Day 5 instruction on ELL Poster 6 to monitor children's understanding of the lesson concept.

Common Core State Standards

Foundational Skills 2.d. Isolate and pronounce the initial, medial vowel, and final sounds (phonemes) in three-phoneme (consonant-vowel-consonant, or CVC) words.* (This does not include CVCs ending with /l/, /r/, or /x/.) **Foundational Skills 3.** Know and apply grade-level phonics and word analysis skills in decoding words.

Access for All

SI Strategic Intervention

Support Phonemic Awareness Have children think of other words that begin with /t/. If they are having difficulty, have children look around the room for things whose names begin with /t/.

Phonemic Awareness

Review /t/

ISOLATE INITIAL AND FINAL /t/ Display the *taxi* Picture Card. What is the first sound in *taxi?* Say the word with me: /t/ /t/ /t/, *taxi.* Review initial /t/ with the following words: *tack, turtle, tub, Tom.*

Picture Card

Display the *hat* Picture Card. What is the last sound in *hat?* Listen carefully: /h/ /a/ /t/. The last sound in *hat* is /t/. Say it with me: *hat,* /t/ /t/ /t/. Continue isolating final /t/ with the following words: *what, wet, net, cat, boat.*

DISCRIMINATE FINAL SOUNDS I am going to say some words. When you hear the same ending sound, I want you to stomp your feet. When you hear different ending sounds, I want you to jump. Listen carefully: *wet, not, rat.* Do these words have the same ending sound or different ending sounds? I hear /t/ at the end of these words, so I will stomp my feet. Continue with the following sets of words: *cat, kit, fat; boat, base, boom; pot, hat, bit.*

Picture Card

Phonics

Review /t/ Spelled *Tt*

TEACH /t/*Tt* Display the *Tt* Alphabet Card. This is a turtle. What sound do you hear at the beginning of *turtle?* What is the letter that spells that sound?

REVIEW HIGH-FREQUENCY WORDS Write the word *a* on the board. This is the word *a.* What is this word? Repeat the routine with the word *to.*

APPLY PHONICS Have children reread one of the books specific to the target letter sound. You may wish to review the rebus words and high-frequency words that appear in each book prior to rereading.

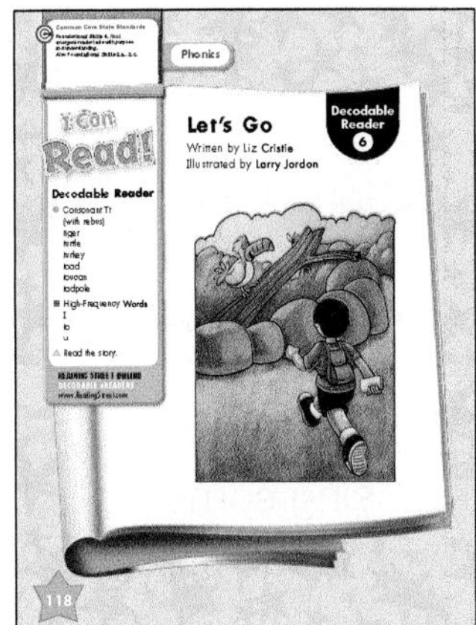

Decodable Reader 6
My Skills Buddy, p. 118

Kindergarten Student Reader K.1.6

Get Set, Roll! Reader 6

Alphabet Card

Concepts of Print Some children's home languages, such as Hebrew, Arabic, and Persian, may be read from right to left. Remind children that English sentences are read from left to right and from top to bottom.

Day 5 SMALL GROUP TIME • Differentiate Close Reading, p. SG•89

OL On-Level
- **Phonics** Spell *t* Words
- **Read** "Simple Machines"

SI Strategic Intervention
- **Phonics** Blend *t* Words
- **Read** "Simple Machines"

A Advanced
- **Phonics** Write Sentences with *t* Words
- **Read** "Simple Machines"

ELL

Place English Language Learners in the groups that correspond to their reading abilities in English.

If... children need more support with **Comprehension,**
then... use the ELL activities on pp. DI•98–DI•99 in the Teacher Resources section of the Digital Path.

Common Core State Standards

Foundational Skills 2. Demonstrate understanding of spoken words, syllables, and sounds (phonemes). **Foundational Skills 3.a.** Demonstrate basic knowledge of one-to-one letter-sound correspondences by producing the primary or many of the most frequent sounds for each consonant. **Foundational Skills 3.c.** Read common high-frequency words by sight. (e.g., *the, of, to, you, she, my, is, are, do, does*).

Assess

- Read letters *Tt.*
- Read high-frequency words.
- Read sentences.

Assessment

Monitor Progress

Review /t/ Spelled *Tt*

WHOLE CLASS Divide a sheet of paper into four equal sections for each child. Have children draw something whose name begins or ends with /t/ in each box. Then have children label each picture with the letter *t.*

MONITOR PROGRESS Check Word and Sentence Reading

If... children cannot complete the whole-class assessment,
then... use the Reteach lesson in *First Stop.*

If... you are unsure of a child's grasp of this week's skills,
then... use the assessment below to obtain a clearer evaluation of the child's progress.

ONE-ON-ONE To facilitate individual progress monitoring, assess some children on Day 4 and the rest on Day 5. While you are assessing some children, have the other children practice identifying /t/ words in the readers.

SOUND DISCRIMINATION Use the pictures on reproducible p. 607 to assess a child's ability to identify initial /t/ words. Say the name of each picture aloud: *taxi, ball, ten, tire, tiger, pig.* Have the child listen for and identify initial /t/ words. Record any problems the child has identifying initial /t/ words.

WORD READING Use the words on reproducible p. 607 to assess a child's ability to read high-frequency words. Record errors and note specific problems.

RECORD SCORES Monitor children's accuracy by recording their scores using the Letter and Word Reading Chart for this unit in *First Stop.*

Name ______________________________

Name the Sounds

Read the Words

to ☐

a ☐

Copyright © Savvas Learning Company LLC. All Rights Reserved.

Note to Teacher: Children listen for and identify initial /t/. Children read each word.

Scoring for Name the Sound/Read the Words: Score 1 point for each correct sound/word.

Name the Sounds (*taxi, ten, tire, tiger*) ______ / 4

High-Frequency Words (*to, a*) ______ / 2

MONITOR PROGRESS

- /t/ Spelled *Tt*
- High-Frequency Words

Common Core State Standards
Literature 1. With prompting and support, ask and answer questions about key details in a text. Also Literature 5.
Let's Practice It!
Folk Tale
Listen to the folk tale.
What can you tell about the third little pig?
What does the wolf say each time he comes to a house?
What lesson do the first two pigs learn?
Why do people like to read or listen to this story?
The Three Little Pigs
1
2
3
4
5
130
131

My Skills Buddy, pp. 130–131

Common Core State Standards

Literature 1. With prompting and support, ask and answer questions about key details in a text. **Literature 3.** With prompting and support, identify characters, settings, and major events in a story. **Literature 5.** Recognize common types of texts (e.g., storybooks, poems).

Let's Practice It!

Folk Tale

TEACH Tell children that today they will listen to a well-known folk tale. A folk tale is a well-known story that can have different versions in different parts of the world. Review the features of a folk tale.

- A folk tale tells a story.
- A folk tale often has repeating words.
- A folk tale teaches a lesson.
- Folk tales sometimes have animal characters that appear often, such as a wolf.

Have children turn to pp. 130–131 of *My Skills Buddy.* I am going to read you a folk tale called "The Three Little Pigs." Look at the pictures as I read. Read the text of "The Three Little Pigs." As you read, direct children to look at the appropriate picture.

GUIDE PRACTICE Discuss the features of a folk tale and the bulleted items on p. 130 of *My Skills Buddy* with children.

- A folk tale tells a story. What happens in this story? (A wolf blows down two pigs' houses. The pigs outsmart him at the third house.)
- A folk tale often has repeating words. What does the wolf say each time he comes to a house? ("Then I'll huff and I'll puff and I'll blow your house down.")
- A folk tale teaches a lesson. What lesson do the two little pigs learn? (It takes hard work to build a safe house, but it is worth it.) When have you learned a lesson about hard work?
- This folk tale has a wolf as a character. What other tales do you know that have a wolf as a character? (Little Red Riding Hood)

Writing to Sources
Use Connect the Texts on pp. 28–29 to guide children in writing text-based responses using two sources.

Teacher Read Aloud

The Three Little Pigs

Three little pigs were building houses to shelter them from the rain, the cold, and the wolf that lived nearby. The first little pig built his house out of straw. The second little pig built his house out of wood. The third little pig built his house out of bricks.

One day the wolf came to the straw house and ordered the first little pig to come out. When the pig refused, the wolf said, "Then I'll huff and I'll puff and I'll blow your house down." He took a deep breath and blew on the straw house. WHOOSH! It fell down, and the first little pig ran to the second little pig's house.

The wolf came to the wooden house and ordered both little pigs to come out. When they refused, the wolf said, "Then I'll huff and I'll puff and I'll blow your house down." He took a very deep breath and blew on the wooden house. WHOOSH! It fell down, and the two little pigs ran to the third little pig's house.

The wolf came to the brick house and ordered all three little pigs to come out. When they refused, the wolf said, "Then I'll huff and I'll puff and I'll blow your house down." He took a VERY deep breath and blew on the brick house. WHOOSH! It did not fall down. The wolf blew a second time and a third time, but the house stood firm.

continued on p. 618a

Access Content Identify the wolf and the pigs in the pictures. Demonstrate the sounds wolves and pigs make.
Visual and Contextual Support To enhance and confirm understanding, have children use the pictures and what they heard in the Read Aloud to answer specific questions about the characters.

Common Core State Standards

Language 5.a. Sort common objects into categories (e.g., shapes, foods) to gain a sense of the concepts the categories represent.

Assess

- Classify and categorize elements of a story.

Assessment

Monitor Progress

REVIEW CLASSIFY AND CATEGORIZE We put things in a group when they are alike in some way. When we put things into groups, we classify and categorize. Good readers pay attention to how things can be grouped together because it helps them better remember and understand what they read.

READ "THE COLOR SONG" Tell children that you are going to read them a song called "The Color Song." The first time, have children listen for different colors. Then have them listen carefully for other ways they can group things in the song. Read "The Color Song" on p. 12 of *Read Aloud Anthology.*

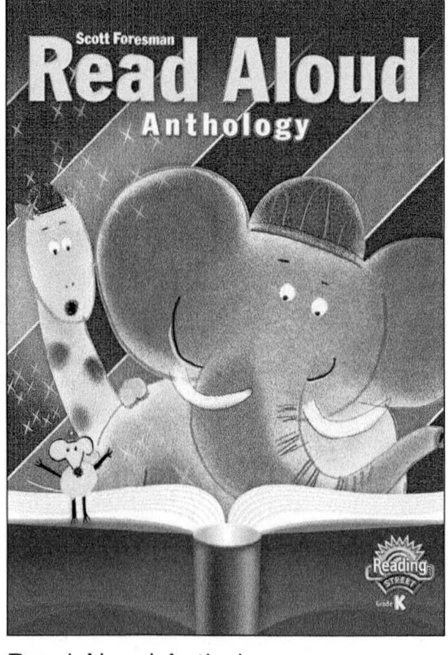

Read Aloud Anthology

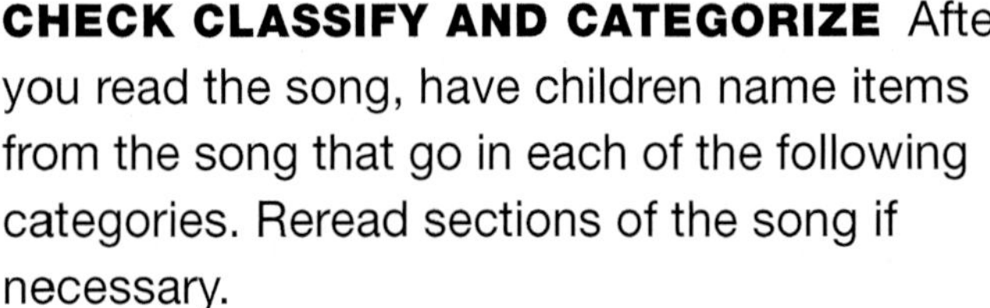

CHECK CLASSIFY AND CATEGORIZE After you read the song, have children name items from the song that go in each of the following categories. Reread sections of the song if necessary.

- colors (red, blue, yellow, green, orange, purple)
- things that are red, blue, yellow, green, orange, or purple
- foods (apple, cherries, strawberries, lemonade, peas, watermelon, oranges, carrots, grapes, grape juice)

Corrective feedback	**If...** children cannot classify and categorize, **then...** reteach classify and categorize using the Reteach lesson in *First Stop.*

ASSESS CLASSIFY AND CATEGORIZE Use the blackline master on p. 611. Make one copy for each child. Have children cut out the pictures. Write the color words *Red* and *Yellow* on the board. On a sheet of paper folded in half, have children copy *Red* on one half and *Yellow* on the other half. Have children glue outlines of red objects under *Red* and color the objects red. Have children glue outlines of yellow objects under *Yellow* and color the objects yellow.

Name ________________________________

Classify and Categorize

Note to Teacher: Distribute another sheet of paper folded in half. Children copy *Red* on one column and *Yellow* on the other. Then they cut out objects, glue red objects under *Red* and yellow objects under *Yellow,* and color the pictures red or yellow.

Copyright © Savvas Learning Company LLC. All Rights Reserved.

MONITOR PROGRESS

- Classify and Categorize

Common Core State Standards

Writing 3. Use a combination of drawing, dictating, and writing to narrate a single event or several loosely linked events, tell about the events in the order in which they occurred, and provide a reaction to what happened. **Language 1.b.** Use frequently occurring nouns and verbs. **Also Writing 6., 7.**

Daily Fix-It

trucks help people work together.
Trucks help people work together.

This week's practice sentences appear on *Teacher Resources DVD-ROM.*

Conventions

Review Nouns for Places and Things

REVIEW Remind children of what they learned about nouns. Nouns are words that name people, animals, places, and things.

MODEL Display the *truck* Picture Card. What is the name of this thing? *Truck* is a word that names this thing. Because the word *truck* names a thing, *truck* is a noun. Pick an object from the classroom, such as a pencil. What is this thing? This thing is a pencil. *Pencil* is a word that names a thing.

GUIDE PRACTICE Review other nouns for things using the *crayon, net,* and *desk* Picture Cards. Continue similarly with nouns for places using the *garden, playground,* and *zoo* Picture Cards. Write each noun on the board as children identify it. Then read the words with children, pointing to each one as you say it.

ON THEIR OWN Have children find an object in the classroom. Tell children to complete this sentence with a noun that names the thing they found in the classroom: *This is a* _______.

Have children draw a picture of a thing from *Dig Dig Digging.* Have children write or dictate a noun label for their picture.

Writing Process: Share a Story

TEACH Display the story you have written together. Now it's time to share our work with other people. But before we share our work, we need to write a clean copy of our story. We will fix any mistakes we found while we were editing our story. We will use our best handwriting. We can add pictures if we choose, and we will make a cover. Then our story will be ready to share with others.

Now I will rewrite our story using my best handwriting. Quickly check spacing between letters and words.

MODEL Work with children as they write or dictate their stories on a separate sheet of paper. Encourage them to personalize their stories by drawing pictures to accompany the text.

GUIDE PRACTICE Children can use p. 79 in *Reader's and Writer's Notebook* to make a cover for their story. Explain that the cover has a picture that goes with the story, a title that tells what the story is about, and the name of the author. With children, think of a title for the class story. After they have drawn a picture, help children write the title and their name on the lines. Place each child's story between the cover and a blank paper and staple the pages together to make a booklet.

If computers are available, and children have the necessary skills, let them use the computers to write the final version of the class story to share with others.

ON THEIR OWN After they have shared their story with others, have children complete p. 80 in *Reader's and Writer's Notebook.* As a group, discuss reviewers' reactions to the stories. Have children save their stories to add to the classroom library.

Name

Dig Dig Digging

Draw Write

Answers will vary.

Title:

Author:

Reader's and Writer's Notebook, pp. 79–80

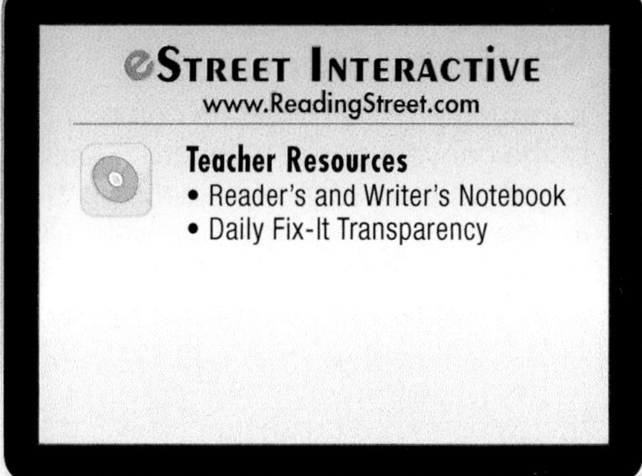

Access for All

Strategic Intervention

Support Writing Remind children to write left-to-right, just as they read.

Bridge to Common Core

PRODUCTION AND DISTRIBUTION OF WRITING

When children write a narrative about a class activity, they are conveying real experiences and events using a structured sequence and well-chosen details. Practicing the steps in the writing process with others will help children as they begin to produce more writing on their own.

ELL

Poster Preview Encourage children to look ahead to next week by previewing ELL Poster 7. Read the Poster Talk-Through to introduce the concept and vocabulary. Ask children to identify and describe objects and actions in the art.

Common Core State Standards

Language 1. Demonstrate command of the conventions of standard English grammar and usage when writing or speaking. **Language 1.b.** Use frequently occurring nouns and verbs. **Language 5.a.** Sort common objects into categories (e.g., shapes, foods) to gain a sense of the concepts the categories represent.

Wrap Up Your Week!

People and Machines Working Together

How do machines help people work?

ILLUSTRATE CLASSIFY AND CATEGORIZE This week we talked about all kinds of machines and how they help people.

- Make a classify and categorize chart like the one shown or use Graphic Organizer 9 and fill it in with children's responses.
- Have children draw a picture of a machine for each category.
- Help children write or dictate a phrase or sentence about their picture.
- Help children put their pictures into appropriate categories.

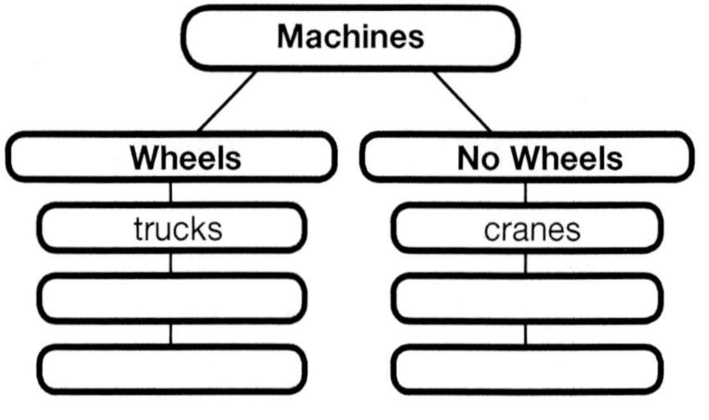

Amazing Words

You've learned 006 words this week!

You've learned 036 words this year!

Next Week's Concept

Looking at Flowers

How are flowers unique?

Discuss next week's question. Guide children in making connections between different machines and different flowers.

Tell children that next week they will read about flowers.

Preview Next Week

Extend Your Day!

Social Studies
On the Job

MATERIALS: construction paper, drawing utensils, scissors, mural paper, glue, Big Book *Dig Dig Digging*

MAKE A WORKERS' MURAL Take a picture walk with children through *Dig Dig Digging,* pointing out the different jobs people have.

- In our community, what jobs do people have?
- Why do people in our community have different jobs?
- What would happen if we didn't have a police officer or a mail carrier?
- What other jobs are important to our community?

Help children expand their ideas about community helpers by talking about other professions, such as bankers or government officials.

Have children draw, color, and cut out a picture of a worker on the job. Glue the people pictures on the mural paper.

Children may add machines and other scenery.

Math
Noun Count

MATERIALS: final class stories from Writing Process activity, chart paper

CREATE A TALLY SHEET Display children's class books. We are going to keep track of the kinds of nouns we used in our class books. Show children how to make a tally sheet with the headings *Person, Animal, Place,* and *Thing.* Start the sheet for them. Have children read pages from the class book and then make a tally mark under the correct heading for each noun they find. Count the marks under each heading with children. Ask them which kind of noun they used most and which kind of noun they used least.

Conventions
We Know Nouns

MATERIALS: large drawing paper, crayons

DRAW NOUNS Give each child a sheet of drawing paper folded in fourths. Have children tell about the kinds of nouns. Write *People, Animals, Places,* and *Things* on the board. Have children copy the labels, one in each box, and draw a picture in each box.

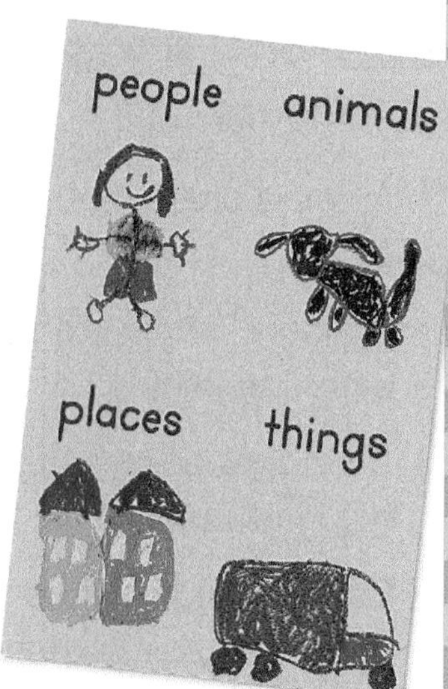

Wrap Up Your Unit! Zoom in on

Discuss Content Knowledge Gained Through Reading

How do we live, work, and play together?

WEEK 1

How do children get to school?

Children understand that riding the bus together

- helps them get to school
- helps them arrive safely

WEEK 2

How do school children work and play together?

Children understand that working together with classmates

- helps them share tools and supplies
- helps them solve problems

WEEK 3

How do families cooperate?

Children understand that support from their families

- helps them take care of themselves
- helps them take care of their friends

How do the characters in the stories live, work, and play together? Possible responses:

- Animals share a bus ride to school and back home again.
- School children work together and have fun making a parade float.
- A girl who always loses her stuffed platypus gets help from others.
- School children go on a field trip and learn about people in their community who help.
- Many different machines help people do their work.

How does it feel to cooperate? Possible responses:

- Cooperating with others can get a lot done.
- It can feel good to share new experiences.

WEEK 4

How do people in a community cooperate?

Children understand that cooperating with others
- helps them have a fun time
- helps them learn new things

WEEK 5

What do you like to do with your friends?

Children understand that playing with others
- helps them share fun experiences
- helps them share a common goal

WEEK 6

How do machines help people work?

Children understand that working with machines
- helps get a lot of work done
- helps with many different jobs

What kinds of activities can use cooperation? Possible responses:

- Children can cooperate by doing jobs and activities at school.
- Families can cooperate by doing chores and playing games at home.
- Friends can cooperate by helping one another with many things.

Amazing Words

You've learned 036 words so far this year!

You've learned 036 words this unit to use as you talk about cooperation.

Assessment Checkpoints for the Week

Weekly Assessment

Use the whole-class assessment on pages 606–607 and 610–611 in this Teacher's Edition to check:

- ✓ **/t/ Spelled *Tt***
- ✓ **Comprehension** *Classify and Categorize*
- ✓ **High-Frequency Words** *a* *to*

Managing Assessment

Use the Assessment Handbook for:

- ✓ **Observation Checklists**
- ✓ **Record-Keeping Forms**
- ✓ **Portfolio Assessment**

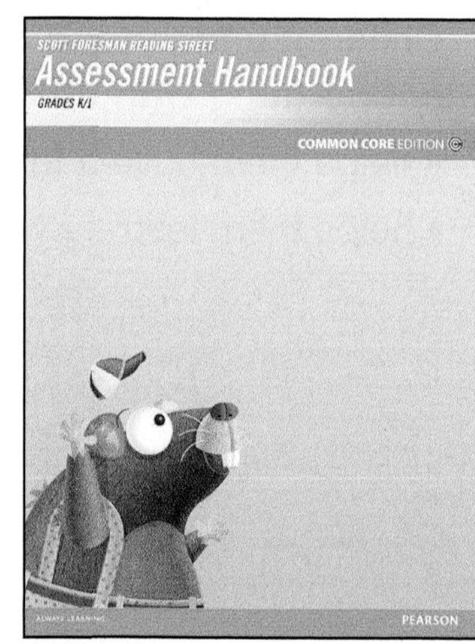

Assessment Handbook

Unit Assessment

Use the Unit 1 Assessment to check progress in:

- ✓ **Letter Recognition**
- ✓ **Phonological/Phonemic Awareness**
- ✓ **Phonics**
- ✓ **High-Frequency Words**
- ✓ **Comprehension** *Character; Sequence; Setting*
- ✓ **Conventions in Writing**

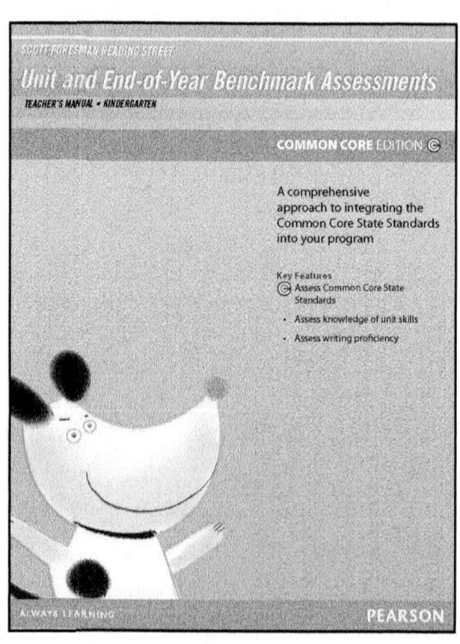

Unit Assessment

Let's Practice It!

Teacher Read Aloud continued from p. 609

The Three Little Pigs

The hungry wolf had an idea. He climbed on the roof of the house. He planned to slide down the chimney. The third little pig thought quickly. He lit a fire in the fireplace. When the wolf came down the chimney, he landed in the fire.

"Ow! Ow!" the wolf cried, jumping out of the fire. "I'll never do that again!" And he ran away as fast he could and was never seen again.

Nevertheless, the first little pig and the second little pig built their new houses out of brick.

TEACHER NOTES

DAY 1 Differentiate Phonics

- Consonant *t*/t/
- Decodable Story
- Advanced Selection "Can We Pat Tim?"

DAY 2 Differentiate Phonics

- Consonant *t*/t/
- Decodable Reader

DAY 3 Differentiate Vocabulary

- Develop Vocabulary: Words for Sizes
- Kindergarten Student Reader

DAY 4 Differentiate Language

- Develop Language
- Get Set, Roll! Reader

DAY 5 Differentiate Close Reading

- Phonics
- "Simple Machines"

Place English Language Learners in the groups that correspond to their reading abilities.
If... children need scaffolding and practice,
then... use the ELL notes on the page.

Independent Practice

Independent Practice Stations

See pp. 526 and 527 for Independent Stations.

Reading Street Digital Path

Independent Practice Activities available in the Digital Path.

Independent Reading

See p. 527 for independent reading suggestions.

On-Level

Common Core State Standards

Literature 1. With prompting and support, ask and answer questions about key details in a text. **Literature 10.** Actively engage in group reading activities with purpose and understanding. **Foundational Skills 2.d.** Isolate and pronounce the initial, medial vowel, and final sounds (phonemes) in three-phoneme (consonant-vowel-consonant, or CVC) words.* (This does not include CVCs ending with /l/, /r/, or /x/.) **Foundational Skills 3.a.** Demonstrate basic knowledge of one-to-one letter-sound correspondences by producing the primary or many of the most frequent sounds for each consonant. **Foundational Skills 3.c.** Read common high-frequency words by sight (e.g., *the, of, to, you, she, my, is, are, do, does*).

1 Build Word Knowledge

Practice Phonemic Awareness

TAP FOR /t/ I am going to tell you a story. When you hear a word that begins with /t/, tap your foot and say the word. Tell the following story, emphasizing and pausing after each /t/ word:

Tim takes a taxi to Aunt *Tammy's* house. Aunt *Tammy tells terrific* stories about *taming tigers* and *teaching turtles. Tim* and Aunt *Tammy talk* a long *time. Tim* plays with a *tiny toy top.* Aunt *Tammy* makes *tasty tomato* soup.

Practice Phonics

MATCH /t/ TO *Tt* Give each child an index card. Ask children to write the letter *t* on it. Retell the story and have children hold up their *t* card when they hear a word that begins with /t/.

2 Read

Decodable Story 6 *Tam!*

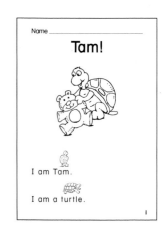

READ Have children read the story. Then have them reread the text to develop automaticity.

HIGH-FREQUENCY WORDS Have children return to the text and identify the high-frequency words *to, am, I,* and *a.* Help children demonstrate their understanding of these words by providing sentence frames such as these: *I walk* _______ *the door.* (to) _______ *am at my desk.* (I)

Name ____________

Tam!

I am Tam.

I am a turtle.

1

3 Reread for Fluency

Have children reread the Decodable Story *Tam!* individually to develop fluency.

Independent Reading Options

Trade Book Library

eStreet Interactive
www.ReadingStreet.com

Teacher's Guides available on the Leveled Reader Database.

On-Level

1 Build Word Knowledge

Practice Phonics

MORE *t* WORDS Distribute paper and crayons to children. Then display the *taxi, ten, mask, tent, tiger, pen, toes, top, tub,* and *box* Picture Cards one at a time. Have one child identify the picture you are displaying. Then have all children write the letter *t* on their paper if the picture name begins with /t/.

Practice High-Frequency Words

CHOOSE AND USE Display the following high-frequency word cards: *I, a, the, is, little, to.* Say the word *little.* Choose a child to point to the word. Have children say the word and use it in a sentence. Continue with the other words.

2 Read

Decodable Reader 6 *Let's Go*

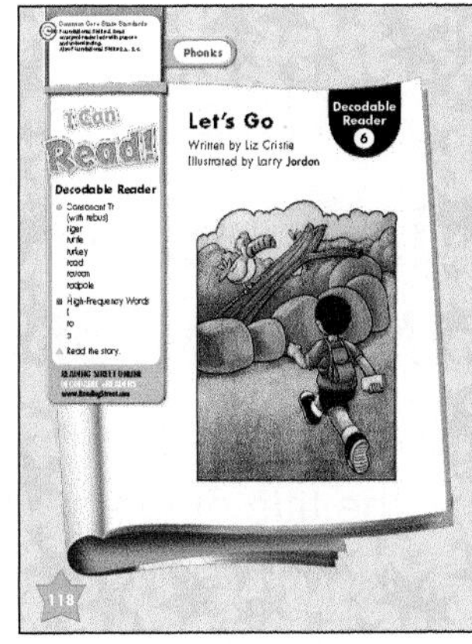

CONCEPTS OF PRINT Display Decodable Reader 6 in *My Skills Buddy.* Show children the illustrations and read aloud the title. What do you think the story is about?

READ Have children take turns reading the Decodable Reader. Pause at the end of each page to ask questions. Who is walking? What does the boy walk to?

3 Reread for Fluency

Have children reread the Decodable Reader *Let's Go* individually to develop fluency.

SMALL GROUP TIME

More Reading for Group Time

CONCEPT LITERACY

- Concept Words
- High-Frequency Words

Use these suggested readers or other text at children's instructional level.

eStreet Interactive
www.ReadingStreet.com

Use the Leveled Reader Database for lesson plans and student pages for *Machines Help.*

If... children need more scaffolding and practice with phonemic awareness and phonics,
then... use the activities on p. DI•97 in the Teacher Resources section of the Digital Path.

Common Core State Standards

Literature 1. With prompting and support, ask and answer questions about key details in a text. **Literature 10.** Actively engage in group reading activities with purpose and understanding. **Foundational Skills 3.c.** Read common high-frequency words by sight (e.g., *the, of, to, you, she, my, is, are, do, does*). **Language 5.a.** Sort common objects into categories (e.g., shapes, foods) to gain a sense of the concepts the categories represent. **Language 5.c.** Identify real-life connections between words and their use (e.g., note places at school that are *colorful*). **Language 6.** Use words and phrases acquired through conversations, reading and being read to, and responding to texts.

1 Build Word Knowledge

Develop Vocabulary

WORDS FOR SIZES Have children return to p. 128 in *My Skills Buddy.* Review the size words *big, little, short,* and *tall.* Point to the pictures of the trucks. Which truck is big? Which truck is little? Point to the pictures of the women. Which woman is short? Which woman is tall? Have children complete the following sentence frames with the words for sizes.

- A whale is _______. (big)
- A giraffe is _______. (tall)
- Ants are _______. (little)
- A dachshund is a dog with very _______ legs. (short)

Team Talk Have children work with a partner to use the words for sizes in sentences.

2 Read

Kindergarten Student Reader *At the Toy Store*

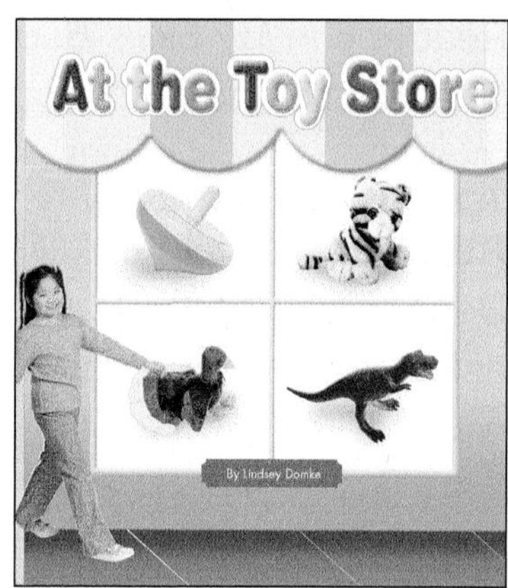

REREAD Display the reader and have children tell the title of the book. Have them tell what they remember about the story. Then have children read the story chorally. After reading each page, ask children to tell what they see. Who is at the toy store? What does she see? To check children's understanding, have them take turns reading the story to a partner and then retelling the story to the partner.

On-Level

1 Build Word Knowledge

Develop Language

Display the Big Book *Dig Dig Digging* and read the text on p. 10.

Garbage trucks are good at gobble,
gobble, gobbling,
crunching messy garbage bags,
squeezing and squashing.

- Ask children to read the text with you as you track the print.
- Point to the line, *crunching messy garbage bags.*
- What does the word *crunching* mean? What is another word for *crunching*? Why do you think the author chose the word *crunching?*
- **Team Talk** Turn to your partner and try some other words in place of *crunching.*
- Continue the routine with the words *messy* and *squashing.*

2 Read

Get Set, Roll! Reader 6 *Ted*

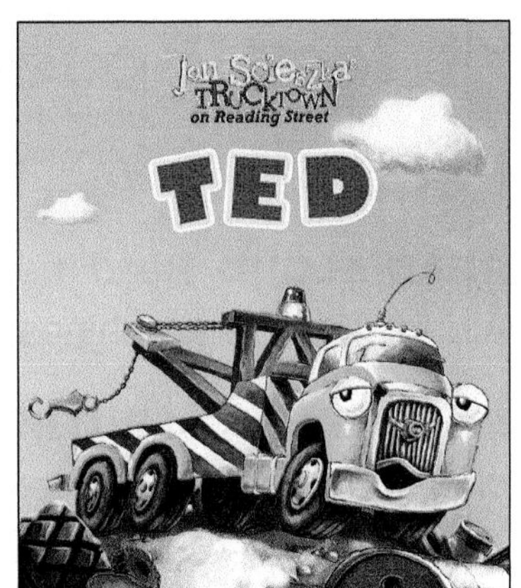

REVIEW HIGH-FREQUENCY WORDS Review the following high-frequency words with children: *I, am, to, the.* Ask children to use each word in a sentence.

REVIEW REBUS WORDS Distribute Letter Tiles to each child or use Letter Tile Drag and Drop in the Digital Path. Write the name *Ted* on a card. Use your letters to build this word. This spells the name of one of our Trucktown friends. What does this spell? Which character is Ted? Continue the routine with the following words: *tows, Rita, Jack, garage.*

REREAD Have children whisper read *Ted* as you listen to each child. Then have children take turns reading the story aloud.

SMALL GROUP TIME

ELL

If... children need more scaffolding and practice with vocabulary,
then... use the ELL activities on p. DI•99 in the Teacher Resources section of the Digital Path.

On-Level

Common Core State Standards

Informational Text 1. With prompting and support, ask and answer questions about key details in a text. **Informational Text 10.** Actively engage in group reading activities with purpose and understanding. **Foundational Skills 3.a.** Demonstrate basic knowledge of one-to-one letter-sound correspondences by producing the primary or many of the most frequent sounds for each consonant. **Language 2.d.** Spell simple words phonetically, drawing on knowledge of sound-letter relationships.

1 Build Word Knowledge

Practice Phonics

SPELL WORDS Distribute Letter Tiles to children. Spell the word *tan* with your tiles and point to the *t.* What is the name of this letter? What is the sound for this letter? Point to *-an* and ask children to name the letters. When these two letters are together, they stand for the sounds /an/. We call them a word family because we can add different letters at the beginning and change the beginning sound, but the middle and ending sounds will stay the same. Let's spell some words with our Letter Tiles. Spell the word *tan.* Watch as children build the word. Have them name the letters in the word and then blend the initial sound and word family to read the word. Continue the routine with these words: *can, fan, man, pan, ran, van.*

Corrective feedback	**If...** children have trouble spelling words, **then...** break the word into individual phonemes and ask children to connect each sound to a letter name.

2 Text-Based Comprehension

Read

READ ALOUD Read the Reading Street Sleuth Read Aloud, "Simple Machines," on p. SG•97 to children.

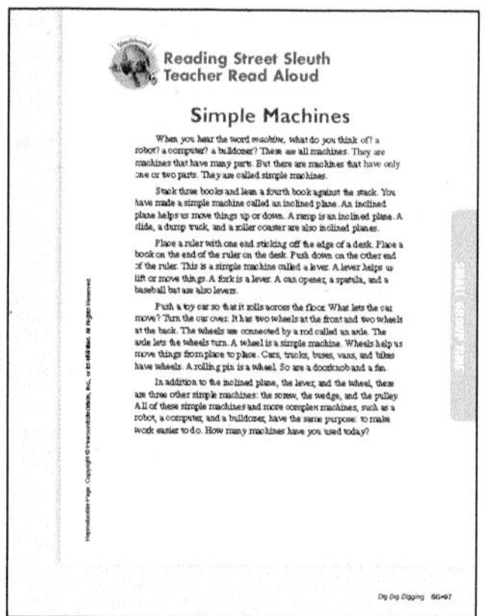

Reading Street Sleuth Teacher Read Aloud

Simple Machines

When you hear the word *machine,* what do you think of? a robot? a computer? a bulldozer? These are all machines. They are machines that have many parts. But there are machines that have only one or two parts. They are called simple machines.

Stack three books and lean a fourth book against the stack. You have made a simple machine called an inclined plane. An inclined plane helps us move things up or down. A ramp is an inclined plane. A slide, a dump truck, and a roller coaster are also inclined planes.

Place a ruler with one end sticking off the edge of a desk. Place a book on the end of the ruler on the desk. Push down on the other end of the ruler. This is a simple machine called a lever. A lever helps us lift or move things. A fork is a lever. A can opener, a spatula, and a baseball bat are also levers.

Push a toy car so that it rolls across the floor. What lets the car move? Turn the car over. It has two wheels at the front and two wheels at the back. The wheels are connected by a rod called an axle. The axle lets the wheels turn. A wheel is a simple machine. Wheels help us move things from place to place. Cars, trucks, buses, vans, and bikes have wheels. A rolling pin is a wheel. So are a doorknob and a fan.

In addition to the inclined plane, the lever, and the wheel, there are three other simple machines: the screw, the wedge, and the pulley. All of these simple machines and more complex machines, such as a robot, a computer, and a bulldozer, have the same purpose: to make work easier to do. How many machines have you used today?

Dig Dig Digging SG•97

READ LIKE A SLEUTH! Encourage children to cite evidence from the text to support their answers. You may wish to reread sections of the text to verify children's answers.

Look for Evidence What simple machines does the author tell about? What can each of these simple machines help us do?

Ask Questions Which simple machine do you think is most interesting? What else would you like to know about that simple machine?

Prove It! Performance Task Have children use a description in the text to draw a picture of one of the simple machines. Ask them to label the picture with one or two key details from the text. Children may write or dictate a short phrase or sentence.

Reading Street Sleuth Teacher Read Aloud

Simple Machines

When you hear the word *machine,* what do you think of? a robot? a computer? a bulldozer? These are all machines. They are machines that have many parts. But there are machines that have only one or two parts. They are called simple machines.

Stack three books and lean a fourth book against the stack. You have made a simple machine called an inclined plane. An inclined plane helps us move things up or down. A ramp is an inclined plane. A slide, a dump truck, and a roller coaster are also inclined planes.

Place a ruler with one end sticking off the edge of a desk. Place a book on the end of the ruler on the desk. Push down on the other end of the ruler. This is a simple machine called a lever. A lever helps us lift or move things. A fork is a lever. A can opener, a spatula, and a baseball bat are also levers.

Push a toy car so that it rolls across the floor. What lets the car move? Turn the car over. It has two wheels at the front and two wheels at the back. The wheels are connected by a rod called an axle. The axle lets the wheels turn. A wheel is a simple machine. Wheels help us move things from place to place. Cars, trucks, buses, vans, and bikes have wheels. A rolling pin is a wheel. So are a doorknob and a fan.

In addition to the inclined plane, the lever, and the wheel, there are three other simple machines: the screw, the wedge, and the pulley. All of these simple machines and more complex machines, such as a robot, a computer, and a bulldozer, have the same purpose: to make work easier to do. How many machines have you used today?

Reproducible Page. Copyright © Pearson Education, Inc., or its affiliates. All Rights Reserved.

Strategic Intervention

Common Core State Standards

Literature 1. With prompting and support, ask and answer questions about key details in a text. **Literature 10.** Actively engage in group reading activities with purpose and understanding. **Foundational Skills 2.d.** Isolate and pronounce the initial, medial vowel, and final sounds (phonemes) in three-phoneme (consonant-vowel-consonant, or CVC) words.* (This does not include CVCs ending with /l/, /r/, or /x/.) **Foundational Skills 3.a.** Demonstrate basic knowledge of one-to-one letter-sound correspondences by producing the primary or many of the most frequent sounds for each consonant. **Foundational Skills 3.c.** Read common high-frequency words by sight (e.g., *the, of, to, you, she, my, is, are, do, does*).

More Reading for Group Time

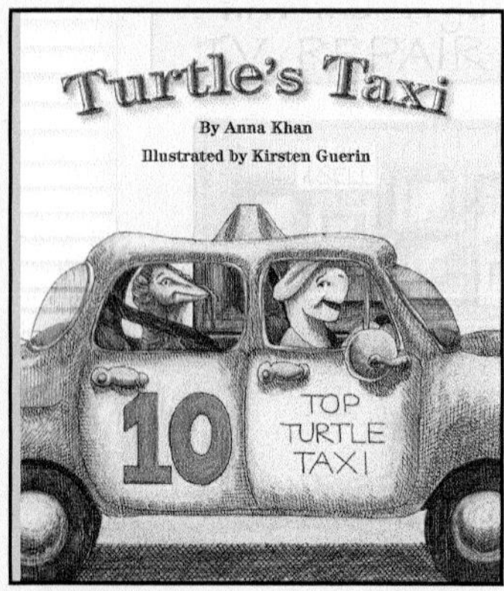

LISTEN TO ME READER

- Concepts of Print

Use these suggested readers or other text at children's instructional level.

eStreet Interactive
www.ReadingStreet.com

Use the Leveled Reader Database to access an online version of *Turtle's Taxi*.

If... children need more scaffolding and practice with phonemic awareness and phonics,
then... use the Phonics Transition lessons beginning on p. 447 in the *ELL Handbook*.

1 Build Word Knowledge

Reteach Phonemic Awareness

ISOLATE /t/ Display the *ten* Picture Card. This is a ten. *Ten* begins with /t/. Say it with me: /t/ /t/ /t/, *ten.* Repeat with the *taxi, tiger, top,* and *tub* Picture Cards.

Reteach Phonics

CONNECT /t/ TO *Tt* I am going to say three words. I want you to tell me which word begins with /t/. Listen carefully: *cap, tent, rug.* Say the words with me: *cap, tent, rug.* Which word begins with /t/? *Tent* begins with /t/. *Cap* and *rug* do not begin with /t/. Display the *Tt* Alphabet Card. The letter *t* stands for /t/. The word *tent* begins with the letter *t.* Continue with these sets of words: *town, map, count; pet, bear, top; rake, teeth, baby; dust, math, touch.*

2 Read

Decodable Story 6 *Tam!*

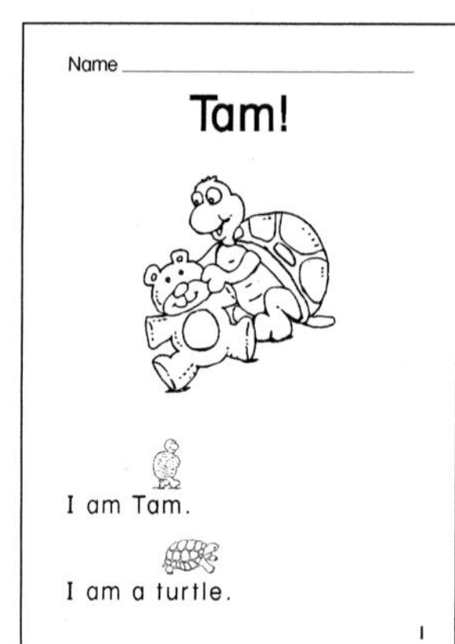

REVIEW HIGH-FREQUENCY WORDS Write *to* on chart paper. This is the word *to.* What word is this? Say the word with me. Listen for the word in the sentence I say. Clap when you hear the word. *I go to the board.* Continue with the high-frequency words *am, I,* and *a.*

Corrective feedback **If...** children have difficulty reading the high-frequency words, **then...** say a word and have children point to the word. Repeat several times, giving assistance as needed.

READ Have children read the story.

3 Reread for Fluency

Have children reread the story *Tam!* chorally. Then have them reread the story several times individually to develop fluency.

1 Build Word Knowledge

Reteach Phonemic Awareness

DISCRIMINATE /t/ Display Phonics Songs and Rhymes Chart 6. Sing "Tick, Tick, Tock" to the tune of "Three Blind Mice" several times with children. Ask them to tap their foot when they hear a /t/ word in the song.

Reteach Phonics

RECOGNIZE *Tt* Ask children to name words that begin with /t/. List the words as children say them. Have children echo read the list of words. Then ask them to take turns circling the *t*'s on the list.

Reteach High-Frequency Words

REVIEW Have children read each previously taught high-frequency word as you point to it on the Word Wall.

I	am	a	to	little	the

Corrective feedback	**If...** children have difficulty reading the words, **then...** say a word and have children point to the word. Repeat several times, giving assistance as needed.

2 Read

Decodable Reader 6 *Let's Go*

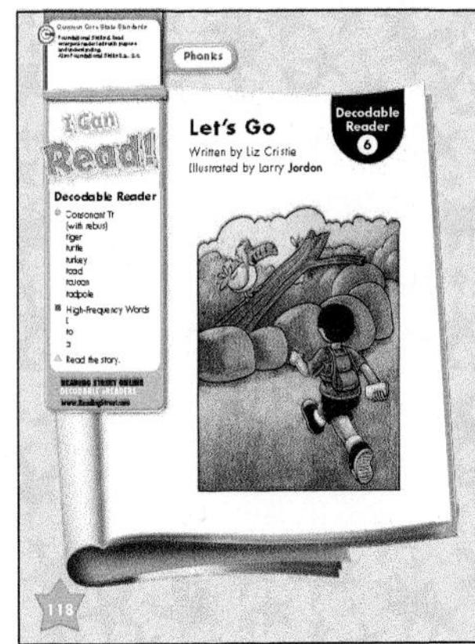

CONCEPTS OF PRINT Display Decodable Reader 6 in *My Skills Buddy.* The title of this story is *Let's Go.* The author is Liz Cristie. The illustrator is Larry Jordon. Look at the picture on the cover. Look at the pictures inside. What do you think the story is about?

READ Let's read the story together. After reading chorally with children, have them reread the story several times with a partner and then independently.

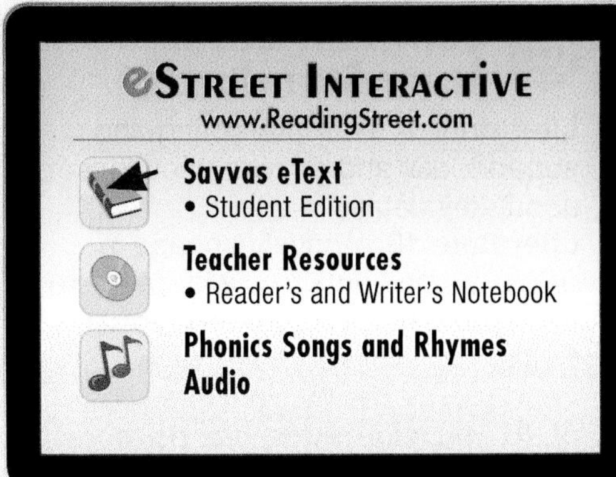

eStreet Interactive
www.ReadingStreet.com
Savvas eText
• Student Edition
Teacher Resources
• Reader's and Writer's Notebook
Phonics Songs and Rhymes Audio

SMALL GROUP TIME

Independent Reading Options

Trade Book Library

eStreet Interactive
www.ReadingStreet.com

Teacher's Guides available on the Leveled Reader Database.

If... children need more support with phonics,
then... use the ELL activities on p. DI•97 in the Teacher Resources section of the Digital Path.

Common Core State Standards

Literature 1. With prompting and support, ask and answer questions about key details in a text. **Literature 10.** Actively engage in group reading activities with purpose and understanding. **Foundational Skills 3.c.** Read common high-frequency words by sight (e.g., *the, of, to, you, she, my, is, are, do, does*). **Language 5.a.** Sort common objects into categories (e.g., shapes, foods) to gain a sense of the concepts the categories represent. **Language 5.c.** Identify real-life connections between words and their use (e.g., note places at school that are *colorful*). **Language 6.** Use words and phrases acquired through conversations, reading and being read to, and responding to texts.

1 Build Word Knowledge

Develop Vocabulary

RETEACH WORDS FOR SIZES Have children return to p. 128 of *My Skills Buddy* to review the size words *big, little, short,* and *tall.*

- Which picture shows a big truck? a little truck?
- Which picture shows a tall woman? a short woman?

Display pairs of classroom objects that are big and little or tall and short. For example, put AlphaBuddy next to a smaller stuffed animal. Have children use the words for sizes to describe the two animals.

2 Read

Kindergarten Student Reader *At the Toy Store*

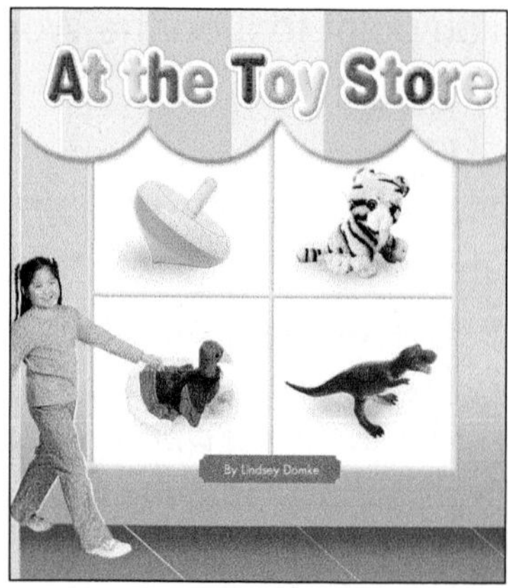

REVIEW STORY WORDS Write *tiger* on chart paper. This word is *tiger.* The word *tiger* is in the story we are going to read. What sound does *tiger* begin with? (/t/) What letter stands for /t/ in *tiger?* (*Tt*) Repeat with the story words *top, turkey, turtle, Tyrannosaurus Rex,* and *teddy bear.* We will read many words that begin with /t/ in our story.

REVIEW HIGH-FREQUENCY WORDS Write *I* on the board. Ask children to read the word with you. Have a volunteer read the word. Continue with the other high-frequency words *am, to, the, little,* and *a.*

REREAD STORY Display the reader. The title of this book is *At the Toy Store.* What do you think the story is about? Read the story chorally with children. Pause at the end of each page to ask: What toy is this? Where is this toy? Have children reread the story several times to build fluency.

If... children need more scaffolding and practice with vocabulary, **then...** use the ELL activities on p. DI•99 in the Teacher Resources section of the Digital Path.

1 Build Word Knowledge

Develop Language

Display the Big Book *Dig Dig Digging* and read the text on p. 10.

> *Garbage trucks are good at gobble,*
> *gobble, gobbling,*
> *crunching messy garbage bags,*
> *squeezing and squashing.*

- Ask children to read the text with you as you track the print.
- Point to the line, *crunching messy garbage bags.*
- What does the word *messy* mean? What is another word that means the same as *messy?*
- I am going to say some words. I want you to tell me which words mean the same as *messy: sloppy, neat, dirty, clean, tidy, filthy, orderly, untidy.*
- Why do you think the author used the word *messy?*
- Continue the routine with the words *crunching* and *squashing.*

2 Read

Get Set, Roll! Reader 6 *Ted*

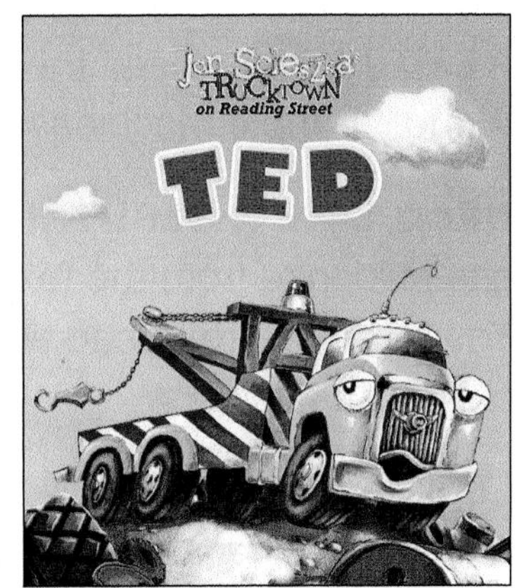

REVIEW HIGH-FREQUENCY AND REBUS WORDS Review the high-frequency and rebus words (*I, am, to, the, Ted, tows, Rita, Jack, garage*) using the following routine.

1. Display and read the word.
2. Name the letters in the word.
3. Read the word. Use it in a sentence.

REREAD Have children chorally read aloud *Ted* several times. Then ask them to take turns reading a page aloud.

eSTREET INTERACTIVE
www.ReadingStreet.com

Savvas eText
- Student Edition
- Kindergarten Student Reader
- Get Set, Roll! Reader

Independent Reading Options

Trade Book Library

eSTREET INTERACTIVE
www.ReadingStreet.com

Teacher's Guides available on the Leveled Reader Database.

Common Core State Standards

Literature 1. With prompting and support, ask and answer questions about key details in a text. **Literature 10.** Actively engage in group reading activities with purpose and understanding. **Informational Text 1.** With prompting and support, ask and answer questions about key details in a text. **Informational Text 10.** Actively engage in group reading activities with purpose and understanding. **Foundational Skills 3.a.** Demonstrate basic knowledge of one-to-one letter-sound correspondences by producing the primary or many of the most frequent sounds for each consonant. **Language 2.d.** Spell simple words phonetically, drawing on knowledge of sound-letter relationships.

1 Build Word Knowledge

Reteach Phonics

BLEND WORDS Distribute Letter Tiles to children. Spell the word *tan* with your tiles and point to the *t.* What is the name of this letter? What is the sound for this letter? Point to *-an* and ask children to name the letters. When these two letters are together, they stand for the sounds /an/. We call them a word family because we can add different letters at the beginning and change the beginning sound, but the middle and ending sounds will stay the same. Find your *t, a, n* Letter Tiles and then spell the word. Let's name the letters and then read the word. Continue the routine with these words: *can, fan, man, pan, ran, van.*

Corrective feedback	**If...** children have trouble blending sounds to read, **then...** have them name the letters in each word.

2 Text-Based Comprehension

Read

READ ALOUD Read the Reading Street Sleuth Read Aloud, "Simple Machines," on p. SG•97 to children.

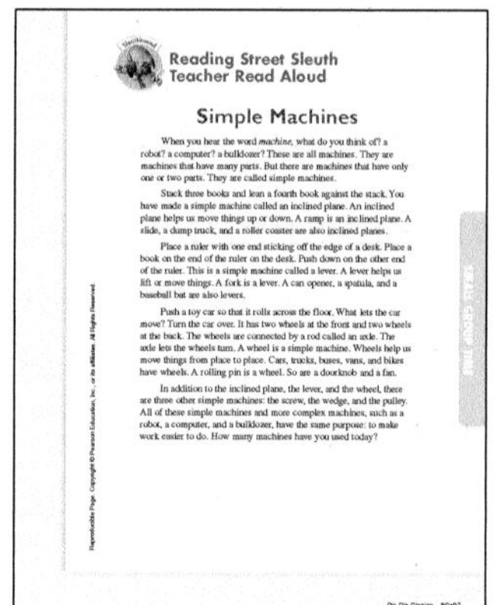
Reading Street Sleuth
Teacher Read Aloud

Simple Machines

When you hear the word *machine,* what do you think of? a robot? a computer? a bulldozer? These are all machines. They are machines that have many parts. But there are machines that have only one or two parts. They are called simple machines.

Stack three books and lean a fourth book against the stack. You have made a simple machine called an inclined plane. An inclined plane helps us move things up or down. A ramp is an inclined plane. A slide, a dump truck, and a roller coaster are also inclined planes.

Place a ruler with one end sticking off the edge of a desk. Place a book on the end of the ruler on the desk. Push down on the other end of the ruler. This is a simple machine called a lever. A lever helps us lift or move things. A fork is a lever. A can opener, a spatula, and a baseball bat are also levers.

Push a toy car so that it rolls across the floor. What lets the car move? Turn the car over. It has two wheels at the front and two wheels at the back. The wheels are connected by a rod called an axle. The axle lets the wheels turn. A wheel is a simple machine. Wheels help us move things from place to place. Cars, trucks, buses, vans, and bikes have wheels. A rolling pin is a wheel. So are a doorknob and a fan.

In addition to the inclined plane, the lever, and the wheel, there are three other simple machines: the screw, the wedge, and the pulley. All of these simple machines and more complex machines, such as a robot, a computer, and a bulldozer, have the same purpose: to make work easier to do. How many machines have you used today?

Reproducible Page. Copyright © Pearson Education, Inc., or its affiliates. All Rights Reserved.

Dig Dig Digging SG•97

READ LIKE A SLEUTH! Encourage children to cite evidence from the text to support their answers. You may wish to reread sections of the text to verify children's answers.

Look for Evidence How many simple machines are there altogether? What are the three simple machines the author tells about?

Ask Questions Which simple machine do you think is most interesting? What else would you like to know about that simple machine?

Prove It! Performance Task Have children use a description in the text to draw a picture of one of the simple machines. Ask them to dictate a phrase or short sentence for the picture using one or two key details from the text. Read children's phrases or sentences to them as you track the print.

Advanced

1 Build Word Knowledge

Extend Phonics

/t/ SPELLED *Tt* Have children write *Tt* on an index card. Ask them to hold up their *Tt* card when they hear a word that begins with /t/. Say longer or more complex words such as these:

teacher	**tulip**	**dozen**	**tender**	**table**
mirror	**tired**	**tennis**	**tuba**	**money**
total	**believe**	**tangle**	**person**	**tiny**

2 Read

"Can We Pat Tim?"

CONCEPTS OF PRINT Read aloud the title of the story, "Can We Pat Tim?" Remember, the title of a story often gives us clues to what the story is about. Ask children what the title tells them about the story. (Two or more characters in the story want to pat another character.)

Can We Pat Tim?

Tim is a pig.
He is *not* a little pig.
Dot and Ted look at Tim.
A pig is not a cat.
A pig is not a dog.
You can pat a cat.
You can pat a dog.
Can you pat a pig?
Look at Dot and Ted.
Dot can pat Tim.
Ted can pat Tim.
They like Tim the pig!

TEACH STORY WORDS Display a picture of a pig and have children identify the animal. Write the word *pig* on chart paper. Present any other story words that children may need help with, such as *look, like, and,* and *pat.* Use the words in sentences that give clues to their meanings. For example, I *pat* the cat. I touch the cat gently with my hand.

READ Distribute copies of "Can We Pat Tim?" from p. SG•104, and have children read it on their own. Then have them take turns reading the story aloud. After reading, have children tell whom the story is about and what happens.

SMALL GROUP TIME

More Reading for Group Time

INDEPENDENT READER

- More Challenging Text

Use the suggested Leveled Reader or other text at children's instructional level.

eStreet Interactive
www.ReadingStreet.com

Use the Leveled Reader Database for lesson plans and student pages for *Two or Three?*

If... children need more practice with phonics,
then... use the Phonics Transition lessons beginning on p. 447 in the *ELL Handbook.*

Can We Pat Tim?

Tim is a pig.
He is *not* a little pig.
Dot and Ted look at Tim.
A pig is not a cat.
A pig is not a dog.
You can pat a cat.
You can pat a dog.
Can you pat a pig?
Look at Dot and Ted.
Dot can pat Tim.
Ted can pat Tim.
They like Tim the pig!

Reproducible Page. Copyright © Pearson Education, Inc., or its affiliates. All Rights Reserved.

Advanced Phonics Selection 6

Advanced

1 Build Word Knowledge

Extend Phonics

 **BLEND *t* WORDS** Write the word *top* on an index card. Display the card and say the word. Point to the *t*. What is the sound for this letter? Yes, the sound for this letter is /t/. Say it with me: /t/ /t/ /t/. The beginning sound in *top* is /t/. *Top* ends with *-op*. Run your finger under the letters *op*. Say the sounds with me: /t/ *-op*. Now let's blend the sounds together: /t/ *-op, top*. Say it with me: /t/ *-op, top*. Now you say it without me.

Listen as I use *top* in a sentence. *He put the book on the top shelf.* Have children use *top* in a sentence.

Continue with the words *tab, tug, ten,* and *tip*.

2 Read

Decodable Reader 6 *Let's Go*

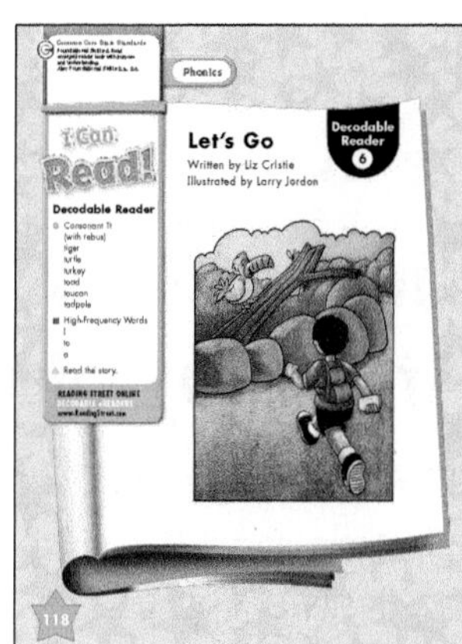

CONCEPTS OF PRINT Display Decodable Reader 6 in *My Skills Buddy.* Ask children to identify the author and illustrator.

READ Have children read the Decodable Reader quietly as you listen to them. Then have them take turns reading aloud one page at a time.

3 Reread for Fluency

Have children reread Decodable Reader 6 *Let's Go* to develop fluency.

SMALL GROUP TIME

Independent Reading Options

Trade Book Library

eStreet Interactive
www.ReadingStreet.com
Teacher's Guides available on the Leveled Reader Database.

If... children need more support with phonics,
then... use the ELL activities on pp. DI•97, DI•100–DI•101 in the Teacher Resources section of the Digital Path.

Advanced

Common Core State Standards

Literature 1. With prompting and support, ask and answer questions about key details in a text. **Literature 10.** Actively engage in group reading activities with purpose and understanding. **Foundational Skills 3.c.** Read common high-frequency words by sight (e.g., *the, of, to, you, she, my, is, are, do, does*). **Language 5.a.** Sort common objects into categories (e.g., shapes, foods) to gain a sense of the concepts the categories represent. **Language 5.c.** Identify real-life connections between words and their use (e.g., note places at school that are *colorful*). **Language 6.** Use words and phrases acquired through conversations, reading and being read to, and responding to texts.

1 Build Word Knowledge

Develop Vocabulary

WORDS FOR SIZES Review the size words *big, little, short,* and *tall* with children. Have them use the words in sentences.

Let's learn more words for sizes. Remember, we can use size words to describe what things look like. Have children identify the size words in these sentences.

- We picked out a *huge* pumpkin.
- A newborn kitten is weak and *tiny.*
- She needed a *long* piece of string.

Team Talk Have children work in pairs to use *huge, tiny,* and *long* in their own sentences. They may then illustrate a size word and write a phrase or sentence to describe their picture.

2 Read

Kindergarten Student Reader *At the Toy Store*

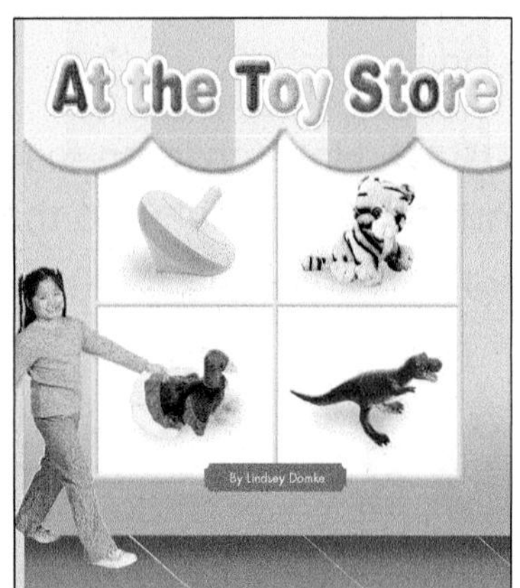

REREAD STORY Display the reader and have children read the title with you. Then have them read the story. Finally, have them reread the story aloud several times to build fluency.

EXTEND STORY Ask children to recall the toys at the toy store in the story. What other toys might the toy store have? Remind children to include at least one *Tt* word. Have them draw a picture and write a phrase or short sentence to go with the picture.

If... children need more scaffolding and practice with vocabulary, **then...** use the ELL activities on p. DI•99 in the Teacher Resources section of the Digital Path.

Advanced

1 Build Word Knowledge

Develop Language

Display the Big Book *Dig Dig Digging* and read the text on p. 10.

Garbage trucks are good at gobble,
gobble, gobbling,
crunching messy garbage bags,
squeezing and squashing.

- Ask children to read the text with you as you track the print.
- Point to the lines, *Garbage trucks are good at gobble, gobble, gobbling.*
- What does the word *gobbling* mean? What is another word that means the same as *gobbling*? Why did the author choose the word *gobbling*?
- Continue the routine with the words *crunching* and *squashing.*
- Team Talk Have children work with a partner to replace key words in a sentence with simpler words or synonyms without changing the meaning of the sentence. Use sentence frames, such as the following.

Garbage trucks are good at ______ and ______.

2 Read

Get Set, Roll! Reader 6 *Ted*

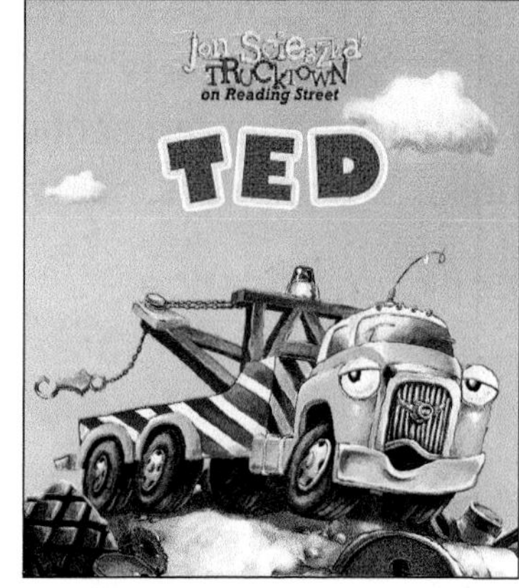

REVIEW HIGH-FREQUENCY AND REBUS WORDS Review the high-frequency and rebus words by asking children to spell the words with Letter Tiles. (*I, am, to, the, Ted, tows, Rita, Jack, garage*)

REREAD Have children whisper read *Ted* as you listen to each child. Then have them take turns reading the story aloud.

3 Reread for Fluency

BUILD FLUENCY Have children read again with expression and accuracy. Encourage them to use self-correction techniques for any mistakes.

SMALL GROUP TIME

Independent Reading Options

Trade Book Library

eStreet Interactive
www.ReadingStreet.com
Teacher's Guides available on the Leveled Reader Database.

Advanced

Common Core State Standards

Informational Text 1. With prompting and support, ask and answer questions about key details in a text. **Informational Text 10.** Actively engage in group reading activities with purpose and understanding. **Foundational Skills 3.a.** Demonstrate basic knowledge of one-to-one letter-sound correspondences by producing the primary or many of the most frequent sounds for each consonant. **Language 1.** Demonstrate command of the conventions of standard English grammar and usage when writing or speaking. **Language 2.** Demonstrate command of the conventions of standard English capitalization, punctuation, and spelling when writing. **Language 2.d.** Spell simple words phonetically, drawing on knowledge of sound-letter relationships.

1 Build Word Knowledge

Extend Phonics

FINISH *t* WORDS Say the word *tag.* Do you hear /t/ in *tag?* Listen carefully: /t/ *-ag.* Use Letter Tiles to spell the middle and ending sounds in *tag.* Have children tell you where to add the *t* Letter Tile to finish the word, or ask a volunteer to add the letter in the correct place. Then say the word together: /t/ *-ag.* Continue with these words: *tub, met, tip, fit, tax, mat, ten, hut, tap, tot.*

WRITE SENTENCES Distribute paper and pencils to children. Today we are going to use what we know about letters and the sounds they stand for to write short sentences. I am going to say a sentence, and I want you to write the sentence. Listen carefully.

1. I am a tan cat. **2.** I ran to the man. **3.** Tap the little pan.

2 Text-Based Comprehension

Read

READ ALOUD Read the Reading Street Sleuth Read Aloud, "Simple Machines," on p. SG•97 to children.

READ LIKE A SLEUTH! Encourage children to cite evidence from the text to support their answers. You may wish to reread sections of the text to verify children's answers.

Reading Street Sleuth
Teacher Read Aloud

Simple Machines

When you hear the word *machine,* what do you think of? a robot? a computer? a bulldozer? These are all machines. They are machines that have many parts. But there are machines that have only one or two parts. They are called simple machines.

Stack three books and lean a fourth book against the stack. You have made a simple machine called an inclined plane. An inclined plane helps us move things up or down. A ramp is an inclined plane. A slide, a dump truck, and a roller coaster are also inclined planes.

Place a ruler with one end sticking off the edge of a desk. Place a book on the end of the ruler on the desk. Push down on the other end of the ruler. This is a simple machine called a lever. A lever helps us lift or move things. A fork is a lever. A can opener, a spatula, and a baseball bat are also levers.

Push a toy car so that it rolls across the floor. What lets the car move? Turn the car over. It has two wheels at the front and two wheels at the back. The wheels are connected by a rod called an axle. The axle lets the wheels turn. A wheel is a simple machine. Wheels help us move things from place to place. Cars, trucks, buses, vans, and bikes have wheels. A rolling pin is a wheel. So are a doorknob and a fan.

In addition to the inclined plane, the lever, and the wheel, there are three other simple machines: the screw, the wedge, and the pulley. All of these simple machines and more complex machines, such as a robot, a computer, and a bulldozer, have the same purpose: to make work easier to do. How many machines have you used today?

Reproducible Page. Copyright © Pearson Education, Inc., or its affiliates. All Rights Reserved.

Look for Evidence What simple machines does the author tell about? What can these simple machines help us do?

Ask Questions Which simple machine do you think is most interesting? What else would you like to know about that simple machine?

Prove It! Performance Task Have children use a description in the text to draw a picture of one of the simple machines. Ask them to write a sentence or two about the simple machine using key details from the text. Have children read their sentences to you.

Teacher's Edition

Grateful acknowledgment is made to the following for copyrighted material:

Holiday House

Plaidypus Lost by Janet Stevens and Susan Stevens Crummel, illustrated by Janet Stevens. Text copyright © 2004 by Janet Stevens and Susan Stevens Crummel. Illustrations copyright © 2004 by Janet Stevens. All rights reserved. Reprinted by permission of Holiday House.

*** North-South**

The Little School Bus by Carol Roth, illustrated by Pamela Paparone, Cheshire Studio Book, 2002. Used by permission.

Henry Holt and Company, LLC

Dig Dig Digging by Margaret Mayo, illustrated by Alex Ayliffe. Text copyright © 2001 by Margaret Mayo. Illustrations copyright © 2001 by Alex Ayliffe.

Penguin Young Readers Group, a division of Penguin Group (USA) Inc.

Miss Bindergarten Takes a Field Trip with Kindergarten by Joseph Slate. Text copyright © 2001 by Joseph Slate. Illustrations copyright © 2001 by Ashley Wolff. Used by permission of Penguin Young Readers Group, a member of Penguin Group (USA) Inc., 345 Hudson Street, New York, NY 10014. All rights reserved.

Simon & Schuster Books for Young Readers, an Imprint of Simon & Schuster Children's Publishing Division

Smash! Crash! by Jon Scieszka. Copyright © 2008 by Jon Scieszka. Trucktown and Jon Scieszka's Trucktown and design trademarks of JRS Worldwide, LLC.

Note: Every effort has been made to locate the copyright owner of material reproduced on this component. Omissions brought to our attention will be corrected in subsequent editions.

* Domestic Edition Only.

KWL Strategy

The KWL Interactive Reading Strategy was developed and is used by permission of Donna Ogle, National-Louis University, Skokie, Illinois, co-author of *Reading Today and Tomorrow,* Holt, Rinehart & Winston Publishers, 1988. (See also the *Reading Teacher,* February 1986, pp. 564–570.)

Photographs

Cover ©William Manning/Corbis

Student Edition

Acknowledgments

Illustrations

Photographs

144

Student Edition, p. 144

TEACHER NOTES

TEACHER NOTES

TEACHER NOTES

TEACHER NOTES

TEACHER NOTES

Looking for Teacher Resources and other important information?

Go online to **SAVVAS** SuccessNet

eStreet Interactive
www.ReadingStreet.com

In the *First Stop* on Reading Street, you will find the following information.

- Research into Practice on Reading Street
- Guide to Reading Street
- Assessment on Reading Street
- Small Group Instruction on Reading Street
- ELL on Reading Street
- Customize Literacy on Reading Street
- 21st Century Skills on Reading Street
- Teacher Resources for Kindergarten
- Index

Looking for Teacher Resources and other important information?

Go online to SAVVAS SuccessNet

eSTREET INTERACTIVE
www.ReadingStreet.com

In the *First Stop* on Reading Street, you will find the following information.

- Research into Practice on Reading Street
- Guide to Reading Street
- Assessment on Reading Street
- Small Group Instruction on Reading Street
- ELL on Reading Street
- Customize Literacy on Reading Street
- 21st Century Skills on Reading Street
- Teacher Resources for Kindergarten
- Index